Maxi Scale
LONDON

CONTENTS

Key to map pages 2-3

Key to map symbols 4-5

Central London maps 6-37

Main London maps 38-207

Theatres and cinemas map 208

Shopping map 208

Index to street names, place names, and places of interest 209-352

Published by Collins
An imprint of HarperCollins*Publishers*
77-85 Fulham Palace Road, Hammersmith, London W6 8JB

www.collins.co.uk

Copyright © HarperCollins*Publishers* Ltd 2005

Collins® is a registered trademark of
HarperCollinsPublishers Limited

Mapping generated from Collins Bartholomew digital
databases

London Underground Map by permission of Transport
Trading Limited
Registered User No. 05/4084

The grid on this map is the National Grid taken from the
Ordnance Survey map with the permission of the
Controller of Her Majesty's Stationery Office.

Printed in China by South China Printing Co. Ltd.

ISBN 0 00 720287 3   SM11996   Imp 001   BDB

e-mail: roadcheck@harpercollins.co.uk

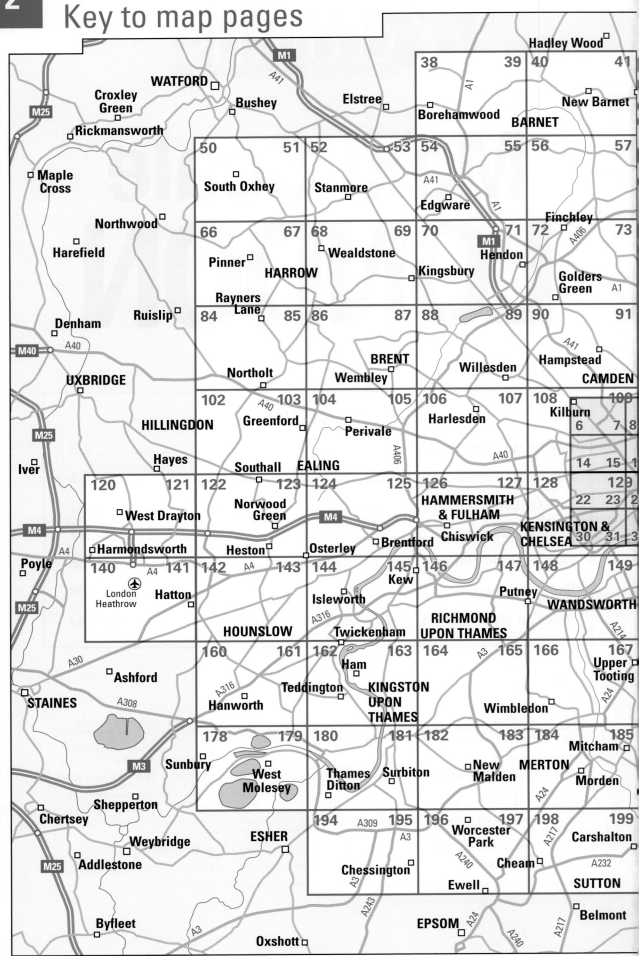

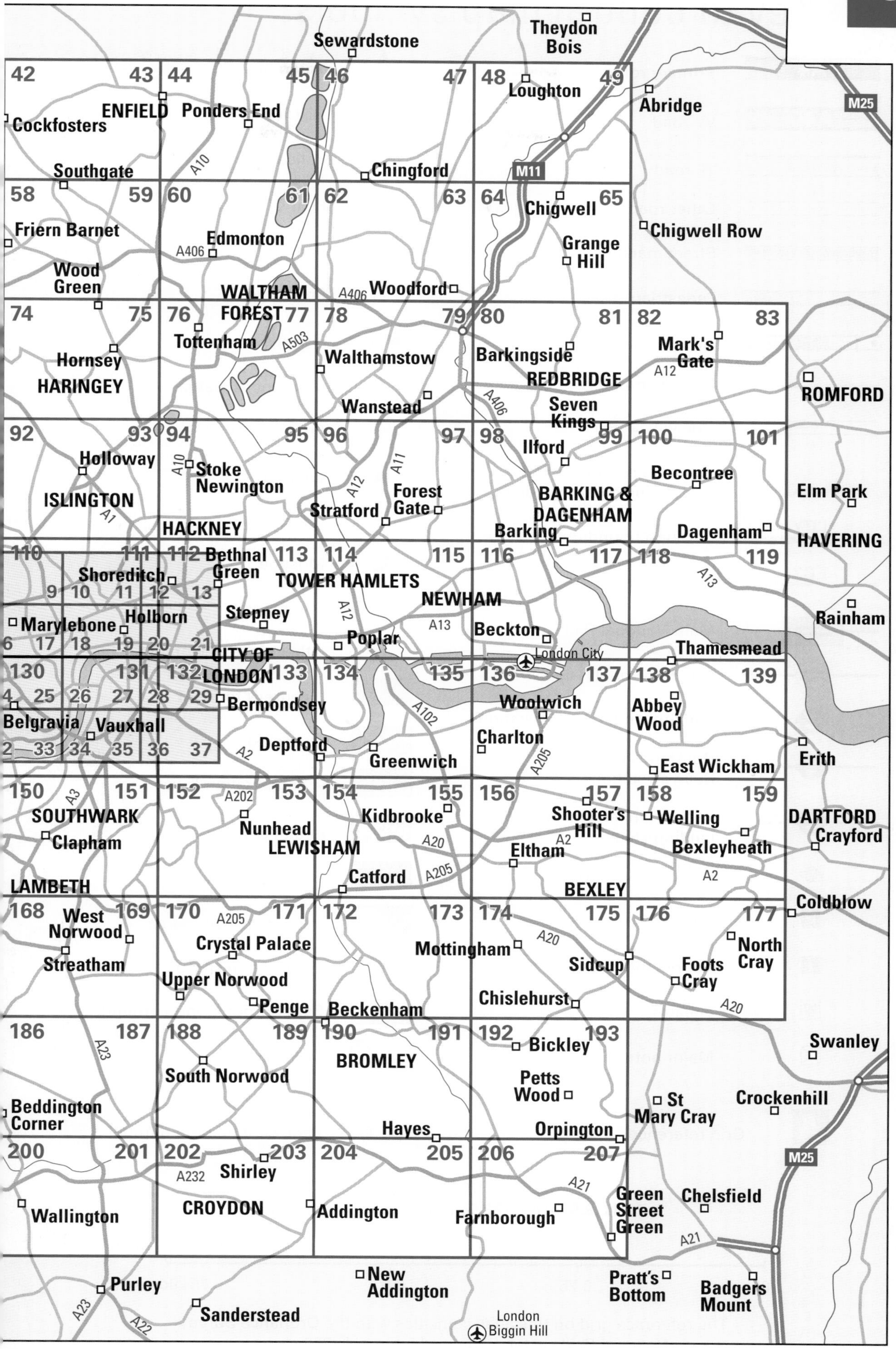

Sewardstone

Theydon Bois

| 42 | 43 | 44 | 45 | 46 | 47 | 48 | 49 |

ENFIELD Ponders End Loughton Abridge

Cockfosters

M25

Southgate Chingford M11

| 58 | 59 | 60 | 61 | 62 | 63 | 64 | 65 |

Friern Barnet Edmonton Chigwell Chigwell Row

A406 Grange Hill

Wood Green WALTHAM

| 74 | 75 | 76 | FOREST 77 | 78 | 79 | 80 | 81 | 82 | 83 |

Hornsey Tottenham A503 Walthamstow Barkingside Mark's Gate

HARINGEY A406 Woodford REDBRIDGE A12 ROMFORD

Wanstead Seven Kings

| 92 | 93 | 94 | 95 | 96 | 97 | 98 | 99 | 100 | 101 |

Holloway Stoke Newington Ilford Becontree Elm Park

A10 Forest Gate

ISLINGTON A1 Stratford BARKING & DAGENHAM

HACKNEY Barking Dagenham HAVERING

| 110 | 111 | 112 | 113 | 114 | 115 | 116 | 117 | 118 | 119 |

Shoreditch Bethnal Green TOWER HAMLETS A13

| 9 | 10 | 11 | 12 | 13 | | | | | |

Marylebone Holborn Stepney NEWHAM Rainham

A12 Beckton

| 6 | 17 | 18 | 19 | 20 | 21 | | | | |

Poplar A13

CITY OF LONDON London City Thamesmead

| 130 | 131 | 132 | 133 | 134 | 135 | 136 | 137 | 138 | 139 |

| 4 | 25 | 26 | 27 | 28 | 29 | | | | |

Bermondsey A102 Woolwich Abbey Wood

Belgravia Vauxhall

| 2 | 33 | 34 | 35 | 36 | 37 | | | | |

Deptford Charlton East Wickham Erith

A2 Greenwich A205

| 150 | 151 | 152 | 153 | 154 | 155 | 156 | 157 | 158 | 159 |

SOUTHWARK A3 Nunhead Kidbrooke Shooter's Hill Welling DARTFORD

Clapham A202 A20 A2 Bexleyheath Crayford

LEWISHAM Eltham A2

LAMBETH Catford A205 BEXLEY Coldblow

| 168 | 169 | 170 | 171 | 172 | 173 | 174 | 175 | 176 | 177 |

West Norwood Crystal Palace A205 Mottingham A20 North Cray

Streatham Sidcup Foots Cray

Upper Norwood Chislehurst A20

Penge Beckenham

| 186 | 187 | 188 | 189 | 190 | 191 | 192 | 193 | | Swanley |

A23 BROMLEY Bickley

South Norwood Petts Wood Crockenhill

Beddington Corner St Mary Cray

Hayes Orpington Green Street Green Chelsfield

| 200 | 201 | 202 | 203 | 204 | 205 | 206 | 207 | | |

A232 Shirley M25

Wallington CROYDON Addington Farnborough A21

Purley New Addington Pratt's Bottom Badgers Mount

Sanderstead London Biggin Hill A21

A23 A22

Key to central map symbols

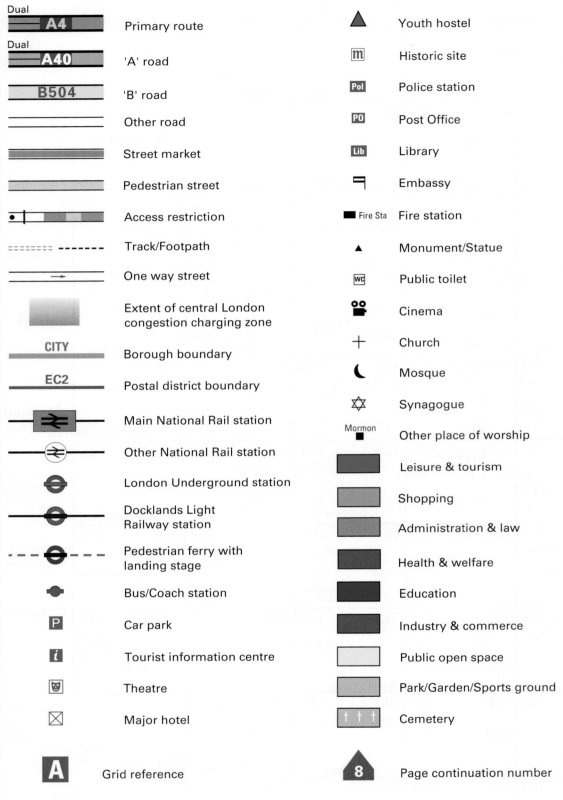

A4 Dual	Primary route
A40 Dual	'A' road
B504	'B' road
	Other road
	Street market
	Pedestrian street
	Access restriction
	Track/Footpath
	One way street
	Extent of central London congestion charging zone
CITY	Borough boundary
EC2	Postal district boundary
	Main National Rail station
	Other National Rail station
	London Underground station
	Docklands Light Railway station
	Pedestrian ferry with landing stage
	Bus/Coach station
P	Car park
i	Tourist information centre
	Theatre
	Major hotel
A	Grid reference

	Youth hostel
m	Historic site
Pol	Police station
PO	Post Office
Lib	Library
	Embassy
Fire Sta	Fire station
	Monument/Statue
WC	Public toilet
	Cinema
	Church
	Mosque
	Synagogue
Mormon	Other place of worship
	Leisure & tourism
	Shopping
	Administration & law
	Health & welfare
	Education
	Industry & commerce
	Public open space
	Park/Garden/Sports ground
✝ ✝ ✝	Cemetery
8	Page continuation number

SCALE
1: 7,143 8.9 inches (22.5cm) to 1 mile/14 cm to 1 km

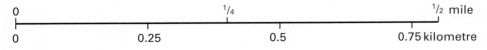

0		¹/₄		¹/₂ mile
0	0.25		0.5	0.75 kilometre

The reference grid on this atlas coincides with the Ordnance Survey
National Grid system. The grid interval is 250 metres.

Key to main map symbols

Symbol	Description
M4	Motorway
Dual A4	Primary route
Dual A40	'A' road
B504	'B' road
→	Other road/One way street
	Toll
	Street market
	Restricted access road
	Pedestrian street
	Cycle path
	Track/Footpath
THAMES PATH	Long distance footpath
LC	Level crossing
V — P	Vehicle/Pedestrian ferry
	County/Borough boundary
	Postal district boundary
	Main National Rail station
	Other National Rail station
	London Underground station
	Docklands Light Railway station
	Tramlink station
	Pedestrian ferry landing stage
	Bus/Coach station

Symbol	Description
	Leisure & tourism
	Shopping
	Administration & law
	Health & welfare
	Education
	Industry & commerce
† † †	Cemetery
↑ ↑	Golf course
	Public open space/Allotments
	Park/Garden/Sports ground
	Wood/Forest
USA	Embassy
Pol	Police station
Fire Sta	Fire station
PO/Lib	Post Office/Library
▲	Youth hostel
i	Tourist information centre
m	Historic Site
P	Car park
	Tower block
H	Heliport
+	Church
☽	Mosque
✡	Synagogue

Extent of London congestion charging zone
For more information see website www.cclondon.com

A Grid reference

38 Page continuation number

SCALE
1:14,286 4.4 inches (11.3cm) to 1 mile/7 cm to 1 km

| 35 | OS National Grid kilometre square |

0   ¼   ½ mile
0   0.25   0.5   0.75   1 kilometre

The reference grid on this atlas coincides with the Ordnance Survey National Grid system. The grid interval is 500 metres.

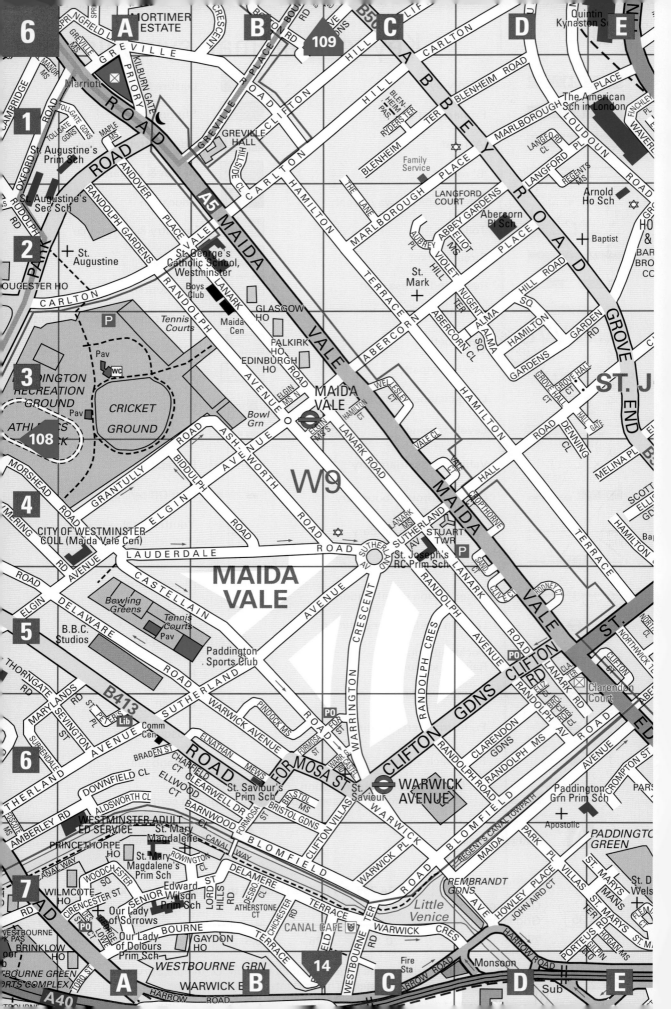

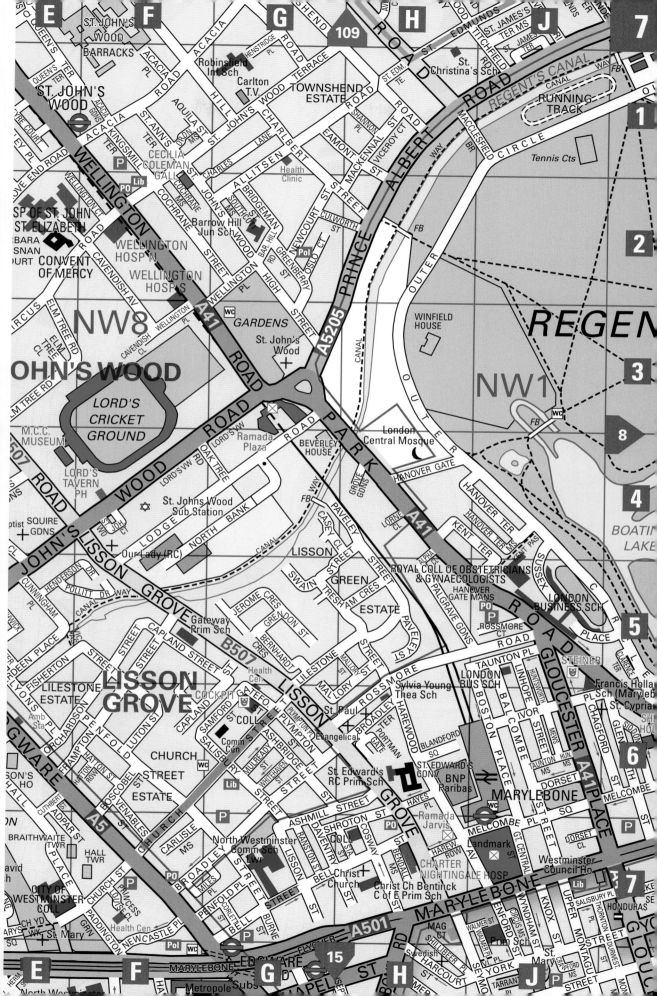

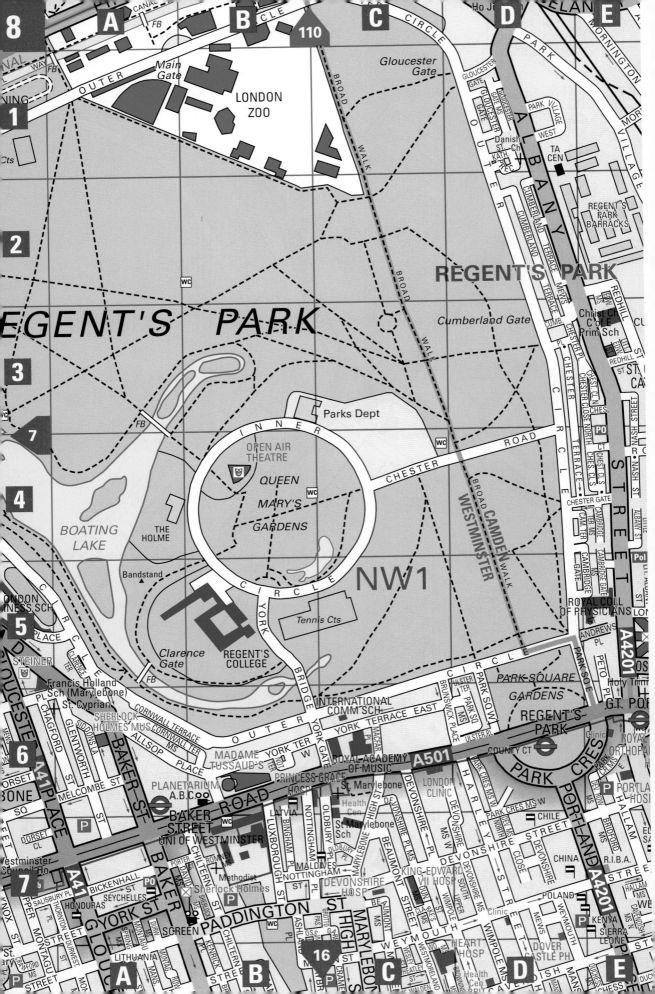

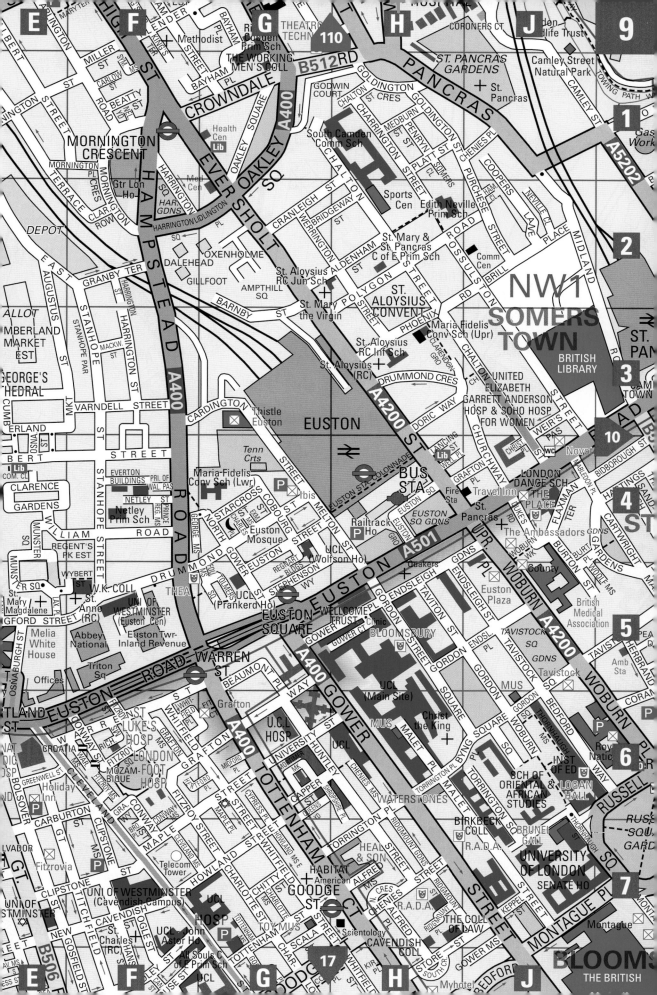

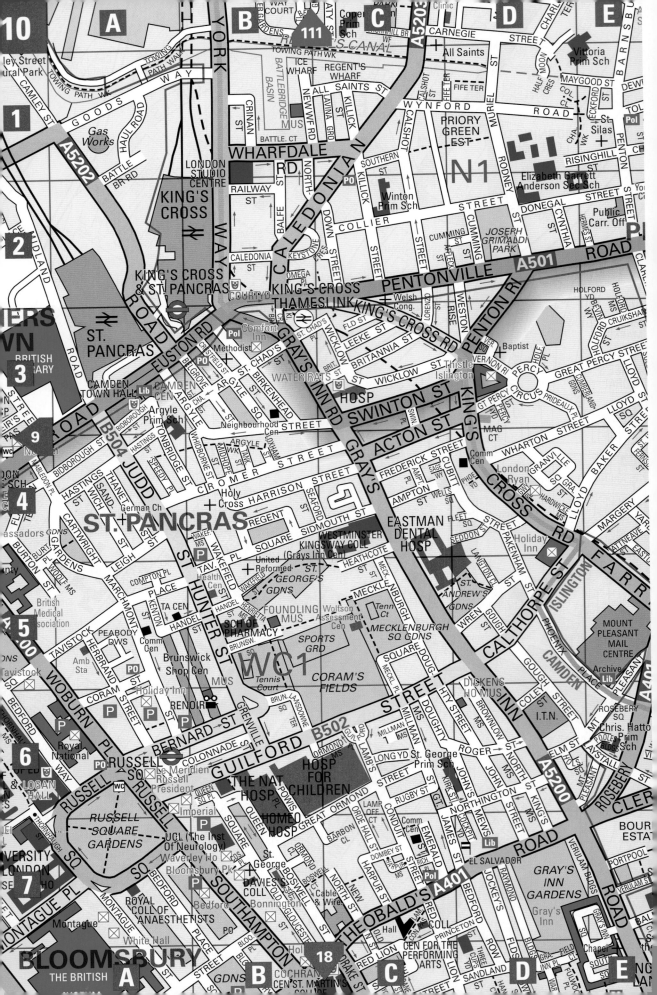

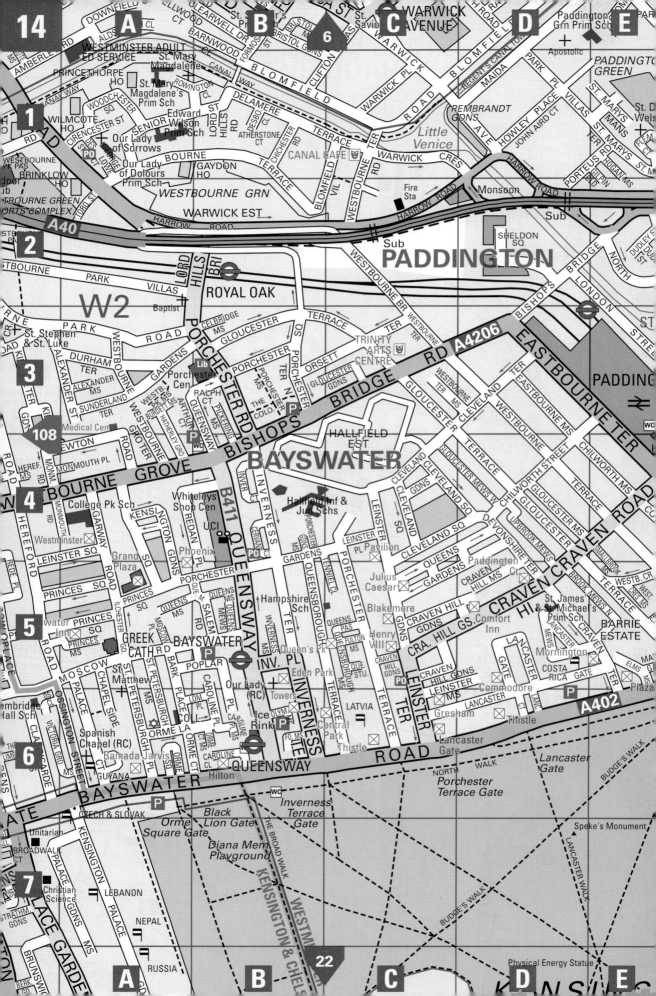

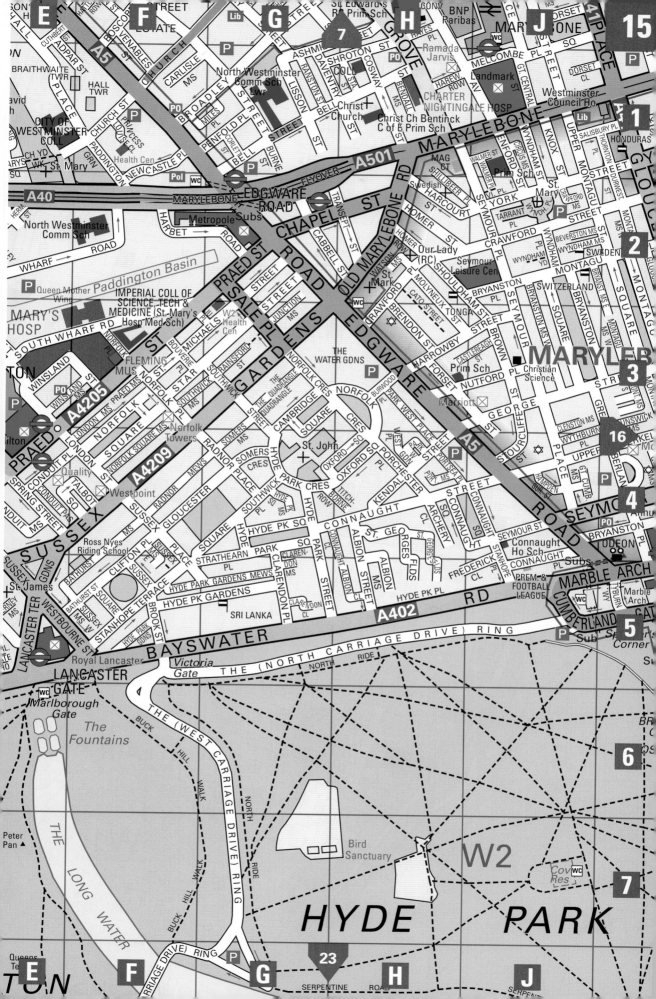

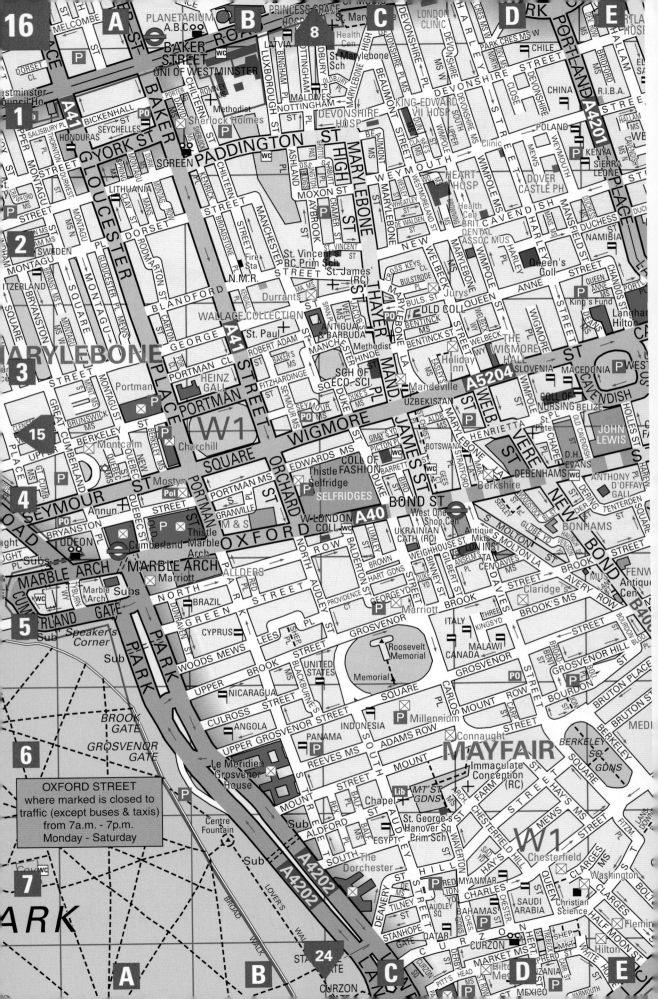

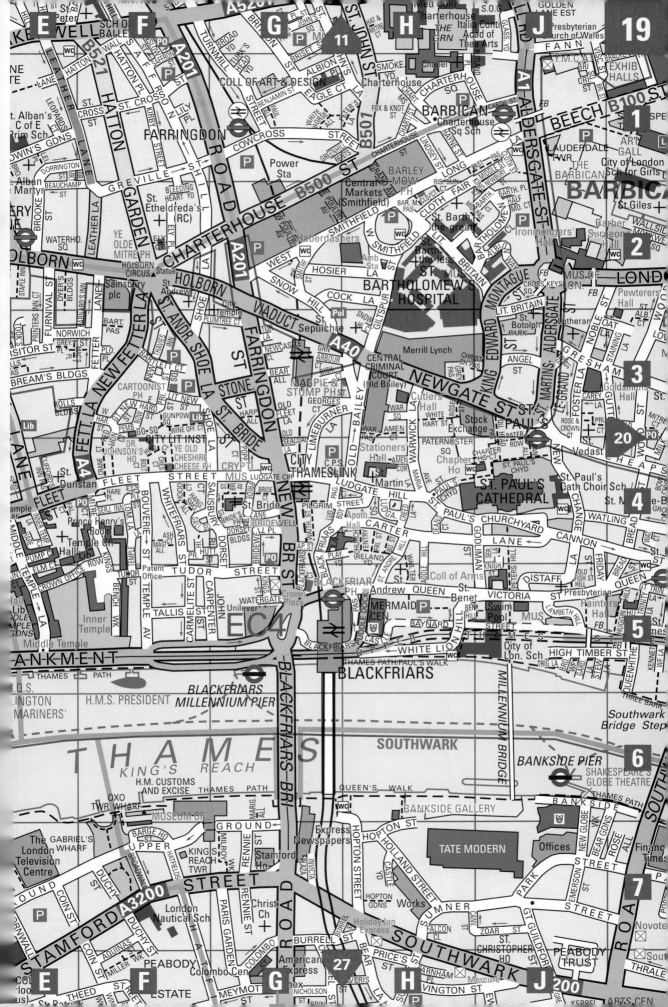

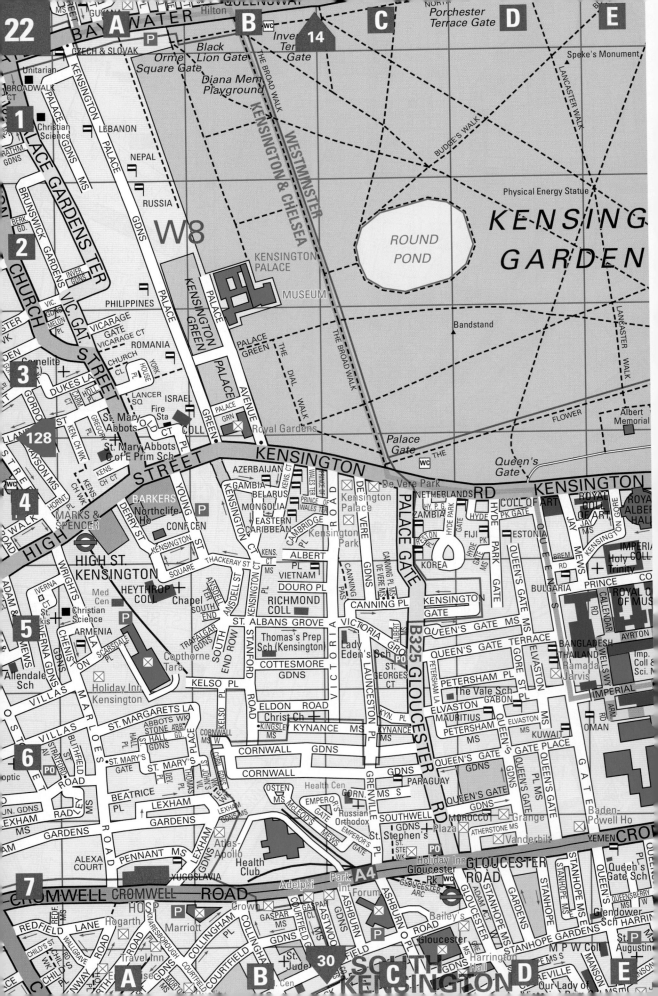

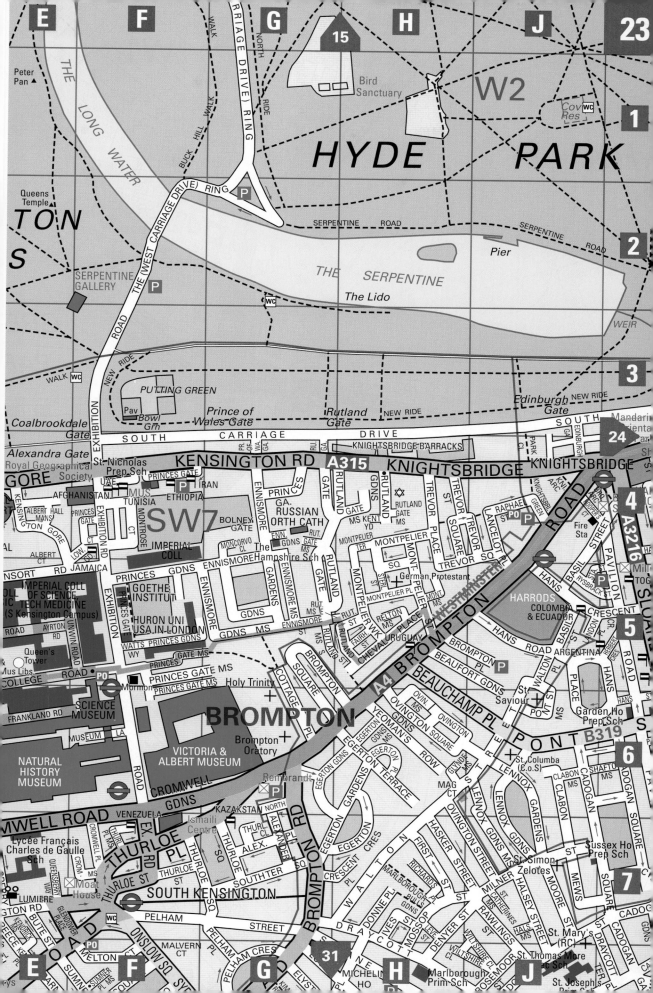

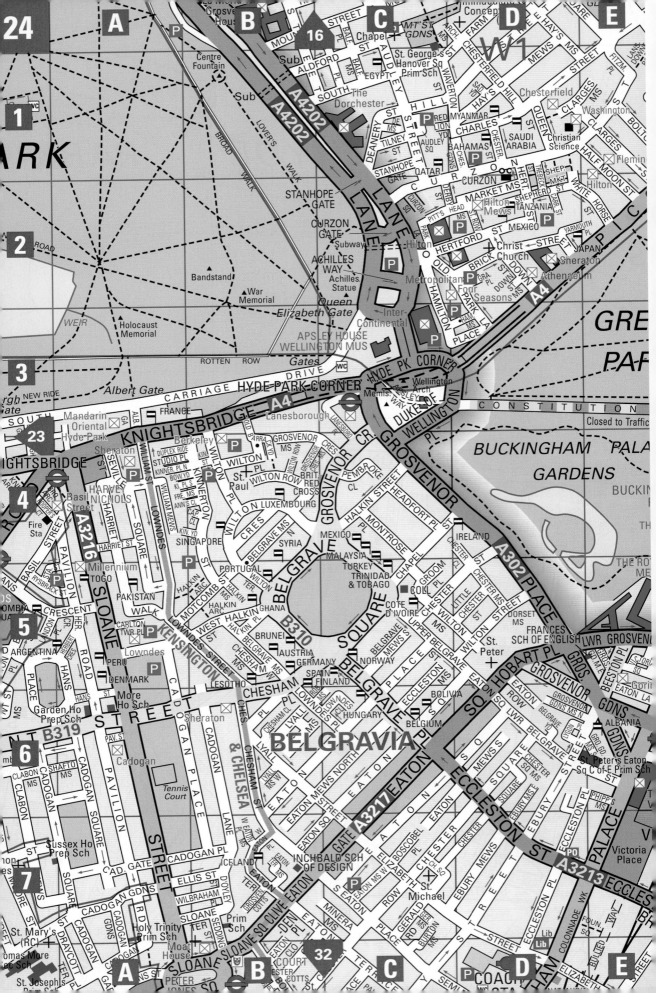

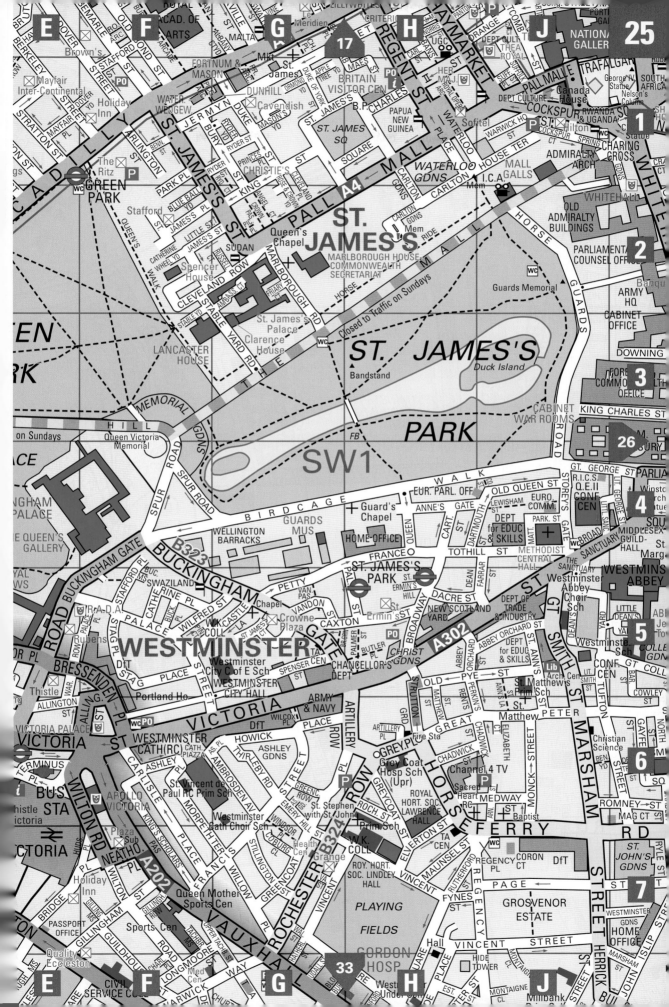

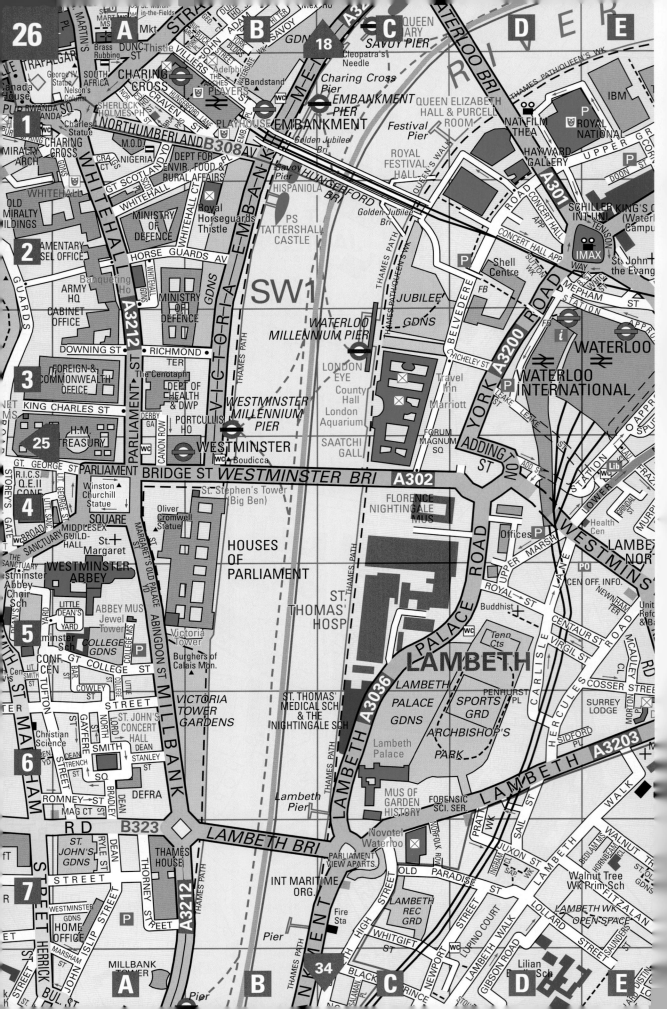

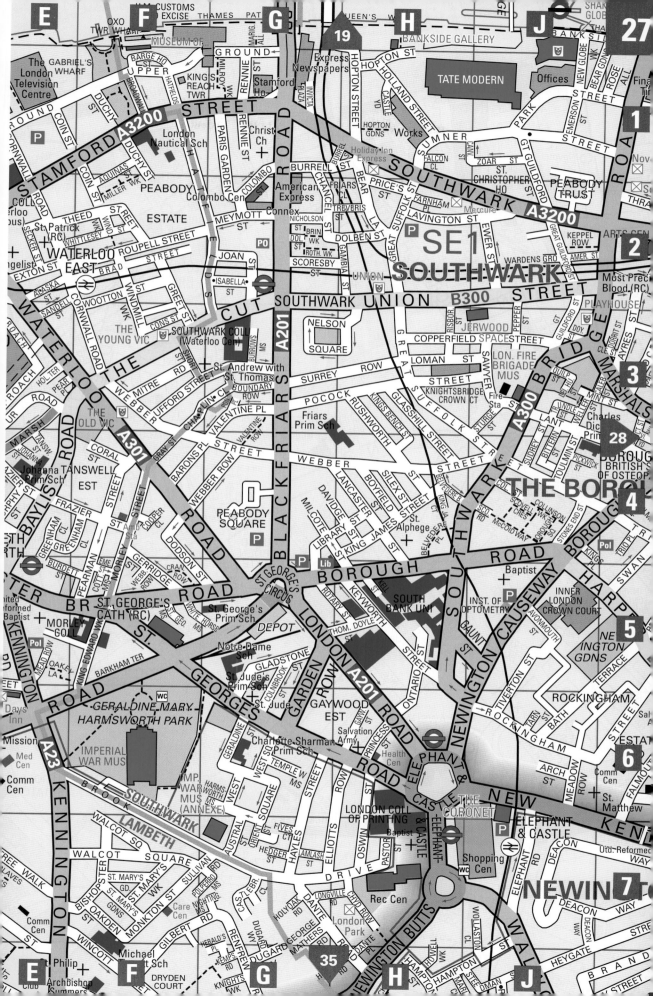

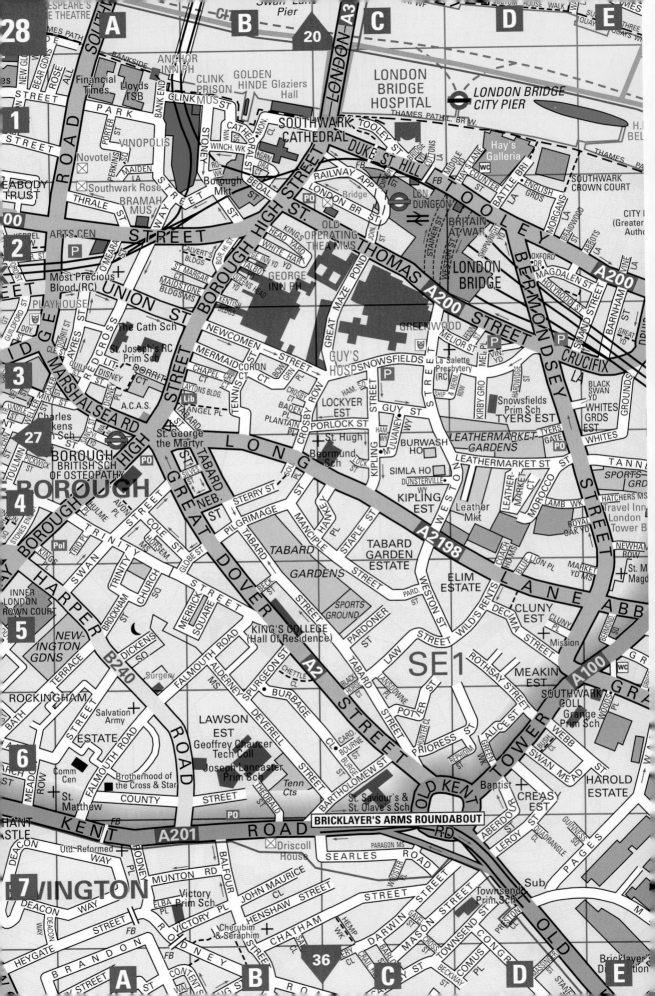

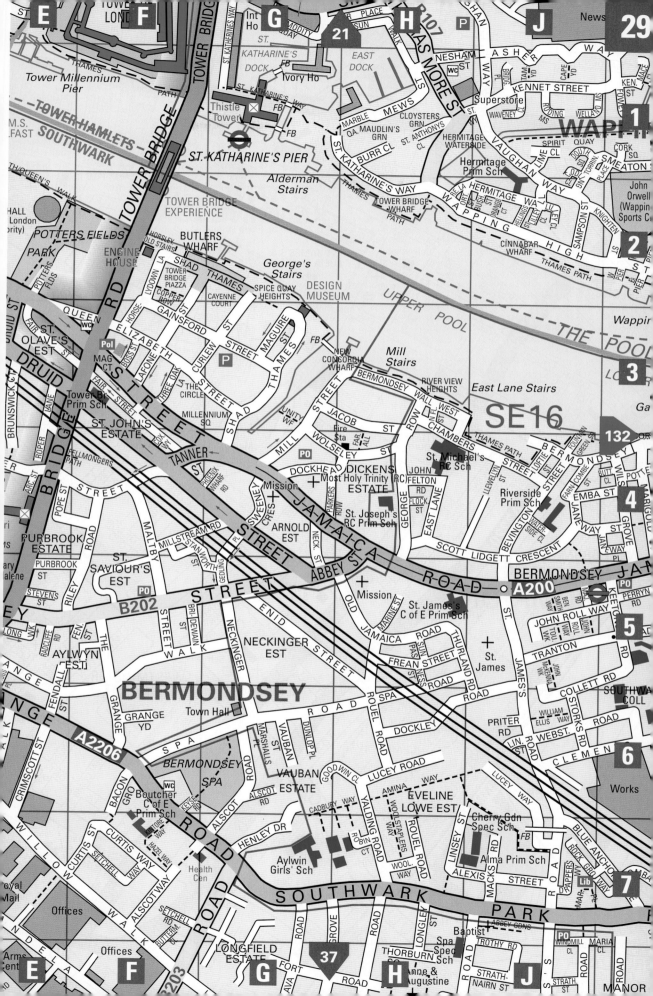

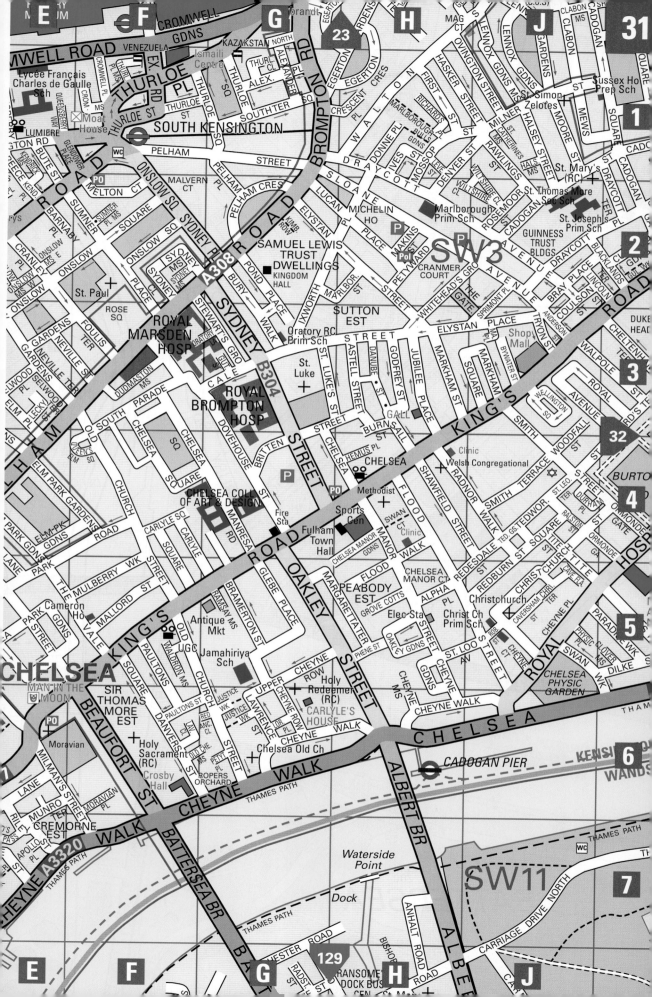

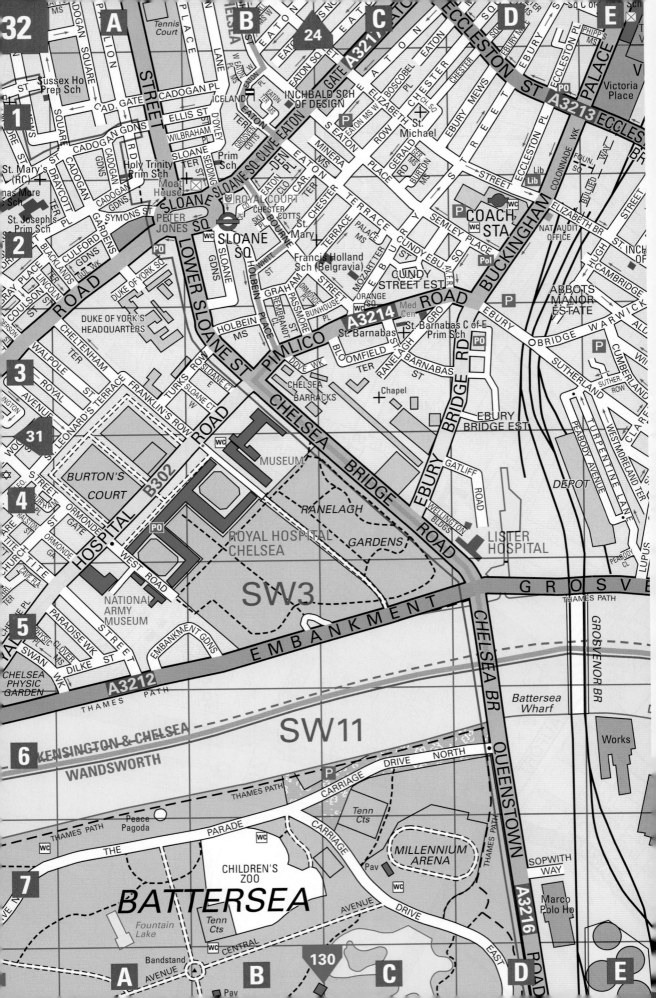

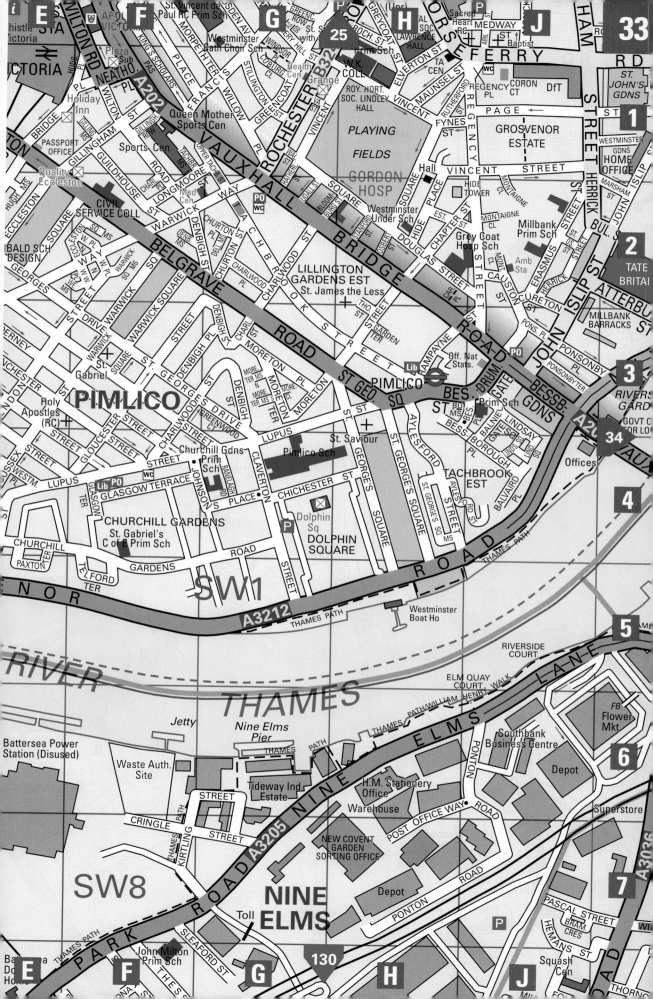

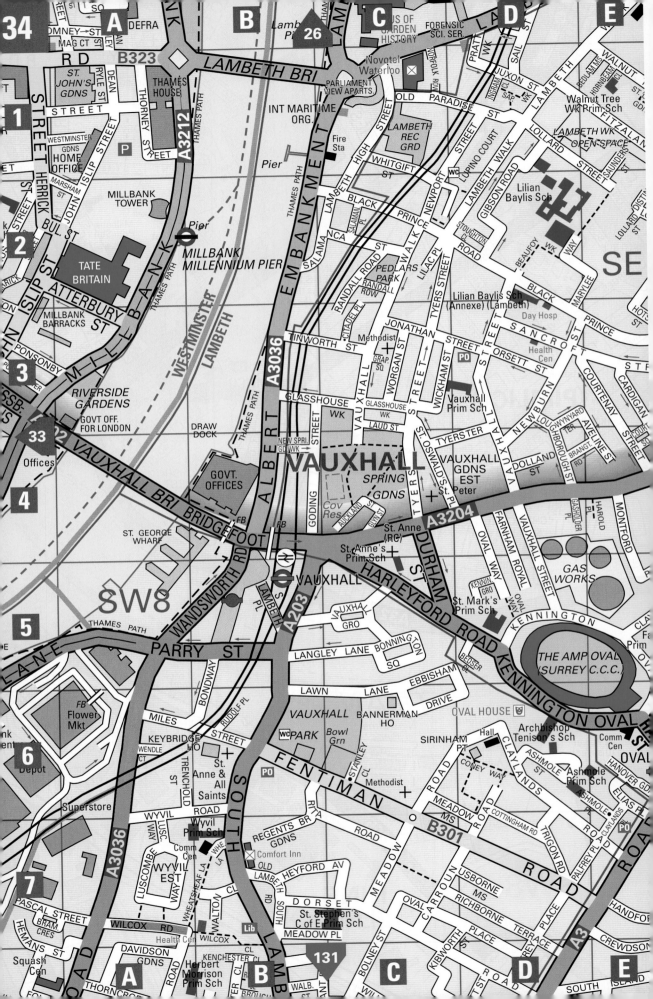

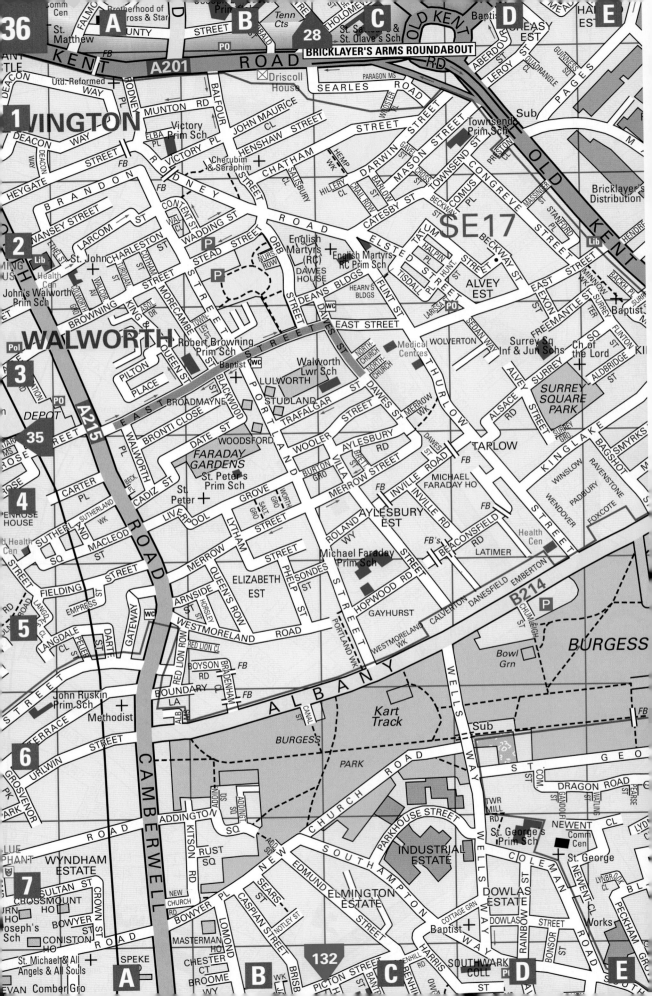

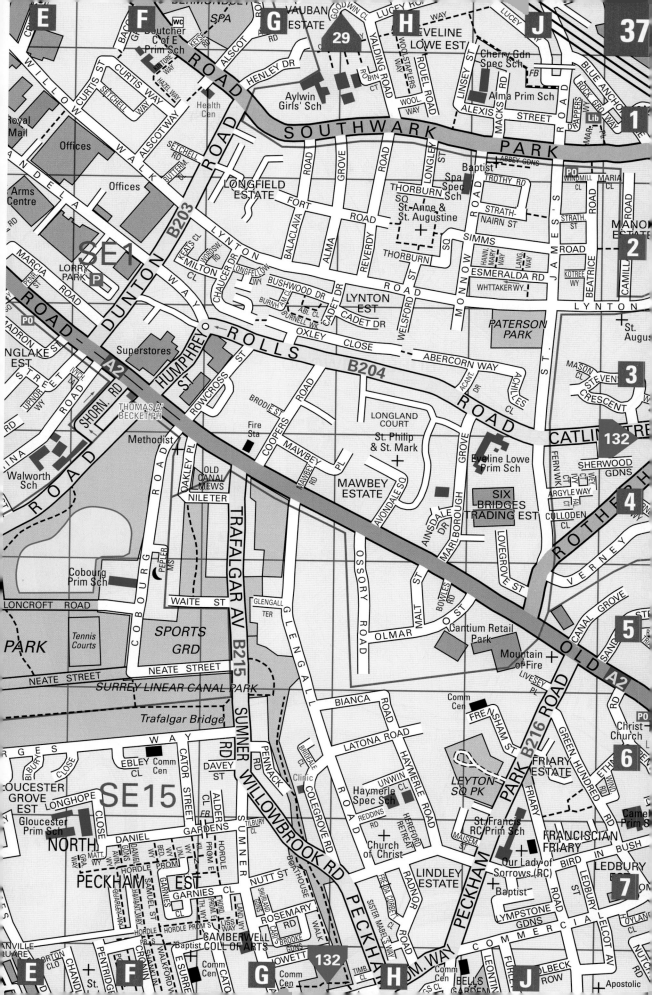

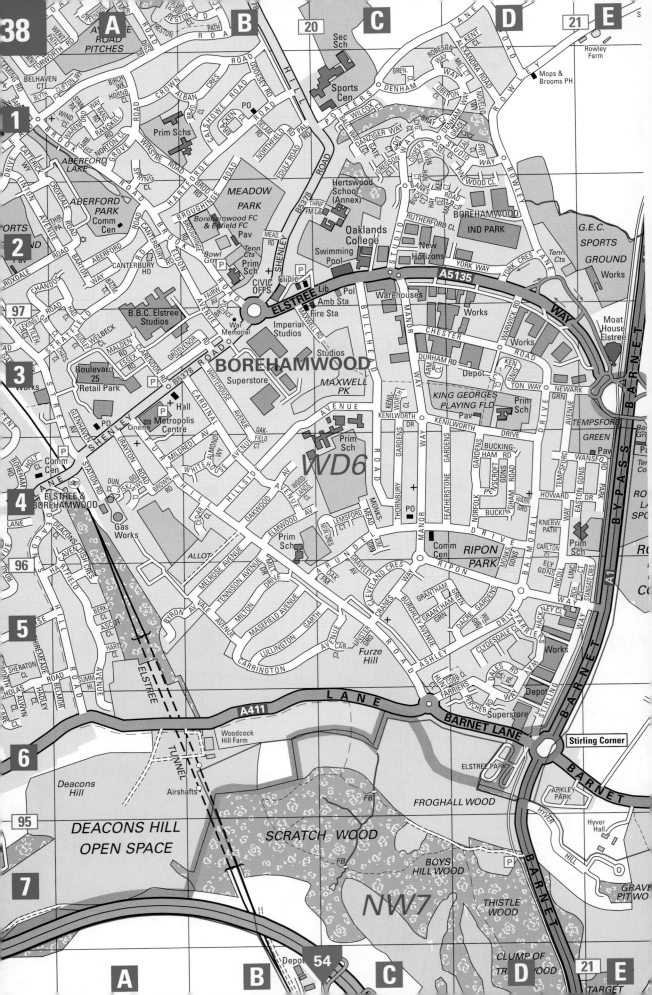

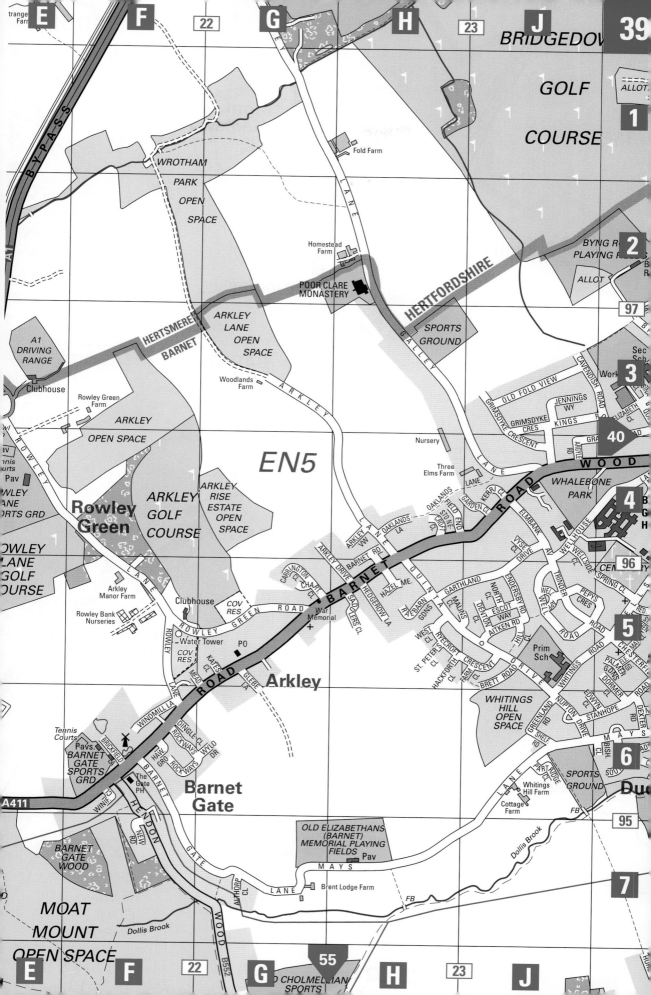

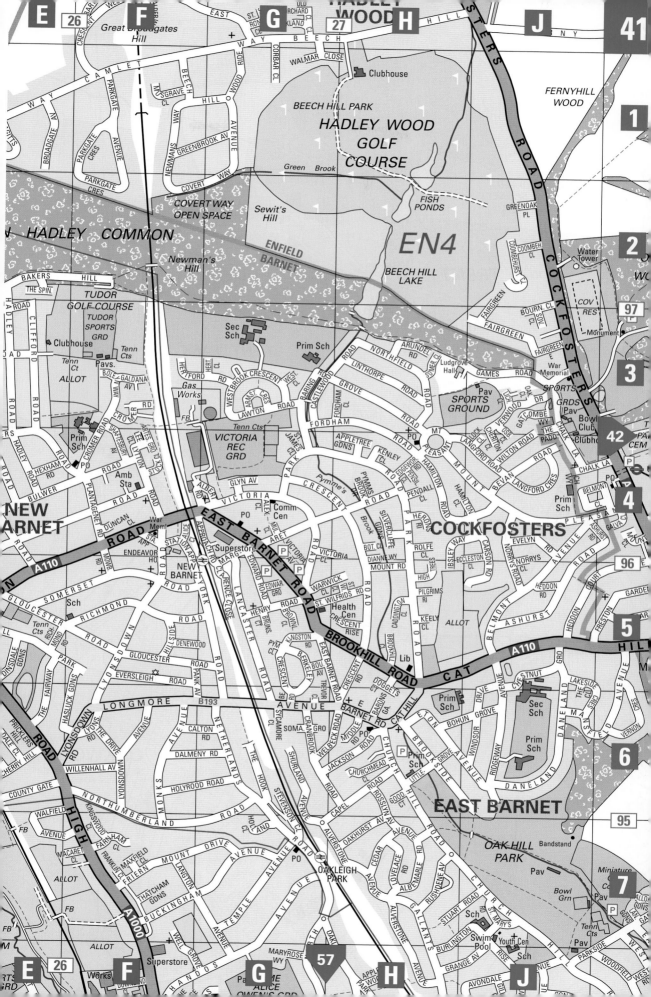

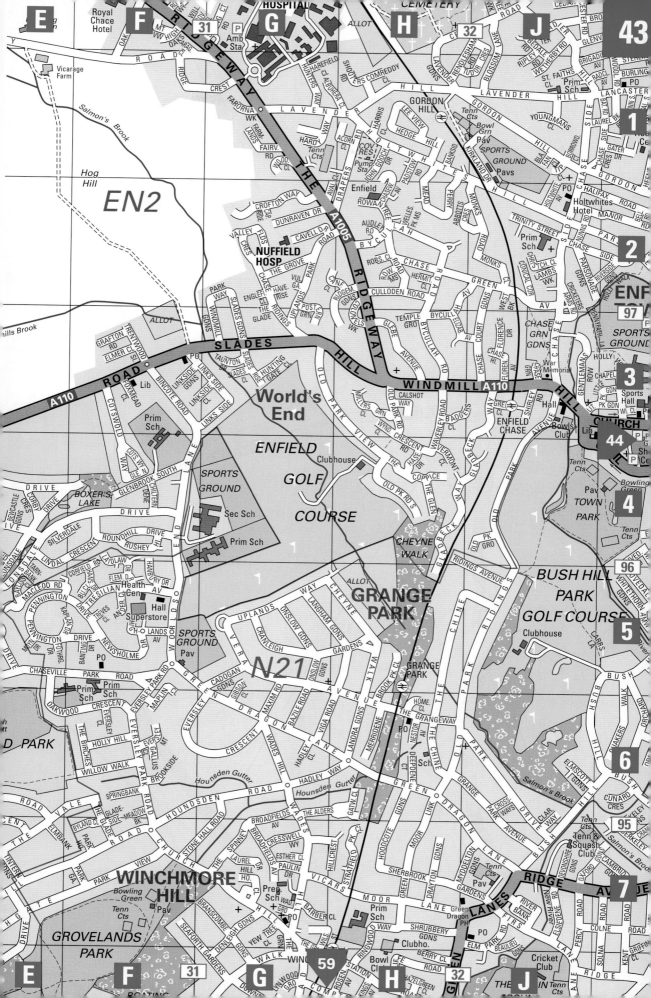

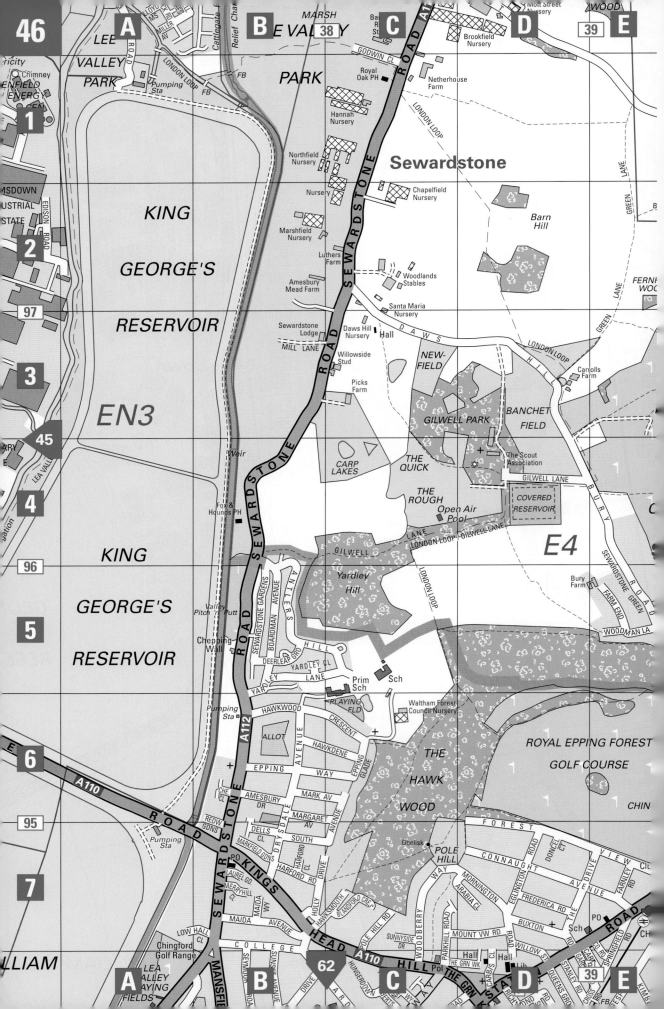

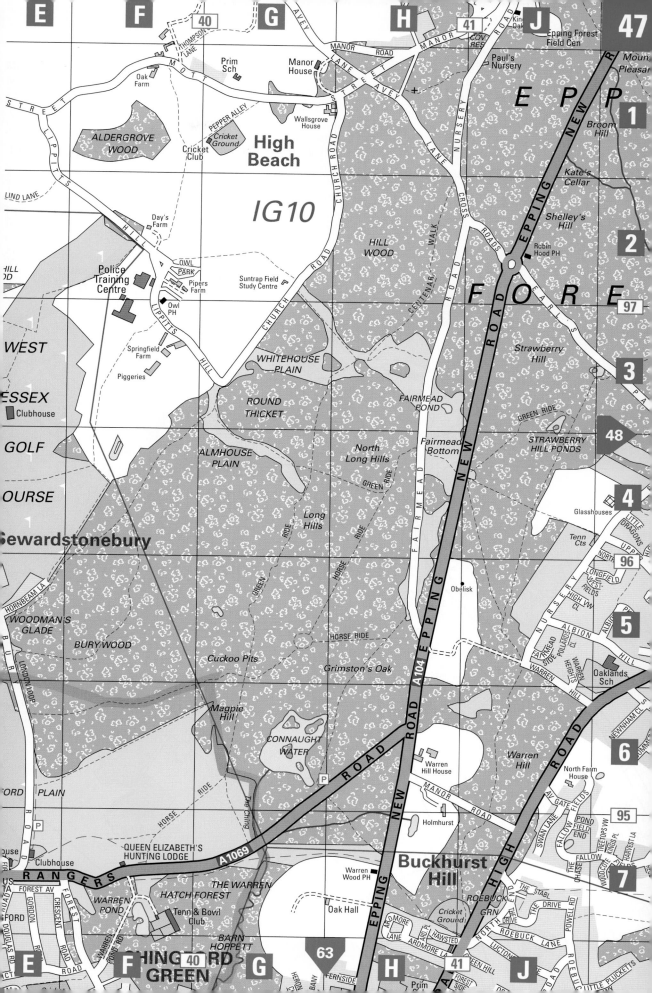

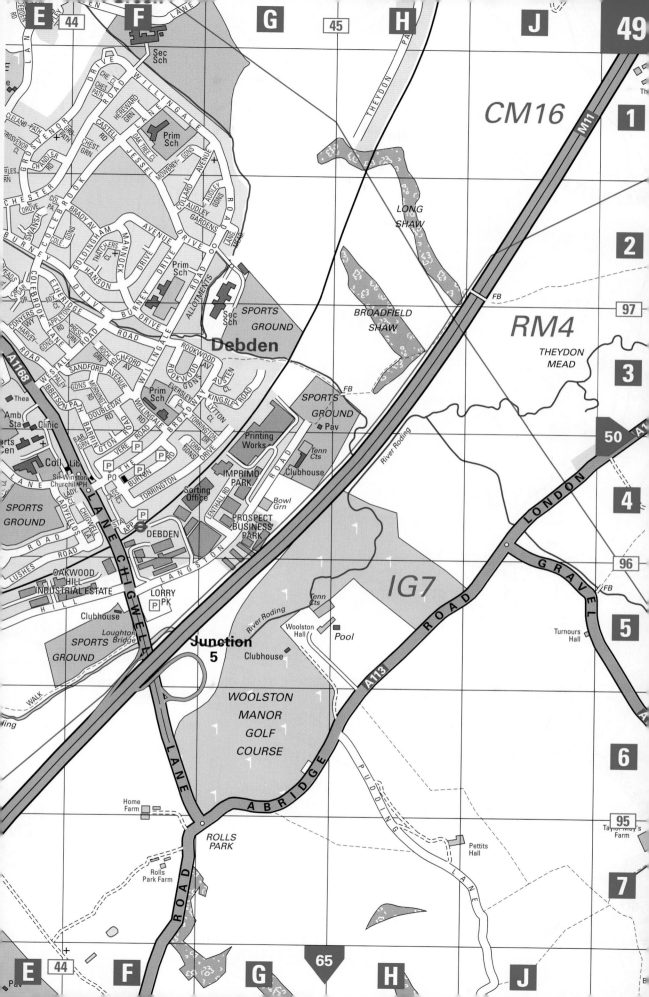

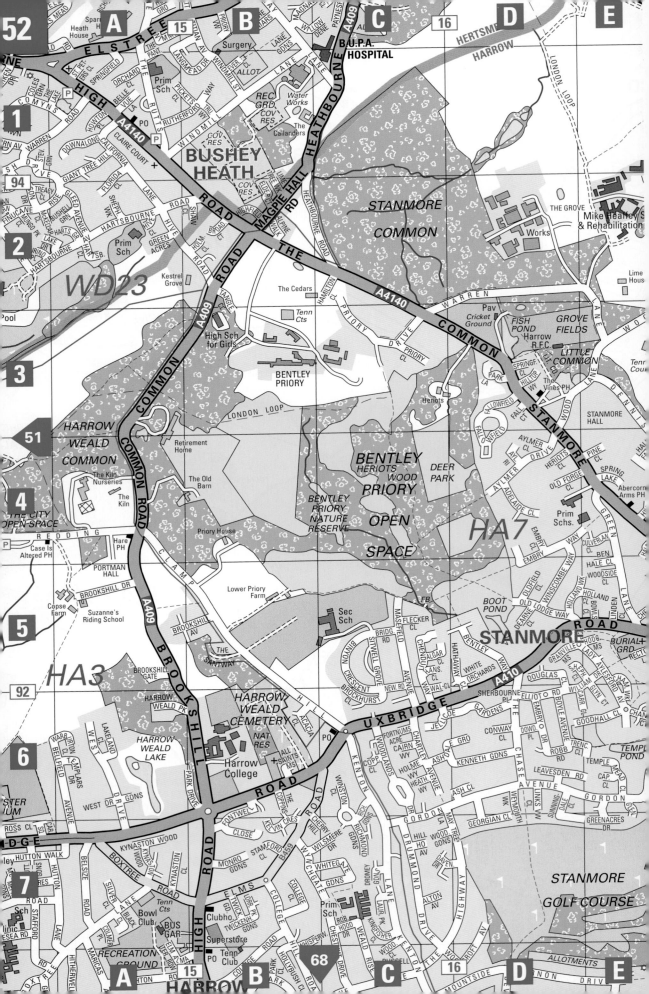

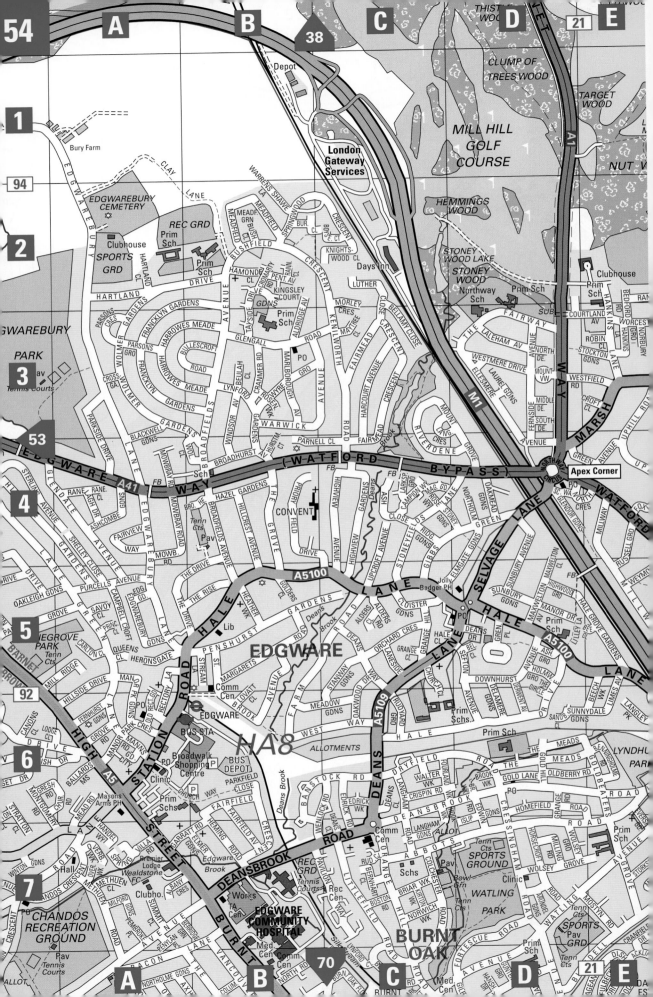

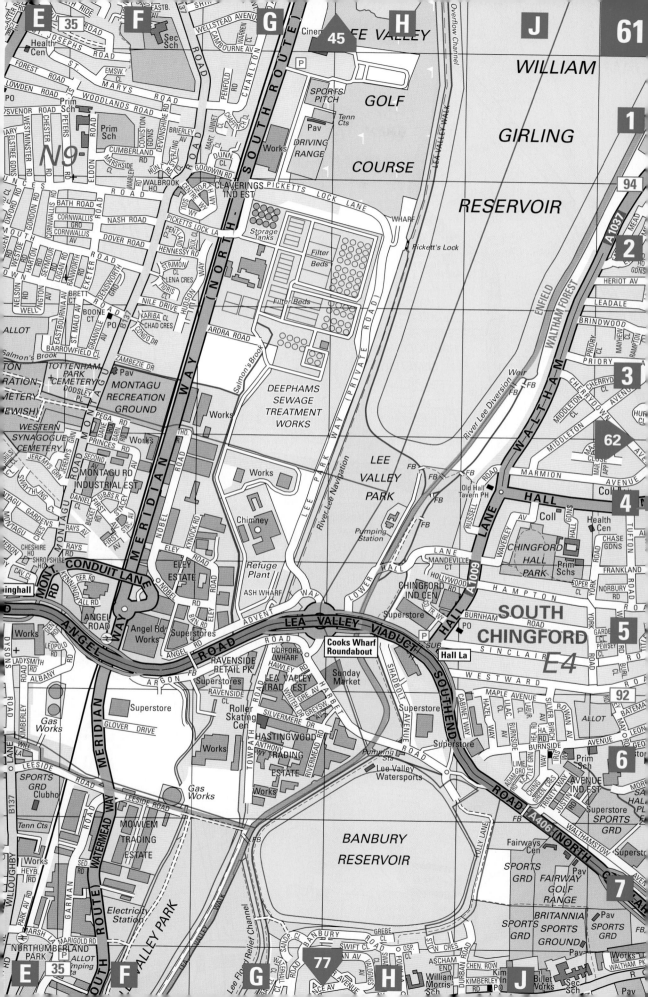

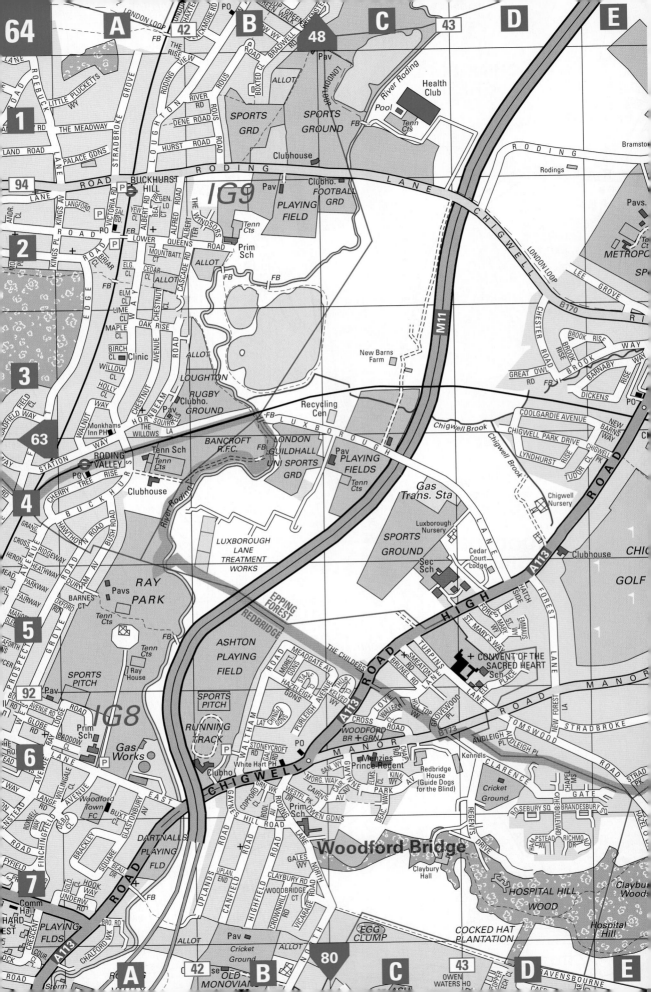

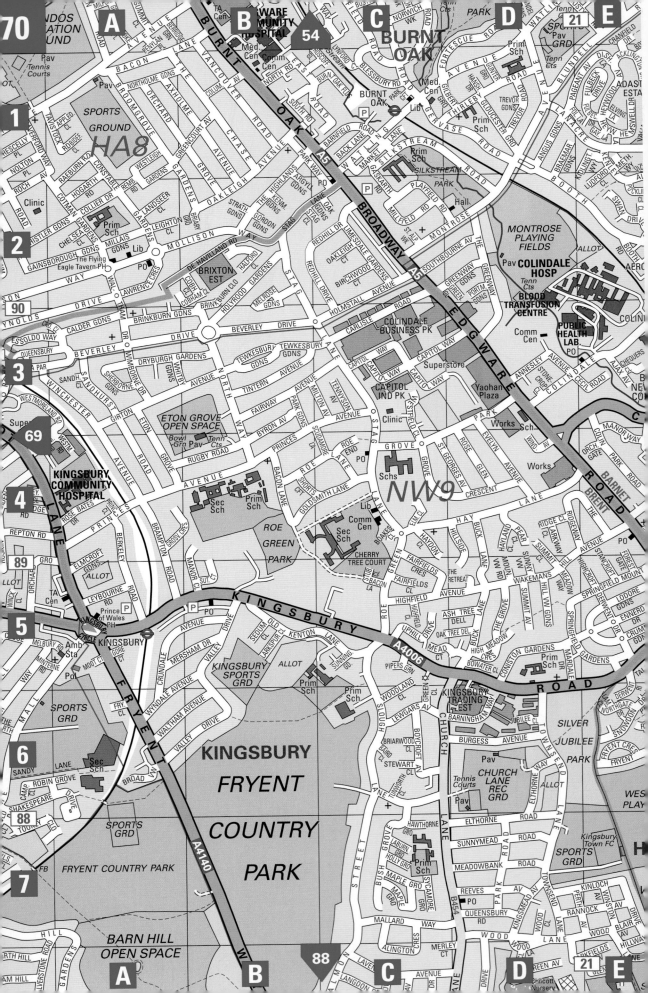

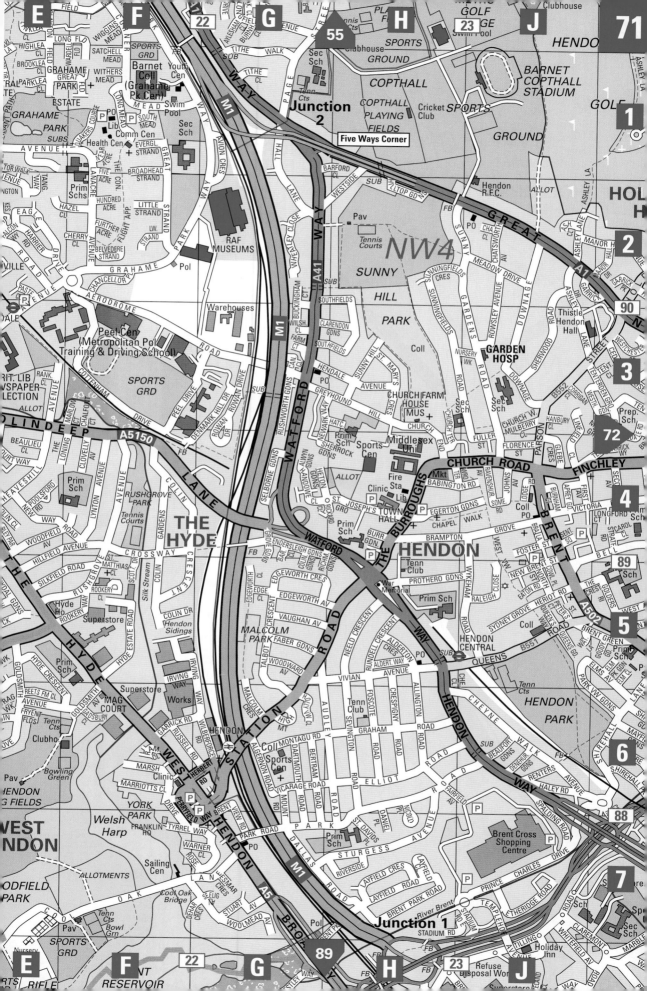

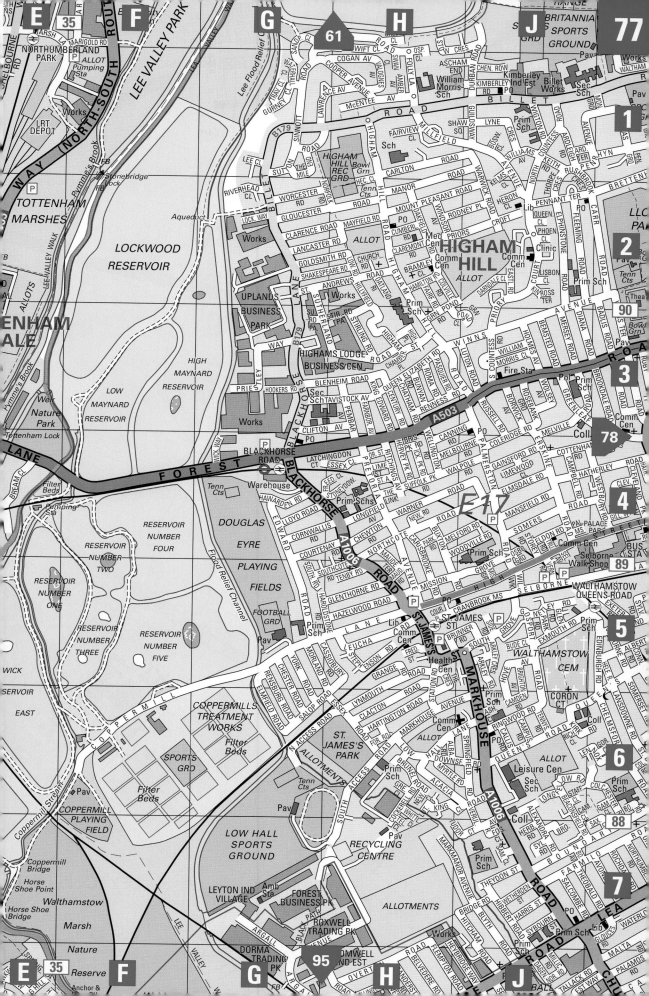

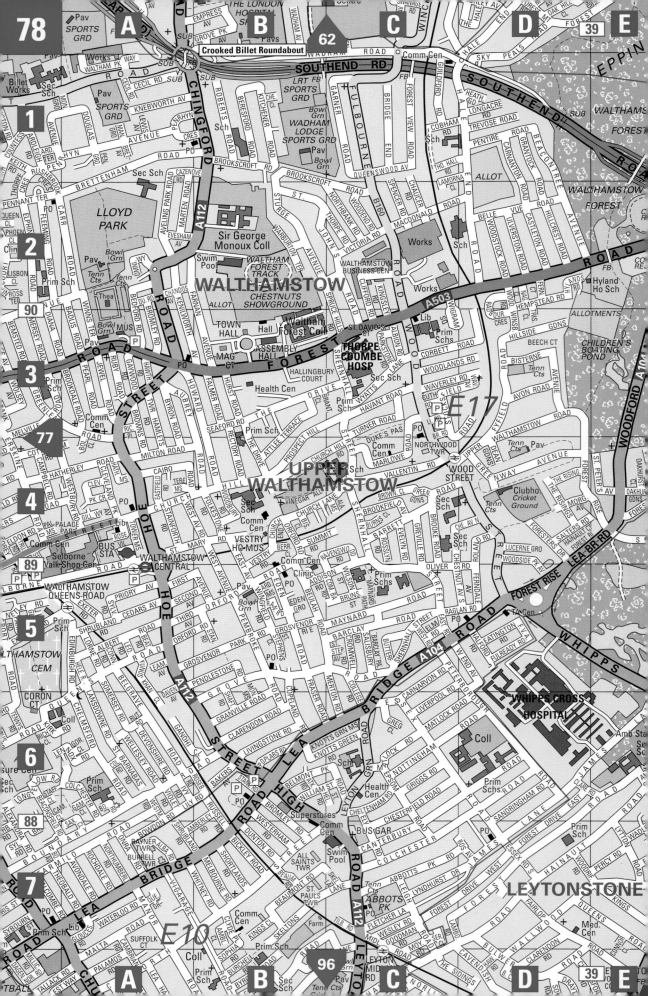

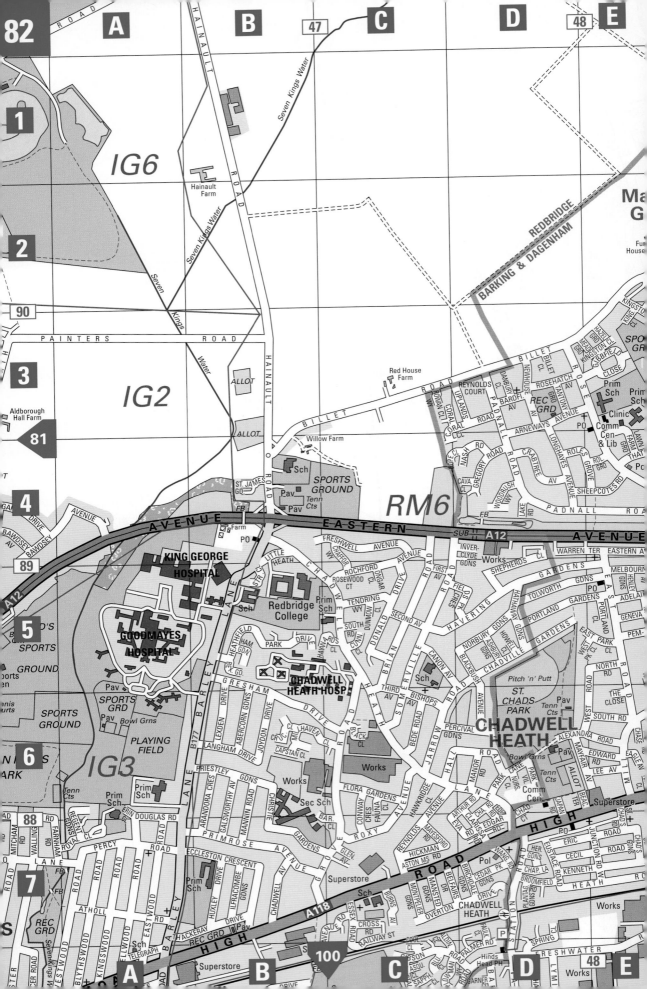

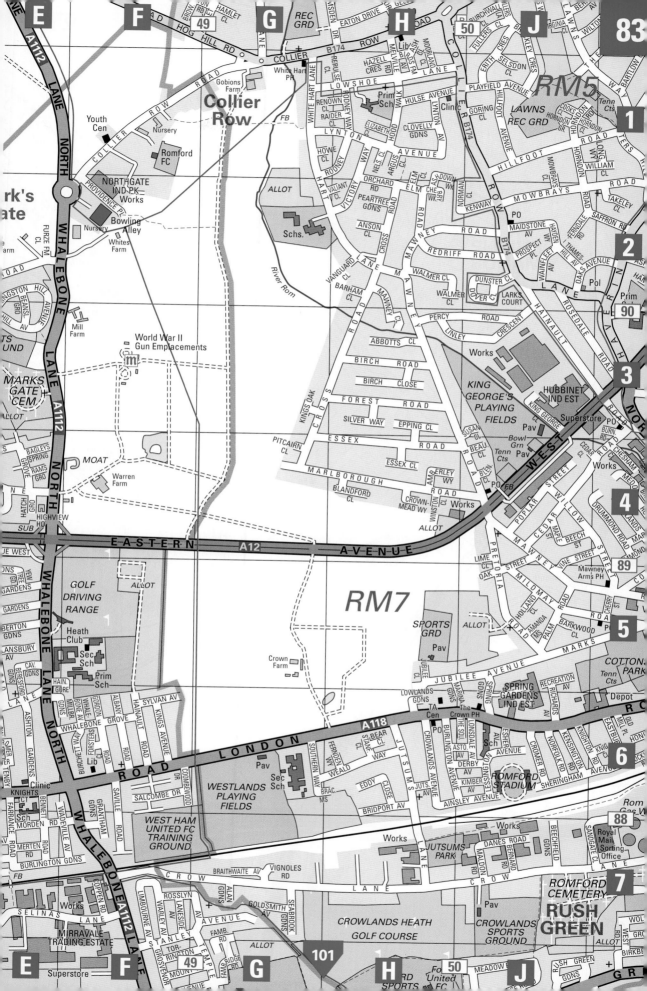

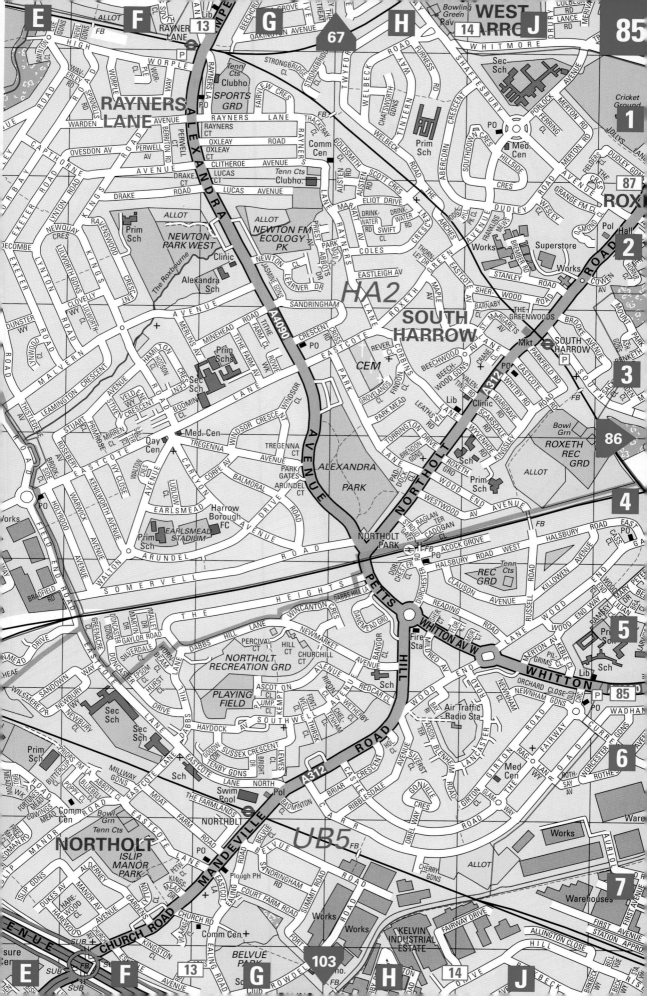

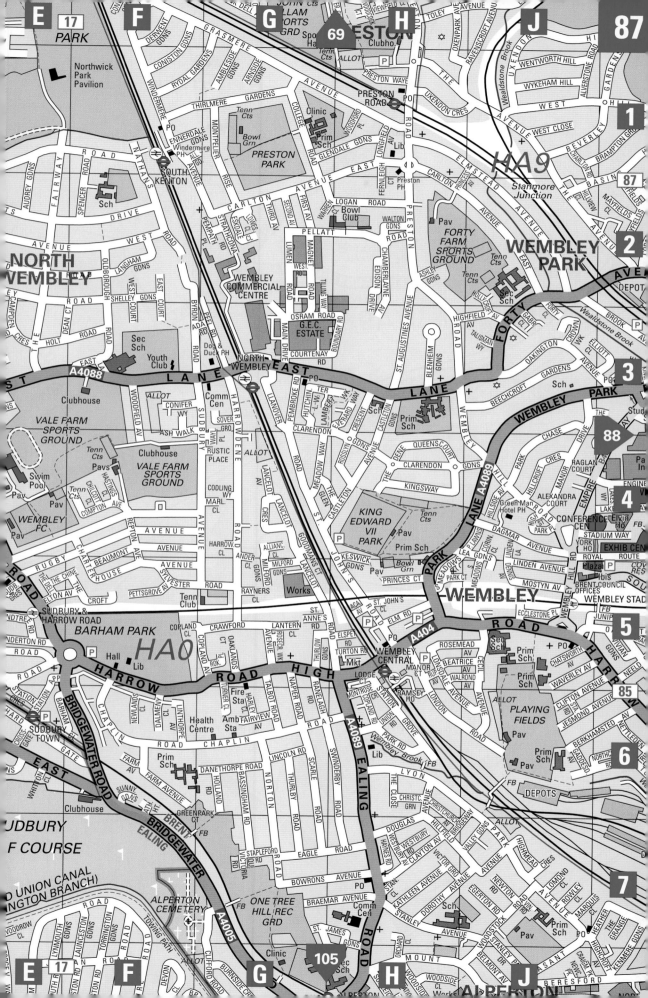

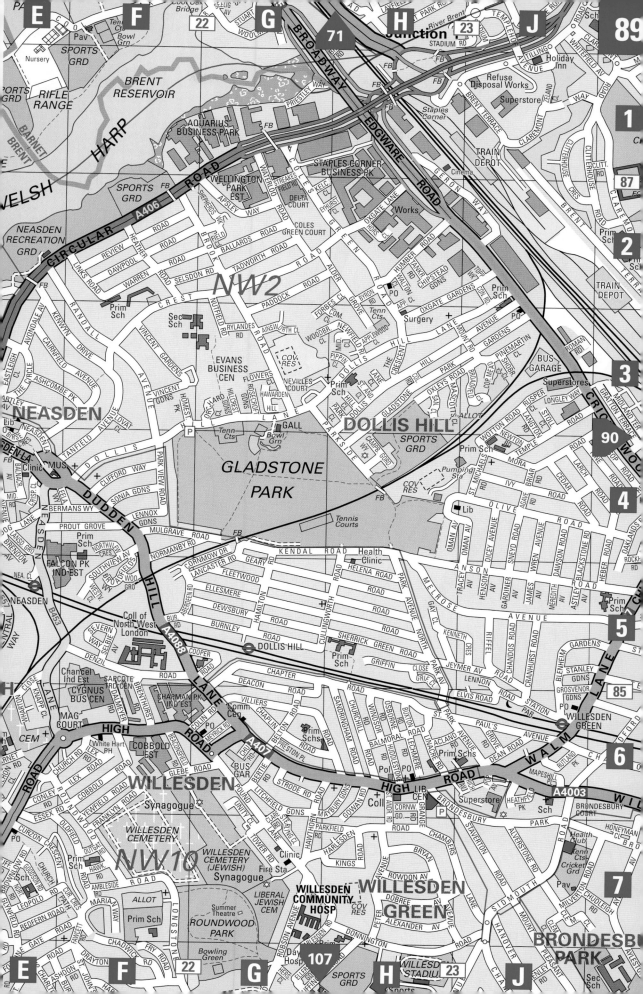

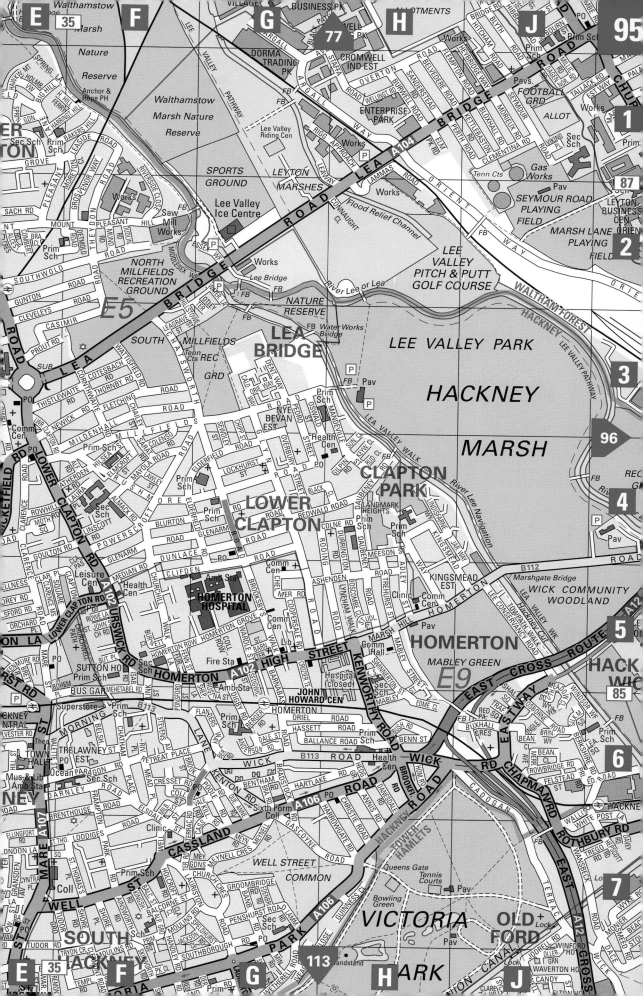

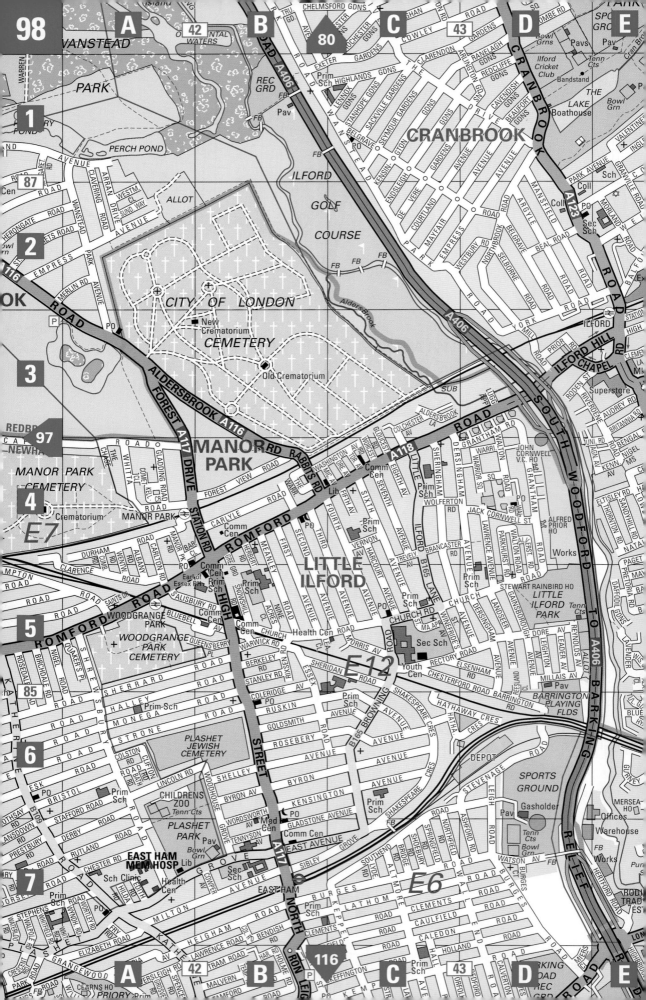

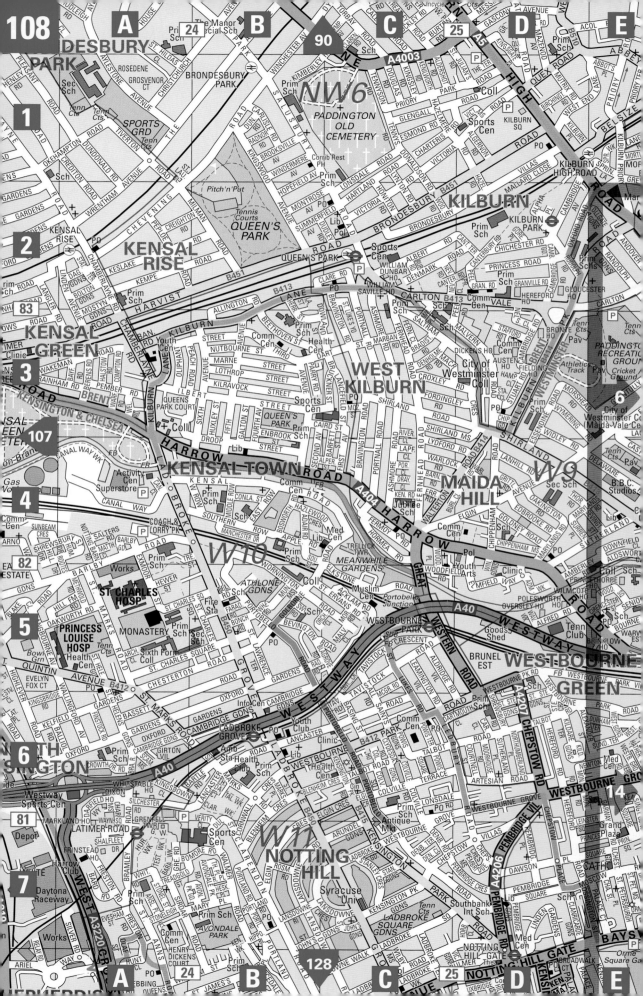

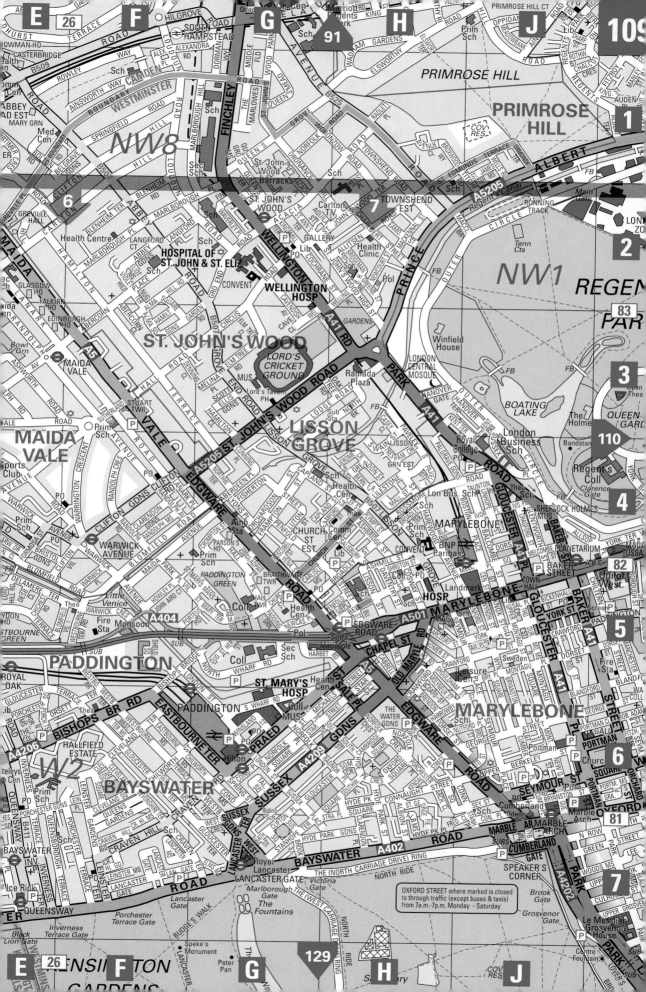

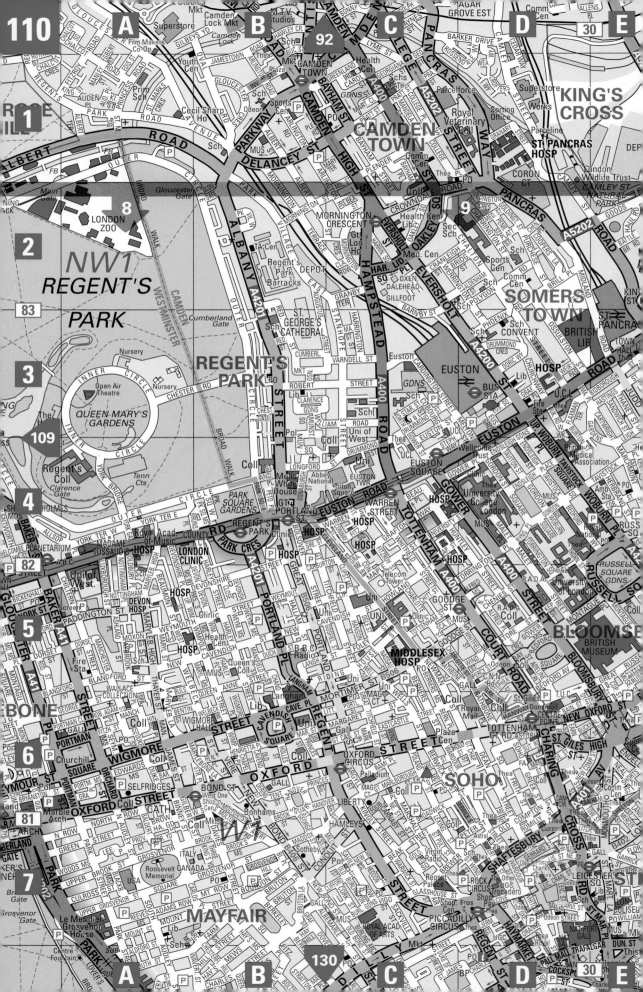

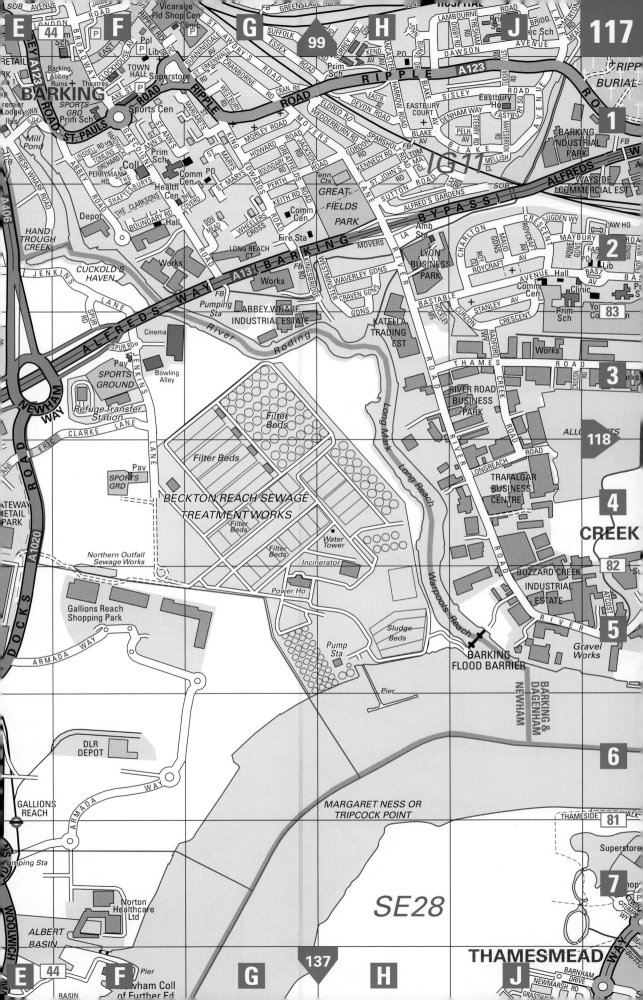

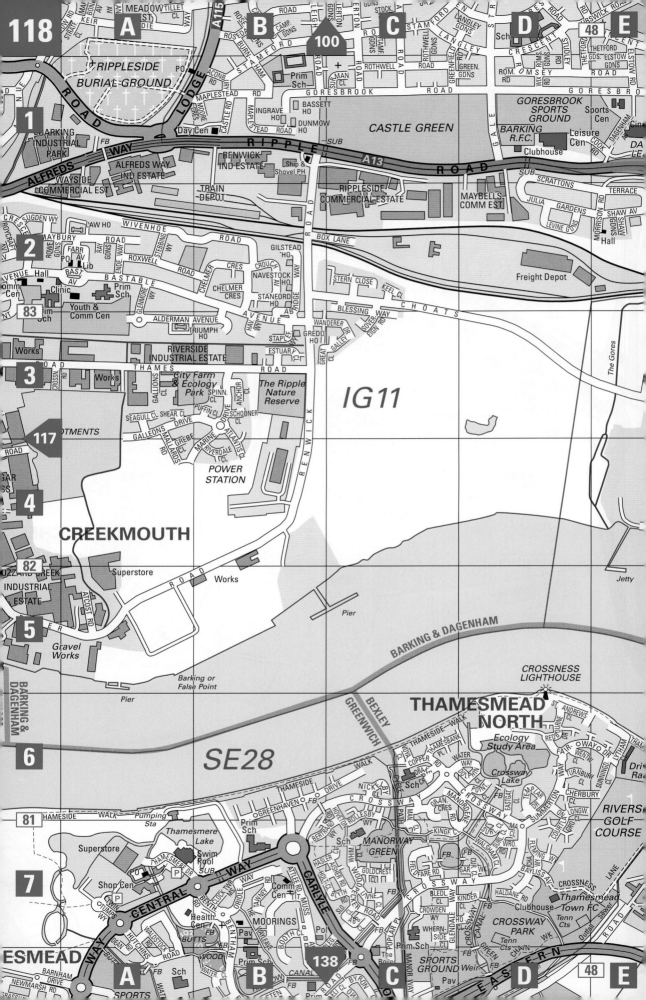

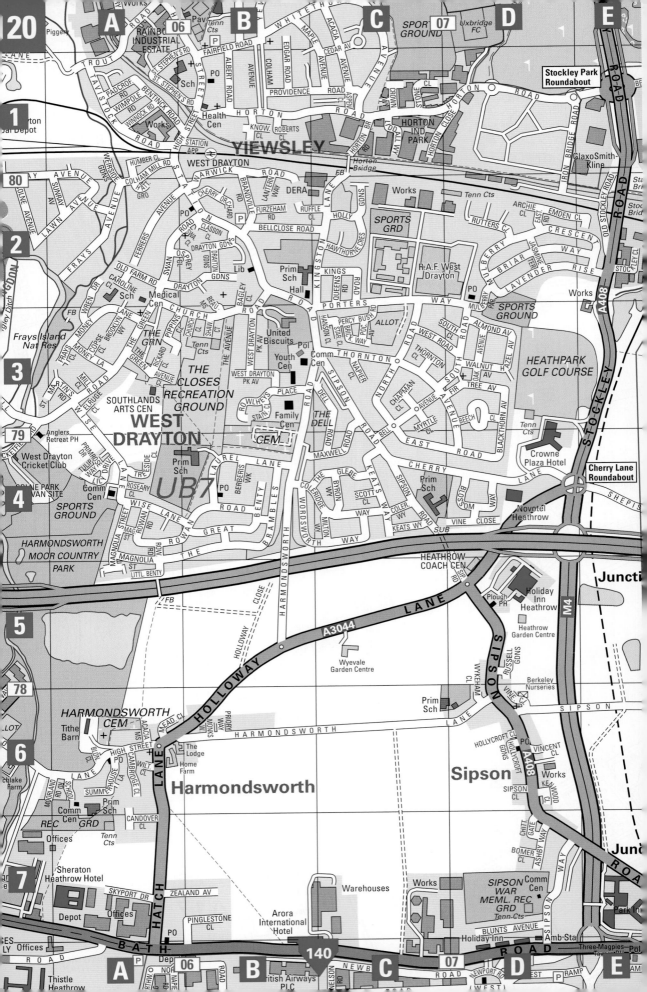

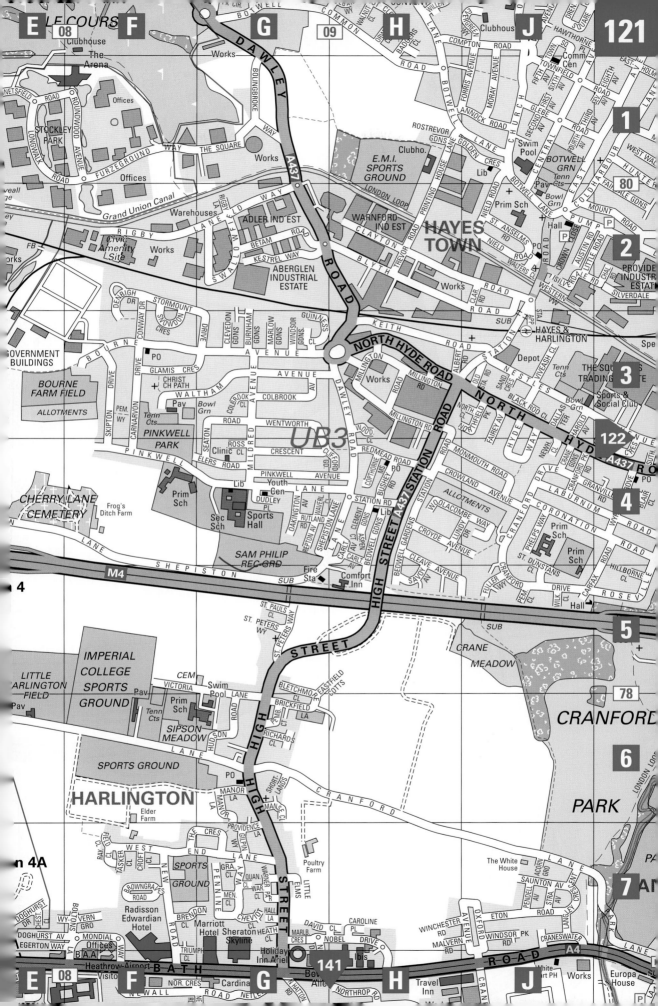

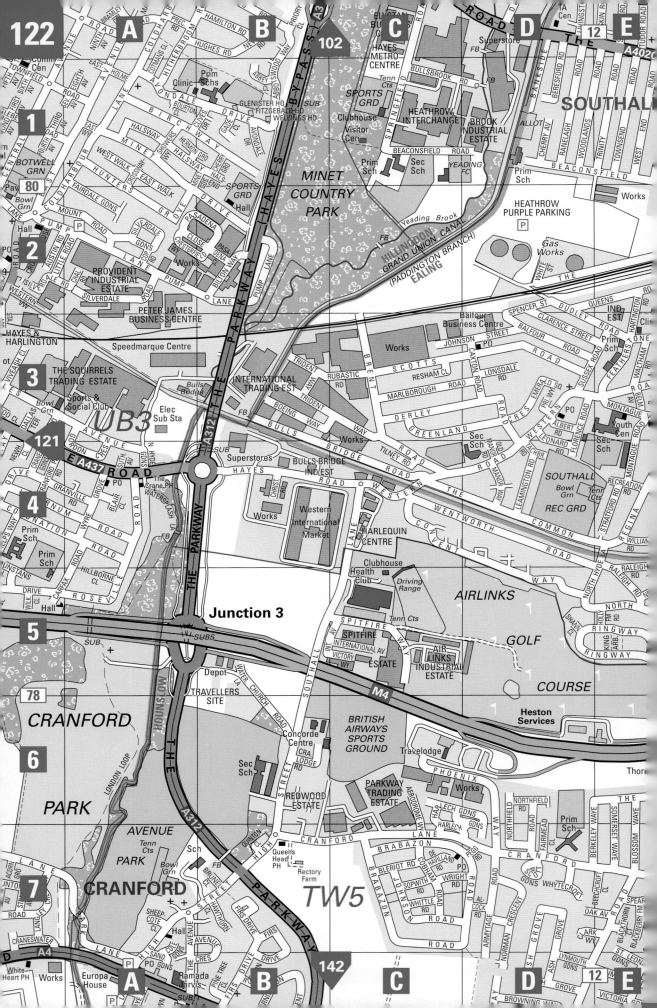

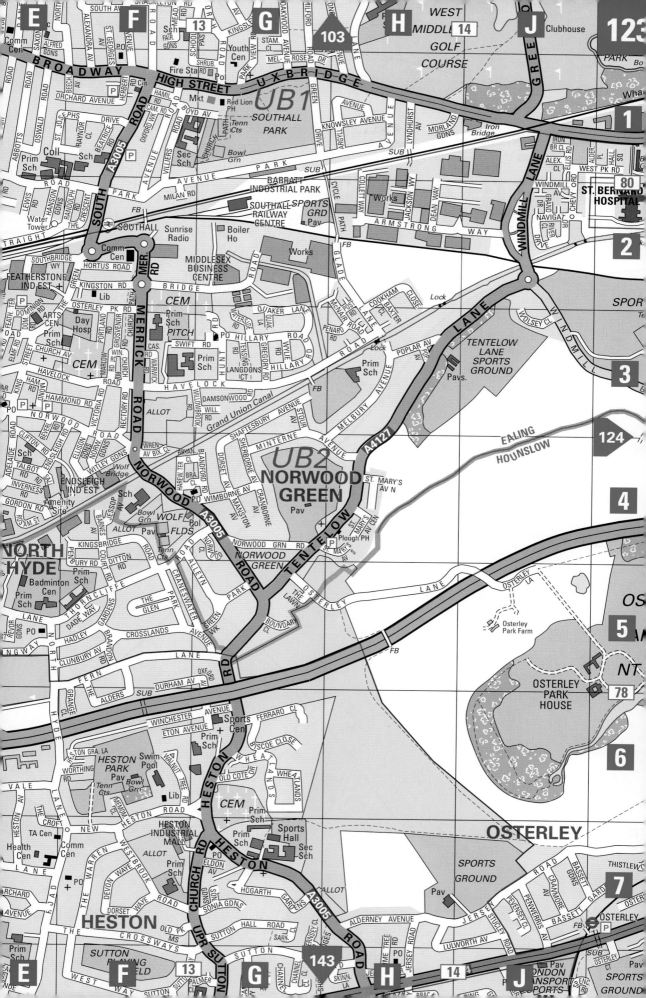

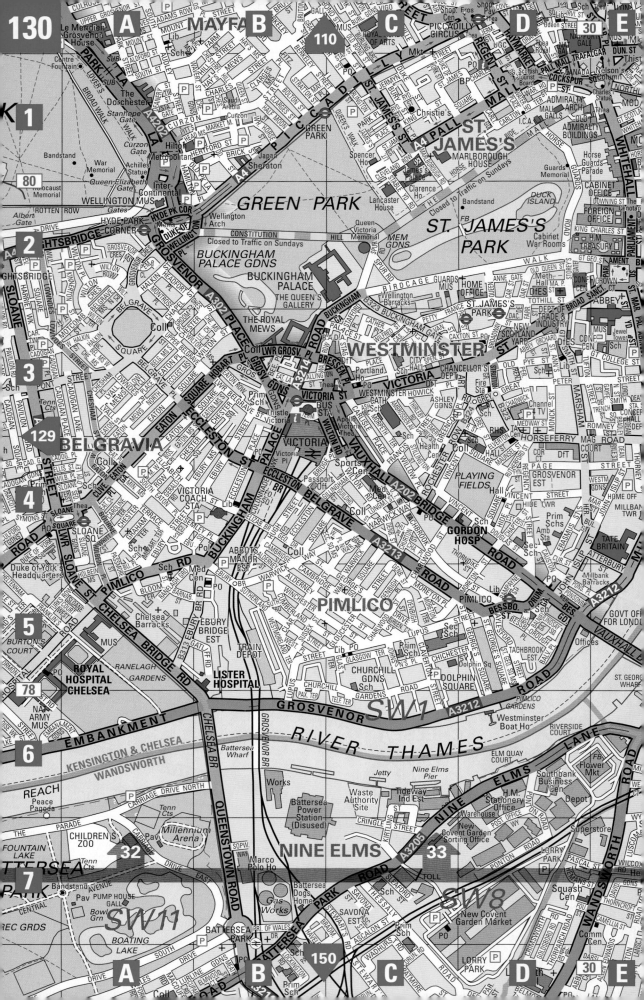

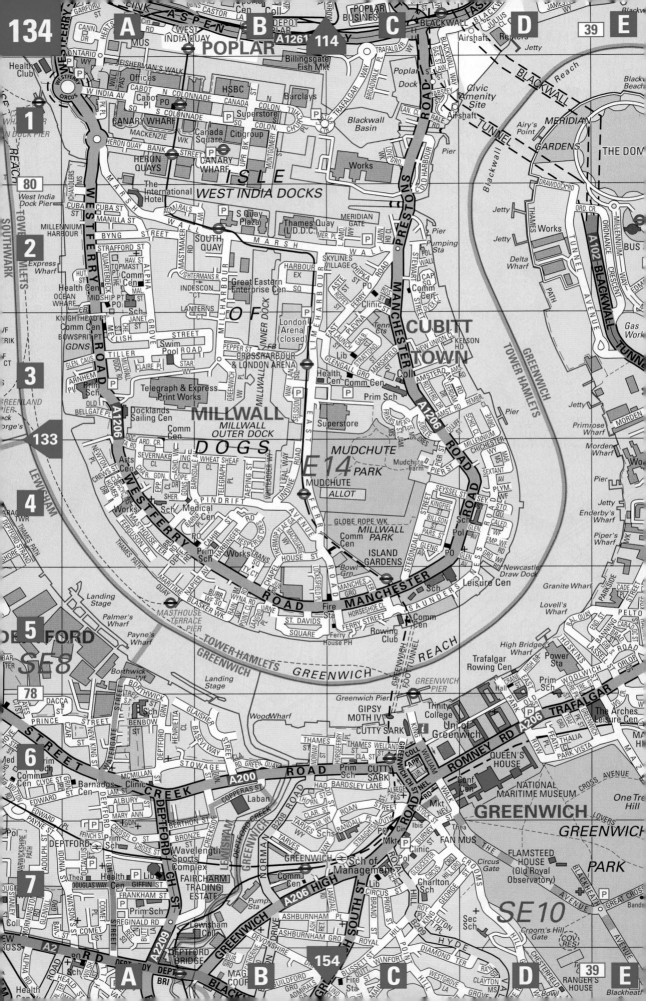

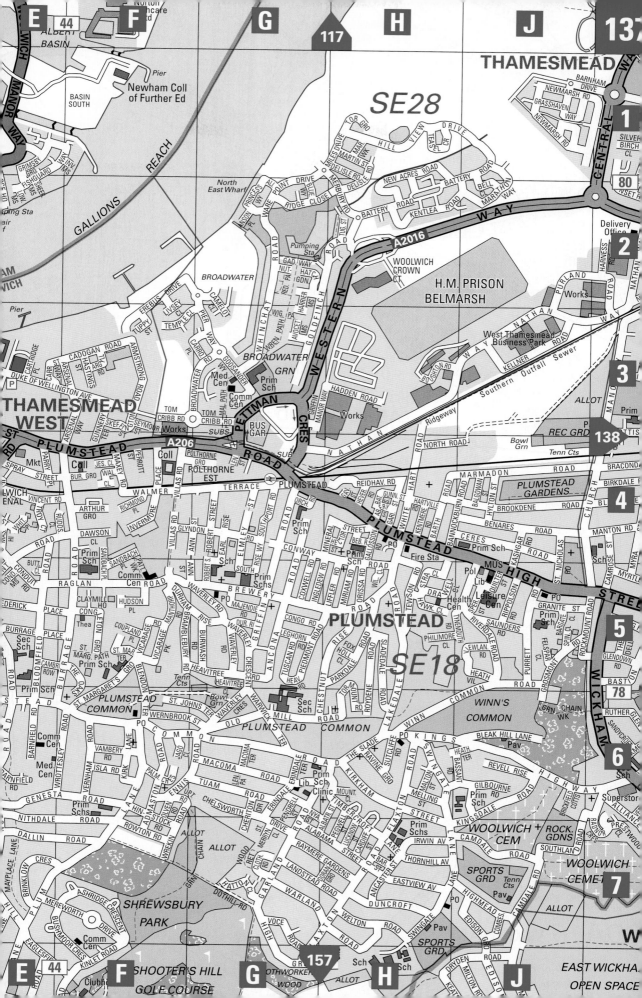

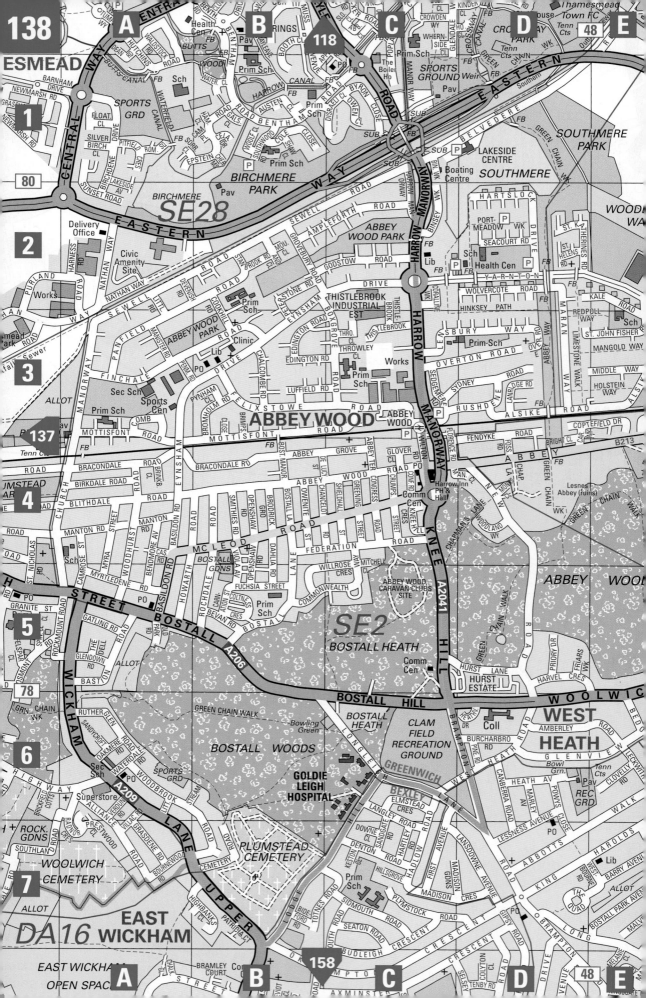

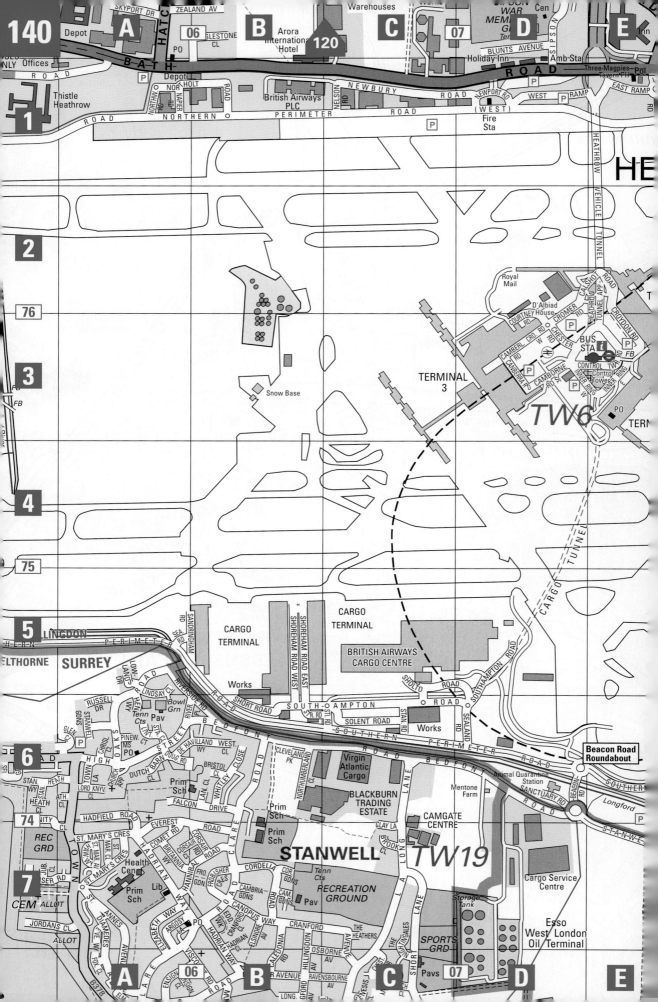

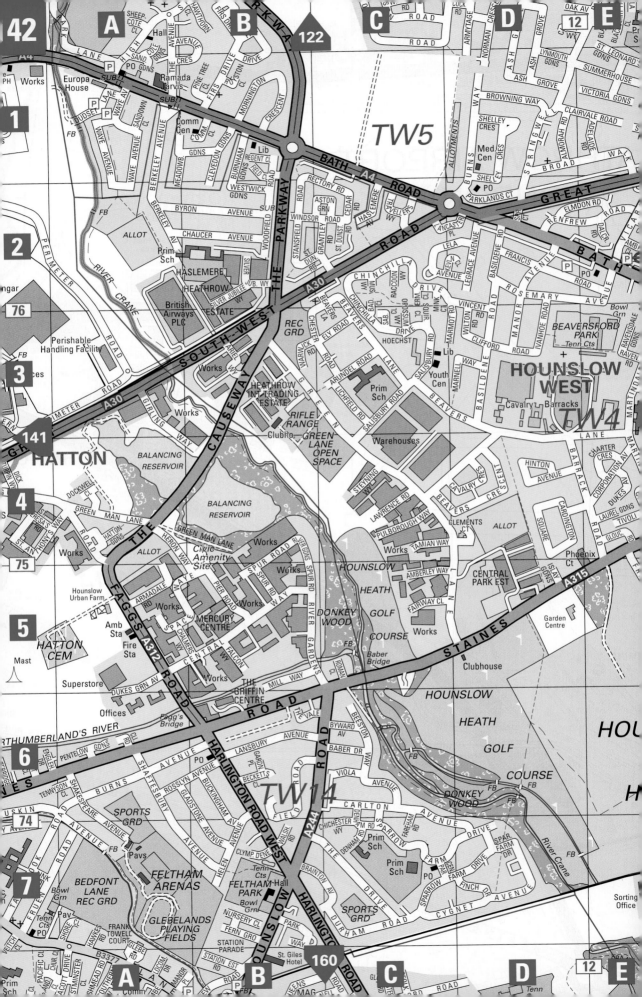

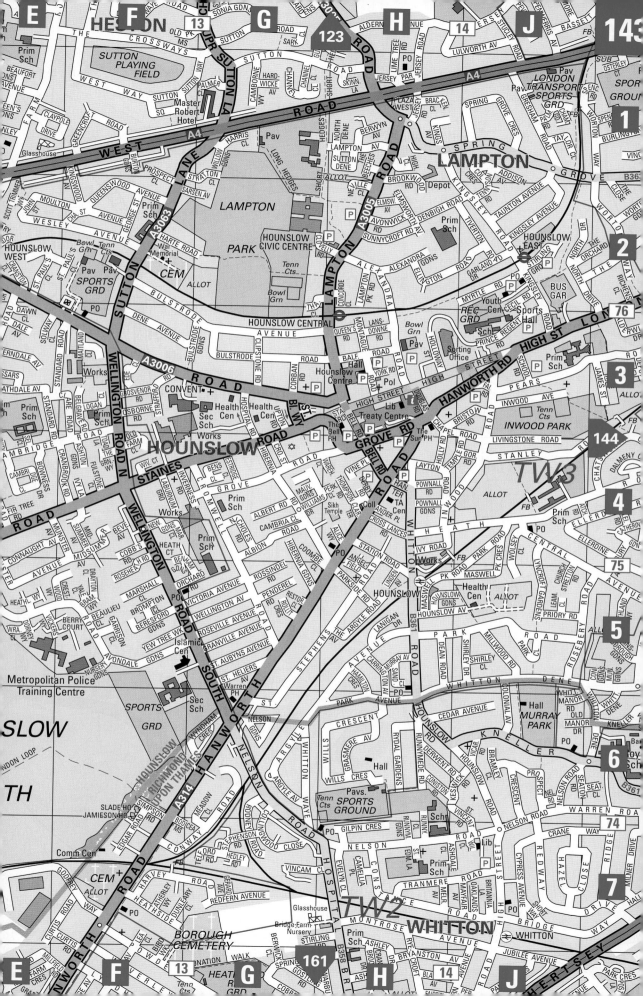

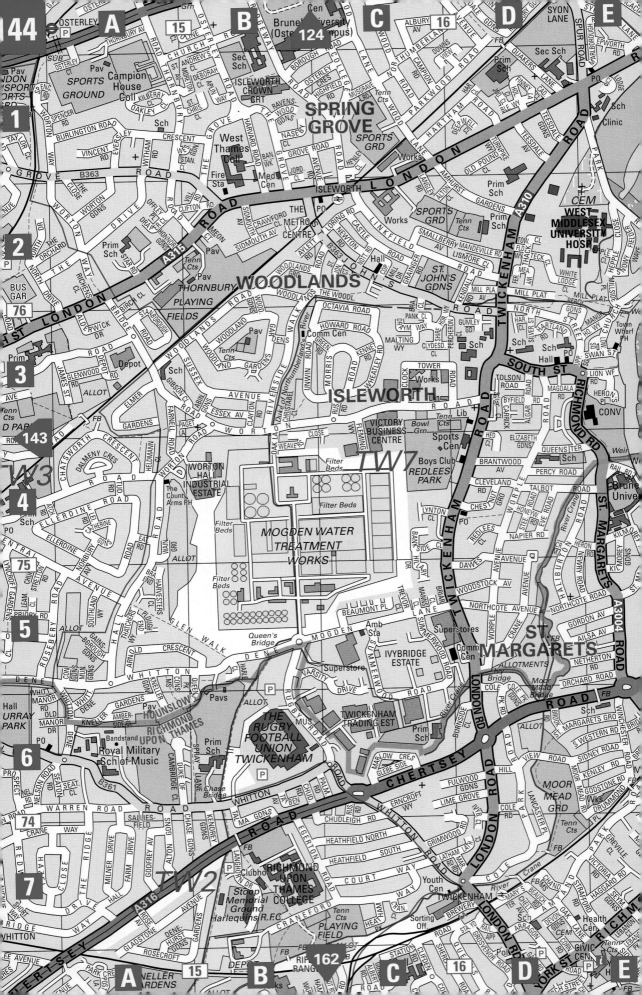

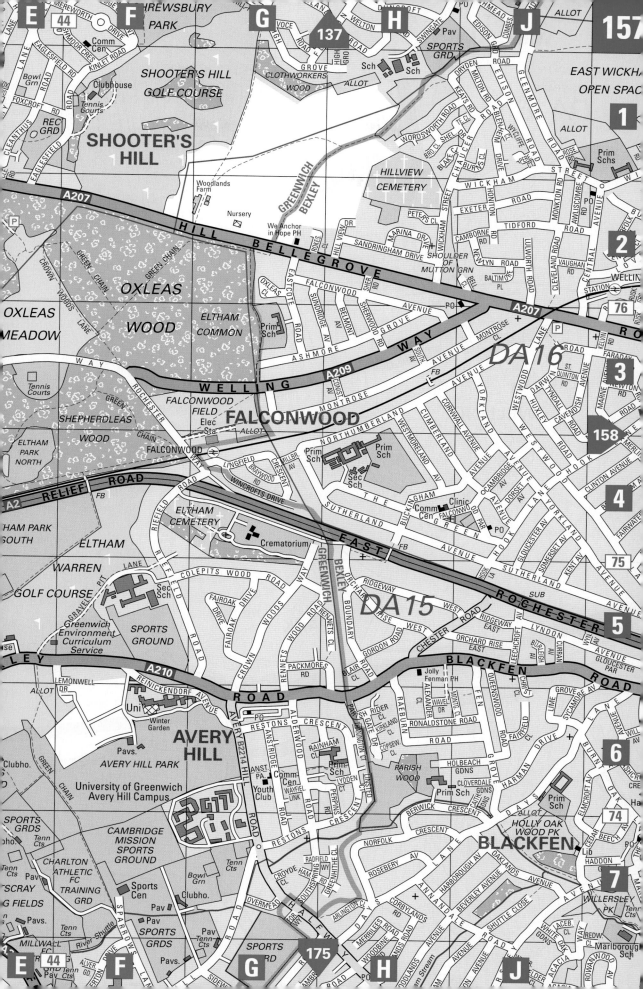

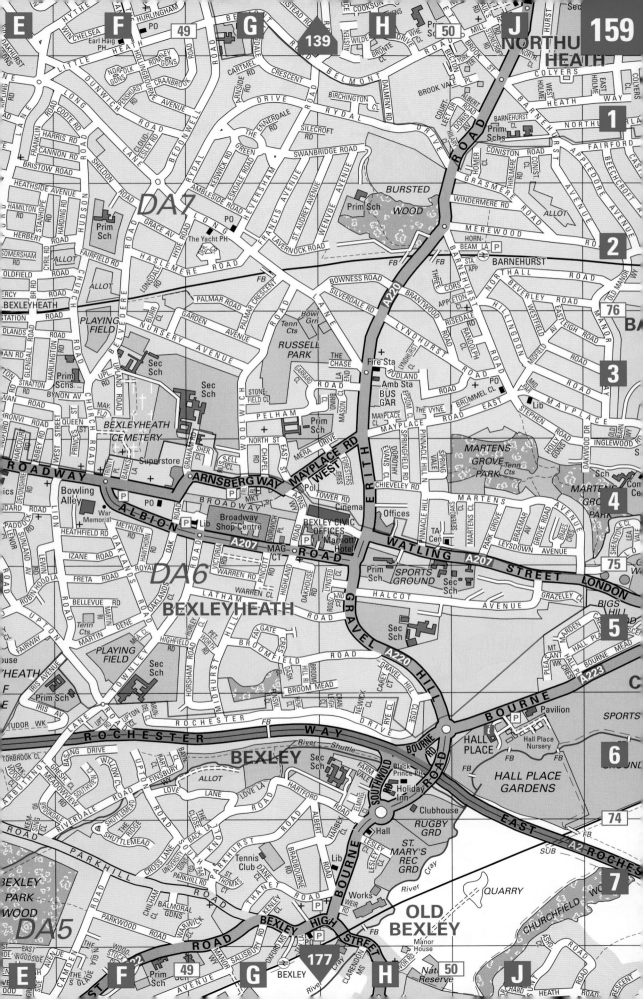

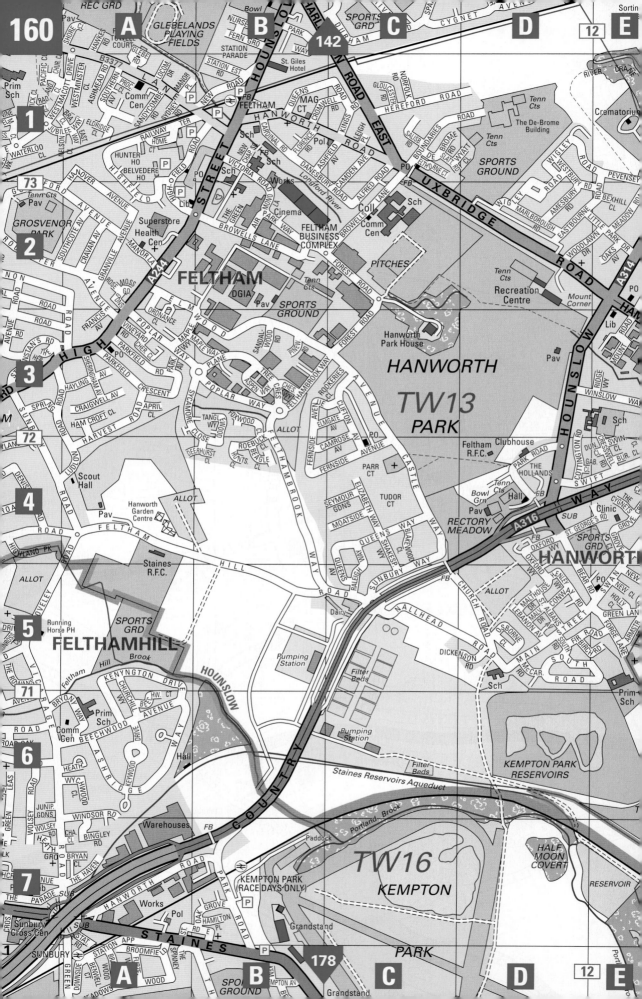

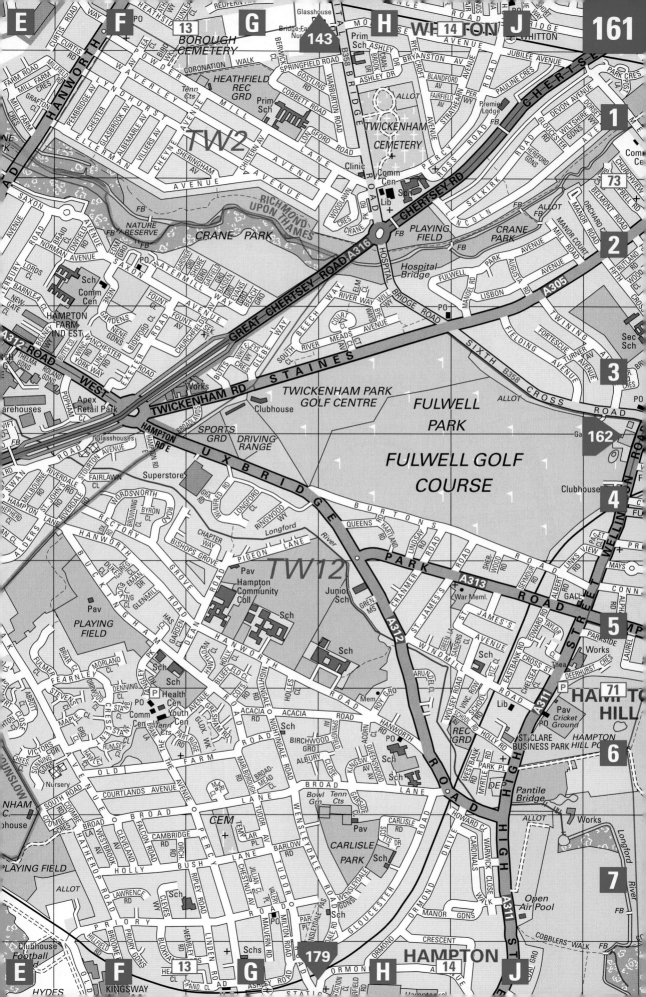

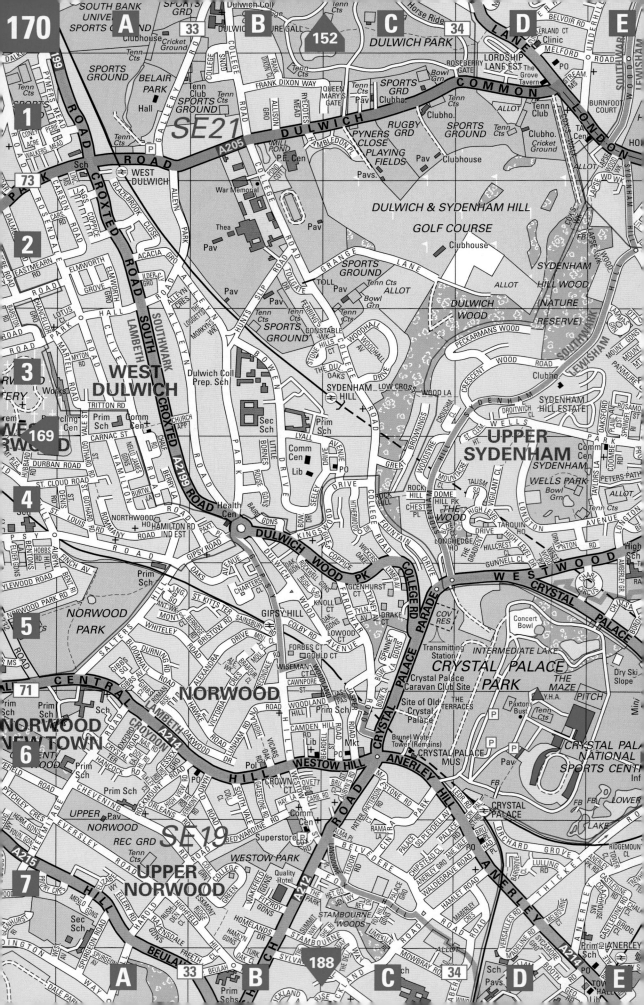

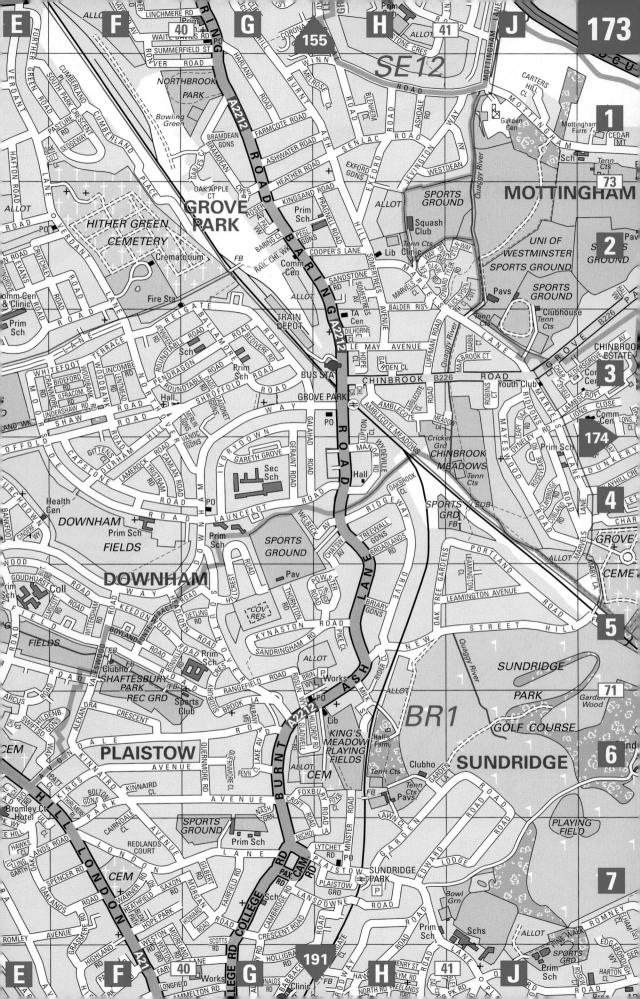

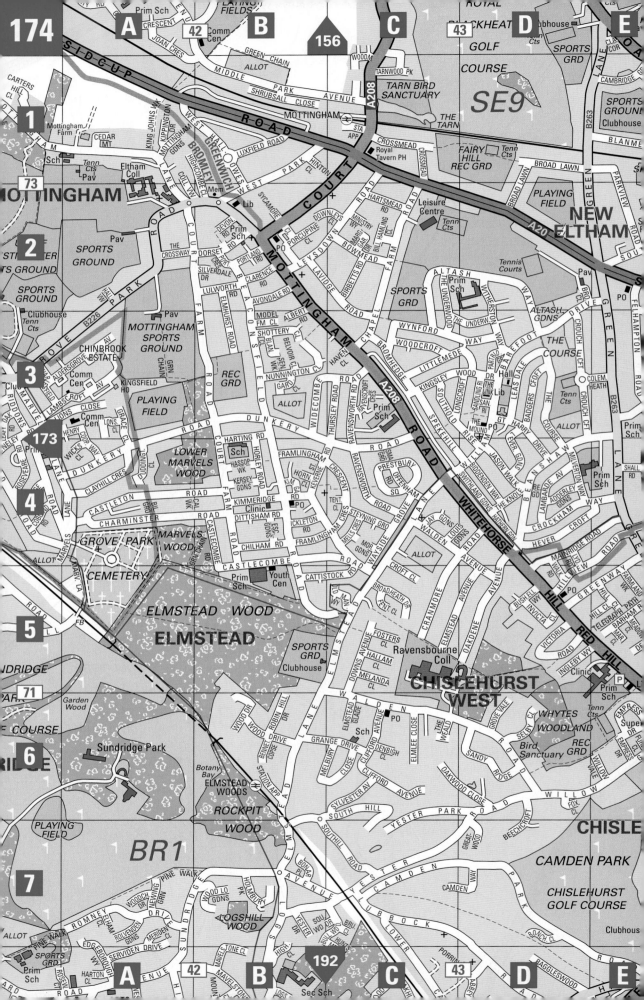

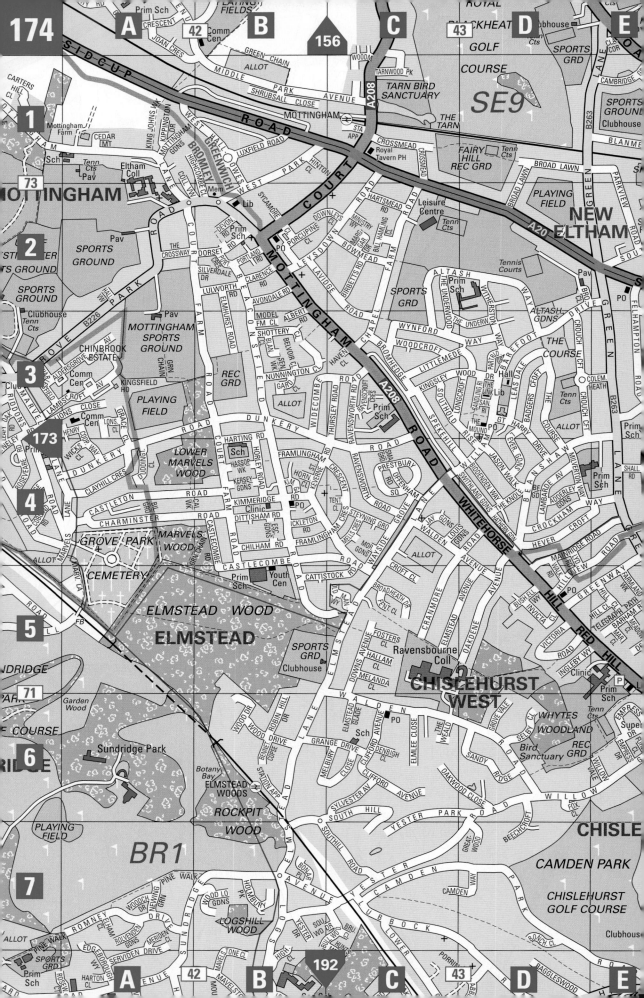

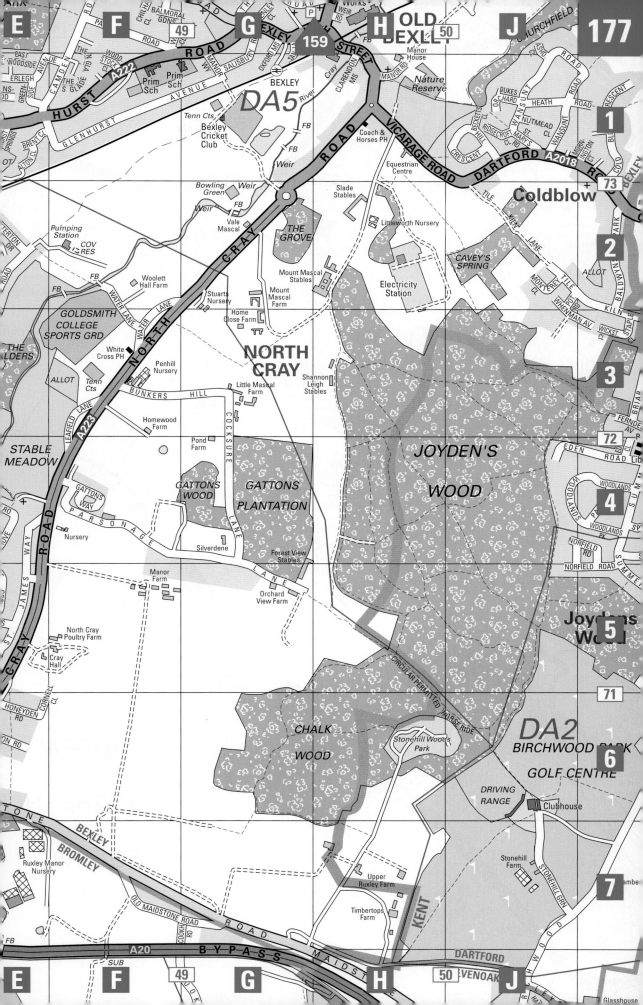

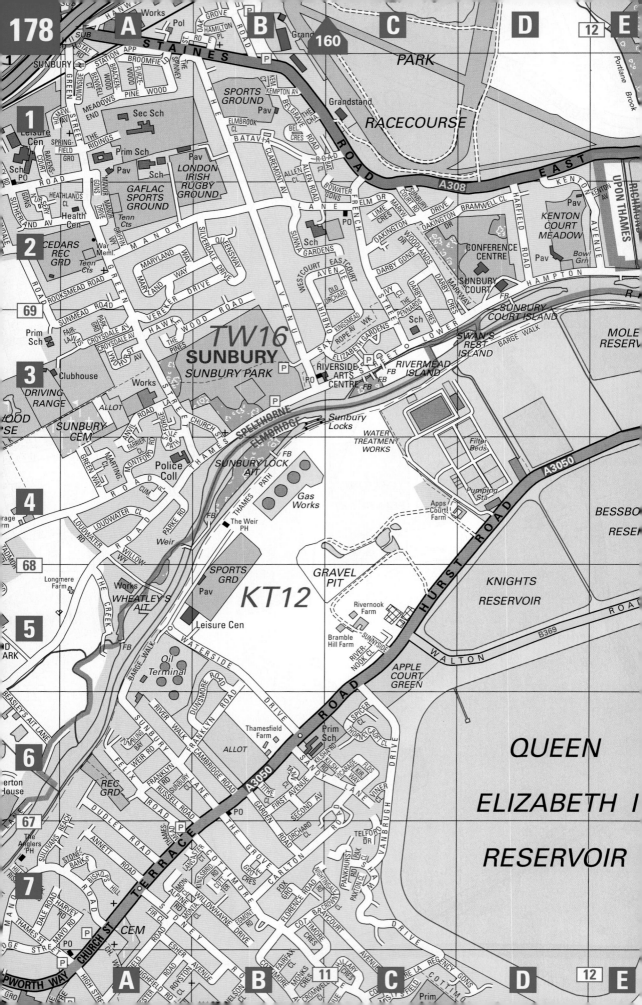

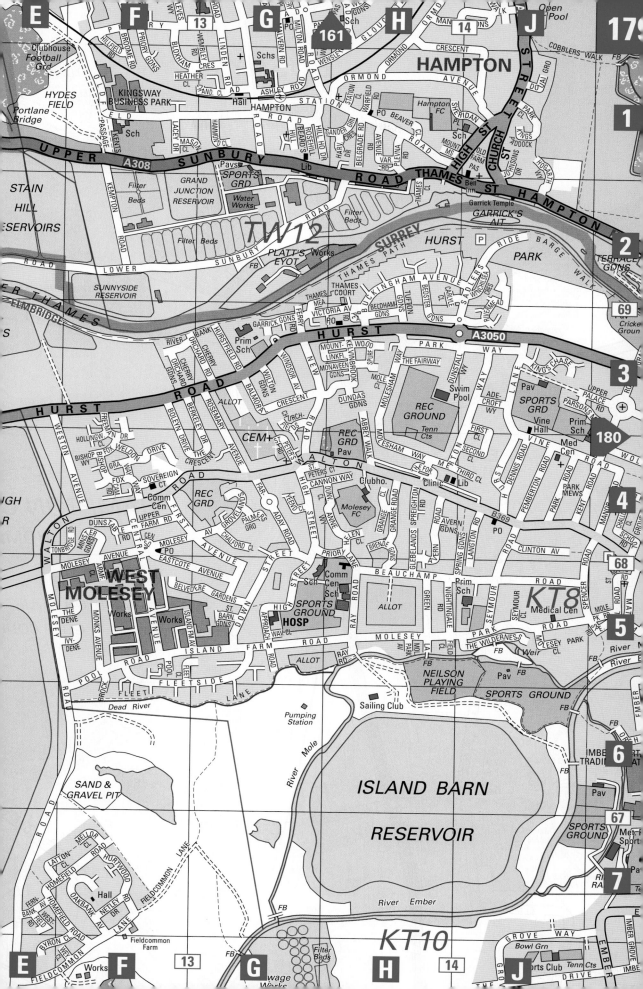

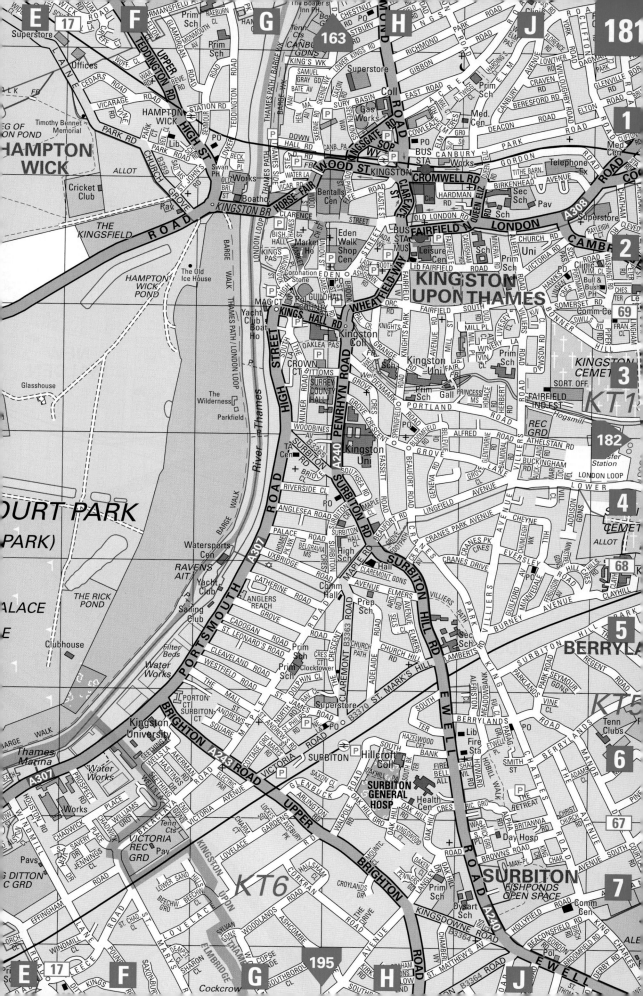

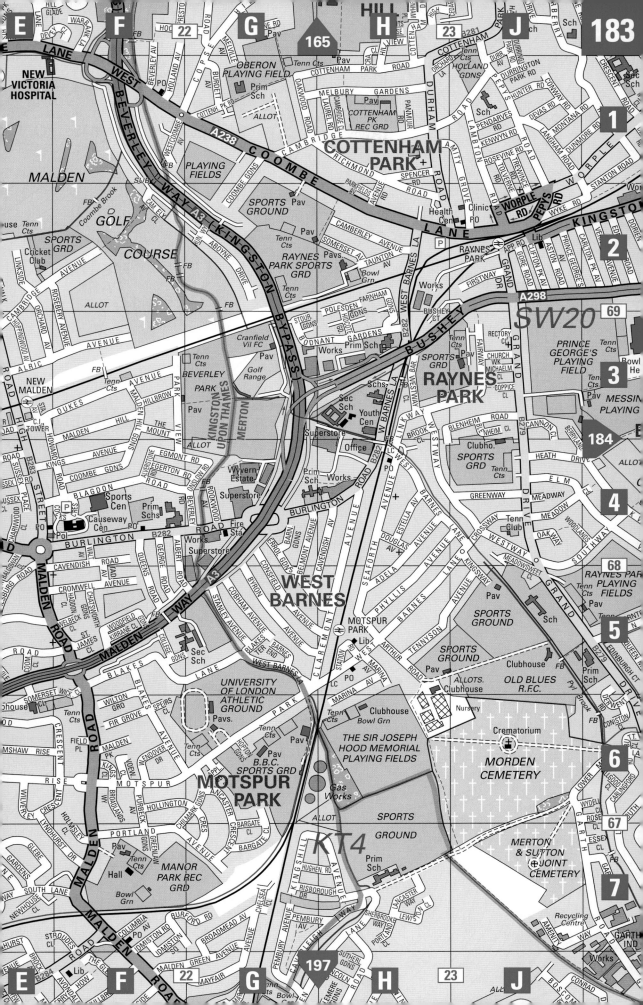

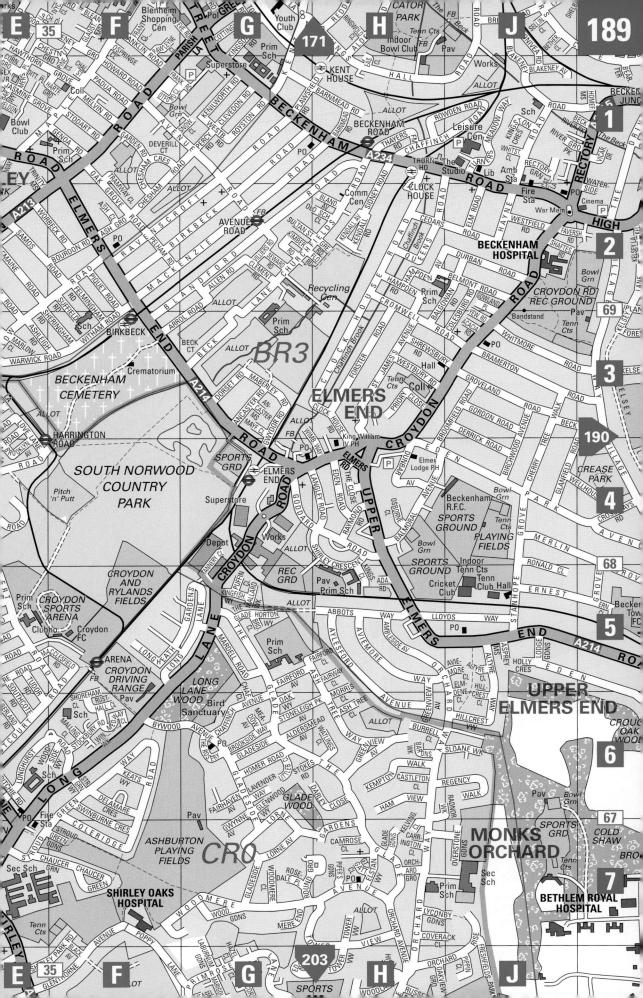

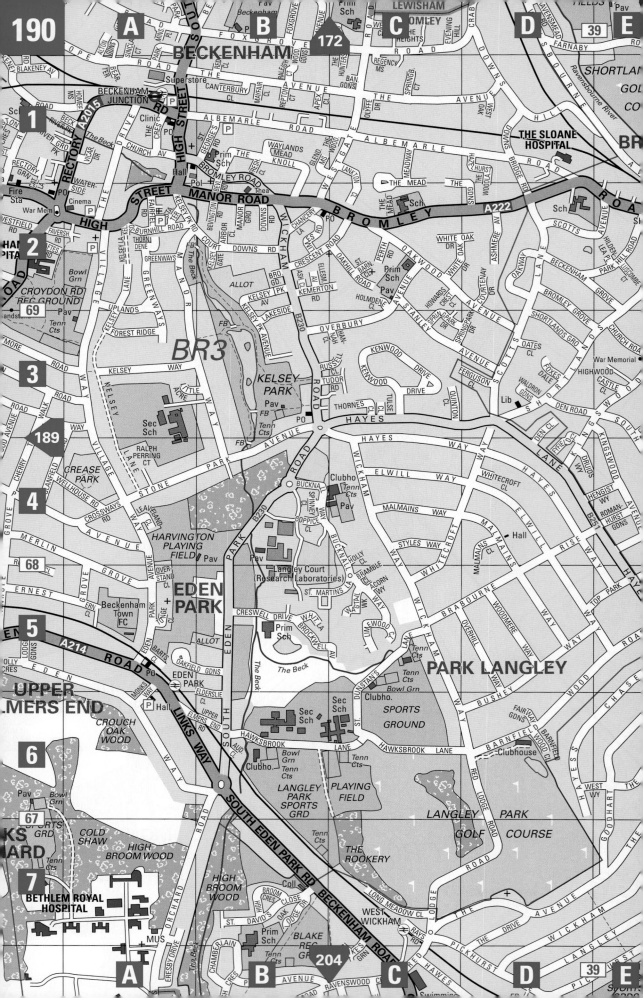

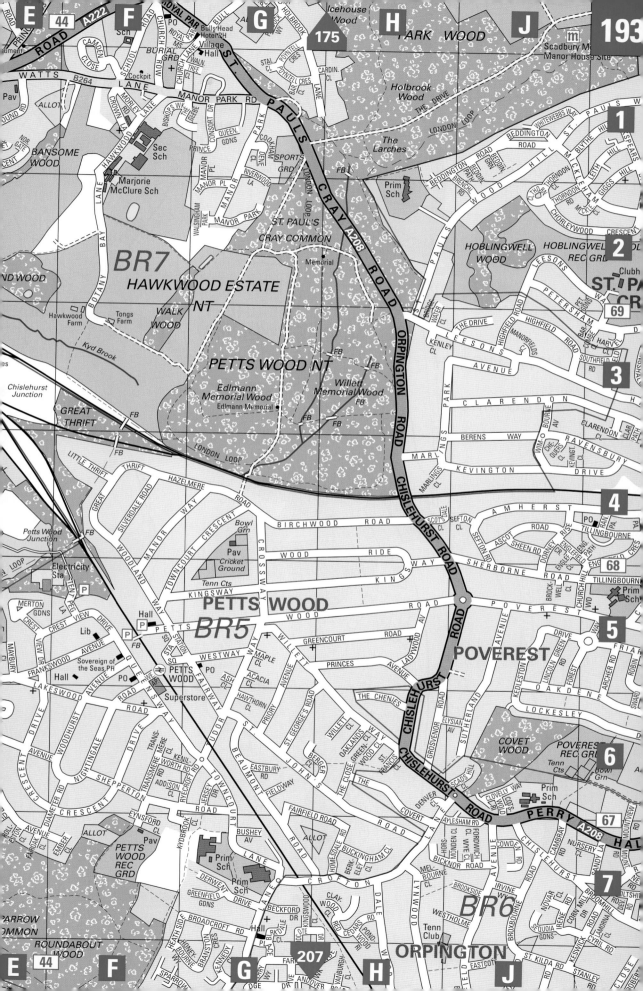

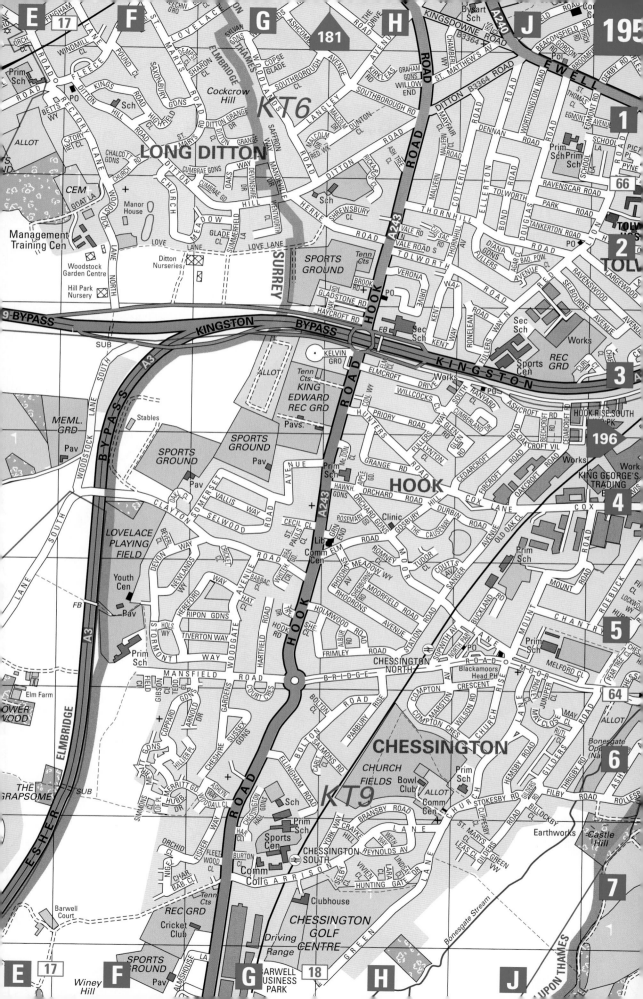

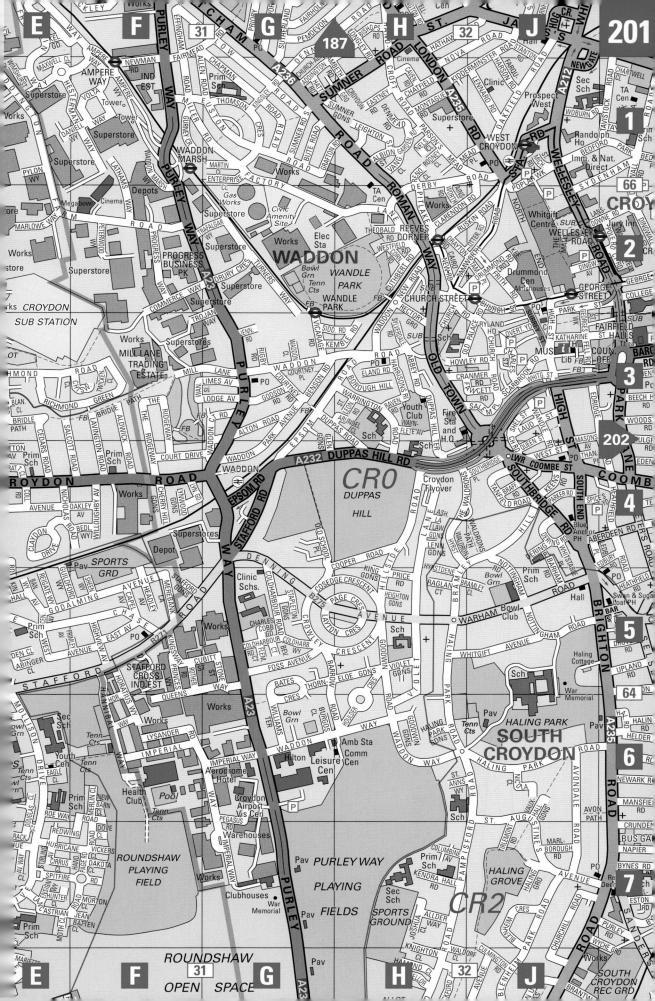

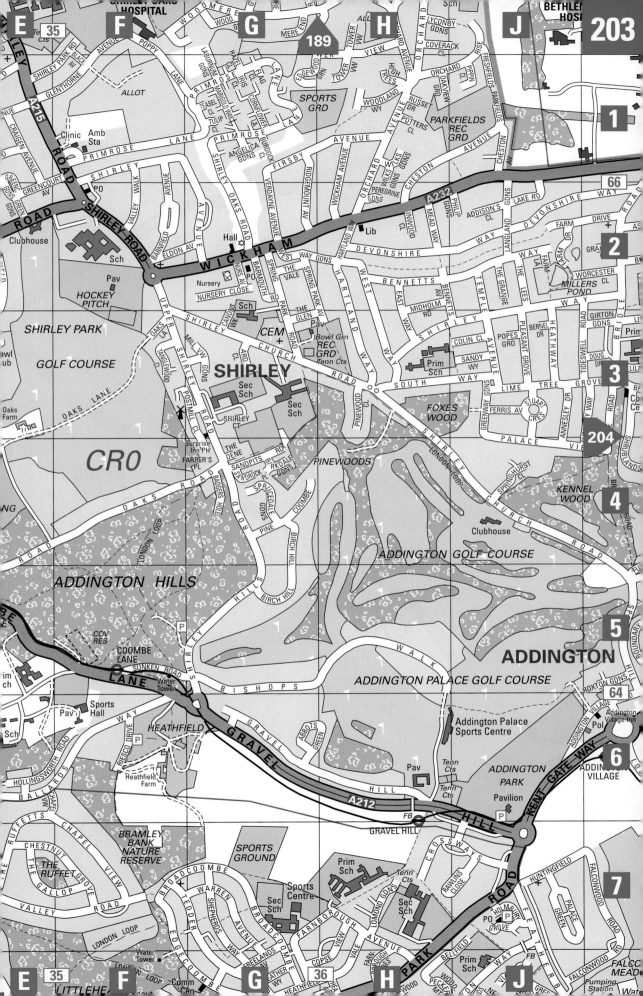

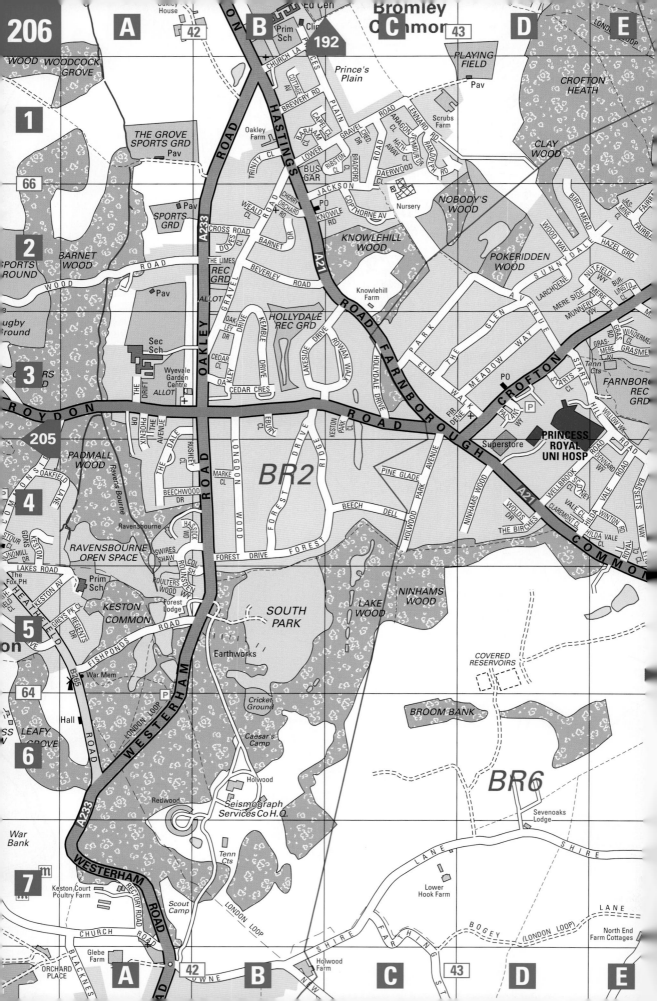

Theatres

Adelphi 0870 403 0303
Albery 0870 060 6621
Aldwych 020 7379 3367
Apollo 020 7494 5070
Arts 020 7836 2132
Cambridge 020 7494 5080
Comedy 0870 060 6637
Criterion 020 7839 8811
Dominion 08706 077400
Donmar Warehouse 0870 060 6624
Duchess 020 7494 5075
Fortune 0870 060 6626
Garrick 020 7494 5085
Gielgud 020 7494 5065
Her Majesty's 020 7494 5400
ICA 020 7930 3647
London Coliseum 020 7632 8300
London Palladium 020 7494 5020
Lyceum 08706 063441
Lyric 020 7494 5045
New London 0870 890 0141
New Players 0870 033 2626
Palace 0870 895 5579
Peacock 020 7863 8222
Phoenix 0870 060 6629
Piccadilly 0870 060 6630
Playhouse 020 7839 4401
Prince Edward 020 7447 5400
Prince of Wales 0870 850 0393
Queen Elizabeth Hall 020 7921 0600
Queen's 020 7494 5040
Royal Court Jerwood Theatre Downstairs
    020 7565 5050
Royal Court Jerwood Theatre Upstairs
    020 7565 5050
Royal Festival Hall 020 7921 0600
Royal National 020 7452 3400
Royal Opera House 020 7304 4000
St. Martin's 020 7836 1443
Savoy 020 7836 8888
Shaftesbury 020 7379 5399
Strand 0870 850 9170
Theatre Royal, Drury Lane 020 7494 5060
Theatre Royal, Haymarket 020 7930 8890
Vaudeville 08708 900511
Whitehall 0870 060 6632
Wyndhams 0870 060 6633

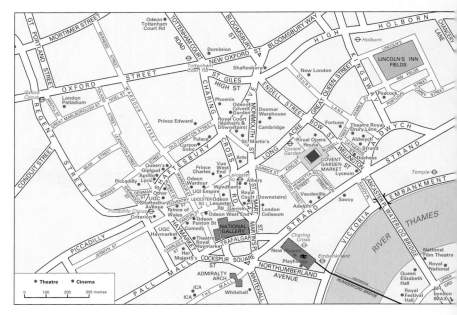

Cinemas

BFI London IMAX
    0870 787 2525
Curzon Soho 020 7734 2255
ICA 020 7930 3647
National Film Theatre
    020 7928 3232
Odeon Leicester Sq
    0871 224 4007
Odeon Panton St
    0871 224 4007

Odeon Covent Garden
    0871 224 4007
Odeon Tottenham Court Rd
    0871 224 4007
Odeon Wardour Street
    0871 224 4007
Odeon West End
    0871 224 4007
Other 020 7437 0757

Prince Charles
    020 7437 7003
UCI Empire Leicester Sq
    08700 102030
UGC Haymarket
    08709 070712
UGC Shaftesbury Avenue
    0871 200 2000
Vue West End 0871 224 0240

West End shopping

Shops

Aquascutum 020 7675 8200
Army & Navy 020 7834 1234
Asprey & Garrard 020 7493 6767
Austin Reed 020 7534 7777
BHS (Oxford St) 020 7629 2011
Bonhams 020 7393 3900
Burberrys 020 7968 0000
Cartier 020 7408 5700
Christie's 020 7839 9060
Covent Garden Market
    020 7836 9136
Debenhams 020 7580 3000
Dickins & Jones 020 7734 7070
Dunhill 020 7355 9500
Fenwick 020 7629 9161
Fortnum & Mason 020 7734 8040
Foyles 020 7437 5660
Habitat (Tottenham Court Rd)
    020 7631 3880
Hamleys 08703 332455
Harrods 020 7730 1234
Harvey Nichols 020 7235 5000
Hatchards 020 7439 9921
Heal's 020 7636 1666
HMV 020 7631 3423
House of Fraser 0870 160 7258
Jaeger 020 7200 4015
John Lewis 020 7629 7711
Laura Ashley (Regent St)
    020 7355 1363
Liberty 020 7734 1234
Lillywhites 0870 333 9602
London Pavilion 020 7439 1791
Marks & Spencer
    (Marble Arch) 020 7935 4422
Marks & Spencer Pantheon
    (Oxford St) 020 7437 7722
Next (Regent St) 020 7434 2515
Plaza Shopping Centre, Oxford St
    020 7637 8811
Selfridges 0870 837 7377
Sotheby's 020 7293 5000
Top Shop & Top Man
    020 7636 7700
Trocadero 09068 881100

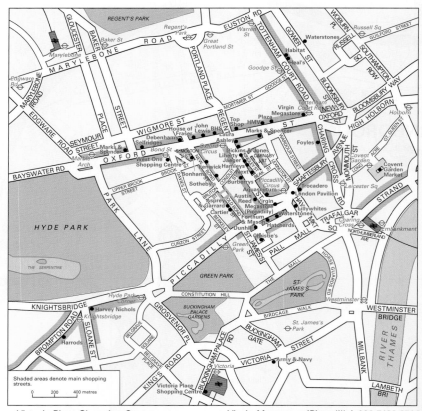

Victoria Place Shopping Centre
    020 7931 8811
Virgin Megastore 020 7631 1234

Virgin Megastore (Piccadilly) 020 7439 2500
Waterstones (Gower St) 020 7636 1577
Waterstones (Piccadilly) 020 7851 2400

How to use this index

This index combines entries for street names, place names and places of interest.

Place names are shown in capital letters,

e.g. **ACTON**, W3 . . . .**126** A1

These include towns, villages and localities within the area covered by this atlas.

Places of interest are shown with a star symbol,

e.g. ★ **British Mus**, WC1 . . . . .**18** A2

These include parks, museums, galleries, and other important buildings or locations of tourist interest.

All other entries are for street names. When there is more than one street with exactly the same name then that name is shown only once in the index. It is then followed by a list of entries for each postal district that contains a street with that same name. For example, there are three streets called Appleby Close in this atlas and the index entry shows that one of these is in London postal district E4, one is in London postal district N15 and one is in Twickenham, TW2.

Appleby Cl, E4 . . . .**62** C6
N15 . . . .**76** A5
Twickenham TW2 . . . . .**162** A2

All entries are followed by the page number and grid reference on which the name will be found. So, in the example above, **Appleby Close**, E4 will be found on page **62** in square C6. All entries are indexed to the largest scale map on which they are shown.

The index also contains some street names which are not actually shown on the maps because there is not enough space to name them. In these cases the adjoining or nearest named thoroughfare to such streets is shown in the index in *italics*, and the reference indicates where the unnamed street is located *off* the named thoroughfare.

e.g. **Bacton St**, E2
off Roman Rd **113** F3

This means that Bacton Street is not named on the map, but it is located *off* Roman Road on page **113** in square F3.

A strict letter-by-letter alphabetical order is followed in this index. All non-alphabetic characters such as spaces, hyphens or apostrophes are not included in the index order. For example Belle Vue Road and Bellevue Road will be found listed together.

Standard terms such as Avenue, Close, Rise and Road are abbreviated in the index but are ordered alphabetically as if given in full. So, for example, **Avondale Ri** comes before **Avondale Rd**.

Names beginning with a definite article (i.e. The) are indexed from their second word onwards with the article being placed at the end of the name,

e.g. **Avenue, The**, E4 . . . .**62** D6

The alphabetical order extends to include postal information so that where two or more streets have exactly the same name, London postal district references are given first in alpha-numeric order and are followed by non-London post town references in alphabetical order, e.g. Appleby Close, E4 is followed by Appleby Close, N15 and then Appleby Close, Twickenham TW2.

In cases where there are two or more streets of the same name in the same postal area, extra information is given in brackets to aid location. For example, High St, Orpington BR6 (Farnborough), and High St, Orpington BR6 (Green St Grn), distinguishes between two streets called High Street which are both in the post town of Orpington, within the same postal district of BR6.

Extra locational information is also given for some localities within large post towns. This is also to aid location.

e.g. **Alford Grn**, Croy. (New Adgtn.) CR0

This street is within the locality of New Addington which is part of the post town of Croydon, and it is within postal district CR0.

A full list of locality and post town abbreviations used in this atlas is given on the next page.

General abbreviations

Acad	Academy	Br	Bridge	Circ	Circus	Cov	Covered
All	Alley	BUPA	British United	Cl	Close	Crem	Crematorium
Allot	Allotments		Provident	Co	County	Cres	Crescent
Amb	Ambulance		Association	Coll	College	Ct	Court
App	Approach	C of E	Church of	Comb	Combined	Cts	Courts
Arc	Arcade		England	Comm	Community	Ctyd	Courtyard
Assoc	Association	Cath	Cathedral	Comp	Comprehensive	Dep	Depot
Av	Avenue	Cem	Cemetery	Conf	Conference	Dept	Department
Bdy	Broadway	Cen	Central, Centre	Cont	Continuing	Dev	Development
Bk	Bank	Cft	Croft	Conv	Convent	Dr	Drive
Bldg	Building	Cfts	Crofts	Cor	Corner	Dws	Dwellings
Bldgs	Buildings	Ch	Church	Coron	Coroners	E	East
Boul	Boulevard	Chyd	Churchyard	Cors	Corners	Ed	Education,
Bowl	Bowling	Cin	Cinema	Cotts	Cottages		Educational

Elec	Electricity	Indep	Independent
Embk	Embankment	Inf	Infant
Est	Estate		Infants
Ex	Exchange	Inst	Institute
Exhib	Exhibition	Int	International
FB	Footbridge	JM	Junior Mixed
FC	Football Club	JMI	Junior Mixed &
Fld	Field		Infant(s)
Flds	Fields	Jun	Junior
Fm	Farm	Junct	Junction
GM	Grant	La	Lane
	Maintained	Las	Lanes
Gall	Gallery	Lib	Library
Gar	Garage	Lit	Literary
Gdn	Garden	Lo	Lodge
Gdns	Gardens	Lwr	Lower
Gen	General	Mag	Magistrates
Govt	Government	Mans	Mansions
Gra	Grange	Med	Medical,
Grad	Graduate		Medicine
Gram	Grammar	Mem	Memorial
Grd	Ground	Met	Metropolitan
Grds	Grounds	Mid	Middle
Grn	Green	Mkt	Market
Grns	Greens	Mkts	Markets
Gro	Grove	Ms	Mews
Gros	Groves	Mt	Mount
Gt	Great	Mus	Museum
HQ	Headquarters	N	North
Ho	House	NHS	National Health
Hos	Houses		Service
Hosp	Hospital	NT	National Trust
Hts	Heights	Nat	National
Ind	Industrial	Nurs	Nursery

PH	Public House	St	Street
PO	Post Office	St.	Saint
PRU	Pupil Referral Unit	Sta	Station
Par	Parade	Sts	Streets
Pas	Passage	Sub	Subway
Pav	Pavilion	Swim	Swimming
Pk	Park	TA	Territorial
Pl	Place		Army
Pol	Police	TH	Town Hall
Poly	Polytechnic	Tech	Technical,
Prec	Precinct		Technology
Prep	Preparatory	Tenn	Tennis
Prim	Primary	Ter	Terrace
Prom	Promenade	Thea	Theatre
Pt	Point	Trd	Trading
Quad	Quadrant	Twr	Tower
RC	Roman Catholic	Twrs	Towers
Rd	Road	Uni	University
Rds	Roads	Upr	Upper
Rec	Recreation	VA	Voluntary
Rehab	Rehabilitation		Aided
Res	Reservoir,	VC	Voluntary
	Residence		Controlled
Ri	Rise	Vet	Veterinary
S	South	Vil	Villa
SM	Secondary		Villas
	Mixed	Vw	View
Sch	School	W	West
Schs	Schools	Wd	Wood
Sec	Secondary	Wds	Woods
Sen	Senior	Wf	Wharf
Shop	Shopping	Wk	Walk
Spec	Special	Wks	Works
Sq	Square	Yd	Yard

Locality and post town abbreviations

In the list of abbreviations shown below, post towns are in **bold** type

Bark.	**Barking**	Har.Wld	Harrow Weald	**Rich.**	**Richmond**
Barn.	**Barnet**	Harm.	Harmondsworth	Rod.Val.	Roding Valley
Barne.	Barnehurst	**Hat.**	**Hatfield**	**Rom.**	**Romford**
Beck.	**Beckenham**	Hatt.Cr.	Hatton Cross	**Ruis.**	**Ruislip**
Bedd.	Beddington	High Barn.	High Barnet	**S.Croy.**	**South Croydon**
Bedd.Cor.	Beddington Corner	Highams Pk	Highams Park	S.Har.	South Harrow
Belv.	**Belvedere**	Hinch.Wd	Hinchley Wood	S.Norwood	South Norwood
Bex.	**Bexley**	Hmptn H.	Hampton Hill	S.Oxhey	South Oxhey
Bexh.	**Bexleyheath**	Hmptn W.	Hampton Wick	S.Ruis.	South Ruislip
Borwd.	**Borehamwood**	Hmptn.	Hampton	Scad.Pk	Scadbury Park
Brent.	**Brentford**	**Houns.**	**Hounslow**	Short.	Shortlands
Brom.	**Bromley**	Houns.W.	Hounslow West	**Sid.**	**Sidcup**
Buck.H.	**Buckhurst Hill**	Hthrw Air.	Heathrow Airport	St.P.Cray	St. Paul's Cray
Bushey Hth	Bushey Heath	Hthrw Air.N.	Heathrow Airport North	**Stai.**	**Staines**
Carp.Pk	Carpenders Park			**Stan.**	**Stanmore**
Cars.	**Carshalton**	**Ilf.**	**Ilford**	Stanw.	Stanwell
Chad.Hth	Chadwell Heath	**Islw.**	**Isleworth**	Sthl Grn	Southall Green
Chess.	**Chessington**	**Kes.**	**Keston**	**Sthl.**	**Southall**
Chig.	**Chigwell**	**Kings.T.**	**Kingston upon**	**Sun.**	**Sunbury-on-Thames**
Chis.	**Chislehurst**		**Thames**	**Surb.**	**Surbiton**
Clay.	Claygate	Long Dit.	Long Ditton	**Sutt.**	**Sutton**
Cockfos.	Cockfosters	**Loug.**	**Loughton**	**T.Ditt.**	**Thames Ditton**
Coll.Row	Collier Row	Lt.Hth	Little Heath	**Tedd.**	**Teddington**
Cran.	Cranford	**Lwr Sydenham**	**Lower Sydenham**	**Th.Hth.**	**Thornton Heath**
Croy.	**Croydon**	**Mitch.**	**Mitcham**	They.B.	Theydon Bois
Dag.	**Dagenham**	Mitch.Com.	Mitcham Common	Tkgtn	Tokyngton
Dart.	**Dartford**	**Mord.**	**Morden**	**Twick.**	**Twickenham**
E.Bed.	East Bedfont	Mots.Pk	Motspur Park	**Uxb.**	**Uxbridge**
E.Croy.	East Croydon	N.Finchley	North Finchley	W.Croy.	West Croydon
E.Mol.	**East Molesey**	N.Har.	North Harrow	W.Ealing	West Ealing
Ealing Com.	Ealing Common	**N.Mal.**	**New Malden**	W.Ewell	West Ewell
Eastcote Vill.	Eastcote Village	New Adgtn	New Addington	**W.Mol.**	**West Molesey**
Edg.	**Edgware**	New Barn.	New Barnet	**W.Wick.**	**West Wickham**
Elm.Wds	Elmstead Woods	Northumb.Hth	Northumberland	**Wall.**	**Wallington**
Enf.	**Enfield**		Heath	**Walt.**	**Walton-on-Thames**
Epp.	**Epping**	Norwood Junct.	Norwood Junction	**Wat.**	**Watford**
Farnboro.	Farnborough	Nthlt.	Northolt	**Wdf.Grn.**	**Woodford Green**
Felt.	**Feltham**	**Nthwd.**	**Northwood**	**Well.**	**Welling**
Grn St Grn	Green Street Green	**Orp.**	**Orpington**	**Wem.**	**Wembley**
Grnf.	**Greenford**	Petts Wd	Petts Wood	**West Dr.**	**West Drayton**
Hackbr.	Hackbridge	**Pnr.**	**Pinner**	Wldste	Wealdstone
Han.	Hanworth	**Pot.B.**	**Potters Bar**	Woodside Pk	Woodside Park
Har.	**Harrow**	**Pur.**	**Purley**	**Wor.Pk.**	**Worcester Park**
Har.Hill	Harrow on the Hill	Rain.	Rainham	Yiew.	Yiewsley

1 Canada Sq, E14 134 B1
30 St. Mary Axe, EC3
off St. Mary Axe 112 B6
99 Bishopsgate, EC2
off Bishopsgate 112 B6

A

Aaron Hill Rd, E6 116 D5
Abberley Ms, SW4
off Cedars Rd 150 B3
Abbess Cl, E6 off Oliver Gdns 116 B5
SW2 169 H1
Abbeville Ms, SW4
off Clapham Pk Rd 150 D4
Abbeville Rd, N8
off Barrington Rd 74 D4
SW4 150 C6
Abbey Av, Wem. HA0 105 H2
Abbey Business Cen, SW8
off Ingate Pl 150 B1
Abbey Cl, E5 94 D4
SW8 150 D1
Hayes UB3 122 B1
Northolt UB5 off Invicta Gro 103 F3
Pinner HA5 66 B3
Abbey Cres, Belv. DA17 139 G4
Abbeydale Rd, Wem. HA0 106 A1
Abbey Dr, SW17 off Church La 168 A5
Abbeyfield Rd, SE16 133 F4
Abbeyfields Cl, NW10 106 A2
Abbey Gdns, NW8 6 C2
SE16 37 J1
W6 128 B6
Chislehurst BR7 192 D1
Abbey Gro, SE2 138 B4
Abbeyhill Rd, Sid. DA15 176 C2
Abbey Ind Est, Mitch. CR4 185 J5
Wembley HA0 105 J1
Abbey La, E15 114 C2
Beckenham BR3 172 A7
Abbey Ms, E17
off Leamington Av 78 A5
Abbey Orchard St, SW1 25 J5
Abbey Par, SW19
off Merton High St 167 F7
W5 off Hanger La 105 J3
Abbey Pk, Beck. BR3 172 A7
Abbey Retail Pk, Bark. IG11 117 E1
Abbey Rd, E15 114 E2
NW6 90 E7
NW8 109 F2
NW10 106 B2
SE2 138 D4
SW19 167 F7
Barking IG11 99 E7
Belvedere DA17 138 D4
Bexleyheath DA7 159 E4
Croydon CR0 201 H3
Enfield EN1 44 B5
Ilford IG2 81 G5
Abbey Rd Est, NW8 109 E1
Abbey St, E13 115 G4
SE1 28 E5
Abbey Ter, SE2 138 C4
Abbey Vw, NW7 55 F3
Abbey Wk, W.Mol. KT8 179 H3
Abbey Way, SE2 138 D3
Abbey Wf Ind Est, Bark. IG11 117 G2
ABBEY WOOD, SE2 138 B3
Abbey Wd Caravan Club Site,
SE2 138 C5
Abbey Wd Rd, SE2 138 B4
Abbotsbury Cl, E15 114 C2
W14 off Abbotsbury Rd 128 C2
Abbotsbury Gdns, Pnr. HA5 66 C6
Abbotsbury Ms, SE15 153 F3
Abbotsbury Rd, W14 128 B2
Bromley BR2 205 F2
Morden SM4 184 E5
Abbots Cl, N1 off Alwyne Rd 93 J6
Orpington BR5 207 F1
Ruislip HA4 84 D3
Abbots Dr, Har. HA2 85 G2
Abbotsford Av, N15 75 J4
Abbotsford Gdns, Wdf.Grn. IG8 63 G7
Abbotsford Rd, Ilf. IG3 100 A2
Abbots Gdns, N2 73 G4
W8 22 A6
Abbots Grn, Croy. CR0 203 G6
Abbotshade Rd, SE16 133 G1
Abbotshall Av, N14 58 C3
Abbotshall Rd, SE6 172 D1
Abbots La, SE1 28 E2
Abbotsleigh Cl, Sutt. SM2 198 E7
Abbotsleigh Rd, SW16 168 C4
Abbots Manor Est, SW1 32 D2
Abbotsmede Cl, Twick. TW1 162 C2
Abbots Pk, SW2 169 G1
Abbot's Pl, NW6 108 E1
Abbot's Rd, E6 116 A1
Abbots Rd, Edg. HA8 54 C7
Abbots Ter, N8 74 E6
Abbotstone Rd, SW15 147 J3
Abbot St, E8 94 C6
Abbots Wk, W8 22 A6
Abbots Way, Beck. BR3 189 H5
Abbotswell Rd, SE4 153 J5
Abbotswood Cl, Belv. DA17
off Coptefield Dr 138/139 E3
Abbotswood Gdns, Ilf. IG5 80 C3
Abbotswood Rd, SE22 152 B4
SW16 168 D3
Abbotswood Way, Hayes UB3 122 B1
Abbott Av, SW20 184 A2
Abbott Cl, Hmptn. TW12 161 E6
Northolt UB5 85 F6
Abbott Rd, E14 114 C5
Abbotts Cl, SE28 118 C7
Romford RM7 83 H3
Abbotts Cres, E4 62 D4
Enfield EN2 43 H2
Abbotts Dr, Wem. HA0 86 E2
Abbotts Pk Rd, E10 78 C7
Abbotts Rd, Barn. EN5 40 E4
Mitcham CR4 186 C4
Southall UB1 123 E1
Sutton SM3 198 C3
Abbotts Wk, Bexh. DA7 138 D7
Abchurch La, EC4 20 C5
Abchurch Yd, EC4 20 B5
Abdale Rd, W12 127 H1
Aberavon Rd, E3 113 H3
Abercairn Rd, SW16 168 C7
Aberconway Rd, Mord. SM4 184 E3
Abercorn Cl, NW7 56 B7
NW8 6 C2
Abercorn Cres, Har. HA2 85 H1
Abercorn Gdns, Har. HA3 69 G7
Romford RM6 82 B6
Abercorn Pl, NW8 6 C3
Abercorn Rd, NW7 56 B7
Stanmore HA7 53 F7
Abercorn Way, SE1 37 H3
Abercrombie Dr, Enf. EN1
off Linwood Cres 44 D1
Abercrombie St, SW11 149 H2
Aberdale Ct, SE16
off Poolmans St 133 G2
Aberdare Cl, W.Wick. BR4 204 C2
Aberdare Gdns, NW6 91 E7
NW7 56 A7
Aberdare Rd, Enf. EN3 45 F4
Aberdeen La, N5 93 H5
Aberdeen Par, N18
off Angel Rd 60/61 E5
Aberdeen Pk, N5 93 H5
Aberdeen Pk Ms, N5 93 J4
Aberdeen Pl, NW8 6 E6
Aberdeen Rd, N5 93 J4
N18 60 E5
NW10 89 F5
Croydon CR0 201 J4
Harrow HA3 68 C2
Aberdeen Sq, E14
off Westferry Circ 133 J1
Aberdeen Ter, SE3 154 D2
Aberdour Rd, Ilf. IG3 100 B3
Aberdour St, SE1 36 D1
Aberfeldy St, E14 114 C6
Aberford Gdns, SE18 156 B1
Aberford Rd, Borwd. WD6 38 A2
Aberfoyle Rd, SW16 168 D6
Abergeldie Rd, SE12 155 H6
Aberglen Ind Est, Hayes UB3 121 G2
Abernethy Rd, SE13 154 E4
Abersham Rd, E8 94 C5
Abery St, SE18 137 H4
Abingdon Cl, NW1
off Camden Sq 92 D6
SE1 37 G3
SW19 167 F6
Abingdon Rd, N3 73 F2
SW16 186 E2
W8 128 D3
Abingdon St, SW1 26 A5
Abingdon Vil, W8 128 D3
Abinger Cl, Bark. IG11 100 A4
Bromley BR1 192 B3
Croydon CR0 204 C6
Wallington SM6 201 E5
Abinger Gdns, Islw. TW7 144 B3
Abinger Gro, SE8 133 J6
Abinger Ms, W9 off Warlock Rd 108 D4
Abinger Rd, W4 127 E3
Ablett St, SE16 133 F5
Abney Gdns, N16
off Stoke Newington High St 94 C2
Aboyne Dr, SW20 183 G2
Aboyne Est, SW17 167 G3
Aboyne Rd, NW10 88 E3
SW17 167 G3
Abraham Cl, Wat. WD19 50 B4
Abridge Rd, Chig. IG7 49 G6
Abridge Way, Bark. IG11 118 B2
Abyssinia Cl, SW11
off Cairns Rd 149 H4
Abyssinia Rd, SW11
off Auckland Rd 149 H4
Acacia Av, N17 60 A7
Brentford TW8 124 E7
Mitcham CR4 off Acacia Rd 186 B2
Ruislip HA4 84 A1
Acacia Av, Wem. HA9 87 H5
Acacia Cl, SE8 133 H4
SE20 off Selby Rd 188 D2
Acacia Cl, Orp. BR5 193 G5
Stanmore HA7 52 B6
Acacia Dr, Sutt. SM3 198 C1
Acacia Gdns, NW8 7 F1
West Wickham BR4 204 C2
Acacia Gro, SE21 170 A2
New Malden KT3 182 D3
Acacia Ms, West Dr. UB7 120 A6
Acacia Pl, NW8 7 F1
Acacia Rd, E11 97 E2
E17 77 H6
N22 75 G1
NW8 7 F1
SW16 187 E1
W3 106 C7
Beckenham BR3 189 J3
Enfield EN2 44 A1
Hampton TW12 161 G6
Mitcham CR4 186 B2
Acacia Way, Sid. DA15 175 J1
Academy Gdns, W8
off Duchess of Bedford's Wk 128 D2
Croydon CR0 202 C1
Northolt UB5 102 D2
Academy Pl, SE18 156 C1
Academy Rd, SE18 156 C1
Acanthus Dr, SE1 37 H3
Acanthus Rd, SW11 150 A3
Accommodation Rd, NW11 72 C7
A.C. Ct, T.Ditt. KT7
off Harvest La 180 D6
Acer Av, Hayes UB4 102 E5
Acfold Rd, SW6 148 E1
Achilles Cl, SE1 37 J3
Achilles Rd, NW6 90 D5
Achilles St, SE14 133 H7
Achilles Way, W1 24 C2
Acklam Rd, W10 108 C5
Acklington Dr, NW9 70 E1
Ackmar Rd, SW6 148 D1
Ackroyd Dr, E3 113 J5
Ackroyd Rd, SE23 153 G7
Acland Cl, SE18
off Clothworkers Rd 137 G7
Acland Cres, SE5 152 A4
Acland Rd, NW2 89 H6
Acle Cl, Ilf. IG6 64 E7
Acock Gro, Nthlt. UB5 85 H4
Acol Cres, Ruis. HA4 84 B5
Acol Rd, NW6 90 D7
Aconbury Rd, Dag. RM9 118 B1
Acorn Cl, E4 62 A5
Chislehurst BR7 175 F5
Enfield EN2 43 H1
Hampton TW12 161 H6
Stanmore HA7 53 E7
Acorn Ct, Ilf. IG2 81 H6
Acorn Gdns, SE19 188 C1
W3 106 D5
Acorn Gro, Hayes UB3 121 J7
Acorn Par, SE15
off Carlton Gro 132/133 E7
Acorns, The, Chig. IG7 65 H4
Acorn Wk, SE16 133 H1
Acorn Way, SE23 171 G3
Beckenham BR3 190 C5
Orpington BR6 207 E4
Acre Dr, SE22 152 D4
Acre La, SW2 150 E4
Carshalton SM5 200 A4
Wallington SM6 200 A4
Acre Path, Nthlt. UB5
off Arnold Rd 84/85 E6
Acre Rd, SW19 167 G6
Dagenham RM10 101 H7
Kingston upon Thames KT2 181 H1
Acris St, SW18 149 F5
ACTON, W3 126 A1
Acton Cl, N9 60 D2
Acton Hill Ms, W3
off Uxbridge Rd 126 B1
Acton La, NW10 106 E2
W3 126 C2
W4 126 D3
Acton Ms, E8 112 C1
Acton Pk Ind Est, W3 126 D2
Acton St, WC1 10 C4
Acuba Rd, SW18 166 E2
Acworth Cl, N9 off Turin Rd 45 F7
Ada Gdns, E14 114 D6
E15 115 F1
Adair Cl, SE25 188 E3
Adair Rd, W10 108 B4
Adair Twr, W10
off Appleford Rd 108 B4
Adam & Eve Ct, W1 17 G3
Adam & Eve Ms, W8 128 D3
Adam Cl, SE6 171 J4
Adam Ct, SW7 30 D1
Adam Pl, N16
off Stoke Newington High St 94 C2
Adam Rd, E4 61 J6
Adams Cl, N3 off Falkland Av 56 D7
NW9 88 B2
Adams Cl, Surb. KT5 181 J6
Adams Ct, EC2 20 C3
Adams Gdns Est, SE16
off St. Marychurch St 133 F2
Adams Ms, N22 58 E7
SW17 167 J2
Adamson Rd, E16 115 G6
NW3 91 G7
Adamson Way, Beck. BR3
off Creswell Dr 190 B5
Adams Pl, N7 off George's Rd 93 F5
Adamsrill Cl, Enf. EN1 44 A6
Adamsrill Rd, SE26 171 H4
Adams Rd, N17 76 A2
Beckenham BR3 189 H5
Adams Row, W1 16 C6
Adams Sq, Bexh. DA6
off Regency Way 158/159 E3
Adam St, WC2 18 B6
Adams Wk, Kings.T. KT1 181 H2
Adams Way, Croy. CR0 188 C6
Adam Wk, SW6 127 J7
Ada Pl, E2 112 D1
Adare Wk, SW16 169 F3
Ada Rd, SE5 132 B7
Wembley HA0 87 G3
Adastral Est, NW9 70 E1
Ada St, E8 112 E1
Adcock Wk, Orp. BR6
off Borkwood Pk 207 J4
Adderley Gdns, SE9 174 D4
Adderley Gro, SW11
off Culmstock Rd 150 A5
Adderley Rd, Har. HA3 68 C1
Adderley St, E14 114 C6
ADDINGTON, Croy. CR0 203 J5
Addington Ct, SW14 146 D3
Addington Dr, N12 57 F6
Addington Gro, SE26 171 H4
Addington Rd, E3 114 A3
E16 115 E4
N4 75 G6
Croydon CR0 201 G1
West Wickham BR4 204 E2
Addington Sq, SE5 36 A7
Addington St, SE1 26 D4
Addington Village Rd, Croy.
CR0 204 A5
Addis Cl, Enf. EN3 45 G1
ADDISCOMBE, Croy. CR0 202 C1
Addiscombe Av, Croy. CR0 188 D7
Addiscombe Cl, Har. HA3 69 F5
Addiscombe Ct Rd, Croy. CR0 202 B1
Addiscombe Gro, Croy. CR0 202 A2
Addiscombe Rd, Croy. CR0 202 B2
Addison Av, N14 42 B6
W11 128 B1
Hounslow TW3 143 J1
Addison Br Pl, W14 128 C4
Addison Cl, Nthwd. HA6 66 A1
Orpington BR5 193 F6
Addison Cres, W14 128 B3
Addison Dr, SE12
off Eltham Rd 155 H5
Addison Gdns, W14 128 A3
Surbiton KT5 181 J4
Addison Gro, W4 127 E3
Addison Pl, W11 128 B1
Southall UB1
off Longford Av 103 G7
Addison Rd, E11 79 G6
E17 78 B5
SE25 188 D4
W14 128 C3
Bromley BR2 191 J5
Enfield EN3 45 F1
Ilford IG6 81 F1
Teddington TW11 162 E6
Addison's Cl, Croy. CR0 203 J2
Addison Way, NW11 72 C4
Hayes UB3 102 A6
Addle Hill, EC4 19 H5
Addle St, EC2 20 A2
Addy Ho, SE16
off Rotherhithe New Rd 133 F4
Adecroft Way, W.Mol. KT8 179 J3
Adela Av, N.Mal. KT3 183 H5
Adelaide Av, SE4 153 J4
Adelaide Cl, SW9
off Broughton Dr 151 G4
Stanmore HA7 52 D4
Adelaide Cotts, W7 124 C2
Adelaide Gdns, Rom. RM6 82 E5
Adelaide Gro, W12 127 G1
Adelaide Rd, E10 96 B3
NW3 91 G7
SW18 off Putney Br Rd 148 D5
W13 124 D1
Chislehurst BR7 175 E5
Hounslow TW5 142 E1
Ilford IG1 99 E2
Richmond TW9 145 J4
Southall UB2 123 E4
Surbiton KT6 181 H5
Teddington TW11 162 C6
Adelaide St, WC2 18 A6
Adelaide Ter, Brent. TW8 125 G5

Adela St, W10 *off Kensal Rd* 108 B4
Adelina Gro, E1 113 F5
Adelina Ms, SW12 *off King's Av* 168 D1
Adeline Pl, WC1 17 J2
Adeliza Cl, Bark. IG11
off North St 98/99 E7
Adelphi Ct, SE16
off Poolmans St 133 G2
Adelphi Ter, WC2 18 B6
Adeney Cl, W6 128 A6
Aden Gro, N16 94 A4
Adenmore Rd, SE6 154 A7
Aden Rd, Enf. EN3 45 H4
Ilford IG1 81 E7
Aden Ter, N16 94 A4
Adie Rd, W6 127 J3
Adine Rd, E13 115 H4
Adler Ind Est, Hayes UB3 121 G2
Adler St, E1 21 H3
Adley St, E5 95 H5
Adlington Cl, N18 60 A5
Admaston Rd, SE18 137 F7
Admiral Ct, NW4 *off Barton Cl* 71 G5
Admiral Ho, Tedd. TW11
off Twickenham Rd 162 D4
Admiral Pl, N8
off Effingham Rd 75 H4
SE16 133 H1
Admirals Cl, E18 79 H4
Admiral Seymour Rd, SE9 156 C4
Admirals Gate, SE10 154 B1
Admiral Sq, SW10 149 G1
Admiral St, SE8 154 A2
Admirals Wk, NW3 91 F3
Admirals Way, E14 134 A2
★ **Admiralty Arch**, SW1 25 J1
Admiralty Cl, SE8
off Reginald Sq 134 A7
Admiralty Way, Tedd. TW11 162 C6
Admiral Wk, W9 108 D5
Adolf St, SE6 172 B4
Adolphus Rd, N4 93 H2
Adolphus St, SE8 133 J7
Adomar Rd, Dag. RM8 100 D3
Adpar St, W2 7 E6
Adrian Av, NW2
off North Circular Rd 89 H1
Adrian Cl, Barn. EN5 40 A6
Adrian Ms, SW10 30 B5
Adriatic Bldg, E14
off Narrow St 113 H7
Adrienne Av, Sthl. UB1 103 F4
Advance Rd, SE27 169 J4
Advent Ct, Wdf.Grn. IG8
off Wood La 63 F5
Adventurers Ct, E14
off Newport Av 114 D7
Advent Way, N18 61 G5
Adys Rd, SE15 152 C3
Aerodrome Rd, NW4 71 F2
NW9 71 F2
Aerodrome Way, Houns. TW5 122 C6
Aeroville, NW9 71 E2
Affleck St, N1 10 D2
Afghan Rd, SW11 149 H2
★ **Africa Cen**, WC2 18 A5
Africa Ho, SE16 133 E3
Agamemnon Rd, NW6 90 C5
Agar Cl, Surb. KT6 195 J2
Agar Gro, NW1 92 C7
Agar Gro Est, NW1 92 D7
Agar Pl, NW1 92 C7
Agar St, WC2 18 A6
Agate Cl, E16 116 A6
Agate Rd, W6 127 J3
Agatha Cl, E1
off Prusom St 132/133 E1
Agaton Rd, SE9 175 F2
Agave Rd, NW2 89 J4
Agdon St, EC1 11 G5
Agincourt Rd, NW3 91 J4
Agnes Av, Ilf. IG1 98 E4
Agnes Cl, E6 116 D7
Agnesfield Cl, N12 57 H6
Agnes Gdns, Dag. RM8 100 D4
Agnes Rd, W3 127 F1
Agnes St, E14 113 J6
Agnew Rd, SE23 153 G7
Agricola Ct, E3 *off Parnell Rd* 113 J1
Agricola Pl, Enf. EN1 44 C5
Aidan Cl, Dag. RM8 100 E4
Aileen Wk, E15 97 F7
Ailsa Av, Twick. TW1 144 D5
Ailsa Rd, Twick. TW1 145 E5
Ailsa St, E14 114 C5
Ainger Ms, NW3 *off Ainger Rd* 91 J7
Ainger Rd, NW3 91 J7
Ainsdale Cl, Orp. BR6 207 G1
Ainsdale Cres, Pnr. HA5 67 G3
Ainsdale Dr, SE1 37 H4
Ainsdale Rd, W5 105 G4
Watford WD19 50 C3
Ainsley Av, Rom. RM7 83 H6
Ainsley Cl, N9 60 B1
Ainsley St, E2 112 E3
Ainslie Wk, SW12 150 B7
Ainslie Wd Cres, E4 62 B5
Ainslie Wd Gdns, E4 62 B4
Ainslie Wd Rd, E4 62 A5
Ainsty Est, SE16 133 G2
Ainsworth Cl, NW2 89 G3
SE15 *off Lyndhurst Gro* 152 B2
Ainsworth Rd, E9 95 F7
Croydon CR0 201 H2
Ainsworth Way, NW8 109 F1
Aintree Av, E6 116 B1
Aintree Cres, Ilf. IG6 81 F2
Aintree Est, SW6 *off Dawes Rd* 128 B7
Aintree Rd, Grnf. UB6 105 E2
Aintree St, SW6 128 B7
Aird Ct, Hmptn. TW12
off Oldfield Rd 179 F1
Airdrie Cl, N1 93 F7
Hayes UB4
off Glencoe Rd 102/103 E5
Airedale Av, W4 127 F4
Airedale Av S, W4
off Netheravon Rd S 127 F5
Airedale Rd, SW12 149 J7
W5 125 F3
Airlie Gdns, W8 128 D2
Ilford IG1 99 E1
Air Links Ind Est, Houns. TW5 122 C5
Air Pk Way, Felt. TW13 160 B2
Airport Roundabout, E16
off Connaught Br 136 A1
Air St, W1 17 G6
Airthrie Rd, Ilf. IG3 100 B2
Aisgill Av, W14 128 C5
Aisher Rd, SE28 118 C7
Aislibie Rd, SE12 155 E4
Aiten Pl, W6 *off Standish Rd* 127 G4
Aitken Cl, E8 *off Pownall Rd* 112 D1
Mitcham CR4 185 J7
Aitken Rd, SE6 172 B2
Barnet EN5 39 J5
Ajax Av, NW9 70 E3
Ajax Rd, NW6 90 D5
Akabusi Cl, Croy. CR0 188 D6
Akehurst St, SW15 147 G6
Akenside Rd, NW3 91 G5
Akerman Rd, SW9 151 H2
Surbiton KT6 181 F6
Alabama St, SE18 137 G7
Alacross Rd, W5 125 F2
Alandale Dr, Pnr. HA5 66 B2
Aland Ct, SE16 *off Finland St* 133 H3
Alander Ms, E17 78 C4
Alan Dr, Barn. EN5 40 B6
Alan Gdns, Rom. RM7 83 G7
Alan Hocken Way, E15 114 E2
Alan Rd, SW19 166 B5
Alanthus Cl, SE12 155 F6
Alaska St, SE1 27 E2
Alba Cl, Hayes UB4
off Ramulis Dr 102 D4
Albacore Cres, SE13 154 B6
Alba Gdns, NW11 72 B6
Alban Cres, Borwd. WD6 38 B1
Alban Highwalk, EC2
off London Wall 111 J5
Albany, W1 17 F6
Albany, The, Wdf.Grn. IG8 63 F4
Albany Cl, N15 75 H4
SW14 146 B4
Bexley DA5 158 C7
Albany Ct, E4 *off Chelwood Cl* 46 B6
Albany Ctyd, W1 17 G6
Albany Cres, Edg. HA8 54 A7
Esher (Clay.) KT10 194 B6
Albany Mans, SW11 129 H7
Albany Ms, N1
off Barnsbury Pk 93 G7
SE5 36 A6
Bromley BR1 173 G6
Kingston upon Thames KT2
off Albany Pk Rd 163 G6
Sutton SM1
off Camden Rd 198/199 E5
Albany Pk Av, Enf. EN3 45 F1
Albany Pk Rd, Kings.T. KT2 163 H6
Albany Pas, Rich. TW10 145 J5
Albany Pl, Brent. TW8
off Albany Rd 125 H6
Albany Rd, E10 78 A7
E12 98 A4
E17 77 H6
N4 75 F6
N18 61 E5
SE5 36 B6
SW19 166 E5
W13 104 E7
Belvedere DA17 139 F6
Bexley DA5 158 C7
Brentford TW8 125 G6
Chislehurst BR7 174 E5
New Malden KT3 182 D4
Richmond TW10
off Albert Rd 145 J5
Romford RM6 83 F6
Albany St, NW1 8 D1
Albany Ter, NW1
off Marylebone Rd 110 B4
Albany Vw, Buck.H. IG9 63 G1
Alba Pl, W11
off Portobello Rd 108 C6
Albatross Cl, E6
off Woolwich Manor Way 116 C4
Albatross St, SE18 137 H7
Albatross Way, SE16 133 G2
Albemarle, SW19 166 A2
Albemarle App, Ilf. IG2 81 E6
Albemarle Av, Twick. TW2 161 F1
Albemarle Gdns, Ilf. IG2 81 E6
New Malden KT3 182 D4
Albemarle Pk, Stan. HA7
off Marsh La 53 F5
Albemarle Rd, Barn. EN4 41 H7
Beckenham BR3 190 B1
Albemarle St, W1 17 E6
Albemarle Way, EC1 11 G6
Alberon Gdns, NW11 72 C4
Alberta Av, Sutt. SM1 198 B4
Alberta Est, SE17 35 H3
Alberta Rd, Enf. EN1 44 C6
Erith DA8 159 J1
Alberta St, SE17 35 G3
Albert Av, E4 62 A4
SW8 131 F7
Albert Br, SW3 31 H6
SW11 31 H6
Albert Br Rd, SW11 31 H7
Albert Carr Gdns, SW16 168 E5
Albert Cl, E9
off Northiam St 112/113 E1
N22 74 D1
Albert Ct, SW7 23 E4
Albert Cres, E4 62 A4
Albert Dr, SW19 166 B2
Albert Embk, SE1 34 B4
Albert Gdns, E1 113 G6
Albert Gate, SW1 24 A3
Albert Gro, SW20 184 A1
Albert Hall Mans, SW7 23 E4
Albert Mans, SW11
off Albert Br Rd 149 J1
★ **Albert Mem**, SW7 22 E3
Albert Ms, E14 *off Narrow St* 113 H7
N4 *off Albert Rd* 93 F1
SE4 *off Arabin Rd* 153 H4
W8 22 C5
Albert Pl, N3 72 D1
N17 *off High Rd* 76 C3
W8 22 B4
Albert Rd, E10 96 C2
E16 136 B1
E17 78 A5
E18 79 H3
N4 93 F1
N15 76 B6
N22 74 C1
NW4 72 A4
NW6 108 C2
NW7 55 F5
SE9 174 B3
SE20 171 G7
SE25 188 D4
W5 105 E4
Barnet EN4 41 F4
Belvedere DA17 139 F5
Bexley DA5 159 G6
Bromley BR2 192 A5
Buckhurst Hill IG9 64 A2
Dagenham RM8 101 G1
Hampton (Hmptn H.) TW12 161 J5
Harrow HA2 67 J3
Hayes UB3 121 H3
Hounslow TW3 143 G4
Ilford IG1 99 E3
Kingston upon Thames KT1 181 J2
Mitcham CR4 185 J3
New Malden KT3 183 F4
Richmond TW10 145 H5
Southall UB2 122 D3
Sutton SM1 199 G5
Teddington TW11 162 C6
Twickenham TW1 162 C1
West Drayton UB7 120 B1
Albert Rd Est, Belv. DA17 139 F5
Albert Sq, E15 97 E5
SW8 131 F7
Albert St, N12 57 F5
NW1 110 B1
Albert Ter, NW1 110 A1
NW10 106 D1
Buckhurst Hill IG9 64 A2
Albert Ter Ms, NW1
off Regents Pk Rd 110 A1
Albert Way, SE15 132 E7
Albion Av, N10 74 A1
SW8 150 D2
Albion Bldgs, EC1
off Bartholomew Cl 111 J5
Albion Cl, W2 15 H5
Albion Dr, E8 94 C7
Albion Est, SE16 133 G2
Albion Gro, N16 94 B4
Albion Hill, Loug. IG10 47 J5
Albion Ms, N1 111 G1
NW6 *off Kilburn High Rd* 90 C7
W2 15 H4
Albion Ms, W6 *off Galena Rd* 127 H4
Albion Par, N16 *off Albion Rd* 94 A4
Albion Pk, Loug. IG10 48 A5
Albion Pl, EC1 19 G1
SE25 *off High St* 188 D3
W6 127 H4
Albion Riverside Bldg, SW11
off Hester Rd 129 H7
Albion Rd, E17 78 C3
N16 94 A4
N17 76 C2
Bexleyheath DA6 159 F4
Hounslow TW3 143 G4
Kingston upon Thames KT2 182 C1
Sutton SM2 199 G6
Twickenham TW2 162 B1
Albion Sq, E8 94 C7
Albion St, SE16 133 F2
W2 15 H4
Croydon CR0 201 H1
Albion Ter, E8 94 C7
Albion Vil Rd, SE26 171 F3
Albion Wk, N1 *off York Way* 110 E2
Albion Way, EC1 19 J2
SE13 154 C4
Wembley HA9
off North End Rd 88 B3
Albion Yd, N1 *off Balfe St* 110 E2
Albon Ho, SW18
off Neville Gill Cl 148 E6
Albrighton Rd, SE22 152 B3
Albuhera Cl, Enf. EN2 43 G1
Albury Av, Bexh. DA7 158 E2
Isleworth TW7 124 C7
Albury Cl, Hmptn. TW12 161 G6
Albury Ct, Sutt. SM1
off Ripley Gdns 199 F4
Albury Dr, Pnr. HA5 50 D7
Albury Ms, E12 97 J1
Albury Rd, Chess. KT9 195 H5
Albury St, SE8 134 A6
Albyfield, Brom. BR1 192 C3
Albyn Rd, SE8 154 A1
Alcester Cres, E5 95 E2
Alcester Rd, Wall. SM6 200 B4
Alcock Cl, Wall. SM6 200 D7
Alcock Rd, Houns. TW5 122 D7
Alconbury Rd, E5 94 D2
Alcorn Cl, Sutt. SM3 198 D2
Alcott Cl, W7 *off Westcott Cres* 104 C5
Alcuin Ct, Stan. HA7
off Old Ch La 53 F7
ALDBOROUGH HATCH, Ilf. IG2 81 H3
Aldborough Rd, Dag. RM10 101 J6
Aldborough Rd N, Ilf. IG2 81 J5
Aldborough Rd S, Ilf. IG3 99 H1
Aldbourne Rd, W12 127 F1
Aldbridge St, SE17 36 E3
Aldburgh Ms, W1 16 C3
Aldbury Av, Wem. HA9 88 B7
Aldbury Ms, N9 44 A7
Aldebert Ter, SW8 131 E7
Aldeburgh Cl, E5
off Southwold Rd 94/95 E2
Aldeburgh Pl, SE10
off Aldeburgh St 135 G4
Woodford Green IG8 63 G4
Aldeburgh St, SE10 135 G5
Alden Av, E15 115 F3
Aldenham St, NW1 9 G2
Aldensley Rd, W6 127 H3
Alderbrook Rd, SW12 150 B6
Alderbury Rd, SW13 127 G6
Alder Cl, SE15 37 G6
Alder Gro, NW2 89 H2
Aldergrove Gdns, Houns. TW3
off Bath Rd 142/143 E2
Alderholt Way, SE15
off Blakes Rd 132 B7
Alderman Av, Bark. IG11 118 A3
Aldermanbury, EC2 20 A3
Aldermanbury Sq, EC2 20 A2
Alderman Judge Mall, Kings.T.
KT1 *off Eden St* 181 H2
Aldermans Hill, N13 58 E4
Alderman's Wk, EC2 20 D2
Aldermary Rd, Brom. BR1 191 G1
Alder Ms, N19 *off Bredgar Rd* 92 C2
Aldermoor Rd, SE6 171 J3
Alderney Av, Houns. TW5 123 H7
Alderney Gdns, Nthlt. UB5 85 F7
Alderney Ms, SE1 28 B5
Alderney Rd, E1 113 G4
Alderney St, SW1 32 E3
Alder Rd, SW14 146 D3
Sidcup DA14 175 J3
Alders, The, N21 43 G6
Feltham TW13 160 E4
Hounslow TW5 123 F6
West Wickham BR4 204 B1
Alders Av, Wdf.Grn. IG8 62 E6
ALDERSBROOK, E12 97 H2
Aldersbrook Av, Enf. EN1 44 B2
Aldersbrook Dr, Kings.T. KT2 163 J6
Aldersbrook La, E12 98 C3
Aldersbrook Rd, E11 97 H2
E12 98 A3

Alders Cl, E11
off Aldersbrook Rd 97 H2
W5 . . . . .125 G3
Edgware HA8 . . . . .54 C5
Aldersey Gdns, Bark. IG11 . . . .99 G5
Aldersford Cl, SE4 . . . . .153 G5
Aldersgate St, EC1 . . . . .19 J3
Aldersgrove Av, SE9 . . . . .173 J3
Aldershot Rd, NW6 . . . . .108 C1
Aldersmead Av, Croy. CR0 . . . .189 G6
Aldersmead Rd, Beck. BR3 . . . .171 H7
Alderson Pl, Sthl. UB2 . . . . . . .123 J1
Alderson St, W10 off Kensal Rd .108 B4
Alders Rd, Edg. HA8 . . . . .54 C5
Alderton Cl, NW10 . . . . .88 D3
Loughton IG10 . . . . .48 D4
Alderton Cres, NW4 . . . . .71 H5
Alderton Hall La, Loug. IG10 . . .48 D4
Alderton Hill, Loug. IG10 . . . . .48 B5
Alderton Ms, Loug. IG10
off Alderton Hall La 48 D4
Alderton Ri, Loug. IG10 . . . . . . .48 D4
Alderton Rd, SE24 . . . . .151 J3
Croydon CR0 . . . . .188 C7
Alderton Way, NW4 . . . . .71 H5
Loughton IG10 . . . . .48 C5
Alderville Rd, SW6 . . . . .148 C2
Alder Wk, Ilf. IG1 . . . . .99 F5
Alderwick Dr, Houns. TW3 . . . .144 A3
Alderwood Rd, SE9 . . . . .157 G6
Aldford St, W1 . . . . .24 B1
Aldgate, EC3 . . . . .21 F4
Aldgate Av, E1 . . . . .21 F3
Aldgate Barrs Shop Cen, E1 . . .21 G3
Aldgate High St, EC3 . . . . .21 F4
Aldine Ct, W12 off Aldine St . . .127 J1
Aldine Pl, W12 off Uxbridge Rd .127 J1
Aldine St, W12 . . . . .127 J2
Aldington Cl, Dag. RM8 . . . . . .82 C7
Aldington Rd, SE18 . . . . .136 A3
Aldis Ms, SW17 off Aldis St . . .167 H5
Aldis St, SW17 . . . . .167 H5
Aldred Rd, NW6 . . . . .90 D5
Aldren Rd, SW17 . . . . .167 F3
Aldriche Way, E4 . . . . .62 C6
Aldrich Gdns, Sutt. SM3 . . . . .198 C3
Aldrich Ter, SW18
off Lidiard Rd 167 F2
Aldridge Av, Edg. HA8 . . . . . . .54 B3
Ruislip HA4 . . . . .84 C4
Stanmore HA7 . . . . .69 H1
Aldridge Ri, N.Mal. KT3 . . . . .182 E7
Aldridge Rd Vil, W11 . . . . .108 C5
Aldridge Wk, N14 . . . . .42 E7
Aldrington Rd, SW16 . . . . .168 C5
Aldsworth Cl, W9 . . . . .6 A6
Aldwick Cl, SE9 . . . . .175 G3
Aldwick Rd, Croy. CR0 . . . . . .201 F3
Aldworth Gro, SE13 . . . . .154 C6
Aldworth Rd, E15 . . . . .96 E7
Aldwych, WC2 . . . . .18 C5
Aldwych Av, Ilf. IG6 . . . . .81 F4
Aldwych Underpass, WC2
off Kingsway 111 F6
Alers Rd, Bexh. DA6 . . . . .158 D5
Alesia Cl, N22
off Nightingale Rd 58/59 E7
Alestan Beck Rd, E16 . . . . . . .116 A5
Alexa Ct, W8 . . . . .30 A1
Sutton SM2 off Mulgrave Rd .198 D6
Alexander Av, NW10 . . . . .89 H7
Alexander Cl, Barn. EN4 . . . . . .41 G4
Bromley BR2 . . . . .205 G1
Sidcup DA15 . . . . .157 H5
Southall UB2 . . . . .123 J1
Twickenham TW2 . . . . . . .162 C2
Alexander Evans Ms, SE23 . . .171 G1
★ Alexander Fleming Laboratory
Mus, W2 . . . . .15 F3
Alexander Ho, Kings.T. KT2
off Kingsgate Rd 181 H1
Alexander Ms, W2 . . . . .14 A3
Alexander Pl, SW7 . . . . .31 G1
Alexander Rd, N19 . . . . .92 E3
Bexleyheath DA7 . . . . . . .158 D2
Chislehurst BR7 . . . . .175 E5
Alexander Sq, SW3 . . . . .31 G1
Alexander St, W2 . . . . .108 D6
Alexandra Av, N22 . . . . .74 D1
SW11 . . . . .150 A1
W4 . . . . .126 D7
Harrow HA2 . . . . .85 F1
Southall UB1 . . . . .103 F7
Sutton SM1 . . . . .198 D3
Alexandra Cl, SE8 . . . . .133 J6
Harrow HA2
off Alexandra Av 85 G3
Alexandra Cotts, SE14 . . . . . .153 J1
Alexandra Ct, N14 . . . . .42 C5
N16 off Belgrade Rd 94 C4
Wembley HA9 . . . . .87 J4
Alexandra Cres, Brom. BR1 . . .173 F6
Alexandra Dr, SE19 . . . . .170 B5
Surbiton KT5 . . . . .182 A7

Alexandra Gdns, N10 . . . . .74 B4
W4 . . . . .126 D7
Hounslow TW3 . . . . .143 H2
Alexandra Gro, N4 . . . . .93 H1
N12 . . . . .57 E5
Alexandra Ms, N2
off Fortis Grn 73 J3
SW19 off Alexandra Rd . . .166 D6
★ Alexandra Palace, N22 . . . . .74 D2
Alexandra Palace Way, N22 . . .74 C3
Alexandra Pk Rd, N10 . . . . . . .74 B2
N22 . . . . .74 D2
Alexandra Pl, NW8 . . . . .109 F1
Croydon CR0
off Alexandra Rd 202 B1
Alexandra Rd, E6 . . . . .116 D3
E10 . . . . .96 C3
E17 . . . . .77 J6
E18 . . . . .79 H3
N8 . . . . .75 G3
N9 . . . . .44 E7
N10 . . . . .58 B6
N15 . . . . .76 A5
NW4 . . . . .72 A4
NW8 . . . . .91 F7
SE26 . . . . .171 G6
SW14 . . . . .146 D3
SW19 . . . . .166 C6
W4 . . . . .126 D2
Brentford TW8 . . . . .125 G6
Croydon CR0 . . . . .202 B1
Enfield EN3 . . . . .45 G4
Hounslow TW3 . . . . .143 H2
Kingston upon Thames KT2 .164 A7
Mitcham CR4 . . . . .167 H7
Richmond TW9 . . . . .145 J2
Romford (Chad.Hth) RM6 . .82 D6
Thames Ditton KT7 . . . . . .180 C5
Twickenham TW1 . . . . . . .145 F6
Alexandra Sq, Mord. SM4 . . . .184 D5
Alexandra St, E16 . . . . .115 G5
SE14 . . . . .133 H7
Alexandra Wk, SE19 . . . . .170 B5
Alexandria Rd, W13 . . . . .104 D7
Alexis St, SE16 . . . . .37 H1
Alfearn Rd, E5 . . . . .95 F4
Alford Grn, Croy. (New Adgtn)
CR0 . . . . .204 D6
Alford Pl, N1 . . . . .12 A2
Alfoxton Av, N15 . . . . .75 H4
Alfreda St, SW11 . . . . .150 B1
Alfred Cl, W4 off Belmont Rd . .126 D4
Alfred Gdns, Sthl. UB1 . . . . . .103 E7
Alfred Ms, W1 . . . . .17 H1
Alfred Pl, WC1 . . . . .17 H1
Alfred Prior Ho, E12 . . . . .98 D4
Alfred Rd, E15 . . . . .97 F5
SE25 . . . . .188 D5
W2 . . . . .108 D5
W3 . . . . .126 C1
Belvedere DA17 . . . . .139 F5
Buckhurst Hill IG9 . . . . . . .64 A2
Feltham TW13 . . . . .160 C2
Kingston upon Thames KT1 .181 H3
Sutton SM1 . . . . .199 F5
Alfred's Gdns, Bark. IG11 . . . .117 H2
Alfred St, E3 . . . . .113 J3
Alfreds Way, Bark. IG11 . . . . . .117 F3
Alfreds Way Ind Est, Bark. IG11 .118 A1
Alfreton Cl, SW19 . . . . .166 A3
Alfriston Av, Croy. CR0 . . . . . .186 E7
Harrow HA2 . . . . .67 G6
Alfriston Cl, Surb. KT5 . . . . . .181 J5
Alfriston Rd, SW11 . . . . .149 J5
Algar Cl, Islw. TW7 off Algar Rd .144 D3
Stanmore HA7 . . . . .52 C5
Algar Rd, Islw. TW7 . . . . .144 D3
Algarve Rd, SW18 . . . . .167 E1
Algernon Rd, NW4 . . . . .71 G6
NW6 . . . . .108 D1
SE13 . . . . .154 B4
Algers Cl, Loug. IG10 . . . . .48 A5
Algers Mead, Loug. IG10 . . . . .48 A5
Algers Rd, Loug. IG10 . . . . . . .48 A5
Algiers Rd, SE13 . . . . .154 A4
Alibon Gdns, Dag. RM10 . . . . .101 G5
Alibon Rd, Dag. RM9, RM10 . . .101 F5
Alice Cl, Barn. EN5 . . . . .41 F4
Alice Ct, SW15 off Deodar Rd . .148 C4
Alice Gilliatt Ct, W14 . . . . .128 C6
Alice La, E3 . . . . .113 J1
Alice Ms, Tedd. TW11
off Luther Rd 162 C5
Alice St, SE1 . . . . .28 D6
Alice Thompson Cl, SE12 . . . .173 J2
Alice Walker Cl, SE24
off Shakespeare Rd 151 H4
Alice Way, Houns. TW3 . . . . . .143 H4
Alicia Av, Har. HA3 . . . . .69 E4
Alicia Cl, Har. HA3 . . . . .69 F4
Alicia Gdns, Har. HA3 . . . . .69 E4
Alie St, E1 . . . . .21 G4
Alington Cres, NW9 . . . . .88 C1
Alison Cl, E6 . . . . .116 D6
Croydon CR0
off Shirley Oaks Rd 203 G1

Aliwal Rd, SW11 . . . . .149 H4
Alkerden Rd, W4 . . . . .127 E5
Alkham Rd, N16 . . . . .94 C2
Allan Barclay Cl, N15
off High Rd 76 C6
Allan Cl, N.Mal. KT3 . . . . .182 D5
Allandale Av, N3 . . . . .72 B3
Allan Way, W3 . . . . .106 C4
Allard Cres, Bushey (Bushey Hth)
WD23 . . . . .51 J1
Allard Gdns, SW4 . . . . .150 D5
Allardyce St, SW4 . . . . .151 F4
Allbrook Cl, Tedd. TW11 . . . . .162 B5
Allcroft Rd, NW5 . . . . .92 A5
Allder Way, S.Croy. CR2 . . . . .201 H7
Allenby Cl, Grnf. UB6 . . . . . . .103 G3
Allenby Rd, SE23 . . . . .171 H3
SE28 off Broadwater Rd . . .137 F3
Southall UB1 . . . . .103 G6
Allen Cl, Mitch. CR4 . . . . .186 B1
Sunbury-on-Thames TW16 .178 B1
Allen Ct, Grnf. UB6 . . . . .86 C5
Allendale Av, Sthl. UB1 . . . . . .103 G6
Allendale Cl, SE5
off Daneville Rd 152 A1
SE26 . . . . .171 G5
Allendale Rd, Grnf. UB6 . . . . . .86 E6
Allen Edwards Dr, SW8 . . . . . .150 E1
Allenford Ho, SW15
off Tunworth Cres 147 F6
Allen Pl, Twick. TW1
off Church St 162 D1
Allen Rd, E3 . . . . .113 J2
N16 . . . . .94 B4
Beckenham BR3 . . . . .189 G2
Croydon CR0 . . . . .187 F7
Sunbury-on-Thames TW16 .178 B1
Allensbury Pl, NW1 . . . . .92 D7
Allens Rd, Enf. EN3 . . . . .45 F5
Allen St, W8 . . . . .128 D3
Allenswood Rd, SE9 . . . . .156 B3
Allerford Ct, Har. HA2 . . . . .67 H5
Allerford Rd, SE6 . . . . .172 B4
Allerton Ct, NW4
off Holders Hill Rd 72 A2
Allerton Rd, N16 . . . . .93 J2
Allerton Wk, N7 off Durham Rd .93 F2
Allestree Rd, SW6 . . . . .128 B7
Alleyn Cres, SE21 . . . . .170 A2
Alleyndale Rd, Dag. RM8 . . . .100 C2
Alleyn Pk, SE21 . . . . .170 A2
Southall UB2 . . . . .123 F4
Alleyn Rd, SE21 . . . . .170 A3
Allfarthing La, SW18 . . . . .149 E6
Allgood Cl, Mord. SM4 . . . . . .184 A6
Allgood St, E2 . . . . .13 G2
Allhallows La, EC4 . . . . .20 B6
★ All Hallows-on-the-Wall
C of E Ch, EC2 . . . . .20 C2
Allhallows Rd, E6 . . . . .116 B5
All Hallows Rd, N17 . . . . .76 B1
Alliance Cl, Wem. HA0 . . . . . . .87 G4
Alliance Ct, W3 off Alliance Rd .106 B4
Alliance Rd, E13 . . . . .115 J4
SE18 . . . . .138 A6
W3 . . . . .106 B4
Allied Way, W3
off Larden Rd 126/127 A2
Allingham Cl, W7 . . . . .104 C7
Allingham Ms, N1 . . . . .11 J1
Allingham St, N1 . . . . .11 J1
Allington Av, N17 . . . . .60 B6
Allington Cl, SW19
off High St Wimbledon . . .166 A5
Greenford UB6 . . . . .85 J7
Allington Ct, Enf. EN3 . . . . .45 G5
Allington Rd, NW4 . . . . .71 H5
W10 . . . . .108 B2
Harrow HA2 . . . . .67 J5
Orpington BR6 . . . . .207 G2
Allington St, SW1 . . . . .25 F6
Allison Cl, SE10
off Dartmouth Hill 154 C1
Allison Gro, SE21 . . . . .170 B1
Allison Rd, N8 . . . . .75 G5
W3 . . . . .106 C6
Allitsen Rd, NW8 . . . . .7 G2
Allnutt Way, SW4 . . . . .150 D5
Alloa Rd, SE8 . . . . .133 G6
Ilford IG3 . . . . .100 A2
Allonby Gdns, Wem. HA9 . . . . .87 F1
Allotment Way, NW2
off Midland Ter 90 A3
Alloway Rd, E3 . . . . .113 H3
Allports Ms, E1 off Stepney Grn .113 F4
All Saints Cl, N9 . . . . .60 C2
SW8
off Lansdowne Way 150/151 E1
All Saints Dr, SE3 . . . . .155 E2
All Saints Ms, Har. HA3 . . . . . .52 B6
All Saints Pas, SW18
off Wandsworth High St .148/149 E5
All Saints Rd, SW19 . . . . .167 F7
W3 . . . . .126 C3
W11 . . . . .108 C5
Sutton SM1 . . . . .199 E3
All Saints St, N1 . . . . .10 C1

All Saints Twr, E10 . . . . .78 B1
Allsop Pl, NW1 . . . . .8 A6
All Souls Av, NW10 . . . . .107 H2
All Souls Pl, W1 . . . . .17 E2
Allum Way, N20 . . . . .57 F1
Allwood Cl, SE26 . . . . .171 G4
Alma Av, E4 . . . . .62 C7
Almack Rd, E5 . . . . .95 F4
Alma Cres, Sutt. SM1 . . . . . . .198 B5
Alma Gro, SE1 . . . . .37 G2
Alma Pl, NW10 off Harrow Rd .107 H3
SE19 . . . . .170 C7
Thornton Heath CR7 . . . . .187 G5
Alma Rd, N10 . . . . .58 A7
SW18 . . . . .149 F5
Carshalton SM5 . . . . .199 H5
Enfield EN3 . . . . .45 H5
Esher KT10 . . . . .194 B3
Sidcup DA14 . . . . .176 A3
Southall UB1 . . . . .102 E7
Alma Row, Har. HA3 . . . . .68 A1
Alma Sq, NW8 . . . . .6 D3
Alma St, E15 . . . . .96 D6
NW5 . . . . .92 B6
Alma Ter, SW18 . . . . .149 G7
W8 off Allen St 128 D3
Almeida St, N1 . . . . .93 H1
Almeric Rd, SW11 . . . . .149 J4
Almer Rd, SW20 . . . . .165 G7
Almington St, N4 . . . . .93 F1
Almond Av, W5 . . . . .125 H3
Carshalton SM5 . . . . .199 J2
West Drayton UB7 . . . . . . .120 D3
Almond Cl, SE15 . . . . .152 D2
Bromley BR2 . . . . .192 D7
Feltham TW13
off Highfield Rd 160 A1
Almond Gro, Brent. TW8 . . . . .124 E7
Almond Rd, N17 . . . . .60 D7
SE16 . . . . .133 F4
Almonds Av, Buck.H. IG9 . . . . .63 G2
Almond Way, Borwd. WD6 . . . .38 B4
Bromley BR2 . . . . .192 D7
Harrow HA2 . . . . .67 H2
Mitcham CR4 . . . . .186 D5
Almorah Rd, N1 . . . . .94 A7
Hounslow TW5 . . . . .142 D1
Alnwick Gro, Mord. SM4
off Bordesley Rd 184/185 E4
Alnwick Rd, E16 . . . . .115 J6
SE12 . . . . .155 H7
ALPERTON, Wem. HA0 . . . . . .105 J1
Alperton La, Grnf. UB6 . . . . . .105 G3
Wembley HA0 . . . . .105 G3
Alperton St, W10 . . . . .108 B4
Alphabet Gdns, Cars. SM5 . . .185 G6
Alphabet Sq, E3
off Hawgood St 114 A5
Alpha Cl, NW1 . . . . .7 H4
Alpha Gro, E14 . . . . .134 A2
Alpha Pl, NW6 . . . . .108 D2
SW3 . . . . .31 H5
Alpha Rd, E4 . . . . .62 B3
N18 . . . . .60 D6
SE14 . . . . .153 J1
Croydon CR0 . . . . .202 B1
Enfield EN3 . . . . .45 H4
Surbiton KT5 . . . . .181 J6
Teddington TW11 . . . . . . .162 A5
Alpha St, SE15 . . . . .152 D2
Alphea Cl, SW19
off Courtney Rd 167 H7
Alpine Av, Surb. KT5 . . . . .196 C2
Alpine Business Cen, E6 . . . . .116 D5
Alpine Cl, Croy. CR0 . . . . .202 B3
Alpine Copse, Brom. BR1 . . . .192 D2
Alpine Gro, E9 . . . . .95 F7
Alpine Rd, E10 . . . . .96 B2
SE16 . . . . .133 F4
Walton-on-Thames KT12 . .178 A7
Alpine Vw, Cars. SM5 . . . . . . .199 H5
Alpine Wk, Stan. HA7 . . . . .52 B2
Alpine Way, E6 . . . . .116 D5
Alric Av, NW10 . . . . .88 D7
New Malden KT3 . . . . . . .183 E3
Alroy Rd, N4 . . . . .75 G7
Alsace Rd, SE17 . . . . .36 D3
Alscot Rd, SE1 . . . . .37 G1
Alscot Way, SE1 . . . . .37 F1
Alsike Rd, SE2 . . . . .138 D3
Erith DA18 . . . . .138 E3
Alsom Av, Wor.Pk. KT4 . . . . . .197 G4
Alston Cl, Surb. KT6 . . . . .181 E7
Alston Rd, N18 . . . . .60 E5
SW17 . . . . .167 G4
Barnet EN5 . . . . .40 B3
Altair Cl, N17 . . . . .60 C6
Altash Way, SE9 . . . . .174 C2
Altenburg Av, W13 . . . . .125 E3
Altenburg Gdns, SW11 . . . . . .149 J4
Alt Gro, SW19
off St. George's Rd 166 C7
Altham Rd, Pnr. HA5 . . . . .51 E7
Althea St, SW6 . . . . .149 E3
Althorne Gdns, E18 . . . . .79 F4
Althorne Way, Dag. RM10 . . . .101 G2

Althorp Cl, Barn. EN5 . . . . .39 G7
Althorpe Gro, SW11
   off Westbridge Rd 149 G1
Althorpe Ms, SW11
   off Battersea High St 149 G1
Althorpe Rd, Har. HA1 . . . . .67 J5
Althorp Rd, SW17 . . . . .167 J1
Altmore Av, E6 . . . . .98 C7
Alton Av, Stan. HA7 . . . . .52 C7
Alton Cl, Bex. DA5 . . . . .177 E1
   Isleworth TW7 . . . . .144 C2
Alton Gdns, Beck. BR3 . . . . . . .172 A7
   Twickenham TW2 . . . . .144 A7
Alton Rd, N17 . . . . .76 A3
   SW15 . . . . .165 G1
   Croydon CR0 . . . . .201 G3
   Richmond TW9 . . . . .145 H4
Alton St, E14 . . . . .114 B5
Altyre Cl, Beck. BR3 . . . . .189 J5
Altyre Rd, Croy. CR0 . . . . .202 A2
Altyre Way, Beck. BR3 . . . . .189 J5
Alvanley Gdns, NW6 . . . . .90 E5
Alva Way, Wat. WD19 . . . . .50 D2
Alverstone Av, SW19 . . . . .166 D2
   Barnet EN4 . . . . .41 H7
Alverstone Gdns, SE9 . . . . .175 F1
Alverstone Rd, E12 . . . . .98 D4
   NW2 . . . . .89 J7
   New Malden KT3 . . . . .183 F4
   Wembley HA9 . . . . .87 J1
Alverston Gdns, SE25 . . . . .188 B5
Alverton St, SE8 . . . . .133 J5
Alveston Av, Har. HA3 . . . . .68 E3
Alvey Est, SE17 . . . . .36 D2
Alvey St, SE17 . . . . .36 D3
Alvia Gdns, Sutt. SM1 . . . . .199 F4
Alvington Cres, E8 . . . . .94 C5
Alway Av, Epsom KT19 . . . . . . .196 C5
Alwold Cres, SE12 . . . . .155 H6
Alwyn Av, W4 . . . . .126 D5
Alwyn Cl, Croy. (New Adgtn)
   CR0 . . . . .204 B7
Alwyne La, N1 off Alwyne Vil . .93 H7
Alwyne Pl, N1 . . . . .93 J6
Alwyne Rd, N1 . . . . .93 J7
   SW19 . . . . .166 C6
   W7 . . . . .104 B7
Alwyne Sq, N1 . . . . .93 J6
Alwyne Vil, N1 . . . . .93 H7
Alwyn Gdns, NW4 . . . . .71 G4
   W3 . . . . .106 B6
Alyth Gdns, NW11 . . . . .72 D6
Alzette Ho, E2 . . . . .113 G3
Amalgamated Dr, Brent. TW8 . .124 D6
Amanda Cl, Chig. IG7 . . . . .65 G6
Amanda Ms, Rom. RM7 . . . . . . .83 J5
Amazon Apartments, N8
   off High St 75 F4
Amazon St, E1
   off Hessel St 112/113 E6
Ambassador Cl, Houns. TW3 . .142 E2
Ambassador Gdns, E6 . . . . .116 C5
Ambassador's Ct, SW1 . . . . .25 G2
Ambassador Sq, E14
   off Cahir St 134 B4
Amber Av, E17 . . . . .77 H1
Amber Ct, SW17
   off Brudenell Rd 168 A4
Amberden Av, N3 . . . . .72 D3
Ambergate St, SE17 . . . . .35 H3
Amber Gro, NW2 off Prayle Gro .90 A1
Amber La, Ilf. IG6 . . . . .64 E7
Amberley Cl, Orp. BR6
   off Warnford Rd 207 J5
   Pinner HA5 . . . . .67 F3
Amberley Ct, Sid. DA14 . . . . . .176 C5
Amberley Gdns, Enf. EN1 . . . . . .44 B7
   Epsom KT19 . . . . .197 F4
Amberley Gro, SE26 . . . . .170 E4
   Croydon CR0 . . . . .188 C7
Amberley Rd, E10 . . . . .78 B7
   N13 . . . . .59 F2
   SE2 . . . . .138 D6
   W9 . . . . .108 C5
   Buckhurst Hill IG9 . . . . .63 J1
   Enfield EN1 . . . . .44 C7
Amberley Way, Houns. TW4 . . .142 C7
   Morden SM4 . . . . .184 C7
   Romford RM7 . . . . .83 H4
Amber Ms, N22
   off Brampton Pk Rd 75 G3
Amberside Cl, Islw. TW7 . . . . . .144 A6
Amber St, E15
   off Great Eastern Rd 96 D6
Amber Wf, E2 off Nursery La . .112 C1
Amberwood Cl, Wall. SM6
   off The Chase 200/201 E5
Amberwood Ri, N.Mal. KT3 . . .182 E6
Amblecote Cl, SE12 . . . . .173 H3
Amblecote Meadows, SE12 . . .173 H3
Amblecote Rd, SE12 . . . . .173 H3
Ambler Rd, N4 . . . . .93 H3
Ambleside, Brom. BR1 . . . . . . .172 D6
Ambleside Av, SW16 . . . . .168 D4
   Beckenham BR3 . . . . .189 H5
Ambleside Cl, E9
   off Churchill Wk 95 F5

Ambleside Cl, E10 . . . . .78 B7
Ambleside Cres, Enf. EN3 . . . . . .45 G3
Ambleside Gdns, SW16 . . . . . .168 D4
   Ilford IG4 . . . . .80 B4
   Sutton SM2 . . . . .199 F6
   Wembley HA9 . . . . .87 G1
Ambleside Pt, SE15
   off Ilderton Rd 133 F7
Ambleside Rd, NW10 . . . . .89 F7
   Bexleyheath DA7 . . . . .159 G2
Ambrooke Rd, Belv. DA17 . . . . .139 G3
Ambrosden Av, SW1 . . . . .25 G6
Ambrose Av, NW11 . . . . .72 B7
Ambrose Cl, E6 off Lovage App .116 B5
   Orpington BR6
   off Stapleton Rd 207 J3
Ambrose Ms, SW11 . . . . .149 H2
Ambrose St, SE16 . . . . .132 E4
Ambrose Wk, E3
   off Malmesbury Rd 114 A2
Amelia Cl, W3 . . . . .126 B1
Amelia St, SE17 . . . . .35 H3
Amen Cor, EC4 . . . . .19 H4
   SW17 . . . . .167 J6
Amen Ct, EC4 . . . . .19 H3
Amenity Way, Mord. SM4 . . . . .183 J7
America Sq, EC3 . . . . .21 F5
America St, SE1 . . . . .27 J2
Amerland Rd, SW18 . . . . .148 C6
Amersham Av, N18 . . . . .60 A6
Amersham Gro, SE14 . . . . .133 J7
Amersham Rd, SE14 . . . . .133 J7
   Croydon CR0 . . . . .187 J6
Amersham Vale, SE14 . . . . .133 J7
Amery Gdns, NW10 . . . . .107 H1
Amery Rd, Har. HA1 . . . . .86 D2
Amesbury Av, SW2 . . . . .169 E2
Amesbury Cl, Wor.Pk. KT4 . . . .197 J1
Amesbury Dr, E4 . . . . .46 B6
Amesbury Rd, Brom. BR1 . . . . .192 A3
   Dagenham RM9 . . . . .100 D7
   Feltham TW13 . . . . .160 D2
Amesbury Twr, SW8
   off Westbury St 150 C2
Amethyst Cl, N11 . . . . .58 D7
Amethyst Rd, E15 . . . . .96 D4
Amherst Av, W13 . . . . .105 F6
Amherst Dr, Orp. BR5 . . . . .193 J4
Amherst Rd, W13 . . . . .105 F6
Amherst Gdns, Islw. TW7 . . . . .144 C1
Amhurst Par, N16
   off Amhurst Pk 76 C7
Amhurst Pk, N16 . . . . .76 A7
Amhurst Pas, E8 . . . . .94 D4
Amhurst Rd, E8 . . . . .94 E5
   N16 . . . . .94 C4
Amhurst Ter, E8 . . . . .94 D4
Amhurst Wk, SE28
   off Pitfield Cres 138 A1
Amidas Gdns, Dag. RM8 . . . . . .100 B4
Amiel St, E1 . . . . .113 F4
Amies St, SW11 . . . . .149 J3
Amina Way, SE16 . . . . .29 H6
Amis Av, Epsom KT19 . . . . .196 B6
Amity Gro, SW20 . . . . .183 J1
Amity Rd, E15 . . . . .115 F1
Ammanford Grn, NW9
   off Ruthin Cl 70/71 E6
Amner Rd, SW11 . . . . .150 A6
Amor Rd, W6 . . . . .127 J3
Amott Rd, SE15 . . . . .152 D3
Amoy Pl, E14 . . . . .114 A6
Ampere Way, Croy. CR0 . . . . . .187 E7
Ampleforth Rd, SE2 . . . . .138 B2
Ampthill Sq, NW1 . . . . .9 G2
Ampton Pl, WC1 . . . . .10 C4
Ampton St, WC1 . . . . .10 C4
Amroth Cl, SE23 . . . . .171 E1
Amroth Grn, NW9
   off Fryent Gro 70/71 E6
Amsterdam Rd, E14 . . . . .134 C3
Amundsen Ct, E14
   off Napier Av 134 A5
Amwell Cl, Enf. EN2 . . . . .44 A5
Amwell Ct Est, N4 . . . . .93 J1
Amwell St, EC1 . . . . .11 E3
Amyand Cotts, Twick. TW1
   off Amyand Pk Rd 144/145 E6
Amyand La, Twick. TW1
   off Marble Hill Gdns 144/145 E7
Amyand Pk Gdns, Twick. TW1
   off Amyand Pk Rd 144/145 E7
Amyand Pk Rd, Twick. TW1 . . . .144 D7
Amy Cl, Wall. SM6
   off Mollison Dr 200/201 E7
Amyruth Rd, SE4 . . . . .154 A5
Amy Warne Cl, E6
   off Evelyn Denington Rd . . .116 B4
Anatola Rd, N19
   off Dartmouth Pk Hill 92 B2
Ancaster Cres, N.Mal. KT3 . . . .183 G6
Ancaster Ms, Beck. BR3 . . . . . .189 G3
Ancaster Rd, Beck. BR3 . . . . . .189 G3
Ancaster St, SE18 . . . . .137 H7
Anchorage Cl, SW19 . . . . .166 D5
Anchorage Pt, E14 off Cuba St . .134 A2
Anchorage Pt Ind Est, SE7 . . . .135 J3

Anchor & Hope La, SE7 . . . . . .135 H3
Anchor Cl, Bark. IG11 . . . . .118 B3
Anchor Ms, N1
   off Balls Pond Rd 94 B6
   SW12 off Hazelbourne Rd . .150 B6
Anchor Retail Pk, E1 . . . . .113 F4
Anchor St, SE16 . . . . .132 E4
Anchor Ter, E1 off Cephas Av . .113 F4
Anchor Wf, E3 off Watts Gro . .114 B5
Anchor Yd, EC1 . . . . .12 A5
Ancill Cl, W6 . . . . .128 B6
Ancona Rd, NW10 . . . . .107 G2
   SE18 . . . . .137 G5
Andace Pk Gdns, Brom. BR1 . .191 J1
Andalus Rd, SW9 . . . . .151 E3
Ander Cl, Wem. HA0 . . . . .87 G4
Anderson Cl, N21 . . . . .43 F5
   W3 . . . . .106 D6
   Sutton SM3 . . . . .198 D1
Anderson Pl, Houns. TW3 . . . . .143 H4
Anderson Rd, E9 . . . . .95 G6
   Woodford Green IG8 . . . . . .80 A3
Andersons Sq, N1 off Gaskin St .111 H1
Anderson St, SW3 . . . . .31 J3
Anderson Way, Belv. DA17 . . . .139 H2
Anderton Cl, SE5 . . . . .152 A3
Andmark Ct, Sthl. UB1
   off Herbert Rd 123 F1
Andover Av, E16
   off King George Av 116 A6
Andover Cl, Grnf. UB6
   off Ruislip Rd 103 H4
Andover Pl, NW6 . . . . .6 A1
Andover Rd, N7 . . . . .93 F2
   Orpington BR6 . . . . .207 H3
   Twickenham TW2 . . . . .162 A1
Andre St, E8 . . . . .94 D5
Andrew Borde St, WC2 . . . . .17 J3
Andrew Cl, Ilf. IG6 . . . . .65 G6
Andrewes Gdns, E6 . . . . .116 B6
Andrewes Ho, EC2 . . . . .20 A2
Andrew Pl, SW8
   off Cowthorpe Rd 150 D1
Andrew Reed Ho, SW18
   off Linstead Way 148 B7
Andrews Cl, E6
   off Linton Gdns 116 B6
   Buckhurst Hill IG9 . . . . .63 J2
   Harrow HA1
   off Bessborough Rd 68 A7
   Worcester Park KT4 . . . . . .198 A2
Andrews Crosse, WC2 . . . . .18 E4
Andrews Pl, SE9 . . . . .156 E6
Andrew's Rd, E8 . . . . .112 E1
Andrew St, E14 . . . . .114 C6
Andrews Wk, SE17 . . . . .35 H6
Andwell Cl, SE2 . . . . .138 B2
ANERLEY, SE20 . . . . .188 E1
Anerley Gro, SE19 . . . . .170 C7
Anerley Hill, SE19 . . . . .170 C6
Anerley Pk, SE20 . . . . .170 D7
Anerley Pk Rd, SE20 . . . . .170 D7
Anerley Pl, SE19 . . . . .170 D7
   SE20 . . . . .170 D7
Anerley Sta Rd, SE20 . . . . .188 E1
Anerley St, SW11 . . . . .149 J2
Anerley Vale, SE19 . . . . .170 C7
Anfield Cl, SW12
   off Belthorn Cres 150 C7
Angel All, E1 . . . . .21 G3
Angel Cl, N18 . . . . .60 C4
Angel Cor Par, N18 off Fore St . .60 D5
Angel Ct, EC2 . . . . .20 C3
   SW1 . . . . .25 G2
   SW17 . . . . .167 J4
Angel Edmonton, N18
   off Angel Rd 60 D5
Angelfield, Houns. TW3 . . . . . .143 H4
Angel Gate, EC1 . . . . .11 H3
Angel Hill, Sutt. SM1
   off Sutton Common Rd .198/199 E3
Angel Hill Dr, Sutt. SM1 . . . . . .199 E3
Angelica Dr, E6 . . . . .116 D5
Angelica Gdns, Croy. CR0 . . . . .203 G1
Angelis Apartments, N1
   off Graham St 111 H2
Angel La, E15 . . . . .96 D6
Angell Pk Gdns, SW9 . . . . .151 G3
Angell Rd, SW9 . . . . .151 G3
Angell Town Est, SW9 . . . . .151 G2
Angel Ms, E1 off Cable St 112 D7
   N1 . . . . .11 F2
   SW15
   off Roehampton High St . . .147 G7
Angel Pas, EC4 . . . . .20 B6
Angel Pl, N18 . . . . .60 D5
   SE1 . . . . .28 B3
Angel Rd, N18 . . . . .60 E5
   Harrow HA1 . . . . .68 B6
   Thames Ditton KT7 . . . . . .180 D7
Angel Rd Wks, N18 . . . . .61 F5
Angel Sq, EC1 . . . . .11 F2
Angel St, EC1 . . . . .19 J3
Angel Wk, W6 . . . . .127 J4
Angerstein La, SE3 . . . . .135 F7

Angle Grn, Dag. RM8 . . . . .100 C1
Anglers Cl, Rich. TW10
   off Locksmeade Rd 163 F4
Angler's La, NW5 . . . . .92 B6
Anglers Reach, Surb. KT6 . . . . .181 G5
Anglesea Av, SE18 . . . . .136 E4
Anglesea Ms, SE18
   off Anglesea Av 136/137 E4
Anglesea Rd, SE18 . . . . .136 E4
   Kingston upon Thames KT1 .181 G4
Anglesea Ter, W6
   off Wellesley Av 127 H3
Anglesey Ct Rd, Cars. SM5 . . . .200 A6
Anglesey Gdns, Cars. SM5 . . . .200 A6
Anglesey Rd, Enf. EN3 . . . . .45 E4
   Watford WD19 . . . . .50 C5
Anglesmede Cres, Pnr. HA5 . . . .67 G3
Anglesmede Way, Pnr. HA5 . . . .67 F3
Angles Rd, SW16 . . . . .169 E4
Anglia Cl, N17 off Park La . . .60/61 E7
Anglia Ct, Dag. RM8
   off Spring Cl 100 D1
Anglia Ho, E14 . . . . .113 H6
Anglian Rd, E11 . . . . .96 D3
Anglia Wk, E6 . . . . .116 C1
Anglo Rd, E3 . . . . .113 J2
Angrave Ct, E8 . . . . .112 C1
Angrave Pas, E8
   off Haggerston Rd 112 C1
Angus Cl, Chess. KT9 . . . . .196 A5
Angus Dr, Ruis. HA4 . . . . .84 C4
Angus Gdns, NW9 . . . . .70 D1
Angus Rd, E13 . . . . .115 J3
Angus St, SE14 . . . . .133 H7
Anhalt Rd, SW11 . . . . .31 H7
Ankerdine Cres, SE18 . . . . .136 D7
Anlaby Rd, Tedd. TW11 . . . . . . .162 B5
Anley Rd, W14 . . . . .128 A2
Anmersh Gro, Stan. HA7 . . . . . .69 G1
Annabel Cl, E14 . . . . .114 B6
Anna Cl, E8 . . . . .112 C1
Annandale Rd, SE10 . . . . .135 F6
   W4 . . . . .126 E4
   Croydon CR0 . . . . .202 D2
   Sidcup DA15 . . . . .157 H7
Anna Neagle Cl, E7
   off Dames Rd 97 G4
Anne Boleyn's Wk, Kings.T. KT2 .163 H5
   Sutton SM3 . . . . .198 A7
Anne Case Ms, N.Mal. KT3
   off Sycamore Gro 182 D3
Anne Compton Ms, SE12 . . . . .155 F7
Annesley Av, NW9 . . . . .70 D3
Annesley Cl, NW10 . . . . .88 E3
Annesley Dr, Croy. CR0 . . . . . . .203 J3
Annesley Rd, SE3 . . . . .155 H1
Annesley Wk, N19 . . . . .92 C2
Anne St, E13 . . . . .115 G4
Annette Cl, Har. HA3
   off Spencer Rd 68 B2
Annette Cres, N1 off Essex Rd . .93 J7
Annette Rd, N7 . . . . .93 F4
Annett Rd, Walt. KT12 . . . . .178 A7
Anne Way, Ilf. IG6 . . . . .65 F6
   West Molesey KT8 . . . . . . .179 H4
Annie Besant Cl, E3 . . . . .113 J1
Annie Taylor Ho, E12
   off Walton Rd 98 D4
Anning St, EC2 . . . . .13 E5
Annington Rd, N2 . . . . .73 J3
Annis Rd, E9 . . . . .95 H6
Ann La, SW10 . . . . .30 E7
Ann Moss Way, SE16 . . . . .133 F3
Ann's Cl, SW1 . . . . .24 A4
Ann's Pl, E1 . . . . .21 F2
Ann St, SE18 . . . . .137 G4
Annsworthy Av, Th.Hth. CR7
   off Grange Pk Rd 188 A3
Annsworthy Cres, SE25
   off Grange Rd 188 A2
Ansdell Rd, SE15 . . . . .153 F2
Ansdell St, W8 . . . . .22 B5
Ansdell Ter, W8 . . . . .22 B5
Ansell Gro, Cars. SM5 . . . . .200 A1
Ansell Rd, SW17 . . . . .167 H3
Anselm Cl, Croy. CR0
   off Park Hill Ri 202 C3
Anselm Rd, SW6 . . . . .128 D6
   Pinner HA5 . . . . .51 F7
Ansford Rd, Brom. BR1 . . . . . . .172 C5
Ansleigh Pl, W11 . . . . .108 A7
Anson Cl, Rom. RM7 . . . . .83 H2
Anson Ho, E1 off Shandy St . . .113 H4
Anson Pl, SE28 . . . . .137 G2
Anson Rd, N7 . . . . .92 C4
   NW2 . . . . .90 A5
Anson Ter, Nthlt. UB5 . . . . .85 H6
Anstey Rd, SE15 . . . . .152 D3
Anstey Wk, N15 . . . . .75 H4
Anstice Cl, W4 . . . . .127 E7
Anstridge Path, SE9 . . . . .157 G6
Anstridge Rd, SE9 . . . . .157 G6
Antelope Rd, SE18 . . . . .136 C3
Anthony Cl, NW7 . . . . .55 E4
   Watford WD19 . . . . .50 C1
★ Anthony d'Offay Gall, W1 . . .16 E4
Anthony Rd, SE25 . . . . .188 D6

Anthony Rd, Grnf. UB6 104 B2
Welling DA16 158 A1
Anthony St, E1
off Commercial Rd 112/113 E6
Anthony Way, N18 61 G6
Antigua Cl, SE19
off Salters Hill 170 A5
Antigua Wk, SE19 170 A5
Antill Rd, E3 113 H3
N15 76 C4
Antill Ter, E1 113 G6
Antlers Hill, E4 46 B5
Anton Cres, Sutt. SM1 198 D3
Antoneys Cl, Pnr. HA5 66 D2
Anton Pl, Wem. HA9 88 B3
Anton St, E8 94 D5
Antrim Gro, NW3 91 J6
Antrim Mans, NW3 91 H6
Antrim Rd, NW3 91 J6
Antrobus Cl, Sutt. SM1 198 C5
Antrobus Rd, W4 126 C4
Anvil Cl, SW16 168 C7
Anvil Rd, Sun. TW16 178 A3
Anworth Cl, Wdf.Grn. IG8 63 H6
Apex Cl, Beck. BR3 190 B1
Apex Cor, NW7 54 D4
Apex Ind Est, NW10
off Hythe Rd 107 G3
Apex Retail Pk, Felt. TW13 161 F3
Apex Twr, N.Mal. KT3 182 E3
Aplin Way, Islw. TW7 144 B1
Apollo, E14 *off Newton Pl* 134 A4
Apollo Av, Brom. BR1
off Rodway Rd 191 H1
Northwood HA6 50 A5
★ **Apollo Hammersmith**, W6 127 J5
Apollo Pl, E11 96 E3
SW10 31 E7
★ **Apollo Thea**, W1 17 H5
★ **Apollo Victoria Thea**, SW1 25 F6
Apollo Way, SE28
off Broadwater Rd 137 G3
Apostle Way, Th.Hth. CR7 187 H2
Apothecary St, EC4 19 G4
Appach Rd, SW2 151 G6
Apple Blossom Ct, SW8
off Pascal St 130 D7
Appleby Cl, E4 62 C6
N15 76 A5
Twickenham TW2 162 A2
Appleby Rd, E8 94 D7
E16 115 F6
Appleby St, E2 13 F1
Appledore Av, Bexh. DA7 159 J1
Ruislip HA4 84 B3
Appledore Cl, SW17 167 J2
Bromley BR2 191 F5
Edgware HA8 70 A1
Appledore Cres, Sid. DA14 175 H3
Appledore Way, NW7
off Tavistock Av 56 A7
Appleford Rd, W10 108 B4
Apple Garth, Brent. TW8 125 G4
Applegarth, Croy. (New Adgtn)
CR0 204 B7
Esher (Clay.) KT10 194 C5
Applegarth Dr, Ilf. IG2 81 J4
Applegarth Rd, SE28 138 B1
W14 128 A3
Apple Gro, Chess. KT9 195 H4
Enfield EN1 44 B3
Apple Mkt, Kings.T. KT1
off Eden St 181 G2
Apple Rd, E11 96 E3
Appleton Cl, Bexh. DA7 159 J2
Appleton Gdns, N.Mal. KT3 183 G6
Appleton Rd, SE9 156 B3
Loughton IG10 49 E3
Appleton Sq, Mitch. CR4
off Silbury Av 185 H1
Appletree Cl, SE20
off Jasmine Gro 188/189 E1
Appletree Gdns, Barn. EN4 41 H4
Apple Tree Yd, SW1 25 G1
Applewood Cl, N20 57 H1
NW2 89 H3
Applewood Dr, E13 115 H4
Appold St, EC2 20 D1
Apprentice Way, E5
off Clarence Rd 94/95 E4
Approach, The, NW4 72 A5
W3 106 D6
Enfield EN1 44 E2
Orpington BR6 207 J2
Approach Cl, N16
off Cowper Rd 94 B4
Approach Rd, E2 113 F2
SW20 183 J2
Barnet EN4 41 G4
West Molesey KT8 179 G5
Aprey Gdns, NW4 71 J4
April Cl, W7 104 B7
Feltham TW13 160 A3
Orpington BR6
off Briarswood Way 207 J5
April Glen, SE23 171 G3
April St, E8 94 C4
Apsley Cl, Har. HA2 67 J5
★ **Apsley Ho, Wellington Mus**,
W1 24 B3
Apsley Rd, SE25 188 E4
New Malden KT3 182 C3
Apsley Way, NW2 89 G2
W1 24 C3
Aquarius Business Pk, NW2 89 G1
Aquarius Way, Nthwd. HA6 50 A5
★ **Aquatic Experience**, Brent.
TW8 145 E1
Aquila St, NW8 7 F1
Aquinas St, SE1 27 F2
Arabella Dr, SW15 147 E4
Arabia Cl, E4 46 D7
Arabin Rd, SE4 153 H4
Aragon Av, T.Ditt. KT7 180 C5
Aragon Cl, Brom. BR2 206 C1
Loughton IG10 48 B6
Aragon Dr, Ilf. IG6 65 F7
Ruislip HA4 84 D1
Aragon Rd, Kings.T. KT2 163 H5
Morden SM4 184 A6
Aragon Twr, SE8 133 J4
Arandora Cres, Rom. RM6 82 B7
Aran Dr, Stan. HA7 53 F4
Arbery Rd, E3 113 H3
Arbor Cl, Beck. BR3 190 B2
Arbor Ct, N16 *off Lordship Rd* 94 A2
Arborfield Cl, SW2 169 F1
Arbor Rd, E4 62 D3
Arbour Rd, Enf. EN3 45 G4
Arbour Sq, E1 113 G6
Arbroath Grn, Wat. WD19 50 A3
Arbroath Rd, SE9 156 B3
Arbury Ter, SE26
off Oaksford Av 170/171 E3
Arbuthnot La, Bex. DA5 159 E6
Arbuthnot Rd, SE14 153 G2
Arbutus St, E8 112 B1
Arcade, The, EC2 20 D2
Croydon CR0 *off High St* 201 J3
Arcadia Av, N3 72 D1
Arcadia Cl, Cars. SM5 200 A4
Arcadian Av, Bex. DA5 158 E6
Arcadian Cl, Bex. DA5 158 E6
Arcadian Gdns, N22 59 F7
Arcadian Pl, SW18
off Sutherland Gro 148 C7
Arcadian Rd, Bex. DA5 158 E6
Arcadia Shop Cen, W5 105 G7
Arcadia St, E14 114 A6
Archangel St, SE16 133 G2
Archbishops Pl, SW2 151 F6
Archdale Pl, N.Mal. KT3 182 B3
Archdale Rd, SE22 152 C5
Archel Rd, W14 128 C6
Archer Cl, Kings.T. KT2 163 H7
Archer Ho, SW11
off Vicarage Cres 149 G1
Archer Ms, Hmptn. (Hmptn H.)
TW12 *off Windmill Rd* 161 J6
Archer Rd, SE25 188 E4
Archers Dr, Enf. EN3 45 F2
Archer Sq, SE14 *off Knoyle St* 133 H6
Archer St, W1 17 H5
Archery Cl, W2 15 H4
Harrow HA3 68 C3
Archery Rd, SE9 156 C5
Arches, The, SW6
off Munster Rd 148 C2
WC2 26 B1
Harrow HA2 85 H2
Archibald Ms, W1 16 C6
Archibald Rd, N7 92 D4
Archibald St, E3 114 A3
Archie Cl, West Dr. UB7 120 D2
Archie St, SE1 29 E4
Arch St, SE1 27 J6
Archway Cl, N19
off St. Johns Way 92 C2
SW19 166 E4
W10 108 A5
Wallington SM6 200 D3
Archway Mall, N19
off Magdala Av 92 C2
Archway Ms, SW15
off Putney Br Rd 148 B4
Archway Rd, N6 73 J6
N19 92 C1
Archway St, SW13 147 E3
Arcola St, E8 94 C5
Arctic St, NW5 *off Gillies St* 92 A5
Arcus Rd, Brom. BR1 173 E6
Ardbeg Rd, SE24 152 A6
Arden Cl, SE28
off Redbourne Dr 118 D6
Harrow HA1 86 A3
Arden Ct Gdns, N2 73 G6
Arden Cres, E14 134 A4
Dagenham RM9 100 C7
Arden Est, N1 12 D2
Arden Gro, Orp. BR6 207 E4
Arden Ho, SW9
off Grantham Rd 150/151 E2
Arden Ms, E17 78 B5
Arden Mhor, Pnr. HA5 66 B4
Arden Rd, N3 72 B3
W13 105 F7
Ardent Cl, SE25 188 B3
Ardfern Av, SW16 187 G3
Ardfillan Rd, SE6 172 D1
Ardgowan Rd, SE6 154 E7
Ardilaun Rd, N5 93 J4
Ardingly Cl, Croy. CR0 203 G3
Ardleigh Gdns, Sutt. SM3 184 D7
Ardleigh Ho, Bark. IG11
off St. Ann's 117 F1
Ardleigh Ms, Ilf. IG1
off Bengal Rd 98/99 E3
Ardleigh Rd, E17 77 J1
N1 94 A6
Ardleigh Ter, E17 77 J1
Ardley Cl, NW10 88 E3
SE6 171 H3
Ardlui Rd, SE27 169 J2
Ardmay Gdns, Surb. KT6 181 H5
Ardmere Rd, SE13 154 D6
Ardmore La, Buck.H. IG9 47 H7
Ardmore Pl, Buck.H. IG9 47 H7
Ardoch Rd, SE6 172 D2
Ardra Rd, N9 61 G3
Ardrossan Gdns, Wor.Pk. KT4 197 G3
Ardshiel Cl, SW15
off Bemish Rd 148 A3
Ardwell Av, Ilf. IG6 81 F5
Ardwell Rd, SW2 168 E2
Ardwick Rd, NW2 90 D4
Arewater Grn, Loug. IG10 48 C1
Argali Ho, Erith DA18
off Kale Rd 138/139 E3
Argall Av, E10 77 G7
Argall Way, E10 95 G1
Argenta Way, NW10 88 B7
Argon Ms, SW6 128 D7
Argon Rd, N18 61 F5
Argosy La, Stai. (Stanw.) TW19 140 A7
Argus Cl, Rom. RM7 83 H1
Argus Way, Nthlt. UB5 102 E3
Argyle Av, Houns. TW3 143 G6
Argyle Cl, W13 104 D4
Argyle Pas, N17 76 C1
Argyle Pl, W6 127 H4
Argyle Rd, E1 113 G4
E15 96 E4
E16 115 J6
N12 56 D5
N17 76 D1
N18 60 D4
W13 104 D5
Barnet EN5 39 J4
Greenford UB6 104 C3
Harrow HA2 67 H6
Hounslow TW3 143 H5
Ilford IG1 98 D2
Teddington TW11 162 B5
Argyle Sq, WC1 10 B3
Argyle St, WC1 10 A3
Argyle Wk, WC1 10 B4
Argyle Way, SE16 37 J4
Argyll Av, Sthl. UB1 123 H1
Argyll Cl, SW9 *off Dalyell Rd* 151 F3
Argyll Gdns, Edg. HA8 70 B2
Argyll Rd, SE18 137 F3
W8 128 D2
Argyll St, W1 17 F4
Arica Rd, SE4 153 H4
Ariel Rd, NW6 90 D6
Ariel Way, W12 127 J1
Hounslow TW4 142 B3
Aristotle Rd, SW4 150 D3
Arkell Gro, SE19 169 H7
Arkindale Rd, SE6 172 C3
ARKLEY, Barn. EN5 39 G5
Arkley Cres, E17 77 J5
Arkley Dr, Barn. EN5 39 G4
Arkley La, Barn. EN5 39 G3
Arkley Pk, Barn. EN5 38 D6
Arkley Rd, E17 77 J5
Arkley Vw, Barn. EN5 39 H4
Arklow Ms, Surb. KT6
off Vale Rd S 195 H2
Arklow Rd, SE14 133 J6
Arkwright Rd, NW3 91 F5
Arlesey Cl, SW15 *off Lytton Gro* 148 B6
Arlesford Rd, SW9 151 E3
Arlingford Rd, SW2 151 G5
Arlington, N12 56 D3
Arlington Av, N1 111 J2
Arlington Cl, SE13 154 D6
Sidcup DA15 157 H7
Sutton SM1 198 D2
Twickenham TW1 145 F6
Arlington Ct, Hayes UB3
off Shepiston La 121 G5
Arlington Dr, Cars. SM5 199 J2
Arlington Gdns, W4 126 C5
Ilford IG1 98 D1
Arlington Grn, NW7 56 A7
Arlington Lo, SW2 151 F4
Arlington Ms, Twick. TW1
off Arlington Rd 145 F6
Arlington Pl, SE10
off Greenwich S St 134 C7
Arlington Rd, N14 58 B2
NW1 110 B1
W13 104 E6
Richmond TW10 163 G2
Surbiton KT6 181 G6
Teddington TW11 162 C4
Twickenham TW1 145 F6
Woodford Green IG8 79 G1
Arlington Sq, N1 111 J1
Arlington St, SW1 25 F1
Arlington Way, EC1 11 F3
Arliss Way, Nthlt. UB5 102 C1
Arlow Rd, N21 59 G1
Armada Ct, SE8
off Watergate St 134 A6
Armadale Cl, N17 76 E4
Armadale Rd, SW6 128 D7
Feltham TW14 142 A5
Armada Way, E6 117 E5
Armagh Rd, E3 113 J1
Armfield Cl, W.Mol. KT8 179 F5
Armfield Cres, Mitch. CR4 185 J2
Armfield Rd, Enf. EN2 44 A1
Arminger Rd, W12 127 H1
Armistice Gdns, SE25
off Penge Rd 188 D3
Armitage Rd, NW11 90 C1
SE10 135 F5
Armour Cl, N7 *off Roman Way* 93 F6
Armoury Rd, SE8 154 B2
Armoury Way, SW18 148 D5
Armstead Wk, Dag. RM10 101 G7
Armstrong Av, Wdf.Grn. IG8 62 E6
Armstrong Cl, E6 *off Porter Rd* 116 C6
Borehamwood WD6 38 C3
Dagenham RM8
off Palmer Rd 100 D1
Pinner HA5 66 A6
Walton-on-Thames KT12
off Sunbury La 178 A6
Armstrong Cres, Barn. EN4 41 G3
Armstrong Rd, SE18 137 F3
SW7 22 E6
W3 127 F1
Feltham TW13 160 E5
Armstrong Way, Sthl. UB2 123 H2
Armytage Rd, Houns. TW5 122 D7
Arnal Cres, SW18 148 B7
Arncliffe Cl, N11
off Kettlewell Cl 58 A6
Arncroft Ct, Bark. IG11
off Renwick Rd 118 B3
Arndale Wk, SW18
off Garratt La 148/149 E5
Arne Gro, Orp. BR6 207 J3
Arne St, WC2 18 B4
Arnett Sq, E4 61 J6
Arne Wk, SE3 155 F4
Arneways Av, Rom. RM6 82 D3
Arneway St, SW1 25 J6
Arnewood Cl, SW15 165 G1
Arney's La, Mitch. CR4 186 A6
Arngask Rd, SE6 154 D7
Arnhem Pl, E14 134 A3
Arnhem Way, SE22
off East Dulwich Gro 152 B5
Arnhem Wf, E14
off Arnhem Pl 134 A3
Arnison Rd, E.Mol. KT8 180 A4
Arnold Bennett Way, N8
off Burghley Rd 75 G3
Arnold Circ, E2 13 F4
Arnold Cl, Har. HA3 69 J7
Arnold Cres, Islw. TW7 144 A5
Arnold Dr, Chess. KT9 195 G6
Arnold Est, SE1 29 G4
Arnold Gdns, N13 59 H5
Arnold Rd, E3 114 A3
N15 76 C3
SW17 167 J7
Dagenham RM9, RM10 101 F7
Northolt UB5 84 D6
Arnos Gro, N14 58 D4
Arnos Rd, N11 58 C5
Arnott Cl, SE28
off Applegarth Rd 118 C7
W4 *off Fishers La* 126 D4
Arnould Av, SE5 152 A4
Arnsberg Way, Bexh. DA7 159 G4
Arnside Gdns, Wem. HA9 87 G1
Arnside Rd, Bexh. DA7 159 G1
Arnside St, SE17 36 A5
Arnulf St, SE6 172 B4
Arnulls Rd, SW16 169 G6
Arodene Rd, SW2 151 F6
Arosa Rd, Twick. TW1 145 G6
Arpley Sq, SE20 *off High St* 171 F7
Arragon Gdns, SW16 168 E7
West Wickham BR4 204 B3
Arragon Rd, E6 116 A1
SW18 166 E1
Twickenham TW1 144 D7
Arran Cl, Wall. SM6 200 B4
Arran Dr, E12 98 A1
Arran Grn, Wat. WD19
off Prestwick Rd 50 C1
Arran Ms, W5 125 J1

Arran Rd, SE6 172   B2
Arran Wk, N1 93   J7
Arras Av, Mord. SM4 185   F5
Arrol Rd, Beck. BR3 189   F3
Arrow Rd, E3 114   B3
Arrowscout Wk, Nthlt. UB5
   off Argus Way 102/103   E3
Arrowsmith Cl, Chig. IG7 65   J5
Arrowsmith Path, Chig. IG7 . . .65   J5
Arrowsmith Rd, Chig. IG7 65   H5
   Loughton IG10 48   B3
★ Arsenal FC, N5 93   H3
Arsenal Rd, SE9 156   C2
Arsenal Way, SE18 137   F3
Arterberry Rd, SW20 165   J7
Artesian Cl, NW10 88   D7
Artesian Gro, Barn. EN5 41   F4
Artesian Rd, W2 108   D6
Artesian Wk, E11 96   E3
Arthingworth St, E15 114   E1
Arthur Ct, W2 14   A3
Arthurdon Rd, SE4 154   A5
Arthur Gro, SE18 137   F4
Arthur Henderson Ho, SW6 . .148   C2
Arthur Horsley Wk, E7
   off Magpie Cl 97   F5
Arthur Rd, E6 116   C2
   N7 93   F4
   N9 60   C2
   SW19 166   B3
   Kingston upon Thames KT2 .164   A7
   New Malden KT3 183   H5
   Romford RM6 82   C7
Arthur St, EC4 20   C6
Arthur Walls Ho, E12
   off Grantham Rd 98   D3
Artichoke Hill, E1
   off Pennington St 112/113   E7
Artichoke Pl, SE5
   off Camberwell Ch St 152   A1
Artillery Cl, Ilf. IG2
   off Horns Rd 81   F6
Artillery La, E1 20   E2
   W12 107   G6
Artillery Pas, E1 21   E2
Artillery Pl, SE18 136   C5
   SW1 25   H6
   Harrow HA3
   off Chicheley Rd 51   J7
Artillery Row, SW1 25   H6
Artington Cl, Orp. BR6 207   F4
Artisan Cl, E6
   off Ferndale St 116/117   E6
Artizan St, E1 21   E3
Arundel Av, Mord. SM4 184   C4
Arundel Cl, E15 97   E4
   SW11 off Chivalry Rd 149   H5
   Bexley DA5 159   F6
   Croydon CR0 201   H3
   Hampton (Hmptn H.) TW12 .161   H5
Arundel Ct, N12 57   H6
   Harrow HA2 85   G4
Arundel Dr, Borwd. WD6 38   C5
   Harrow HA2 85   F4
   Woodford Green IG8 63   G7
Arundel Gdns, N21 59   G1
   W11 108   C7
   Edgware HA8 54   D7
   Ilford IG3 100   A2
Arundel Gt Ct, WC2 18   D5
Arundel Gro, N16 94   B5
Arundel Pl, N1 93   G6
Arundel Rd, Barn. EN4 41   H4
   Croydon CR0 188   A6
   Hounslow TW4 142   C3
   Kingston upon Thames KT1 .182   B2
   Sutton SM2 198   C7
Arundel Sq, N7 93   G6
Arundel St, WC2 18   D5
Arundel Ter, SW13 127   H6
Arvon Rd, N5 93   G5
Asbaston Ter, Ilf. IG1
   off Buttsbury Rd 99   F5
Ascalon St, SW8 130   C7
Ascham Dr, E4 off Rushcroft Rd .62   B7
Ascham End, E17 77   H1
Ascham St, NW5 92   C5
Aschurch Rd, Croy. CR0 188   C7
Ascot Cl, Borwd. (Elstree) WD6 .38   A5
   Ilford IG6 65   H6
   Northolt UB5 85   G5
Ascot Gdns, Sthl. UB1 103   F5
Ascot Rd, E6 116   C3
   N15 76   A5
   N18 60   D4
   SW17 168   A6
   Orpington BR5 193   J4
Ascott Av, W5 125   H2
Ashanti Ms, E8
   off Lower Clapton Rd . . .94/95   E5
Ashbourne Av, E18 79   H4
   N20 57   J2
   NW11 72   C5
   Bexleyheath DA7 139   E7
   Harrow HA2 86   A2
Ashbourne Cl, N12 57   E4
   W5 106   A5

Ashbourne Ct, E5
   off Daubeney Rd 95   H4
Ashbourne Gro, NW7 54   D5
   SE22 152   C5
   W4 127   E5
Ashbourne Par, W5
   off Ashbourne Rd 105   J4
Ashbourne Ri, Orp. BR6 207   G2
Ashbourne Rd, W5 105   J5
   Mitcham CR4 168   A6
Ashbourne Ter, SW19 166   D7
Ashbourne Way, NW11
   off Ashbourne Av 72   C5
Ashbridge Rd, E11 79   F7
Ashbridge St, NW8 7   G6
Ashbrook Rd, N19 92   D1
   Dagenham RM10 101   H3
Ashburn Gdns, SW7 30   C1
Ashburnham Av, Har. HA1 68   C6
Ashburnham Cl, N2 73   G3
   Watford WD19
   off Ashburnham Dr 50   A3
Ashburnham Dr, Wat. WD19 . . .50   A3
Ashburnham Gdns, Har. HA1 . .68   C6
Ashburnham Gro, SE10 134   B7
Ashburnham Pl, SE10 134   B7
Ashburnham Retreat, SE10 . .134   B7
Ashburnham Rd, NW10 107   J3
   SW10 129   F7
   Belvedere DA17 139   J4
   Richmond TW10 163   E3
Ashburn Pl, SW7 30   C1
Ashburton Av, Croy. CR0 202   E1
   Ilford IG3 99   H4
Ashburton Cl, Croy. CR0 202   D1
Ashburton Ct, Pnr. HA5 66   D3
Ashburton Gdns, Croy. CR0 . . .202   D2
Ashburton Rd, E16 115   G6
   Croydon CR0 202   D1
   Ruislip HA4 84   A2
Ashburton Ter, E13
   off Grasmere Rd 115   G2
Ashbury Gdns, Rom. RM6 82   D5
Ashbury Pl, SW19 167   F6
Ashbury Rd, SW11 149   J3
Ashby Av, Chess. KT9 196   A6
Ashby Gro, N1 93   J7
Ashby Ms, SE4 153   J2
   SW2 off Prague Pl 150/151   A5
Ashby Rd, N15 76   D5
   SE4 153   J2
Ashby St, EC1 11   H4
Ashby Wk, Croy. CR0 187   J6
Ashby Way, West Dr. UB7 . . .120   D7
Ashchurch Gro, W12 127   G2
Ashchurch Pk Vil, W12 127   G3
Ashchurch Ter, W12 127   G3
Ash Cl, SE20 189   F2
   Carshalton SM5 199   J2
   Edgware HA8 54   C4
   New Malden KT3 182   D2
   Orpington BR5 193   G6
   Sidcup DA14 176   B3
   Stanmore HA7 52   D6
Ashcombe Av, Surb. KT6 181   G7
Ashcombe Gdns, Edg. HA8 . . .54   A4
Ashcombe Ho, Enf. EN3 45   G3
Ashcombe Pk, NW2 89   E3
Ashcombe Rd, SW19 166   D5
   Carshalton SM5 200   A6
Ashcombe Sq, N.Mal. KT3 . . .182   C3
Ashcombe St, SW6 148   E2
Ash Ct, Epsom KT19 196   C4
Ashcroft, Pnr. HA5 51   H7
Ashcroft Av, Sid. DA15 158   A6
Ashcroft Ct, N20
   off Oakleigh Rd N 57   G2
Ashcroft Cres, Sid. DA15 158   A6
Ashcroft Rd, E3 113   H3
   Chessington KT9 195   J3
Ashcroft Sq, W6 off King St . . .127   J4
Ashdale Cl, Twick. TW2 143   J7
Ashdale Gro, Stan. HA7 52   C6
Ashdale Rd, SE12 173   H1
Ashdale Way, Twick. TW2
   off Ashdale Cl 143   J7
Ashdene, SE15 152   E1
   Pinner HA5 66   C3
Ashdon Cl, Wdf.Grn. IG8 63   H6
Ashdon Rd, NW10 107   E1
Ashdown Cl, Beck. BR3 190   B2
   Bexley DA5 159   J7
Ashdown Cres, NW5
   off Queen's Cres 92   A5
Ashdown Est, E11
   off High Rd Leytonstone .96/97   E4
Ashdown Pl, T.Ditt. KT7 180   D7
Ashdown Rd, Enf. EN3 45   F3
   Kingston upon Thames KT1 .181   H2
Ashdown Wk, E14 134   A4
   Romford RM7 83   H2
Ashdown Way, SW17 168   A2
Ashen, E6 off Downings 116   D6
Ashenden Rd, E5 95   G5
Ashen Gro, SW19 166   D3
Ashentree Ct, EC4 19   F4
Asher Loftus Way, N11 57   J6

Asher Way, E1 29   J1
Ashfield Av, Felt. TW13 160   B1
Ashfield Cl, Beck. BR3 172   A7
   Richmond TW10 163   H1
Ashfield La, Chis. BR7 175   F6
Ashfield Par, N14 58   D1
Ashfield Rd, N4 75   J6
   N14 58   C3
   W3 127   F1
Ashfields, Loug. IG10 48   C2
Ashfield St, E1 112   E5
Ashfield Yd, E1
   off Ashfield St 112/113   E5
Ashford Av, N8 74   E4
   Hayes UB4 102   D6
Ashford Cl, E17 77   J6
Ashford Cres, Enf. EN3 45   F2
Ashford Grn, Wat. WD19 50   D5
Ashford Ms, N17
   off Vicarage Rd 76   D1
Ashford Rd, E6 98   D6
   E18 79   H2
   NW2 90   A4
Ashford St, N1 12   D3
Ash Gro, E8 113   E1
   N13 59   J3
   NW2 90   A4
   SE20 189   F2
   W5 125   H2
   Enfield EN1 44   B7
   Hounslow TW5 142   D1
   Southall UB1 103   G5
   Wembley HA0 86   D4
   West Wickham BR4 204   C2
Ashgrove Rd, Brom. BR1 172   D6
   Ilford IG3 99   J1
Ash Hill Cl, Bushey WD23 51   H1
Ash Hill Dr, Pnr. HA5 66   C3
Ashingdon Cl, E4 62   C3
Ashington Rd, SW6 148   C2
Ash Island, E.Mol. KT8 180   A3
Ashlake Rd, SW16 168   E4
Ashland Pl, W1 16   B1
Ashlar Pl, SE18
   off Masons Hill 136/137   E4
Ashleigh Gdns, Sutt. SM1 . . .198   E2
Ashleigh Pt, SE23
   off Dacres Rd 171   G3
Ashleigh Rd, SE20 188   E3
   SW14 146   E3
Ashley Av, Ilf. IG6 81   E2
   Morden SM4 184   D5
Ashley Cl, NW4 71   J2
   Pinner HA5 66   B2
Ashley Cres, N22 75   G2
   SW11 150   A3
Ashley Dr, Borwd. WD6 38   C5
   Isleworth TW7 124   B6
   Twickenham TW2 143   H7
Ashley Gdns, N13 59   J4
   SW1 25   G6
   Orpington BR6 207   H5
   Richmond TW10 163   G3
   Wembley HA9 87   H2
Ashley Gro, Loug. IG10
   off Staples Rd 48   B3
Ashley La, NW4 71   J2
   Croydon CR0 201   H4
Ashley Pl, SW1 25   F6
Ashley Rd, E4 62   A5
   E7 97   J7
   N17 76   D3
   N19 92   E1
   SW19 166   E6
   Enfield EN3 45   F2
   Hampton TW12 179   G1
   Richmond TW9
   off Jocelyn Rd 145   H3
   Thames Ditton KT7 180   C6
   Thornton Heath CR7 187   F4
Ashley Wk, NW7 55   J7
Ashling Rd, Croy. CR0 202   D1
Ashlin Rd, E15 96   D4
Ashlone Rd, SW15 147   J3
Ashlyns Way, Chess. KT9 195   G6
Ashmead, N14 42   C5
Ashmead Gate, Brom. BR1 . . .191   J1
Ashmead Ho, E9
   off Kingsmead Way 95   H5
Ashmead Rd, SE8 154   A2
   Feltham TW14 160   A1
Ashmere Av, Beck. BR3 190   D2
Ashmere Cl, Sutt. SM3 197   J5
Ashmere Gro, SW2 150   E4
Ashmill St, NW1 15   G1
Ashmole Pl, SW8 34   E6
Ashmole St, SW8 34   D6
Ashmore Cl, SE15
   off Lisford St 152   C1
Ashmore Ct, Houns. TW5
   off Wheatlands 123   G6
Ashmore Gro, Well. DA16 157   G3
Ashmore Rd, W9 108   C4
Ashmount Est, N19
   off Ashmount Rd 74   D7
Ashmount Rd, N15 76   C5
   N19 74   C7

Ashmount Ter, W5
   off Murray Rd 125   G4
Ashneal Gdns, Har. HA1 86   A3
Ashness Gdns, Grnf. UB6 86   E6
Ashness Rd, SW11 149   J5
Ashridge Cl, Har. HA3 69   F6
Ashridge Cres, SE18 137   F7
Ashridge Dr, Wat. WD19 50   C5
Ashridge Gdns, N13 58   D5
   Pinner HA5 66   E4
Ashridge Way, Mord. SM4 . . .184   C3
   Sunbury-on-Thames TW16 .160   A6
Ash Rd, E15 97   E5
   Croydon CR0 204   A2
   Orpington BR6 207   J7
   Sutton SM3 184   B7
Ash Row, Brom. BR2 192   D5
Ashstead Rd, E5 76   D7
Ashton Cl, Sutt. SM1 198   D4
Ashton Ct, E4
   off Connington Cres 62   E3
Ashton Gdns, Houns. TW4 . . .143   F4
   Romford RM6 83   E6
Ashton Rd, E15 96   D5
Ashton St, E14 114   C7
Ashtree Av, Mitch. CR4 185   H2
Ash Tree Cl, Croy. CR0 189   H6
Ashtree Cl, Orp. BR6
   off Broadwater Gdns . . .206/207   E4
Ash Tree Cl, Surb. KT6 195   H1
Ash Tree Dell, NW9 70   C5
Ash Tree Way, Croy. CR0 189   H5
Ashurst Cl, SE20 189   E1
Ashurst Dr, Ilf. IG2, IG6 81   E6
Ashurst Rd, N12 57   H5
   Barnet EN4 41   J5
Ashurst Wk, Croy. CR0 202   E2
Ashvale Rd, SW17 167   J5
Ashville Rd, E11 96   D2
Ash Wk, SW2 169   F1
   Wembley HA0 87   F4
Ashwater Rd, SE12 173   G1
Ashwell Cl, E6
   off Northumberland Rd 116   B6
Ashwin St, E8 94   C6
Ashwood Gdns, Croy. (New Adgtn)
   CR0 204   B6
   Hayes UB3 off Cranford Dr .121   J4
Ashwood Rd, E4 62   D3
Ashworth Cl, SE5 off Love Wk .152   A2
Ashworth Rd, W9 6   B3
Askern Cl, Bexh. DA6 158   D4
Aske St, N1 12   D3
Askew Cres, W12 127   F2
Askew Rd, W12 127   F1
Askham Ct, W12 127   G1
Askham Rd, W12 127   G1
Askill Dr, SW15
   off Keswick Rd 148   B5
Asland Rd, E15 114   E1
Aslett St, SW18 149   E7
Asmara Rd, NW2 90   B5
Asmuns Hill, NW11 72   D5
Asmuns Pl, NW11 72   C5
Asolando Dr, SE17 36   A2
Aspen Cl, N19 off Hargrave Pk .92   C2
   W5 125   J2
   West Drayton UB7 120   C1
Aspen Copse, Brom. BR1 192   C2
Aspen Ct, Hayes UB3 121   H4
Aspen Dr, Wem. HA0 86   D4
Aspen Gdns, W6 127   H5
   Mitcham CR4 186   A5
Aspen Grn, Erith DA18 139   F3
Aspen La, Nthlt. UB5 102   E3
Aspenlea Rd, W6 128   A6
Aspen Way, E14 114   A7
   Feltham TW13 160   B3
Aspern Gro, NW3 91   H5
Aspinall Rd, SE4 153   G3
Aspinden Rd, SE16 133   E4
Aspley Rd, SW18 149   E5
Asplins Rd, N17 76   D1
Asprey Ms, Beck. BR3 189   J5
Asprey Pl, Brom. BR1
   off Chislehurst Rd 192   A2
Asquith Cl, Dag. RM8 100   C1
Assam St, E1 21   H3
Assata Ms, N1 off St. Paul's Rd . .93   H6
Assembly Pas, E1 113   F5
Assembly Wk, Cars. SM5 185   H7
Ass Ho La, Har. HA3 51   H4
Assurance Cotts, Belv. DA17
   off Heron Hill 139   F5
Astall Cl, Har. HA3 68   B1
Astbury Business Pk, SE15
   off Station Pas 153   F1
Astbury Rd, SE15 153   F1
Astell St, SW3 31   H3
Aste St, E14 134   C2
Asteys Row, N1 off River Pl . . .93   H7
Asthall Gdns, Ilf. IG6 81   F4
Astle St, SW11 150   A2
Astley Av, NW2 89   J5
Aston Av, Har. HA3 69   F7
Aston Cl, Sid. DA14 176   A3
Aston Grn, Houns. TW4 142   C2

Aston Ms, Rom. RM6 . . . . .82 C7
Aston Pl, SW16 off Averil Gro . .169 H6
Aston Rd, SW20 . . . . . .183 J2
  W5 . . . . . .105 G6
  Esher (Clay.) KT10 . . . .194 B5
Aston St, E14 . . . .113 H6
Aston Ter, SW12 off Cathles Rd .150 B6
Astonville St, SW18 . . . .166 D1
Astor Av, Rom. RM7 . . . .83 J6
Astor Cl, Kings.T. KT2 . . .164 B6
Astoria Wk, SW9 . . . .151 G3
Astrop Ms, W6 . . . .127 J3
Astrop Ter, W6 . . . .127 J3
Astwood Ms, SW7 . . . .30 C1
Asylum Rd, SE15 . . . .133 E7
Atalanta St, SW6 . . . .148 A1
Atbara Ct, Tedd. TW11 . . .163 E6
Atbara Rd, Tedd. TW11 . . .163 E6
Atcham Rd, Houns. TW3 . . .143 J4
Atcost Rd, Bark. IG11 . . .118 A5
Atheldene Rd, SW18 . . . .167 E1
Athelney St, SE6 . . . .172 A3
Athelstane Gro, E3 . . . .113 J2
Athelstane Ms, N4
  off Stroud Grn Rd 93 G1
Athelstan Ho, E9
  off Kingsmead Way 95 J5
Athelstan Rd, Kings.T. KT1 .181 J4
Athelstone Rd, Har. HA3 . . .68 A2
Athena Cl, Har. HA2
  off Byron Hill Rd 86 B2
  Kingston upon Thames KT1 .181 J3
Athenaeum Pl, N10
  off Fortis Grn Rd 74 B3
Athenaeum Rd, N20 . . . .57 F1
Athenlay Rd, SE15 . . . .153 G5
Athens Gdns, W9
  off Harrow Rd 108 D4
Atherden Rd, E5 . . . .95 F4
Atherfold Rd, SW9 . . . .150 E3
Atherley Way, Houns. TW4 . .143 F7
Atherstone Ct, W2 . . . .14 B1
Atherstone Ms, SW7 . . . .30 D1
Atherton Cl, Stai. (Stanw.)
  TW19 . . . .140 A6
Atherton Dr, SW19 . . . .166 A4
Atherton Hts, Wem. HA0 . . .87 F6
Atherton Ms, E7 . . . .97 F6
Atherton Pl, Har. HA2 . . . .68 A3
  Southall UB1 . . . .103 H7
Atherton Rd, E7 . . . .97 F5
  SW13 . . . .127 G7
  Ilford IG5 . . . .80 B2
Atherton St, SW11 . . . .149 H2
Athlone, Esher (Clay.) KT10 .194 B6
Athlone Cl, E5
  off Goulton Rd 94/95 E4
Athlone Rd, SW2 . . . .151 F7
Athlone St, NW5 . . . .92 A6
Athlon Rd, Wem. HA0 . . .105 G2
Athol Cl, Pnr. HA5 . . . .66 B1
Athole Gdns, Enf. EN1 . . . .44 B5
Athol Gdns, Pnr. HA5 . . . .66 B1
Atholl Rd, Ilf. IG3 . . . .82 A7
Athol Rd, Erith DA8 . . . .139 J5
Athol Sq, E14 . . . .114 C6
Atkins Dr, W.Wick. BR4 . . .204 D2
Atkinson Rd, E16 . . . .115 J5
Atkins Rd, E10 . . . .78 B6
  SW12 . . . .150 D7
Atlantic Rd, SW9 . . . .151 G4
Atlantis Cl, Bark. IG11 . . .118 B3
Atlas Gdns, SE7 . . . .135 J4
Atlas Ms, E8 off Tyssen St . . .94 C6
  N7 . . . .93 F6
Atlas Rd, E13 . . . .115 G2
  N11 . . . .58 B6
  NW10 . . . .107 E3
  Wembley HA9 . . . .88 C4
Atley Rd, E3 . . . .114 A1
Atlip Rd, Wem. HA0 . . .105 H1
Atney Rd, SW15 . . . .148 B4
Atria Rd, Nthwd. HA6 . . . .50 A5
Attenborough Cl, Wat. WD19
  off Harrow Way 50/51 E3
Atterbury Rd, N4 . . . .75 G6
Atterbury St, SW1 . . . .33 J2
Attewood Av, NW10 . . . .88 E3
Attewood Rd, Nthlt. UB5 . . .85 E6
Attfield Cl, N20 . . . .57 G2
Attlee Cl, Hayes UB4 . . .102 C4
  Thornton Heath CR7 . . .187 J6
Attlee Rd, SE28 . . . .118 B7
  Hayes UB4 . . . .102 A4
Attlee Ter, E17 . . . .78 B4
Attneave St, WC1 . . . .10 E4
Atwater Cl, SW2 . . . .169 G1
Atwell Cl, E10 off Belmont Pk Rd .78 B6
Atwell Pl, T.Ditt. KT7 . . .194 C1
Atwell Rd, SE15 off Rye La . .152 D2
Atwood Av, Rich. TW9 . . .146 A2
Atwood Rd, W6 . . . .127 H4
Atwoods All, Rich. TW9
  off Leyborne Pk 146 A1
Aubert Pk, N5 . . . .93 H4
Aubert Rd, N5 . . . .93 H4
Aubrey Pl, NW8 . . . .6 C2

Aubrey Rd, E17 . . . .78 A3
  N8 . . . .75 E5
  W8 . . . .128 C1
Aubrey Wk, W8 . . . .128 C1
Auburn Cl, SE14 . . . .133 H7
Aubyn Hill, SE27 . . . .169 J4
Aubyn Sq, SW15 . . . .147 G4
Auckland Cl, SE19 . . . .188 C1
Auckland Gdns, SE19 . . . .188 B1
Auckland Hill, SE27 . . . .169 J4
Auckland Ri, SE19 . . . .188 B1
Auckland Rd, E10 . . . .96 B3
  SE19 . . . .188 C1
  SW11 . . . .149 H4
  Ilford IG1 . . . .99 E1
  Kingston upon Thames KT1 .181 J4
Auckland St, SE11 . . . .34 C4
Auden Pl, NW1 . . . .110 A1
  Sutton SM3
  off Wordsworth Dr 197 J4
Audleigh Pl, Chig. IG7 . . . .64 D6
Audley Cl, N10 . . . .58 B7
  SW11 . . . .150 A3
  Borehamwood WD6 . . . .38 A3
Audley Ct, E18 . . . .79 F4
  Pinner HA5
  off Rickmansworth Rd 66 C2
Audley Dr, E16 off Wesley Av . .135 H1
Audley Gdns, Ilf. IG3 . . . .99 J2
  Loughton IG10 . . . .49 F2
Audley Rd, NW4 . . . .71 H6
  W5 . . . .105 J5
  Enfield EN2 . . . .43 H2
  Richmond TW10 . . . .145 J5
Audley Sq, W1 . . . .24 C1
Audrey Cl, Beck. BR3 . . .190 B6
Audrey Gdns, Wem. HA0 . . .87 E2
Audrey Rd, Ilf. IG1 . . . .98 E3
Audrey St, E2 . . . .13 H1
Audric Cl, Kings.T. KT2 . . .182 A1
Augers La, E13 . . . .115 H3
Augusta Cl, W.Mol. KT8
  off Freeman Dr 179 F3
Augusta Rd, Twick. TW2 . . .161 J2
Augusta St, E14 . . . .114 B6
Augustine Rd, W14 . . . .128 A3
  Harrow HA3 . . . .67 H1
Augustus Cl, W12
  off Goldhawk Rd 127 H2
  Brentford TW8 . . . .125 F7
Augustus Rd, SW19 . . . .166 B1
Augustus St, NW1 . . . .9 E2
Aultone Way, Cars. SM5 . . .199 J3
  Sutton SM1 . . . .199 E2
Aulton Pl, SE11 . . . .35 F4
Aurelia Gdns, Croy. CR0 . . .187 F5
Aurelia Rd, Croy. CR0 . . .187 G6
Auriga Ms, N16 . . . .94 A5
Auriol Cl, Wor.Pk. KT4
  off Auriol Pk Rd 196/197 E3
Auriol Dr, Grnf. UB6 . . . .86 A7
Auriol Pk Rd, Wor.Pk. KT4 . .197 E3
Auriol Rd, W14 . . . .128 B4
Austell Gdns, NW7 . . . .55 E3
Austen Cl, SE28 . . . .138 B1
  Loughton IG10 . . . .49 G3
Austen Ho, NW6 . . . .108 D3
Austen Rd, Erith DA8 . . . .139 H7
  Harrow HA2 . . . .85 H2
Austin Av, Brom. BR2 . . .192 B5
Austin Cl, SE23 . . . .153 J7
  Twickenham TW1 . . . .145 F5
Austin Ct, E6 off Kings Rd . .115 J1
Austin Friars, EC2 . . . .20 C3
Austin Friars Pas, EC2 . . . .20 C3
Austin Friars Sq, EC2 . . . .20 C3
Austin Rd, SW11 . . . .150 A1
  Hayes UB3 . . . .121 J2
Austin St, E2 . . . .13 F4
Austral Cl, Sid. DA15 . . .175 J3
Australia Rd, W12 . . . .107 H7
Austral St, SE11 . . . .35 G1
Austyn Gdns, Surb. KT6 . . .196 B1
Autumn Cl, SW19 . . . .167 F6
  Enfield EN1 . . . .44 D1
Autumn St, E3 . . . .114 A1
Avalon Cl, SW20 . . . .184 B2
  W13 . . . .104 D5
  Enfield EN2 . . . .43 G2
Avalon Rd, SW6 . . . .148 E1
  W13 . . . .104 D4
Avard Gdns, Orp. BR6 . . .207 F4
Avarn Rd, SW17 . . . .167 J6
Avebury Ct, N1 off Poole St . .112 A1
Avebury Pk, Surb. KT6 . . .181 G7
Avebury Rd, E11
  off Southwest Rd 96 D1
  SW19 . . . .184 C1
  Orpington BR6 . . . .207 G3
Avebury St, N1 off Poole St . .112 A1
Aveline St, SE11 . . . .34 E3
Aveling Pk Rd, E17 . . . .78 A2
Ave Maria La, EC4 . . . .19 H4
Avenell Rd, N5 . . . .93 H3
Avening Rd, SW18
  off Brathway Rd 148 D7

Avening Ter, SW18 . . . .148 D6
Avenons Rd, E13 . . . .115 G4
Avenue, The, E4 . . . .62 D6
  E11 (Leytonstone) 97 F2
  E11 (Wanstead) 79 H6
  N3 . . . .72 D2
  N8 . . . .75 G3
  N10 . . . .74 C2
  N11 . . . .58 B4
  N17 . . . .76 B3
  NW6 . . . .108 A1
  SE10 . . . .134 D7
  SW4 . . . .150 A5
  SW11 . . . .149 H7
  SW18 . . . .149 H7
  W4 . . . .126 E3
  W13 . . . .104 E7
  Barnet EN5 . . . .40 B3
  Beckenham BR3 . . . .190 B1
  Bexley DA5 . . . .158 D7
  Bromley BR1 . . . .192 D5
  Carshalton SM5 . . . .200 A7
  Croydon CR0 . . . .202 B3
  Epsom KT17 . . . .197 H7
  Esher (Clay.) KT10 . . . .194 B6
  Hampton TW12 . . . .161 F6
  Harrow HA3 . . . .68 C1
  Hounslow TW3 . . . .143 H5
  Hounslow (Cran.) TW5 . . .142 A1
  Isleworth TW7 . . . .124 A6
  Keston BR2 . . . .206 A3
  Loughton IG10 . . . .48 A6
  Orpington BR6 . . . .207 J2
  Orpington (St.P.Cray) BR5 . .176 B7
  Pinner HA5 . . . .67 F6
  Pinner (Hatch End) HA5 . . .51 G7
  Richmond TW9 . . . .145 J2
  Sunbury-on-Thames TW16 . .178 B1
  Surbiton KT5 . . . .181 J6
  Sutton (Cheam) SM3 . . .197 J7
  Twickenham TW1 . . . .145 F5
  Wembley HA9 . . . .87 J2
  West Drayton UB7 . . . .120 B3
  West Wickham BR4 . . . .190 C7
  Worcester Park KT4 . . . .197 F2
Avenue Cl, N14 . . . .42 C6
  NW8 . . . .109 H1
  Hounslow TW5
  off The Avenue 142 A1
  West Drayton UB7 . . . .120 A3
Avenue Cres, W3 . . . .126 B2
  Hounslow TW5 . . . .122 B7
Avenue Elmers, Surb. KT6 . .181 H5
Avenue Gdns, SE25 . . . .188 D3
  SW14 . . . .146 E3
  W3 . . . .126 B2
  Hounslow TW5
  off The Avenue 122 A7
  Teddington TW11 . . . .162 C7
Avenue Gate, Loug. IG10 . . .47 J6
Avenue Ind Est, E4 . . . .61 J6
Avenue Ms, N10 . . . .74 B3
Avenue Pk Rd, SE27 . . . .169 H2
Avenue Rd, E7 . . . .97 H5
  N6 . . . .74 C7
  N12 . . . .57 F4
  N14 . . . .42 B7
  N15 . . . .76 A5
  NW3 . . . .91 G7
  NW8 . . . .91 G7
  NW10 . . . .107 F2
  SE20 . . . .189 F1
  SE25 . . . .188 D2
  SW16 . . . .186 D2
  SW20 . . . .183 H2
  W3 . . . .126 B2
  Beckenham BR3 . . . .189 F1
  Belvedere DA17 . . . .139 J4
  Bexleyheath DA7 . . . .158 E3
  Brentford TW8 . . . .125 F5
  Erith DA8 . . . .139 J7
  Hampton TW12 . . . .179 H1
  Isleworth TW7 . . . .144 C1
  Kingston upon Thames KT1 .181 H3
  New Malden KT3 . . . .182 E4
  Pinner HA5 . . . .66 E3
  Romford (Chad.Hth) RM6 . .82 B7
  Southall UB1 . . . .123 F2
  Teddington TW11 . . . .162 D7
  Wallington SM6 . . . .200 C7
  Woodford Green IG8 . . . .63 J6
Avenue S, Surb. KT5 . . . .181 J7
Avenue Ter, N.Mal. KT3
  off Kingston Rd 182 C3
Averil Gro, SW16 . . . .169 H6
Averill St, W6 . . . .128 A6
Avern Gdns, W.Mol. KT8 . . .179 H4
Avern Rd, W.Mol. KT8 . . . .179 H4
Avery Fm Row, SW1 . . . .32 C2
Avery Gdns, Ilf. IG2 . . . .80 C5
AVERY HILL, SE9 . . . .157 F6
  ★ Avery Hill Pk, SE9 . . . .157 F6
Avery Hill Rd, SE9 . . . .157 G6
Avery Row, W1 . . . .16 D5
Avey La, Loug. IG10 . . . .47 H1
Aviary Cl, E16 . . . .115 F5
Aviemore Cl, Beck. BR3 . . .189 J5

Aviemore Way, Beck. BR3 . .189 H5
Avignon Rd, SE4 . . . .153 G3
Avington Ct, SE1
  off Old Kent Rd 132 B4
Avington Gro, SE20 . . . .171 F7
Avington Way, SE15 . . . .37 F7
Avion Cres, NW9 . . . .71 G1
Avis Sq, E1 . . . .113 G6
Avoca Rd, SW17 . . . .168 A4
Avocet Ms, SE28 . . . .137 G3
Avon Cl, Hayes UB4 . . . .102 C4
  Sutton SM1 . . . .199 F4
  Worcester Park KT4 . . . .197 G2
Avon Ct, Grnf. UB6
  off Braund Av 103 H4
  NW2 . . . .89 E3
  Barnet EN4 . . . .57 J1
  Esher KT10 . . . .194 D3
  Worcester Park KT4 . . . .197 F1
Avondale Cl, Loug. IG10 . . .48 C7
Avondale Ct, E11 . . . .96 E1
  E16 off Avondale Rd . . .114/115 E5
  E18 . . . .79 H1
Avondale Cres, Enf. EN3 . . .45 H3
  Ilford IG4 . . . .80 A5
Avondale Dr, Hayes UB3 . . .122 A1
  Loughton IG10 . . . .48 C7
Avondale Gdns, Houns. TW4 .143 F5
Avondale Ms, Brom. BR1
  off Avondale Rd 173 G6
Avondale Pk Gdns, W11 . . .108 B7
Avondale Pk Rd, W11 . . . .108 B7
Avondale Pavement, SE1
  off Avondale Sq 132 D5
Avondale Ri, SE15 . . . .152 C3
Avondale Rd, E16 . . . .115 E5
  E17 . . . .78 A7
  N3 . . . .73 F1
  N13 . . . .59 G2
  N15 . . . .75 H5
  SE9 . . . .174 B2
  SW14 . . . .146 D3
  SW19 . . . .166 E5
  Bromley BR1 . . . .173 E6
  Harrow HA3 . . . .68 C3
  South Croydon CR2 . . . .201 J6
  Welling DA16 . . . .158 C2
Avondale Sq, SE1 . . . .37 H4
Avonley Rd, SE14 . . . .133 F7
Avon Ms, Pnr. HA5 . . . .67 F1
Avonmore Gdns, W14
  off Avonmore Rd 128 C4
Avonmore Pl, W14
  off Avonmore Rd 128 B4
Avonmore Rd, W14 . . . .128 C4
Avonmouth St, SE1 . . . .27 J5
Avon Path, S.Croy. CR2 . . .201 J6
Avon Pl, SE1 . . . .28 A4
Avon Rd, E17 . . . .78 D3
  SE4 . . . .154 A3
  Greenford UB6 . . . .103 G4
Avonstowe Cl, Orp. BR6 . . .207 F3
Avon Way, E18 . . . .79 G3
Avonwick Rd, Houns. TW3 . .143 H2
Avril Way, E4 . . . .62 C5
Avro Way, Wall. SM6 . . . .201 E7
Awlfield Av, N17 . . . .76 A1
Awliscombe Rd, Well. DA16 .157 J2
Axe St, Bark. IG11 . . . .117 F1
Axholme Av, Edg. HA8 . . . .70 A1
Axminster Cres, Well. DA16 .158 C1
Axminster Rd, N7 . . . .93 E3
Aybrook St, W1 . . . .16 B2
Aycliffe Cl, Brom. BR1 . . .192 C4
Aycliffe Rd, W12 . . . .127 F1
Aylands Rd, Wem. HA9
  off Preston Rd 87 H2
Aylesbury Cl, E7
  off Atherton Rd 97 F6
Aylesbury Ct, Sutt. SM1
  off Benhill Wd Rd 199 F3
Aylesbury Est, SE17 . . . .36 C4
Aylesbury Rd, SE17 . . . .36 C4
  Bromley BR2 . . . .191 G3
Aylesbury St, EC1 . . . .11 G6
  NW10 . . . .88 D3
Aylesford Av, Beck. BR3 . . .189 H5
Aylesford St, SW1 . . . .33 H3
Aylesham Cen, The, SE15 . .152 D1
Aylesham Cl, NW7 . . . .55 G7
Aylesham Rd, Orp. BR6 . . .193 J7
Ayles Rd, Hayes UB4 . . . .102 B3
Aylestone Av, NW6 . . . .108 A1
Aylett Rd, SE25 . . . .188 E4
  Isleworth TW7 . . . .144 B2
Ayley Cft, Enf. EN1 . . . .44 D5
Aylmer Cl, Stan. HA7 . . . .52 D4
Aylmer Dr, Stan. HA7 . . . .52 D4
Aylmer Par, N2 . . . .73 J5
Aylmer Rd, E11 . . . .97 F1
  N2 . . . .73 H5
  W12 . . . .127 E2
  Dagenham RM8 . . . .100 E3
Ayloffe Rd, Dag. RM9 . . . .101 F6

Aylton Est, SE16
off Renforth St 133 F2
Aylward Rd, SE23 171 G2
SW20 184 C2
Aylwards Ri, Stan. HA7 52 D4
Aylward St, E1 113 F6
Aylwyn Est, SE1 29 F5
Aynhoe Rd, W14 128 A4
Aynscombe La, SW14 146 C3
Aynscombe Path, SW14
off Thames Bk 146 C2
Ayr Ct, W3 *off Monks Dr* 106 A5
Ayres Cl, E13 115 G3
Ayres Cres, NW10 88 D7
Ayres St, SE1 28 A3
Ayrsome Rd, N16 94 B3
Ayrton Rd, SW7 23 E5
Aysgarth Ct, Sutt. SM1
off Sutton Common Rd 198/199 E3
Aysgarth Rd, SE21 152 B6
Aytoun Pl, SW9 151 F2
Aytoun Rd, SW9 151 F2
Azalea Cl, W7 124 C1
Ilford IG1 98 E5
Azalea Ct, Wdf.Grn. IG8
off The Bridle Path 62/63 E7
Azalea Wk, Pnr. HA5 66 B5
Southall UB2
off Navigator Dr 123 J2
Azania Ms, NW5 92 B5
Azenby Rd, SE15 152 C2
Azile Everitt Ho, SE18
off Blendon Ter 137 F5
Azof St, SE10 135 E4

B

Baalbec Rd, N5 93 H5
Babbacombe Cl, Chess. KT9 195 G5
Babbacombe Gdns, Ilf. IG4 80 B4
Babbacombe Rd, Brom. BR1 191 G1
Baber Dr, Felt. TW14 142 C6
Babington Ri, Wem. HA9 88 A6
Babington Rd, NW4 71 H4
SW16 168 D5
Dagenham RM8 100 C5
Babmaes St, SW1 17 G6
Bacchus Wk, N1 12 D2
Baches St, N1 12 C4
Back Ch La, E1 21 H5
Back Hill, EC1 11 E6
Backhouse Pl, SE17 36 E2
Back La, N8 74 E5
NW3 *off Heath St* 91 F4
Bexley DA5 159 G7
Brentford TW8 125 G6
Edgware HA8 70 C1
Richmond TW10 163 F3
Romford RM6
off St. Chad's Rd 82/83 E7
Backley Gdns, SE25 188 D6
Back Rd, Sid. DA14 176 A4
Bacon Gro, SE1 29 F6
Bacon La, NW9 70 B4
Edgware HA8 70 A1
Bacons La, N6 92 A1
Bacon St, E1 13 G5
E2 13 G5
Bacon Ter, Dag. RM8
off Fitzstephen Rd 100 B5
Bacton, NW5 92 A5
Bacton St, E2 *off Roman Rd* 113 F3
Baddow Cl, Dag. RM10 119 G1
Woodford Green IG8 64 A6
Baddow Wk, N1 111 J1
Baden Pl, SE1 28 B3
Baden Powell Cl, Dag. RM9 119 E1
Surbiton KT6 195 J2
Baden Rd, N8 74 D4
Ilford IG1 98 E5
Badger Cl, Felt. TW13
off Sycamore Cl 160 A3
Hounslow TW4 142 C3
Ilford IG2 81 F7
Badgers Cl, Enf. EN2 43 H3
Harrow HA1 68 A6
Badgers Copse, Orp. BR6 207 J2
Worcester Park KT4 197 F2
Badgers Cft, N20 56 B1
SE9 174 D3
Badgers Hole, Croy. CR0 203 G4
Badgers Wk, N.Mal. KT3 182 E2
Badlis Rd, E17 78 A2
Badma Cl, N9 *off Hudson Way* 61 F3
Badminton Cl, Borwd. WD6 38 A2
Harrow HA1 68 B4
Northolt UB5 85 G6
Badminton Ms, E16
off Hanameel St 135 G1
Badminton Rd, SW12 150 A6
Badric Ct, SW11
off Yelverton Rd 149 G2
Badsworth Rd, SE5 131 J7
Baffin Way, E14 *off Prestons Rd* 114 C7
Bagley Cl, West Dr. UB7 120 B2
Bagley's La, SW6 149 E1
Bagleys Spring, Rom. RM6 83 E4
Bagshot Ct, SE18
off Prince Imperial Rd 156 D1
Bagshot Rd, Enf. EN1 44 C7
Bagshot St, SE17 36 E4
Baildon St, SE8 133 J7
Bailey Cl, E4 62 C4
N11 58 D7
Bailey Cres, Chess. KT9
off Nigel Fisher Way 195 G6
Bailey Ms, SW2 151 G5
Bailey Pl, SE26 171 G6
Baillies Wk, W5
off Liverpool Rd 125 G2
Bainbridge Cl, Rich. (Ham) TW10
off Latchmere Cl 163 H5
Bainbridge Rd, Dag. RM9 101 F4
Bainbridge St, WC1 17 J3
Baines Cl, S.Croy. CR2
off Brighton Rd 201 J5
Baird Av, Sthl. UB1 103 H7
Baird Cl, E10 *off Marconi Rd* 96 A1
NW9 70 C6
Baird Gdns, SE19 170 B4
Baird Rd, Enf. EN1 44 E4
Baird St, EC1 12 A5
Bairny Wd App, Wdf.Grn. IG8
off Broadway Cl 63 H6
Baizdon Rd, SE3 154 E2
Baker La, Mitch. CR4 186 A2
Baker Pas, NW10
off Acton La 106/107 E1
Baker Rd, NW10 106 E1
SE18 136 B7
Bakers Av, E17 78 B6
Bakers Ct, SE25 188 B3
Bakers End, SW20 184 B2
Bakers Fld, N7 *off Crayford Rd* 92 D4
Bakers Gdns, Cars. SM5 199 H2
Bakers Hall Ct, EC3 20 E6
Bakers Hill, E5 95 F1
Barnet EN5 41 E2
Bakers La, N6 73 J5
Baker's Ms, W1 16 B3
Bakers Ms, Orp. BR6 207 J6
Bakers Pas, NW3 *off Heath St* 91 F4
Baker's Rents, E2 13 F4
Bakers Row, E15 114 E2
Baker's Row, EC1 11 E6
Baker St, NW1 8 A6
W1 16 A1
Enfield EN1 44 A3
Baker's Yd, EC1
off Baker's Row 111 G4
Bakery Cl, SW9 151 F1
Bakery Path, Edg. HA8
off Station Rd 54 B6
Bakery Pl, SW11
off Altenburg Gdns 149 J4
Bakewell Way, N.Mal. KT3 182 E2
Balaams La, N14 58 D2
Balaam St, E13 115 G3
Balaclava Rd, SE1 37 G2
Surbiton KT6 181 F7
Bala Grn, NW9
off Snowdon Dr 70/71 E6
Balcaskie Rd, SE9 156 C5
Balchen Rd, SE3 156 A2
Balchier Rd, SE22 152 E6
Balcombe Cl, Bexh. DA6 158 D4
Balcombe St, NW1 7 J6
Balcon Ct, W5 *off Boileau Rd* 105 J6
Balcon Way, Borwd. WD6 38 C1
Balcorne St, E9 95 F7
Balder Ri, SE12 173 H2
Balderton St, W1 16 C4
Baldock St, E3 114 B2
Baldry Gdns, SW16 169 E6
Baldwin Cres, SE5 151 J1
Baldwin Gdns, Houns. TW3
off Chamberlain Gdns 143 J1
Baldwin's Gdns, EC1 18 E1
Baldwins Hill, Loug. IG10 48 C2
Baldwin St, EC1 12 B4
Baldwin Ter, N1 11 J1
Baldwyn Gdns, W3 106 C7
Bale Rd, E1 113 H5
Balfern Gro, W4 127 E5
Balfern St, SW11 149 H1
Balfe St, N1 10 B2
Balfour Av, W7 124 C1
Balfour Business Cen, Sthl.
UB2 122 D3
Balfour Gro, N20 57 J3
Balfour Ho, W10
off St. Charles Sq 108 A5
Balfour Ms, N9
off The Broadway 60 D3
W1 24 C1
Balfour Pl, SW15 147 H4
W1 16 C6
Balfour Rd, N5 93 J4
SE25 188 D4
SW19 166 E7
W3 106 C5
W13 124 D2
Bromley BR2 192 A5
Balfour Rd, Cars. SM5 199 J7
Harrow HA1 68 A5
Hounslow TW3 143 H3
Ilford IG1 98 E2
Southall UB2 122 D3
Balfour St, SE17 36 B1
Balfron Twr, E14
off St. Leonards Rd 114 C6
Balgonie Rd, E4 62 D1
Balgowan Cl, N.Mal. KT3 183 E5
Balgowan Rd, Beck. BR3 189 H3
Balgowan St, SE18 137 J4
BALHAM, SW12 167 J1
Balham Continental Mkt, SW12
off Shipka Rd 168 B1
Balham Gro, SW12 150 A7
Balham High Rd, SW12 168 A1
SW17 168 A2
Balham Hill, SW12 150 B7
Balham New Rd, SW12 150 B7
Balham Pk Rd, SW12 167 J1
Balham Rd, N9 60 D2
Balham Sta Rd, SW12 168 B1
Balkan Wk, E1
off Pennington St 112/113 E7
Balladier Wk, E14 114 B5
Ballamore Rd, Brom. BR1 173 G3
Ballance Rd, E9 95 G6
Ballantine St, SW18 149 F4
Ballard Cl, Kings.T. KT2 164 D7
Ballards Cl, Dag. RM10 119 H1
Ballards Fm Rd, Croy. CR0 202 D6
South Croydon CR2 202 D6
Ballards La, N3 72 D1
N12 72 D1
Ballards Ms, Edg. HA8 54 A6
Ballards Ri, S.Croy. CR2 202 D6
Ballards Rd, NW2 89 G2
Dagenham RM10 119 H1
Ballards Way, Croy. CR0 203 E6
South Croydon CR2 202 D6
Ballast Quay, SE10 134 D5
Ballater Cl, Wat. WD19 50 C4
Ballater Rd, SW2 151 E4
South Croydon CR2 202 C5
Ball Ct, EC3 *off Cornhill* 112 A6
Ballina St, SE23 153 G6
Ballingdon Rd, SW11 150 A6
Ballinger Pt, E3
off Bromley High St 114 B3
Balliol Av, E4 62 D4
Balliol Rd, N17 76 B1
W10 107 J6
Welling DA16 158 B2
Balloch Rd, SE6 172 D1
Ballogie Av, NW10 89 E4
Ballow Cl, SE5 *off Harris St* 132 B7
Balls Pond Pl, N1
off Balls Pond Rd 94 A6
Balls Pond Rd, N1 94 A6
Balmain Cl, W5 125 G1
Balmer Rd, E3 113 J2
Balmes Rd, N1 112 A1
Balmoral Apartments, W2
off Praed St 109 H5
Balmoral Av, N11 58 A5
Beckenham BR3 189 H4
Balmoral Cl, SW15
off Westleigh Av 148 A6
Balmoral Ct, Wor.Pk. KT4 197 H2
Balmoral Cres, W.Mol. KT8 179 G3
Balmoral Dr, Borwd. WD6 38 D5
Southall UB1 103 F4
Balmoral Gdns, W13 124 D3
Bexley DA5 159 F7
Ilford IG3 99 J1
Balmoral Gro, N7 93 F6
Balmoral Ms, W12 127 F2
Balmoral Rd, E7 97 J4
E10 96 B2
NW2 89 H6
Harrow HA2 85 G4
Kingston upon Thames KT1 181 J4
Worcester Park KT4 197 H3
Balmore Cl, E14 114 C6
Balmore Cres, Barn. EN4 42 A5
Balmore St, N19 92 B2
Balmuir Gdns, SW15 147 J4
Balnacraig Av, NW10 89 E4
Balniel Gate, SW1 33 J3
Baltic Cl, SW19 167 G7
Baltic Ct, SE16
off Timber Pond Rd 133 G2
Baltic Pl, N1 *off Kingsland Rd* 112 B1
Baltic St E, EC1 11 J6
Baltic St W, EC1 11 J6
Baltimore Pl, Well. DA16 157 J2
Balvaird Pl, SW1 33 J4
Balvernie Gro, SW18 148 C7
Bamber Ho, Bark. IG11
off St. Margarets 117 F1
Bamber Rd, SE15
off Moody Rd 152 C1
Bamborough Gdns, W12 127 J2
Bamford Av, Wem. HA0 105 J1
Bamford Ct, E15 *off Clays La* 96 B5
Bamford Rd, Bark. IG11 99 F6
Bamford Rd, Brom. BR1 172 C5
Bampfylde Cl, Wall. SM6 200 C3
Bampton Dr, NW7 55 G7
Bampton Rd, SE23 171 G3
Banavie Gdns, Beck. BR3 190 C1
Banbury Cl, Enf. EN2
off Holtwhites Hill 43 H1
Banbury Ct, WC2 18 A5
Sutton SM2 198 D7
Banbury Enterprise Cen, Croy. CR0
off Factory La 201 H2
Banbury Rd, E9 95 G7
E17 61 G7
Banbury St, SW11 149 H2
Banbury Wk, Nthlt. UB5
off Brabazon Rd 103 G2
Banchory Rd, SE3 135 H7
Bancroft Av, N2 73 H5
Buckhurst Hill IG9 63 G2
Bancroft Ct, Nthlt. UB5 102 C1
Bancroft Gdns, Har. HA3 67 J1
Orpington BR6 207 J1
Bancroft Rd, E1 113 F3
Harrow HA3 67 J2
Bandon Ri, Wall. SM6 200 D5
Banfield Rd, SE15 152 E4
Bangalore St, SW15 147 J3
Bangor Cl, Nthlt. UB5 85 H5
Banim St, W6 127 H3
Banister Rd, W10 108 A3
Bank, The, N6 *off Cholmeley Pk* 92 B1
Bank Av, Mitch. CR4 185 G2
Bank End, SE1 28 A1
Bankfoot Rd, Brom. BR1 173 E4
Bankhurst Rd, SE6 153 J7
Bank La, SW15 146 E5
Kingston upon Thames KT2 163 H7
Bank Ms, Sutt. SM1
off Sutton Ct Rd 199 F6
★ **Bank of England**, EC2 20 B4
★ **Bank of England Mus**, EC2 20 C4
Banksian Wk, Islw. TW7 144 B1
Banksia Rd, N18 61 F5
Bankside, SE1 19 J6
Enfield EN2 43 H1
South Croydon CR2 202 C6
Southall UB1 122 D1
Bankside Av, Nthlt. UB5
off Townson Av 102 A2
Bankside Cl, Cars. SM5 199 H6
Isleworth TW7 144 C4
Bankside Dr, T.Ditt. KT7 194 E1
★ **Bankside Gall**, SE1 19 H6
Bankside Rd, Ilf. IG1 99 F5
Bankside Way, SE19
off Lunham Rd 170 B6
Banks La, Bexh. DA6 159 F4
Banks Rd, Borwd. WD6 38 C2
Bank St, E14 134 A1
Banks Way, E12
off Grantham Rd 98 D4
Bankton Rd, SW2 151 G4
Bankwell Rd, SE13 155 E4
Bannerman Ho, SW8 34 C6
Banner St, EC1 12 A6
Banning St, SE10 134 E5
Bannister Cl, SW2
off Ewen Cres 169 G1
Greenford UB6 86 A5
Bannister Ho, E9
off Homerton High St 95 G5
Bannockburn Rd, SE18 137 H4
Bannow Cl, Epsom KT19 196 E4
★ **Banqueting Ho**, SW1 26 A2
Banstead Gdns, N9 60 B3
Banstead Rd, Cars. SM5 199 H6
Banstead St, SE15 153 F3
Banstead Way, Wall. SM6 201 E5
Banstock Rd, Edg. HA8 54 B6
Banting Dr, N21 43 F5
Banton Cl, Enf. EN1
off Central Av 44/45 E2
Bantry St, SE5 132 A7
Banwell Rd, Bex. DA5
off Woodside La 158 D6
Banyard Rd, SE16
off Southwark Pk Rd 132/133 E3
Baptist Gdns, NW5
off Queen's Cres 92 A6
Barandon Wk, W11 108 A7
Barbara Brosnan Ct, NW8 7 E2
Barbara Hucklesby Cl, N22
off The Sandlings 75 H2
Barbauld Rd, N16 94 B3
Barber Cl, N21 43 G7
Barber's All, E13 115 H3
Barbers Rd, E15 114 B2
BARBICAN, EC2 19 J2
★ **Barbican Arts & Conf Cen**,
EC2 20 A1
Barbican Rd, Grnf. UB6 103 H6
Barb Ms, W6 127 J3
Barbon Cl, WC1 18 C1
Barbot Cl, N9 60 D3
Barchard St, SW18 148 E5
Barchester Cl, W7 124 C1
Barchester Rd, Har. HA3 68 A2

Barchester St, E14 114 B5
Barclay Cl, SW6 128 D7
Barclay Oval, Wdf.Grn. IG8 63 G4
Barclay Path, E17 78 C5
Barclay Rd, E11 97 E1
E13 115 J4
E17 78 C5
N18 60 A6
SW6 128 D7
Croydon CR0 202 A3
Barclay Way, SE22
off Lordship La 152 D7
Barcombe Av, SW2 169 E2
Barcombe Cl, Orp. BR5 193 J3
Barden St, SE18 137 H7
Bardfield Av, Rom. RM6 82 D3
Bardney Rd, Mord. SM4 185 E4
Bardolph Rd, N7 92 E4
Richmond TW9
off St. Georges Rd 145 J3
Bard Rd, W10 108 A7
Bardsey Pl, E1 *off Mile End Rd* 113 F5
Bardsey Wk, N1
off Clephane Rd 93 J6
Bardsley Cl, Croy. CR0 202 C3
Bardsley La, SE10 134 C6
Barfett St, W10 108 C4
Barfield Av, N20 57 H2
Barfield Rd, E11 97 F1
Bromley BR1 192 D3
Barfields, Loug. IG10 48 D4
Barfields Gdns, Loug. IG10
off Barfields 48 D4
Barfields Path, Loug. IG10 48 D4
Barford Cl, NW4 71 G1
Barford St, N1 111 G1
Barforth Rd, SE15 153 E3
Barfreston Way, SE20 189 E1
Bargate Cl, SE18 137 J5
New Malden KT3 183 G6
Barge Ho Rd, E16 136 E1
Barge Ho St, SE1 27 F1
Bargery Rd, SE6 172 B1
Barge Wk, E.Mol. KT8 181 G2
Kingston upon Thames KT1 181 G1
Walton-on-Thames KT12 178 D3
Bargrove Cl, SE20 170 D7
Bargrove Cres, SE6 *off Elm La* 171 J2
Barham Cl, Brom. BR2 206 B1
Chislehurst BR7 174 E5
Romford RM7 83 H2
Wembley HA0 87 E6
Barham Rd, SW20 165 G7
Chislehurst BR7 174 E5
South Croydon CR2 201 J5
Baring Cl, SE12 173 G2
Baring Rd, SE12 155 G7
Barnet EN4 41 G3
Croydon CR0 202 D1
Baring St, N1 112 A1
Barkantine Shop Par, The, E14
off The Quarterdeck 134 A2
Barker Cl, N.Mal. KT3 182 B4
Barker Dr, NW1 92 C7
Barker Ms, SW4 150 B4
Barker St, SW10 30 C5
Barker Wk, SW16 168 D3
Barker Way, SE22
off Dulwich Common 170 D1
Barkham Rd, N17 60 A7
Barkham Ter, SE1 27 F5
BARKING, IG11 117 E1
Barking Ind Pk, Bark. IG11 117 J1
Barking Rd, E6 116 A2
E13 115 H4
E16 115 F5
BARKINGSIDE, Ilf. IG6 81 E3
Bark Pl, W2 14 A5
Barkston Gdns, SW5 30 A3
Barkwood Cl, Rom. RM7 83 J5
Barkworth Rd, SE16 133 E5
Barlborough St, SE14 133 F7
Barlby Gdns, W10 108 A4
Barlby Rd, W10 108 A5
Barleycorn Way, E14 113 J7
Barleyfields Cl, Rom. RM6 82 B7
Barley La, Ilf. IG3 100 A1
Romford RM6 82 B6
Barley Mow Pas, EC1 19 H2
W4 126 D5
Barley Shotts Business Pk, W10
off St. Ervans Rd 108 C5
Barlow Cl, Wall. SM6 200 E7
Barlow Dr, SE18 156 B1
Barlow Pl, W1 17 E6
Barlow Rd, NW6 90 C6
W3 126 B1
Hampton TW12 161 G7
Barlow St, SE17 36 C2
Barmeston Rd, SE6 172 B2
Barmor Cl, Har. HA2 67 H2
Barmouth Av, Grnf. UB6 104 C2
Barmouth Rd, SW18 149 F6
Croydon CR0 203 G2
Barnabas Ct, N21
off Cheyne Wk 43 G5
Barnabas Rd, E9 95 G5
Barnaby Cl, Har. HA2 85 J2
Barnaby Pl, SW7 31 E2
Barnaby Way, Chig. IG7 64 E3
Barnard Cl, SE18 136 D4
Chislehurst BR7 193 G1
Sunbury-on-Thames TW16
off Oak Gro 160 B7
Wallington SM6 200 D7
Barnard Gdns, Hayes UB4 102 B4
New Malden KT3 183 G4
Barnard Gro, E15
off Vicarage La 97 F7
Barnard Hill, N10 74 A2
Barnard Ms, SW11 149 H4
Barnardo Dr, Ilf. IG6 81 F4
Barnardo Gdns, E1
off Devonport St 113 G7
Barnardo St, E1
off Devonport St 113 G6
Barnardos Village, Ilf. IG6 81 F3
Barnard Rd, SW11 149 H4
Enfield EN1 45 E2
Mitcham CR4 186 A3
Barnard's Inn, EC1 19 F3
Barnby Sq, E15
off Barnby St 114/115 E1
Barnby St, E15 114 E1
NW1 9 G2
Barn Cl, Nthlt. UB5 102 C2
Barn Cres, Stan. HA7 53 F6
Barncroft Cl, Loug. IG10 48 D5
Barncroft Grn, Loug. IG10 48 D5
Barncroft Rd, Loug. IG10 48 D5
Barneby Cl, Twick. TW2
off Rowntree Rd 162 B1
Barnehurst Av, Bexh. DA7 159 J1
Erith DA8 159 J1
Barnehurst Cl, Erith DA8 159 J1
Barnehurst Rd, Bexh. DA7 159 J2
Barn Elms Pk, SW15 147 J2
BARNES, SW13 147 G2
Barnes All, Hmptn. TW12
off Hampton Ct Rd 179 J2
Barnes Av, SW13 127 G7
Southall UB2 123 F4
Barnes Br, SW13 147 E2
W4 147 E2
Barnesbury Ho, SW4 150 D5
Barnes Cl, E12 98 A4
★ **Barnes Common**, SW13 147 G3
Barnes Ct, E16 *off Ridgwell Rd* 115 J5
Woodford Green IG8 64 A5
Barnes End, N.Mal. KT3 183 G5
Barnes High St, SW13 147 F2
Barnes Ho, Bark. IG11
off St. Marys 117 G1
Barnes Pikle, W5 105 G7
Barnes Rd, N18 61 F4
Ilford IG1 99 F5
Barnes St, E14 113 H6
Barnes Ter, SE8 133 J5
BARNET, EN4 & EN5 40 C3
Barnet Bypass, Barn. EN5 38 E3
Barnet Dr, Brom. BR2 206 B2
BARNET GATE, Barn. EN5 39 F6
Barnet Gate La, Barn. EN5 39 F6
Barnet Gro, E2 13 H3
Barnet Hill, Barn. EN5 40 D4
Barnet Ho, N20 57 F2
Barnet La, N20 56 C1
Barnet EN5 40 C6
★ **Barnet Mus**, Barn. EN5
off Wood St 40 B4
Barnet Rd, Barn. EN5 39 H5
Barnet Trd Est, Barn. EN5 40 C3
Barnett St, E1
off Cannon St Rd 112/113 E6
Barnet Way, NW7 38 D7
Barnet Wd Rd, Brom. BR2 205 J2
Barney Cl, SE7 135 J5
Barnfield, N.Mal. KT3 182 E6
Barnfield Av, Croy. CR0 203 F2
Kingston upon Thames KT2 163 H5
Mitcham CR4 186 B4
Barnfield Cl, N4
off Crouch Hill 74/75 E7
SW17 167 F3
Barnfield Gdns, SE18
off Plumstead Common Rd 136/137 E6
Kingston upon Thames KT2 163 H4
Barnfield Pl, E14 134 A4
Barnfield Rd, SE18 137 E6
W5 105 F4
Belvedere DA17 139 F6
Edgware HA8 70 C1
Barnfield Wd Cl, Beck. BR3 190 D6
Barnfield Wd Rd, Beck. BR3 190 D6
Barnham Dr, SE28 137 J1
Barnham Rd, Grnf. UB6 103 J3
Barnham St, SE1 28 E3
Barnhill, Pnr. HA5 66 C5
Barn Hill, Wem. HA9 88 B2
Barnhill Av, Brom. BR2 191 F5
Barnhill La, Hayes UB4 102 B3
Barnhill Rd, Hayes UB4 102 B4
Wembley HA9 88 C3
Barnhurst Path, Wat. WD19 50 C5
Barningham Way, NW9 70 D6
Barnlea Cl, Felt. TW13 161 E2
Barnmead Gdns, Dag. RM9 101 F5
Barnmead Rd, Beck. BR3 189 H1
Dagenham RM9 101 F5
Barn Ri, Wem. HA9 88 A1
BARNSBURY, N1 93 F7
Barnsbury Cl, N.Mal. KT3 182 C4
Barnsbury Cres, Surb. KT5 196 C1
Barnsbury Est, N1
off Barnsbury Rd 111 G1
Barnsbury Gro, N7 93 F7
Barnsbury La, Surb. KT5 196 B2
Barnsbury Pk, N1 93 G7
Barnsbury Rd, N1 10 E1
Barnsbury Sq, N1 93 G7
Barnsbury St, N1 93 G7
Barnsbury Ter, N1 93 F7
Barnscroft, SW20 183 H3
Barnsdale Av, E14 134 A4
Barnsdale Rd, W9 108 C4
Barnsley St, E1 113 E4
Barnstaple Rd, Ruis. HA4 84 C3
Barnston Wk, N1 *off Popham St* 111 J1
Barn St, N16
off Stoke Newington Ch St 94 B3
Barn Way, Wem. HA9 88 A1
Barnwell Rd, SW2 151 G5
Barnwood Cl, N20 56 C1
W9 6 A6
Baron Cl, N11 *off Balmoral Av* 58 A5
Baroness Rd, E2 13 G3
Baronet Gro, N17
off St. Paul's Rd 76 D1
Baronet Rd, N17 76 D1
Baron Gdns, Ilf. IG6 81 F3
Baron Gro, Mitch. CR4 185 H4
Baron Rd, Dag. RM8 100 D1
Barons, The, Twick. TW1 145 E6
Barons Ct, Wall. SM6
off Whelan Way 200 D3
Barons Ct Rd, W14 128 B5
Baronsfield Rd, Twick. TW1 145 E6
Barons Gate, Barn. EN4 41 H6
Barons Keep, W14 128 B5
Barons Mead, Har. HA1 68 B4
Baronsmead Rd, SW13 147 G1
Baronsmede, W5 125 J2
Baronsmere Rd, N2 73 H4
Barons Pl, SE1 27 F4
Baron St, N1 11 E1
Barons Wk, Croy. CR0 189 H6
Baron Wk, E16 115 F5
Mitcham CR4 185 H4
Barque Ms, SE8
off Watergate St 134 A6
Barrack Rd, Houns. TW4 142 D4
Barracks La, Barn. EN5
off High St 40 B3
Barratt Av, N22 75 F2
Barratt Ind Pk, Sthl. UB1 123 G2
Barratt Way, Har. HA3
off Tudor Rd 68 A3
Barrenger Rd, N10 73 J1
Barrett Rd, E17 78 C4
Barretts Grn Rd, NW10 106 C2
Barretts Gro, N16 94 B5
Barrett St, W1 16 C4
Barrhill Rd, SW2 169 E2
Barriedale, SE14 153 H1
Barrie Est, W2 14 E5
Barrier App, SE7 136 A3
Barrier Pt Rd, E16 135 J1
Barrier Pt Twr, E16
off Barrier Pt Rd 135 J2
Barringer Sq, SW17 168 A4
Barrington Cl, NW5 92 A5
Ilford IG5 80 C1
Loughton IG10
off Barrington Rd 49 F4
Barrington Grn, Loug. IG10 49 F4
Barrington Rd, E12 98 D6
N8 74 D5
SW9 151 H3
Bexleyheath DA7 158 D2
Loughton IG10 49 F3
Sutton SM3 198 D1
Barrington Vil, SE18 156 D1
Barrow Av, Cars. SM5 199 J7
Barrow Cl, N21 59 H3
Barrowdene Cl, Pnr. HA5
off Paines La 66/67 E2
Barrowell Grn, N21 59 H2
Barrowfield Cl, N9 61 E3
Barrowgate Rd, W4 126 C5
Barrow Hedges Cl, Cars. SM5 199 H7
Barrow Hedges Way, Cars. SM5 199 H7
Barrow Hill, Wor.Pk. KT4 196 E2
Barrow Hill Cl, Wor.Pk. KT4
off Barrow Hill 196/197 E2
Barrow Hill Est, NW8
off Barrow Hill Rd 109 H2
Barrow Hill Rd, NW8 7 G2
Barrow Pt Av, Pnr. HA5 66 E2
Barrow Pt La, Pnr. HA5 66 E2
Barrow Rd, SW16 168 D6
Barrow Rd, Croy. CR0 201 G5
Barrow Wk, Brent. TW8
off Glenhurst Rd 125 F5
Barrs Rd, NW10 88 D7
Barry Av, N15 *off Craven Pk Rd* 76 C6
Bexleyheath DA7 138 E7
Barry Cl, Orp. BR6 207 H3
Barry Rd, E6 116 B6
NW10 88 C7
SE22 152 D6
Barset Rd, SE15 153 F3
Barson Cl, SE20 171 F7
Barston Rd, SE27 169 J3
Barstow Cres, SW2 169 F1
Barter St, WC1 18 B2
Barters Wk, Pnr. HA5
off High St 66/67 E3
Barth Ms, SE18 *off Barth Rd* 137 H4
Bartholomew Cl, EC1 19 J2
SW18 149 F4
Bartholomew Ct, E14
off Newport Av 114 D7
Bartholomew La, EC2 20 C4
Bartholomew Pl, EC1 19 J2
Bartholomew Rd, NW5 92 C6
Bartholomew Sq, E1
off Coventry Rd 112/113 E4
EC1 12 A5
Bartholomew St, SE1 28 B6
Bartholomew Vil, NW5 92 C6
Barth Rd, SE18 137 H4
Bartle Av, E6 116 B2
Bartle Rd, W11 108 B6
Bartlett Cl, E14 114 A6
Bartlett Ct, EC4 19 F3
Bartletts Pas, EC4 19 F3
Bartlett St, S.Croy. CR2 202 A5
Barton Av, Rom. RM7 101 H1
Barton Cl, E6 116 C6
E9 *off Churchill Wk* 95 F5
NW4 71 G5
SE15 *off Kirkwood Rd* 152/153 E3
Bexleyheath DA6 158 E5
Chigwell IG7 65 F2
Barton Grn, N.Mal. KT3 182 D2
Barton Ho, SW6
off Wandsworth Br Rd 148/149 E3
Barton Meadows, Ilf. IG6 81 F4
Barton Rd, W14 128 B5
Sidcup DA14 177 E6
Barton St, SW1 26 A5
Bartonway, NW8
off Queen's Ter 109 G2
Barton Way, Borwd. WD6 38 A2
Bartram Rd, SE4 153 H5
Barts Cl, Beck. BR3 190 A5
Barville Cl, SE4
off St. Norbert Rd 153 H4
Barwick Rd, E7 97 H4
Barwood Av, W.Wick. BR4 204 B1
Bascombe St, SW2 151 G6
Basden Gro, Felt. TW13 161 G2
Basedale Rd, Dag. RM9 100 B7
Baseing Cl, E6 116 D7
Basevi Way, SE8 134 B6
Bashley Rd, NW10 106 D4
Basil Av, E6 116 B2
Basildene Rd, Houns. TW4 142 D2
Basildon Av, Ilf. IG5 80 D1
Basildon Rd, SE2 138 A5
Basil Gdns, SE27 169 J5
Croydon CR0
off Primrose La 203 G1
Basilon Rd, Bexh. DA7 158 E2
Basil St, SW3 23 J5
Basin App, E14
off Commercial Rd 113 H6
Basing Cl, T.Ditt. KT7 180 C7
Basing Ct, SE15 152 C1
Basingdon Way, SE5 152 A4
Basing Dr, Bex. DA5 159 F6
Basingfield Rd, T.Ditt. KT7 180 C7
Basinghall Av, EC2 20 B2
Basinghall St, EC2 20 B3
Basing Hill, NW11 90 C1
Wembley HA9 87 J2
Basing Ho, Bark. IG11
off St. Margarets 117 G1
Basing Ho Yd, E2 13 E3
Basing Pl, E2 13 E3
Basing St, W11 108 C6
Basing Way, N3 72 D3
Thames Ditton KT7 180 C7
Basire St, N1 111 J1
Baskerville Rd, SW18 149 H7
Basket Gdns, SE9 156 B5
Baslow Cl, Har. HA3 68 A1
Baslow Wk, E5 *off Overbury St* 95 G4
Basnett Rd, SW11 150 A3
Basque Ct, SE16
off Poolmans St 133 G2
Bassano St, SE22 152 C5
Bassant Rd, SE18 137 J6
Bassein Pk Rd, W12 127 F2
Bassett Gdns, Islw. TW7 123 J7
Bassett Ho, Dag. RM9 118 B1
Bassett Rd, W10 108 A6

Bassetts Cl, Orp. BR6 . . . . .206 E4
Bassett St, NW5 . . . . .92 A6
Bassetts Way, Orp. BR6 . . . . .206 E4
Bassett Way, Grnf. UB6 . . . . .103 H6
Bassingham Rd, SW18 . . . . .149 F7
   Wembley HA0 . . . . .87 G6
Bassishaw Highwalk, EC2
   off London Wall 111 J5
Bastable Av, Bark. IG11 . . . . .117 H2
Bastion Highwalk, EC2
   off London Wall 111 J5
Bastion Ho, EC2
   off London Wall 111 J5
Bastion Rd, SE2 . . . . .138 A5
Baston Manor Rd, Brom. BR2 . .205 H3
Baston Rd, Brom. BR2 . . . . .205 H1
Bastwick St, EC1 . . . . .11 J5
Basuto Rd, SW6 . . . . .148 D1
Batavia Cl, Sun. TW16 . . . . .178 C1
Batavia Ms, SE14
   off Goodwood Rd 133 H7
Batavia Rd, SE14 . . . . .133 H7
   Sunbury-on-Thames TW16 . . . .178 B1
Batchelor St, N1 . . . . .11 E1
Bateman Cl, Bark. IG11
   off Glenny Rd 99 F6
Bateman Ho, SE17 . . . . .35 G6
Bateman Rd, E4 . . . . .62 A6
Bateman's Bldgs, W1 . . . . .17 H4
Bateman's Row, EC2 . . . . .12 E5
Bateman St, W1 . . . . .17 H4
Bates Cres, SW16 . . . . .168 C7
   Croydon CR0 . . . . .201 G4
Bateson St, SE18 . . . . .137 H4
Bates Pt, E13 off Pelly Rd 115 G1
Bate St, E14 off Three Colt St . . .113 J7
Bath Cl, SE15
   off Asylum Rd 132/133 E7
Bath Ct, EC1 . . . . .11 E4
Bathgate Rd, SW19 . . . . .166 A3
Bath Ho Rd, Croy. CR0 . . . . .200 E1
Bath Pas, Kings.T. KT1
   off St. James Rd 181 G2
Bath Pl, EC2 . . . . .12 E4
   Barnet EN5 . . . . .40 C3
Bath Rd, E7 . . . . .98 A6
   N9 . . . . .61 E2
   W4 . . . . .126 E4
   Hayes UB3 . . . . .141 F1
   Hounslow TW3, TW4, TW5,
   TW6 .142 D2
   Mitcham CR4 . . . . .185 G3
   Romford RM6 . . . . .82 E6
   West Drayton UB7 . . . . .140 A1
Baths Rd, Brom. BR2 . . . . .192 A4
Bath St, EC1 . . . . .12 A4
Bath Ter, SE1 . . . . .27 J6
Bathurst Av, SW19
   off Brisbane Av 184/185 E1
Bathurst Gdns, NW10 . . . . .107 H2
Bathurst Ms, W2 . . . . .15 E5
Bathurst Rd, Ilf. IG1 . . . . .98 E1
Bathurst St, W2 . . . . .15 E5
Bathway, SE18 . . . . .136 D4
Batley Cl, Mitch. CR4 . . . . .185 J7
Batley Pl, N16 . . . . .94 C3
Batley Rd, N16
   off Stoke Newington High St . .94 C3
   Enfield EN2 . . . . .43 J1
Batman Cl, W12 . . . . .127 H1
Batoum Gdns, W6 . . . . .127 J3
Batson St, W12 . . . . .127 G2
Batsworth Rd, Mitch. CR4 . . . . . .185 G3
Battenburg Wk, SE19
   off Brabourne Cl 170 B5
Batten Cl, E6 off Savage Gdns . .116 C6
Batten St, SW11 . . . . .149 H3
Battersby Rd, SE6 . . . . .172 D2
BATTERSEA, SW11 . . . . .150 B1
Battersea Br, SW3 . . . . .31 F7
   SW11 . . . . .31 F7
Battersea Br Rd, SW11 . . . . .129 H7
Battersea Ch Rd, SW11 . . . . .149 G1
★ Battersea Dogs Home,
   SW8 .130 B7
Battersea High St, SW11 . . . . . . .149 G1
★ Battersea Park, SW11 . . . . . . .32 A7
Battersea Pk Rd, SW8 . . . . .150 B1
   SW11 . . . . .149 H2
Battersea Ri, SW11 . . . . .149 H5
Battersea Sq, SW11
   off Battersea High St 149 G1
Battery Rd, SE28 . . . . .137 H2
Battishill Gdns, N1
   off Waterloo Ter 93 H7
Battishill St, N1
   off Waterloo Ter 93 H7
Battlebridge Ct, N1 . . . . .10 B1
Battle Br La, SE1 . . . . .28 D2
Battle Br Rd, NW1 . . . . .10 A2
Battle Cl, SW19 off North Rd . . .167 F6
Battledean Rd, N5 . . . . .93 H5
Battle Rd, Belv. DA17 . . . . .139 J4
   Erith DA8 . . . . .139 J4
Batty St, E1 . . . . .21 J3
Baudwin Rd, SE6 . . . . .172 E2
Baugh Rd, Sid. DA14 . . . . .176 C5

Baulk, The, SW18 . . . . .148 D7
Bavant Rd, SW16 . . . . .187 E2
Bavaria Rd, N19 . . . . .92 E2
Bavdene Ms, NW4
   off The Burroughs 71 H4
Bavent Rd, SE5 . . . . .151 J2
Bawdale Rd, SE22 . . . . .152 C5
Bawdsey Av, Ilf. IG2 . . . . .81 J4
Bawtree Rd, SE14 . . . . .133 H7
Bawtry Rd, N20 . . . . .57 J3
Baxendale, N20 . . . . .57 F2
Baxendale St, E2 . . . . .13 H3
Baxter Cl, Sthl. UB2 . . . . .123 H2
Baxter Rd, E16 . . . . .115 J6
   N1 . . . . .94 A6
   N18 . . . . .60 E4
   NW10 . . . . .106 E4
   Ilford IG1 . . . . .98 E5
Bay Ct, W5 off Popes La 125 H4
Baycroft Cl, Pnr. HA5 . . . . .66 C3
Baydon Ct, Brom. BR2 . . . . .191 F3
Bayes Cl, SE26 . . . . .171 F5
Bayfield Rd, SE9 . . . . .156 A4
Bayford Ms, E8
   off Bayford St 94/95 E7
Bayford Rd, NW10 . . . . .108 A3
Bayford St, E8 . . . . .95 E7
Bayham Pl, NW1 . . . . .9 F1
Bayham Rd, W4 . . . . .126 D3
   W13 .104 E7
   Morden SM4 . . . . .185 E4
Bayham St, NW1 . . . . .110 C1
Bayley St, WC1 . . . . .17 H2
Bayley Wk, SE2
   off Woolwich Rd 138/139 E5
Baylin Rd, SW18
   off Garratt La 148/149 E6
Baylis Ms, Twick. TW1
   off Amyand Pk Rd 144 D7
Baylis Rd, SE1 . . . . .27 E4
Bayliss Av, SE28 . . . . .118 D7
Bayliss Cl, N21 . . . . .43 E5
   Southall UB1 . . . . .103 H6
Bayne Cl, E6 off Savage Gdns . . .116 C6
Baynes Cl, Enf. EN1 . . . . .44 D2
Baynes Ms, NW3 off Belsize La . .91 G6
Baynes St, NW1 . . . . .92 C7
Baynham Cl, Bex. DA5 . . . . .159 F6
Bayonne Rd, W6 . . . . .128 B6
Bayshill Ri, Nthlt. UB5 . . . . .85 H6
Bayston Rd, N16 . . . . .94 C3
BAYSWATER, W2 . . . . .14 B4
Bayswater Rd, W2 . . . . .15 F5
Baythorne St, E3 . . . . .113 J5
Bay Tree Cl, Brom. BR1 . . . . .191 J1
   Ilford IG6 off Hazel La 64/65 E7
Baytree Cl, Sid. DA15 . . . . .175 J1
Baytree Ho, E4 off Dells Cl 46 B7
Baytree Rd, SW2 . . . . .151 F4
Bazalgette Cl, N.Mal. KT3 . . . . . .182 D5
Bazalgette Gdns, N.Mal. KT3 . . .182 D5
Bazely St, E14 . . . . .114 C7
Bazile Rd, N21 . . . . .43 G6
Beacham Cl, SE7 . . . . .136 A5
Beachborough Rd, Brom. BR1 . . .172 C4
Beachcroft Rd, E11 . . . . .97 E3
Beachcroft Way, N19 . . . . .92 D1
Beach Gro, Felt. TW13 . . . . .161 G2
Beachy Rd, E3 . . . . .96 A7
Beacon Gate, SE14 . . . . .153 G3
Beacon Gro, Cars. SM5 . . . . .200 A4
Beacon Hill, N7 . . . . .92 E5
Beacon Rd, SE13 . . . . .154 D6
   Hounslow (Hthrw Air.) TW6 . . .140 D6
Beacon Rd Roundabout, Houns.
   (Hthrw Air.) TW6 . . . . .140 E6
Beacons Cl, E6
   off Oliver Gdns 116 B5
Beaconsfield Cl, N11 . . . . .58 A4
   SE3 .135 G6
   W4 . . . . .126 C5
Beaconsfield Gdns, Esher (Clay.)
   KT10 .194 B7
Beaconsfield Par, SE9
   off Beaconsfield Rd 174 B4
Beaconsfield Rd, E10 . . . . .96 C2
   E16 . . . . .115 F4
   E17 . . . . .77 J6
   N9 . . . . .60 D4
   N11 . . . . .58 A3
   N15 . . . . .76 B4
   NW10 . . . . .89 F6
   SE3 .135 F7
   SE9 .174 B2
   SE17 .36 C4
   W4 . . . . .126 D3
   W5 . . . . .125 F2
   Bromley BR1 . . . . .192 A3
   Croydon CR0 . . . . .188 A6
   Esher (Clay.) KT10 . . . . .194 B7
   Hayes UB4 . . . . .122 C1
   New Malden KT3 . . . . .182 D3
   Southall UB1 . . . . .122 D1
   Surbiton KT5 . . . . .181 J7
   Twickenham TW1 . . . . .144 E6
Beaconsfield Ter, Rom. RM6 . . . .82 D6
Beaconsfield Ter Rd, W14 . . . . . .128 B3

Beaconsfield Wk, E6
   off East Ham Manor Way . . .116 D6
   SW6 .148 C1
Beacontree Av, E17 . . . . .78 D1
Beacontree Rd, E11 . . . . .79 F7
Beadlow Cl, Cars. SM5
   off Olveston Wk 185 G6
Beadman Pl, SE27
   off Norwood High St 169 H4
Beadman St, SE27 . . . . .169 H4
Beadnell Rd, SE23 . . . . .171 G1
Beadon Rd, W6 . . . . .127 J4
   Bromley BR2 . . . . .191 G4
Beaford Gro, SW20 . . . . .184 B3
Beagle Cl, Felt. TW13 . . . . .160 B4
Beak St, W1 . . . . .17 G5
Beal Cl, Well. DA16 . . . . .158 A1
Beale Cl, N13 . . . . .59 H5
Beale Pl, E3 . . . . .113 J2
Beale Rd, E3 . . . . .113 J1
Beal Rd, Ilf. IG1 . . . . .98 D2
Beam Av, Dag. RM10 . . . . .119 H1
Beaminster Gdns, Ilf. IG6 . . . . . .80 E2
Beamish Dr, Bushey (Bushey Hth)
   WD23 . . . . .51 J1
Beamish Rd, N9 . . . . .60 D1
Beanacre Cl, E9 . . . . .95 J6
Bean Rd, Bexh. DA6 . . . . .158 D4
Beanshaw, SE9 . . . . .174 D4
Beansland Gro, Rom. RM6 . . . . . .83 E2
Bear All, EC4 . . . . .19 G3
Bear Cl, Rom. RM7 . . . . .83 H6
Beardell St, SE19 . . . . .170 C6
Beardow Gro, N14 . . . . .42 C6
Beard Rd, Kings.T. KT2 . . . . .163 J5
Beardsfield, E13 off Valetta Gro . .115 J5
Beard's Hill, Hmptn. TW12 . . . . .179 G1
Beard's Hill Cl, Hmptn. TW12
   off Beard's Hill 179 G1
Beardsley Ter, Dag. RM8
   off Fitzstephen Rd 100 B5
Beardsley Way, W3 . . . . .126 D2
Bearfield Rd, Kings.T. KT2 . . . . . .163 H7
Bear Gdns, SE1 . . . . .27 J1
Bear La, SE1 . . . . .27 H1
Bear Rd, Felt. TW13 . . . . .160 D5
Bearstead Ri, SE4 . . . . .153 J5
Bearsted Ter, Beck. BR3 . . . . . . .190 A1
Bear St, WC2 . . . . .17 J5
Beaton Cl, SE15 . . . . .152 C1
Beatrice Av, SW16 . . . . .187 F3
   Wembley HA9 . . . . .87 H5
Beatrice Cl, E13
   off Chargeable La 115 G4
   Pinner HA5 off Reid Cl 66 A4
Beatrice Ct, Buck.H. IG9 . . . . . . .64 A2
Beatrice Pl, W8 . . . . .22 A6
Beatrice Rd, E17 . . . . .78 A5
   N4 . . . . .75 G7
   N9 . . . . .45 F7
   SE1 . . . . .37 J2
   Richmond TW10
   off Albert Rd 145 J5
   Southall UB1 . . . . .123 F1
Beatson Wk, SE16 . . . . .133 G1
Beattock Ri, N10 . . . . .74 B4
Beatty Rd, N16 . . . . .94 B4
   Stanmore HA7 . . . . .53 F6
Beatty St, NW1 . . . . .9 F1
Beattyville Gdns, Ilf. IG6 . . . . . . .80 D3
Beauchamp Cl, W4
   off Church Path 126 C3
Beauchamp Ct, Stan. HA7
   off Hardwick Cl 53 F5
Beauchamp Pl, SW3 . . . . .23 H5
Beauchamp Rd, E7 . . . . .97 H7
   SE19 .188 A1
   SW11 . . . . .149 H4
   East Molesey KT8 . . . . .179 H5
   Sutton SM1 . . . . .198 D5
   Twickenham TW1 . . . . .144 D7
   West Molesey KT8 . . . . .179 H5
Beauchamp St, EC1 . . . . .19 E2
Beauchamp Ter, SW15
   off Dryburgh Rd 147 H3
Beauclerc Rd, W6 . . . . .127 H3
Beauclerk Cl, Felt. TW13
   off Florence Rd 160 B1
Beaudesert Ms, West Dr. UB7 . . .120 B2
Beaufort, E6 off Newark Knok . . .116 D6
Beaufort Av, Har. HA3 . . . . .68 D4
Beaufort Cl, E4
   off Higham Sta Av 62 B6
   SW15 . . . . .147 H7
   W5 . . . . .105 J5
   Romford RM7 . . . . .83 J4
Beaufort Ct, Rich. TW10
   off Beaufort Rd 163 F4
Beaufort Dr, NW11 . . . . .72 D4
Beaufort Gdns, NW4 . . . . .71 J6
   SW3 .23 H5
   SW16 . . . . .169 F7
   Hounslow TW5 . . . . .143 E1
   Ilford IG1 . . . . .98 D1
Beaufort Ms, SW6 off Lillie Rd . .128 C6
Beaufort Pk, NW11 . . . . .72 D4
Beaufort Rd, W5 . . . . .105 J5

Beaufort Rd, Kings.T. KT1 . . . . . .181 H4
   Richmond TW10 . . . . .163 F4
   Twickenham TW1 . . . . .145 F7
Beaufort St, SW3 . . . . .31 F6
Beaufort Way, Epsom KT17 . . . . .197 G2
Beaufoy Rd, N17 . . . . .60 B7
Beaufoy Wk, SE11 . . . . .34 D2
Beaulieu Av, E16 . . . . .135 H1
   SE26 .170 E4
Beaulieu Cl, NW9 . . . . .71 E4
   SE5 .152 A3
   Hounslow TW4 . . . . .143 F5
   Mitcham CR4 . . . . .186 A1
   Twickenham TW1 . . . . .145 G7
   Watford WD19 . . . . .50 C1
Beaulieu Dr, Pnr. HA5 . . . . .66 D6
Beaulieu Gdns, N21 . . . . .43 J7
Beaulieu Pl, W4
   off Rothschild Rd 126 C3
Beaumanor Gdns, SE9 . . . . .174 D4
Beaumaris Dr, Wdf.Grn. IG8 . . . .64 A7
Beaumaris Grn, NW9
   off Goldsmith Av 70/71 E6
Beaumont Av, W14 . . . . .128 C5
   Harrow HA2 . . . . .67 H6
   Richmond TW9 . . . . .145 J3
   Wembley HA0 . . . . .87 F5
Beaumont Cl, Kings.T. KT2 . . . . .164 A7
Beaumont Cres, W14 . . . . .128 C5
Beaumont Gdns, NW3 . . . . .90 D3
Beaumont Gro, E1 . . . . .113 G4
Beaumont Ms, W1 . . . . .16 C1
   Pinner HA5 . . . . .66 E3
Beaumont Pl, W1 . . . . .9 G5
   Barnet EN5 . . . . .40 C1
   Isleworth TW7 . . . . .144 C5
Beaumont Ri, N19 . . . . .92 D1
Beaumont Rd, E10 . . . . .78 B7
   E13 . . . . .115 H3
   SE19 .169 J6
   SW19 . . . . .148 B7
   W4 . . . . .126 C3
   Orpington BR5 . . . . .193 G6
Beaumont Sq, E1 . . . . .113 G4
Beaumont St, W1 . . . . .16 C1
Beaumont Wk, NW3 . . . . .91 J7
Beauvais Ter, Nthlt. UB5 . . . . . . .102 D3
Beauval Rd, SE22 . . . . .152 C6
Beaverbank Rd, SE9 . . . . .175 G1
Beaver Cl, SE20
   off Lullington Rd 170 D7
   Hampton TW12 . . . . .179 H1
Beaver Gro, Nthlt. UB5
   off Jetstar Way 102/103 E3
Beavers Cres, Houns. TW4 . . . . .142 C4
Beavers La, Houns. TW4 . . . . . . .142 C3
Beavers La Camp, Houns. TW4
   off Beavers La 142 C3
Beaverwood Rd, Chis. BR7 . . . . .175 H6
Beavor Gro, W6 off Beavor La . . .127 G4
Beavor La, W6 . . . . .127 G4
Bebbington Rd, SE18 . . . . .137 H4
Bebletts Cl, Orp. BR6 . . . . .207 J5
Beccles Dr, Bark. IG11 . . . . .99 H6
Beccles St, E14 . . . . .113 J7
Bec Cl, Ruis. HA4 . . . . .84 D3
Beck Cl, SE13 . . . . .154 B1
Beck Ct, Beck. BR3 . . . . .189 G3
BECKENHAM, BR3 . . . . .190 A1
Beckenham Business Cen, Beck.
   BR3 . . . . .171 H6
Beckenham Gdns, N9 . . . . .60 B3
Beckenham Gro, Brom. BR2 . . . .190 D2
Beckenham Hill Rd, SE6 . . . . . . .172 B5
   Beckenham BR3 . . . . .172 B5
Beckenham La, Brom. BR2 . . . . .191 F2
Beckenham Pl Pk, Beck. BR3 . . . .172 B7
Beckenham Rd, Beck. BR3 . . . . . .189 G1
   West Wickham BR4 . . . . .190 B7
Beckers, The, N16
   off Rectory Rd 94 D3
Becket Av, E6 . . . . .116 D3
Becket Cl, SE25 . . . . .188 D6
Becket Fold, Har. HA1
   off Courtfield Cres 68 C5
Becket Rd, N18 . . . . .61 F4
Becket St, SE1 . . . . .28 B5
Beckett Cl, NW10 . . . . .88 D6
   SW16 . . . . .168 D2
   Belvedere DA17
   off Tunstock Way 138/139 E3
Becketts Cl, Bex. DA5 . . . . .177 J1
   Feltham TW14 . . . . .142 B6
   Orpington BR6 . . . . .207 J4
Becketts Pl, Kings.T. (Hmptn W.)
   KT1 . . . . .181 G1
Beckett Wk, Beck. BR3 . . . . .171 H6
Beckford Dr, Orp. BR5 . . . . .193 G7
Beckford Pl, SE17 . . . . .36 A4
Beckford Rd, Croy. CR0 . . . . .188 C6
Beck La, Beck. BR3 . . . . .189 G3
Becklow Gdns, W12
   off Becklow Rd 127 G2
Becklow Ms, W12
   off Becklow Rd 127 F2
Becklow Rd, W12 . . . . .127 G2
Beck River Pk, Beck. BR3 . . . . . .189 J1

Beck Rd, E8 . . . 112 E1
Becks Rd, Sid. DA14 . . . 176 A3
BECKTON, E6 . . . 116 D5
Beckton Pk Roundabout, E16
  off Royal Albert Way . . . 116 C7
Beckton Retail Pk, E6 . . . 116 D5
Beckton Rd, E16 . . . 115 F5
Beckton Triangle Retail Pk, E6 . . . 116 D4
Beck Way, Beck. BR3 . . . 189 J3
Beckway Rd, SW16 . . . 186 D2
Beckway St, SE17 . . . 36 C2
Beckwith Rd, SE24 . . . 152 A6
Beclands Rd, SW17 . . . 168 A6
Becmead Av, SW16 . . . 168 D4
  Harrow HA3 . . . 68 E5
Becondale Rd, SE19 . . . 170 B5
BECONTREE, Dag. RM8 . . . 100 C3
Becontree Av, Dag. RM8 . . . 100 B4
BECONTREE HEATH, Dag. RM8 . . . 101 G1
Bective Pl, SW15
  off Bective Rd . . . 148 C4
Bective Rd, E7 . . . 97 G4
  SW15 . . . 148 C4
Becton Pl, Erith DA8 . . . 139 H7
Bedale St, SE1 . . . 28 B2
BEDDINGTON, Croy. CR0 . . . 200 D2
BEDDINGTON CORNER, Mitch.
  CR4 . . . 186 A7
Beddington Cross, Croy. CR0 . . . 200 D1
Beddington Fm Rd, Croy. CR0 . . 200 E1
Beddington Gdns, Cars. SM5 . . 200 A6
  Wallington SM6 . . . B6
Beddington Grn, Orp. BR5 . . . 193 J1
Beddington Gro, Wall. SM6 . . . 200 D5
Beddington La, Croy. CR0 . . . 186 C5
Beddington Path, Orp. BR5 . . . 193 J1
Beddington Rd, Ilf. IG3 . . . J7
  Orpington BR5 . . . 193 H2
Beddington Trd Pk W, Croy.
  CR0 . . . 200 E1
Bede Cl, Pnr. HA5 . . . 66 D1
Bedenham Way, SE15 . . . 37 F7
Bedens Rd, Sid. DA14 . . . 176 E6
Bede Rd, Rom. RM6 . . . 82 C6
Bedevere Rd, N9
  off Salisbury Rd . . . 60 D3
Bedfont Cl, Felt. TW14 . . . 141 F6
  Mitcham CR4 . . . 186 A2
Bedfont La, Felt. TW13, TW14 . . 141 J7
Bedfont Rd, Stai. (Stanw.) TW19 . 140 B6
Bedford Av, WC1 . . . 17 J2
  Barnet EN5 . . . 40 C5
  Hayes UB4 . . . 102 B6
Bedfordbury, WC2 . . . 18 A5
Bedford Cl, N10 . . . 58 A7
  W4 . . . 127 E6
Bedford Cor, W4
  off The Avenue . . . 126/127 E4
Bedford Ct, WC2 . . . 18 A6
Bedford Gdns, W8 . . . 128 D1
Bedford Hill, SW12 . . . 168 B1
  SW16 . . . 168 B1
Bedford Ho, SW4 . . . 150 E4
Bedford Ms, N2 off Bedford Rd . . 73 H3
  SE6 off Aitken Rd . . . 172 B2
BEDFORD PARK, W4 . . . 126 D3
Bedford Pk, Croy. CR0 . . . 201 J1
Bedford Pk Cor, W4
  off Bath Rd . . . 126/127 E4
Bedford Pas, SW6
  off Dawes Rd . . . 128 B7
Bedford Pl, WC1 . . . 18 A1
  Croydon CR0 . . . 202 A1
Bedford Rd, E6 . . . 116 D1
  E17 . . . 78 A2
  E18 . . . 79 G2
  N2 . . . 73 H3
  N8 . . . 74 D6
  N9 . . . 44 E7
  N15 . . . 76 B4
  N22 . . . 74 E1
  NW7 . . . 54 E3
  SW4 . . . 150 E3
  W4 . . . 126 D3
  W13 . . . 104 E7
  Harrow HA1 . . . 67 J6
  Ilford IG1 . . . 99 E3
  Sidcup DA15 . . . 175 H3
  Twickenham TW2 . . . 162 A3
  Worcester Park KT4 . . . 197 J2
Bedford Row, WC1 . . . 18 D1
Bedford Sq, WC1 . . . 17 J2
Bedford St, WC2 . . . 18 A5
Bedford Ter, SW2
  off Lyham Rd . . . 150/151 E5
Bedford Way, WC1 . . . 9 J6
Bedgebury Gdns, SW19 . . . 166 B2
Bedgebury Rd, SE9 . . . 156 A4
Bedivere Rd, Brom. BR1 . . . 173 G3
Bedlam Ms, SE11 . . . 34 D1
Bedlow Way, Croy. CR0 . . . 201 F4
Bedonwell Rd, SE2 . . . 138 E6
  Belvedere DA17 . . . 139 G6
  Bexleyheath DA7 . . . 139 G6
Bedser Cl, SE11 . . . 34 D5
  Thornton Heath CR7 . . . 187 J3
Bedser Dr, Grnf. UB6 . . . 86 A5

Bedster Gdns, W.Mol. KT8 . . . 179 H2
Bedwardine Rd, SE19 . . . 170 B7
Bedwell Gdns, Hayes UB3 . . . 121 H5
Bedwell Rd, N17 . . . 76 B1
  Belvedere DA17 . . . 139 G5
Beeby Rd, E16 . . . 115 H5
Beech Av, N20 . . . 57 H1
  W3 . . . 126 E1
  Brentford TW8 . . . 125 E7
  Buckhurst Hill IG9 . . . 63 H2
  Ruislip HA4 . . . 84 B1
  Sidcup DA15 . . . 158 A3
Beech Cl, N9 . . . 44 D6
  SE8 off Clyde St . . . 133 J6
  SW15 . . . 147 G5
  SW19 . . . 165 J6
  Carshalton SM5 . . . 199 J2
  Loughton IG10
    off Cedar Dr . . . 48/49 E2
  Staines (Stanw.) TW19
    off St. Mary's Cres . . . 140 A7
  Sunbury-on-Thames TW16
    off Harfield Rd . . . 178 D2
  West Drayton UB7 . . . 120 D3
Beech Copse, Brom. BR1 . . . 192 C2
  South Croydon CR2 . . . 202 B5
Beech Ct, E17 . . . 78 B5
  SE9 . . . 156 B6
  Ilford IG1 off Riverdene Rd . . 98 D3
Beechcroft, Chis. BR7 . . . 174 D7
Beechcroft Av, NW11 . . . 72 C7
  Harrow HA2 . . . 67 G7
  New Malden KT3 . . . 182 C1
  Southall UB1 . . . 123 F1
Beechcroft Cl, Houns. TW5 . . . 122 E7
  Orpington BR6 . . . 207 G4
Beechcroft Gdns, Wem. HA9 . . . 87 J3
Beechcroft Lo, Sutt. SM2
  off Devonshire Rd . . . 199 F7
Beechcroft Rd, E18 . . . 79 H2
  SW14 off Elm Rd . . . 146 C3
  SW17 . . . 167 H2
  Chessington KT9 . . . 195 J3
  Orpington BR6 . . . 207 G4
Beechdale, N21 . . . 59 F2
Beechdale Rd, SW2 . . . 151 F6
Beech Dell, Kes. BR2 . . . 206 C4
Beech Dr, N2 . . . 73 J3
Beechen Cliff Way, Islw. TW7
  off Henley Cl . . . 144 C1
Beechen Gro, Pnr. HA5 . . . 67 F3
Beeches, The, Houns. TW3 . . . 143 H1
Beeches Av, Cars. SM5 . . . 199 H7
Beeches Cl, SE20 off Genoa Rd . 189 F1
Beeches Rd, SW17 . . . 167 H3
  Sutton SM3 . . . 198 B1
Beechfield Cotts, Brom. BR1
  off Widmore Rd . . . 191 J2
Beechfield Gdns, Rom. RM7 . . . 83 J7
Beechfield Rd, N4 . . . 75 J6
  SE6 . . . 171 J1
  Bromley BR1 . . . 191 J2
Beech Gdns, EC2
  off Aldersgate St . . . 111 J5
  W5 . . . 125 H2
  Dagenham RM10 . . . 101 H7
Beech Gro, Ilf. IG6 . . . 65 H6
  Mitcham CR4 . . . 186 D4
  New Malden KT3 . . . 182 D3
Beech Hall Cres, E4 . . . 62 D7
Beech Hall Rd, E4 . . . 62 C7
Beech Hill, Barn. EN4 . . . 41 F1
Beechhill Rd, SE9 . . . 156 D5
Beech Ho, Croy. CR0 . . . 204 B6
Beech Ho Rd, Croy. CR0 . . . 202 A3
Beech La, Buck.H. IG9 . . . 63 H2
Beech Lawns, N12 . . . 57 G5
Beechmont Cl, Brom. BR1 . . . 172 E5
Beechmore Gdns, Sutt. SM3 . . . 198 A2
Beechmore Rd, SW11 . . . 149 J1
Beechmount Av, W7 . . . 104 A5
Beecholme Av, Mitch. CR4 . . . 186 B1
Beecholme Est, E5
  off Prout Rd . . . 94/95 E3
Beech Rd, N11 . . . 59 E6
  SW16 . . . 187 E2
  Feltham TW14 . . . 141 H7
Beech Row, Rich. TW10 . . . 163 H4
Beech St, EC2 . . . 19 J1
  Romford RM7 . . . 83 J4
Beech Tree Cl, Stan. HA7 . . . 53 F5
Beech Tree Glade, E4 . . . 63 F1
Beech Tree Pl, Sutt. SM1
  off St. Nicholas Way . . . 198/199 E5
Beechvale Cl, N12 . . . 57 H5
Beech Wk, NW7 . . . 54 E6
Beech Way, NW10 . . . 88 D7
  Twickenham TW2 . . . 161 G3
Beechwood Av, N3 . . . 72 C3
  Greenford UB6 . . . 103 H3
  Harrow HA2 . . . 85 H3
  Orpington BR6 . . . 207 H5
  Richmond TW9 . . . 146 A1
  Sunbury-on-Thames TW16 . . . 160 A6
  Thornton Heath CR7 . . . 187 H4

Beechwood Circle, Har. HA2
  off Beechwood Gdns . . . 85 H3
Beechwood Cl, NW7 . . . 54 D5
  Surbiton KT6 . . . 181 F7
Beechwood Ct, Cars. SM5 . . . 199 J4
  Sunbury-on-Thames TW16 . . . 160 A6
Beechwood Cres, Bexh. DA7 . . . 158 D3
Beechwood Dr, Kes. BR2 . . . 206 A4
  Woodford Green IG8 . . . 63 F5
Beechwood Gdns, NW10
  off St. Annes Gdns . . . 105 J3
  Harrow HA2 . . . 85 H3
  Ilford IG5 . . . 80 C5
Beechwood Gro, W3
  off East Acton La . . . 106/107 E7
  Surbiton KT6 . . . 181 F7
Beechwood Ms, N9 . . . 60 D2
Beechwood Pk, E18 . . . 79 G3
Beechwood Ri, Chis. BR7 . . . 175 E4
Beechwood Rd, E8 . . . 94 C6
  N8 . . . 74 D4
Beechwoods Ct, SE19
  off Crystal Palace Par . . . 170 C5
Beechworth Cl, NW3 . . . 90 D2
Beecroft La, SE4
  off Beecroft Rd . . . 153 H5
Beecroft Ms, SE4
  off Beecroft Rd . . . 153 H5
Beecroft Rd, SE4 . . . 153 H5
Beehive Cl, E8 . . . 94 C7
Beehive La, Ilf. IG1, IG4 . . . 80 C6
Beehive Pas, EC3 . . . 20 D4
Beehive Pl, SW9 . . . 151 G3
Beeken Dene, Orp. BR6
  off Isabella Dr . . . 207 F4
Beeleigh Rd, Mord. SM4 . . . 185 E4
Beeston Cl, E8 off Ferncliff Rd . . 94 D5
  Watford WD19 . . . 50 D4
Beeston Pl, SW1 . . . 24 E6
Beeston Rd, Barn. EN4 . . . 41 G6
Beeston Way, Felt. TW14 . . . 142 C6
Beethoven St, W10 . . . 108 B3
Beeton Cl, Pnr. HA5 . . . 51 G7
Begbie Rd, SE3 . . . 155 J1
Beggars Hill, Epsom KT17 . . . 197 F7
Beggars Roost La, Sutt. SM1 . . . 198 D6
Begonia Cl, E6 . . . 116 B5
Begonia Pl, Hmptn. TW12
  off Gresham Rd . . . 161 G6
Begonia Wk, W12
  off Du Cane Rd . . . 107 F6
Beira St, SW12 . . . 150 B7
Bekesbourne St, E14
  off Ratcliffe La . . . 113 H6
Belcroft Cl, Brom. BR1
  off Hope Pk . . . 173 F7
Beldham Gdns, W.Mol. KT8 . . . 179 H3
Belfairs Dr, Rom. RM6 . . . 82 C7
Belfairs Grn, Wat. WD19
  off Heysham Dr . . . 50 D5
Belfast Rd, N16 . . . 94 C2
  SE25 . . . 188 E4
Belfont Wk, N7 . . . 93 E4
Belford Gro, SE18 . . . 136 D4
Belfort Rd, SE15 . . . 153 F2
Belfour Ter, N3 . . . 72 E2
Belfry Cl, SE16
  off Masters Dr . . . 132/133 E5
Belgrade Rd, N16 . . . 94 B4
  Hampton TW12 . . . 179 H1
Belgrave Cl, N14
  off Prince George Av . . . 42 C5
  NW7 . . . 54 D5
  W3 off Avenue Rd . . . 126 C2
Belgrave Ct, E14
  off Westferry Circ . . . 134 A1
Belgrave Cres, Sun. TW16 . . . 178 B1
Belgrave Gdns, N14 . . . 42 D5
  NW8 . . . 109 E1
  Stanmore HA7
    off Copley Rd . . . 53 F5
Belgrave Hts, E11 . . . 97 G1
Belgrave Ms N, SW1 . . . 24 B4
Belgrave Ms S, SW1 . . . 24 C4
Belgrave Ms W, SW1 . . . 24 B5
Belgrave Pl, SW1 . . . 24 C5
Belgrave Rd, E10 . . . 96 C1
  E11 . . . 97 G2
  E13 . . . 115 J4
  E17 . . . 78 A5
  SE25 . . . 188 C4
  SW1 . . . 33 F2
  SW13 . . . 127 F7
  Hounslow TW4 . . . 143 F3
  Ilford IG1 . . . 98 C1
  Mitcham CR4 . . . 185 G3
  Sunbury-on-Thames TW16 . . . 178 B1
Belgrave Sq, SW1 . . . 24 B5
Belgrave St, E1 . . . 113 G6
Belgrave Ter, Wdf.Grn. IG8 . . . 63 G3
Belgrave Wk, Mitch. CR4 . . . 185 G3
Belgrave Yd, SW1 . . . 24 D6
BELGRAVIA, SW1 . . . 24 B6
Belgravia Cl, Barn. EN5 . . . 40 C3
Belgravia Gdns, Brom. BR1 . . . 172 E6
Belgravia Ho, SW4 . . . 150 D6
Belgravia Ms, Kings.T. KT1 . . . 181 G4

Belgrove St, WC1 . . . 10 A3
Belham Wk, SE5
  off D'Eynsford Rd . . . 152 A1
Belinda Rd, SW9 . . . 151 H3
Belitha Vil, N1 . . . 93 F7
Bellamy Cl, E14 off Byng St . . . 134 A2
  W14 off Aisgill Av . . . 128 C5
  Edgware HA8 . . . 54 C3
Bellamy Dr, Stan. HA7 . . . 68 E7
Bellamy Rd, E4 . . . 62 B6
  Enfield EN2 . . . 44 A2
Bellamy St, SW12 . . . 150 B7
Bellarmine Cl, SE28 . . . 137 J2
Bellasis Av, SW2 . . . 168 E2
Bell Av, West Dr. UB7 . . . 120 C4
Bell Cl, Pnr. HA5 . . . 66 C3
Bellclose Rd, West Dr. UB7 . . . 120 B2
Bell Ct, Surb. KT5
  off Barnsbury La . . . 196 B2
Bell Dr, SW18 . . . 148 B7
Bellefields Rd, SW9 . . . 151 F3
Bellegrove Cl, Well. DA16 . . . 157 J2
Bellegrove Par, Well. DA16
  off Bellegrove Rd . . . 157 J3
Bellegrove Rd, Well. DA16 . . . 157 G2
Bellenden Rd, SE15 . . . 152 C2
Bellestaines Pleasaunce, E4 . . . 62 A2
Belleville Rd, SW11 . . . 149 J5
Belle Vue, Grnf. UB6 . . . 104 A1
Belle Vue Est, NW4 off Bell La . . 71 J4
Belle Vue La, Bushey (Bushey Hth)
  WD23 . . . 52 A1
Bellevue Ms, N11
  off Bellevue Rd . . . 58 A5
Bellevue Par, SW17
  off Bellevue Rd . . . 167 H1
Belle Vue Pk, Th.Hth. CR7 . . . 187 J3
Bellevue Pl, E1 . . . 113 F4
Belle Vue Rd, E17 . . . 78 D2
Bellevue Rd, N11 . . . 58 A4
Belle Vue Rd, NW4 off Bell La . . 71 J4
Bellevue Rd, SW13 . . . 147 G2
  SW17 . . . 167 H1
  W13 . . . 104 E4
  Bexleyheath DA6 . . . 159 F5
  Kingston upon Thames KT1 . . 181 H3
Bellew St, SW17 . . . 167 F3
Bell Fm Av, Dag. RM10 . . . 101 J3
Bellfield Av, Har. HA3 . . . 51 J6
Bellfield Cl, SE3
  off Charlton Rd . . . 135 G7
Bellflower Cl, E6
  off Sorrel Gdns . . . 116 B5
Bell Gdns, E10 off Church Rd . . . 96 A1
  E17 off Markhouse Rd . . . 77 J5
Bellgate Ms, NW5 off York Ri . . 92 B3
BELL GREEN, SE6 . . . 171 J3
Bell Grn, SE26 . . . 171 J3
Bell Grn La, SE26 . . . 171 H5
Bell Hill, Croy. CR0
  off Surrey St . . . 201 J3
Bell Ho Rd, Rom. RM7 . . . 101 J1
BELLINGHAM, SE6 . . . 172 B3
Bellingham Ct, Bark. IG11
  off Renwick Rd . . . 118 B3
Bellingham Grn, SE6 . . . 172 A3
Bellingham Rd, SE6 . . . 172 B3
Bell Inn Yd, EC3 . . . 20 C4
Bell La, E1 . . . 21 F2
  E16 . . . 135 G1
  NW4 . . . 72 A4
  Twickenham TW1
    off The Embankment . . . 162 D1
  Wembley HA9
    off Magnet Rd . . . 87 G2
Bellmaker Ct, E3
  off St. Pauls Way . . . 114 A5
Bell Meadow, SE19
  off Dulwich Wd Av . . . 170 B4
Bello Cl, SE24 . . . 151 H7
Bellot Gdns, SE10
  off Bellot St . . . 134/135 E5
Bellot St, SE10 . . . 135 E5
Bellring Cl, Belv. DA17 . . . 139 G6
Bell Rd, E.Mol. KT8 . . . 180 A5
  Enfield EN1 . . . 44 A1
  Hounslow TW3 . . . 143 H4
Bells All, SW6 . . . 148 D2
Bells Gdn Est, SE15
  off Buller Cl . . . 132 D7
Bells Hill, Barn. EN5 . . . 40 A5
Bell St, NW1 . . . 15 G1
  SE18 . . . 156 B1
Belltrees Gro, SW16 . . . 169 F5
Bell Water Gate, SE18 . . . 136 D3
Bell Wf La, EC4 . . . 20 A5
Bellwood Rd, SE15 . . . 153 G4
Bell Yd, WC2 . . . 18 E3
Bell Yd Ms, SE1
  off Bermondsey St . . . 132 B2
Belmarsh Rd, SE28
  off Western Way . . . 137 H2
BELMONT, Har. HA3 . . . 68 D2
Belmont Av, N9 . . . 60 D1
  N13 . . . 59 E6
  N17 . . . 75 J3
  Barnet EN4 . . . 41 J5

Belmont Av, N.Mal. KT3 .183 G5
Southall UB2 .122 E3
Welling DA16 .157 H3
Wembley HA0 .105 J1
Belmont Circle, Har. HA3 .68 E1
Belmont Cl, E4 .62 D5
N20 .56 E1
SW4 .150 C3
Barnet EN4 .41 J4
Woodford Green IG8 .63 H4
Belmont Ct, NW11 .72 C5
Belmont Gro, SE13 .154 D3
W4 off Belmont Rd .126 D4
Belmont Hall Ct, SE13
off Belmont Gro .154 D3
Belmont Hill, SE13 .154 D3
Belmont La, Chis. BR7 .175 F5
Stanmore HA7 .53 F7
Belmont Ms, SW19
off Chapman Sq .166 A2
Belmont Pk, SE13 .154 D4
Belmont Pk Cl, SE13
off Belmont Pk .154 D4
Belmont Pk Rd, E10 .78 B6
Belmont Ri, Sutt. SM2 .198 C6
Belmont Rd, N15 .75 J4
N17 .75 J4
SE25 .188 E5
SW4 .150 C3
W4 .126 D4
Beckenham BR3 .189 J2
Chislehurst BR7 .175 E5
Erith DA8 .139 G7
Harrow HA3 .68 C3
Ilford IG1 .99 F3
Twickenham TW2 .162 A2
Wallington SM6 .200 B5
Belmont St, NW1 .92 A7
Belmont Ter, W4
off Belmont Rd .126 D4
Belmor, Borwd. (Elstree) WD6 .38 A5
Belmore Av, Hayes UB4 .102 A6
Belmore La, N7 .92 D5
Belmore St, SW8 .150 D1
Beloe Cl, SW15 .147 G3
Belper Ct, E5 off Pedro St .95 G4
Belsham St, E9 .95 F6
Belsize Av, N13 .59 F6
NW3 .91 G6
W13 .125 E3
Belsize Ct, NW3 off Belsize La .91 H5
Belsize Cres, NW3 .91 G5
Belsize Gdns, Sutt. SM1 .199 E4
Belsize Gro, NW3 .91 H6
Belsize La, NW3 .91 G6
Belsize Ms, NW3 off Belsize La .91 G6
BELSIZE PARK, NW3 .91 H6
Belsize Pk, NW3 .91 G6
Belsize Pk Gdns, NW3 .91 H6
Belsize Pk Ms, NW3
off Belsize La .91 G6
Belsize Pl, NW3 off Belsize La .91 G6
Belsize Rd, NW6 .108 E1
Harrow HA3 .52 A7
Belsize Sq, NW3 .91 G6
Belsize Ter, NW3 .91 G6
Belson Rd, SE18 .136 C4
Beltane Dr, SW19 .166 A3
Belthorn Cres, SW12 .150 C7
Belton Rd, E7 .97 H7
E11 .96 E4
N17 .76 B3
NW2 .89 G6
Sidcup DA14 .176 A4
Belton Way, E3 .114 A5
Beltran Rd, SW6 .148 E2
Beltwood Rd, Belv. DA17 .139 J4
BELVEDERE, DA17 .139 H4
Belvedere Av, SW19 .166 B5
Ilford IG5 .80 E2
Belvedere Bldgs, SE1 .27 H4
Belvedere Cl, Tedd. TW11 .162 B5
Belvedere Ct, N2 .73 G5
Belvedere Dr, SW19 .166 B5
Belvedere Gdns, W.Mol. KT8 .179 F5
Belvedere Gro, SW19 .166 B5
Belvedere Ho, Felt. TW13 .160 A1
Belvedere Ind Est, Belv. DA17 .139 J3
Belvedere Ms, SE3
off Langton Way .155 F1
SE15 .153 E3
Belvedere Pl, SE1 .27 H4
SW2 off Acre La .151 F4
Belvedere Rd, E10 .95 H1
SE1 .26 D3
SE2 .138 D1
SE19 .170 C7
W7 .124 C3
Bexleyheath DA7 .159 F3
Belvedere Sq, SW19 .166 B5
Belvedere Strand, NW9 .71 F2
Belvedere Twr, The, SW10 .149 F1
Belvedere Way, Har. HA3 .69 H6
Belvoir Cl, SE9 .174 B3
Belvoir Rd, SE22 .152 D7
Belvue Cl, Nthlt. UB5 .85 G7
Belvue Rd, Nthlt. UB5 .85 G7
Bembridge Cl, NW6 .90 B7
Bemerton Est, N1 .93 F7
Bemerton St, N1 .111 F1
Bemish Rd, SW15 .148 A3
Bempton Dr, Ruis. HA4 .84 B2
Bemsted Rd, E17 .77 J3
Benares Rd, SE18 .137 J4
Benbow Rd, W6 .127 H3
Benbow St, SE8 .134 A6
Benbury Cl, Brom. BR1 .172 C5
Bench Fld, S.Croy. CR2 .202 C6
Bencroft Rd, SW16 .168 C7
Bencurtis Pk, W.Wick. BR4 .204 D3
Bendall Ms, NW1 .15 H1
Bendemeer Rd, SW15 .148 A3
Bendish Rd, E6 .98 B7
Bendmore Av, SE2 .138 A5
Bendon Valley, SW18 .148 E7
Benedict Cl, Belv. DA17
off Tunstock Way .138/139 E3
Orpington BR6 .207 H3
Benedict Dr, Felt. TW14 .141 G7
Benedict Rd, SW9 .151 F3
Mitcham CR4 .185 G3
Benedict Way, N2 .73 F3
Benenden Grn, Brom. BR2 .191 G5
Benett Gdns, SW16 .186 E2
Benfleet Cl, Sutt. SM1 .199 F3
Benfleet Way, N11 .58 A2
Bengal Ct, EC3 off Birchin La .112 A6
Bengal Rd, Ilf. IG1 .98 E4
Bengarth Dr, Har. HA3 .68 A2
Bengarth Rd, Nthlt. UB5 .102 D1
Bengeworth Rd, SE5 .151 J3
Harrow HA1 .86 D2
Ben Hale Cl, Stan. HA7 .52 E4
Benham Cl, SW11 .149 G3
Chessington KT9
off Merritt Gdns .195 F6
Benham Gdns, Houns. TW4 .143 F5
Benham Rd, W7 .104 B5
Benhams Pl, NW3 off Holly Wk .91 F4
Benhill Av, Sutt. SM1 .199 E4
Benhill Rd, SE5 .132 A7
Sutton SM1 .199 F3
Benhill Wd Rd, Sutt. SM1 .199 F3
BENHILTON, Sutt. SM1 .199 E2
Benhilton Gdns, Sutt. SM1 .199 E3
Benhurst Ct, SW16 .169 G5
Benhurst La, SW16 .169 G5
Benin St, SE13 .154 D7
Benjafield Cl, N18
off Brettenham Rd .60/61 E4
Benjamin Cl, E8 .112 D1
Benjamin St, EC1 .19 G1
Ben Jonson Rd, E1 .113 H5
Benledi St, E14 .114 D6
Bennelong Cl, W12 .107 H7
Bennerley Rd, SW11 .149 H5
Bennetsfield Rd, Uxb. UB11 .120 E1
Bennet's Hill, EC4 .19 H5
Bennett Cl, Kings.T. (Hmptn W.)
KT1 .181 F1
Welling DA16 .158 A2
Bennett Gro, SE13 .154 B1
Bennett Pk, SE3 .155 F3
Bennett Rd, E13 .115 J4
N16 .94 B4
Romford RM6 .83 E6
Bennetts Av, Croy. CR0 .203 H2
Greenford UB6 .104 B1
Bennetts Castle La, Dag. RM8 .100 C4
Bennetts Cl, N17 .60 C6
Mitcham CR4 .186 B1
Bennetts Copse, Chis. BR7 .174 B6
Bennett St, SW1 .25 F1
W4 .126 E6
Bennetts Way, Croy. CR0 .203 H2
Bennetts Yd, SW1 .25 J6
Benningholme Rd, Edg. HA8 .54 E6
Bennington Rd, N17 .76 B1
Woodford Green IG8 .62 E7
Benn St, E9 .95 H6
Benn's Wk, Rich. TW9
off Rosedale Rd .145 H4
Benrek Cl, Ilf. IG6 .81 F1
Bensbury Cl, SW15 .147 H7
Bensham Cl, Th.Hth. CR7 .187 J4
Bensham Gro, Th.Hth. CR7 .187 J2
Bensham La, Croy. CR0 .187 H7
Thornton Heath CR7 .187 H4
Bensham Manor Rd, Th.Hth.
CR7 .187 J4
Bensington Ct, Felt. TW14 .141 G6
Bensley Cl, N11 .57 J5
Ben Smith Way, SE16 .29 J5
Benson Av, E6 .115 J2
Benson Cl, Houns. TW3 .143 G4
Benson Quay, E1 off Garnet St .113 F7
Benson Rd, SE23 .171 F1
Croydon CR0 .201 G3
Bentalls Cen, Kings.T. KT1 .181 G2
Bentfield Gdns, SE9
off Aldersgrove Av .173 J3
Benthal Rd, N16 .94 D2
Bentham Ct, N1
off Rotherfield St .93 J7
Bentham Rd, E9 .95 G6
SE28 .118 B7
Bentham Wk, NW10 .88 C5
Ben Tillet Cl, Bark. IG11 .100 A7
Ben Tillett Cl, E16
off Newland St .136 C1
Bentinck Ms, W1 .16 C3
Bentinck Rd, West Dr. UB7 .120 A1
Bentinck St, W1 .16 C3
Bentley Dr, NW2 .90 C3
Ilford IG2 .81 F6
Bentley Ms, Enf. EN1 .44 A6
★ Bentley Priory, Stan. HA7 .52 B3
Bentley Rd, N1
off Tottenham Rd .94 B6
Bentley Way, Stan. HA7 .52 D5
Woodford Green IG8 .63 G3
Benton Rd, Ilf. IG1 .99 G1
Watford WD19 .50 D5
Bentons La, SE27 .169 J4
Bentons Ri, SE27 .170 A5
Bentry Cl, Dag. RM8 .101 E2
Bentry Rd, Dag. RM8 .101 E2
Bentworth Rd, W12 .107 H6
Benwell Ct, Sun. TW16 .178 A1
Benwell Rd, N7 .93 G4
Benwick Cl, SE16
off Aspinden Rd .132/133 E3
Benworth St, E3 .113 J3
Benyon Rd, N1
off Southgate Rd .112 A1
Berberis Wk, West Dr. UB7 .120 B4
Berber Pl, E14 off Birchfield St .114 A7
Berber Rd, SW11 .149 J5
Berberry Cl, Edg. HA8
off Larkspur Gro .54 C4
Bercta Rd, SE9 .175 F2
Berenger Wk, SW10 .30 E7
Berens Rd, NW10 .108 A3
Berens Way, Chis. BR7 .193 J4
Beresford Av, N20 .57 J2
W7 .104 A5
Surbiton KT5 .196 B1
Twickenham TW1 .145 F6
Wembley HA0 .105 J1
Beresford Dr, Brom. BR1 .192 A3
Woodford Green IG8 .63 J4
Beresford Gdns, Enf. EN1 .44 B4
Hounslow TW4 .143 F5
Romford RM6 .83 E5
Beresford Rd, E4 .62 E1
E17 .78 B1
N2 .73 H3
N5 .93 J5
N8 .75 G5
Harrow HA1 .68 A5
Kingston upon Thames KT2 .181 J1
New Malden KT3 .182 C4
Southall UB1 .122 D1
Sutton SM2 .198 C7
Beresford Sq, SE18 .136 E4
Beresford St, SE18 .136 E3
Beresford Ter, N5 .93 J5
Berestede Rd, W6 .127 F5
Bere St, E1 off Cranford St .113 G7
Bergen Sq, SE16
off Norway Gate .133 H3
Berger Cl, Orp. BR5 .193 G6
Berger Rd, E9 .95 G6
Berghem Ms, W14
off Blythe Rd .128 A3
Bergholt Av, Ilf. IG4 .80 B5
Bergholt Cres, N16 .76 B7
Bergholt Ms, NW1
off Rossendale Way .92 C7
Berglen Ct, E14 off Branch Rd .113 H6
Bering Sq, E14 off Napier Av .134 A5
Bering Wk, E16 .116 A6
Berisford Ms, SW18 .149 F6
Berkeley Av, Bexh. DA7 .158 D1
Greenford UB6 .86 B6
Hounslow TW4 .142 A2
Ilford IG5 .80 D2
Berkeley Cl, Borwd. (Elstree)
WD6 .38 A5
Kingston upon Thames KT2 .163 H7
Orpington BR5 .193 H7
Ruislip HA4 .84 A3
Berkeley Ct, N14 .42 C6
Wallington SM6 .200 C3
Berkeley Cres, Barn. EN4 .41 G5
Berkeley Dr, W.Mol. KT8 .179 F3
Berkeley Gdns, N21 .44 A7
W8 off Brunswick Gdns .128 D1
Esher (Clay.) KT10 .194 D6
Berkeley Ho, E3 .114 A4
Berkeley Ms, W1 .16 A3
Berkeley Pl, SW19 .166 A6
Berkeley Rd, E12 .98 B5
N8 .74 D5
N15 .76 A6
NW9 .70 A4
SW13 .147 G1
Berkeley Sq, W1 .16 E6
Berkeley St, W1 .17 E6
Berkeley Twr, E14
off Westferry Circ .133 J1
Berkeley Wk, N7
off Durham Rd .93 F2
Berkeley Waye, Houns. TW5 .122 D7
Berkhampstead Rd, Belv. DA17 .139 G5
Berkhamsted Av, Wem. HA9 .87 J6
Berkley Gro, NW1
off Berkley Rd .91 J7
Berkley Rd, NW1 .91 J7
Berkshire Gdns, N13 .59 G6
N18 .60 E5
Berkshire Rd, E9 .95 J6
Berkshire Sq, Mitch. CR4
off Berkshire Way .186/187 E4
Berkshire Way, Mitch. CR4 .186 E4
Bermans Way, NW10 .89 E4
BERMONDSEY, SE1 .29 F6
Bermondsey Sq, SE1 .28 E5
Bermondsey St, SE1 .28 D2
Bermondsey Wall E, SE16 .29 J4
Bermondsey Wall W, SE16 .29 H3
Bernal Cl, SE28 off Haldane Rd .118 D7
Bernard Ashley Dr, SE7 .135 H5
Bernard Av, W13 .125 E3
Bernard Cassidy St, E16 .115 F5
Bernard Gdns, SW19 .166 C5
Bernard Rd, N15 .76 C5
Romford RM7 .83 J7
Wallington SM6 .200 B4
Bernards Cl, Ilf. IG6 .65 F6
Bernard St, WC1 .10 A6
Bernays Cl, Stan. HA7 .53 F6
Bernays Gro, SW9 .151 F4
Bernel Dr, Croy. CR0 .203 J3
Berne Rd, Th.Hth. CR7 .187 J5
Berners Dr, W13 .104 D6
Bernersmede, SE3
off Blackheath Pk .155 G3
Berners Ms, W1 .17 G2
Berners Pl, W1 .17 G3
Berners Rd, N1 .11 F1
N22 .75 G1
Berners St, W1 .17 G2
Berney Rd, Croy. CR0 .188 A7
Bernhardt Cres, NW8 .7 G5
Bernhart Cl, Edg. HA8 .54 C7
Bernville Way, Har. HA3
off Kenton Rd .69 J5
Bernwell Rd, E4 .63 E3
Berridge Grn, Edg. HA8 .54 A7
Berridge Ms, NW6
off Hillfield Rd .90 D5
Berridge Rd, SE19 .170 A5
Berriman Rd, N7 .93 F3
Berriton Rd, Har. HA2 .85 F1
Berrybank Cl, E4
off Greenbank Cl .62 C2
Berry Cl, N21 .59 H1
NW10 .88 E7
Dagenham RM10 .101 G5
Berry Ct, Houns. TW4 .143 F5
Berrydale Rd, Hayes UB4 .102 E4
Berryfield Cl, E17 .78 B4
Bromley BR1 .192 B1
Berryfield Rd, SE17 .35 H3
Berryhill, SE9 .156 E4
Berry Hill, Stan. HA7 .53 G4
Berryhill Gdns, SE9 .156 E4
BERRYLANDS, Surb. KT5 .181 J5
Berrylands, SW20 .183 J3
Surbiton KT5 .182 A5
Berrylands Rd, Surb. KT5 .181 J6
Berry La, SE21 .170 A4
Berryman Cl, Dag. RM8
off Bennetts Castle La .100 C3
Berrymans La, SE26 .171 G4
Berrymead Gdns, W3 .126 C1
Berrymede Rd, W4 .126 D3
Berry Pl, EC1 .11 H4
Berry St, EC1 .11 H5
Berry Way, W5 .125 H3
Bertal Rd, SW17 .167 G4
Berthon St, SE8 .134 A7
Bertie Rd, NW10 .89 G6
SE26 .171 G6
Bertram Cotts, SW19
off Hartfield Rd .166 D7
Bertram Rd, NW4 .71 G6
Enfield EN1 .44 D4
Kingston upon Thames KT2 .164 A7
Bertram St, N19 .92 B2
Bertram Way, Enf. EN1 .44 C4
Bertrand St, SE13 .154 B3
Bertrand Way, SE28 .118 B7
Bert Rd, Th.Hth. CR7 .187 J5
Berwick Av, Hayes UB4 .102 D6
Berwick Cl, Stan. HA7
off Gordon Av .52 C7
Twickenham TW2 .161 G1
Berwick Cres, Sid. DA15 .157 H6
Berwick Gdns, Sutt. SM1
off Woodside Rd .199 F3
Berwick Rd, E16 .115 H6
N22 .75 H1
Welling DA16 .158 B1
Berwick St, W1 .17 H4
Berwyn Av, Houns. TW3 .143 H1
Berwyn Rd, SE24 .169 H1

Berwyn Rd, Rich. TW10 . . . . . . .146 B4
Beryl Av, E6 . . . . .116 B5
Beryl Ho, SE18 off Spinel Cl 137 J5
Beryl Rd, W6 . . . . .128 A5
Berystede, Kings.T. KT2 . . . . . . .164 B7
Besant Ct, N1
  off Newington Grn Rd 94 A5
Besant Rd, NW2 . . . . .90 B4
Besant Wk, N7
  off Newington Barrow Way 93 F2
Besant Way, NW10 . . . . .88 C5
Besley St, SW16 . . . . .168 C6
Bessant Dr, Rich. TW9 . . . . .146 B1
Bessborough Gdns, SW1 . . . . . . .33 J3
Bessborough Pl, SW1 . . . . .33 H3
Bessborough Rd, SW15 . . . . . . .165 G1
  Harrow HA1 . . . . .86 A1
Bessborough St, SW1 . . . . .33 H3
Bessemer Rd, SE5 . . . . .151 J2
Bessie Lansbury Cl, E6 . . . . .116 D6
Bessingby Rd, Ruis. HA4 . . . . . . .84 A2
Bessingham Wk, SE4
  off Frendsbury Rd 153 G4
Besson St, SE14 . . . . .153 F1
Bessy St, E2 off Roman Rd 113 F3
Bestwood St, SE8 . . . . .133 G4
Beswick Ms, NW6
  off Lymington Rd 90/91 E6
Betam Rd, Hayes UB3 . . . . .121 G2
Beta Pl, SW4
  off Santley St 150/151 E4
Betchworth Cl, Sutt. SM1 . . . . . .199 G5
  off Turnpike La
Betchworth Rd, Ilf. IG3 . . . . .99 H2
Betham Rd, Grnf. UB6 . . . . .104 A3
Bethany Waye, Felt. TW14 . . . . .141 H7
Bethecar Rd, Har. HA1 . . . . .68 B5
Bethell Av, E16 . . . . .115 F4
  Ilford IG1 . . . . .80 C1
Bethel Rd, Well. DA16 . . . . .158 C3
Bethersden Cl, Beck. BR3 . . . . . .171 J7
BETHNAL GREEN, E2 . . . . .112 D2
Bethnal Grn Est, E2 . . . . .113 F3
★ Bethnal Grn Mus of
  Childhood, E2 . . . . .113 E3
Bethnal Grn Rd, E1 . . . . .13 F5
  E2 . . . . .13 F5
Bethune Av, N11 . . . . .57 J4
Bethune Rd, N16 . . . . .76 A7
  NW10 . . . . .106 D4
Bethwin Rd, SE5 . . . . .35 H7
Betjeman Cl, Pnr. HA5 . . . . .67 G4
Betony Cl, Croy. CR0
  off Primrose La 203 G1
Betoyne Av, E4 . . . . .62 E4
Betstyle Circ, N11 . . . . .58 B4
Betstyle Rd, N11 . . . . .58 B4
Betterton Dr, Sid. DA14 . . . . . . .177 E2
Betterton St, WC2 . . . . .18 A4
Bettons Pk, E15 . . . . .115 E1
Bettridge Rd, SW6 . . . . .148 C2
Betts Cl, Beck. BR3
  off Kendall Rd 189 H2
Betts Ms, E17 off Queen's Rd 77 J6
Betts Rd, E16
  off Victoria Dock Rd 115 H7
Betts St, E1
  off The Highway 112/113 E7
Betts Way, SE20 . . . . .189 E1
  Surbiton KT6 . . . . .195 E1
Beulah Av, Th.Hth. CR7
  off Beulah Rd 187 J2
Beulah Cl, Edg. HA8 . . . . .54 B3
Beulah Cres, Th.Hth. CR7 . . . . . .187 J2
Beulah Gro, Croy. CR0 . . . . .187 J6
Beulah Hill, SE19 . . . . .169 H6
Beulah Path, E17
  off Addison Rd 78 B5
Beulah Rd, E17 . . . . .78 B5
  SW19 . . . . .166 C7
  Sutton SM1 . . . . .198 D4
  Thornton Heath CR7 . . . . .187 J3
Bevan Av, Bark. IG11 . . . . .100 A7
Bevan Ct, Croy. CR0 . . . . .201 G5
Bevan Rd, SE2 . . . . .138 B5
  Barnet EN4 . . . . .41 J4
Bevan St, N1 . . . . .111 J1
Bev Callender Cl, SW8
  off Daley Thompson Way . . .150 B3
Bevenden St, N1 . . . . .12 C3
Bevercote Wk, Belv. DA17
  off Osborne Rd 139 F6
Beveridge Rd, NW10
  off Curzon Cres 88/89 E7
Beverley Av, SW20 . . . . .183 F1
  Hounslow TW4 . . . . .143 F4
  Sidcup DA15 . . . . .157 J7
Beverley Cl, N21 . . . . .59 J1
  SW11 off Maysoule Rd 149 G4
  SW13 . . . . .147 F2
  Chessington KT9 . . . . .195 F4
  Enfield EN1 . . . . .44 B4
Beverley Cotts, SW15
  off Kingston Vale 164 D4
Beverley Cres, N14 . . . . .42 C7
  N20 off Farnham Cl 41 F7
  SE4 .153 J3

Beverley Cres, Wdf.Grn. IG8 . . . .79 H1
Beverley Dr, Edg. HA8 . . . . .70 B3
Beverley Gdns, NW11 . . . . .72 B7
  SW13 . . . . .147 F3
  Stanmore HA7 . . . . .68 D1
  Wembley HA9 . . . . .87 J1
  Worcester Park KT4
    off Green La 197 G1
Beverley Ho, NW8 . . . . .7 G4
Beverley La, SW15 . . . . .165 F3
  Kingston upon Thames KT2 . .165 E7
Beverley Ms, E4
  off Beverley Rd 62 D6
Beverley Path, SW13 . . . . .147 F2
Beverley Rd, E4 . . . . .62 D6
  E6 . . . . .116 A3
  SE20 off Wadhurst Cl . . .188/189 A2
  SW13 . . . . .147 F3
  W4 .127 F5
  Bexleyheath DA7 . . . . .159 J2
  Bromley BR2 . . . . .206 B2
  Dagenham RM9 . . . . .101 E4
  Kingston upon Thames KT1 . .181 F1
  Mitcham CR4 . . . . .186 D4
  New Malden KT3 . . . . .183 G4
  Ruislip HA4 . . . . .84 A2
  Southall UB2 . . . . .123 E3
  Worcester Park KT4 . . . . .197 J2
Beverley Trd Est, Mord. SM4
  off Garth Rd 184 A7
Beverley Way, SW20 . . . . .183 F1
  New Malden KT3 . . . . .183 F1
Beversbrook Rd, N19 . . . . .92 D3
Beverstone Rd, SW2 . . . . .151 F5
  Thornton Heath CR7 . . . . .187 G4
Beverston Ms, W1 . . . . .15 J2
Bevill Allen Cl, SW17 . . . . .167 J5
Bevill Cl, SE25 . . . . .188 D3
Bevin Cl, SE16 off Stave Yd Rd . .133 H1
Bevin Ct, WC1 off Holford St 111 G3
Bevington Path, SE1
  off Tanner St 132 C2
Bevington Rd, W10 . . . . .108 B5
  Beckenham BR3 . . . . .190 B2
Bevington St, SE16 . . . . .29 J4
Bevin Rd, Hayes UB4 . . . . .102 A3
Bevin Sq, SW17 . . . . .167 J3
Bevin Way, WC1 . . . . .10 E3
Bevis Marks, EC3 . . . . .20 E3
Bewcastle Gdns, Enf. EN2 . . . . . .43 E4
Bew Ct, SE22 off Lordship La . . .152 D7
Bewdley St, N1 . . . . .93 G7
Bewick Ms, SE15 . . . . .132 E7
Bewick St, SW8 . . . . .150 B2
Bewley St, E1
  off Dellow St 112/113 E7
  SW19 . . . . .167 F6
Bewlys Rd, SE27 . . . . .169 H5
Bexhill Cl, Felt. TW13 . . . . .160 E2
Bexhill Rd, N11 . . . . .58 D5
  SE4 .153 J7
  SW14 . . . . .146 C3
Bexhill Wk, E15
  off Mitre Rd 114/115 E2
BEXLEY, DA5 . . . . .159 G6
Bexley Gdns, N9 . . . . .60 A3
  Romford (Chad.Hth) RM6 . . . . .82 B5
BEXLEYHEATH, DA6 & DA7 . . . . .159 F5
Bexley High St, Bex. DA5 . . . . . .159 G7
Bexley La, Sid. DA14 . . . . .176 C3
Bexley Rd, SE9 . . . . .156 E5
  Erith DA8 . . . . .139 J7
Beynon Rd, Cars. SM5 . . . . .199 J5
Bianca Ho, N1 off Crondall St 112 B2
Bianca Rd, SE15 . . . . .37 H6
Bibsworth Rd, N3 . . . . .72 C2
Bibury Cl, SE15 . . . . .37 E6
Bicester Rd, Rich. TW9 . . . . .146 A3
Bickenhall St, W1 . . . . .16 A1
Bickersteth Rd, SW17 . . . . .167 J6
Bickerton Rd, N19 . . . . .92 C2
BICKLEY, Brom. BR1 . . . . .192 C3
Bickley Cres, Brom. BR1 . . . . . . .192 B4
Bickley Pk Rd, Brom. BR1 . . . . . .192 B3
Bickley Rd, E10 . . . . .78 B7
  Bromley BR1 . . . . .192 A2
Bickley St, SW17 . . . . .167 H5
Bicknell Rd, SE5 . . . . .151 J3
Bicknoller Rd, Enf. EN1 . . . . .44 C1
Bicknor Rd, Orp. BR6 . . . . .193 H7
Bidborough Cl, Brom. BR2 . . . . . .191 F5
Bidborough St, WC1 . . . . .10 A4
Biddenden Way, SE9 . . . . .174 D4
Bidder St, E16 . . . . .114 E5
Biddestone Rd, N7 . . . . .93 F4
Biddulph Rd, W9 . . . . .6 A4
Bideford Av, Grnf. UB6 . . . . .104 D2
Bideford Cl, Edg. HA8 . . . . .70 A1
  Feltham TW13 . . . . .161 F3
Bideford Gdns, Enf. EN1 . . . . . . .44 B7
Bideford Rd, Brom. BR1 . . . . . . .173 F3
  Ruislip HA4 . . . . .84 B3
  Welling DA16 . . . . .138 B7
Bidwell Gdns, N11 . . . . .58 C7
Bidwell St, SE15 . . . . .153 E1
★ Big Ben (St. Stephens Tower),
  SW1 . . . . .26 B4

Bigbury Cl, N17 . . . . .60 B7
Biggerstaff Rd, E15 . . . . .114 C1
Biggerstaff St, N4 . . . . .93 G2
Biggin Av, Mitch. CR4 . . . . .185 J1
Biggin Hill, SE19 . . . . .169 H7
Biggin Hill Cl, Kings.T. KT2 . . . . .163 F5
Biggin Way, SE19 . . . . .169 H7
Bigginwood Rd, SW16 . . . . .169 H7
Biggs Row, SW15
  off Felsham Rd 148 A3
Big Hill, E5 . . . . .95 E1
Bigland St, E1 . . . . .112 E6
Bignell Rd, SE18 . . . . .136 E5
Bignold Rd, E7 . . . . .97 G4
Bigwood Rd, NW11 . . . . .72 E5
Billet Cl, Rom. RM6 . . . . .82 D3
Billet Rd, E17 . . . . .77 G2
  Romford RM6 . . . . .82 B3
Billets Hart Cl, W7 . . . . .124 B2
Billet Wks, E17 . . . . .77 J1
Billingford Cl, SE4 . . . . .153 G4
Billing Pl, SW10 . . . . .30 B7
Billing Rd, SW10 . . . . .30 B7
Billings Cl, Dag. RM9
  off Ellerton Rd 100 C7
★ Billingsgate Mkt, E14 . . . . . . .134 B1
Billing St, SW10 . . . . .30 B7
Billington Ms, W3 off High St 126 B1
Billington Rd, SE14 . . . . .133 G7
Billiter Sq, EC3 . . . . .20 E5
Billiter St, EC3 . . . . .20 E4
Bill Nicholson Way, N17
  off High Rd 60 C7
Billockby Cl, Chess. KT9 . . . . . . .195 J6
Billson St, E14 . . . . .134 C4
Bilsby Gro, SE9 . . . . .174 A4
Bilton Rd, Grnf. UB6 . . . . .105 E1
Bilton Way, Enf. EN3 . . . . .45 H1
  Hayes UB3 . . . . .122 B2
Bina Gdns, SW5 . . . . .30 C2
Bincote Rd, Enf. EN2 . . . . .43 F3
Binden Rd, W12 . . . . .127 F3
Bindon Grn, Mord. SM4 . . . . . . .185 E4
Binfield Rd, SW4 . . . . .151 E1
  South Croydon CR2 . . . . .202 C5
Bingfield St, N1 . . . . .111 E1
Bingham Ct, N1 off Halton Rd 93 H7
Bingham Pl, W1 . . . . .16 B1
Bingham Pt, SE18
  off Whitworth Pl 136/137 E4
Bingham Rd, Croy. CR0 . . . . . . .202 D1
Bingham St, N1 . . . . .94 A6
Bingley Rd, E16 . . . . .115 J6
  Greenford UB6 . . . . .103 J5
  Sunbury-on-Thames TW16 . . .160 A7
Binley Ho, SW15
  off Highcliffe Dr 147 G6
Binney St, W1 . . . . .16 C5
Binns Rd, W4 . . . . .126 E5
Binns Ter, W4 off Binns Rd . .126/127 E5
Binsey Wk, SE2 . . . . .138 C1
Binstead Cl, Hayes UB4 . . . . . . .102 E5
Binyon Cres, Stan. HA7 . . . . .52 C5
Birbetts Rd, SE9 . . . . .174 C2
Bircham Path, SE4
  off St. Norbert Rd 153 G4
Birchanger Rd, SE25 . . . . .188 D5
Birch Av, N13 . . . . .59 J3
Birch Cl, E16 . . . . .115 E5
  N19 off Hargrave Pk 92 C2
  SE15 off Bournemouth Rd . . .152 D2
  Brentford TW8 . . . . .124 E7
  Buckhurst Hill IG9 . . . . .64 A3
  Hounslow TW3 . . . . .144 A3
  Romford RM7 . . . . .83 H3
  Teddington TW11 . . . . .162 D5
Birchdale Gdns, Rom. RM6 . . . . .82 D7
Birchdale Rd, E7 . . . . .97 J5
Birchdene Dr, SE28 . . . . .138 A2
Birchen Cl, NW9 . . . . .88 D2
Birchend Cl, S.Croy. CR2 . . . . . .202 A6
Birchen Gro, NW9 . . . . .88 D2
Birches, The, N21 . . . . .43 F6
  SE7 . . . . .135 H6
  Orpington BR6 . . . . .206 D4
Birches Cl, Mitch. CR4 . . . . .185 J3
  Pinner HA5 . . . . .66 E5
Birchfield St, E14 . . . . .114 A7
Birch Gdns, Dag. RM10 . . . . . . .101 J3
Birch Grn, NW9
  off Clayton Fld 54/55 E7
Birch Gro, E11 . . . . .96 E3
  SE12 . . . . .155 F7
  W3 .126 A1
  Welling DA16 . . . . .158 A4
Birch Hill, Croy. CR0 . . . . .203 G5
Birchington Cl, Bexh. DA7 . . . . .159 H1
Birchington Rd, N8 . . . . .74 D6
  NW6 . . . . .108 D1
  Surbiton KT5 . . . . .181 J7
Birchin La, EC3 . . . . .20 C4
Birchlands Av, SW12 . . . . .149 J7
Birch Mead, Orp. BR6 . . . . .206 D2
Birchmead Av, Pnr. HA5 . . . . .66 C4
Birchmere Business Pk, SE28
  off Eastern Way 138 A2

Birchmere Row, SE3 . . . . .155 F2
Birchmore Wk, N5 . . . . .93 J3
Birch Pk, Har. HA3 . . . . .51 J7
Birch Rd, Felt. TW13 . . . . .160 D5
  Romford RM7 . . . . .83 H3
Birch Row, Brom. BR2 . . . . .192 D7
Birch Tree Av, W.Wick. BR4 . . . .205 F5
Birch Tree Way, Croy. CR0 . . . . .202 E2
Birchville Ct, Bushey (Bushey Hth)
  WD23 off Heathbourne Rd 52 B1
Birch Wk, Borwd. WD6 . . . . .38 C1
  Erith DA8 . . . . .139 J2
  Mitcham CR4 . . . . .186 B1
Birchway, Hayes UB3 . . . . .122 A1
Birchwood Av, N10 . . . . .74 A3
  Beckenham BR3 . . . . .189 J4
  Sidcup DA14 . . . . .176 B2
  Wallington SM6 . . . . .200 A3
Birchwood Cl, Mord. SM4 . . . . . .184 E4
Birchwood Ct, N13 . . . . .59 H5
  Edgware HA8 . . . . .70 C2
Birchwood Dr, NW3 . . . . .91 E3
Birchwood Gro, Hmptn. TW12 . .161 G6
Birchwood Rd, SW17 . . . . .168 B5
  Orpington BR5 . . . . .193 G4
Birdbrook Cl, Dag. RM10 . . . . . .101 J7
Birdbrook Rd, SE3 . . . . .155 J3
Birdcage Wk, SW1 . . . . .25 G4
Birdham Cl, Brom. BR1 . . . . .192 B5
Birdhurst Av, S.Croy. CR2 . . . . . .202 A4
Birdhurst Gdns, S.Croy. CR2 . . . .202 A4
Birdhurst Ri, S.Croy. CR2 . . . . . .202 B5
Birdhurst Rd, SW18 . . . . .149 F4
  SW19 . . . . .167 H6
  South Croydon CR2 . . . . .202 B5
Bird in Bush Rd, SE15 . . . . .37 J7
Bird-in-Hand La, Brom. BR1 . . . .192 A2
Bird-in-Hand Pas, SE23
  off Dartmouth Rd 171 F2
Birds Fm Av, Rom. RM5 . . . . .83 H1
Birdsfield La, E3 . . . . .113 J1
Bird St, W1 . . . . .16 C4
Bird Wk, Twick. TW2 . . . . .161 F1
Birdwood Cl, Tedd. TW11 . . . . . .162 B4
Birkbeck Av, W3 . . . . .106 C1
  Greenford UB6 . . . . .103 J1
Birkbeck Gdns, Wdf.Grn. IG8 . . . .63 F2
Birkbeck Gro, W3 . . . . .126 D2
Birkbeck Hill, SE21 . . . . .169 H2
Birkbeck Ms, E8
  off Sandringham Rd 94 C5
  W3 off Birkbeck Rd 126 D1
Birkbeck Pl, SE21 . . . . .169 J1
Birkbeck Rd, E8 . . . . .94 C5
  N8 . . . . .75 E4
  N12 .57 F5
  N17 .76 C1
  NW7 .55 F5
  SW19 . . . . .167 E6
  W3 .126 D1
  W5 .125 F4
  Beckenham BR3 . . . . .189 F2
  Enfield EN2 . . . . .44 A1
  Ilford IG2 . . . . .81 G5
  Sidcup DA14 . . . . .176 A3
Birkbeck St, E2 . . . . .113 E3
Birkbeck Way, Grnf. UB6 . . . . . .103 J1
Birkdale Av, Pnr. HA5 . . . . .67 G3
Birkdale Cl, SE16
  off Masters Dr 132/133 E5
  SE28 off Redbourne Dr 118 D6
  Orpington BR6 . . . . .193 G7
Birkdale Gdns, Croy. CR0 . . . . . .203 G4
  Watford WD19 . . . . .50 D3
Birkdale Rd, SE2 . . . . .138 A4
  W5 .105 H4
Birkenhead Av, Kings.T. KT2 . . . .181 J2
Birkenhead St, WC1 . . . . .10 B3
Birkhall Rd, SE6 . . . . .172 D1
Birkwood Cl, SW12 . . . . .150 D7
Birley Rd, N20 . . . . .57 F2
Birley St, SW11 . . . . .150 A2
Birnam Rd, N4 . . . . .93 F2
Birrell Ho, SW9
  off Stockwell Rd 151 F2
Birse Cres, NW10 . . . . .89 E4
Birstall Grn, Wat. WD19 . . . . .50 D4
Birstall Rd, N15 . . . . .76 B5
Biscay Rd, W6 . . . . .128 A5
Biscoe Cl, Houns. TW5 . . . . .123 G6
Biscoe Way, SE13 . . . . .154 D3
Bisenden Rd, Croy. CR0 . . . . . . .202 B2
Bisham Cl, Cars. SM5 . . . . .199 J1
Bisham Gdns, N6 . . . . .92 A1
Bishop Butt Cl, Orp. BR6
  off Stapleton Rd 207 J3
Bishop Cl, W4 . . . . .126 C5
Bishop Fox Way, W.Mol. KT8 . . .179 F4
Bishop Ken Rd, Har. HA3 . . . . . . .68 C2
Bishop Kings Rd, W14 . . . . .128 B4
Bishop Rd, N14 . . . . .42 B7
Bishop's Av, E13 . . . . .115 H1
  SW6 . . . . .148 A2
Bishops Av, Brom. BR1 . . . . .191 J2
  Romford RM6 . . . . .82 C6
Bishops Av, The, N2 . . . . .73 G7
Bishops Br, W2 . . . . .14 D3

Bishops Br Rd, W2 . . . . .14 B4
Bishops Cl, E17 . . . . .78 B4
  N19 off Wyndham Cres 92 C3
  SE9 .175 F2
  Barnet EN5 . . . . .40 A6
  Enfield EN1 off Central Av .44/45 E2
  Richmond TW10 . . . . .163 G3
Bishop's Cl, Sutt. SM1 . . . . .198 D3
Bishop's Ct, EC4 . . . . .19 G5
  WC2 .18 E3
Bishops Dr, Felt. TW14 . . . . .141 G4
  Northolt UB5 . . . . .103 E1
Bishopsford Rd, Mord. SM4 . . . .185 F7
Bishopsgate, EC2 . . . . .20 D4
Bishopsgate Arc, EC2 . . . . .20 D4
Bishopsgate Chyd, EC2 . . . . .20 D2
Bishops Gro, N2 . . . . .73 G6
  Hampton TW12 . . . . .161 F4
Bishop's Hall, Kings.T. KT1 . . . .181 G2
Bishops Hill, Walt. KT12 . . . . . .178 A7
Bishop's Pk, SW6 . . . . .148 A2
Bishop's Pk Rd, SW6 . . . . .148 A2
Bishops Pk Rd, SW16 . . . . .187 E1
Bishops Pl, Sutt. SM1
  off Lind Rd 199 F5
Bishops Rd, N6 . . . . .74 A6
  SW6 . . . . .148 C1
Bishop's Rd, SW11 . . . . .129 H7
Bishops Rd, W7 . . . . .124 B2
  Croydon CR0 . . . . .187 H7
Bishops Ter, SE11 . . . . .35 F1
Bishopsthorpe Rd, SE26 . . . . . . .171 G4
Bishop St, N1 . . . . .111 J1
Bishops Wk, Chis. BR7 . . . . .193 F1
  Croydon CR0 . . . . .203 G5
Bishop's Wk, Pnr. HA5
  off High St 66/67 E3
Bishops Way, E2 . . . . .113 J2
Bishopswood Rd, N6 . . . . .73 J7
Bishop Way, NW10 . . . . .88 E7
Bishop Wilfred Wd Cl, SE15
  off Moncrieff St 152 D2
Bisley Cl, Wor.Pk. KT4 . . . . .197 J1
Bisley Ho, SW19 . . . . .166 A2
Bispham Rd, NW10 . . . . .105 J3
Bisson Rd, E15 . . . . .114 C2
Bisterne Av, E17 . . . . .78 D3
Bittacy Cl, NW7 . . . . .56 A6
Bittacy Hill, NW7 . . . . .56 A6
Bittacy Pk Av, NW7 . . . . .56 A6
Bittacy Ri, NW7 . . . . .55 J6
Bittacy Rd, NW7 . . . . .56 A6
Bittern Cl, Hayes UB4 . . . . .102 D5
Bittern Pl, N22 off Coburg Rd 75 F2
Bittern St, SE1 . . . . .27 J4
Bittoms, The, Kings.T. KT1 . . . . .181 G3
Bixley Cl, Sthl. UB2 . . . . .123 F4
Blackall St, EC2 . . . . .12 D5
Blackberry Fm Cl, Houns. TW5 . .122 E7
Blackbird Hill, NW9 . . . . .88 C2
Blackbird Yd, E2 . . . . .13 G4
Blackborne Rd, Dag. RM10 . . . . .101 G6
Black Boy La, N15 . . . . .75 J5
Blackbrook La, Brom. BR1, BR2 .192 D3
Blackburne's Ms, W1 . . . . .16 B5
Blackburn Rd, NW6 . . . . .90 E6
Blackburn Trd Est, Stai. (Stanw.)
  TW19 . . . . .140 C4
Blackbush Av, Rom. RM6 . . . . . . .82 D5
Blackbush Cl, Sutt. SM2 . . . . . . .199 E7
Blackdown Cl, N2 . . . . .73 F2
Blackdown Ter, SE18
  off Prince Imperial Rd 136 D7
Blackett St, SW15 . . . . .148 A3
BLACKFEN, Sid. DA15 . . . . .157 J7
Blackfen Rd, Sid. DA15 . . . . .157 H5
Blackford Rd, Wat. WD19 . . . . . . .50 D5
Blackford's Path, SW15
  off Roehampton High St 147 G7
Blackfriars Br, EC4 . . . . .19 G5
  SE1 .19 G5
Blackfriars Ct, EC4 . . . . .19 G5
Black Friars La, EC4 . . . . .19 G5
Blackfriars Pas, EC4 . . . . .19 G5
Blackfriars Rd, SE1 . . . . .27 G4
Black Gates, Pnr. HA5
  off Church La 67 F3
BLACKHEATH, SE3 . . . . .155 E1
★ Blackheath, SE3 . . . . .154 D1
Blackheath Av, SE10 . . . . .134 D7
Blackheath Gro, SE3 . . . . .155 F2
Blackheath Hill, SE10 . . . . .154 C1
BLACKHEATH PARK, SE3 . . . . .155 H4
Blackheath Pk, SE3 . . . . .155 F3
Blackheath Ri, SE13 . . . . .154 C2
Blackheath Rd, SE10 . . . . .154 B1
Blackheath Vale, SE3 . . . . .155 E2
Blackheath Village, SE3 . . . . . . .155 F2
Black Horse Ct, SE1 . . . . .28 C5
Blackhorse La, E17 . . . . .77 G4
  Croydon CR0 . . . . .188 D7
Blackhorse Ms, E17
  off Blackhorse La 77 G3
Blackhorse Rd, E17 . . . . .77 G4
  SE8 .133 H5
  Sidcup DA14 . . . . .176 A4

Blacklands Rd, SE6 . . . . .172 C4
Blacklands Ter, SW3 . . . . .31 J2
Black Lion La, W6 . . . . .127 G4
Black Lion Ms, W6
  off Black Lion La 127 G4
Blackmore Av, Sthl. UB1 . . . . . .124 A1
Blackmore Rd, Buck.H. IG9 . . . . .48 B7
Blackmores Gro, Tedd. TW11 . . .162 D6
Blackmore Twr, W3 . . . . .126 C2
Black Path, E10 . . . . .77 G7
Blackpool Rd, SE15 . . . . .152 E2
Black Prince Rd, SE1 . . . . .34 C2
  SE11 . . . . .34 D2
Black Rod Cl, Hayes UB3 . . . . . .121 J3
Blackshaw Pl, N1
  off Hertford Rd 94 B7
Blackshaw Rd, SW17 . . . . .167 G4
Blacksmiths Cl, Rom. RM6 . . . . . .82 C6
Blacks Rd, W6
  off Queen Caroline St 127 J4
Blackstock Ms, N4
  off Blackstock Rd 93 H2
Blackstock Rd, N4 . . . . .93 H2
  N5 . . . . .93 H2
Blackstone Est, E8 . . . . .94 E7
Blackstone Rd, NW2 . . . . .89 J5
Black Swan Yd, SE1 . . . . .28 E3
Blackthorn Av, West Dr. UB7 . . .120 D4
Blackthorn Ct, Houns. TW5 . . . .122 E7
Blackthorne Av, Croy. CR0 . . . . .189 F7
Blackthorne Dr, E4 . . . . .62 D4
Blackthorn Gro, Bexh. DA7 . . . .158 D3
Blackthorn St, E3 . . . . .114 A4
Blacktree Ms, SW9 . . . . .151 G3
Blackwall La, SE10 . . . . .135 E5
Blackwall Pier, E14 . . . . .114 E7
Blackwall Trd Est, E14 . . . . .114 D5
Blackwall Tunnel, E14 . . . . .134 D1
Blackwall Tunnel App, SE10 . . . .134 E2
Blackwall Tunnel Northern App,
  E3 . . . . .114 A2
  E14 .114 A2
Blackwall Way, E14 . . . . .114 C7
Blackwater Cl, E7 . . . . .97 F4
Blackwater Rd, Sutt. SM1
  off High St 198/199 E4
Blackwater St, SE22 . . . . .152 C5
Blackwell Cl, E5 . . . . .95 G4
  Harrow HA3 . . . . .52 A7
Blackwell Gdns, Edg. HA8 . . . . . .54 A3
Blackwood Av, N18
  off Harbet Rd 61 G5
Blackwood St, SE17 . . . . .36 B3
Blade Ms, SW15 off Deodar Rd .148 C4
Blades Ct, SW15 off Deodar Rd .148 C4
Bladindon Dr, Bex. DA5 . . . . . . .158 C7
Bladon Gdns, Har. HA2 . . . . .67 H6
Blagdens Cl, N14 . . . . .58 C2
Blagdens La, N14 . . . . .58 D2
Blagdon Rd, SE13 . . . . .154 B6
  New Malden KT3 . . . . .183 F4
Blagdon Wk, Tedd. TW11 . . . . . .163 F6
Blagrove Rd, W10 . . . . .108 B5
Blair Av, NW9 . . . . .70 E7
Blair Cl, N1 . . . . .93 J6
  Hayes UB3 . . . . .122 A4
  Sidcup DA15 . . . . .157 H5
Blairderry Rd, SW2 . . . . .169 E2
Blairhead Dr, Wat. WD19 . . . . . . .50 B3
Blair St, E14 . . . . .114 C6
Blake Apartments, N8
  off High St 75 F4
Blake Av, Bark. IG11 . . . . .117 H1
Blake Cl, W10 . . . . .107 J5
  Carshalton SM5 . . . . .185 H7
  Welling DA16 . . . . .157 H1
Blakeden Dr, Esher (Clay.) KT10 .194 C6
Blake Gdns, SW6 . . . . .148 E1
Blake Hall Cres, E11 . . . . .97 G1
Blake Hall Rd, E11 . . . . .79 G1
Blakehall Rd, Cars. SM5 . . . . . . .199 J6
Blake Ho, Beck. BR3 . . . . .172 A6
Blake Ms, Rich. TW9
  off High Pk Rd 146 A1
Blakemore Rd, SW16 . . . . .168 E3
  Thornton Heath CR7 . . . . . . .187 F5
Blakemore Way, Belv. DA17 . . . .139 E3
Blakeney Av, Beck. BR3 . . . . . . .189 J1
Blakeney Cl, E8 off Ferncliff Rd .94 D5
  N20 .57 F1
  NW1 off Rossendale Way 92 D7
Blakeney Rd, Beck. BR3 . . . . . . .171 J7
Blakenham Rd, SW17 . . . . .167 J4
Blaker Ct, SE7 off Fairlawn 135 J7
Blaker Rd, E15 . . . . .114 C1
Blakes Av, N.Mal. KT3 . . . . .183 F5
Blake's Grn, W.Wick. BR4 . . . . .204 C1
Blakes La, N.Mal. KT3 . . . . .183 F5
Blakesley Av, W5 . . . . .105 F5
Blakesley Ho, E12
  off Grantham Rd 98 D3
Blakesley Wk, SW20
  off Kingston Rd 184 C2

Blakes Rd, SE15 . . . . .36 E7
Blakes Ter, N.Mal. KT3 . . . . .183 G5
Blake St, SE8 off Watergate St .134 A6
Blakesware Gdns, N9 . . . . .44 A7
Blakewood Cl, Felt. TW13 . . . . . .160 C4
Blanchard Cl, SE9 . . . . .174 B3
Blanchard Way, E8 . . . . .94 D6
Blanch Cl, SE15 off Culmore Rd .133 F7
Blanchedowne, SE5 . . . . .152 A4
Blanche St, E16 . . . . .115 F4
Blanchland Rd, Mord. SM4 . . . .184 E5
Blandfield Rd, SW12 . . . . .150 A6
Blandford Av, Beck. BR3 . . . . . .189 H2
  Twickenham TW2 . . . . .161 H1
Blandford Cl, N2 . . . . .73 F4
  Croydon CR0 . . . . .201 E3
  Romford RM7 . . . . .83 H4
Blandford Cres, E4 . . . . .46 C7
Blandford Rd, W4 . . . . .126 E3
  W5 .125 G2
  Beckenham BR3 . . . . .189 E2
  Southall UB2 . . . . .123 G4
  Teddington TW11 . . . . .162 A5
Blandford Sq, NW1 . . . . .7 H6
Blandford St, W1 . . . . .16 A3
Blandford Waye, Hayes UB4 . . . .102 C6
Bland St, SE9 . . . . .156 A4
Blaney Cres, E6 . . . . .116 E3
Blanmerle Rd, SE9 . . . . .174 E1
Blann Cl, SE9 . . . . .156 A6
Blantyre St, SW10 . . . . .30 E7
Blantyre Wk, SW10 . . . . .30 E7
Blashford, NW3 . . . . .91 J7
Blashford St, SE13 . . . . .154 D7
Blasker Wk, E14 . . . . .134 A5
Blawith Rd, Har. HA1 . . . . .68 B4
Blaydon Cl, N17 . . . . .60 E7
Blaydon Wk, N17 . . . . .60 E7
Bleak Hill La, SE18 . . . . .137 J6
Blean Gro, SE20 . . . . .171 F7
Bleasdale Av, Grnf. UB6 . . . . . . .104 D2
Blechynden St, W10
  off Bramley Rd 108 A7
Bleddyn Cl, Sid. DA15 . . . . .158 C6
Bledlow Cl, SE28 . . . . .118 C7
Bledlow Ri, Grnf. UB6 . . . . .103 J2
Bleeding Heart Yd, EC1 . . . . .19 F2
Blegborough Rd, SW16 . . . . . . .168 C6
Blendon Dr, Bex. DA5 . . . . .158 D6
Blendon Path, Brom. BR1 . . . . . .173 F7
Blendon Rd, Bex. DA5 . . . . .158 D6
Blendon Ter, SE18 . . . . .137 F5
Blendworth Pt, SW15
  off Wanborough Dr 165 H1
Blendworth Way, SE15
  off Blakes Rd 132 B7
Blenheim Av, Ilf. IG2 . . . . .80 E6
Blenheim Cl, N21 off Elm Pk Rd . .59 J1
  SE12 . . . . .173 H1
  SW20 . . . . .183 J3
  Greenford UB6
    off Leaver Gdns 104 A2
  Romford RM7 . . . . .83 J4
  Wallington SM6 . . . . .200 C7
Blenheim Ct, N19
  off Marlborough Rd . . .92/93 E2
  Sidcup DA14 . . . . .175 G3
  Sutton SM2
    off Wellesley Rd 199 F6
  Woodford Green IG8
    off Navestock Cres 63 J7
Blenheim Cres, W11 . . . . .108 B6
  South Croydon CR2 . . . . . . .201 J4
Blenheim Dr, Well. DA16 . . . . . .157 J1
Blenheim Gdns, NW2 . . . . .89 J5
  SW2 . . . . .151 F6
  Kingston upon Thames KT2 . .164 B7
  Wallington SM6 . . . . .200 C6
  Wembley HA9 . . . . .87 H3
Blenheim Gro, SE15 . . . . .152 D2
Blenheim Pas, NW8 . . . . .6 C1
Blenheim Pl, Tedd. TW11 . . . . . .162 C5
Blenheim Ri, N15 off Talbot Rd . .76 C4
Blenheim Rd, E6 . . . . .116 A3
  E15 . . . . .97 E4
  E17 . . . . .77 G3
  NW8 . . . . .6 C1
  SE20 off Maple Rd 171 F7
  SW20 . . . . .183 J3
  W4 .126 A3
  Barnet EN5 . . . . .40 A3
  Bromley BR1 . . . . .192 B4
  Harrow HA2 . . . . .67 H4
  Northolt UB5 . . . . .85 H6
  Sidcup DA15 . . . . .176 C1
  Sutton SM1 . . . . .198 D3
Blenheim Shop Cen, SE20 . . . . .171 F7
Blenheim St, W1 . . . . .16 D4
Blenheim Ter, NW8 . . . . .6 C1
Blenheim Way, Islw. TW7 . . . . . .144 D1
Blenkarne Rd, SW11 . . . . .149 J6
Bleriot Rd, Houns. TW5 . . . . . . .122 C7
Blessbury Rd, Edg. HA8 . . . . .70 C1
Blessington Cl, SE13 . . . . .154 D3
Blessington Rd, SE13 . . . . .154 D3
Blessing Way, Bark. IG11 . . . . . .118 C3
Bletchingley Cl, Th.Hth. CR7 . . .187 H4

Bletchley Ct, N1 . . . . .12 B2
Bletchley St, N1 . . . . .12 A2
Bletchmore Cl, Hayes UB3 . . . . .121 G5
Bletsoe Wk, N1 . . . . .12 A1
Blewbury Ho, SE2
  off Yarnton Way 138 D2
Blincoe Cl, SW19 . . . . .166 A2
Blind La, Loug. (High Beach)
  IG10 .46 E2
Bliss Cres, SE13 . . . . .154 B2
Blissett St, SE10 . . . . .154 C1
Bliss Ms, W10 off Third Av 108 B3
Blisworth Cl, Hayes UB4
  off Braunston Dr 102/103 E4
Blithbury Rd, Dag. RM9 . . . . . . .100 B6
Blithdale Rd, SE2 . . . . .138 A4
Blithfield St, W8 . . . . .22 A6
Blockley Rd, Wem. HA0 . . . . .86 E2
Bloemfontein Av, W12 . . . . .127 H1
Bloemfontein Rd, W12 . . . . .107 H7
Blomfield Rd, W9 . . . . .14 C1
Blomfield St, EC2 . . . . .20 C2
Blomfield Vil, W2 . . . . .14 B2
Blomville Rd, Dag. RM8 . . . . . . .101 E3
Blondell Cl, West Dr. UB7 . . . . . .120 A6
Blondel St, SW11 . . . . .150 A2
Blondin Av, W5 . . . . .125 F4
Blondin St, E3 . . . . .114 A2
Bloomburg St, SW1 . . . . .33 G2
Bloomfield Cres, Ilf. IG2 . . . . .81 E6
Bloomfield Pl, W1 . . . . .16 E5
Bloomfield Rd, N6 . . . . .74 A6
  SE18 . . . . .137 E5
  Bromley BR2 . . . . .192 A5
  Kingston upon Thames KT1 . .181 H4
Bloomfield Ter, SW1 . . . . .32 C3
Bloom Gro, SE27 . . . . .169 H3
Bloomhall Rd, SE19 . . . . .170 A5
Bloom Pk Rd, SW6 . . . . .128 C7
BLOOMSBURY, WC1 . . . . .17 J2
Bloomsbury Cl, NW7 . . . . .55 G7
  W5 .105 J7
Bloomsbury Ct, WC1 . . . . .18 B2
  Pinner HA5 . . . . .67 F3
Bloomsbury Ho, SW4 . . . . .150 D6
Bloomsbury Pl, SW18
  off Fullerton Rd 149 F5
  WC1 .18 B1
Bloomsbury Sq, WC1 . . . . .18 B2
Bloomsbury St, WC1 . . . . .17 J2
Bloomsbury Way, WC1 . . . . .18 A3
Blore Cl, SW8 off Thessaly Rd . .150 D1
Blore Ct, W1 . . . . .17 H4
Blossom Cl, W5 off Almond Av . .125 H2
  Dagenham RM9 . . . . .119 F1
  South Croydon CR2 . . . . . . .202 C5
Blossom La, Enf. EN2 . . . . .43 J1
Blossom St, E1 . . . . .21 E1
Blossom Way, West Dr. UB7 . . . .120 D4
Blossom Waye, Houns. TW5 . . . .122 E7
Blount St, E14 . . . . .113 H6
Bloxam Gdns, SE9 . . . . .156 B5
Bloxhall Rd, E10 . . . . .95 J1
Bloxham Cres, Hmptn. TW12 . . .161 F7
Bloxworth Cl, Wall. SM6 . . . . . . .200 C3
Blucher Rd, SE5 . . . . .131 J7
Blue Anchor All, Rich. TW9
  off Kew Rd 145 H4
Blue Anchor La, SE16 . . . . .37 J1
Blue Anchor Yd, E1 . . . . .21 H5
Blue Ball Yd, SW1 . . . . .25 F2
Bluebell Av, E12 . . . . .98 A5
Bluebell Cl, E9 off Moulins Rd . .113 F1
  SE26 . . . . .170 C4
  Northolt UB5 . . . . .85 F6
  Orpington BR6 . . . . .207 F2
  Wallington SM6 . . . . .200 B1
Bluebell Way, Ilf. IG1 . . . . .98 E6
Blueberry Cl, Wdf.Grn. IG8 . . . . .63 G6
Bluebird La, Dag. RM10 . . . . . . .101 G6
Bluebird Way, SE28 . . . . .137 G2
Bluefield Cl, Hmptn. TW12 . . . . .161 G5
Bluegates, Epsom (Ewell) KT17 .197 G7
Bluehouse Rd, E4 . . . . .63 E3
Bluelion Pl, SE1 . . . . .28 D5
Blueprint Apartments, SW12
  off Balham Gro 150 B7
Bluewater Ho, SW18
  off Smugglers Way 148/149 E4
Blundell Cl, E8 off Amhurst Rd . .94 D5
Blundell Rd, Edg. HA8 . . . . .70 D1
Blundell St, N7 . . . . .92 E7
Blunden Cl, Dag. RM8 . . . . .100 C1
Blunt Rd, S.Croy. CR2 . . . . .202 A5
Blunts Av, West Dr. UB7 . . . . . . .120 D7
Blunts Rd, SE9 . . . . .156 D5
Blurton Rd, E5 . . . . .95 F4
Blyth Cl, E14
  off Manchester Rd 134 D4
  Twickenham TW1
    off Grimwood Rd 144 C6
Blythe Cl, SE6 . . . . .153 J7
Blythe Hill, SE6 . . . . .153 J7
  Orpington BR5 . . . . .193 J1
Blythe Hill La, SE6 . . . . .153 J7
Blythe Hill Pl, SE23
  off Brockley Pk 153 H7

Blythe Ms, W14 *off Blythe Rd* . . .128 A3
Blythe Rd, W14 . . . . .128 A3
Blythe St, E2 . . . . .112 C3
Blythe Vale, SE6 . . . . .171 J1
Blyth Rd, E17 . . . . .77 J7
SE28 . . . . .118 C7
Bromley BR1 . . . . .191 F1
Hayes UB3 . . . . .121 H2
Blyth's Wf, E14 *off Narrow St* . . .113 H7
Blythswood Rd, Ilf. IG3 . . . . . . .100 A1
Blyth Wd Pk, Brom. BR1
off Blyth Rd 191 F1
Blythwood Rd, N4 . . . . .75 E7
Pinner HA5 . . . . .66 D1
Boades Ms, NW3 *off New End* . .91 G4
Boadicea St, N1
off Copenhagen St 111 F1
Boakes Cl, NW9 . . . . .70 C4
Boardman Av, E4 . . . . .46 B5
Boardman Cl, Barn. EN5 . . . . . . .40 A5
Boardwalk Pl, E14 . . . . .134 C1
Boar's Head Yd, Brent. TW8
off Brent Way 125 G7
Boathouse Wk, SE15 . . . . .37 G7
Richmond TW9 . . . . .145 H1
Boat Lifter Way, SE16
off Sweden Gate 133 H4
Boat Quay, E16
off Royal Albert Way 115 J7
Bob Anker Cl, E13
off Chesterton Rd 115 G3
Bobbin Cl, SW4 . . . . .150 C3
Bobby Moore Way, N10 . . . . . . .57 J7
Bob Marley Way, SE24
off Mayall Rd 151 G4
Bockhampton Rd, Kings.T. KT2 . .163 J7
Bocking St, E8 . . . . .112 E1
Boddicott Cl, SW19 . . . . .166 B2
Bodiam Cl, Enf. EN1 . . . . .44 A2
Bodiam Rd, SW16 . . . . .168 D7
Bodicea Ms, Houns. TW4 . . . . . .143 F7
Bodley Cl, N.Mal. KT3 . . . . . . .182 E5
Bodley Manor Way, SW2
off Papworth Way 151 G7
Bodley Rd, N.Mal. KT3 . . . . . . .182 D6
Bodmin Cl, Har. HA2 . . . . .85 F3
Bodmin Gro, Mord. SM4 . . . . . .185 E5
Bodmin St, SW18 . . . . .166 D1
Bodnant Gdns, SW20 . . . . .183 G3
Bodney Rd, E8 . . . . .94 E5
Boeing Way, Sthl. UB2 . . . . . . .122 B3
Boevey Path, Belv. DA17 . . . . . .139 F6
Bogey La, Orp. BR6 . . . . .206 D7
Bognor Gdns, Wat. WD19
off Bowring Grn 50 C5
Bognor Rd, Well. DA16 . . . . . . .158 D1
Bohemia Pl, E8 . . . . .95 E6
Bohn Rd, E1 . . . . .113 H5
Bohun Gro, Barn. EN4 . . . . .41 H6
Boileau Par, W5 *off Boileau Rd* . .105 J6
Boileau Rd, SW13 . . . . .127 G7
W5 . . . . .105 J6
Bolden St, SE8 . . . . .154 B2
Bolderwood Way, W.Wick. BR4 . .204 B2
Boldmere Rd, Pnr. HA5 . . . . .66 C7
Boleyn Av, Enf. EN1 . . . . .44 E1
Boleyn Cl, E17 . . . . .78 A4
Loughton IG10
off Roding Gdns 48 B6
Boleyn Ct, Buck.H. IG9 . . . . .63 G1
Boleyn Dr, Ruis. HA4 . . . . .84 D2
West Molesey KT8 . . . . .179 F3
Boleyn Gdns, Dag. RM10 . . . . .101 J7
West Wickham BR4 . . . . .204 B2
Boleyn Gro, W.Wick. BR4 . . . . . .204 C2
Boleyn Rd, E6 . . . . .116 A2
E7 .97 G7
N16 . . . . .94 B5
Boleyn Way, Barn. EN5 . . . . . . .41 F3
Ilford IG6 . . . . .65 F6
Bolina Rd, SE16 . . . . .133 F5
Bolingbroke Gro, SW11 . . . . . . .149 H4
Bolingbroke Rd, W14 . . . . .128 A3
Bolingbroke Wk, SW11 . . . . . . .129 G7
Bolingbroke Way, Hayes UB3 . . .121 G1
Bolliger Ct, NW10
off Park Royal Rd 106 C4
Bollo Br Rd, W3 . . . . .126 B3
Bollo La, W3 . . . . .126 B2
W4 . . . . .126 C4
Bolney Gate, SW7 . . . . .23 G4
Bolney St, SW8 . . . . .131 F7
Bolney Way, Felt. TW13 . . . . . . .161 E3
Bolsover St, W1 . . . . .9 E6
Bolstead Rd, Mitch. CR4 . . . . . .186 B1
Bolt Ct, EC4 . . . . .19 F4
Boltmore Cl, NW4 . . . . .72 A3
Bolton Cl, SE20 *off Selby Rd* . . .188 D2
Chessington KT9 . . . . .195 G6
Bolton Cres, SE5 . . . . .35 F6
Bolton Gdns, NW10 . . . . .108 A2
SW5 . . . . .30 A3
Bromley BR1 . . . . .173 F6
Teddington TW11 . . . . .162 D6
Bolton Gdns Ms, SW10 . . . . .30 C3
Bolton Rd, E15 . . . . .97 F6
N18 . . . . .60 C5

Bolton Rd, NW8 . . . . .109 E1
NW10 . . . . .107 E1
W4 . . . . .126 C7
Chessington KT9 . . . . .195 G6
Harrow HA1 . . . . .67 J4
Boltons, The, SW10 . . . . .30 C4
Wembley HA0 . . . . .86 C4
Woodford Green IG8 . . . . .63 G4
Boltons La, Hayes UB3 . . . . . . .121 F7
Boltons Pl, SW5 . . . . .30 C3
Bolton St, W1 . . . . .24 E1
Bolton Wk, N7 *off Durham Rd* . . .93 F2
Bombay St, SE16 . . . . .132 E4
Bomer Cl, West Dr. UB7 . . . . . .120 D7
Bomore Rd, W11 . . . . .108 A7
Bonar Pl, Chis. BR7 . . . . .174 B7
Bonar Rd, SE15 . . . . .132 D7
Bonchester Cl, Chis. BR7 . . . . . .174 D7
Bonchurch Cl, Sutt. SM2 . . . . . .199 E7
Bonchurch Rd, W10 . . . . .108 B5
W13 . . . . .124 E1
Bond Ct, EC4 . . . . .20 B4
Bondfield Av, Hayes UB4 . . . . . .102 A3
Bondfield Rd, E6
off Lovage App 116 B5
Bond Gdns, Wall. SM6 . . . . . . .200 C4
Bonding Yd Wk, SE16
off Finland St 133 H3
Bond Rd, Mitch. CR4 . . . . .185 H2
Surbiton KT6 . . . . .195 J2
Bond St, E15 . . . . .96 E5
W4 . . . . .126 E4
W5 . . . . .105 G7
Bondway, SW8 . . . . .34 B6
Boneta Rd, SE18 . . . . .136 C3
Bonfield Rd, SE13 . . . . .154 C4
Bonham Gdns, Dag. RM8 . . . . .100 D2
Bonham Rd, SW2 . . . . .151 F5
Dagenham RM8 . . . . .100 D2
Bonheur Rd, W4 . . . . .126 D2
Bonhill St, EC2 . . . . .12 C6
Boniface Gdns, Har. HA3 . . . . . . .51 H7
Boniface Wk, Har. HA3 . . . . .51 H7
Bonington Ho, Enf. EN1
off Ayley Cft 44 D5
Bonita Ms, SE4 . . . . .153 G3
Bon Marche Ter Ms, SE27
off Gipsy Rd 170 B4
Bonner Hill Rd, Kings.T. KT1 . . .181 J3
Bonner Rd, E2 . . . . .113 F2
Bonnersfield Cl, Har. HA1 . . . . . .68 C6
Bonnersfield La, Har. HA1 . . . . . .68 D6
Bonner St, E2 . . . . .113 F2
Bonneville Gdns, SW4 . . . . . . .150 C6
Bonnington Sq, SW8 . . . . .34 C5
Bonnington Twr, Brom. BR2 . . . .192 B6
Bonny St, NW1 . . . . .92 C7
Bonser Rd, Twick. TW1 . . . . . . .162 C2
Bonsor St, SE5 . . . . .132 B7
Bonville Gdns, NW4
off Handowe Cl 71 G4
Bonville Rd, Brom. BR1 . . . . . . .173 F5
Bookbinders' Cotts, N20
off Manor Dr 57 J3
Booker Cl, E14 *off Wallwood St* . .113 J5
Booker Rd, N18 . . . . .60 D5
Book Ms, WC2 . . . . .17 J4
Boone Ct, N9 . . . . .61 F3
Boones Rd, SE13 . . . . .155 E4
Boone St, SE13 . . . . .155 E4
Boord St, SE10 . . . . .135 E3
Boothby Rd, N19 . . . . .92 D2
Booth Cl, E9
off Victoria Pk Rd 112/113 E1
SE28 . . . . .118 B7
Booth Rd, NW9 . . . . .70 E2
Croydon CR0
off Waddon New Rd 201 H2
Booth's Pl, W1 . . . . .17 G2
Boot St, N1 . . . . .12 D4
Bordars Rd, W7 . . . . .104 B5
Bordars Wk, W7 . . . . .104 B5
Borden Av, Enf. EN1 . . . . .44 A6
Border Cres, SE26 . . . . .170 E5
Border Gdns, Croy. CR0 . . . . . .204 B4
Bordergate, Mitch. CR4 . . . . . . .185 H1
Border Rd, SE26 . . . . .171 E5
Borders La, Loug. IG10 . . . . .48 D4
Bordesley Rd, Mord. SM4 . . . . .185 E4
Bordon Wk, SW15 . . . . .147 G7
Boreas Wk, N1 . . . . .11 H2
Boreham Av, E16 . . . . .115 G6
Boreham Cl, E11
off Hainault Rd 96 C1
Boreham Rd, N22 . . . . .75 J2
BOREHAMWOOD, WD6 . . . . . . .38 B3
Borehamwood Ind Pk, Borwd.
WD6 . . . . .38 D2
Borgard Rd, SE18 . . . . .136 C4
Borkwood Pk, Orp. BR6 . . . . . . .207 J4
Borkwood Way, Orp. BR6 . . . . . .207 H4
Borland Rd, SE15 . . . . .153 F4
Teddington TW11 . . . . .162 E6
Borneo St, SW15 . . . . .147 J3
BOROUGH, THE, SE1 . . . . .27 J4
Borough High St, SE1 . . . . .27 J4
Borough Hill, Croy. CR0 . . . . . . .201 H3

★ Borough Mkt, SE1 . . . . .28 B2
Borough Rd, SE1 . . . . .27 G5
Isleworth TW7 . . . . .144 B1
Kingston upon Thames KT2 . .182 A1
Mitcham CR4 . . . . .185 H2
Borough Sq, SE1 . . . . .27 J4
Borrett Cl, SE17 . . . . .35 J4
Borrodaile Rd, SW18 . . . . .149 E6
Borrowdale Av, Har. HA3 . . . . . . .68 D2
Borrowdale Cl, Ilf. IG4 . . . . .80 B4
Borrowdale Ct, Enf. EN2 . . . . . . .43 J1
Borthwick Ms, E15
off Borthwick Rd 96/97 E4
Borthwick Rd, E15 . . . . .96 E4
NW9 *off West Hendon Bdy* . . .71 F6
Borthwick St, SE8 . . . . .134 A5
Borwick Av, E17 . . . . .77 J3
Bosbury Rd, SE6 . . . . .172 C3
Boscastle Rd, NW5 . . . . .92 B3
Boscobel Cl, Brom. BR1 . . . . . .192 C2
Boscobel Pl, SW1 . . . . .32 C1
Boscobel St, NW8 . . . . .7 F6
Bosco Cl, Orp. BR6
off Strickland Way 207 J4
Boscombe Av, E10 . . . . .78 D7
Boscombe Cl, E5 . . . . .95 H5
Boscombe Gdns, SW16 . . . . . . .169 E6
Boscombe Rd, SW17 . . . . .168 A6
SW19 . . . . .184 E1
W12 . . . . .127 G1
Worcester Park KT4 . . . . .197 J1
Bose Cl, N3 *off Claremont Pk* . . .72 B1
Bosgrove, E4 . . . . .62 C1
Boss Ho, SE1 . . . . .29 F3
Boss St, SE1 . . . . .29 F3
Bostall Heath, SE2 . . . . .138 C5
Bostall Hill, SE2 . . . . .138 A5
Bostall La, SE2 . . . . .138 B5
Bostall Manorway, SE2 . . . . . . .138 B4
Bostall Pk Av, Bexh. DA7 . . . . . .138 E7
Bostall Rd, Orp. BR5 . . . . .176 B7
Bostal Row, Bexh. DA7
off Harlington Rd 159 F3
Boston Gdns, W4 . . . . .127 E6
W7 . . . . .124 D4
Brentford TW8 . . . . .124 D4
★ Boston Manor, Brent. TW8 . . .125 F5
Boston Manor Rd, Brent. TW8 . .124 E4
Boston Pk Rd, Brent. TW8 . . . . .125 F5
Boston Pl, NW1 . . . . .7 J6
Boston Rd, E6 . . . . .116 B3
E17 . . . . .78 A6
W7 . . . . .124 B1
Croydon CR0 . . . . .187 F6
Edgware HA8 . . . . .54 C7
Boston St, E2 . . . . .13 H1
Bostonthorpe Rd, W7 . . . . .124 B2
Boston Vale, W7 . . . . .124 D4
Bosun Cl, E14 *off Byng St* 134 A2
Boswell Ct, WC1 . . . . .18 B1
Boswell Path, Hayes UB3
off Croyde Av 121 J4
Boswell Rd, Th.Hth. CR7 . . . . . .187 J4
Boswell St, WC1 . . . . .18 B1
Bosworth Cl, E17 . . . . .77 J1
Bosworth Rd, N11 . . . . .58 D6
W10 . . . . .108 B4
Barnet EN5 . . . . .40 D3
Dagenham RM10 . . . . .101 G4
Botany Bay La, Chis. BR7 . . . . . .193 F3
Botany Cl, Barn. EN4 . . . . .41 H4
Boteley Cl, E4 . . . . .62 D2
Botham Cl, Edg. HA8
off Pavilion Way 54 C7
Botha Rd, E13 . . . . .115 H5
Bothwell Cl, E16 . . . . .115 F5
Bothwell St, W6
off Delorme St 128 A6
Botolph All, EC3 . . . . .20 D5
Botolph La, EC3 . . . . .20 D5
Botsford Rd, SW20 . . . . .184 B2
Botts Ms, W2 *off Chepstow Rd* . .108 D6
Botts Pas, W2
off Chepstow Rd 108 D6
Botwell La, Hayes UB3 . . . . . . .121 H1
Boucher Cl, Tedd. TW11 . . . . . .162 C5
Boughton Av, Brom. BR2 . . . . . .191 F7
Boughton Rd, SE28 . . . . .137 H3
Boulcott St, E1 . . . . .113 G6
Boulevard, The, SW6 . . . . .149 F1
SW17
off Balham High Rd 168 A2
SW18
off Smugglers Way 148/149 E4
Pinner HA5 *off Pinner Rd* 67 G4
Woodford Green IG8 . . . . .64 D7
Boulevard 25 Retail Pk, Borwd.
WD6 . . . . .38 A3
Boulogne Rd, Croy. CR0 . . . . . .187 J6
Boulton Ho, Brent. TW8
off Green Dragon La 125 H5
Boulton Rd, Dag. RM8 . . . . . . .101 E3
Boultwood Rd, E6 . . . . .116 B6
Bounces La, N9 . . . . .60 E2
Bounces Rd, N9 . . . . .60 E1
Boundaries Rd, SW12 . . . . .167 J2
Feltham TW13 . . . . .160 C1

Boundary Av, E17 . . . . .77 J7
Boundary Cl, SE20
off Haysleigh Gdns 188 D2
Barnet EN5 . . . . .40 C1
Ilford IG3 *off Loxford La* 99 H4
Kingston upon Thames KT1 . .182 B3
Southall UB2 . . . . .123 G5
Boundary La, E13 . . . . .116 A3
SE17 . . . . .36 A6
Boundary Pas, E2 . . . . .13 F5
Boundary Rd, E13 . . . . .115 J2
E17 .77 J7
N9 .45 F6
N22 . . . . .75 H3
NW8 . . . . .109 E1
SW19 . . . . .167 G6
Barking IG11 . . . . .117 F2
Carshalton SM5 . . . . .200 B6
Pinner HA5 . . . . .66 D6
Sidcup DA15 . . . . .157 H5
Wallington SM6 . . . . .200 B6
Wembley HA9 . . . . .87 H3
Boundary Row, SE1 . . . . .27 G3
Boundary St, E2 . . . . .13 F4
Boundary Way, Croy. CR0 . . . . . .204 A5
Boundfield Rd, SE6 . . . . .172 E3
Bounds Grn Rd, N11 . . . . .58 C6
N22 . . . . .58 C6
Bourchier St, W1 . . . . .17 H5
Bourdon Pl, W1 . . . . .16 E5
Bourdon Rd, SE20 . . . . .189 F2
Bourdon St, W1 . . . . .16 E5
Bourke Cl, NW10
off Mayo Rd 88/89 E6
SW4 . . . . .150 E6
Bourlet Cl, W1 . . . . .17 F2
Bourn Av, N15 . . . . .76 A4
Barnet EN4 . . . . .41 G5
Bournbrook Rd, SE3 . . . . .156 A3
Bourne, The, N14 . . . . .58 D1
Bourne Av, N14 . . . . .58 E2
Hayes UB3 . . . . .121 F3
Ruislip HA4 . . . . .84 C5
Bourne Cl, T.Ditt. KT7 . . . . .194 C2
Bourne Ct, Ruis. HA4 . . . . .84 B5
Bourne Dr, Mitch. CR4 . . . . . . .185 G2
Bourne Est, EC1 . . . . .18 E1
Bourne Gdns, E4 . . . . .62 B4
Bourne Hill, N13 . . . . .58 E1
Bourne Hill Cl, N13
off Bourne Hill 59 F2
Bournemead Av, Nthlt. UB5 . . . .102 A2
Bournemead Cl, Nthlt. UB5 . . . .102 A2
Bournemead Way, Nthlt. UB5 . . .102 B2
Bournemouth Cl, SE15 . . . . . . .152 D2
Bournemouth Rd, SE15 . . . . . . .152 D2
SW19 . . . . .184 D1
Bourne Pl, W4 *off Dukes Av* . . .126 D5
Bourne Rd, E7 . . . . .97 F3
N8 .75 E6
Bexley DA5 . . . . .159 H6
Bromley BR2 . . . . .192 A4
Dartford DA1 . . . . .159 J6
Bourneside Cres, N14 . . . . .58 D1
Bourneside Gdns, SE6 . . . . .172 C5
Bourne St, SW1 . . . . .32 B2
Croydon CR0
off Waddon New Rd 201 H2
Bourne Ter, W2 . . . . .14 A1
Bourne Vale, Brom. BR2 . . . . . .191 G7
Bournevale Rd, SW16 . . . . .168 E4
Bourne Vw, Grnf. UB6 . . . . .86 C6
Bourne Way, Brom. BR2 . . . . . . .205 F2
Epsom KT19 . . . . .196 C5
Sutton SM1 . . . . .198 C5
Bournewood Rd, SE18 . . . . .138 A7
Bournville Rd, SE6 . . . . .154 A7
Bournwell Cl, Barn. EN4 . . . . . . .41 J3
Bourton Cl, Hayes UB3 . . . . . . .122 A1
Bousfield Rd, SE14 . . . . .153 G2
Boutflower Rd, SW11 . . . . .149 H4
Bouverie Gdns, Har. HA3 . . . . . . .69 G6
Bouverie Ms, N16
off Bouverie Rd 94 B2
Bouverie Pl, W2 . . . . .15 F3
Bouverie Rd, N16 . . . . .94 B2
Harrow HA1 . . . . .67 J7
Bouverie St, EC4 . . . . .19 F4
Boveney Rd, SE23 . . . . .153 G7
Bovill Rd, SE23 . . . . .153 G7
Bovingdon Av, Wem. HA9 . . . . . .88 A6
Bovingdon Cl, N19
off Brookside Rd 92 C2
Bovingdon La, NW9 . . . . .71 E1
Bovingdon Rd, SW6 . . . . .148 E1
Bovingdon Sq, Mitch. CR4
off Leicester Av 186/187 E4
BOW, E3 . . . . .113 J2
Bowater Cl, NW9 . . . . .70 D5
SW2 . . . . .150 E6
Bowater Gdns, Sun. TW16 . . . . .178 B2
Bowater Pl, SE3 . . . . .135 H7
Bowater Rd, SE18 . . . . .136 A3
Wembley HA9
off Chalkhill Rd 88 B3
Bow Back Rivers Wk, E15 . . . . . .96 B3
Bow Br Est, E3 . . . . .114 B3

Bow Chyd, EC4	.20	A4
Bow Common La, E3	.113	J4
Bowden St, SE11	.35	F4
Bowditch, SE8	.133	J5
Bowdon Rd, E17	.78	A7
Bowen Dr, SE21	.170	B3
Bowen Rd, Har. HA1	.67	J7
Bowen St, E14	.114	B6
Bower Av, SE10	.154	E1
Bower Cl, Nthlt. UB5	.102	C2
Bowerdean St, SW6	.148	E1
Bowerman Av, SE14	.133	H6
Bower St, E1	.113	G6
Bowers Wk, E6	.116	B6
Bowes Cl, Sid. DA15	.158	B6
BOWES PARK, N22	.59	E6
Bowes Rd, N11	.58	B5
N13	.58	E5
W3	.106	C4
Dagenham RM8	.100	C4
Bowfell Rd, W6	.127	J6
Bowford Av, Bexh. DA7	.158	E1
Bowhill Cl, SW9	.35	F7
Bowie Cl, SW4	.150	D7
Bow Ind Pk, E15	.96	A7
Bowland Rd, SW4	.150	D4
Woodford Green IG8	.63	J6
Bowland Yd, SW1	.24	A4
Bow La, EC4	.20	A4
N12	.73	F1
Morden SM4	.184	B6
Bowl Ct, EC2	.12	E6
Bowles Rd, SE1	.37	H5
Bowley Cl, SE19	.170	C6
Bowley La, SE19	.170	C5
Bowling Grn Cl, SW15	.147	H4
Bowling Grn La, EC1	.11	F5
Bowling Grn Pl, SE1	.28	B3
Bowling Grn Row, SE18		
off Samuel St	.136	C3
Bowling Grn St, SE11	.35	F5
Bowling Grn Wk, N1	.12	D3
Bowls, The, Chig. IG7	.65	H4
Bowls Cl, Stan. HA7	.52	E5
Bowman Av, E16	.115	F7
Bowman Ms, SW18	.166	C1
Bowmans Cl, W13	.124	E1
Bowmans Lea, SE23	.153	F7
Bowmans Meadow, Wall. SM6	.200	B4
Bowmans Ms, E1	.21	H5
N7 off Seven Sisters Rd	.92/93	E3
Bowmans Pl, N7		
off Holloway Rd	.92/93	E3
Bowman's Trd Est, NW9		
off Westmoreland Rd	.69	J3
Bowmead, SE9	.174	C2
Bowmore Wk, NW1		
off St. Paul's Cres	.92	D7
Bowness Cl, E8		
off Beechwood Rd	.94	C6
Bowness Cres, SW15	.164	E5
Bowness Dr, Houns. TW4	.143	E4
Bowness Rd, SE6	.154	B7
Bexleyheath DA7	.159	H2
Bowood Rd, SW11	.150	A4
Enfield EN3	.45	G2
Bowring Grn, Wat. WD19	.50	C5
Bow Rd, E3	.113	J3
Bowrons Av, Wem. HA0	.87	G7
Bowsley Ct, Felt. TW13		
off Highfield Rd	.160	A1
Bowsprit Pt, E14	.134	A3
Bow St, E15	.96	E5
WC2	.18	B4
Bowyer Cl, E6	.116	C5
Bowyer Pl, SE5	.36	A7
Bowyer St, SE5	.35	J7
Boxall Rd, SE21	.152	B6
Box La, Bark. IG11	.118	B2
Boxley Rd, Mord. SM4	.185	F4
Boxley St, E16	.135	H1
Boxmoor Rd, Har. HA3	.68	E4
Boxoll Rd, Dag. RM9	.101	F4
Boxted Cl, Buck.H. IG9	.64	B1
Boxtree La, Har. HA3	.67	J1
Boxtree Rd, Har. HA3	.52	A7
Boxwood Cl, West Dr. UB7		
off Hawthorne Cres	.120	C2
Boxworth Cl, N12	.57	G5
Boxworth Gro, N1		
off Richmond Av	.111	F1
Boyard Rd, SE18	.136	E5
Boyce St, SE1	.26	D2
Boyce Way, E13	.115	G4
Boycroft Av, NW9	.70	C6
Boyd Av, Sthl. UB1	.123	F1
Boyd Cl, Kings.T. KT2		
off Crescent Rd	.164	A7
Boydell Ct, NW8		
off St. John's Wd Pk	.91	G7
Boyd Rd, SW19	.167	G6
Boyd St, E1	.21	H4
Boyfield St, SE1	.27	H4
Boyland Rd, Brom. BR1	.173	F5
Boyle Av, Stan. HA7	.52	D6
Boyle Fm Island, T.Ditt. KT7	.180	D6
Boyle Fm Rd, T.Ditt. KT7	.180	D6
Boyle St, W1	.17	F5
Boyne Av, NW4	.72	A4
Boyne Rd, SE13	.154	C3
Dagenham RM10	.101	G3
Boyne Ter Ms, W11	.128	C1
Boyseland Ct, Edg. HA8	.54	C2
Boyson Rd, SE17	.36	B5
Boyton Cl, E1 off Stayner's Rd	.113	G4
N8	.75	E3
Boyton Rd, N8	.75	E3
Brabant Ct, EC3	.20	D5
Brabant Rd, N22	.75	F2
Brabazon Av, Wall. SM6	.200	E7
Brabazon Rd, Houns. TW5	.122	C7
Northolt UB5	.103	G2
Brabazon St, E14	.114	B6
Brabourne Cl, SE19	.170	B5
Brabourne Cres, Bexh. DA7	.139	F6
Brabourne Hts, NW7	.55	E3
Brabourne Ri, Beck. BR3	.190	C5
Brabourn Gro, SE15	.153	F2
Bracewell Av, Grnf. UB6	.86	C5
Bracewell Rd, W10	.107	J5
Bracewood Gdns, Croy. CR0	.202	C3
Bracey Ms, N4 off Bracey St	.92/93	E2
Bracey St, N4	.93	E2
Bracken, The, E4 off Hortus Rd	.62	C2
Bracken Av, SW12	.150	A6
Croydon CR0	.204	B3
Brackenbridge Dr, Ruis. HA4	.84	D3
Brackenbury Gdns, W6	.127	H3
Brackenbury Rd, N2	.73	F3
W6	.127	H3
Bracken Cl, E6	.116	C5
Borehamwood WD6	.38	B1
Twickenham TW2		
off Hedley Rd	.143	G7
Brackendale, N21	.59	F2
Brackendale Cl, Houns. TW3	.143	H1
Bracken Dr, Chig. IG7	.65	G6
Bracken End, Islw. TW7	.144	A5
Brackenfield Cl, E5		
off Tiger Way	.94/95	E4
Bracken Gdns, SW13	.147	G2
Bracken Hill Cl, Brom. BR1		
off Bracken Hill La	.191	F1
Bracken Hill La, Brom. BR1	.191	F1
Bracken Ind Est, Ilf. IG6	.65	J7
Bracken Ms, E4 off Hortus Rd	.62	C2
Romford RM7	.83	G6
Brackens, The, Enf. EN1	.44	B7
Brackenwood, Sun. TW16	.178	A1
Brackley Av, SE15		
off Linden Gro	.152	D3
Brackley Cl, Wall. SM6	.201	E7
Brackley Rd, W4	.127	E5
Beckenham BR3	.171	J7
Brackley Sq, Wdf.Grn. IG8	.64	A7
Brackley St, EC1	.19	J1
Brackley Ter, W4	.127	E5
Bracklyn Cl, N1	.12	B1
Bracklyn Ct, N1	.12	B1
Bracklyn St, N1	.12	B1
Bracknell Cl, N22	.75	G1
Bracknell Gdns, NW3	.90	E4
Bracknell Gate, NW3	.90	E5
Bracknell Way, NW3	.90	E4
Bracondale Rd, SE2	.138	A4
Bradbourne Rd, Bex. DA5	.159	G7
Bradbourne St, SW6	.148	D2
Bradbury Cl, Borwd. WD6	.38	B1
Southall UB2	.123	F4
Bradbury Ms, N16		
off Bradbury St	.94	B5
Bradbury St, N16	.94	B5
Braddock Cl, Islw. TW7	.144	C3
Braddon Rd, Rich. TW9	.145	J3
Braddyll St, SE10	.134	E5
Bradenham Av, Well. DA16	.158	A4
Bradenham Cl, SE17	.36	B5
Bradenham Rd, Har. HA3	.68	E4
Braden St, W9	.6	A6
Bradfield Dr, Bark. IG11	.100	A5
Bradfield Rd, E16	.135	G2
Ruislip HA4	.85	E5
Bradford Cl, N17		
off Commercial Rd	.60	B6
SE26 off Coombe Rd	.170/171	E4
Bromley BR2	.206	C1
Bradford Dr, Epsom KT19	.197	F6
Bradford Rd, W3		
off Warple Way	.126/127	E2
Ilford IG1	.99	G1
Bradgate Rd, SE6	.154	A6
Brading Cres, E11	.97	H2
Brading Rd, SW2	.151	F7
Croydon CR0	.187	F6
Brading Ter, W12	.127	H3
Bradiston Rd, W9	.108	C3
Bradley Cl, N1	.11	H1
N7 off Sutterton St	.93	F6
Bradley Gdns, W13	.104	E6
Bradley Ms, SW17		
off Bellevue Rd	.167	J1
Bradley Rd, N22	.75	F2
SE19	.169	J6
Bradley Stone Rd, E6	.116	C5
Bradman Row, Edg. HA8		
off Pavilion Way	.54	C7
Bradmead, SW8	.130	B7
Bradmore Pk Rd, W6	.127	H3
Bradshaw Cl, SW19	.166	D6
Bradshaw Dr, NW7	.56	A7
Bradshaws, SE25	.188	D3
Bradstock Rd, E9	.95	G6
Epsom KT17	.197	G5
Brad St, SE1	.27	F2
Bradwell Av, Dag. RM10	.101	G2
Bradwell Cl, E18	.79	F4
Bradwell Ms, N18		
off Lyndhurst Rd	.60	D4
Bradwell Rd, Buck.H. IG9	.64	B1
Bradwell St, E1	.113	G3
Brady Av, Loug. IG10	.49	F2
Bradymead, E6	.116	D6
Brady St, E1	.112	E4
Braemar Av, N22	.75	E1
NW10	.88	D3
SW19	.166	D2
Bexleyheath DA7	.159	J4
Thornton Heath CR7	.187	G3
Wembley HA0	.87	G3
Braemar Cl, SE16		
off Masters Dr	.132/133	E5
Braemar Gdns, NW9	.70	D1
Sidcup DA15	.175	G3
West Wickham BR4	.204	C1
Braemar Rd, E13	.115	F4
N15	.76	B5
Brentford TW8	.125	H6
Worcester Park KT4	.197	H3
Braeside, Beck. BR3	.172	A5
Braeside Av, SW19	.184	B1
Braeside Cl, Pnr. HA5		
off The Avenue	.51	G7
Braeside Cres, Bexh. DA7	.159	J4
Braeside Rd, SW16	.168	C7
Braes St, N1	.93	H7
Braesyde Cl, Belv. DA17	.139	F4
Brafferton Rd, Croy. CR0	.201	J4
Braganza St, SE17	.35	G3
Bragg Cl, Dag. RM8		
off Porters Av	.100	B6
Braham St, E1	.21	G4
Braid Av, W3	.106	E6
Braid Cl, Felt. TW13	.161	F2
Braid Ct, W4 off Lawford Rd	.126	C7
Braidwood Pas, EC1		
off Aldersgate St	.111	J5
Braidwood Rd, SE6	.172	D1
Braidwood St, SE1	.28	D2
Brailsford Cl, Mitch. CR4	.167	H7
Brailsford Rd, SW2	.151	G5
Brainton Av, Felt. TW14	.142	B7
Braintree Av, Ilf. IG4	.80	B4
Braintree Ind Est, Ruis. HA4	.84	B4
Braintree Rd, Dag. RM10	.101	G3
Ruislip HA4	.84	B4
Braintree St, E2	.113	F3
Braithwaite Av, Rom. RM7	.83	G7
Braithwaite Gdns, Stan. HA7	.69	F1
Braithwaite Ho, EC1		
off Bunhill Row	.112	A4
Braithwaite Rd, Enf. EN3	.45	J3
Braithwaite Twr, W2	.15	E1
Bramah Grn, SW9	.151	G1
★ Bramah Mus, SE1	.28	A2
Bramalea Cl, N6	.74	A6
Bramall Cl, E15 off Idmiston Rd	.97	F5
Bramber Ct, Brent. TW8		
off Sterling Pl	.125	H4
Bramber Ho, Kings.T. KT2		
off Kingsgate Rd	.181	H1
Bramber Rd, N12	.57	H5
W14	.128	C6
Brambleacres Cl, Sutt. SM2	.198	D7
Bramblebury Rd, SE18	.137	F5
Bramble Cl, N15 off Broad La	.76	D4
Beckenham BR3	.190	C5
Chigwell IG7 off High Rd	.65	F1
Croydon CR0	.204	A4
Stanmore HA7	.53	G7
Bramble Cft, Erith DA8	.139	J4
Brambledown Rd, Cars. SM5	.200	A7
South Croydon CR2	.202	B7
Wallington SM6	.200	B7
Bramble Gdns, W12		
off Wallflower St	.107	F7
Bramble La, Hmptn. TW12	.161	F6
Brambles, The, Chig. IG7		
off Clayside	.65	F5
West Drayton UB7	.120	B4
Brambles Cl, Islw. TW7	.124	E7
Bramblewood Cl, Cars. SM5	.199	H1
Bramblings, The, E4	.62	D4
Bramcote Av, Mitch. CR4	.185	J4
Bramcote Ct, Mitch. CR4		
off Bramcote Av	.185	J4
Bramcote Gro, SE16	.133	F5
Bramcote Rd, SW15	.147	H4
Bramdean Cres, SE12	.173	G1
Bramdean Gdns, SE12	.173	G1
Bramerton Rd, Beck. BR3	.189	J3
Bramerton St, SW3	.31	G5
Bramfield Ct, N4 off Queens Dr	.93	J2
Bramfield Rd, SW11	.149	H6
Bramford Ct, N14	.58	D2
Bramford Rd, SW18	.149	F4
Bramham Gdns, SW5	.30	A3
Chessington KT9	.195	G4
Bramhope La, SE7	.135	H6
Bramlands Cl, SW11	.149	H3
Bramley Cl, E17	.77	H2
N14	.42	B5
Hayes UB3	.102	A7
Orpington BR6	.207	E1
South Croydon CR2	.201	H5
Twickenham TW2	.143	J6
Woodford Green IG8		
off Orsett Ter	.63	J7
Bramley Ct, Well. DA16	.158	B1
Bramley Cres, SW8	.33	J7
Ilford IG2	.80	C6
Bramley Gdns, Wat. WD19	.50	C5
Bramley Hill, S.Croy. CR2	.201	H5
Bramley Ho, SW15		
off Tunworth Cres	.147	F6
Bramley Rd, N14	.42	B5
W5	.125	F3
W10	.108	A7
Sutton SM1	.199	G5
Bramley Way, Houns. TW4	.143	F5
West Wickham BR4	.204	B2
Brampton Cl, E5	.95	E2
Brampton Gdns, N15		
off Brampton Rd	.75	J5
Brampton Gro, NW4	.71	J4
Harrow HA3	.68	D4
Wembley HA9	.88	A1
Brampton La, NW4	.71	J4
Brampton Pk Rd, N22	.75	G3
Brampton Rd, E6	.116	A3
N15	.75	J5
NW9	.70	A4
SE2	.138	C6
Bexleyheath DA7	.138	D7
Croydon CR0	.188	C7
Watford WD19	.50	A3
Bramshaw Gdns, Wat. WD19	.50	D5
Bramshaw Ri, N.Mal. KT3	.183	E6
Bramshaw Rd, E9	.95	G6
Bramshill Cl, Chig. IG7		
off Tine Rd	.65	H5
Bramshill Gdns, NW5	.92	B3
Bramshill Rd, NW10	.107	F2
Bramshot Av, SE7	.135	G6
Bramshot Way, Wat. WD19	.50	A2
Bramston Cl, Ilf. IG6	.65	J6
Bramston Rd, NW10	.107	G2
SW17	.167	F3
Bramwell Cl, Sun. TW16	.178	D2
Bramwell Ms, N1	.111	F1
Brancaster Dr, NW7	.55	F7
Brancaster Pl, Loug. IG10	.48	C3
Brancaster Rd, E12	.98	C4
SW16	.168	E3
Ilford IG2	.81	G6
Brancepeth Gdns, Buck.H. IG9	.63	G2
Branch Hill, NW3	.91	F3
Branch Pl, N1	.112	A1
Branch Rd, E14	.113	H7
Branch St, SE15	.132	B7
Brancker Cl, Wall. SM6		
off Brown Cl	.200/201	E7
Brancker Rd, Har. HA3	.69	G3
Brancroft Way, Enf. EN3	.45	H1
Brand Cl, N4	.93	H1
Brandesbury Sq, Wdf.Grn. IG8	.64	C7
Brandlehow Rd, SW15	.148	C4
Brandon Est, SE17	.35	H6
Brandon Ms, EC2		
off The Barbican	.111	J5
Brandon Rd, E17	.78	C3
N7	.92	E7
Southall UB2	.123	F5
Sutton SM1	.198	E4
Brandon St, SE17	.35	J2
Brandram Ms, SE13		
off Brandram Rd	.154/155	E3
Brandram Rd, SE13	.154	E3
Brandreth Rd, E6	.116	C6
SW17	.168	B2
Brandries, The, Wall. SM6	.200	D3
Brand St, SE10	.134	C7
Brandville Gdns, Ilf. IG6	.81	E4
Brandville Rd, West Dr. UB7	.120	B2
Brandy Way, Sutt. SM2	.198	D7
Brangbourne Rd, Brom. BR1	.172	C5
Brangton Rd, SE11	.34	D4
Brangwyn Cres, SW19	.185	G1
Branksea St, SW6	.128	B7
Branksome Av, N18	.60	C5
Branksome Cl, Tedd. TW11	.162	A4
Branksome Rd, SW2	.151	E5
SW19	.184	D1
Branksome Way, Har. HA3	.69	H6
New Malden KT3	.182	C1
Bransby Rd, Chess. KT9	.195	H6
Branscombe Gdns, N21	.43	G7

Branscombe St, SE13 . . . . .154 B3
Bransdale CI, NW6
  off West End La 108/109 E1
Bransgrove Rd, Edg. HA8 . . . .69 J1
Branston Cres, Orp. BR5 . . . .207 G1
Branstone Rd, Rich. TW9 . . . .145 J1
Brants Wk, W7 . . . . .104 B4
Brantwood Av, Erith DA8 . . . .139 J7
  Isleworth TW7 . . . . .144 D4
Brantwood CI, E17 . . . . .78 B3
Brantwood Gdns, Enf. EN2 . . .42 E4
  Ilford IG4 . . . . .80 B4
Brantwood Rd, N17 . . . . .60 C6
  SE24 . . . . .151 J5
  Bexleyheath DA7 . . . . . . .159 H2
Brasenose Dr, SW13 . . . . . . .127 J6
Brasher CI, Grnf. UB6 . . . . . . .86 A5
Brassett Pt, E15 . . . . .114 E1
Brassey CI, Felt. TW14 . . . . . .160 A1
Brassey Rd, NW6 . . . . .90 C6
Brassey Sq, SW11 . . . . .150 A3
Brassie Av, W3 . . . . .106 E6
Brass Tally All, SE16
  off Middleton Dr 133 G2
Brasted CI, SE26 . . . . .171 F4
  Bexleyheath DA6 . . . . . . .158 D5
Brathway Rd, SW18 . . . . . . .148 D7
Bratley St, E1 . . . . .13 H6
Braund Av, Grnf. UB6 . . . . . .103 H4
Braundton Av, Sid. DA15 . . . .175 J1
Braunston Dr, Hayes UB4 . . .102 E4
Bravington PI, W9
  off Bravington Rd 108 C4
Bravington Rd, W9 . . . . .108 C2
Bravingtons Wk, N1
  off Pentonville Rd 110 E2
Brawne Ho, SE17 . . . . .35 G6
Braxfield Rd, SE4 . . . . .153 H4
Braxted Pk, SW16 . . . . .169 F6
Bray, NW3 . . . . .91 H7
Brayards Rd, SE15 . . . . .152 E2
Braybourne Dr, Islw. TW7 . . .124 C7
Braybrooke Gdns, SE19
  off Fox Hill 170 C7
Braybrook St, W12 . . . . .107 F5
Brayburne Av, SW4 . . . . . . .150 C2
Bray CI, Borwd. WD6 . . . . . . .38 C1
Braycourt Av, Walt. KT12 . . . .178 B7
Bray Cres, SE16
  off Marlow Way 133 G2
Braydon Rd, N16 . . . . .94 C1
Bray Dr, E16 . . . . .115 F7
Brayfield Ter, N1 off Lofting Rd .93 G7
Brayford Sq, E1
  off Summercourt Rd 113 F6
Bray Pas, E16 . . . . .115 G7
Bray PI, SW3 . . . . .31 J2
Bray Rd, NW7 . . . . .56 A6
Brayton Gdns, Enf. EN2 . . . . .42 D4
Braywood Rd, SE9 . . . . .157 G4
Brazil CI, Croy. (Bedd.) CR0 . .186 E7
Breach La, Dag. RM9 . . . . . .119 G3
Bread St, EC4 . . . . .20 A4
Breakspears Ms, SE4
  off Breakspears Rd 154 A2
Breakspears Rd, SE4 . . . . . .153 J3
Bream CI, N17 . . . . .77 E4
Bream Gdns, E6 . . . . .116 D3
Breamore CI, SW15 . . . . . . .165 G1
Breamore Rd, Ilf. IG3 . . . . . . .99 J2
Bream's Bldgs, EC4 . . . . .18 E3
Bream St, E3 . . . . .96 A7
Breamwater Gdns, Rich. TW10 .163 E3
Brearley CI, Edg. HA8
  off Pavilion Way 54 C7
Breasley CI, SW15 . . . . .147 H4
Brechin PI, SW7 . . . . .30 D2
Brecknock Rd, N7 . . . . .92 C4
  N19 . . . . .92 C4
Brecknock Rd Est, N7 . . . . . . .92 C4
Breckonmead, Brom. BR1
  off Wanstead Rd 191 J2
Brecon CI, Mitch. CR4 . . . . . .186 E3
  Worcester Park KT4 . . . . . .197 J2
Brecon Grn, NW9
  off Goldsmith Av 70/71 E6
  Enfield EN3 . . . . .45 F4
Brede CI, E6 . . . . .116 D3
Bredgar, SE13 . . . . .154 C5
Bredgar Rd, N19 . . . . .92 C2
Bredhurst CI, SE20 . . . . .171 F6
Bredon Rd, Croy. CR0 . . . . . .188 C7
Breer St, SW6 . . . . .148 E3
Breezers Hill, E1 . . . . .21 H6
Brember Rd, Har. HA2 . . . . . . .85 J2
Bremer Ms, E17 off Church La .78 B4
Bremner Rd, SW7 . . . . .22 D4
Brenchley CI, Brom. BR2 . . . .191 F6
  Chislehurst BR7 . . . . .192 D1
Brenchley Gdns, SE23 . . . . . .153 F6
Brenchley Rd, Orp. BR5 . . . .193 J1
Brenda Rd, SW17 . . . . .167 J2
Brende Gdns, W.Mol. KT8 . . .179 H4
Brendon Av, NW10 . . . . .89 E4
Brendon CI, Hayes UB3 . . . . .121 F7
Brendon Gdns, Har. HA2 . . . . .85 H4

Brendon Gdns, Ilf. IG2 . . . . . .81 H5
Brendon Gro, N2 . . . . .73 F2
Brendon Rd, SE9 . . . . .175 G2
  Dagenham RM8 . . . . .101 F1
Brendon St, W1 . . . . .15 H3
Brendon Way, Enf. EN1 . . . . . .44 B7
Brenley CI, Mitch. CR4 . . . . . .186 A3
Brenley Gdns, SE9 . . . . .156 A4
Brent CI, Bex. DA5 . . . . .177 E1
Brentcot CI, W13 . . . . .104 E4
Brent Cres, NW10 . . . . .105 J2
Brent Cross Gdns, NW4
  off Haley Rd 72 A6
Brent Cross Shop Cen, NW4 . .71 J7
Brentfield, NW10 . . . . .88 B7
Brentfield CI, NW10
  off Normans Mead 88 D6
Brentfield Gdns, NW2
  off Hendon Way 72 A7
Brentfield Rd, NW10 . . . . .88 D6
BRENTFORD, TW8 . . . . .125 G6
Brentford Business Cen, Brent.
  TW8 . . . . .125 F7
Brentford CI, Hayes UB4 . . . .102 D4
Brent Gm, NW4 . . . . .71 J5
Brent Gm Wk, Wem. HA9 . . . .88 C3
Brentham Way, W5 . . . . .105 G4
Brenthouse Rd, E9 . . . . .95 E7
Brenthurst Rd, NW10 . . . . . . .89 F5
Brent Lea, Brent. TW8 . . . . . .125 F7
Brentmead CI, W7 . . . . .104 B7
Brentmead Gdns, NW10 . . . .105 J2
Brentmead PI, NW11
  off North Circular Rd 72 A6
Brenton St, E14 . . . . .113 H6
Brent Pk, NW10 . . . . .88 D5
Brent Pk Rd, NW4 . . . . .71 H7
  NW9 . . . . .89 G1
Brent PI, Barn. EN5 . . . . .40 D5
Brent Rd, E16 . . . . .115 G5
  SE18 . . . . .136 E7
  Brentford TW8 . . . . .125 F6
  Southall UB2 . . . . .122 C3
Brent Side, Brent. TW8 . . . . .125 F6
Brentside CI, W13 . . . . .104 D4
Brentside Executive Cen, Brent.
  TW8 . . . . .125 E6
Brent St, NW4 . . . . .71 J4
Brent Ter, NW2 . . . . .89 J2
Brentvale Av, Sthl. UB1 . . . . .124 A1
  Wembley HA0 . . . . .88 J1
Brent Vw Rd, NW9 . . . . .71 G7
Brent Way, N3 . . . . .56 D6
  Brentford TW8 . . . . .125 G7
  Wembley HA9 . . . . .88 B6
Brentwick Gdns, Brent. TW8 . .125 H4
Brentwood CI, SE9 . . . . .175 F1
Brentwood Ho, SE18
  off Shooter's Hill Rd 136 A7
Brereton Rd, N17 . . . . .60 C7
Bressenden PI, SW1 . . . . .25 E5
Bressey Av, Enf. EN1 . . . . . . .44 D1
Bressey Gro, E18 . . . . .79 F2
Brett CI, N16 off Yoakley Rd . .94 B2
  Northolt UB5
  off Broomcroft Av 102 D3
Brett Ct, N9 . . . . .61 F2
Brett Cres, NW10 . . . . .88 D7
Brettell St, SE17 . . . . .36 C4
Brettenham Av, E17 . . . . .78 A1
Brettenham Rd, E17 . . . . .78 A2
  N18 . . . . .60 E4
Brett Gdns, Dag. RM9 . . . . . .100 E7
Brett Ho CI, SW15
  off Putney Heath La 148 A6
Brett Pas, E8
  off Kenmure Rd 94/95 E5
Brett Rd, E8 . . . . .95 E5
  Barnet EN5 . . . . .39 J5
Brewer's Grn, SW1 . . . . .25 H5
Brewers Hall Gdns, EC2 . . . . .20 A2
Brewers La, Rich. TW9 . . . . . .145 G5
Brewer St, W1 . . . . .17 G5
★ Brewery, The, EC1 . . . . . . .20 A1
Brewery CI, Wem. HA0 . . . . . .86 D5
Brewery La, Twick. TW1 . . . . .144 C7
Brewery Rd, N7 . . . . .92 E7
  SE18 . . . . .137 G5
  Bromley BR2 . . . . .206 B1
Brewery Sq, EC1 . . . . .11 H5
  SE1 off Horselydown La . . .132 C1
Brewhouse La, E1 . . . . .133 E1
  SW15 . . . . .148 B3
Brewhouse Rd, SE18 . . . . . . .136 C4
Brewhouse Wk, SE16 . . . . . .133 H1
Brewhouse Yd, EC1 . . . . .11 H5
Brewood Rd, Dag. RM8 . . . . .100 B6
Brewster Gdns, W10 . . . . . . .107 J5
Brewster Ho, E14 . . . . .113 J7
Brewster Rd, E10 . . . . .96 B1
Brian Rd, Rom. RM6 . . . . .82 C5
Briants CI, Pnr. HA5 . . . . .67 F2
Briant St, SE14 . . . . .153 G1
Briar Av, SW16 . . . . .169 F7
Briarbank Rd, W13 . . . . .104 D6
Briar CI, N2 . . . . .73 E3

Briar CI, N13 . . . . .59 J3
  Buckhurst Hill IG9 . . . . .64 A2
  Hampton TW12 . . . . .161 F5
  Isleworth TW7 . . . . .144 C5
Briar Ct, Sutt. SM3 . . . . .197 J4
Briar Cres, Nthlt. UB5 . . . . . . .85 H6
Briardale Gdns, NW3 . . . . . . .90 D3
Briarfield Av, N3 . . . . .72 E2
Briarfield CI, Bexh. DA7
  off Palmar Rd 159 G2
Briar Gdns, Brom. BR2 . . . . .205 F1
Briaris CI, N17 . . . . .60 E7
Briar La, Croy. CR0 . . . . .204 B4
Briar Pas, SW16 . . . . .187 E3
Briar PI, SW16 . . . . .187 F3
Briar Rd, NW2 . . . . .89 J4
  SW16 . . . . .187 E3
  Harrow HA3 . . . . .69 F5
  Twickenham TW2 . . . . .162 B1
Briarswood Way, Orp. BR6 . . .207 J5
Briar Wk, SW15 . . . . .147 H4
  W10 off Droop St 108 B4
  Edgware HA8 . . . . .54 C7
Briar Way, West Dr. UB7 . . . .120 D2
Briarwood CI, NW9 . . . . .70 C6
Briarwood Dr, Nthwd. HA6 . . . .66 A2
Briarwood Rd, SW4 . . . . .150 D5
  Epsom KT17 . . . . .197 G3
Briary CI, NW3 off Fellows Rd . .91 H7
Briary Ct, E16 off Turner St . . .115 F6
  Sidcup DA14 . . . . .176 B5
Briary Gdns, Brom. BR1 . . . . .173 H5
Briary Gro, Edg. HA8 . . . . . . .70 B2
Briary La, N9 . . . . .60 C3
Brick Ct, EC4 . . . . .18 E4
Brick Fm CI, Rich. TW9 . . . . .146 B1
Brickfield CI, Brent. TW8 . . . .125 F7
Brickfield Cotts, SE18 . . . . . .137 J6
Brickfield Fm Gdns, Orp. BR6 .207 F4
Brickfield La, Barn. EN5 . . . . . .39 F6
  Hayes UB3 . . . . .121 G6
Brickfield Rd, SW19 . . . . . . .167 E4
  Thornton Heath CR7 . . . . .187 H1
Brickfields, Har. HA2 . . . . .86 A2
Brickfields Way, West Dr. UB7 .120 C3
Brick La, E1 . . . . .13 G5
  E2 . . . . .13 G4
  Enfield EN1, EN3 . . . . .44 E2
  Stanmore HA7
  off Honeypot La 53 G7
Bricklayer's Arms Distribution Cen,
  SE1 . . . . .36 E2
Bricklayer's Arms Roundabout,
  SE1 . . . . .36 B1
Brick St, W1 . . . . .24 D2
Brickwood CI, SE26 . . . . .171 E3
Brickwood Rd, Croy. CR0 . . . .202 B2
Brideale CI, SE15 . . . . .37 G6
Bride Ct, EC4 . . . . .19 G4
Bride La, EC4 . . . . .19 G4
Bridel Ms, N1
  off Colebrooke Row 111 H1
Brides PI, N1
  off De Beauvoir Rd 94 B7
Bride St, N7 . . . . .93 F6
Bridewain St, SE1 . . . . .29 F5
Bridewell PI, E1
  off Brewhouse La 132/133 E1
  EC4 . . . . .19 G4
Bridford Ms, W1 . . . . .16 E1
Bridge, The, Har. HA3 . . . . . . .68 B3
Bridge App, NW1 . . . . .92 A7
Bridge Av, W6 . . . . .127 J5
  W7 . . . . .104 A5
Bridge CI, W10
  off Kingsdown CI 108 A6
  Enfield EN1 . . . . .45 E1
  Teddington TW11
  off Shacklegate La 162 C4
Bridge Ct, E14 off Newport Av .114 D7
Bridge Dr, N13 . . . . .59 F4
Bridge End, E17 . . . . .78 C1
Bridgefield Rd, Sutt. SM1 . . . .198 D6
Bridgefoot, SE1 . . . . .34 A4
Bridge Gdns, N16
  off Green Las 94 A4
  East Molesey KT8 . . . . . . .180 A4
Bridge Gate, N21 off Ridge Av .43 J7
Bridge Ho Quay, E14
  off Prestons Rd 134 C1
Bridgeland Rd, E16 . . . . .115 G7
Bridge La, NW11 . . . . .72 B5
  SW11 . . . . .149 H1
Bridgeman Rd, N1 . . . . .93 F7
  Teddington TW11 . . . . .162 D6
Bridgeman St, NW8 . . . . .7 G2
Bridge Meadows, SE14 . . . . .133 G6
Bridgend Rd, SW18 . . . . .149 F4
Bridgenhall Rd, Enf. EN1 . . . . .44 C1
Bridgen Rd, Bex. DA5 . . . . . .158 E6
Bridge Pk, SW18 . . . . .148 D5
Bridge PI, SW1 . . . . .33 E1
  Croydon CR0 . . . . .188 A7
Bridgeport PI, E1 . . . . .29 J1
Bridge Rd, E6 . . . . .98 C7
  E15 . . . . .96 D7
  E17 . . . . .77 J7

Bridge Rd, N9 off The Broadway .60 D3
  N22 . . . . .74 E1
  NW10 . . . . .88 E6
  Beckenham BR3 . . . . .171 J7
  Bexleyheath DA7 . . . . .159 E2
  Chessington KT9 . . . . .195 H5
  East Molesey KT8 . . . . . . .180 B4
  Hounslow TW3 . . . . .144 A3
  Isleworth TW7 . . . . .144 A3
  Southall UB2 . . . . .123 F2
  Sutton SM2 . . . . .199 E6
  Twickenham TW1 . . . . .144 E6
  Wallington SM6 . . . . .200 C5
  Wembley HA9 . . . . .88 A3
Bridge Row, Croy. CR0
  off Cross Rd 202 A1
Bridges Ct, SW11 . . . . .149 G3
Bridges La, Croy. CR0 . . . . . .200 E4
Bridges PI, SW6 . . . . .148 C1
Bridges Rd, SW19 . . . . .166 E6
  Stanmore HA7 . . . . .52 C5
Bridges Rd Ms, SW19
  off Bridges Rd 166/167 E6
Bridge St, SW1 . . . . .26 A4
  W4 . . . . .126 D4
  Pinner HA5 . . . . .66 D3
  Richmond TW9 . . . . .145 G5
Bridge Ter, E15 off Bridge Rd . .96 D7
  SE13 off Mercator Rd 154 D4
Bridgetown CI, SE19
  off St. Kitts Ter 170 B5
Bridge Vw, W6 . . . . .127 J5
Bridgeview Ct, Ilf. IG6 . . . . . . .65 G6
Bridgewater CI, Chis. BR7 . . . .193 H3
Bridgewater Gdns, Edg. HA8 . .69 J2
Bridgewater Rd, Ruis. HA4 . . . .84 A4
  Wembley HA0 . . . . .87 F7
Bridgewater Sq, EC2 . . . . .19 J1
Bridgewater St, EC2 . . . . .19 J1
Bridge Way, N11
  off Pymmes Grn Rd 58 C3
  NW11 . . . . .72 C5
Bridgeway, Bark. IG11 . . . . . . .99 J7
Bridge Way, Twick. TW2 . . . . .143 J7
Bridgeway, Wem. HA0 . . . . . . .87 H7
Bridgeway St, NW1 . . . . .9 H2
Bridge Wf Rd, Islw. TW7
  off Church St 144/145 E3
Bridgewood CI, SE20 . . . . . . .170 E7
Bridgewood Rd, SW16 . . . . . .168 D7
  Worcester Park KT4 . . . . . .197 G4
Bridge Yd, SE1 . . . . .28 C1
Bridgford St, SW18 . . . . .167 F3
Bridgman Rd, W4 . . . . .126 C3
Bridgwater Rd, E15 . . . . .114 C1
Bridle CI, Epsom KT19 . . . . . .196 C6
  Kingston upon Thames KT1 . .181 G4
  Sunbury-on-Thames TW16
  off Forge La 178 A3
Bridle La, W1 . . . . .17 G5
  Twickenham TW1
  off Crown Rd 144/145 E6
Bridle Path, Croy. CR0 . . . . . .201 F3
Bridle Path, The, Wdf.Grn. IG8 . .62 E1
Bridle Rd, Croy. CR0 . . . . . . .204 A3
  Esher (Clay.) KT10 . . . . . . .194 E6
  Pinner HA5 . . . . .66 C6
Bridle Way, Croy. CR0 . . . . . .204 A5
  Orpington BR6 . . . . .207 F4
Bridle Way, The, Wall. SM6 . . .200 C4
Bridlington Rd, N9 . . . . .44 E7
  Watford WD19 . . . . .50 D3
Bridport Av, Rom. RM7 . . . . . .83 H6
Bridport PI, N1 . . . . .12 C1
Bridport Rd, N18 . . . . .60 B5
  Greenford UB6 . . . . .103 H1
  Thornton Heath CR7 . . . . .187 G3
Bridport Ter, SW8
  off Wandsworth Rd 150 D1
Bridstow PI, W2 off Talbot Rd . .108 D6
Brief St, SE5 . . . . .151 H1
Brierley, Croy. (New Adgtn)
  CR0 . . . . .204 B6
Brierley Av, N9 . . . . .61 F1
Brierley CI, SE25 . . . . .188 D4
Brierley Rd, E11 . . . . .96 D4
  SW12 . . . . .168 C2
Brierly Gdns, E2
  off Royston St 113 F2
Brigade CI, Har. HA2 . . . . .86 A2
Brigade St, SE3 off Royal Par . .155 F2
Brigadier Av, Enf. EN2 . . . . . . .43 J1
Briggeford CI, E5
  off Geldeston Rd 94 D2
Briggs CI, Mitch. CR4 . . . . . . .186 B1
Bright CI, Belv. DA17 . . . . . . .138 D4
Brightfield Rd, SE12 . . . . .155 F5
Brightling Rd, SE4 . . . . .153 J6
Brightlingsea PI, E14 . . . . . . .113 J7
Brightman Rd, SW18 . . . . . . .167 G1
Brighton Av, E17 . . . . .77 J5
Brighton Dr, Nthlt. UB5 . . . . . .85 G6
Brighton Gro, SE14
  off Harts La 153 H1
Brighton Rd, E6 . . . . .116 D3
  N2 . . . . .73 F2
  N16 . . . . .94 B4

Brighton Rd, S.Croy. CR2 . . . . .201 J5
Surbiton KT6 . . . . .181 F6
Brighton Ter, SW9 . . . . .151 F4
Brightside, The, Enf. EN3 . . . . . . .45 G1
Brightside Rd, SE13 . . . . .154 D6
Bright St, E14 . . . . .114 B6
Brightwell Cl, Croy. CR0
off Sumner Rd 201 G1
Brightwell Cres, SW17 . . . . .167 J5
Brig Ms, SE8 off Watergate St . . .134 A6
Brigstock Rd, Belv. DA17 . . . . . .139 H4
Thornton Heath CR7 . . . . .187 G5
Brill Pl, NW1 . . . . .9 J2
Brim Hill, N2 . . . . .73 F4
Brimpsfield Cl, SE2 . . . . .138 B3
BRIMSDOWN, Enf. EN3 . . . . .45 H2
Brimsdown Av, Enf. EN3 . . . . .45 H2
Brimsdown Ind Est, Enf. EN3 . . . .45 J2
Brindle Gate, Sid. DA15 . . . . . . .175 H1
Brindley Cl, Bexh. DA7 . . . . .159 H3
Wembley HA0 . . . . .105 F1
Brindley Ho, SW2
off New Pk Rd 150/151 E7
Brindley St, SE14 . . . . .153 J1
Brindley Way, Brom. BR1 . . . . . . .173 G5
Southall UB1 . . . . .103 H7
Brindwood Rd, E4 . . . . .61 J3
Brinkburn Cl, SE2 . . . . .138 A4
Edgware HA8 . . . . .70 B2
Brinkburn Gdns, Edg. HA8 . . . . . .70 A3
Brinkley, Kings.T. KT1
off Burritt Rd 182 A2
Brinkley Rd, Wor.Pk. KT4 . . . . . .197 J2
Brinklow Cres, SE18 . . . . .137 E7
Brinklow Ho, W2 . . . . .14 A1
Brinkworth Rd, Ilf. IG5 . . . . .80 B3
Brinkworth Way, E9 . . . . .95 J6
Brinsdale Rd, NW4 . . . . .72 A4
Brinsley Rd, Har. HA3 . . . . .68 A2
Brinsley St, E1
off Watney St 112/113 E6
Brinsworth Cl, Twick. TW2 . . . . . .162 A2
Brinton Wk, SE1 . . . . .27 G2
Brion Pl, E14 . . . . .114 C5
Brisbane Av, SW19 . . . . .184 E1
Brisbane Ct, N10 off Sydney Rd . . .58 B7
Brisbane Rd, E10 . . . . .96 B2
W13 . . . . .124 D2
Ilford IG1 . . . . .81 E7
Brisbane St, SE5 . . . . .132 A7
Briscoe Cl, E11 . . . . .97 F2
Briscoe Rd, SW19 . . . . .167 G6
Briset Rd, SE9 . . . . .156 A3
Briset St, EC1 . . . . .19 G1
Briset Way, N7 . . . . .93 F2
Bristol Cl, Stai. (Stanw.) TW19 . . .140 B6
Wallington SM6 . . . . .200 E7
Bristol Gdns, SW15
off Portsmouth Rd 147 J7
W9 . . . . .6 B6
Bristol Ms, W9 . . . . .6 B6
Bristol Pk Rd, E17 . . . . .77 H4
Bristol Rd, E7 . . . . .97 J6
Greenford UB6 . . . . .103 H1
Morden SM4 . . . . .185 F5
Briston Gro, N8 . . . . .75 E6
Briston Ms, NW7 . . . . .55 G7
Bristowe Cl, SW2 off Tulse Hill . .151 G6
Bristow Rd, SE19 . . . . .170 B5
Bexleyheath DA7 . . . . .159 E1
Croydon CR0 . . . . .200 E4
Hounslow TW3 . . . . .143 J3
★ Britain at War Experience,
SE1 .28 D2
Britannia Cl, SW4
off Bowland Rd 150 D4
Northolt UB5 . . . . .102 D3
Britannia Gate, E16 . . . . .135 G1
Britannia La, Twick. TW2 . . . . . . .143 H7
Britannia Rd, E14 . . . . .134 A4
N12 .57 F3
SW6 . . . . .128 E7
Ilford IG1 . . . . .98 E3
Surbiton KT5 . . . . .181 J7
Britannia Row, N1 . . . . .111 H1
Britannia St, WC1 . . . . .10 C3
Britannia Wk, N1 . . . . .12 B3
Britannia Way, NW10 . . . . .106 A4
SW6 off Britannia Rd 148/149 E1
Staines (Stanw.) TW19 . . . . . .140 A7
★ British Dental Assoc Mus,
W1 . . . . .16 D2
British Gro, W4 . . . . .127 F5
British Gro Pas, W4 . . . . .127 F5
British Gro S, W4
off British Gro Pas 127 F5
British Legion Rd, E4 . . . . .63 F2
★ British Lib, NW1 . . . . .9 J3
★ British Lib Newspaper Collection,
NW9 .70 E3
★ British Med Assoc, WC1 . . . . . .9 J5
★ British Mus, WC1 . . . . .18 A2
★ British Red Cross Mus & Archives,
SW1 .24 B4
British St, E3 . . . . .113 J3
Brittain Rd, Dag. RM8 . . . . .101 E3
Britten Cl, NW11 . . . . .90 E1

Brittenden Cl, Orp. BR6 . . . . . . .207 H6
Brittenden Par, Orp. BR6
off Glentrammon Rd 207 J6
Britten Dr, Sthl. UB1 . . . . .103 G6
Britten St, SW3 . . . . .31 G4
Britton Cl, SE6
off Brownhill Rd 154 D7
Britton St, EC1 . . . . .11 G6
Brixham Cres, Ruis. HA4 . . . . .84 A1
Brixham Gdns, Ilf. IG3 . . . . .99 H5
Brixham Rd, Well. DA16 . . . . .158 D1
Brixham St, E16 . . . . .136 C1
BRIXTON, SW2 . . . . .151 E4
★ Brixton Acad, The, SW9 . . . . .151 F3
Brixton Est, Edg. HA8 . . . . .70 B2
Brixton Hill, SW2 . . . . .151 E7
Brixton Hill Pl, SW2
off Brixton Hill 150/151 E7
Brixton Oval, SW2 . . . . .151 G4
Brixton Rd, SW9 . . . . .151 G2
Brixton Sta Rd, SW9 . . . . .151 G4
Brixton Water La, SW2 . . . . .151 F5
Broadbent Cl, N6 . . . . .92 B1
Broadbent St, W1 . . . . .16 D5
Broadberry Ct, N18 . . . . .60 E5
Broadbridge Cl, SE3 . . . . .135 G7
Broadcoombe, S.Croy. CR2 . . . . .203 F7
Broad Ct, WC2 . . . . .18 B4
Broadcroft Av, Stan. HA7 . . . . . . .69 G2
Broadcroft Rd, Orp. BR5 . . . . . . .193 G7
Broadeaves Cl, S.Croy. CR2 . . . . .202 B5
Broadfield Cl, NW2 . . . . .89 J3
Croydon CR0
off Progress Way 201 F2
Broadfield Ct, Bushey (Bushey Hth)
WD23 . . . . .52 B2
Broadfield La, NW1 . . . . .92 E7
Broadfield Rd, SE6 . . . . .154 E7
Broadfields, E.Mol. KT8 . . . . .180 A6
Harrow HA2 . . . . .67 H2
Broadfields Av, N21 . . . . .43 G7
Edgware HA8 . . . . .54 B4
Broadfields Hts, Edg. HA8 . . . . . .54 B4
Broadfields La, Wat. WD19 . . . . . .50 B1
Broadfield Sq, Enf. EN1 . . . . .45 E2
Broadfields Way, NW10 . . . . .89 F5
Broadfield Way, Buck.H. IG9 . . . . .63 J3
BROADGATE, EC2 . . . . .20 C1
Broadgate, E13 . . . . .115 J2
EC2 off Liverpool St 112 B5
Broadgate Circle, EC2 . . . . .20 D1
Broadgate Rd, E16 . . . . .116 A6
Broadgates Av, Barn. EN4 . . . . . . .41 E1
Broadgates Rd, SW18
off Ellerton Rd 167 G1
BROAD GREEN, Croy. CR0 . . . . . .187 G6
Broad Grn Av, Croy. CR0 . . . . . . .187 H7
Broadhead Strand, NW9 . . . . .71 F1
Broadheath Dr, Chis. BR7 . . . . . . .174 C5
Broadhinton Rd, SW4 . . . . .150 B3
Broadhurst Av, Edg. HA8 . . . . . . .54 B4
Ilford IG3 . . . . .99 J4
Broadhurst Cl, NW6
off Broadhurst Gdns 91 F6
Richmond TW10
off Lower Gro Rd 145 J5
Broadhurst Gdns, NW6 . . . . .90 E6
Chigwell IG7 . . . . .65 F4
Ruislip HA4 . . . . .84 C2
Broadlands, Felt. TW13 . . . . .161 F3
Broadlands Av, SW16 . . . . .168 E2
Enfield EN3 . . . . .45 E3
Broadlands Cl, N6 . . . . .74 A7
SW16 . . . . .168 E2
Enfield EN3 . . . . .45 E3
Broadlands Rd, N6 . . . . .73 J7
Bromley BR1 . . . . .173 H4
Broadlands Way, N.Mal. KT3 . . . .183 F6
Broad La, EC2 . . . . .20 D1
N8 off Tottenham La 75 F5
N15 . . . . .76 C4
Hampton TW12 . . . . .161 G6
Broad Lawn, SE9 . . . . .174 D2
Broadlawns Ct, Har. HA3 . . . . . . .68 C1
Broadley St, NW8 . . . . .15 F1
Broadley Ter, NW1 . . . . .7 H6
Broadmayne, SE17 . . . . .36 B3
Broadmead, SE6 . . . . .172 A3
Broadmead Av, Wor.Pk. KT4 . . . .183 G7
Broadmead Cl, Hmptn. TW12 . . . .161 G6
Pinner HA5 . . . . .51 E7
Broadmead Rd, Hayes UB4 . . . . .102 E4
Northolt UB5 . . . . .102 E4
Woodford Green IG8 . . . . .63 G6
Broad Oak, Wdf.Grn. IG8 . . . . . . .63 H5
Broad Oak Cl, E4 . . . . .62 A5
Broadoaks, Surb. KT6 . . . . .196 B1
Broadoaks Way, Brom. BR2 . . . . .191 F5
Broad Sanctuary, SW1 . . . . .25 J4
Broadstone Pl, W1 . . . . .16 B2
Broad St, Dag. RM10 . . . . .101 G7
Teddington TW11 . . . . .162 C6
Broad St Av, EC2 . . . . .20 D2
Broad St Pl, EC2 . . . . .20 C2
Broad Vw, NW9 . . . . .70 A6
Broadview Rd, SW16 . . . . .168 D7
Broadwalk, E18 . . . . .79 F3

Broad Wk, N21 . . . . .59 F2
NW1 . . . . .8 D4
SE3 .155 J3
W1 . . . . .24 B1
Broadwalk, Har. HA2 . . . . .67 G5
Broad Wk, Houns. TW5 . . . . .142 D1
Richmond TW9 . . . . .125 J7
Broad Wk, The, W8 . . . . .14 B6
East Molesey KT8 . . . . .180 C3
Broadwalk Ct, W8 . . . . .128 D1
Broad Wk La, NW11 . . . . .72 C7
Broadwalk Shop Cen, Edg. HA8 . . .54 B6
Broadwall, SE1 . . . . .27 F1
Broadwater Fm Est, N17 . . . . .76 A2
Broadwater Gdns, Orp. BR6 . . . . .207 E4
Broadwater Rd, N17 . . . . .76 B1
SE28 . . . . .137 G3
SW17 . . . . .167 H4
Broadway, E15 . . . . .96 D7
SW1 .25 H5
Barking IG11 . . . . .99 F7
Bexleyheath DA6 . . . . .159 E4
Broadway, The, E4 . . . . .62 C6
E13 .115 H2
N8 . . . . .74 E6
N9 . . . . .60 D3
N14 off Winchmore Hill Rd 58 D1
N22 . . . . .75 G2
NW7 .55 F5
SW13 off The Terrace 146/147 E2
SW19 . . . . .166 C6
W5 . . . . .105 G7
W7 off Cherington Rd 124 B1
W7 (W.Ealing) 124 D1
W13 .124 D1
Croydon CR0
off Croydon Rd 200/201 E4
Dagenham RM8 . . . . .101 F2
Greenford UB6 . . . . .103 J4
Harrow HA2 . . . . .68 B2
Loughton IG10 . . . . .49 F4
Pinner HA5 . . . . .51 F7
Southall UB1 . . . . .102 D7
Stanmore HA7 . . . . .53 F5
Sutton SM1 off Manor La 199 F5
Sutton (Cheam) SM3 . . . . .198 B6
Thames Ditton KT7
off Hampton Ct Way 194 B1
Wembley HA9 off East La 87 H3
Woodford Green IG8 . . . . .63 H6
Broadway Av, Croy. CR0 . . . . . . .188 A5
Twickenham TW1 . . . . .144 E6
Broadway Cl, Wdf.Grn. IG8 . . . . . .63 H6
Broadway Ct, SW19
off The Broadway 166 D6
Broadway Gdns, Mitch. CR4 . . . . .185 H4
Broadway Ho, Brom. BR1
off Elmfield Pk 191 G3
Broadway Mkt, E8 . . . . .112 E1
Broadway Mkt Ms, E8
off Regents Row 112 D1
Broadway Ms, E5 . . . . .76 C2
N13 off Elmdale Rd 59 F5
N21 off Compton Rd 59 H1
Broadway Par, N8 . . . . .74 E6
Hayes UB3
off Coldharbour La 122 A1
Broadway Pl, SW19
off Hartfield Rd 166 C6
Broadway Shop Cen, W6
off Hammersmith Bdy 127 J4
Bexleyheath DA6 . . . . .159 G4
Broadwick St, W1 . . . . .17 G5
Broadwood Ter, W8
off Pembroke Rd 128 C4
Broad Yd, EC1 . . . . .11 G6
Brocas Cl, NW3 off Fellows Rd . . .91 H7
Brockbridge Ho, SW15
off Tangley Gro 147 F6
Brockdish Av, Bark. IG11 . . . . .99 J5
Brockenhurst, W.Mol. KT8 . . . . . .179 F6
Brockenhurst Av, Wor.Pk. KT4 . . .197 E1
Brockenhurst Gdns, NW7 . . . . . . .55 E5
Ilford IG1 . . . . .99 F5
Brockenhurst Ms, N18
off Lyndhurst Rd 60 D4
Brockenhurst Rd, Croy. CR0 . . . . .188 D7
Brockenhurst Way, SW16 . . . . . . .186 D2
Brocket Cl, Chig. IG7
off Burrow Rd 65 J5
Brocket Way, Chig. IG7 . . . . .65 H5
Brockham Cl, SW19 . . . . .166 C5
Brockham Cres, Croy. (New Adgtn)
CR0 . . . . .204 D7
Brockham Dr, SW2
off Fairview Pl 151 F7
Ilford IG2 . . . . .81 E6
Brockham St, SE1 . . . . .28 A5
Brockhurst Cl, Stan. HA7 . . . . . . .52 C6
Brockill Cres, SE4 . . . . .153 H4
Brocklebank Rd, SE7 . . . . .135 H4
SW18 . . . . .149 F7
Brocklehurst St, SE14 . . . . .133 G7
Brocklesby Rd, SE25 . . . . .188 E4
BROCKLEY, SE4 . . . . .153 H5
Brockley Av, Stan. HA7 . . . . .53 H3
Brockley Cl, Stan. HA7 . . . . .53 H4

Brockley Cross, SE4
off Endwell Rd 153 H3
Brockley Footpath, SE15 . . . . . . .153 F4
Brockley Gdns, SE4 . . . . .153 J2
Brockley Gro, SE4 . . . . .153 J5
Brockley Hall Rd, SE4 . . . . .153 H6
Brockley Hill, Stan. HA7 . . . . .53 F1
Brockley Ms, SE4 . . . . .153 H5
Brockley Pk, SE23 . . . . .153 H7
Brockley Ri, SE23 . . . . .153 H6
Brockley Rd, SE4 . . . . .153 J3
Brockleyside, Stan. HA7 . . . . .53 G4
Brockley Vw, SE23 . . . . .153 H7
Brockley Way, SE4 . . . . .153 G5
Brockman Ri, Brom. BR1 . . . . . . .172 D4
Brock Pl, E3 . . . . .114 B4
Brock Rd, E13 . . . . .115 H5
Brocks Dr, Sutt. SM3 . . . . .198 B3
Brockshot Cl, Brent. TW8 . . . . . . .125 G6
Brock St, SE15 off Evelina Rd . . .153 F3
Brockway Cl, E11 . . . . .97 E1
Brockwell Av, Beck. BR3 . . . . . . .190 B5
Brockwell Cl, Orp. BR5 . . . . .193 J5
★ Brockwell Park, SE24 . . . . . . .151 H6
Brockwell Pk Gdns, SE24 . . . . . .151 G7
Brockwell Pk Row, SW2 . . . . .151 G6
Brodewater Rd, Borwd. WD6 . . . . .38 B2
Brodia Rd, N16 . . . . .94 B3
Brodie Rd, E4 . . . . .62 C1
Enfield EN2 . . . . .43 J1
Brodie St, SE1 . . . . .37 G3
Brodlove La, E1 . . . . .113 G7
Brodrick Gro, SE2 . . . . .138 B4
Brodrick Rd, SW17 . . . . .167 H2
Brograve Gdns, Beck. BR3 . . . . . .190 B2
Broken Wf, EC4 . . . . .19 J5
Brokesley St, E3 . . . . .113 J4
Broke Wk, E8 . . . . .112 C1
Bromar Rd, SE5 . . . . .152 B3
Bromborough Grn, Wat. WD19 . . .50 C5
Bromefield, Stan. HA7 . . . . .69 F1
Bromehead Rd, E1 . . . . .113 F6
Bromehead St, E1
off Commercial Rd 113 F6
Bromell's Rd, SW4 . . . . .150 C4
Brome Rd, SE9 . . . . .156 C3
Bromfelde Rd, SW4 . . . . .150 D2
Bromfelde Wk, SW4 . . . . .150 D2
Bromfield St, N1 . . . . .11 F1
Bromhall Rd, Dag. RM8, RM9 . . . .100 B6
Bromhedge, SE9 . . . . .174 C3
Bromholm Rd, SE2 . . . . .138 B3
Bromleigh Ct, SE23
off Lapse Wd Wk 170/171 E2
BROMLEY, E3 . . . . .114 B4
BROMLEY, BR1 & BR2 . . . . .191 F2
Bromley Av, Brom. BR1 . . . . .173 E7
BROMLEY COMMON, Brom.
BR2 . . . . .192 C7
Bromley Common, Brom. BR2 . . .191 J4
Bromley Cres, Brom. BR2 . . . . . . .191 F3
Bromley Gdns, Brom. BR2 . . . . . .191 F3
Bromley Gro, Brom. BR2 . . . . . . .190 D2
Bromley Hall Rd, E14 . . . . .114 C5
Bromley High St, E3 . . . . .114 B3
Bromley Hill, Brom. BR1 . . . . . . .172 E5
Bromley La, Chis. BR7 . . . . .175 F7
Bromley Mall, The, Brom. BR1 . . .191 G3
BROMLEY PARK, Brom. BR1 . . . .190 E1
Bromley Pk, Brom. BR1
off London Rd 191 F1
Bromley Pl, W1 . . . . .17 F1
Bromley Rd, E10 . . . . .78 B6
E17 . . . . .78 A2
N17 . . . . .76 C1
N18 . . . . .60 A3
SE6 .172 B1
Beckenham BR3 . . . . .190 B1
Bromley (Downham) BR1 . . . . .172 C4
Bromley (Short.) BR2 . . . . .190 C2
Chislehurst BR7 . . . . .192 E1
Bromley St, E1 . . . . .113 G5
BROMPTON, SW3 . . . . .23 H4
Brompton Arc, SW3 . . . . .23 J4
Brompton Cl, SE20
off Selby Rd 188 D2
Hounslow TW4 . . . . .143 F5
Brompton Gro, N2 . . . . .73 H4
★ Brompton Oratory, SW7 . . . . .23 G6
Brompton Pk Cres, SW6 . . . . .30 A6
Brompton Pl, SW3 . . . . .23 H5
Brompton Rd, SW1 . . . . .23 H5
SW3 .31 G1
SW7 .23 H5
Brompton Sq, SW3 . . . . .23 G5
Brompton Ter, SE18
off Prince Imperial Rd 156 D1
Bromwich Av, N6 . . . . .92 A2
Bromyard Av, W3 . . . . .127 E1
Bromyard Ho, SE15 . . . . .132 E7
BRONDESBURY, NW2 . . . . .90 B7
Brondesbury Ct, NW2 . . . . .89 J6
Brondesbury Ms, NW6
off Willesden La 90 D7
BRONDESBURY PARK, NW6 . . . .89 J7
Brondesbury Pk, NW2 . . . . .89 H6
NW6 .90 A7
Brondesbury Rd, NW6 . . . . .108 C2

Brondesbury Vil, NW6 . . . . .108 C2
Bronsart Rd, SW6 . . . . .128 B7
Bronson Rd, SW20 . . . . .184 A2
Bronte Cl, E7 off Bective Rd 97 G4
   Erith DA8 . . . . .139 H7
   Ilford IG2 . . . . .80 D5
Bronte Ho, NW6 . . . . .108 D3
Bronti Cl, SE17 . . . . .36 A4
Bronze Age Way, Belv. DA17 . . . .139 J3
   Erith DA8 . . . . .139 J3
Bronze St, SE8 . . . . .134 A7
Brook Av, Dag. RM10 . . . . .101 H2
   Edgware HA8 . . . . .54 B6
   Wembley HA9 . . . . .88 A3
Brookbank Av, W7 . . . . .104 A5
Brookbank Rd, SE13 . . . . .154 A3
Brook Cl, NW7 off Frith Ct 56 B7
   SW17 . . . . .168 A2
   SW20 . . . . .183 H3
   W3 off West La Av 126 A4
   Borehamwood WD6 . . . . .38 B3
   Staines (Stanw.) TW19 . . . . . .140 C7
Brook Cres, E4 . . . . .62 A4
   N9 . . . . .60 E4
Brookdale, N11 . . . . .58 C4
Brookdale Rd, E17 . . . . .78 A3
   SE6 . . . . .154 B6
   Bexley DA5 . . . . .159 E6
Brookdene Rd, SE18 . . . . .137 J4
Brook Dr, SE11 . . . . .27 F4
   Harrow HA1 . . . . .67 J4
Brooke Av, Har. HA2 . . . . .85 J3
Brookehowse Rd, SE6 . . . . .172 B3
Brookend Rd, Sid. DA15 . . . . . . .175 H1
Brooke Rd, E5 . . . . .94 D3
   E17 . . . . .78 C4
   N16 . . . . .94 C3
Brooke's Ct, EC1 . . . . .19 E1
Brookes Mkt, EC1 . . . . .19 F1
Brooke St, EC1 . . . . .19 E2
Brookfield, N6 . . . . .92 A3
Brookfield Av, E17 . . . . .78 C4
   NW7 . . . . .55 H6
   W5 . . . . .105 G4
   Sutton SM1 . . . . .199 G4
Brookfield Cl, NW7 . . . . .55 H6
Brookfield Ct, Grnf. UB6 . . . . . . .103 J3
   Harrow HA3 . . . . .69 G5
Brookfield Cres, NW7 . . . . .55 H6
   Harrow HA3 . . . . .69 H5
Brookfield Gdns, Esher (Clay.)
   KT10 . . . . .194 C6
Brookfield Pk, NW5 . . . . .92 B3
Brookfield Path, Wdf.Grn. IG8 . . . .62 E6
Brookfield Rd, E9 . . . . .95 H6
   N9 . . . . .60 D3
   W4 . . . . .126 D2
Brookfields, Enf. EN3 . . . . .45 G4
Brookfields Av, Mitch. CR4 . . . . .185 H5
Brook Gdns, E4 . . . . .62 B4
   SW13 . . . . .147 F3
   Kingston upon Thames KT2 . . . .182 C1
Brook Gate, W1 . . . . .16 A6
Brook Grn, W6 . . . . .128 A4
Brookhill Cl, SE18 . . . . .136 E5
   Barnet EN4 . . . . .41 H5
Brookhill Rd, SE18 . . . . .136 E5
   Barnet EN4 . . . . .41 H5
Brookhouse Gdns, E4 . . . . .62 E4
Brook Ind Est, Hayes UB4 . . . . . .122 D1
Brooking Cl, Dag. RM8 . . . . .100 C4
Brooking Rd, E7 . . . . .97 G5
Brookland Cl, NW11 . . . . .72 D4
Brookland Garth, NW11 . . . . .72 E4
Brookland Hill, NW11 . . . . .72 D4
Brookland Ri, NW11 . . . . .72 D4
Brooklands Av, SW19 . . . . .166 E2
   Sidcup DA15 . . . . .175 G2
Brooklands Dr, Grnf. UB6 . . . . . .105 G1
Brooklands Pk, SE3 . . . . .155 G3
Brooklands Pas, SW8
   off Belmore St 150 D1
Brooklands Rd, T.Ditt. KT7 . . . . .194 C1
Brook La, SE3 . . . . .155 H2
   Bexley DA5 . . . . .158 D6
   Bromley BR1 . . . . .173 G6
Brook La N, Brent. TW8 . . . . . . .125 G6
Brooklea Cl, NW9 . . . . .71 E1
Brooklyn Av, SE25 . . . . .188 E4
   Loughton IG10 . . . . .48 B4
Brooklyn Cl, Cars. SM5 . . . . .199 H2
Brooklyn Gro, SE25 . . . . .188 E4
Brooklyn Rd, SE25 . . . . .188 E4
   Bromley BR2 . . . . .192 A5
Brooklyn Way, West Dr. UB7 . . . .120 A3
Brookmarsh Ind Est, SE10
   off Norman St 134 B7
Brook Mead, Epsom KT19 . . . . . .197 E6
Brookmead Av, Brom. BR1 . . . . .192 C5
Brook Meadow, N12 . . . . .56 E4
Brook Meadow Cl, Wdf.Grn.
   IG8 . . . . .62 E6
Brookmead Rd, Croy. CR0 . . . . . .186 C6
Brook Ms N, W2 . . . . .14 D5
Brookmill Rd, SE8 . . . . .154 A1

Brook Par, Chig. IG7
   off High Rd 64/65 E3
Brook Pk Cl, N21 . . . . .43 H6
Brook Path, Loug. IG10 . . . . .48 B4
Brook Pl, Barn. EN5 . . . . .40 D5
Brook Ri, Chig. IG7 . . . . .64 D3
Brook Rd, N8 . . . . .74 E4
   N22 . . . . .75 F3
   NW2 . . . . .89 G2
   Borehamwood WD6 . . . . .38 A2
   Buckhurst Hill IG9 . . . . .63 G2
   Ilford IG2 . . . . .81 H6
   Loughton IG10 . . . . .48 B5
   Surbiton KT6 . . . . .195 H2
   Thornton Heath CR7 . . . . .187 J4
   Twickenham TW1 . . . . .144 D6
Brook Rd S, Brent. TW8 . . . . . . .125 G6
Brooksbank Ms, N1 . . . . .93 G7
   off Brooksby St
Brooksby Ms, N1 . . . . .93 G7
Brooksby's Wk, E9 . . . . .95 G5
Brooks Av, E6 . . . . .116 C4
Brooks Cl, SE9 . . . . .174 D2
Brooks Ct, E15 off Clays La 96 B5
Brookscroft Rd, E17 . . . . .78 B1
Brookshill, Har. HA3 . . . . .52 A5
Brookshill Av, Har. HA3 . . . . .52 A5
Brookshill Dr, Har. HA3 . . . . .52 A5
Brookshill Gate, Har. (Har.Wld)
   HA3 . . . . .52 A5
Brookside, N21 . . . . .43 F6
   Barnet EN4 . . . . .41 H6
   Carshalton SM5 . . . . .200 A5
   Ilford IG6 . . . . .65 F6
   Orpington BR6 . . . . .193 J7
Brookside Cl, Barn. EN5 . . . . .40 B6
   Feltham TW13
   off Sycamore Cl 160 A3
   Harrow (Kenton) HA2 . . . . . . .69 G5
   Harrow (S.Har.) HA3 . . . . .85 E4
Brookside Cres, Wor.Pk. KT4
   off Green La 197 G1
Brookside Rd, N9 . . . . .60 E4
   N19 . . . . .92 C2
   NW11 . . . . .72 B6
   Hayes UB4 . . . . .102 C7
Brookside S, Barn. EN4 . . . . .42 A7
Brookside Wk, N3 . . . . .72 B2
   N12 . . . . .56 D6
   NW4 . . . . .72 B4
   NW11 . . . . .72 B4
Brookside Way, Croy. CR0 . . . . . .189 G6
Brooks La, W4 . . . . .126 A6
Brook's Ms, W1 . . . . .16 D5
Brook Sq, SE18
   off Shooter's Hill Rd 156 B1
Brooks Rd, E13 . . . . .115 G1
   W4 . . . . .126 A5
Brook St, N17 off High Rd 76 C2
   W1 . . . . .16 C5
   W2 . . . . .15 F5
   Belvedere DA17 . . . . .139 H5
   Erith DA8 . . . . .139 H6
   Kingston upon Thames KT1 . . . .181 H2
Brooksville Av, NW6 . . . . .108 B1
Brook Vale, Erith DA8 . . . . .159 H1
Brookview Rd, SW16 . . . . .168 C5
Brookville Rd, SW6 . . . . .128 C7
Brook Wk, N2 . . . . .73 G1
   Edgware HA8 . . . . .54 D6
Brookway, SE3 . . . . .155 G3
Brook Way, Chig. IG7 . . . . .64 D3
Brookwood Av, SW13 . . . . .147 F3
Brookwood Cl, Brom. BR2 . . . . . .191 F4
Brookwood Rd, SW18 . . . . .166 C1
   Hounslow TW3 . . . . .143 H1
Broom Cl, Brom. BR2 . . . . .192 B6
   Teddington TW11 . . . . .163 G7
Broomcroft Av, Nthlt. UB5 . . . . . .102 C3
Broome Rd, Hmptn. TW12 . . . . . .161 F7
Broome Way, SE5 . . . . .131 J7
Broomfield, E17 . . . . .77 J7
   Sunbury-on-Thames TW16 . . . .178 A1
Broomfield Av, N13 . . . . .59 F5
   Loughton IG10 . . . . .48 C6
Broomfield La, N13 . . . . .59 F4
Broomfield Pl, W13
   off Broomfield Rd 124/125 E1
Broomfield Rd, N13 . . . . .59 E5
   W13 . . . . .125 E1
   Beckenham BR3 . . . . .189 H3
   Bexleyheath DA6 . . . . .159 G5
   Richmond TW9 . . . . .145 J1
   Romford RM6 . . . . .82 D7
   Surbiton KT5 . . . . .195 J1
   Teddington TW11
   off Melbourne Rd 163 F6
Broomfield St, E14 . . . . .114 A5
Broom Gdns, Croy. CR0 . . . . . . .204 A3
Broomgrove Gdns, Edg. HA8 . . . . .70 A1
Broomgrove Rd, SW9 . . . . .151 F2
Broomhill Ct, Wdf.Grn. IG8
   off Broomhill Rd 63 G6
Broomhill Ri, Bexh. DA6 . . . . . . .159 G5
Broomhill Rd, SW18 . . . . .148 D5
   Ilford IG3 . . . . .100 A2

Broomhill Rd, Wdf.Grn. IG8 . . . . . .63 G6
Broomhill Wk, Wdf.Grn. IG8 . . . . .63 F7
Broomhouse La, SW6 . . . . .148 D2
Broomhouse Rd, SW6 . . . . .148 D2
Broomloan La, Sutt. SM1 . . . . . . .198 D2
Broom Lock, Tedd. TW11 . . . . . . .163 F6
Broom Mead, Bexh. DA6 . . . . . . .159 G5
Broom Pk, Tedd. TW11 . . . . .163 G7
Broom Rd, Croy. CR0 . . . . .204 A3
   Teddington TW11 . . . . .163 F6
Broomsleigh St, NW6 . . . . .90 C5
Broom Water, Tedd. TW11 . . . . . .163 F6
Broom Water W, Tedd. TW11 . . . .163 F5
Broomwood Cl, Croy. CR0 . . . . . .189 G5
Broomwood Rd, SW11 . . . . .149 J6
Broseley Gro, SE26 . . . . .171 H5
Broster Gdns, SE25 . . . . .188 C3
Brougham Rd, E8 . . . . .112 D1
   W3 . . . . .106 C6
Brougham St, SW11 . . . . .149 J2
Brough Cl, SW8
   off Kenchester Cl 130/131 E7
   Kingston upon Thames KT2 . . . .163 G5
Broughinge Rd, Borwd. WD6 . . . . .38 B2
Broughton Av, N3 . . . . .72 B3
   Richmond TW10 . . . . .163 E3
Broughton Dr, SW9 . . . . .151 G4
Broughton Gdns, N6 . . . . .74 C6
Broughton Rd, SW6 . . . . .148 E2
   W13 . . . . .105 E7
   Orpington BR6 . . . . .207 G2
   Thornton Heath CR7 . . . . .187 G6
Broughton Rd App, SW6
   off Wandsworth Br Rd . .148/149 E2
Broughton St, SW8 . . . . .150 A2
Brouncker Rd, W3 . . . . .126 C2
Browells La, Felt. TW13 . . . . .160 B2
Brown Cl, Wall. SM6 . . . . .200 E7
Brownfield St, E14 . . . . .114 B6
Browngraves Rd, Hayes UB3 . . . .121 F7
Brown Hart Gdns, W1 . . . . .16 C5
Brownhill Rd, SE6 . . . . .154 B7
Browning Av, W7 . . . . .104 C6
   Sutton SM1 . . . . .199 H4
   Worcester Park KT4 . . . . .197 H1
Browning Cl, E17 . . . . .78 C4
   W9 .6 D6
   Hampton TW12 . . . . .161 F4
   Welling DA16 . . . . .157 H1
Browning Ho, W12 off Wood La . . .107 J6
Browning Ms, W1 . . . . .16 D2
Browning Rd, E11 . . . . .79 F7
   E12 . . . . .98 C6
Browning St, SE17 . . . . .36 A3
Browning Way, Houns. TW5 . . . . .142 D1
Brownlea Gdns, Ilf. IG3 . . . . .100 A2
Brownlow Cl, Barn. EN4 . . . . .41 G5
Brownlow Ms, WC1 . . . . .10 D6
Brownlow Rd, E7
   off Woodford Rd 97 H4
   E8 . . . . .112 C1
   N3 . . . . .56 E7
   N11 . . . . .58 E6
   NW10 . . . . .89 E7
   W13 . . . . .124 D1
   Borehamwood WD6 . . . . .38 A4
   Croydon CR0 . . . . .202 B4
Brownlow St, WC1 . . . . .18 D2
Brown's Bldgs, EC3 . . . . .20 E4
Brownsea Wk, NW7
   off Sanders La 56 A6
Browns La, NW5 . . . . .92 B5
Brownspring Dr, SE9 . . . . .175 E4
Browns Rd, E17 . . . . .78 A3
   Surbiton KT5 . . . . .181 J7
Brown St, W1 . . . . .15 J3
Brownswell Rd, N2 . . . . .73 G2
Brownswood Rd, N4 . . . . .93 H3
Broxash Rd, SW11 . . . . .150 A6
Broxbourne Av, E18 . . . . .79 H4
Broxbourne Rd, E7 . . . . .97 G3
   Orpington BR6 . . . . .193 J7
Broxholm Rd, SE27 . . . . .169 G3
Broxted Rd, SE6 . . . . .171 J2
Broxwood Way, NW8 . . . . .109 H1
★ Bruce Castle Mus, N17 . . . . . . .76 B1
Bruce Castle Rd, N17 . . . . .76 C1
Bruce Cl, W10
   off Ladbroke Gro 108 B5
   Welling DA16 . . . . .158 B1
Bruce Gdns, N20
   off Balfour Gro 57 J3
Bruce Gro, N17 . . . . .76 B1
Bruce Hall Ms, SW17
   off Brudenell Rd 168 A4
Bruce Rd, E3 . . . . .114 B3
   NW10 . . . . .88 D7
   SE25 . . . . .188 A4
   Barnet EN5 off St. Albans Rd . . .40 B3
   Harrow HA3 . . . . .68 B2
   Mitcham CR4 . . . . .168 A7
Bruckner St, W10 . . . . .108 C3
Brudenell Rd, SW17 . . . . .167 J3
Bruffs Meadow, Nthlt. UB5 . . . . . .85 E6
Bruford Ct, SE8 off Creekside 134 B6
Bruges Pl, NW1
   off Randolph St 92 C7

Brumfield Rd, Epsom KT19 . . . . . .196 C5
Brummel Cl, Bexh. DA7 . . . . .159 J3
★ Brunei Gall, WC1 . . . . .17 J1
Brunel Cl, SE19 . . . . .170 C6
   Hounslow TW5 . . . . .122 B7
   Northolt UB5 . . . . .103 F3
★ Brunel Engine Ho, SE16 . . . . . .133 F2
Brunel Est, W2 . . . . .108 D5
Brunel Pl, Sthl. UB1 . . . . .103 H6
Brunel Rd, E17 . . . . .77 H6
   SE16 . . . . .133 F2
   W3 . . . . .106 E5
   Woodford Green IG8 . . . . .64 C5
Brunel St, E16
   off Victoria Dock Rd 115 F6
Brunel Wk, N15 . . . . .76 B4
   Twickenham TW2
   off Stephenson Rd 143 G7
Brune St, E1 . . . . .21 F2
Brunner Cl, NW11 . . . . .73 F5
Brunner Rd, E17 . . . . .77 J5
   W5 . . . . .105 G4
Bruno Pl, NW9 . . . . .88 C2
Brunswick Av, N11 . . . . .58 A3
Brunswick Cl, Bexh. DA6 . . . . . . .158 D4
   Pinner HA5 . . . . .67 E6
   Thames Ditton KT7 . . . . .194 C1
   Twickenham TW2 . . . . .162 A3
Brunswick Ct, EC1
   off Northampton Sq 111 H3
   SE1 . . . . .29 E4
   Barnet EN4 . . . . .41 G5
Brunswick Cres, N11 . . . . .58 A3
Brunswick Gdns, W5 . . . . .105 H3
   W8 . . . . .128 D1
   Ilford IG6 . . . . .65 F7
Brunswick Gro, N11 . . . . .58 A3
Brunswick Ind Pk, N11 . . . . .58 B4
Brunswick Ms, SW16 . . . . .168 D6
   off Potters La
   W1 . . . . .16 A3
BRUNSWICK PARK, N11 . . . . .57 J7
Brunswick Pk, SE5 . . . . .152 A1
Brunswick Pk Gdns, N11 . . . . .58 A2
Brunswick Pk Rd, N11 . . . . .58 A2
Brunswick Pl, N1 . . . . .12 C4
   NW1 . . . . .8 C5
   SE19 . . . . .170 D7
Brunswick Quay, SE16 . . . . .133 G3
Brunswick Rd, E10 . . . . .96 C1
   E14 off Blackwall Tunnel Northern
   App 114 C6
   N15 . . . . .76 B5
   W5 . . . . .105 G4
   Bexleyheath DA6 . . . . .158 D4
   Kingston upon Thames KT2 . . . .182 A1
   Sutton SM1 . . . . .199 E4
Brunswick Shop Cen, WC1 . . . . . .10 A4
Brunswick Sq, N17 . . . . .60 C6
   WC1 . . . . .10 B5
Brunswick St, E17 . . . . .78 C5
Brunswick Vil, SE5 . . . . .152 B1
Brunswick Way, N11 . . . . .58 B4
Brunton Pl, E14 . . . . .113 H6
Brushfield St, E1 . . . . .21 E2
Brussels Rd, SW11 . . . . .149 G4
Bruton Cl, Chis. BR7 . . . . .174 C7
Bruton La, W1 . . . . .16 E6
Bruton Pl, W1 . . . . .16 E6
Bruton Rd, Mord. SM4 . . . . .185 F5
Bruton St, W1 . . . . .16 E6
Bruton Way, W13 . . . . .104 D5
Bryan Av, NW10 . . . . .89 H7
Bryan Cl, Sun. TW16 . . . . .160 A7
Bryan Rd, SE16 . . . . .133 J2
Bryan's All, SW6
   off Wandsworth Br Rd . .148/149 E2
Bryanston Av, Twick. TW2 . . . . . .161 H1
Bryanston Cl, Sthl. UB2 . . . . .123 F4
Bryanstone Ct, Sutt. SM1
   off Oakhill Rd 199 F4
Bryanstone Rd, N8 . . . . .74 D5
Bryanston Ms E, W1 . . . . .15 J2
Bryanston Ms W, W1 . . . . .15 J2
Bryanston Pl, W1 . . . . .15 J2
Bryanston Sq, W1 . . . . .15 J2
Bryanston St, W1 . . . . .15 J4
Bryant Cl, Barn. EN5 . . . . .40 C5
Bryant Ct, E2 . . . . .13 F1
Bryant Rd, Nthlt. UB5 . . . . .102 C3
Bryant St, E15 . . . . .96 D7
Bryantwood Rd, N7 . . . . .93 G5
Brycedale Cres, N14 . . . . .58 D4
Bryce Rd, Dag. RM8 . . . . .100 C4
Brydale Ho, SE16
   off Rotherhithe New Rd 133 G4
Bryden Cl, SE26 . . . . .171 H5
Brydges Pl, WC2 . . . . .18 A6
Brydges Rd, E15 . . . . .96 D5
Brydon Wk, N1
   off Outram Pl 110/111 E1
Bryer Cl, EC2 off Aldersgate St . . .111 J5
Bryett Rd, N7 . . . . .93 E3
Brymay Cl, E3 . . . . .114 A2
Brynmaer Rd, SW11 . . . . .149 J1
Bryn-y-Mawr Rd, Enf. EN1 . . . . . .44 C4
Bryony Cl, Loug. IG10 . . . . .48 E4

Bryony Rd, W12 . . . . .107 G7
Buchanan Cl, N21 . . . . .43 F5
Buchanan Ct, Borwd. WD6 . . . . . .38 C2
Buchanan Gdns, NW10 . . . . . .107 H2
Buchan Rd, SE15 . . . . .153 F3
Bucharest Rd, SW18 . . . . .149 F7
Buckden Cl, N2 off Southern Rd .73 J4
  SE12 off Upwood Rd 155 F6
Buckfast Ct, W13
  off Romsey Rd 104 D7
Buckfast Rd, Mord. SM4 . . . . . .185 E4
Buckfast St, E2 . . . . .13 J4
Buck Hill Wk, W2 . . . . .15 F6
Buckhold Rd, SW18 . . . . .148 D6
Buckhurst Av, Cars. SM5 . . . . .199 H1
BUCKHURST HILL, IG9 . . . . .47 H7
Buckhurst St, E1 . . . . .13 E4
Buckhurst Way, Buck.H. IG9 . . . .64 A4
Buckingham Arc, WC2 . . . . .18 B6
Buckingham Av, N20 . . . . .41 F7
  Feltham TW14 . . . . .142 B6
  Greenford UB6 . . . . .104 D1
  Thornton Heath CR7 . . . . . . .187 G1
  Welling DA16 . . . . .157 H4
  West Molesey KT8 . . . . .179 H3
Buckingham Cl, W5 . . . . .105 F5
  Enfield EN1 . . . . .44 B2
  Hampton TW12 . . . . .161 F5
  Orpington BR5 . . . . .193 H7
Buckingham Ct, NW4 . . . . .71 G3
  Loughton IG10
   off Rectory La 48 D2
Buckingham Dr, Chis. BR7 . . . .175 E5
Buckingham Gdns, Edg. HA8 . . .53 J7
  Thornton Heath CR7 . . . . . . .187 G2
  West Molesey KT8
   off Buckingham Av 179 H2
Buckingham Gate, SW1 . . . . . . .25 F4
Buckingham La, SE23 . . . . .153 H7
Buckingham Ms, N1
  off Buckingham Rd 94 B6
  NW10 off Buckingham Rd 107 F2
  SW1 . . . . .25 F4
★ Buckingham Palace, SW1 . . .24 E4
Buckingham Palace Rd, SW1 . . .32 D2
Buckingham Pl, SW1 . . . . .25 F4
Buckingham Rd, E10 . . . . .96 B3
  E11 .79 J5
  E15 .97 F5
  E18 .79 F1
  N1 . . . . .94 B6
  N22 .74 E1
  NW10 . . . . .107 F2
  Borehamwood WD6 . . . . .38 D4
  Edgware HA8 . . . . .53 J7
  Hampton TW12 . . . . .161 F4
  Harrow HA1 . . . . .68 A5
  Ilford IG1 . . . . .99 G2
  Kingston upon Thames KT1 . . .181 J4
  Mitcham CR4 . . . . .186 E5
  Richmond TW10 . . . . .163 G2
Buckingham St, WC2 . . . . .18 B6
Buckland Cres, NW3 . . . . .91 G7
Buckland Ri, Pnr. HA5 . . . . .66 C1
Buckland Rd, E10 . . . . .96 C2
  Chessington KT9 . . . . .195 J5
  Orpington BR6 . . . . .207 H4
Bucklands Rd, Tedd. TW11 . . . .163 F6
Buckland St, N1 . . . . .12 C2
Buckland Wk, W3 . . . . .126 C2
  Morden SM4 . . . . .185 F4
Buck La, NW9 . . . . .70 D5
Buckleigh Av, SW20 . . . . .184 B3
Buckleigh Rd, SW16 . . . . .168 D6
Buckleigh Way, SE19 . . . . .188 C1
Buckler Gdns, SE9
  off Southold Ri 174 C3
Bucklers All, SW6 . . . . .128 C6
Bucklersbury, EC4 . . . . .20 B4
Bucklersbury Pas, EC4 . . . . .20 B4
Bucklers Way, Cars. SM5 . . . . .199 J3
Buckles Ct, Belv. DA17
  off Fendyke Rd 138 D3
Buckle St, E1 . . . . .21 G3
Buckley Cl, SE23 . . . . .153 E7
Buckley Rd, NW6 . . . . .90 C7
Buckley St, SE1
  off Mepham St 131 G1
Buckmaster Cl, SW9
  off Stockwell Pk Rd 151 F3
Buckmaster Rd, SW11 . . . . . . .149 H4
Bucknall St, WC2 . . . . .17 J3
Bucknall Way, Beck. BR3 . . . . .190 B4
Bucknell Cl, SW2 . . . . .151 F4
Buckner Rd, SW2 . . . . .151 F4
Buckrell Rd, E4 . . . . .62 D2
Buckstone Cl, SE23 . . . . .153 F6
Buckstone Rd, N18 . . . . .60 D6
Buck St, NW1 . . . . .92 B7
Buckters Rents, SE16 . . . . .133 H1
Buckthorne Rd, SE4 . . . . .153 H6
Buck Wk, E17 off Wood St 78 D4
Budd Cl, N12 . . . . .57 E4
Buddings Circle, Wem. HA9 . . . .88 C3
Budd's All, Twick. TW1
  off Arlington Cl 145 F5

Bude Cl, E17 . . . . .77 J5
Budge La, Mitch. CR4 . . . . .185 J7
Budge Row, EC4 . . . . .20 B5
Budge's Wk, W2 . . . . .22 C1
Budleigh Cres, Well. DA16 . . . .158 C1
Budoch Ct, Ilf. IG3 . . . . .100 A2
Budoch Dr, Ilf. IG3 . . . . .100 A2
Buer Rd, SW6 . . . . .148 B2
Bugsby's Way, SE7 . . . . .135 G4
  SE10 . . . . .135 F4
Bulganak Rd, Th.Hth. CR7 . . . .187 J4
Bulinga St, SW1 . . . . .33 J2
Bullace Row, SE5 . . . . .132 A7
Bull All, Well. DA16
  off Welling High St 158 B3
Bullards Pl, E2 . . . . .113 G3
Bullbanks Rd, Belv. DA17 . . . . .139 J4
Bullen St, SW11 . . . . .149 H2
Buller Cl, SE15 . . . . .132 D7
Buller Rd, N17 . . . . .76 D2
  N22 .75 G2
  NW10 off Chamberlayne Rd . .108 A3
  Barking IG11 . . . . .99 H7
  Thornton Heath CR7 . . . . . . .188 A2
Bullers Cl, Sid. DA14 . . . . .176 E5
Bullers Wd Dr, Chis. BR7 . . . . .174 B7
Bullescroft Rd, Edg. HA8 . . . . . .54 A3
Bullhead Rd, Borwd. WD6 . . . . .38 C3
Bullied Way, SW1 . . . . .32 E2
Bull Inn Ct, WC2 . . . . .18 B6
Bullivant St, E14 . . . . .114 C7
Bull La, N18 . . . . .60 B5
  Chislehurst BR7 . . . . .175 G7
  Dagenham RM10 . . . . .101 H3
Bull Rd, E15 . . . . .115 F2
Bullrush Cl, Croy. CR0 . . . . . . .188 B6
Bull's All, SW14 . . . . .146 D2
Bullsbrook Rd, Hayes UB4 . . . .122 C1
Bulls Br Ind Est, Sthl. UB2 . . . .122 B4
Bulls Br Rd, Sthl. UB2 . . . . . . .122 B3
Bull's Head Pas, EC3 . . . . .20 D4
Bull Yd, SE15
  off Peckham High St 152 D1
Bulmer Gdns, Har. HA3 . . . . . . .69 G7
Bulmer Ms, W11
  off Ladbroke Rd 108 D1
Bulmer Pl, W11 . . . . .128 D1
Bulow Est, SW6
  off Broughton Rd 148/149 E2
Bulrush Cl, Cars. SM5 . . . . . . .199 H2
Bulstrode Av, Houns. TW3 . . . .143 F2
Bulstrode Gdns, Houns. TW3 . .143 F3
Bulstrode Pl, W1 . . . . .16 C2
Bulstrode Rd, Houns. TW3 . . . .143 G3
Bulstrode St, W1 . . . . .16 C3
Bulwer Ct Rd, E11 . . . . .96 D1
Bulwer Gdns, Barn. EN5
  off Bulwer Rd 41 F4
Bulwer Rd, E11 . . . . .78 D7
  N18 .60 B4
  Barnet EN5 . . . . .41 E4
Bulwer St, W12 . . . . .127 J1
Bunces La, Wdf.Grn. IG8 . . . . . .63 F7
Bungalow Rd, SE25 . . . . .188 B4
Bungalows, The, SW16 . . . . . . .168 B7
  Wallington SM6 . . . . .200 B5
Bunhill Row, EC1 . . . . .12 B5
Bunhouse Pl, SW1 . . . . .32 B3
Bunkers Hill, NW11 . . . . .73 F7
  Belvedere DA17 . . . . .139 G4
  Sidcup DA14 . . . . .177 F3
Bunning Way, N7 . . . . .93 E7
Bunns La, NW7 . . . . .55 F6
Bunsen St, E3
  off Kenilworth Rd 113 H2
Buntingbridge Rd, Ilf. IG2 . . . . . .81 G5
Bunting Cl, N9 off Dunnock Cl . .61 G1
  Mitcham CR4 . . . . .185 J5
Bunton St, SE18 . . . . .136 D3
Bunyan Ct, EC2 off Beech St . .111 J5
Bunyan Rd, E17 . . . . .77 H3
Buonaparte Ms, SW1 . . . . .33 H3
Burbage Cl, SE1 . . . . .28 B6
Burbage Rd, SE21 . . . . .152 A6
  SE24 . . . . .152 A6
Burberry Cl, N.Mal. KT3 . . . . . .183 E2
Burbridge Way, N17 . . . . .76 C2
Burcham St, E14 . . . . .114 B6
Burcharbro Rd, SE2 . . . . .138 D6
Burchell Rd, E10 . . . . .96 B1
  SE15 . . . . .153 E1
Burchett Way, Rom. RM6 . . . . . .83 F6
Burcote Rd, SW18 . . . . .167 G1
Burden Cl, Brent. TW8 . . . . . . .125 F5
Burdenshott Av, Rich. TW10 . . .146 B4
Burden Way, E11
  off Brading Cres 97 H2
Burder Cl, N1 . . . . .94 B6
Burder Rd, N1
  off Balls Pond Rd 94 B6
Burdett Cl, W7
  off Cherington Rd 124 C2
  Sidcup DA14 . . . . .176 E5
Burdett Ms, NW3
  off Belsize Cres 91 G6

Burdett Ms, W2 . . . . .14 A3
Burdett Rd, E3 . . . . .113 J4
  E14 .113 J4
  Croydon CR0 . . . . .188 A6
  Richmond TW9 . . . . .145 J3
Burdetts Rd, Dag. RM9 . . . . . . .119 F7
Burdett St, SE1 . . . . .27 E5
Burdock Cl, Croy. CR0 . . . . . . .203 G1
Burdock Rd, N17 . . . . .76 D3
Burdon La, Sutt. SM2 . . . . .198 B7
Burfield Cl, SW17 . . . . .167 G4
Burford Cl, Dag. RM8 . . . . .100 C4
  Ilford IG6 . . . . .81 F4
Burford Gdns, N13 . . . . .59 F3
Burford Rd, E6 . . . . .116 B3
  E15 .96 D7
  SE6 . . . . .171 J2
  Brentford TW8 . . . . .125 H5
  Bromley BR1 . . . . .192 B4
  Sutton SM1 . . . . .198 D2
  Worcester Park KT4 . . . . .183 F7
Burford Wk, SW6
  off Cambria St 128/129 E7
Burford Way, Croy. (New Adgtn)
  CR0 . . . . .204 C6
Burges Ct, E6 . . . . .98 D7
Burges Gro, SW13 . . . . .127 H7
Burges Rd, E6 . . . . .98 B7
Burgess Av, NW9 . . . . .70 D6
Burgess Cl, Felt. TW13 . . . . . . .160 E4
Burgess Hill, NW2 . . . . .90 D4
Burgess Rd, E15 . . . . .96 E4
  Sutton SM1 . . . . .198 E4
Burgess St, E14 . . . . .114 A5
Burge St, SE1 . . . . .28 C6
★ Burgh Ho (Hampstead Mus),
  NW3 off New End Sq 91 G4
Burghill Rd, SE26 . . . . .171 H4
Burghley Av, Borwd. WD6 . . . . . .38 C5
  New Malden KT3 . . . . .182 D1
Burghley Hall Cl, SW19 . . . . . .148 B7
Burghley Ho, SW19 . . . . .166 B3
Burghley Pl, Mitch. CR4 . . . . . .186 A5
Burghley Rd, E11 . . . . .97 E1
  N8 . . . . .75 G3
  NW5 . . . . .92 B5
  SW19 . . . . .166 A4
Burghley Twr, W3 . . . . .107 F7
Burgh St, N1 . . . . .11 H1
Burgon St, EC4 . . . . .19 H4
Burgos Cl, Croy. CR0 . . . . .201 G6
Burgos Gro, SE10 . . . . .154 B1
Burgoyne Rd, N4 . . . . .75 H6
  SE25 . . . . .188 C4
  SW9 . . . . .151 F3
Burham Cl, SE20 off Maple Rd . .171 F7
Burhill Gro, Pnr. HA5 . . . . .66 E2
Burke Cl, SW15 . . . . .147 E4
Burke St, E16 . . . . .115 F6
Burket Cl, Sthl. UB2
  off Kingsbridge Rd 123 F4
Burland Rd, SW11 . . . . .149 J5
Burleigh Av, Sid. DA15 . . . . . . .157 J5
  Wallington SM6 . . . . .200 A3
Burleigh Gdns, N14 . . . . .58 C1
Burleigh Ho, W10
  off St. Charles Sq 108 A5
Burleigh Pl, SW15 . . . . .148 A5
Burleigh Rd, Enf. EN1 . . . . .44 B4
  Sutton SM3 . . . . .198 B1
Burleigh St, WC2 . . . . .18 C5
Burleigh Wk, SE6
  off Muirkirk Rd 172 C1
Burleigh Way, Enf. EN2
  off Church St 44 A3
Burley Cl, E4 . . . . .62 A5
  SW16 . . . . .186 D2
Burley Rd, E16 . . . . .115 J6
Burlington Arc, W1 . . . . .17 F6
Burlington Av, Rich. TW9 . . . . .146 A1
  Romford RM7 . . . . .83 H6
Burlington Cl, E6
  off Northumberland Rd 116 B6
  W9 .108 C4
  Feltham TW14 . . . . .141 G7
  Orpington BR6 . . . . .206 E2
  Pinner HA5 . . . . .66 B3
Burlington Gdns, W1 . . . . .17 F6
  W3 .126 C1
  W4 .126 C5
  Romford RM6 . . . . .83 E7
Burlington La, W4 . . . . .126 E7
Burlington Ms, SW15 . . . . .148 C5
  W3 .126 C1
Burlington Pl, SW6
  off Burlington Rd 148 B2
  Woodford Green IG8 . . . . .63 G3
Burlington Ri, Barn. EN4 . . . . . . .57 H1
Burlington Rd, N10
  off Tetherdown 74 A2
  N17 .76 D1
  SW6 . . . . .148 B2
  W4 .126 C5
  Enfield EN2 . . . . .44 A1
  Isleworth TW7 . . . . .144 A1
  New Malden KT3 . . . . .183 G4
  Thornton Heath CR7 . . . . . . .187 J2

Burma Rd, N16 . . . . .94 A4
Burmester Rd, SW17 . . . . .167 F3
Burnaby Cres, W4 . . . . .126 B6
Burnaby Gdns, W4 . . . . .126 C6
Burnaby St, SW10 . . . . .129 F7
Burnbrae Cl, N12 . . . . .57 E6
Burnbury Rd, SW12 . . . . .168 C1
Burncroft Av, Enf. EN3 . . . . .45 F2
Burndell Way, Hayes UB4 . . . . .102 E5
Burne Jones Ho, W14 . . . . .128 C4
Burnell Av, Rich. TW10 . . . . . . .163 F5
  Welling DA16 . . . . .158 A2
Burnell Gdns, Stan. HA7 . . . . . .69 G1
Burnell Rd, Sutt. SM1 . . . . .199 E4
Burnell Wk, SE1 . . . . .37 G3
Burnels Av, E6 . . . . .116 D3
Burness Cl, N7 off Roman Way . .93 F6
Burne St, NW1 . . . . .15 G1
Burnett Cl, E9 . . . . .95 F5
Burney Av, Surb. KT5 . . . . .181 J5
Burney Dr, Loug. IG10 . . . . .49 E2
Burney St, SE10 . . . . .134 C7
Burnfoot Av, SW6 . . . . .148 B1
Burnfoot Ct, SE22 . . . . .170 E1
Burnham, NW3 . . . . .91 H7
Burnham Cl, NW7 . . . . .55 G7
  SE1 .37 G2
  Harrow (Wldste) HA3 . . . . .68 D4
Burnham Ct, NW4 . . . . .71 J4
Burnham Cres, E11 . . . . .79 J4
  Dartford DA1 . . . .
Burnham Dr, Wor.Pk. KT4 . . . . .198 A2
Burnham Gdns, Croy. CR0 . . . .188 C7
  Hayes UB3 . . . . .121 G3
  Hounslow TW4 . . . . .142 B1
Burnham Rd, E4 . . . . .61 J5
  Dagenham RM9 . . . . .100 B7
  Morden SM4 . . . . .185 E4
  Sidcup DA14 . . . . .176 E2
Burnham St, E2 . . . . .113 F3
  Kingston upon Thames KT2 . .182 A1
Burnham Way, SE26 . . . . .171 J5
  W13 . . . . .124 E4
Burnhill Cl, SE15
  off Gervase St 132/133 E7
Burnhill Rd, Beck. BR3 . . . . . . .190 A2
Burnley Cl, Wat. WD19 . . . . .50 C5
Burnley Rd, NW10 . . . . .89 G5
  SW9 . . . . .151 F2
Burnsall St, SW3 . . . . .31 H3
Burns Av, Felt. TW14 . . . . .142 A6
  Romford (Chad.Hth) RM6 . . . . .82 C7
  Sidcup DA15 . . . . .158 B6
  Southall UB1 . . . . .103 G7
Burns Cl, E17 . . . . .78 C4
  SW19 . . . . .167 G6
  Welling DA16 . . . . .157 J1
Burns Ct, NW10 . . . . .107 F1
  SW11 . . . . .149 J3
  W13 . . . . .124 E2
  Wembley HA0 . . . . .105 G2
Burns Way, Houns. TW5 . . . . . .142 D2
Burnt Ash Hill, SE12 . . . . .155 F6
Burnt Ash La, Brom. BR1 . . . . .173 G6
Burnt Ash Rd, SE12 . . . . .155 F5
Burnthwaite Rd, SW6 . . . . .128 D7
BURNT OAK, Edg. HA8 . . . . .54 C7
Burnt Oak Bdy, Edg. HA8 . . . . . .54 B7
Burnt Oak Flds, Edg. HA8 . . . . . .70 C1
Burnt Oak La, Sid. DA15 . . . . . .158 A6
Burntwood Cl, SW18 . . . . .167 G1
Burntwood Gra Rd, SW18 . . . . .167 G1
Burntwood La, SW17 . . . . .167 H2
Burntwood Vw, SE19
  off Bowley La 170 C5
Buross St, E1
  off Commercial Rd 112/113 E6
Burpham Cl, Hayes UB4 . . . . . .102 D5
Burrage Gro, SE18 . . . . .137 G4
Burrage Pl, SE18 . . . . .137 E5
Burrage Rd, SE18 . . . . .137 G6
Burrard Rd, E16 . . . . .115 H6
  NW6 .90 D5
Burr Cl, E1 . . . . .29 H1
  Bexleyheath DA7 . . . . .159 F3
Burrell Cl, Croy. CR0 . . . . .189 H6
  Edgware HA8 . . . . .54 B2
Burrell Row, Beck. BR3
  off High St 190 A2
Burrell St, SE1 . . . . .27 G1
Burrell Twr, E10 . . . . .78 A7
Burrett Rd, Kings.T. KT1 . . . . . .182 A2
Burroughs, The, NW4 . . . . .71 H5
Burroughs Gdns, NW4 . . . . .71 H4
Burroughs Par, NW4
  off The Burroughs 71 H4
Burrow Cl, Chig. IG7
  off Burrow Rd 65 J5
Burrow Grn, Chig. IG7 . . . . .65 J5
Burrow Rd, SE22 . . . . .152 B4
  Chigwell IG7 . . . . .65 J5

Burrows Ms, SE1 27 G3
Burrows Rd, NW10 107 J3
Burrow Wk, SE21
off Rosendale Rd 151 J7
Burr Rd, SW18 148 D7
Bursdon Cl, Sid. DA15 175 J2
Bursland Rd, Enf. EN3 45 G4
Burslem St, E1 21 J4
Burstock Rd, SW15 148 B4
Burston Rd, SW15 148 A5
Burston Vil, SW15
off St. John's Av 148 A5
Burstow Rd, SW20 184 B1
Burtenshaw Rd, T.Ditt. KT7 180 D7
Burtley Cl, N4 93 J1
Burton Cl, Chess. KT9 195 G7
Thornton Heath CR7 188 A3
Burton Ct, SW3
off Franklin's Row 129 J5
Burton Gdns, Houns. TW5 143 F1
Burton Gro, SE17 36 B4
Burtonhole Cl, NW7 56 A4
Burtonhole La, NW7 56 B4
Burton La, SW9 151 G2
Burton Ms, SW1 32 C2
Burton Pl, WC1 9 J4
Burton Rd, E18 79 H3
NW6 90 C7
SW9 151 H2
Kingston upon Thames KT2 163 H7
Loughton IG10 49 F4
Burtons Rd, Hmptn. (Hmptn H.)
TW12 161 H4
Burton St, WC1 9 J4
Burt Rd, E16 135 J1
Burtwell La, SE27 170 A4
Burwash Ho, SE1 28 C4
Burwash Rd, SE18 137 G5
Burwell Av, Grnf. UB6 86 B6
Burwell Cl, E1
off Bigland St 112/113 E6
Burwell Rd, E10 95 H1
Burwell Wk, E3 114 A4
Burwood Av, Brom. BR2 205 H2
Pinner HA5 66 C5
Burwood Cl, Surb. KT6 196 A1
Burwood Pl, W2 15 H3
Bury Cl, SE16
off Rotherhithe St 133 G1
Bury Ct, EC3 20 E3
Bury Gro, Mord. SM4 184 E5
Bury Pl, WC1 18 A2
Bury Rd, E4 47 E5
N22 75 G3
Dagenham RM10 101 H5
Buryside Cl, Ilf. IG2 81 J4
Bury St, EC3 20 E4
N9 60 D1
SW1 25 F1
Bury St W, N9 44 A7
Bury Wk, SW3 31 G2
Busbridge Ho, E14
off Brabazon St 114 A5
Busby Pl, NW5 92 D6
Busby St, E2 13 G5
Bushbaby Cl, SE1 28 D6
Bushberry Rd, E9 95 H6
Bush Cl, Ilf. IG2 81 G5
Bush Cotts, SW18
off Putney Br Rd 148 D5
Bush Ct, W12
off Shepherds Bush Grn 128 A2
Bushell Cl, SW2 169 F2
Bushell Grn, Bushey (Bushey Hth)
WD23 52 A2
Bushell St, E1 29 J2
Bushell Way, Chis. BR7 174 D5
Bushey Av, E18 79 F3
Orpington BR5 193 G7
Bushey Cl, E4 62 C3
Bushey Ct, SW20 183 H2
Bushey Down, SW12
off Bedford Hill 168 B2
BUSHEY HEATH, Bushey WD23 52 B1
Bushey Hill Rd, SE5 152 B1
Bushey La, Sutt. SM1 198 D4
Bushey Lees, Sid. DA15
off Fen Gro 157 J6
BUSHEY MEAD, SW20 184 A3
Bushey Rd, E13 115 J2
N15 76 B6
SW20 183 H3
Croydon CR0 204 A2
Hayes UB3 121 H4
Sutton SM1 198 E4
Bushey Way, Beck. BR3 190 D6
Bushfield Cl, Edg. HA8 54 B2
Bushfield Cres, Edg. HA8 54 B2
Bushfields, Loug. IG10 48 D5
Bush Gro, NW9 70 C7
Stanmore HA7 69 G1
Bushgrove Rd, Dag. RM8 100 D4
Bush Hill, N21 43 J7
BUSH HILL PARK, Enf. EN1 44 B5
Bush Hill Rd, N21 44 A6
Harrow HA3 69 J6
Bush Ind Est, NW10 106 D4
Bush La, EC4 20 B5
Bushmead Cl, N15
off Copperfield Dr 76 C4
Bushmoor Cres, SE18 137 F7
Bushnell Rd, SW17 168 B2
Bush Rd, E8 112 E1
E11 79 F7
SE8 133 G4
Buckhurst Hill IG9 64 A4
Richmond TW9 125 J6
Bushway, Dag. RM8 100 D4
Bushwood, E11 97 F1
Bushwood Dr, SE1 37 G2
Bushwood Rd, Rich. TW9 126 A6
★ **Bushy Park**, Tedd. TW11 180 C1
Bushy Pk, Hmptn. (Hmptn H.)
TW12 180 C1
Teddington TW11 180 C1
Bushy Pk Gdns, Tedd. TW11 162 A5
Bushy Pk Rd, Tedd. TW11 163 E7
Bushy Rd, Tedd. TW11 162 C6
★ **Business Design Cen**, N1 111 G1
Butcher Row, E1 113 G7
E14 113 G7
Butchers Rd, E16 115 G6
Bute Av, Rich. TW10 163 H2
Bute Ct, Wall. SM6 *off Bute Rd* 200 C5
Bute Gdns, W6 128 A4
Wallington SM6 200 C5
Bute Gdns W, Wall. SM6 200 C5
Bute Ms, NW11
off Northway 72/73 E5
Bute Rd, Croy. CR0 201 G1
Ilford IG6 81 E5
Wallington SM6 200 C4
Bute St, SW7 31 E1
Bute Wk, N1 *off Marquess Rd* 94 A6
Butler Av, Har. HA1 68 A7
Butler Ct, Wem. HA0
off Harrow Rd 86 D4
Butler Pl, SW1 25 H5
Butler Rd, NW10
off Curzon Cres 89 F7
Dagenham RM8 100 B4
Harrow HA1 67 J7
Butler St, E2 *off Knottisford St* 113 F3
Butlers Wf, SE1 29 G2
Buttercup Cl, Nthlt. UB5 85 F6
Butterfield Cl, N17
off Devonshire Rd 59 J6
SE16 *off Wilson Gro* 132/133 E2
Twickenham TW1
off Rugby Rd 144 C6
Butterfields, E17 78 C5
Butterfield Sq, E6 *off Harper Rd* 116 C6
Butterfly La, SE9 156 E6
Butterfly Wk, SE5
off Denmark Hill 152 A1
Butter Hill, Cars. SM5 200 A3
Wallington SM6 200 A3
Butteridges Cl, Dag. RM9 119 F1
Buttermere Cl, E15 96 D4
SE1 37 F1
Morden SM4 184 A6
Buttermere Dr, SW15 148 B5
Buttermere Wk, E8 94 C6
Butterwick, W6 127 J4
Butterworth Gdns, Wdf.Grn.
IG8 63 G6
Buttesland St, N1 12 C3
Buttfield Cl, Dag. RM10 101 H6
Buttmarsh Cl, SE18 137 E5
Butts, The, Brent. TW8 125 G6
Sunbury-on-Thames TW16
off Elizabeth Gdns 178 C3
Buttsbury Rd, Ilf. IG1 99 F5
Butts Cotts, Felt. TW13 161 F3
Butts Cres, Felt. TW13 161 G3
Butts Piece, Nthlt. UB5
off Longhook Gdns 102 B2
Butts Rd, Brom. BR1 173 E5
Buxhall Cres, E9 95 J6
Buxted Rd, E8 94 C7
N12 57 H5
SE22 152 B4
Buxton Cl, N9 61 F2
Woodford Green IG8 64 A6
Buxton Ct, N1 12 A3
Buxton Cres, Sutt. SM3 198 B4
Buxton Dr, E11 79 E4
New Malden KT3 182 D2
Buxton Gdns, W3 106 B7
Buxton Ms, SW4
off Larkhall La 150 D2
Buxton Path, Wat. WD19 50 C3
Buxton Rd, E4 46 D7
E6 116 B3
E15 96 E5
E17 77 H4
N19 92 D1
NW2 89 H6
SW14 147 E3
Ilford IG2 81 H6
Thornton Heath CR7 187 H5
Buxton St, E1 13 G6
Buzzard Creek Ind Est, Bark.
IG11 117 J5
Byam St, SW6 149 F2
Byards Cft, SW16 186 D1
Byatt Wk, Hmptn. TW12
off Victors Dr 160/161 E6
Bychurch End, Tedd. TW11
off Church Rd 162 C5
Bycroft Rd, Sthl. UB1 103 G4
Bycroft St, SE20 *off Parish La* 171 G7
Byculla Av, Enf. EN2 43 H3
Bycullah Rd, Enf. EN2 43 H3
Bye, The, W3 107 E6
Byegrove Rd, SW19 167 G6
Byeway, The, SW14 146 C3
Bye Way, The, Har. HA3 68 B1
Byeways, Twick. TW2 161 H3
Byeways, The, Surb. KT5 182 A5
Byfeld Gdns, SW13 147 G1
Byfield Cl, SE16 133 H2
Byfield Pas, Islw. TW7 144 D3
Byfield Rd, Islw. TW7 144 D3
Byford Cl, E15 97 E7
Bygrove, Croy. (New Adgtn)
CR0 204 B6
Bygrove St, E14 114 B6
Byland Cl, N21 43 F7
Bylands Cl, SE2
off Finchale Rd 138 B3
SE16 *off Rotherhithe St* 133 G1
Byne Rd, SE26 171 F6
Carshalton SM5 199 H2
Bynes Rd, S.Croy. CR2 202 A7
Byng Pl, WC1 9 H6
Byng Rd, Barn. EN5 40 A3
Byng St, E14 134 A2
Bynon Av, Bexh. DA7 159 E3
Byre, The, N14 *off Farm La* 42 B6
Byre Rd, N14 *off Farm La* 42 A6
Byrne Rd, SW12 168 B1
Byron Av, E12 98 B6
E18 79 F3
NW9 70 B4
Borehamwood WD6 38 A5
Hounslow TW4 142 A2
New Malden KT3 183 G5
Sutton SM1 199 G4
Byron Av E, Sutt. SM1 199 G4
Byron Cl, E8 112 D1
SE26 *off Porthcawe Rd* 171 H4
SE28 138 C1
Hampton TW12 161 F4
Byron Ct, W9 *off Lanhill Rd* 108 D4
Enfield EN2 *off Bycullah Rd* 43 H2
Harrow HA1 68 B6
Byron Dr, N2 73 G6
Erith DA8 139 H7
Byron Gdns, Sutt. SM1 199 G4
Byron Hill Rd, Har. HA2 86 A1
Byron Ho, Beck. BR3 172 A6
Byron Ms, NW3 91 H5
W9 *off Shirland Rd* 108 D4
Byron Rd, E10 96 B1
E17 78 A3
NW2 89 H2
NW7 55 G5
W5 125 J1
Harrow HA1 68 B6
Harrow (Wldste) HA3 68 C2
Wembley HA0 87 F3
Byron St, E14
off St. Leonards Rd 114 C6
Byron Ter, N9 45 F7
Byron Way, Nthlt. UB5 102 E3
West Drayton UB7 120 C4
Bysouth Cl, N15 76 A4
Ilford IG5 80 E1
By the Wd, Wat. WD19 50 D2
Bythorn St, SW9 151 F3
Byton Rd, SW17 167 J6
Byward Av, Felt. TW14 142 C6
Byward St, EC3 20 E6
Bywater Pl, SE16 133 H1
Bywater St, SW3 31 J3
Byway, The, Epsom KT19 197 F4
Bywell Pl, W1 17 F2
Bywood Av, Croy. CR0 189 F6
Byworth Wk, N19
off Courtauld Rd 92 D1

C

Cabbell St, NW1 15 G2
★ **Cabinet War Rooms**, SW1 25 J3
Cabinet Way, E4 61 J6
Cable Pl, SE10 *off Diamond Ter* 154 C1
Cable St, E1 21 H5
Cable Trade Pk, SE7 135 J4
Cabot Pl, E14 134 A1
Cabot Sq, E14 134 A1
Cabot Way, E6 *off Parr Rd* 116 A1
Cabul Rd, SW11 149 H2
Cactus Cl, SE15
off Lyndhurst Gro 152 B2
Cactus Wk, W12
off Du Cane Rd 107 F6
Cadbury Cl, Islw. TW7 144 D1
Cadbury Way, SE16 29 G6
Caddington Cl, Barn. EN4 41 H5
Caddington Rd, NW2 90 B3
Caddis Cl, Stan. HA7
off Daventer Dr 52 C7
Cadell Cl, E2 13 G2
Cade Rd, SE10 154 D1
Cader Rd, SW18 149 F6
Cadet Dr, SE1 37 G3
Cadet Pl, SE10 134 E5
Cadiz Rd, Dag. RM10 101 J7
Cadiz St, SE17 36 A4
Cadley Ter, SE23 171 F2
Cadman Cl, SW9
off Langton Rd 131 H7
Cadmer Cl, N.Mal. KT3 182 E4
Cadmus Cl, SW4
off Aristotle Rd 150 D3
Cadnam Pt, SW15
off Dilton Gdns 165 H1
Cadogan Cl, E9 *off Cadogan Ter* 95 J7
Beckenham BR3
off Albemarle Rd 190 D1
Harrow HA2 85 H4
Teddington TW11 162 B5
Cadogan Ct, Sutt. SM2 199 E6
Cadogan Gdns, E18 79 H3
N3 72 E1
N21 43 G5
SW3 32 A1
Cadogan Gate, SW1 32 A1
Cadogan La, SW1 24 B6
Cadogan Pl, SW1 24 A5
Cadogan Rd, SE18 137 F3
Surbiton KT6 181 G5
Cadogan Sq, SW1 24 A6
Cadogan St, SW3 31 J2
Cadogan Ter, E9 95 J6
Cadoxton Av, N15 76 C6
Cadwallon Rd, SE9 175 E2
Caedmon Rd, N7 93 F4
Caerleon Cl, Esher (Clay.) KT10 194 E7
Sidcup DA14 176 C5
Caerleon Ter, SE2
off Blithdale Rd 138 B4
Caernarvon Cl, Mitch. CR4 186 E3
Caernarvon Dr, Ilf. IG5 80 D1
Caesars Wk, Mitch. CR4 185 J5
Cahill St, EC1 12 A6
Cahir St, E14 134 B4
Cains La, Felt. TW14 141 H5
Caird St, W10 108 B3
Cairn Av, W5 125 G1
Cairndale Cl, Brom. BR1 173 F7
Cairnes Ms, SE18
off Shooter's Hill Rd 156 B1
Cairnfield Av, NW2 89 E3
Cairngorm Cl, Tedd. TW11
off Vicarage Rd 162 D5
Cairns Av, Wdf.Grn. IG8 64 B6
Cairns Rd, SW11 149 H5
Cairn Way, Stan. HA7 52 C6
Cairo New Rd, Croy. CR0 201 H2
Cairo Rd, E17 78 A4
Caishowe Rd, Borwd. WD6 38 B1
Caistor Ms, SW12
off Caistor Rd 150 B7
Caistor Pk Rd, E15 115 F1
Caistor Rd, SW12 150 B7
Caithness Gdns, Sid. DA15 157 J6
Caithness Rd, W14 128 A4
Mitcham CR4 168 B7
Calabria Rd, N5 93 H6
Calais Gate, SE5 *off Calais St* 151 H1
Calais St, SE5 151 H1
Calbourne Rd, SW12 149 J7
Calcott Wk, SE9 174 A4
Caldbeck Av, Wor.Pk. KT4 197 G2
Caldecot Rd, SE5 151 J2
Caldecott Way, E5 95 G3
Calder Av, Grnf. UB6 104 C2
Calder Cl, Enf. EN1 44 B3
Calder Gdns, Edg. HA8 70 A3
Calderon Pl, W10
off St. Quintin Gdns 107 J5
Calderon Rd, E11 96 C4
Calder Rd, Mord. SM4 185 F5
Caldervale Rd, SW4 150 D5
Calderwood St, SE18 136 D4
Caldicot Grn, NW9
off Snowdon Dr 70/71 E6
Caldwell Rd, Wat. WD19 50 D4
Caldwell St, SW9 131 F7
Caldwell Yd, EC4
off Upper Thames St 111 J7
Caldy Rd, Belv. DA17 139 H3
Caldy Wk, N1 *off Clephane Rd* 93 J6
Caleb St, SE1 27 J3
Caledonian Cl, Ilf. IG3 100 B1
Caledonian Rd, N1 10 B2
N7 93 F5
Caledonian Wf, E14 134 D4
Caledonia St, N1 10 B2
Caledon Rd, E6 116 B1
Wallington SM6 200 A4
Cale St, SW3 31 G3
Caletock Way, SE10 135 F5
Calico Row, SW11 *off York Pl* 149 F3

Calidore Cl, SW2
   off Endymion Rd 151 F6
California La, Bushey (Bushey Hth)
   WD23 ....52 A1
California Rd, N.Mal. KT3 ....182 C4
Callaby Ter, N1 off Wakeham St ..94 A6
Callaghan Cl, SE13
   off Glenton Rd 154/155 E4
Callander Rd, SE6 ....172 B2
Callard Av, N13 ....59 H5
Callcott Rd, NW6 ....90 C7
Callcott St, W8 off Hillgate Pl ..128 D1
Callendar Rd, SW7 ......22 E5
Callingham Cl, E14
   off Wallwood St 113 J5
Callis Fm Cl, Stai. (Stanw.) TW19
   off Bedfont Rd 140 B6
Callis Rd, E17 ....77 J6
Callow St, SW3 ....30 D5
Calmont Rd, Brom. BR1 ....172 D6
Calne Av, Ilf. IG5 ....80 E1
Calonne Rd, SW19 ....166 A4
Calshot Rd, Houns. (Hthrw Air.)
   TW6 ....140 D2
Calshot St, N1 ....10 C1
Calshot Way, Enf. EN2 ......43 H3
   Hounslow (Hthrw Air.) TW6
   off Calshot Rd 140/141 E2
Calthorpe Gdns, Edg. HA8
   off Jesmond Way 53 H5
   Sutton SM1 ....199 F3
Calthorpe St, WC1 ....10 D5
Calton Av, SE21 ....152 B5
Calton Rd, Barn. EN5 ......41 F6
Calverley Cl, Beck. BR3 ....172 B6
Calverley Cres, Dag. RM10 ..101 G2
Calverley Gdns, Har. HA3 ....69 G7
Calverley Gro, N19 ....92 D1
Calverley Rd, Epsom KT17 ..197 G6
Calvert Av, E2 ....13 E4
Calvert Cl, Belv. DA17 ......139 G4
   Sidcup DA14 ....176 E6
Calverton, SE5 ....36 C5
Calverton Rd, E6 ....116 D1
Calvert Rd, SE10 ....135 F5
   Barnet EN5 ....40 A2
Calvert's Bldgs, SE1 ......28 B2
Calvert St, NW1 off Chalcot Rd ..110 A1
Calvin St, E1 ....13 F6
Calydon Rd, SE7 ....135 H5
Calypso Cres, SE15
   off Samuel St 132 C7
Calypso Way, SE16 ....133 J3
Camac Rd, Twick. TW2 ......162 A1
Cambalt Rd, SW15 ....148 A5
Camberley Av, SW20 ....183 H2
   Enfield EN1 ....44 B4
Camberley Cl, Sutt. SM3 ....198 A3
Camberley Rd, Houns. (Hthrw Air.)
   TW6 ....140 D3
Cambert Way, SE3 ....155 H4
CAMBERWELL, SE5 ....131 J7
Camberwell Ch St, SE5 ....152 A1
Camberwell Glebe, SE5 ....152 A1
Camberwell Grn, SE5 ......152 A1
Camberwell Gro, SE5 ......152 A1
Camberwell New Rd, SE5 ....35 E6
Camberwell Pas, SE5
   off Camberwell Grn 151 J1
Camberwell Rd, SE5 ......36 A6
Camberwell Sta Rd, SE5 ....151 J1
Cambeys Rd, Dag. RM10 ....101 H5
Camborne Av, W13 ....125 E2
Camborne Cl, Houns. (Hthrw Air.)
   TW6 off Camborne Rd S ..140 D3
Camborne Ms, W11
   off St. Marks Rd 108 B6
Camborne Rd, SW18 ......148 D7
   Croydon CR0 ....188 D7
   Morden SM4 ....184 A5
   Sidcup DA14 ....176 C3
   Sutton SM2 ....198 D7
   Welling DA16 ....157 J2
Camborne Rd N, Houns. (Hthrw Air.)
   TW6 off Camborne Rd S ..140 D3
Camborne Rd S, Houns. (Hthrw Air.)
   TW6 ....140 D3
Camborne Way, Houns. TW5 ..143 G1
   Hounslow (Hthrw Air.) TW6
   off Camborne Rd S 140 D3
Cambourne Av, N9 ....45 G7
Cambray Rd, SW12 ....168 C1
   Orpington BR6 ....193 J7
Cambria Cl, Houns. TW3 ....143 G4
   Sidcup DA15 ....175 G1
Cambria Ct, Felt. TW14
   off Hounslow Rd 142 B7
Cambria Gdns, Stai. TW19 ..140 B7
Cambria Ho, SE26
   off High Level Dr 170 D4
Cambrian Av, Ilf. IG2 ......81 H5
Cambrian Cl, SE27 ....169 H3
Cambrian Grn, NW9
   off Snowdon Dr 70/71 E5
Cambrian Rd, E10 ....78 A7
   Richmond TW10 ....145 J6
Cambria Rd, SE5 ....151 J3

Cambria St, SW6 ....129 E7
Cambridge Av, NW6 ....108 D2
   Greenford UB6 ....86 C5
   New Malden KT3 ....183 F2
   Welling DA16 ....157 J4
Cambridge Barracks Rd, SE18 ..136 C4
Cambridge Circ, WC2 ......17 J4
Cambridge Cl, E17 ....77 J6
   N22 off Pellatt Gro 75 G1
   NW10 off Lawrence Way ..88 C3
   SW20 ....183 H1
   Hounslow TW4 ....143 E4
   West Drayton UB7 ......120 A6
Cambridge Cotts, Rich. TW9 ..126 A6
Cambridge Cres, E2 ....112 E2
   Teddington TW11 ....162 D5
Cambridge Dr, SE12 ......155 G5
   Ruislip HA4 ....84 C2
Cambridge Gdns, N10 ......74 B1
   N13 ....59 H5
   N17 off Great Cambridge Rd ..60 A7
   N21 ....44 A7
   NW6 ....108 D2
   W10 ....108 B6
   Enfield EN1 ....44 D4
   Kingston upon Thames KT1 ..182 A2
Cambridge Gate, NW1 ......8 E4
Cambridge Gate Ms, NW1 ....8 E4
Cambridge Grn, SE9 ......174 E1
Cambridge Gro, SE20 ......188 E1
   W6 ....127 H4
Cambridge Gro Rd, Kings.T.
   KT1 ....182 A2
Cambridge Heath Rd, E1 ....113 E2
   E2 ....113 E2
Cambridge Mans, SW11
   off Cambridge Rd 149 J1
Cambridge Par, Enf. EN1
   off Great Cambridge Rd 44 D1
Cambridge Pk, E11 ....79 G7
   Twickenham TW1 ....145 F7
Cambridge Pk Rd, E11
   off Cambridge Pk 79 F7
Cambridge Pl, W8 ....22 B4
Cambridge Rd, E4 ....62 D1
   E11 ....79 F6
   NW6 ....108 D3
   SE20 ....188 E3
   SW11 ....149 J1
   SW13 ....147 F2
   SW20 ....183 G1
   W7 ....124 C2
   Barking IG11 ....99 F7
   Bromley BR1 ....173 G7
   Carshalton SM5 ....199 H6
   Hampton TW12 ....161 F7
   Harrow HA2 ....67 G5
   Hounslow TW4 ....143 E4
   Ilford IG3 ....99 H1
   Kingston upon Thames KT1 ..181 J2
   Mitcham CR4 ....186 C3
   New Malden KT3 ....182 E4
   Richmond TW9 ....126 A7
   Sidcup DA14 ....175 H4
   Southall UB1 ....123 F1
   Teddington TW11 ....162 C4
   Twickenham TW1 ....145 G6
   Walton-on-Thames KT12 ..178 B6
   West Molesey KT8 ......179 F4
Cambridge Rd N, W4 ......126 B5
Cambridge Rd S, W4 ......126 B5
Cambridge Row, SE18 ......137 E5
Cambridge Sq, W2 ....15 G3
Cambridge St, SW1 ....32 E2
Cambridge Ter, N13 ....59 G5
   NW1 ....8 E4
Cambridge Ter Ms, NW1 ....8 E4
Cambstone Cl, N11 ....58 A2
Cambus Cl, Hayes UB4 ....103 E5
Cambus Rd, E16 ....115 G5
Camdale Rd, SE18 ....137 J7
★ Camden Arts Cen, NW3 ....91 F5
Camden Av, Felt. TW13 ....160 C2
   Hayes UB4 ....102 C7
Camden Cl, Chis. BR7 ......175 F7
Camden Gdns, NW1
   off Kentish Town Rd 92 B7
   Sutton SM1 ....198 E5
   Thornton Heath CR7 ......187 H3
Camden Gro, Chis. BR7 ....175 E6
Camden High St, NW1 ......110 B1
Camden Hill Rd, SE19 ......170 B6
Camdenhurst St, E14 ......113 H6
Camden La, N7
   off Rowstock Gdns 92 D6
★ Camden Lock Mkt & Waterbuses,
   NW1 ....92 B7
Camden Lock Pl, NW1
   off Chalk Fm Rd 92 B7
Camden Ms, NW1 ....92 D6
Camden Pk Rd, NW1 ......92 D6
   Chislehurst BR7 ....174 C7
Camden Pas, N1 ....111 H1
Camden Rd, E11 ....79 H6
   E17 ....77 J6
   N7 ....92 D5
   NW1 ....110 C1

Camden Rd, Bex. DA5 ......177 F1
   Carshalton SM5 ....199 J4
   Sutton SM1 ....198 D5
Camden Row, SE3 ....155 E2
Camden Sq, NW1 ....92 D6
   SE15 off Watts St 152 C1
Camden St, NW1 ....92 B7
Camden Ter, NW1 off North Vil ..92 D6
CAMDEN TOWN, NW1 ....110 C1
Camden Wk, N1 ....111 H1
Camden Way, Chis. BR7 ....174 C7
   Thornton Heath CR7 ......187 H3
Camelford Wk, W11
   off Lancaster Rd 108 B6
Camel Gro, Kings.T. KT2 ....163 G5
Camellia Ct, Wdf.Grn. IG8
   off The Bridle Path 62/63 E7
Camellia Pl, Twick. TW2 ....143 H7
Camellia St, SW8 ....130 E7
Camelot Cl, SE28 ....137 G2
   SW19 ....166 D4
Camelot St, SE15
   off Bird in Bush Rd 132/133 E7
Camel Rd, E16 ....136 A1
Camera Pl, SW10 ....30 E6
Cameron Cl, N18 ....61 E4
   N20 off Myddelton Pk 57 H2
Cameron Pl, E1
   off Varden St 112/113 E6
Cameron Rd, SE6 ....171 J2
   Bromley BR2 ....191 G4
   Croydon CR0 ....187 H6
   Ilford IG3 ....99 H1
Cameron Sq, Mitch. CR4 ....185 H1
Camerton Cl, E8
   off Buttermere Wk 94 C6
Camgate Cen, Stai. (Stanw.)
   TW19 ....140 C6
Camilla Rd, SE16 ....132 E4
Camille Cl, SE25 ....188 D3
Camlan Rd, Brom. BR1 ....173 F4
Camlet St, E2 ....13 F5
Camlet Way, Barn. EN4 ....40 D2
Camley St, NW1 ....9 J1
★ Camley St Natural Pk, NW1 ..9 J1
Camm Gdns, Kings.T. KT1
   off Church Rd 181 J2
   Thames Ditton KT7 ......180 B7
Camms Ter, Dag. RM10 ....101 J5
Camomile Av, Mitch. CR4 ....185 J1
Camomile St, EC3 ....20 D3
Campana Rd, SW6 ....148 D1
Campbell Av, Ilf. IG6 ......81 F4
Campbell Cl, SE18
   off Moordown 156 D1
   SW16 ....168 D4
   Ruislip HA4 ....66 A4
   Twickenham TW2 ....162 A2
Campbell Ct, N17 ....76 C1
   SE22 off Lordship La 152 D7
Campbell Cft, Edg. HA8 ....54 A5
Campbell Gordon Way, NW2 ..89 H4
Campbell Rd, E3 ....114 A3
   E6 ....116 B1
   E15 off Trevelyan Rd 97 F4
   E17 ....77 J4
   N17 ....76 D1
   W7 ....104 B7
   Croydon CR0 ....187 H7
   East Molesey KT8
   off Hampton Ct Rd 180 C3
   Twickenham TW2 ....162 A2
Campbell Wk, N1
   off Outram Pl 110/111 E1
Campdale Rd, N7 ....92 D3
Campden Cres, Dag. RM8 ..100 B4
   Wembley HA0 ....87 E2
Campden Gro, W8 ....128 D2
Campden Hill Ct, W8
   off Campden Hill Rd 128 D2
Campden Hill Gdns, W8 ....128 D1
Campden Hill Gate, W8
   off Duchess of Bedford's Wk ..128 D2
Campden Hill Pl, W11
   off Holland Pk Av 128 C1
Campden Hill Rd, W8 ......128 D1
Campden Hill Sq, W8 ......128 C1
Campden Hill Twrs, W11
   off Notting Hill Gate 128 D1
Campden Ho Cl, W8
   off Hornton St 128 D2
Campden Rd, S.Croy. CR2 ..202 B5
Campden St, W8 ....128 D1
Campen Cl, SW19 ....166 B2
Camperdown St, E1 ......21 G4
Campfield Rd, SE9 ....156 A7
Campion Cl, E6 ....116 C7
   Croydon CR0 ....202 B4
   Harrow HA3 ....69 J6
Campion Gdns, Wdf.Grn. IG8 ..63 G5
Campion Pl, SE28 ....138 B1
Campion Rd, SW15 ....147 J4
   Isleworth TW7 ....144 C1
Campion Ter, NW2 ....90 A3
Campion Way, Edg. HA8 ....54 C4
Camplin Rd, Har. HA3 ......69 H5
Camplin St, SE14 ....133 G7

Camp Rd, SW19 ....165 J5
Campsbourne, The, N8
   off High St 74/75 F4
Campsbourne Rd, N8 ......75 E3
Campsey Gdns, Dag. RM9 ..100 B7
Campsey Rd, Dag. RM9 ....100 B7
Campsfield Rd, N8
   off Campsbourne Rd 74/75 E3
Campshill Pl, SE13
   off Campshill Rd 154 C5
Campshill Rd, SE13 ......154 C5
Campus Rd, E17 ....77 J6
Campus Way, NW4
   off Greyhound Hill 71 J3
Camp Vw, SW19 ....165 H5
Cam Rd, E15 ....114 D1
Camrose Av, Edg. HA8 ....69 J2
   Erith DA8 ....139 H6
   Feltham TW13 ....160 B4
Camrose Cl, Croy. CR0 ....189 H7
   Morden SM4 ....184 D4
Camrose St, SE2 ....138 A5
Canada Av, N18 ....59 J6
Canada Cres, W3 ....106 C5
Canada Est, SE16 ....133 F3
Canada Gdns, SE13 ......154 C5
Canada Rd, W3 ....106 C4
Canada Sq, E14 ....134 B1
Canada St, SE16 ....133 G2
Canada Way, W12 ....107 H7
Canadian Av, SE6 ....172 B1
Canal App, SE8 ....133 H6
Canal Cl, E1 ....113 H4
   W10 ....108 A4
Canal Gro, SE15 ....37 J5
Canal Path, E2 ....112 C1
Canal St, SE5 ....36 B6
Canal Wk, N1 ....112 A1
   SE26 ....171 F5
   Croydon CR0 ....188 B6
Canal Way, N1 ....12 A1
   NW1 ....7 H3
   NW8 ....7 G4
   NW10 ....107 F4
   W10 ....108 A4
Canal Way Wk, W10 ......108 A4
Canberra Cl, NW4 ....71 G3
Canberra Dr, Hayes UB4 ..102 C3
   Northolt UB5 ....102 C3
Canberra Rd, E6
   off Barking Rd 116 C1
   SE7 ....135 J6
   W13 ....124 D1
   Bexleyheath DA7 ....138 D6
   Hounslow (Hthrw Air.) TW6 ..140 D3
Canbury Av, Kings.T. KT2 ..181 J1
Canbury Ms, SE26
   off Wells Pk Rd 170 D3
Canbury Pk Rd, Kings.T. KT2 ..181 H1
Canbury Pas, Kings.T. KT2 ..181 G1
Cancell Rd, SW9 ....151 G1
Candahar Rd, SW11 ......149 H2
Candle Gro, SE15 ....153 E3
Candlemakers Apartments, SW18
   off York Rd 149 G3
Candler St, N15 ....76 A6
Candover Cl, West Dr. UB7 ..120 A7
Candover St, W1 ....17 F2
Candy St, E3 ....113 J1
Caney Ms, NW2
   off Claremont Rd 90 A2
Canfield Dr, Ruis. HA4 ....84 B5
Canfield Gdns, NW6 ......91 F7
Canfield Pl, NW6
   off Canfield Gdns 91 F6
Canfield Rd, Wdf.Grn. IG8 ..64 B7
Canford Av, Nthlt. UB5 ....103 E1
Canford Cl, Enf. EN2 ......43 G2
Canford Gdns, N.Mal. KT3 ..182 D6
Canford Pl, Tedd. TW11 ....163 E6
Canford Rd, SW11 ....150 A5
Canham Rd, SE25 ....188 B3
   W3 ....126 E2
Canmore Gdns, SW16 ....168 C7
Cann Hall Rd, E11 ....96 E4
Canning Cres, N22 ....75 F1
Canning Cross, SE5 ......152 B2
Canning Pas, W8 ....22 C5
Canning Pl, W8 ....22 C5
Canning Pl Ms, W8 ......22 C4
Canning Rd, E15 ....114 E2
   E17 ....77 H4
   N5 ....93 H3
   Croydon CR0 ....202 C2
   Harrow HA3 ....68 C3
Cannington Rd, Dag. RM9 ..100 C6
CANNING TOWN, E16 ......115 G6
Cannizaro Rd, SW19 ......165 J6
Cannonbury Av, Pnr. HA5 ..66 D6
Cannon Cl, SW20 ....183 J3
   Hampton TW12
   off Hanworth Rd 161 H6
Cannon Ct, EC1 off St. John St ..111 H4
Cannon Dr, E14 ....114 A7
Cannon Hill, N14 ....58 D3
   NW6 ....90 D5
Cannon Hill La, SW20 ....184 B3

Cannon La, NW3 . . . . .91 G3
Pinner HA5 . . . . .84 E1
Cannon PI, NW3 . . . . .91 G3
SE7 . . . . .136 B5
Cannon Rd, N14 . . . . .58 E3
Bexleyheath DA7 . . . . .159 E1
Cannon St, EC4 . . . . .19 J4
Cannon St Rd, E1 . . . . .112 E6
Cannon Trd Est, Wem. HA9 . . .88 B4
Cannon Way, W.Mol. KT8 . . . .179 G4
Cannon Wf Business Cen, SE8 .133 H4
Cannon Workshops, E14
off Cannon Dr 114 A7
Canon Av, Rom. RM6 . . . . . . .82 C5
Canon Beck Rd, SE16 . . . . . .133 F2
Canonbie Rd, SE23 . . . . .153 F7
CANONBURY, N1 . . . . .93 J6
Canonbury Cres, N1 . . . . .93 J7
Canonbury Gro, N1 . . . . .93 J7
Canonbury La, N1 . . . . .93 H7
Canonbury Pk N, N1 . . . . .93 J6
Canonbury Pk S, N1 . . . . .93 J6
Canonbury PI, N1 . . . . .93 H6
Canonbury Rd, N1 . . . . .93 H6
Enfield EN1 . . . . .44 B1
Canonbury Sq, N1 . . . . .93 H7
Canonbury St, N1 . . . . .93 J7
Canonbury Vil, N1 . . . . .93 H7
Canonbury Yd, N1
off New N Rd 111 J1
Canonbury Yd W, N1
off Compton Rd 93 H6
Canon Mohan Cl, N14
off Farm La 42 B6
Canon Rd, Brom. BR1 . . . . . .191 J3
Canon Row, SW1 . . . . .26 A4
Canons Cl, N2 . . . . .73 G7
Edgware HA8 . . . . .53 J6
Canons Cor, Edg. HA8 . . . . . .53 H4
Canons Dr, Edg. HA8 . . . . . . .53 H6
Canonsleigh Rd, Dag. RM9 . . .100 B7
CANONS PARK, Edg. HA8 . . . .53 H7
Canons Pk Cl, Edg. HA8
off Donnefield Av 53 H7
Canon St, N1 . . . . .111 J1
Canons Wk, Croy. CR0 . . . . . .203 G3
Canopus Way, Nthwd. HA6 . . . .50 A4
Staines TW19 . . . . .140 B7
Canrobert St, E2 . . . . .112 E3
Cantelowes Rd, NW1 . . . . . . .92 D6
Canterbury Av, Ilf. IG1 . . . . . .80 B7
Sidcup DA15 . . . . .176 C2
Canterbury Cl, E6
off Harper Rd 116 C6
Beckenham BR3 . . . . .190 B1
Chigwell IG7 . . . . .65 J3
Greenford UB6 . . . . .103 H6
Canterbury Cres, SW9 . . . . . .151 G3
Canterbury Gro, SE27 . . . . . .169 H3
Canterbury Ho, Borwd. WD6 . . .38 A2
Canterbury PI, SE17 . . . . .35 H2
Canterbury Rd, E10 . . . . .78 C7
NW6 . . . . .108 D2
Borehamwood WD6 . . . . . . .38 A2
Croydon CR0 . . . . .187 F7
Feltham TW13 . . . . .161 E2
Harrow HA1, HA2 . . . . .67 H5
Morden SM4 . . . . .185 F5
Canterbury Ter, NW6 . . . . . . .108 D2
Cantium Retail Pk, SE1 . . . . . .37 J5
Cantley Gdns, SE19 . . . . . . .188 C1
Ilford IG2 . . . . .81 F6
Cantley Rd, W7 . . . . .124 D3
Canton St, E14 . . . . .114 A6
Cantrell Rd, E3 . . . . .113 J4
Cantwell Rd, SE18 . . . . .136 E7
Canute Gdns, SE16 . . . . .133 G4
Canvey St, SE1 . . . . .27 H1
Cape Cl, Bark. IG11 off North St . .99 F6
Capel Av, Wall. SM6 . . . . . . .201 F5
Capel Cl, N20 . . . . .57 F3
Bromley BR2 . . . . .206 B1
Capel Ct, EC2 . . . . .20 C4
SE20 off Melvin Rd 189 F1
Capel Gdns, Ilf. IG3 . . . . .99 J4
Pinner HA5 . . . . .67 F4
Capel Pt, E7 . . . . .97 H4
Capel Rd, E7 . . . . .97 H4
E12 . . . . .97 J4
Barnet EN4 . . . . .41 H6
Capener's Cl, SW1 . . . . .24 B4
Capern Rd, SW18
off Cargill Rd 167 F1
Cape Rd, N17
off High Cross Rd 76 D3
Cape Yd, E1 . . . . .29 J1
Capital Business Cen, Wem.
HA0 . . . . .105 G2
Capital Ind Est, Mitch. CR4
off Willow La 185 J5
Capital Interchange Way, Brent.
TW8 . . . . .126 A5
Capitol Ind Pk, NW9 . . . . .70 C3
Capitol Way, NW9 . . . . .70 C3
Capland St, NW8 . . . . .7 F5
Caple Par, NW10
off Harley Rd 106/107 E2

Caple Rd, NW10 . . . . .107 F2
Capper St, WC1 . . . . .9 G6
Caprea Cl, Hayes UB4
off Triandra Way 102 D5
Capri Rd, Croy. CR0 . . . . . . .202 C1
Capstan Cl, Rom. RM6 . . . . . .82 B6
Capstan Ride, Enf. EN2 . . . . . .43 G2
Capstan Rd, SE8 . . . . .133 J4
Capstan Sq, E14 . . . . .134 C2
Capstan Way, SE16 . . . . .133 H1
Capstone Rd, Brom. BR1 . . . .173 F4
Capthorne Av, Har. HA2 . . . . . .85 E1
Capulet Ms, E16
off Hanover Av 135 G1
Capworth St, E10 . . . . .96 A1
Caradoc Cl, W2 . . . . .108 D6
Caradoc St, SE10 . . . . .134 E5
Caradon Cl, E11
off Brockway Cl 96/97 E2
Caradon Way, N15 . . . . .76 A4
Caravel Cl, E14 off Tiller Rd . . .134 A3
Caravelle Gdns, Nthlt. UB5
off Javelin Way 102 D3
Caravel Ms, SE8
off Watergate St 134 A6
Caraway Cl, E13 . . . . .115 H5
Caraway PI, Wall. SM6 . . . . . .200 B3
Carberry Rd, SE19 . . . . .170 B6
Carbery Av, W3 . . . . .125 J2
Carbis Cl, E4 . . . . .62 D1
Carbis Rd, E14 . . . . .113 J6
Carbuncle Pas Way, N17 . . . . .76 D2
Carburton St, W1 . . . . .17 E1
Cardale St, E14 off Plevna St . . .134 C3
Carden Rd, SE15 . . . . .152 E3
Cardiff Rd, W7 . . . . .124 D3
Enfield EN3 . . . . .45 E4
Cardiff St, SE18 . . . . .137 H7
Cardigan Gdns, Ilf. IG3 . . . . .100 A2
Cardigan Rd, E3 . . . . .113 J2
SW13 . . . . .147 G2
SW19 off Haydons Rd 167 F6
Richmond TW10 . . . . .145 H6
Cardigan St, SE11 . . . . .34 E3
Cardigan Wk, N1 off Ashby Gro . .93 J7
Cardinal Av, Borwd. WD6 . . . . .38 B3
Kingston upon Thames KT2 . .163 H5
Morden SM4 . . . . .184 B6
Cardinal Bourne St, SE1 . . . . . .28 C6
Cardinal Cl, Chis. BR7 . . . . . .193 G1
Edgware HA8 off Abbots Rd . . .54 D7
Morden SM4 . . . . .184 B7
Worcester Park KT4 . . . . . . .197 G4
Cardinal Ct, Borwd. WD6
off Cardinal Av 38 B3
Cardinal Cres, N.Mal. KT3 . . . .182 C2
Cardinal Dr, Ilf. IG6 . . . . .65 F6
Cardinal Hinsley Cl, NW10 . . . .107 G2
Cardinal PI, SW15 . . . . .148 A4
Cardinal Rd, Felt. TW13 . . . . .160 B1
Ruislip HA4 . . . . .84 D1
Cardinals Wk, Hmptn. TW12 . . .161 J7
Cardinals Way, N19 . . . . .92 D1
Cardinal Way, Har. HA3
off Wolseley Rd 68 B3
Cardine Ms, SE15 . . . . .132 E7
Cardington Sq, Houns. TW4 . . .142 D4
Cardington St, NW1 . . . . .9 F3
Cardinham Rd, Orp. BR6 . . . . .207 J4
Cardozo Rd, N7 . . . . .93 E5
Cardrew Av, N12 . . . . .57 G5
Cardrew Cl, N12 . . . . .57 H5
Cardross St, W6 . . . . .127 H3
Cardwell Rd, N7 . . . . .92 E4
Carew Cl, N7 . . . . .93 F2
Carew Rd, N17 . . . . .76 D2
W13 . . . . .125 F2
Mitcham CR4 . . . . .186 A2
Thornton Heath CR7 . . . . . .187 H3
Wallington SM6 . . . . .200 C6
Carew St, SE5 . . . . .151 J2
Carew Way, Wat. WD19 . . . . . .51 F3
Carey Ct, Bexh. DA6 . . . . . . .159 H5
Carey Gdns, SW8 . . . . .150 C1
Carey La, EC2 . . . . .19 J3
Carey PI, SW1 . . . . .33 H2
Carey Rd, Dag. RM9 . . . . . . .101 E4
Carey St, WC2 . . . . .18 D4
Carey Way, Wem. HA9 . . . . . . .88 B4
Carfax PI, SW4 off Holwood PI . .150 D4
Carfax Rd, Hayes UB3 . . . . . .121 J5
Carfree Cl, N1 off Bewdley St . . .93 G7
Cargill Rd, SW18 . . . . .167 E1
Cargreen PI, SE25
off Cargreen Rd 188 C4
Cargreen Rd, SE25 . . . . .188 C4
Carholme Rd, SE23 . . . . .171 J1
Carisbrooke Av, Bex. DA5 . . . .176 D1
Carisbrooke Cl, Enf. EN1 . . . . .44 C1
Stanmore HA7 . . . . .69 G2
Carisbrooke Gdns, SE15 . . . . . .37 G7
Carisbrooke Ho, Kings.T. KT2
off Kingsgate Rd 181 H1
Carisbrooke Rd, E17 . . . . .77 H4
Bromley BR2 . . . . .191 J4
Mitcham CR4 . . . . .186 D4

Carker's La, NW5 . . . . .92 B5
Carleton Cl, Esher KT10 . . . . .194 A1
Carleton Rd, N7 . . . . .92 D5
Carleton Vil, NW5
off Leighton Gro 92 C5
Carlile Cl, E3 . . . . .113 J2
Carlina Gdns, Wdf.Grn. IG8 . . . .63 H5
Carlingford Gdns, Mitch. CR4 . .167 J7
Carlingford Rd, N15 . . . . .75 H3
NW3 . . . . .91 G4
Morden SM4 . . . . .184 A6
Carlisle Av, EC3 . . . . .21 E4
W3 . . . . .106 E6
Carlisle Cl, Kings.T. KT2 . . . . .182 A1
Pinner HA5 . . . . .66 E7
Carlisle Gdns, Har. HA3 . . . . . .69 G7
Ilford IG1 . . . . .80 B6
Carlisle La, SE1 . . . . .26 D6
Carlisle Ms, NW8 . . . . .15 F1
Carlisle PI, N11 . . . . .58 B4
SW1 . . . . .25 F6
Carlisle Rd, E10 . . . . .96 A2
N4 . . . . .75 G7
NW6 . . . . .108 B1
NW9 . . . . .70 C3
Hampton TW12 . . . . .161 H7
Sutton SM1 . . . . .198 C5
Carlisle St, W1 . . . . .17 H4
Carlisle Wk, E8 off Laurel St 94 C6
Carlisle Way, SW17 . . . . .168 A5
Carlos PI, W1 . . . . .16 C6
Carlow St, NW1 . . . . .9 F1
Carlton Av, N14 . . . . .42 D5
Feltham TW14 . . . . .142 C6
Harrow HA3 . . . . .68 E5
Hayes UB3 . . . . .121 H4
South Croydon CR2 . . . . . .202 B7
Carlton Av E, Wem. HA9 . . . . . .87 H1
Carlton Av W, Wem. HA0 . . . . .86 E2
Carlton Cl, NW3 . . . . .90 D2
Borehamwood WD6 . . . . . . .38 D4
Chessington KT9 . . . . .195 G6
Edgware HA8 . . . . .54 A5
Northolt UB5
off Whitton Av W 85 J5
Carlton Ct, SW9 . . . . .151 H1
Ilford IG6 . . . . .81 G3
Carlton Cres, Sutt. SM3 . . . . .198 B4
Carlton Dr, SW15 . . . . .148 B5
Ilford IG6 . . . . .81 G3
Carlton Gdns, SW1 . . . . .25 H2
W5 . . . . .105 F6
Carlton Gro, SE15 . . . . .152 E1
Carlton Hill, NW8 . . . . .109 E2
Carlton Ho, Felt. TW14 . . . . . .141 J7
Carlton Ho Ter, SW1 . . . . .25 H2
Carlton Pk Av, SW20 . . . . . . .183 J2
Carlton Rd, E11 . . . . .97 F1
E12 . . . . .98 A4
E17 . . . . .77 H1
N4 . . . . .75 G7
N11 . . . . .58 A5
SW14 . . . . .146 C3
W4 . . . . .126 D2
W5 . . . . .105 F7
Erith DA8 . . . . .139 H6
New Malden KT3 . . . . .182 E2
Sidcup DA14 . . . . .175 J5
South Croydon CR2 . . . . . .202 A6
Walton-on-Thames KT12 . . .178 B7
Welling DA16 . . . . .158 B3
Carlton Sq, E1 off Argyle Rd . . .113 G4
Carlton St, SW1 . . . . .17 H6
Carlton Ter, E11 . . . . .79 H5
N18 . . . . .60 A3
SE26 . . . . .171 F3
Carlton Twr PI, SW1 . . . . .24 A5
Carlton Vale, NW6 . . . . .108 E2
Carlton Vil, SW15
off St. John's Av 147 J5
Carlwell St, SW17 . . . . .167 H5
Carlyle Av, Brom. BR1 . . . . . .192 A3
Southall UB1 . . . . .103 F7
Carlyle Cl, N2 . . . . .73 F6
West Molesey KT8 . . . . . . .179 H2
Carlyle Gdns, Sthl. UB1 . . . . .103 F7
Carlyle Lo, Barn. (New Barn.) EN5
off Richmond Rd 41 F5
Carlyle Ms, E1 off Alderney Rd . .113 G4
Carlyle PI, SW15 . . . . .148 A4
Carlyle Rd, E12 . . . . .98 B4
NW10 . . . . .106 D1
SE28 . . . . .118 B7
W5 . . . . .125 F5
Croydon CR0 . . . . .202 D2
★ Carlyle's Ho, SW3 . . . . .31 G6
Carlyle Sq, SW3 . . . . .31 F4
Carlyon Av, Har. HA2 . . . . .85 F4
Carlyon Cl, Wem. HA0 . . . . . .105 H1
Carlyon Rd, Hayes UB4 . . . . . .102 C6
Wembley HA0 . . . . .105 H2
Carmalt Gdns, SW15 . . . . . . .147 J4
Carmarthen Grn, NW9
off Snowdon Dr 70/71 E6
Carmarthen PI, SE1
off Bermondsey St 132 B2
Carmel Ct, W8 . . . . .22 A3

Carmel Ct, Wem. HA9 . . . . . . .88 B2
Carmelite Cl, Har. HA3 . . . . . . .67 J1
Carmelite Rd, Har. HA3 . . . . . .67 J1
Carmelite St, EC4 . . . . .19 F5
Carmelite Wk, Har. HA3 . . . . . .67 J1
Carmelite Way, Har. HA3 . . . . .67 J2
Carmen St, E14 . . . . .114 B6
Carmichael Cl, SW11
off Darien Rd 149 G3
Ruislip HA4 . . . . .84 A4
Carmichael Ms, SW18 . . . . . .149 G7
Carmichael Rd, SE25 . . . . . . .188 D5
Carminia Rd, SW17 . . . . .168 B2
Carnaby St, W1 . . . . .17 F4
Carnac St, SE27 . . . . .170 A4
Carnanton Rd, E17 . . . . .78 D1
Carnarvon Av, Enf. EN1 . . . . . .44 C3
Carnarvon Dr, Hayes UB3 . . . .121 F3
Carnarvon Rd, E10 . . . . .78 C6
E15 . . . . .97 F6
E18 . . . . .79 F1
Barnet EN5 . . . . .40 B3
Carnation St, SE2 . . . . .138 B5
Carnbrook Rd, SE3 . . . . .156 A3
Carnecke Gdns, SE9 . . . . . . .156 B5
Carnegie Cl, Surb. KT6
off Fullers Av 195 J2
Carnegie PI, SW19 . . . . .166 A3
Carnegie St, N1 . . . . .111 F1
Carnforth Cl, Epsom KT19 . . . .196 B6
Carnforth Rd, SW16 . . . . .168 D7
Carnie Lo, SW17
off Manville Rd 168 B3
Carnoustie Cl, SE28
off Redbourne Dr 118 D6
Carnoustie Dr, N1 . . . . .93 F7
Carnwath Rd, SW6 . . . . .148 D3
Carol Cl, NW4 . . . . .72 A4
Carolina Cl, E15 . . . . .96 E5
Carolina Rd, Th.Hth. CR7 . . . .187 H2
Caroline Cl, N10
off Alexandra Pk Rd 74 B2
SW16 . . . . .169 F4
W2 . . . . .14 B6
Croydon CR0 . . . . .202 B4
Isleworth TW7 . . . . .124 A7
West Drayton UB7 . . . . . . .120 A2
Caroline Ct, Stan. HA7
off The Chase 52 D6
Caroline Gdns, SE15 . . . . .37 E7
Caroline PI, SW11 . . . . .150 A2
W2 . . . . .14 B5
Hayes UB3 . . . . .121 H7
Caroline PI Ms, W2 . . . . .14 B6
Caroline Rd, SW19 . . . . .166 C7
Caroline St, E1 . . . . .113 G6
Caroline Ter, SW1 . . . . .32 B2
Caroline Wk, W6 . . . . .128 B6
Carol St, NW1 . . . . .110 C1
Carpenders Av, Wat. WD19 . . . .50 E3
CARPENDERS PARK, Wat. WD19 .51 F2
Carpenders Pk, Wat. WD19 . . . .51 E2
Carpenter Gdns, N21 . . . . .59 H2
Carpenters Arms Path, SE9
off Eltham High St 156 C6
Carpenters Ct, Twick. TW2 . . . .162 B2
Carpenters Ms, N7 off North Rd . .92 E5
Carpenters PI, SW4 . . . . .150 D4
Carpenters Rd, E15 . . . . .96 B6
Carpenter St, W1 . . . . .16 D6
Carrara Cl, SW9 off Eaton Dr . . .151 H4
Carrara Ms, E8 . . . . .94 D5
Carrara Wf, SW6 . . . . .148 B3
Carr Cl, Stan. HA7 . . . . .52 E6
Carr Gro, SE18 . . . . .136 B4
Carriage Dr E, SW11 . . . . .32 B7
Carriage Dr N, SW11 . . . . .32 C6
Carriage Dr S, SW11 . . . . .149 J1
Carriage Dr W, SW11 . . . . . . .129 J7
Carriage Ms, Ilf. IG1 . . . . .99 F2
Carriage PI, N16 . . . . .94 A3
SW16 off Eardley Rd 168 C5
Carriage St, SE18 . . . . .137 E3
Carrick Cl, Islw. TW7 . . . . . . .144 D3
Carrick Dr, Ilf. IG6 . . . . .81 F1
Carrick Gdns, N17
off Flexmere Rd 60 B7
Carrick Ms, SE8
off Watergate St 134 A6
Carrill Way, Belv. DA17 . . . . . .138 D4
Carrington Av, Borwd. WD6 . . . .38 B5
Hounslow TW3 . . . . .143 H5
Carrington Cl, Barn. EN5 . . . . .39 G5
Borehamwood WD6 . . . . . . .38 C5
Croydon CR0 . . . . .189 H7
Kingston upon Thames KT2 . .164 C5
Carrington Gdns, E7
off Woodford Rd 97 H4
Carrington Rd, Rich. TW10 . . . .146 A4
Carrington Sq, Har. HA3 . . . . . .51 J7
Carrington St, W1 . . . . .24 D2
Carrol Cl, NW5 . . . . .92 B4
Carroll Cl, E15 . . . . .97 F5
Carroll Hill, Loug. IG10 . . . . . . .48 C3
Carronade PI, SE28 . . . . .137 F3
Carron Cl, E14 . . . . .114 B6
Carroun Rd, SW8 . . . . .34 C7

Carroway La, Grnf. UB6
  off Cowgate Rd 104 A3
Carrow Rd, Dag. RM9 . . . . . . .100 B7
Carr Rd, E17 . . . . .77 J2
  Northolt UB5 . . . . .85 G6
Carrs La, N21 . . . . .43 J5
Carr St, E14 . . . . .113 H5
CARSHALTON, Sutt. SM5 . . . . .199 G4
Carshalton Gro, Sutt. SM1 . . . .199 G4
Carshalton Pk Rd, Cars. SM5 . .199 J5
Carshalton Pl, Cars. SM5 . . . . .200 A4
Carshalton Rd, Cars. SM5 . . . . .199 F5
  Mitcham CR4 . . . . .186 A4
  Sutton SM1 . . . . .199 F5
Carslake Rd, SW15 . . . . .147 J6
Carson Rd, E16 . . . . .115 G4
  SE21 . . . . .170 A2
  Barnet EN4 . . . . .41 J4
Carstairs Rd, SE6 . . . . .172 C3
Carston Cl, SE12 . . . . .155 F5
Carswell Cl, Ilf. IG4
  off Roding La S 80 A4
Carswell Rd, SE6 . . . . .154 C7
Carter Cl, Wall. SM6 . . . . .200 D4
Carter Ct, EC4 off Carter La . .111 H6
Carteret St, SW1 . . . . .25 H4
Carteret Way, SE8 . . . . .133 H4
Carterhatch La, Enf. EN1 . . . . .44 D2
Carterhatch Rd, Enf. EN3 . . . . .45 F2
Carter La, EC4 . . . . .19 H4
Carter Pl, SE17 . . . . .36 A4
Carter Rd, E13 . . . . .115 H1
  SW19 . . . . .167 G6
Carters Cl, Wor.Pk. KT4 . . . . . .198 A2
Carters Hill Cl, SE9 . . . . .173 J1
Carters La, SE23 . . . . .171 H2
Carter St, SE17 . . . . .35 J5
Carters Yd, SW18
  off Wandsworth High St . . .148 D5
Carthew Rd, W6 . . . . .127 H3
Carthew Vil, W6 . . . . .127 H3
Carthusian St, EC1 . . . . .19 J1
Cartier Circle, E14 . . . . .134 B7
Carting La, WC2 . . . . .18 B6
Cart La, E4 . . . . .46 D7
Cartmel, N17
  off Heybourne Rd 60/61 E7
Cartmel Gdns, Mord. SM4 . . . .185 F5
Cartmel Rd, Bexh. DA7 . . . . . .159 G3
Carton St, W1 . . . . .16 A3
Cartridge Pl, SE18 . . . . .137 E3
Cartwright Gdns, WC1 . . . . . . .10 A4
Cartwright Rd, Dag. RM9 . . . .101 F7
Cartwright St, E1 . . . . .21 G5
Cartwright Way, SW13 . . . . . . .127 H7
Carver Cl, W4 . . . . .126 C3
Carver Rd, SE24 . . . . .151 J6
Carville Cres, Brent. TW8 . . . . .125 H4
Cary Rd, E11 . . . . .97 E4
Carysfort Rd, N8 . . . . .74 D5
  N16 . . . . .94 A3
Cascade Av, N10 . . . . .74 C4
Cascade Cl, Buck.H. IG9
  off Cascade Rd 64 A2
Cascade Rd, Buck.H. IG9 . . . . .64 A2
Casella Rd, SE14 . . . . .133 G7
Casewick Rd, SE27 . . . . .169 H4
Casey Cl, NW8 . . . . .7 G4
Casimir Rd, E5 . . . . .95 E3
Casino Av, SE24 . . . . .151 J5
Caspian St, SE5 . . . . .36 B7
Caspian Wk, E16 . . . . .116 A6
Caspian Wf, E3 off Violet Rd . .114 B5
Cassandra Cl, Nthlt. UB5 . . . . .86 A4
Casselden Rd, NW10 . . . . .88 D7
Cassidy Rd, SW6 . . . . .128 D7
Cassilda Rd, SE2 . . . . .138 A4
Cassilis Rd, Twick. TW1 . . . . . .145 E5
Cassiobury Av, Felt. TW14 . . . .141 J6
Cassiobury Rd, E17 . . . . .77 G5
Cassis Ct, Loug. IG10 . . . . .49 F4
Cassland Rd, E9 . . . . .95 F7
  Thornton Heath CR7 . . . . . .188 A4
Casslee Rd, SE6 . . . . .153 J7
Casson St, E1 . . . . .21 H2
Castalia Sq, E14
  off Roserton St 134 C2
Castalia St, E14 off Plevna St . .134 C2
Castellain Rd, W9 . . . . .6 C6
Castellane Cl, Stan. HA7
  off Daventer Dr 52 C7
Castello Av, SW15 . . . . .147 J5
Castell Rd, Loug. IG10 . . . . . . .49 F1
CASTELNAU, SW13 . . . . .127 G6
Castelnau, SW13 . . . . .127 H6
Castelnau Gdns, SW13
  off Arundel Ter 127 H6
Castelnau Pl, SW13
  off Castelnau 127 H6
Castelnau Row, SW13
  off Lonsdale Rd 127 H6
Casterbridge, NW6 . . . . .109 E1
Casterbridge Rd, SE3 . . . . . . .155 G3
Casterton St, E8
  off Wilton Way 94/95 E6
Castile Rd, SE18 . . . . .136 D4
Castillon Rd, SE6 . . . . .172 E2

Castlands Rd, SE6 . . . . .171 J2
Castle Av, E4 . . . . .62 D5
Castlebar Hill, W5 . . . . .105 E5
Castlebar Ms, W5 . . . . .105 F5
Castlebar Pk, W5 . . . . .105 E4
Castlebar Rd, W5 . . . . .105 F5
Castle Baynard St, EC4 . . . . . .19 H5
Castlebrook Cl, SE11 . . . . .35 G1
Castle Cl, E9 off Swinnerton St .95 H5
  SW19 . . . . .166 A3
  W3 . . . . .126 B2
  Bromley BR2 . . . . .190 E3
Castlecombe Dr, SW19 . . . . . .148 A3
Castlecombe Rd, SE9 . . . . . . .174 B4
Castle Ct, EC3 . . . . .20 C4
  SE26 off Champion Rd 171 H4
  SW15 off Brewhouse La . . .148 B3
Castledine Rd, SE20 . . . . .170 E7
Castle Dr, Ilf. IG4 . . . . .80 B6
Castleford Av, SE9 . . . . .174 E1
Castleford Cl, N17 . . . . .60 C6
Castlegate, Rich. TW9 . . . . . . .145 J3
Castlehaven Rd, NW1 . . . . . . .92 B7
Castleleigh Ct, Enf. EN2 . . . . . .44 A5
Castlemaine Av, S.Croy. CR2 . .202 C5
Castlemaine Twr, SW11 . . . . . .149 J1
Castle Ms, N12 off Castle Rd . .57 F5
  NW1 off Castle Rd 92 B6
  Hampton TW12
    off Station Rd 179 H1
Castle Par, Epsom KT17
  off Ewell Bypass 197 G7
Castle Pl, NW1 . . . . .92 B6
  W4 off Windmill Rd . . .126/127 E4
Castle Pt, E13 . . . . .115 J2
Castlereagh St, W1 . . . . .15 J3
Castle Rd, N12 . . . . .57 F5
  NW1 . . . . .92 B6
  Dagenham RM9 . . . . .118 B1
  Enfield EN3 . . . . .45 H1
  Isleworth TW7 . . . . .144 C2
  Northolt UB5 . . . . .85 H6
  Southall UB2 . . . . .123 F3
Castle St, E6 . . . . .115 J2
  Kingston upon Thames KT1 .181 H2
Castleton Av, Wem. HA9 . . . . . .87 H4
Castleton Cl, Croy. CR0 . . . . . .189 H6
Castleton Gdns, Wem. HA9 . . .87 H3
Castleton Rd, E17 . . . . .78 D2
  SE9 . . . . .174 A4
  Ilford IG3 . . . . .100 A1
  Mitcham CR4 . . . . .186 D4
  Ruislip HA4 . . . . .84 D1
Castletown Rd, W14 . . . . .128 B5
Castleview Cl, N4 . . . . .93 J1
Castleview Gdns, Ilf. IG1 . . . . .80 B6
Castle Wk, Sun. TW16
  off Elizabeth Gdns 178 C3
Castle Way, SW19 . . . . .166 A3
  Feltham TW13 . . . . .160 C4
Castlewood Dr, SE9 . . . . .156 C2
Castlewood Rd, N15 . . . . .76 D6
  N16 . . . . .76 D7
  Barnet EN4 . . . . .41 G3
Castle Yd, N6 off North Rd 74 A7
  SE1 . . . . .27 H1
  Richmond TW10 off Hill St . .145 G5
Castor La, E14 . . . . .114 B7
Caterham Av, Ilf. IG5 . . . . .80 C2
Caterham Rd, SE13 . . . . .154 C3
Catesby St, SE17 . . . . .36 C2
CATFORD, SE6 . . . . .172 B1
Catford Bdy, SE6 . . . . .154 B7
Catford Hill, SE6 . . . . .171 J2
Catford Ms, SE6
  off Holbeach Rd 154 B7
Catford Rd, SE6 . . . . .172 A1
Cathall Rd, E11 . . . . .96 D3
Cathay St, SE16 . . . . .133 E2
Cathay Wk, Nthlt. UB5
  off Brabazon St 103 G2
Cathcart Dr, Orp. BR6 . . . . . . .207 H2
Cathcart Hill, N19 . . . . .92 C3
Cathcart Rd, SW10 . . . . .30 B5
Cathcart St, NW5 . . . . .92 B6
Cathedral Piazza, SW1 . . . . . . .25 F6
Cathedral St, SE1 . . . . .28 B1
Catherall Rd, N5 . . . . .93 J3
Catherine Ct, Loug. IG10
  off Roding Gdns 48 C6
Catherine Ct, N14
  off Conisbee Ct 42 C5
Catherine Dr, Rich. TW9 . . . . . .145 H4
Catherine Gdns, Houns. TW3 . .144 A4
Catherine Griffiths Ct, EC1 . . . .11 F5
Catherine Gro, SE10 . . . . .154 B1
Catherine Pl, SW1 . . . . .25 F5
  Harrow HA1 . . . . .68 C5
Catherine Rd, Surb. KT6 . . . . . .181 G5
Catherine's Cl, West Dr. UB7
  off Money La 120 A3
Catherine St, WC2 . . . . .18 C5
Catherine Wheel All, E1 . . . . . .20 E2
Catherine Wheel Rd, Brent.
  TW8 . . . . .125 G7
Catherine Wheel Yd, SW1 . . . .25 F2

Cat Hill, Barn. EN4 . . . . .41 H6
Cathles Rd, SW12 . . . . .150 B6
Cathnor Rd, W12 . . . . .127 H2
Catling Cl, SE23 . . . . .171 F3
Catlins La, Pnr. HA5 . . . . .66 B3
Catlin St, SE16 . . . . .37 J4
Cator La, Beck. BR3 . . . . .189 J2
Cato Rd, SW4 . . . . .150 D3
Cator Rd, SE26 . . . . .171 G6
  Carshalton SM5 . . . . .199 J5
Cator St, SE15 . . . . .37 F6
Cato St, W1 . . . . .15 H2
Catterick Cl, N11 . . . . .58 A6
Cattistock Rd, SE9 . . . . .174 B5
Cattley Cl, Barn. EN5
  off Wood St 40 B4
Catton St, WC1 . . . . .18 C2
Caughley Ho, SE11
  off Denny St . . . .
Caulfield Rd, E6 . . . . .98 C7
  SE15 . . . . .153 E2
Causeway, The, N2 . . . . .73 H4
  SW18 . . . . .148 E4
  SW19 . . . . .166 A5
  Carshalton SM5 . . . . .200 A3
  Chessington KT9 . . . . .195 H4
  Esher (Clay.) KT10 . . . . . . .194 C7
  Feltham TW14 . . . . .142 A4
  Hounslow TW4 . . . . .142 A4
  Teddington TW11
    off Broad St 162 C6
Causeyware Rd, N9 . . . . .45 E7
Causton Rd, N6 . . . . .74 B7
Causton Sq, Dag. RM10 . . . . . .101 G7
Causton St, SW1 . . . . .33 J2
Cautley Av, SW4 . . . . .150 C5
Cavalier Cl, Rom. RM6 . . . . . . .82 D4
Cavalry Barracks, Houns. TW4 .142 D3
Cavalry Cres, Houns. TW4 . . . .142 D4
Cavalry Gdns, SW15 . . . . .148 B5
Cavan Pl, Pnr. HA5 . . . . .67 F1
Cavaye Pl, SW10 . . . . .30 C4
Cavell Dr, Enf. EN2 . . . . .43 G2
Cavell Rd, N17 . . . . .60 A7
Cavell St, E1 . . . . .113 E5
Cavendish Av, N3 . . . . .72 D2
  NW8 . . . . .7 F3
  W13 . . . . .104 D5
  Erith DA8 . . . . .139 J6
  Harrow HA1 . . . . .86 A4
  New Malden KT3 . . . . .183 H5
  Ruislip HA4 . . . . .84 B5
  Sidcup DA15 . . . . .158 A7
  Welling DA16 . . . . .157 J3
  Woodford Green IG8 . . . . . .79 H4
Cavendish Cl, N18 . . . . .61 E5
  NW6 off Cavendish Rd 90 C7
  NW8 . . . . .7 F3
Cavendish Ct, EC3 . . . . .20 E3
Cavendish Cres, Borwd. (Elstree)
  WD6 . . . . .38 A4
Cavendish Dr, E11 . . . . .96 D1
  Edgware HA8 . . . . .53 J6
  Esher (Clay.) KT10 . . . . . . .194 B5
Cavendish Gdns, Bark. IG11 . . .99 H5
  Ilford IG1 . . . . .98 D1
  Romford RM6 . . . . .83 E5
Cavendish Ms N, W1 . . . . .16 E1
Cavendish Ms S, W1 . . . . .16 E2
Cavendish Par, Houns. TW4
  off Bath Rd 142/143 E2
Cavendish Pl, W1 . . . . .16 E3
  N4 . . . . .75 G6
  N18 . . . . .60 E5
  NW6 . . . . .90 B7
  SW12 . . . . .150 B6
  SW19 . . . . .167 G7
  W4 . . . . .146 C1
  Barnet EN5 . . . . .39 J3
  Croydon CR0 . . . . .201 H1
  New Malden KT3 . . . . .183 F5
  Sutton SM2 . . . . .199 F7
Cavendish Sq, W1 . . . . .16 E3
Cavendish St, N1 . . . . .12 B2
Cavendish Ter, Felt. TW13
  off High St 160 A2
Cavendish Way, W.Wick. BR4 . .204 B1
Cavenham Gdns, Ilf. IG1 . . . . . .99 G3
Caverleigh Way, Wor.Pk. KT4 . .197 G1
Cave Rd, E13 . . . . .115 H2
  Richmond TW10 . . . . .163 F4
Caversham Av, N13 . . . . .59 G3
  Sutton SM3 . . . . .198 B2
Caversham Ct, N11 . . . . .58 A3
Caversham Flats, SW3 . . . . . . .31 J5
Caversham Rd, N15 . . . . .75 J4
  NW5 . . . . .92 C6
  Kingston upon Thames KT1 .181 J2
Caversham St, SW3 . . . . .31 J5
Caverswall St, W12 . . . . .107 J6
Caveside Cl, Chis. BR7 . . . . . . .192 D1
Cawdor Cres, W7 . . . . .124 D4
Cawnpore St, SE19 . . . . .170 B5
Caxton Gro, E3 . . . . .114 A3
Caxton Ms, Brent. TW8
  off The Butts 125 G6
Caxton Rd, N22 . . . . .75 F2
  SW19 . . . . .167 F5

Caxton Rd, W12 . . . . .128 A2
  Southall UB2 . . . . .122 D3
Caxton St, SW1 . . . . .25 G5
Caxton St N, E16
  off Victoria Dock Rd 115 F7
Cayenne Ct, SE1 . . . . .29 G7
Caygill Cl, Brom. BR2 . . . . . . .191 F4
Cayley Cl, Wall. SM6 . . . . .200 E7
Cayley Rd, Sthl. UB2
  off McNair Rd 123 H3
Cayton Pl, EC1 . . . . .12 B4
Cayton Rd, Grnf. UB6 . . . . . . .104 C2
Cayton St, EC1 . . . . .12 B4
Cazenove Rd, E17 . . . . .78 A1
  N16 . . . . .94 C2
Cearns Ho, E6 . . . . .116 A1
Cecil Av, Bark. IG11 . . . . .99 G7
  Enfield EN1 . . . . .44 C4
  Wembley HA9 . . . . .87 J5
Cecil Cl, W5 off Helena Rd 105 G5
  Chessington KT9 . . . . .195 G4
Cecil Ct, WC2 . . . . .17 J6
  Barnet EN5 . . . . .40 A3
Cecile Pk, N8 . . . . .75 E6
Cecilia Cl, N2 . . . . .73 F3
★ Cecilia Coleman Gall, NW8 . .7 F1
Cecilia Rd, E8 . . . . .94 D5
Cecil Pk, Pnr. HA5 . . . . .67 E4
Cecil Pl, Mitch. CR4 . . . . .185 J5
Cecil Rd, E11 . . . . .97 E3
  E13 . . . . .115 G1
  E17 . . . . .78 A1
  N10 . . . . .74 B2
  N14 . . . . .58 C1
  NW9 . . . . .70 E3
  NW10 . . . . .106 E1
  SW19 . . . . .166 E7
  W3 . . . . .106 C5
  Croydon CR0 . . . . .187 F6
  Enfield EN2 . . . . .44 A4
  Harrow HA3 . . . . .68 B3
  Hounslow TW3 . . . . .143 J2
  Ilford IG1 . . . . .98 E3
  Romford RM6 . . . . .82 D7
  Sutton SM1 . . . . .198 C6
Cecil Sharp Ho, NW1 . . . . . . .110 A1
Cecil Way, Brom. BR2 . . . . . . .205 G1
Cedar Av, Barn. EN4 . . . . .41 H7
  Enfield EN3 . . . . .45 F2
  Hayes UB3 . . . . .102 A6
  Romford RM6 . . . . .82 E5
  Ruislip HA4 . . . . .84 C6
  Sidcup DA15 . . . . .158 A7
  Twickenham TW2 . . . . .143 H6
  West Drayton UB7 . . . . . . .120 C1
Cedar Cl, E3 . . . . .113 J1
  SE21 . . . . .169 J1
  SW15 . . . . .164 D4
  Borehamwood WD6 . . . . . .38 A3
  Bromley BR2 . . . . .206 B3
  Buckhurst Hill IG9 . . . . .64 A2
  Carshalton SM5 . . . . .199 J6
  East Molesey KT8
    off Cedar Rd 180 B4
  Romford RM7 . . . . .83 J4
Cedar Copse, Brom. BR1 . . . . .192 C2
Cedar Ct, E11 off Grosvenor Rd .79 H5
  N1 off Essex Rd 93 J7
  SE9 . . . . .156 B6
  SW19 . . . . .166 A3
Cedar Cres, Brom. BR2 . . . . . .206 B3
Cedarcroft Rd, Chess. KT9 . . . .195 J4
Cedar Dr, N2 . . . . .73 H4
  Loughton IG10 . . . . .49 E2
  Pinner HA5 . . . . .51 G6
Cedar Gdns, Sutt. SM2 . . . . . .199 F6
Cedar Gro, W5 . . . . .125 H3
  Bexley DA5 . . . . .158 C6
  Southall UB1 . . . . .103 G5
Cedar Hts, Rich. TW10 . . . . . . .163 H1
Cedar Ho, Croy. CR0 . . . . .204 B6
Cedarhurst, Brom. BR1
  off Elstree Hill 172/173 E7
Cedarhurst Dr, SE9 . . . . .155 J5
Cedar Lawn Av, Barn. EN5 . . . .40 B5
Cedar Mt, SE9 . . . . .174 A1
Cedarne Rd, SW6 . . . . .128 E7
Cedar Pk, Chig. IG7
  off High Rd 64/65 E4
Cedar Pk Gdns, Rom. RM6 . . . .82 D7
Cedar Pl, SE7 off Floyd Rd 135 J5
Cedar Ri, N14 . . . . .42 A7
Cedar Rd, N17 . . . . .76 C1
  NW2 . . . . .89 J4
  Bromley BR1 . . . . .191 J2
  Croydon CR0 . . . . .202 B2
  East Molesey KT8 . . . . . . .180 B4
  Hounslow TW4 . . . . .142 C2
  Romford RM7 . . . . .83 J4
  Sutton SM2 . . . . .199 F6
  Teddington TW11 . . . . .162 D5
Cedars, The, E15 off Portway . .115 F1
  W13 off Heronsforde 105 F6
  Buckhurst Hill IG9 . . . . .63 G1
  Teddington TW11
    off Adelaide Rd 162 C6
Cedars Av, E17 . . . . .78 A5

Cedars Av, Mitch. CR4 . . . . .186 A4
Cedars Cl, NW4 . . . . .72 A3
SE13 .154 D3
Cedars Ct, N9 off Church St 60 B2
Cedars Ms, SW4 off Cedars Rd .150 B4
Cedars Rd, E15 . . . . .97 E6
N9 off Church St 60 D2
N21 . . . . .59 H2
SW4 .150 B3
SW13 . . . . .147 A5
W4 . . . . .126 C5
Beckenham BR3 . . . . .189 H2
Croydon CR0 . . . . .201 E3
Kingston upon Thames (Hmptn W.)
KT1 .181 F1
Morden SM4 . . . . .184 D4
Cedar Ter, Rich. TW9 . . . . .145 H4
Cedar Tree Gro, SE27 . . . . .169 H5
Cedarville Gdns, SW16 . . . . .169 F6
Cedar Vista, Rich. TW9 . . . . .145 H1
off Kew Rd 145 H1
Cedar Wk, Esher (Clay.) KT10 . .194 C6
Cedar Way, NW1 . . . . .92 D7
Cedra Ct, N16 . . . . .94 D1
Cedric Rd, SE9 . . . . .175 F3
Celadon Cl, Enf. EN3 . . . . .45 H3
Celandine Cl, E14 . . . . .114 A5
Celandine Dr, E8 . . . . .94 C7
SE28 .138 B1
Celandine Way, E15 . . . . .115 E3
Celbridge Ms, W2 . . . . .14 B3
Celestial Gdns, SE13 . . . . .154 D4
Celia Rd, N19 . . . . .92 C4
Celtic Av, Brom. BR2 . . . . .190 E3
Celtic St, E14 . . . . .114 B5
Cemetery La, SE7 . . . . .136 B6
Cemetery Rd, E7 . . . . .97 F4
N17 . . . . .60 B7
SE2 . . . . .138 B7
Cenacle Cl, NW3 . . . . .90 D3
★ Cenotaph, The, SW1 . . . . .26 A3
Centaurs Business Cen, Islw.
TW7 .124 D6
Centaur St, SE1 . . . . .26 D5
Centenary Est, Enf. EN3 . . . . .45 J4
Centenary Rd, Enf. EN3 . . . . .45 J4
Centenary Wk, Loug. IG10 . . . . . .47 H3
Central Av, E11 . . . . .96 D2
N2 . . . . .73 G2
N9 . . . . .60 B3
SW11 . . . . .129 J7
Enfield EN1 . . . . .44 E2
Hayes UB3 . . . . .102 A7
Hounslow TW3 . . . . .143 J4
Pinner HA5 . . . . .67 F6
Wallington SM6 . . . . .201 E5
Welling DA16 . . . . .157 J2
West Molesey KT8 . . . . .179 F4
Central Circ, NW4
off Hendon Way 71 H5
★ Central Criminal Ct (Old Bailey),
EC4 . . . . .19 H3
Central Gdns, Mord. SM4
off Central Rd 184/185 E5
Central Hill, SE19 . . . . .170 A5
Central Ho, E15 off High St 114 C2
Barking IG11
off Cambridge Rd 99 F7
Central Par, Felt. TW14 . . . . .142 C7
Greenford UB6 . . . . .104 D3
Hounslow TW5
off Heston Rd 123 G7
Surbiton KT6
off St. Mark's Hill 181 H6
Central Pk Av, Dag. RM10 . . . . . .101 H4
Central Pk Est, Houns. TW4 . . . . .142 D5
Central Pk Rd, E6 . . . . .116 A2
Central Pl, SE25
off Portland Rd 188/189 E4
Central Rd, Mord. SM4 . . . . .184 D5
Wembley HA0 . . . . .86 E5
Worcester Park KT4 . . . . .197 G2
Central Sch Footpath, SW14 . . . .146 C3
Central Sq, NW11 . . . . .72 E6
Wembley HA9
off Station Gro 87 H5
West Molesey KT8 . . . . .179 F4
Central St, EC1 . . . . .11 J4
Central Way, NW10 . . . . .106 C2
SE28 .138 A1
Carshalton SM5 . . . . .199 H7
Feltham TW14 . . . . .142 B5
Centre, The, Felt. TW13 . . . . .160 A2
Centre at the Circ, W1 . . . . .17 G6
Centre Av, W3 . . . . .126 D1
W10 off Harrow Rd 107 J3
Centre Common Rd, Chis. BR7 . .175 F6
Centre Ct Shop Cen, SW19 . . . . .166 C6
Centrepoint, WC1 . . . . .17 J3
Centre Rd, E7 . . . . .97 G2
E11 . . . . .97 G2
Dagenham RM10 . . . . .119 H2
Centre St, E2 . . . . .113 E2
Centre Way, E17 . . . . .62 C7
N9 . . . . .61 F2
Centreway, Ilf. IG1 . . . . .99 F2
Centric Cl, NW1 off Oval Rd 110 B1

Centurion Cl, N7 . . . . .93 F7
Centurion Ct, Wall. SM6
off Wandle Rd 200 B2
Centurion La, E3 off Libra Rd . . .113 J2
Centurion Way, Erith DA18 . . . . .139 G3
Century Cl, NW4 . . . . .72 A5
Century Ms, E5
off Lower Clapton Rd 95 F4
Century Rd, E17 . . . . .77 H3
Century Yd, SE23 . . . . .171 F2
Cephas Av, E1 . . . . .113 F4
Cephas St, E1 . . . . .113 F4
Ceres Rd, SE18 . . . . .137 J4
Cerise Rd, SE15 . . . . .152 D1
Cerne Cl, Hayes UB4 . . . . .102 D7
Cerne Rd, Mord. SM4 . . . . .185 F6
Cerney Ms, W2 . . . . .15 C5
Cervantes Ct, W2 . . . . .14 B4
Cester St, E2 off Whiston Rd 112 D1
Ceylon Rd, W14 . . . . .128 A3
Chabot Dr, SE15
off Linden Gro 152 D3
Chadacre Av, Ilf. IG5 . . . . .80 C3
Chadacre Rd, Epsom KT17 . . . . .197 H6
Chadbourn St, E14 . . . . .114 B5
Chad Cres, N9 . . . . .61 F3
Chadd Dr, Brom. BR1 . . . . .192 B3
Chadd Grn, E13 . . . . .115 G1
Chadview Ct, Rom. (Chad.Hth)
RM6 . . . . .82 D7
Chadville Gdns, Rom. RM6 . . . . . .82 D5
Chadway, Dag. RM8 . . . . .100 C1
Chadwell Av, Rom. RM6 . . . . .82 B7
CHADWELL HEATH, Rom. RM6 . .82 D6
Chadwell Heath La, Rom. RM6 . . .82 B5
Chadwell St, EC1 . . . . .11 F3
Chadwick Av, E4 . . . . .62 D4
N21 off Laidlaw Dr 43 F5
SW19 . . . . .166 D6
Chadwick Cl, SW15 . . . . .147 F7
W7 off Westcott Cres 104 C5
Teddington TW11 . . . . .162 D6
Chadwick Ms, W4
off Thames Rd 126 B6
Chadwick Pl, Surb. KT6 . . . . .181 F7
Chadwick Rd, E11 . . . . .79 E7
NW10 . . . . .107 F1
SE15 .152 C2
Ilford IG1 . . . . .99 E3
Chadwick St, SW1 . . . . .25 J6
Chadwick Way, SE28 . . . . .118 D7
Chadwin Rd, E13 . . . . .115 H5
Chadworth Way, Esher (Clay.)
KT10 .194 A5
Chaffinch Av, Croy. CR0 . . . . .189 G6
Chaffinch Cl, N9 . . . . .61 G1
Croydon CR0 . . . . .189 G6
Surbiton KT6 . . . . .196 A3
Chaffinch Rd, Beck. BR3 . . . . . . .189 H1
Chafford Way, Rom. RM6 . . . . . . .82 C4
Chagford St, NW1 . . . . .7 J6
Chailey Av, Enf. EN1 . . . . .44 C2
Chailey Cl, Houns. TW5
off Springwell Rd 142 D1
Chailey St, E5 . . . . .95 F3
Chalbury Wk, N1 . . . . .10 D1
Chalcombe Rd, SE2 . . . . .138 B3
Chalcot Cl, Sutt. SM2 . . . . .198 D7
Chalcot Cres, NW1 . . . . .109 J1
Chalcot Gdns, NW3 . . . . .91 J6
Chalcot Ms, SW16 . . . . .168 E3
Chalcot Rd, NW1 . . . . .92 A7
Chalcot Sq, NW1 . . . . .92 A7
Chalcott Gdns, Surb. KT6 . . . . . .195 F1
Chalcroft Rd, SE13 . . . . .154 E5
Chaldon Path, Th.Hth. CR7 . . . . .187 H4
Chaldon Rd, SW6 . . . . .128 B7
Chale Rd, SW2 . . . . .150 E6
Chalet Est, NW7 . . . . .55 G4
Chalfont Av, Wem. HA9 . . . . .88 B6
Chalfont Ct, NW9 . . . . .71 F3
Chalfont Grn, N9 . . . . .60 B3
Chalfont Ms, SW19
off Augustus Rd 166 C1
Chalfont Rd, N9 . . . . .60 B3
SE25 .188 C3
Hayes UB3 . . . . .122 A2
Chalfont Wk, Pnr. HA5
off Willows Cl 66 C2
Chalfont Way, W13 . . . . .124 E3
Chalford Cl, W.Mol. KT8 . . . . .179 G4
Chalford Rd, SE21 . . . . .170 A4
Chalford Wk, Wdf.Grn. IG8 . . . . . .80 A1
Chalgrove Av, Mord. SM4 . . . . . .184 D5
Chalgrove Cres, Ilf. IG5 . . . . .80 B2
Chalgrove Gdns, N3 . . . . .72 B3
Chalgrove Rd, N17 . . . . .76 E1
Sutton SM2 . . . . .199 G7
Chalice Cl, Wall. SM6
off Lavender Vale 200 D6
Chalkenden Cl, SE20 . . . . .170 E7
Chalk Fm Rd, NW1 . . . . .92 A7
Chalk Hill Rd, W6
off Shortlands 128 A4
Chalkhill Rd, Wem. HA9 . . . . .88 B3
Chalklands, Wem. HA9 . . . . .88 C3
Chalk La, Barn. EN4 . . . . .41 J4

Chalkley Cl, Mitch. CR4 . . . . .185 J2
Chalkmill Dr, Enf. EN1 . . . . .44 E3
Chalk Pit Way, Sutt. SM1 . . . . . . .199 F5
Chalk Rd, E13 . . . . .115 H5
Chalkstone Cl, Well. DA16 . . . . . .158 A1
Chalkwell Pk Av, Enf. EN1 . . . . . . .44 B4
Challice Way, SW2 . . . . .169 F1
Challin St, SE20 . . . . .189 F1
Challis Rd, Brent. TW8 . . . . .125 G5
Challoner Cl, N2 . . . . .73 G2
Challoner Cres, W14
off Challoner St 128 C5
Challoners Cl, E.Mol. KT8 . . . . . . .180 A4
Challoner St, W14 . . . . .128 C5
Chalmers Ho, SW11 off York Rd .149 F3
Chalmers Wk, SE17 . . . . .35 H6
Chalmers Way, Felt. TW14 . . . . . .142 A5
Chaloner Ct, SE1 . . . . .28 B3
Chalsey Rd, SE4 . . . . .153 J4
Chalton Dr, N2 . . . . .73 F6
Chalton St, NW1 . . . . .9 J3
Chamberlain Cl, SE28
off Broadwater Rd 137 G3
Chamberlain Cotts, SE5
off Camberwell Gro 152 A1
Chamberlain Cres, W.Wick.
BR4 .204 B1
Chamberlain Gdns, Houns.
TW3 .143 J1
Chamberlain La, Pnr. HA5 . . . . . . .66 A4
Chamberlain Pl, E17 . . . . .77 H3
Chamberlain Rd, N2 . . . . .73 F2
N9 . . . . .60 D3
W13 off Midhurst Rd 124 D2
Chamberlain St, NW1
off Regents Pk Rd 91 J7
Chamberlain Wk, Felt. TW13
off Burgess Cl 160/161 E4
Chamberlayne Av, Wem. HA9 . . . .87 H2
Chamberlayne Rd, NW10 . . . . . . .108 A3
Chambers Gdns, N2 . . . . .73 G1
Chambers La, NW10 . . . . .89 H7
Chambers Pl, S.Croy. CR2
off Rolleston Rd 202 A7
Chambers Rd, N7 . . . . .92 E4
Chambers St, SE16 . . . . .29 H3
Chamber St, E1 . . . . .21 G5
Chambers Wk, Stan. HA7 . . . . . . .52 E6
Chambon Pl, W6
off Beavor La 127 G4
Chambord St, E2 . . . . .13 G4
Champion Cres, SE26 . . . . .171 H4
Champion Gro, SE5 . . . . .152 A3
Champion Hill, SE5 . . . . .152 A3
Champion Hill Est, SE5 . . . . .152 B3
Champion Pk, SE5 . . . . .152 A2
Champion Pk Est, SE5
off Denmark Hill 152 A3
Champion Rd, SE26 . . . . .171 H4
Champness Cl, SE27
off Rommany Rd 170 A4
Champness Rd, Bark. IG11 . . . . . .99 J6
Champneys Cl, Sutt. SM2 . . . . . .198 C7
Chancellor Gro, SE21 . . . . .169 J2
Chancellor Pas, E14
off South Colonnade 134 A1
Chancellor Pl, NW9 . . . . .71 F2
Chancellors Rd, W6 . . . . .127 J5
Chancellors St, W6 . . . . .127 J5
Chancelot Rd, SE2 . . . . .138 B4
Chancel St, SE1 . . . . .27 G1
Chancery La, WC2 . . . . .18 E3
Beckenham BR3 . . . . .190 B2
Chancery Ms, SW17 . . . . .167 H2
Chance St, E1 . . . . .13 F5
E2 . . . . .13 F5
Chanctonbury Cl, SE9 . . . . .175 E3
Chanctonbury Gdns, Sutt.
SM2 .198 E7
Chanctonbury Way, N12 . . . . .56 C4
Chandler Av, E16 . . . . .115 G5
Chandler Cl, Hmptn. TW12 . . . . .179 G1
Chandler Ms, Twick. TW1 . . . . . .144 D7
Chandler Rd, Loug. IG10 . . . . .49 E1
Chandlers Cl, Felt. TW14 . . . . . . .141 J7
Chandlers Ms, E14 . . . . .134 A2
Chandler St, E1
off Wapping La 132/133 E1
Chandlers Way, SW2 . . . . .151 G7
Chandler Way, SE15 . . . . .132 C7
Chandon Lo, Sutt. SM2
off Devonshire Rd 199 F7
Chandos Av, E17 . . . . .78 A2
N14 . . . . .58 C3
N20 . . . . .57 F1
W5 . . . . .125 F4
Chandos Cl, Buck.H. IG9 . . . . .63 H2
Chandos Ct, Stan. HA7 . . . . .52 E6
Chandos Cres, Edg. HA8 . . . . .53 J7
Chandos Par, Edg. HA8
off Chandos Cres 53 J7
Chandos Pl, WC2 . . . . .18 A6
Chandos Rd, E15 . . . . .96 D5
N2 . . . . .73 G2
N17 . . . . .76 B2

Chandos Rd, NW2 . . . . .89 J5
NW10 .106 E4
Harrow HA1 . . . . .67 J5
Pinner HA5 . . . . .66 C7
Chandos St, W1 . . . . .16 E2
Chandos Way, NW11 . . . . .90 E1
Change All, EC3 . . . . .20 C4
Channel Cl, Houns. TW5 . . . . . . .143 G1
Channel Gate Rd, NW10
off Old Oak La 107 F3
Channelsea Rd, E15 . . . . .114 D1
Chantress Cl, Dag. RM10 . . . . . . .119 J1
Chantrey Rd, SW9 . . . . .151 F3
Chantry Cl, NW7
off Hendon Wd La 39 F6
SE2 off Felixstowe Rd 138 C3
W9 off Elgin Av 108 C4
Harrow HA3 . . . . .69 J5
Sidcup DA14
off Ellenborough Rd 176/177 E5
Sunbury-on-Thames TW16 . . . .160 A7
Chantry Ct, Cars. SM5 . . . . .199 H3
Chantry La, Brom. BR2
off Bromley Common 192 A5
Chantry Pl, Har. HA3 . . . . .67 H1
Chantry Rd, Chess. KT9 . . . . .195 J5
Harrow HA3 . . . . .67 H1
Chantry Sq, W8
off St. Mary's Pl 128/129 E3
Chantry St, N1 . . . . .111 H1
Chantry Way, Mitch. CR4 . . . . . . .185 G3
Chant Sq, E15 . . . . .96 D7
Chant St, E15 . . . . .96 D7
Chapel Ct, N2 . . . . .73 H3
SE1 . . . . .28 B3
Chapel Fm Rd, SE9 . . . . .174 C3
Chapel Gate Ms, SW4
off Bedford Rd 150 E3
Chapel Ho St, E14 . . . . .134 B5
Chapelier Ho, SW18
off Point Pleasant 148 D4
Chapel La, Chig. IG7 . . . . .65 J3
Pinner HA5 . . . . .66 D3
Romford RM6 . . . . .82 D7
Chapel Mkt, N1 . . . . .10 E1
Chapel Ms, Wdf.Grn. IG8 . . . . . . .64 D6
Chapelmount Rd, Wdf.Grn. IG8 . .64 C6
Chapel Path, E11 . . . . .79 G6
Chapel Pl, EC2 . . . . .12 D4
N1 . . . . .11 F1
N17 off White Hart La 60 C7
W1 . . . . .16 D4
Chapel Rd, SE27 . . . . .169 H4
W13 . . . . .125 E1
Bexleyheath DA7 . . . . .159 G4
Hounslow TW3 . . . . .143 H3
Ilford IG1 . . . . .98 D3
Twickenham TW1 . . . . .145 E7
Chapel Side, W2 . . . . .14 A5
Chapel Stones, N17 . . . . .76 C1
Chapel St, NW1 . . . . .15 G2
SW1 . . . . .24 C5
Enfield EN2 . . . . .43 J3
Chapel Ter, Loug. IG10
off Forest Rd 48 B4
Chapel Vw, S.Croy. CR2 . . . . .203 E6
Chapel Wk, NW4 . . . . .71 H4
Croydon CR0
off Wellesley Rd 201 J2
Chapel Way, N7 off Sussex Way . .93 F3
Chapel Yd, SW18
off Wandsworth High St 148 D5
Chaplin Cl, SE1 . . . . .27 F3
Chaplin Rd, E15 . . . . .115 E2
N17 . . . . .76 C3
NW2 . . . . .89 G6
Dagenham RM9 . . . . .101 E7
Wembley HA0 . . . . .87 F6
Chaplin Sq, N12 . . . . .57 G7
Chapman Cl, West Dr. UB7 . . . . .120 C3
Chapman Cres, Har. HA3 . . . . .69 H5
Chapman Pk Ind Est, NW10 . . . . .89 F6
Chapman Pl, N4 . . . . .93 H2
Chapman Rd, E9 . . . . .95 J6
Belvedere DA17 . . . . .139 G5
Croydon CR0 . . . . .201 G1
Chapman's La, SE2 . . . . .138 C4
Belvedere DA17 . . . . .138 D4
Chapman Sq, SW19 . . . . .166 A2
Chapman St, E1 . . . . .112 E7
Chapone Pl, W1 . . . . .17 H4
Chapter Cl, W4
off Beaumont Rd 126 C3
Chapter Ho Ct, EC4 . . . . .19 J4
Chapter Rd, NW2 . . . . .89 G5
SE17 . . . . .35 H4
Chapter St, SW1 . . . . .33 H2
Chapter Way, Hmptn. TW12 . . . . .161 G4
Chara Pl, W4 . . . . .126 D6
Charcot Ho, SW15
off Highcliffe Dr 147 F6
Charcroft Gdns, Enf. EN3 . . . . . . .45 G4
Chardin Rd, W4
off Elliott Rd 126/127 E4
Chardmore Rd, N16 . . . . .94 D1
Chard Rd, Houns. (Hthrw Air.) TW6
off Heathrow Tunnel App 140 D3

Chardwell Cl, E6
  off Northumberland Rd 116 B6
Charecroft Way, W12 ....128 A2
Charfield Ct, W9 ....6 A6
Charford Rd, E16 ....115 G5
Chargeable La, E13 ....115 F4
Chargeable St, E16 ....115 F4
Chargrove Cl, SE16
  off Marlow Way 133 G2
Charing Cl, Orp. BR6 ....207 J4
Charing Cross, SW1 ....26 A1
Charing Cross Rd, WC2 ......17 J3
Charlbert St, NW8 ....7 G1
Charlbury Av, Stan. HA7 ......53 G5
Charlbury Gdns, Ilf. IG3 ......99 J2
Charlbury Gro, W5 ....105 F6
Charlbury Ho, E12
  off Grantham Rd 98 D3
Charldane Rd, SE9 ....174 E3
Charlecote Gro, SE26 ....171 E3
Charlecote Rd, Dag. RM8 ....100 E3
Charlemont Rd, E6 ....116 C3
Charles Babbage Cl, Chess.
  KT9 ....195 F7
Charles Barry Cl, SW4 ....150 C3
Charles Burton Ct, E5
  off Ashenden Rd 95 H5
Charles Cl, Sid. DA14 ....176 B4
Charles Cobb Gdns, Croy. CR0 .201 G5
Charles Coveney Rd, SE15 ....152 C1
Charles Cres, Har. HA1 ....68 A7
Charles Dickens Ho, E2 ......112 E3
Charles Dickens Ter, SE20
  off Maple Rd 171 F7
Charlesfield, SE9 ....173 J3
Charles Flemwell Ms, E16
  off Hanameel St 135 G1
Charles Grinling Wk, SE18 ....136 D4
Charles Haller St, SW2
  off Tulse Hill 151 G7
Charles Ho, N17 off Love La 60 C7
Charles La, NW8 ....7 F2
Charlesmere Gdns, SE28
  off Battery Rd 137 H2
Charles Pl, NW1 ....9 G4
Charles Rd, E7 off Lens Rd 97 J7
  SW19 ....184 D1
  W13 ....104 D6
  Romford RM6 ....82 D7
Charles II Pl, SW3
  off King's Rd 129 J5
Charles II St, SW1 ....25 H1
Charles Sevright Dr, NW7 ......56 A5
Charles Sq, N1 ....12 C4
Charles Sq Est, N1
  off Pitfield St 112 A3
Charles St, E16 ....136 A1
  SW13 ....147 E2
  W1 ....24 D1
  Croydon CR0 ....201 J3
  Enfield EN1 ....44 C5
  Hounslow TW3 ....143 F2
Charleston Cl, Felt. TW13
  off Vineyard Rd 160 A3
Charleston St, SE17 ....36 A2
Charles Townsend Ho, EC1 ....11 F4
Charles Whincup Rd, E16 ....135 H1
Charleville Circ, SE26 ....170 D5
Charleville Ms, Islw. TW7
  off Railshead Rd 144/145 E4
Charleville Rd, W14 ....128 B5
Charlie Chaplin Wk, SE1
  off Waterloo Rd 131 G1
Charlieville Rd, Erith DA8
  off Northumberland Pk 139 J7
Charlmont Rd, SW17 ....167 J6
Charlotte Cl, Bexh. DA6 ......158 E5
Ilford IG6 off Connor Cl 81 F1
Charlotte Ct, W6
  off Goldhawk Rd 127 G3
Charlotte Despard Av, SW11 ..150 A1
Charlotte Ms, W1 ....17 G1
  W10 ....108 A6
  W14 off Munden St 128 B4
Charlotte Pl, NW9 off Uphill Dr ..70 C3
  SW1 ....33 F2
  W1 ....17 G2
Charlotte Rd, EC2 ....12 D3
  SW13 ....147 F1
  Dagenham RM10 ....101 H6
  Wallington SM6 ....200 C6
Charlotte Row, SW4 ....150 C3
Charlotte Sq, Rich. TW10
  off Greville Rd 145 J6
Charlotte St, W1 ....17 G1
Charlotte Ter, N1 ....111 F1
Charlow Cl, SW6
  off Townmead Rd 149 F2
CHARLTON, SE7 ....135 J6
★ Charlton Athletic FC, SE7 ..135 J5
Charlton Ch La, SE7 ....135 J5
Charlton Cres, Bark. IG11 ....117 J2
Charlton Dene, SE7 ....135 J7
Charlton Kings Rd, NW5 ......92 D5
Charlton La, SE7 ....136 A5
Charlton Pk La, SE7 ....136 A7
Charlton Pk Rd, SE7 ....136 A6

Charlton Pl, N1 ....11 G1
Charlton Rd, N9 ....61 G1
  NW10 ....107 E1
  SE3 ....135 G7
  SE7 ....135 H7
  Harrow HA3 ....69 G4
  Wembley HA9 ....87 J1
Charlton Way, SE3 ....154 E1
Charlwood Cl, Har. HA3
  off Kelvin Cres 52 B7
Charlwood Pl, SW1 ....33 G2
Charlwood Rd, SW15 ....148 A3
Charlwood Sq, Mitch. CR4 ....185 G3
Charlwood St, SW1 ....33 G2
Charlwood Ter, SW15
  off Cardinal Pl 148 A4
Charmian Av, Stan. HA7 ......69 G3
Charminster Av, SW19 ....184 E2
Charminster Ct, Surb. KT6 ....181 G7
Charminster Rd, SE9 ....174 A4
  Worcester Park KT4 ....198 A1
Charmouth Rd, Well. DA16 ....158 C1
Charnock Rd, E5 ....94 E3
Charnwood Av, SW19 ....184 D2
Charnwood Cl, N.Mal. KT3 ....183 E4
Charnwood Dr, E18 ....79 H3
Charnwood Gdns, E14 ....134 A4
Charnwood Pl, N20 ....57 F3
Charnwood Rd, SE25 ....188 A5
Charnwood St, E5 ....94 D2
Charrington Rd, Croy. CR0
  off Drayton Rd 201 H2
Charrington St, NW1 ....9 H1
Charsley Rd, SE6 ....172 B2
Chart Cl, Brom. BR2 ....191 E1
  Croydon CR0
   off Stockbury Rd 189 F6
Charter Av, Ilf. IG2 ....99 G1
Charter Ct, N.Mal. KT3 ......182 E3
Charter Cres, Houns. TW4 ....142 E4
Charter Dr, Bex. DA5 ....158 E7
Charteris Rd, N4 ....93 G1
  NW6 ....108 C1
  Woodford Green IG8 ....63 H7
Charter Rd, Kings.T. KT1 ....182 B3
Charter Rd, The, Wdf.Grn. IG8 ..62 E6
Charters Cl, SE19 ....170 B5
Charter Sq, Kings.T. KT1 ....182 B2
Charter Way, N3 ....72 C4
  N14 ....42 C6
Chartfield Av, SW15 ....147 H5
Chartfield Sq, SW15 ....148 A5
Chartham Gro, SE27
  off Royal Circ 169 G3
Chartham Rd, SE25 ....188 E3
Chart Hills Cl, SE28
  off Fairway Dr 118/119 E6
Chartley Av, NW2 ....88 E3
  Stanmore HA7 ....52 C6
Charton Cl, Belv. DA17
  off Nuxley Rd 139 F6
Chartridge Cl, Barn. EN5 ......39 G5
Chart St, N1 ....12 C3
Chartwell Cl, SE9 ....175 F2
  Croydon CR0 ....202 A1
  Greenford UB6 ....103 H1
Chartwell Gdns, Sutt. SM3 ..198 B4
Chartwell Pl, Har. HA2 ......86 A2
  Sutton SM3 ....198 C4
Chartwell Way, SE20 ....188 E1
Charwood, SW16 ....169 G4
Chase, The, E12 ....98 A4
  SW4 ....150 B3
  SW16 ....169 F7
  SW20 ....184 B1
  Bexleyheath DA7 ....159 H3
  Bromley BR1 ....191 H3
  Chigwell IG7 ....65 F4
  Edgware HA8 ....70 B1
  Loughton IG10 ....47 J7
  Pinner HA5 ....67 F4
  Pinner (Eastcote) HA5 ......66 C6
  Romford (Chad.Hth) RM6 ....82 E6
  Stanmore HA7 ....52 D5
  Sunbury-on-Thames TW16 ..178 B1
  Wallington SM6 ....200 E5
Chase Ct Gdns, Enf. EN2 ......43 J3
Chasefield Rd, SW17 ....167 J4
Chase Gdns, E4 ....62 A4
  Twickenham TW2 ....144 A6
Chase Grn, Enf. EN2 ....43 J3
Chase Grn Av, Enf. EN2 ....43 H2
Chase Hill, Enf. EN2 ....43 J3
Chase La, Ilf. IG6 ....81 G5
Chaseley Dr, W4 ....126 B5
Chaseley St, E14 ....113 H6
Chasemore Cl, Mitch. CR4 ....185 J7

Chasemore Gdns, Croy. CR0
  off Thorneloe Gdns 201 H5
Chase Ridings, Enf. EN2 ......43 G2
Chase Rd, N14 ....42 C6
  NW10 ....106 D4
  W3 ....106 D4
Chase Side, N14 ....42 A6
  Enfield EN2 ....43 J3
Chase Side Av, SW20 ....184 B1
  Enfield EN2 ....43 J2
Chase Side Cres, Enf. EN2 ....43 J1
Chase Side Pl, Enf. EN2
  off Chase Side 43 J2
Chaseville Pk Rd, N21 ....43 E5
Chase Way, N14 ....58 B2
Chasewood Av, Enf. EN2 ......43 H2
Chasewood Pk, Har. HA1 ......86 C3
Chatfield Rd, SW11 ....149 F3
  Croydon CR0 ....201 H1
Chatham Av, Brom. BR2 ......191 F7
Chatham Cl, NW11 ....72 D5
  SE18 off Cadogan Rd 136 E3
  Sutton SM3 ....184 C7
Chatham Pl, E9 ....95 F6
Chatham Rd, E17 ....77 H3
  E18 off Grove Hill 79 F2
  SW11 ....149 J6
  Kingston upon Thames KT1 ..182 A2
  Orpington BR6 ....207 F5
Chatham St, SE17 ....36 B1
Chatsfield Pl, W5 ....105 H6
Chatsworth Av, NW4 ....71 J2
  SW20 ....184 B1
  Bromley BR1 ....173 H4
  Sidcup DA15 ....176 A1
  Wembley HA9 ....87 J5
Chatsworth Cl, NW4 ....71 J2
  Borehamwood WD6 ....38 A3
  West Wickham BR4 ....205 F2
Chatsworth Ct, W8 ....128 D4
  Stanmore HA7 off Marsh La ..53 F5
Chatsworth Cres, Houns. TW3 ..144 A4
Chatsworth Dr, Enf. EN1 ......44 D7
Chatsworth Est, E5
  off Elderfield Rd 95 G4
Chatsworth Gdns, W3 ....106 B7
  Harrow HA2 ....85 H1
  New Malden KT3 ....183 F5
Chatsworth Par, Orp. BR5
  off Queensway 193 F5
Chatsworth Pl, Mitch. CR4 ....185 J3
  Teddington TW11 ....162 D4
Chatsworth Ri, W5 ....105 J4
Chatsworth Rd, E5 ....95 F3
  E15 ....97 F5
  NW2 ....90 A6
  W4 ....126 C6
  W5 ....105 J4
  Croydon CR0 ....202 A4
  Hayes UB4 ....102 B4
  Sutton SM3 ....198 A5
Chatsworth Way, SE27 ......169 H3
Chatterton Ms, N4
  off Chatterton Rd 93 H3
Chatterton Rd, N4 ....93 H3
  Bromley BR2 ....192 A4
Chatto Rd, SW11 ....149 J5
Chaucer Av, Hayes UB4 ......102 A5
  Hounslow TW4 ....142 B2
  Richmond TW9 ....146 A2
Chaucer Cl, N11 ....58 C5
Chaucer Ct, N16 ....94 B4
Chaucer Dr, SE1 ....37 G2
Chaucer Gdns, Sutt. SM1 ....198 D3
Chaucer Grn, Croy. CR0 ......189 E7
Chaucer Ho, Sutt. SM1 ......198 D3
Chaucer Rd, E7 ....97 G6
  E11 ....79 G6
  E17 ....78 C2
  SE24 ....151 G5
  W3 ....126 C1
  Sidcup DA15 ....176 C1
  Sutton SM1 ....198 D4
  Welling DA16 ....157 H1
Chaucer Way, SW19 ....167 G6
Chauncey Cl, N9 ....60 D3
Chaundrye Cl, SE9 ....156 C6
Chauntler Cl, E16 ....115 H7
CHEAM, Sutt. SM3 ....198 A6
Cheam Common Rd, Wor.Pk.
  KT4 ....197 H2
Cheam Mans, Sutt. SM3 ......198 B7
Cheam Pk Way, Sutt. SM3 ....198 B6
Cheam Rd, Sutt. SM1 ....198 C6
Cheam St, SE15
  off Evelina Rd 152/153 E3
Cheapside, EC2 ....20 A4
  N13 off Taplow Rd 59 J4
Cheddar Cl, N11
  off Martock Gdns 58 A6
Cheddar Rd, Houns. (Hthrw Air.)
  TW6 off Cromer Rd 140 D2
Cheddar Waye, Hayes UB4 ....102 B6
Cheddington Rd, N18 ....60 B3
Chedworth Cl, E16
  off Hallsville Rd 115 F6
Cheeseman Cl, Hmptn. TW12 ..161 E6

Cheesemans Ter, W14 ....128 C5
Cheldon Av, NW7 ....56 A7
Chelford Rd, Brom. BR1 ......172 D5
Chelmer Cres, Bark. IG11 ....118 B2
Chelmer Rd, E9 ....95 G5
Chelmsford Cl, E6
  off Guildford Rd 116 C6
  W6 ....128 A6
Chelmsford Gdns, Ilf. IG1 ....80 B3
Chelmsford Rd, E11 ....96 D1
  E17 ....78 A6
  E18 ....79 F1
  N14 ....42 C7
Chelmsford Sq, NW10 ....107 J1
CHELSEA, SW3 ....31 E5
★ Chelsea Antique Mkt, SW3 ..31 F5
Chelsea Br, SW1 ....32 D5
  SW8 ....32 D5
Chelsea Br Rd, SW1 ....32 B3
Chelsea Cloisters, SW3
  off Lucan Pl 129 H4
Chelsea Cl, NW10
  off Winchelsea Rd 106 D1
  Edgware HA8 ....70 A2
  Hampton (Hmptn H.) TW12 ..161 J5
  Worcester Park KT4 ....183 G7
Chelsea Cres, SW10
  off Harbour Av 149 F1
Chelsea Embk, SW3 ....31 H6
★ Chelsea FC, SW6 ....30 A7
Chelsea Gdns, W13
  off Hathaway Gdns 104 C5
  Sutton SM3 ....198 B4
Chelsea Harbour, SW10 ......149 F1
Chelsea Harbour Dr, SW10 ....149 F1
Chelsea Manor Ct, SW3 ......31 H5
Chelsea Manor Gdns, SW3 ....31 G5
Chelsea Manor St, SW3 ......31 G4
Chelsea Pk Gdns, SW3 ......30 E5
★ Chelsea Physic Gdn, SW3 ..31 J5
Chelsea Sq, SW3 ....31 F3
Chelsea Vista, SW6
  off The Boulevard 149 F1
Chelsea Wf, SW10 ....129 G7
Chelsfield Av, N9 ....45 G7
Chelsfield Gdns, SE26 ....171 F3
Chelsfield Grn, N9
  off Chelsfield Av 45 G7
Chelsham Rd, SW4 ....150 D3
  South Croydon CR2 ....202 A6
Chelston App, Ruis. HA4 ......84 A2
Chelston Rd, Ruis. HA4 ......84 A1
Chelsworth Dr, SE18 ....137 G6
Cheltenham Av, Twick. TW1 ..144 D7
Cheltenham Cl, N.Mal. KT3
  off Northcote Rd 182 C3
  Northolt UB5 ....85 H6
Cheltenham Gdns, E6 ....116 B2
  Loughton IG10 ....48 B6
Cheltenham Pl, W3 ....126 B1
  Harrow HA3 ....69 H4
Cheltenham Rd, E10 ....78 C6
  SE15 ....153 F4
Cheltenham Ter, SW3 ....32 A3
Chelverton Rd, SW15 ....148 A4
Chelwood, N20
  off Oakleigh Rd N 57 G2
Chelwood Cl, E4 ....46 B6
Chelwood Gdns, Rich. TW9 ..146 A2
Chelwood Gdns Pas, Rich. TW9
  off Chelwood Gdns 146 A2
Chelwood Wk, SE4 ....153 H4
Chenappa Cl, E13 ....115 G3
Chenduit Way, Stan. HA7 ....52 C5
Cheney Row, E17 ....77 J1
Cheneys Rd, E11 ....97 E3
Cheney St, Pnr. HA5 ....66 C5
Chenies, The, Orp. BR6 ......193 H6
Chenies Ms, WC1 ....9 H6
Chenies Pl, NW1 ....9 H1
Chenies St, WC1 ....17 H1
Cheniston Gdns, W8 ....22 A5
Chepstow Cl, SW15
  off Lytton Gro 148 B6
Chepstow Cres, W11 ....108 D7
  Ilford IG3 ....81 H6
Chepstow Gdns, Sthl. UB1 ....103 F6
Chepstow Pl, W2 ....108 D6
Chepstow Ri, Croy. CR0 ......202 B3
Chepstow Rd, W2 ....108 D6
  W7 ....124 D3
  Croydon CR0 ....202 B3
Chepstow Vil, W11 ....108 C7
Chepstow Way, SE15 ....132 C7
Chequers, Buck.H. IG9
  off Hills Rd 63 H1
Chequers Cl, NW9 ....70 E3
  Orpington BR5 ....193 J4
Chequers Gdns, N13 ....59 H5
Chequers La, Dag. RM9 ......119 F4
Chequers Par, SE9
  off Eltham High St 156 C6
Chequers Rd, Loug. IG10 ....48 D5
Chequer St, EC1 ....12 A6
Chequers Way, N13 ....59 J5
Cherbury Cl, SE28 ....118 D6
Cherbury Ct, N1 ....12 C2

Cherbury St, N1 ...12 C2
Cherchefelle Ms, Stan. HA7 ...52 E5
Cherimoya Gdns, W.Mol. KT8
　off Kelvinbrook ...179 H3
Cherington Rd, W7 ...124 C1
Cheriton Av, Brom. BR2 ...191 F5
　Ilford IG5 ...80 C2
Cheriton Cl, W5 ...105 F5
　Barnet EN4 ...41 J3
Cheriton Rd, SE18 ...137 G7
Cheriton Sq, SW17 ...168 A2
Cherry Av, Sthl. UB1 ...122 D1
Cherry Blossom Cl, N13 ...59 H5
Cherry Cl, E17 off Eden Rd ...78 B4
　NW9 ...71 E2
　SW2 off Tulse Hill ...151 G7
　W5 ...125 G3
　Carshalton SM5 ...199 J2
　Morden SM4 ...184 B4
Cherrycot Hill, Orp. BR6 ...207 G4
Cherrycot Ri, Orp. BR6 ...207 F4
Cherry Cres, Brent. TW8 ...124 E7
Cherrycroft Gdns, Pnr. HA5
　off Westfield Pk ...51 F7
Cherrydown Av, E4 ...61 J3
Cherrydown Cl, E4 ...61 J3
Cherrydown Rd, Sid. DA14 ...176 D2
Cherry Gdns, Dag. RM9 ...101 F5
　Northolt UB5 ...85 H7
Cherry Gdn St, SE16 ...132 E2
Cherry Garth, Brent. TW8 ...125 G4
Cherry Gro, Hayes UB3 ...122 B1
　Harrow HA3 ...52 B6
Cherry Hill, Barn. EN5 ...41 E6
Cherry Hill Gdns, Croy. CR0 ...201 F4
Cherry Hills, Wat. WD19 ...50 E5
Cherrylands Cl, NW9 ...88 C2
Cherry La, West Dr. UB7 ...120 C4
Cherry La Roundabout, West Dr.
　UB7 ...120 E4
Cherry Laurel Wk, SW2
　off Beechdale Rd ...151 F6
Cherry Orchard, West Dr. UB7 ...120 B2
Cherry Orchard Gdns, Croy. CR0
　off Oval Rd ...202 A2
　West Molesey KT8 ...179 F3
Cherry Orchard Rd, Brom. BR2 ...206 B2
　Croydon CR0 ...202 A2
　West Molesey KT8 ...179 G3
Cherry Tree Cl, E9
　off Moulins Rd ...113 F1
　Wembley HA0 ...86 C4
Cherry Tree Ct, NW9 ...70 C4
Cherry Tree Dr, SW16 ...169 E3
Cherry Tree Ri, Buck.H. IG9 ...63 J4
Cherry Tree Rd, E15
　off Wingfield Rd ...96/97 E4
　N2 ...73 J4
Cherry Tree Wk, EC1 ...12 A6
　Beckenham BR3 ...189 J4
　West Wickham BR4 ...205 F4
Cherry Tree Way, Stan. HA7 ...53 E6
Cherry Wk, Brom. BR2 ...205 G1
Cherry Way, Epsom KT19 ...196 D6
Cherrywood Cl, E3 ...113 H3
　Kingston upon Thames KT2 ...164 A7
Cherrywood Dr, SW15 ...148 A5
Cherrywood La, Mord. SM4 ...184 B4
Cherry Wd Way, W5
　off Hanger Vale La ...106 A5
Cherston Gdns, Loug. IG10
　off Cherston Rd ...48 D4
Cherston Rd, Loug. IG10 ...48 D4
Chertsey Dr, Sutt. SM3 ...198 B2
Chertsey Rd, E11 ...96 D2
　Ilford IG1 ...99 G4
　Twickenham TW1, TW2 ...144 C6
Chertsey St, SW17 ...168 A5
Chervil Cl, Felt. TW13 ...160 A3
Chervil Ms, SE28 ...138 B1
Cherwell Ct, Epsom KT19 ...196 C4
Cheryls Cl, SW6 ...149 E1
Cheseman St, SE26 ...171 E3
Chesfield Rd, Kings.T. KT2 ...163 H7
Chesham Av, Orp. BR5 ...192 E6
Chesham Cl, SW1 ...24 B6
Chesham Cres, SE20 ...189 F2
Chesham Ms, SW1 ...24 B5
Chesham Pl, SW1 ...24 B6
Chesham Rd, SE20 ...189 F2
　SW19 ...167 G6
　Kingston upon Thames KT1 ...182 A1
Chesham St, NW10 ...88 D3
　SW1 ...24 B6
Chesham Ter, W13 ...124 E2
Cheshire Cl, E17 ...78 B1
　SE4 ...153 J2
　Mitcham CR4 ...186 E3
Cheshire Ct, EC4 ...19 F4
Cheshire Gdns, Chess. KT9 ...195 G6
Cheshire Ho, N18 ...61 E4
Cheshire Rd, N22 ...59 F7
Cheshire St, E2 ...13 G5
Chesholm Rd, N16 ...94 B3
Cheshunt Rd, E7 ...97 H6
　Belvedere DA17 ...139 G5

Chesil Ct, E2 ...113 F2
Chesilton Rd, SW6 ...148 C1
Chesley Gdns, E6 ...116 A2
Chesney Cres, Croy. (New Adgtn)
　CR0 ...204 C7
Chesney St, SW11 ...150 A1
Chesnut Est, N17 ...76 C3
Chesnut Gro, N17 ...76 C3
　off Chesnut Rd ...76 C3
Chesnut Rd, N17 ...76 C3
Chessell Cl, Th.Hth. CR7 ...187 H4
CHESSINGTON, KT9 ...195 H6
Chessington Av, N3 ...72 B3
　Bexleyheath DA7 ...139 E7
Chessington Cl, Epsom KT19 ...196 C6
Chessington Ct, Pnr. HA5 ...67 F4
Chessington Hall Gdns, Chess.
　KT9 ...195 G7
Chessington Hill Pk, Chess.
　KT9 ...196 A5
Chessington Lo, N3 ...72 C3
Chessington Way, W.Wick. BR4 ...204 B2
Chesson Rd, W14 ...128 C6
Chesswood Way, Pnr. HA5 ...66 C2
Chester Av, Rich. TW10 ...145 J5
　Twickenham TW2 ...161 F1
Chester Cl, SW1 ...24 C4
　SW13 ...147 H3
　Loughton IG10 ...49 F1
　Sutton SM1 ...198 D2
Chester Cl N, NW1 ...8 E3
Chester Cl S, NW1 ...8 E4
Chester Cotts, SW1 ...32 B2
Chester Ct, NW1 ...8 E3
　SE5 ...132 A7
Chester Cres, E8 off Ridley Rd ...94 C6
Chester Dr, Har. HA2 ...67 F6
Chesterfield Dr, Esher KT10 ...194 D2
Chesterfield Gdns, N4 ...75 H5
　SE10 off Crooms Hill ...134 D7
　W1 ...24 D1
Chesterfield Gro, SE22 ...152 C5
Chesterfield Hill, W1 ...16 D6
Chesterfield Ms, N4
　off Chesterfield Gdns ...75 H5
Chesterfield Rd, E10 ...78 C6
　N3 ...56 D6
　W4 ...126 C6
　Barnet EN5 ...40 A5
　Epsom KT19 ...196 D7
Chesterfield St, W1 ...24 D1
Chesterfield Wk, SE10 ...154 D1
Chesterfield Way, SE15 ...133 F7
　Hayes UB3 ...122 A2
Chesterford Gdns, NW3 ...91 E4
Chesterford Ho, SE18
　off Shooter's Hill Rd ...136 A7
Chesterford Rd, E12 ...98 C5
Chester Gdns, W13 ...104 D6
　Enfield EN3 ...45 E6
　Morden SM4 ...185 F6
Chester Gate, NW1 ...8 D4
Chester Grn, Loug. IG10 ...49 F1
Chester Ms, E17
　off Chingford Rd ...78 A2
　SW1 ...24 D5
Chester Path, Loug. IG10 ...49 F1
Chester Pl, NW1 ...8 D3
Chester Rd, E7 ...98 A7
　E11 ...79 H6
　E16 ...115 E4
　E17 ...77 G5
　N9 ...61 E1
　N17 ...76 A3
　N19 ...92 B2
　NW1 ...8 C4
　SW19 ...165 J6
　Borehamwood WD6 ...38 C3
　Chigwell IG7 ...64 D3
　Hounslow TW4 ...142 B3
　Hounslow (Hthrw Air.) TW6 ...140 D3
　Ilford IG3 ...99 J1
　Loughton IG10 ...48 E2
　Sidcup DA15 ...157 H5
Chester Row, SW1 ...32 B2
Chesters, The, N.Mal. KT3 ...182 E1
Chester Sq, SW1 ...32 D1
Chester Sq Ms, SW1 ...24 D6
Chester St, E2 ...13 J5
　SW1 ...24 C5
Chester Ter, NW1 ...8 D3
Chesterton Cl, SW18
　off Ericcson Cl ...148 D5
　Greenford UB6 ...103 H2
Chesterton Ho, SW11
　off Ingrave St ...149 G3
Chesterton Rd, E13 ...115 G3
　W10 ...108 A5
Chesterton Sq, W8
　off Pembroke Rd ...128 C4
Chesterton Ter, E13 ...115 G3
　Kingston upon Thames KT1 ...182 A2
Chester Way, SE11 ...35 F2
Chesthunte Rd, N17 ...75 J1
Chestnut All, SW6 off Lillie Rd ...128 C6
Chestnut Av, E7 ...97 H4
　N8 ...74 E5

Chestnut Av, SW14
　off Thornton Rd ...146 D3
　Brentford TW8 ...125 G4
　Buckhurst Hill IG9 ...64 A3
　East Molesey KT8 ...180 C3
　Edgware HA8 ...53 H6
　Epsom KT19 ...196 E4
　Esher KT10 ...180 A7
　Hampton TW12 ...161 G7
　Teddington TW11 ...180 C2
　Wembley HA0 ...86 E5
　West Wickham BR4 ...205 E5
Chestnut Av N, E17 ...78 C4
Chestnut Av S, E17 ...78 C4
Chestnut Cl, N14 ...42 C5
　N16 off Lordship Gro ...94 A2
　SE6 ...172 C5
　SE14 ...153 J1
　SW16 ...169 G4
　Buckhurst Hill IG9 ...64 A2
　Carshalton SM5 ...199 J1
　Sidcup DA15 ...176 A1
　West Drayton UB7 ...121 E7
Chestnut Ct, SW6
　off North End Rd ...128 C6
　Surbiton KT6
　off Penners Gdns ...181 H7
Chestnut Dr, E11 ...79 G6
　Bexleyheath DA7 ...158 D3
　Harrow HA3 ...52 C7
　Pinner HA5 ...66 D6
Chestnut Gro, SE20 ...171 E7
　SW12 ...150 A7
　W5 ...125 G3
　Barnet EN4 ...41 J5
　Ilford IG6 ...65 H6
　Isleworth TW7 ...144 D4
　Mitcham CR4 ...186 D4
　New Malden KT3 ...182 D3
　South Croydon CR2 ...203 E7
　Wembley HA0 ...86 E5
Chestnut La, N20 ...56 B1
Chestnut Pl, SE26 ...170 C4
Chestnut Ri, SE18 ...137 G5
Chestnut Rd, SE27 ...169 H3
　SW20 ...184 A2
　Kingston upon Thames KT2 ...163 H7
　Twickenham TW2 ...162 B2
Chestnut Row, N3
　off Nether St ...56 D7
Chestnut Wk, Wdf.Grn. IG8 ...63 G5
Chestnut Way, Felt. TW13 ...160 B3
Cheston Av, Croy. CR0 ...203 H2
Chettle Cl, SE1 ...28 B5
Chettle Ct, N8 ...75 G6
Chetwode Rd, SW17 ...167 J3
Chetwood Wk, E6 ...116 B6
Chetwynd Av, Barn. EN4 ...57 J1
Chetwynd Rd, NW5 ...92 B4
Chevalier Cl, Stan. HA7 ...53 H4
Cheval Pl, SW7 ...23 H5
Cheval St, E14 ...134 A3
Cheveney Wk, Brom. BR2
　off Marina Cl ...191 G3
Chevening Rd, NW6 ...108 A2
　SE10 ...135 F5
　SE19 ...170 A6
Chevenings, The, Sid. DA14 ...176 C3
Cheverton Rd, N19 ...92 D1
Chevet St, E9 off Kenworthy Rd ...95 H5
Cheviot Cl, Enf. EN1 ...44 A2
　Hayes UB3 ...121 G7
Cheviot Gdns, NW2 ...90 A2
　SE27 ...169 H4
Cheviot Gate, NW2 ...90 B2
Cheviot Rd, SE27 ...169 G5
Cheviot Way, Ilf. IG2 ...81 H4
Chevron Cl, E16 ...115 G6
Chevy Rd, Sthl. UB2 ...123 J2
Chewton Rd, E17 ...77 H4
Cheyne Av, E18 ...79 F3
　Twickenham TW2 ...161 F1
Cheyne Cl, NW4 ...71 J5
　Bromley BR2 off Cedar Cres ...206 B3
Cheyne Ct, SW3 ...31 J5
Cheyne Gdns, SW3 ...31 H5
Cheyne Hill, Surb. KT5 ...181 J4
Cheyne Ms, SW3 ...31 H5
Cheyne Path, W7 ...104 C5
Cheyne Pl, SW3 ...31 J5
Cheyne Row, SW3 ...31 G6
Cheyne Wk, N21 ...43 H5
　NW4 ...71 J6
　SW3 ...31 H6
　SW10 ...30 E7
　Croydon CR0 ...202 D2
Cheyneys Av, Edg. HA8 ...53 G6
Chichele Gdns, Croy. CR0 ...202 B4
Chichele Rd, NW2 ...90 A5
Chicheley Gdns, Har. HA3 ...51 J7
Chicheley Rd, Har. HA3 ...51 J7
Chicheley St, SE1 ...26 D3
Chichester Cl, E6 ...116 B6
　SE3 ...155 J1
　Hampton TW12 off Maple Cl ...161 F6
Chichester Ct, Stan. HA7 ...69 H3
Chichester Gdns, Ilf. IG1 ...80 B7

Chichester Ms, SE27 ...169 G4
Chichester Rents, WC2 ...18 E3
Chichester Rd, E11 ...97 E3
　N9 ...60 D1
　NW6 ...108 D2
　W2 ...14 B1
　Croydon CR0 ...202 B3
Chichester St, SW1 ...33 G4
Chichester Way, E14 ...134 D4
　Feltham TW14 ...142 B7
Chicksand St, E1 ...21 G2
Chiddingfold, N12 ...56 D3
Chiddingstone Av, Bexh. DA7 ...139 F7
Chiddingstone St, SW6 ...148 D2
Chieveley Rd, Bexh. DA7 ...159 H4
Chignell Pl, W13
　off The Broadway ...124 D1
CHIGWELL, IG7 ...65 G3
Chigwell Hill, E1
　off Pennington St ...112/113 E7
Chigwell Hurst Ct, Pnr. HA5 ...66 D3
Chigwell La, Loug. IG10 ...49 F5
Chigwell Pk, Chig. IG7 ...64 E3
Chigwell Pk Dr, Chig. IG7 ...64 D3
Chigwell Ri, Chig. IG7 ...64 D2
Chigwell Rd, E18 ...79 H3
　Woodford Green IG8 ...79 J2
Chilcombe Ho, SW15
　off Fontley Way ...147 G7
Chilcot Cl, E14 off Grundy St ...114 B6
Chilcott Cl, Wem. HA0 ...87 F4
Childebert Rd, SW17 ...168 B2
Childeric Rd, SE14 ...133 H7
Childerley, Kings.T. KT1
　off Burritt Rd ...182 A3
Childerley St, SW6
　off Fulham Palace Rd ...148 A1
Childers, The, Wdf.Grn. IG8 ...64 C5
Childers St, SE8 ...133 H6
Child La, SE10 ...135 F3
CHILDS HILL, NW2 ...90 D2
Childs Hill Wk, NW2 ...90 C3
Childs La, SE19 off Westow St ...170 B6
Child's Ms, SW5 off Child's Pl ...128 D4
Child's Pl, SW5 ...128 D4
Child's St, SW5 ...128 D4
Child's Wk, SW5 off Child's St ...128 D4
Childs Way, NW11 ...72 C5
Chilham Cl, Bex. DA5 ...159 F7
　Greenford UB6 ...104 D2
Chilham Rd, SE9 ...174 B4
Chilham Way, Brom. BR2 ...191 G7
Chillerton Rd, SW17 ...168 A5
Chillingford Dr, SW11
　off Wynter St ...149 F3
Chillingworth Gdns, Twick. TW1
　off Tower Rd ...162 C3
Chillingworth Rd, N7 ...93 F5
Chilmark Gdns, N.Mal. KT3 ...183 F7
Chilmark Rd, SW16 ...186 D2
Chiltern Av, Twick. TW2 ...161 G1
Chiltern Cl, Croy. CR0 ...202 B3
　Worcester Park KT4
　off Cotswold Way ...197 J2
Chiltern Dene, Enf. EN2 ...43 F4
Chiltern Dr, Surb. KT5 ...182 B5
Chiltern Gdns, NW2 ...90 A3
　Bromley BR2 ...191 F4
Chiltern Rd, E3 ...114 A4
　Ilford IG2 ...81 H4
　Pinner HA5 ...66 C5
Chiltern St, W1 ...16 B1
Chiltern Way, Wdf.Grn. IG8 ...63 G3
Chilthorne Cl, SE6
　off Ravensbourne Pk Cres ...153 J7
Chilton Av, W5 ...125 G4
Chilton Gro, SE8 ...133 G4
Chiltonian Ind Est, SE12 ...155 F6
Chilton Rd, Edg. HA8
　off Manor Pk Cres ...54 A6
　Richmond TW9 ...146 A3
Chiltons, The, E18
　off Grove Hill ...79 G2
Chilton St, E2 ...13 G5
Chilver St, SE10 ...135 F5
Chilwell Gdns, Wat. WD19 ...50 C4
Chilworth Ct, SW19
　off Windlesham Gro ...166 A1
Chilworth Gdns, Sutt. SM1 ...199 F3
Chilworth Ms, W2 ...14 D4
Chilworth St, W2 ...14 D4
Chimes Av, N13 ...59 G5
China Hall Ms, SE16
　off Lower Rd ...133 G3
China Ms, SW2 off Craster Rd ...151 F7
★ Chinatown, W1
　off Gerrard St ...17 H5
Chinbrook Cres, SE12 ...173 H3
Chinbrook Est, SE9 ...174 A3
Chinbrook Rd, SE12 ...173 H3
Chinchilla Dr, Houns. TW4 ...142 C2
Chine, The, N10 ...74 C4
　N21 ...43 H6
　Wembley HA0 ...87 E5
Ching Ct, WC2 ...18 A4
Chingdale Rd, E4 ...62 E3
CHINGFORD, E4 ...62 B1

Chingford Av, E4 62 B3
CHINGFORD GREEN, E4 63 F1
CHINGFORD HATCH, E4 62 C4
Chingford Ind Cen, E4 61 H5
Chingford La, Wdf.Grn. IG8 62 E4
Chingford Mt Rd, E4 62 A4
Chingford Rd, E4 62 A6
E17 78 B1
Chingley Cl, Brom. BR1 173 E6
Ching Way, E4 61 J6
Chinnor Cres, Grnf. UB6 103 H2
Chipka St, E14 134 C2
Chipley St, SE14 133 H6
Chipmunk Gro, Nthlt. UB5
off Argus Way 102/103 E3
Chippendale St, E5 95 G3
Chippenham Av, Wem. HA9 88 B5
Chippenham Gdns, NW6 108 D3
Chippenham Ms, W9 108 D4
Chippenham Rd, W9 108 D4
CHIPPING BARNET, Barn. EN5 40 B4
Chipping Cl, Barn. EN5
off St. Albans Rd 40 B3
Chipstead Av, Th.Hth. CR7 187 H4
Chipstead Cl, SE19 170 C7
Chipstead Gdns, NW2 89 H2
Chipstead St, SW6 148 D1
Chip St, SW4 150 D3
Chirk Cl, Hayes UB4
off Braunston Dr 102/103 E4
Chisenhale Rd, E3 113 H2
Chisholm Rd, Croy. CR0 202 B2
Richmond TW10 145 J6
Chisledon Wk, E9
off Southmoor Way 95 J6
CHISLEHURST, BR7 174 D7
Chislehurst Av, N12 57 F7
★ **Chislehurst Caves**, Chis. BR7
off Caveside Cl 192 D1
Chislehurst Rd, Brom. BR1 192 A2
Chislehurst BR7 192 A2
Orpington BR5, BR6 193 H4
Richmond TW10 145 H6
Sidcup DA14 176 A5
CHISLEHURST WEST, Chis.
BR7 174 C5
Chislet Cl, Beck. BR3
off Abbey La 172 A7
Chisley Rd, N15 76 B6
Chiswell Sq, SE3 *off Brook La* 155 H2
Chiswell St, EC1 20 A1
CHISWICK, W4 126 D6
Chiswick Br, SW14 146 C2
W4 146 C2
Chiswick Cl, Croy. CR0 201 F3
Chiswick Common Rd, W4 126 D4
Chiswick Ct, Pnr. HA5 67 F3
Chiswick Grn Studios, W4
off Evershed Wk 126 C4
Chiswick High Rd, W4 126 D4
Brentford TW8 125 J5
★ **Chiswick Ho**, W4 126 E6
Chiswick Ho Grds, W4 126 D6
Chiswick La, W4 127 E5
Chiswick La S, W4 127 F5
Chiswick Mall, W4 127 F6
W6 127 F6
Chiswick Pk, W4 126 B4
Chiswick Quay, W4 146 C1
Chiswick Rd, N9 60 D2
W4 126 C4
Chiswick Roundabout, W4
off Chiswick High Rd 126 A5
Chiswick Sq, W4
off Hogarth
Roundabout 126/127 E6
Chiswick Staithe, W4 146 C1
Chiswick Ter, W4 *off Acton La* 126 C4
Chiswick Village, W4 126 B5
Chiswick Wf, W4 127 F6
Chitterfield Gate, West Dr. UB7 120 D7
Chitty's La, Dag. RM8 100 D2
Chitty St, W1 17 G1
Chivalry Rd, SW11 149 H5
Chivenor Gro, Kings.T. KT2 163 G5
Chivers Rd, E4 62 B3
Choats Manor Way, Dag. RM9 118 E2
Choats Rd, Bark. IG11 118 C2
Dagenham RM9 118 C2
Chobham Gdns, SW19 166 A2
Chobham Rd, E15 96 D5
Cholmeley Cres, N6 74 B7
Cholmeley Pk, N6 92 B1
Cholmley Gdns, NW6
off Fortune Grn Rd 90 D5
Cholmley Rd, T.Ditt. KT7 180 E6
Cholmondeley Av, NW10 107 G2
Cholmondeley Wk, Rich. TW9 145 F5
Choppins Ct, E1
off Wapping La 132/133 E1
Chopwell Cl, E15
off Bryant St 96 D7
Chorleywood Cres, Orp. BR5 193 J2
Choumert Gro, SE15 152 D2
Choumert Ms, SE15 152 D2
Choumert Rd, SE15 152 C3
Choumert Sq, SE15 152 D2
Chow Sq, E8 *off Arcola St* 94 C5
Chrislaine Cl, Stai. (Stanw.)
TW19 140 A6
Chrisp St, E14 114 B5
Christabel Cl, Islw. TW7 144 B3
Christchurch Av, N12 57 F6
NW6 90 B7
Harrow HA3 69 E4
Teddington TW11 162 D5
Wembley HA0 87 H6
Christchurch Cl, N12
off Summers La 57 G7
SW19 167 G7
Enfield EN2 43 J2
Christchurch Ct, NW6 90 B7
Christchurch Gdns, Har. HA3 68 D4
Christchurch Grn, Wem. HA0 87 H6
Christchurch Hill, NW3 91 G3
Christchurch La, Barn. EN5 40 B2
Christchurch Pk, Sutt. SM2 199 F7
Christ Ch Pas, EC1 19 H3
Christchurch Pas, NW3 91 F3
Barnet EN5 40 B3
Christ Ch Path, Hayes UB3 121 F3
Christchurch Rd, N8 74 E6
SW2 169 F1
SW14 146 B5
SW19 185 G1
Christ Ch Rd, Beck. BR3
off Fairfield Rd 190 A2
Christchurch Rd, Houns. (Hthrw Air.)
TW6 *off Courtney Rd* 140 D3
Ilford IG1 99 E1
Sidcup DA15 175 J4
Christ Ch Rd, Surb. KT5 181 J6
Christchurch Sq, E9
off Victoria Pk Rd 113 F1
Christchurch St, SW3 31 J5
Christchurch Ter, SW3 31 J5
Christchurch Way, SE10 135 E4
Christian Ct, SE16 133 J1
Christian Flds, SW16 169 G7
Christian St, E1 21 J3
Christie Dr, Croy. CR0 188 D5
Christie Gdns, Rom. RM6 82 B6
Christie Rd, E9 95 H6
Christina Sq, N4
off Adolphus Rd 93 H1
Christina St, EC2 12 D5
Christine Worsley Cl, N21
off Highfield Rd 59 H2
Christopher Av, W7 124 D3
Christopher Cl, SE16 133 G2
Sidcup DA15 157 J5
Christopher Gdns, Dag. RM9
off Wren Rd 100 D5
Christopher Pl, NW1 9 J4
Christopher Rd, Sthl. UB2 122 B4
Christopher's Ms, W11
off Penzance St 128 B1
Christopher St, EC2 12 C6
Chryssell Rd, SW9 131 G7
Chubworthy St, SE14 133 H6
Chudleigh Cres, Ilf. IG3 99 H4
Chudleigh Gdns, Sutt. SM1 199 F3
Chudleigh Rd, NW6 90 A7
SE4 153 J5
Twickenham TW2 144 C7
Chudleigh St, E1 113 G6
Chudleigh Way, Ruis. HA4 84 A1
Chulsa Rd, SE26 170 E5
Chumleigh St, SE5 36 D5
Chumleigh Wk, Surb. KT5 181 J4
Church All, Croy. CR0 201 G1
Church App, SE21 170 A3
Staines (Stanw.) TW19 140 A6
Church Av, E4 62 D6
NW1 *off Kentish Town Rd* 92 B6
SW14 146 D3
Beckenham BR3 190 A1
Northolt UB5 85 F7
Pinner HA5 67 E6
Sidcup DA14 176 A5
Southall UB2 123 E3
Churchbury Cl, Enf. EN1 44 B2
Churchbury La, Enf. EN1 44 A3
Churchbury Rd, SE9 156 A7
Enfield EN1 44 A2
Church Cl, N20 57 H3
W8 22 A3
Edgware HA8 54 C5
Hounslow TW3 *off Bath Rd* 143 F3
Loughton IG10 48 C2
West Drayton UB7 120 B3
Church Ct, Rich. TW9
off George St 145 G5
Church Cres, E9 95 G7
N3 72 C1
N10 74 B4
N20 57 H3
Churchcroft Cl, SW12
off Endlesham Rd 150 A7
Churchdown, Brom. BR1 173 E4
Church Dr, NW9 88 D1
Harrow HA2 67 F6
West Wickham BR4 205 E3
Church Elm La, Dag. RM10 101 G6
CHURCH END, N3 72 C1
CHURCH END, NW10 88 E6
Church End, E17 78 B4
NW4 71 H3
Church Entry, EC4 19 H4
★ **Church Farm Ho Mus**, NW4 71 H3
Church Fm La, Sutt. SM3 198 B6
Churchfield Av, N12 57 F6
Churchfield Cl, Har. HA2 67 J4
Churchfield Rd, W3 126 C1
W7 124 B2
W13 125 E1
Welling DA16 158 A3
Churchfields, E18 79 G1
SE10 *off Roan St* 134 C6
Loughton IG10 48 B4
West Molesey KT8 179 G3
Churchfields Av, Felt. TW13 161 F3
Churchfields Rd, Beck. BR3 189 G2
Church Gdns, W5 125 G2
Wembley HA0 86 D4
Church Gate, SW6 148 B3
Church Gro, SE13 154 B4
Kingston upon Thames KT1 181 F1
Church Hill, E17 78 A4
N21 43 F7
SE18 136 C3
SW19 166 C5
Carshalton SM5 199 J5
Harrow HA1 86 B1
Loughton IG10 48 B3
Church Hill Rd, E17 78 B4
Barnet EN4 41 J7
Surbiton KT6 181 H5
Sutton SM3 198 A4
Church Hill Wd, Orp. BR5 193 J5
Church Hyde, SE18
off Old Mill Rd 137 H6
Churchill Av, Har. HA3 68 E6
Churchill Ct, W5 105 J4
Northolt UB5 85 G5
Churchill Gdns, SW1 33 F4
W3 106 A6
Churchill Gdns Rd, SW1 33 E4
Churchill Ms, Wdf.Grn. IG8
off High Rd Woodford Grn 63 F6
Churchill Pl, E14 134 B1
Harrow HA1
off Sandridge Cl 68 B4
Churchill Rd, E16 115 J6
NW2 89 H6
NW5 92 B4
Edgware HA8 53 J6
South Croydon CR2 201 J7
Churchill Ter, E4 62 A4
Churchill Wk, E9 95 F5
Churchill Way, Brom. BR1
off Ethelbert Rd 191 G3
Sunbury-on-Thames TW16 160 A5
Church La, E11 97 E1
E17 78 B4
N2 73 G3
N8 75 F4
N9 60 D2
N17 76 B1
NW9 88 C2
SW17 168 B4
SW19 184 C1
W5 125 F2
Bromley BR2 206 B1
Chessington KT9 195 J6
Chislehurst BR7 193 F1
Dagenham RM10 101 H6
Enfield EN1 44 A3
Harrow HA3 68 C1
Loughton IG10 48 C3
Pinner HA5 67 E3
Richmond TW10 163 H1
Teddington TW11 162 C5
Thames Ditton KT7 180 C6
Twickenham TW1 162 D1
Wallington SM6 200 D3
Churchley Rd, SE26 171 E4
Church Manor Est, SW9
off Vassall Rd 131 G7
Church Manorway, SE2 137 J4
Church Manorway Ind Est, Erith
DA8 139 J3
Churchmead Cl, Barn. EN4 41 H6
Church Meadow, Surb. KT6 195 F2
Churchmead Rd, NW10 89 G6
Churchmore Rd, SW16 186 C1
Church Mt, N2 73 G5
Church Paddock Ct, Wall. SM6 200 D3
Church Pas, EC2
off Gresham St 111 J6
Barnet EN5 *off Wood St* 40 C4
Surbiton KT6 181 H5
Church Path, E11 79 G5
E17 *off St. Mary Rd* 78 B4
N5 93 H5
N12 57 F5
N17 *off White Hart La* 60 B7
N20 57 F4
NW10 89 E7
SW14 146 D3
SW19 184 D2
Church Path, W4 126 C3
W7 124 B1
Mitcham CR4 185 H3
Southall UB1 123 G1
Southall (Sthl Grn) UB2 123 F3
Church Pl, SW1 17 G6
W5 *off Church Gdns* 125 G2
Mitcham CR4 185 H3
Twickenham TW1
off Church St 162/163 E1
Church Ri, SE23 171 G1
Chessington KT9 195 J6
Church Rd, E10 96 B2
E12 98 B5
E17 77 H2
N1 93 J6
N6 74 A6
N17 76 B1
NW4 71 H4
NW10 89 E6
SE19 188 B1
SW13 147 F2
SW19 (Wimbledon) 166 B4
W3 126 C2
W7 124 C1
Barking IG11 99 F6
Bexleyheath DA7 159 F2
Bromley BR2 191 G2
Bromley (Short.) BR2 190 E3
Buckhurst Hill IG9 63 H1
Croydon CR0 201 H3
East Molesey KT8 180 A4
Enfield EN3 45 F6
Epsom (W.Ewell) KT19 196 D7
Esher (Clay.) KT10 194 C6
Feltham TW13 160 D5
Hayes UB3 121 J1
Hounslow (Cran.) TW5 122 B5
Hounslow (Heston) TW5 123 G7
Ilford IG2 81 G6
Isleworth TW7 144 A1
Keston BR2 206 A7
Kingston upon Thames KT1 181 J2
Loughton (High Beach) IG10 47 H2
Mitcham CR4 185 G2
Northolt UB5 85 F7
Orpington (Farnboro.) BR6 207 F5
Richmond TW9, TW10 145 H5
Richmond (Ham) TW10 163 J5
Sidcup DA14 176 A4
Southall UB2 123 F3
Stanmore HA7 53 E5
Surbiton KT6 195 F2
Sutton SM3 198 B6
Teddington TW11 162 B4
Wallington SM6 200 C3
Welling DA16 158 B2
West Drayton UB7 120 A3
Worcester Park KT4 196 E1
Church Rd Merton, SW19 185 G1
Church Rd Twr Block, Stan. HA7
off Church Rd 53 F5
Church Row, NW3 91 F4
Chislehurst BR7 175 F7
Church St, E15 115 E1
E16 136 E1
N9 60 B2
NW8 15 F1
W2 15 F1
W4 127 E6
Croydon CR0 201 J2
Dagenham RM10 101 H6
Enfield EN2 44 A3
Hampton TW12 179 J1
Isleworth TW7 144 E3
Kingston upon Thames KT1 181 G2
Sunbury-on-Thames TW16 178 B3
Sutton SM1 *off High St* 198/199 E5
Twickenham TW1 162 D1
Church St Est, NW8 7 F6
Church St N, E15 115 E1
Church St Pas, E15
off Church St 114/115 E1
Church Stretton Rd, Houns.
TW3 143 J5
Church Ter, NW4 71 H3
SE13 154 E3
SW8 150 D2
Richmond TW10 145 G5
Church Vale, N2 73 J3
SE23 171 F2
Churchview Rd, Twick. TW2 162 A1
Church Wk, N6 *off Swains La* 92 A3
N16 94 A4
NW2 90 C3
NW4 71 J3
NW9 88 D2
SW13 147 G1
SW15 147 H5
SW16 186 C2
SW20 183 J3
Brentford TW8 125 F6
Enfield EN2 *off Church La* 44 A3
Richmond TW9
off Red Lion St 145 G5
Thames Ditton KT7 180 C6
Church Way, N20 57 G3

Churchway, NW1 . . . . .9 J3
Church Way, Barn. EN4 . . . . .41 J4
   Edgware HA8 . . . . .54 A6
Churchwell Path, E9 . . . . .95 F5
Churchyard Row, SE11 . . . . .35 H1
Church Yd Wk, W2 . . . . .15 E1
Churston Av, E13 . . . . .115 H1
Churston Cl, SW2 off Tulse Hill .169 H1
Churston Dr, Mord. SM4 . . . . . .184 A5
Churston Gdns, N11 . . . . .58 C6
Churton Pl, SW1 . . . . .33 G2
Churton St, SW1 . . . . .33 G2
Chusan Pl, E14
   off Commercial Rd 113 J6
Chyngton Cl, Sid. DA15 . . . . . . .175 J3
Cibber Rd, SE23 . . . . .171 G2
Cicada Rd, SW18 . . . . .149 F5
Cicely Rd, SE15 . . . . .152 D1
Cinderella Path, NW11
   off North End Rd 90/91 E1
Cinderford Way, Brom. BR1 . . . .173 E4
Cinema Par, W5
   off Ashbourne Rd 105 J4
Cinnabar Wf, E1 . . . . .29 J2
Cinnamon Cl, SE15
   off Pentridge St 132 C7
   Croydon CR0 . . . . .186 E7
Cinnamon Row, SW11 . . . . .149 F3
Cinnamon St, E1 . . . . .133 E1
Cintra Pk, SE19 . . . . .170 C7
Circle, The, NW2 . . . . .89 E3
   NW7 . . . . .54 D5
   SE1 . . . . .29 F3
Circle Gdns, SW19 . . . . .184 D2
Circuits, The, Pnr. HA5 . . . . .66 C4
Circular Rd, N17 . . . . .76 C3
Circular Way, SE18 . . . . .136 C6
Circus Ms, W1 . . . . .15 J1
Circus Pl, EC2 . . . . .20 C2
Circus Rd, NW8 . . . . .6 E3
Circus St, SE10 . . . . .134 C7
Cirencester St, W2 . . . . .14 A1
Cirrus Cl, Wall. SM6 . . . . .200 E7
Cissbury Ring N, N12 . . . . .56 C5
Cissbury Ring S, N12 . . . . .56 C5
Cissbury Rd, N15 . . . . .76 A5
Citadel Pl, SE11 . . . . .34 C3
Citizen Ho, N7 off Harvist Est . . .93 G4
Citizen Rd, N7 . . . . .93 G4
C.I. Twr, N.Mal. KT3 . . . . .183 E3
Citron Ter, SE15
   off Nunhead La 152/153 E3
City Cross Business Pk, SE10
   off Salutation Rd 134/135 E4
City Forum, EC1 . . . . .11 J3
City Gdn Row, N1 . . . . .11 H2
City Gate Ho, Ilf. IG2 . . . . .80 E6
City Ho, Croy. CR0 . . . . .187 H7
★ City of Westminster Archives Cen,
   SW1 off St. Ann's St 25 J5
City Pt, EC2 . . . . .20 B1
City Rd, EC1 . . . . .11 G2
★ City Uni, EC1 . . . . .11 G4
Civic Way, Ilf. IG6 . . . . .81 F4
   Ruislip HA4 . . . . .84 D5
Clabon Ms, SW1 . . . . .23 J6
Clack St, SE16 . . . . .133 F2
Clacton Rd, E6 . . . . .116 A3
   E17 . . . . .77 H6
   N17 off Sperling Rd 76 C2
Claigmar Gdns, N3 . . . . .72 E1
Claire Ct, N12 . . . . .57 F3
   Bushey (Bushey Hth) WD23 . .52 A1
   Pinner HA5 off Westfield Pk . . .51 F7
Claire Gdns, Stan. HA7 . . . . .53 F5
Claire Pl, E14 . . . . .134 A3
Clairvale Rd, Houns. TW5 . . . . . .142 D1
Clairview Rd, SW16 . . . . .168 B5
Clairville Gdns, W7 . . . . .124 C1
Clairville Pt, SE23 . . . . .171 G3
Clamp Hill, Stan. HA7 . . . . .52 A4
Clancarty Rd, SW6 . . . . .148 D2
Clandon Cl, W3 off Avenue Rd . .126 B2
   Epsom KT17 . . . . .197 F6
Clandon Gdns, N3 . . . . .72 D3
Clandon Rd, Ilf. IG3 . . . . .99 H2
Clandon St, SE8 . . . . .154 A2
Clanfield Way, SE15
   off Blakes Rd 132 B7
Clanricarde Gdns, W2 . . . . .108 D7
CLAPHAM, SW4 . . . . .150 B3
★ Clapham Common, SW4 . . . .150 A4
Clapham Common N Side,
   SW4 . . . . .150 B4
Clapham Common S Side,
   SW4 . . . . .150 B6
Clapham Common W Side,
   SW4 . . . . .150 A4
Clapham Cres, SW4 . . . . .150 D4
Clapham Est, SW11 . . . . .149 H4
Clapham High St, SW4 . . . . .150 D4
Clapham Manor St, SW4 . . . . . . .150 C3
CLAPHAM PARK, SW4 . . . . .150 D6
Clapham Pk Est, SW4 . . . . .150 D6

Clapham Pk Rd, SW4 . . . . .150 D4
Clapham Rd, SW9 . . . . .150 E3
Clapham Rd Est, SW4 . . . . .150 D4
Clap La, Dag. RM10 . . . . .101 H3
Claps Gate La, E6 . . . . .116 E4
Clapton Common, E5 . . . . .76 C7
CLAPTON PARK, E5 . . . . .95 H4
Clapton Pk Est, E5
   off Blackwell Cl 95 H4
Clapton Pas, E5 . . . . .95 F5
Clapton Sq, E5 . . . . .95 F5
Clapton Ter, N16 off Oldhill St . . .94 D1
Clapton Way, E5 . . . . .94 D4
Clara Pl, SE18 . . . . .136 D4
Clare Cl, N2
   off Thomas More Way 73 F3
Clare Cor, SE9 . . . . .156 E7
Claredale St, E2 . . . . .13 J2
Clare Gdns, E7 . . . . .97 G4
   W11 off Westbourne Pk Rd . . .108 B6
   Barking IG11 . . . . .99 J6
Clare Ho, E3 . . . . .113 J1
Clare La, N1 . . . . .93 J7
Clare Lawn Av, SW14 . . . . .146 D5
Clare Mkt, WC2 . . . . .18 C4
Clare Ms, SW6
   off Waterford Rd 128/129 E7
Claremont Av, Har. HA3 . . . . .69 H5
   New Malden KT3 . . . . .183 G5
   Sunbury-on-Thames TW16 . . .178 B1
Claremont Cl, E16 . . . . .136 D1
   N1 . . . . .11 F2
   SW2 off Streatham Hill . .168/169 A1
   Orpington BR6 . . . . .206 D4
Claremont Ct, Surb. KT6
   off St. James Rd 181 G6
Claremont Gdns, Ilf. IG3 . . . . . . .99 H2
   Surbiton KT6 . . . . .181 H5
Claremont Gro, W4
   off Edensor Gdns 126/127 E7
   Woodford Green IG8 . . . . . . .63 J6
Claremont Pk, N3 . . . . .72 B1
Claremont Rd, E7 . . . . .97 H5
   E17 . . . . .77 H1
   N6 .74 C7
   NW2 . . . . .90 A3
   W9 . . . . .108 B2
   W13 . . . . .104 D5
   Bromley BR1 . . . . .192 B4
   Croydon CR0 . . . . .202 D1
   Esher (Clay.) KT10 . . . . .194 B7
   Harrow HA3 . . . . .68 B2
   Surbiton KT6 . . . . .181 H6
   Teddington TW11 . . . . .162 C5
   Twickenham TW1 . . . . .145 F6
Claremont Sq, N1 . . . . .10 E2
Claremont St, E16 . . . . .136 D1
   N18 . . . . .60 D6
   SE10 . . . . .134 B6
Claremont Way, NW2 . . . . .89 J1
Clarence Av, SW4 . . . . .150 D6
   Bromley BR1 . . . . .192 B4
   Ilford IG2 . . . . .80 D6
   New Malden KT3 . . . . .182 C2
Clarence Cl, Barn. EN4 . . . . .41 G5
Clarence Cres, SW4 . . . . .150 D6
   Sidcup DA14 . . . . .176 B3
Clarence Gdns, NW1 . . . . .9 E4
Clarence Gate, Wdf.Grn. IG8 . . . .64 D6
Clarence Gate Gdns, NW1
   off Glentworth St 109 J4
★ Clarence Ho, SW1 . . . . .25 G3
Clarence La, SW15 . . . . .147 E6
Clarence Ms, E5 . . . . .95 E5
   SE16 . . . . .133 G1
   SW12 . . . . .150 B7
Clarence Pl, E5 . . . . .95 E5
Clarence Rd, E5 . . . . .95 E4
   E12 . . . . .98 A5
   E16 . . . . .115 E4
   E17 . . . . .77 G2
   N15 . . . . .75 J5
   N22 . . . . .59 E7
   NW6 . . . . .90 C7
   SE8 . . . . .134 B6
   SE9 . . . . .174 B2
   SW19 . . . . .166 E6
   W4 . . . . .126 A5
   Bexleyheath DA6 . . . . .158 E4
   Bromley BR1 . . . . .192 A3
   Croydon CR0 . . . . .188 A7
   Enfield EN3 . . . . .45 E5
   Richmond TW9 . . . . .145 J1
   Sidcup DA14 . . . . .176 B3
   Sutton SM1 . . . . .198 E4
   Teddington TW11 . . . . .162 C6
   Wallington SM6 . . . . .200 B5
Clarence St, Kings.T. KT1 . . . . . .181 H2
   Richmond TW9 . . . . .145 H4
   Southall UB2 . . . . .122 D3
Clarence Ter, NW1 . . . . .8 A5
   Hounslow TW3 . . . . .143 H4
Clarence Wk, SW4 . . . . .150 E2
Clarence Way, NW1 . . . . .92 B7
Clarence Way Est, NW1 . . . . .92 B7
Clarendon Cl, E9 . . . . .95 F7
   W2 . . . . .15 G5

Clarendon Cres, Twick. TW2 . . . .162 A3
Clarendon Cross, W11
   off Portland Rd 108 B7
Clarendon Dr, SW15 . . . . .147 J4
Clarendon Gdns, NW4 . . . . .71 H3
   W9 .6 D6
   Ilford IG1 . . . . .98 C1
   Wembley HA9 . . . . .87 H4
Clarendon Gro, NW1 . . . . .9 H3
   Mitcham CR4 . . . . .185 J3
Clarendon Ms, W2 . . . . .15 G4
   Bexley DA5 . . . . .177 H1
   Borehamwood WD6
   off Clarendon Rd 38 A3
Clarendon Pl, W2 . . . . .15 G5
Clarendon Ri, SE13 . . . . .154 C3
Clarendon Rd, E11 . . . . .96 D1
   E17 . . . . .78 B6
   E18 . . . . .79 G3
   N8 .75 F3
   N15 . . . . .75 H4
   N18 . . . . .60 D6
   N22 . . . . .75 F2
   SW19 . . . . .167 H7
   W5 . . . . .105 H4
   W11 . . . . .108 B7
   Borehamwood WD6 . . . . .38 A3
   Croydon CR0 . . . . .201 H2
   Harrow HA1 . . . . .68 B6
   Hayes UB3 . . . . .121 J2
   Wallington SM6 . . . . .200 C6
Clarendon St, SW1 . . . . .32 E4
Clarendon Ter, W9 . . . . .6 D5
Clarendon Wk, W11 . . . . .108 B6
Clarendon Way, N21 . . . . .43 J6
   Chislehurst BR7 . . . . .193 J3
   Orpington BR5 . . . . .193 J3
Clarens St, SE6 . . . . .171 J2
Clare Pl, SW15
   off Minstead Gdns 147 F7
Clare Pt, NW2
   off Claremont Rd 90 A1
Clare Rd, E11 . . . . .78 D6
   NW10 . . . . .89 G7
   SE14 . . . . .153 J1
   Greenford UB6 . . . . .86 A6
   Hounslow TW4 . . . . .143 F3
   Staines (Stanw.) TW19 . . . . .140 B7
Clare St, E2 . . . . .113 E2
Claret Gdns, SE25 . . . . .188 B4
Clareville Gro, SW7 . . . . .30 D2
Clareville Rd, Orp. BR5 . . . . . . .207 F2
Clareville St, SW7 . . . . .30 D2
Clare Way, Bexh. DA7 . . . . .158 E1
Clarewood Wk, SW9 . . . . .151 H4
Clarges Ms, W1 . . . . .24 D1
Clarges St, W1 . . . . .24 E1
Claribel Rd, SW9 . . . . .151 H2
Claridge Rd, Dag. RM8 . . . . . . .100 D1
Clarina Rd, SE20
   off Evelina Rd 171 G7
Clarissa Rd, Rom. RM6 . . . . .82 D7
Clarissa St, E8 . . . . .112 C1
Clarke Ms, N9 off Plevna Rd . .60/61 E3
Clarke Path, N16 . . . . .94 D1
Clarkes Av, Wor.Pk. KT4 . . . . . .198 A1
Clarke's Ms, W1 . . . . .16 C1
Clark Lawrence Ct, SW11
   off Winstanley Rd 149 G3
Clarkson Rd, E16 . . . . .115 F6
Clarkson Row, NW1 . . . . .9 F2
Clarksons, The, Bark. IG11 . . . . .117 F2
Clarkson St, E2 . . . . .112 E3
Clarks Pl, EC2 . . . . .20 D3
Clarks Rd, Ilf. IG1 . . . . .99 G2
Clark St, E1 . . . . .113 E5
Clark Way, Houns. TW5 . . . . . . .122 N7
Classon Cl, West Dr. UB7 . . . . . .120 B2
Claude Rd, E10 . . . . .96 C2
   E13 . . . . .115 H1
   SE15 . . . . .152 E2
Claude St, E14 . . . . .134 A4
Claudia Jones Way, SW2 . . . . . .150 E6
Claudia Pl, SW19 . . . . .166 B1
Claughton Rd, E13 . . . . .115 J2
Clauson Av, Nthlt. UB5 . . . . .85 H5
Clavell St, SE10 . . . . .134 C6
Claverdale Rd, SW2 . . . . .151 F7
Clavering Av, SW13 . . . . .127 H6
Clavering Cl, Twick. TW1 . . . . . .162 D4
Clavering Rd, E12 . . . . .98 A1
Claverings Ind Est, N9 . . . . .61 G2
Claverley Gro, N3 . . . . .56 D7
Claverley Vil, N3
   off Claverley Gro 56/57 E7
Claverton St, SW1 . . . . .33 G4
Clave St, E1
   off Cinnamon St 132/133 E1
Claxton Gro, W6 . . . . .128 A5
Clay Av, Mitch. CR4 . . . . .186 B2
Claybank Gro, SE13
   off Algernon Rd 154 B3
Claybourne Ms, SE19
   off Church Rd 170 B7
Claybridge Rd, SE12 . . . . .173 J4
Claybrook Cl, N2 . . . . .73 G3
Claybrook Rd, W6 . . . . .128 A6

Claybury Bdy, Ilf. IG5 . . . . .80 B3
Claybury Hall, Wdf.Grn. IG8
   off Regents Dr 64 C7
Claybury Rd, Wdf.Grn. IG8 . . . . .64 B7
Claydon Dr, Croy. CR0 . . . . .201 E4
Claydown Ms, SE18
   off Woolwich New Rd 136 D5
Clayfarm Rd, SE9 . . . . .175 F2
CLAYGATE, Esher KT10 . . . . . . .194 B7
Claygate Cres, Croy. (New Adgtn)
   CR0 . . . . .204 C6
Claygate La, Esher KT10 . . . . . .194 D2
   Thames Ditton KT7 . . . . . . .194 D1
Claygate Lo Cl, Esher (Clay.)
   KT10 . . . . .194 B7
Claygate Rd, W13 . . . . .124 E3
CLAYHALL, Ilf. IG5 . . . . .80 C2
Clayhall Av, Ilf. IG5 . . . . .80 B5
Clayhill, Surb. KT5 . . . . .182 A5
Clayhill Cres, SE9 . . . . .174 A4
Claylands Pl, SW8 . . . . .34 D6
Claylands Rd, SW8 . . . . .34 D6
Clay La, Edg. HA8 . . . . .54 A1
   Staines (Stanw.) TW19 . . . . .140 C7
Claymill Ho, SE18 . . . . .137 F5
Claymore Cl, Mord. SM4 . . . . . .184 D7
Claymore Ct, E17 off Billet Rd . . .77 H1
Claypole Dr, Houns. TW5 . . . . . .143 E1
Claypole Rd, E15 . . . . .114 C2
Clayponds Av, Brent. TW8 . . . . .125 H4
Clayponds Gdns, W5 . . . . .125 G4
Clayponds La, Brent. TW8 . . . . .125 H5
Clay Rd, The, Loug. IG10 . . . . . . .48 B3
Clayside, Chig. IG7 . . . . .65 F6
Clays La, E15 . . . . .96 B5
Clay's La, Loug. IG10 . . . . .48 D1
Clays La Cl, E15 . . . . .96 B5
Clay St, W1 . . . . .16 A2
Clayton Av, Wem. HA0 . . . . .87 H7
Clayton Cl, E6
   off Brandreth Rd 116 C6
Clayton Cres, N1 . . . . .111 E1
   Brentford TW8 . . . . .125 G5
Clayton Dr, SE8
   off Sapphire Rd 133 H5
Clayton Fld, NW9 . . . . .55 E7
Clayton Ms, SE10 . . . . .154 D1
Clayton Rd, SE15 . . . . .152 D1
   Chessington KT9 . . . . .195 F4
   Hayes UB3 . . . . .121 H2
   Isleworth TW7 . . . . .144 B3
   Romford RM7 . . . . .101 J1
Clayton St, SE11 . . . . .34 F4
Clayton Ter, Hayes UB4
   off Jollys La 102 D5
Claywood Cl, Orp. BR6 . . . . . . .193 H7
Clayworth Cl, Sid. DA15 . . . . . .158 B6
Cleanthus Cl, SE18
   off Cleanthus Rd 156/157 E1
Cleanthus Rd, SE18 . . . . .157 E1
Clearbrook Way, E1
   off West Arbour St 113 G6
Clearwater Ter, W11
   off Lorne Gdns 128 A2
Clearwell Dr, W9 . . . . .6 A6
Cleave Av, Hayes UB3 . . . . .121 H4
   Orpington BR6 . . . . .207 H4
Cleaveland Rd, Surb. KT6 . . . . .181 G5
Cleaverholme Cl, SE25 . . . . . . .188 E6
Cleaver Sq, SE11 . . . . .35 F3
Cleaver St, SE11 . . . . .35 F3
Cleeve Hill, SE23 . . . . .171 E1
Cleeve Pk Gdns, Sid. DA14 . . . .176 B2
Cleeve Way, SW15
   off Danebury Av 147 F7
Clegg Ho, SE3 off Pinto Way . . .155 H4
Clegg St, E1 off Prusom St . .132/133 E1
   E13 . . . . .115 G2
Cleland Path, Loug. IG10 . . . . . . .49 E1
Clematis Gdns, Wdf.Grn. IG8 . . . .63 G5
Clematis St, W12 . . . . .107 F7
Clem Attlee Ct, SW6 . . . . .128 C6
Clem Attlee Est, SW6
   off Lillie Rd 128 C6
Clem Attlee Par, SW6
   off North End Rd 128 C6
Clemence Rd, Dag. RM10 . . . . . .119 J1
Clemence St, E14 . . . . .113 J5
Clement Av, SW4 . . . . .150 D4
Clement Cl, NW6 . . . . .89 J7
   W4 off Acton La 126 D4
Clement Gdns, Hayes UB3 . . . . .121 H4
Clementhorpe Rd, Dag. RM9 . . . .100 C6
Clementina Rd, E10 . . . . .95 J1
Clementine Cl, W13
   off Balfour Rd 124/125 E2
Clementine Wk, Wdf.Grn. IG8
   off Salway Cl 63 G7
Clement Rd, SW19 . . . . .166 B5
   Beckenham BR3 . . . . .189 G2
Clements Av, E16 . . . . .115 G7
Clements Ct, Houns. TW4 . . . . . .142 C4
   Ilford IG1
   off Clements La 98/99 E3
Clement's Inn, WC2 . . . . .18 D4
Clement's Inn Pas, WC2 . . . . . . .18 D4
Clements La, EC4 . . . . .20 C5

Clements La, Ilf. IG1 98 E3
Clements Pl, Brent. TW8 125 G5
Clements Rd, E6 98 C7
SE16 29 J6
Ilford IG1 98 E3
Clendon Way, SE18
off Polthorne Gro 137 G4
Clennam St, SE1 28 A3
Clensham Ct, Sutt. SM1
off Sutton Common Rd 198 D2
Clensham La, Sutt. SM1 198 D2
Clenston Ms, W1 15 J3
★ **Cleopatra's Needle**, WC2 26 C1
Clephane Rd, N1 93 J6
Clere St, EC2 12 C5
CLERKENWELL, EC1 11 G6
Clerkenwell Cl, EC1 11 F5
Clerkenwell Grn, EC1 11 F6
Clerkenwell Rd, EC1 10 E6
Clerks Piece, Loug. IG10 48 C3
Clermont Rd, E9 113 F1
Clevedon Cl, N16
off Smalley Cl 94 C3
Clevedon Gdns, Hayes UB3 121 G3
Hounslow TW5 142 B1
Clevedon Rd, SE20 189 G1
Kingston upon Thames KT1 182 A2
Twickenham TW1 145 G6
Cleveland Av, SW20 184 C2
W4 127 F4
Hampton TW12 161 F7
Cleveland Cres, Borwd. WD6 38 C5
Cleveland Gdns, N4 75 J5
NW2 90 A2
SW13 147 F2
W2 14 C4
Worcester Park KT4 197 E2
Cleveland Gro, E1
off Cleveland Way 113 F4
Cleveland Ms, W1 17 F1
Cleveland Pk, Stai. TW19 140 B6
Cleveland Pk Av, E17 78 A4
Cleveland Pk Cres, E17 78 A4
Cleveland Pl, SW1 25 G1
Cleveland Ri, Mord. SM4 184 A7
Cleveland Rd, E18 79 G3
N1 94 A7
N9 45 E7
SW13 147 F2
W4 *off Antrobus Rd* 126 C3
W13 104 E5
Ilford IG1 99 E3
Isleworth TW7 144 D4
New Malden KT3 182 E4
Welling DA16 157 J2
Worcester Park KT4 197 E2
Cleveland Row, SW1 25 F2
Cleveland Sq, W2 14 C4
Cleveland St, W1 9 F6
Cleveland Ter, W2 14 D3
Cleveland Way, E1 113 F4
Cleveley Cl, SE7 136 A4
Cleveley Cres, W5 105 H2
Cleveleys Rd, E5 95 E3
Cleverly Est, W12 127 G1
Cleve Rd, NW6 90 D7
Sidcup DA14 176 D3
Cleves Cl, Loug. IG10 48 B6
Cleves Rd, E6 116 A1
Richmond TW10 163 F3
Cleves Wk, Ilf. IG6 65 F7
Cleves Way, Hmptn. TW12 161 F7
Ruislip HA4 84 D1
Clewer Cres, Har. HA3 68 A1
Clewer Ho, SE2
off Wolvercote Rd 138 D2
Clichy Est, E1 113 F5
Clifden Rd, E5 95 F5
Brentford TW8 125 G6
Twickenham TW1 162 C1
Cliffe Rd, S.Croy. CR2 202 A5
Cliffe Wk, Sutt. SM1
off Turnpike La 199 F5
Clifford Av, SW14 146 B3
Chislehurst BR7 174 C6
Ilford IG5 80 E1
Wallington SM6 200 C4
Clifford Cl, Nthlt. UB5 103 E1
Clifford Dr, SW9 151 H4
Clifford Gdns, NW10 107 J2
Hayes UB3 121 G4
Clifford Rd, E16 115 F4
E17 78 C2
N9 45 F6
SE25 188 D4
Barnet EN5 41 E3
Hounslow TW4 142 D3
Richmond TW10 163 G2
Wembley HA0 105 G1
Clifford's Inn Pas, EC4 19 E4
Clifford St, W1 17 F6
Clifford Way, NW10 89 F4
Cliff Rd, NW1 92 D6
Cliff Ter, SE8 154 A2
Cliffview Rd, SE13 154 A3
Cliff Vil, NW1 92 D6
Cliff Wk, E16 115 F5
Clifton Av, E17 77 G3
N3 72 C1
W12 127 F1
Feltham TW13 160 C3
Stanmore HA7 69 E2
Wembley HA9 87 J6
Clifton Cl, Orp. BR6 207 F5
Clifton Ct, N4 *off Biggerstaff St* 93 G2
NW8 6 E5
Woodford Green IG8
off Snakes La W 63 G6
Clifton Cres, SE15 133 E7
Clifton Est, SE15
off Consort Rd 152/153 E1
Clifton Gdns, N15 76 C6
NW11 72 C6
W4 *off Dolman Rd* 126 D4
W9 6 C6
Enfield EN2 42 E4
Clifton Gro, E8 94 D6
Clifton Hill, NW8 109 E2
Clifton Pk Av, SW20 183 J2
Clifton Pl, SE16
off Canon Beck Rd 133 F2
W2 15 F5
Clifton Ri, SE14 133 H7
Clifton Rd, E7 98 A6
E16 115 E5
N1 93 J6
N3 73 F1
N8 74 D6
N22 74 C1
NW10 107 G2
SE25 188 B4
SW19 166 A6
W9 6 D5
Greenford UB6 103 J4
Harrow HA3 69 J5
Hounslow (Hthrw Air.) TW6
off Inner Ring E 140/141 E3
Ilford IG2 81 G6
Isleworth TW7 144 A2
Kingston upon Thames KT2 163 J7
Loughton IG10 48 B4
Sidcup DA14 175 H4
Southall UB2 123 E4
Teddington TW11 162 B4
Wallington SM6 200 B5
Welling DA16 158 C3
Clifton St, EC2 20 D1
Clifton Ter, N4 93 G2
Clifton Vil, W9 14 B1
Clifton Wk, E6 116 B6
W6 *off Galena Rd* 127 H4
Clifton Way, SE15 133 E7
Borehamwood WD6 38 A1
Wembley HA0 105 H1
Clinch Ct, E16 115 G5
Cline Rd, N11 58 C6
Clinger Ct, N1 *off Pitfield St* 112 B1
★ **Clink Prison Mus**, SE1 28 B1
Clink St, SE1 28 A1
Clinton Av, E.Mol. KT8 179 J4
Welling DA16 157 J4
Clinton Cres, Ilf. IG6 65 H6
Clinton Rd, E3 113 H3
E7 97 G4
N15 76 A4
Clinton Ter, Sutt. SM1
off Manor La 199 F4
Clipper Cl, SE16 *off Kinburn St* 133 G2
Clipper Way, SE13 154 C4
Clippesby Cl, Chess. KT9 195 J7
Clipstone Ms, W1 9 F6
Clipstone Rd, Houns. TW3 143 G3
Clipstone St, W1 17 E1
Clissold Cl, N2 73 J3
Clissold Ct, N4 93 J2
Clissold Cres, N16 94 A3
Clissold Rd, N16 94 A3
Clitheroe Av, Har. HA2 85 G1
Clitheroe Gdns, Wat. WD19 50 D3
Clitheroe Rd, SW9 151 E2
Clitherow Av, W7 124 D3
Clitherow Pas, Brent. TW8 125 F5
Clitherow Rd, Brent. TW8 125 F5
Clitterhouse Cres, NW2 89 J1
Clitterhouse Rd, NW2 89 J1
Clive Av, N18 *off Claremont St* 60 D6
Clive Ct, W9 6 D5
Cliveden Cl, N12
off Woodside Av 57 F4
Cliveden Pl, SW1 32 B1
Cliveden Rd, SW19 184 C1
Clivedon Ct, W13 104 E5
Clivedon Rd, E4 62 E5
Clive Pas, SE21 *off Clive Rd* 170 A3
Clive Rd, SE21 170 A3
SW19 167 H6
Belvedere DA17 139 G4
Enfield EN1 44 D4
Feltham TW14 142 A6
Twickenham TW1 162 C4
Clivesdale Dr, Hayes UB3 122 B1
Clive Way, Enf. EN1 44 D4
Cloak La, EC4 20 A5
Clockhouse Av, Bark. IG11 117 F1
Clockhouse Cl, SW19 165 J3
Clockhouse Pl, SW15 148 B5
Clock Ho Rd, Beck. BR3 189 H3
★ **Clockmakers Company Collection, The, Guildhall Lib**, EC2 20 A3
Clock Twr Ms, N1
off Arlington Av 111 J1
SE28 118 B7
Clock Twr Pl, N7 92 E6
Clock Twr Rd, Islw. TW7 144 C3
Cloister Cl, Tedd. TW11 162 E5
Cloister Gdns, SE25 188 E6
Edgware HA8 54 C5
Cloister Rd, NW2 90 C3
W3 106 C5
Cloisters Av, Brom. BR2 192 C5
Cloisters Business Cen, SW8
off Battersea Pk Rd 130 B7
Cloisters Mall, Kings.T. KT1
off Union St 181 G2
Clonard Way, Pnr. HA5 51 G6
Clonbrock Rd, N16 94 B4
Cloncurry St, SW6 148 A2
Clonmel Cl, Har. HA2 86 A1
Clonmell Rd, N17 76 A3
Clonmel Rd, SW6 128 C7
Teddington TW11 162 A4
Clonmore St, SW18 166 C1
Cloonmore Av, Orp. BR6 207 J4
Clorane Gdns, NW3 90 D3
Close, The, E4 *off Beech Hall Rd* 62 C7
N14 58 D2
N20 56 C2
SE3 *off Heath La* 154 D2
Barnet EN4 41 J6
Beckenham BR3 189 H4
Bexley DA5 159 G6
Harrow HA2 67 J2
Isleworth TW7 144 A2
Mitcham CR4 185 J4
New Malden KT3 182 C2
Orpington BR5 193 H6
Pinner (Eastcote) HA5 66 C7
Pinner (Rayners La) HA5 67 F7
Richmond TW9 146 B3
Romford RM6 82 E6
Sidcup DA14 176 B5
Sutton SM3 184 C7
Wembley (Barnhill Rd) HA9 88 C3
Wembley (Lyon Pk Av) HA0 87 H6
Cloth Ct, EC1 19 H2
Cloth Fair, EC1 19 H2
Clothier St, E1 21 E3
Cloth St, EC1 19 J1
Clothworkers Rd, SE18 137 G7
Cloudesdale Rd, SW17 168 B2
Cloudesley Pl, N1 111 G1
Cloudesley Rd, N1 111 G1
Bexleyheath DA7 159 F1
Cloudesley Sq, N1 111 G1
Cloudesley St, N1 111 G1
Clouston Cl, Wall. SM6 200 E5
Clova Rd, E7 97 F6
Clove Cres, E14 114 D7
Clove Hitch Quay, SW11 149 F3
Clovelly Av, NW9 71 F4
Clovelly Cl, Pnr. HA5 66 B3
Clovelly Gdns, SE19 188 C1
Enfield EN1 44 B7
Romford RM7 83 H1
Clovelly Rd, N8 74 D4
W4 126 C2
W5 125 F2
Bexleyheath DA7 138 E6
Hounslow TW3 143 G2
Clovelly Way, E1 *off Jamaica St* 113 F6
Harrow HA2 85 F2
Orpington BR6 193 J6
Clover Cl, E11 *off Norman Rd* 96 D2
Cloverdale Gdns, Sid. DA15 157 J6
Cloverleys, Loug. IG10 48 A5
Clover Ms, SW3 31 J5
Clover Way, Wall. SM6 200 A1
Clove St, E13 *off Barking Rd* 115 G4
Clowders Rd, SE6 171 J3
Clowser Cl, Sutt. SM1
off Turnpike La 199 F5
Cloysters Grn, E1 29 H1
Cloyster Wd, Edg. HA8 53 G7
Club Gdns Rd, Brom. BR2 191 G7
Club Row, E1 13 F5
E2 13 F5
Clunbury Av, Sthl. UB2 123 F5
Clunbury St, N1 12 C2
Cluny Est, SE1 28 D5
Cluny Ms, SW5 128 D4
Cluny Pl, SE1 28 D5
Cluse Ct, N1 11 J1
Clutton St, E14 114 B5
Clydach Rd, Enf. EN1 44 C4
Clyde Circ, N15 76 B4
Clyde Pl, E10 78 B7
Clyde Rd, N15 76 B4
N22 74 D1
Croydon CR0 202 C1
Sutton SM1 198 D5
Clyde Rd, Wall. SM6 200 C5
Clydesdale, Enf. EN3 45 G4
Clydesdale Av, Stan. HA7 69 G3
Clydesdale Cl, Borwd. WD6 38 D5
Isleworth TW7 144 C3
Clydesdale Gdns, Rich. TW10 146 B4
Clydesdale Ho, Erith DA18
off Kale Rd 138/139 E2
Clydesdale Rd, W11 108 C6
Clyde St, SE8 133 J6
Clyde Ter, SE23 171 F2
Clyde Vale, SE23 171 F2
Clymping Dene, Felt. TW14 142 B7
Clyston St, SW8 150 C2
Coach & Horses Yd, W1 17 E5
Coach Ho La, N5
off Highbury Hill 93 H4
SW19 166 A4
Coach Ho Ms, SE1 28 D5
SE14 *off Waller Rd* 153 G2
Coachhouse Ms, SE20 170 E7
Coach Ho Ms, SE23 153 G6
Coach Ho Yd, SW18
off Ebner St 148/149 E4
Coachmaker Ms, SW4
off Fenwick Pl 150/151 E3
Coach Yd Ms, N19
off Trinder Rd 92/93 E1
Coaldale Wk, SE21
off Lairdale Cl 151 J7
Coalecroft Rd, SW15 147 J4
Coal Wf Rd, W12 *off Sterne St* 128 A2
Coates Av, SW18 149 H6
Coates Hill Rd, Brom. BR1 192 D2
Coate St, E2 13 J2
Coates Wk, Brent. TW8 125 H5
Cobb Cl, Borwd. WD6 38 C5
Cobbett Rd, SE9 156 B3
Twickenham TW2 161 G1
Cobbetts Av, Ilf. IG4 80 A5
Cobbett St, SW8 131 F7
Cobble La, N1 *off Edwards Ms* 93 H7
Cobble Ms, N5 93 J3
Cobblers Wk, E.Mol. KT8 180 D1
Hampton TW12 161 J7
Kingston upon Thames KT2 180 D1
Teddington TW11 180 D1
Cobblestone Pl, Croy. CR0
off Oakfield Rd 201 J1
Cobbold Est, NW10 89 F6
Cobbold Ms, W12
off Cobbold Rd 127 F2
Cobbold Rd, E11 97 F3
NW10 89 F6
W12 127 E2
Cobb's Ct, EC4 *off Ludgate Hill* 111 H6
Cobb's Rd, Houns. TW4 143 F4
Cobb St, E1 21 F2
Cobden Rd, E11 97 E3
SE25 188 D5
Orpington BR6 207 G4
Cobham Av, N.Mal. KT3 183 G5
Cobham Cl, SW11 149 H6
Bromley BR2 192 B7
Edgware HA8 70 B2
Enfield EN1 44 D3
Sidcup DA15 *off Park Mead* 158 B6
Wallington SM6 200 E6
Cobham Ho, Bark. IG11
off St. Margarets 117 F1
Cobham Ms, NW1 *off Agar Gro* 92 D7
Cobham Pl, Bexh. DA6 158 D5
Cobham Rd, E17 78 C1
N22 75 H3
Hounslow TW5 122 C7
Ilford IG3 99 H2
Kingston upon Thames KT1 182 A1
Cobland Rd, SE12 173 J4
Coborn Rd, E3 113 J3
Coborn St, E3 113 J3
Cobourg Rd, SE5 37 F5
Cobourg St, NW1 9 G4
Coburg Cl, SW1 33 G1
Coburg Cres, SW2 169 F1
Coburg Gdns, Ilf. IG5 80 A2
Coburg Rd, N22 75 F3
Cochrane Ms, NW8 7 F2
Cochrane Rd, SW19 166 C7
Cochrane St, NW8 7 F2
Cockayne Way, SE8 133 H5
Cockerell Rd, E17 77 H7
COCKFOSTERS, Barn. EN4 41 H4
Cockfosters Par, Barn. EN4
off Cockfosters Rd 42 A4
Cockfosters Rd, Barn. EN4 41 J2
Cock Hill, E1 21 E2
Cock La, EC1 19 G2
Cockpit Steps, SW1 25 J4
Cockpit Yd, WC1 18 D1
Cocks Cres, N.Mal. KT3 183 F4
Cocksett Av, Orp. BR6 207 H6
Cockspur Ct, SW1 25 J1
Cockspur St, SW1 25 J1
Cocksure La, Sid. DA14 177 G3
Coda Cen, The, SW6 148 B1
Code St, E1 13 G6
Codicote Ter, N4 *off Green Las* 93 J2

Codling Cl, E1 . . . . .29 J1
Codling Way, Wem. HA0 . . . . . . .87 G4
Codrington Hill, SE23 . . . . .153 H7
Codrington Ms, W11
  off Blenheim Cres 108 B6
Cody Cl, Har. HA3 . . . . .69 G3
  Wallington SM6
  off Alcock Cl 200 D7
Cody Rd, E16 . . . . .114 D4
Cody Rd Business Cen, E16 . . .114 D4
Coe Av, SE25 . . . . .188 D6
Coe's All, Barn. EN5 off Wood St . .40 B4
Cogan Av, E17 . . . . .77 H1
Coin St, SE1 . . . . .27 L1
Coity Rd, NW5 . . . . .92 A6
Cokers La, SE21 off Perifield . . .170 A1
Coke St, E1 . . . . .21 H3
Colas Ms, NW6
  off Birchington Rd 108 D1
Colbeck Ms, SW7 . . . . .30 B2
Colbeck Rd, Har. HA1 . . . . .67 J7
Colberg Pl, N16 . . . . .76 B7
Colborne Way, Wor.Pk. KT4 . . . .197 J3
Colbrook Av, Hayes UB3 . . . . . .121 G3
Colbrook Cl, Hayes UB3 . . . . . .121 G3
Colburn Av, Pnr. HA5 . . . . .51 E6
Colburn Way, Sutt. SM1 . . . . . .199 G3
Colby Ms, SE19 off Gipsy Hill . .170 B5
Colby Rd, SE19 . . . . .170 B5
Colchester Av, E12 . . . . .98 C3
Colchester Dr, Pnr. HA5 . . . . . . .66 D5
Colchester Rd, E10 . . . . .78 C7
  E17 . . . . .78 A6
  Edgware HA8 . . . . .54 C7
  Northwood HA6 . . . . .66 A2
Colchester St, E1 . . . . .21 G3
Coldbath Sq, EC1 . . . . .11 E5
Coldbath St, SE13 . . . . .154 B1
COLDBLOW, Bex. DA5 . . . . . . .177 J2
Cold Blow La, SE14 . . . . .133 G7
Cold Blows, Mitch. CR4 . . . . . .186 A3
Coldershaw Rd, W13 . . . . .124 D1
Coldfall Av, N10 . . . . .73 J2
Cold Harbour, E14 . . . . .134 C2
Coldharbour Crest, SE9
  off Great Harry Dr 174 D3
Coldharbour La, SE5 . . . . .151 G4
  SW9 . . . . .151 G4
  Hayes UB3 . . . . .102 A7
Coldharbour Pl, SE5
  off Denmark Hill 151 J2
Coldharbour Rd, Croy. CR0 . . . .201 G5
Coldharbour Way, Croy. CR0 . . .201 G5
Coldstream Gdns, SW18 . . . . . .148 C6
Colebeck Ms, N1 . . . . .93 H6
Colebert Av, E1 . . . . .113 F4
Colebrook Cl, NW7 . . . . .56 A7
  SW15 off West Hill 148 A7
Colebrooke Av, W13 . . . . .104 E6
Colebrooke Dr, E11 . . . . .79 H7
Colebrooke Pl, N1
  off St. Peters St 111 H1
Colebrooke Ri, Brom. BR2 . . . . .191 E2
Colebrooke Row, N1 . . . . .11 G2
Colebrook Gdns, Loug. IG10 . . . .49 E2
Colebrook Ho, E14 . . . . .114 B6
  off Brabazon St 114 B6
Colebrook La, Loug. IG10 . . . . . .49 E2
Colebrook Path, Loug. IG10 . . . .49 E2
Colebrook Rd, SW16 . . . . .187 E1
Colebrook Way, N11 . . . . .58 B5
Coleby Path, SE5 off Harris St . .132 A7
Cole Cl, SE28 . . . . .138 B1
Coledale Dr, Stan. HA7 . . . . .69 F1
Coleford Rd, SW18 . . . . .149 F5
Cole Gdns, Houns. TW5 . . . . . .122 A7
Colegrave Rd, E15 . . . . .96 D5
Colegrove Rd, SE15 . . . . .37 G6
Coleherne Ct, SW5 . . . . .30 B4
Coleherne Ms, SW10 . . . . .30 A4
Coleherne Rd, SW10 . . . . .30 A4
Colehill Gdns, SW6
  off Fulham Palace Rd 148 B2
Colehill La, SW6 . . . . .148 B1
Coleman Cl, SE25 . . . . .188 D2
Coleman Flds, N1 . . . . .111 J1
Coleman Rd, SE5 . . . . .36 D7
  Belvedere DA17 . . . . .139 G4
  Dagenham RM9 . . . . .101 E6
Colemans Heath, SE9 . . . . .174 E3
Coleman St, EC2 . . . . .20 B3
Colenso Dr, NW7 . . . . .55 G7
Colenso Rd, E5 . . . . .95 F4
  Ilford IG2 . . . . .99 H1
Cole Pk Gdns, Twick. TW1 . . . . .144 D6
Cole Pk Rd, Twick. TW1 . . . . . .144 D6
Cole Pk Vw, Twick. TW1
  off Hill Vw Rd 144 D6
Colepits Wd Rd, SE9 . . . . .157 F5
Coleraine Rd, N8 . . . . .75 G3
  SE3 . . . . .135 F6
Coleridge Av, E12 . . . . .98 B6
  Sutton SM1 . . . . .199 H4
Coleridge Cl, SW8 . . . . .150 B2
Coleridge Ct, W6
  off Fairhazel Gdns 91 F7
  SW10 . . . . .30 B7

Coleridge La, N8
  off Coleridge Rd 74/75 E6
Coleridge Rd, E17 . . . . .77 J4
  N4 .93 G2
  N8 .74 D6
  N12 . . . . .57 F5
  Croydon CR0 . . . . .189 F7
Coleridge Sq, SW10 . . . . .30 C7
  W13 off Berners Dr 104 D6
Coleridge Wk, NW11 . . . . .72 D4
Coleridge Way, Hayes UB4 . . . .102 A6
  West Drayton UB7 . . . . .120 C1
Cole Rd, Twick. TW1 . . . . .144 D6
Colesburg Rd, Beck. BR3 . . . . .189 J3
Coles Cres, Har. HA2 . . . . .85 H2
Coles Grn, Bushey (Bushey Hth)
  WD23 . . . . .51 J1
  Loughton IG10 . . . . .48 D1
Coles Grn Ct, NW2 . . . . .89 G2
Coles Grn Rd, NW2 . . . . .89 G1
Coleshill Rd, Tedd. TW11 . . . . . .162 B6
Colestown St, SW11 . . . . .149 H2
Cole St, SE1 . . . . .28 A4
Colet Cl, N13 . . . . .59 H6
Colet Gdns, W14 . . . . .128 A4
Coley St, WC1 . . . . .10 D6
Colfe Rd, SE23 . . . . .171 H1
Colham Av, West Dr. UB7 . . . . . .120 B1
Colham Mill Rd, West Dr. UB7 . .120 A2
Colina Ms, N15
  off Harringay Rd 75 H5
Colina Rd, N15 . . . . .75 H5
Colin Cl, NW9 . . . . .71 E4
  Croydon CR0 . . . . .203 J3
  West Wickham BR4 . . . . .205 F3
Colin Cres, NW9 . . . . .71 F4
Colindale Av, NW9 . . . . .70 D3
Colindale Business Pk, NW9 . . . .70 C3
Colindeep Gdns, NW4 . . . . .71 G5
Colindeep La, NW4 . . . . .70 E3
  NW9 . . . . .70 E3
Colin Dr, NW9 . . . . .71 F5
Colinette Rd, SW15 . . . . .147 J4
Colin Gdns, NW9 . . . . .71 F5
Colin Par, NW9
  off Edgware Rd 70/71 E4
Colin Pk Rd, NW9 . . . . .70 E4
Colin Rd, NW10 . . . . .89 G6
Colinton Rd, Ilf. IG3 . . . . .100 B2
Coliston Pas, SW18
  off Coliston Rd 148 D7
Coliston Rd, SW18 . . . . .148 D7
Collamore Av, SW18 . . . . .167 H1
Collapit Cl, Har. HA1 . . . . .67 H5
Collard Av, Loug. IG10 . . . . .49 F2
Collard Grn, Loug. IG10
  off Collard Av 49 F2
Collard Pl, NW1
  off Harmood St 92 B7
College App, SE10 . . . . .134 C6
College Av, Har. HA3 . . . . .68 B1
College Cl, E9 off Median Rd 95 F5
  N18 . . . . .60 C5
  Harrow HA3 . . . . .52 B7
  Twickenham TW2
  off Meadway 162 A1
College Cres, NW3 . . . . .91 G6
College Cross, N1 . . . . .93 G7
College Dr, Ruis. HA4 . . . . .66 A7
  Thames Ditton KT7 . . . . .180 B7
College Gdns, E4 . . . . .46 B7
  N18 . . . . .60 C5
  SE21 . . . . .170 B1
  SW17 . . . . .167 H2
  Enfield EN2 . . . . .44 A1
  Ilford IG4 . . . . .80 B5
  New Malden KT3 . . . . .183 F5
College Grn, SE19 . . . . .170 B7
College Gro, NW1
  off St. Pancras Way 110 D1
College Hill, EC4 . . . . .20 A5
College Hill Rd, Har. HA3 . . . . . . .68 C1
College La, NW5 . . . . .92 B4
College Ms, SW1 . . . . .26 A5
  SW18 off St. Ann's Hill . .148/149 E5
★ College of Arms, EC4 . . . . . . .19 H5
College Pk Cl, SE13 . . . . .154 D4
College Pk Rd, N17
  off College Rd 60 C6
College Pl, E17 . . . . .78 E4
  NW1 . . . . .110 C1
  SW10 . . . . .30 C7
College Pt, E15 . . . . .97 F6
College Rd, E17 . . . . .78 C5
  N17 . . . . .60 C6
  N21 . . . . .59 G2
  NW10 . . . . .107 J2
  SE19 . . . . .170 C5
  SE21 . . . . .152 B7
  SW19 . . . . .167 G6
  W13 . . . . .104 E6
  Bromley BR1 . . . . .173 G7
  Croydon CR0 . . . . .202 A2
  Enfield EN2 . . . . .44 A2
  Harrow (Har.Hill) HA1 . . . . . . .68 B6
  Harrow (Har.Wld) HA3 . . . . . . .68 B1

College Rd, Islw. TW7 . . . . .144 C1
  Wembley HA9 . . . . .87 G1
College Row, E9 . . . . .95 G5
College Slip, Brom. BR1 . . . . . .191 G1
College St, EC4 . . . . .20 A5
College Ter, E3 . . . . .113 J3
  N3 off Hendon La 72 C2
College Vw, SE9 . . . . .174 A1
College Wk, Kings.T. KT1
  off Grange Rd 181 H2
College Way, Hayes UB3 . . . . . .102 A1
College Yd, NW5 off College La . .92 B4
Collent St, E9 . . . . .95 F6
Colless Rd, N15 . . . . .76 C5
Collett Rd, SE16 . . . . .29 J6
Collett Way, Sthl. UB2 . . . . .123 H1
Collier Cl, E6 off Trader Rd . .116/117 E6
  Epsom KT19 . . . . .196 A6
Collier Dr, Edg. HA8 . . . . .70 A2
COLLIER ROW, Rom. RM5 . . . . . .83 G1
Collier Row La, Rom. RM5 . . . . . .83 F1
Colliers Shaw, Kes. BR2 . . . . . .206 A4
Collier St, N1 . . . . .10 C2
Colliers Water La, Th.Hth. CR7 . .187 G5
COLLIER'S WOOD, SW19 . . . . .167 G7
Collindale Av, Erith DA8 . . . . . . .139 H6
  Sidcup DA15 . . . . .176 A1
Collingbourne Rd, W12 . . . . . . .127 H1
Collingham Gdns, SW5 . . . . .30 B2
Collingham Pl, SW5 . . . . .30 A2
Collingham Rd, SW5 . . . . .30 B1
Collings Cl, N22
  off Whittington Rd 59 F6
Collington St, SE10
  off Hoskins St 134 D5
Collingtree Rd, SE26 . . . . .171 F4
Collingwood Av, N10 . . . . .74 A3
  Surbiton KT5 . . . . .196 C1
Collingwood Cl, SE20 . . . . .189 E1
  Twickenham TW2 . . . . .143 G6
Collingwood Rd, E17 . . . . .78 A6
  N15 . . . . .76 B4
  Mitcham CR4 . . . . .185 H2
  Sutton SM1 . . . . .198 D3
Collingwood St, E1 . . . . .113 E4
Collins Av, Stan. HA7 . . . . .69 H2
Collins Dr, Ruis. HA4 . . . . .84 C2
Collinson St, SE1 . . . . .27 J4
Collinson Wk, SE1 . . . . .27 J4
Collins Rd, N5 . . . . .93 J4
Collins Sq, SE3
  off Tranquil Vale 155 F2
Collins St, SE3 . . . . .155 E2
Collin's Yd, N1
  off Islington Grn 111 H1
Collinwood Av, Enf. EN3 . . . . . . .45 F3
Collinwood Gdns, Ilf. IG5 . . . . . .80 C5
Collis All, Twick. TW2
  off The Green 162 B1
Collison Pl, N16 . . . . .94 B2
Colls Rd, SE15 . . . . .153 F1
Collyer Av, Croy. CR0 . . . . .200 E4
Collyer Pl, SE15
  off Peckham High St 152 D1
Collyer Rd, Croy. CR0 . . . . .201 E4
Colman Rd, E16 . . . . .115 J5
Colmar Cl, E1 off Alderney Rd . .113 G4
Colmer Pl, Har. HA3 . . . . .52 A7
Colmer Rd, SW16 . . . . .187 E1
Colmore Ms, SE15 . . . . .153 E1
Colmore Rd, Enf. EN3 . . . . .45 F4
Colnbrook St, SE1 . . . . .27 G6
Colne Ct, Epsom KT19 . . . . . . .196 C4
Colne Ho, Bark. IG11 . . . . .99 E6
Colne Rd, E5 . . . . .95 H4
  N21 . . . . .44 A7
  Twickenham TW1, TW2 . . . . .162 B1
Colne St, E13 off Grange Rd 115 G3
Colney Hatch La, N10 . . . . .58 A7
  N11 . . . . .57 J6
Cologne Rd, SW11 . . . . .149 G4
Colombo Rd, Ilf. IG1 . . . . .99 F1
Colombo St, SE1 . . . . .27 G2
Colomb St, SE10 . . . . .135 E5
Colonels Wk, Enf. EN2 . . . . .43 H3
Colonial Av, Twick. TW2 . . . . . . .143 J5
Colonial Dr, W4 . . . . .126 C4
Colonial Rd, Felt. TW14 . . . . . . .141 H7
Colonnade, WC1 . . . . .10 A6
Colonnades, The, W2 . . . . .14 B3
Colonnade Wk, SW1 . . . . .32 D2
Colosseum Ter, NW1
  off Albany St 110 B4
Colson Gdns, Loug. IG10
  off Colson Rd 48/49 E4
Colson Path, Loug. IG10 . . . . . . .48 D4
Colson Rd, Croy. CR0 . . . . .202 B2
  Loughton IG10 . . . . .48 D4
Colson Way, SW16 . . . . .168 C4
Colsterworth Rd, N15 . . . . .76 C4
Colston Av, Cars. SM5 . . . . .199 H4
Colston Cl, Cars. SM5
  off West St 199 J4
Colston Rd, E7 . . . . .98 A6
  SW14 . . . . .146 C4
Colthurst Cres, N4 . . . . .93 J2
Colthurst Dr, N9 . . . . .60 E3

Coltness Cres, SE2 . . . . .138 B5
Colton Gdns, N17 . . . . .75 J3
Colton Rd, Har. HA1 . . . . .68 B5
Columbia Av, Edg. HA8 . . . . .70 B1
  Ruislip HA4 . . . . .84 B1
  Worcester Park KT4 . . . . .183 F7
Columbia Pt, SE16
  off Moodkee St 133 F3
Columbia Rd, E2 . . . . .13 F3
  E13 . . . . .115 F4
Columbia Sq, SW14
  off Upper Richmond Rd W . .146 C4
Columbine Av, E6 . . . . .116 B5
  South Croydon CR2 . . . . .201 H7
Columbine Way, SE13 . . . . .154 C2
Columbus Ct, SE16
  off Rotherhithe St 133 F1
Columbus Ctyd, E14
  off West India Av 134 A1
Columbus Gdns, Nthwd. HA6 . . . .66 A1
Colva Wk, N19 off Chester Rd 92 B2
Colvestone Cres, E8 . . . . .94 C5
Colview Ct, SE9
  off Mottingham La 174 A1
Colville Est, N1 . . . . .112 B1
Colville Gdns, W11 . . . . .108 C6
Colville Hos, W11 . . . . .108 C6
Colville Ms, W11
  off Lonsdale Rd 108 C6
Colville Pl, W1 . . . . .17 G2
Colville Rd, E11 . . . . .96 C5
  E17 . . . . .77 H2
  N9 .60 E1
  W3 . . . . .126 B3
  W11 . . . . .108 C6
Colville Sq, W11 . . . . .108 C6
Colville Ter, W11 . . . . .108 C6
Colvin Cl, SE26 . . . . .171 F5
Colvin Gdns, E4 . . . . .62 C3
  E11 . . . . .79 H4
  Ilford IG6 . . . . .81 F1
Colvin Rd, E6 . . . . .98 B7
  Thornton Heath CR7 . . . . .187 G5
Colwall Gdns, Wdf.Grn. IG8 . . . . .63 G5
Colwell Rd, SE22 . . . . .152 C5
Colwick Cl, N6 . . . . .74 D7
Colwith Rd, W6 . . . . .127 J6
Colwood Gdns, SW19 . . . . .167 G7
Colworth Gro, SE17 . . . . .36 A2
Colworth Rd, E11 . . . . .78 E6
  Croydon CR0 . . . . .202 D1
Colwyn Av, Grnf. UB6 . . . . .104 C2
Colwyn Cl, SW16 . . . . .168 C5
Colwyn Cres, Houns. TW3 . . . . .143 J1
Colwyn Grn, NW9
  off Snowdon Dr 70/71 E6
Colwyn Rd, NW2 . . . . .89 H3
Colyer Cl, N1 . . . . .10 C1
  SE9 . . . . .175 E2
Colyers La, Erith DA8 . . . . .159 J1
Colyton Cl, Well. DA16 . . . . .158 D1
  Wembley HA0
  off Bridgewater Rd 87 F6
Colyton Rd, SE22 . . . . .153 E5
Colyton Way, N18 . . . . .60 D5
Combe Av, SE3 . . . . .135 F7
Combedale Rd, SE10 . . . . .135 G5
Combe Lo, SE7
  off Elliscombe Rd 135 J6
Combemartin Rd, SW18 . . . . . .148 B7
Combe Ms, SE3 . . . . .135 F7
Comber Cl, NW2 . . . . .89 H3
Comber Gro, SE5 . . . . .151 J1
Combermere Rd, SW9 . . . . .151 F3
  Morden SM4 . . . . .185 E6
Comberton Rd, E5 . . . . .95 E2
Combeside, SE18 . . . . .137 J7
Combwell Cres, SE2 . . . . .138 A3
Comely Bk Rd, E17 . . . . .78 C5
Comeragh Ms, W14 . . . . .128 B5
Comeragh Rd, W14 . . . . .128 B5
Comer Cres, Sthl. UB2
  off Windmill Av 123 J2
Comerford Rd, SE4 . . . . .153 H4
Comet Cl, E12 . . . . .98 A4
Comet Pl, SE8 . . . . .134 A7
Comet Rd, Stai. (Stanw.) TW19 . .140 A7
Comet St, SE8 . . . . .134 A7
Comfort St, SE15 . . . . .36 D6
Commerce Rd, N22 . . . . .75 F1
  Brentford TW8 . . . . .125 F7
Commerce Way, Croy. CR0 . . . .201 F2
Commercial Rd, E1 . . . . .21 H3
  E14 . . . . .113 F6
  N17 . . . . .60 B6
  N18 . . . . .60 B5
Commercial St, E1 . . . . .13 F6
Commercial Way, NW10 . . . . . .106 B2
  SE15 . . . . .132 C7
Commerell St, SE10 . . . . .135 E5
Commodity Quay, E1 . . . . .21 G6
Commodore St, E1 . . . . .113 H4
Common, The, E15 . . . . .97 E6
  W5 . . . . .105 H7
  Richmond TW10 . . . . .163 G3
  Southall UB2 . . . . .122 C4

Common, The, Stan. HA7 . . . . . .52 B2
Commondale, SW15 . . . . . . .147 J3
Common La, Esher (Clay.) KT10 .194 D7
Common Mile Cl, SW4 . . . . .150 D5
Common Rd, SW13 . . . . . . .147 G3
  Esher (Clay.) KT10 . . . . . .194 D6
  Stanmore HA7 . . . . .52 A4
Commonside, Kes. BR2 . . . . .205 J4
Commonside E, Mitch. CR4 . . . .185 J3
Commonside W, Mitch. CR4 . . . .185 J3
Commonwealth Av, W12 . . . . .107 H7
★ Commonwealth Inst, W8 . . . .128 C3
Commonwealth Rd, N17 . . . . . .60 D7
Commonwealth Way, SE2 . . . .138 B5
Community Cl, Houns. TW5 . . . .142 B1
Community La, N7 . . . . .92 D5
Community Rd, E15 . . . . .96 D5
  Greenford UB6 . . . . .103 J1
Como Rd, SE23 . . . . .171 H2
Compass Hill, Rich. TW10 . . . .145 G6
Compass Ho, SW18
  off Smugglers Way 148/149 E4
Companye Gdns, NW6 . . . . . . .90 E7
Compton Av, E6 . . . . .116 A2
  N1 . . . . .93 H6
  N6 . . . . .73 H7
  Wembley HA0 . . . . .87 F4
Compton Cl, E3 . . . . .114 A4
  NW1 . . . . .9 E4
  NW11 off The Vale 90 A3
  W13 . . . . .104 D6
  Edgware HA8
    off Pavilion Way 54 C7
Compton Ct, SE19
  off Victoria Cres 170 B5
Compton Cres, N17 . . . . .59 J7
  W4 . . . . .126 C6
  Chessington KT9 . . . . . . .195 H6
  Northolt UB5 . . . . .102 D1
Compton Ho, SW11
  off Parkham St 149 H1
Compton Pas, EC1 . . . . .11 H5
Compton Pl, WC1 . . . . .10 A5
  Watford WD19 . . . . .50 E3
Compton Ri, Pnr. HA5 . . . . . .67 E5
Compton Rd, N1 . . . . .93 H6
  N21 . . . . .59 G1
  NW10 . . . . .108 A3
  SW19 . . . . .166 C6
  Croydon CR0 . . . . .202 E1
Compton St, EC1 . . . . .11 G5
Compton Ter, N1 . . . . .93 H6
Computer Ho, Brent. TW8 . . . .125 F6
Comreddy Cl, Enf. EN2 . . . . . .43 H1
Comus Pl, SE17 . . . . .36 D2
Comyn Rd, SW11 . . . . .149 H4
Comyns, The, Bushey (Bushey Hth)
  WD23 . . . . .51 J1
Comyns Cl, E16 . . . . .115 F5
Comyns Rd, Dag. RM9 . . . . . .101 G7
Conant Ms, E1 . . . . .21 H5
Concanon Rd, SW2 . . . . . . .151 F4
Concert Hall App, SE1 . . . . . .26 D2
Concord Cl, Nthlt. UB5 . . . . .102 E3
Concorde Cl, Houns. TW3 . . . .143 H2
Concorde Dr, E6 . . . . .116 C5
Concord Rd, W3 . . . . .106 B4
  Enfield EN3 . . . . .45 F5
Concord Ter, Har. HA2
  off Coles Cres 85 H2
Concourse, The, N9 off New Rd . .60 D2
  NW9 . . . . .71 F1
Condell Rd, SW8 . . . . .150 C1
Conder St, E14 off Salmon La . .113 H6
Condor Path, Nthlt. UB5
  off Brabazon Rd 103 G2
Condover Cres, SE18 . . . . . .136 E7
Condray Pl, SW11 . . . . .129 H7
Conduit Av, SE10
  off Crooms Hill 154 D1
Conduit Ct, WC2 . . . . .18 A5
Conduit La, N18 . . . . .61 F5
  Croydon CR0 . . . . .202 D5
  Enfield EN3 off Morson Rd . .45 H6
  South Croydon CR2 . . . . . .202 D5
Conduit Ms, SE18 . . . . .137 E5
  W2 . . . . .14 E4
Conduit Pas, W2 . . . . .15 E4
Conduit Pl, W2 . . . . .15 E4
Conduit Rd, SE18 . . . . .137 E5
Conduit St, W1 . . . . .17 E5
Conduit Way, NW10 . . . . .88 C7
Conewood St, N5 . . . . .93 H3
Coney Acre, SE21 . . . . .169 J1
Coney Burrows, E4
  off Wyemead Cres 62/63 E2
Coneygrove Path, Nthlt. UB5
  off Arnold Rd 84/85 E6
CONEY HALL, W.Wick. BR4 . . . .205 F3
Coney Hill Rd, W.Wick. BR4 . . . .205 E2
Coney Way, SW8 . . . . .34 D6
Conference Cl, E4
  off Greenbank Cl 62 C2
★ Conference Forum, The, E1 . .21 H3
Conference Rd, SE2 . . . . . . .138 C4
Congleton Gro, SE18 . . . . . .137 F5
Congo Dr, N9 . . . . .61 F3

Congo Rd, SE18 . . . . .137 G5
Congress Rd, SE2 . . . . .138 C4
Congreve Rd, SE9 . . . . .156 C3
Congreve St, SE17 . . . . .36 D1
Congreve Wk, E16 . . . . .116 A5
Conical Cor, Enf. EN2 . . . . . .43 J2
Conifer Cl, Orp. BR6 . . . . . .207 G4
Conifer Gdns, SW16 . . . . . . .169 E3
  Enfield EN1 . . . . .44 B6
  Sutton SM1 . . . . .198 E2
Conifers Cl, Tedd. TW11 . . . . .163 E7
Conifer Way, Wem. HA0 . . . . . .87 F3
Coniger Rd, SW6 . . . . .148 D2
Coningham Ms, W12
  off Percy Rd 127 G1
Coningham Rd, W12 . . . . . . .127 H2
Coningsby Cotts, W5
  off Coningsby Rd 125 G2
Coningsby Gdns, E4 . . . . .62 B6
Coningsby Rd, N4 . . . . .75 H1
  W5 . . . . .125 F2
Conington Rd, SE13 . . . . . . .154 B2
Conisbee Ct, N14 . . . . .42 C5
Conisborough Cres, SE6 . . . . .172 C3
Coniscliffe Cl, Chis. BR7 . . . .192 D1
Coniscliffe Rd, N13 . . . . .59 J3
Coniston Av, Bark. IG11 . . . . . .99 H7
  Greenford UB6 . . . . .105 E3
  Welling DA16 . . . . .157 H3
Coniston Cl, N20 . . . . .57 F3
  SW13 off Lonsdale Rd 127 F7
  SW20 . . . . .184 A6
  W4 . . . . .146 C1
  Barking IG11 off Coniston Av . .99 H7
  Bexleyheath DA7 . . . . . . .159 J1
Conistone Way, N7 . . . . .93 E7
Coniston Gdns, N9 . . . . .61 F1
  NW9 . . . . .70 D5
  Ilford IG4 . . . . .80 B4
  Pinner HA5 . . . . .66 A4
  Sutton SM2 . . . . .199 G6
  Wembley HA9 . . . . .87 F1
Coniston Ho, SE5 . . . . .35 J7
Coniston Rd, N10 . . . . .74 B2
  N17 . . . . .60 D6
  Bexleyheath DA7 . . . . . . .159 J1
  Bromley BR1 . . . . .172 E6
  Croydon CR0 . . . . .188 D7
  Twickenham TW2 . . . . . . .143 H6
Coniston Wk, E9 off Clifden Rd . .95 F5
Coniston Way, Chess. KT9 . . . .195 H3
Conlan St, W10 . . . . .108 B4
Conley Rd, NW10 . . . . .89 E6
Conley St, SE10
  off Pelton Rd 134/135 E5
Connaught Av, E4 . . . . .46 D7
  SW14 . . . . .146 C3
  Barnet EN4 . . . . .57 J1
  Enfield EN1 . . . . .44 B2
  Hounslow TW4 . . . . .143 E5
  Loughton IG10 . . . . .48 A4
Connaught Br, E16 . . . . .136 A1
Connaught Business Cen, Mitch.
  CR4 off Wandle Way 185 J5
Connaught Cl, E10 . . . . .95 H2
  W2 . . . . .15 G4
  Enfield EN1 . . . . .44 B2
  Sutton SM1 . . . . .199 G2
Connaught Ct, E17
  off Orford Rd 78 B4
  Buckhurst Hill IG9 . . . . . .63 H1
Connaught Dr, NW11 . . . . . . .72 D4
Connaught Gdns, N10 . . . . . . .74 B5
  N13 . . . . .59 H4
  Morden SM4 . . . . .185 F4
Connaught Hill, Loug. IG10 . . . .48 A4
Connaught La, Ilf. IG1
  off Connaught Rd 99 G2
Connaught Ms, SE18 . . . . . . .136 D5
  Ilford IG1 off Connaught Rd . .99 G2
Connaught Pl, W2 . . . . .15 J5
Connaught Rd, E4 . . . . .46 E7
  E11 . . . . .96 D1
  E16 . . . . .136 A1
  E17 . . . . .78 A5
  N4 . . . . .75 G7
  NW10 . . . . .107 E1
  SE18 . . . . .136 D5
  W13 . . . . .104 E7
  Barnet EN5 . . . . .40 A6
  Harrow HA3 . . . . .68 C1
  Ilford IG1 . . . . .99 G2
  New Malden KT3 . . . . . . .183 E4
  Richmond TW10
    off Albert Rd 145 J5
  Sutton SM1 . . . . .199 G2
  Teddington TW11 . . . . . . .162 A5
Connaught Roundabout, E16
  off Connaught Br 116 A7
Connaught Sq, W2 . . . . .15 J4
Connaught St, W2 . . . . .15 G4
Connaught Way, N13 . . . . . . .59 H4
Connell Cres, W5 . . . . .105 J4
Connemara Cl, Borwd. WD6
  off Percheron Rd 38 D6
Connington Cres, E4 . . . . . . .62 D3
Connor Cl, E11 . . . . .78 E7

Connor Cl, Ilf. IG6 . . . . .81 E1
Connor Rd, Dag. RM9 . . . . . .101 F4
Connor St, E9 off Lauriston Rd . .113 G1
Conolly Rd, W7 . . . . .124 B1
Conrad Dr, Wor.Pk. KT4 . . . . .197 J1
Conrad Ho, N16 . . . . .94 B5
Consfield Av, N.Mal. KT3 . . . .183 G4
Consort Ms, Islw. TW7 . . . . .144 A5
Consort Rd, SE15 . . . . .152 E1
Cons St, SE1 . . . . .27 F3
Constable Av, E16
  off Wesley Av 135 H1
Constable Cl, NW11 . . . . . . .73 E6
Constable Cres, N15 . . . . . . .76 D5
Constable Gdns, Edg. HA8 . . . .70 A1
  Isleworth TW7 . . . . .144 A5
Constable Ho, Dag. RM8
  off Stonard Rd 100 B4
Constable Wk, SE21 . . . . . . .170 C3
Constance Cres, Brom. BR2 . . . .191 F7
Constance Rd, Croy. CR0 . . . .187 H1
  Enfield EN1 . . . . .44 B6
  Sutton SM1 . . . . .199 F4
  Twickenham TW2 . . . . . . .143 H7
Constance St, E16
  off Albert Rd 136 B1
Constantine Rd, NW3 . . . . . . .91 H4
Constitution Hill, SW1 . . . . . .24 D3
Constitution Ri, SE18 . . . . . .156 D1
Consul Av, Dag. RM9 . . . . . .119 J3
Content St, SE17 . . . . .36 A2
Contessa Cl, Orp. BR6 . . . . .207 H5
Control Twr Rd, Houns. (Hthrw. Air.)
  TW6 . . . . .140 D3
Convair Wk, Nthlt. UB5
  off Kittiwake Rd 102 D3
Convent Cl, Beck. BR3 . . . . .172 C7
Convent Gdns, W5 . . . . .125 F4
  W11 off Kensington Pk Rd . .108 C6
Convent Hill, SE19 . . . . .169 J6
Convent Way, Sthl. UB2 . . . . .122 C4
Conway Cl, Stan. HA7 . . . . . .52 D6
Conway Cres, Grnf. UB6 . . . .104 B2
  Romford RM6 . . . . .82 C7
Conway Dr, Hayes UB3 . . . . .121 F3
  Sutton SM2 . . . . .198 E6
Conway Gdns, Mitch. CR4 . . . .186 D4
  Wembley HA9 . . . . .69 G7
Conway Gro, W3 . . . . .106 D5
Conway Ms, W1 . . . . .9 F6
Conway Rd, N14 . . . . .59 E3
  N15 . . . . .75 H5
  NW2 . . . . .89 J2
  SE18 . . . . .137 G4
  SW20 . . . . .183 J1
  Feltham TW13 . . . . .160 D5
  Hounslow TW4 . . . . .143 F7
  Hounslow (Hthrw. Air.) TW6
    off Inner Ring E 140/141 E3
Conway St, E13 . . . . .115 G4
  W1 . . . . .9 F6
Conway Wk, Hmptn. TW12
  off Fearnley Cres 161 F6
Conybeare, NW3
  off King Henry's Rd 91 H7
Conyers Cl, Wdf.Grn. IG8 . . . .62 E6
Conyers Rd, SW16 . . . . .168 D5
Conyer St, E3 . . . . .113 H2
Conyers Way, Loug. IG10 . . . .49 E3
Cooden Cl, Brom. BR1
  off Plaistow La 173 H7
Cook Ct, SE16
  off Rotherhithe St 133 F1
Cooke Cl, E14 off Cabot Sq 134 A1
Cookes Cl, E11 . . . . .97 F2
Cookes La, Sutt. SM3 . . . . . .198 B6
Cookham Cl, Sthl. UB2 . . . . .123 H2
Cookham Cres, SE16
  off Marlow Way 133 G2
Cookham Dene Cl, Chis. BR7 . . . .193 G1
Cookham Rd, Sid. DA14 . . . . .177 D3
Cookhill Rd, SE2 . . . . .138 B2
Cook Rd, Dag. RM9 . . . . . . .118 E1
Cooks Cl, Rom. RM5 . . . . . . .83 J1
Cookson Gro, Erith DA8 . . . . .139 H7
Cook's Rd, E15 . . . . .114 B2
Cooks Rd, SE17 . . . . .35 G5
Cooks Wf Roundabout, N18 . . . .61 G3
Coolfin Rd, E16 . . . . .115 G6
Coolgardie Av, E4 . . . . .62 C5
  Chigwell IG7 . . . . .64 D3
Coolhurst Rd, N8 . . . . .74 D6
Cool Oak La, NW9 . . . . .71 E7
Coomassie Rd, W9
  off Bravington Rd 108 C4
COOMBE, Kings.T. KT2 . . . . .164 C7
Coombe Av, Croy. CR0 . . . . .202 B4
Coombe Bk, Kings.T. KT2 . . . .182 E1
Coombe Cl, Edg. HA8 . . . . . .69 J2
  Hounslow TW3 . . . . .143 G4
Coombe Cor, N21 . . . . .59 H1
Coombe Cres, Hmptn. TW12 . . . .161 E7
Coombe Dr, Kings.T. KT2 . . . .164 D7
  Ruislip HA4 . . . . .84 B1
Coombe End, Kings.T. KT2 . . . .164 E7
Coombefield Cl, N.Mal. KT3 . . . .183 E5
Coombe Gdns, SW20 . . . . . .183 G2

Coombe Gdns, N.Mal. KT3 . . . .183 F4
Coombe Hts, Kings.T. KT2 . . . .165 E7
Coombe Hill Glade, Kings.T. KT2 165 E7
Coombe Hill Rd, Kings.T. KT2 . . . .164 E7
Coombe Ho Chase, N.Mal. KT3 .182 D1
Coombehurst Cl, Barn. EN4 . . . .41 J2
Coombe La, SW20 . . . . .183 G1
  Croydon CR0 . . . . .202 E5
Coombe La W, Kings.T. KT2 . . . .164 E7
Coombe Lea, Brom. BR1 . . . .192 B3
Coombe Neville, Kings.T. KT2 . .164 D7
Coombe Pk, Kings.T. KT2 . . . .164 D5
Coombe Ridings, Kings.T. KT2 . .164 C5
Coombe Ri, Kings.T. KT2 . . . .182 C1
Coombe Rd, N22 . . . . .75 G1
  NW10 . . . . .88 D3
  SE26 . . . . .170 E4
  W4 . . . . .127 E5
  W13 off Northcroft Rd . .124/125 E3
  Croydon CR0 . . . . .202 A4
  Hampton TW12 . . . . .161 F6
  Kingston upon Thames KT2 . .182 A1
  New Malden KT3 . . . . . . .182 E2
Coombes Rd, Dag. RM9 . . . . .119 F3
Coombe Wk, Sutt. SM1 . . . . .198 E3
Coombewood Dr, Rom. RM6 . . . .83 F6
Coombe Wd Rd, Kings.T. KT2 . .164 C5
Coombs St, N1 . . . . .11 H2
Coomer Ms, SW6
  off Coomer Pl 128 C6
Coomer Pl, SW6 . . . . .128 C6
Coomer Rd, SW6
  off Coomer Pl 128 C6
Cooms Wk, Edg. HA8 off East Rd .70 C1
Cooperage Cl, N17
  off Brantwood Rd 60 C6
Cooper Av, E17 . . . . .77 G1
Cooper Cl, SE1 . . . . .27 F4
Cooper Ct, E15 off Clays La 96 B5
Cooper Cres, Cars. SM5 . . . . .199 J3
Cooper Rd, NW4 . . . . .72 A6
  NW10 . . . . .89 F5
  Croydon CR0 . . . . .201 G4
Coopersale Cl, Wdf.Grn. IG8
  off Navestock Cres 63 J7
Coopersale Rd, E9 . . . . .95 G5
Coopers Cl, E1 . . . . .113 F4
  Dagenham RM10 . . . . . . .101 H6
Coopers Cres, Borwd. WD6 . . . .38 C1
Coopers La, E10 . . . . .96 B1
  NW1 . . . . .9 J1
Cooper's La, SE12 . . . . .173 H2
Coopers Rd, SE1 . . . . .37 G4
Cooper's Row, EC3 . . . . .21 F5
Cooper St, E16
  off Lawrence St 115 F5
Coopers Wk, E15
  off Maryland St 96 D5
Coopers Yd, N1 off Upper St 93 H7
Cooper's Yd, SE19
  off Westow Hill 170 B6
Coote Gdns, Dag. RM8 . . . . .101 F3
Coote Rd, Bexh. DA7 . . . . . .159 F1
  Dagenham RM8 . . . . .101 F3
Copeland Dr, E14 . . . . .134 A4
Copeland Rd, E17 . . . . .78 B5
  SE15 . . . . .152 D2
Copeman Cl, SE26 . . . . .171 F5
Copenhagen Gdns, W4 . . . . . .126 C2
Copenhagen Pl, E14 . . . . . . .113 J6
Copenhagen St, N1 . . . . . . .111 E1
Cope Pl, W8 . . . . .128 D3
Copers Cope Rd, Beck. BR3 . . . .171 J6
Cope St, SE16 . . . . .133 G4
Copford Cl, Wdf.Grn. IG8 . . . .64 B6
Copford Wk, N1 off Popham St . .111 J1
Copgate Path, SW16 . . . . . . .169 F6
Copinger Wk, Edg. HA8
  off North Rd 70 B1
Copland Av, Wem. HA0 . . . . . .87 G5
Copland Cl, Wem. HA0 . . . . . .87 F5
Copland Ms, Wem. HA0
  off Copland Rd 87 H6
Copland Rd, Wem. HA0 . . . . . .87 H6
Copleston Ms, SE15
  off Copleston Rd 152 C2
Copleston Pas, SE15 . . . . . .152 C3
Copleston Rd, SE15 . . . . . . .152 C3
Copley Cl, SE17 . . . . .35 H6
  W7 . . . . .104 C5
Copley Dene, Brom. BR1 . . . .192 A1
Copley Pk, SW16 . . . . .169 F6
Copley Rd, Stan. HA7 . . . . . .53 F5
Copley St, E1 . . . . .113 G5
Copnor Way, SE15
  off Blakes Rd 132 B7
Coppard Gdns, Chess. KT9 . . . .195 F6
Copped Hall, SE21
  off Glazebrook Cl 170 A2
Coppelia Rd, SE3 . . . . .155 F4
Copperas St, SE8 . . . . .134 B6
Copper Beech Cl, Ilf. IG5 . . . .80 D1
Copper Beeches, Islw. TW7
  off Eversley Cres 144 A1

Copper Cl, SE19
  off Auckland Rd 170 C7
Copperdale Rd, Hayes UB3 ..122 A2
Copperfield, Chig. IG7 ......65 G6
Copperfield App, Chig. IG7 ...65 G6
Copperfield Ct, Pnr. HA5
  off Copperfield Way 67 F4
Copperfield Dr, N15 ....76 C4
Copperfield Ms, N18 ....60 B5
Copperfield Rd, E3 ....113 H4
  SE28 ....118 C6
Copperfield St, SE1 ....27 H3
Copperfield Way, Chis. BR7 ..175 F6
  Pinner HA5 ....67 F4
Coppergate Cl, Brom. BR1 ...191 H1
Copper Mead Cl, NW2 ....89 J3
Copper Mill Dr, Islw. TW7 ...144 C2
Coppermill La, E17 ....77 F6
Copper Mill La, SW17 ....167 F4
Copper Row, SE1 ....29 F2
Coppetts Cl, N12 ....57 H7
Coppetts Rd, N10 ....74 A2
Coppice, The, Enf. EN2 ....43 H4
Coppice Cl, SW20 ....183 J3
  Beckenham BR3 ....190 B4
  Stanmore HA7 ....52 C6
Coppice Dr, SW15 ....147 H6
Coppice Wk, N20 ....56 D3
Coppice Way, E18 ....79 F4
Coppies Gro, N11 ....58 A4
Copping Cl, Croy. CR0 ......202 B4
Coppins, The, Croy. (New Adgtn)
  CR0 ....204 B6
  Harrow HA3 ....52 B6
Coppock Cl, SW11 ....149 H2
Coppsfield, W.Mol. KT8
  off Hurst Rd 179 G3
Copse, The, E4 ....63 F1
Copse Av, W.Wick. BR4 ......204 B3
Copse Cl, SE7 ....135 H6
  West Drayton UB7 ....120 A3
Copse Glade, Surb. KT6 .....195 G1
COPSE HILL, SW20 ....165 G7
Copse Hill, SW20 ....165 H7
  Sutton SM2 ....199 E7
Copsewood Cl, Sid. DA15 ...157 H6
Coptefield Dr, Belv. DA17 ...138 D3
Copthall Av, EC2 ....20 C3
Copthall Bldgs, EC2 ....20 B3
Copthall Cl, EC2 ....20 B3
Copthall Ct, EC2 ....20 B3
Copthall Dr, NW7 ....55 G7
Copthall Gdns, NW7 ....55 G7
  Twickenham TW1 ....162 C1
Copthorne Av, SW12 ....150 D7
  Bromley BR2 ....206 C2
  Ilford IG6 ....65 E6
Copthorne Ms, Hayes UB3 ...121 H4
Coptic St, WC1 ....18 A2
Copwood Cl, N12 ....57 G4
Coral Cl, Rom. RM6 ....82 C4
Coraline Cl, Sthl. UB1 ....103 F3
Coralline Wk, SE2 ....138 C2
Coral Row, SW11
  off Gartons Way 149 F3
Coral St, SE1 ....27 F4
Coram St, WC1 ....10 A6
Coran Cl, N9 ....45 G7
Corban Rd, Houns. TW3 .....143 G3
Corbden Cl, SE15 ....152 C1
Corbet Cl, Wall. SM6 ....200 A1
Corbet Ct, EC3 ....20 C4
Corbet Pl, E1 ....21 F1
Corbett Gro, N22 ....58 E7
Corbett Ho, Wat. WD19 ......50 C3
Corbett Rd, E11 ....79 J6
  E17 ....78 C3
Corbetts La, SE16
  off Rotherhithe New Rd 133 F4
Corbetts Pas, SE16
  off Rotherhithe New Rd 133 F4
Corbicum, E11 ....79 E7
Corbidge Ct, SE8
  off Glaisher St 134 B6
Corbiere Ct, SW19
  off Thornton Rd 166 A6
Corbiere Ho, N1 ....112 B1
Corbins La, Har. HA2 ....85 H3
Corbridge Cres, E2 ....112 E2
Corby Cres, Enf. EN2 ....43 E4
Corbylands Rd, Sid. DA15 ...157 H7
Corbyn St, N4 ....93 E1
Corby Rd, NW10 ....106 D2
Corby Way, E3 off Knapp Rd ..114 A4
Cordelia Cl, SE24 ....151 H4
Cordelia Gdns, Stai. TW19 ..140 B7
Cordelia Rd, Stai. TW19 .....140 B7
Cordelia St, E14 ....114 B6
Cordell Ho, N15 off Newton Rd ..76 C5
Cording St, E14 off Chrisp St ..114 B5
Cordwainers Wk, E13
  off Richmond St 115 G2
Cord Way, E14 off Mellish St ..134 A3
Cordwell Rd, SE13 ....154 E5
Corefield Cl, N11
  off Benfleet Way 58 A2
Corelli Rd, SE3 ....156 B2

Corfe Av, Har. HA2 ....85 G4
Corfe Cl, Borwd. WD6
  off Chester Rd 38 D3
  Hayes UB4 ....102 C6
Corfe Twr, W3 ....126 B2
Corfield Rd, N21 ....43 F5
Corfield St, E2 ....113 E3
Corfton Rd, W5 ....105 H6
Coriander Av, E14 ....114 D6
Cories Cl, Dag. RM8 ....100 D2
Corinium Cl, Wem. HA9 ......87 J4
Corinne Rd, N19 ....92 C4
Corinthian Way, Stai. (Stanw.) TW19
  off Clare Rd 140 A7
Corker Wk, N7 ....93 F2
Corkran Rd, Surb. KT6 ......181 G7
Corkscrew Hill, W.Wick. BR4 ..204 D2
Cork Sq, E1
  off Smeaton St 132/133 E1
Cork St, W1 ....17 F6
Cork St Ms, W1 ....17 F6
Cork Tree Way, E4 ....61 H6
Corlett St, NW1 ....15 G1
Cormont Rd, SE5 ....151 H1
Cormorant Cl, E17
  off Banbury Rd 77 G1
Cormorant Ho, Enf. EN3
  off Alma Rd 45 G5
Cormorant Pl, Sutt. SM1
  off Sandpiper Rd 198 C5
Cormorant Rd, E7 ....97 F4
Cornbury Rd, Edg. HA8 ....53 G7
Cornelia Dr, Hayes UB4 .....102 C4
Cornelia St, N7 ....93 F6
Cornell Cl, Sid. DA14 ....177 E6
Corner Grn, SE3 ....155 G2
Corner Ho St, WC2 ....26 A1
Corner Mead, NW9 ....55 F7
Corney Reach Way, W4 ......127 E7
Corney Rd, W4 ....127 E6
Cornflower La, Croy. CR0 ....203 G1
Cornflower Ter, SE22 ....152 E6
Cornford Cl, Brom. BR2 .....191 G5
Cornford Gro, SW12 ....168 B2
Cornhill, EC3 ....20 C4
Cornish Ct, N9 ....44 E7
Cornish Gro, SE20 ....171 E7
Cornish Ho, SE17 ....35 G6
  Brentford TW8
  off Green Dragon La 125 J5
Corn Mill Dr, Orp. BR6 ......193 J7
Cornmill La, SE13 ....154 B3
Cornmow Dr, NW10 ....89 F5
Cornshaw Rd, Dag. RM8 .....100 D1
Cornthwaite Rd, E5 ....95 F3
Cornwall Av, E2 ....113 F3
  N3 ....56 D7
  N22 ....75 E1
  Esher (Clay.) KT10
  off The Causeway 194 C7
  Southall UB1 ....103 F5
  Welling DA16 ....157 H3
Cornwall Cl, Bark. IG11 ......99 J6
Cornwall Cres, W11 ....108 B7
Cornwall Dr, Orp. BR5 ......176 C7
Cornwall Gdns, NW10 ....89 H6
  SW7 ....22 B6
Cornwall Gdns Wk, SW7 .....22 B6
Cornwall Gro, W4 ....127 E5
Cornwallis Av, N9 ....61 E2
  SE9 ....175 G2
Cornwallis Gro, N9 ....61 E2
Cornwallis Rd, E17 ....77 G4
  N9 ....61 E2
  N19 ....92 E2
  SE18
  off Duke of Wellington Av ..137 F3
  Dagenham RM9 ....100 D4
Cornwallis Sq, N19 ....92 E2
Cornwallis Wk, SE9 ....156 C3
Cornwall Ms S, SW7 ....22 C6
Cornwall Ms W, SW7 ....22 B6
Cornwall Rd, N4 ....75 G7
  N15 ....76 A5
  N18 off Fairfield Rd 60 D5
  SE1 ....26 E1
  Croydon CR0 ....201 H2
  Esher (Clay.) KT10 ....194 D7
  Harrow HA1 ....67 J6
  Pinner HA5 ....51 F7
  Sutton SM2 ....198 C7
  Twickenham TW1 ....162 D1
Cornwall Sq, SE11 ....35 G3
Cornwall St, E1
  off Watney St 112/113 E7
Cornwall Ter, NW1 ....8 A6
Cornwall Ter Ms, NW1 ....8 A6
Corn Way, E11 ....96 D3
Cornwood Cl, N2 ....73 G5
Cornwood Dr, E1 ....113 F6
Cornworthy Rd, Dag. RM8 ...100 C5
Corona Rd, SE12 ....155 G7
Coronation Av, N16
  off Victorian Rd 94 C3
Coronation Cl, Bex. DA5 ....158 D6
  Ilford IG6 ....81 F4
Coronation Rd, E13 ....115 J3

Coronation Rd, NW10 ....105 J3
  Hayes UB3 ....121 J4
Coronation Wk, Twick. TW2 ..161 F1
Coronet St, N1 ....12 D4
Corporation Av, Houns. TW4 ..142 E4
Corporation Row, EC1 ....11 F5
Corporation St, E15 ....115 E2
  N7 ....92 E5
Corrance Rd, SW2 ....151 E4
Corri Av, N14 ....58 D4
Corrib Dr, Sutt. SM1 ....199 H5
Corrigan Cl, NW4 ....71 J3
Corringham Ct, NW11
  off Corringham Rd 72/73 E7
Corringham Rd, NW11 ....72 D7
  Wembley HA9 ....88 A2
Corringway, NW11 ....72 E7
  W5 ....106 A4
Corris Grn, NW9
  off Snowdon Dr 70/71 E6
Corry Dr, SW9 ....151 H4
Corsair Cl, Stai. TW19 ......140 A7
Corsair Rd, Stai. TW19 .....140 A7
Corscombe Cl, Kings.T. KT2 ..164 C5
Corsehill St, SW16 ....168 C6
Corsham St, N1 ....12 C4
Corsica St, N5 ....93 H6
Cortayne Rd, SW6 ....148 C2
Cortina Dr, Dag. RM9 ....119 J3
Cortis Rd, SW15 ....147 H6
Cortis Ter, SW15 ....147 H6
Corunna Rd, SW8 ....150 C1
Corunna Ter, SW8 ....150 C1
Corvette Sq, SE10
  off Feathers Pl 134 D6
Coryton Path, W9
  off Ashmore Rd 108 C4
Cosbycote Av, SE24 ....151 J5
Cosdach Av, Wall. SM6 .....200 D7
Cosedge Cres, Croy. CR0 ...201 G5
Cosgrove Cl, N21 ....59 J2
  Hayes UB4
  off Kingsash Dr 102/103 E4
Cosmo Pl, WC1 ....18 B1
Cosmur Cl, W12 ....127 F3
Cossall Wk, SE15 ....153 E1
Cossar Ms, SW2 off Tulse Hill ..151 G5
Cosser St, SE1 ....26 E5
Costa St, SE15 ....152 D2
Costons Av, Grnf. UB6 ......104 A3
Costons La, Grnf. UB6 ......104 A3
Coston Wk, SE4
  off Hainford Cl 153 G4
Cosway St, NW1 ....15 H1
Cotall St, E14 ....114 A6
Coteford Cl, Loug. IG10 ......48 E2
  Pinner HA5 ....66 A5
Coteford St, SW17 ....167 J4
Cotelands, Croy. CR0 ....202 B3
Cotesbach Rd, E5 ....95 F3
Cotesmore Gdns, Dag. RM8 ..100 C4
Cotford Rd, Th.Hth. CR7 ....187 J4
Cotham St, SE17 ....36 A2
Cotherstone Rd, SW2 ....169 F1
Cotleigh Av, Bex. DA5 ......176 D2
Cotleigh Rd, NW6 ....90 D7
Cotman Cl, NW11 ....73 F6
  SW15 off Westleigh Av 148 A6
Cotman Gdns, Edg. HA8 ......70 A2
Cotman Ms, Dag. RM8
  off Highgrove Rd 100 C5
Cotmans Cl, Hayes UB3 .....122 A1
Coton Rd, Well. DA16 ....158 A3
Cotsford Av, N.Mal. KT3 ....182 C5
Cotswold Cl, Esher KT10 ....194 C3
  Kingston upon Thames KT2 ..164 B6
Cotswold Ct, EC1 ....11 J5
  N11 ....58 A4
Cotswold Gdns, E6 ....116 A3
  NW2 ....90 A2
  Ilford IG2 ....81 G7
Cotswold Gate, NW2
  off Cotswold Gdns 90 B1
Cotswold Grn, Enf. EN2
  off Cotswold Way 43 F4
Cotswold Ms, SW11
  off Battersea High St 149 G1
Cotswold Ri, Orp. BR6 ......193 J6
Cotswold Rd, Hmptn. TW12 ..161 G6
Cotswold St, SE27
  off Norwood High St 169 H4
Cotswold Way, Enf. EN2 ......43 F4
  Worcester Park KT4 ......197 J2
Cottage Av, Brom. BR2 .....206 B1
Cottage Fld Cl, Sid. DA14 ...176 C1
Cottage Grn, SE5 ....36 C7
Cottage Gro, SW9 ....150 E3
  Surbiton KT6 ....181 G6
Cottage Homes, NW7 ....55 G4
Cottage Pl, SW3 ....23 G5
Cottage Rd, Epsom KT19 ....196 D6
Cottage St, E14 ....114 B7
Cottage Wk, N16 off Smalley Cl ..94 C3
Cottenham Dr, NW9 ....71 F3
  SW20 ....165 H7
Cottenham Par, SW20
  off Durham Rd 183 H2

COTTENHAM PARK, SW20 ....183 H1
Cottenham Pk Rd, SW20 ....165 H7
Cottenham Pl, SW20 ....165 H7
Cottenham Rd, E17 ....77 J4
Cotterill Rd, Surb. KT6 .....195 H2
Cottesbrook St, SE14
  off Nynehead St 133 H7
Cottesloe Ms, SE1 ....27 F5
Cottesmore Av, Ilf. IG5 ......80 D2
Cottesmore Gdns, W8 ....22 B5
Cottimore Cres, Walt. KT12 ..178 B7
Cottimore Ter, Walt. KT12 ...178 B7
Cottingham Chase, Ruis. HA4 ..84 A3
Cottingham Rd, SE20 ....171 G7
  SW8 ....34 D6
Cottington Rd, Felt. TW13 ...160 D4
Cottington St, SE11 ....35 F3
Cottle Way, SE16
  off St. Marychurch St 133 F2
Cotton Av, W3 ....106 D6
Cotton Cl, Dag. RM9
  off Flamstead Rd 100 C7
Cottongrass Cl, Croy. CR0 ...203 G1
  off Cornflower La 203 G1
Cotton Hill, Brom. BR1 .....172 D4
Cotton Row, SW11 ....149 F3
Cottons Gdns, E2 ....13 E3
Cottons La, SE1 ....28 C1
Cotton St, E14 ....114 C7
Cottrell Ct, SE10
  off Greenroof Way 135 F3
Cotts Cl, W7 off Westcott Cres ..104 C5
Couchmore Av, Esher KT10 ..194 B2
  Ilford IG5 ....80 C2
Coulgate St, SE4 ....153 H3
Coulson Cl, Dag. RM8 ....82 C7
Coulson St, SW3 ....31 J3
Coulter Cl, Hayes UB4
  off Berrydale Rd 102/103 E4
Coulter Rd, W6 ....127 H3
Councillor St, SE5 ....131 J7
Counter Ct, SE1
  off Southwark St 132 A1
Counter St, SE1 ....28 D2
Countess Rd, NW5 ....92 C5
Countisbury Av, Enf. EN1 .....44 C7
Country Way, Felt. TW13 ....160 B7
  Sunbury-on-Thames TW16 ..160 B7
County Gate, SE9 ....175 F3
  Barnet EN5 ....41 E6
County Gro, SE5 ....151 J1
★ County Hall, SE1 ....26 C3
County Rd, E6 ....116 E5
  Thornton Heath CR7 ......187 H2
County St, SE1 ....28 A6
Coupland Pl, SE18 ....137 F5
Courcy Rd, N8 ....75 G3
Courier Rd, Dag. RM9 ....119 J4
Courland Gro, SW8 ....150 D1
Courland Gro Hall, SW8 ....150 D2
Courland St, SW8 ....150 D1
Course, The, SE9 ....174 D3
Court, The, Ruis. HA4 ....84 E4
Courtauld Cl, SE28
  off Pitfield Cres 138 A1
★ Courtauld Inst of Art, WC2 ..18 C5
Courtauld Rd, N19 ....92 D1
Court Av, Belv. DA17 ....139 F5
Court Cl, Har. HA3 ....69 H3
  Twickenham TW2 ....161 H3
  Wallington SM6 ....200 D7
Court Cl Av, Twick. TW2 ....161 H3
Court Cres, Chess. KT9 .....195 G5
Court Downs Rd, Beck. BR3 ..190 B2
★ Court Dress Collection,
  Kensington Palace, W8 .....22 B2
Court Dr, Croy. CR0 ....201 F4
  Stanmore HA7 ....53 H4
  Sutton SM1 ....199 H4
Courtenay Av, N6 ....73 H6
  Harrow HA3 ....67 J1
Courtenay Dr, Beck. BR3 ....190 D2
Courtenay Gdns, Har. HA3 ...67 J2
Courtenay Ms, E17
  off Cranbrook Ms 77 H5
Courtenay Pl, E17 ....77 H5
Courtenay Rd, E11 ....97 F3
  E17 ....77 G4
  SE20 ....171 G7
  Wembley HA9 ....87 G3
  Worcester Park KT4 ......197 J3
Courtenay Sq, SE11 ....34 E4
Courtenay St, SE11 ....34 E3
Courtens Ms, Stan. HA7 .....53 F7
Court Fm Av, Epsom KT19 ...196 D5
Court Fm Rd, SE9 ....174 A2
  Northolt UB5 ....85 G7
Courtfield, W5
  off Castlebar Hill 105 F5
Courtfield Av, Har. HA1 ......68 C5
Courtfield Cres, Har. HA1 ....68 C5
Courtfield Gdns, SW5 ....30 B1
  W13 ....104 D6
Courtfield Ms, SW5 ....30 C2
Courtfield Ri, W.Wick. BR4 ..204 D3
Courtfield Rd, SW7 ....30 B2
Court Gdns, N7 ....93 G6

Courtgate Cl, NW7 . . . . .55 F6
Courthill Rd, SE13 . . . . .154 C4
Courthope Rd, NW3 . . . . .91 J4
  SW19 . . . . .166 B5
  Greenford UB6 . . . . .104 A2
Courthope Vil, SW19 . . . . .166 B7
Court Ho Gdns, N3 . . . . .56 D6
Courthouse Rd, N12 . . . . .56 E6
Courtland Av, E4 . . . . .63 F2
  NW7 . . . . .54 D3
  SW16 . . . . .169 F7
  Ilford IG1 . . . . .98 C2
Courtland Cl, Wdf.Grn. IG8 . . . . .79 J1
Courtland Dr, Chig. IG7 . . . . .65 E3
Courtland Gro, SE28 . . . . .118 D7
Courtland Rd, E6 off Harrow Rd .116 B1
Courtlands, Rich. TW10 . . . . . . .146 A4
Courtlands Av, SE12 . . . . .155 H5
  Bromley BR2 . . . . .205 F1
  Hampton TW12 . . . . .161 F4
  Richmond TW9 . . . . .146 B2
Courtlands Dr, Epsom KT19 . . . .197 E6
Courtlands Rd, Surb. KT5 . . . . . .182 A7
Court La, SE21 . . . . .152 B6
Court La Gdns, SE21 . . . . .152 B7
Courtleet Dr, Erith DA8 . . . . .159 H1
Courtleigh Gdns, NW11 . . . . .72 B4
Courtman Rd, N17 . . . . .59 J7
Court Mead, Nthlt. UB5 . . . . .103 F3
Courtmead Cl, SE24 . . . . .151 J6
Courtnell St, W2 . . . . .108 D6
Courtney Cl, SE19 . . . . .170 B6
Courtney Cres, Cars. SM5 . . . . . .199 J7
Courtney Pl, Croy. CR0 . . . . .201 G3
Courtney Rd, N7 . . . . .93 G5
  off Bryantwood Rd 93 G5
  SW19 . . . . .167 H7
  Croydon CR0 . . . . .201 G3
  Hounslow (Hthrw Air.) TW6 . .140 D3
Courtney Way, Houns. (Hthrw Air.)
  TW6 off Courtney Rd 140 D2
Court Par, Wem. HA0 . . . . .86 C3
Courtrai Rd, SE23 . . . . .153 H6
Court Rd, SE9 . . . . .174 B2
  SE25 .188 C2
  Southall UB2 . . . . .123 F4
Courtside, N8 . . . . .74 D6
Court St, E1
  off Durward St 112/113 E5
  Bromley BR1 . . . . .191 G2
Court Way, NW9 . . . . .71 E4
  W3 . . . . .106 C5
  Ilford IG6 . . . . .81 F3
  Twickenham TW2 . . . . .144 C7
Courtway, Wdf.Grn. IG8 . . . . .63 J5
Courtway, The, Wat. WD19 . . . . . .51 F2
Court Yd, SE9 . . . . .156 B6
Courtyard, The, N1 . . . . .93 F7
Cousin La, EC4 . . . . .20 A6
Couthurst Rd, SE3 . . . . .135 H6
Coutts Av, Chess. KT9 . . . . .195 H5
Coutts Cres, NW5 . . . . .92 A3
Coval Gdns, SW14 . . . . .146 B4
Coval La, SW14 . . . . .146 B4
Coval Rd, SW14 . . . . .146 B4
Covelees Wall, E6 . . . . .116 D6
Covell Ct, SE8 off Reginald Sq . .134 A7
★ Covent Garden, WC2 . . . . .18 B5
Coventry Cl, E6 off Harper Rd . . .116 C6
  NW6 off Kilburn High Rd 108 D1
Coventry Cross, E3
  off Gillender St 114 C4
Coventry Rd, E1 . . . . .113 E4
  E2 . . . . .113 E4
  SE25 .188 D4
  Ilford IG1 . . . . .98 E1
Coventry St, W1 . . . . .17 H6
Coverack Cl, N14 . . . . .42 C6
  Croydon CR0 . . . . .189 H7
Coverdale Cl, Stan. HA7 . . . . .53 E5
Coverdale Gdns, Croy. CR0
  off Park Hill Ri 202 C3
Coverdale Rd, N11 . . . . .58 A6
  NW2 . . . . .90 A7
  W12 . . . . .127 H1
Coverdales, The, Bark. IG11 . . . .117 F2
Coverley Cl, E1 . . . . .21 J1
Covert, The, Orp. BR6 . . . . .193 H6
Coverton Rd, SW17 . . . . .167 H5
Covert Rd, Ilf. IG6 . . . . .65 J6
Covert Way, Barn. EN4 . . . . .41 F2
Covet Wd Cl, Orp. BR5
  off Lockesley Dr 193 J6
Covey Cl, SW19 . . . . .184 E2
Covington Gdns, SW16 . . . . .169 H7
Covington Way, SW16 . . . . .169 F6
Cowan Cl, E6 off Oliver Gdns . . .116 B5
Cowbridge La, Bark. IG11 . . . . . . .98 E7
Cowbridge Rd, Har. HA3 . . . . .69 J4
Cowcross St, EC1 . . . . .19 G1
Cowden Rd, Orp. BR6 . . . . .193 J7
Cowden St, SE6 . . . . .172 A4
Cowdenbeath Path, N1 . . . . .111 F1
Cowdray Cl, Enf. EN1 . . . . .44 B2
Cowdrey Rd, SW19 . . . . .167 E5
Cowdry Rd, E9 off Wick Rd 95 H6
Cowen Av, Har. HA2 . . . . .85 J2

Cowgate Rd, Grnf. UB6 . . . . .104 A2
Cowick Rd, SW17 . . . . .167 J4
Cowings Mead, Nthlt. UB5 . . . . . .85 E7
Cowland Av, Enf. EN3 . . . . .45 F4
Cow La, Grnf. UB6 . . . . .104 A2
Cow Leaze, E6 . . . . .116 D6
Cowleaze Rd, Kings.T. KT2 . . . . .181 H1
Cowley La, E11
  off Cathall Rd 96/97 E3
Cowley Pl, NW4 . . . . .71 J5
Cowley Rd, E11 . . . . .79 H5
  SW9 .151 G1
  SW14 . . . . .146 E3
  W3 . . . . .127 F1
  Ilford IG1 . . . . .80 C7
Cowley St, SW1 . . . . .26 A5
Cowling Cl, W11 off Wilsham St .128 B1
Cowper Av, E6 . . . . .98 B7
  Sutton SM1 . . . . .199 G4
Cowper Cl, Brom. BR2 . . . . .192 A4
  Welling DA16 . . . . .158 A4
Cowper Gdns, N14 . . . . .42 C6
  Wallington SM6 . . . . .200 C6
Cowper Rd, N14 . . . . .58 B1
  N16 . . . . .94 B5
  N18 . . . . .60 D5
  SW19 . . . . .167 F6
  W3 . . . . .126 D1
  W7 . . . . .104 C1
  Belvedere DA17 . . . . .139 G4
  Bromley BR2 . . . . .192 A4
  Kingston upon Thames KT2 . .163 J5
Cowpers Ct, EC3
  off Birchin La 112 A6
Cowper St, EC2 . . . . .12 C5
Cowper Ter, W10
  off St. Marks Rd 108 A5
Cowslip Rd, E18 . . . . .79 H2
Cowthorpe Rd, SW8 . . . . .150 D1
Coxe Pl, Har. (Wldste) HA3 . . . . . .68 D4
Cox La, Chess. KT9 . . . . .195 J4
  Epsom KT19 . . . . .196 B5
Coxmount Rd, SE7 . . . . .136 A5
Coxson Way, SE1 . . . . .29 F4
Cox's Wk, SE21 . . . . .170 D1
Coxwell Rd, SE18 . . . . .137 G5
  SE19 .170 B7
Coxwold Path, Chess. KT9
  off Garrison La 195 H7
Crabbs Cft Cl, Orp. BR6
  off Ladycroft Way 207 F5
Crab Hill, Beck. BR3 . . . . .172 D7
Crabtree Av, Rom. RM6 . . . . .82 D4
  Wembley HA0 . . . . .105 H2
Crabtree Cl, E2 . . . . .13 F2
Crabtree Ct, E15 off Clays La 96 B5
Crabtree La, SW6 . . . . .128 A7
Crabtree Manorway Ind Est, Belv.
  DA17 . . . . .139 H3
Crabtree Manorway N, Belv.
  DA17 . . . . .139 J2
Crabtree Manorway S, Belv.
  DA17 . . . . .139 J3
Craddock Rd, Enf. EN1 . . . . .44 C3
Craddock St, NW5
  off Prince of Wales Rd 92 A6
Cradley Rd, SE9 . . . . .175 G1
★ Crafts Council, N1 . . . . .11 F2
Craigen Av, Croy. CR0 . . . . .203 E1
Craigerne Rd, SE3 . . . . .135 H7
Craig Gdns, E18 . . . . .79 F2
Craigholm, SE18 . . . . .156 D2
Craigmuir Pk, Wem. HA0 . . . . . .105 J1
Craignair Rd, SW2 . . . . .151 G7
Craignish Av, SW16 . . . . .187 F2
Craig Pk Rd, N18 . . . . .60 E5
Craig Rd, Rich. TW10 . . . . .163 F4
Craigs Ct, SW1 . . . . .26 A1
Craigton Rd, SE9 . . . . .156 C4
Craigweil Cl, Stan. HA7 . . . . .53 G5
Craigweil Dr, Stan. HA7 . . . . .53 G5
Craigwell Av, Felt. TW13 . . . . . . .160 A3
Craik Ct, NW6 off Carlton Vale . .108 C2
Crail Row, SE17 . . . . .36 C2
Cramer Ct, N.Mal. KT3
  off Warwick Rd 182 C3
Cramer St, W1 . . . . .16 C2
Cramond Cl, W6 . . . . .128 B6
Crampton Rd, SE20 . . . . .171 F6
Crampton St, SE17 . . . . .35 J2
Cranberry Cl, Nthlt. UB5
  off Parkfield Av 102 D2
Cranberry La, E16 . . . . .114 E4
Cranborne Av, Sthl. UB2 . . . . . . .123 G4
  Surbiton KT6 . . . . .196 A3
Cranborne Rd, Bark. IG11 . . . . . .117 G1
Cranborne Waye, Hayes UB4 . . .102 C7
Cranbourn All, WC2 . . . . .17 J5
Cranbourne Av, E11 . . . . .79 H4
Cranbourne Cl, SW16 . . . . .187 E3
  Ilford IG6 . . . . .81 F3
Cranbourne Dr, Pnr. HA5 . . . . . . .66 D5
Cranbourne Gdns, NW11 . . . . . . .72 B5
  Ilford IG6 . . . . .81 F3
Cranbourne Pas, SE16
  off Marigold St 132/133 E2
Cranbourne Rd, E12
  off High St N 98 B5

Cranbourne Rd, E15 . . . . .96 C4
  N10 . . . . .74 B2
Cranbourn St, WC2 . . . . .17 J5
CRANBROOK, Ilf. IG1 . . . . .98 C1
Cranbrook Cl, Brom. BR2 . . . . . .191 G6
Cranbrook Dr, Twick. TW2 . . . . . .161 H1
Cranbrook Ms, E17 . . . . .77 H5
Cranbrook Pk, N22 . . . . .75 F1
Cranbrook Ri, Ilf. IG1 . . . . .80 C7
Cranbrook Rd, SE8 . . . . .154 A1
  SW19 . . . . .166 B7
  W4 . . . . .127 E5
  Barnet EN4 . . . . .41 G6
  Bexleyheath DA7 . . . . .159 F1
  Hounslow TW4 . . . . .143 F4
  Ilford IG1, IG2, IG6 . . . . .80 D7
  Thornton Heath CR7 . . . . .187 J2
Cranbrook St, E2 off Mace St . . .113 G2
Cranbury Rd, SW6 . . . . .149 E2
Crane Av, W3 . . . . .106 C7
  Isleworth TW7 . . . . .144 D5
Cranebank Ms, Twick. TW1 . . . . .144 D4
Cranebrook, Twick. TW2
  off Manor Rd 161 J2
Crane Cl, Dag. RM10 . . . . .101 G6
  Harrow HA2 . . . . .85 J3
Crane Ct, EC4 . . . . .19 F4
  Epsom KT19 . . . . .196 C4
Craneford Cl, Twick. TW2 . . . . . .144 C7
Craneford Way, Twick. TW2 . . . . .144 B7
Crane Gdns, Hayes UB3 . . . . . . .121 J4
Crane Gro, N7 . . . . .93 G6
Crane Lo Rd, Houns. TW5 . . . . . .122 B6
Crane Mead, SE16 . . . . .133 G4
Crane Pk Rd, Twick. TW2 . . . . . .161 H2
Crane Rd, Twick. TW2 . . . . .162 B1
Cranesbill Cl, NW9
  off Colindale Av 70 D3
Cranes Dr, Surb. KT5 . . . . .181 H4
Cranes Pk, Surb. KT5 . . . . .181 H4
Cranes Pk Av, Surb. KT5 . . . . . . .181 H4
Cranes Pk Cres, Surb. KT5 . . . . .181 J4
Crane St, SE10 . . . . .134 D5
  SE15 .152 C1
Craneswater, Hayes UB3 . . . . . . .121 J7
Craneswater Pk, Sthl. UB2 . . . . .123 F5
Cranes Way, Borwd. WD6 . . . . . . .38 C5
Crane Way, Twick. TW2 . . . . .143 J7
Cranfield Cl, SE27
  off Dunelm Gro 169 J3
Cranfield Dr, NW9 . . . . .54 E7
Cranfield Rd, SE4 . . . . .153 J3
Cranfield Row, SE1 . . . . .27 F5
CRANFORD, Houns. TW5 . . . . . .122 A7
Cranford Av, N13 . . . . .59 E5
  Staines TW19 . . . . .140 B7
Cranford Cl, SW20 . . . . .183 H1
  Staines TW19 . . . . .140 B7
Cranford Cotts, E1
  off Cranford St 113 G7
Cranford Dr, Hayes UB3 . . . . . . .121 J4
Cranford La, Hayes UB3 . . . . . . .121 G6
  Hounslow (Hthrw Air.) TW6 . .141 J3
  Hounslow (Hthrw Air.N.)
  TW6 . . . . .141 J1
  Hounslow (Heston) TW5 . . . .122 D7
Cranford Pk Rd, Hayes UB3 . . . .121 J4
Cranford St, E1 . . . . .113 G7
Cranford Way, N8 . . . . .75 F5
Cranhurst Rd, NW2 . . . . .89 J5
Cranleigh Cl, SE20 . . . . .188 E2
  Bexley DA5 . . . . .159 H6
Cranleigh Gdns, N21 . . . . .43 G5
  SE25 .188 B3
  Barking IG11 . . . . .99 G7
  Harrow HA3 . . . . .69 H5
  Kingston upon Thames KT2 . .163 J6
  Loughton IG10 . . . . .48 C6
  Southall UB1 . . . . .103 F6
  Sutton SM1 . . . . .198 E2
Cranleigh Gdns Ind Est, Sthl. UB1
  off Cranleigh Gdns 103 F6
Cranleigh Ms, SW11 . . . . .149 H2
Cranleigh Rd, N15 . . . . .75 J5
  SW19 . . . . .184 D3
Cranleigh St, NW1 . . . . .9 G2
Cranley Dene Ct, N10 . . . . .74 B4
Cranley Dr, Ilf. IG2 . . . . .81 F7
Cranley Gdns, N10 . . . . .74 C4
  N13 . . . . .59 F3
  SW7 . . . . .30 D3
  Wallington SM6 . . . . .200 C7
Cranley Ms, SW7 . . . . .30 D3
Cranley Par, SE9
  off Beaconsfield Rd 174 B4
Cranley Pl, SW7 . . . . .31 E2
Cranley Rd, E13 . . . . .115 H5
  Ilford IG2 . . . . .81 F6
Cranmer Av, W13 . . . . .124 E3
Cranmer Cl, Mord. SM4 . . . . . . .184 A6
  Ruislip HA4 . . . . .84 D1
  Stanmore HA7 . . . . .53 F7
Cranmer Ct, SW3 . . . . .31 H2
  SW4 .150 D3
  Hampton (Hmptn H.) TW12
  off Cranmer Rd 161 H5
Cranmer Fm Cl, Mitch. CR4 . . . .185 J4

Cranmer Gdns, Dag. RM10 . . . . .101 J4
Cranmer Ho, SW11
  off Surrey La 149 H1
Cranmer Rd, E7 . . . . .97 H4
  SW9 . . . . .35 H7
  Croydon CR0 . . . . .201 H3
  Edgware HA8 . . . . .54 B3
  Hampton (Hmptn H.) TW12 . .161 H5
  Kingston upon Thames KT2 . .163 H5
  Mitcham CR4 . . . . .185 J4
Cranmer Ter, SW17 . . . . .167 G5
Cranmore Av, Islw. TW7 . . . . . . .123 J7
Cranmore Rd, Brom. BR1 . . . . . .173 E3
  Chislehurst BR7 . . . . .174 C5
Cranmore Way, N10 . . . . .74 C4
Cranston Cl, Houns. TW3 . . . . . .143 E2
Cranston Est, N1 . . . . .12 C2
Cranston Gdns, E4 . . . . .62 B5
Cranston Rd, SE23 . . . . .171 H1
Cranswick Rd, SE16 . . . . .133 E5
Crantock Rd, SE6 . . . . .172 B2
Cranwell Cl, E3 . . . . .114 B4
Cranwich Av, N21 . . . . .44 A7
Cranwich Rd, N16 . . . . .76 A7
Cranwood St, EC1 . . . . .12 B4
Cranworth Cres, E4 . . . . .62 D1
Cranworth Gdns, SW9 . . . . .151 G1
Craster Rd, SW2 . . . . .151 F7
Crathie Rd, SE12 . . . . .155 H6
Cravan Av, Felt. TW13 . . . . .160 A2
Craven Av, W5 . . . . .105 F7
  Southall UB1 . . . . .103 F5
Craven Cl, Hayes UB4 . . . . .102 A4
Craven Gdns, SW19 . . . . .166 D5
  Barking IG11 . . . . .117 H2
  Ilford IG6 . . . . .81 G2
Craven Hill, W2 . . . . .14 D5
Craven Hill Gdns, W2 . . . . .14 C5
Craven Hill Ms, W2 . . . . .14 D5
Craven Ms, SW11
  off Taybridge Rd 150 A3
Craven Pk, NW10 . . . . .106 E1
Craven Pk Ms, NW10 . . . . .106 E1
Craven Pk Rd, N15 . . . . .76 C6
  NW10 . . . . .106 E1
Craven Pas, WC2 . . . . .26 A1
Craven Rd, NW10 . . . . .106 D1
  W2 . . . . .14 D5
  W5 . . . . .105 F7
  Croydon CR0 . . . . .202 D1
  Kingston upon Thames KT2 . .181 J1
Craven St, WC2 . . . . .26 A1
Craven Ter, W2 . . . . .14 D5
Craven Wk, N16 . . . . .76 D7
Crawford Av, Wem. HA0 . . . . .87 G5
Crawford Cl, Islw. TW7 . . . . .144 B2
Crawford Est, SE5 . . . . .151 J2
Crawford Gdns, N13 . . . . .59 H3
  Northolt UB5 . . . . .103 F3
Crawford Ms, W1 . . . . .15 J2
Crawford Pas, EC1 . . . . .11 E6
Crawford Pl, W1 . . . . .15 H3
Crawford Rd, SE5 . . . . .151 J1
Crawford St, NW10
  off Fawood Av 88 D7
  W1 . . . . .15 H3
Crawley Rd, E10 . . . . .96 B1
  N22 . . . . .75 J2
  Enfield EN1 . . . . .44 C7
Crawshay Ct, SW9
  off Eythorne Rd 151 G1
Crawthew Gro, SE22 . . . . .152 C4
Craybrooke Rd, Sid. DA14 . . . . . .176 B4
Craybury End, SE9 . . . . .175 F2
Crayford Cl, E6
  off Neatscourt Rd 116 B5
Crayford Rd, N7 . . . . .92 D4
Crayke Hill, Chess. KT9 . . . . .195 H7
Cray Rd, Belv. DA17 . . . . .139 G6
  Sidcup DA14 . . . . .176 C7
Crealock Gro, Wdf.Grn. IG8 . . . . .63 F5
Crealock St, SW18 . . . . .149 E6
Creasy Est, SE1 . . . . .28 D6
Crebor St, SE22 . . . . .152 D6
Credenhall Dr, Brom. BR2 . . . . . .206 C1
Credenhill St, SW16 . . . . .168 C6
Crediton Hill, NW6 . . . . .90 E5
Crediton Rd, E16 off Pacific Rd . .115 G6
  NW10 . . . . .108 A1
Crediton Way, Esher (Clay.)
  KT10 . . . . .194 D5
Credon Rd, E13 . . . . .115 J2
  SE16 .133 E5
Creechurch La, EC3 . . . . .20 E4
Creechurch Pl, EC3 . . . . .21 E4
Creed Ct, EC4 off Ludgate Hill . .111 H6
Creed La, EC4 . . . . .19 H4
Creek, The, Sun. TW16 . . . . .178 A4
CREEKMOUTH, Bark. IG11 . . . . .118 A4
Creek Rd, SE8 . . . . .134 A6
  SE10 .134 A6
  Barking IG11 . . . . .117 J3
  East Molesey KT8 . . . . .180 B4
Creekside, SE8 . . . . .134 B7
Creeland Gro, SE6
  off Catford Hill 171 J1
Crefeld Cl, W6 . . . . .128 A6

Creffield Rd, W3 . . . . .105 J7
  W5 . . . . .105 J7
Creighton Av, E6 . . . . .116 A2
  N2 . . . . .73 H3
  N10 . . . . .74 A2
Creighton Cl, W12 . . . . .107 H7
Creighton Rd, N17 . . . . .60 B7
  NW6 .108 A2
  W5 . . . . .125 G3
Cremer St, E2 . . . . .13 F2
Cremorne Est, SW10 . . . . .31 E7
Cremorne Rd, SW10 . . . . .129 F7
Crescent, EC3 . . . . .21 F5
Crescent, The, E17 . . . . .77 H5
  N11 . . . . .57 J4
  NW2 . . . . .89 H3
  SW13 . . . . .147 F2
  SW19 . . . . .166 D3
  W3 . . . . .106 A6
  Barnet EN5 . . . . .40 E3
  Beckenham BR3 . . . . .190 A1
  Bexley DA5 . . . . .158 C7
  Croydon CR0 . . . . .188 A5
  Harrow HA2 . . . . .86 A1
  Hayes UB3 . . . . .121 F7
  Ilford IG2 . . . . .80 D6
  Loughton IG10 . . . . .48 A5
  New Malden KT3 . . . . .182 C2
  Sidcup DA14 . . . . .175 J4
  Southall UB1 . . . . .123 F2
  Surbiton KT6 . . . . .181 H5
  Sutton SM1 . . . . .199 G4
  Wembley HA0 . . . . .86 C2
  West Molesey KT8 . . . . .179 G4
  West Wickham BR4 . . . . .190 E6
Crescent Arc, SE10
  off Creek Rd 134 C6
Crescent Ct, Surb. KT6 . . . . .181 G5
Crescent Dr, Orp. BR5 . . . . .193 E6
Crescent Gdns, SW19 . . . . .166 D3
  Ruislip HA4 . . . . .66 B6
Crescent Gro, SW4 . . . . .150 C4
  Mitcham CR4 . . . . .185 H4
Crescent Ho, SE13
  off Ravensbourne Pl 154 B2
Crescent La, SW4 . . . . .150 D5
Crescent Ms, N22
  off Palace Gates Rd 74/75 E1
Crescent Pl, SW3 . . . . .31 G1
Crescent Ri, N22 . . . . .74 D1
  Barnet EN4 . . . . .41 H5
Crescent Rd, E4 . . . . .47 E7
  E6 . . . . .115 J1
  E10 . . . . .96 B2
  E13 .115 G1
  E18 . . . . .79 J2
  N3 . . . . .72 C1
  N8 . . . . .74 D7
  N9 . . . . .60 D1
  N11 . . . . .57 J4
  N15 off Carlingford Rd 75 H3
  N22 . . . . .74 D1
  SE18 . . . . .136 E5
  SW20 . . . . .184 A1
  Barnet EN4 . . . . .41 H5
  Beckenham BR3 . . . . .190 B2
  Bromley BR1 . . . . .173 G7
  Dagenham RM10 . . . . .101 H4
  Enfield EN2 . . . . .43 H3
  Kingston upon Thames KT2 . .164 A7
  Sidcup DA15 . . . . .175 J3
Crescent Row, EC1 . . . . .11 J6
Crescent Stables, SW15
  off Upper Richmond Rd 148 B4
Crescent St, N1 . . . . .93 F7
Crescent Vw, Loug. IG10 . . . . .48 A6
Crescent Way, N12 . . . . .57 H6
  SE4 .154 A3
  SW16 . . . . .169 F7
  Orpington BR6 . . . . .207 H5
Crescent Wd Rd, SE26 . . . . .170 D3
Cresford Rd, SW6 . . . . .148 E1
Crespigny Rd, NW4 . . . . .71 H6
Cressage Cl, Sthl. UB1 . . . . .103 G4
Cresset Rd, E9 . . . . .95 F6
Cresset St, SW4 . . . . .150 D3
Cressfield Cl, NW5 . . . . .92 A5
Cressida Rd, N19 . . . . .92 C1
Cressingham Gro, Sutt. SM1 . . . .199 F4
Cressingham Rd, SE13 . . . . .154 C3
  Edgware HA8 . . . . .54 D6
Cressington Cl, N16
  off Wordsworth Rd 94 B5
Cress Ms, Brom. BR1 . . . . .172 D5
Cresswell Gdns, SW5 . . . . .30 C3
Cresswell Pk, SE3 . . . . .155 F3
Cresswell Pl, SW10 . . . . .30 C3
Cresswell Rd, SE25 . . . . .188 D4
  Feltham TW13 . . . . .160 E4
  Twickenham TW1 . . . . .145 G6
Cresswell Way, N21 . . . . .43 G7
Cressy Ct, E1 off Cressy Pl 113 F5
  W6 . . . . .127 H3
Cressy Pl, E1 . . . . .113 F5
Cressy Rd, NW3 . . . . .91 J5
Crest, The, N13 . . . . .59 G4
  NW4 . . . . .71 J5

Crest, The, Surb. KT5 . . . . .182 A5
Crestbrook Av, N13 . . . . .59 H3
Crestbrook Pl, N13 . . . . .59 H3
Crestfield St, WC1 . . . . .10 B3
Crest Gdns, Ruis. HA4 . . . . .84 C3
Creston Way, Wor.Pk. KT4 . . . . . .198 A1
Crest Rd, NW2 . . . . .89 F3
  Bromley BR2 . . . . .191 F7
  South Croydon CR2 . . . . .202 E7
Crest Vw, Pnr. HA5 . . . . .66 D4
Crest Vw Dr, Orp. BR5 . . . . .193 E5
Crestway, SW15 . . . . .147 H6
Crestwood Way, Houns. TW4 . . . .143 F5
Creswell Dr, Beck. BR3 . . . . .190 B5
Creswick Rd, W3 . . . . .106 B7
Creswick Wk, E3
  off Malmesbury Rd 114 A3
  NW11 .72 C4
Creton St, SE18 . . . . .136 D3
Crewdson Rd, SW9 . . . . .131 G7
Crewe Pl, NW10 . . . . .107 F3
Crews St, E14 . . . . .134 A4
Crewys Rd, NW2 . . . . .90 C2
  SE15 . . . . .153 E2
Crichton Av, Wall. SM6 . . . . .200 D5
Crichton Rd, Cars. SM5 . . . . .199 J6
Crichton St, SW8
  off Westbury St 150 C2
Cricketers Arms Rd, Enf. EN2 . . . .43 J2
Cricketers Cl, N14 . . . . .42 C7
  Chessington KT9 . . . . .195 G4
Cricketers Ct, SE11 . . . . .35 G2
Cricketers Ms, SW18
  off East Hill 148/149 E5
Cricketers Ter, Cars. SM5
  off Wrythe La 199 H3
Cricketfield Rd, E5 . . . . .94 E4
Cricket Grn, Mitch. CR4 . . . . .185 J3
Cricket Grd Rd, Chis. BR7 . . . . . .192 E1
Cricket La, Beck. BR3 . . . . .171 H6
Cricklade Av, SW2 . . . . .169 E2
CRICKLEWOOD, NW2 . . . . .90 A3
Cricklewood Bdy, NW2 . . . . .89 J3
Cricklewood La, NW2 . . . . .90 A4
Cridland St, E15 off Church St . . .115 F1
Crieff Ct, Tedd. TW11 . . . . .163 F7
Crieff Rd, SW18 . . . . .149 F6
Criffel Av, SW2 . . . . .168 D2
Crimscott St, SE1 . . . . .29 E6
Crimsworth Rd, SW8 . . . . .150 D1
Crinan St, N1 . . . . .10 B1
Cringle St, SW8 . . . . .33 F7
Cripplegate St, EC2 . . . . .19 J1
Cripps Grn, Hayes UB4
  off Stratford Rd 102 B4
Crispe Ho, Bark. IG11
  off Dovehouse Mead 117 G2
Crispen Rd, Felt. TW13 . . . . .160 E4
Crispian Cl, NW10 . . . . .89 E4
Crispin Cl, Croy. CR0
  off Harrington Cl 200/201 E2
Crispin Cres, Croy. CR0 . . . . .200 D3
Crispin Rd, Edg. HA8 . . . . .54 C6
Crispin St, E1 . . . . .21 E2
Crisp Rd, W6 . . . . .127 J5
Cristowe Rd, SW6 . . . . .148 C2
Criterion Ms, N19 . . . . .92 D2
Crittall's Cor, Sid. DA14 . . . . .176 C7
Crockerton Rd, SW17 . . . . .167 J2
Crockham Way, SE9 . . . . .174 D4
Crocus Cl, Croy. CR0
  off Cornflower La 203 G1
Crocus Fld, Barn. EN5 . . . . .40 C6
Croft, The, E4 . . . . .62 E2
  NW10 . . . . .107 F2
  W5 . . . . .105 H5
  Barnet EN5 . . . . .40 A4
  Hounslow TW5 . . . . .123 E6
  Loughton IG10 . . . . .48 D2
  Pinner HA5 off Rayners La 67 F7
  Ruislip HA4 . . . . .84 C4
  Wembley HA0 . . . . .87 F5
Croft Av, W.Wick. BR4 . . . . .204 C1
Croft Cl, NW7 . . . . .54 E3
  Belvedere DA17 . . . . .139 F5
  Chislehurst BR7 . . . . .174 C4
  Hayes UB3 . . . . .121 F7
Croft Ct, Borwd. WD6
  off Kensington Way 38 D3
Croftdown Rd, NW5 . . . . .92 A3
Croft End Cl, Chess. KT9
  off Ashcroft Rd 195 J3
Crofters Cl, Islw. TW7
  off Ploughmans End 144 A5
Crofters Ct, SE8 off Croft St 133 H4
Crofters Way, NW1 . . . . .110 D1
Croft Gdns, W7 . . . . .124 D2
Croft Lo Cl, Wdf.Grn. IG8 . . . . . . .63 H6
Croft Ms, N12 . . . . .57 F3
Crofton Av, W4 . . . . .126 D7
  Bexley DA5 . . . . .158 D7
  Orpington BR6 . . . . .207 F2
Croftongate Way, SE4 . . . . .153 H5
Crofton Gro, E4 . . . . .62 D4
Crofton La, Orp. BR5, BR6 . . . . . .193 G7
Crofton Pk Rd, SE4 . . . . .153 J6
Crofton Rd, E13 . . . . .115 H4

Crofton Rd, SE5 . . . . .152 B1
  Orpington BR6 . . . . .206 D3
Crofton Ter, E5 off Studley Cl 95 H5
  Richmond TW9 . . . . .145 J4
Crofton Way, Barn. EN5
  off Wycherley Cres 40/41 E6
  Enfield EN2 . . . . .43 G2
Croft Rd, SW16 . . . . .187 G1
  SW19 . . . . .167 F7
  Bromley BR1 . . . . .173 G6
  Enfield EN3 . . . . .45 H1
  Sutton SM1 . . . . .199 H5
Croftside, SE25 off Sunny Bk 188 D3
Crofts La, N22 off Glendale Av 59 G2
Crofts Rd, Har. HA1 . . . . .68 D6
Crofts St, E1 . . . . .21 H6
Croft St, SE8 . . . . .133 H4
Croftway, NW3 . . . . .90 D4
  Richmond TW10 . . . . .163 E3
Croft Way, Sid. DA15 . . . . .175 H3
Crogsland Rd, NW1 . . . . .92 A7
Croham Cl, S.Croy. CR2 . . . . .202 B6
Croham Manor Rd, S.Croy.
  CR2 .202 B5
Croham Mt, S.Croy. CR2 . . . . . . .202 B7
Croham Pk Av, S.Croy. CR2 . . . . .202 C5
Croham Rd, S.Croy. CR2 . . . . . . .202 A5
Croham Valley Rd, S.Croy. CR2 . . .202 C6
Croindene Rd, SW16 . . . . .187 E1
Cromartie Rd, N19 . . . . .74 D1
Cromarty Rd, Edg. HA8 . . . . .54 B2
Crombie Cl, Ilf. IG4 . . . . .80 C5
Crombie Rd, Sid. DA15 . . . . .175 G1
Crome Rd, NW10 . . . . .88 E6
Cromer Pl, Orp. BR6
  off Andover Rd 207 G1
Cromer Rd, E10 off James La 78 D6
  N17 . . . . .76 D2
  SE25 . . . . .188 E3
  SW17 . . . . .168 A6
  Barnet EN5 . . . . .41 F4
  Hounslow (Hthrw Air.) TW6 . . .140 D3
  Romford RM7 . . . . .83 J6
  Romford (Chad.Hth) RM6 . . . . .83 E6
  Woodford Green IG8 . . . . .63 G4
Cromer Rd W, Houns. (Hthrw Air.)
  TW6 .140 D3
Cromer St, WC1 . . . . .10 B4
Cromer Ter, E8 off Ferncliff Rd 94 D5
Cromer Vil Rd, SW18 . . . . .148 C6
Cromford Cl, Orp. BR6 . . . . .207 H3
Cromford Path, E5
  off Overbury St 95 G4
Cromford Rd, SW18 . . . . .148 D5
Cromford Way, N.Mal. KT3 . . . . . .182 D1
Cromlix Cl, Chis. BR7 . . . . .192 E2
Crompton St, W2 . . . . .6 E6
Cromwell Av, N6 . . . . .92 B1
  W6 . . . . .127 H5
  Bromley BR2 . . . . .191 H4
  New Malden KT3 . . . . .183 F5
Cromwell Cl, E1
  off Vaughan Way 132 D1
  N2 . . . . .73 G4
  W3 off High St 126 C1
  Bromley BR2 . . . . .191 H4
Cromwell Cres, SW5 . . . . .128 C4
Cromwell Gdns, SW7 . . . . .23 F6
Cromwell Gro, W6 . . . . .127 J3
Cromwell Highwalk, EC2
  off Beech St 111 J5
Cromwell Ind Est, E10 . . . . .95 H1
Cromwell Ms, SW7 . . . . .31 F1
Cromwell Pl, N6 . . . . .92 B1
  SW7 . . . . .31 F1
  SW14 . . . . .146 C3
  W3 off Grove Pl 126 C1
Cromwell Rd, E7 . . . . .97 J7
  E17 . . . . .78 C5
  N3 . . . . .73 F1
  N10 . . . . .58 A7
  SW5 .128 E4
  SW7 . . . . .30 E1
  SW9 .151 H1
  SW19 . . . . .166 D5
  Beckenham BR3 . . . . .189 H2
  Croydon CR0 . . . . .188 A7
  Feltham TW13 . . . . .160 B1
  Hounslow TW3 . . . . .143 G4
  Kingston upon Thames KT2 . . .181 H1
  Teddington TW11 . . . . .162 D6
  Wembley HA0 . . . . .105 H2
  Worcester Park KT4 . . . . .196 D3
Cromwell St, Houns. TW3 . . . . . . .143 G4
Cromwell Twr, EC2 . . . . .20 A1
Crondace Rd, SW6 . . . . .148 D1
Crondall Ct, N1 . . . . .12 D2
Crondall Ho, SW15
  off Fontley Way 165 G1
Crondall St, N1 . . . . .12 C2
Cronin St, SE15 . . . . .132 C7
Crooked Billet, SW19
  off Woodhayes Rd 165 J6
Crooked Billet Roundabout,
  E17 . . . . .62 A7
Crooked Billet Yd, E2
  off Kingsland Rd 112 B3

Crooked Usage, N3 . . . . .72 B3
Crooke Rd, SE8 . . . . .133 H5
Crookham Rd, SW6 . . . . .148 C1
Crook Log, Bexh. DA6 . . . . .158 D3
Crookston Rd, SE9 . . . . .156 D3
Croombs Rd, E16 . . . . .115 J5
Crooms Hill, SE10 . . . . .134 D7
Crooms Hill Gro, SE10 . . . . .134 C7
Cropley Ct, N1 . . . . .12 B1
Cropley St, N1 . . . . .12 B1
Croppath Rd, Dag. RM10 . . . . . . .101 G4
Cropthorne Ct, W9 . . . . .6 D4
Crosby Cl, Felt. TW13 . . . . .160 E4
Crosby Ct, SE1 . . . . .28 B3
Crosby Rd, E7 . . . . .97 G6
  Dagenham RM10 . . . . .119 H2
Crosby Row, SE1 . . . . .28 B4
Crosby Sq, EC3 . . . . .20 D4
Crosby Wk, E8 off Laurel St 94 C6
  SW2 .151 G7
Crosier Cl, SE3 . . . . .156 B1
Crosland Pl, SW11
  off Taybridge Rd 150 A3
Cross Av, SE10 . . . . .134 D6
Crossbow Rd, Chig. IG7 . . . . .65 J5
Crossbrook Rd, SE3 . . . . .156 B2
Cross Cl, SE15
  off Gordon Rd 152/153 E1
Cross Deep, Twick. TW1 . . . . .162 C2
Cross Deep Gdns, Twick. TW1 . . . .162 C2
Crossfield Rd, N17 . . . . .75 J3
  NW3 . . . . .91 G7
Crossfields, Loug. IG10 . . . . .48 D5
Crossfield St, SE8 . . . . .134 A7
Crossford St, SW9 . . . . .151 F2
Crossgate, Edg. HA8 . . . . .54 A3
  Greenford UB6 . . . . .87 E6
Cross Keys Cl, N9
  off Balham Rd 60 D2
  W1 . . . . .16 C2
Cross Keys Sq, EC1 . . . . .19 J2
Cross Lances Rd, Houns. TW3 . . .143 H4
Crossland Rd, Th.Hth. CR7 . . . . . .187 H6
Crosslands Av, W5 . . . . .125 J1
  Southall UB2 . . . . .123 F5
Crosslands Rd, Epsom KT19 . . . . .196 D6
Cross La, EC3 . . . . .20 D6
  N8 . . . . .75 F3
  Bexley DA5 . . . . .159 F7
Crosslet St, SE17 . . . . .36 C1
Crosslet Vale, SE10 . . . . .154 B1
Crossley St, N7 . . . . .93 G6
Crossmead, SE9 . . . . .174 C1
Crossmead Av, Grnf. UB6 . . . . . . .103 G3
Crossmount Ho, SE5 . . . . .35 J7
Crossness La, SE28 . . . . .118 D7
★ Crossness Pumping Sta,
  SE2 .119 E6
Crossness Rd, Bark. IG11 . . . . . . .117 J3
Cross Rd, E4 . . . . .62 E1
  N11 . . . . .58 B5
  N22 . . . . .59 G7
  SE5 .152 B2
  SW19 . . . . .166 D7
  Bromley BR2 . . . . .206 B2
  Croydon CR0 . . . . .202 A1
  Enfield EN1 . . . . .44 B4
  Feltham TW13 . . . . .160 E4
  Harrow HA1 . . . . .68 A4
  Harrow (S.Har.) HA2 . . . . .85 H3
  Harrow (Wldste) HA3 . . . . .68 D2
  Kingston upon Thames KT2 . . .163 J7
  Romford RM7 . . . . .83 G3
  Romford (Chad.Hth) RM6 . . . . .82 C7
  Sidcup DA14 off Sidcup Hill . . .176 B4
  Sutton SM2 . . . . .199 G5
  Woodford Green IG8 . . . . .64 C6
Cross Rds, Loug. (High Beach)
  IG10 .47 H2
Cross St, N1 . . . . .111 H1
  SW13 . . . . .147 E2
  Hampton (Hmptn H.) TW12 . . .161 J5
Crossthwaite Av, SE5 . . . . .152 A4
Crosswall, EC3 . . . . .21 F5
Crossway, N12 . . . . .57 G6
  N16 . . . . .94 B5
  NW9 . . . . .71 F4
  SE28 .118 C6
  SW20 . . . . .183 J4
  W13 .104 D3
  Dagenham RM8 . . . . .100 C3
  Enfield EN1 . . . . .44 B7
  Hayes UB3 . . . . .122 A1
  Orpington BR5 . . . . .193 G4
  Pinner HA5 . . . . .66 B2
  Ruislip HA4 . . . . .84 C4
  Woodford Green IG8 . . . . .63 J4
Crossway, The, N22 . . . . .59 H7
  SE9 .174 A2
Cross Way, The, Har. HA3 . . . . .68 B2
Crossways, N21 . . . . .43 J6
  South Croydon CR2 . . . . .203 H7
Crossways, The, Houns. TW5 . . . .123 F7
  Wembley HA9 . . . . .88 A2
Crossways Rd, Beck. BR3 . . . . . . .190 A4
  Mitcham CR4 . . . . .186 B3
Croston St, E8 . . . . .112 D1

Crothall Cl, N13 . . . . .59 F3
Crouch Av, Bark. IG11 . . . . . . .118 B2
Crouch Cl, Beck. BR3
   off Abbey La 172 A6
Crouch Cft, SE9 . . . . .174 D7
CROUCH END, N8 . . . . .74 C6
Crouch End Hill, N8 . . . . .74 D7
Crouch Hall Rd, N8 . . . . .74 D6
Crouch Hill, N4 . . . . .74 E6
  N8 . . . . .74 E6
Crouchman's Cl, SE26 . . . . . . .170 C3
Crouch Rd, NW10 . . . . .88 D7
Crowborough Path, Wat. WD19
   off Prestwick Rd 50 D4
Crowborough Rd, SW17 . . . . . .168 A6
Crowden Way, SE28 . . . . .118 C7
Crowder St, E1 . . . . .112 E7
Crowfoot Cl, E9
   off Lee Conservancy Rd 95 J5
  SE28 off Hill Vw Dr 137 H1
Crowhurst Cl, SW9 . . . . .151 G2
Crowland Av, Hayes UB3 . . . . .121 H4
Crowland Gdns, N14 . . . . .42 E7
Crowland Rd, N15 . . . . .76 C5
  Thornton Heath CR7 . . . . . . .188 A4
Crowlands Av, Rom. RM7 . . . . .83 H6
Crowland Ter, N1 . . . . .94 A7
Crowland Wk, Mord. SM4 . . . . .185 E6
Crow La, Rom. RM7 . . . . .83 F7
Crowley Cres, Croy. CR0 . . . . .201 G5
Crowline Wk, N1
   off St. Paul's Rd 94 A6
Crowmarsh Gdns, SE23
   off Tyson Rd 153 F7
Crown Arc, Kings.T. KT1
   off Union St 181 G2
Crown Cl, E3 . . . . .114 A1
  N22 off Winkfield Rd 75 G1
  NW6 . . . . .90 E6
  NW7 . . . . .55 F2
  Hayes UB3 . . . . .121 J2
  Walton-on-Thames KT12 . . . .178 C7
Crown Ct, EC2 . . . . .20 A4
  SE12 . . . . .155 H6
  WC2 . . . . .18 B4
  Bromley BR2
   off Victoria Rd 192 A5
Crown Dale, SE19 . . . . .169 H6
Crowndale Rd, NW1 . . . . .9 F1
Crownfield Av, Ilf. IG2 . . . . .81 H5
Crownfield Rd, E15 . . . . .96 D5
Crown Hill, Croy. CR0
   off Church St 201 J2
Crownhill Rd, NW10 . . . . .107 F1
  Woodford Green IG8 . . . . . . .64 B7
Crown Ho, Bark. IG11
   off Linton Rd 99 F7
Crown La, N14 . . . . .58 C1
  SW16 . . . . .169 G5
  Bromley BR2 . . . . .192 A5
  Chislehurst BR7 . . . . .193 F1
  Morden SM4 . . . . .184 E3
Crown La Gdns, SW16
   off Crown La 169 G5
Crown La Spur, Brom. BR2 . . . .192 A6
Crownmead Way, Rom. RM7 . . .83 H4
Crown Ms, E13
   off Waghorn Rd 115 J1
  W6 . . . . .127 G4
Crown Office Row, EC4 . . . . . . .19 E5
Crown Pas, SW1 . . . . .25 G2
  Kingston upon Thames KT1
   off Church St 181 G2
Crown Pl, EC2 . . . . .20 D1
  NW5 off Kentish Town Rd 92 B6
  SE16 off Varcoe Rd 132 E5
Crown Pt Par, SE19
   off Beulah Hill 169 H6
Crown Reach, SW1
   off Grosvenor Rd 130 D5
Crown Rd, N10 . . . . .58 A7
  Borehamwood WD6 . . . . . . .38 A1
  Enfield EN1 . . . . .44 E4
  Ilford IG6 . . . . .81 G4
  Morden SM4 . . . . .184 E4
  New Malden KT3 . . . . .182 C1
  Ruislip HA4 . . . . .84 D5
  Sutton SM1 . . . . .198 E4
  Twickenham TW1 . . . . .145 E6
Crownstone Rd, SW2 . . . . .151 G5
Crown St, SE5 . . . . .36 A7
  W3 . . . . .126 B1
  Dagenham RM10 . . . . .101 J6
  Harrow HA2 . . . . .86 A1
Crown Ter, Rich. TW9 . . . . . . .145 J4
Crowntree Cl, Islw. TW7 . . . . . .124 C6
Crown Wk, Wem. HA9 . . . . .87 J3
Crown Way, West Dr. UB7 . . . . .120 C1
Crown Wds La, SE9 . . . . .157 E2
  SE18 . . . . .157 E2
Crown Wds Way, SE9 . . . . .157 G5
Crown Wks, E2
   off Temple St 112/113 E2
Crown Yd, Houns. TW3
   off High St 143 J3
Crowshott Av, Stan. HA7 . . . . . .69 F1
Crows Rd, E15 . . . . .114 D3

Crows Rd, Bark. IG11 . . . . .99 E6
Crowther Av, Brent. TW8 . . . . .125 H4
Crowther Rd, SE25 . . . . .188 D4
Crowthorne Cl, SW18 . . . . .166 C1
Crowthorne Rd, W10 . . . . .108 A6
Croxden Cl, Edg. HA8 . . . . .69 J3
Croxden Wk, Mord. SM4 . . . . . .185 F6
Croxford Gdns, N22 . . . . .59 H7
Croxley Rd, W9 . . . . .108 C3
Croxted Cl, SE21 . . . . .151 J7
Croxted Ms, SE24
   off Croxted Rd 151 J6
Croxted Rd, SE21 . . . . .151 J7
  SE24 . . . . .151 J7
Croyde Av, Grnf. UB6 . . . . .103 J3
  Hayes UB3 . . . . .121 H4
Croyde Cl, Sid. DA15 . . . . .157 G7
CROYDON, CR0 . . . . .202 A2
Croydon Flyover, Croy. CR0 . . . .201 H4
Croydon Gro, Croy. CR0 . . . . . .201 H1
★ Croydon Mus, Croy. CR0 . . .201 J2
Croydon Rd, E13 . . . . .115 F4
  SE20 . . . . .188 E2
  Beckenham BR3 . . . . .189 H4
  Bromley BR2 . . . . .205 F3
  Croydon (Bedd.) CR0 . . . . . .201 E4
  Croydon (Mitch.Com.) CR0 . . .186 A4
  Hounslow (Hthrw Air.) TW6 . . .140 E2
  Keston BR2 . . . . .205 J3
  Mitcham CR4 . . . . .186 A4
  Wallington SM6 . . . . .200 B4
  West Wickham BR4 . . . . . . .204 B4
Croyland Rd, N9 . . . . .60 D1
Croylands Dr, Surb. KT6 . . . . . .181 H7
Croysdale Av, Sun. TW16 . . . . .178 A3
Crozier Ho, SE3
   off Ebdon Way 155 H3
Crozier Ter, E9 . . . . .95 G5
Crucible Cl, Rom. RM6 . . . . . . .82 B6
Crucifix La, SE1 . . . . .28 D3
Cruden Ho, SE17 . . . . .35 G6
Cruden St, N1 . . . . .111 H1
Cruikshank Rd, E15 . . . . .97 E4
Cruikshank St, WC1 . . . . .10 E3
Crummock Gdns, NW9 . . . . . . .70 E5
Crumpsall St, SE2 . . . . .138 C4
Crundale Av, NW9 . . . . .70 A5
Crunden Rd, S.Croy. CR2 . . . . .202 A7
Crusader Gdns, Croy. CR0
   off Cotelands 202 B3
Crusoe Ms, N16 . . . . .94 A2
Crusoe Rd, Mitch. CR4 . . . . . . .167 J7
Crutched Friars, EC3 . . . . .21 E5
Crutchley Rd, SE6 . . . . .173 E2
Crystal Ct, SE19
   off College Rd 170 C5
Crystal Ho, SE18
   off Spinel Cl 137 J5
Crystal Palace Caravan Club,
  SE19 . . . . .170 C5
★ Crystal Palace FC, SE25 . . . .188 B4
★ Crystal Palace Nat Sport Cen,
  SE19 . . . . .170 D6
Crystal Palace Par, SE19 . . . . . .170 C6
★ Crystal Palace Pk, SE19 . . . .170 C5
Crystal Palace Pk Rd, SE26 . . . .170 D5
Crystal Palace Rd, SE22 . . . . . .152 D4
Crystal Palace Sta Rd, SE19 . . .170 D6
Crystal Ter, SE19 . . . . .170 A6
Crystal Vw Ct, Brom. BR1
   off Winlaton Rd 172 D4
Crystal Way, Dag. RM8 . . . . . . .100 C1
  Harrow HA1 . . . . .68 C5
Crystal Wf, N1 off Graham Rd . . .111 H2
Cuba Dr, Enf. EN3 . . . . .45 F2
Cuba St, E14 . . . . .134 A2
Cubitt Sq, Sthl. UB2
   off Windmill Av 123 J1
Cubitt Steps, E14
   off Cabot Sq 134 A1
Cubitt St, WC1 . . . . .10 C4
  Croydon CR0 . . . . .201 F5
Cubitts Yd, WC2 . . . . .18 B5
Cubitt Ter, SW4 . . . . .150 C3
CUBITT TOWN, E14 . . . . .134 C3
Cuckoo Av, W7 . . . . .104 B4
Cuckoo Dene, W7 . . . . .104 A5
Cuckoo Hall La, N9 . . . . .45 F7
Cuckoo Hill, Pnr. HA5 . . . . .66 C3
Cuckoo Hill Dr, Pnr. HA5 . . . . . .66 C3
Cuckoo Hill Rd, Pnr. HA5 . . . . . .66 C4
Cuckoo La, W7 . . . . .104 B7
Cudas Cl, Epsom KT19 . . . . . . .197 F4
Cuddington Av, Wor.Pk. KT4 . . .197 F3
Cudham St, SE6 . . . . .154 C7
Cudworth St, E1 . . . . .113 E4
Cuff Cres, SE9 . . . . .156 A6
Cuff Pt, E2 . . . . .13 F3
Culford Gdns, SW3 . . . . .32 A2
Culford Gro, N1 . . . . .94 B6
Culford Ms, N1 off Culford Rd . .94 B6
Culford Rd, N1 . . . . .94 B7
Culgaith Gdns, Enf. EN2 . . . . . .42 E4
Cullen Way, NW10 . . . . .106 C4
Culling Rd, SE16
   off Lower Rd 133 F3
Cullington Cl, Har. HA3 . . . . . . .68 D4

Cullingworth Rd, NW10 . . . . . . .89 G5
Culloden Cl, SE16 . . . . .37 J4
Culloden Rd, Enf. EN2 . . . . .43 H2
Culloden St, E14 . . . . .114 C6
Cullum St, EC3 . . . . .20 D5
Culmington Rd, W13 . . . . .125 F2
  South Croydon CR2 . . . . . . .133 E7
Culmore Rd, SE15 . . . . .133 E7
Culmstock Rd, SW11 . . . . .150 A5
Culpeper Cl, Ilf. IG6 . . . . .65 E6
Culpepper Cl, N18
   off Dysons Rd 60 E5
Culross Cl, N15 . . . . .75 J4
Culross St, W1 . . . . .16 B6
Culsac Rd, Surb. KT6 . . . . .195 H2
Culverden Rd, SW12 . . . . .168 C2
  Watford WD19 . . . . .50 B3
Culver Gro, Stan. HA7 . . . . .69 F2
Culverhouse Gdns, SW16 . . . . .169 F3
Culverlands Cl, Stan. HA7 . . . . .52 E4
Culverley Rd, SE6 . . . . .172 B1
Culvers Av, Cars. SM5 . . . . . . .199 J2
Culvers Retreat, Cars. SM5 . . . .199 J1
Culverstone Cl, Brom. BR2 . . . .191 F6
Culvers Way, Cars. SM5 . . . . . .199 J2
Culvert Pl, SW11 . . . . .150 A2
Culvert Rd, N15 . . . . .76 B5
  SW11 . . . . .149 J2
Culworth St, NW8 . . . . .7 G2
Cumberland Av, NW10 . . . . . . .106 B3
  Welling DA16 . . . . .157 H3
Cumberland Cl, E8 . . . . .94 C6
  SW20 off Lansdowne Rd 166 A7
  Ilford IG6 . . . . .81 F1
  Twickenham TW1
   off Westmorland Cl 144/145 E6
Cumberland Ct, Well. DA16
   off Bellegrove Rd 157 H2
Cumberland Cres, W14 . . . . . . .128 B4
Cumberland Dr, Bexh. DA7 . . . .138 E7
  Chessington KT9 . . . . .195 J3
  Esher KT10 . . . . .194 D2
Cumberland Gdns, NW4 . . . . . .72 B2
  WC1 . . . . .10 D3
Cumberland Gate, W1 . . . . .15 J5
Cumberland Mkt, NW1 . . . . .9 E3
Cumberland Mkt Est, NW1 . . . . .9 E3
Cumberland Mills Sq, E14
   off Saunders Ness Rd 134 D5
Cumberland Pk, NW10 . . . . . . .107 G3
  W3 . . . . .106 C7
Cumberland Pl, NW1 . . . . .8 D3
  SE6 . . . . .173 F1
  Sunbury-on-Thames TW16 . . .178 A4
Cumberland Rd, E12 . . . . .98 A4
  E13 . . . . .115 H5
  E17 . . . . .77 H2
  N9 .61 F1
  N22 . . . . .75 F2
  SE25 . . . . .189 E6
  SW13 . . . . .147 F1
  W3 . . . . .106 C7
  W7 . . . . .124 C2
  Bromley BR2 . . . . .190 E4
  Harrow HA1 . . . . .67 H5
  Richmond TW9 . . . . .126 A7
  Stanmore HA7 . . . . .69 J3
Cumberland St, SW1 . . . . .32 E3
Cumberland Ter, NW1 . . . . .8 D2
Cumberland Ter Ms, NW1 . . . . .8 D2
Cumberland Vil, W3
   off Cumberland Rd 106 C7
Cumberlow Av, SE25 . . . . .188 C3
Cumberton Rd, N17 . . . . .76 A1
Cumbrae Gdns, Surb. KT6 . . . . .195 G2
Cumbrian Gdns, NW2 . . . . .90 A2
★ Cuming Mus, SE17 . . . . .35 J2
Cumming St, N1 . . . . .10 C2
Cumnor Gdns, Epsom KT17 . . . .197 G6
Cumnor Rd, Sutt. SM2 . . . . . . .199 F6
Cunard Cres, N21 . . . . .44 A6
Cunard Pl, EC3 . . . . .20 E4
Cunard Rd, NW10 . . . . .106 D3
Cunard St, SE5 off Albany Rd . .132 B6
Cunard Wk, SE16 . . . . .133 H4
Cundy Rd, E16 . . . . .115 J6
Cundy St, SW1 . . . . .32 C2
Cundy St Est, SW1 . . . . .32 C2
Cunliffe Rd, Epsom KT19 . . . . . .197 F4
Cunliffe St, SW16 . . . . .168 C6
Cunningham Cl, Rom. RM6 . . . .82 C5
  West Wickham BR4 . . . . . . .204 B2
Cunningham Pk, Har. HA1 . . . . .67 J5
Cunningham Pl, NW8 . . . . .7 E5
Cunningham Rd, N15 . . . . .76 D4
Cunnington St, W4 . . . . .126 C3
Cupar Rd, SW11 . . . . .150 A1
Cupola Cl, Brom. BR1 . . . . .173 H5
Cureton St, SW1 . . . . .33 J2
Curfew Ho, Bark. IG11
   off St. Ann's 117 F1
Curie Gdns, NW9
   off Pasteur Cl 70/71 E2
Curlew Cl, SE28 . . . . .118 D7
Curlew Ct, Surb. KT6 . . . . .195 J3
Curlew Ho, Enf. EN3
   off Allington Ct 45 G5
Curlew St, SE1 . . . . .29 F3

Curlew Ter, Ilf. IG5
   off Tiptree Cres 80 D3
Curlew Way, Hayes UB4 . . . . . .102 D5
Curness St, SE13
   off Lewisham High St 154 C4
Curnick's La, SE27
   off Chapel Rd 169 J4
Curnock Est, NW1
   off Plender St 110 C1
Curran Av, Sid. DA15 . . . . .157 J5
  Wallington SM6 . . . . .200 A3
Currey Rd, Grnf. UB6 . . . . .86 A6
Curricle St, W3 . . . . .126 E1
Currie Hill Cl, SW19 . . . . .166 C4
Curry Ri, NW7 . . . . .56 A6
Cursitor St, EC4 . . . . .18 E3
Curtain Pl, EC2 off Curtain Rd . .112 B3
Curtain Rd, EC2 . . . . .12 D6
Curthwaite Gdns, Enf. EN2 . . . .42 D4
Curtis Dr, W3 . . . . .106 D6
Curtis Fld Rd, SW16 . . . . .169 F4
Curtis La, Wem. HA0
   off Montrose Cres 87 H6
Curtis Rd, Epsom KT19 . . . . . . .196 C4
  Hounslow TW4 . . . . .143 F7
Curtis St, SE1 . . . . .37 F1
Curtis Way, SE1 . . . . .37 F1
  SE28 off Tawney Rd 118 B7
Curve, The, W12 . . . . .107 G7
Curwen Av, E7
   off Woodford Rd 97 H4
Curwen Rd, W12 . . . . .127 G2
Curzon Av, Enf. EN3 . . . . .45 G5
  Stanmore HA7 . . . . .68 D7
Curzon Cl, Orp. BR6 . . . . .207 G4
  Barking IG11 . . . . .117 J2
Curzon Cres, NW10 . . . . .89 F7
  Barking IG11 . . . . .117 J2
Curzon Gate, W1 . . . . .24 C2
Curzon Pl, Pnr. HA5 . . . . .66 C5
Curzon Rd, N10 . . . . .74 B2
  W5 . . . . .105 E4
  Thornton Heath CR7 . . . . . . .187 G6
Curzon Sq, W1 . . . . .24 C2
Curzon St, W1 . . . . .24 C2
Cusack Cl, Twick. TW1
   off Waldegrave Rd 162 C4
CUSTOM HOUSE, E16 . . . . . . .116 A6
Custom Ho Reach, SE16 . . . . . .133 J2
Custom Ho Wk, EC3 . . . . .20 D6
Cut, The, SE1 . . . . .27 F3
Cutcombe Rd, SE5 . . . . .151 J2
Cuthberga Cl, Bark. IG11
   off George St 99 F7
Cuthbert Gdns, SE25 . . . . .188 B3
Cuthbert Rd, E17 . . . . .78 C3
  N18 off Fairfield Rd 60 D5
  Croydon CR0 . . . . .201 H2
Cuthbert St, W2 . . . . .15 E1
Cuthill Wk, SE5 . . . . .152 A1
Cutlers Gdns, E1 . . . . .21 E3
Cutlers Gdns Arc, EC2
   off Cutler St 112 B6
Cutlers Sq, E14
   off Britannia Rd 134 A4
Cutlers Ter, N1
   off Balls Pond Rd 94 A6
Cutler St, E1 . . . . .21 E3
Cutthroat All, Rich. TW10
   off Ham St 163 F2
★ Cutty Sark, SE10 . . . . .134 C6
Cutty Sark Gdns, SE10
   off King William Wk 134 C6
Cuxton Cl, Bexh. DA6 . . . . .158 E5
Cyclamen Cl, Hmptn. TW12
   off Gresham Rd 161 G6
Cyclamen Way, Epsom KT19 . . .196 B5
Cyclops Ms, E14 . . . . .134 A4
Cygnet Av, Felt. TW14 . . . . . . .142 C7
Cygnet Cl, NW10 . . . . .88 D5
  Borehamwood WD6 . . . . . . .38 C1
Cygnets, The, Felt. TW13 . . . . .160 E4
Cygnet St, E1 . . . . .13 G5
Cygnet Way, Hayes UB4 . . . . . .102 D5
Cygnus Business Cen, NW10 . . .89 F6
Cymbeline Ct, Har. HA1 . . . . . . .68 C6
Cynthia St, N1 . . . . .10 D2
Cyntra Pl, E8 . . . . .95 E7
Cypress Av, Twick. TW2 . . . . . .143 J7
Cypress Gdns, SE4 . . . . .153 H5
Cypress Gro, Ilf. IG6 . . . . .65 H6
Cypress Pl, W1 . . . . .9 G6
Cypress Rd, SE25 . . . . .188 B2
  Harrow HA3 . . . . .68 A2
Cypress Tree Cl, Sid. DA15
   off White Oak Gdns 157 J7
Cyprus, N3 . . . . .72 B2
Cyprus Cl, N4 off Atterbury Rd . .75 H6
Cyprus Gdns, N3 . . . . .72 B2
Cyprus Pl, E2 . . . . .113 F2
  E6 . . . . .116 D7
Cyprus Rd, N3 . . . . .72 C2
  N9 .60 C2
Cyprus Roundabout, E16
   off Royal Albert Way 116 D7
Cyprus St, E2 . . . . .113 F2
Cyrena Rd, SE22 . . . . .152 C6
Cyril Mans, SW11 . . . . .149 J1

Cyril Rd, Bexh. DA7 ....159 E2
Cyrus St, EC1 ....11 H5
Czar St, SE8 ....134 A6

D

Dabbs Hill La, Nthlt. UB5 ..85 H5
Dabin Cres, SE10 ....154 C1
Dacca St, SE8 ....133 J4
Dace Av, Ilf. IG5 ....80 D2
Dace Rd, E3 ....96 A7
Dacre Cl, Chig. IG7 ....65 F4
  Greenford UB6 ....103 H2
Dacre Gdns, SE13 ....154 E4
  Borehamwood WD6 ....38 D5
  Chigwell IG7 ....65 F4
Dacre Pk, SE13 ....155 E3
Dacre Pl, SE13 ....154 E3
Dacre Rd, E11 ....97 F1
  E13 ....115 H1
  Croydon CR0 ....187 E7
Dacres Rd, SE23 ....171 G3
Dacre St, SW1 ....25 H5
Dade Way, Sthl. UB2 ....123 F5
Daerwood Cl, Brom. BR2 ....206 C1
Daffodil Cl, Croy. CR0
  off Primrose La 203 G1
Daffodil Gdns, Ilf. IG1 ....98 E5
Daffodil Pl, Hmptn. TW12
  off Gresham Rd 161 G6
Daffodil St, W12 ....107 F7
Dafforne Rd, SW17 ....168 A3
DAGENHAM, RM8 - RM10 ....101 G6
Dagenham Av, Dag. RM9 ....118 E1
Dagenham Rd, E10 ....95 J1
  Dagenham RM10 ....101 J4
Dagmar Av, Wem. HA9 ....87 J4
Dagmar Gdns, NW10 ....108 A2
Dagmar Ms, Sthl. UB2
  off Dagmar Rd 122/123 E3
Dagmar Pas, N1 off Cross St 111 H1
Dagmar Rd, N4 ....75 G7
  N15 off Cornwall Rd 76 A4
  N22 ....74 D1
  SE5 ....152 B1
  SE25 ....188 B5
  Dagenham RM10 ....101 J7
  Kingston upon Thames KT2 ....181 J1
  Southall UB2 ....122 E3
Dagmar Ter, N1 ....111 H1
Dagnall Pk, SE25 ....188 B6
Dagnall Rd, SE25 ....188 B5
Dagnall St, SW11 ....149 J2
Dagnan Rd, SW12 ....150 B7
Dagonet Gdns, Brom. BR1 ....173 G3
Dagonet Rd, Brom. BR1 ....173 G3
Dahlia Gdns, Ilf. IG1 ....99 E6
  Mitcham CR4 ....186 D4
Dahlia Rd, SE2 ....138 B4
Dahomey Rd, SW16 ....168 C6
Daimler Way, Wall. SM6 ....200 E7
Daines Cl, E12
  off Colchester Av 98 C3
Dainford Cl, Brom. BR1 ....172 D5
Dainton Cl, Brom. BR1 ....191 H1
Daintry Cl, Har. HA3 ....68 D4
Daintry Way, E9 off Osborne Rd ..95 J6
Dairsie Rd, SE9 ....156 D3
Dairy Cl, NW10 ....107 G1
  Thornton Heath CR7 ....187 J2
Dairy Fm Pl, SE15
  off Queens Rd 153 F1
Dairy La, SE18 ....136 C4
Dairyman Cl, NW2
  off Claremont Rd 90 B3
Dairy Ms, SW9 ....151 E3
Dairy Wk, SW19 ....166 B4
Daisy Cl, Croy. CR0
  off Primrose La 203 G1
Daisy Dobbins Wk, N19
  off Hillrise Rd 74/75 E7
Daisy La, SW6 ....148 D3
Daisy Rd, E16
  off Cranberry La 114/115 E4
  E18 ....79 H2
Dakota Cl, Wall. SM6 ....201 F7
Dakota Gdns, E6 ....116 B4
  Northolt UB5
  off Argus Way 102/103 E3
Dalberg Rd, SW2 ....151 G4
Dalberg Way, SE2
  off Lanridge Rd 138 D3
Dalby Rd, SW18 ....149 F4
Dalby St, NW5 ....92 B6
Dalcross Rd, Houns. TW4 ....142 E2
Dale, The, Kes. BR2 ....206 A4
Dale Av, Edg. HA8 ....69 J1
  Hounslow TW4 ....143 E3
Dalebury Rd, SW17 ....167 H2
Dale Cl, SE3 ....155 G3
  Barnet EN5 ....41 E6
  Pinner HA5 ....66 B1
Dale Gdns, Wdf.Grn. IG8 ....63 H4
Dale Grn Rd, N11 ....58 B3
Dale Gro, N12 ....57 F5
Daleham Gdns, NW3 ....91 G5

Daleham Ms, NW3 ....91 G6
Dalehead, NW1 ....9 F2
Dalemain Ms, E16
  off Hanover Av 135 G1
Dale Pk Av, Cars. SM5 ....199 J2
Dale Pk Rd, SE19 ....187 J1
Dale Rd, NW5 off Grafton Rd 92 A5
  SE17 ....35 H4
  Greenford UB6 ....103 H5
  Sutton SM1 ....198 C4
Dale Row, W11
  off St. Marks Rd 108 B6
Daleside, Chig. IG7 ....65 F3
Daleside Gdns, SW16 ....168 B5
  Epsom KT19 ....196 D6
Dales Path, Borwd. WD6
  off Farriers Way 38 D5
Dales Rd, Borwd. WD6 ....38 D5
Dale St, W4 ....126 E5
Dale Vw Av, E4 ....62 C2
Dale Vw Cres, E4 ....62 C2
Dale Vw Gdns, E4 ....62 D3
Daleview Rd, N15 ....76 B6
Dalewood Gdns, Wor.Pk. KT4 ....197 H2
Dale Wd Rd, Orp. BR6 ....193 H7
Daley St, E9 ....95 G6
Daley Thompson Way, SW8 ....150 B2
Dalgarno Gdns, W10 ....107 J5
Dalgarno Way, W10 ....107 J4
Dalgleish St, E14 ....113 H6
Daling Way, E3 ....113 H1
Dalkeith Gro, Stan. HA7 ....53 G5
Dalkeith Rd, SE21 ....169 J1
  Ilford IG1 ....99 F3
Dallas Rd, NW4 ....71 G7
  SE26 ....170 E4
  W5 ....105 J5
  Sutton SM3 ....198 B6
Dallas Ter, Hayes UB3 ....121 J3
Dallinger Rd, SE12 ....155 F6
Dalling Rd, W6 ....127 H3
Dallington Sq, EC1
  off Dallington St 111 H4
Dallington St, EC1 ....11 H5
Dallin Rd, SE18 ....137 E7
  Bexleyheath DA6 ....158 D4
Dalmain Rd, SE23 ....171 G1
Dalmally Rd, Croy. CR0 ....188 C7
Dalmeny Av, N7 ....92 D4
  SW16 ....187 G2
Dalmeny Cl, Wem. HA0 ....87 F6
Dalmeny Cres, Houns. TW3 ....144 A4
Dalmeny Rd, N7 ....92 D3
  Barnet EN5 ....41 F6
  Carshalton SM5 ....200 A7
  Erith DA8 ....159 H1
  Worcester Park KT4 ....197 H3
Dalmeyer Rd, NW10 ....89 F6
Dalmore Av, Esher (Clay.) KT10 ..194 C6
Dalmore Rd, SE21 ....169 J2
Dalrymple Cl, N14 ....42 D7
Dalrymple Rd, SE4 ....153 H4
DALSTON, E8 ....94 D7
Dalston Gdns, Stan. HA7 ....69 H1
Dalston La, E8 ....94 C6
Dalton Av, Mitch. CR4 ....185 H2
Dalton Cl, Orp. BR6 ....207 H3
Dalton Rd, Har. (Har.Wld) HA3 ..68 A2
Dalton St, SE27 ....169 H2
Dalwood St, SE5 ....152 B1
Daly Ct, E15 off Clays La 96 C5
Dalyell Rd, SW9 ....151 F3
Damascene Wk, SE21
  off Lovelace Rd 169 J1
Damask Cres, E16
  off Cranberry La 114/115 E4
Damer Ter, SW10
  off Tadema Rd 129 F7
Dames Rd, E7 ....97 G3
Dame St, N1 ....11 J1
Damien St, E1 ....113 E6
Damon Cl, Sid. DA14 ....176 B3
Damson Dr, Hayes UB3 ....102 A7
Damsonwood Rd, Sthl. UB2 ....123 G3
Danbrook Rd, SW16 ....187 E1
Danbury Cl, Rom. RM6 ....82 D3
Danbury Ms, Wall. SM6 ....200 B4
Danbury Rd, Loug. IG10 ....48 B7
Danbury St, N1 ....11 H1
Danbury Way, Wdf.Grn. IG8 ....63 J6
Danby St, SE15 ....152 C3
Dancer Rd, SW6 ....148 C1
  Richmond TW9 ....146 A3
Dando Cres, SE3 ....155 H3
Dandridge Cl, SE10 ....135 F5
Danebury, Croy. (New Adgtn)
  CR0 ....204 B6
Danebury Av, SW15 ....147 E6
Daneby Rd, SE6 ....172 B2
Dane Cl, Bex. DA5 ....159 G7
  Orpington BR6 ....207 G5
Danecourt Gdns, Croy. CR0 ....202 C3
Danecroft Rd, SE24 ....151 J5
Danehill Wk, Sid. DA14
  off Hatherley Rd 176 A3
Danehurst Gdns, Ilf. IG4 ....80 B5
Danehurst St, SW6 ....148 B1

Daneland, Barn. EN4 ....41 J6
Danemead Gro, Nthlt. UB5 ....85 H5
Danemere St, SW15 ....147 J3
Dane Pl, E3 off Roman Rd 113 H2
Dane Rd, N18 ....61 F3
  SW19 ....185 F1
  W13 ....125 F1
  Ilford IG1 ....99 F5
  Southall UB1 ....103 E7
Danesbury Rd, Felt. TW13 ....160 B1
Danescombe, SE12
  off Winn Rd 173 G1
Danes Ct, Wem. HA9 ....88 B3
Danescourt Cres, Sutt. SM1 ....199 F2
Danescroft, NW4 ....72 A5
Danescroft Av, NW4 ....72 A5
Danescroft Gdns, NW4 ....72 A5
Danesdale Rd, E9 ....95 H6
Danesfield, SE5 ....36 D5
Danes Gate, Har. HA1 ....68 B3
Danes Rd, Rom. RM7 ....83 J7
Dane St, WC1 ....18 C2
Daneswood Av, SE6 ....172 C3
Danethorpe Rd, Wem. HA0 ....87 G6
Danetree Cl, Epsom KT19 ....196 C7
Danetree Rd, Epsom KT19 ....196 C7
Danette Gdns, Dag. RM10 ....101 F2
Daneville Rd, SE5 ....152 A1
Dangan Rd, E11 ....79 G6
Daniel Bolt Cl, E14
  off Uamvar St 114 B5
Daniel Cl, N18 ....61 F4
  SW17 ....167 H6
  Hounslow TW4
  off Harvey Rd 143 F7
Daniel Gdns, SE15 ....37 F7
Daniell Way, Croy. CR0 ....201 E1
Daniel Pl, NW4 ....71 H6
Daniel Rd, W5 ....105 J7
Daniels Rd, SE15 ....153 F3
Dan Leno Wk, SW6
  off Britannia Rd 128/129 E7
Dan Mason Dr, W4
  off Great Chertsey Rd 146 C2
Dansey Pl, W1 ....17 H5
Dansington Rd, Well. DA16 ....158 A4
Danson Cres, Well. DA16 ....158 B3
Danson La, Well. DA16 ....158 A4
Danson Mead, Well. DA16 ....158 C3
★ Danson Park, Well. DA16 ....158 C4
Danson Pk, Bexh. DA6 ....158 C4
Danson Rd, Bex. DA5 ....158 D5
  Bexleyheath DA6 ....158 D5
Danson Underpass, Sid. DA15
  off Danson Rd 158 C6
Dante Pl, SE11 ....35 H1
Dante Rd, SE11 ....35 G1
Danube St, SW3 ....31 H3
Danvers Rd, N8 ....74 D4
Danvers St, SW3 ....31 F6
Danziger Way, Borwd. WD6 ....38 C1
Daphne Gdns, E4
  off Gunners Gro 62 C3
Daphne St, SW18 ....149 F6
Daplyn St, E1 ....21 H1
D'Arblay St, W1 ....17 G4
Darby Cres, Sun. TW16 ....178 C2
Darby Gdns, Sun. TW16 ....178 C2
Darcy Av, Wall. SM6 ....200 C4
Darcy Cl, N20 ....57 G2
D'Arcy Dr, Har. HA3 ....69 G4
Darcy Gdns, Dag. RM9 ....119 F1
D'Arcy Gdns, Har. HA3 ....69 H4
D'Arcy Pl, Brom. BR2 ....191 G4
Darcy Rd, SW16 ....186 E2
  Isleworth TW7
  off London Rd 144 D1
D'Arcy Rd, Sutt. SM3 ....198 A4
Dare Gdns, Dag. RM8
  off Grafton Rd 100/101 E3
Darell Rd, Rich. TW9 ....146 A3
Darenth Rd, N16 ....76 C7
  Welling DA16 ....158 A1
Darfield Rd, SE4 ....153 J5
Darfield Way, W10 ....108 A6
Darfur St, SW15 ....148 A3
Dargate Cl, SE19
  off Chipstead Cl 170 C7
Darien Rd, SW11 ....149 G3
Dark Ho Wk, EC3
  off King William St 112 B7
Darlands Dr, Barn. EN5 ....40 A5
Darlan Rd, SW6 ....128 C7
Darlaston Rd, SW19 ....166 A7
Darley Cl, Croy. CR0 ....189 H6
Darley Dr, N.Mal. KT3 ....182 D2
Darley Gdns, Mord. SM4 ....185 E6
Darley Rd, N9 ....60 C1
  SW11 ....149 J6
Darling Rd, SE4 ....154 A3
Darling Row, E1 ....113 E4
Darlington Rd, SE27 ....169 H5
Darmaine Cl, S.Croy. CR2
  off Churchill Rd 201 J7
Darnaway Pl, E14 off Abbott Rd ..114 C6
Darndale Cl, E17 ....77 J2
Darnley Ho, E14 ....113 H6

Darnley Rd, E9 ....95 E6
  Woodford Green IG8 ....79 G1
Darnley Ter, W11
  off St. James's Gdns 128 B1
Darrell Rd, SE22 ....152 D5
Darren Cl, N4 ....75 F7
Darrick Wd Rd, Orp. BR6 ....207 G2
Darris Cl, Hayes UB4 ....103 E4
Darsley Dr, SW8 ....150 E1
Dartford Av, N9 ....45 F6
Dartford Gdns, Rom. (Chad.Hth)
  RM6 off Heathfield Pk Dr 82 B6
Dartford Rd, Bex. DA5 ....177 J1
Dartford St, SE17 ....36 A5
Dartmoor Wk, E14
  off Charnwood Gdns 134 A4
Dartmouth Cl, W11 ....108 C6
Dartmouth Gro, SE10 ....154 C1
Dartmouth Hill, SE10 ....154 C1
Dartmouth Ho, Kings.T. KT2
  off Kingsgate Rd 181 H1
DARTMOUTH PARK, NW5 ....92 B3
Dartmouth Pk Av, NW5 ....92 B3
Dartmouth Pk Hill, N19 ....92 B1
  NW5 ....92 B1
Dartmouth Pk Rd, NW5 ....92 B4
Dartmouth Pl, SE23
  off Dartmouth Rd 171 F2
  W4 ....127 E6
Dartmouth Rd, E16
  off Fords Pk Rd 115 G6
  NW2 ....90 A6
  NW4 ....71 G6
  SE23 ....171 F3
  SE26 ....171 F3
  Bromley BR2 ....191 G7
  Ruislip HA4 ....84 A3
Dartmouth Row, SE10 ....154 C1
Dartmouth St, SW1 ....25 H4
Dartmouth Ter, SE10 ....154 D1
Dartnell Rd, Croy. CR0 ....188 C7
Dartrey Wk, SW10 ....30 D7
Dart St, W10 ....108 B3
Darville Rd, N16 ....94 C3
Darwell Cl, E6 ....116 D2
Darwin Cl, N11 ....58 B3
  Orpington BR6 ....207 G5
Darwin Dr, Sthl. UB1 ....103 H6
Darwin Gdns, Wat. WD19
  off Barnhurst Path 50 C5
Darwin Rd, N22 ....75 H1
  W5 ....125 F5
  Welling DA16 ....157 J3
Darwin St, SE17 ....36 C1
Daryngton Dr, Grnf. UB6 ....104 A2
Dashwood Cl, Bexh. DA6 ....159 G5
Dashwood Rd, N8 ....75 F6
Dassett Rd, SE27 ....169 H5
Datchelor Pl, SE5 ....152 A1
Datchet Rd, SE6 ....171 J3
Datchworth Ct, N4
  off Queens Dr 93 J3
Date St, SE17 ....36 B4
Daubeney Gdns, N17 ....59 J4
Daubeney Rd, E5 ....95 H4
  N17 ....59 J4
Daubeney Twr, SE8 ....133 J4
Dault Rd, SW18 ....149 F6
Davema Cl, Chis. BR7
  off Brenchley Cl 192 D1
Davenant Rd, N19 ....92 D2
  Croydon CR0
  off Duppas Hill Rd 201 H4
Davenant St, E1 ....21 J2
Davenport Cl, Tedd. TW11 ....162 D6
Davenport Rd, SE6 ....154 B6
  Sidcup DA14 ....176 D2
Daventer Dr, Stan. HA7 ....52 C7
Daventry Av, E17 ....78 A5
Daventry St, NW1 ....15 G1
Davern Cl, SE10 ....135 F4
Davey Cl, N7 ....93 F6
Davey Rd, E9 ....96 A7
Davey St, SE15 ....37 G6
David Av, Grnf. UB6 ....104 B3
David Cl, Hayes UB3 ....121 G7
Davidge St, SE1 ....27 G4
David Lee Pt, E15 ....115 E1
David Ms, W1 ....16 A1
David Rd, Dag. RM8 ....100 E2
Davidson Gdns, SW8 ....130 E7
Davidson La, Har. HA1
  off Grove Hill 68 C7
Davidson Rd, Croy. CR0 ....188 C6
Davids Rd, SE23 ....171 F1
David St, E15 ....96 D6
David's Way, Ilf. IG6 ....65 H6
David Twigg Cl, Kings.T. KT2 ....181 H1
Davies Cl, Croy. CR0 ....188 D6
Davies La, E11 ....97 E2
Davies Ms, W1 ....16 D5
Davies St, W1 ....16 D5
Davington Gdns, Dag. RM8 ....100 B5
Davington Rd, Dag. RM8 ....100 B6
Davinia Cl, Wdf.Grn. IG8
  off Deacon Way 64 C6
Davis Rd, W3 ....127 F1

Davis Rd, Chess. KT9 . . . . .196 A4
Davis St, E13 . . . . .115 H2
Davisville Rd, W12 . . . . .127 G2
Dawes Av, Islw. TW7 . . . . .144 D5
Dawes Ho, SE17 . . . . .36 C2
Dawes Rd, SW6 . . . . .128 B7
Dawes St, SE17 . . . . .36 C3
Dawley Rd, Hayes UB3 . . . . . . .121 H1
Dawlish Av, N13 . . . . .58 E4
  SW18 . . . . .166 E2
  Greenford UB6 . . . . .104 D2
Dawlish Dr, Ilf. IG3 . . . . .99 H4
  Pinner HA5 . . . . .67 E5
  Ruislip HA4 . . . . .84 A2
Dawlish Rd, E10 . . . . .96 C2
  N17 .76 D3
  NW2 . . . . .90 A6
Dawnay Gdns, SW18 . . . . .167 G2
Dawnay Rd, SW18 . . . . .167 F2
Dawn Cl, Houns. TW4 . . . . .143 E3
Dawn Cres, E15 off Bridge Rd . .114 D1
Dawpool Rd, NW2 . . . . .89 F2
Daws Hill, E4 . . . . .46 C3
Daws La, NW7 . . . . .55 F5
Dawson Av, Bark. IG11 . . . . . . .99 H1
Dawson Cl, SE18 . . . . .137 F4
Dawson Gdns, Bark. IG11
  off Dawson Av 99 J7
Dawson Hts Est, SE22 . . . . . . .152 D7
Dawson Pl, W2 . . . . .108 D7
Dawson Rd, NW2 . . . . .89 J5
  Kingston upon Thames KT1 . .181 J3
Dawson St, E2 . . . . .13 G2
Dax Ct, Sun. TW16
  off Thames St 178 C3
Daybrook Rd, SW19 . . . . .184 E2
Daylesford Av, SW15 . . . . .147 G4
Daymer Gdns, Pnr. HA5 . . . . . . .66 B4
Daysbrook Rd, SW2 . . . . .169 F2
Days La, Sid. DA15 . . . . .157 H7
Dayton Gro, SE15 . . . . .153 F1
Deacon Ms, N1 . . . . .94 A7
Deacon Rd, NW2 . . . . .89 G5
  Kingston upon Thames KT2 . .181 J1
Deacons Cl, Borwd. (Elstree)
  WD6 . . . . .38 A2
  Pinner HA5 . . . . .66 B2
Deacons Leas, Orp. BR6 . . . . . .207 G4
Deacons Ri, N2 . . . . .73 G5
Deacons Wk, Hmptn. TW12
  off Bishops Gro 161 F4
Deacon Way, SE17 . . . . .35 J1
  Woodford Green IG8 . . . . . . .64 C7
Deal Ms, W5 off Darwin Rd 125 G4
Deal Porters Way, SE16 . . . . . .133 F3
Deal Rd, SW17 . . . . .168 A6
Deal's Gateway, SE10
  off Blackheath Rd 154 B1
Deal St, E1 . . . . .21 H1
Dealtry Rd, SW15 . . . . .147 J4
Deal Wk, SW9 off Mandela St . .131 G7
Dean Bradley St, SW1 . . . . .26 A6
Dean Cl, E9 off Churchill Wk 95 F5
  SE16 off Surrey Water Rd . . .133 G1
Dean Ct, Wem. HA0 . . . . .87 B4
Deancross St, E1 . . . . .113 F6
Dean Dr, Stan. HA7 . . . . .69 H2
Deane Av, Ruis. HA4 . . . . .84 C5
Deane Cft Rd, Pnr. HA5 . . . . . . .66 B6
Deanery Cl, N2 . . . . .73 H4
Deanery Ms, W1 . . . . .24 C1
Deanery Rd, E15 . . . . .97 E6
Deanery St, W1 . . . . .24 C1
Deane Way, Ruis. HA4 . . . . .66 B6
Dean Farrar St, SW1 . . . . .25 H5
Dean Gdns, E17 . . . . .78 D4
  W13 off Northfield Av 124/125 E1
Deanhill Rd, SW14 . . . . .146 B4
Dean Rd, NW2 . . . . .89 J6
  SE28 . . . . .118 A7
  Croydon CR0 . . . . .202 A4
  Hampton TW12 . . . . .161 G5
  Hounslow TW3 . . . . .143 H5
Dean Ryle St, SW1 . . . . .34 A1
Deansbrook Cl, Edg. HA8 . . . . . .54 C7
Deansbrook Rd, Edg. HA8 . . . . .54 C6
Deans Bldgs, SE17 . . . . .36 B2
Deans Cl, W4 . . . . .126 B6
Dean's Cl, Croy. CR0 . . . . .202 C3
Deans Cl, Edg. HA8 . . . . .54 C6
Deans Ct, EC4 . . . . .19 H4
Deanscroft Av, NW9 . . . . .88 C2
Deans Dr, N13 . . . . .59 H6
  Edgware HA8 . . . . .54 D5
Dean's Gate Cl, SE23 . . . . .171 G3
Deans La, W4 . . . . .126 B6
  Edgware HA8 . . . . .54 C6
Deans Ms, W1 . . . . .16 E3
Deans Rd, W7 . . . . .124 C1
  Sutton SM1 . . . . .198 D3
Dean Stanley St, SW1 . . . . .26 A6
Dean St, E7 . . . . .97 G5
  W1 . . . . .17 H3
Deansway, N2 . . . . .73 G4
  N9 .60 B3
Deans Way, Edg. HA8 . . . . .54 C5
Dean's Yd, SW1 . . . . .25 J5

Dean Trench St, SW1 . . . . .26 A6
Dean Wk, Edg. HA8
  off Deansbrook Rd 54 C6
Dean Way, Sthl. UB2 . . . . .123 H2
Dearne Cl, Stan. HA7 . . . . .52 D5
De'Arn Gdns, Mitch. CR4 . . . . .185 H3
Dearsley Rd, Enf. EN1 . . . . .44 D3
Deason St, E15 off High St 114 C1
De Barowe Ms, N5
  off Leigh Rd 93 H4
DEBDEN, Loug. IG10 . . . . .49 G3
Debden Cl, Kings.T. KT2 . . . . . .163 G5
  Woodford Green IG8 . . . . . . .63 J7
De Beauvoir Cres, N1 . . . . .112 A1
De Beauvoir Est, N1 . . . . .112 A1
De Beauvoir Rd, N1 . . . . .112 B1
De Beauvoir Sq, N1 . . . . .94 B7
DE BEAUVOIR TOWN, N1 . . . . .112 A1
Debnams Rd, SE16
  off Rotherhithe New Rd 133 F4
De Bohun Av, N14 . . . . .42 B6
Deborah Cl, Islw. TW7 . . . . . . .144 B1
De Brome Rd, Felt. TW13 . . . . .160 C1
Deburgh Rd, SW19 . . . . .167 F7
Decima St, SE1 . . . . .28 D5
Deck Cl, SE16 off Thame Rd . . .133 G2
Decoy Av, NW11 . . . . .72 B5
De Crespigny Pk, SE5 . . . . .152 A2
Deeley Rd, SW8 . . . . .150 D1
Deena Cl, W3 . . . . .105 J6
Deepdale, SW19 . . . . .166 A4
Deepdale Av, Brom. BR2 . . . . . .191 F4
Deepdale Cl, N11
  off Ribblesdale Av 58 A6
Deepdene, W5 . . . . .105 J4
Deepdene Av, Croy. CR0 . . . . . .202 C3
Deepdene Cl, E11 . . . . .79 G4
Deepdene Ct, N21 . . . . .43 H6
Deepdene Gdns, SW2 . . . . .151 F7
Deepdene Path, Loug. IG10 . . . .48 D4
Deepdene Pt, SE23
  off Dacres Rd 171 G3
Deepdene Rd, SE5 . . . . .152 A4
  Loughton IG10 . . . . .48 D4
  Welling DA16 . . . . .158 A3
Deepwell Cl, Islw. TW7 . . . . . . .144 D1
Deepwood La, Grnf. UB6
  off Cowgate Rd 104 A3
Deerbrook Rd, SE24 . . . . .169 H1
Deerdale Rd, SE24 . . . . .151 J4
Deerfield Cl, NW9
  off Rookery Cl 71 F5
Deerhurst Cl, Felt. TW13 . . . . . .160 A4
Deerhurst Cres, Hmptn. (Hmptn H.)
  TW12 . . . . .161 J5
Deerhurst Rd, NW2 . . . . .90 A6
  SW16 . . . . .169 F5
Deerings Dr, Pnr. HA5 . . . . .66 A5
Deerleap Gro, E4 . . . . .46 B5
Dee Rd, Rich. TW9 . . . . .145 J4
Deer Pk Cl, Kings.T. KT2 . . . . . .164 B7
Deer Pk Gdns, Mitch. CR4 . . . . .185 G3
Deer Pk Rd, SW19 . . . . .185 E2
Deer Pk Way, W.Wick. BR4 . . . .205 F2
Deeside Rd, SW17 . . . . .167 G3
Dee St, E14 . . . . .114 C6
Defiance Wk, SE18 . . . . .136 C3
Defiant Way, Wall. SM6 . . . . . .200 E7
Defoe Av, Rich. TW9 . . . . .126 A7
Defoe Cl, SE16 off Vaughan St . .133 J2
  SW17 . . . . .167 H6
Defoe Ho, EC2 . . . . .20 A1
Defoe Pl, EC2 off Beech St 111 J5
  SW17 off Lessingham Av 167 J4
Defoe Rd, N16 . . . . .94 B2
De Frene Rd, SE26 . . . . .171 G4
De Gama Pl, E14
  off Maritime Quay 134 A5
Degema Rd, Chis. BR7 . . . . . . .174 E5
Dehar Cres, NW9 . . . . .71 F7
Dehavilland Cl, Nthlt. UB5 . . . . .102 D3
De Havilland Dr, SE18
  off Cambridge Row 136 E5
De Havilland Rd, Edg. HA8 . . . . .70 B2
  Hounslow TW5 . . . . .122 C7
De Havilland Way, Stai. (Stanw.)
  TW19 . . . . .140 A6
Dekker Rd, SE21 . . . . .152 B6
Delacourt Rd, SE3
  off Old Dover Rd 135 H7
Delafield Rd, SE7 . . . . .135 H5
Delaford Rd, SE16 . . . . .133 E5
Delaford St, SW6 . . . . .128 B7
Delamare Cres, Croy. CR0 . . . . .189 F6
Delamere Gdns, NW7 . . . . .54 D6
Delamere Rd, SW20 . . . . .184 A1
  W5 . . . . .125 H1
  Borehamwood WD6 . . . . . . .38 B1
  Hayes UB4 . . . . .102 D7
Delamere Ter, W2 . . . . .14 B1
Delancey Pas, NW1
  off Delancey St 110 B1
Delancey St, NW1 . . . . .110 B1
De Laune St, SE17 . . . . .35 G4
Delaware Rd, W9 . . . . .6 A5
Delawyk Cres, SE24 . . . . .151 J6
Delcombe Av, Wor.Pk. KT4 . . . .197 J1

Delft Way, SE22
  off East Dulwich Gro 152 B5
Delhi Rd, Enf. EN1 . . . . .44 C7
Delhi St, N1 . . . . .111 E1
Delia St, SW18 . . . . .149 E7
Delisle Rd, SE28 . . . . .137 H1
Delius Gro, E15 . . . . .114 D2
Dell, The, SE2 . . . . .138 A5
  SE19 . . . . .188 C1
  Brentford TW8 . . . . .125 F6
  Feltham TW14
    off Harlington Rd W 142 B7
  Pinner HA5 . . . . .66 D2
  Wembley HA0 . . . . .87 E5
  Woodford Green IG8 . . . . . . .63 H3
Della Path, E5 . . . .
  off Napoleon Rd 94/95 E3
Dellbow Rd, Felt. TW14
  off Central Way 142 B5
Dell Cl, E15 . . . . .114 D1
  Wallington SM6 . . . . .200 C4
  Woodford Green IG8 . . . . . . .63 H3
Dellfield Cl, Beck. BR3
  off Foxgrove Rd 172 C7
Dell La, Epsom KT17 . . . . .197 G5
Dellors Cl, Barn. EN5 . . . . .40 A5
Dellow Cl, Ilf. IG2 . . . . .81 G7
Dellow St, E1 . . . . .113 E7
Dell Rd, Epsom KT17 . . . . .197 G6
  West Drayton UB7 . . . . .120 C3
Dells Cl, E4 . . . . .46 B7
  Teddington TW11
    off Middle La 162 C6
Dell's Ms, SW1 . . . . .33 G2
Dell Wk, N.Mal. KT3 . . . . .183 E2
Dell Way, W13 . . . . .105 F6
Dellwood Gdns, Ilf. IG5 . . . . . . .80 D3
Delmare Cl, SW9
  off Brighton Ter 151 F4
Delme Cres, SE3 . . . . .155 H2
Delmey Cl, Croy. CR0
  off Radcliffe Rd 202 C3
Deloraine St, SE8 . . . . .154 A1
Delorme St, W6 . . . . .128 A6
Delta Cl, Wor.Pk. KT4 . . . . .197 F3
Delta Ct, NW2 . . . . .89 G2
Delta Gain, Wat. WD19 . . . . . . .50 D2
Delta Gro, Nthlt. UB5 . . . . .102 D3
Delta Rd, Wor.Pk. KT4 . . . . . . .197 E3
Delta St, E2 . . . . .13 H3
De Luci Rd, Erith DA8 . . . . .139 J5
De Lucy St, SE2 . . . . .138 B4
Delvan Cl, SE18
  off Ordnance Rd 136 D7
Delvers Mead, Dag. RM10 . . . .101 J4
Delverton Rd, SE17 . . . . .35 H4
Delvino Rd, SW6 . . . . .148 D1
De Mandeville Gate, Enf. EN1
  off Southbury Rd 44 D4
Demesne Rd, Wall. SM6 . . . . . .200 D5
Demeta Cl, Wem. HA9 . . . . .88 C3
De Montfort Par, SW16
  off Streatham High Rd . .168/169 E3
De Montfort Rd, SW16 . . . . . . .168 E3
De Morgan Rd, SW6 . . . . .149 E3
Dempster Cl, Surb. KT6 . . . . . .195 F1
Dempster Rd, SW18 . . . . .149 F5
Denbar Par, Rom. RM7
  off Mawney Rd 83 J4
Denberry Dr, Sid. DA14 . . . . . . .176 B3
Denbigh Cl, NW10 . . . . .88 E7
  W11 . . . . .108 C7
  Chislehurst BR7 . . . . .174 C6
  Southall UB1 . . . . .103 F6
  Sutton SM1 . . . . .198 C5
Denbigh Dr, Hayes UB3 . . . . . . .121 F2
Denbigh Gdns, Rich. TW10 . . . .145 J5
Denbigh Ms, SW1 . . . . .33 F2
Denbigh Pl, SW1 . . . . .33 F3
Denbigh Rd, E6 . . . . .116 A3
  W11 . . . . .108 C7
  W13 . . . . .105 E7
  Hounslow TW3 . . . . .143 H2
  Southall UB1 . . . . .103 F6
Denbigh St, SW1 . . . . .33 F2
Denbigh Ter, W11 . . . . .108 C7
Denbridge Rd, Brom. BR1 . . . . .192 C2
Den Cl, Beck. BR3 . . . . .190 D3
Dene, The, W13 . . . . .104 E5
  Croydon CR0 . . . . .203 G4
  Wembley HA9 . . . . .87 H4
  West Molesey KT8 . . . . .179 F5
Dene Av, Houns. TW3 . . . . .143 F3
  Sidcup DA15 . . . . .158 B7
Dene Cl, SE4 . . . . .153 H3
  Bromley BR2 . . . . .205 F1
  Worcester Park KT4 . . . . . . .197 F2
Dene Ct, Stan. HA7
  off Marsh La 53 F5
Dene Gdns, Stan. HA7 . . . . .53 F5
  Thames Ditton KT7 . . . . .194 D2
Denehurst Gdns, NW4 . . . . .71 J6
  W3 . . . . .126 B1
  Richmond TW10 . . . . .146 A4
  Twickenham TW2 . . . . .144 A7
  Woodford Green IG8 . . . . . . .63 H4
Dene Rd, N11 . . . . .57 J1

Dene Rd, Buck.H. IG9 . . . . .64 A1
Denewood, Barn. EN5 . . . . .41 F5
Denewood Rd, N6 . . . . .73 J6
Denford St, SE10
  off Woolwich Rd 135 F5
Dengie Wk, N1 off Basire St . . .111 J1
Denham Cl, Well. DA16
  off Park Vw Rd 158 C3
Denham Cres, Mitch. CR4 . . . . .185 J4
Denham Dr, Ilf. IG2 . . . . .81 F6
Denham Rd, N20 . . . . .57 J3
  Feltham TW14 . . . . .142 C6
Denham St, SE10 . . . . .135 G5
Denham Way, Bark. IG11 . . . . . .117 H1
  Borehamwood WD6 . . . . . . .38 D1
Denholme Rd, W9 . . . . .108 C3
Denison Cl, N2 . . . . .73 F3
Denison Rd, SW19 . . . . .167 G6
  W5 . . . . .105 F4
Deniston Av, Bex. DA5 . . . . . . .176 E1
Denis Way, SW4
  off Gauden Rd 150 D3
Denleigh Gdns, N21 . . . . .59 G1
  Thames Ditton KT7 . . . . .180 B6
Denman Dr, NW11 . . . . .72 D5
  Esher (Clay.) KT10 . . . . . . .194 D5
Denman Dr N, NW11 . . . . .72 D5
Denman Dr S, NW11 . . . . .72 D5
Denman Pl, W1
  off Great Windmill St 110 D7
Denman Rd, SE15 . . . . .152 C1
Denman St, W1 . . . . .17 H6
Denmark Av, SW19 . . . . .166 B7
Denmark Ct, Mord. SM4 . . . . . .184 D5
Denmark Gdns, Cars. SM5 . . . .199 J3
Denmark Gro, N1 . . . . .11 E1
Denmark Hill, SE5 . . . . .152 A1
Denmark Hill Dr, NW9 . . . . .71 F4
Denmark Hill Est, SE5 . . . . .152 A4
Denmark Pl, WC2 . . . . .17 J3
Denmark Rd, N8 . . . . .75 G4
  NW6 . . . . .108 C2
  SE5 . . . . .151 J1
  SE25 . . . . .188 D5
  SW19 . . . . .166 A6
  W13 . . . . .105 E7
  Bromley BR1 . . . . .191 H1
  Carshalton SM5 . . . . .199 J3
  Kingston upon Thames KT1 . .181 H3
  Twickenham TW2 . . . . .162 A3
Denmark St, E11
  off High Rd Leytonstone . .96/97 E3
  E13 . . . . .115 H5
  N17 . . . . .76 E1
  WC2 . . . . .17 J4
Denmark Wk, SE27 . . . . .169 J4
Denmead Ho, SW15
  off Highcliffe Dr 147 F6
Denmead Rd, Croy. CR0 . . . . . .201 H1
Denmead Way, SE15
  off Pentridge St 132 C7
Dennan Rd, Surb. KT6 . . . . .195 J1
Dennard Way, Orp. BR6 . . . . . .206 E4
Denner Rd, E4 . . . . .62 A2
Denne Ter, E8 . . . . .112 C1
Dennett Rd, Croy. CR0 . . . . . . .201 G1
Dennetts Gro, SE14
  off Dennetts Rd 153 G2
Dennetts Rd, SE14 . . . . .153 F1
Denning Av, Croy. CR0 . . . . . . .201 G4
Denning Cl, NW8 . . . . .6 D3
  Hampton TW12 . . . . .161 F6
Denning Rd, NW3 . . . . .91 G4
Dennington Cl, E5
  off Detmold Rd 94/95 E2
Dennington Pk Rd, NW6 . . . . . . .90 D6
Denningtons, The, Wor.Pk. KT4 .197 E2
Dennis Av, Wem. HA9 . . . . .87 J5
Dennis Gdns, Stan. HA7 . . . . . . .53 F5
Dennis La, Stan. HA7 . . . . .52 E3
Dennison Pt, E15 . . . . .96 C7
Dennis Pk Cres, SW20 . . . . . . .184 B1
Dennis Reeve Cl, Mitch. CR4 . . .185 J1
Dennis Rd, E.Mol. KT8 . . . . . . .179 J4
Denny Cl, E6 off Linton Gdns . . .116 B5
Denny Cres, SE11 . . . . .35 F2
Denny Gdns, Dag. RM9
  off Canonsleigh Rd 100 B7
Denny Rd, N9 . . . . .60 E1
Denny St, SE11 . . . . .35 F3
Den Rd, Brom. BR2 . . . . .190 D3
Densham Rd, E15 . . . . .115 E1
Densole Cl, Beck. BR3
  off Kings Hall Rd 189 H1
Densworth Gro, N9 . . . . .61 F2
Denton Cl, Barn. EN5 . . . . .39 J5
Denton Rd, N8 . . . . .75 F5
  N18 . . . . .60 B4
  Twickenham TW1 . . . . .145 G4
  Welling DA16 . . . . .138 C7
Denton St, SW18 . . . . .149 E6
Denton Way, E5 . . . . .95 G3
Dents Rd, SW11 . . . . .149 J6
Denver Cl, Orp. BR6 . . . . .193 H6
Denver Rd, N16 . . . . .76 B7
Denyer St, SW3 . . . . .31 H2
Denzil Rd, NW10 . . . . .89 F5

Deodara Cl, N20 . . . . .57 H3
Deodar Rd, SW15 . . . . .148 B4
★ Department for Environment,
   Food & Rural Affairs (D.E.F.R.A.),
   SW1 .26 A1
★ Department for Transport (D.f.T.),
   SW1 .33 J1
★ Department of Health & Dept for
   Work & Pensions (D.W.P.),
   SW1 .26 A3
Depot App, NW2 . . . . .90 A4
Depot Rd, W12 off Wood La 107 J7
   Hounslow TW3 . . . . .144 A4
DEPTFORD, SE8 . . . . .133 J5
Deptford Br, SE8 . . . . .154 A1
Deptford Bdy, SE8 . . . . .154 A1
Deptford Ch St, SE8 . . . . .134 A6
Deptford Ferry Rd, E14 . . . . . . .134 A4
Deptford Grn, SE8 . . . . .134 A6
Deptford High St, SE8 . . . . .134 A6
Deptford Strand, SE8 . . . . .133 J4
Deptford Wf, SE8 . . . . .133 J4
De Quincey Ms, E16
   off Wesley Av 135 G1
De Quincey Rd, N17 . . . . .76 A1
Derby Av, N12 . . . . .57 F5
   Harrow HA3 . . . . .68 A1
   Romford RM7 . . . . .83 J6
Derby Ct, E5 off Overbury St 95 G4
Derby Gate, SW1 . . . . .26 A3
Derby Hill, SE23 . . . . .171 F2
Derby Hill Cres, SE23 . . . . .171 F2
Derby Rd, E7 . . . . .97 J7
   E9 .113 G1
   E18 .79 F1
   N18 .61 F5
   SW14 . . . . .146 B4
   SW19 off Russell Rd 166 D7
   Croydon CR0 . . . . .201 H4
   Enfield EN3 . . . . .45 E5
   Greenford UB6 . . . . .103 H1
   Hounslow TW3 . . . . .143 H4
   Surbiton KT5 . . . . .196 A1
   Sutton SM1 . . . . .198 C6
Derby Rd Ind Est, Houns. TW3
   off Derby Rd 143 H4
Derbyshire St, E2 . . . . .13 J4
Derby St, W1 . . . . .24 C2
Dereham Pl, EC2 . . . . .12 E4
Dereham Rd, Bark. IG11 . . . . . . .99 J6
Derek Av, Epsom KT19 . . . . . . .196 A5
   Wallington SM6 . . . . .200 B4
   Wembley HA9 . . . . .88 D7
Derek Cl, Epsom (Ewell) KT19 . .196 B5
Derek Walcott Cl, SE24
   off Shakespeare Rd 151 H5
Dericote St, E8 . . . . .112 D1
Deridene Cl, Stai. (Stanw.) TW19
   off Bedfont Rd 140 B6
Derifall Cl, E6 . . . . .116 C5
Dering Pl, Croy. CR0 . . . . .201 J4
Dering Rd, Croy. CR0 . . . . .201 J4
Dering St, W1 . . . . .16 D4
Derinton Rd, SW17 . . . . .167 J4
Derley Rd, Sthl. UB2 . . . . .122 C3
Dermody Gdns, SE13 . . . . .154 D5
Dermody Rd, SE13 . . . . .154 D5
Deronda Rd, SE24 . . . . .169 H1
Deroy Cl, Cars. SM5 . . . . .199 J6
Derrick Gdns, SE7
   off Anchor & Hope La 135 J4
Derrick Rd, Beck. BR3 . . . . .189 J3
Derry Rd, Croy. CR0 . . . . .200 E3
Derry St, W8 . . . . .22 A4
Dersingham Av, E12 . . . . .98 C5
Dersingham Rd, NW2 . . . . .90 B3
Derwent Av, N18 . . . . .60 A5
   NW7 . . . . .54 D5
   SW15 . . . . .164 E4
   Barnet EN4 . . . . .57 J1
   Pinner HA5 . . . . .51 E6
Derwent Cl, Esher (Clay.) KT10 .194 B6
Derwent Cres, N20 . . . . .57 F3
   Bexleyheath DA7 . . . . .159 G2
   Stanmore HA7 . . . . .69 F2
Derwent Dr, NW9 . . . . .70 E5
   Orpington BR5 . . . . .193 G7
Derwent Gdns, Ilf. IG4 . . . . .80 B4
   Wembley HA9 . . . . .69 F7
Derwent Gro, SE22 . . . . .152 C4
Derwent Ri, NW9 . . . . .70 E6
Derwent Rd, N13 . . . . .59 F4
   SE20 . . . . .188 D2
   SW20 . . . . .184 A6
   W5 . . . . .125 F3
   Southall UB1 . . . . .103 G6
   Twickenham TW2 . . . . .143 H6
Derwent St, SE10 . . . . .134 E5
Derwent Wk, Wall. SM6 . . . . . . .200 B7
Derwentwater Rd, W3 . . . . .126 C1
Derwent Yd, W5
   off Northfield Av 125 F3
Desborough Cl, W2 . . . . .14 B1
Desborough St, W2 . . . . .14 A1
Desenfans Rd, SE21 . . . . .152 B6
Desford Ms, E16
   off Desford Rd 114/115 E4

Desford Rd, E16 . . . . .115 E4
★ Design Mus, SE1 . . . . .29 G2
Desmond St, SE14 . . . . .133 H6
Desmond Tutu Dr, SE23
   off St. Germans Rd 171 H1
Despard Rd, N19 . . . . .92 C1
Detling Rd, Brom. BR1 . . . . .173 G5
Detmold Rd, E5 . . . . .95 F2
Devalls Cl, E6 . . . . .116 D7
Devana End, Cars. SM5 . . . . . . .199 J3
Devas Rd, SW20 . . . . .183 J1
Devas St, E3 . . . . .114 B4
Devenay Rd, E15 . . . . .97 F7
Devenish Rd, SE2 . . . . .138 A2
Deventer Cres, SE22 . . . . .152 B5
Deveraux Cl, Beck. BR3
   off Creswell Dr 190 B5
Deverell St, SE1 . . . . .28 B6
Devereux Ct, WC2 . . . . .18 E4
Devereux La, SW13 . . . . .127 H7
Devereux Rd, SW11 . . . . .149 J6
Deverill Ct, SE20 . . . . .189 F1
Devey Cl, Kings.T. KT2 . . . . .165 E7
Devizes St, N1 off Poole St 112 A1
Devon Av, Twick. TW2 . . . . .161 J1
Devon Cl, N17 . . . . .76 C3
   Buckhurst Hill IG9 . . . . .63 H1
   Greenford UB6 . . . . .105 F1
Devon Ct, Buck.H. IG9 . . . . .63 H1
Devoncroft Gdns, Twick. TW1 . .144 D7
Devon Gdns, N4 . . . . .75 H6
Devonhurst Pl, W4
   off Heathfield Ter 126 D5
Devonia Gdns, N18 . . . . .59 J6
Devonia Rd, N1 . . . . .11 H1
Devonport Gdns, Ilf. IG1 . . . . . . .80 C6
Devonport Ms, W12
   off Devonport Rd 127 H1
Devonport Rd, W12 . . . . .127 H2
Devonport St, E1 . . . . .113 F6
Devon Ri, N2 . . . . .73 G4
Devon Rd, Bark. IG11 . . . . .117 H1
Devons Est, E3 . . . . .114 B3
Devonshire Av, Sutt. SM2 . . . . .199 F7
Devonshire Cl, E15 . . . . .97 E4
   N13 .59 G4
   W1 .16 D1
Devonshire Cres, NW7 . . . . .56 A7
Devonshire Dr, SE10 . . . . .134 B7
   Surbiton KT6 . . . . .195 G1
Devonshire Gdns, N17 . . . . .59 J6
   N21 .43 J7
   W4 . . . . .126 C7
Devonshire Gro, SE15 . . . . .133 E6
Devonshire Hill La, N17 . . . . . . .59 J6
Devonshire Ho, Sutt. SM2
   off Devonshire Av 199 F7
Devonshire Ms, SW10
   off Park Wk 129 G6
   W4 off Glebe St 126/127 E5
Devonshire Ms N, W1 . . . . .16 D1
Devonshire Ms S, W1 . . . . .16 D1
Devonshire Ms W, W1 . . . . .8 D6
Devonshire Pas, W4 . . . . .126 E5
Devonshire Pl, NW2 . . . . .90 D3
   W1 .8 C6
   W8 .22 A6
Devonshire Pl Ms, W1 . . . . .8 C6
Devonshire Rd, E16 . . . . .115 H6
   E17 .78 A6
   N9 . . . . .61 F1
   N13 .59 F4
   N17 .59 J6
   NW7 . . . . .56 A7
   SE9 . . . . .174 B2
   SE23 . . . . .171 F1
   SW19 . . . . .167 H7
   W4 . . . . .126 E5
   W5 . . . . .125 F3
   Bexleyheath DA6 . . . . .159 E4
   Carshalton SM5 . . . . .200 A4
   Croydon CR0 . . . . .188 A7
   Feltham TW13 . . . . .160 E3
   Harrow HA1 . . . . .68 A6
   Ilford IG2 . . . . .81 G7
   Pinner (Eastcote) HA5 . . . . . .66 C6
   Pinner (Hatch End) HA5 . . . . .67 F1
   Southall UB1 . . . . .103 G5
   Sutton SM2 . . . . .199 F7
Devonshire Row, EC2 . . . . .20 E2
Devonshire Row Ms, W1 . . . . . . .8 E6
Devonshire Sq, EC2 . . . . .20 E3
   Bromley BR2 . . . . .191 H4
Devonshire St, W1 . . . . .16 C1
   W4 . . . . .126 E5
Devonshire Ter, W2 . . . . .14 D4
Devonshire Way, Croy. CR0 . . . .203 H2
   Hayes UB4 . . . . .102 B6
Devons Rd, E3 . . . . .114 A5
Devon St, SE15 . . . . .132 E6
Devon Way, Chess. KT9 . . . . . . .195 F5
   Epsom KT19 . . . . .196 B5

Devon Waye, Houns. TW5 . . . . .123 F7
De Walden St, W1 . . . . .16 C2
Dewar St, SE15 . . . . .152 D3
Dewberry Gdns, E6 . . . . .116 B5
Dewberry St, E14 . . . . .114 C5
Dewey Rd, N1 . . . . .10 E1
   Dagenham RM10 . . . . .101 H6
Dewey St, SW17 . . . . .167 J5
Dewhurst Rd, W14 . . . . .128 A3
Dewlands Ct, NW4
   off Holders Hill Rd 72 A2
Dewsbury Cl, Pnr. HA5 . . . . .67 F6
Dewsbury Ct, W4
   off Chiswick Rd 126 C4
Dewsbury Gdns, Wor.Pk. KT4 . .197 G3
Dewsbury Rd, NW10 . . . . .89 G5
Dewsbury Ter, NW1
   off Camden High St 110 B1
Dexter Ho, Erith DA18
   off Kale Rd 138/139 E3
Dexter Rd, Barn. EN5 . . . . .40 A6
Deyncourt Rd, N17 . . . . .75 J1
Deynecourt Gdns, E11 . . . . .79 J4
D'Eynsford Rd, SE5 . . . . .152 A1
Diadem Ct, W1 . . . . .17 H4
Dial Wk, The, W8 . . . . .22 B3
Diamedes Av, Stai. (Stanw.)
   TW19 . . . . .140 A7
Diameter Rd, Orp. BR5 . . . . . . .193 E7
Diamond Cl, Dag. RM8 . . . . . . .100 C1
Diamond Rd, Ruis. HA4 . . . . .84 D4
Diamond St, NW10 . . . . .88 D7
   SE15 . . . . .132 B7
Diamond Ter, SE10 . . . . .154 C1
Diamond Way, SE8
   off Deptford High St 134 A7
Diana Cl, E18 . . . . .79 H1
   SE8 off Staunton St 133 J6
Diana Gdns, Surb. KT6 . . . . . . .195 J2
Diana Ho, SW13 . . . . .147 F1
★ Diana Princess of Wales Mem,
   W2 .23 F2
Diana Rd, E17 . . . . .77 J3
Dianne Way, Barn. EN4 . . . . .41 H5
Dianthus Cl, SE2
   off Carnation St 138 B5
Dibden Row, SE1
   off Gerridge St 131 G3
Dibden St, N1 . . . . .111 H1
Dibdin Cl, Sutt. SM1 . . . . .198 D3
Dibdin Rd, Sutt. SM1 . . . . .198 D3
Dicey Av, NW2 . . . . .89 J5
Dickens Av, N3 . . . . .73 F1
Dickens Cl, Erith DA8 . . . . .139 H7
   Hayes UB3 off Croyde Av 121 H4
   Richmond TW10 . . . . .163 H2
Dickens Dr, Chis. BR7 . . . . .175 F6
Dickens Est, SE1 . . . . .29 H4
   SE16 . . . . .29 H4
Dickens Ho, NW6 . . . . .108 D3
★ Dickens Ho Mus, WC1 . . . . . . .10 D6
Dickens La, N18 . . . . .60 B5
Dickenson Cl, N9
   off Croyland Rd 60 D1
Dickenson Rd, N8 . . . . .75 E7
   Feltham TW13 . . . . .160 C5
Dickensons La, SE25 . . . . .188 D5
Dickensons Pl, SE25 . . . . .188 D6
Dickenson St, NW5 off Dalby St .92 B6
Dickens Ri, Chig. IG7 . . . . .64 D3
Dickens Rd, E6 . . . . .116 A2
Dickens Sq, SE1 . . . . .28 A5
Dickens St, SW8 . . . . .150 B2
Dickenswood Cl, SE19 . . . . .169 H7
Dickerage La, N.Mal. KT3 . . . . .182 C3
Dickerage Rd, Kings.T. KT1 . . . .182 C1
   New Malden KT3 . . . . .182 C1
Dickinson Ct, EC1
   off St. John St 111 H4
Dickson Fold, Pnr. HA5 . . . . .66 D4
Dickson Rd, SE9 . . . . .156 B3
Dick Turpin Way, Felt. TW14 . . .141 J4
Didsbury Cl, E6 off Barking Rd . .116 C1
Dieppe Cl, W14 off Gibbs Grn . .128 C5
Digby Cres, N4 . . . . .93 J2
Digby Gdns, Dag. RM10 . . . . . .119 G1
Digby Pl, Croy. CR0 . . . . .202 C3
Digby Rd, E9 . . . . .95 G6
   Barking IG11 . . . . .99 J7
Digby St, E2 . . . . .113 F3
Diggon St, E1
   off Stepney Way 113 G5
Dighton Ct, SE5 . . . . .35 J6
Dighton Rd, SW18 . . . . .149 F5
Dignum St, N1 . . . . .11 E1
Digswell St, N7
   off Holloway Rd 93 G6
Dilhorne Cl, SE12 . . . . .173 H3
Dilke St, SW3 . . . . .32 A5
Dilloway Yd, Sthl. UB2
   off The Green 122/123 E2
Dillwyn Cl, SE26 . . . . .171 H4
Dilston Cl, Nthlt. UB5
   off Yeading La 102 C3
Dilston Gro, SE16
   off Abbeyfield Rd 133 F4
Dilton Gdns, SW15 . . . . .165 G1

Dilwyn Ct, E17 off Hillyfield 77 H3
Dimes Pl, W6 off King St 127 H4
Dimmock Dr, Grnf. UB6 . . . . .86 A5
Dimond Cl, E7 . . . . .97 G4
Dimsdale Dr, NW9 . . . . .88 C1
   Enfield EN1 . . . . .44 D6
Dimsdale Wk, E13
   off Stratford Rd 115 G1
Dimson Cres, E3 . . . . .114 A4
Dingle Cl, Barn. EN5 . . . . .39 F6
Dingle Gdns, E14 . . . . .114 A7
Dingley La, SW16 . . . . .168 D2
Dingley Pl, EC1 . . . . .12 A4
Dingley Rd, EC1 . . . . .11 J4
Dingwall Av, Croy. CR0 . . . . . . .201 J2
Dingwall Gdns, NW11 . . . . .72 D6
Dingwall Rd, SW18 . . . . .149 F7
   Croydon CR0 . . . . .202 A2
Dinmont St, E2
   off Coate St 112/113 E2
Dinsdale Gdns, SE25 . . . . .188 B5
   Barnet EN5 . . . . .41 E5
Dinsdale Rd, SE3 . . . . .135 F6
Dinsmore Rd, SW12 . . . . .150 B7
Dinton Rd, SW19 . . . . .167 G6
   Kingston upon Thames KT2 . .163 J7
Diploma Av, N2 . . . . .73 H4
Diploma Ct, N2 off Diploma Av . . .73 H4
Dirleton Rd, E15 . . . . .115 F1
Disbrowe Rd, W6 . . . . .128 B6
Discovery Business Pk, SE16
   off St. James's Rd 132 D3
Discovery Wk, E1 . . . . .132 E1
Dishforth La, NW9 . . . . .70 E1
Disney Ms, N4
   off Chesterfield Gdns 75 H5
Disney Pl, SE1 . . . . .28 A3
Disney St, SE1 . . . . .28 A3
Dison Cl, Enf. EN3 . . . . .45 G1
Disraeli Cl, SE28 . . . . .138 C1
   W4 off Acton La 126 D4
Disraeli Gdns, SW15
   off Fawe Pk Rd 148 C4
Disraeli Rd, E7 . . . . .97 G6
   NW10 . . . . .106 C2
   SW15 . . . . .148 B4
   W5 . . . . .125 G1
Diss St, E2 . . . . .13 F3
Distaff La, EC4 . . . . .19 J5
Distillery La, W6
   off Fulham Palace Rd 127 J5
Distillery Rd, W6 . . . . .127 J5
Distillery Wk, Brent. TW8 . . . . . .125 H6
Distin St, SE11 . . . . .34 E2
District Rd, Wem. HA0 . . . . .86 E5
Ditch All, SE10 . . . . .154 B1
Ditchburn St, E14 . . . . .114 C7
Ditchfield Rd, Hayes UB4 . . . . . .102 E4
Dittisham Rd, SE9 . . . . .174 B4
Ditton Cl, T.Ditt. KT7 . . . . .180 D7
Dittoncroft Cl, Croy. CR0 . . . . . .202 B4
Ditton Gra Cl, Surb. KT6 . . . . . .195 G1
Ditton Gra Dr, Surb. KT6 . . . . . .195 G1
Ditton Hill, Surb. KT6 . . . . .195 F1
Ditton Hill Rd, Surb. KT6 . . . . . .195 F1
Ditton Lawn, T.Ditt. KT7 . . . . . . .194 D1
Ditton Pl, SE20 . . . . .189 E1
Ditton Reach, T.Ditt. KT7 . . . . . .180 E6
Ditton Rd, Bexh. DA6 . . . . .158 D5
   Southall UB2 . . . . .123 F4
   Surbiton KT6 . . . . .195 H1
Divis Way, SW15 . . . . .147 H6
Dixon Clark Ct, N1
   off Canonbury Rd 93 H6
Dixon Cl, E6 off Brandreth Rd . . .116 C6
Dixon Ho, W10 . . . . .108 A6
Dixon Pl, W.Wick. BR4 . . . . .204 B1
Dixon Rd, SE14 . . . . .153 H1
   SE25 . . . . .188 B3
Dixon's All, SE16 . . . . .132 E2
Dobbin Cl, Har. HA3 . . . . .68 D2
Dobell Path, SE9 off Dobell Rd . .156 C5
Dobell Rd, SE9 . . . . .156 C5
Dobree Av, NW10 . . . . .89 H7
Dobson Cl, NW6 . . . . .91 G7
Doby Ct, EC4 . . . . .20 A5
Dockers Tanner Rd, E14 . . . . . .134 A3
Dockhead, SE1 . . . . .29 G4
Dock Hill Av, SE16 . . . . .133 G2
Dockland St, E16 . . . . .136 D1
Dockley Rd, SE16 . . . . .29 H6
Dock Rd, E16 . . . . .115 F7
   Brentford TW8 . . . . .125 G7
Dockside Rd, E16 . . . . .116 A7
Dock St, E1 . . . . .21 H5
Dockwell Cl, Felt. TW14 . . . . . . .142 A4
Dockyard Ind Est, SE18
   off Woolwich Ch St 136 B3
Doctor Johnson Av, SW17 . . . . .168 B3
★ Doctor Johnson's Ho, EC4 . . . .19 F4
Doctors Cl, SE26 . . . . .171 F5
Docwra's Bldgs, N1 . . . . .94 B6
Dodbrooke Rd, SE27 . . . . .169 G3
Doddington Gro, SE17 . . . . .35 G5
Doddington Pl, SE17 . . . . .35 G5
Dodsley Pl, N9 . . . . .61 F3
Dodson St, SE1 . . . . .27 F4

Dod St, E14 . . . . .113 J6
Doebury Wk, SE18
   off Prestwood Cl 138 A6
Doel Cl, SW19 . . . . .167 F7
Doggets Ct, Barn. EN4 . . . . . . .41 H5
Doggett Rd, SE6 . . . . .154 A7
Doghurst Av, Hayes UB3 . . . . . .121 E7
Doghurst Dr, West Dr. UB7 . . . .121 E7
Dog Kennel Hill, SE22 . . . . . . .152 B3
Dog Kennel Hill Est, SE22 . . . . .152 B3
Dog La, NW10 . . . . .89 E4
Doherty Rd, E13 . . . . .115 G4
Dokal Ind Est, Sthl. UB2
   off Hartington Rd 122/123 E3
Dolben St, SE1 . . . . .27 G2
Dolby Rd, SW6 . . . . .148 C2
Dolland St, SE11 . . . . .34 D4
Dollis Av, N3 . . . . .72 C1
Dollis Brook Wk, Barn. EN5 . . . .40 B6
Dollis Cres, Ruis. HA4 . . . . . . .84 C1
DOLLIS HILL, NW2 . . . . .89 H3
Dollis Hill Av, NW2 . . . . .89 H3
Dollis Hill La, NW2 . . . . .89 H3
Dollis Ms, N3 off Dollis Pk 72 C1
Dollis Pk, N3 . . . . .72 C1
Dollis Rd, N3 . . . . .56 B7
   NW7 . . . . .56 B7
Dollis Valley Dr, Barn. EN5 . . . .40 C6
Dollis Valley Grn Wk, N20
   off Totteridge La 57 F2
   Barnet EN5 . . . . .40 B6
Dollis Valley Way, Barn. EN5 . . .40 C6
Dolman Cl, N3 off Avondale Rd . .73 F2
Dolman Rd, W4 . . . . .126 D4
Dolman St, SW4 . . . . .151 F4
Dolphin Cl, SE16
   off Kinburn St 133 G2
   SE28 . . . . .118 D6
   Surbiton KT6 . . . . .181 G6
Dolphin Ct, NW11 . . . . .72 B6
Dolphin Ho, SW18
   off Smugglers Way 148/149 E4
Dolphin La, E14 . . . . .114 B7
Dolphin Rd, Nthlt. UB5 . . . . . .103 F2
Dolphin Sq, SW1 . . . . .33 G4
   W4 . . . . .126 E7
Dolphin Rd, Kings.T. KT1 . . . . .181 H1
Dolphin Twr, SE8
   off Abinger Gro 133 J6
Dombey St, WC1 . . . . .18 C1
★ Dome, The, SE10 . . . . .134 E1
Dome Hill Pk, SE26 . . . . .170 C4
Domett Cl, SE5 . . . . .152 A4
Domfe Pl, E5 off Rushmore Rd . . .95 F4
Domingo St, EC1 . . . . .11 J5
Dominica Cl, E13 . . . . .115 J2
Dominion Rd, Croy. CR0 . . . . . .188 C2
   Southall UB2 . . . . .123 E3
Dominion St, EC2 . . . . .20 C1
★ Dominion Thea, W1 . . . . . . .17 J3
Domonic Dr, SE9 . . . . .174 E4
Domville Cl, N20 . . . . .57 G2
Donald Dr, Rom. RM6 . . . . .82 C5
Donald Rd, E13 . . . . .115 H1
   Croydon CR0 . . . . .187 F6
Donaldson Rd, NW6 . . . . .108 C1
   SE18 . . . . .156 D1
Donald Wds Gdns, Surb. KT5 . . .196 B2
Donato Dr, SE15
   off Wells Way 132 B7
Doncaster Dr, Nthlt. UB5 . . . . . .85 F5
Doncaster Gdns, N4
   off Stanhope Gdns 75 J6
   Northolt UB5 . . . . .85 F5
Doncaster Grn, Wat. WD19 . . . . .50 C5
Doncaster Rd, N9 . . . . .44 E7
Doncel Ct, E4 . . . . .46 D7
Donegal St, N1 . . . . .10 D2
Doneraile St, SW6 . . . . .148 A2
Dongola Rd, E1 . . . . .113 H5
   E13 . . . . .115 H3
   N17 . . . . .76 B3
Dongola Rd W, E13
   off Balaam St 115 H3
Donington Av, Ilf. IG6 . . . . .81 F5
Donkey All, SE22 . . . . .152 D7
Donkey La, Enf. EN1 . . . . .44 D2
Donne Ct, SE24 . . . . .151 J6
Donnefield Av, Edg. HA8 . . . . . .53 H7
Donne Pl, SW3 . . . . .31 H1
   Mitcham CR4 . . . . .186 B4
Donne Rd, Dag. RM8 . . . . .100 C3
Donnington Rd, NW10 . . . . .89 H7
   Harrow HA3 . . . . .69 G5
   Worcester Park KT4 . . . . . .197 G2
Donnybrook Rd, SW16 . . . . . . .168 C7
Donovan Av, N10 . . . . .74 B2
Don Phelan Cl, SE5 . . . . .152 A1
Doone Cl, Tedd. TW11 . . . . . . .162 D6
Doon St, SE1 . . . . .26 E2
Doral Way, Cars. SM5 . . . . . . .199 J5
Dorando Cl, W12 . . . . .107 H7
Doran Gro, SE18 . . . . .137 H7
Doran Wk, E15 . . . . .96 C7
Dora Rd, SW19 . . . . .166 D5
Dora St, E14 . . . . .113 J6
Dorchester Av, N13 . . . . .59 J4

Dorchester Av, Bex. DA5 . . . . .176 D1
   Harrow HA2 . . . . .67 J6
Dorchester Cl, Nthlt. UB5 . . . . .85 H5
   Orpington BR5
   off Grovelands Rd 176 A7
Dorchester Ct, N14 . . . . .42 B7
   SE24 . . . . .151 J5
Dorchester Dr, SE24 . . . . .151 J5
   Feltham TW14 . . . . .141 H6
Dorchester Gdns, E4 . . . . .62 A4
   NW11 . . . . .72 D4
Dorchester Gro, W4 . . . . .127 E5
Dorchester Ms, N.Mal. KT3
   off Elm Rd 182 D4
   Twickenham TW1 . . . . .145 F7
Dorchester Rd, Mord. SM4 . . . .185 E7
   Northolt UB5 . . . . .85 H5
   Worcester Park KT4 . . . . . .197 J1
Dorchester Way, Har. HA3 . . . . .69 J6
Dorchester Waye, Hayes UB4 . . .102 C6
Dorcis Av, Bexh. DA7 . . . . . . .158 E2
Dordrecht Rd, W3 . . . . .127 E1
Dore Av, E12 . . . . .98 D5
Doreen Av, NW9 . . . . .88 D1
Dore Gdns, Mord. SM4 . . . . . . .185 E7
Dorell Cl, Sthl. UB1 . . . . .103 F5
Doria Rd, SW6 . . . . .148 C2
Doric Way, NW1 . . . . .9 H3
Dorien Rd, SW20 . . . . .184 A2
Doris Av, Erith DA8 . . . . .159 J1
Doris Rd, E7 . . . . .97 G7
Dorking Cl, SE8 . . . . .133 J6
   Worcester Park KT4 . . . . . .198 A2
Dorlcote Rd, SW18 . . . . .149 G7
Dorman Pl, N9 off Balham Rd . . .60 D2
Dorman Wk, NW10
   off Garden Way 88 D5
Dorman Way, NW8 . . . . .109 G1
Dorma Trd Pk, E10 . . . . .95 G1
Dormay St, SW18 . . . . .148 E5
Dormer Cl, E15 . . . . .97 F6
   Barnet EN5 . . . . .40 A5
Dormers Av, Sthl. UB1 . . . . . . .103 G6
Dormers Ri, Sthl. UB1 . . . . . . .103 H6
DORMER'S WELLS, Sthl. UB1 . . .103 H7
Dormers Wells La, Sthl. UB1 . . .103 G6
Dornberg Cl, SE3 . . . . .135 G7
Dornberg Rd, SE3
   off Banchory Rd 135 H7
Dorncliffe Rd, SW6 . . . . .148 B2
Dorney, NW3 . . . . .91 H7
Dorney Ri, Orp. BR5 . . . . .193 J4
Dorney Way, Houns. TW4 . . . . .143 E5
Dornfell St, NW6 . . . . .90 C5
Dornton Rd, SW12 . . . . .168 B2
   South Croydon CR2 . . . . . .202 A5
Dorothy Av, Wem. HA0 . . . . .87 H6
Dorothy Evans Cl, Bexh. DA7 . . .159 H4
Dorothy Gdns, Dag. RM8 . . . . .100 B4
Dorothy Rd, SW11 . . . . .149 J3
Dorrell Pl, SW9 off Brixton Rd . .151 G4
Dorrien Wk, SW16 . . . . .168 D2
Dorrington Pt, E3
   off Bromley High St 114 B3
Dorrington St, EC1 . . . . .19 E1
Dorrington Way, Beck. BR3
   off Creswell Dr 190 B5
Dorrit Ms, N18 . . . . .60 B4
Dorrit St, SE1 . . . . .28 A3
Dorrit Way, Chis. BR7 . . . . . . .175 F6
Dors Cl, NW9 . . . . .88 D1
Dorset Av, Sthl. UB2 . . . . .123 G4
   Welling DA16 . . . . .157 J4
Dorset Bldgs, EC4 . . . . .19 G4
Dorset Cl, NW1 . . . . .15 J1
Dorset Dr, Edg. HA8 . . . . .53 J6
Dorset Est, E2 . . . . .13 G3
Dorset Gdns, Mitch. CR4 . . . . .187 F4
Dorset Ms, N3 . . . . .72 D1
   SW1 . . . . .24 D5
Dorset Pl, E15 . . . . .96 D6
Dorset Ri, EC4 . . . . .19 G4
Dorset Rd, E7 . . . . .97 J7
   N15 . . . . .76 A4
   N22 . . . . .75 E1
   SE9 . . . . .174 B2
   SW8 . . . . .34 B7
   SW19 . . . . .184 D1
   W5 . . . . .125 F3
   Beckenham BR3 . . . . .189 G3
   Harrow HA1 . . . . .67 J6
   Mitcham CR4 . . . . .185 H2
Dorset Sq, NW1 . . . . .7 J6
Dorset St, W1 . . . . .16 A2
Dorset Way, Twick. TW2 . . . . . .162 A1
Dorset Waye, Houns. TW5 . . . . .123 F7
Dorton Cl, SE15
   off Chandler Way 132 C7
Dorville Cres, W6 . . . . .127 H3
Dorville Rd, SE12 . . . . .155 F5
Dothill Rd, SE18 . . . . .137 G7
Douai Gro, Hmptn. TW12 . . . . .179 J1
Doubleday Rd, Loug. IG10 . . . . .49 F3
Doughty Ms, WC1 . . . . .10 C6
Doughty St, WC1 . . . . .10 C5
Douglas Av, E17 . . . . .78 A1

Douglas Av, N.Mal. KT3 . . . . . .183 H4
   Wembley HA0 . . . . .87 H7
Douglas Cl, Stan. HA7 . . . . .52 D5
   Wallington SM6 . . . . .201 E5
Douglas Cres, Hayes UB4 . . . . .102 C4
Douglas Dr, Croy. CR0 . . . . . . .204 A3
Douglas Ms, NW2 . . . . .90 B3
Douglas Path, E14
   off Manchester Rd 134 C5
Douglas Rd, E4 . . . . .47 E1
   E16 . . . . .115 G5
   N1 . . . . .93 J7
   N22 . . . . .75 G1
   NW6 . . . . .108 C1
   Hounslow TW3 . . . . .143 H3
   Ilford IG3 . . . . .82 A6
   Kingston upon Thames KT1 . .182 B2
   Staines (Stanw.) TW19 . . . .140 A6
   Surbiton KT6 . . . . .195 J2
   Welling DA16 . . . . .158 B1
Douglas Sq, Mord. SM4 . . . . . .184 D6
Douglas St, SW1 . . . . .33 H2
Douglas Ter, E17
   off Douglas Av 78 A1
Douglas Way, SE8 . . . . .133 J7
Doulton Ms, NW6
   off Lymington Rd 90/91 E6
Dounesforth Gdns, SW18 . . . . .166 E1
Douro Pl, W8 . . . . .22 B5
Douro St, E3 . . . . .114 A2
Douthwaite Sq, E1 . . . . .29 J1
Dove App, E6 . . . . .116 B5
Dove Cl, NW7 off Bunns La 55 F7
   Northolt UB5
   off Wayfarer Rd 102 D4
   Wallington SM6 . . . . .201 F7
Dovecot Cl, Pnr. HA5 . . . . .66 B5
Dovecote Av, N22 . . . . .75 G3
Dovecote Gdns, SW14
   off Avondale Rd 146 D3
Dove Ct, EC2 . . . . .20 B4
Dovedale Av, Har. HA3 . . . . .69 F6
   Ilford IG5 . . . . .80 D2
Dovedale Cl, Well. DA16 . . . . . .158 A2
Dovedale Ri, Mitch. CR4 . . . . . .167 J7
Dovedale Rd, SE22 . . . . .153 E5
Dovedon Cl, N14 . . . . .58 E2
Dove Ho Gdns, E4 . . . . .62 A2
Dovehouse Mead, Bark. IG11 . . .117 G2
Dovehouse St, SW3 . . . . .31 G3
Dove Ms, SW5 . . . . .30 C2
Dove Pk, Pnr. HA5 . . . . .51 G7
Dover Cl, NW2 off Brent Ter 90 A2
   Romford RM5 . . . . .83 J2
Dovercourt Av, Th.Hth. CR7 . . . .187 G4
Dovercourt Est, N1 . . . . .94 A6
Dovercourt Gdns, Stan. HA7 . . . .53 H5
Dovercourt La, Sutt. SM1 . . . . .199 F3
Dovercourt Rd, SE22 . . . . .152 B6
Doverfield Rd, SW2 . . . . .151 E6
Dover Flats, SE1
   off Old Kent Rd 132 B4
Dover Gdns, Cars. SM5 . . . . . .199 J3
Dover Ho Rd, SW15 . . . . .147 G4
Doveridge Gdns, N13 . . . . .59 H4
Dove Rd, N1 . . . . .94 A6
Dove Row, E2 . . . . .112 D1
Dover Pk Dr, SW15 . . . . .147 H6
Dover Patrol, SE3
   off Kidbrooke Way 155 H2
Dover Rd, E12 . . . . .97 J2
   N9 . . . . .61 F2
   SE19 . . . . .170 A6
   Romford RM6 . . . . .82 E6
Dover St, W1 . . . . .17 E6
Dover Yd, W1 . . . . .25 F1
Doves Cl, Brom. BR2 . . . . .206 B2
Doves Yd, N1 . . . . .111 G1
Doveton Rd, S.Croy. CR2 . . . . .202 A5
Doveton St, E1
   off Malcolm Rd 113 F4
Dove Wk, SW1 . . . . .32 B3
Dowanhill Rd, SE6 . . . . .172 D1
Dowdeswell Cl, SW15 . . . . . . .147 E4
Dowding Pl, Stan. HA7 . . . . .52 D6
Dowdney Cl, NW5 . . . . .92 C5
Dowgate Hill, EC4 . . . . .20 B5
Dowland St, W10 . . . . .108 B2
Dowlas Est, SE5 . . . . .36 D7
Dowlas St, SE5 . . . . .36 D7
Dowlerville Rd, Orp. BR6 . . . . . .207 J6
Dowman Cl, SW19
   off Nelson Gro Rd 184/185 E1
Downage, NW4 . . . . .71 J3
Downalong, Bushey (Bushey Hth)
   WD23 . . . . .52 A1
Downbarns Rd, Ruis. HA4 . . . . . .84 D3
Downbury Ms, SW18
   off Merton Rd 148 D6
Down Cl, Nthlt. UB5 . . . . .102 B2
Downderry Rd, Brom. BR1 . . . . .172 D3
Downe Cl, Well. DA16 . . . . .138 C7
Downend, SE18
   off Moordown 136/137 E7
Downe Rd, Mitch. CR4 . . . . . . .185 J2
Downers Cotts, SW4
   off The Pavement 150 C4

Downes Cl, Twick. TW1
   off St. Margarets Rd 144/145 E6
Downes Ct, N21 . . . . .59 G1
Downfield, Wor.Pk. KT4 . . . . . .197 F1
Downfield Cl, W9 . . . . .6 A6
Down Hall Rd, Kings.T. KT2 . . . .181 G1
DOWNHAM, Brom. BR1 . . . . . .173 F5
Downham La, Brom. BR1
   off Downham Way 172 D5
Downham Rd, N1 . . . . .94 A7
Downham Way, Brom. BR1 . . . .172 D5
Downhills Av, N17 . . . . .76 A3
Downhills Pk Rd, N17 . . . . .75 J3
Downhills Way, N17 . . . . .75 J3
Downhurst Av, NW7 . . . . .54 D5
Downing Cl, Har. HA2 . . . . .67 J3
Downing Dr, Grnf. UB6 . . . . . . .104 A1
Downing Rd, Dag. RM9 . . . . . . .119 F1
Downings, E6 . . . . .116 D6
Downing St, SW1 . . . . .26 A3
Downland Cl, N20 . . . . .57 F1
Downleys Cl, SE9 . . . . .174 B2
Downman Rd, SE9 . . . . .156 B3
Down Pl, W6 . . . . .127 H4
Down Rd, Tedd. TW11 . . . . . . .163 E6
Downs, The, SW20 . . . . .166 A7
Downs Av, Chis. BR7 . . . . .174 C5
   Pinner HA5 . . . . .67 F6
Downs Br Rd, Beck. BR3 . . . . . .190 D1
Downsbury Ms, SW18
   off Merton Rd 148 D6
Downsell Rd, E15 . . . . .96 C4
Downsfield Rd, E17 . . . . .77 H6
Downshall Av, Ilf. IG3 . . . . .81 H6
Downs Hill, Beck. BR3 . . . . . . .172 D7
Downshire Hill, NW3 . . . . .91 G4
Downside, Sun. TW16 . . . . .178 A1
   Twickenham TW1 . . . . .162 C3
Downside Cl, SW19 . . . . .167 F6
Downside Cres, NW3 . . . . .91 H5
   W13 . . . . .104 D4
Downside Rd, Sutt. SM2 . . . . . .199 G6
Downside Wk, Nthlt. UB5 . . . . .103 F3
Downs La, E5 off Downs Rd . .94/95 E4
Downs Pk Rd, E5 . . . . .94 D5
   E8 . . . . .94 C5
Downs Rd, E5 . . . . .94 D4
   Beckenham BR3 . . . . .190 B2
   Enfield EN1 . . . . .44 B4
   Thornton Heath CR7 . . . . . .187 J1
Down St, W1 . . . . .24 D2
   West Molesey KT8 . . . . . . .179 G5
Down St Ms, W1 . . . . .24 D2
Downs Vw, Islw. TW7 . . . . .124 C7
Downsview Gdns, SE19 . . . . . . .169 H7
Downsview Rd, SE19 . . . . .169 J7
Downsway, Orp. BR6 . . . . .207 H5
Downton Av, SW2 . . . . .169 E2
Downtown Rd, SE16 . . . . .133 H2
Down Way, Nthlt. UB5 . . . . . . .102 B3
Dowrey St, N1
   off Richmond Av 111 G1
Dowsett Rd, N17 . . . . .76 C2
Dowson Cl, SE5 . . . . .152 A4
Doyce St, SE1 . . . . .27 J3
Doyle Gdns, NW10 . . . . .107 G1
Doyle Rd, SE25 . . . . .188 D4
D'Oyley St, SW1 . . . . .32 B1
Doynton St, N19 . . . . .92 B2
Draco St, SE17 . . . . .35 J5
Dragonfly Cl, E13
   off Hollybush St 115 H3
Dragon Rd, SE15 . . . . .36 D6
Dragoon Rd, SE8 . . . . .133 J5
Dragor Rd, NW10 . . . . .106 C4
Drake Cl, SE16
   off Middleton Dr 133 G2
Drake Ct, SE19 . . . . .170 C5
   W12 . . . . .127 J2
   Harrow HA2 . . . . .85 F1
Drake Cres, SE28 . . . . .118 C6
Drakefell Rd, SE4 . . . . .153 G2
   SE14 . . . . .153 G2
Drakefield Rd, SW17 . . . . .168 A3
Drakeley Ct, N5
   off Highbury Hill 93 H4
Drake Rd, SE4 . . . . .154 A3
   Chessington KT9 . . . . .196 A5
   Croydon CR0 . . . . .187 F7
   Harrow HA2 . . . . .85 F2
   Mitcham CR4 . . . . .186 A6
Drakes Ctyd, NW6 . . . . .90 C7
Drake St, WC1 . . . . .18 C2
   Enfield EN2 . . . . .44 A1
Drakes Wk, E6 . . . . .116 C1
Drakewood Rd, SW16 . . . . .168 D7
Draper Cl, Belv. DA17 . . . . .139 F4
   Isleworth TW7 . . . . .144 A2
Draper Ho, SE1
   off Newington Butts 131 H4
Draper Pl, N1 off Dagmar Ter . . .111 H1
Drapers Gdns, EC2
   off Copthall Av 112 A6
Drapers Rd, E15 . . . . .96 D4
   N17 . . . . .76 C3
   Enfield EN2 . . . . .43 H2
Drappers Way, SE16 . . . . .37 J1

Draven Cl, Brom. BR2 . . . . .191 F7
Drawdock Rd, SE10 . . . . .134 D7
Drawell Cl, SE18 . . . . .137 H5
Drax Av, SW20 . . . . .165 H7
Draxmont, SW19 . . . . .166 B6
Draycot Rd, E11 . . . . .79 H6
  Surbiton KT6 . . . . .196 A1
Draycott Av, SW3 . . . . .31 H1
  Harrow HA3 . . . . .69 E6
Draycott Cl, NW2 . . . . .90 A3
  SE5 off Edmund St 132 A7
  Harrow HA3 . . . . .69 E6
Draycott Ms, SW6
  off New Kings Rd 148 C2
Draycott Pl, SW3 . . . . .31 J2
Draycott Ter, SW3 . . . . .32 A1
Drayford Cl, W9 . . . . .108 C4
Dray Gdns, SW2 . . . . .151 F5
Draymans Ms, SE15
  off Chadwick Rd 152 C2
Draymans Way, Islw. TW7 . . .144 C3
Drayside Ms, Sthl. UB2
  off Kingston Rd 123 F2
Drayson Ms, W8 . . . . .128 D2
Drayton Av, W13 . . . . .104 D7
  Loughton IG10 . . . . .48 C3
  Orpington BR6 . . . . . . .207 E1
Drayton Br Rd, W7 . . . . . . .104 C7
  W13 . . . . .104 C7
Drayton Cl, Houns. TW4 . . . .143 F5
  Ilford IG1 . . . . .99 G1
Drayton Gdns, N21 . . . . . . .43 H7
  SW10 . . . . .30 D3
  W13 . . . . .104 D7
  West Drayton UB7 . . . . .120 B2
Drayton Grn, W13 . . . . . . .104 D7
Drayton Grn Rd, W13 . . . . . .104 E7
Drayton Gro, W13 . . . . . . .104 D7
Drayton Pk, N5 . . . . .93 G5
Drayton Pk Ms, N5
  off Drayton Pk 93 G5
Drayton Rd, E11 . . . . .96 D1
  N17 . . . . .76 B2
  NW10 . . . . .107 F1
  W13 . . . . .104 D7
  Borehamwood WD6 . . . . .38 A4
  Croydon CR0 . . . . . . .201 H2
Drayton Waye, Har. HA3 . . . .69 E6
Dresden Cl, NW6 . . . . .91 E6
Dresden Rd, N19 . . . . .92 D1
Dressington Av, SE4 . . . . . .154 A6
Drew Av, NW7 . . . . .56 B6
Drew Gdns, Grnf. UB6 . . . . . .86 C6
Drew Rd, E16 . . . . .136 B1
Drewstead Rd, SW16 . . . . . .168 D2
Driffield Rd, E3 . . . . .113 H2
Drift, The, Brom. BR2 . . . . . .206 A3
Drift Way, Rich. TW10 . . . . .163 J1
Driftway, The, Mitch. CR4 . . .186 A1
Drinkwater Rd, Har. HA2 . . . .85 H2
Drive, The, E4 . . . . .46 D7
  E17 . . . . .78 B4
  E18 . . . . .79 G3
  N3 . . . . .56 D7
  N6 . . . . .73 J5
  N11 . . . . .58 C6
  NW10 off Longstone Av . . .107 F1
  NW11 . . . . .72 B7
  SW6 off Fulham Rd 148 B2
  SW16 . . . . .187 F3
  SW20 . . . . .165 J7
  W3 . . . . .106 C6
  Barking IG11 . . . . .99 J7
  Barnet (High Barn.) EN5 . . .40 B3
  Barnet (New Barn.) EN5 . . .41 F6
  Beckenham BR3 . . . . . .190 A2
  Bexley DA5 . . . . .158 C6
  Buckhurst Hill IG9 . . . . . .47 J7
  Chislehurst BR7 . . . . . .193 J3
  Chislehurst (Scad.Pk) BR7 . .193 H1
  Edgware HA8 . . . . .54 A4
  Enfield EN2 . . . . .44 A1
  Epsom KT19 . . . . .197 F6
  Erith DA8 . . . . .139 H7
  Feltham TW14 . . . . . . .142 C7
  Harrow HA2 . . . . .67 G7
  Hounslow TW3 . . . . . . .144 A2
  Ilford IG1 . . . . .98 C1
  Isleworth TW7 . . . . . . .144 A2
  Kingston upon Thames KT2 .164 C7
  Loughton IG10 . . . . .48 B3
  Morden SM4 . . . . .185 G5
  Orpington BR6 . . . . . . .207 J2
  Romford (Coll.Row) RM5 . . .83 J1
  Sidcup DA14 . . . . .176 B3
  Surbiton KT6 . . . . .181 H7
  Thornton Heath CR7 . . . .188 A4
  Wembley HA9 . . . . .88 C2
  West Wickham BR4 . . . . .190 D7
Driveway, The, E17 off Hoe St . .78 B6
Droitwich Cl, SE26 . . . . . . .170 D3
Dromey Gdns, Har. HA3 . . . .52 C7
Dromore Rd, SW15 . . . . . . .148 B6
Dronfield Gdns, Dag. RM8 . . .100 C5
Droop St, W10 . . . . .108 B4
Drovers Pl, SE15 . . . . .133 E7
Drovers Rd, S.Croy. CR2 . . . .202 A5

Droveway, Loug. IG10 . . . . . . .49 E2
Druce Rd, SE21 . . . . .152 B6
Druid St, SE1 . . . . .28 E3
Druids Way, Brom. BR2 . . . . .190 D4
Drumaline Ridge, Wor.Pk. KT4 .197 E2
Drummond Cen, Croy. CR0 . . .201 J2
Drummond Cres, NW1 . . . . . . .9 H3
Drummond Dr, Stan. HA7 . . . .52 C7
Drummond Gate, SW1 . . . . . .33 J3
Drummond Pl, Twick. TW1 . . .144 E7
Drummond Rd, E11 . . . . .79 H6
  SE16 . . . . .132 E3
  Croydon CR0 . . . . . . .201 J2
Drummonds, The, Buck.H. IG9 . .63 H2
Drummonds Pl, Rich. TW9 . . .145 H4
Drummond St, NW1 . . . . .9 F5
Drum St, E1 . . . . .21 G3
Drury Cres, Croy. CR0 . . . . .201 G2
Drury La, WC2 . . . . .18 B4
Drury Rd, Har. HA1 . . . . . . .67 J7
Drury Way, NW10 . . . . .88 C4
Drury Way Ind Est, NW10 . . . .88 C5
Dryad St, SW15 . . . . .148 A3
Dryburgh Gdns, NW9 . . . . . . .70 A3
Dryburgh Rd, SW15 . . . . . . .147 H3
Drydell St, NW1 . . . . .9 H4
Dryden Av, W7 . . . . .104 C6
Dryden Cl, Ilf. IG6 . . . . .65 J6
Dryden Ct, SE11 . . . . .35 F2
Dryden Rd, SW19 . . . . . . .167 F6
  Enfield EN1 . . . . .44 B6
  Harrow HA3 . . . . .68 C1
  Welling DA16 . . . . . . .157 H1
Dryden St, WC2 . . . . .18 B4
Dryfield Cl, NW10 . . . . .88 C6
Dryfield Rd, Edg. HA8 . . . . . .54 C6
Dryfield Wk, SE8
  off New King St 134 A6
Dryhill Rd, Belv. DA17 . . . . .139 F6
Dryland Av, Orp. BR6 . . . . . .207 J4
Drylands Rd, N8 . . . . .75 E6
Drysdale Av, E4 . . . . .46 B7
Drysdale Pl, N1 . . . . .12 E3
Drysdale St, N1 . . . . .12 E4
Dublin Av, E8 . . . . .112 D1
Du Burstow Ter, W7 . . . . . .124 B2
Ducal St, E2 . . . . .13 G4
Du Cane Cl, W12 . . . . . . .107 J6
Du Cane Ct, SW17 . . . . . . .168 A1
Du Cane Rd, W12 . . . . . . .107 F6
Duchess Cl, N11 . . . . .58 B5
  Sutton SM1 . . . . .199 F4
Duchess Gro, Buck.H. IG9 . . . .63 H2
Duchess Ms, W1 . . . . .16 E2
Duchess of Bedford's Wk, W8 . .128 D2
Duchess St, W1 . . . . .16 E2
Duchy Pl, SE1 . . . . .27 F1
Duchy St, SE1 . . . . .27 F1
Ducie St, SW4 . . . . .151 F4
Duckett Ms, N4 off Duckett Rd . .75 H6
Duckett Rd, N4 . . . . .75 H6
Duckett St, E1 . . . . .113 G4
Duck La, W1 . . . . .17 H4
Duck Lees La, Enf. EN3 . . . . . .45 H4
DUCKS ISLAND, Barn. EN5 . . . .40 A6
Ducks Wk, Twick. TW1 . . . . .145 F5
Du Cros Dr, Stan. HA7 . . . . . .53 G6
Du Cros Rd, W3
  off The Vale 126/127 E1
Dudden Hill La, NW10 . . . . . .89 F4
Duddington Cl, SE9 . . . . . . .174 A4
Dudley Av, Har. HA3 . . . . . . .69 F3
Dudley Ct, NW11 . . . . .72 C4
  Ruislip HA4 . . . . .84 B5
Dudley Dr, Mord. SM4 . . . . .184 B7
  Ruislip HA4 . . . . .84 B5
Dudley Gdns, W13 . . . . . . .125 E2
  Harrow HA2 . . . . .86 A1
Dudley Ms, SW2
  off Bascombe St 151 G6
Dudley Pl, Hayes UB3 . . . . . .121 G4
Dudley Rd, E17 . . . . .78 A2
  N3 . . . . .72 E2
  NW6 . . . . .108 B2
  SW19 . . . . .166 D6
  Harrow HA2 . . . . .85 J2
  Ilford IG1 . . . . .99 E4
  Kingston upon Thames KT1 .181 J3
  Richmond TW9 . . . . . . .145 J2
  Southall UB2 . . . . . . .122 D2
  Walton-on-Thames KT12 . . .178 A6
Dudley St, W2 . . . . .14 E2
Dudlington Rd, E5 . . . . .95 F2
Dudmaston Ms, SW3 . . . . . . .31 F3
Dudrich Ms, SE22
  off Melbourne Gro 152 C5
Dudsbury Rd, Sid. DA14 . . . .176 B6
Dudset La, Houns. TW5 . . . . .142 A1
Dufferin Av, EC1 . . . . .12 B6
Dufferin St, EC1 . . . . .12 A6
Duffield Cl, Har. HA1 . . . . . .68 C5
Duffield Dr, N15
  off Copperfield Dr 76 C4
Duff St, E14 . . . . .114 B6
Dufour's Pl, W1 . . . . .17 G4
Dugard Way, SE11 . . . . .35 G1
Duggan Dr, Chis. BR7
  off Wood Dr 174 B6
Dugolly Av, Wem. HA9
  off Chalkhill Rd 88 B3

Duke Gdns, Ilf. IG6 off Duke Rd . .81 G4
Duke Humphrey Rd, SE3 . . . . .155 E1
Duke of Cambridge Cl, Twick.
  TW2 . . . . .144 A6
Duke of Edinburgh Rd, Sutt.
  SM1 . . . . .199 G2
Duke of Wellington Av, SE18 . .137 E3
Duke of Wellington Pl, SW1 . . .24 C4
Duke of York Sq, SW3 . . . . . .32 A2
Duke of York St, SW1 . . . . . .25 G1
Duke Rd, W4 . . . . .126 D5
  Ilford IG6 . . . . .81 G4
Dukes Av, N3 . . . . .72 E1
  N10 . . . . .74 C3
  W4 . . . . .126 D5
  Edgware HA8 . . . . .53 J6
  Harrow HA1 . . . . .68 B4
  Harrow (N.Har.) HA2 . . . . .67 F6
  Hounslow TW4 . . . . . . .143 E4
  Kingston upon Thames KT2 .163 F4
  New Malden KT3 . . . . . .183 F3
  Northolt UB5 . . . . .85 E7
  Richmond TW10 . . . . . .163 F4
Dukes Cl, Hmptn. TW12 . . . .161 F5
Dukes Ct, E6 . . . . .116 D1
Dukes Gate, W4 off Acton La . .126 C4
Dukes Grn Av, Felt. TW14 . . . .142 A5
Dukes Head Yd, N6
  off Highgate High St 92 B1
Dukes La, W8 . . . . .128 D2
Duke's Meadows, W4
  off Great Chertsey Rd 146 C2
Dukes Ms, N10 off Dukes Av . . .74 B3
Duke's Ms, W1 . . . . .16 C3
Dukes Orchard, Bex. DA5 . . . .177 J1
Duke's Pas, E17 . . . . .78 C4
Dukes Pl, EC3 . . . . .21 E4
Dukes Rd, E6 . . . . .116 D1
  W3 . . . . .106 A5
Duke's Rd, WC1 . . . . .9 J4
Dukesthorpe Rd, SE26 . . . . .171 G4
Duke St, SW1 . . . . .25 G1
  W1 . . . . .16 C3
  Richmond TW9 . . . . . . .145 G4
  Sutton SM1 . . . . .199 G4
Duke St Hill, SE1 . . . . .28 C1
Dukes Way, W.Wick. BR4 . . . .205 E3
Duke's Yd, W1 . . . . .16 C5
Dulas St, N4 off Everleigh St . . .93 F1
Dulford St, W11 . . . . .108 B7
Dulka Rd, SW11 . . . . .149 J5
Dulverton Rd, SE9 . . . . . . .175 F2
  Ruislip HA4 . . . . .84 A1
DULWICH, SE21 . . . . .152 B7
★ Dulwich Coll Picture Gall,
  SE21 . . . . .152 B7
Dulwich Common, SE21 . . . . .170 B1
  SE22 . . . . .170 B1
Dulwich Lawn Cl, SE22
  off Colwell Rd 152 C5
Dulwich Oaks, The, SE21 . . . .170 B3
Dulwich Rd, SE24 . . . . . . .151 F4
Dulwich Village, SE21 . . . . . .152 B6
Dulwich Wd Av, SE19 . . . . . .170 B4
Dulwich Wd Pk, SE19 . . . . . .170 B4
Dumbarton Rd, SW2 . . . . . . .151 E6
Dumbleton Cl, Kings.T. KT1
  off Gloucester Rd 182 B1
Dumbreck Rd, SE9 . . . . . . .156 C4
Dumont Rd, N16 . . . . .94 B3
Dumpton Pl, NW1
  off Gloucester Av 92 A7
Dunbar Av, SW16 . . . . . . .187 G2
  Beckenham BR3 . . . . . .189 H4
  Dagenham RM10 . . . . . .101 G3
Dunbar Cl, Hayes UB4 . . . . .102 A5
Dunbar Ct, Sutt. SM1 . . . . . .199 G5
Dunbar Gdns, Dag. RM10 . . . .101 G5
Dunbar Rd, E7 . . . . .97 G6
  N22 . . . . .75 G1
  New Malden KT3 . . . . . .182 C4
Dunbar St, SE27 . . . . .169 J3
Dunblane Cl, Edg. HA8
  off Tayside Dr 54 B2
Dunblane Rd, SE9 . . . . . . .156 B3
Dunboyne Rd, NW3 . . . . .91 J5
Dunbridge Ho, SW15
  off Highcliffe Dr 147 F6
Dunbridge St, E2 . . . . .13 J5
Duncan Cl, Barn. EN5 . . . . . .41 F4
Duncan Gro, W3 . . . . .106 E6
Duncannon St, WC2 . . . . . . .18 A6
Duncan Rd, E8 . . . . .112 E1
  Richmond TW9 . . . . . . .145 H4
Duncan St, N1 . . . . .11 G1
Duncan Ter, N1 . . . . .11 G2
Dunch St, E1
  off Watney St 112/113 E6
Duncombe Hill, SE23 . . . . . .153 H7
Duncombe Rd, N19 . . . . .92 D1
Duncrievie Rd, SE13 . . . . . . .154 D6
Duncroft, SE18 . . . . .137 H7
Dundalk Rd, SE4 . . . . .153 H3

Dundas Gdns, W.Mol. KT8 . . .179 H3
Dundas Rd, SE15 . . . . .153 F2
Dundee Rd, E13 . . . . .115 H2
  SE25 . . . . .188 E5
Dundee St, E1 . . . . .132 E1
Dundee Way, Enf. EN3 . . . . . .45 H3
Dundela Gdns, Wor.Pk. KT4 . . .197 H4
Dundonald Cl, E6
  off Northumberland Rd . . .116 B6
Dundonald Rd, NW10 . . . . . .108 A1
  SW19 . . . . .166 B7
Dunedin Ho, E16
  off Manwood St 136 C1
Dunedin Rd, E10 . . . . .96 B3
  Ilford IG1 . . . . .99 F1
Dunedin Way, Hayes UB4 . . . .102 C4
Dunelm Gro, SE27 . . . . . . .169 J4
Dunelm St, E1 . . . . .113 G6
Dunfield Gdns, SE6 . . . . . . .172 B5
Dunfield Rd, SE6 . . . . .172 B5
Dunford Rd, N7 . . . . .93 F4
Dungarvan Av, SW15 . . . . . .147 G4
Dunheved Cl, Th.Hth. CR7 . . .187 G6
Dunheved Rd N, Th.Hth. CR7 . .187 G6
Dunheved Rd S, Th.Hth. CR7 . .187 G6
Dunheved Rd W, Th.Hth. CR7 . .187 G6
Dunhill Pt, SW15
  off Dilton Gdns 165 H1
Dunholme Grn, N9 . . . . .60 C3
Dunholme La, N9
  off Dunholme Rd 60 C3
Dunholme Rd, N9 . . . . .60 C3
Dunkeld Rd, SE25 . . . . . . .188 A4
  Dagenham RM8 . . . . . .100 C1
Dunkery Rd, SE9 . . . . .174 A4
Dunkirk St, SE27
  off Waring St 169 J4
Dunlace Rd, E5 . . . . .95 F4
Dunleary Cl, Houns. TW4 . . . .143 F7
Dunley Dr, Croy. (New Adgtn)
  CR0 . . . . .204 B7
Dunlin Ho, W13 . . . . .104 C4
Dunloe Av, N17 . . . . .76 A3
Dunloe St, E2 . . . . .13 F2
Dunlop Pl, SE16 . . . . .29 G3
Dunmore Pt, E2 . . . . .13 F4
Dunmore Rd, NW6 . . . . . . .108 B1
  SW20 . . . . .183 J1
Dunmow Cl, Felt. TW13 . . . . .160 E4
  Loughton IG10 . . . . .48 B6
  Romford RM6 . . . . .82 C5
Dunmow Ho, Dag. RM9 . . . . .118 B1
Dunmow Rd, E15 . . . . .96 D4
Dunmow Wk, N1
  off Popham St 111 J1
Dunnage Cres, SE16
  off Plough Way 133 H4
Dunn Mead, NW9
  off Field Mead 55 F7
Dunnock Cl, N9 . . . . .61 G1
  Borehamwood WD6 . . . . .38 A4
Dunnock Rd, E6 . . . . .116 B6
Dunns Pas, WC1 . . . . .18 B3
Dunn St, E8 . . . . .94 C5
Dunollie Pl, NW5
  off Dunollie Rd 92 C5
Dunollie Rd, NW5 . . . . .92 C5
Dunoon Rd, SE23 . . . . .153 F7
Dunraven Dr, Enf. EN2 . . . . . .43 G2
Dunraven Rd, W12 . . . . . . .127 G1
Dunraven St, W1 . . . . .16 A5
Dunsany Rd, W14 . . . . .128 A3
Dunsfold Way, Croy. (New Adgtn)
  CR0 . . . . .204 B7
Dunsford Way, SW15
  off Dover Pk Dr 147 H6
Dunsmore Cl, Hayes UB4 . . . .102 D4
Dunsmore Rd, Walt. KT12 . . . .178 B6
Dunsmure Rd, N16 . . . . .94 B1
Dunspring La, Ilf. IG5 . . . . . . .80 E2
Dunstable Ms, W1 . . . . .16 C1
Dunstable Rd, Rich. TW9 . . . .145 H4
  West Molesey KT8 . . . . . .179 F4
Dunstall Rd, SW20 . . . . . . .165 H6
Dunstall Way, W.Mol. KT8 . . . .179 H3
Dunstan Cl, N2
  off Thomas More Way 73 F3
Dunstan Rd, NW11 . . . . .90 C1
Dunstans Gro, SE22 . . . . . . .152 E6
Dunstans Rd, SE22 . . . . . . .152 D7
Dunster Av, Mord. SM4 . . . . .198 A1
Dunster Cl, Barn. EN5 . . . . . .40 A4
  Romford RM5 . . . . .83 J2
Dunster Ct, EC3 . . . . .20 D5
  Borehamwood WD6
  off Kensington Way 38 D3
Dunster Dr, NW9 . . . . .88 C1
Dunster Gdns, NW6 . . . . .90 C7
Dunsterville Way, SE1 . . . . . .28 C4
Dunster Way, Har. HA2 . . . . . .85 E3
  Wallington SM6
  off Helios Rd 200 A1
Dunston Rd, E8 . . . . .112 C1
  SW11 . . . . .150 A2
Dunston St, E8 . . . . .112 C1
Dunton Cl, Surb. KT6 . . . . . .195 H1
Dunton Rd, E10 . . . . .78 B7

Dunton Rd, SE1 . . . . .37 F3
Duntshill Rd, SW18 . . . . . . .167 E1
Dunvegan Cl, W.Mol. KT8 . . .179 H4
Dunvegan Rd, SE9 . . . . .156 C4
Dunwich Rd, Bexh. DA7 . . . .159 F1
Dunworth Ms, W11
    off Portobello Rd 108 C6
Duplex Ride, SW1 . . . . .24 A4
Dupont Rd, SW20 . . . . .184 A2
Duppas Av, Croy. CR0
    off Violet La 201 H4
Duppas Hill La, Croy. CR0 . . .201 H4
Duppas Hill Rd, Croy. CR0 . . .201 H4
Duppas Hill Ter, Croy. CR0 . . .201 H3
Duppas Rd, Croy. CR0 . . . . .201 G3
Dupree Rd, SE7 . . . . .135 H5
Dura Den Cl, Beck. BR3 . . . .172 B1
Durand Cl, Cars. SM5 . . . . . .199 J1
Durand Gdns, SW9 . . . . . . .151 F1
Durands Wk, SE16 . . . . .133 J2
Durand Way, NW10 . . . . . . .88 C7
Durants Pk Av, Enf. EN3 . . . .45 G4
Durants Rd, Enf. EN3 . . . . . .45 F4
Durant St, E2 . . . . .13 H3
Durban Gdns, Dag. RM10 . . .101 J7
Durban Rd, E15 . . . . .114 E3
    E17 . . . . .77 J1
    N17 . . . . .60 B6
    SE27 . . . . .169 J4
    Beckenham BR3 . . . . . . .189 J2
    Ilford IG2 . . . . .99 H1
Durbin Rd, Chess. KT9 . . . . .195 H4
Durdans Rd, Sthl. UB1 . . . . .103 F6
Durell Gdns, Dag. RM9 . . . . .100 D5
Durell Rd, Dag. RM9 . . . . . .100 D5
Durford Cres, SW15 . . . . . . .165 G1
Durham Av, Brom. BR2 . . . . .191 F4
    Hounslow TW5 . . . . .123 F5
    Woodford Green IG8 . . . . .64 A5
Durham Cl, SW20
    off Durham Rd 183 H2
Durham Hill, Brom. BR1 . . . .173 F4
Durham Ho St, WC2 . . . . . . .18 B6
Durham Pl, SW3 . . . . .31 J4
    Ilford IG1 off Eton Rd 99 F4
Durham Ri, SE18 . . . . .137 F5
Durham Rd, E12 . . . . .98 A4
    E16 . . . . .115 E4
    N2 . . . . .73 H3
    N7 . . . . .93 F2
    N9 . . . . .60 D2
    SW20 . . . . .183 H1
    W5 . . . . .125 G3
    Borehamwood WD6 . . . . .38 C3
    Bromley BR2 . . . . .191 F3
    Dagenham RM10 . . . . . .101 J5
    Feltham TW14 . . . . .142 C7
    Harrow HA1 . . . . .67 H5
    Sidcup DA14 . . . . .176 B5
Durham Row, E1 . . . . .113 H5
Durham St, SE11 . . . . .34 C4
Durham Ter, W2 . . . . .14 A3
Durham Wf, Brent. TW8
    off London Rd 125 F7
Durham Yd, E2
    off Teesdale St 112/113 E3
Durley Av, Pnr. HA5 . . . . . . .67 E7
Durley Rd, N16 . . . . .76 B7
Durlston Rd, E5 . . . . .94 D2
    Kingston upon Thames KT2 .163 H6
Durnell Way, Loug. IG10 . . . .48 D3
Durnford St, N15 . . . . .76 B5
    SE10 off Greenwich Ch St . .134 C6
Durning Rd, SE19 . . . . .170 A5
Durnsford Av, SW19 . . . . . . .166 D2
Durnsford Rd, N11 . . . . .74 D1
    SW19 . . . . .166 D2
Durrant Way, Orp. BR6 . . . . .207 G5
Durrell Rd, SW6 . . . . .148 C1
Durrington Av, SW20 . . . . . .183 J1
Durrington Pk Rd, SW20 . . . .165 J7
Durrington Rd, E5 . . . . .95 H4
Durrington Twr, SW8
    off Westbury St 150 C2
Dursley Cl, SE3 . . . . .155 J2
Dursley Gdns, SE3 . . . . .156 A1
Dursley Rd, SE3 . . . . .155 J2
Durward St, E1 . . . . .112 E5
Durweston Ms, W1 . . . . .16 A1
Durweston St, W1 . . . . .16 A1
Dury Rd, Barn. EN5 . . . . . . .40 C1
Dutch Barn Cl, Stai. (Stanw.)
    TW19 . . . . .140 A6
Dutch Gdns, Kings.T. KT2
    off Windmill Ri 164 B6
Dutch Yd, SW18
    off Wandsworth High St . . .148 D5
Dutton St, SE10 . . . . .154 C1
Duxberry Cl, Brom. BR2
    off Southborough La 192 B5
Duxford Ho, SE2
    off Wolvercote Rd 138 D2
Dwight Ct, SW6
    off Burlington Rd 148 B2
Dye Ho La, E3 . . . . .114 A1
Dyer's Bldgs, EC1 . . . . .19 E2

Dyers Hall Rd, E11 . . . . .96 E1
Dyers La, SW15 . . . . .147 H4
Dykes Way, Brom. BR2 . . . . .191 F3
Dylan Rd, SE24 . . . . .151 H4
    Belvedere DA17 . . . . . . .139 G3
Dylways, SE5 . . . . .152 A4
Dymchurch Cl, Ilf. IG5 . . . . . .80 D2
    Orpington BR6 . . . . .207 H4
Dymes Path, SW19
    off Queensmere Rd 166 A2
Dymock St, SW6 . . . . .148 E3
Dymond Est, SW17
    off Glenburnie Rd 167 H3
Dyneley Rd, SE12 . . . . .173 J4
Dyne Rd, NW6 . . . . .90 C7
Dynevor Rd, N16 . . . . .94 B3
    Richmond TW10 . . . . . . .145 H5
Dynham Rd, NW6 . . . . .90 D7
Dyott St, WC1 . . . . .18 A3
Dysart Av, Kings.T. KT2 . . . .163 F5
Dysart St, EC2 . . . . .12 D6
Dyson Rd, E11 . . . . .79 E6
    E15 . . . . .97 F6
Dysons Rd, N18 . . . . .61 E5

E

Eade Rd, N4 . . . . .75 J7
Eagans Cl, N2 off Market Pl . .73 H3
Eagle Av, Rom. RM6 . . . . . . .82 E6
Eagle Cl, SE16 off Varcoe Rd .133 F5
    Enfield EN3 . . . . .45 H4
    Wallington SM6 . . . . .201 E6
Eagle Ct, EC1 . . . . .19 G1
Eagle Dr, NW9 . . . . .71 E2
Eagle Hts, SW11
    off Bramlands Cl 149 H3
Eagle Hill, SE19 . . . . .170 A6
Eagle La, E11 . . . . .79 G4
Eagle Ms, N1 off Tottenham Rd .94 B6
Eagle Pl, SW1 . . . . .17 G6
    SW7 . . . . .30 D3
Eagle St, WC1 . . . . .18 C2
Eagle Ter, Wdf.Grn. IG8 . . . . .63 H7
Eagle Trd Est, Mitch. CR4
    off Willow La 185 J6
Eagle Wf, E14 off Broomfield St .114 B5
Eagle Wf Rd, N1 . . . . .12 A1
Ealdham Sq, SE9 . . . . .155 J4
EALING, W5 . . . . .105 F7
Ealing Bdy Shop Cen, W5 . . .105 G7
Ealing Cl, Borwd. WD6 . . . . . .38 D1
★ Ealing Common, W5 . . . . .125 H1
Ealing Downs Ct, Grnf. UB6
    off Perivale La 104 D3
Ealing Grn, W5 . . . . .125 G1
Ealing Pk Gdns, W5 . . . . . . .125 F4
Ealing Rd, Brent. TW8 . . . . .125 G5
    Northolt UB5 . . . . .85 G7
    Wembley HA0 . . . . .105 G1
Ealing Village, W5 . . . . .105 H6
Eamont St, NW8 . . . . .7 G1
Eardley Cres, SW5 . . . . .128 D5
Eardley Pt, SE18
    off Wilmount St 136/137 E4
Eardley Rd, SW16 . . . . .168 C5
    Belvedere DA17 . . . . . . .139 G5
Earl Cl, N11 . . . . .58 B5
Earldom Rd, SW15 . . . . .147 J4
Earle Gdns, Kings.T. KT2 . . . .163 H6
Earlham Gro, E7 . . . . .97 F5
    N22 . . . . .59 F7
Earlham St, WC2 . . . . .17 J4
Earl Ri, SE18 . . . . .137 G4
Earl Rd, SW14 off Elm Rd . . .146 C4
EARLS COURT, SW5 . . . . . . .128 C5
★ Earls Court Exhib Cen, SW5 .128 C5
Earls Ct Gdns, SW5 . . . . . . .30 A2
Earls Ct Rd, SW5 . . . . .128 D4
    W8 . . . . .128 D4
Earls Ct Sq, SW5 . . . . .30 A3
Earls Cres, Har. HA1 . . . . . . .68 B4
Earlsdown Ho, Bark. IG11
    off Wheelers Cross 117 G2
Earlsferry Way, N1 . . . . .93 F7
EARLSFIELD, SW18 . . . . . . .167 F1
Earlsfield Ho, Kings.T. KT2
    off Kingsgate Rd 181 H1
Earlsfield Rd, SW18 . . . . . . .167 F1
Earlshall Rd, SE9 . . . . .156 C4
Earlsmead, Har. HA2 . . . . . . .85 F4
Earlsmead Rd, N15 . . . . .76 C5
    NW10 . . . . .107 J2
Earl's Path, Loug. IG10 . . . . . .47 J2
Earls Ter, W8 . . . . .128 C3
Earlsthorpe Ms, SW12 . . . . .150 A6
Earlsthorpe Rd, SE26 . . . . . .171 G4
Earlstoke St, EC1 . . . . .11 G3
Earlston Gro, E9 . . . . .113 E1
Earl St, EC2 . . . . .20 D1
Earls Wk, W8 . . . . .128 D3
    Dagenham RM8 . . . . . . .100 B4
Earls Way, Orp. BR6
    off Station Rd 207 J2

Earlswood Av, Th.Hth. CR7 . . .187 G5
Earlswood Gdns, Ilf. IG5 . . . . .80 D3
Earlswood St, SE10 . . . . . . .135 E5
Early Ms, NW1 off Arlington Rd .110 B1
Earnshaw St, WC2 . . . . .17 J3
Earsby St, W14 . . . . .128 B4
Easby Cres, Mord. SM4 . . . . .185 E6
Easebourne Rd, Dag. RM8 . . .100 C5
Easedale Ho, Islw. TW7
    off Summerwood Rd 144 C5
Eashing Pt, SW15
    off Wanborough Dr 165 H1
Easley's Ms, W1 . . . . .16 C3
EAST ACTON, W3 . . . . .126 D1
East Acton La, W3 . . . . .106 E7
East Arbour St, E1 . . . . .113 G6
East Av, E12 . . . . .98 B7
    E17 . . . . .78 B4
    Hayes UB3 . . . . .121 J2
    Southall UB1 . . . . .103 F7
    Wallington SM6 . . . . .201 F5
East Bk, N16 . . . . .76 B7
Eastbank Rd, Hmptn. (Hmptn H.)
    TW12 . . . . .161 J5
EAST BARNET, Barn. EN4 . . . .41 H6
East Barnet Rd, Barn. EN4 . . .41 H6
Eastbourne Av, W3 . . . . .106 D6
Eastbourne Gdns, SW14 . . . .146 C3
Eastbourne Ms, W2 . . . . . . .14 D3
Eastbourne Rd, E6 . . . . .116 D3
    E15 . . . . .115 E1
    N15 . . . . .76 B6
    SW17 . . . . .168 A6
    W4 . . . . .126 C6
    Brentford TW8 . . . . .125 F5
    Feltham TW13 . . . . .160 D2
Eastbourne Ter, W2 . . . . . . .14 D3
Eastbournia Av, N9 . . . . .61 E3
Eastbrook Av, N9 . . . . .45 F7
    Dagenham RM10 . . . . . .101 J4
Eastbrook Rd, SE3 . . . . .135 H7
Eastbury Av, Bark. IG11 . . . .117 H1
    Enfield EN1 . . . . .44 B1
Eastbury Ct, Bark. IG11 . . . .117 H1
Eastbury Gro, W4 . . . . .127 E5
★ Eastbury Ho, Bark. IG11 . . .117 J1
Eastbury Rd, E6 . . . . .116 D4
    Kingston upon Thames KT2 .163 H7
    Orpington BR5 . . . . .193 G6
Eastbury Sq, Bark. IG11 . . . .117 J1
Eastbury Ter, E1 . . . . .113 G4
Eastcastle St, W1 . . . . .17 F3
Eastcheap, EC3 . . . . .20 C5
East Churchfield Rd, W3 . . . .126 D1
Eastchurch Rd, Houns. (Hthrw Air.)
    TW6 . . . . .141 H2
East Cl, W5 . . . . .106 A4
    Barnet EN4 . . . . .42 A4
    Greenford UB6 . . . . .103 J2
Eastcombe Av, SE7 . . . . . . .135 H6
EASTCOTE, Pnr. HA5 . . . . . . .66 C6
Eastcote, Orp. BR6 . . . . . . .207 J1
Eastcote Av, Grnf. UB6 . . . . .86 D5
    Harrow HA2 . . . . .85 H2
    West Molesey KT8 . . . . . .179 F5
Eastcote La, Har. HA2 . . . . . .85 G3
    Northolt UB5 . . . . .85 G7
Eastcote La N, Nthlt. UB5 . . . .85 F6
Eastcote Pl, Pnr. HA5 . . . . . .66 B6
Eastcote Rd, Har. HA2 . . . . . .85 J3
    Pinner HA5 . . . . .66 C6
    Pinner (Eastcote Vill.) HA5 . .66 A6
    Welling DA16 . . . . .157 G2
Eastcote St, SW9 . . . . .151 F2
Eastcote Vw, Pnr. HA5 . . . . . .66 C4
EASTCOTE VILLAGE, Pnr. HA5 .66 B5
Eastcourt, Sun. TW16 . . . . . .178 C2
East Ct, Wem. HA0 . . . . .87 F2
East Cres, N11 . . . . .57 J4
    Enfield EN1 . . . . .44 C5
Eastcroft Rd, Epsom KT19 . . .197 E7
East Cross Cen, E15 . . . . . . .96 A6
East Cross Route, E3 . . . . . . .95 J7
    E9 . . . . .95 J7
Eastdown Pk, SE13 . . . . . . .154 D4
East Duck Lees La, Enf. EN3 . .45 H4
EAST DULWICH, SE22 . . . . . .152 D6
East Dulwich Gro, SE22 . . . .152 B6
East Dulwich Rd, SE15 . . . . .152 C4
    SE22 . . . . .152 C4
East End Rd, N2 . . . . .73 F3
    N3 . . . . .72 D2
East End Way, Pnr. HA5 . . . . .67 E3
East Entrance, Dag. RM10 . . .119 H2
Eastern Av, E11 . . . . .79 J6
    Ilford IG2, IG4 . . . . .80 B6
    Pinner HA5 . . . . .66 D7
    Romford RM6 . . . . .82 C4
Eastern Av W, Rom. RM1, RM5,
    RM6, RM7 . . . . .82 E4
Eastern Gateway, E16 . . . . . .115 J7
Eastern Ind Est, Erith DA18 . .139 G2
Eastern Perimeter Rd, Houns.
    (Hthrw Air.) TW6 . . . . . . .141 J3
Eastern Quay Apartments, E16
    off Rayleigh Rd 135 H1
Eastern Rd, E13 . . . . .115 H2

Eastern Rd, E17 . . . . .78 C5
    N2 . . . . .73 J3
    N22 . . . . .75 E1
    SE4 . . . . .154 A4
Easternville Gdns, Ilf. IG2 . . . .81 F6
Eastern Way, SE2 . . . . .138 D1
    SE28 . . . . .138 A2
    Belvedere DA17 . . . . . . .139 H2
    Erith DA18 . . . . .138 D1
East Ferry Rd, E14 . . . . .134 B4
Eastfield Cotts, Hayes UB3 . . .121 H5
Eastfield Gdns, Dag. RM10 . . .101 G3
Eastfield Rd, E17 . . . . .78 A4
    N8 . . . . .74 E3
    Dagenham RM9, RM10 . . .101 G3
Eastfields, Pnr. HA5 . . . . .66 C5
Eastfields Av, SW18
    off Point Pleasant 148 D4
Eastfields Rd, W3 . . . . .106 C5
    Mitcham CR4 . . . . .186 A2
Eastfield St, E14 . . . . .113 H5
EAST FINCHLEY, N2 . . . . . . .73 G4
East Gdns, SW17 . . . . .167 H6
Eastgate Cl, SE28 . . . . .118 D6
Eastglade, Pnr. HA5 . . . . .67 E3
EAST HAM, E6 . . . . .116 B2
Eastham Cl, Barn. EN5 . . . . . .40 B5
East Ham Ind Est, E6 . . . . . .116 B4
East Ham Manor Way, E6 . . . .116 D6
East Ham Shop Hall, E6
    off Myrtle Rd 116 B1
East Harding St, EC4 . . . . . . .19 F3
East Heath Rd, NW3 . . . . . . .91 G3
East Hill, SW18 . . . . .149 E5
    Wembley HA9 . . . . .88 A2
Eastholm, NW11 . . . . .73 E4
Eastholme, Hayes UB3 . . . . .122 A1
East India Dock Rd, E14 . . . .114 A6
East India Way, Croy. CR0 . . .202 C1
Eastlake Rd, SE5 . . . . .151 H2
Eastlands Cres, SE21 . . . . . .152 C6
East La, SE16 . . . . .29 H4
    Kingston upon Thames KT1
        off High St 181 G3
    Wembley HA0, HA9 . . . . . .87 G3
Eastlea Ms, E16
    off Desford Rd 114/115 E4
Eastleigh Av, Har. HA2 . . . . . .85 H2
Eastleigh Cl, NW2 . . . . .89 E3
    Sutton SM2 . . . . .199 E7
Eastleigh Rd, E17 . . . . .77 J2
    Bexleyheath DA7 . . . . . . .159 J2
    Hounslow (Hthrw Air.) TW6
        off Cranford La 141 J3
Eastleigh Wk, SW15 . . . . . . .147 G7
Eastleigh Way, Felt. TW14 . . .160 A1
Eastman Rd, W3 . . . . .126 D1
East Mascalls, SE7
    off Mascalls Rd 135 J6
East Mead, Ruis. HA4 . . . . . .84 D3
Eastmead Av, Grnf. UB6 . . . .103 H3
Eastmead Cl, Brom. BR1 . . . .192 B2
Eastmearn Rd, SE21 . . . . . . .169 J2
EAST MOLESEY, KT8 . . . . . .180 A4
Eastmont Rd, Esher KT10 . . . .194 B2
Eastmoor Pl, SE7
    off Eastmoor St 136 A3
Eastmoor St, SE7 . . . . .136 A3
East Mt St, E1 . . . . .113 E5
Eastney Rd, Croy. CR0 . . . . .201 H1
Eastney St, SE10 . . . . .134 D5
Eastnor Rd, SE9 . . . . .175 F1
Easton Gdns, Borwd. WD6 . . .38 D3
Easton St, WC1 . . . . .10 E4
East Pk Cl, Rom. RM6 . . . . . .82 D5
East Parkside, SE10 . . . . . . .135 E2
East Pas, EC1 . . . . .19 H1
East Pier, E1
    off Wapping High St . . .132/133 E1
East Pl, SE27 off Pilgrim Hill . .169 J4
East Poultry Av, EC1 . . . . . . .19 G2
East Ramp, Houns. (Hthrw Air.)
    TW6 . . . . .140 E1
East Rd, E15 . . . . .115 G1
    N1 . . . . .12 B4
    SW19 . . . . .167 F6
    Barnet EN4 . . . . .58 A1
    Edgware HA8 . . . . .70 B1
    Feltham TW14 . . . . .141 G7
    Kingston upon Thames KT2 .181 H1
    Romford (Chad.Hth) RM6 . .82 E5
    Welling DA16 . . . . .158 B2
    West Drayton UB7 . . . . . .120 C4
East Rochester Way, SE9 . . . .157 H4
    Bexley DA5 . . . . .158 D6
    Sidcup DA15 . . . . .157 H4
East Row, E11 . . . . .79 G6
    W10 . . . . .108 B4
Eastry Av, Brom. BR2 . . . . . .191 F6
Eastry Rd, Erith DA8 . . . . . .139 G7
EAST SHEEN, SW14 . . . . . . .146 D4
East Sheen Av, SW14 . . . . . .146 D4
Eastside Rd, NW11 . . . . .72 C4
East Smithfield, E1 . . . . .21 G6
East St, SE17 . . . . .36 A3
    Barking IG11 . . . . .99 F7
    Bexleyheath DA7 . . . . . . .159 G4

East St, Brent. TW8 . . . . .125 F7
Bromley BR1 . . . . .191 G2
East Surrey Gro, SE15 . . . . . . .132 C2
East Tenter St, E1 . . . . .21 G4
East Twrs, Pnr. HA5 . . . . .66 D5
East Vw, E4 . . . . .62 C5
Barnet EN5 . . . . .40 C3
Eastview Av, SE18 . . . . .137 H4
Eastville Av, NW11 . . . . .72 C6
East Wk, Barn. EN4 . . . . .42 A7
Hayes UB3 . . . . .122 A1
Eastway, E9 . . . . .95 J6
East Way, E11 . . . . .79 H5
Bromley BR2 . . . . .191 G2
Croydon CR0 . . . . .203 H2
Hayes UB3 . . . . .122 A1
Eastway, Mord. SM4 . . . . .184 A5
East Way, Ruis. HA4 . . . . .84 A5
Eastway, Wall. SM6 . . . . .200 C4
Eastway Commercial Cen, E9 . .96 A5
Eastway Cres, Har. HA2
off Eliot Dr 85 H2
Eastwell Cl, Beck. BR3 . . . . . . .189 H1
Eastwick Ct, SW19
off Victoria St 166 A1
EAST WICKHAM, Well. DA16 . . .138 A7
Eastwood Cl, E18 off George La . .79 G2
N7 off Eden Gro 93 G5
N17
off Northumberland Gro . .60/61 E7
Eastwood Rd, E18 . . . . .79 G2
N10 . . . . .74 A2
Ilford IG3 . . . . .82 A7
West Drayton UB7 . . . . .120 D2
East Woodside, Bex. DA5 . . . . .177 E1
Eastwood St, SW16 . . . . .168 C6
Eatington Rd, E10 . . . . .78 D5
Eaton Cl, SW1 . . . . .32 B2
Stanmore HA7 . . . . .53 E4
Eaton Dr, SW9 . . . . .151 H4
Kingston upon Thames KT2 . .164 A7
Eaton Gdns, Dag. RM9 . . . . . . .100 E7
Eaton Gate, SW1 . . . . .32 B1
Eaton Ho, E14
off Westferry Circ 134 A1
Eaton La, SW1 . . . . .24 E6
Eaton Ms N, SW1 . . . . .32 B1
Eaton Ms S, SW1 . . . . .32 C1
Eaton Ms W, SW1 . . . . .32 C1
Eaton Pk Rd, N13 . . . . .59 G2
Eaton Pl, SW1 . . . . .24 B6
Eaton Ri, E11 . . . . .79 J5
W5 . . . . .105 G6
Eaton Rd, NW4 . . . . .71 J5
Enfield EN1 . . . . .44 B3
Hounslow TW3 . . . . .144 A4
Sidcup DA14 . . . . .176 D2
Sutton SM2 . . . . .199 G6
Eaton Row, SW1 . . . . .24 D6
Eatons Mead, E4 . . . . .62 A2
Eaton Sq, SW1 . . . . .24 D5
Eaton Ter, SW1 . . . . .32 B1
Eaton Ter Ms, SW1 . . . . .32 B1
Eatonville Rd, SW17 . . . . .167 J2
Eatonville Vil, SW17
off Eatonville Rd 167 J2
Ebbisham Dr, SW8 . . . . .34 C5
Ebbisham Rd, Wor.Pk. KT4 . . . .197 J2
Ebbsfleet Rd, NW2 . . . . .90 B4
Ebdon Way, SE3 . . . . .155 H3
Ebenezer Ho, SE11 . . . . .35 F2
Ebenezer St, N1 . . . . .12 B3
Ebenezer Wk, SW16 . . . . .186 C1
Ebley Cl, SE15 . . . . .37 F6
Ebner St, SW18 . . . . .149 E5
Ebor St, E1 . . . . .13 F5
Ebrington Rd, Har. HA3 . . . . . . .69 G6
Ebsworth St, SE23 . . . . .153 G7
Eburne Rd, N7 . . . . .93 E3
Ebury Br, SW1 . . . . .32 D3
Ebury Br Est, SW1 . . . . .32 D3
Ebury Br Rd, SW1 . . . . .32 C4
Ebury Cl, Kes. BR2 . . . . .206 B3
Ebury Ms, SE27 . . . . .169 H3
SW1 . . . . .32 C1
Ebury Ms E, SW1 . . . . .32 D1
Ebury Sq, SW1 . . . . .32 C2
Ebury St, SW1 . . . . .32 D1
Ecclesbourne Cl, N13 . . . . .59 G5
Ecclesbourne Gdns, N13 . . . . . .59 G5
Ecclesbourne Rd, N1 . . . . .93 J7
Thornton Heath CR7 . . . . . . .187 J5
Eccles Rd, SW11 . . . . .149 J4
Eccleston Br, SW1 . . . . .32 E1
Eccleston Cl, Barn. EN4 . . . . . . .41 J4
Orpington BR6 . . . . .207 G1
Eccleston Cres, Rom. RM6 . . . . .82 A7
Ecclestone Ct, Wem. HA9
off St. John's Rd 87 H5
Ecclestone Pl, Wem. HA9 . . . . .87 J5
Eccleston Ms, SW1 . . . . .24 C6
Eccleston Pl, SW1 . . . . .32 D1
Eccleston Rd, W13 . . . . .104 D7
Eccleston Sq, SW1 . . . . .32 E2
Eccleston Sq Ms, SW1 . . . . . . .33 F2
Eccleston St, SW1 . . . . .24 D6
Echo Hts, E4 off Mount Echo Dr . .62 B1

Eckersley St, E1 off Buxton St . .112 D4
Eckford St, N1 . . . . .10 E1
Eckington Ho, N15
off Fladbury Rd 76 A6
Eckstein Rd, SW11 . . . . .149 H4
Eclipse Rd, E13 . . . . .115 H5
Ector Rd, SE6 . . . . .172 E2
Edbrooke Rd, W9 . . . . .108 D4
Eddiscombe Rd, SW6 . . . . . . .148 C2
Eddy Cl, Rom. RM7 . . . . .83 H4
Eddystone Rd, SE4 . . . . .153 H5
Eddystone Twr, SE8 . . . . .133 H4
Eddystone Wk, Stai. TW19 . . . .140 B7
Ede Cl, Houns. TW3 . . . . .143 F3
Edenbridge Cl, SE16
off Masters Dr 132/133 E5
Edenbridge Rd, E9 . . . . .95 G7
Enfield EN1 . . . . .44 B6
Eden Cl, NW3 . . . . .90 D2
W8 off Adam & Eve Ms 128 D3
Wembley HA0 . . . . .105 G1
Edencourt Rd, SW16 . . . . .168 B6
Edenfield Gdns, Wor.Pk. KT4 . . .197 F3
Edenhurst Av, SW6 . . . . .148 C3
Eden Ms, SW17
off Huntspill St 167 F3
EDEN PARK, Beck. BR3 . . . . . .190 A5
Eden Pk Av, Beck. BR3 . . . . . . .189 H4
Eden Rd, E17 . . . . .78 B5
SE27 . . . . .169 H5
Beckenham BR3 . . . . .189 H4
Bexley DA5 . . . . .177 J4
Croydon CR0 . . . . .202 A4
Edensor Gdns, W4 . . . . .127 E7
Edensor Rd, W4 . . . . .126 E7
Eden St, Kings.T. KT1 . . . . . . .181 G2
Edenvale Cl, Mitch. CR4
off Edenvale Rd 168 A7
Edenvale Rd, Mitch. CR4 . . . . .168 A7
Edenvale St, SW6 . . . . .149 E2
Eden Wk, Kings.T. KT1
off Eden St 181 H2
Eden Wk Shop Cen, Kings.T.
KT1 . . . . .181 H2
Eden Way, Beck. BR3 . . . . . . .189 J5
Ederline Av, SW16 . . . . .187 F3
Edgar Kail Way, SE22 . . . . . . .152 B4
Edgarley Ter, SW6 . . . . .148 B1
Edgar Rd, E3 . . . . .114 B3
Hounslow TW4 . . . . .143 F7
Romford RM6 . . . . .82 D7
Edgbaston Rd, Wat. WD19 . . . . .50 B3
Edgeborough Way, Brom. BR1 . .174 A7
Edgebury, Chis. BR7 . . . . .175 E4
Edgebury Wk, Chis. BR7 . . . . .175 F4
Edgecombe Ho, SW19 . . . . . . .166 B1
Edgecoombe, S.Croy. CR2 . . . .203 F7
Edgecoombe Cl, Kings.T. KT2 . . .164 D7
Edgecote Cl, W3
off Cheltenham Pl 126 C1
Edgecot Gro, N15
off Oulton Rd 76 A5
Edgefield Av, Bark. IG11 . . . . . .99 J7
Edge Hill, SE18 . . . . .136 E6
SW19 . . . . .166 A7
Edge Hill Av, N3 . . . . .72 D3
Edge Hill Ct, SW19 . . . . .166 A7
Edgehill Gdns, Dag. RM10 . . . .101 G4
Edgehill Rd, W13 . . . . .105 F5
Chislehurst BR7 . . . . .175 F3
Mitcham CR4 . . . . .186 B1
Edgeley La, SW4
off Edgeley Rd 150 D3
Edgeley Rd, SW4 . . . . .150 D3
Edgel St, SW18
off Ferrier St 148/149 E4
Edgepoint Cl, SE27
off Knights Hill 169 H5
Edge St, W8
off Kensington Ch St 128 D1
Edgewood Dr, Orp. BR6 . . . . . .207 J5
Edgewood Grn, Croy. CR0 . . . .203 G1
Edgeworth Av, NW4 . . . . .71 G5
Edgeworth Cl, NW4 . . . . .71 G5
Edgeworth Cres, NW4 . . . . . . .71 G5
Edgeworth Rd, SE9 . . . . .155 J4
Barnet EN4 . . . . .41 H4
Edgington Rd, SW16 . . . . .168 D6
Edgington Way, Sid. DA14 . . . .176 C7
EDGWARE, HA8 . . . . .54 B5
Edgwarebury Gdns, Edg. HA8 . . .54 A5
Edgwarebury La, Edg. HA8 . . . . .54 A4
Edgware Ct, Edg. HA8
off Cavendish Dr 54 A6
Edgware Rd, NW2 . . . . .89 H1
NW9 . . . . .70 D3
W2 . . . . .15 H3
Edgware Rd Sub, W2
off Edgware Rd 109 H5
Edgware Way, Edg. HA8 . . . . . .53 J4
Edinburgh Cl, E2 off Russia La . .113 F2
Pinner HA5 . . . . .66 D7
Edinburgh Ct, SW20 . . . . .184 A5

Edinburgh Dr, Rom. RM7
off Eastern Av W 83 J4
Edinburgh Gate, SW1 . . . . .23 J7
Edinburgh Ho, W9 . . . . .6 B3
Edinburgh Rd, E13 . . . . .115 H2
E17 . . . . .78 A5
N18 . . . . .60 D5
W7 . . . . .124 C2
Sutton SM1 . . . . .199 F2
Edington Rd, SE2 . . . . .138 B3
Enfield EN3 . . . . .45 F2
Edison Cl, E17 off Exeter Rd 78 A5
Edison Ct, SE10
off Greenroof Way 135 F3
Edison Dr, Sthl. UB1 . . . . .103 H6
Wembley HA9 . . . . .87 H2
Edison Gro, SE18 . . . . .137 J7
Edison Rd, N8 . . . . .74 D6
Bromley BR2 . . . . .191 G2
Enfield EN3 . . . . .45 J2
Welling DA16 . . . . .157 J1
Edis St, NW1 . . . . .110 A1
Edith Cavell Cl, N19
off Hornsey Ri Gdns 74 D7
Edith Cavell Way, SE18
off Shooter's Hill Rd 156 B1
Edith Gdns, Surb. KT5 . . . . . . .182 B7
Edith Gro, SW10 . . . . .30 C6
Edithna St, SW9 . . . . .151 E3
Edith Nesbit Wk, SE9
off Westhorne Av 156 B4
Edith Rd, E6 . . . . .98 A7
E15 off Chandos Rd 96 D5
N11 . . . . .58 D7
SE25 . . . . .188 A5
SW19 . . . . .167 E6
W14 . . . . .128 B4
Romford RM6 . . . . .82 D6
Edith Row, SW6 . . . . .149 E1
Edith St, E2 . . . . .13 H1
Edith Summerskill Ho, SW6
off Clem Attlee Ct 128 C7
Edith Ter, SW10 . . . . .30 C7
Edith Vil, SW15 off Bective Rd . .148 B4
W14 . . . . .128 C4
Edith Yd, SW10 . . . . .30 D7
Edmansons Cl, N17
off Bruce Gro 76 B1
Edmeston Cl, E9 . . . . .95 H6
Edmond Halley Way, SE10 . . . .134 E2
Edmonds Ct, W.Mol. KT8
off Avern Rd 179 H4
EDMONTON, N9 . . . . .60 D4
Edmonton Grn, N9
off Hertford Rd 60/61 E2
Edmonton Grn Shop Cen, N9 . . .60 E2
Edmund Gro, Felt. TW13 . . . . .161 F2
Edmund Hurst Dr, E6 . . . . .116 E5
Edmund Rd, Mitch. CR4 . . . . . .185 H3
Welling DA16 . . . . .158 A3
Edmunds Cl, Hayes UB4 . . . . . .102 C5
Edmund St, SE5 . . . . .36 B7
Edmunds Wk, N2 . . . . .73 H4
Edna Rd, SW20 . . . . .184 A2
Edna St, SW11 . . . . .149 H1
Edrich Ho, SW4 . . . . .150 E1
Edrick Rd, Edg. HA8 . . . . .54 C6
Edrick Wk, Edg. HA8 . . . . .54 C6
Edric Rd, SE14 . . . . .133 G7
Edridge Rd, Croy. CR0 . . . . . . .201 J3
Edulf Rd, Borwd. WD6 . . . . .38 B1
Edward Av, E4 . . . . .62 B6
Morden SM4 . . . . .185 G5
Edward Cl, N9 . . . . .44 C7
NW2 . . . . .90 A4
Hampton (Hmptn H.) TW12
off Edward Rd 161 J5
Northolt UB5 . . . . .102 C2
Edward Ct, E16
off Alexandra St 115 G5
Edwardes Pl, W8
off Edwardes Sq 128 C3
Edwardes Sq, W8 . . . . .128 D3
Edward Gro, Barn. EN4 . . . . . . .41 G5
Edward Ms, NW1 . . . . .8 E2
Edward Pl, SE8 . . . . .133 J6
Edward Rd, E17 . . . . .77 G4
SE20 . . . . .171 G7
Barnet EN4 . . . . .41 G5
Bromley BR1 . . . . .173 H7
Chislehurst BR7 . . . . .175 E5
Croydon CR0 . . . . .188 B7
Feltham TW14 . . . . .141 G6
Hampton (Hmptn H.) TW12 . .161 J5
Harrow HA2 . . . . .67 J3
Northolt UB5 . . . . .102 C2
Romford RM6 . . . . .82 E6
Edward's Av, Ruis. HA4 . . . . . . .84 B6
Edwards Cl, Wor.Pk. KT4 . . . . .198 A2
Edwards Cotts, N1
off Compton Av 93 H6
Edwards Dr, N11 off Gordon Rd . .58 D7
Edwards La, N16 . . . . .94 A2
Edwards Ms, N1 . . . . .93 G7
W1 . . . . .16 B4
Edward Sq, N1
off Caledonian Rd 111 F1

Edward Sq, SE16
off Rotherhithe St 133 H1
Edwards Rd, Belv. DA17 . . . . . .139 G4
Edward St, E16 . . . . .115 G4
SE8 . . . . .133 J6
SE14 . . . . .133 H7
Edward's Way, SE4
off Adelaide Av 154 A5
Edwards Yd, Wem. HA0
off Mount Pleasant 105 H1
Edward Temme Av, E15 . . . . . . .97 F7
Edward Tyler Rd, SE12 . . . . . . .173 H2
Edwina Gdns, Ilf. IG4 . . . . .80 B5
Edwin Av, E6 . . . . .116 D2
Edwin Cl, Bexh. DA7 . . . . .139 F6
Edwin Pl, Croy. CR0
off Cross Rd 202 A1
Edwin Rd, Edg. HA8 . . . . .54 D6
Twickenham TW1, TW2 . . . . .162 C1
Edwin's Mead, E9
off Lindisfarne Way 95 H4
Edwin St, E1 . . . . .113 F4
E16 . . . . .115 G5
Edwyn Cl, Barn. EN5 . . . . .39 J6
Edwyn Ho, SW18
off Neville Gill Cl 148 E6
Eel Brook Cl, SW6
off King's Rd 148 E1
Eel Brook Studios, SW6
off Moore Pk Rd 128 D7
Eel Pie Island, Twick. TW1 . . . .162 E1
Effie Pl, SW6 . . . . .128 D7
Effie Rd, SW6 . . . . .128 D7
Effingham Cl, Sutt. SM2 . . . . . .199 E7
Effingham Rd, N8 . . . . .75 G5
SE12 . . . . .155 E5
Croydon CR0 . . . . .187 F7
Surbiton KT6 . . . . .181 E7
Effort St, SW17 . . . . .167 H5
Effra Par, SW2 . . . . .151 G5
Effra Rd, SW2 . . . . .151 G4
SW19 . . . . .166 E6
Egbert St, NW1 . . . . .110 A1
Egbury Ho, SW15
off Tangley Gro 147 F6
Egerton Cl, Pnr. HA5 . . . . .66 A4
Egerton Cres, SW3 . . . . .31 H1
Egerton Dr, SE10 . . . . .154 B1
Egerton Gdns, NW4 . . . . .71 H4
NW10 . . . . .107 J1
SW3 . . . . .23 G6
W13 . . . . .105 E6
Ilford IG3 . . . . .99 J5
Egerton Gdns Ms, SW3 . . .23 H6
Egerton Pl, SW3 . . . . .23 H6
Egerton Rd, N16 . . . . .76 C7
SE25 . . . . .188 B3
New Malden KT3 . . . . .183 F4
Twickenham TW2 . . . . .144 B7
Wembley HA0 . . . . .87 J7
Egerton Ter, SW3 . . . . .23 H6
Egerton Way, Hayes UB3 . . . . .121 E7
Eggardon Ct, Nthlt. UB5
off Lancaster Rd 85 J6
Egham Cl, SW19
off Winterfold Cl 166 B2
Sutton SM3 . . . . .198 B2
Egham Cres, Sutt. SM3 . . . . . .198 A3
Egham Rd, E13 . . . . .115 H5
Eglantine Rd, SW18 . . . . .149 F5
Egleston Rd, Mord. SM4 . . . . . .184 E6
Eglington Ct, SE17 . . . . .35 J5
Eglington Rd, E4 . . . . .46 D7
Eglinton Hill, SE18 . . . . .137 E6
Eglinton Rd, SE18 . . . . .136 D6
Egliston Ms, SW15 . . . . .147 J3
Egliston Rd, SW15 . . . . .147 J3
Eglon Ms, NW1 off Berkley Rd . .91 J7
Egmont Av, Surb. KT6 . . . . . . .195 J1
Egmont Rd, N.Mal. KT3 . . . . . .183 F4
Surbiton KT6 . . . . .195 J1
Sutton SM2 . . . . .199 F7
Walton-on-Thames KT12 . . . .178 B7
Egmont St, SE14 . . . . .133 G7
Egremont Ho, SE13
off Conington Rd 154 B2
Egremont Rd, SE27 . . . . .169 G3
Egret Way, Hayes UB4 . . . . . . .102 D5
Eider Cl, E7 . . . . .97 F5
Hayes UB4 off Cygnet Way . .102 D5
Eighteenth Rd, Mitch. CR4 . . . .186 E4
Eighth Av, E12 . . . . .98 C4
Hayes UB3 . . . . .122 A1
Eileen Rd, SE25 . . . . .188 A5
Eindhoven Cl, Cars. SM5 . . . . .200 A1
Eisenhower Dr, E6 . . . . .116 B5
Elaine Gro, NW5 . . . . .92 A5
Elam Cl, SE5 . . . . .151 H2
Elam St, SE5 . . . . .151 H2
Eland Pl, Croy. CR0
off Eland Rd 201 H3
Eland Rd, SW11 . . . . .149 J3
Croydon CR0 . . . . .201 H3
Elba Pl, SE17 . . . . .36 A1
Elberon Av, Croy. CR0 . . . . . . .186 C6
Elbe St, SW6 . . . . .149 F2
Elborough Rd, SE25 . . . . .188 D5

Elborough St, SW18 166 D1
Elbury Dr, E16 115 G6
Elcho St, SW11 129 H7
Elcot Av, SE15 132 E7
Elder Av, N8 74 E5
Elderberry Cl, Ilf. IG6
off Hazel La 64/65 E7
Elderberry Gro, SE27
off Linton Gro 169 J5
Elderberry Rd, W5 125 H2
Elderberry Way, E6
off Vicarage La 116 C3
Elder Cl, N20 56 E2
Sidcup DA15 175 J1
Elder Ct, Bushey (Bushey Hth)
WD23 52 B2
Elderfield Pl, SW17 168 B4
Elderfield Rd, E5 95 F4
Elderfield Wk, E11 79 H5
Elderflower Way, E15 96 E7
Elder Gdns, SE27 169 J4
Elder Oak Cl, SE20 188 E1
Elder Rd, SE27 169 J5
Elderslie Cl, Beck. BR3 190 B5
Elderslie Rd, SE9 156 D5
Elder St, E1 21 F1
Elderton Rd, SE26 171 H4
Eldertree Pl, Mitch. CR4
off Eldertree Way 186 C1
Eldertree Way, Mitch. CR4 186 B1
Elder Wk, N1 *off Essex Rd* 111 H1
Elderwood Pl, SE27
off Elder Rd 169 J5
Eldon Av, Borwd. WD6 38 A2
Croydon CR0 203 F2
Hounslow TW5 123 G7
Eldon Gro, NW3 91 G5
Eldon Pk, SE25 188 E4
Eldon Rd, E17 77 J4
N9 61 F2
N22 75 H1
W8 22 B6
Eldon St, EC2 20 C2
Eldon Way, NW10 106 B2
Eldred Rd, Bark. IG11 117 H1
Eldridge Cl, Felt. TW14 160 A1
Eleanor Cl, N15 *off Arnold Rd* 76 C3
SE16 133 G2
Eleanor Cres, NW7 56 A4
Eleanor Gdns, Barn. EN5 40 A5
Dagenham RM8 101 F3
Eleanor Gro, SW13 147 E3
Eleanor Rd, E8 94 E7
E15 97 F6
N11 58 E6
Eleanor St, E3 114 A3
Eleanor Wk, SE18
off Samuel St 136 C4
Electra Business Pk, E16
off Bidder St 114 D5
Electric Av, SW9 151 G4
Electric La, SW9 151 G4
Electric Par, E18 *off George La* 79 G2
Surbiton KT6 181 G6
Elektron Ho, E14
off Blackwall Way 114 D7
Elephant & Castle, SE1 27 H6
Elephant & Castle Shop Cen, SE1
off Elephant & Castle 131 J4
Elephant La, SE16 133 F2
Elephant Rd, SE17 35 J1
Elers Rd, W13 125 F2
Hayes UB3 121 G4
Eleven Acre Ri, Loug. IG10 48 C3
Eley Est, N18 61 F5
Eley Rd, N18 61 G5
Elfindale Rd, SE24 151 J5
Elfin Gro, Tedd. TW11
off Broad St 162 C5
Elford Cl, SE3 155 H4
Elfort Rd, N5 93 G4
Elfrida Cres, SE6 172 A4
Elf Row, E1 113 F7
Elfwine Rd, W7 104 B5
Elgal Cl, Orp. BR6
off Orchard Rd 206/207 E5
Elgar Av, NW10
off Mitchellbrook Way 88 D6
SW16 186 E3
W5 125 H2
Surbiton KT5 182 B7
Elgar Cl, E13 *off Bushey Rd* 115 J2
SE8 *off Comet St* 134 A7
Buckhurst Hill IG9 64 A2
Elgar St, SE16 133 H3
Elgin Av, W9 6 A4
W12 127 G2
Harrow HA3 68 E2
Elgin Cl, W12 127 H2
Elgin Cres, W11 108 C6
Hounslow (Hthrw Air.) TW6
off Eastern Perimeter Rd 141 H2
Elgin Ms, W11 *off Ladbroke Gro* 108 B6
Elgin Ms N, W9 6 B3
Elgin Ms S, W9 6 B3
Elgin Rd, N22 74 C2
Croydon CR0 202 C1
Elgin Rd, Ilf. IG3 99 H1
Sutton SM1 199 F3
Wallington SM6 200 C6
Elgood Av, Nthwd. HA6 50 A6
Elgood Cl, W11
off Avondale Pk Rd 108 B7
Elham Cl, Brom. BR1 174 A7
Elia Ms, N1 11 G2
Elias Pl, SW8 34 E6
Elia St, N1 11 G2
Elibank Rd, SE9 156 D4
Elim Est, SE1 28 D5
Elim Way, E13 115 F3
Eliot Bk, SE23 170 E2
Eliot Cotts, SE3
off Eliot Pl 154/155 E2
Eliot Ct, N15 *off Tynemouth Rd* 76 C4
Eliot Dr, Har. HA2 85 H2
Eliot Gdns, SW15 147 G4
Eliot Hill, SE13 154 C2
Eliot Ms, NW8 6 D2
Eliot Pk, SE13 154 C3
Eliot Pl, SE3 154 E2
Eliot Rd, Dag. RM9 100 D4
Eliot Vale, SE3 154 D2
Elizabethan Cl, Stai. (Stanw.) TW19
off Elizabethan Way 140 A7
Elizabethan Way, Stai. (Stanw.)
TW19 140 A7
Elizabeth Av, N1 93 J7
Enfield EN2 43 H3
Ilford IG1 99 G2
Elizabeth Blackwell Ho, N22
off Progress Way 75 G1
Elizabeth Br, SW1 32 D2
Elizabeth Cl, E14
off Grundy St 114 B6
W9 6 D5
Barnet EN5 40 A3
Romford RM7 83 H1
Sutton SM1 198 C4
Elizabeth Clyde Cl, N15 76 B4
Elizabeth Cotts, Rich. TW9 145 J1
Elizabeth Ct, SW1 25 J6
Woodford Green IG8
off Navestock Cres 63 J7
Elizabeth Est, SE17 36 B5
Elizabeth Fry Pl, SE18 156 B1
Elizabeth Fry Rd, E8
off Lamb La 94/95 E7
Elizabeth Gdns, W3 127 F1
Isleworth TW7 144 D4
Stanmore HA7 53 F6
Sunbury-on-Thames TW16 178 C3
Elizabeth Ms, NW3 91 H6
Elizabeth Pl, N15 76 A4
Elizabeth Ride, N9 45 E7
Elizabeth Rd, E6 116 A1
N15 76 B5
Elizabeth Sq, SE16
off Rotherhithe St 113 H7
Elizabeth St, SW1 32 C1
Elizabeth Ter, SE9 156 C6
Elizabeth Way, SE19 170 A7
Feltham TW13 160 C4
Elkanette Ms, N20
off Ridgeview Rd 57 F2
Elkington Rd, E13 115 H4
Elkstone Rd, W10 108 C5
Ellaline Rd, W6 128 A6
Ellanby Cres, N18 60 E5
Elland Rd, SE15 153 F4
Ella Rd, N8 75 E7
Ellement Cl, Pnr. HA5 66 D5
Ellenborough Pl, SW15 147 G4
Ellenborough Rd, N22 75 J1
Sidcup DA14 176 D5
Ellen Cl, Brom. BR1 192 A3
Ellen Ct, N9 *off Densworth Gro* 61 F2
Ellen St, E1 21 J4
Ellen Webb Dr, Har. (Wldste)
HA3 68 B3
Elleray Rd, Tedd. TW11 162 C6
Ellerby St, SW6 148 A1
Ellerdale Cl, NW3
off Ellerdale Rd 91 F4
Ellerdale Rd, NW3 91 F5
Ellerdale St, SE13 154 B4
Ellerdine Rd, Houns. TW3 143 J4
Ellerker Gdns, Rich. TW10 145 H6
Ellerman Av, Twick. TW2 161 F1
Ellerslie Gdns, NW10 107 G1
Ellerslie Rd, W12 127 H1
Ellerslie Sq Ind Est, SW2 150 E5
Ellerton Gdns, Dag. RM9 100 C7
Ellerton Rd, SW13 147 G1
SW18 167 G1
SW20 165 G7
Dagenham RM9 100 C7
Surbiton KT6 195 J2
Ellery Rd, SE19 170 A7
Ellery St, SE15 152 E2
Ellesborough Cl, Wat. WD19 50 C5
Ellesmere Av, NW7 54 D3
Beckenham BR3 190 B2
Ellesmere Cl, E11 79 F5
Ellesmere Gdns, Ilf. IG4 80 B5
Ellesmere Gro, Barn. EN5 40 C5
Ellesmere Rd, E3 113 H2
NW10 89 G5
W4 126 D6
Greenford UB6 103 J4
Twickenham TW1 145 F6
Ellesmere St, E14 114 B6
Ellingfort Rd, E8 95 E7
Ellingham Rd, E15 96 D4
W12 127 G2
Chessington KT9 195 G6
Ellington Rd, N10 74 B4
Hounslow TW3 143 H2
Ellington St, N7 93 G6
Elliot Cl, E15 96 E7
Elliot Rd, NW4 71 H6
Stanmore HA7 52 D6
Elliott Av, Ruis. HA4 84 B2
Elliott Cl, Wem. HA9 87 J3
Elliott Rd, SW9 131 H7
W4 126 E4
Bromley BR2 192 A4
Thornton Heath CR7 187 H4
Elliott's Pl, N1 *off St. Peters St* 111 H1
Elliott Sq, NW3 91 H7
Elliotts Row, SE11 35 G1
Ellis Cl, NW10 *off High Rd* 89 H6
SE9 175 F2
Elliscombe Rd, SE7 135 J5
Ellis Ct, W7 104 C5
Ellisfield Dr, SW15 147 F7
Ellison Gdns, Sthl. UB2 123 F4
Ellison Ho, SE13
off Lewisham Rd 154 C2
Ellison Rd, SW13 147 F2
SW16 168 D7
Sidcup DA15 175 G1
Ellis Rd, Mitch. CR4 185 J6
Southall UB2 123 J1
Ellis St, SW1 32 A1
Elliston Ho, SE18 136 D4
Ellora Rd, SW16 168 D5
Ellsworth St, E2 113 E3
Ellwood Ct, W9 6 A6
Elmar Rd, N15 76 A4
Elm Av, W5 125 H1
Ruislip HA4 84 A1
Elmbank, N14 43 E7
Elmbank Av, Barn. EN5 39 J4
Elm Bk Dr, Brom. BR1 192 A2
Elm Bk Gdns, SW13 147 E2
Elmbank Way, W7 104 A5
Elmbourne Dr, Belv. DA17 139 H4
Elmbourne Rd, SW17 168 A3
Elmbridge Av, Surb. KT5 182 B5
Elmbridge Cl, Ruis. HA4 66 A6
Elmbridge Wk, E8
off Wilman Gro 94 D7
Elmbrook Cl, Sun. TW16 178 B1
Elmbrook Gdns, SE9 156 B4
Elmbrook Rd, Sutt. SM1 198 C4
Elm Cl, E11 79 H6
N19 *off Hargrave Pk* 92 C2
NW4 72 A5
SW20 *off Grand Dr* 183 J4
Buckhurst Hill IG9 64 A2
Carshalton SM5 199 J1
Harrow HA2 67 H6
Hayes UB3 102 A6
Romford RM7 83 H2
South Croydon CR2 202 B6
Surbiton KT5 182 C7
Twickenham TW2 161 H2
Elm Ct, EC4 19 E5
Mitcham CR4
off Armfield Cres 185 J2
Elmcourt Rd, SE27 169 H2
Elm Cres, W5 125 H1
Kingston upon Thames KT2 181 H1
Elmcroft, N8 75 F5
Elmcroft Av, E11 79 H5
N9 44 E6
NW11 72 C7
Sidcup DA15 157 J6
Elmcroft Cl, E11 79 H4
W5 105 G6
Chessington KT9 195 H3
Feltham TW14 141 J6
Elmcroft Cres, NW11 72 B7
Harrow HA2 67 G3
Elmcroft Dr, Chess. KT9 195 H3
Elmcroft Gdns, NW9 70 A5
Elmcroft St, E5 95 F4
Elmdale Rd, N13 59 F5
Elmdene, Surb. KT5 196 C1
Elmdene Cl, Beck. BR3 189 J5
Elmdene Rd, SE18 136 E5
Elmdon Rd, Houns. TW4 142 D2
Hounslow (Hatt.Cr.) TW6 141 J3
Elm Dr, Har. HA2 67 H6
Sunbury-on-Thames TW16 178 C2
Elmer Cl, Enf. EN2 43 F3
Elmer Gdns, Edg. HA8 54 B7
Isleworth TW7 144 A3
Elmer Rd, SE6 154 C7
Elmers Dr, Tedd. TW11
off Kingston Rd 162/163 E6
ELMERS END, Beck. BR3 189 H3
Elmers End Rd, SE20 189 F2
Beckenham BR3 189 F2
Elmerside Rd, Beck. BR3 189 H4
Elmers Rd, SE25 188 D7
Elmfield Av, N8 74 E5
Mitcham CR4 186 A1
Teddington TW11 162 C5
Elmfield Cl, Har. HA1 86 B2
Elmfield Pk, Brom. BR1 191 G3
Elmfield Rd, E4 62 C2
E17 77 G6
N2 73 G3
SW17 168 A2
Bromley BR1 191 G3
Southall UB2 123 E3
Elmfield Way, W9 108 D5
Elm Friars Wk, NW1 92 D7
Elm Gdns, N2 73 F3
Esher (Clay.) KT10 194 C6
Mitcham CR4 186 D4
Elmgate Av, Felt. TW13 160 B3
Elmgate Gdns, Edg. HA8 54 D5
Elm Grn, W3 106 E6
Elmgreen Cl, E15
off Church St N 114/115 E1
Elm Gro, N8 75 E6
NW2 90 A4
SE15 152 C2
SW19 166 B7
Harrow HA2 67 G7
Kingston upon Thames KT2 181 H1
Orpington BR6 207 J1
Sutton SM1 199 E4
Woodford Green IG8 63 F5
Elmgrove Cres, Har. HA1 68 C5
Elmgrove Gdns, Har. HA1 68 D5
Elm Gro Par, Wall. SM6
off Butter Hill 200 A3
Elm Gro Rd, SW13 147 G2
W5 125 H2
Elmgrove Rd, Croy. CR0 188 E7
Harrow HA1 68 C5
Elm Hall Gdns, E11 79 H5
Elmhurst, Belv. DA17 139 E6
Elmhurst Av, N2 73 G3
Mitcham CR4 168 B7
Elmhurst Dr, E18 79 G2
Elmhurst Gdns, E18
off Elmhurst Dr 79 H1
Elmhurst Mans, SW4
off Edgeley Rd 150 D3
Elmhurst Rd, E7 97 H7
N17 76 C2
SE9 174 B2
Elmhurst St, SW4 150 D3
Elmhurst Vil, SE15
off Cheltenham Rd 153 F4
Elmhurst Way, Loug. IG10 48 C7
Elmington Cl, Bex. DA5 159 H6
Elmington Est, SE5 36 C7
Elmington Rd, SE5 152 A1
Elmira St, SE13 154 B3
Elm La, SE6 171 J2
Elmlee Cl, Chis. BR7 174 C6
Elmley Cl, E6
off Northumberland Rd 116 B5
Elmley St, SE18 137 G4
Elm Ms, Rich. TW10
off Grove Rd 145 J6
Elmore Cl, Wem. HA0 105 H2
Elmore Rd, E11 96 C3
Enfield EN3 45 G1
Elmores, Loug. IG10 48 D3
Elmore St, N1 93 J7
Elm Pk, SW2 151 F6
Stanmore HA7 53 E5
Elm Pk Av, N15 76 C5
Elm Pk Ct, Pnr. HA5 66 C3
Elm Pk Gdns, NW4 72 A5
SW10 31 E4
Elm Pk La, SW3 30 E4
Elm Pk Mans, SW10 30 D5
Elm Pk Rd, E10 95 H1
N3 56 C7
N21 43 J7
SE25 188 C3
SW3 30 E5
Pinner HA5 66 C2
Elm Pl, SW7 31 E3
Elm Quay Ct, SW8 33 H5
Elm Rd, E7 97 F6
E11 96 D2
E17 78 C5
N22 *off Granville Rd* 75 H1
SW14 146 C3
Barnet EN5 40 C4
Beckenham BR3 189 J2
Chessington KT9 195 H4
Epsom KT17 197 F6
Esher (Clay.) KT10 194 C6
Kingston upon Thames KT2 181 J1
New Malden KT3 182 D4
Romford RM7 83 H2
Sidcup DA14 176 A4
Thornton Heath CR7 188 A4
Wallington SM6 200 A1

Elm Rd, Wembley HA9 . . . . .87 H5
Elm Rd W, Sutt. SM3 . . . . .184 C7
Elm Row, NW3 . . . . .91 F3
Elms, The, SW13 . . . . .147 F3
Elms Av, N10 . . . . .74 B3
NW4 . . . . .72 A5
Elmscott Gdns, N21 . . . . .43 J6
Elmscott Rd, Brom. BR1 . . . . . .173 F5
Elms Ct, Wem. HA0 . . . . .86 C4
Elms Cres, SW4 . . . . .150 C6
Elmsdale Rd, E17 . . . . .77 J4
Elms Gdns, Dag. RM9 . . . . .101 F4
Wembley HA0 . . . . .86 D4
Elmshaw Rd, SW15 . . . . .147 G5
Elmshurst Cres, N2 . . . . .73 G4
Elmside, Croy. (New Adgtn)
CR0 . . . . .204 B6
Elmside Rd, Wem. HA9 . . . . .88 A3
Elms La, Wem. HA0 . . . . .86 D4
Elmsleigh Av, Har. HA3 . . . . .69 G4
Elmsleigh Ct, Sutt. SM1 . . . . . .198 E3
Elmsleigh Rd, Twick. TW2 . . . . .162 A2
Elmslie Cl, Wdf.Grn. IG8 . . . . . . .64 C6
Elmslie Pt, E3 . . . . .113 J5
Elms Ms, W2 . . . . .14 E5
Elms Pk Av, Wem. HA0 . . . . .86 D4
Elms Rd, SW4 . . . . .150 C5
Harrow HA3 . . . . .52 B7
ELMSTEAD, Chis. BR7 . . . . . . .174 A5
Elmstead Av, Chis. BR7 . . . . . . .174 C5
Wembley HA9 . . . . .87 H1
Elmstead Cl, N20 . . . . .56 D2
Epsom KT19 . . . . .197 E5
Elmstead Cres, Well. DA16 . . . .138 C6
Elmstead Gdns, Wor.Pk. KT4 . . .197 G3
Elmstead Glade, Chis. BR7 . . . .174 C6
Elmstead La, Chis. BR7 . . . . . . .174 C5
Elmstead Rd, Ilf. IG3 . . . . .99 H2
Elmstone Rd, SW6 . . . . .148 D1
Elm St, WC1 . . . . .10 D6
Elmsworth Av, Houns. TW3 . . . .143 H2
Elm Ter, NW2 . . . . .90 D1
SE9 . . . . .156 D6
Harrow HA3 . . . . .52 A7
Elmton Way, E5
off Rendlesham Rd 94 D3
Elm Tree Av, Esher KT10 . . . . . .180 A5
Elm Tree Cl, NW8 . . . . .7 E3
Northolt UB5 . . . . .103 F2
Elm Tree Rd, NW8 . . . . .7 E3
Elmtree Rd, Tedd. TW11 . . . . . .162 B4
Elm Wk, NW3 . . . . .90 D2
SW20 . . . . .183 J4
Orpington BR6 . . . . .206 C3
Elm Way, N11 . . . . .58 A6
NW10 . . . . .88 E4
Epsom KT19 . . . . .196 D5
Worcester Park KT4 . . . . . . .197 J3
Elmwood Av, N13 . . . . .59 E5
Borehamwood WD6 . . . . .38 B4
Feltham TW13 . . . . .160 A2
Harrow HA3 . . . . .68 D5
Elmwood Cl, Epsom KT17 . . . . .197 G6
Wallington SM6 . . . . .200 A2
Elmwood Ct, SW11 . . . . .150 B1
Wembley HA0 . . . . .86 D3
Elmwood Cres, NW9 . . . . .70 C4
Elmwood Dr, Bex. DA5 . . . . . . .158 E7
Epsom KT17 . . . . .197 G6
Elmwood Gdns, W7 . . . . .104 B6
Elmwood Rd, SE24 . . . . .152 A5
W4 .126 C6
Croydon CR0 . . . . .187 H7
Mitcham CR4 . . . . .185 J3
Elmworth Gro, SE21 . . . . .170 A2
Elnathan Ms, W9 . . . . .6 B6
Elphinstone Rd, E17 . . . . .77 J2
Elphinstone St, N5
off Avenell Rd 93 H4
Elrington Rd, E8 . . . . .94 D6
Woodford Green IG8 . . . . . . .63 G5
Elruge Cl, West Dr. UB7 . . . . . . .120 A3
Elsa Rd, Well. DA16 . . . . .158 B2
Elsa St, E1 . . . . .113 H5
Elsdale St, E9 . . . . .95 F6
Elsden Ms, E2 off Old Ford Rd . .113 F2
Elsden Rd, N17 . . . . .76 C1
Elsenham Rd, E12 . . . . .98 D5
Elsenham St, SW18 . . . . .166 C1
Elsham Rd, E11 . . . . .96 E3
W14 . . . . .128 B2
Elsham Ter, W14 . . . . .128 B2
Elsiedene Rd, N21 . . . . .43 J7
Elsiemaud Rd, SE4 . . . . .153 J5
Elsie Rd, SE22 . . . . .152 C4
Elsinore Av, Stai. TW19 . . . . . . .140 B7
Elsinore Gdns, NW2 . . . . .90 B3
Elsinore Rd, SE23 . . . . .171 H1
Elsinore Way, Rich. TW9
off Lower Richmond Rd 146 B3
Elsley Rd, SW11 . . . . .149 J3
Elspeth Rd, SW11 . . . . .149 J4
Wembley HA0 . . . . .87 H5
Elsrick Av, Mord. SM4 . . . . .184 D5
Elstan Way, Croy. CR0 . . . . .189 H7
Elstead Ct, Sutt. SM3
off Stonecot Hill 198 B1

Elsted St, SE17 . . . . .36 C2
Elstow Cl, SE9 . . . . .156 D5
Ruislip HA4 . . . . .66 D7
Elstow Gdns, Dag. RM9 . . . . . .118 E1
Elstow Rd, Dag. RM9 . . . . .100 E7
Elstree Gdns, N9 . . . . .61 E1
Belvedere DA17 . . . . .139 E4
Ilford IG1 . . . . .99 F5
Elstree Hill, Brom. BR1 . . . . . . .172 E7
Elstree Pk, Borwd. WD6 . . . . . . .38 D6
Elstree Way, Borwd. WD6 . . . . . .38 B3
Elswick Rd, SE13 . . . . .154 B2
Elswick St, SW6 . . . . .149 F2
Elsworthy, T.Ditt. KT7 . . . . .180 B6
Elsworthy Ri, NW3 . . . . .91 H7
Elsworthy Rd, NW3 . . . . .109 H1
Elsworthy Ter, NW3 . . . . .91 H7
Elsynge Rd, SW18 . . . . .149 G5
ELTHAM, SE9 . . . . .156 A6
Eltham Grn, SE9 . . . . .155 J5
Eltham Grn Rd, SE9 . . . . .155 J4
Eltham High St, SE9 . . . . .156 C6
Eltham Hill, SE9 . . . . .156 A5
★ Eltham Palace, SE9 . . . . . . .156 B7
Eltham Palace Rd, SE9 . . . . . . .155 J6
Eltham Pk Gdns, SE9 . . . . .156 C4
Eltham Rd, SE9 . . . . .155 J5
SE12 . . . . .155 F5
Elthiron Rd, SW6 . . . . .148 D1
Elthorne Av, W7 . . . . .124 C2
Elthorne Ct, Felt. TW13 . . . . . . .160 C1
Elthorne Pk Rd, W7 . . . . .124 C2
Elthorne Rd, N19 . . . . .92 D2
NW9 . . . . .70 D7
Elthorne Way, NW9 . . . . .70 D6
Elthruda Rd, SE13 . . . . .154 D6
Eltisley Rd, Ilf. IG1 . . . . .98 E4
Elton Av, Barn. EN5 . . . . .40 C5
Greenford UB6 . . . . .86 C6
Wembley HA0 . . . . .87 E5
Elton Cl, Kings.T. KT1 . . . . .163 F7
Elton Ho, E3 . . . . .113 J1
Elton Pl, N16 . . . . .94 B5
Elton Rd, Kings.T. KT2 . . . . .181 J1
Eltringham St, SW18 . . . . .149 F4
Elvaston Ms, SW7 . . . . .22 C6
Elvaston Pl, SW7 . . . . .22 C6
Elveden Pl, NW10 . . . . .106 A2
Elveden Rd, NW10 . . . . .106 A2
Elvendon Rd, N13 . . . . .58 E6
Elver Gdns, E2 . . . . .13 J3
Elverson Ms, SE8 . . . . .154 B2
Elverson Rd, SE8 . . . . .154 B2
Elverton St, SW1 . . . . .33 H1
Elvington Grn, Brom. BR2 . . . . .191 F5
Elvington La, NW9 . . . . .70 E1
Elvino Rd, SE26 . . . . .171 H5
Elvis Rd, NW2 . . . . .89 J6
Elwill Way, Beck. BR3 . . . . .190 C4
Elwin St, E2 . . . . .13 H3
Elwood St, N5 . . . . .93 H3
Elwyn Gdns, SE12 . . . . .155 G7
Ely Cl, N.Mal. KT3 . . . . .183 F2
Ely Ct, EC1 . . . . .19 F2
Ely Gdns, Borwd. WD6 . . . . .38 D5
Dagenham RM10 . . . . .101 J3
Ilford IG1 off Canterbury Av . .80 B7
Elyne Rd, N4 . . . . .75 G6
Ely Pl, EC1 . . . . .19 F2
Woodford Green IG8 . . . . . . .64 D6
Ely Rd, E10 . . . . .78 C6
Croydon CR0 . . . . .188 A5
Hounslow (Hthrw Air.) TW6
off Eastern Perimeter Rd . .141 J2
Hounslow (Houns.W.) TW4 . .142 C3
Elysian Av, Orp. BR5 . . . . .193 J6
Elysium Pl, SW6
off Fulham Pk Gdns 148 C2
Elysium St, SW6
off Fulham Pk Gdns 148 C2
Elystan Business Cen, Hayes
UB4 . . . . .102 C7
Elystan Pl, SW3 . . . . .31 H3
Elystan St, SW3 . . . . .31 G2
Elystan Wk, N1
off Cloudesley Rd 111 G1
Emanuel Av, W3 . . . . .106 C6
Emanuel Dr, Hmptn. TW12 . . . .161 F5
Embankment, SW15 . . . . .148 A2
Embankment, The, Twick. TW1 . .162 D1
Embankment Gdns, SW3 . . . . . .32 A5
Embankment Pl, WC2 . . . . .26 B1
Embassy Ct, Sid. DA14 . . . . . . .176 B3
Welling DA16
off Welling High St 158 B3
Embassy Gdns, Beck. BR3
off Blakeney Rd 189 J1
Emba St, SE16 . . . . .29 J4
Ember Cl, Orp. BR5 . . . . .193 F7
Embercourt Rd, T.Ditt. KT7 . . . .180 B6
Ember Fm Av, E.Mol. KT8 . . . . .180 A6
Ember Fm Way, E.Mol. KT8 . . . .180 A6
Ember Gdns, T.Ditt. KT7 . . . . . .180 B7
Ember La, E.Mol. KT8 . . . . .180 A7
Esher KT10 . . . . .180 A7

Embleton Rd, Wat. WD19 . . . . . .50 A3
Embleton Wk, Hmptn. TW12
off Fearnley Cres 161 F6
Embry Cl, Stan. HA7 . . . . .52 D4
Embry Dr, Stan. HA7 . . . . .52 D6
Embry Way, Stan. HA7 . . . . .52 D5
Emden Cl, West Dr. UB7 . . . . . .120 D2
Emden St, SW6 . . . . .149 E1
Emerald Cl, E16 . . . . .116 B6
Emerald Gdns, Dag. RM8 . . . . .101 G1
Emerald Sq, Sthl. UB2 . . . . . . .122 D3
Emerald St, WC1 . . . . .18 C1
Emerson Gdns, Har. HA3 . . . . . . .69 J6
Emerson Rd, Ilf. IG1 . . . . .80 D7
Emerson St, SE1 . . . . .27 J1
Emerton Cl, Bexh. DA6 . . . . . . .159 E4
Emery Hill St, SW1 . . . . .25 G6
Emery St, SE1 . . . . .27 F5
Emes Rd, Erith DA8 . . . . .139 J7
Emilia Cl, Enf. EN3 . . . . .45 E5
Emlyn Gdns, W12 . . . . .127 E2
Emlyn Rd, W12 . . . . .127 E2
Emmanuel Rd, SW12 . . . . .168 C1
Emma Rd, E13 . . . . .115 F2
Emma St, E2 . . . . .112 E2
Emmaus Way, Chig. IG7 . . . . . . .64 D5
Emmott Av, Ilf. IG6 . . . . .81 F5
Emmott Cl, E1 . . . . .113 H4
NW11 . . . . .73 F6
Emms Pas, Kings.T. KT1
off High St 181 G2
Emperor's Gate, SW7 . . . . .22 B6
Empire Av, N18 . . . . .59 J5
Empire Ct, Wem. HA9 . . . . .88 B3
Empire Rd, Grnf. UB6 . . . . .105 F1
Empire Sq, N7 . . . . .93 E3
SE20 off High St 171 G7
Empire Way, Wem. HA9 . . . . .87 J4
Empire Wf Rd, E14 . . . . .134 D4
Empress Av, E4 . . . . .62 A7
E12 . . . . .97 J2
Ilford IG1 . . . . .98 C2
Woodford Green IG8 . . . . . . .63 F7
Empress Dr, Chis. BR7 . . . . . . .174 E6
Empress Ms, SE5 . . . . .151 J2
Empress Pl, SW6 . . . . .128 D5
Empress St, SE17 . . . . .36 A5
Empson St, E3 . . . . .114 B4
Emsworth Cl, N9 . . . . .61 F1
Emsworth Rd, Ilf. IG6 . . . . .81 E2
Emsworth St, SW2 . . . . .169 F2
Emu Rd, SW8 . . . . .150 B2
Ena Rd, SW16 . . . . .186 E3
Enbrook St, W10 . . . . .108 B3
Endale Cl, Cars. SM5 . . . . .199 J2
Endeavour Ho, Barn. EN5 . . . . . .41 F4
Endeavour Way, SW19 . . . . .166 E4
Barking IG11 . . . . .118 A2
Croydon CR0 . . . . .186 D7
Endell St, WC2 . . . . .18 A3
Enderby St, SE10 . . . . .134 E5
Enderley Cl, Har. HA3
off Enderley Rd 68 B1
Enderley Rd, Har. HA3 . . . . .68 B1
Endersby Rd, Barn. EN5 . . . . . . .39 J5
Endersleigh Gdns, NW4 . . . . . . .71 G4
Endlebury Rd, E4 . . . . .62 B2
Endlesham Rd, SW12 . . . . .150 A7
Endsleigh Gdns, WC1 . . . . .9 H4
Ilford IG1 . . . . .98 C2
Surbiton KT6 . . . . .181 F6
Endsleigh Ind Est, Sthl. UB2 . . .123 F4
Endsleigh Pl, WC1 . . . . .9 J5
Endsleigh Rd, W13 . . . . .104 D7
Southall UB2 . . . . .123 E4
Endsleigh St, WC1 . . . . .9 H5
Endway, Surb. KT5 . . . . .182 A7
Endwell Rd, SE4 . . . . .153 H2
Endymion Rd, N4 . . . . .75 G7
SW2 . . . . .151 F6
Energen Cl, NW10 . . . . .88 E6
ENFIELD, Enf. EN1 - EN3 . . . . . .44 C3
ENFIELD HIGHWAY, Enf. EN3 . . .45 F3
Enfield Retail Pk, Enf. EN1 . . . . .44 E3
Enfield Rd, N1 . . . . .94 B7
W3 .126 B2
Brentford TW8 . . . . .125 G5
Enfield EN2 . . . . .42 D4
Hounslow (Hthrw Air.) TW6
off Eastern Perimeter Rd . .141 H2
ENFIELD TOWN, Enf. EN2 . . . . . .44 A2
Enfield Wk, Brent. TW8 . . . . . . .125 G5
Enford St, W1 . . . . .15 J1
Engadine Cl, Croy. CR0 . . . . . . .202 C3
Engadine St, SW18 . . . . .166 C1
Engate St, SE13 . . . . .154 C4
Engel Pk, NW7 . . . . .55 J6
Engineer Cl, SE18 . . . . .136 D6
Engineers Way, Wem. HA9 . . . . . .88 A4
Englands La, NW3 . . . . .91 J6
Loughton IG10 . . . . .48 D1
England Way, N.Mal. KT3 . . . . . .182 B4
Englefield Cl, Croy. CR0
off Queen's Rd 187 J6
Enfield EN2 . . . . .43 G2
Orpington BR5 . . . . .193 J4
Englefield Cres, Orp. BR5 . . . . .193 J4

Englefield Path, Orp. BR5 . . . . .193 J4
Englefield Rd, N1 . . . . .94 A6
Engleheart Dr, Felt. TW14 . . . . .141 J6
Engleheart Rd, SE6 . . . . .154 B7
Englewood Rd, SW12 . . . . .150 B6
English Grds, SE1 . . . . .28 D2
English St, E3 . . . . .113 J4
Enid St, SE16 . . . . .29 G5
Enmore Av, SE25 . . . . .188 D5
Enmore Gdns, SW14 . . . . .146 D5
Enmore Rd, SE25 . . . . .188 D5
SW15 . . . . .147 J4
Southall UB1 . . . . .103 G4
Ennerdale Av, Stan. HA7 . . . . . . .69 F3
Ennerdale Cl, Sutt. SM1 . . . . . .198 C4
Ennerdale Dr, NW9 . . . . .70 E5
Ennerdale Gdns, Wem. HA9 . . . .87 G1
Ennerdale Ho, E3 . . . . .113 J4
Ennerdale Rd, Bexh. DA7 . . . . .159 G1
Richmond TW9 . . . . .145 J2
Ennersdale Rd, SE13 . . . . .154 D5
Ennis Av, W4 . . . . .127 F4
Greenford UB6 . . . . .86 B6
Ennismore Gdns, SW7 . . . . .23 G4
Thames Ditton KT7 . . . . . . .180 B6
Ennismore Gdns Ms, SW7 . . . . .23 G5
Ennismore Ms, SW7 . . . . .23 G5
Ennismore St, SW7 . . . . .23 G5
Ennis Rd, N4 . . . . .93 G1
SE18 . . . . .137 F6
Ensign Dr, N13 . . . . .59 J3
Ensign St, E1 . . . . .21 H5
Ensign Way, Wall. SM6 . . . . . . .200 E7
Enslin Rd, SE9 . . . . .156 D6
Ensor Ms, SW7 . . . . .30 E3
Enstone Rd, Enf. EN3 . . . . .45 H3
Enterprise Cl, Croy. CR0 . . . . . .201 G1
Enterprise Pk, E10 . . . . .95 H1
Enterprise Way, NW10 . . . . . . .107 G3
SW18 . . . . .148 D4
Teddington TW11 . . . . .162 C5
Enterprize Way, SE8 . . . . .133 J4
Epirus Ms, SW6 . . . . .128 D7
Epirus Rd, SW6 . . . . .128 C7
Epping Cl, E14 . . . . .134 A4
Romford RM7 . . . . .83 H3
★ Epping Forest, Epp. & Loug. . .47 J1
Epping Glade, E4 . . . . .46 C6
Epping New Rd, Buck.H. IG9 . . . .63 H2
Loughton IG10 . . . . .47 H5
Epping Pl, N1 off Liverpool Rd . . .93 G6
Epping Way, E4 . . . . .46 B6
Epple Rd, SW6 . . . . .148 C1
Epsom Cl, Bexh. DA7 . . . . .159 H3
Northolt UB5 . . . . .85 F5
Epsom Rd, E10 . . . . .78 C6
Croydon CR0 . . . . .201 G4
Ilford IG3 . . . . .81 J6
Morden SM4 . . . . .184 C7
Sutton SM3 . . . . .184 C7
Epsom Sq, Houns. (Hthrw Air.) TW6
off Eastern Perimeter Rd . . .141 J2
Epstein Rd, SE28 . . . . .138 A1
Epworth Rd, Islw. TW7 . . . . . . .124 D7
Epworth St, EC2 . . . . .12 C6
Equity Sq, E2 . . . . .13 G4
Erasmus St, SW1 . . . . .33 J2
Erconwald St, W12 . . . . .107 F6
Erebus Dr, SE28 . . . . .137 F3
Eresby Dr, Beck. BR3 . . . . .204 A3
Eresby Pl, NW6 . . . . .90 D7
Erica Gdns, Croy. CR0 . . . . .204 B4
Erica St, W12 . . . . .107 G7
Eric Clarke La, Bark. IG11 . . . . .117 E4
Eric Cl, E7 . . . . .97 G4
Ericcson Cl, SW18 . . . . .148 D5
Eric Rd, E7 . . . . .97 G4
NW10 off Church Rd 89 F6
Romford RM6 . . . . .82 D7
Eric St, E3 . . . . .113 J4
Eridge Rd, W4 . . . . .126 D3
Erin Cl, Brom. BR1 . . . . .172 E7
Ilford IG3 . . . . .82 A6
Erindale, SE18 . . . . .137 G6
Erindale Ter, SE18 . . . . .137 G6
Erith Cres, Rom. RM5 . . . . .83 J1
Erith Rd, Belv. DA17 . . . . .139 G4
Bexleyheath DA7 . . . . .159 H4
Erith DA8 . . . . .159 H4
Erlanger Rd, SE14 . . . . .153 G1
Erlesmere Gdns, W13 . . . . .124 D3
Ermine Cl, Houns. TW4 . . . . . . .142 C2
Ermine Ho, N17 off Moselle St . . .60 C7
Ermine Rd, N15 . . . . .76 C6
SE13 . . . . .154 B3
Ermine Side, Enf. EN1 . . . . .44 D5
Ermington Rd, SE9 . . . . .175 F2
Ernald Av, E6 . . . . .116 B2
Erncroft Way, Twick. TW1 . . . . .144 C6
Ernest Av, SE27 . . . . .169 H4
Ernest Cl, Beck. BR3 . . . . .190 A5
Ernest Gdns, W4 . . . . .126 B6
Ernest Gro, Beck. BR3 . . . . .189 J5
Ernest Rd, Kings.T. KT1 . . . . . . .182 B2
Ernest Sq, Kings.T. KT1 . . . . . . .182 B2
Ernest St, E1 . . . . .113 G4
Ernle Rd, SW20 . . . . .165 H7

Ernshaw Pl, SW15
  off Carlton Dr 148 B5
★ Eros, W1 . . . . .17 H6
Erpingham Rd, SW15 . . . . . . .147 J3
Erridge Rd, SW19 . . . . .184 D2
Errington Rd, W9 . . . . .108 C4
Errol Gdns, Hayes UB4 . . . . . .102 B4
  New Malden KT3 . . . . .183 G4
Errol St, EC1 . . . . .12 A6
Erskine Cl, Sutt. SM1 . . . . . . .199 H3
Erskine Cres, N17 . . . . .76 E4
Erskine Hill, NW11 . . . . .72 D5
Erskine Ms, NW3
  off Erskine Rd 91 J7
Erskine Rd, E17 . . . . .77 J4
  NW3 . . . . .91 J7
  Sutton SM1 . . . . .199 G4
  Watford WD19 . . . . .50 C3
Erwood Rd, SE7 . . . . .136 B5
Esam Way, SW16 . . . . .169 G5
Escott Gdns, SE9 . . . . .174 B4
Escot Way, Barn. EN5 . . . . . . .39 J5
Escreet Gro, SE18 . . . . .136 D4
Esher Av, Rom. RM7 . . . . .83 J6
  Sutton SM3 . . . . .198 A3
  Walton-on-Thames KT12 . . . .178 A7
Esher Bypass, Chess. KT9 . . . .195 E7
  Esher KT10 . . . . .195 E7
Esher Cl, Bex. DA5 . . . . .176 E1
Esher Cres, Houns. (Hthrw.Air.) TW6
  off Eastern Perimeter Rd . . .141 H2
Esher Gdns, SW19 . . . . .166 A2
Esher Ms, Mitch. CR4 . . . . . . .185 J3
Esher Rd, E.Mol. KT8 . . . . . . .180 A6
  Ilford IG3 . . . . .99 H3
Eskdale Av, Nthlt. UB5 . . . . . . .103 F1
Eskdale Cl, Wem. HA9 . . . . . . .87 G1
Eskdale Rd, Bexh. DA7 . . . . . .159 G2
Eskmont Ridge, SE19 . . . . . . .170 B7
Esk Rd, E13 . . . . .115 G4
Esmar Cres, NW9 . . . . .71 G1
Esme Ho, SW15 . . . . .147 F4
Esmeralda Rd, SE1 . . . . .37 J2
Esmond Rd, NW6 . . . . .108 C1
  W4 . . . . .126 D4
Esmond St, SW15 . . . . .148 B4
Esparto St, SW18 . . . . .149 E7
Essenden Rd, Belv. DA17 . . . . .139 G5
  South Croydon CR2 . . . . .202 B7
Essendine Rd, W9 . . . . .108 D4
Essex Av, Islw. TW7 . . . . .144 B3
Essex Cl, E17 . . . . .77 H4
  Morden SM4 . . . . .184 A7
  Romford RM7 . . . . .83 H4
  Ruislip HA4 . . . . .84 D1
Essex Ct, EC4 . . . . .18 E4
  SW13 . . . . .147 F2
Essex Gdns, N4 . . . . .75 H6
Essex Gro, SE19 . . . . .170 A6
Essex Ho, E14 *off Giraud St* . .114 B6
Essex Pk, N3 . . . . .56 E4
Essex Pk Ms, W3 . . . . .126 E1
Essex Pl, W4 . . . . .126 C4
Essex Pl Sq, W4
  off Chiswick High Rd 126 D4
Essex Rd, E4 . . . . .62 E1
  E10 .78 C6
  E12 .98 B5
  E17 .77 H6
  E18 .79 H2
  N1 .111 H1
  NW10 . . . . .89 E7
  W3 .106 C7
  W4 *off Belmont Rd* 126 D4
  Barking IG11 . . . . .99 G7
  Borehamwood WD6 . . . . .38 A3
  Dagenham RM10 . . . . .101 J5
  Enfield EN2 . . . . .44 A4
  Romford RM7 . . . . .83 H4
  Romford (Chad.Hth) RM6 . . . .82 C7
Essex Rd S, E11 . . . . .78 D7
Essex St, E7 . . . . .97 G5
  WC2 . . . . .18 E5
Essex Twr, SE20 . . . . .189 E1
Essex Vil, W8 . . . . .128 D2
Essex Wf, E5 . . . . .95 F2
Essian St, E1 . . . . .113 H5
Essoldo Way, Edg. HA8 . . . . . . .69 J3
Estate Way, E10 . . . . .95 J1
Estcourt Rd, SE25 . . . . .189 E6
  SW6 . . . . .128 C7
Estella Av, N.Mal. KT3 . . . . . .183 H4
Estelle Rd, NW3 . . . . .91 J4
Esterbrooke St, SW1 . . . . .33 H2
Este Rd, SW11 . . . . .149 H3
Esther Cl, N21 . . . . .43 G7
Esther Rd, E11 . . . . .78 E7
Estoria Cl, SW2 . . . . .151 G7
★ Estorick Collection of Modern
  Italian Art, N1 . . . . .93 H6
Estreham Rd, SW16 . . . . .168 D6
Estridge Cl, Houns. TW3 . . . . .143 G4
Estuary Cl, Bark. IG11 . . . . . . .118 B3
Eswyn Rd, SW17 . . . . .167 J4
Etchingham Pk Rd, N3 . . . . . . .57 E7
Etchingham Rd, E15 . . . . .96 C4
Eternit Wk, SW6 . . . . .147 J1

Etfield Gro, Sid. DA14 . . . . . . .176 B5
Ethelbert Cl, Brom. BR1 . . . . .191 G3
Ethelbert Gdns, Ilf. IG2 . . . . . .80 C5
Ethelbert Rd, SW20 . . . . .184 A1
  Bromley BR1 . . . . .191 G3
  Erith DA8 . . . . .139 J7
Ethelbert St, SW12
  off Fernlea Rd 168 B1
Ethelburga St, SW11 . . . . . . .149 H1
Etheldene Av, N10 . . . . .74 C4
Ethelden Rd, W12 . . . . .127 H1
Ethel Rd, E16 . . . . .115 H6
Ethel St, SE17 . . . . .35 J2
Etheridge Grn, Loug. IG10
  off Etheridge Rd 49 F3
Etheridge Rd, NW2 . . . . .71 J7
  Loughton IG10 . . . . .49 E2
Etherley Rd, N15 . . . . .75 J5
Etherow St, SE22 . . . . .152 D6
Etherstone Grn, SW16 . . . . . .169 G4
Etherstone Rd, SW16 . . . . . . .169 G4
Ethnard Rd, SE15 . . . . .132 E6
Ethronvi Rd, Bexh. DA7 . . . . .159 E3
Etloe Rd, E10 . . . . .96 A2
Eton Av, N12 . . . . .57 F7
  NW3 . . . . .91 G7
  Barnet EN4 . . . . .41 H6
  Hounslow TW5 . . . . .123 F7
  New Malden KT3 . . . . .182 D5
  Wembley HA0 . . . . .87 G4
Eton Cl, SW18 . . . . .149 E7
Eton Coll Rd, NW3 . . . . .91 J6
Eton Ct, NW3 *off Eton Av* 91 G7
  Wembley HA0 *off Eton Av* . . .87 F4
Eton Garages, NW3
  off Lambolle Pl 91 H6
Eton Gro, NW9 . . . . .70 A3
  SE13 . . . . .154 E3
Eton Hall, NW3
  off Eton Coll Rd 91 J6
Eton Pl, NW3
  off Haverstock Hill 92 A7
Eton Ri, NW3 *off Eton Coll Rd* .91 J6
Eton Rd, NW3 . . . . .91 J7
  Hayes UB3 . . . . .121 J7
  Ilford IG1 . . . . .99 F5
Eton St, Rich. TW9 . . . . .145 H5
Eton Vil, NW3 . . . . .91 J6
Etta St, SE8 . . . . .133 H6
Ettrick St, E14 . . . . .114 C6
Etwell Pl, Surb. KT5 . . . . .181 J6
Euesden Cl, N9 . . . . .60 E3
Eugenia Rd, SE16 . . . . .133 F4
Eureka Rd, Kings.T. KT1
  off Washington Rd 182 A2
Europa Pl, EC1 . . . . .11 J4
Europe Rd, SE18 . . . . .136 C3
Eustace Pl, SE18
  off Borgard Rd 136 C4
Eustace Rd, E6 . . . . .116 B3
  SW6 . . . . .128 D7
  Romford RM6 . . . . .82 D7
Euston Cen, NW1 *off Triton Sq* .110 C4
Euston Gro, NW1 . . . . .9 H4
Euston Rd, N1 . . . . .10 A3
  NW1 .9 E6
  Croydon CR0 . . . . .201 G1
Euston Sq, NW1 . . . . .9 H4
Euston Sta Colonnade, NW1 . . . .9 H4
Euston St, NW1 . . . . .9 G5
Euston Twr, NW1 . . . . .9 F5
Evandale Rd, SW9 . . . . .151 G2
Evangelist Rd, NW5 . . . . .92 B4
Evans Business Cen, NW2 . . . . .89 G3
Evans Cl, E8
  off Buttermere Wk 94 C6
Evans Gro, Felt. TW13 . . . . . .161 G2
Evans Rd, SE6 . . . . .173 E2
Evanston Av, E4 . . . . .62 C7
Evanston Gdns, Ilf. IG4 . . . . . . .80 B6
Eva Rd, Rom. RM6 . . . . .82 C7
Evelina Rd, SE15 . . . . .153 F3
  SE20 . . . . .171 G7
Eveline Lowe Est, SE16 . . . . . .29 H6
Eveline Rd, Mitch. CR4 . . . . . .185 J1
Evelyn Av, NW9 . . . . .70 D4
Evelyn Cl, Twick. TW2 . . . . . . .143 H7
Evelyn Ct, N1 . . . . .12 B2
Evelyn Denington Rd, E6 . . . . .116 B4
Evelyn Dr, Pnr. HA5 . . . . .50 D7
Evelyn Fox Ct, W10 . . . . .107 J5
Evelyn Gdns, SW7 . . . . .30 E4
  Richmond TW9 *off Kew Rd* .145 H4
Evelyn Gro, W5 . . . . .125 J1
  Southall UB1 . . . . .103 F6
Evelyn Rd, E16 . . . . .135 H1
  E17 .78 C4
  SW19 . . . . .166 E5
  W4 .126 D3
  Barnet EN4 . . . . .41 J4
  Richmond TW9 . . . . .145 H4
  Richmond (Ham) TW10 . . . . .163 F3
Evelyn St, SE8 . . . . .133 H5
Evelyn Ter, Rich. TW9 . . . . . . .145 H4
Evelyn Wk, N1 . . . . .12 B2
Evelyn Way, Wall. SM6 . . . . . .200 D4
Evelyn Yd, W1 . . . . .17 H3

Evening Hill, Beck. BR3 . . . . . .172 C7
Evenwood Cl, SW15 . . . . .148 B5
Everard Av, Brom. BR2 . . . . . .205 G1
Everard Way, Wem. HA9 . . . . . .87 H3
Everatt Cl, SW18
  off Amerland Rd 148 C6
Everdon Rd, SW13 . . . . .127 G6
Everest Pl, E14 . . . . .114 C5
  SW16 . . . . .168 C5
Everest Rd, SE9 . . . . .156 C5
  Staines (Stanw.) TW19 . . . . .140 A7
Everett Wk, Belv. DA17
  off Osborne Rd 139 F5
Everglade Strand, NW9 . . . . . . .71 F1
Evergreen Ct, Stai. (Stanw.) TW19
  off Evergreen Way 140 A7
Evergreen Sq, E8 . . . . .94 C7
Evergreen Way, Stai. (Stanw.)
  TW19 . . . . .140 A7
Everilda St, N1 . . . . .111 F1
Evering Rd, E5 . . . . .94 C3
  N16 .94 C3
Everington Rd, N10 . . . . .73 J2
Everington St, W6 . . . . .128 A6
Everitt Rd, NW10 . . . . .106 D3
Everleigh St, N4 . . . . .93 F1
Eve Rd, E11 . . . . .96 E4
  E15 . . . . .115 E2
  N17 .76 B3
  Isleworth TW7 . . . . .144 D4
Eversfield Gdns, NW7 . . . . .54 E7
Eversfield Rd, Rich. TW9 . . . . .145 J2
Evershed Wk, W4 . . . . .126 D4
Eversholt St, NW1 . . . . .9 G1
Evershot Rd, N4 . . . . .93 F1
Eversleigh Rd, E6 . . . . .116 A1
  N3 . . . . .56 C7
  SW11 . . . . .149 J3
  Barnet EN5 . . . . .41 F5
Eversley Av, Wem. HA9 . . . . . . .88 A2
Eversley Cl, N21 . . . . .43 F6
  Loughton IG10 . . . . .49 F3
Eversley Cres, N21 . . . . .43 F6
  Isleworth TW7 . . . . .144 A1
Eversley Mt, N21 . . . . .43 F6
Eversley Pk, SW19 . . . . .165 H5
Eversley Pk Rd, N21 . . . . .43 F6
Eversley Rd, SE7 . . . . .135 H6
  SE19 . . . . .170 A7
  Surbiton KT5 . . . . .181 J4
Eversley Way, Croy. CR0 . . . . .204 A4
Everthorpe Rd, SE15 . . . . .152 C3
Everton Bldgs, NW1 . . . . .9 F4
Everton Dr, Stan. HA7 . . . . .69 J3
Everton Rd, Croy. CR0 . . . . . . .202 D1
Evesham Av, E17 . . . . .78 A2
Evesham Cl, Grnf. UB6 . . . . . .103 H2
  Sutton SM2 . . . . .198 D7
Evesham Ct, W13
  off Tewkesbury Rd 124 D1
Evesham Grn, Mord. SM4 . . . .184 E6
Evesham Rd, E15 . . . . .115 F1
  N11 .58 C5
  Morden SM4 . . . . .185 E6
Evesham St, W11 . . . . .108 A7
Evesham Wk, SE5 *off Love Wk* .152 A2
  SW9 . . . . .151 G2
Evesham Way, SW11 . . . . .150 A3
  Ilford IG5 . . . . .80 D3
Evry Rd, Sid. DA14 . . . . .176 C6
Ewald Rd, SW6 . . . . .148 C2
Ewanrigg Ter, Wdf.Grn. IG8 . . . .63 J5
Ewart Gro, N22 . . . . .75 G1
Ewart Pl, E3 *off Roman Rd* . . .113 J2
Ewart Rd, SE23 . . . . .153 G7
Ewe Cl, N7 . . . . .93 E6
Ewell Bypass, Epsom KT17 . . .197 G7
Ewell Ct Av, Epsom KT19 . . . .197 E5
Ewellhurst Rd, Ilf. IG5 . . . . . . .80 B2
Ewell Pk Gdns, Epsom KT17 . .197 G7
Ewell Pk Way, Epsom (Ewell)
  KT17 . . . . .197 G6
Ewell Rd, Surb. KT6 . . . . .181 H6
  Surbiton (Long Dit.) KT6 . . . .180 E7
  Sutton SM3 . . . . .198 B6
Ewelme Rd, SE23 . . . . .171 F1
Ewen Cres, SW2 . . . . .151 G1
Ewer St, SE1 . . . . .27 J2
Ewhurst Cl, E1 . . . . .113 F5
  Sutton SM2 . . . . .197 J5
Ewhurst Rd, SE4 . . . . .153 J6
Exbury Rd, SE6 . . . . .172 A2
★ ExCeL, E16 . . . . .115 H7
Excel Ct, WC2 . . . . .17 J6
ExCeL Marina, E16
  off Western Gateway 115 H7
Excelsior Cl, Kings.T. KT1
  off Washington Rd 182 A2
Excelsior Gdns, SE13 . . . . . . .154 C2
ExCeL Waterfront, E16
  off Western Gateway 115 H7
Exchange Arc, EC2 . . . . .20 E1
Exchange Bldgs, E1
  off Cutler St 112 B6
Exchange Cl, N11
  off Benfleet Way 58 A2
Exchange Ct, WC2 . . . . .18 B6

Exchange Ho, N8
  off Crouch End Hill 74 E6
Exchange Mall, The, Ilf. IG1 . . . .98 E2
Exchange Pl, EC2 . . . . .20 D1
Exchange Sq, EC2 . . . . .20 D1
Exchange Wk, Pnr. HA5 . . . . . . .66 E7
Exeter Cl, E6 *off Harper Rd* . .116 C6
Exeter Gdns, Ilf. IG1 . . . . .98 B1
Exeter Ho, SW15
  off Putney Heath 147 J6
Exeter Ms, NW6
  off West Hampstead Ms . .90/91 E6
  SW6 *off Farm La* 128 D7
Exeter Rd, E16 . . . . .115 G5
  E17 .78 A5
  N9 . . . . .61 F2
  N14 .58 B1
  NW2 . . . . .90 B5
  Croydon CR0 . . . . .188 B7
  Dagenham RM10 . . . . .101 H6
  Enfield EN3 . . . . .45 G3
  Feltham TW13 . . . . .161 F3
  Harrow HA2 . . . . .85 E2
  Hounslow (Hthrw.Air.) TW6 . .141 H2
  Welling DA16 . . . . .157 J2
Exeter St, WC2 . . . . .18 B5
Exeter Way, SE14 . . . . .133 J7
  Hounslow (Hthrw.Air.) TW6 . .141 H3
Exford Gdns, SE12 . . . . .173 H1
Exford Rd, SE12 . . . . .173 H2
Exhibition Cl, W12 . . . . .107 J7
Exhibition Rd, SW7 . . . . .23 F4
Exmoor Cl, Ilf. IG6 . . . . .81 F1
Exmoor St, W10 . . . . .108 A4
Exmouth Mkt, EC1 . . . . .11 E5
Exmouth Ms, NW1 . . . . .9 G4
Exmouth Pl, E8 . . . . .94 E7
Exmouth Rd, E17 . . . . .77 J5
  Bromley BR2 . . . . .191 H3
  Ruislip HA4 . . . . .84 C3
  Welling DA16 . . . . .158 C1
Exmouth St, E1
  off Commercial Rd 113 F6
Exning Rd, E16 . . . . .115 F4
Exon St, SE17 . . . . .36 D3
Express Dr, Ilf. IG3 . . . . .100 B1
Exton Cres, NW10 . . . . .88 C7
Exton Gdns, Dag. RM8 . . . . . .100 C5
Exton Rd, NW10 . . . . .88 C7
Exton St, SE1 . . . . .27 E2
Eyebright Cl, Croy. CR0
  off Primrose La 203 G1
Eyhurst Cl, NW2 . . . . .89 G2
Eylewood Rd, SE27 . . . . .169 J5
Eynella Rd, SE22 . . . . .152 C7
Eynham Rd, W12 . . . . .107 J6
Eynsford Cl, Orp. BR5 . . . . . . .193 F7
Eynsford Cres, Bex. DA5 . . . . .176 C1
Eynsford Rd, Ilf. IG3 . . . . .99 H2
Eynsham Dr, SE2 . . . . .138 A4
Eynswood Dr, Sid. DA14 . . . . .176 B5
Eyot Gdns, W6 . . . . .127 F5
Eyot Grn, W4 *off Chiswick Mall* .127 F6
Eyre Ct, NW8 . . . . .6 E1
Eyre St Hill, EC1 . . . . .11 E6
Eythorne Rd, SW9 . . . . .151 G1
Ezra St, E2 . . . . .13 G3

F

Faber Gdns, NW4 . . . . .71 G5
Fabian Rd, SW6 . . . . .128 C7
Fabian St, E6 . . . . .116 C4
Factory La, N17 . . . . .76 C2
  Croydon CR0 . . . . .201 G1
Factory Rd, E16 . . . . .136 B1
Factory Sq, SW16 . . . . .168 E6
Factory Yd, W7
  off Uxbridge Rd 124 B1
Faggs Rd, Felt. TW14 . . . . . . .142 A5
Fairacre, N.Mal. KT3 . . . . .182 E3
Fairacres, SW15 . . . . .147 G4
Fair Acres, Brom. BR2 . . . . . . .191 G5
Fairbairn Grn, SW9 . . . . .151 G1
Fairbank Av, Orp. BR6 . . . . . . .206 E2
Fairbank Est, N1 *off East Rd* . .112 A2
Fairbanks Rd, N17 . . . . .76 C3
Fairbourne Rd, N17 . . . . .76 B3
Fairbridge Rd, N19 . . . . .92 D2
Fairbrook Cl, N13 . . . . .59 G5
Fairbrook Rd, N13 . . . . .59 G6
Fairburn Cl, Borwd. WD6 . . . . .38 A1
Fairburn Ct, SW15
  off Mercier Rd 148 B5
Fairby Rd, SE12 . . . . .155 H5
Faircharm Trd Est, SE8 . . . . . .134 B7
Fairchild Cl, SW11 *off Wye St* .149 G2
Fairchild Pl, EC2 . . . . .13 E6
Fairchild St, EC2 . . . . .13 E6
Fairclough St, E1 . . . . .21 J4
Faircross Av, Bark. IG11 . . . . . .99 F6
Fairdale Gdns, SW15 . . . . .147 H4
  Hayes UB3 . . . . .122 A1
Fairey Av, Hayes UB3 . . . . . . .121 J4
Fairfax Gdns, SE3 . . . . .156 A1
Fairfax Ms, E16 *off Wesley Av* .135 H1

Fairfax Ms, SW15 . . . . .147 J4
Fairfax Pl, NW6 . . . . .91 F7
  W14 . . . . .128 B3
Fairfax Rd, N8 . . . . .75 G4
  NW6 .91 F7
  W4 .127 E3
  Teddington TW11 . . . . .162 D6
Fairfax Way, N10
  off Cromwell Rd 58 A7
Fairfield Av, NW4 . . . . .71 H6
  Edgware HA8 . . . . .54 B6
  Twickenham TW2 . . . . .161 H1
  Watford WD19 . . . . .50 C3
Fairfield Cl, N12 . . . . .57 F4
  Enfield EN3
  off Scotland Grn Rd N 45 H4
  Epsom (Ewell) KT19 . . . . .196 E5
  Mitcham CR4 . . . . .167 H7
  Sidcup DA15 . . . . .157 J6
Fairfield Ct, NW10 . . . . .107 G1
  Northwood HA6
  off Windsor Cl 66 A2
Fairfield Cres, Edg. HA8 . . . . . . .54 B6
Fairfield Dr, SW18 . . . . .149 E5
  Greenford UB6 . . . . .105 F1
  Harrow HA2 . . . . .67 J3
Fairfield E, Kings.T. KT1 . . . . . . .181 H2
Fairfield Gdns, N8
  off Elder Av 74/75 E5
Fairfield Gro, SE7 . . . . .136 A5
★ Fairfield Halls, Croy. CR0 . . . .202 A3
Fairfield N, Kings.T. KT1 . . . . . . .181 H2
Fairfield Path, Croy. CR0 . . . . . .202 A3
Fairfield Pl, Kings.T. KT1 . . . . . .181 H3
Fairfield Rd, E3 . . . . .114 A2
  E17 . . . . .77 H2
  N8 . . . . .75 E5
  N18 . . . . .60 D4
  W7 . . . . .124 D3
  Beckenham BR3 . . . . .190 A4
  Bexleyheath DA7 . . . . .159 F2
  Bromley BR1 . . . . .173 G7
  Croydon CR0 . . . . .202 B3
  Ilford IG1 . . . . .99 E6
  Kingston upon Thames KT1 . . .181 H2
  Orpington BR5 . . . . .193 G6
  Southall UB1 . . . . .103 F6
  West Drayton UB7 . . . . .120 B1
  Woodford Green IG8 . . . . .63 G6
Fairfields Cl, NW9 . . . . .70 C5
Fairfields Cres, NW9 . . . . .70 C4
Fairfield S, Kings.T. KT1 . . . . . . .181 H2
Fairfields Rd, Houns. TW3 . . . . .143 J3
Fairfield St, SW18 . . . . .149 E5
Fairfield Trade Pk, Kings.T. KT1 .181 J3
Fairfield Way, Barn. EN5 . . . . . . .40 D5
  Epsom KT19 . . . . .196 E5
Fairfield W, Kings.T. KT1 . . . . . . .181 H2
Fairfoot Rd, E3 . . . . .114 A4
Fairford Av, Croy. CR0 . . . . .189 G5
Fairford Cl, Croy. CR0 . . . . .189 H5
Fairford Ct, Sutt. SM2
  off Grange Rd 198/199 E7
Fairford Gdns, Wor.Pk. KT4 . . . .197 F3
Fairford Ho, SE11 . . . . .35 F2
Fairgreen, Barn. EN4 . . . . .41 J3
Fairgreen E, Barn. EN4 . . . . .41 J3
Fairgreen Par, Mitch. CR4
  off London Rd 185 J3
Fairgreen Rd, Th.Hth. CR7 . . . . .187 H5
Fairhaven Av, Croy. CR0 . . . . . . .189 G6
Fairhaven Cres, Wat. WD19 . . . . .50 A3
Fairhazel Gdns, NW6 . . . . .91 E6
Fairholme, Felt. TW14 . . . . .141 G7
Fairholme Cl, N3 . . . . .72 B4
Fairholme Gdns, N3 . . . . .72 B3
Fairholme Rd, W14 . . . . .128 B5
  Croydon CR0 . . . . .187 G7
  Harrow HA1 . . . . .68 C5
  Ilford IG1 . . . . .80 C7
  Sutton SM1 . . . . .198 C6
Fairholt Cl, N16 . . . . .94 B1
Fairholt Rd, N16 . . . . .94 A1
Fairholt St, SW7 . . . . .23 H5
Fairland Rd, E15 . . . . .97 F6
Fairlands Av, Buck.H. IG9 . . . . . .63 G2
  Sutton SM1 . . . . .198 D2
  Thornton Heath CR7 . . . . .187 F4
Fairlands Ct, SE9 off North Pk . .156 D6
Fairlawn, SE7 . . . . .135 J6
Fairlawn Av, N2 . . . . .73 H4
  W4 .126 C4
  Bexleyheath DA7 . . . . .158 D2
Fairlawn Cl, N14 . . . . .42 C6
  Esher (Clay.) KT10 . . . . .194 C6
  Feltham TW13 . . . . .161 F4
  Kingston upon Thames KT2 . . .164 C6
Fairlawn Dr, Wdf.Grn. IG8 . . . . . .63 G7
Fairlawnes, Wall. SM6
  off Maldon Rd 200 B5
Fairlawn Gdns, Sthl. UB1 . . . . . .103 F7
Fairlawn Gro, W4 . . . . .126 C4
Fairlawn Pk, SE26 . . . . .171 H5
Fairlawn Rd, SW19 . . . . .166 C7
Fairlawns, Pnr. HA5 . . . . .66 C2
  Sunbury-on-Thames TW16 . . .178 A3
  Twickenham TW1 . . . . .145 F6

Fairlea Pl, W5 . . . . .105 G4
Fairlie Gdns, SE23 . . . . .153 F7
Fairlight Av, E4 . . . . .62 D2
  NW10 . . . . .107 E2
  Woodford Green IG8 . . . . .63 G6
Fairlight Cl, E4 . . . . .62 D2
  Worcester Park KT4 . . . . .197 J4
Fairlight Rd, SW17 . . . . .167 G4
Fairlop Gdns, Ilf. IG6 . . . . .65 F7
Fairlop Rd, E11 . . . . .78 D7
  Ilford IG6 . . . . .81 F2
Fairmead, Brom. BR1 . . . . .192 C4
  Surbiton KT5 . . . . .196 B1
Fairmead Cl, Brom. BR1 . . . . . . .192 C4
  Hounslow TW5 . . . . .122 D7
  New Malden KT3 . . . . .182 D3
Fairmead Cres, Edg. HA8 . . . . . . .54 C3
Fairmead Gdns, Ilf. IG4 . . . . .80 B5
Fairmead Ho, E9
  off Kingsmead Way 95 H4
Fairmead Rd, N19 . . . . .92 D3
  Croydon CR0 . . . . .201 F1
  Loughton IG10 . . . . .47 H4
Fairmeads, Loug. IG10 . . . . .48 C2
Fairmead Side, Loug. IG10 . . . . . .47 J5
Fairmile Av, SW16 . . . . .168 D5
Fairmile Ho, Tedd. TW11
  off Twickenham Rd 162 D4
Fairmont Av, E14
  off Blackwall Way 134 D1
Fairmont Cl, Belv. DA17 . . . . . . .139 F5
Fairmont Rd, SW2 . . . . .151 F6
Fairoak Cl, Orp. BR5 . . . . .193 E7
Fairoak Dr, SE9 . . . . .157 G5
Fairseat Cl, Bushey (Bushey Hth)
  WD23 off Hive Rd 52 B2
Fairstead Wk, N1
  off Popham Rd 111 J1
Fair St, SE1 . . . . .29 E3
  Hounslow TW3 off High St 143 J3
Fairthorn Rd, SE7 . . . . .135 G5
Fairview Av, Wem. HA0 . . . . .87 G6
Fairview Cl, E17 . . . . .77 H1
  Chigwell IG7 . . . . .65 H4
Fairview Cres, Har. HA2 . . . . .85 G1
Fairview Dr, Chig. IG7 . . . . .65 H4
  Orpington BR6 . . . . .207 G4
Fairview Gdns, Wdf.Grn. IG8 . . . .79 H1
Fairview Pl, SW2 . . . . .151 F7
Fairview Rd, N15 . . . . .76 C5
  SW16 . . . . .187 F1
  Chigwell IG7 . . . . .65 H4
  Enfield EN2 . . . . .43 G1
  Sutton SM1 . . . . .199 G5
Fairview Way, Edg. HA8 . . . . .54 A4
Fairwater Av, Well. DA16 . . . . . .158 A4
Fairway, SW20 . . . . .183 J3
  Bexleyheath DA6 . . . . .159 E5
  Orpington BR5 . . . . .193 G5
  Woodford Green IG8 . . . . .63 J5
Fairway, The, N13 . . . . .59 J3
  N14 . . . . .42 B6
  NW7 .54 D3
  W3 . . . . .106 E6
  Barnet EN5 . . . . .41 E6
  Bromley BR1 . . . . .192 C5
  New Malden KT3 . . . . .182 D1
  Northolt UB5 . . . . .85 J6
  Ruislip HA4 . . . . .84 D3
  Wembley HA0 . . . . .87 E3
  West Molesey KT8 . . . . .179 H3
Fairway Av, NW9 . . . . .70 B3
  Borehamwood WD6 . . . . .38 B2
Fairway Cl, NW11 . . . . .73 F7
  Croydon CR0 . . . . .189 H5
  Epsom KT19 . . . . .196 C4
  Hounslow TW4 . . . . .142 C5
Fairway Ct, NW7
  off The Fairway 54 D3
Fairway Dr, SE28 . . . . .118 D6
  Greenford UB6 . . . . .85 H7
Fairway Gdns, Beck. BR3 . . . . . .190 D6
  Ilford IG1 . . . . .99 F5
Fairways, Stan. HA7 . . . . .69 H2
  Teddington TW11 . . . . .163 G7
Fairweather Cl, N15 . . . . .76 B4
Fairweather Rd, N16 . . . . .76 D6
Fairwyn Rd, SE26 . . . . .171 H4
Fakenham Cl, NW7 . . . . .55 G7
  Northolt UB5
  off Goodwood Dr 85 G6
Fakruddin St, E1 . . . . .13 J6
Falcon Av, Brom. BR1 . . . . .192 B4
Falconberg Ct, W1 . . . . .17 J3
Falconberg Ms, W1 . . . . .17 H3
Falcon Cl, SE1 . . . . .27 H1
  W4 off Sutton La S 126 C6
Falcon Ct, EC4 . . . . .19 E4
Falcon Cres, Enf. EN3 . . . . .45 G5
Falcon Dr, Stai. (Stanw.) TW19 . .140 A6
Falconer Wk, N7
  off Newington Barrow Way 93 F3
Falcon Gro, SW11 . . . . .149 H3
Falcon Ho, W13 . . . . .104 C4
Falcon La, SW11 . . . . .149 H3
Falcon Pk Ind Est, NW10 . . . . . . .89 F5
Falcon Rd, SW11 . . . . .149 H2

Falcon Rd, Enf. EN3 . . . . .45 G5
  Hampton TW12 . . . . .161 F7
Falcon St, E13 . . . . .115 G4
Falcon Ter, SW11 . . . . .149 H3
Falcon Way, E11 . . . . .79 G4
  E14 .134 B4
  NW9 .71 E2
  Feltham TW14 . . . . .142 B5
  Harrow HA3 . . . . .69 H5
FALCONWOOD, Well. DA16 . . . .157 G3
Falconwood Av, Well. DA16 . . . . .157 G2
Falconwood Par, Well. DA16 . . . .157 H4
Falconwood Rd, Croy. CR0 . . . . .204 A7
Falcourt Cl, Sutt. SM1 . . . . .198 E5
Falkirk Gdns, Wat. WD19
  off Blackford Rd 50 D5
Falkirk Ho, W9 . . . . .6 B3
Falkirk St, N1 . . . . .12 E2
Falkland Av, N3 . . . . .56 D7
  N11 . . . . .58 A4
Falkland Pk Av, SE25 . . . . .188 B3
Falkland Pl, NW5
  off Falkland Rd 92 C5
Falkland Rd, N8 . . . . .75 G4
  NW5 .92 C5
  Barnet EN5 . . . . .40 B2
Fallaize Av, Ilf. IG1
  off Riverdene Rd 98/99 E4
Fallodon Way, NW11 . . . . .72 D4
Fallow Cl, Chig. IG7 . . . . .65 J5
Fallow Ct, SE16 . . . . .37 J4
Fallow Ct Av, N12 . . . . .57 F7
Fallowfield, Stan. HA7 . . . . .52 D3
Fallowfield Ct, Stan. HA7 . . . . . . .52 D3
Fallow Flds, Loug. IG10 . . . . .47 J7
Fallowfields Dr, N12 . . . . .57 H6
Fallows Cl, N2 . . . . .73 F2
Fallsbrook Rd, SW16 . . . . .168 C7
Falman Cl, N9 off Croyland Rd . . .60 D1
Falmer Rd, E17 . . . . .78 B3
  N15 . . . . .75 J5
  Enfield EN1 . . . . .44 B4
Falmouth Av, E4 . . . . .62 D5
Falmouth Cl, N22 off Truro Rd . . .59 F7
  SE12 . . . . .155 F5
Falmouth Gdns, Ilf. IG4 . . . . .80 B5
Falmouth Ho, Kings.T. KT2
  off Kingsgate Rd 181 H1
Falmouth Rd, SE1 . . . . .28 A5
Falmouth St, E15 . . . . .96 D5
Falmouth Way, E17
  off Gosport Rd 77 J5
Falstaff Ms, Hmptn. (Hmptn H.)
  TW12 off Hampton Rd 162 A5
Fambridge Cl, SE26 . . . . .171 J4
Fambridge Rd, Dag. RM8 . . . . . .101 G1
★ Family Records Cen, Public
  Record Office, EC1 . . . . .11 F4
Fane St, W14 off North End Rd . .128 C6
★ Fan Mus, SE10 . . . . .134 C7
Fann St, EC1 . . . . .11 J6
  EC2 . . . . .11 J6
Fanshawe Av, Bark. IG11 . . . . . . .99 F6
Fanshawe Cres, Dag. RM9 . . . . .101 E5
Fanshawe Rd, Rich. TW10 . . . . .163 F4
Fanshaw St, N1 . . . . .12 D3
Fanthorpe St, SW15 . . . . .147 J3
Faraday Av, Sid. DA14 . . . . .176 A2
Faraday Cl, N7 off Bride St 93 F6
★ Faraday Mus, W1 . . . . .17 F5
Faraday Rd, E15 . . . . .97 F6
  SW19 . . . . .166 D6
  W3 . . . . .106 C7
  W10 .108 B5
  Southall UB1 . . . . .103 H7
  Welling DA16 . . . . .158 A3
  West Molesey KT8 . . . . .179 G4
Faraday Way, SE18 . . . . .136 A3
  Croydon CR0
  off Ampere Way 201 F1
Fareham Rd, Felt. TW14 . . . . . . .142 C7
Fareham St, W1 . . . . .17 H3
Farewell Pl, Mitch. CR4 . . . . . . .185 H1
Faringdon Av, Brom. BR2 . . . . . .192 E6
Faringford Rd, E15 . . . . .96 E7
Farjeon Rd, SE3 . . . . .156 A1
Farleigh Av, Brom. BR2 . . . . .191 F6
Farleigh Pl, N16 off Farleigh Rd . .94 C4
Farleigh Rd, N16 . . . . .94 C4
Farley Dr, Ilf. IG3 . . . . .99 H1
Farley Ms, SE6 . . . . .154 C7
Farley Pl, SE25 . . . . .188 D4
Farley Rd, SE6 . . . . .154 B7
  South Croydon CR2 . . . . .202 E7
Farlington Pl, SW15
  off Roehampton La 147 H7
Farlow Rd, SW15 . . . . .148 A3
Farlton Rd, SW18 . . . . .149 E7
Farman Gro, Nthlt. UB5
  off Wayfarer Rd 102 D3
Farm Av, NW2 . . . . .90 B3
  SW16 . . . . .169 E4
  Harrow HA2 . . . . .67 F7
  Wembley HA0 . . . . .87 F6
Farmborough Cl, Har. HA1
  off Pool Rd 68 A7
Farm Cl, SW6 off Farm La 128 D7

Farm Cl, Barn. EN5 . . . . .39 J5
  Buckhurst Hill IG9 . . . . .63 J3
  Dagenham RM10 . . . . .101 J7
  Southall UB1 . . . . .103 H7
  Sutton SM2 . . . . .199 G7
  West Wickham BR4 . . . . .205 E3
Farmcote Rd, SE12 . . . . .173 G1
Farm Ct, NW4 . . . . .71 G3
Farmdale Rd, SE10 . . . . .135 G5
  Carshalton SM5 . . . . .199 H7
Farm Dr, Croy. CR0 . . . . .203 J2
Farm End, E4 . . . . .46 E5
Farmer Rd, E10 . . . . .96 B1
Farmers Rd, SE5 . . . . .35 H7
Farmer St, W8 off Uxbridge St . .128 D1
Farmfield Rd, Brom. BR1 . . . . . . .172 E5
Farmhouse Rd, SW16 . . . . .168 C7
Farmilo Rd, E17 . . . . .77 J7
Farmington Av, Sutt. SM1 . . . . . .199 G3
Farmlands, Enf. EN2 . . . . .43 G1
  Pinner HA5 . . . . .66 A4
Farmlands, The, Nthlt. UB5 . . . . .85 F6
Farmland Wk, Chis. BR7 . . . . . . .174 E5
Farm La, N14 . . . . .42 A6
  SW6 .128 D6
  Croydon CR0 . . . . .203 J2
Farm La Trd Cen, SW6
  off Farm La 128 D6
Farmleigh, N14 . . . . .42 C7
Farm Pl, W8 off Uxbridge St 128 D1
Farm Rd, N21 . . . . .59 H1
  NW10 . . . . .106 D1
  Edgware HA8 . . . . .54 B6
  Hounslow TW4 . . . . .161 E1
  Morden SM4 . . . . .185 E5
  Sutton SM2 . . . . .199 G7
Farmstead Rd, SE6 . . . . .172 B4
  Harrow HA3 . . . . .68 A1
Farm St, W1 . . . . .16 D6
Farm Vale, Bex. DA5 . . . . .159 H6
Farm Wk, NW11 . . . . .72 C5
Farm Way, Buck.H. IG9 . . . . .63 J4
Farmway, Dag. RM8 . . . . .100 C4
Farm Way, Wor.Pk. KT4 . . . . . . .197 J3
Farnaby Rd, SE9 . . . . .155 G4
  Bromley BR1, BR2 . . . . .172 D7
Farnan Av, E17 . . . . .78 A2
Farnan Rd, SW16 . . . . .169 E5
FARNBOROUGH, Orp. BR6 . . . .206 E5
Farnborough Av, E17 . . . . .77 H3
  South Croydon CR2 . . . . .203 G7
Farnborough Cl, Wem. HA9
  off Chalkhill Rd 88 B2
Farnborough Common, Orp.
  BR6 .206 C5
Farnborough Cres, Brom. BR2
  off Saville Row 205 F1
Farnborough Hill, Orp. BR6 . . . . .207 G5
Farnborough Ho, SW15
  off Fontley Way 165 G1
Farnborough Way, SE15
  off Blakes Rd 132 B7
  Orpington BR6 . . . . .207 F4
Farncombe St, SE16 . . . . .29 J4
Farndale Av, N13 . . . . .59 H3
Farndale Cres, Grnf. UB6 . . . . . .103 J3
Farnell Ms, SW5 . . . . .30 A3
Farnell Pl, W3 . . . . .106 B7
Farnell Rd, Islw. TW7 . . . . .144 A3
Farnham Cl, N20 . . . . .41 F7
Farnham Gdns, SW20 . . . . .183 H2
Farnham Pl, SE1 . . . . .27 H2
Farnham Rd, Ilf. IG3 . . . . .81 J7
  Welling DA16 . . . . .158 C2
Farnham Royal, SE11 . . . . .34 D4
Farningham Rd, N17 . . . . .60 D7
Farnley Rd, E4 . . . . .46 E1
  SE25 . . . . .188 A4
Faro Cl, Brom. BR1 . . . . .192 D2
Faroe Rd, W14 . . . . .128 A3
Farorna Wk, Enf. EN2 . . . . .43 G1
Farquhar Rd, SE19 . . . . .170 C5
  SW19 . . . . .166 D2
Farquharson Rd, Croy. CR0 . . . . .201 J2
Farrance Rd, Rom. RM6 . . . . . . .83 E6
Farrance St, E14 . . . . .113 J6
Farrans Ct, Har. HA3 . . . . .69 E7
Farrant Av, N22 . . . . .75 G2
Farr Av, Bark. IG11 . . . . .118 A2
Farrell Ho, E1 . . . . .113 F6
Farren Rd, SE23 . . . . .171 H2
Farrer Ms, N8 off Farrer Rd 74 C4
Farrer Rd, N8 . . . . .74 C4
  Harrow HA3 . . . . .69 H5
Farrer's Pl, Croy. CR0 . . . . .203 G4
Farrier Cl, Sun. TW16 . . . . .178 A4
Farrier Rd, Nthlt. UB5 . . . . .103 G2
Farriers Ct, Sutt. SM3
  off Forge La 198 B7
Farriers Ms, SE15
  off Machell Rd 153 F3
Farrier St, NW1 . . . . .92 B7
Farriers Way, Borwd. WD6 . . . . . .38 C6
Farrier Wk, SW10 . . . . .30 C5
Farringdon La, EC1 . . . . .11 F6
Farringdon Rd, EC1 . . . . .10 E5
Farringdon St, EC4 . . . . .19 G3

Farringale Pl, Chis. BR7 ....175 G7
Farrins Rents, SE16 ....133 H1
Farrow La, SE14 ....133 F7
Farrow Pl, SE16
  off Ropemaker Rd 133 H3
Farr Rd, Enf. EN2 ....44 A1
Farthingale Wk, E15 ....96 D7
Farthing All, E1 ....29 H4
Farthing Flds, E1
  off Raine St 132/133 E1
Farthings, The, Kings.T. KT2
  off Brunswick Rd 182 A1
Farthings, E4 ....63 E3
  Pinner HA5 ....66 B6
Farthing St, Orp. BR6 ....206 C7
Farwell Rd, Sid. DA14 ....176 B3
Farwig La, Brom. BR1 ....191 F1
Fashion St, E1 ....21 F1
Fashoda Rd, Brom. BR2 ....192 A4
Fassett Rd, E8 ....94 D6
  Kingston upon Thames KT1 .181 H1
Fassett Sq, E8 ....94 D6
Fauconberg Rd, W4 ....126 C6
Faulkner Cl, Dag. RM8 ....82 D7
Faulkner's All, EC1 ....19 G1
Faulkner St, SE14 ....153 F1
Fauna Cl, Rom. RM6 ....82 C7
Faunce St, SE17 ....35 G5
Favart Rd, SW6 ....148 D1
Faversham Av, E4 ....63 E1
  Enfield EN1 ....44 A6
Faversham Rd, SE6 ....153 J7
  Beckenham BR3 ....189 J2
  Morden SM4 ....185 E6
Fawcett Cl, SW11 ....149 G2
  SW16 ....169 G4
Fawcett Est, E5 ....94 D1
Fawcett Rd, NW10 ....107 F1
  Croydon CR0 ....201 J3
Fawcett St, SW10 ....30 C5
Fawcus Cl, Esher (Clay.) KT10
  off Dalmore Av 194 C6
Fawe Pk Rd, SW15 ....148 C4
Fawe St, E14 ....114 B5
Fawley Rd, NW6 ....90 E5
Fawnbrake Av, SE24 ....151 H5
Fawn Rd, E13 ....115 J2
  Chigwell IG7 ....65 J5
Fawood Av, NW10 ....88 D7
Faygate Cres, Bexh. DA6 ......159 G5
Faygate Rd, SW2 ....169 F2
Fayland Av, SW16 ....168 C5
Fearnley Cres, Hmptn. TW12 ..161 E5
Fearon St, SE10 ....135 G5
Featherbed La, Croy. CR0 ......203 J7
Feathers Pl, SE10 ....134 D6
Featherstone Av, SE23 ....171 E2
Featherstone Gdns, Borwd.
  WD6 ....38 C4
Featherstone Ind Est, Sthl. UB2 .123 E2
  Southall UB2 ....122 E3
Featherstone Rd, NW7 ....55 H6
  Southall UB2 ....123 E3
Featherstone St, EC1 ....12 B5
Featherstone Ter, Sthl. UB2 ....123 E3
Featley Rd, SW9 ....151 H3
Federal Rd, Grnf. UB6 ....105 F2
Federation Rd, SE2 ....138 B4
Fee Fm Rd, Esher (Clay.) KT10 .194 C7
Felbridge Av, Stan. HA7 ....68 D1
Felbridge Cl, SW16 ....169 G4
Felbrigge Rd, Ilf. IG3 ....99 J2
Felday Rd, SE13 ....154 B6
Felden Cl, Pnr. HA5 ....51 E7
Felden St, SW6 ....148 C1
Feldman Cl, N16 ....94 D1
Felgate Ms, W6 ....127 H4
Felhampton Rd, SE9 ....174 E2
Felhurst Cres, Dag. RM10 .....101 H4
Felix Av, N8 ....74 E6
Felix Rd, W13 ....104 D7
  Walton-on-Thames KT12 ...178 A6
Felixstowe Ct, E16
  off Fishguard Way 136/137 E2
Felixstowe Rd, N9 ....60 D4
  N17 ....76 C3
  NW10 ....107 H3
  SE2 ....138 B3
Fellbrigg Rd, SE22 ....152 C5
Fellbrigg St, E1
  off Headlam St 112/113 E4
Fellbrook, Rich. TW10 ....163 E3
Fellmongers Path, SE1 ....29 E4
Fellmongers Yd, Croy. CR0
  off Surrey St 201 J2
Fellowes Cl, Hayes UB4
  off Paddington Cl 102 D4
Fellowes Rd, Cars. SM5 ....199 H3
Fellows Ct, E2 ....13 F2
Fellows Rd, NW3 ....91 G7
Fell Rd, Croy. CR0 ....201 J3
Felltram Way, SE7
  off Woolwich Rd 135 G5
Fell Wk, Edg. HA8 off East Rd ..70 B1
Felmersham Cl, SW4
  off Haselrigge Rd 150 D4
Felmingham Rd, SE20 ....189 F2
Felnex Trd Est, Wall. SM6 .....200 A2

Felsberg Rd, SW2 ....151 E6
Fels Cl, Dag. RM10 ....101 H3
Fels Fm Av, Dag. RM10 ....101 J3
Felsham Rd, SW15 ....148 A3
Felspar Cl, SE18 ....137 J5
Felstead Av, Ilf. IG5 ....80 D1
Felstead Gdns, E14 off Ferry Rd .134 C5
Felstead Rd, E11 ....79 G7
  Loughton IG10 ....48 B7
Felstead St, E9 ....95 J6
Felsted Rd, E16 ....116 A6
FELTHAM, TW13 & TW14 .....160 A2
Feltham Av, E.Mol. KT8 ....180 B4
Felthambrook Way, Felt. TW13 .160 B3
Feltham Business Complex, Felt.
  TW13 ....160 B2
Feltham Hill Rd, Felt. TW13 ....160 A4
Feltham Rd, Mitch. CR4 ....185 J2
Felton Cl, Orp. BR5 ....192 E6
Felton Gdns, Bark. IG11
  off Sutton Rd 117 H1
Felton Ho, SE3 off Ryan Cl 155 H4
Felton Lea, Sid. DA14 ....175 J5
Felton Rd, W13
  off Camborne Av 125 F2
  Barking IG11 off Sutton Rd ..117 H2
Felton St, N1 ....112 A1
Fencepiece Rd, Chig. IG7 ....65 F5
  Ilford IG6 ....65 F5
Fenchurch Av, EC3 ....20 D4
Fenchurch Bldgs, EC3 ....20 E4
Fenchurch Pl, EC3 ....20 E5
Fenchurch St, EC3 ....20 D5
Fen Ct, EC3 ....20 D5
Fendall Rd, Epsom KT19 ......196 C5
Fendall St, SE1 ....29 E6
Fendt Cl, E16 off Bowman Av ..115 F7
Fendyke Rd, Belv. DA17 ....138 D3
Fenelon Pl, W14 ....128 C4
Fen Gro, Sid. DA15 ....157 J6
Fenham Rd, SE15 ....132 D7
Fenman Ct, N17
  off Shelbourne Rd 76/77 E1
Fenman Gdns, Ilf. IG3 ....100 B1
Fenn Cl, Brom. BR1 ....173 G6
Fennel Cl, E16
  off Cranberry La 114/115 E4
  Croydon CR0
  off Primrose La 203 G1
Fennel St, SE18 ....136 D6
Fenner Cl, SE16
  off Layard Rd 132/133 E4
Fenner Sq, SW11
  off Thomas Baines Rd 149 G3
Fenning St, SE1 ....28 D3
Fenn St, E9 ....95 F5
Fenstanton Av, N12 ....57 G5
Fen St, E16
  off Victoria Dock Rd 115 F7
Fenswood Cl, Bex. DA5 ....159 G5
Fentiman Rd, SW8 ....34 B6
Fenton Cl, E8 off Laurel St 94 C6
  SW9 ....151 F2
  Chislehurst BR7 ....174 C5
★ Fenton Ho, NW3 ....91 F3
Fenton Rd, N17 ....59 J7
Fentons Av, E13 ....115 H2
Fenwick Cl, SE18 off Ritter Rd .136 D6
Fenwick Gro, SE15 ....152 D3
Fenwick Pl, SW9 ....150 E3
  South Croydon CR2
  off Columbine Av 201 H7
Fenwick Rd, SE15 ....152 D3
Ferdinand Pl, NW1
  off Ferdinand St 92 A7
Ferdinand St, NW1 ....92 A6
Ferguson Av, Surb. KT5 ....181 J5
Ferguson Cl, E14 ....134 A4
  Bromley BR2 ....190 C3
Ferguson Dr, W3 ....106 D6
Fergus Rd, N5 off Calabria Rd ..93 H5
Ferme Pk Rd, N4 ....75 E5
  N8 ....75 E5
Fermor Rd, SE23 ....171 H1
Fermoy Rd, W9 ....108 C4
  Greenford UB6 ....103 H4
Fern Av, Mitch. CR4 ....186 D4
Fernbank, Buck.H. IG9 ....63 H1
Fernbank Av, Walt. KT12 ......179 E7
  Wembley HA0 ....86 C4
Fernbank Ms, SW12 ....150 C6
Fernbrook Av, Sid. DA15
  off Blackfen Rd 157 H5
Fernbrook Cres, SE13 ....154 E6
Fernbrook Dr, Har. HA2 ....67 H7
Fernbrook Rd, SE13 ....154 E6
Ferncliff Rd, E8 ....94 D5
Fern Cl, N1 ....12 D1
Ferncroft Av, N12 ....57 H6
  NW3 ....90 D3
  Ruislip HA4 ....84 C2
Ferndale, Brom. BR1 ....191 J2
Ferndale Av, E17 ....78 D5
  Hounslow TW4 ....143 F3
Ferndale Cl, Bexh. DA7 ....158 E1
Ferndale Ct, SE3 ....135 F7
Ferndale Rd, E7 ....97 H7

Ferndale Rd, E11 ....97 E2
  N15 ....76 C6
  SE25 ....188 E5
  SW4 ....150 E4
  SW9 ....151 F3
  Romford RM5 ....83 J2
Ferndale St, E6 ....116 E7
Ferndale Ter, Har. HA1 ....68 C4
Ferndale Way, Orp. BR6 ....207 G5
Fern Dene, W13
  off Templewood 104/105 E5
Ferndene Rd, SE24 ....151 J4
Fernden Way, Rom. RM7 ....83 H6
Ferndown, Nthwd. HA6 ....66 A2
Ferndown Av, Orp. BR6 ....207 G5
Ferndown Cl, Pnr. HA5 ....50 E7
  Sutton SM2 ....199 G6
Ferndown Rd, SE9 ....156 A7
  Watford WD19 ....50 C3
Ferney Meade Way, Islw. TW7 .144 D2
Ferney Rd, Barn. EN4 ....42 A7
Fern Gro, Felt. TW14 ....142 B7
Fernhall Dr, Ilf. IG4 ....80 A5
Fernhead Rd, W9 ....108 C4
Fernhill Ct, E17 ....78 D2
Fernhill Gdns, Kings.T. KT2 ....163 G5
Fernhill St, E16 ....136 C1
Fernholme Rd, SE15 ....153 G5
Fernhurst Gdns, Edg. HA8 ......54 A6
Fernhurst Rd, SW6 ....148 B1
  Croydon CR0 ....188 D7
Fern La, Houns. TW5 ....123 F5
Fernlea Rd, SW12 ....168 B1
  Mitcham CR4 ....186 A2
Fernleigh Cl, W9 ....108 C3
  Croydon CR0
  off Stafford Rd 201 G4
Fernleigh Ct, Har. HA2 ....67 H2
  Wembley HA9 ....87 H2
Fernleigh Rd, N21 ....59 G2
Fernsbury St, WC1 ....10 E3
Fernshaw Rd, SW10 ....30 C6
Fernside, NW11 off Finchley Rd .90 D2
  Buckhurst Hill IG9 ....63 H1
Fernside Av, NW7 ....54 D3
  Feltham TW13 ....160 B4
Fernside Rd, SW12 ....167 J1
Ferns Rd, E15 ....97 F6
Fern St, E3 ....114 A4
Fernthorpe Rd, SW16 ....168 C6
Ferntower Rd, N5 ....94 A5
Fern Wk, SE16 ....37 J4
Fernways, Ilf. IG1
  off Cecil Rd 98/99 E4
Fernwood Av, SW16 ....168 D4
  Wembley HA0
  off Bridgewater Rd 87 F5
Fernwood Cl, Brom. BR1 ......191 J2
Fernwood Cres, N20 ....57 J3
Ferranti Cl, SE18 ....136 A3
Ferraro Cl, Houns. TW5 ....123 G6
Ferrers Av, Wall. SM6 ....200 D4
  West Drayton UB7 ....120 A2
Ferrers Rd, SW16 ....168 D5
Ferrestone Rd, N8 ....75 F4
Ferrey Ms, SW9 ....151 G2
Ferriby Cl, N1 off Bewdley St ..93 G7
Ferrier Pt, E16
  off Forty Acre La 115 H5
Ferrier St, SW18 ....149 E4
Ferring Cl, Har. HA2 ....85 J1
Ferrings, SE21 ....170 B2
Ferris Av, Croy. CR0 ....203 J3
Ferris Rd, SE22 ....152 D4
Ferron Rd, E5 ....94 E3
Ferrour Ct, N2 ....73 G3
Ferryhills Cl, Wat. WD19 ....50 C3
Ferry La, N17 ....76 D4
  SW13 ....127 F6
  Brentford TW8 ....125 H6
  Richmond TW9 ....125 J6
Ferryman's Quay, SW6 ....149 F2
Ferrymead Av, Grnf. UB6 ......103 G3
Ferrymead Dr, Grnf. UB6 ......103 G2
Ferrymead Gdns, Grnf. UB6 ...103 H2
Ferrymoor, Rich. TW10 ....163 E3
Ferry Pl, SE18
  off Woolwich High St 136 D3
Ferry Rd, SW13 ....127 G7
  Teddington TW11 ....162 E5
  Thames Ditton KT7 ....180 E6
  Twickenham TW1 ....162 E1
  West Molesey KT8 ....179 G3
Ferry Sq, Brent. TW8 ....125 H6
Ferry St, E14 ....134 C5
Festing Rd, SW15 ....148 A3
Festival Cl, Bex. DA5 ....176 D1
Festival Wk, Cars. SM5 ....199 J5
Festoon Way, E16 ....116 A7
Fetter La, EC4 ....19 F4
Ffinch St, SE8 ....134 A7
Field Cl, E4 ....62 B6
  NW2 ....89 G2
  Bromley BR1 ....191 J2
  Buckhurst Hill IG9 ....63 J3
  Chessington KT9 ....195 F5

Field Cl, Hayes UB3 ....121 F7
  Hounslow TW4 ....142 B1
  West Molesey KT8 ....179 H5
Fieldcommon La, Walt. KT12 ...179 F7
Field Ct, WC1 ....18 D2
Field End, Barn. EN5 ....39 H4
  Northolt UB5 ....84 D6
  Ruislip HA4 ....84 C6
Fieldend, Twick. TW1 ....162 C4
Fieldend Rd, SW16 ....186 C1
Field End Rd, Pnr. HA5 ....66 B6
  Ruislip HA4 ....85 E4
Fielders Cl, Enf. EN1
  off Woodfield Cl 44 B4
  Harrow HA2 ....85 J1
Fieldfare Rd, SE28 ....118 C7
Fieldgate La, Mitch. CR4 ......185 H3
Fieldgate St, E1 ....21 J2
Fieldhouse Cl, E18 ....79 G1
Fieldhouse Rd, SW12 ....168 C1
Fielding Av, Twick. TW2 ....161 J3
Fielding Ho, NW6 ....108 D3
Fielding Ms, SW13
  off Castelnau 127 H6
Fielding Rd, W4 ....126 D3
  W14 ....128 A3
Fieldings, The, SE23 ....171 F1
Fielding St, SE17 ....35 J5
Fielding Wk, W13 ....124 E3
Field La, Brent. TW8 ....125 F7
  Teddington TW11 ....162 D5
Field Mead, NW7 ....55 E7
  NW9 ....55 E7
Field Pl, N.Mal. KT3 ....183 F6
Field Rd, E7 ....97 F4
  N17 ....76 A3
  W6 ....128 B5
  Feltham TW14 ....142 B6
Fieldsend Rd, Sutt. SM3 ......198 B5
Fields Est, E8 ....94 D7
Fieldside Cl, Orp. BR6
  off State Fm Av 207 F4
Fieldside Rd, Brom. BR1 ......172 D5
Fields Pk Cres, Rom. RM6 ......82 D5
Field St, WC1 ....10 C3
Fieldview, SW18 ....167 G1
Field Way, NW10
  off Twybridge Way 88 C7
  Croydon CR0 ....204 B6
Fieldway, Dag. RM8 ....100 B4
Field Way, Grnf. UB6 ....103 H1
Fieldway, Orp. BR5 ....193 G6
Fieldway Cres, N5 ....93 G5
Fiennes Cl, Dag. RM8 ....100 C1
Fiesta Dr, Dag. RM9 ....119 J4
Fife Rd, E16 ....115 G5
  N22 ....59 H7
  SW14 ....146 C5
  Kingston upon Thames KT1 .181 H2
Fife Ter, N1 ....10 D1
Fifield Path, SE23
  off Bampton Rd 171 G3
Fifth Av, E12 ....98 C4
  W10 ....108 B3
  Hayes UB3 ....121 J1
Fifth Cross Rd, Twick. TW2 ....162 A2
Fifth Way, Wem. HA9 ....88 B4
Figges Rd, Mitch. CR4 ....168 A7
Fig Tree Cl, NW10
  off Craven Pk 106/107 E1
Filby Rd, Chess. KT9 ....195 J6
Filey Av, N16 ....94 D1
Filey Cl, Sutt. SM2 ....199 F7
Filey Waye, Ruis. HA4 ....84 A2
Filigree Ct, SE16
  off Silver Wk 133 J1
Fillebrook Av, Enf. EN1 ....44 B2
Fillebrook Rd, E11 ....96 D1
Filmer Rd, SW6 ....148 B1
Filston Rd, Erith DA8
  off Riverdale Rd 139 H5
Finborough Rd, SW10 ....30 A5
  SW17 ....167 J6
Finchale Rd, SE2 ....138 A3
Finch Av, SE27 ....170 A4
Finch Cl, NW10 ....88 D5
  Barnet EN5 ....40 D5
Finchdean Ho, SW15
  off Tangley Gro 147 F7
Finch Dr, Felt. TW14 ....142 D7
Finch Gdns, E4 ....62 A5
Finchingfield Av, Wdf.Grn. IG8 ..63 J7
Finch La, EC3 ....20 C4
FINCHLEY, N3 ....72 E1
Finchley Ct, N3 ....57 E6
Finchley La, NW4 ....71 J4
Finchley Pk, N12 ....57 F4
Finchley Pl, NW8 ....6 C2
Finchley Rd, NW2 ....90 D3
  NW3 ....91 F6
  NW8 ....109 G1
  NW11 ....72 C6
Finchley Way, N3 ....56 D7
Finch Ms, SE15 ....132 C7
Finden Rd, E7 ....97 H5
Findhorn Av, Hayes UB4 ......102 C3
Findhorn St, E14 ....114 C6

Findon Cl, SW18
  off Wimbledon Pk Rd **148** D6
  Harrow HA2 ....**85** H3
Findon Rd, N9 ....**60** E1
  W12 ....**127** G2
Fingal St, SE10 ....**135** F5
Finland Quay, SE16
  off Finland St **133** H3
Finland Rd, SE4 ....**153** H3
Finland St, SE16 ....**133** H3
Finlays Cl, Chess. KT9 ......**196** A5
Finlay St, SW6 ....**148** A1
Finney La, Islw. TW7 ....**144** D1
Finnis St, E2 ....**113** E3
Finnymore Rd, Dag. RM9 ....**101** E7
FINSBURY, EC1 ....**11** F3
Finsbury Av, EC2 ....**20** C2
Finsbury Av Sq, EC2 ....**20** C2
Finsbury Circ, EC2 ....**20** C2
Finsbury Cotts, N22
  off Clarence Rd **58/59** E7
Finsbury Est, EC1 ....**11** G4
Finsbury Ho, N22 ....**75** E1
Finsbury Mkt, EC2 ....**12** D6
FINSBURY PARK, N4 ....**93** G1
★ Finsbury Park, N4 ....**75** H7
Finsbury Pk Av, N4 ....**75** J6
Finsbury Pk Rd, N4 ....**93** H2
Finsbury Pavement, EC2 ......**20** C1
Finsbury Rd, N22 ....**75** F1
Finsbury Sq, EC2 ....**20** C1
Finsbury St, EC2 ....**20** B1
Finsbury Twr, EC1 ....**12** B6
Finsbury Way, Bex. DA5 .....**159** F6
Finsen Rd, SE5 ....**151** J3
Finstock Rd, W10 ....**108** A6
Finucane Ri, Bushey (Bushey Hth)
  WD23 ....**51** J2
Firbank Cl, E16 ....**116** A5
  Enfield EN2
    off Gladbeck Way **43** J4
Firbank Rd, SE15 ....**153** E2
Fir Cl, Walt. KT12 ....**178** A7
Fircroft Gdns, Har. HA1 ......**86** B3
Fircroft Rd, SW17 ....**167** J2
  Chessington KT9 ....**195** J4
Fir Dene, Orp. BR6 ....**206** C3
Firdene, Surb. KT5 ....**196** C1
Fire Bell All, Surb. KT6 ......**181** H6
Firecrest Dr, NW3 ....**91** E3
Firefly Cl, Wall. SM6 ....**200** E7
Firefly Gdns, E6
  off Jack Dash Way **116** B4
★ Firepower, SE18 ....**136** E3
Fire Sta All, Barn. EN5
  off Christchurch La **40** C2
Firethorn Cl, Edg. HA8
  off Larkspur Gro **54** C4
Fir Gro, N.Mal. KT3 ....**183** F6
Fir Gro Rd, SW9
  off Marcella Rd **151** G2
Firhill Rd, SE6 ....**172** A4
Fir Rd, Felt. TW13 ....**160** D5
  Sutton SM3 ....**198** C1
Firs, The, E17 off Leucha Rd ...**77** H5
  N20 ....**57** G1
  W5 ....**105** G5
Firs Av, N10 ....**74** A3
  N11 ....**58** A6
  SW14 ....**146** C4
Firsby Av, Croy. CR0 ....**203** G1
Firsby Rd, N16 ....**94** C1
Firs Cl, N10 off Firs Av **74** A3
  SE23 ....**153** G7
  Esher (Clay.) KT10 ....**194** B6
  Mitcham CR4 ....**186** B2
Firscroft, N13 ....**59** J3
Firs Dr, Houns. TW5 ....**122** B7
  Loughton IG10 ....**48** D1
Firside Gro, Sid. DA15 ......**175** J1
Firs La, N13 ....**59** J3
  N21 ....**59** J2
Firs Pk Av, N21 ....**60** A1
Firs Pk Gdns, N21 ....**59** J1
First Av, E12 ....**98** B4
  E13 ....**115** G3
  E17 ....**78** A5
  N18 ....**61** F4
  NW4 ....**71** J4
  SW14 ....**146** E4
  W3 ....**127** F1
  W10 ....**108** C4
  Bexleyheath DA7 ....**138** C7
  Dagenham RM10 ....**119** H2
  Enfield EN1 ....**44** C6
  Greenford UB6 ....**86** A7
  Hayes UB3 ....**121** J1
  Romford RM6 ....**82** C5
  Walton-on-Thames KT12 ...**178** B6
  Wembley HA9 ....**87** G2
  West Molesey KT8 ....**179** F4
First Cl, W.Mol. KT8 ....**179** J3
First Cross Rd, Twick. TW2 ...**162** B2
First Dr, NW10 ....**88** C7
First St, SW3 ....**31** H1
Firstway, SW20 ....**183** J2
First Way, Wem. HA9 ....**88** B4

Firs Wk, Wdf.Grn. IG8 ....**63** G5
Firswood Av, Epsom KT19 ...**197** F5
Firth Gdns, SW6 ....**148** B1
Fir Tree Av, Mitch. CR4 ......**186** A2
  West Drayton UB7 ....**120** D3
Fir Tree Cl, SW16 ....**168** C5
  W5 ....**105** H6
  Epsom (Ewell) KT19 ......**197** F4
  Orpington BR6
    off Highfield Av **207** J5
Fir Tree Gdns, Croy. CR0 ....**204** A4
Fir Tree Gro, Cars. SM5 .....**199** J7
Fir Tree Rd, Houns. TW4 ....**143** E4
Fir Trees Cl, SE16 ....**133** H1
Fir Tree Wk, Dag. RM10
  off Wheel Fm Dr **101** J3
  Enfield EN1 ....**44** A3
Fisher Cl, Croy. CR0
  off Grant Rd **202** C1
  Greenford UB6 ....**103** G3
Fisherman Cl, Rich. TW10
  off Locksmeade Rd **163** F4
Fishermans Dr, SE16 ....**133** G2
Fisherman's Wk, E14 ....**134** A1
Fishermans Wk, SE28
  off Tugboat St **137** H2
Fisher Rd, Har. HA3 ....**68** C2
Fishers Cl, SW16
  off Garrad's Rd **168** D3
Fishers Ct, SE14 off Besson St ...**153** G1
Fishersdene, Esher (Clay.) KT10 .**194** D7
Fishers La, W4 ....**126** D4
Fisher St, E16 ....**115** G5
  WC1 ....**18** B2
Fishers Way, Belv. DA17 .....**139** J1
Fisherton St, NW8 ....**7** E6
Fishguard Way, E16 ....**137** E2
Fishponds Rd, SW17 ....**167** H4
  Keston BR2 ....**206** A5
Fish St Hill, EC3 ....**20** C5
Fitzalan Rd, N3 ....**72** B3
  Esher (Clay.) KT10 ....**194** B7
Fitzalan St, SE11 ....**34** E1
Fitzgeorge Av, W14 ....**128** B4
  New Malden KT3 ....**182** D1
Fitzgerald Av, SW14 ....**147** E3
Fitzgerald Cl, E11
  off Fitzgerald Rd **79** G5
Fitzgerald Ho, E14 ....**114** B6
  Hayes UB3 ....**122** B1
Fitzgerald Rd, E11 ....**79** G5
  SW14 ....**146** D3
  Thames Ditton KT7 ....**180** D6
Fitzhardinge St, W1 ....**16** B3
Fitzherbert Ho, Rich. TW10
  off Kingsmead **145** J6
Fitzhugh Gro, SW18 ....**149** G6
Fitzjames Av, W14 ....**128** B4
  Croydon CR0 ....**202** D2
Fitzjohn Av, Barn. EN5 ......**40** B5
Fitzjohn's Av, NW3 ....**91** F5
Fitzmaurice Pl, W1 ....**24** E1
Fitzneal St, W12 ....**107** F6
Fitzroy Cl, N6 ....**91** J1
Fitzroy Ct, W1 ....**9** G6
Fitzroy Cres, W4 ....**126** D7
Fitzroy Ms, W1 ....**9** F6
Fitzroy Pk, N6 ....**91** J1
Fitzroy Rd, NW1 ....**110** A1
Fitzroy Sq, W1 ....**9** F6
Fitzroy St, W1 ....**9** F6
Fitzroy Yd, NW1 off Fitzroy Rd ..**110** A1
Fitzstephen Rd, Dag. RM8 ...**100** B5
Fitzwarren Gdns, N19 ....**92** C1
Fitzwilliam Av, Rich. TW9 ...**145** J2
Fitzwilliam Ms, E16
  off Hanover Av **135** G1
Fitzwilliam Rd, SW4 ....**150** C3
Fitzwygram Cl, Hmptn. (Hmptn H.)
  TW12 ....**161** J5
Five Acre, NW9 ....**71** F1
Five Bell All, E14
  off Three Colt St **113** J7
Five Elms Rd, Brom. BR2 ....**205** H3
  Dagenham RM9 ....**101** F3
Five Flds Cl, Wat. WD19 .....**51** F3
Fives Ct, SE11 ....**35** G1
Five Ways Cor, NW4 ....**71** H1
Fiveways Rd, SW9 ....**151** G2
Fladbury Rd, N15 ....**76** A6
Fladgate Rd, E11 ....**79** E6
Flag Cl, Croy. CR0 ....**203** G1
Flag Wk, Pnr. HA5
  off Eastcote Rd **66** A6
Flambard Rd, Har. HA1 ......**68** D6
Flamborough Rd, Ruis. HA4 ..**84** A3
Flamborough St, E14 ....**113** H6
Flamborough Wk, E14
  off Flamborough St **113** H6
Flamingo Gdns, Nthlt. UB5
  off Jetstar Way **102/103** E3
Flamstead Gdns, Dag. RM9
  off Flamstead Rd **100** C7
Flamstead Rd, Dag. RM9 ....**100** C7
Flamsted Av, Wem. HA9 .....**88** A6

★ Flamsteed Ho Mus, SE10 ...**134** D7
Flamsteed Rd, SE7 ....**136** B5
Flanchford Rd, W12 ....**127** F3
Flanders Cres, SW17 ....**167** J7
Flanders Rd, E6 ....**116** C2
  W4 ....**127** E4
Flanders Way, E9 ....**95** G6
Flank St, E1 ....**21** H5
Flask Cotts, NW3
  off New End Sq **91** G4
Flask Wk, NW3 ....**91** G4
Flat Iron Sq, SE1 off Union St ...**131** J1
Flavell Ms, SE10 ....**135** E5
Flaxen Cl, E4 off Flaxen Rd ...**62** B3
Flaxen Rd, E4 ....**62** B3
Flaxley Rd, Mord. SM4 ......**184** E6
Flaxman Ct, W1 ....**17** H4
Flaxman Rd, SE5 ....**151** H2
Flaxman Ter, WC1 ....**9** J4
Flaxton Rd, SE18 ....**157** G1
Flecker Cl, Stan. HA7 ....**52** C5
Fleece Dr, N9 ....**60** D4
Fleece Rd, Surb. KT6 ....**195** F1
Fleece Wk, N7
  off Manger Rd **92/93** E6
Fleeming Cl, E17
  off Pennant Ter **77** J2
Fleeming Rd, E17 ....**77** J2
Fleet Cl, W.Mol. KT8 ....**179** F5
Fleet La, W.Mol. KT8 ....**179** F6
Fleet Pl, EC4 off Farringdon St ...**111** G6
Fleet Rd, NW3 ....**91** H5
Fleetside, W.Mol. KT8 ....**179** F6
Fleet Sq, WC1 ....**10** C4
Fleet St, EC4 ....**19** E4
Fleet St Hill, E1 ....**13** H6
Fleetway Business Pk, Grnf.
  UB6 ....**105** G2
Fleetwood Cl, E16 ....**116** A5
  Chessington KT9 ....**195** G7
  Croydon CR0 ....**202** C3
Fleetwood Ct, E6
  off Evelyn Denington Rd ...**116** C5
Fleetwood Gro, W3
  off East Acton La **106/107** E7
Fleetwood Rd, NW10 ....**89** G5
  Kingston upon Thames KT1 ..**182** B3
Fleetwood Sq, Kings.T. KT1 ...**182** B3
Fleetwood St, N16
  off Stoke Newington Ch St ...**94** B2
Fleetwood Way, Wat. WD19 ...**50** C4
Fleming Cl, W9
  off Chippenham Rd **108** D4
Fleming Ct, W2
  off Pasteur Cl **70/71** E2
  Croydon CR0 ....**201** G5
Fleming Dr, N21 ....**43** F5
Fleming Mead, Mitch. CR4 ...**167** H7
Fleming Rd, SE17 ....**35** H5
  Southall UB1 ....**103** H6
Fleming Wk, NW9
  off Pasteur Cl **70/71** E2
Fleming Way, SE28 ....**118** D7
  Isleworth TW7 ....**144** C3
Flemming Av, Ruis. HA4 .....**84** B1
Flempton Rd, E10 ....**77** H7
Fletcher Cl, E6
  off Trader Rd **116/117** E6
Fletcher La, E10 ....**78** C7
Fletcher Path, SE8
  off New Butt La **134** A7
Fletcher Rd, W4 ....**126** C3
  Chigwell IG7 ....**65** J5
Fletchers Cl, Brom. BR2 .....**191** H4
Fletcher St, E1 ....**21** J5
Fletching Rd, E5 ....**95** F3
  SE7 ....**135** J6
Fletton Rd, N11 ....**58** E7
Fleur de Lis St, E1 ....**13** E6
Fleur Gates, SW19
  off Princes Way **148** A7
Flexmere Gdns, N17
  off Flexmere Rd **76** A1
Flexmere Rd, N17 ....**76** A1
Flight App, NW9 ....**71** F2
Flimwell Cl, Brom. BR1 ......**172** E5
Flint Cl, E15 off Vicarage La ...**96** E7
Flintmill Cres, SE3 ....**156** B2
Flinton St, SE17 ....**36** E3
Flint St, SE17 ....**36** C2
Flitcroft St, WC2 ....**17** J3
Floathaven Cl, SE28 ....**138** A1
Flock Mill Pl, SW18 ....**166** E1
Flockton St, SE16 ....**29** H4
Flodden Rd, SE5 ....**151** J1
Flood La, Twick. TW1
  off Church La **162** D1
Flood Pas, SE18 off Samuel St ..**136** C4
Flood St, SW3 ....**31** H4
Flood Wk, SW3 ....**31** H5
Flora Cl, E14 ....**114** B6
Flora Gdns, W6 ....**127** H4
  Romford RM6 ....**82** C6
Floral St, WC2 ....**18** A5
Flora St, Belv. DA17
  off Victoria St **139** F5
Florence Av, Enf. EN2 ....**43** J3
  Morden SM4 ....**185** F5

Florence Cantwell Wk, N19
  off Hillrise Rd **74/75** E7
Florence Cl, Walt. KT12
  off Florence Rd **178** B7
Florence Dr, Enf. EN2 ....**43** J3
Florence Elson Cl, E12
  off Grantham Rd **98** D4
Florence Gdns, W4 ....**126** C6
  Romford RM6 off Roxy Av ...**82** C7
★ Florence Nightingale Mus,
  SE1 ....**26** C4
Florence Rd, E6 ....**115** J1
  E13 ....**115** F2
  N4 ....**93** G1
  SE2 ....**138** C3
  SE14 ....**153** J1
  SW19 ....**166** E6
  W4 ....**126** D3
  W5 ....**105** H7
  Beckenham BR3 ....**189** G7
  Bromley BR1 ....**191** G1
  Feltham TW13 ....**160** B1
  Kingston upon Thames KT2 ..**163** J7
  Southall UB2 ....**122** D4
  Walton-on-Thames KT12 ...**178** B7
Florence St, E16 ....**115** F4
  N1 ....**93** H7
  NW4 ....**71** J4
Florence Ter, SE14 ....**153** J1
Florence Way, SW12 ....**167** J1
Florey Sq, N21
  off Highlands Av **43** F5
Florfield Pas, E8
  off Reading La **94/95** E6
Florfield Rd, E8
  off Reading La **94/95** E6
Florian Av, Sutt. SM1 ....**199** G4
Florian Rd, SW15 ....**148** B4
Florida Cl, Bushey (Bushey Hth)
  WD23 ....**52** A2
Florida Rd, Th.Hth. CR7 .....**187** H1
Florida St, E2 ....**13** H4
Florin Ct, SE1 off Tanner St ...**132** C2
Floris Pl, SW4
  off Fitzwilliam Rd **150** C3
Floriston Cl, Stan. HA7 ......**69** E1
Floriston Ct, Nthlt. UB5 .....**85** H5
Floriston Gdns, Stan. HA7 ...**69** E1
Floss St, SW15 ....**147** J2
Flower & Dean Wk, E1 ......**21** G2
Flower La, NW7 ....**55** F5
Flower Ms, NW11 ....**72** B6
Flower Pot Cl, N15
  off St. Ann's Rd **76** C6
Flowers Cl, NW2 ....**89** G3
Flowersmead, SW17 ....**168** A2
Flowers Ms, N19
  off Archway Rd **92** C2
Flower Wk, The, SW7 ....**22** C4
Floyd Rd, SE7 ....**135** J5
Floyer Cl, Rich. TW10
  off Queens Rd **145** J5
Fludyer St, SE13 ....**154** E4
Foley Ms, Esher (Clay.) KT10 ..**194** B7
Foley Rd, Esher (Clay.) KT10 ..**194** B7
Foley St, W1 ....**17** F2
Folgate St, E1 ....**21** E1
Foliot St, W12 ....**107** F6
Folkestone Rd, E6 ....**116** C2
  E17 ....**78** B4
  N18 ....**60** D4
Folkingham La, NW9 ....**70** D1
Folkington Cor, N12 ....**56** C5
Follett St, E14 ....**114** C6
Folly La, E4 ....**61** J7
  E17 ....**77** H1
Folly Ms, W11 off Portobello Rd ..**108** C6
Folly Wall, E14 ....**134** C2
Fontaine Rd, SW16 ....**169** F7
Fontarabia Rd, SW11 ....**150** A4
Fontayne Av, Chig. IG7 .....**65** F4
Fontenoy Rd, SW12 ....**168** B2
Fonteyne Gdns, Wdf.Grn. IG8
  off Lechmere Av **80** A2
Fonthill Cl, SE20 off Selby Rd ..**188** D2
Fonthill Ms, N4 off Lennox Rd ...**93** F2
Fonthill Rd, N4 ....**93** F1
Font Hills, N2 ....**73** F2
Fontley Way, SW15 ....**147** G7
Fontwell Cl, Har. HA3 ....**52** B7
  Northolt UB5 ....**85** G6
Fontwell Dr, Brom. BR2 .....**192** D5
Football La, Har. HA1 ....**86** B1
Footpath, The, SW15 ....**147** G5
FOOTS CRAY, Sid. DA14 ....**176** B6
Foots Cray High St, Sid. DA14 .**176** C6
Foots Cray La, Sid. DA14 ....**176** C1
Footscray Rd, SE9 ....**156** D6
Forbes Cl, NW2 ....**89** G3
Forbes Ct, SE19 ....**170** B5
Forbes St, E1 ....**21** J4
Forbes Way, Ruis. HA4 .....**84** B2
Forburg Rd, N16 ....**94** D1
Ford Cl, E3 off Roman Rd ...**113** H2
  Harrow HA1 ....**68** A7
  Thornton Heath CR7 ......**187** H6
Forde Av, Brom. BR1 ....**191** J3

Fordel Rd, SE6 ....172 D1
Ford End, Wdf.Grn. IG8 ....63 H6
Fordham Cl, Barn. EN4 .....41 H3
Fordham Rd, Barn. EN4 .....41 G3
Fordham St, E1 ....21 J3
Fordhook Av, W5 ....105 J4
Fordingley Rd, W9 ....108 C3
Fordington Ho, SE26
    off Sydenham Hill 170 D3
Fordington Rd, N6 ....73 J5
Fordmill Rd, SE6 ....172 A2
Ford Rd, E3 ....113 H1
    Dagenham RM9, RM10 ....101 F7
Fords Gro, N21 ....59 J1
Fords Pk Rd, E16 ....115 G6
Ford Sq, E1 ....113 E5
Ford St, E3 ....113 H1
    E16 ....115 F6
Fordwich Cl, Orp. BR6 .....193 J7
Fordwych Rd, NW2 ....90 B4
Fordyce Ho, SW16
    off Colson Way 168 C4
Fordyce Rd, SE13 ....154 C6
Fordyke Rd, Dag. RM8 .....101 F2
★ Foreign & Commonwealth
    Office, SW1 ....26 A3
Foreign St, SE5 ....151 H2
Foreland Ct, NW4 ....72 B1
Foreland St, SE18
    off Plumstead Rd 137 G4
Foreman Ct, W6
    off Hammersmith Bdy ...127 J4
Foremark Cl, Ilf. IG6 ......65 J5
Foreshore, SE8 ....133 J4
Forest, The, E11 ....79 E4
Forest App, E4 ....47 E7
    Woodford Green IG8 ....63 F7
Forest Av, E4 ....47 E7
    Chigwell IG7 ....64 D5
Forest Business Pk, E17 ....77 G7
Forest Cl, E11 ....79 F5
    Chislehurst BR7 ....192 D1
    Woodford Green IG8 ....63 H3
Forest Ct, E4 ....63 F1
    E11 ....79 E4
Forest Cft, SE23 ....171 E2
Forestdale, N14 ....58 D4
Forest Dr, E12 ....98 A3
    Keston BR2 ....206 B4
    Woodford Green IG8 ....62 D7
Forest Dr E, E11 ....78 D7
Forest Dr W, E11 ....78 C7
Forest Edge, Buck.H. IG9 ...63 J4
Forester Rd, SE15 ....153 E4
Foresters Cl, Wall. SM6 ....200 D7
Foresters Cres, Bexh. DA7 ..159 H4
Foresters Dr, E17 ....78 D4
    Wallington SM6 ....200 D7
Forest Gdns, N17 ....76 C2
FOREST GATE, E7 ....97 G5
Forest Gate, NW9 ....70 E5
Forest Glade, E4 ....62 E4
    E11 ....79 E6
Forest Gro, E8 ....94 C7
Forest Hts, Buck.H. IG9 ....63 G2
FOREST HILL, SE23 ....171 G1
Forest Hill Business Cen, SE23 ..171 F2
Forest Hill Ind Est, SE23
    off Perry Vale 171 F2
Forest Hill Rd, SE22 ......152 E5
    SE23 ....152 E5
Forestholme Cl, SE23 ......171 F2
Forest Ind Pk, Ilf. IG6 .....81 H1
Forest La, E7 ....97 E5
    E15 ....97 E5
    Chigwell IG7 ....64 D5
Forest Mt Rd, Wdf.Grn. IG8 ..62 D7
Fore St, EC2 ....20 A2
    N9 ....60 D5
    N18 ....60 C6
    Pinner HA5 ....66 A5
Fore St Av, EC2 ....20 B2
Forest Ridge, Beck. BR3 ....190 A3
    Keston BR2 ....206 B4
Forest Ri, E17 ....78 D5
Forest Rd, E7 ....97 G4
    E8 ....94 C6
    E11 ....78 D7
    E17 ....77 F4
    N9 ....61 E1
    N17 ....77 H4
    Feltham TW13 ....160 C2
    Ilford IG6 ....81 H1
    Loughton IG10 ....48 A3
    Richmond TW9 ....126 A7
    Romford RM7 ....83 H3
    Sutton SM3 ....198 D1
    Woodford Green IG8 ....63 G3
Forest Side, E4 ....47 F7
    E7 off Capel Rd 97 H4
    Buckhurst Hill IG9 .....63 J1
    Worcester Park KT4 ....197 F1
Forest St, E7 ....97 G5
Forest Vw, E4 ....46 D7
    E11 off High Rd Leytonstone ..79 F7
Forest Vw Av, E10 ....78 D5
Forest Vw Rd, E12 ....98 B4

Forest Vw Rd, E17 ....78 C1
    Loughton IG10 ....48 A4
Forest Wk, N10 ....74 B1
Forest Way, N19
    off Hargrave Pk 92 C2
    Loughton IG10 ....48 B3
    Orpington BR5 ....193 J5
    Sidcup DA15 ....157 G7
    Woodford Green IG8 ....63 H4
Forfar Rd, N22 ....75 H1
    SW11 ....150 A1
Forge Cl, Brom. BR2 ......205 G1
    Hayes UB3 off High St ..121 G6
Forge Cotts, W5 off Ealing Grn ..125 G1
Forge Dr, Esher (Clay.) KT10 ..194 D7
Forge La, Felt. TW13 ......160 E5
    Sunbury-on-Thames TW16 ..178 A3
    Sutton SM3 ....198 B7
Forge Ms, Croy. CR0
    off Addington Village Rd ..204 A5
    Sunbury-on-Thames TW16
    off Forge La 178 A3
Forge Pl, NW1 off Malden Cres ..92 A6
Forlong Path, Nthlt. UB5
    off Arnold Rd 84/85 E6
Forman Pl, N16 off Farleigh Rd ..94 C4
Formation, The, E16
    off Woolwich Manor
    Way 136/137 E2
Formby Av, Stan. HA7 .....69 F3
Formosa St, W9 ....6 C6
Formunt Cl, E16 off Vincent St ..115 F5
Forres Gdns, NW11 ....72 D6
Forrester Path, SE26 ......171 G4
Forrest Gdns, SW16 ......187 F3
Forris Av, Hayes UB3 .....121 J1
Forset St, W1 ....15 H3
Forstal Cl, Brom. BR2
    off Ridley Rd 191 G3
Forster Cl, E17 ....62 D7
Forster Rd, E17 ....77 H6
    N17 ....76 C3
    SW2 ....150 E7
    Beckenham BR3 ....189 H3
    Croydon CR0
    off Windmill Rd 187 J7
Forsters Cl, Rom. RM6 .....83 F6
Forster's Way, SW18 ......166 E1
Forsters Way, Hayes UB4 ...102 B6
Forston St, N1 ....12 B1
Forsyte Cres, SE19 ....188 B1
Forsyth Gdns, SE17 ....35 H5
Forsythia Cl, Ilf. IG1 ......98 E5
Forsyth Pl, Enf. EN1 ......44 B5
Forterie Gdns, Ilf. IG3 .....100 A3
Fortescue Av, E8
    off Mentmore Ter 94/95 E7
    Twickenham TW2 ......161 J3
Fortescue Rd, SW19 ......167 G7
    Edgware HA8 ....70 D1
Fortess Gro, NW5
    off Fortess Rd 92 B5
Fortess Rd, NW5 ....92 B5
Fortess Wk, NW5 off Fortess Rd ..92 B5
Forthbridge Rd, SW11 .....150 A4
Fortis Cl, E16 ....115 J6
FORTIS GREEN, N2 ....73 J4
Fortis Grn, N2 ....73 H4
    N10 ....73 H4
Fortis Grn Av, N2 ....73 J3
Fortis Grn Rd, N10 ....74 A3
Fortismere Av, N10 ....74 A3
Fortnam Rd, N19 ....92 D2
★ Fortnum & Mason, W1 ....25 F1
Fortnums Acre, Stan. HA7 ..52 C6
Fort Rd, SE1 ....37 G2
    Northolt UB5 ....85 G7
Fortrose Gdns, SW2
    off New Pk Rd 168 D1
Fort St, E1 ....21 E2
    E16 ....135 H1
Fortuna Cl, N7 off Vulcan Way ..93 F6
Fortune Gate Rd, NW10 ....107 E1
Fortune Grn Rd, NW6 ......90 D4
Fortunes Mead, Nthlt. UB5 ..85 E6
Fortune St, EC1 ....12 A6
Fortune Wk, SE28
    off Broadwater Rd 137 G3
Fortune Way, NW10 ....107 G3
Forty Acre La, E16 ....115 G5
Forty Av, Wem. HA9 ....87 J3
Forty Cl, Wem. HA9 ....87 J2
Forty Footpath, SW14 .....146 C3
Forty La, Wem. HA9 ....88 B2
Forum, The, W.Mol. KT8 ....179 H4
★ Forum Club, NW5 ....92 B5
Forum Magnum Sq, SE1 ....26 C3
Forumside, Edg. HA8
    off High St 54 A6
Forum Way, Edg. HA8
    off High St 54 A6
Forval Cl, Mitch. CR4 .....185 J5
Forward Dr, Har. HA3 .....68 C4
Fosbury Ms, W2 ....14 B6
Foscote Ms, W9
    off Amberley Rd 108 D5
Foscote Rd, NW4 ....71 H6

Foskett Rd, SW6 ....148 C2
Foss Av, Croy. CR0 ....201 G5
Fossdene Rd, SE7 ....135 H5
Fossdyke Cl, Hayes UB4 ...103 E5
Fosse Way, W13 ....104 D5
Fossil Rd, SE13 ....154 A3
Fossington Rd, Belv. DA17 ..138 D4
Foss Rd, SW17 ....167 G4
Fossway, Dag. RM8 ....100 C2
Foster La, EC2 ....19 J3
Foster Rd, E13 ....115 G4
    W3 ....106 E7
    W4 ....126 D5
Fosters Cl, E18 ....79 H1
    Chislehurst BR7 ....174 C5
Foster St, NW4 ....71 J4
Foster Wk, NW4
    off New Brent St 71 J4
Fothergill Cl, E13 ....115 G2
Fothergill Dr, N21 ....43 E5
Fotheringham Rd, Enf. EN1 ..44 C4
Foubert's Pl, W1 ....17 F4
Foulden Rd, N16 ....94 C4
Foulden Ter, N16
    off Foulden Rd 94 C4
Foulis Ter, SW7 ....31 F3
Foulser Rd, SW17 ....167 J3
Foulsham Rd, Th.Hth. CR7 ..187 J3
Founder Cl, E6
    off Trader Rd 116/117 E6
Founders Ct, EC2 ....20 B3
Founders Gdns, SE19 ......169 J7
★ Foundling Mus, WC1 .....10 B5
Foundry Cl, SE16 ....133 H1
Foundry Ms, NW1 ....9 G5
Fountain Ct, EC4 ....19 E5
Fountain Dr, SE19 ....170 C4
Fountain Grn Sq, SE16 ....29 J3
Fountain Ms, N5
    off Highbury Gra 93 J4
    NW3 ....91 J6
Fountain Pl, SW9 ....151 G1
Fountain Rd, SW17 ....167 G5
    Thornton Heath CR7 ...187 J2
Fountains, The, Loug. IG10
    off Fallow Flds 48 A7
Fountains Av, Felt. TW13 ..161 F3
Fountains Cl, Felt. TW13 ..161 F2
Fountains Cres, N14 ......42 E7
Fountain Sq, SW1 ....32 D1
Fountain St, E2
    off Columbia Rd 112 C3
Fountayne Rd, N15 ....76 D4
    N16 ....94 D2
Fount St, SW8 ....130 D7
Fouracres, SW12
    off Little Dimocks 168 B2
    Enfield EN3 ....45 H1
Fourland Wk, Edg. HA8 ....54 C6
Fournier St, E1 ....21 F1
Four Seasons Cl, E3 ......114 A2
Four Seasons Cres, Sutt. SM3 ..198 C2
Fourth Av, E12 ....98 C4
    W10 ....108 B4
    Hayes UB3 ....121 J1
Fourth Cross Rd, Twick. TW2 ..162 A2
Fourth Way, Wem. HA9 ....88 C4
Four Wents, The, E4
    off Kings Rd 62 D2
Fowey Av, Ilf. IG4 ....80 A5
Fowey Cl, E1
    off Kennet St 132/133 E1
Fowler Cl, SW11 ....149 G3
Fowler Rd, E7 ....97 G4
    N1 off Halton Rd 93 H7
    Mitcham CR4 ....186 A2
Fowlers Cl, Sid. DA14
    off Thursland Rd 176/177 E5
Fowlers Wk, W5 ....105 G4
Fownes St, SW11 ....149 H3
Fox & Knot St, EC1 ....19 H1
Foxberry Rd, SE4 ....153 H3
Foxborough Gdns, SE4 ....154 A6
Foxbourne Rd, SW17 .....168 A2
Foxbury Av, Chis. BR7 ....175 G6
Foxbury Cl, Brom. BR1 ....173 H6
Foxbury Rd, Brom. BR1 ....173 G6
Fox Cl, E1 ....113 F4
    E16 ....115 G5
Foxcombe, Croy. (New Adgtn)
    CR0 ....204 B6
Foxcombe Cl, E6
    off Boleyn Rd 116 A2
Foxcombe Rd, SW15
    off Alton Rd 165 G1
Foxcote, SE5 ....36 E4
Foxcroft Rd, SE18 ....157 E1
Foxes Dale, SE3 ....155 G3
    Bromley BR2 ....190 D3
Foxfield Rd, Orp. BR6 ....207 G2
Foxglove Cl, Sid. DA15
    off Wellington Av 158 A6
    Southall UB1 ....103 E7
Foxglove Gdns, E11 ......79 J4
Foxglove La, Chess. KT9 ...196 A4
Foxglove Path, SE28
    off Hill Vw Dr 137 H1

Foxglove St, W12 ....107 F7
Foxglove Way, Wall. SM6 ..200 B7
Foxgrove, N14 ....58 E3
Fox Gro, Walt. KT12 ......178 B7
Foxgrove Av, Beck. BR3 ...172 B7
Foxgrove Path, Wat. WD19 ..50 D5
Foxgrove Rd, Beck. BR3 ...172 B7
Foxham Rd, N19 ....92 D3
Fox Hill, SE19 ....170 C7
    Keston BR2 ....205 J5
Fox Hill Gdns, SE19 ......170 C7
Foxhole Rd, SE9 ....156 B5
Fox Hollow Cl, SE18 .....137 H5
Fox Hollow Dr, Bexh. DA7 ..158 D3
Foxholt Gdns, NW10 ......88 C7
Foxhome Cl, Chis. BR7 ....174 D6
Fox Ho Rd, Belv. DA17 ....139 H4
Foxlands Cres, Dag. RM10 ..101 J5
Foxlands La, Dag. RM10 ...101 J5
Foxlands Rd, Dag. RM10 ...101 J5
Fox La, N13 ....59 F3
    W5 ....105 H4
    Keston BR2 ....205 H5
Foxlees, Wem. HA0 ....86 D4
Foxley Cl, E8 off Ferncliff Rd ..94 D5
    Loughton IG10 ....49 E2
Foxley Ct, Sutt. SM2 ......199 F7
Foxley Rd, SW9 ....35 F7
    Thornton Heath CR7 ...187 H4
Foxleys, Wat. WD19 ......51 E3
Foxley Sq, SW9 off Cancell Rd ..131 H7
Foxmead Cl, Enf. EN2 .....43 F3
Foxmore St, SW11 ....149 J1
Fox Rd, E16 ....115 F5
Fox's Path, Mitch. CR4 ....185 H2
Foxton Gro, Mitch. CR4 ...185 G2
Foxwell Ms, SE4 off Foxwell St ..153 H3
Foxwell St, SE4 ....153 H3
Foxwood Cl, NW7 ....54 E4
    Feltham TW13 ....160 B3
Foxwood Grn Cl, Enf. EN1 ..44 B6
Foxwood Rd, SE3 ....155 F4
Foyle Rd, N17 ....76 D1
    SE3 ....135 F6
Framfield Cl, N12 ....56 D3
Framfield Ct, Enf. EN1 ....44 B6
Framfield Rd, N5 ....93 H5
    W7 ....104 B6
    Mitcham CR4 ....168 A7
Framlingham Cl, E5
    off Detmold Rd 95 F2
Framlingham Cres, SE9 ....174 B4
Frampton Cl, Sutt. SM2 ...198 D7
Frampton Pk Rd, E9 ......95 F6
Frampton Rd, Houns. TW4 ..142 E5
Frampton St, NW8 ....7 E6
Francemary Rd, SE4 ......154 A5
Frances Rd, E4 ....62 A6
Frances St, SE18 ....136 C4
Franche Ct Rd, SW17 .....167 F3
Francis Av, Bexh. DA7 ....159 G2
    Feltham TW13 ....160 A3
    Ilford IG1 ....99 G2
Francis Barber Cl, SW16
    off Well Cl 169 F4
Franciscan Rd, SW17 .....167 J5
Francis Chichester Way, SW11 ..150 A1
Francis Cl, E14
    off Saunders Ness Rd ..134 D4
    Epsom KT19 ....196 D4
Francis Gro, SW19 ....166 C6
Francis Rd, E10 ....96 C1
    N2 off Lynmouth Rd ...73 J4
    Croydon CR0 ....187 H7
    Greenford UB6 ....105 J1
    Harrow HA1 ....68 D5
    Hounslow TW4 ....142 D2
    Ilford IG1 ....99 G2
    Pinner HA5 ....66 C5
    Wallington SM6 ....200 C6
Francis St, E15 ....96 E5
    SW1 ....33 F1
    Ilford IG1 ....99 G2
Francis Ter, N19 off Junction Rd ..92 C3
Francis Wk, N1 off Bingfield St ..111 F1
Francklyn Gdns, Edg. HA8 ..54 A3
Franconia Rd, SW4 ....150 C5
Frank Bailey Wk, E12
    off Gainsborough Av ...98 D5
Frank Burton Cl, SE7
    off Victoria Way 135 H5
Frank Dixon Cl, SE21 .....170 B1
Frank Dixon Way, SE21 ...170 B1
Frankfurt Rd, SE24 ....151 J5
Frankham St, SE8 ....134 A7
Frankland Cl, SE16 ....133 E3
    Woodford Green IG8 ....63 H5
Frankland Rd, E4 ....62 A6
    SW7 ....23 E6
Franklin Cl, N20 ....41 F7
    SE13 ....154 B1
    SE27 ....169 H3
    Kingston upon Thames KT1 ..182 A3
Franklin Cres, Mitch. CR4 ..186 C4
Franklin Ho, NW9 ....71 H7
Franklin Pas, SE9 ....156 B3
Franklin Pl, SE13 ....154 B1

Franklin Rd, SE20 . . . . .171 F7
Bexleyheath DA7 . . . . .159 E1
Franklins Ms, Har. HA2 . . . . . . .85 J2
Franklin Sq, W14
off Marchbank Rd 128 C5
Franklin's Row, SW3 . . . . .32 A3
Franklin St, E3
off St. Leonards St 114 B3
N15 . . . . .76 B6
Franklin Way, Croy. CR0 . . . . . .187 E7
Franklyn Gdns, Ilf. IG6 . . . . . . .65 G6
Franklyn Rd, NW10 . . . . .89 F7
Walton-on-Thames KT12 . . . .178 A6
Franks Av, N.Mal. KT3 . . . . . . .182 C4
Frank St, E13 . . . . .115 G4
Frankswood Av, Orp. BR5 . . . . .193 E5
Frank Towell Ct, Felt. TW14
off Glebelands Rd 160 A1
Franlaw Cres, N13 . . . . .59 J4
Fransfield Gro, SE26 . . . . .171 E3
Frant Cl, SE20 . . . . .171 F7
Franthorne Way, SE6 . . . . .172 B2
Frant Rd, Th.Hth. CR7 . . . . . . .187 H5
Fraser Cl, E6 off Linton Gdns . .116 B6
Bexley DA5 off Dartford Rd . .177 J1
Fraser Ho, Brent. TW8
off Green Dragon La 125 J5
Fraser Rd, E17 . . . . .78 B5
N9 .60 E3
Erith DA8 . . . . .139 J5
Greenford UB6 . . . . .105 E1
Fraser St, W4 . . . . .126 E5
Frating Cres, Wdf.Grn. IG8 . . . . .63 G6
Frays Av, West Dr. UB7 . . . . . . .120 A2
Frays Cl, West Dr. UB7 . . . . . . .120 A3
Frazer Av, Ruis. HA4 . . . . .84 C5
Frazier St, SE1 . . . . .26 E4
Frean St, SE16 . . . . .29 H5
Freda Corbett Cl, SE15 . . . . . . .37 H7
Frederica Rd, E4 . . . . .46 D7
Frederica St, N7
off Caledonian Rd 93 F7
Frederick Cl, W2 . . . . .15 J5
Sutton SM1 . . . . .198 C4
Frederick Ct, NW2
off Douglas Rd 90 B3
Frederick Cres, SW9 . . . . .131 H7
Enfield EN3 . . . . .45 F2
Frederick Gdns, Croy. CR0 . . . .187 H6
Sutton SM1 . . . . .198 C5
Frederick Pl, SE18 . . . . .137 E5
Frederick Rd, SE17 . . . . .35 H5
Sutton SM1 . . . . .198 C5
Frederick's Pl, EC2 . . . . .20 B4
Fredericks Pl, N12 . . . . .57 F4
Frederick Sq, SE16
off Rotherhithe St 113 H7
Frederick's Row, EC1 . . . . .11 G3
Frederick St, WC1 . . . . .10 C4
Frederick Ter, E8
off Haggerston Rd 112 C1
Frederick Vil, W7
off Lower Boston Rd 124 B1
Frederic Ms, SW1 . . . . .24 A4
Frederic St, E17 . . . . .77 H5
Fred White Wk, N7
off Market Rd 92/93 E6
Fred Wigg Twr, E11 . . . . .97 F2
Freedom Cl, E17 . . . . .77 H4
Freedom Rd, N17 . . . . .76 A2
Freedom St, SW11 . . . . .149 J2
Freegrove Rd, N7 . . . . .93 E5
Freeland Pk, NW4 . . . . .72 B2
Freeland Rd, W5 . . . . .105 J7
Freelands Gro, Brom. BR1 . . . .191 H1
Freelands Rd, Brom. BR1 . . . . .191 H1
Freeling St, N1
off Caledonian Rd 93 F7
Freeman Cl, Nthlt. UB5 . . . . . . .85 E7
Freeman Ct, N7
off Tollington Way 92/93 E3
Freeman Dr, W.Mol. KT8 . . . . . .179 F3
Freeman Rd, Mord. SM4 . . . . . .185 G5
Freemantle Av, Enf. EN3 . . . . . .45 G5
Freemantle St, SE17 . . . . .36 D3
★ Freemason's Hall (United Grand
Lo of England), WC2 . . . . . . .18 B3
Freemasons Rd, E16 . . . . .115 H5
Croydon CR0 . . . . .202 B1
Freesia Cl, Orp. BR6
off Briarswood Way 207 J5
Freethorpe Cl, SE19 . . . . .188 A1
Free Trade Wf, E1
off The Highway 113 G7
★ Freightliners City Fm, N7 . . .93 F6
Freke Rd, SW11 . . . . .150 A3
Fremantle Rd, Belv. DA17 . . . . .139 G4
Ilford IG6 . . . . .81 F2
Fremont St, E9 . . . . .113 F1
French Ordinary Ct, EC3 . . . . . .21 E5
French Pl, E1 . . . . .13 E5
French St, Sun. TW16 . . . . . . .178 C2
Frendsbury Rd, SE4 . . . . .153 H4
Frensham Cl, Sthl. UB1 . . . . . .103 F4
Frensham Ct, Mitch. CR4
off Phipps Br Rd 185 G3
Frensham Dr, SW15 . . . . .165 G2

Frensham Dr, Croy. (New Adgtn)
CR0 . . . . .204 C7
Frensham Rd, SE9 . . . . .175 G2
Frensham St, SE15 . . . . .37 J6
Frere St, SW11 . . . . .149 H2
Freshfield Av, E8 . . . . .94 C7
Freshfield Cl, SE13
off Marischal Rd 154 D4
Freshfield Dr, N14 . . . . .42 B7
Freshfields, Croy. CR0 . . . . . . .189 J7
Freshford St, SW18 . . . . .167 F3
Freshwater Cl, SW17 . . . . .168 A6
Freshwater Rd, SW17 . . . . .168 A6
Dagenham RM8 . . . . .100 D1
Freshwell Av, Rom. RM6 . . . . . .82 C4
Fresh Wf Rd, Bark. IG11 . . . . . .117 E1
Freshwood Cl, Beck. BR3 . . . . .190 B1
Freston Gdns, Barn. EN4 . . . . . .42 A5
Freston Pk, N3 . . . . .72 C2
Freston Rd, W10 . . . . .108 A7
W11 . . . . .108 A7
Freta Rd, Bexh. DA6 . . . . .159 F5
★ Freud Mus, NW3 . . . . .91 F6
Frewin Rd, SW18 . . . . .167 G1
Friar Ms, SE27 off Prioress Rd .169 H3
Friar Rd, Hayes UB4 . . . . .102 D4
Friars, The, Chig. IG7 . . . . .65 H4
Friars Av, N20 . . . . .57 H3
SW15 . . . . .165 F3
Friars Cl, E4 . . . . .62 C3
N2 .73 G4
SE1 . . . . .27 H2
Ilford IG1 . . . . .99 G1
Northolt UB5
off Broomcroft Av 102 D3
Friars Gdns, W3
off St. Dunstans Av 106 D6
Friars Gate Cl, Wdf.Grn. IG8 . . . .63 G4
Friars La, Rich. TW9 . . . . .145 G5
Friars Mead, E14 . . . . .134 C3
Friars Ms, SE9 . . . . .156 D5
Friars Pl La, W3 . . . . .106 D7
Friars Rd, E6 . . . . .116 A1
Friars Stile Pl, Rich. TW10
off Friars Stile Rd 145 H6
Friars Stile Rd, Rich. TW10 . . . .145 H6
Friar St, EC4 . . . . .19 H4
Friars Wk, N14 . . . . .58 B1
SE2 . . . . .138 D5
Friars Way, W3 . . . . .106 D6
Friary Cl, N12 . . . . .57 H5
Friary Ct, SW1 . . . . .25 G2
Friary Est, SE15 . . . . .37 J6
Friary La, Wdf.Grn. IG8 . . . . . . .63 G4
Friary Rd, N12 . . . . .57 G4
SE15 . . . . .37 J6
W3 . . . . .106 D6
Friary Way, N12 . . . . .57 H4
FRIDAY HILL, E4 . . . . .62 D2
Friday Hill, E4 . . . . .62 E2
Friday Hill E, E4 . . . . .62 E3
Friday Hill W, E4 . . . . .62 E2
Friday Rd, Mitch. CR4 . . . . .167 J7
Friday St, EC4 . . . . .19 J4
Frideswide Pl, NW5 off Islip St . .92 C5
Friendly Pl, SE13
off Lewisham Rd 154 B1
Friendly St, SE8 . . . . .154 A1
Friendly St Ms, SE8
off Friendly St 154 A2
Friendship Wk, Nthlt. UB5
off Wayfarer Rd 102 D3
Friendship Way, E15
off Carpenters Rd 114 C1
Friends Rd, Croy. CR0 . . . . . . .202 A3
Friend St, EC1 . . . . .11 G3
FRIERN BARNET, N11 . . . . .57 H4
Friern Barnet La, N11 . . . . .57 H4
N20 . . . . .57 H4
Friern Barnet Rd, N11 . . . . .57 J5
Friern Br Retail Pk, N11 . . . . . . .58 B6
Friern Ct, N20 . . . . .57 G3
Friern Mt Dr, N20 . . . . .41 F7
Friern Pk, N12 . . . . .57 F5
Friern Rd, SE22 . . . . .152 D6
Friern Watch Av, N12 . . . . .57 F4
Frigate Ms, SE8
off Watergate St 134 A6
Frimley Av, Wall. SM6 . . . . .201 E5
Frimley Cl, SW19 . . . . .166 B2
Croydon (New Adgtn) CR0 . . .204 C7
Frimley Ct, Sid. DA14 . . . . .176 B5
Frimley Cres, Croy. (New Adgtn)
CR0 . . . . .204 C7
Frimley Gdns, Mitch. CR4 . . . . .185 H3
Frimley Rd, Chess. KT9 . . . . . .195 H5
Ilford IG3 . . . . .99 H3
Frimley Way, E1 . . . . .113 G4
Frinstead Ho, W10 . . . . .108 A7
Frinton Cl, Wat. WD19 . . . . .50 B2
Frinton Dr, Wdf.Grn. IG8 . . . . . .62 D7
Frinton Ms, Ilf. IG2
off Bramley Cres 80 D6
Frinton Rd, E6 . . . . .116 A3
N15 . . . . .76 B6
SW17 . . . . .168 A6
Sidcup DA14 . . . . .176 E2

Friston Path, Chig. IG7 . . . . . . .65 H5
Friston St, SW6 . . . . .148 E2
Friswell Pl, Bexh. DA6 . . . . . . .159 G4
Fritham Cl, N.Mal. KT3 . . . . . . .182 E6
Frith Ct, NW7 . . . . .56 B7
Frith La, NW7 . . . . .56 B7
Frith Rd, E11 . . . . .96 C4
Croydon CR0 . . . . .201 J2
Frith St, W1 . . . . .17 H4
Frithville Gdns, W12 . . . . .127 J1
Frizlands La, Dag. RM10 . . . . . .101 H4
Frobisher Cl, Pnr. HA5 . . . . .66 D7
Frobisher Cres, EC2
off Beech St 111 J5
Staines TW19 . . . . .140 B7
Frobisher Gdns, Stai. TW19 . . . .140 B7
Frobisher Pas, E14
off North Colonnade 134 A1
N8 .75 G4
Frobisher Rd, E6 . . . . .116 C6
N8 .75 G4
Frobisher St, SE10 . . . . .135 E6
Froghall La, Chig. IG7 . . . . .65 G4
Frogley Rd, SE22 . . . . .152 C4
Frogmore, SW18 . . . . .148 D5
Frogmore Cl, Sutt. SM3 . . . . . .198 A3
Frogmore Est, Ruis. HA4 . . . . . .84 D5
Frogmore Gdns, Sutt. SM3 . . . .198 B4
Frogmore Ind Est, NW10 . . . . . .106 C3
Frognal, NW3 . . . . .91 F5
Frognal Av, Har. HA1 . . . . .68 C4
Sidcup DA14 . . . . .176 A5
Frognal Cl, NW3 . . . . .91 F5
Frognal Ct, NW3 . . . . .91 F6
Frognal Gdns, NW3 . . . . .91 F4
Frognal La, NW3 . . . . .90 E5
Frognal Par, NW3
off Frognal Ct 91 F6
Frognal Pl, Sid. DA14 . . . . .176 A5
Frognal Ri, NW3 . . . . .91 F4
Frognal Way, NW3 . . . . .91 F4
Froissart Rd, SE9 . . . . .156 A5
Frome Rd, N22 off Westbury Av .75 H3
Frome St, N1 . . . . .11 J1
Fromondes Rd, Sutt. SM3 . . . . .198 B5
Frostic Wk, E1 . . . . .21 G2
Froude St, SW8 . . . . .150 B2
Fruen Rd, Felt. TW14 . . . . .141 J7
Fruiterers Pas, EC4
off Southwark Br 111 J7
Fryatt Rd, N17 . . . . .60 A7
Fryday Gro Ms, SW12
off Weir Rd 150 C7
Fryent Cl, NW9 . . . . .70 A6
Fryent Cres, NW9 . . . . .70 E6
Fryent Flds, NW9 . . . . .71 E6
Fryent Gro, NW9 . . . . .70 E6
Fryent Way, NW9 . . . . .70 A5
Frying Pan All, E1 . . . . .21 F2
Fry Rd, E6 . . . . .98 A7
NW10 . . . . .107 F1
Fryston Av, Croy. CR0 . . . . .202 D2
Fuchsia St, SE2 . . . . .138 B5
Fulbeck Dr, NW9 . . . . .70 E1
Fulbeck Wk, Edg. HA8
off Knightswood Cl 54 B2
Fulbeck Way, Har. HA2 . . . . .67 J2
Fulbourne Rd, E17 . . . . .78 C1
Fulbourne St, E1
off Durward St 112/113 E5
Fulbrook Ms, N19
off Junction Rd 92 C4
Fulford Gro, Wat. WD19 . . . . . . .50 B2
Fulford Rd, Epsom KT19 . . . . . .196 D7
Fulford St, SE16 . . . . .133 E2
FULHAM, SW6 . . . . .148 B2
Fulham Bdy, SW6 . . . . .128 D7
Fulham Ct, SW6
off Shottendane Rd 128 D7
★ Fulham FC, SW6 . . . . .148 A1
Fulham High St, SW6 . . . . .148 B2
★ Fulham Palace Mus, SW6 . . .148 A2
Fulham Palace Rd, SW6 . . . . . .128 A7
W6 . . . . .127 J5
Fulham Pk Gdns, SW6 . . . . . . .148 C2
Fulham Pk Rd, SW6 . . . . .148 C2
Fulham Rd, SW3 . . . . .30 E4
SW6 . . . . .30 B7
SW10 . . . . .30 A4
Fullbrooks Av, Wor.Pk. KT4 . . . .197 F1
Fuller Cl, E2 . . . . .13 H5
Orpington BR6 . . . . .207 J5
Fuller Rd, Dag. RM8 . . . . .100 B3
Fullers Av, Surb. KT6 . . . . .195 J2
Woodford Green IG8 . . . . .63 F7
★ Fuller's Griffin Brewery, W4 .127 F6
Fullers Rd, E18 . . . . .79 F1
Fuller St, NW4 . . . . .71 J4
Fullers Way N, Surb. KT6 . . . . .195 J3
Fullers Way S, Chess. KT9 . . . .195 H4
Fullers Wd, Croy. CR0 . . . . . . .204 A5
Fuller Ter, Ilf. IG1
off Oaktree Gro 99 F5
Fullerton Rd, SW18 . . . . .149 F5
Croydon CR0 . . . . .188 C7
Fuller Way, Hayes UB3 . . . . . . .121 J5
Fullwell Av, Ilf. IG5, IG6 . . . . . . .80 C1
FULLWELL CROSS, Ilf. IG6 . . . .81 G1

Fullwell Cross Roundabout, Ilf. IG6
off High St 81 G2
Fullwoods Ms, N1 . . . . .12 C3
Fulmar Cl, Surb. KT5 . . . . .181 J6
Fulmead St, SW6 . . . . .149 E1
Fulmer Cl, Hmptn. TW12 . . . . . .161 E5
Fulmer Rd, E16 . . . . .116 A5
Fulmer Way, W13 . . . . .124 E3
Fulready Rd, E10 . . . . .78 D5
Fulstone Cl, Houns. TW4 . . . . . .143 F4
Fulthorp Rd, SE3 . . . . .155 F2
Fulton Ms, W2 . . . . .14 C5
Fulton Rd, Wem. HA9 . . . . .88 A3
Fulwell Pk Av, Twick. TW2 . . . . .161 H2
Fulwell Rd, Tedd. TW11 . . . . . . .162 A4
Fulwood Av, Wem. HA0 . . . . . . .105 J1
Fulwood Gdns, Twick. TW1 . . . .144 C6
Fulwood Pl, WC1 . . . . .18 D2
Fulwood Wk, SW19 . . . . .166 B1
Furber St, W6 . . . . .127 H3
Furham Feild, Pnr. HA5 . . . . . . .51 G7
Furley Rd, SE15 . . . . .132 D7
Furlong Cl, Wall. SM6 . . . . .200 A1
Furlong Rd, N7 . . . . .93 G6
Furmage St, SW18 . . . . .149 E7
Furneaux Av, SE27 . . . . .169 H5
Furness Rd, NW10 . . . . .107 G2
SW6 . . . . .149 E2
Harrow HA2 . . . . .67 H7
Morden SM4 . . . . .185 E7
Furnival St, EC4 . . . . .19 E3
Furrow La, E9 . . . . .95 F5
Fursby Av, N3 . . . . .56 D6
Further Acre, NW9 . . . . .71 F2
Furtherfield Cl, Croy. CR0 . . . . .187 G6
Further Grn Rd, SE6 . . . . .155 E7
Furze Cl, Wat. WD19 . . . . .50 C5
FURZEDOWN, SW17 . . . . .168 A5
Furzedown Dr, SW17 . . . . .168 B5
Furzedown Hall, SW17
off Spalding Rd 168 B5
Furzedown Rd, SW17 . . . . .168 B5
Furze Fm Cl, Rom. RM6 . . . . . . .83 E2
Furzefield Cl, Chis. BR7 . . . . . .174 E6
Furzefield Rd, SE3 . . . . .135 H6
Furzeground Way, Uxb. UB11 . . .121 F1
Furzeham Rd, West Dr. UB7 . . . .120 B2
Furzehill Rd, Borwd. WD6 . . . . . .38 A4
Furze Rd, Th.Hth. CR7 . . . . . . .187 J3
Furze St, E3 . . . . .114 A5
Furzewood, Sun. TW16 . . . . . . .178 A1
Fuschia Ct, Wdf.Grn. IG8
off The Bridle Path 62/63 E7
Fyfe Way, Brom. BR1
off Widmore Rd 191 G2
Fyfield Cl, Brom. BR2 . . . . .190 D4
Fyfield Ct, E7 . . . . .97 G6
Fyfield Rd, E17 . . . . .78 D3
SW9 . . . . .151 G3
Enfield EN1 . . . . .44 B3
Woodford Green IG8 . . . . .63 J7
Fynes St, SW1 . . . . .33 H1

G

Gable Cl, Pnr. HA5 . . . . .51 G7
Gable Ct, SE26
off Lawrie Pk Av 170/171 E5
Gables, The, Wem. HA9 . . . . . . .87 J3
Gables Cl, SE5 . . . . .152 B1
SE12 . . . . .173 G1
Gabriel Cl, Felt. TW13 . . . . .160 D4
Gabrielle Cl, Wem. HA9 . . . . . . .87 J3
Gabrielle Ct, NW3 . . . . .91 G6
Gabriel St, SE23 . . . . .153 G7
Gabriel's Wf, SE1 . . . . .27 E1
Gad Cl, E13 . . . . .115 H3
Gaddesden Av, Wem. HA9 . . . . .87 J6
Gade Cl, Hayes UB3 . . . . .122 B1
Gadesden Rd, Epsom KT19 . . . .196 C6
Gadsbury Cl, NW9 . . . . .71 F6
Gadwall Cl, E16
off Freemasons Rd 115 H6
Gadwall Way, SE28 . . . . .137 G2
Gage Rd, E16
off Malmesbury Rd 114/115 E5
Gage St, WC1 . . . . .18 B1
Gainford St, N1
off Richmond Av 111 G1
Gainsboro Gdns, Grnf. UB6 . . . .86 C5
Gainsborough Av, E12 . . . . .98 D5
Gainsborough Cl, Beck. BR3 . . .172 A7
Esher KT10 off Lime Tree Av .194 B1
Gainsborough Ct, N12 . . . . .57 E5
W12 off Lime Gro 127 J2
Bromley BR2 . . . . .191 J4
Gainsborough Gdns, NW3 . . . . .91 G3
NW11 . . . . .72 C7
Edgware HA8 . . . . .69 J2
Isleworth TW7 . . . . .144 A5
Gainsborough Ho, Enf. EN1
off Ayley Cft 44 D5
Gainsborough Ms, SE26
off Panmure Rd 170/171 E3
Gainsborough Pl, Chig. IG7 . . . .65 J3
Gainsborough Rd, E11 . . . . .79 E7

Gainsborough Rd, E15 ....114 E3
   N12 ....57 E5
   W4 ....127 E4
   Dagenham RM8 ....100 B4
   New Malden KT3 ......182 D7
   Richmond TW9 ....145 J3
   Woodford Green IG8 ....64 B6
Gainsborough Sq, Bexh. DA6
   off Regency Way 158 D3
Gainsborough St, E9
   off Trowbridge Rd 95 J6
Gainsborough Studios, N1
   off Poole St 112 A1
Gainsford Rd, E17 ....77 J4
Gainsford St, SE1 ....29 F3
Gairloch Rd, SE5 ....152 B2
Gaisford St, NW5 ....92 C6
Gaitskell Ct, SW11 ....149 H2
Gaitskell Rd, SE9 ....175 F1
Galahad Rd, N9
   off Salisbury Rd 60 D3
   Bromley BR1 ....173 G3
Galata Rd, SW13 ....127 G7
Galatea Sq, SE15
   off Scylla Rd 152/153 E2
Galaxy, E14 off Crews St ...134 A4
Galba Ct, Brent. TW8
   off Augustus Cl 125 G7
Galbraith St, E14 ....134 C3
Galdana Av, Barn. EN5 ......41 F3
Galeborough Av, Wdf.Grn. IG8 ..62 D7
Gale Cl, Hmptn. TW12
   off Stewart Cl 160/161 E6
   Mitcham CR4 ....185 G3
Galena Ho, SE18
   off Grosmont Rd 137 J5
Galena Rd, W6 ....127 H4
Galen Pl, WC1 ....18 B2
Galesbury Rd, SW18 ....149 F6
Gale St, E3 ....114 A5
   Dagenham RM9 ....118 D1
Gales Way, Wdf.Grn. IG8 .....64 B7
Galgate Cl, SW19 ....166 B1
Gallants Fm Rd, Barn. EN4 ...41 H7
Galleon Cl, SE16
   off Kinburn St 133 G2
Galleons Dr, Bark. IG11 ....118 A3
Gallery Gdns, Nthlt. UB5 ...102 D2
Gallery Rd, SE21 ....170 A1
Galley La, Barn. EN5 ....39 H3
Galleywall Rd, SE16 ....132 E4
Galliard Cl, N9 ....45 F6
Galliard Rd, N9 ....60 D1
Gallia Rd, N5 ....93 H5
Gallions Cl, Bark. IG11 .....118 A3
Gallions Reach Shop Pk, E6 .117 F5
Gallions Rd, SE7 ....135 H4
Gallions Roundabout, E16 ...116 E7
Gallions Vw Rd, SE28
   off Goldfinch Rd 137 H2
Gallon Cl, SE7 ....135 J4
Gallop, The, S.Croy. CR2 ...203 F7
   Sutton SM2 ....199 F7
Gallosson Rd, SE18 ....137 H4
Galloway Path, Croy. CR0 ...202 A4
Galloway Rd, W12 ....127 G1
Gallus Cl, N21 ....43 F6
Gallus Sq, SE3 ....155 H3
Galpins Rd, Th.Hth. CR7 ....187 F4
Galsworthy Av, E14 ....113 H5
   Romford RM6 ....82 B7
Galsworthy Cl, SE28 ....138 B1
Galsworthy Cres, SE3
   off Merriman Rd 155 J1
Galsworthy Rd, NW2 ....90 B4
   Kingston upon Thames KT2 ..164 B7
Galsworthy Ter, N16
   off Hawksley Rd 94 B3
Galton St, W10 ....108 B4
Galva Cl, Barn. EN4 ....42 A4
Galvani Way, Croy. CR0
   off Ampere Way 201 F1
Galveston Rd, SW15 ....148 C5
Galway Cl, SE16
   off Masters Dr 132/133 E5
Galway St, EC1 ....12 A4
Gambetta St, SW8 ....150 B2
Gambia St, SE1 ....27 H2
Gambier Ho, EC1 off Mora St ..111 J3
Gambole Rd, SW17 ....167 H4
Games Rd, Barn. EN4 ....41 J3
Gamlen Rd, SW15 ....148 A4
Gamuel Cl, E17 ....78 A6
Gander Grn Cres, Hmptn. TW12 ..179 G1
Gander Grn La, Sutt. SM1, SM3 ..198 B2
Gandhi Cl, E17 ....78 A6
Gandolfi St, SE15 ....36 D6
Ganton St, W1 ....17 F5
Ganton Wk, Wat. WD19
   off Woodhall La 50/51 E4
GANTS HILL, Ilf. IG2 ....80 D5
Gants Hill, Ilf. IG2
   off Eastern Av 80 D6
Gantshill Cres, Ilf. IG2 ......80 D5
Gap Rd, SW19 ....166 D5
Garage Rd, W3 ....106 A6

Garbutt Pl, W1 ....16 C1
Garden Av, Bexh. DA7 ......159 G3
   Mitcham CR4 ....168 B7
Garden City, Edg. HA8 ....54 A6
Garden Cl, E4 ....62 A5
   SE12 ....173 H3
   SW15 ....147 H7
   Barnet EN5 ....39 J4
   Hampton TW12 ......161 F5
   Northolt UB5 ....103 E1
   Wallington SM6 ......200 E5
Garden Ct, EC4 ....18 E5
   N12 off Holden Rd ..56/57 E5
   Richmond TW9
   off Lichfield Rd 145 J1
   Stanmore HA7
   off Marsh La 53 F5
   West Molesey KT8
   off Avern Rd 179 H4
Gardeners Cl, N11 ....58 A2
   SE9 ....174 B3
Gardeners Rd, Croy. CR0 ....201 H1
Gardenia Rd, Enf. EN1 ....44 B6
Gardenia Way, Wdf.Grn. IG8 ..63 G5
Garden La, SW2
   off Christchurch Rd ...169 F1
   Bromley BR1 ....173 H6
Garden Ms, W2
   off Linden Gdns 108 D7
Garden Pl, E8
   off Haggerston Rd 112 C1
Garden Rd, NW8 ....6 D3
   SE20 ....189 F1
   Bromley BR1 ....173 H7
   Richmond TW9 ....146 A3
   Walton-on-Thames KT12 ..178 B6
Garden Row, SE1 ....27 G6
Gardens, The, SE22 ....152 D4
   Beckenham BR3 ......190 C2
   Feltham TW14 ....141 G5
   Harrow HA1 ....67 J6
   Pinner HA5 ....67 F6
Garden St, E1 ....113 G5
Garden Ter, SW1 ....33 H3
Garden Wk, EC2 ....12 D4
   Beckenham BR3
   off Hayne Rd 189 J1
Garden Way, NW10 ....88 C6
Gardiner Av, NW2 ....89 J5
Gardiner Cl, Dag. RM8 ......100 D4
   Enfield EN3 ....45 G6
Gardner Cl, E11 ....79 H6
Gardner Ct, EC1 off St. John St ..111 H4
Gardner Gro, Felt. TW13 ....161 F2
Gardner Pl, Felt. TW14 .....142 B6
Gardner Rd, E13 ....115 H4
Gardners La, EC4 ....19 J5
Gardnor Rd, NW3 off Flask Wk ..91 G4
Gard St, EC1 ....11 H3
Garendon Gdns, Mord. SM4 ..184 E7
Garendon Rd, Mord. SM4 ....184 E7
Gareth Cl, Wor.Pk. KT4
   off Burnham Dr 198 A2
Gareth Gro, Brom. BR1 .....173 G4
Garfield Ms, SW11
   off Garfield Rd 150 A3
Garfield Rd, E4 ....62 D1
   E13 ....115 F4
   SW11 ....150 A3
   SW19 ....167 F5
   Enfield EN3 ....45 F4
   Twickenham TW1 ....162 D1
Garford St, E14 ....114 A7
Garganey Wk, SE28 ....118 D7
Garibaldi St, SE18 ....137 H4
Garland Dr, Houns. TW3 ....143 J2
Garland Ho, Kings.T. KT2
   off Kingsgate Rd 181 H1
Garland Rd, SE18 ....137 G7
   Stanmore HA7 ....69 H1
Garlands Ct, Croy. CR0
   off Chatsworth Rd ...202 A4
Garlick Hill, EC4 ....20 A5
Garlies Rd, SE23 ....171 H3
Garlinge Rd, NW2 ....90 C6
Garman Cl, N18 ....60 A5
Garman Rd, N17 ....61 F7
Garnault Ms, EC1 ....11 F4
Garnault Pl, EC1 ....11 F4
Garner Cl, Dag. RM8 ....100 D1
Garner Rd, E17 ....78 C1
Garner St, E2 ....13 J2
Garnet Rd, NW10 ....89 E6
   Thornton Heath CR7 ..188 A4
Garnet St, E1 ....113 F7
Garnett Cl, SE9 ....156 C3
Garnett Rd, NW3 ....91 J5
Garnett Way, E17
   off McEntee Av 77 H1
Garnet Wk, E6
   off Kingfisher St 116 B5
Garnham Cl, N16
   off Garnham St 94 C2
Garnham St, N16 ....94 C2
Garnies Cl, SE15 ....37 F7
Garrad's Rd, SW16 ....168 D3
Garrard Cl, Bexh. DA7 ......159 G3

Garrard Cl, Chis. BR7 ......175 E5
Garrard Wk, NW10
   off Garnet Rd 88/89 E6
Garratt Cl, Croy. CR0 ......200 E4
Garratt La, SW17 ....167 G4
   SW18 ....148 E5
Garratt Rd, Edg. HA8 ....54 A7
Garratt Ter, SW17 ....167 H4
Garrett Cl, W3 off Jenner Av ..106 D5
Garrett St, EC1 ....12 A5
Garrick Av, NW11 ....72 B6
Garrick Cl, SW18 ....149 F4
   W5 ....105 H4
   Richmond TW9
   off The Green 145 G5
Garrick Cres, Croy. CR0 ....202 B2
Garrick Dr, NW4 ....71 J2
   SE28 off Broadwater Rd ..137 G3
Garrick Gdns, W.Mol. KT8 ..179 G3
Garrick Pk, NW4 ....72 A2
Garrick Rd, NW9 ....71 F6
   Greenford UB6 ......103 H4
   Richmond TW9 ....146 A2
Garricks Ho, Kings.T. KT1
   off Wadbrook St 181 G2
Garrick St, WC2 ....18 A5
Garrick Way, NW4 ....72 A4
Garrison Cl, SE18
   off Red Lion La 136 D7
   Hounslow TW4 ....143 F5
Garrison La, Chess. KT9 ....195 G7
Garsdale Cl, N11 ....58 A6
Garside Cl, SE28
   off Goosander Way ...137 G3
   Hampton TW12 ......161 H6
Garsington Ms, SE4 ....153 J3
Garter Way, SE16
   off Poolmans St 133 G2
Garth, The, N12
   off Holden Rd 56/57 E5
   Hampton (Hmptn H.) TW12
   off Uxbridge Rd 161 H6
   Harrow HA3 ....69 J6
Garth Cl, W4 ....126 D5
   Kingston upon Thames KT2 ..163 J5
   Morden SM4 ....184 A7
   Ruislip HA4 ....84 D1
Garth Ct, W4 off Garth Rd ..126 D5
Garthland Dr, Barn. EN5 .....39 H5
Garth Ms, W5
   off Greystoke Gdns ...105 H4
Garthorne Rd, SE23 ....153 G7
Garth Rd, NW2 ....90 C2
   W4 ....126 D6
   Kingston upon Thames KT2 ..163 J5
   Morden SM4 ....183 J6
Garth Rd Ind Cen, Mord. SM4 ..184 A7
Garthside, Rich. TW10 ......163 H5
Garthway, N12 ....57 H6
Gartmoor Gdns, SW19 ......166 C1
Gartmore Rd, Ilf. IG3 ....99 J1
Garton Pl, SW18 ....149 F6
Gartons Cl, Enf. EN3 ....45 F5
Gartons Way, SW11 ....149 F3
Garvary Rd, E16 ....115 H6
Garway Rd, W2 ....14 A4
Garwood Cl, N17 ....76 E1
Gascoigne Gdns, Wdf.Grn. IG8 ..63 E7
Gascoigne Pl, E2 ....13 F4
Gascoigne Rd, Bark. IG11 ...117 F1
Gascony Av, NW6 ....90 D7
Gascoyne Rd, E9 ....95 G7
Gaselee St, E14 ....114 C7
Gasholder Pl, SE11 ....34 D4
Gaskarth Rd, SW12 ....150 B6
   Edgware HA8 ....70 C1
Gaskell Rd, N6 ....73 J6
Gaskell St, SW4 ....150 E2
Gaskin St, N1 ....111 H1
Gaspar Cl, SW5 ....30 B1
Gaspar Ms, SW5 ....30 B1
Gassiot Rd, SW17 ....167 J4
Gassiot Way, Sutt. SM1 ....199 G3
Gastein Rd, W6 ....128 A6
Gaston Bell Cl, Rich. TW9 ..145 J3
Gaston Rd, Mitch. CR4 .....186 A3
Gataker St, SE16 ....133 E3
Gatcombe Ms, W5 ....105 J7
Gatcombe Rd, E16 ....135 G1
   N19 ....92 D3
Gatcombe Way, Barn. EN4 ...41 J3
Gate Cl, Borwd. WD6 ....38 C1
Gate End, Nthwd. HA6 ....50 A7
Gateforth St, NW8 ....7 G6
Gatehouse Cl, Kings.T. KT2 ..164 C7
Gatehouse Sq, SE1
   off Southwark Br Rd ..131 J1
Gateley Rd, SW9 ....151 F3
Gate Ms, SW7 ....23 H4
Gater Dr, Enf. EN2 ....44 A1
Gatesborough St, EC2 ....12 D5
Gates Grn Rd, Kes. BR2 ....205 G4
   West Wickham BR4 ...205 F3
Gateside Rd, SW17 ....167 J3
Gatestone Rd, SE19 ....170 B6
Gate St, WC2 ....18 C3
Gateway, SE17 ....36 A5

Gateway Arc, N1
   off Islington High St ..111 H2
Gateway Ho, Bark. IG11
   off St. Ann's 117 F1
Gateway Ind Est, NW10 ....107 F3
Gateway Ms, E8
   off Shacklewell La 94 C5
Gateway Retail Pk, E6 .....117 E4
Gateway Rd, E10 ....96 B3
Gateways, The, SW3 ....31 H2
Gatfield Gro, Felt. TW13 ...161 G2
Gathorne Rd, N22 ....75 G2
Gathorne St, E2 off Mace St ..113 G2
Gatley Av, Epsom KT19 ....196 B5
Gatliff Rd, SW1 ....32 C4
Gatling Rd, SE2 ....138 A5
Gatonby St, SE15 ....152 C1
Gatting Cl, Edg. HA8
   off Pavilion Way 54 C7
Gatton Rd, SW17 ....167 H4
Gattons Way, Sid. DA14 ...177 F4
Gatward Cl, N21 ....43 H6
Gatward Grn, N9 ....60 B2
Gatwick Rd, SW18 ....148 C7
Gauden Cl, SW4 ....150 D3
Gauden Rd, SW4 ....150 D2
Gaumont Ter, W12 off Lime Gro ..127 J2
Gauntlet Cl, Nthlt. UB5 .....84 E7
Gauntlett Ct, Wem. HA0 .....86 C5
Gauntlett Rd, Sutt. SM1 ....199 G5
Gaunt St, SE1 ....27 H5
Gautrey Rd, SE15 ....153 F2
Gautrey Sq, E6 ....116 C6
Gavel St, SE17 ....36 C1
Gaverick Ms, E14
   off Westferry Rd 134 A4
Gavestone Cres, SE12 .....155 H7
Gavestone Rd, SE12 ....155 H7
Gaviller Pl, E5
   off Clarence Rd 94/95 E4
Gavina Cl, Mord. SM4 .....185 H5
Gavin St, SE18 ....137 H4
Gawain Wk, N9
   off Salisbury Rd 60 D3
Gawber St, E2 ....113 F3
Gawsworth Cl, E15
   off Ash Rd 96/97 E5
Gawthorne Av, NW7
   off Lane App 56 B5
Gawthorne Ct, E3
   off Mostyn Gro 114 A2
Gay Cl, NW2 ....89 H5
Gaydon Ho, W2 ....14 B1
Gaydon La, NW9 ....70 E1
Gayfere Rd, Epsom KT17 ...197 G5
   Ilford IG5 ....80 C3
Gayfere St, SW1 ....26 A6
Gayford Rd, W12 ....127 F2
Gay Gdns, Dag. RM10 ......101 J4
Gayhurst, SE17 ....36 C5
Gayhurst Rd, E8 ....94 D7
Gaylor Rd, Nthlt. UB5 ......85 F5
Gaynesford Rd, SE23 ......171 G2
   Carshalton SM5 ......199 J7
Gaynes Hill Rd, Wdf.Grn. IG8 ..64 B6
Gay Rd, E15 ....114 D2
Gaysham Av, Ilf. IG2 ....80 D5
Gaysham Hall, Ilf. IG5 ......80 E3
Gay St, SW15 ....148 A3
Gayton Ct, Har. HA1 ....68 C6
Gayton Cres, NW3 ....91 G4
Gayton Ho, E3
   off Blackthorn St 114 A4
Gayton Rd, NW3 ....91 G4
   SE2 off Florence Rd ..138 C3
   Harrow HA1 ....68 C6
Gayville Rd, SW11 ....149 J6
Gaywood Cl, SW2 ....169 F1
Gaywood Est, SE1 ....27 H6
Gaywood Rd, E17 ....78 A3
Gaywood St, SE1 ....27 H6
Gaza St, SE17 ....35 G4
Geariesville Gdns, Ilf. IG6 ..81 E4
Geary Rd, NW10 ....89 G5
Geary St, N7 ....93 F5
G.E.C. Est, Wem. HA9 ......87 G3
Geddes Pl, Bexh. DA6
   off Market Pl 159 G4
Gedeney Rd, N17 ....75 J1
Gedling Pl, SE1 ....29 G5
Geere Rd, E15 ....115 F1
Gees Ct, W1 ....16 C4
Gee St, EC1 ....11 J5
Geffrye Ct, N1 ....12 E2
Geffrye Est, N1 off Stanway St ..112 B2
★ Geffrye Mus, E2 ....13 E2
Geffrye St, E2 ....13 F1
Geldart Rd, SE15 ....132 E7
Geldeston Rd, E5 ....94 D2
Gellatly Rd, SE14 ....153 F2
Gemini Gro, Nthlt. UB5
   off Javelin Way ...102/103 E3
General Gordon Pl, SE18 ...136 E4
General Wolfe Rd, SE10 ....154 D1
Genesta Rd, SE18 ....137 E6
Geneva Dr, SW9 ....151 G4
Geneva Gdns, Rom. RM6 ....82 E5

Geneva Rd, Kings.T. KT1 181 H4
Thornton Heath CR7 187 J5
Genever Cl, E4 62 A5
Genista Rd, N18 61 E5
Genoa Av, SW15 147 J5
Genoa Rd, SE20 189 F1
Genotin Rd, Enf. EN1 44 A3
Genotin Ter, Enf. EN1
off Genotin Rd 44 A3
Gentian Row, SE13
off Sparta St 154 C1
Gentlemans Row, Enf. EN2 43 J3
Gentry Gdns, E13
off Whitwell Rd 115 G4
Geoffrey Cl, SE5 151 J2
Geoffrey Gdns, E6 116 B2
Geoffrey Rd, SE4 153 J3
George Beard Rd, SE8 133 J4
George Comberton Wk, E12
off Gainsborough Av 98 D5
George Ct, WC2 18 B6
George Cres, N10 58 A7
George Downing Est, N16
off Cazenove Rd 94 C2
George V Av, Pnr. HA5 67 G3
George V Cl, Pnr. HA5
off George V Av 67 G3
George V Way, Grnf. UB6 105 E1
George Gange Way, Har. (Wldste)
HA3 68 B3
George Gro Rd, SE20 188 D1
★ **George Inn**, SE1 28 B2
George Inn Yd, SE1 28 B2
George La, E18 79 G2
SE13 154 C6
Bromley BR2 205 H1
George Lansbury Ho, N22
off Progress Way 75 G1
George Loveless Ho, E2 13 G3
George Lowe Ct, W2 14 A1
George Mathers Rd, SE11 35 G1
George Ms, NW1 9 F4
Enfield EN2 *off Sydney Rd* 44 A3
George Pl, N17
off Dongola Rd 76 B3
George Rd, E4 62 A6
Kingston upon Thames KT2 164 B7
New Malden KT3 183 F4
George Row, SE16 29 H4
George Sq, SW19
off Mostyn Rd 184 C3
George's Rd, N7 93 F5
Georges Sq, SW6
off North End Rd 128 C6
George St, E16 115 F6
W1 16 A3
W7 *off The Broadway* 124 B1
Barking IG11 99 F7
Croydon CR0 202 A2
Hounslow TW3 143 F2
Richmond TW9 145 G5
Southall UB2 122 E4
Georgetown Cl, SE19
off St. Kitts Ter 170 A5
Georgette Pl, SE10
off King George St 134 C7
Georgeville Gdns, Ilf. IG6 81 E4
George Wyver Cl, SW19
off Beaumont Rd 148 B7
George Yd, EC3 20 C4
W1 16 C5
Georgiana St, NW1 110 C1
Georgian Cl, Brom. BR2 191 H7
Stanmore HA7 52 D7
Georgian Ct, SW16
off Gleneldon Rd 168/169 E4
Wembley HA9 88 A6
Georgian Way, Har. HA1 86 A2
Georgia Rd, N.Mal. KT3 182 C4
Thornton Heath CR7 187 H1
Georgina Gdns, E2 13 G3
Geraint Rd, Brom. BR1 173 G4
Geraldine Rd, SW18 149 F5
W4 126 A6
Geraldine St, SE11 27 G6
Gerald Ms, SW1 32 C1
Gerald Rd, E16 115 F4
SW1 32 C1
Dagenham RM8 101 F2
Gerard Av, Houns. TW4 143 G7
Gerard Pl, E9
off Groombridge Rd 95 G7
Gerard Rd, SW13 147 F1
Harrow HA1 68 D6
Gerards Cl, SE16 133 F5
Gerda Rd, SE9 175 F2
Germander Way, E15 115 E3
Gernigan Ho, SW18
off Fitzhugh Gro 149 G6
Gernon Rd, E3 113 H2
Geron Way, NW2 89 H1
Gerrard Gdns, Pnr. HA5 66 A5
Gerrard Pl, W1 17 J5
Gerrard Rd, N1 11 H1
Gerrards Cl, N14 42 C5
Gerrard St, W1 17 H5
Gerridge St, SE1 27 F4
Gerry Raffles Sq, E15
off Great Eastern Rd 96 D6
Gertrude Rd, Belv. DA17 139 G4
Gertrude St, SW10 30 D6
Gervase Cl, Wem. HA9 88 C3
Gervase Rd, Edg. HA8 70 C1
Gervase St, SE15 133 E7
Ghent St, SE6 172 A2
Ghent Way, E8 *off Tyssen St* 94 C6
Giant Arches Rd, SE24 151 J7
Giant Tree Hill, Bushey (Bushey Hth)
WD23 52 A1
Gibbard Ms, SW19 166 A5
Gibbfield Cl, Rom. RM6 82 E3
Gibbins Rd, E15 96 C7
Gibbon Rd, SE15 153 F2
W3 106 E7
Kingston upon Thames KT2 181 H1
Gibbons Ms, NW11
off Hayes Cres 72 C5
Gibbons Rents, SE1
off Magdalen St 132 B1
Gibbons Rd, NW10 88 D6
Gibbon Wk, SW15
off Swinburne Rd 147 G4
Gibbs Av, SE19 170 A5
Gibbs Cl, SE19 170 A5
Gibbs Couch, Wat. WD19 50 D3
Gibbs Grn, W14 128 C5
Edgware HA8 54 C5
Gibbs Rd, N18 61 F4
Gibbs Sq, SE19 170 A5
Gibraltar Wk, E2 13 G4
Gibson Cl, E1 *off Colebert Av* 113 F4
N21 43 G6
Chessington KT9 195 F6
Isleworth TW7 144 A3
Gibson Gdns, N16
off Northwold Rd 94 C2
Gibson Ms, Twick. TW1
off Richmond Rd 145 F7
Gibson Rd, SE11 34 D2
Dagenham RM8 100 C1
Sutton SM1 198 E5
Gibson's Hill, SW16 169 G6
Gibson Sq, N1 111 G1
Gibson St, SE10 134 E5
Gideon Cl, Belv. DA17 139 H4
Gideon Ms, W5 125 G2
Gideon Rd, SW11 150 A3
Giesbach Rd, N19 92 C2
Giffard Rd, N18 60 B5
Giffin St, SE8 134 A7
Gifford Gdns, W7 104 A5
Gifford St, N1 93 E7
Gift La, E15 115 E1
Giggs Hill Gdns, T.Ditt. KT7 194 D1
Giggs Hill Rd, T.Ditt. KT7 180 D7
Gilbert Cl, SE18 156 C1
Gilbert Gro, Edg. HA8 70 D1
Gilbert Ho, EC2
off The Barbican 111 J5
SE8 *off McMillan St* 134 A6
Gilbert Pl, WC1 18 A2
Gilbert Rd, SE11 35 F2
SW19 167 F7
Belvedere DA17 139 G3
Bromley BR1 173 G7
Pinner HA5 66 D4
Gilbert St, E15 96 E4
W1 16 C4
Hounslow TW3 *off High St* 143 J3
Gilbert Way, Croy. CR0
off Beddington Fm Rd 200/201 E1
Gilbey Rd, SW17 167 H4
Gilbeys Yd, NW1 92 A7
Gilbourne Rd, SE18 137 J6
Gilda Av, Enf. EN3 45 H5
Gilda Cres, N16 94 D1
Gildea Cl, Pnr. HA5 51 G7
Gildea St, W1 17 E2
Gilden Cres, NW5 92 A5
Gildersome St, SE18
off Nightingale Vale 136 D6
Gilders Rd, Chess. KT9 195 J6
Giles Coppice, SE19 170 C4
Gilkes Cres, SE21 152 B6
Gilkes Pl, SE21 152 B6
Gillan Grn, Bushey (Bushey Hth)
WD23 51 J2
Gillards Ms, E17
off Gillards Way 78 A4
Gillards Way, E17 78 A4
Gill Av, E16 115 G6
Gillender St, E3 114 C4
E14 114 C4
Gillespie Rd, N5 93 G3
Gillett Av, E6 116 B2
Gillette Cor, Islw. TW7 124 D7
Gillett Pl, N16 *off Gillett St* 94 B5
Gillett Rd, Th.Hth. CR7 188 A4
Gillett St, N16 94 B5
Gillfoot, NW1 9 F2
Gillham Ter, N17 60 D6
Gillian Pk Rd, Sutt. SM3 198 C1
Gillian St, SE13 154 B5
Gillies St, NW5 92 A5
Gilling Ct, NW3 91 H6
Gillingham Ms, SW1 33 F1
Gillingham Rd, NW2 90 B3
Gillingham Row, SW1 33 F1
Gillingham St, SW1 33 E1
Gillison Wk, SE16 29 J5
Gillman Dr, E15 115 F1
Gill St, E14 113 J6
Gillum Cl, Barn. EN4 57 J1
Gilmore Rd, SE13 154 D4
Gilpin Av, SW14 146 D4
Gilpin Cl, W2 14 E1
Mitcham CR4 185 H2
Gilpin Cres, N18 60 C5
Twickenham TW2 143 H7
Gilpin Rd, E5 95 H4
Gilpin Way, Hayes UB3 121 G7
Gilsland Rd, Th.Hth. CR7 188 A4
Gilstead Ho, Bark. IG11 118 B2
Gilstead Rd, SW6 149 E2
Gilston Rd, SW10 30 D4
Gilton Rd, SE6 173 E3
Giltspur St, EC1 19 H3
Gilwell Cl, E4 *off Antlers Hill* 46 B4
Gilwell La, E4 46 C4
Gilwell Pk, E4 46 C3
Gippeswyck Cl, Pnr. HA5
off Uxbridge Rd 66 D1
Gipsy Hill, SE19 170 B4
Gipsy La, SW15 147 G3
★ **Gipsy Moth IV**, SE10 134 C6
Gipsy Rd, SE27 169 J4
Welling DA16 158 D1
Gipsy Rd Gdns, SE27 169 J4
Giralda Cl, E16 *off Fulmer Rd* 116 A5
Giraud St, E14 114 B6
Girdlers Rd, W14 128 A4
Girdlestone Wk, N19 92 C2
Girdwood Rd, SW18 148 B7
Girling Way, Felt. TW14 142 A3
Gironde Rd, SW6 128 C7
Girton Av, NW9 70 A3
Girton Cl, Nthlt. UB5 85 J6
Girton Gdns, Croy. CR0 204 A3
Girton Rd, SE26 171 G5
Northolt UB5 85 J6
Girton Vil, W10 108 A6
Gisbourne Cl, Wall. SM6 200 D3
Gisburn Rd, N8 75 F4
Gissing Wk, N1 *off Lofting Rd* 93 G7
Gittens Cl, Brom. BR1 173 F4
Given Wilson Wk, E13 115 F2
Glacier Way, Wem. HA0 105 G2
Gladbeck Way, Enf. EN2 43 H4
Gladding Rd, E12 98 A4
Glade, The, N21 43 F6
SE7 135 J7
Bromley BR1 192 A2
Croydon CR0 189 G5
Enfield EN2 43 G3
Epsom KT17 197 G5
Ilford IG5 80 C1
West Wickham BR4 204 B3
Woodford Green IG8 63 H3
Glade Cl, Surb. KT6 195 G2
Glade Ct, Ilf. IG5 *off The Glade* 80 C1
Glade Gdns, Croy. CR0 189 H7
Glade La, Sthl. UB2 123 H2
Gladeside, N21 43 F6
Croydon CR0 189 G6
Gladesmore Rd, N15 76 C6
Glades Shop Cen, The, Brom.
BR1 191 G2
Gladeswood Rd, Belv. DA17 139 H4
Gladiator St, SE23 153 H6
Glading Ter, N16 94 C3
Gladioli Cl, Hmptn. TW12
off Gresham Rd 161 G6
Gladsdale Dr, Pnr. HA5 66 A4
Gladsmuir Rd, N19 92 C1
Barnet EN5 40 B2
Gladstone Av, E12 98 B7
N22 75 G2
Feltham TW14 142 A6
Twickenham TW2 144 A7
Gladstone Ct, SW19
off Gladstone Rd 166 D7
Gladstone Gdns, Houns. TW3
off Palmerston Rd 143 J1
Gladstone Ms, N22
off Pelham Rd 75 G2
NW6 *off Cavendish Rd* 90 C7
SE20 171 F7
Gladstone Par, NW2
off Edgware Rd 89 H1
Gladstone Pk Gdns, NW2 89 H3
Gladstone Pl, E3 *off Roman Rd* 113 J2
Barnet EN5 40 A4
Gladstone Rd, SW19 166 D7
W4 *off Acton La* 126 D3
Buckhurst Hill IG9 63 H1
Croydon CR0 188 A7
Kingston upon Thames KT1 182 A3
Orpington BR6 207 F5
Southall UB2 122 E3
Surbiton KT6 195 G2
Gladstone St, SE1 27 G5
Gladstone Ter, SE27
off Bentons La 169 J4
Gladstone Way, Har. (Wldste)
HA3 68 B3
Gladwell Rd, N8 75 F6
Bromley BR1 173 G6
Gladwyn Rd, SW15 148 A3
Gladys Rd, NW6 90 D7
Glaisher St, SE8 134 A6
Glamis Cres, Hayes UB3 121 F3
Glamis Pl, E1 113 F7
Glamis Rd, E1 113 F7
Glamis Way, Nthlt. UB5 85 J6
Glamorgan Cl, Mitch. CR4 186 E3
Glamorgan Rd, Kings.T. KT1 163 F7
Glanfield Rd, Beck. BR3 189 J4
Glanleam Rd, Stan. HA7 53 G4
Glanville Ms, Stan. HA7 52 D5
Glanville Rd, SW2 151 E5
Bromley BR2 191 H3
Glasbrook Av, Twick. TW2 161 F1
Glasbrook Rd, SE9 156 A7
Glaserton Rd, N16 76 B7
Glasford St, SW17 167 J6
Glasgow Ho, W9 6 B3
Glasgow Rd, E13 115 H2
N18 *off Aberdeen Rd* 60/61 E5
Glasgow Ter, SW1 33 F4
Glasse Cl, W13 104 D7
Glasshill St, SE1 27 H3
Glasshouse Flds, E1 113 G7
Glasshouse St, W1 17 G6
Glasshouse Wk, SE11 34 B3
Glasshouse Yd, EC1 11 J6
Glasslyn Rd, N8 74 D5
Glassmill La, Brom. BR2 191 F2
Glass St, E2
off Coventry Rd 112/113 E4
Glass Yd, SE18
off Woolwich High St 136 D3
Glastonbury Av, Wdf.Grn. IG8 64 A7
Glastonbury Pl, E1
off Sutton St 113 F6
Glastonbury Rd, N9 60 D1
Morden SM4 184 D7
Glastonbury St, NW6 90 C5
Glaucus St, E3 114 B5
Glazbury Rd, W14 128 B4
Glazebrook Cl, SE21 170 A2
Glazebrook Rd, Tedd. TW11 162 C7
Glebe, The, SE3 154 E3
SW16 168 D4
Chislehurst BR7 193 F1
West Drayton UB7 120 C4
Worcester Park KT4 197 F1
Glebe Av, Enf. EN2 43 H3
Harrow HA3 69 H3
Mitcham CR4 185 H2
Ruislip HA4 84 B6
Woodford Green IG8 63 G6
Glebe Cl, W4 *off Glebe St* 126/127 E5
Glebe Cotts, Sutt. SM1
off Vale Rd 198/199 E4
Glebe Ct, W7 104 A7
Mitcham CR4 185 J3
Stanmore HA7 53 F5
Glebe Cres, NW4 71 J4
Harrow HA3 69 H3
Glebe Gdns, N.Mal. KT3 183 E7
Glebe Ho Dr, Brom. BR2 205 H1
Glebe Hyrst, SE19
off Giles Coppice 170 C4
Glebelands, W.Mol. KT8 179 H5
Glebelands Av, E18 79 G2
Ilford IG2 81 G7
Glebelands Cl, SE5
off Grove Hill Rd 152 B3
Glebelands Rd, Felt. TW14 142 A7
Glebe La, Barn. EN5 39 G5
Harrow HA3 69 H4
Glebe Path, Mitch. CR4 185 H3
Glebe Pl, SW3 31 G5
Glebe Rd, E8 *off Middleton Rd* 94 C7
N3 73 F1
N8 75 F4
NW10 89 F6
SW13 147 G2
Bromley BR1 191 G1
Carshalton SM5 199 J6
Dagenham RM10 101 H6
Hayes UB3 121 J1
Stanmore HA7 53 F5
Glebe Side, Twick. TW1 144 C6
Glebe St, W4 126 E5
Glebe Ter, E3 *off Bow Rd* 114 A3
Glebe Way, Felt. TW13 161 G3
West Wickham BR4 204 C2
Glebeway, Wdf.Grn. IG8 63 J5
Gledhow Gdns, SW5 30 C2
Gledstanes Rd, W14 128 B5
Gleed Av, Bushey (Bushey Hth)
WD23 52 A2
Gleeson Dr, Orp. BR6 207 J5
Glegg Pl, SW15 148 A4
Glen, The, Brom. BR2 190 E2
Croydon CR0 203 G2
Enfield EN2 43 H4

Glen, The, Orp. BR6 . . . . .206 C3
Pinner HA5 . . . . .67 E7
Pinner (Eastcote) HA5 . . . . . .66 B5
Southall UB2 . . . . .123 F5
Wembley HA9 . . . . .87 G4
Glenaffric Av, E14 . . . . .134 D4
Glen Albyn Rd, SW19 . . . . .166 A2
Glenalmond Rd, Har. HA3 . . . . . .69 H4
Glenalvon Way, SE18 . . . . .136 A6
Glena Mt, Sutt. SM1 . . . . .199 F4
Glenarm Rd, E5 . . . . .95 F5
Glenavon Cl, Esher (Clay.) KT10 .194 D7
Glenavon Rd, E15 . . . . .97 E7
Glenbarr Cl, SE9
off Dumbreck Rd 156/157 E3
Glenbow Rd, Brom. BR1 . . . . . .172 E6
Glenbrook N, Enf. EN2 . . . . . . .43 F4
Glenbrook Rd, NW6 . . . . .90 D5
Glenbrook S, Enf. EN2 . . . . . . .43 F4
Glenbuck Ct, Surb. KT6
off Glenbuck Rd 181 G6
Glenbuck Rd, Surb. KT6 . . . . . .181 G6
Glenburnie Rd, SW17 . . . . .167 J3
Glencairn Dr, W5 . . . . .105 A4
Glencairne Cl, E16 . . . . .116 A5
Glencairn Rd, SW16 . . . . .186 E1
Glencoe Av, Ilf. IG2 . . . . .81 G7
Glencoe Dr, Dag. RM10 . . . . . .101 G4
Glencoe Rd, Hayes UB4 . . . . . .102 D5
Glencorse Grn, Wat. WD19
off Caldwell Rd 50 D4
Glen Cres, Wdf.Grn. IG8 . . . . . .63 H6
Glendale Av, N22 . . . . .59 G7
Edgware HA8 . . . . .53 J4
Romford RM6 . . . . .82 C7
Glendale Cl, SE9
off Dumbreck Rd 156 D3
Glendale Dr, SW19 . . . . .166 C5
Glendale Gdns, Wem. HA9 . . . . .87 G1
Glendale Ms, Beck. BR3 . . . . . .190 B1
Glendale Rd, Erith DA8 . . . . . . .139 J4
Glendale Way, SE28 . . . . .118 C7
Glendall St, SW9 . . . . .151 F4
Glendarvon St, SW15 . . . . .148 A3
Glendevon Cl, Edg. HA8
off Tayside Dr 54 B4
Glendish Rd, N17 . . . . .76 D1
Glendor Gdns, NW7 . . . . .54 D4
Glendower Gdns, SW14
off Glendower Rd 146 D3
Glendower Pl, SW7 . . . . .31 E1
Glendower Rd, E4 . . . . .62 D1
SW14 . . . . .146 D3
Glendown Rd, SE2 . . . . .138 A5
Glendun Rd, W3 . . . . .107 E7
Gleneagle Ms, SW16
off Ambleside Av 168 D5
Gleneagle Rd, SW16 . . . . .168 D5
Gleneagles, Stan. HA7 . . . . . . .52 E6
Gleneagles Cl, SE16
off Ryder Dr 132/133 E5
Orpington BR6 . . . . .207 G1
Staines (Stanw.) TW19 . . . . .140 A6
Watford WD19 . . . . .50 D4
Gleneagles Grn, Orp. BR6
off Tandridge Dr 207 G1
Gleneagles Twr, Sthl. UB1 . . . . .103 J6
Gleneldon Ms, SW16 . . . . .168 E4
Gleneldon Rd, SW16 . . . . .168 E4
Glenelg Rd, SW2 . . . . .151 E5
Glenesk Rd, SE9 . . . . .156 D3
Glenfarg Rd, SE6 . . . . .172 D1
Glenfield Rd, SW12 . . . . .168 C1
W13 . . . . .125 E2
Glenfield Ter, W13 . . . . .124 E2
Glenfinlas Way, SE5 . . . . .35 H7
Glenforth St, SE10 . . . . .135 F5
Glengall Causeway, E14 . . . . . .134 A3
Glengall Gro, E14 . . . . .134 B3
Glengall Rd, NW6 . . . . .108 C1
SE15 . . . . .37 G5
Bexleyheath DA7 . . . . .159 E3
Edgware HA8 . . . . .54 B3
Woodford Green IG8 . . . . . . .63 G6
Glengall Ter, SE15 . . . . .37 G5
Glen Gdns, Croy. CR0 . . . . . . .201 G3
Glengarnock Av, E14 . . . . .134 C4
Glengarry Rd, SE22 . . . . .152 B5
Glenham Dr, Ilf. IG2 . . . . .80 E5
Glenhaven Av, Borwd. WD6 . . . .38 A3
Glenhead Cl, SE9
off Dumbreck Rd 156/157 E3
Glenhill Cl, N3 . . . . .72 D2
Glenhouse Rd, SE9 . . . . .156 D5
Glenhurst Av, NW5 . . . . .92 A4
Bexley DA5 . . . . .177 F1
Glenhurst Ct, SE19 . . . . .170 C5
Glenhurst Ri, SE19 . . . . .169 J7
Glenhurst Rd, N12 . . . . .57 F5
Brentford TW8 . . . . .125 F6
Glenilla Rd, NW3 . . . . .91 H6
Glenister Ho, Hayes UB3 . . . . .122 B1
Glenister Pk Rd, SW16 . . . . . . .168 D7
Glenister Rd, SE10 . . . . .135 F5
Glenister St, E16 . . . . .136 D1
Glenkerry Ho, E14
off Burcham St 114 C6

Glenlea Path, SE9
off Well Hall Rd 156 C5
Glenlea Rd, SE9 . . . . .156 C5
Glenloch Rd, NW3 . . . . .91 H6
Enfield EN3 . . . . .45 F2
Glenluce Rd, SE3 . . . . .135 G7
Glenlyon Rd, SE9 . . . . .156 D5
Glenmere Av, NW7 . . . . .55 G7
Glen Ms, E17 off Glen Rd 77 J5
Glenmill, Hmptn. TW12 . . . . . .161 F5
Glenmore Rd, NW3 . . . . .91 H6
Welling DA16 . . . . .157 J1
Glenmore Way, Bark. IG11 . . . . .118 A3
Glenmount Path, SE18
off Raglan Rd 137 F5
Glennie Rd, SE27 . . . . .169 G3
Glenny Rd, Bark. IG11 . . . . . . .99 F6
Glenorchy Cl, Hayes UB4 . . . . .103 E5
Glenparke Rd, E7 . . . . .97 H6
Glen Ri, Wdf.Grn. IG8 . . . . . . .63 H6
Glen Rd, E13 . . . . .115 J4
E17 . . . . .77 J5
Chessington KT9 . . . . .195 H3
Glenrosa St, SW6 . . . . .149 F2
Glenrose Ct, Sid. DA14 . . . . . . .176 B5
Glenroy St, W12 . . . . .107 J6
Glensdale Rd, SE4 . . . . .153 J3
Glenshiel Rd, SE9 . . . . .156 D5
Glenside, Chig. IG7 . . . . .65 E6
Glentanner Way, SW17
off Aboyne Rd 167 G3
Glen Ter, E14
off Manchester Rd 134 C2
Glentham Gdns, SW13
off Glentham Rd 127 H6
Glentham Rd, SW13 . . . . .127 G6
Glenthorne Av, Croy. CR0 . . . . .203 E1
Glenthorne Cl, Sutt. SM3 . . . . .198 D1
Glenthorne Gdns, Ilf. IG6 . . . . .80 D3
Sutton SM3 . . . . .198 D1
Glenthorne Ms, W6
off Glenthorne Rd 127 H4
Glenthorne Rd, E17 . . . . .77 H5
N11 . . . . .57 J5
W6 . . . . .127 J4
Kingston upon Thames KT1 . . .181 J4
Glenthorpe Rd, Mord. SM4 . . . .184 A5
Glenton Rd, SE13 . . . . .154 E4
Glentrammon Av, Orp. BR6 . . . .207 J6
Glentrammon Cl, Orp. BR6 . . . .207 J6
Glentrammon Gdns, Orp. BR6 . .207 J6
Glentrammon Rd, Orp. BR6 . . . .207 J6
Glentworth St, NW1 . . . . .8 A6
Glenure Rd, SE9 . . . . .156 D5
Glenview, SE2 . . . . .138 D6
Glenview Rd, Brom. BR1 . . . . . .192 A2
Glenville Gro, SE8 . . . . .133 J7
Glenville Ms, SW18 . . . . .148 E7
Glenville Rd, Kings.T. KT2 . . . . .182 A1
Glen Wk, Islw. TW7 . . . . .144 A5
Glenwood Av, NW9 . . . . .88 E1
Glenwood Cl, Har. HA1 . . . . . . .68 C5
Glenwood Ct, E18
off Clarendon Rd 79 G3
Glenwood Gdns, Ilf. IG2 . . . . . .80 D5
Glenwood Gro, NW9 . . . . .88 C1
Glenwood Rd, N15 . . . . .75 H5
NW7 . . . . .55 F5
SE6 . . . . .171 J1
Epsom KT17 . . . . .197 G6
Hounslow TW3 . . . . .144 A3
Glenwood Way, Croy. CR0 . . . . .189 G6
Glenworth Av, E14 . . . . .134 D4
Gliddon Dr, E5 . . . . .94 E4
Gliddon Rd, W14 . . . . .128 B4
Glimpsing Grn, Erith DA18 . . . . .139 E3
Global App, E3 off Hancock Rd . .114 B2
Globe Pond Rd, SE16 . . . . .133 H1
Globe Rd, E1 . . . . .113 F3
E2 . . . . .113 F3
E15 . . . . .97 F5
Woodford Green IG8 . . . . . . .63 J6
Globe Rope Wk, E14 . . . . .134 C4
Globe St, SE1 . . . . .28 A5
Globe Ter, E2 off Globe Rd 113 F3
Globe Wf, SE16
off Rotherhithe St 133 G1
Globe Yd, W1 . . . . .16 D4
Gloster Rd, N.Mal. KT3 . . . . . .182 E4
Gloucester Arc, SW7 . . . . .30 C1
Gloucester Av, NW1 . . . . .92 A7
Sidcup DA15 . . . . .175 H2
Welling DA16 . . . . .157 J4
Gloucester Circ, SE10 . . . . . . .134 C7
Gloucester Cl, NW10 . . . . .88 D7
Thames Ditton KT7 . . . . . .194 D1
Gloucester Ct, EC3 . . . . .21 E6
Richmond TW9 . . . . .126 A7
Gloucester Cres, NW1 . . . . . . .110 B1
Gloucester Dr, N4 . . . . .93 H2
NW11 . . . . .72 D4
Gloucester Gdns, NW11 . . . . . .72 C7
W2 . . . . .14 B3
Barnet EN4 . . . . .42 A4
Ilford IG1 . . . . .80 B7
Sutton SM1 . . . . .199 E2
Gloucester Gate, NW1 . . . . .8 D1

Gloucester Gate Ms, NW1 . . . . . .8 D1
Gloucester Gro, Edg. HA8 . . . . .70 D1
Gloucester Gro Est, SE15 . . . . .37 E6
Gloucester Ho, NW6 . . . . .108 D2
Gloucester Ms, E10
off Gloucester Rd 78 A7
W2 . . . . .14 D4
Gloucester Ms W, W2 . . . . .14 C4
Gloucester Par, Sid. DA15 . . . . .158 A5
Gloucester Pk, SW7 . . . . .30 C1
Gloucester Pl, NW1 . . . . .7 J5
W1 . . . . .16 A1
Gloucester Pl Ms, W1 . . . . .16 A2
Gloucester Rd, E10 . . . . .78 A7
E11 . . . . .79 H5
E12 . . . . .98 C3
E17 . . . . .77 G2
N17 . . . . .76 A2
N18 . . . . .60 C5
SW7 . . . . .22 C5
W3 . . . . .126 C2
W5 . . . . .125 F2
Barnet EN5 . . . . .41 F5
Belvedere DA17 . . . . .139 F5
Croydon CR0 . . . . .188 A6
Feltham TW13 . . . . .160 C1
Hampton TW12 . . . . .161 H7
Harrow HA1 . . . . .67 H5
Hounslow TW4 . . . . .142 E4
Kingston upon Thames KT1 . . .182 B2
Richmond TW9 . . . . .126 A7
Teddington TW11 . . . . . . .162 B5
Twickenham TW2 . . . . . . .161 J1
Gloucester Sq, E2
off Whiston Rd 112 D1
W2 . . . . .15 F4
Gloucester Sq, E2 . . . . .13 F4
Gloucester St, SW1 . . . . .33 F4
Gloucester Ter, W2 . . . . .14 C3
Gloucester Wk, W8 . . . . .128 D2
Gloucester Way, EC1 . . . . .11 F4
Glover Cl, SE2 . . . . .138 C4
Glover Dr, N18 . . . . .61 F6
Glover Rd, Pnr. HA5 . . . . .66 D6
Gloxinia Wk, Hmptn. TW12 . . . .161 G6
Glycena Rd, SW11 . . . . .149 J3
Glyn Av, Barn. EN4 . . . . .41 G4
Glyn Cl, SE25 . . . . .188 B2
Glyn Ct, SW16 . . . . .169 G3
Stanmore HA7 . . . . .52 E6
Glyndebourne Pk, Orp. BR6 . . . .207 E2
Glynde Ms, SW3 . . . . .23 H6
Glynde Rd, Bexh. DA7 . . . . . . .158 D3
Glynde St, SE4 . . . . .153 J6
Glyndon Rd, SE18 . . . . .137 F4
Glyn Dr, Sid. DA14 . . . . .176 B4
Glynfield Rd, NW10 . . . . .89 E7
Glynne Rd, N22 . . . . .75 G2
Glyn Rd, E5 . . . . .95 G3
Enfield EN3 . . . . .45 F4
Worcester Park KT4 . . . . . .198 A2
Glyn St, SE11 . . . . .34 C4
Glynwood Ct, SE23 . . . . .171 F2
Goaters All, SW6 . . . . .128 C7
Goat La, Surb. KT6 . . . . .195 F2
Goat Rd, Mitch. CR4 . . . . .186 A7
Goat Wf, Brent. TW8 . . . . .125 H6
Godalming Av, Wall. SM6 . . . . .201 E5
Godalming Rd, E14 . . . . .114 B5
Godbold Rd, E15 . . . . .114 E3
Goddard Pl, N19 . . . . .92 C3
Goddard Rd, Beck. BR3 . . . . . .189 G4
Goddards Way, Ilf. IG1 . . . . . . .99 G1
Godfrey Av, Nthlt. UB5 . . . . . . .102 E1
Twickenham TW2 . . . . . . .144 A7
Godfrey Hill, SE18 . . . . .136 B4
Godfrey Rd, SE18 . . . . .136 C4
Godfrey St, E15 . . . . .114 C2
SW3 . . . . .31 H4
Godfrey Way, Houns. TW4 . . . . .143 E7
Goding St, SE11 . . . . .34 B4
Godley Cl, SE14 off Kender St . .153 F1
Godley Rd, SW18 . . . . .167 G1
Godliman St, EC4 . . . . .19 J4
Godman Rd, SE15 . . . . .152 E2
Godolphin Cl, N13 . . . . .59 H6
Godolphin Pl, W3 off Vyner Rd . .106 D7
Godolphin Rd, W12 . . . . .127 H2
Godson Rd, Croy. CR0 . . . . . . .201 G3
Godson St, N1 . . . . .11 E1
Godstone Rd, Sutt. SM1 . . . . . .199 F4
Twickenham TW1 . . . . . . .144 D6
Godstow Rd, SE2 . . . . .138 C2
Godwin Cl, N1 . . . . .12 A1
Epsom KT19 . . . . .196 C6
Godwin Ct, NW1 . . . . .9 G1
Godwin Rd, E7 . . . . .97 H4
Bromley BR2 . . . . .191 J3
Goffers Rd, SE3 . . . . .154 D1
Goidel Cl, Wall. SM6 . . . . .200 D4
Golborne Gdns, W10
off Golborne Rd 108 C4
Golborne Ms, W10
off Portobello Rd 108 B5
Golborne Rd, W10 . . . . .108 B5
Golda Cl, Barn. EN5 . . . . .40 A6
Goldbeaters Gro, Edg. HA8 . . . .54 E6
Goldcliff Cl, Mord. SM4 . . . . . .184 D6

Goldcrest Cl, E16 . . . . .116 A5
off Sheerwater Rd
SE28 . . . . .118 C7
Goldcrest Ms, W5
off Montpelier Av 105 G5
Goldcrest Way, Bushey WD23 . .51 J1
Golden Ct, Rich. TW9
off George St 145 G5
Golden Cres, Hayes UB3 . . . . .121 J1
Golden Cross Ms, W11
off Basing St 108 C6
★ Golden Hinde, SE1 . . . . .28 B1
Golden Jubilee Br, SE1 . . . . . . .26 C2
WC2 . . . . .26 C1
Golden La, EC1 . . . . .11 J6
Golden La Est, EC1 . . . . .11 J6
Golden Manor, W7 . . . . .104 B7
Golden Plover Cl, E16
off Maplin Rd 115 H6
Golden Sq, W1 . . . . .17 G5
Golden Yd, NW3 off Heath St . . .91 F4
Golders Cl, Edg. HA8 . . . . .54 B5
Golders Gdns, NW11 . . . . .72 B7
GOLDERS GREEN, NW11 . . . . .72 D7
Golders Grn Cres, NW11 . . . . . .72 C7
Golders Grn Rd, NW11 . . . . . . .72 B6
Golders Manor Dr, NW11 . . . . . .72 A6
Golders Pk Cl, NW11 . . . . .90 E1
Golders Ri, NW4 . . . . .72 A5
Golders Way, NW11 . . . . .72 C7
Goldfinch Rd, SE28 . . . . .137 G3
Goldfinch Way, Borwd. WD6 . . . .38 A4
Goldhawk Ms, W12
off Devonport Rd 127 H2
Goldhawk Rd, W6 . . . . .127 F4
W12 . . . . .127 G3
Goldhaze Cl, Wdf.Grn. IG8 . . . . .64 A7
Gold Hill, Edg. HA8 . . . . .54 D6
Goldhurst Ter, NW6 . . . . .90 E7
Golding Cl, Chess. KT9
off Coppard Gdns 195 F6
Goldingham Av, Loug. IG10 . . . .49 F2
Goldings Hill, Loug. IG10 . . . . . .48 D1
Goldings Ri, Loug. IG10 . . . . . .48 D1
Goldings Rd, Loug. IG10 . . . . . .48 D1
Golding St, E1 . . . . .21 J4
Golding Ter, SW11
off Longhedge St 150 A2
Goldington Cres, NW1 . . . . .9 H1
Goldington St, NW1 . . . . .9 H1
Gold La, Edg. HA8 . . . . .54 D6
Goldman Cl, E2 . . . . .13 H5
Goldmark Ho, SE3
off Lebrun Sq 155 H3
Goldney Rd, W9 . . . . .108 D4
Goldrill Dr, N11 . . . . .58 A2
Goldsboro Rd, SW8 . . . . .150 D1
Goldsborough Cres, E4 . . . . . . .62 C2
Goldsdown Cl, Enf. EN3 . . . . . .45 H2
Goldsdown Rd, Enf. EN3 . . . . . .45 G2
Goldsmid St, SE18
off Sladedale Rd 137 H5
Goldsmith Av, E12 . . . . .98 B6
NW9 . . . . .71 F6
W3 . . . . .106 D7
Romford RM7 . . . . .83 G7
Goldsmith Cl, W3
off East Acton La 126/127 E1
Harrow HA2 . . . . .85 H1
Goldsmith La, NW9 . . . . .70 B4
Goldsmith Rd, E10 . . . . .96 A1
E17 . . . . .77 G2
N11 . . . . .57 J5
SE15 . . . . .152 D1
W3 . . . . .126 D1
★ Goldsmiths' Hall, EC2 . . . . . .20 A3
Goldsmith's Row, E2 . . . . .13 H2
Goldsmith's Sq, E2 . . . . .13 J1
Goldsmith St, EC2 . . . . .20 A3
Goldsworthy Gdns, SE16 . . . . . .133 F4
Goldwell Rd, Th.Hth. CR7 . . . . .187 F4
Goldwin Cl, SE14 . . . . .153 F1
Goldwing Cl, E16 . . . . .115 G6
Golf Cl, Stan. HA7 . . . . .53 F7
Thornton Heath CR7
off Kensington Av 187 G1
Golf Club Dr, Kings.T. KT2 . . . . .164 D7
Golfe Rd, Ilf. IG1 . . . . .99 G3
Golf Rd, W5 off Boileau Rd 105 J6
Bromley BR1 . . . . .192 D3
Golf Side, Twick. TW2 . . . . . . .162 A3
Golfside Cl, N20 . . . . .57 H3
New Malden KT3 . . . . . . .183 E2
Goliath Cl, Wall. SM6 . . . . .200 E7
Gollogly Ter, SE7 . . . . .135 J5
Gomer Gdns, Tedd. TW11 . . . . .162 D6
Gomer Pl, Tedd. TW11 . . . . . . .162 D6
Gomm Rd, SE16 . . . . .133 F3
Gomshall Av, Wall. SM6 . . . . . .200 E5
Gondar Gdns, NW6 . . . . .90 C5
Gonson St, SE8 . . . . .134 B6
Gonston Cl, SW19 . . . . .166 B2
Gonville Cres, Nthlt. UB5 . . . . . .85 H6
Gonville Rd, Th.Hth. CR7 . . . . .187 F5
Gonville St, SW6
off Putney Br App 148 B3
Gooch Ho, E5 . . . . .95 E3

Goodall Rd, E11 . . . . .96 C3
Gooden Ct, Har. HA1 . . . . .86 B3
Goodenough Rd, SW19 . . . . . .166 C7
Goodey Rd, Bark. IG11 . . . . . . .99 J7
Goodge Pl, W1 . . . . .17 G2
Goodge St, W1 . . . . .17 G2
Goodhall Cl, Stan. HA7 . . . . . . .52 E6
Goodhall St, NW10 . . . . .107 E3
Goodhart Pl, E14 . . . . .113 H7
Goodhart Way, W.Wick. BR4 . .190 E1
Goodhew Rd, Croy. CR0 . . . . . .188 D6
Gooding Cl, N.Mal. KT3 . . . . . .182 C4
Goodinge Cl, N7 . . . . .92 E5
Goodman Cres, SW2 . . . . .168 D2
Goodman Rd, E10 . . . . .78 C7
Goodmans Ct, E1 . . . . .21 F5
   Wembley HA0 . . . . .87 G4
Goodman's Stile, E1 . . . . .21 H4
Goodmans Yd, E1 . . . . .21 F5
GOODMAYES, Ilf. IG3 . . . . . . .100 B2
Goodmayes Av, Ilf. IG3 . . . . . .100 A1
Goodmayes La, Ilf. IG3 . . . . . .100 A4
Goodmayes Rd, Ilf. IG3 . . . . . .100 A1
Goodrich Rd, SE22 . . . . .152 C6
Goodson Rd, NW10 . . . . .89 E7
Goods Way, NW1 . . . . .10 A1
Goodway Gdns, E14 . . . . .114 D6
Goodwin Cl, SE16 . . . . .29 G6
   Mitcham CR4 . . . . .185 G3
Goodwin Ct, Barn. EN4 . . . . . . .41 H6
Goodwin Dr, Sid. DA14 . . . . . .176 D3
Goodwin Gdns, Croy. CR0 . . . .201 H6
Goodwin Rd, N9 . . . . .61 F1
   W12 . . . . .127 G2
   Croydon CR0 . . . . .201 H5
Goodwins Ct, WC2 . . . . .18 A5
Goodwin St, N4 off Fonthill Rd . .93 G2
Goodwood Cl, Mord. SM4 . . . .184 D4
   Stanmore HA7 . . . . .53 F5
Goodwood Dr, Nthlt. UB5 . . . . .85 G6
Goodwood Path, Borwd. WD6
   off Stratfield Rd 38 A3
Goodwood Rd, SE14 . . . . .133 H7
Goodwyn Av, NW7 . . . . .55 E5
Goodwyns Vale, N10 . . . . .74 A1
Goodyers Gdns, NW4 . . . . .72 A5
Goosander Way, SE28 . . . . . . .137 G3
Gooseacre La, Har. HA3 . . . . . .69 G5
Gooseley La, E6 . . . . .116 D3
Goosens Cl, Sutt. SM1
   off Turnpike La 199 F5
Goose Sq, E6 off Harper Rd 116 C6
Gophir La, EC4 . . . . .20 B5
Gopsall St, N1 . . . . .112 A1
Gordon Av, E4 . . . . .62 E6
   SW14 . . . . .146 E4
   Stanmore HA7 . . . . .52 E6
   Twickenham TW1 . . . . .144 D5
Gordonbrook Rd, SE4 . . . . . . .154 A3
Gordon Cl, E17 . . . . .78 A6
   N19 off Highgate Hill 92 C1
Gordon Ct, W12 . . . . .107 J6
Gordon Cres, Croy. CR0 . . . . . .202 B1
   Hayes UB3 . . . . .122 A3
Gordondale Rd, SW19 . . . . . . .166 D2
Gordon Gdns, Edg. HA8 . . . . . .70 B2
Gordon Gro, SE5 . . . . .151 H2
Gordon Hill, Enf. EN2 . . . . .43 J1
Gordon Ho, E1 off Glamis Rd . . .113 F7
Gordon Ho Rd, NW5 . . . . .92 A4
Gordon Pl, W8 . . . . .128 D2
Gordon Rd, E4 . . . . .47 E7
   E11 . . . . .79 G6
   E15 . . . . .96 C4
   E18 . . . . .79 H1
   N3 .56 C7
   N9 .61 E2
   N11 . . . . .58 D7
   SE15 . . . . .152 E2
   W4 . . . . .126 B6
   W5 . . . . .105 F7
   W13 . . . . .104 E7
   Barking IG11 . . . . .117 H1
   Beckenham BR3 . . . . .189 J3
   Belvedere DA17 . . . . .139 J4
   Carshalton SM5 . . . . .199 J6
   Enfield EN2 . . . . .43 J1
   Esher (Clay.) KT10 . . . . . . .194 B6
   Harrow HA3 . . . . .68 B3
   Hounslow TW3 . . . . .143 J4
   Ilford IG1 . . . . .99 G3
   Kingston upon Thames KT2 .181 J1
   Richmond TW9 . . . . .145 J2
   Romford RM6 . . . . .83 F6
   Sidcup DA15 . . . . .157 H5
   Southall UB2 . . . . .123 E4
   Surbiton KT5 . . . . .181 J7
Gordon Sq, WC1 . . . . .9 J6
Gordon St, E13 off Grange Rd . .115 G3
   WC1 . . . . .9 H5
Gordon Way, Barn. EN5 . . . . . .40 C4
   Bromley BR1 . . . . .191 G1
Gore Ct, NW9 . . . . .70 A5
Gorefield Pl, NW6 . . . . .108 D2
Gore Rd, E9 . . . . .113 F1
   SW20 . . . . .183 J2
Goresbrook Rd, Dag. RM9 . . . .118 B1

Goresbrook Village, Dag. RM9
   off Goresbrook Rd 118 B1
Gore St, SW7 . . . . .22 D5
Gorham Pl, W11 off Mary Pl . . .108 B7
Goring Cl, Rom. RM5 . . . . .83 J1
Goring Gdns, Dag. RM8 . . . . . .100 C4
Goring Rd, N11 . . . . .58 E6
Goring St, EC3 . . . . .21 E3
Goring Way, Grnf. UB6 . . . . . . .103 J2
Gorleston Rd, N15 . . . . .76 A5
Gorleston St, W14 . . . . .128 B4
Gorman Rd, SE18 . . . . .136 C4
Gorringe Pk Av, Mitch. CR4 . . .167 J7
Gorse Cl, E16 . . . . .115 G6
Gorse Ri, SW17 . . . . .168 A5
Gorse Rd, Croy. CR0 . . . . .204 A4
Gorst Rd, NW10 . . . . .106 C4
   SW11 . . . . .149 J6
Gorsuch Pl, E2 . . . . .13 F3
Gorsuch St, E2 . . . . .13 F3
Gosberton Rd, SW12 . . . . .168 A1
Gosbury Hill, Chess. KT9 . . . . .195 H4
Gosfield Rd, Dag. RM8 . . . . . .101 G2
Gosfield St, W1 . . . . .17 F1
Gosford Gdns, Ilf. IG4 . . . . .80 C5
Gosforth La, Wat. WD19 . . . . . .50 C3
Gosforth Path, Wat. WD19 . . . . .50 A3
Goslett Yd, WC2 . . . . .17 J4
Gosling Cl, Grnf. UB6 . . . . .103 G3
Gosling Way, SW9 . . . . .151 G1
Gospatrick Rd, N17 . . . . .59 J7
GOSPEL OAK, NW5 . . . . .92 A4
Gospel Oak Est, NW5 . . . . .91 J5
Gosport Rd, E17 . . . . .77 J5
Gosport Wk, N17
   off Yarmouth Cres 76/77 E5
Gosport Way, SE15
   off Blakes La 132 C7
Gossage Rd, SE18
   off Ancona Rd 137 G5
Gosset St, E2 . . . . .13 G3
Gosshill Rd, Chis. BR7 . . . . . . .192 D2
Gossington Cl, Chis. BR7
   off Beechwood Ri 174/175 E4
Gosterwood St, SE8 . . . . .133 H6
Gostling Rd, Twick. TW2 . . . . . .161 G1
Goston Gdns, Th.Hth. CR7 . . . .187 G3
Goswell Rd, EC1 . . . . .11 J6
Gothic Ct, Hayes UB3
   off Sipson La 121 G6
Gothic Rd, Twick. TW2 . . . . . . .162 A2
Gottfried Ms, NW5
   off Fortess Rd 92 C4
Goudhurst Rd, Brom. BR1 . . . .173 E5
Gough Rd, E15 . . . . .97 F4
   Enfield EN1 . . . . .44 E2
Gough Sq, EC4 . . . . .19 F3
Gough St, WC1 . . . . .10 D5
Gough Wk, E14 off Saracen St . .114 A6
Gould Ct, SE19 . . . . .170 C5
Goulden Ho App, SW11 . . . . . .149 H2
Goulding Gdns, Th.Hth. CR7 . . .187 H2
Gould Rd, Felt. TW14 . . . . .141 H7
   Twickenham TW2 . . . . .162 B1
Gould Ter, E8
   off Kenmure Rd 94/95 E5
Goulston St, E1 . . . . .21 F3
Goulton Rd, E5 . . . . .95 E4
Gourley Pl, N15 off Gourley St . .76 B5
Gourley St, N15 . . . . .76 B5
Gourock Rd, SE9 . . . . .156 D5
Govan St, E2 off Whiston Rd . . .112 D1
Govier Cl, E15 . . . . .97 E7
Gowan Av, SW6 . . . . .148 B1
Gowan Rd, NW10 . . . . .89 H6
Gower Cl, SW4 . . . . .150 C6
Gower Ct, WC1 . . . . .9 H5
Gower Ms, WC1 . . . . .17 H2
Gower Pl, WC1 . . . . .9 G5
Gower Rd, E7 . . . . .97 G6
   Isleworth TW7 . . . . .124 C6
Gower St, WC1 . . . . .9 G5
Gower's Wk, E1 . . . . .21 H3
Gowland Pl, Beck. BR3 . . . . . . .189 J2
Gowlett Rd, SE15 . . . . .152 D3
Gowlland Cl, Croy. CR0 . . . . . .188 D7
Gowrie Rd, SW11 . . . . .150 A3
Graburn Way, E.Mol. KT8 . . . . .180 A3
Grace Av, Bexh. DA7 . . . . .159 F2
Grace Business Cen, Mitch.
   CR4 . . . . .185 J5
Gracechurch St, EC3 . . . . .20 C5
Grace Cl, SE9 . . . . .174 A3
   Borehamwood WD6 . . . . . . .38 D1
   Edgware HA8
      off Pavilion Way 54 C7
   Ilford IG6 . . . . .65 J6
Gracedale Rd, SW16 . . . . .168 B5
Gracefield Gdns, SW16 . . . . . .169 E3
Grace Jones Cl, E8
   off Parkholme Rd 94 D6
Grace Path, SE26 . . . . .171 F4
Grace Pl, E3
   off St. Leonards St 114 B3
Grace Rd, Croy. CR0 . . . . .187 J6
Grace's All, E1 . . . . .21 H5
Graces Ms, SE5 . . . . .152 B2

Graces Rd, SE5 . . . . .152 B2
Grace St, E3 . . . . .114 B3
Gradient, The, SE26 . . . . .170 D4
Graduate Pl, SE1 off Long La . .132 B3
Graeme Rd, Enf. EN1 . . . . .44 A2
Graemesdyke Av, SW14 . . . . . .146 B3
Grafton Cl, W13 . . . . .104 D6
   Hounslow TW4 . . . . .161 E1
   Worcester Park KT4 . . . . . .197 E3
Grafton Cres, NW1 . . . . .92 B6
Grafton Gdns, N4 . . . . .75 J6
   Dagenham RM8 . . . . .101 E2
Grafton Ho, E3 . . . . .114 A3
Grafton Ms, W1 . . . . .9 F6
Grafton Pk Rd, Wor.Pk. KT4 . . .196 E2
Grafton Pl, NW1 . . . . .9 H4
Grafton Rd, NW5 . . . . .92 A5
   W3 . . . . .106 C7
   Croydon CR0 . . . . .201 G1
   Dagenham RM8 . . . . .101 E2
   Enfield EN2 . . . . .43 F3
   Harrow HA1 . . . . .67 J5
   New Malden KT3 . . . . .182 E3
   Worcester Park KT4 . . . . . .196 D3
Graftons, The, NW2
   off Hermitage La 90 D3
Grafton Sq, SW4 . . . . .150 C3
Grafton St, W1 . . . . .17 E6
Grafton Ter, NW5 . . . . .91 J5
Grafton Way, W1 . . . . .9 F6
   WC1 . . . . .9 F6
   West Molesey KT8 . . . . . . .179 F4
Grafton Yd, NW5
   off Prince of Wales Rd 92 B6
Graham Av, W13 . . . . .124 E2
   Mitcham CR4 . . . . .186 A1
Graham Cl, Croy. CR0 . . . . . . .204 A2
Grahame Pk Est, NW9 . . . . .71 E1
Grahame Pk Way, NW7 . . . . . . .55 F7
   NW9 . . . . .71 F2
Graham Gdns, Surb. KT6 . . . . .195 H1
Graham Rd, E8 . . . . .94 C6
   E13 . . . . .115 G4
   N15 . . . . .75 H3
   NW4 . . . . .71 H6
   SW19 . . . . .166 C7
   W4 . . . . .126 D3
   Bexleyheath DA6 . . . . .159 G4
   Hampton TW12 . . . . .161 G4
   Harrow HA3 . . . . .68 B3
   Mitcham CR4 . . . . .186 A1
Graham St, N1 . . . . .11 H2
Graham Ter, SW1 . . . . .32 B2
Grainger Cl, Nthlt. UB5
   off Lancaster Rd 85 J5
Grainger Rd, N22 . . . . .75 J1
   Isleworth TW7 . . . . .144 C2
Gramer Cl, E11 off Norman Rd . .96 D2
Grampian Cl, Hayes UB3 . . . . .121 G7
   Orpington BR6
      off Cotswold Ri 193 J6
   Sutton SM2
      off Devonshire Rd 199 F7
Grampian Gdns, NW2 . . . . .90 B1
Grampian Ho, N9
   off Plevna Rd 60/61 E2
Granard Av, SW15 . . . . .147 H5
Granard Rd, SW12 . . . . .149 J7
Granary Cl, N9 off Turin Rd 45 E7
Granary Rd, E1 . . . . .112 E4
Granary Sq, N1
   off Liverpool Rd 93 G6
Granary St, NW1 . . . . .110 D1
Granby Pl, SE1 . . . . .26 E4
Granby Rd, SE9 . . . . .156 C2
Granby St, E2 . . . . .13 G5
Granby Ter, NW1 . . . . .9 F2
Grand Arc, N12 off Ballards La . .57 F5
Grand Av, EC1 . . . . .19 H1
   N10 . . . . .74 A4
   Surbiton KT5 . . . . .182 B5
   Wembley HA9 . . . . .88 A5
Grand Av E, Wem. HA9 . . . . . . .88 B5
Grand Dep Rd, SE18 . . . . .136 D5
Grand Dr, SW20 . . . . .183 J2
   Southall UB2 . . . . .123 J2
Granden Rd, SW16 . . . . .187 E2
Grandison Rd, SW11 . . . . .149 J5
   Worcester Park KT4 . . . . . .197 J2
Grand Junct Wf, N1 . . . . .11 J2
Grand Par Ms, SW15
   off Upper Richmond Rd 148 B5
Grand Union Canal Wk, W7 . . . .124 B3
Grand Union Cl, W9
   off Woodfield Rd 108 C5
Grand Union Cres, E8 . . . . .94 D7
Grand Union Ind Est, NW10 . . .106 B2
Grand Union Wk, NW1 . . . . .92 B7
Grand Wk, E1 off Solebay St . . .113 H4
Granfield St, SW11 . . . . .149 G1
Grange, The, N2 off Central Av . .73 G2
   N20 . . . . .57 F1
   SE1 . . . . .29 F5
   SW19 . . . . .166 A6
   Croydon CR0 . . . . .203 J2
   Wembley HA0 . . . . .88 A7
   Worcester Park KT4 . . . . . .196 D3

Grange Av, N12 . . . . .57 F5
   N20 . . . . .40 B7
   SE25 . . . . .188 B2
   Barnet EN4 . . . . .57 H1
   Stanmore HA7 . . . . .69 E2
   Twickenham TW2 . . . . .162 B2
   Woodford Green IG8 . . . . . . .63 G6
Grangecliffe Gdns, SE25 . . . . .188 B2
Grange Cl, Edg. HA8 . . . . .54 C5
   Hounslow TW5 . . . . .123 F6
   Sidcup DA15 . . . . .176 A3
   West Molesey KT8 . . . . . . .179 H4
   Woodford Green IG8 . . . . . . .63 G7
Grange Ct, WC2 . . . . .18 C4
   Chigwell IG7 . . . . .65 F2
   Loughton IG10 . . . . .48 A3
   Northolt UB5 . . . . .102 C2
Grangecourt Rd, N16 . . . . .94 B1
Grange Cres, SE28 . . . . .118 C6
   Chigwell IG7 . . . . .65 G5
Grange Dr, Chis. BR7 . . . . .174 B6
Grange Fm Cl, Har. HA2 . . . . . . .85 J2
Grange Gdns, N14 . . . . .58 D1
   NW3 . . . . .91 E3
   SE25 . . . . .188 B2
   Pinner HA5 . . . . .67 F4
Grange Gro, N1 . . . . .93 H6
GRANGE HILL, Chig. IG7 . . . . .65 G6
Grange Hill, SE25 . . . . .188 B2
   Edgware HA8 . . . . .54 C5
Grangehill Pl, SE9
   off Westmount Rd 156 C3
Grangehill Rd, SE9 . . . . .156 C3
Grange Ho, Bark. IG11
   off St. Margarets 117 G1
Grange La, SE21 . . . . .170 C2
Grange Mans, Epsom KT17 . . .197 F7
Grangemill Rd, SE6 . . . . .172 A3
Grangemill Way, SE6 . . . . .172 A2
★ Grange Mus of Comm History,
   NW10 off Neasden La 89 E4
GRANGE PARK, N21 . . . . .43 H5
Grange Pk, W5 . . . . .125 H1
Grange Pk Av, N21 . . . . .43 H6
Grange Pk Pl, SW20 . . . . .165 H7
Grange Pk Rd, E10 . . . . .96 B1
   Thornton Heath CR7 . . . . . .188 A4
Grange Pl, NW6 . . . . .90 D7
Grange Rd, E10 . . . . .96 A1
   E13 . . . . .115 F3
   E17 . . . . .77 H5
   N6 .74 A6
   N17 . . . . .60 D6
   N18 . . . . .60 D6
   NW10 . . . . .89 H6
   SE1 . . . . .28 E5
   SE19 . . . . .188 A4
   SE25 . . . . .188 A4
   SW13 . . . . .147 G1
   W4 . . . . .126 B5
   W5 . . . . .125 G1
   Chessington KT9 . . . . .195 H4
   Edgware HA8 . . . . .54 D6
   Harrow HA1 . . . . .68 D6
   Harrow (S.Har.) HA2 . . . . . . .86 A2
   Ilford IG1 . . . . .99 E4
   Kingston upon Thames KT1 .181 H3
   Orpington BR6 . . . . .207 F2
   Southall UB1 . . . . .122 E4
   Sutton SM2 . . . . .198 D7
   Thornton Heath CR7 . . . . . .188 A4
   West Molesey KT8 . . . . . . .179 H4
Grange St, N1 . . . . .112 A1
Grange Vale, Sutt. SM2 . . . . . .199 E7
Grange Vw Rd, N20 . . . . .57 F1
Grange Wk, SE1 . . . . .28 E5
Grangeway, N12 . . . . .57 E4
   NW6 off Messina Av 90 D7
   Woodford Green IG8 . . . . . . .63 J4
Grangeway, The, N21 . . . . .43 H6
Grangeway Gdns, Ilf. IG4 . . . . . .80 B5
Grangewood, Bex. DA5
   off Hurst Rd 177 F1
Grangewood Cl, Pnr. HA5 . . . . .66 A5
Grangewood La, Beck. BR3 . . . .171 J6
Grangewood St, E6 . . . . .115 J1
Grangewood Ter, SE25
   off Grange Rd 188 A3
Grange Yd, SE1 . . . . .29 F6
Granham Gdns, N9 . . . . .60 C2
Granite St, SE18 . . . . .137 J4
Granleigh Rd, E11 . . . . .96 E2
Gransden Av, E8 . . . . .95 E7
Gransden Rd, W12
   off Wendell Rd 127 F2
Grantbridge St, N1 . . . . .11 H1
Grantchester Cl, Har. HA1 . . . . .86 C3
Grant Cl, N14 . . . . .42 C7
Grantham Cen, The, SW9 . . . . .151 G2
Grantham Cl, Edg. HA8 . . . . . . .53 H3
Grantham Gdns, Rom. RM6 . . . .83 F6
Grantham Grn, Borwd. WD6 . . . .38 C5
Grantham Pl, W1 . . . . .24 D2
Grantham Rd, E12 . . . . .98 D4
   SW9 . . . . .151 E2
   W4 . . . . .126 E7
Grantley Rd, Houns. TW4 . . . . .142 C2

Grantley St, E1 . . . . .113 G3
Grantock Rd, E17 . . . . .78 D1
Granton Rd, SW16 . . . . .186 C1
  Ilford IG3 . . . . .100 A1
  Sidcup DA14 . . . . .176 C6
Grant Pl, Croy. CR0 . . . . .202 C1
Grant Rd, SW11 . . . . .149 G4
  Croydon CR0 . . . . .202 C1
  Harrow HA3 . . . . .68 B3
Grants Cl, N17 . . . . .76 B2
  NW7 . . . . .55 J7
Grant's Quay Wf, EC3 . . . . .20 C6
Grant St, E13 . . . . .115 G3
  N1 . . . . .11 E1
Grantully Rd, W9 . . . . .6 A4
Grant Way, Islw. TW7 . . . . .124 D6
Granville Av, N9 . . . . .61 F3
  Feltham TW13 . . . . .160 A2
  Hounslow TW3 . . . . .143 G5
Granville Cl, Croy. CR0 . . . . . . .202 B2
Granville Ct, N1 . . . . .112 A1
Granville Gdns, SW16 . . . . .187 F1
  W5 .125 J1
Granville Gro, SE13 . . . . .154 C3
Granville Ms, Sid. DA14 . . . . . .176 A4
Granville Pk, SE13 . . . . .154 C3
Granville Pl, N12 (N.Finchley)
  off Granville Rd 57 F7
  SW6 off Maxwell Rd 128/129 E7
  W1 . . . . .16 A4
  Pinner HA5 . . . . .66 D3
Granville Rd, E17 . . . . .78 B6
  E18 .79 H2
  N4 . . . . .75 F6
  N12 .57 E7
  N13 off Russell Rd 59 F6
  N22 .75 H1
  NW2 .90 C2
  NW6 . . . . .108 D2
  SW18 . . . . .148 D7
  SW19 off Russell Rd 166 D7
  Barnet EN5 . . . . .39 J4
  Hayes UB3 . . . . .121 J4
  Ilford IG1 . . . . .98 C1
  Sidcup DA14 . . . . .176 A4
  Welling DA16 . . . . .158 C3
Granville Sq, SE15 . . . . .132 B7
Granville St, WC1 . . . . .10 D4
Grape St, WC2 . . . . .18 A3
Graphite Sq, SE11 . . . . .34 C3
Grapsome Cl, Chess. KT9
  off Nigel Fisher Way 195 F7
Grasdene Rd, SE18 . . . . .138 A7
Grasgarth Cl, W3
  off Creswick Rd 106 C7
Grasmere Av, SW15 . . . . .164 C4
  SW19 . . . . .184 D3
  W3 .106 C7
  Hounslow TW3 . . . . .143 H6
  Orpington BR6 . . . . .206 E3
  Wembley HA9 . . . . .69 G7
Grasmere Cl, Loug. IG10 . . . . . . .48 C2
Grasmere Ct, N22
  off Palmerston Rd 59 F6
Grasmere Gdns, Har. HA3 . . . . . .68 D2
  Ilford IG4 . . . . .80 C5
  Orpington BR6 . . . . .206 E3
Grasmere Pt, SE15
  off Ilderton Rd 133 F7
Grasmere Rd, E13 . . . . .115 G2
  N10 .74 B1
  N17 .60 D6
  SE25 . . . . .189 E6
  SW16 . . . . .169 F5
  Bexleyheath DA7 . . . . .159 J1
  Bromley BR1 . . . . .191 F1
  Orpington BR6 . . . . .206 E3
Grasshaven Way, SE28 . . . . . . .137 J1
Grassington Cl, N11
  off Ribblesdale Av 58 A6
Grassington Rd, Sid. DA14 . . . .176 A4
Grassmount, SE23 . . . . .171 E2
Grass Pk, N3 . . . . .72 C1
Grassway, Wall. SM6 . . . . .200 C4
Grasvenor Av, Barn. EN5 . . . . . . .40 D6
Grately Way, SE15 . . . . .37 F7
Gratton Rd, W14 . . . . .128 B3
Gratton Ter, NW2 . . . . .90 A3
Graveley, Kings.T. KT1
  off Willingham Way 182 A2
Graveley Av, Borwd. WD6 . . . . . .38 C4
Gravel Hill, N3 . . . . .72 C2
  Bexleyheath DA6 . . . . .159 H5
  Croydon CR0 . . . . .203 G6
Gravel Hill Cl, Bexh. DA6 . . . . .159 H5
Gravel La, E1 . . . . .21 F3
Gravelly Ride, SW19 . . . . .165 H4
Gravel Pit La, SE9 . . . . .157 F5
Gravel Rd, Brom. BR2 . . . . .206 B2
  Twickenham TW2 . . . . .162 B1
Gravelwood Cl, Chis. BR7 . . . . .175 F3
Graveney Gro, SE20 . . . . .171 F7
Graveney Rd, SW17 . . . . .167 H4
Gravesend Rd, W12 . . . . .107 G7
Gray Av, Dag. RM8 . . . . .101 F1
Grayham Cres, N.Mal. KT3 . . . .182 D4

Grayham Rd, N.Mal. KT3 . . . . .182 D4
Grayland Cl, Brom. BR1 . . . . . .192 A1
Grayling Cl, E16
  off Cranberry La 114/115 E4
Grayling Rd, N16 . . . . .94 A2
Grayling Sq, E2 . . . . .13 J3
Grayscroft Rd, SW16 . . . . .168 D7
Grayshott Rd, SW11 . . . . .150 A2
★ Gray's Inn, WC1 . . . . .18 D1
Gray's Inn Pl, WC1 . . . . .18 D2
Gray's Inn Rd, WC1 . . . . .10 C4
Gray's Inn Sq, WC1 . . . . .18 E1
Gray St, SE1 . . . . .27 F4
Grayswood Gdns, SW20
  off Farnham Gdns 183 H2
Grayswood Pt, SW15
  off Norley Vale 165 G1
Gray's Yd, W1 . . . . .16 C4
Graywood Ct, N12 . . . . .57 F7
Grazebrook Rd, N16 . . . . .94 A2
Grazeley Cl, Bexh. DA6 . . . . . . .159 J5
Grazeley Ct, SE19
  off Gipsy Hill 170 B4
Great Acre Ct, SW4
  off St. Alphonsus Rd 150 D4
Great Arthur Ho, EC1
  off Fann St 111 J4
Great Bell All, EC2 . . . . .20 B3
Great Benty, West Dr. UB7 . . . .120 B4
Great Brownings, SE21 . . . . . . .170 C4
Great Bushey Dr, N20 . . . . .57 E1
Great Cambridge Junct, N18
  off North Circular Rd 60 A4
Great Cambridge Rd, N9 . . . . . . .60 B1
  N17 .60 A5
  N18 .60 A5
  Enfield EN1 . . . . .44 D4
Great Castle St, W1 . . . . .17 E3
Great Cen Av, Ruis. HA4 . . . . . . .84 C5
Great Cen St, NW1 . . . . .15 J1
Great Cen Way, NW10 . . . . .88 E5
  Wembley HA9 . . . . .88 C5
Great Chapel St, W1 . . . . .17 H3
Great Chart St, SW11
  off Wynter St 149 F4
Great Chertsey Rd, W4 . . . . . . .146 C2
  Feltham TW13 . . . . .161 G3
Great Ch La, W6 . . . . .128 A5
Great Coll St, SW1 . . . . .26 A5
Great Cross Av, SE10 . . . . .134 E7
Great Cumberland Ms, W1 . . . . .15 J4
Great Cumberland Pl, W1 . . . . . .15 J3
Great Dover St, SE1 . . . . .28 A4
Greatdown Rd, W7 . . . . .104 C4
Great Eastern Enterprise Cen, E14
  off Millharbour 134 B2
Great Eastern Rd, E15 . . . . .96 D7
Great Eastern St, EC2 . . . . .12 D4
Great Eastern Wk, EC2 . . . . .20 E2
Great Elms Rd, Brom. BR2 . . . .191 J4
Great Fld, NW9 . . . . .71 E1
Greatfield Av, E6 . . . . .116 C4
Greatfield Cl, N19
  off Warrender Rd 92 C4
  SE4 . . . . .154 A4
Greatfields Rd, Bark. IG11 . . . . .117 G1
Great Fleete Way, Bark. IG11
  off Choats Rd 118 C2
Great Galley Cl, Bark. IG11 . . . .118 B3
Great Gatton Cl, Croy. CR0 . . . .189 H7
Great George St, SW1 . . . . .25 J4
Great Guildford St, SE1 . . . . . . .27 J1
Greatham Wk, SW15 . . . . .165 G1
Great Harry Dr, SE9 . . . . .174 D3
Great James St, WC1 . . . . .10 C6
Great Marlborough St, W1 . . . . .17 F4
Great Maze Pond, SE1 . . . . .28 C3
Great Newport St, WC2
  off Cranbourn St 110 D7
Great New St, EC4 . . . . .19 F3
Great N Leisure Pk, N12 . . . . . . .57 G7
Great N Rd, N2 . . . . .73 H4
  N6 . . . . .73 H4
  Barnet (New Barn.) EN5 . . . . .40 D5
Great N Way, NW4 . . . . .71 J2
Great Oaks, Chig. IG7 . . . . .65 F4
Greatorex St, E1 . . . . .21 H1
Great Ormond St, WC1 . . . . .18 B1
Great Owl Rd, Chig. IG7 . . . . . . .64 D3
Great Percy St, WC1 . . . . .10 D3
Great Peter St, SW1 . . . . .25 H6
Great Portland St, W1 . . . . .17 E1
Great Pulteney St, W1 . . . . .17 G5
Great Queen St, WC2 . . . . .18 B4
Great Russell St, WC1 . . . . .17 J3
Great St. Helens, EC3 . . . . .20 D3
Great St. Thomas Apostle, EC4 . .20 A5
Great Scotland Yd, SW1 . . . . . . .26 A2
Great Smith St, SW1 . . . . .25 J5
Great South-West Rd, Felt.
  TW14 . . . . .141 F7
  Hounslow TW4 . . . . .141 J4
Great Spilmans, SE22 . . . . .152 B5
Great Strand, NW9 . . . . .71 F1
Great Suffolk St, SE1 . . . . .27 H2
Great Sutton St, EC1 . . . . .11 H6
Great Swan All, EC2 . . . . .20 B3

Great Thrift, Orp. BR5 . . . . .193 F4
Great Titchfield St, W1 . . . . .17 F3
Great Twr St, EC3 . . . . .20 D5
Great Trinity La, EC4 . . . . .20 A5
Great Turnstile, WC1 . . . . .18 D2
Great Western Rd, W2 . . . . .108 C5
  W9 .108 C5
  W11 . . . . .108 C5
Great W Rd, W4 . . . . .126 B5
  W6 .127 F5
  Brentford TW8 . . . . .126 B5
  Hounslow TW5 . . . . .142 D2
  Isleworth TW7 . . . . .124 B7
Great Wf Rd, E14
  off Churchill Pl 134 B1
Great Winchester St, EC2 . . . . . .20 C3
Great Windmill St, W1 . . . . .17 H5
Greatwood, Chis. BR7 . . . . .174 D7
Great Yd, SE1 . . . . .28 E3
Greaves Cl, Bark. IG11
  off Norfolk Rd 99 H7
Greaves Pl, SW17 . . . . .167 H4
Grebe Av, Hayes UB4
  off Cygnet Way 102 D6
Grebe Cl, E7 off Cormorant Rd . .97 F5
  E17 .61 H7
  Barking IG11 . . . . .118 A4
Grebe Ct, Sutt. SM1 . . . . .198 C5
Grecian Cres, SE19 . . . . .169 H6
Gredo Ho, Bark. IG11 . . . . .118 B3
Greek Ct, W1 . . . . .17 J4
★ Greek Orthodox Cath of the
  Divine Wisdom (St. Sophia),
  W2 . . . . .14 A5
Greek St, W1 . . . . .17 J4
Greek Yd, WC2 . . . . .18 A5
Green, The, E4 . . . . .62 C1
  E11 .79 H6
  E15 .97 E6
  N9 . . . . .60 D2
  N14 .58 D3
  N21 .43 G7
  SW14 . . . . .146 C3
  SW19 . . . . .166 A5
  W3 .107 E6
  W5 off High St 125 G1
  Bexleyheath DA7 . . . . .159 G1
  Bromley BR1
    off Downham Way 173 G3
  Bromley (Hayes) BR2 . . . . . .191 G7
  Carshalton SM5 . . . . .200 A4
  Esher (Clay.) KT10 . . . . .194 C6
  Feltham TW13 . . . . .160 B2
  Hounslow TW5
    off Heston Rd 123 G6
  Morden SM4 . . . . .184 B4
  New Malden KT3 . . . . .182 C3
  Orpington (St.P.Cray) BR5
    off The Avenue 176 B7
  Richmond TW9 . . . . .145 G5
  Sidcup DA14 . . . . .176 A4
  Southall UB2 . . . . .123 E3
  Sutton SM1 . . . . .198 E3
  Twickenham TW2 . . . . .162 B1
  Welling DA16 . . . . .157 H4
  Wembley HA0 . . . . .86 D2
  West Drayton UB7 . . . . .120 A3
  Woodford Green IG8 . . . . . . .63 G5
Greenacre Cl, Nthlt. UB5 . . . . . . .85 F5
Greenacre Gdns, E17 . . . . .78 C4
Greenacre Pl, Wall. (Hackbr.) SM6
  off Park Rd 200 B2
Greenacres, N3 . . . . .72 B2
  SE9 . . . . .156 D6
  Bushey (Bushey Hth) WD23 . .52 A2
Green Acres, Croy. CR0 . . . . . . .202 C3
Greenacres Cl, Orp. BR6 . . . . . .207 F4
Greenacres Dr, Stan. HA7 . . . . . .52 E7
Greenacre Sq, SE16
  off Fishermans Dr 133 G2
Greenacre Wk, N14 . . . . .58 E3
Green Arbour Ct, EC1 . . . . .19 G3
Green Av, NW7 . . . . .54 D4
  W13 . . . . .125 E3
Greenaway Av, N18 . . . . .61 G6
Greenaway Gdns, NW3 . . . . .90 E4
Green Bk, E1 . . . . .132 E1
  N12 .57 E4
Greenbank Av, Wem. HA0 . . . . . .86 D5
Greenbank Cl, E4 . . . . .62 C2
Greenbank Cres, NW4 . . . . .72 B4
Greenbay Rd, SE7 . . . . .136 A7
Greenberry St, NW8 . . . . .7 G2
Greenbrook Av, Barn. EN4 . . . . . .41 F1
Green Cl, NW9 . . . . .70 C6
  NW11 . . . . .73 F7
  Bromley BR2 . . . . .190 E3
  Carshalton SM5 . . . . .199 J2
  Feltham TW13 . . . . .160 E5
Greencoat Pl, SW1 . . . . .33 G1
Greencoat Row, SW1 . . . . .25 G6
Greencourt Av, Croy. CR0 . . . . .203 E2
  Edgware HA8 . . . . .70 B1
Greencourt Gdns, Croy. CR0 . . .203 E1
Greencourt Rd, Orp. BR5 . . . . . .193 G5
Greencrest Pl, NW2
  off Dollis Hill La 89 G3

Green Cft, Edg. HA8
  off Deans La 54 C5
Greencroft Av, Ruis. HA4 . . . . . . .84 C2
Greencroft Cl, E6
  off Neatscourt Rd 116 B5
Greencroft Gdns, NW6 . . . . .91 E7
  Enfield EN1 . . . . .44 B3
Greencroft Rd, Houns. TW5 . . . .143 F1
Green Dale, SE5 . . . . .152 A4
  SE22 . . . . .152 B5
Green Dale Cl, SE22
  off Green Dale 152 B5
Green Dragon Ct, SE1 . . . . .28 B1
Green Dragon La, N21 . . . . .43 H6
  Brentford TW8 . . . . .125 H5
Green Dragon Yd, E1 . . . . .21 H2
Green Dr, Sthl. UB1 . . . . .123 G1
Green End, N21 . . . . .59 H2
  Chessington KT9 . . . . .195 H4
Greenend Rd, W4 . . . . .126 E2
Greenfarm Cl, Orp. BR6 . . . . . . .207 J5
Greenfell Mans, SE8
  off Glaisher St 134 B6
Greenfield Av, Surb. KT5 . . . . . .182 B7
  Watford WD19 . . . . .50 D2
Greenfield Dr, N2 . . . . .73 J4
Greenfield Gdns, NW2 . . . . .90 B2
  Dagenham RM9 . . . . .118 D1
  Orpington BR5 . . . . .193 G5
Greenfield Rd, E1 . . . . .21 J2
  N15 .76 B5
  Dagenham RM9 . . . . .118 C1
Greenfields, Loug. IG10 . . . . .48 D4
Greenfields Cl, Loug. IG10 . . . . . .48 D4
Greenfield Way, Har. HA2 . . . . . .67 H3
GREENFORD, UB6 . . . . .103 H3
Greenford Av, W7 . . . . .104 B4
  Southall UB1 . . . . .103 F7
Greenford Gdns, Grnf. UB6 . . . .103 H3
Greenford Rd, Grnf. UB6 . . . . . .103 J5
  Harrow HA1 . . . . .86 B5
  Southall UB1 . . . . .123 H1
  Sutton SM1 . . . . .198 E4
Green Gdns, Orp. BR6 . . . . .207 F5
Greengate, Grnf. UB6 . . . . .86 E6
Greengate St, E13 . . . . .115 H2
Greenhalgh Wk, N2 . . . . .73 F4
Greenham Cl, SE1 . . . . .27 E4
Greenham Cres, E4 . . . . .61 J6
Greenham Rd, N10 . . . . .74 A2
Greenhaven Dr, SE28 . . . . .118 B6
Greenheys Dr, E18 . . . . .79 F3
Greenhill, NW3
  off Hampstead High St 91 G4
  SE18 . . . . .136 C5
Green Hill, Buck.H. IG9 . . . . .63 J1
Greenhill, Sutt. SM1 . . . . .199 F2
  Wembley HA9 . . . . .88 B2
Greenhill Gdns, Nthlt. UB5 . . . .103 F2
Greenhill Gro, E12 . . . . .98 B4
Greenhill Pk, NW10 . . . . .106 E1
  Barnet EN5 . . . . .40 E5
Greenhill Rd, NW10 . . . . .106 E1
  Harrow HA1 . . . . .68 B6
Greenhill's Rents, EC1 . . . . .19 H1
Greenhills Ter, N1 off Baxter Rd . .94 A6
Greenhill Ter, SE18 . . . . .136 C5
  Northolt UB5 . . . . .103 F2
Greenhill Way, Har. HA1 . . . . . . .68 B6
  Wembley HA9 . . . . .88 B2
Greenhithe Cl, Sid. DA15 . . . . . .157 H7
Greenholm Rd, SE9 . . . . .156 E5
Green Hundred Rd, SE15 . . . . . . .37 J6
Greenhurst Rd, SE27 . . . . .169 G5
Greening St, SE2 . . . . .138 C4
Greenland Cres, Sthl. UB2 . . . . .122 C3
Greenland Ms, SE8
  off Trundleys Rd 133 G5
Greenland Pl, NW1
  off Greenland Rd 110 B1
Greenland Quay, SE16 . . . . .133 G4
Greenland Rd, NW1 . . . . .110 C1
  Barnet EN5 . . . . .39 J6
Greenland St, NW1
  off Camden High St 110 B1
Green La, E4 . . . . .46 E3
  NW4 .72 A5
  SE9 . . . . .174 D2
  SE20 . . . . .171 G4
  SW16 . . . . .169 F7
  W7 .124 B2
  Chigwell IG7 . . . . .65 G2
  Chislehurst BR7 . . . . .174 E4
  Dagenham RM8 . . . . .100 A1
  Edgware HA8 . . . . .54 A5
  Feltham TW13 . . . . .160 E5
  Harrow HA1 . . . . .86 B1
  Hounslow TW4 . . . . .142 B3
  Ilford IG1, IG3 . . . . .99 F2
  Morden SM4 . . . . .184 E6
  New Malden KT3 . . . . .182 C5
  Stanmore HA7 . . . . .52 E4
  Thornton Heath CR7 . . . . . . .187 G1
  Watford WD19 . . . . .50 C1
  West Molesey KT8 . . . . .179 H5
  Worcester Park KT4 . . . . . . .197 G1
Green La Gdns, Th.Hth. CR7 . . .187 J2

Green Las, N4 .....93 J1
N8 .....75 H1
N13 .....59 F6
N15 .....75 H1
N16 .....93 J3
N21 .....59 H1
Greenlaw Gdns, N.Mal. KT3 ..183 F7
Greenlawn La, Brent. TW8
off Ealing Rd 125 G4
Green Lawns, Ruis. HA4 .....84 C1
Greenlaw St, SE18 .....136 D3
Green Leaf Av, Wall. SM6 .....200 D4
Greenleaf Cl, SW2 off Tulse Hill .151 G7
Greenleafe Dr, Ilf. IG6 .....81 E4
Greenleaf Rd, E6
off Redclyffe Rd 115 J1
E17 .....77 J3
Greenlea Pk, SW19 .....185 G1
Green Man Gdns, W13 .....104 D7
Green Man La, W13 .....124 D1
Feltham TW14 .....142 A4
Green Man Pas, W13 .....104 D7
Green Man Roundabout, E11 .....79 F7
Greenman St, N1 .....93 J7
Greenmead Cl, SE25 .....188 D5
Green Moor Link, N21 .....43 H7
Greenmoor Rd, Enf. EN3 .....45 F2
Greenoak Pl, Barn. EN4 .....41 J2
Greenoak Way, SW19 .....166 A4
Greenock Rd, SW16 .....186 D1
W3 .....126 B3
★ Green Park, SW1 .....24 C4
Greenpark Ct, Wem. HA0 .....87 F7
Green Pk Way, Grnf. UB6 .....104 B1
Green Pt, E15 .....97 E6
Green Pond Cl, E17 .....77 J3
Green Pond Rd, E17 .....77 H3
Green Ride, Loug. IG10 .....47 G5
Green Rd, N14 .....42 B6
N20 .....57 F3
Greenroof Way, SE10 .....135 F3
Greens Cl, The, Loug. IG10 .....48 D2
Green's Ct, W1 .....17 H5
Green's End, SE18 .....136 E4
Greenshank Cl, E17
off Banbury Rd 61 H7
Greenshields Ind Est, E16 .....135 H1
Greenside, Bex. DA5 .....177 E1
Dagenham RM8 .....100 C1
Greenside Cl, N20 .....57 G2
SE6 .....172 D2
Greenside Rd, W12 .....127 G3
Croydon CR0 .....187 G7
Greenslade Rd, Bark. IG11 .....99 G7
Green Slip Rd, Barn. EN5 .....40 C2
Greenstead Av, Wdf.Grn. IG8 .....63 J7
Greenstead Cl, Wdf.Grn. IG8
off Greenstead Gdns 63 J6
Greenstead Gdns, SW15 .....147 G5
Woodford Green IG8 .....63 J6
Greensted Rd, Loug. IG10 .....48 B7
Greenstone Ms, E11 .....79 G6
Green St, E7 .....97 H6
E13 .....115 J1
W1 .....16 A5
Enfield EN3 .....45 F2
Sunbury-on-Thames TW16 .178 A1
GREEN STREET GREEN, Orp.
BR6 .....207 H6
Green Ter, EC1 .....11 F4
Green Vale, W5 .....105 J6
Bexleyheath DA6 .....158 D5
Greenvale Rd, SE9 .....156 C4
Green Verges, Stan. HA7 .....53 G7
Green Vw, Chess. KT9 .....195 J7
Greenview Av, Beck. BR3 .....189 H6
Croydon CR0 .....189 H6
Greenview Cl, W3 .....126 E1
Green Wk, NW4 .....72 A5
SE1 .....28 D6
Buckhurst Hill IG9 .....48 B7
Hampton TW12
off Orpwood Cl 161 F6
Southall UB2 .....123 G5
Woodford Green IG8 .....64 B6
Green Wk, The, E4 .....62 C1
Greenway, N14 .....58 E2
N20 .....56 D2
Green Way, SE9 .....156 A4
Greenway, SW20 .....183 J4
Green Way, Brom. BR2 .....192 B6
Greenway, Chis. BR7 .....174 D6
Dagenham RM8 .....100 C2
Harrow HA3 .....69 H5
Hayes UB4 .....102 B4
Pinner HA5 .....66 B2
Green Way, Sun. TW16 .....178 A4
Greenway, Wall. SM6 .....200 C4
Woodford Green IG8 .....63 J5
Greenway, The, NW9 .....70 D2
Harrow HA3 .....68 B1
Hounslow TW4 .....143 F4
Pinner HA5 .....67 G6
Greenway Av, E17 .....78 D4
Greenway Cl, N4 .....93 J2
N11 .....58 A6
N15 off Copperfield Dr .76 C4

Greenway Cl, N20 .....56 D2
NW9 .....70 D2
Greenway Gdns, NW9 .....70 D2
Croydon CR0 .....203 J3
Greenford UB6 .....103 G3
Harrow HA3 .....68 B2
Greenways, Beck. BR3 .....190 A4
Esher KT10 .....194 B4
Greenways, The, Twick. TW1
off South Western Rd 144 D6
Greenwell St, W1 .....9 E6
GREENWICH, SE10 .....134 D6
Greenwich Ch St, SE10 .....134 C6
Greenwich Cres, E6
off Swan App 116 B5
SE10 .....134 C5
Greenwich Foot Tunnel, E14 .134 C5
Greenwich High Rd, SE10 .....154 B1
Greenwich Ind Est, SE7 .....135 H4
Greenwich Mkt, SE10
off King William Wk 134 C6
★ Greenwich Park, SE10 .....134 D7
Greenwich Pk St, SE10 .....134 D5
★ Greenwich Pier, SE10 .....134 C6
Greenwich Quay, SE8 .....134 B6
Greenwich Shop Pk, SE7
off Bugsby's Way 135 H4
Greenwich S St, SE10 .....154 B1
Greenwich Vw Pl, E14 .....134 B3
Greenwood Av, Dag. RM10 .....101 H4
Enfield EN3 .....45 H2
Greenwood Cl, Mord. SM4 .....184 B4
Orpington BR5 .....193 H6
Sidcup DA15 off Hurst Rd ...176 A2
Thames Ditton KT7 .....194 D1
Greenwood Ct, SW1 .....33 F3
Greenwood Dr, E4 off Avril Way .62 C5
Greenwood Gdns, N13 .....59 H3
Ilford IG6 .....65 F7
Greenwood La, Hmptn. (Hmptn H.)
TW12 .....161 H5
Greenwood Pk, Kings.T. KT2 ...165 E7
Greenwood Pl, NW5
off Highgate Rd 92 B5
Greenwood Rd, E8 .....94 D6
E13 off Valetta Gro 115 F2
Croydon CR0 .....187 H7
Isleworth TW7 .....144 B3
Mitcham CR4 .....186 D3
Thames Ditton KT7 .....194 D1
Greenwoods, The, Har. (S.Har.)
HA2 .....85 J2
Greenwood Ter, NW10 .....106 D1
Green Wrythe Cres, Cars. SM5 ..199 H1
Green Wrythe La, Cars. SM5 ...185 G6
Greer Rd, Har. HA3 .....67 J1
Greet St, SE1 .....27 F2
Greg Cl, E10 .....78 C6
Gregor Ms, SE3 .....135 G7
Gregory Cres, SE9 .....156 A7
Gregory Pl, W8 .....22 A3
Gregory Rd, Rom. RM6 .....82 D4
Southall UB2 .....123 G3
Gregson Cl, Borwd. WD6 .....38 C1
Greig Cl, N8 .....74 E5
Greig Ter, SE17 .....35 H5
Grenaby Av, Croy. CR0 .....188 A7
Grenaby Rd, Croy. CR0 .....188 A7
Grenada Rd, SE7 .....135 J7
Grenade St, E14 .....113 J7
Grenadier St, E16 .....136 D1
Grena Gdns, Rich. TW9 .....145 J4
Grenard Cl, SE15 off Lisford St .152 C1
Grena Rd, Rich. TW9 .....145 J4
Grendon Gdns, Wem. HA9 .....88 A2
Grendon St, NW8 .....7 G5
Grenfell Cl, Borwd. WD6 .....38 C1
Grenfell Gdns, Har. HA3 .....69 H7
Grenfell Rd, W11 .....108 A7
Mitcham CR4 .....167 J6
Grenfell Twr, W11 .....108 A7
Grenfell Wk, W11 .....108 A7
Grennell Cl, Sutt. SM1 .....199 G2
Grennell Rd, Sutt. SM1 .....199 F2
Grenoble Gdns, N13 .....59 G6
Grenville Cl, N3 .....72 C1
Surbiton KT5 .....196 C1
Grenville Ct, SE19 off Lymer Av .170 C5
Grenville Gdns, Wdf.Grn. IG8 ...79 J1
Grenville Ms, N19
off Grenville Rd 92 E1
SW7 .....30 D1
Hampton TW12 .....161 H5
Grenville Pl, NW7 .....54 D5
SW7 .....22 C6
Grenville Rd, N19 .....92 E1
Grenville St, WC1 .....10 B6
Gresham Av, N20 .....57 J4
Gresham Cl, Bex. DA5 .....159 E6
Enfield EN2 .....43 J3
Gresham Dr, Rom. RM6 .....82 B5
Gresham Gdns, NW11 .....90 B1
Gresham Pl, N19 .....92 D2
Gresham Rd, E6 .....116 C2
E16 .....115 H6
NW10 .....88 D5
SE25 .....188 D4

Gresham Rd, SW9 .....151 G3
Beckenham BR3 .....189 H2
Edgware HA8 .....53 J6
Hampton TW12 .....161 G6
Hounslow TW3 .....143 J1
Gresham St, EC2 .....19 J3
Gresham Way, SW19 .....166 D3
Gresley Cl, E17 .....77 H6
N15 off Clinton Rd 76 A4
Gresley Rd, N19 .....92 C1
Gressenhall Rd, SW18 .....148 C6
Gresse St, W1 .....17 H2
Gresswell Cl, Sid. DA14 .....176 A3
Greswell St, SW6 .....148 A1
Gretton Rd, N17 .....60 B7
Greville Cl, Twick. TW1 .....144 E7
Greville Hall, NW6 .....6 B1
Greville Ms, NW6
off Greville Rd 108/109 E2
Greville Pl, NW6 .....6 B1
Greville Rd, E17 .....78 C4
NW6 .....6 A1
Richmond TW10 .....145 J6
Greville St, EC1 .....19 F2
Grey Cl, NW11 .....73 F6
Greycoat Pl, SW1 .....25 H6
Greycoat St, SW1 .....25 H6
Greycot Rd, Beck. BR3 .....172 A5
Grey Eagle St, E1 .....21 F1
Greyfell Cl, Stan. HA7
off Coverdale Cl 52/53 E5
Greyfriars Pas, EC1 .....19 H3
Greyhound Hill, NW4 .....71 G3
Greyhound La, SW16 .....168 D6
Greyhound Rd, N17 .....76 B3
NW10 .....107 H3
W6 .....128 A6
W14 .....128 A6
Sutton SM1 .....199 F5
Greyhound Ter, SW16 .....186 C1
Greys Pk Cl, Kes. BR2 .....205 J5
Greystead Rd, SE23 .....153 F7
Greystoke Av, Pnr. HA5 .....67 G3
Greystoke Gdns, W5 .....105 H4
Enfield EN2 .....42 D4
Greystoke Pk Ter, W5 .....105 G3
Greystoke Pl, EC4 .....19 E3
Greystone Gdns, Har. HA3 .....69 F6
Ilford IG6 .....81 F2
Greystone Path, E11
off Grove Rd 79 F7
Greyswood Av, N18 .....61 G6
Greyswood St, SW16 .....168 B6
Grierson Rd, SE23 .....153 G7
Griffin Cen, The, Felt. TW14 .142 B5
Griffin Cl, NW10 .....89 H5
Griffin Manor Way, SE28 .....137 G3
Griffin Rd, N17 .....76 B2
SE18 .....137 G5
Griffins Cl, N21 .....44 A7
Griffin Way, Sun. TW16 .....178 A2
Griffith Cl, Dag. RM8
off Gibson Rd 100 C1
Griffiths Cl, Wor.Pk. KT4 .....197 H2
Griffiths Rd, SW19 .....166 D7
Griggs App, Ilf. IG1 .....99 F2
Griggs Pl, SE1 .....28 E6
Griggs Rd, E10 .....78 C6
Grilse Cl, N9 .....61 E4
Grimsby Gro, E16 .....137 E1
Grimsby St, E2 .....13 G6
Grimsdyke Cres, Barn. EN5 .....39 J3
Grimsdyke Rd, Pnr. HA5 .....51 E7
Grimsel Path, SE5 .....35 H7
Grimshaw Cl, N6 .....74 A7
Grimston Rd, SW6 .....148 C2
Grimwade Av, Croy. CR0 .....202 D3
Grimwade Cl, SE15 .....153 F3
Grimwood Rd, Twick. TW1 .....144 C7
Grindall Cl, Croy. CR0
off Hillside Rd 201 H4
Grindal St, SE1 .....26 E4
Grindleford Av, N11 .....58 A2
Grindley Gdns, Croy. CR0 .....188 C6
Grinling Pl, SE8 .....134 A6
Grinstead Rd, SE8 .....133 H5
Grittleton Av, Wem. HA9 .....88 B6
Grittleton Rd, W9 .....108 D4
Grizedale Ter, SE23 .....171 E2
Grocer's Hall Ct, EC2 .....20 B4
Grogan Cl, Hmptn. TW12 .....161 F6
Groombridge Cl, Well. DA16 .158 A5
Groombridge Rd, E9 .....95 G2
Groom Cl, Brom. BR2 .....191 H4
Grooms Cres, SW18 .....149 G5
Groomfield Cl, SW17 .....168 A4
Groom Pl, SW1 .....24 C5
Grooms Dr, Pnr. HA5 .....66 A5
Grosmont Rd, SE18 .....137 J5
Grosse Way, SW15 .....147 H6
Grosvenor Av, N5 .....93 J5
SW14 .....146 E3
Carshalton SM5 .....199 J6
Harrow HA2 .....67 H6
Richmond TW10
off Grosvenor Rd 145 H5
Grosvenor Cl, Loug. IG10 .....48 E1

Grosvenor Cotts, SW1 .....32 B1
Grosvenor Ct, N14 .....42 C7
NW6 .....108 A1
Grosvenor Cres, NW9 .....70 A4
SW1 .....24 C4
Grosvenor Cres Ms, SW1 .....24 B4
Grosvenor Dr, Loug. IG10 .....49 E1
Grosvenor Est, SW1 .....33 J1
Grosvenor Gdns, E6 .....116 A3
N10 .....74 C3
N14 .....42 D5
NW2 .....89 J5
NW11 .....72 C6
SW1 .....24 D5
SW14 .....146 E3
Kingston upon Thames KT2 ..163 G6
Wallington SM6 .....200 C7
Woodford Green IG8 .....63 G6
Grosvenor Gdns Ms E, SW1 .....24 C5
Grosvenor Gdns Ms N, SW1 .....24 D6
Grosvenor Gdns Ms S, SW1 .....24 E6
Grosvenor Gate, W1 .....16 A6
Grosvenor Hill, SW19 .....166 B6
W1 .....16 D5
Grosvenor Pk, SE5 .....35 J6
Grosvenor Pk Rd, E17 .....78 A5
Grosvenor Path, Loug. IG10 .....49 E1
Grosvenor Pl, SW1 .....24 C4
Grosvenor Ri E, E17 .....78 B5
Grosvenor Rd, E6 .....116 A1
E7 .....97 H6
E10 .....96 C1
E11 .....79 G5
N3 .....56 C7
N9 .....60 E1
N10 .....74 B1
SE25 .....188 D4
SW1 .....32 D5
W4 .....126 B5
W7 .....124 D1
Belvedere DA17 .....139 G6
Bexleyheath DA6 .....158 D5
Borehamwood WD6 .....38 A3
Brentford TW8 .....125 G6
Dagenham RM8 .....101 F3
Hounslow TW3 .....143 F3
Ilford IG1 .....99 F3
Orpington BR5 .....193 H6
Richmond TW10 .....145 H5
Southall UB2 .....123 F3
Twickenham TW1 .....144 D7
Wallington SM6 .....200 B6
West Wickham BR4 .....204 B1
Grosvenor Sq, W1 .....16 C5
Grosvenor St, W1 .....16 D5
Grosvenor Ter, SE5 .....35 H7
Grosvenor Way, E5 .....95 F2
Grosvenor Wf Rd, E14 .....134 D4
Grote's Bldgs, SE3 .....155 E2
Grote's Pl, SE3 .....154 E2
Groton Rd, SW18 .....167 E2
Grotto Pas, W1 .....16 C1
Grotto Rd, Twick. TW1 .....162 C2
Grove, The, E15 .....96 E6
N3 .....72 D1
N4 .....75 F7
N6 .....92 A1
N8 .....74 D5
N13 .....59 G5
N14 .....42 C5
NW9 .....70 D5
NW11 .....72 B7
W5 .....125 G1
Bexleyheath DA6 .....158 D4
Edgware HA8 .....54 B4
Enfield EN2 .....43 G2
Greenford UB6 .....103 H4
Isleworth TW7 .....144 B1
Sidcup DA14 .....177 E4
Stanmore HA7 .....52 D2
Teddington TW11 .....162 D4
Twickenham TW1
off Bridge Rd 144/145 E6
Walton-on-Thames KT12 ...178 B7
West Wickham BR4 .....204 B3
Grove Av, N3 .....56 D7
N10 .....74 C2
W7 .....104 B6
Pinner HA5 .....67 E4
Sutton SM1 .....198 D6
Twickenham TW1 .....162 C1
Grove Bk, Wat. WD19 .....50 D1
Grovebury Rd, SE2 .....138 B2
Grove Cl, N14 off Avenue Rd 42 B7
SE23 .....171 G1
Bromley BR2 .....205 G2
Feltham TW13 .....160 E4
Kingston upon Thames KT1 ..181 J4
Grove Cotts, SW3 .....31 H5
Grove Ct, SE3 .....155 F2
Barnet EN5 off High St 40 C3
East Molesey KT8
off Walton Rd 180 A5
Grove Cres, E18 .....79 F2
NW9 .....70 C4
Feltham TW13 .....160 E4
Kingston upon Thames KT1 ..181 H3

Grove Cres, Walt. KT12 ....178 B7
Grove Cres Rd, E15 ....96 D6
Grovedale Rd, N19 ....92 D2
Grove End, E18 *off Grove Hill* ..79 F2
  NW5 *off Chetwynd Rd* 92 B4
Grove End Gdns, NW8
  off Grove End Rd 109 G2
Grove End La, Esher KT10 ....194 A1
Grove End Rd, NW8 ....6 E2
Grove Fm Ct, Mitch. CR4
  off Brookfields Av 185 J4
Grove Footpath, Surb. KT5 ...181 H4
Grove Gdns, NW4 ....71 J4
  NW8 ....7 H4
  Dagenham RM10 ....101 J3
  Enfield EN3 ....45 G1
  Teddington TW11 ....162 D4
Grove Grn Rd, E11 ....96 C3
Grove Hall Ct, NW8 ....6 D1
Grove Hill, E18 ....79 F2
  Harrow HA1 ....68 B7
Grove Hill Rd, SE5 ....152 B3
  Harrow HA1 ....68 B7
Grove Ho Rd, N8 ....74 E4
Groveland Av, SW16 ....169 F7
Groveland Ct, EC4 ....20 A4
Groveland Rd, Beck. BR3 ....189 J3
Grovelands, W.Mol. KT8 .....179 G4
Grovelands Cl, SE5 ....152 B2
  Harrow HA2 ....85 H3
Grovelands Ct, N14 ....42 D7
Grovelands Rd, N13 ....59 F4
  N15 ....76 D6
  Orpington BR5 ....176 A7
Groveland Way, N.Mal. KT3 ..182 C5
Grove La, SE5 ....152 A1
  Chigwell IG7 ....65 J3
  Kingston upon Thames KT1 ..181 H4
Grove La Ter, SE5 *off Grove La* ..152 B3
Grove Mkt Pl, SE9 ....156 C6
Grove Ms, W6 ....127 J3
  W11 *off Portobello Rd* 108 C6
Grove Mill Pl, Cars. SM5 ....200 A3
GROVE PARK, SE12 ....173 G2
GROVE PARK, W4 ....126 B7
Grove Pk, E11 ....79 H6
  NW9 ....70 C4
  SE5 ....152 B2
Grove Pk Av, E4 ....62 B7
Grove Pk Br, W4 ....126 C7
Grove Pk Gdns, W4 ....126 B6
Grove Pk Ms, W4 ....126 C7
Grove Pk Rd, N15 ....76 B4
  SE9 ....173 J3
  W4 ....126 B7
Grove Pk Ter, W4 ....126 B6
Grove Pas, E2 ....113 E2
  Teddington TW11 ....162 D5
Grove Pl, NW3
  off Christchurch Hill 91 G4
  SW12 *off Cathles Rd* 150 B6
  W3 ....126 C1
  W5 *off The Grove* 125 G7
  Barking IG11
  off Clockhouse Av 117 F1
Grove Rd, E3 ....113 G1
  E4 ....62 B4
  E11 ....79 F7
  E17 ....78 B6
  E18 ....79 F2
  N11 ....58 B5
  N12 ....57 G5
  N15 ....76 B5
  NW2 ....89 J6
  SW13 ....147 F2
  SW19 ....167 F7
  W3 ....126 C1
  W5 ....105 G7
  Barnet EN4 ....41 H3
  Belvedere DA17 ....139 F6
  Bexleyheath DA7 ....159 J4
  Borehamwood WD6 ....38 A1
  Brentford TW8 ....125 F5
  East Molesey KT8 ....180 A4
  Edgware HA8 ....54 A6
  Hounslow TW3 ....143 H4
  Isleworth TW7 ....144 A1
  Mitcham CR4 ....186 B2
  Pinner HA5 ....67 F5
  Richmond TW10 ....145 J4
  Romford RM6 ....82 B7
  Surbiton KT6 ....181 G5
  Sutton SM1 ....199 E6
  Thornton Heath CR7 .....187 G4
  Twickenham TW2 ....162 A2
Groveside Cl, W3 ....106 A6
  Carshalton SM5 ....199 H2
Groveside Rd, E4 ....62 E2
Grovestile Waye, Felt. TW14 ..141 G7
Grove St, N18 ....60 C6
  SE8 ....133 J4
Grove Ter, NW5 ....92 B3
  Teddington TW11 ....162 D4
Grove Ter Ms, NW5
  off Grove Ter 92 B3
Grove Vale, SE22 ....152 B4
  Chislehurst BR7 ....174 D6

Grove Vil, E14 ....114 B7
Groveway, SW9 ....151 F1
  Dagenham RM8 ....100 D4
Grove Way, Esher KT10 .....179 J7
  Wembley HA9 ....88 B5
Grovewood, Rich. TW9
  off Sandycombe Rd 146 A1
Grovewood Pl, Wdf.Grn. IG8 ..64 C6
Grummant Rd, SE15 ....152 C1
Grundy St, E14 ....114 B6
Gruneisen Rd, N3 ....56 E7
★ Guards Mus, SW1 ....25 G4
Gubyon Av, SE24 ....151 H5
Guerin Sq, E3 ....113 J3
Guernsey Cl, Houns. TW5 ....143 G1
Guernsey Gro, SE24 ....151 J7
Guernsey Rd, E11 ....96 D1
Guibal Rd, SE12 ....155 H7
Guildersfield Rd, SW16 .....168 E7
Guildford Gro, SE10 ....154 B1
Guildford Rd, E6 ....116 B6
  E17 ....78 C1
  SW8 ....151 E1
  Croydon CR0 ....188 A4
  Ilford IG3 ....99 H2
Guildford Way, Wall. SM6 ...201 E5
★ Guildhall, The, EC2 ....20 B3
★ Guildhall Art Gall, Guildhall Lib,
  EC2 ....20 A3
Guildhall Bldgs, EC2
  off Basinghall St 112 A6
Guildhall Yd, EC2 ....20 B3
Guildhouse St, SW1 ....33 F1
Guild Rd, SE7 ....136 A5
  Erith DA8 .... (note)
Guildsway, E17 ....77 J1
Guilford Av, Surb. KT5 .....181 J5
Guilford Pl, WC1 ....10 B5
Guilford St, WC1 ....10 B6
Guilford Vil, Surb. KT5
  off Alpha Rd 181 J6
Guilsborough Cl, NW10 ....88 E7
Guinness Cl, E9 ....95 H7
  Hayes UB3 ....121 G3
Guinness Sq, SE1 ....36 D1
Guinness Trust Bldgs, SE1
  off Snowsfields 132 B2
  SE11 ....35 H3
  SW3 ....31 J2
  SW9 ....151 H4
Guinness Trust Est, N16
  off Holmleigh Rd 94 B1
Guion Rd, SW6 ....148 C2
Gulland Wk, N1
  off Clephane Rd 93 J6
Gull Cl, Wall. SM6 ....200 E7
Gulliver Rd, Nthlt. UB5 ....103 F1
Gulliver Rd, Sid. DA15 .....175 H3
Gulliver St, SE16 ....133 J3
Gulston Wk, SW3 ....32 A2
Gumleigh Rd, W5 ....125 F4
Gumley Gdns, Islw. TW7 ....144 D3
Gumping Rd, Orp. BR5 .....207 F2
Gundulph Rd, Brom. BR2 ....191 J3
Gunmakers La, E3 ....113 H1
Gunnell Cl, SE26 ....170 D6
  Croydon CR0 ....188 D6
Gunner La, SE18 ....136 D5
GUNNERSBURY, W4 ....126 B4
Gunnersbury Av, W3 ....126 A3
  W4 ....126 A3
  W5 ....125 J1
Gunnersbury Cl, W4
  off Grange Rd 126 B5
Gunnersbury Ct, W3
  off Bollo La 126 B2
Gunnersbury Cres, W3 ....126 A2
Gunnersbury Dr, W5 ....125 J2
Gunnersbury Gdns, W3 ....126 A2
Gunnersbury La, W3 ....126 A3
Gunnersbury Ms, W4
  off Chiswick High Rd 126 B5
★ Gunnersbury Park, W3 .....125 J4
Gunnersbury Pk, W3 ....125 J4
  W5 ....125 J4
★ Gunnersbury Park Mus & Art Cen,
  W3 ....126 A3
Gunners Gro, E4 ....62 C3
Gunners Rd, SW18 ....167 G2
Gunnery Ter, SE18 ....137 F4
Gunning St, SE18 ....137 H4
Gunpowder Sq, EC4 ....19 F3
Gunstor Rd, N16 ....94 B4
Gun St, E1 ....21 E2
Gunter Gro, SW10 ....30 C6
  Edgware HA8 ....70 D1
Gunterstone Rd, W14 ....128 B4
Gunthorpe St, E1 ....21 G2
Gunton Rd, E5 ....95 E3
  SW17 ....168 A6
Gunwhale Cl, SE16 ....133 G1
Gurdon Rd, SE7 ....135 G5
Gurnell Gro, W13 ....104 C4
Gurney Cl, E15
  off Gurney Rd 96/97 E5
  E17 ....77 G1
  Barking IG11 ....98 E6

Gurney Cres, Croy. CR0 .....201 F1
Gurney Dr, N2 ....73 F5
Gurney Rd, E15 ....96 E5
  SW6 ....149 F3
  Carshalton SM5 ....200 A4
  Northolt UB5 ....102 B3
Guthrie St, SW3 ....31 G3
Gutter La, EC2 ....20 A3
Guyatt Gdns, Mitch. CR4
  off Ormerod Gdns 186 A2
Guy Barnett Gro, SE3
  off Casterbridge Rd 155 G3
Guy Rd, Wall. SM6 ....200 D3
Guyscliff Rd, SE13 ....154 C5
Guy St, SE1 ....28 C3
Gwalior Rd, SW15
  off Felsham Rd 148 A3
Gwendolen Av, SW15 ....148 A5
Gwendolen Cl, SW15 ....148 A5
Gwendoline Av, E13 ....115 H1
Gwendwr Rd, W14 ....128 B5
Gwillim Cl, Sid. DA15 .....158 A5
Gwydor Rd, Beck. BR3 .....189 G4
Gwydyr Rd, Brom. BR2 .....191 F3
Gwyn Cl, SW6 ....129 F7
Gwynne Av, Croy. CR0 .....189 G7
Gwynne Cl, W4
  off Pumping Sta Rd 127 F6
Gwynne Pk Av, Wdf.Grn. IG8 ..64 C6
Gwynne Pl, WC1 ....10 D4
Gwynne Rd, SW11 ....149 G2
Gylcote Cl, SE5 ....152 A4
Gyles Pk, Stan. HA7 ....69 F1
Gyllyngdune Gdns, Ilf. IG3 ..99 J2
Gypsy Cor, W3 ....106 D5

H

Haarlem Rd, W14 ....128 A3
Haberdasher Est, N1
  off Haberdasher St 112 A3
Haberdasher Pl, N1 ....12 C3
Haberdasher St, N1 ....12 C3
Habgood Rd, Loug. IG10 ....48 B3
Haccombe Rd, SW19
  off Haydons Rd 167 F6
HACKBRIDGE, Wall. SM6 .....200 B2
Hackbridge Grn, Wall. SM6 ..200 A2
Hackbridge Pk Gdns, Cars.
  SM5 ....200 A2
Hackbridge Rd, Wall. SM6 ...200 A2
Hackford Rd, SW9 ....151 F1
Hackford Wk, SW9 ....151 F1
Hackforth Cl, Barn. EN5 ....39 H5
Hackington Cres, Beck. BR3 ..172 A6
HACKNEY, E8 ....94 E6
★ Hackney City Fm, E2 ....13 H2
Hackney Cl, Borwd. WD6 ....38 D5
Hackney Gro, E8
  off Reading La 94/95 E6
★ Hackney Marsh, E9 ....95 H1
★ Hackney Mus, E8 ....95 E6
Hackney Rd, E2 ....13 F4
HACKNEY WICK, E9 ....96 A5
Hackworth Pt, E3
  off Rainhill Way 114 B3
Hadar Cl, N20 ....56 E1
Hadden Rd, SE28 ....137 H3
Hadden Way, Grnf. UB6 ....86 A6
Haddington Rd, Brom. BR1 ...172 D3
Haddon Cl, Borwd. WD6 ....38 A3
  Enfield EN1 ....44 D6
  New Malden KT3 ....183 F5
Haddonfield, SE8 ....133 G4
Haddon Gro, Sid. DA15 .....158 A7
Haddon Rd, Sutt. SM1 .....198 E4
Haddo St, SE10 ....134 B6
Hadfield Cl, Sthl. UB1
  off Adrienne Av 103 F3
Hadfield Rd, Stai. (Stanw.)
  TW19 ....140 A6
Hadleigh Cl, E1 *off Mantus Rd* ..113 F4
  SW20 ....184 C2
Hadleigh Rd, N9 ....44 E7
Hadleigh St, E2 ....113 F4
Hadleigh Wk, E6 ....116 B6
HADLEY, Barn. EN5 ....40 C2
Hadley Cl, N21 ....43 G6
Hadley Common, Barn. EN5 ....40 D2
Hadley Gdns, W4 ....126 D5
  Southall UB2 ....123 F5
Hadley Grn, Barn. EN5 ....40 C2
Hadley Grn Rd, Barn. EN5 .....40 C2
Hadley Grn W, Barn. EN5 .....40 C2
Hadley Gro, Barn. EN5 ....40 B2
Hadley Highstone, Barn. EN5 ..40 C1
Hadley Ridge, Barn. EN5 .....40 C3
Hadley Rd, Barn. (New Barn.)
  EN5 ....41 H4
  Belvedere DA17 ....139 F4
  Mitcham CR4 ....186 D4
Hadley St, NW1 ....92 B6
Hadley Way, N21 ....43 G6
Hadlow Pl, SE19 ....170 D7
Hadlow Rd, Sid. DA14 .....176 A4
  Welling DA16 ....138 C7

Hadrian Ct, Sutt. SM2
  off Stanley Rd 198/199 E7
Hadrian Est, E2 ....13 J2
Hadrian Ms, N7 *off Roman Way* ..93 F7
Hadrians Ride, Enf. EN1 ....44 C5
Hadrian St, SE10 ....134 E5
Hadrian Way, Stai. (Stanw.)
  TW19 ....140 B7
Hadyn Pk Rd, W12 ....127 G2
Hafer Rd, SW11 ....149 J4
Hafton Rd, SE6 ....173 E1
Haggard Rd, Twick. TW1 ....144 E7
HAGGERSTON, E2 ....13 G1
Haggerston Rd, E8 ....94 C7
Hague St, E2 ....13 J4
Ha-Ha Rd, SE18 ....136 C6
Haig Pl, Mord. SM4
  off Green La 184 D6
Haig Rd, Stan. HA7 ....53 F5
Haig Rd E, E13 ....115 J3
Haig Rd W, E13 ....115 J3
Haigville Gdns, Ilf. IG6 ....81 E4
Hailes Cl, SW19 *off North Rd* ..167 F6
Haileybury Av, Enf. EN1 ....44 C6
Hailey Rd, Erith DA18 ....139 G2
Hailsham Av, SW2 ....169 F2
Hailsham Cl, Surb. KT6 .....181 G7
Hailsham Dr, Har. HA1 ....68 A3
Hailsham Rd, SW17 ....168 A6
Hailsham Ter, N18 ....59 J5
Haimo Rd, SE9 ....156 A5
HAINAULT, Ilf. IG6 ....65 H7
Hainault Ct, E17 ....78 D4
Hainault Gore, Rom. RM6 ....83 E5
Hainault Gro, Chig. IG7 ....65 F4
Hainault Rd, E11 ....96 C1
  Chigwell IG7 ....65 G3
  Romford RM5 ....83 J2
  Romford (Chad.Hth) RM6 ....83 F6
  Romford (Lt.Hth) RM6 .....82 B3
Hainault St, SE9 ....175 E1
  Ilford IG1 ....99 E2
Haines Wk, Mord. SM4
  off Dorchester Rd 184/185 E7
Hainford Cl, SE4 ....153 G4
Haining Cl, W4
  off Wellesley Rd 126 A5
Hainthorpe Rd, SE27 ....169 H3
Hainton Cl, E1 ....113 E6
Halberd Ms, E5
  off Knightland Rd 94/95 E2
Halbutt Gdns, Dag. RM9 .....101 F3
Halbutt St, Dag. RM9 .....101 F4
Halcomb St, N1 ....112 B1
Halcot Av, Bexh. DA6 ....159 H5
Halcrow St, E1
  off Newark St 112/113 E5
Haldane Cl, N10 ....58 B7
Haldane Pl, SW18 ....166 E1
Haldane Rd, E6 ....116 A3
  SE28 ....118 D7
  SW6 ....128 C7
  Southall UB1 ....103 J6
Haldan Rd, E4 ....62 C6
Haldon Cl, Chig. IG7
  off Arrowsmith Rd 65 H5
Haldon Rd, SW18 ....148 C5
Hale, The, E4 ....62 D7
  N17 ....76 D3
Hale Cl, E4 ....62 C3
  Edgware HA8 ....54 C5
  Orpington BR6 ....207 F4
Hale Dr, NW7 ....54 C6
HALE END, E4 ....62 D6
Hale End Cl, Ruis. HA4 ....66 A6
Hale End Rd, E4 ....62 D6
  E17 ....78 D1
  Woodford Green IG8 ....62 D7
Halefield Rd, N17 ....76 D1
Hale Gdns, N17 ....76 D3
  W3 ....126 A1
Hale Gro Gdns, NW7 ....54 D5
Hale La, NW7 ....54 D5
  Edgware HA8 ....54 B4
Hale Path, SE27 ....169 H4
Hale Rd, E6 ....116 B4
  N17 ....76 D3
Halesowen Rd, Mord. SM4 ...184 E7
Hales St, SE8
  off Deptford High St 134 A7
Hale St, E14 ....114 B7
Halesworth Cl, E5
  off Theydon Rd 95 F2
Halesworth Rd, SE13 ....154 B3
Hale Wk, W7 ....104 B5
Haley Rd, NW4 ....71 J6
Half Acre, Brent. TW8 .....125 G6
Half Acre Rd, W7 ....124 B1
Half Moon Ct, EC1 ....19 J2
Half Moon Cres, N1 ....10 D1
Half Moon La, SE24 ....151 J6
Half Moon Pas, E1 ....21 G4
Half Moon St, W1 ....24 E1
Halford Cl, Edg. HA8 ....70 B2
Halford Rd, E10 ....78 D5
  SW6 ....128 D6
  Richmond TW10 ....145 H5

Halfway St, Sid. DA15 **157** G7
Haliburton Rd, Twick. TW1 **144** D5
Haliday Wk, N1
off Balls Pond Rd **94** A6
Halidon Cl, E9 *off Urswick Rd* **95** F5
Halifax Rd, Enf. EN2 **43** J2
Greenford UB6 **103** H1
Halifax St, SE26 **171** E4
Halifield Dr, Belv. DA17 **138** E3
Haling Gro, S.Croy. CR2 **201** J7
Haling Pk, S.Croy. CR2 **201** J6
Haling Pk Gdns, S.Croy. CR2 **201** H6
Haling Pk Rd, S.Croy. CR2 **201** H5
Haling Rd, S.Croy. CR2 **202** A6
Halkin Arc, SW1 **24** B5
Halkin Ms, SW1 **24** B5
Halkin Pl, SW1 **24** B5
Halkin St, SW1 **24** C4
Hall, The, SE3 **155** G3
Hallam Cl, Chis. BR7 **174** C5
Hallam Gdns, Pnr. HA5 **51** E7
Hallam Ms, W1 **16** E1
Hallam Rd, N15 **75** H4
SW13 **147** H3
Hallam St, W1 **8** E6
Hall Av, N18 *off Weir Hall Av* **60** A6
Hall Cl, W5 **105** H5
Hall Ct, Tedd. TW11 **162** C5
Hall Dr, SE26 **171** F5
W7 **104** B6
Halley Gdns, SE13 **154** D4
Halley Rd, E7 **97** J6
E12 **98** A6
Halley St, E14 **113** H5
Hall Fm Cl, Stan. HA7 **52** E4
Hall Fm Dr, Twick. TW2 **144** A7
Hallfield Est, W2 **14** C4
Hall Gdns, E4 **61** J4
Hall Gate, NW8 **6** D3
Halliards, The, Walt. KT12
off Felix Rd **178** A6
Halliday Sq, Sthl. UB2 **124** A1
Halliford St, N1 **93** J7
Hallingbury Ct, E17 **78** B3
Halliwell Rd, SW2 **151** F6
Halliwick Rd, N10 **74** A1
Hall La, E4 **61** H5
E4 (Junct) **61** H5
NW4 **71** G1
Hayes UB3 **121** G7
Hallmark Trd Est, NW10
off Great Cen Way **88** C4
Hallmead Rd, Sutt. SM1 **198** E3
Hall Oak Wk, NW6
off Barlow Rd **90** C6
Hallowell Av, Croy. CR0 **200** E4
Hallowell Cl, Mitch. CR4 **186** A3
Hallowes Cres, Wat. WD19
off Hayling Rd **50** A3
Hallowfield Way, Mitch. CR4 **185** G4
★ **Hall Pl**, Bex. DA5 **159** J6
Hall Pl, W2 **6** E6
Hall Pl Cres, Bex. DA5 **159** J5
Hall Rd, E6 **116** C1
E15 **96** D4
NW8 **6** D4
Isleworth TW7 **144** A5
Romford (Chad.Hth) RM6 **82** C6
Hall St, EC1 **11** H3
N12 **57** F5
Hallsville Rd, E16 **115** F6
Hallswelle Rd, NW11 **72** C5
Hall Twr, W2 **15** F1
Hall Vw, SE9 **174** A2
Hallywell Cres, E6 **116** C5
Halons Rd, SE9 **156** D7
Halpin Pl, SE17 **36** C2
Halsbrook Rd, SE3 **156** A3
Halsbury Cl, Stan. HA7 **52** E4
Halsbury Rd, W12 **127** H1
Halsbury Rd E, Nthlt. UB5 **85** J4
Halsbury Rd W, Nthlt. UB5 **85** H5
Halsend, Hayes UB3 **122** B1
Halsey Ms, SW3 **31** J1
Halsey St, SW3 **31** J1
Halsham Cres, Bark. IG11 **99** J6
Halsmere Rd, SE5 **151** H1
Halstead Cl, Croy. CR0
off Charles St **201** J3
Halstead Ct, N1 **12** C2
Halstead Gdns, N21 **60** A1
Halstead Rd, E11 **79** G5
N21 **59** J1
Enfield EN1 **44** B4
Halston Cl, SW11 **149** J6
Halstow Rd, NW10 **108** A3
SE10 **135** G5
Halsway, Hayes UB3 **122** A1
Halter Cl, Borwd. WD6
off Clydesdale Cl **38** D5
Halton Cl, N11
off Colney Hatch La **57** J6
Halton Cross St, N1 **111** H1
Halton Pl, N1 *off Dibden St* **111** J1
Halton Rd, N1 **93** H7
Halt Robin La, Belv. DA17
off Halt Robin Rd **139** H4
Halt Robin Rd, Belv. DA17 **139** G4
HAM, Rich. TW10 **163** G3
Ham, The, Brent. TW8 **125** F7
Hambalt Rd, SW4 **150** C5
Hamble Ct, Tedd. TW11 **163** G7
Hambledon Gdns, SE25 **188** C3
Hambledon Pl, SE21 **170** B1
Hambledon Rd, SW18 **148** C7
Hambledown Rd, Sid. DA15 **157** G7
Hamble St, SW6 **149** E3
Hambleton Cl, Wor.Pk. KT4
off Cotswold Way **197** J2
Hamble Wk, Nthlt. UB5
off Brabazon Rd **103** G2
Hambridge Way, SW2 **151** G7
Hambro Av, Brom. BR2 **205** G1
Hambrook Rd, SE25 **188** E3
Hambro Rd, SW16 **168** D6
Hambrough Rd, Sthl. UB1 **122** E1
Ham Cl, Rich. TW10 **163** F3
Ham Common, Rich. TW10 **163** J4
Ham Cft Cl, Felt. TW13 **160** A3
Hamden Cres, Dag. RM10 **101** H3
Hamel Cl, Har. HA3 **69** G3
Hamelin St, E14
off St. Leonards Rd **114** C6
Hameway, E6 **116** D4
Ham Fm Rd, Rich. TW10 **163** G4
Hamfrith Rd, E15 **97** F6
Ham Gate Av, Rich. TW10 **163** G3
★ **Ham Ho**, Rich. TW10 **163** F1
Hamilton Av, N9 **44** D7
Ilford IG6 **81** E4
Surbiton KT6 **196** B1
Sutton SM3 **198** B2
Hamilton Cl, N17 **76** C3
NW8 **6** E4
SE16 *off Somerford Way* **133** H2
Barnet EN4 **41** H4
Stanmore HA7 **52** C2
Hamilton Ct, W5 **105** J7
W9 **6** C3
Hamilton Cres, N13 **59** G4
Harrow HA2 **85** F3
Hounslow TW3 **143** H5
Hamilton Gdns, NW8 **6** D3
Hamilton La, N5
off Hamilton Pk **93** H4
Hamilton Ms, SW18
off Merton Rd **166** D1
W1 **24** D3
Hamilton Pk, N5 **93** H4
Hamilton Pk W, N5 **93** H4
Hamilton Pl, N19
off Wedmore St **92** D3
W1 **24** C2
Sunbury-on-Thames TW16 **160** B7
Hamilton Rd, E15 **115** E3
E17 **77** H2
N2 **73** F3
N9 **44** D7
NW10 **89** G5
NW11 **72** A7
SE27 **170** A4
SW19 **167** E7
W4 **126** E2
W5 **105** H7
Barnet EN4 **41** H4
Bexleyheath DA7 **159** E2
Brentford TW8 **125** G6
Harrow HA1 **68** B5
Hayes UB3 **102** B7
Ilford IG1 **98** E4
Sidcup DA15 **176** A4
Southall UB1 **123** F1
Thornton Heath CR7 **188** A3
Twickenham TW2 **162** B1
Watford WD19 **50** B3
Hamilton Rd Ind Est, SE27 **170** A4
Hamilton Sq, N12
off Sandringham Gdns **57** G6
SE1 **28** C3
Hamilton St, SE8
off Deptford High St **134** A6
Hamilton Ter, NW8 **6** D3
Hamilton Way, N3 **56** D6
N13 **59** H4
Hamlea Cl, SE12 **155** F5
Hamlet, The, SE5 **152** A3
Hamlet Cl, SE13
off Old Rd **154/155** E4
Hamlet Gdns, W6 **127** G4
Hamleton Ter, Dag. RM9
off Flamstead Rd **100** C7
Hamlet Rd, SE19 **170** C7
Hamlet Sq, NW2 **90** B3
Hamlets Way, E3 **113** J4
Hamlet Way, SE1 **28** C3
★ **Hamleys**, W1 **17** F5
Hamlin Cres, Pnr. HA5 **66** C5
Hamlyn Cl, Edg. HA8 **53** H3
Hamlyn Gdns, SE19 **170** B7
Hammelton Grn, SW9
off Cromwell Rd **151** H1
Hammelton Rd, Brom. BR1 **191** F1
Hammers La, NW7 **55** G5
HAMMERSMITH, W6 **127** J5
Hammersmith Br, SW13 **127** H6
W6 **127** H6
Hammersmith Br Rd, W6 **127** J5
Hammersmith Bdy, W6 **127** J4
Hammersmith Flyover, W6 **127** J5
Hammersmith Gro, W6 **127** J3
Hammersmith Rd, W6 **128** A4
W14 **128** A4
Hammersmith Ter, W6 **127** G5
Hammet Cl, Hayes UB4 **102** D5
Hammett St, EC3 **21** F5
Hammond Av, Mitch. CR4 **186** B2
Hammond Cl, Barn. EN5 **40** B5
Greenford UB6
off Lilian Board Way **86** A5
Hampton TW12 **179** G1
Hammond Rd, Enf. EN1 **45** E2
Southall UB2 **123** E3
Hammonds Cl, Dag. RM8 **100** C3
Hammond St, NW5 **92** C6
Hammond Way, SE28
off Oriole Way **118** B7
Hamonde Cl, Edg. HA8 **54** B2
Hamond Sq, N1 *off Hoxton St* **112** B2
Ham Pk Rd, E7 **97** F7
E15 **97** F7
Hampden Av, Beck. BR3 **189** H2
Hampden Cl, NW1 **9** J2
Hampden Gurney St, W1 **15** J4
Hampden La, N17 **76** C1
Hampden Rd, N8 **75** G4
N10 **58** A7
N17 **76** D1
N19 *off Holloway Rd* **92** D2
Beckenham BR3 **189** H2
Harrow HA3 **67** J1
Kingston upon Thames KT1 **182** A3
Hampden Sq, N14
off Osidge La **58** B1
Hampden Way, N14 **58** B2
Hampshire Cl, N18
off Berkshire Gdns **60/61** E5
Hampshire Hog La, W6
off King St **127** H4
Hampshire Rd, N22 **59** F7
Hampshire St, NW5
off Torriano Av **92** D6
Hampson Way, SW8 **151** F1
HAMPSTEAD, NW3 **91** G4
Hampstead Av, Wdf.Grn. IG8 **64** D7
Hampstead Cl, SE28 **138** B1
Hampstead Gdns, NW11 **72** D6
Romford (Chad.Hth) RM6 **82** B5
HAMPSTEAD GARDEN SUBURB,
N2 **73** F5
Hampstead Grn, NW3 **91** H5
Hampstead Gro, NW3 **91** F3
★ **Hampstead Heath**, NW3 **91** G2
Hampstead Hts, N2 **73** F4
Hampstead High St, NW3 **91** F4
Hampstead Hill Gdns, NW3 **91** G4
Hampstead La, N6 **73** G7
NW3 **73** G7
Hampstead Rd, NW1 **9** F1
Hampstead Sq, NW3 **91** F3
Hampstead Wk, E3
off Waterside Cl **113** J1
Hampstead Way, NW11 **91** F1
HAMPTON, TW12 **179** H1
Hampton Cl, N11
off Balmoral Av **58** B5
NW6 **108** D3
SW20 **165** J7
Hampton Ct, N1 *off Upper St* **93** H6
Hampton Ct Av, E.Mol. KT8 **180** A5
Hampton Ct Cres, E.Mol. KT8 **180** A3
★ **Hampton Court Palace & Pk**,
E.Mol. KT8 **180** B3
Hampton Ct Par, E.Mol. KT8
off Creek Rd **180** B4
Hampton Ct Rd, E.Mol. KT8 **180** C3
Hampton TW12 **179** J2
Kingston upon Thames KT1 **180** C3
Hampton Ct Way, E.Mol. KT8 **180** B6
Thames Ditton KT7 **194** B2
Hampton Fm Ind Est, Felt.
TW13 **161** F3
HAMPTON HILL, Hmptn. TW12 **161** J6
Hampton Hill Business Pk, Hmptn.
TW12 *off Wellington Rd* **161** J5
Hampton La, Felt. TW13 **161** E4
Hampton Mead, Loug. IG10 **48** E3
Hampton Ms, NW10
off Minerva Rd **106** D3
Hampton Ri, Har. HA3 **69** H6
Hampton Rd, E4 **61** J5
E7 **97** H5
E11 **96** D1
Croydon CR0 **187** J6
Hampton (Hmptn H.) TW12 **162** A5
Ilford IG1 **99** E4
Teddington TW11 **162** A5
Twickenham TW2 **162** A3
Worcester Park KT4 **197** G2
Hampton Rd E, Felt. TW13 **161** F3
Hampton Rd W, Felt. TW13 **160** E2
Hampton St, SE1 **35** H2
Hampton St, SE17 **35** H2
HAMPTON WICK, Kings.T. KT1 **181** E1
Ham Ridings, Rich. TW10 **163** J5
Hamshades Cl, Sid. DA15 **175** J3
Ham St, Rich. TW10 **163** F2
Ham Vw, Croy. CR0 **189** H6
Ham Yd, W1 **17** H5
Hanah Ct, SW19 **166** A7
Hanameel St, E16 **135** G1
Hana Ms, E5 *off Goulton Rd* **95** F4
Hanbury Cl, NW4 **71** J3
Hanbury Dr, E11
off High Rd Leytonstone **79** F7
N21 **43** F5
Hanbury Ms, N1 *off Mary St* **111** J1
Hanbury Rd, N17 **76** E2
W3 **126** B2
Hanbury St, E1 **21** F1
Hancock Ct, Borwd. WD6 **38** C1
Hancock Rd, E3 **114** C3
SE19 **170** A6
Handa Wk, N1 *off Clephane Rd* **94** A6
Hand Ct, WC1 **18** D2
Handcroft Rd, Croy. CR0 **187** H7
Handel Cl, Edg. HA8 **53** J6
Handel Pl, NW10
off Mitchellbrook Way **88** D6
Handel St, WC1 **10** A5
Handel Way, Edg. HA8 **54** A7
Handen Rd, SE12 **155** E5
Handforth Rd, SW9 **34** E7
Ilford IG1
off Winston Way **98/99** E3
Handley Gro, NW2 **90** A3
Handley Page Rd, Wall. SM6 **201** F7
Handley Rd, E9 **95** F7
Handowe Cl, NW4 **71** G4
Handside Cl, Wor.Pk. KT4
off Carters Cl **198** A1
Hands Wk, E16 **115** G6
Handsworth Av, E4 **62** D6
Handsworth Rd, N17 **76** A3
Handsworth Way, Wat. WD19
off Hayling Rd **50** A3
Handtrough Way, Bark. IG11
off Fresh Wf Rd **116/117** E2
Hanford Cl, SW18 **166** D1
Hanford Row, SW19 **165** J6
Hangar Ruding, Wat. WD19 **51** F3
Hanger Grn, W5 **106** A4
Hanger La, W5 **105** J4
Hanger Vale La, W5 **105** J6
Hanger Vw Way, W3 **106** A6
Hanging Sword All, EC4 **19** F4
Hankey Pl, SE1 **28** C4
Hankins La, NW7 **54** E3
Hanley Gdns, N4 **93** F1
Hanley Pl, Beck. BR3 **172** A7
Hanley Rd, N4 **93** E1
Hanmer Wk, N7
off Newington Barrow Way **93** F3
Hannah Cl, NW10 **88** C4
Beckenham BR3 **190** C3
Hannah Ct, N13 **59** F2
Hannah Mary Way, SE1 **37** J2
Hannah Ms, Wall. SM6 **200** C7
Hannay La, N8 **74** D7
Hannay Wk, SW16 **168** D2
Hannell Rd, SW6 **128** B7
Hannen Rd, SE27
off Norwood High St **169** H3
Hannibal Rd, E1 **113** F5
Staines (Stanw.) TW19 **140** A7
Hannibal Way, Croy. CR0 **201** F5
Hannington Rd, SW4 **150** B3
Hanover Av, E16 **135** G1
Feltham TW13 **160** A1
Hanover Cl, Rich. TW9 **126** A7
Sutton SM3 **198** C4
Hanover Ct, SE19
off Anerley Rd **170** D7
W12 *off Uxbridge Rd* **127** G1
Hanover Dr, Chis. BR7 **175** F4
Hanover Gdns, SE11 **34** E6
Ilford IG6 **65** F7
Hanover Gate, NW1 **7** H4
Hanover Gate Mans, NW1 **7** H5
Hanover Ho, Surb. KT6
off Lenelby Rd **196** A1
Hanover Pk, SE15 **152** D1
Hanover Pl, E3 *off Brokesley St* **113** J3
WC2 **18** B4
Hanover Rd, N15 **76** C4
NW10 **89** J7
SW19 **167** F7
Hanover Sq, W1 **17** E4
Hanover St, W1 **17** E4
Croydon CR0 *off Abbey Rd* **201** H3
Hanover Ter, NW1 **7** H4
Hanover Ter Ms, NW1 **7** H4
Hanover Way, Bexh. DA6 **158** D3
Hanover W Ind Est, NW10 **106** D2
Hanover Yd, N1 **11** H1
Hansard Ms, W14
off Holland Rd **128** A2
Hansart Way, Enf. EN2
off The Ridgeway **43** G1

Hanscomb Ms, SW4
  off Bromell's Rd 150 C4
Hans Cres, SW1 . . . . .23 J5
Hanselin Cl, Stan. HA7 . . . . . .52 C5
Hansen Dr, N21 . . . . .43 F5
Hanshaw Dr, Edg. HA8 . . . . . .70 D1
Hansler Gro, E.Mol. KT8 . . . .180 A4
Hansler Rd, SE22 . . . . .152 C5
Hansol Rd, Bexh. DA6 . . . . . .158 E5
Hanson Cl, SW12 . . . . .150 B7
  SW14 . . . . .146 C3
  Beckenham BR3 . . . . .172 B6
  Loughton IG10
    off Hanson Dr 49 F2
  West Drayton UB7 . . . . . . .120 C3
Hanson Dr, Loug. IG10 . . . . . .49 F2
Hanson Gdns, Sthl. UB1 . . . .123 E2
Hanson Grn, Loug. IG10
  off Hanson Dr 49 F2
Hanson St, W1 . . . . .17 F1
Hans Pl, SW1 . . . . .24 A5
Hans Rd, SW3 . . . . .23 J5
Hans St, SW1 . . . . .24 A6
Hanway Pl, W1 . . . . .17 H3
Hanway Rd, W7 . . . . .104 A6
Hanway St, W1 . . . . .17 H3
HANWELL, W7 . . . . .124 C1
HANWORTH, Felt. TW13 . . . .160 D4
Hanworth Rd, Felt. TW13 . . .160 B1
  Hampton TW12 . . . . .161 H6
  Hounslow TW3, TW4 . . . . .143 H3
  Sunbury-on-Thames TW16 . .160 A7
Hanworth Ter, Houns. TW3 . .143 H4
Hanworth Trd Est, Felt. TW13 161 E3
Hapgood Cl, Grnf. UB6 . . . . . .86 A5
Harads Pl, E1 . . . . .21 J1
Harben Rd, NW6 . . . . .91 F7
Harberson Rd, E15 . . . . .115 F1
  SW12 . . . . .168 B1
Harberton Rd, N19 . . . . .92 C1
Harbet Rd, E4 . . . . .61 G5
  N18 . . . . .61 G5
  W2 . . . . .15 F2
Harbex Cl, Bex. DA5 . . . . . . .159 H7
Harbinger Rd, E14 . . . . .134 B4
Harbledown Rd, SW6 . . . . . .148 D1
Harbord Cl, SE5
  off De Crespigny Pk 152 A2
Harbord St, SW6 . . . . .148 A1
Harborne Cl, Wat. WD19 . . . . .50 C5
Harborough Av, Sid. DA15 . . .157 H7
Harborough Rd, SW16 . . . . . .169 F4
Harbour Av, SW10 . . . . .149 F1
Harbour Ex Sq, E14 . . . . .134 B2
Harbour Reach, SW6
  off The Boulevard 149 F1
Harbour Rd, SE5 . . . . .151 J3
Harbour Yd, SW10
  off Harbour Av 149 F1
Harbridge Av, SW15 . . . . . . .147 F7
Harbut Rd, SW11 . . . . .149 G4
Harcombe Rd, N16 . . . . .94 B3
Harcourt Av, E12 . . . . .98 C4
  Edgware HA8 . . . . .54 C3
  Sidcup DA15 . . . . .158 C6
  Wallington SM6 . . . . .200 B4
Harcourt Cl, Islw. TW7 . . . . . .144 D3
Harcourt Fld, Wall. SM6 . . . . .200 B4
Harcourt Lo, Wall. SM6
  off Croydon Rd 200 B4
Harcourt Rd, E15 . . . . .115 F2
  N22 . . . . .74 D1
  SE4 . . . . .153 H4
  SW19 off Russell Rd 166 D7
  Bexleyheath DA6 . . . . .159 E4
  Thornton Heath CR7 . . . . .187 F6
  Wallington SM6 . . . . .200 B4
Harcourt St, W1 . . . . .15 H2
Harcourt Ter, SW10 . . . . .30 B4
Hardcastle Cl, Croy. CR0 . . . .188 D6
Hardcourts Cl, W.Wick. BR4 . .204 B3
Hardel Ri, SW2 . . . . .169 H2
Hardel Wk, SW2
  off Papworth Way 151 G7
Hardens Manorway, SE7 . . . .136 A3
Harders Rd, SE15 . . . . .152 E2
Hardess St, SE24
  off Herne Hill Rd 151 J3
Hardie Cl, NW10 . . . . .88 D5
Hardie Rd, Dag. RM10 . . . . . .101 J3
Harding Cl, SE17 . . . . .35 J5
  Croydon CR0 . . . . .202 C3
Hardinge Cres, SE18
  off Armstrong Rd 137 F3
Hardinge Rd, N18 . . . . .60 B5
  NW10 . . . . .107 H1
Hardinge St, E1 . . . . .113 F6
Harding Ho, Hayes UB3 . . . . .102 B6
Harding Rd, Bexh. DA7 . . . . .159 F2
Harding's Cl, Kings.T. KT2 . . .181 J1
Hardings La, SE20 . . . . .171 G6
Hardman Rd, SE7 . . . . .135 H5
  Kingston upon Thames KT2 .181 H2
Hardwick Cl, Stan. HA7 . . . . . .53 F5
Hardwicke Av, Houns. TW5 . .143 G1
Hardwicke Ms, WC1 . . . . .10 D4
Hardwicke Rd, N13 . . . . .58 E6

Hardwicke Rd, W4 . . . . .126 D4
  Richmond TW10 . . . . .163 F4
Hardwicke St, Bark. IG11 . . . .117 F1
Hardwick Grn, W13 . . . . .105 E5
Hardwick St, EC1 . . . . .11 F4
Hardwicks Way, SW18
  off Buckhold Rd 148 D5
Hardwidge St, SE1 . . . . .28 D3
Hardy Av, E16 off Wesley Av . .135 G1
  Ruislip HA4 . . . . .84 B5
Hardy Cl, SE16
  off Middleton Dr 133 G2
  Barnet EN5 . . . . .40 B6
  Pinner HA5 . . . . .66 D7
Hardy Rd, E4 . . . . .61 J6
  SE3 . . . . .135 F7
  SW19 . . . . .167 E7
Hardys Cl, E.Mol. KT8
  off Feltham Av 180 B4
Hardy Way, Enf. EN2 . . . . .43 G1
Hare & Billet Rd, SE3 . . . . . . .154 D1
Harebell Dr, E6 . . . . .116 D5
Harecastle Cl, Hayes UB4 . . . .102 E4
Hare Ct, EC4 . . . . .19 E4
Harecourt Rd, N1 . . . . .93 J6
Haredale Rd, SE24 . . . . .151 J4
Haredon Cl, SE23 . . . . .153 F7
Harefield, Esher KT10 . . . . . .194 B4
Harefield Cl, Enf. EN2 . . . . . . .43 G1
Harefield Ms, SE4 . . . . .153 J3
Harefield Rd, N8 . . . . .74 D5
  SE4 . . . . .153 J3
  SW16 . . . . .169 F7
  Sidcup DA14 . . . . .176 D2
Hare La, Esher (Clay.) KT10 . .194 B6
Hare Marsh, E2 . . . . .13 H5
Hare Pl, EC4 . . . . .19 F4
Hare Row, E2 . . . . .113 E2
Haresfield Rd, Dag. RM10 . . .101 G6
Hare St, SE18 . . . . .136 D3
Hare Wk, N1 . . . . .12 E2
Harewood Av, NW1 . . . . .7 H6
  Northolt UB5 . . . . .85 E7
Harewood Cl, Nthlt. UB5 . . . . .85 F7
Harewood Dr, Ilf. IG5 . . . . . . .80 C2
Harewood Pl, W1 . . . . .16 E4
Harewood Rd, SW19 . . . . . . .167 H6
  Isleworth TW7 . . . . .124 C7
  South Croydon CR2 . . . . . .202 B6
  Watford WD19 . . . . .50 B3
Harewood Row, NW1 . . . . . . .15 H1
Harewood Ter, Sthl. UB2 . . . .123 F4
Harfield Gdns, SE5 . . . . .152 B3
Harfield Rd, Sun. TW16 . . . . .178 D2
Harford Cl, E4 . . . . .46 B7
Harford Ms, N19
  off Wedmore St 92 D3
Harford Rd, E4 . . . . .46 B7
Harford St, E1 . . . . .113 H4
Harford Wk, N2 . . . . .73 G5
Hargood Cl, Har. HA3 . . . . .69 H6
Hargood Rd, SE3 . . . . .155 J1
Hargrave Pk, N19 . . . . .92 C2
Hargrave Pl, N7
  off Brecknock Rd 92 D5
Hargrave Rd, N19 . . . . .92 C2
Hargwyne St, SW9 . . . . .151 F3
Haringey Pk, N8 . . . . .74 E6
Haringey Pas, N4 . . . . .75 H6
  N8 . . . . .75 G4
Haringey Rd, N8 . . . . .74 E4
Harington Ter, N9 . . . . .60 A3
  N18 . . . . .60 A3
Harkett Cl, Har. HA3
  off Byron Rd 68 C2
Harkett Ct, Har. HA3 . . . . .68 C2
Harland Av, Croy. CR0 . . . . . .202 C3
  Sidcup DA15 . . . . .175 G3
Harland Cl, SW19 . . . . .184 E3
Harland Rd, SE12 . . . . .173 G1
Harlands Gro, Orp. BR6
  off Pinecrest Gdns 206/207 E4
Harlech Gdns, Houns. TW5 . .122 C6
  Pinner HA5 . . . . .66 D7
Harlech Rd, N14 . . . . .59 E3
Harlech Twr, W3 . . . . .126 B2
Harlequin Av, Brent. TW8 . . . .124 D6
Harlequin Cl, Hayes UB4
  off Cygnet Way 102 D5
  Isleworth TW7 . . . . .144 B5
Harlequin Ho, Erith DA18
  off Kale Rd 138/139 E3
Harlequin Rd, Tedd. TW11 . . .162 E7
★ Harlequins F.C. (Rugby), Twick.
  TW2 . . . . .144 B7
Harlescott Rd, SE15 . . . . .153 G4
HARLESDEN, NW10 . . . . . . .107 E2
Harlesden Gdns, NW10 . . . . .107 F1
Harlesden La, NW10 . . . . . . .107 G1
Harlesden Rd, NW10 . . . . . . .107 G1
Harleston Cl, E5
  off Theydon Rd 95 F2
Harley Cl, Wem. HA0 . . . . .87 G6
Harley Ct, E11 off Blake Hall Rd .79 G7
Harley Cres, Har. HA1 . . . . . . .68 A4
Harleyford, Brom. BR1 . . . . . .191 H1
Harleyford Rd, SE11 . . . . .34 C5

Harleyford St, SE11 . . . . .34 E6
Harley Gdns, SW10 . . . . .30 D4
  Orpington BR6 . . . . .207 H4
Harley Gro, E3 . . . . .113 J3
Harley Pl, W1 . . . . .16 D2
Harley Rd, NW3 . . . . .91 G7
  NW10 . . . . .106 E2
  Harrow HA1 . . . . .68 A4
Harley St, W1 . . . . .16 D2
Harling Ct, SW11
  off Latchmere Rd 149 J2
Harlinger St, SE18 . . . . .136 B3
HARLINGTON, Hayes UB3 . . .121 F6
Harlington Cl, Hayes UB3
  off New Rd 121 F7
Harlington Rd, Bexh. DA7 . . . .159 E3
  Hounslow (Hthrw Air.) TW6 .141 J4
Harlington Rd E, Felt. TW13,
  TW14 . . . . .142 B7
Harlington Rd W, Felt. TW14 . .142 B6
Harlow Rd, N13 . . . . .60 A3
Harlyn Dr, Pnr. HA5 . . . . .66 B3
Harman Av, Wdf.Grn. IG8 . . . .63 F7
Harman Cl, E4 . . . . .62 D4
  NW2 . . . . .90 B3
Harman Dr, NW2 . . . . .90 B3
  Sidcup DA15 . . . . .157 J6
Harman Rd, Enf. EN1 . . . . .44 C5
HARMONDSWORTH, West Dr.
  UB7 . . . . .120 A6
Harmondsworth La, West Dr.
  UB7 . . . . .120 B6
Harmondsworth Rd, West Dr.
  UB7 . . . . .120 B5
Harmony Cl, NW11 . . . . .72 B5
Harmony Ter, Har. HA2
  off Goldsmith Cl 85 H1
Harmony Way, NW4
  off Victoria Rd 71 J4
Harmood Gro, NW1
  off Clarence Way 92 B7
Harmood Pl, NW1
  off Harmood St 92 B7
Harmood St, NW1 . . . . .92 B7
Harmsworth Ms, SE11 . . . . . . .27 G6
Harmsworth St, SE17 . . . . . . .35 G4
Harmsworth Way, N20 . . . . . .56 C1
Harness Rd, SE28 . . . . .138 A2
Harold Av, Belv. DA17 . . . . . .139 F5
  Hayes UB3 . . . . .121 J3
Harold Est, SE1 . . . . .28 E6
Harold Gibbons Ct, SE7 . . . . .135 J6
Harold Laski Ho, EC1 . . . . .11 G4
Harold Pl, SE11 . . . . .34 E4
Harold Rd, E4 . . . . .62 C4
  E11 . . . . .96 E1
  E13 . . . . .115 H1
  N8 . . . . .75 F5
  N15 . . . . .76 C5
  NW10 . . . . .106 D3
  SE19 . . . . .170 B6
  Sutton SM1 . . . . .199 G4
  Woodford Green IG8 . . . . . .79 G1
Haroldstone Rd, E17 . . . . .77 G5
Harp All, EC4 . . . . .19 G3
Harpenden Rd, E12 . . . . .97 J2
  SE27 . . . . .169 H3
Harpenmead Pt, NW2
  off Granville Rd 90 C2
Harper Cl, N14 off Alexandra Ct .42 C5
Harper Ms, SW17 . . . . .167 F3
Harper Rd, E6 . . . . .116 C6
  SE1 . . . . .27 J5
Harpers Yd, N17 off Ruskin Rd .76 C1
Harp Island Cl, NW10 . . . . . . .88 D2
Harp La, EC3 . . . . .20 D6
Harpley Sq, E1 . . . . .113 F3
Harpour Rd, Bark. IG11 . . . . . .99 F6
Harp Rd, W7 . . . . .104 C4
Harpsden St, SW11 . . . . .150 A1
Harpur Ms, WC1 . . . . .18 C1
Harpur St, WC1 . . . . .18 C1
Harraden Rd, SE3 . . . . .155 J1
Harrap St, E14 . . . . .114 C7
Harrier Av, E11 off Eastern Av . .79 H6
Harrier Ms, SE28 . . . . .137 G3
Harrier Rd, NW9 . . . . .71 E2
Harriers Cl, W5 . . . . .105 H7
Harrier Way, E6 . . . . .116 C4
Harries Rd, Hayes UB4 . . . . . .102 C4
Harriet Cl, E8 . . . . .112 D1
Harriet Gdns, Croy. CR0 . . . . .202 D1
Harriet St, SW1 . . . . .24 A4
Harriet Tubman Cl, SW2 . . . . .151 G7
Harriet Wk, SW1 . . . . .24 A4
HARRINGAY, N8 . . . . .75 G5
Harringay Gdns, N8 . . . . .75 H4
Harringay Rd, N15 . . . . .75 H5
Harrington Cl, NW10 . . . . .88 D2
  Croydon CR0 . . . . .200 E2
Harrington Ct, W10 off Dart St .108 C3
Harrington Gdns, SW7 . . . . . . .30 B2
Harrington Hill, E5 . . . . .95 E1
Harrington Rd, E11 . . . . .97 E1
  SE25 . . . . .188 D4
  SW7 . . . . .30 E1
Harrington Sq, NW1 . . . . .9 F2

Harrington St, NW1 . . . . .9 F3
Harrington Way, SE18 . . . . . . .136 A3
Harriott Cl, SE10 . . . . .135 F4
Harris Cl, Enf. EN2 . . . . .43 H1
  Hounslow TW3 . . . . .143 H1
Harrison Cl, N20 . . . . .57 H1
Harrison Rd, Dag. RM10 . . . . .101 H6
Harrisons Ri, Croy. CR0 . . . . .201 H3
Harrison St, WC1 . . . . .10 B4
Harris Rd, Bexh. DA7 . . . . . . .159 E1
  Dagenham RM9 . . . . .101 F5
Harris St, E17 . . . . .77 J7
  SE5 . . . . .132 A7
★ Harrods, SW1 . . . . .23 J5
Harrogate Ct, N11
  off Coverdale Rd 58 A6
Harrogate Rd, Wat. WD19 . . . .50 C3
Harrold Rd, Dag. RM8 . . . . . .100 B5
HARROW, HA1 - HA3 . . . . . . .68 A7
★ Harrow Arts Cen, Pnr. HA5 .51 H7
Harrow Av, Enf. EN1 . . . . .44 C6
Harroway Rd, SW11 . . . . .149 G2
Harrowby St, W1 . . . . .15 H3
Harrow Cl, Chess. KT9 . . . . . .195 G7
Harrowdene Cl, Wem. HA0 . . . .87 G4
Harrowdene Gdns, Tedd. TW11 162 D6
Harrowdene Rd, Wem. HA0 . . .87 G3
Harrow Dr, N9 . . . . .60 C1
Harrowes Meade, Edg. HA8 . . .54 A3
Harrow Flds Gdns, Har. HA1 . .86 B2
Harrowgate Rd, E9 . . . . .95 H6
Harrow Grn, E11
  off Harrow Rd 96/97 E3
Harrow La, E14 . . . . .114 C7
Harrow Manorway, SE2 . . . . .138 C1
★ Harrow Mus & Heritage Cen,
  Har. HA2 . . . . .67 J3
HARROW ON THE HILL, Har.
  HA1 . . . . .86 B2
Harrow Pk, Har. HA1 . . . . .86 B2
Harrow Pas, Kings.T. KT1
  off Market Pl 181 G2
Harrow Pl, E1 . . . . .21 E3
Harrow Rd, E6 . . . . .116 B1
  E11 . . . . .97 E3
  NW10 . . . . .107 H3
  W2 . . . . .14 A2
  W9 . . . . .108 C4
  W10 . . . . .108 A4
  Barking IG11 . . . . .117 H1
  Carshalton SM5 . . . . .199 H5
  Ilford IG1 . . . . .99 F4
  Wembley HA0 . . . . .87 F5
  Wembley (Tkgtn) HA9 . . . . .87 J5
★ Harrow Sch, Har. HA1 . . . . .86 B1
Harrow Vw, Har. HA1, HA2 . . . .68 A4
  Hayes UB3 . . . . .102 A6
Harrow Vw Rd, W5 . . . . .105 C4
Harrow Way, Wat. WD19 . . . . .50 E3
HARROW WEALD, Har. HA3 . .68 A1
Harrow Weald Pk, Har. HA3 . . .52 A4
Hart Cres, Chig. IG7 . . . . .65 J5
Harte Rd, Houns. TW3 . . . . . .143 F2
Hartfield Av, Borwd. (Elstree)
  WD6 . . . . .38 A5
  Northolt UB5 . . . . .102 B2
Hartfield Cl, Borwd. (Elstree)
  WD6 . . . . .38 A5
Hartfield Cres, SW19 . . . . . . .166 C7
  West Wickham BR4 . . . . . .205 G3
Hartfield Gro, SE20 . . . . .189 E1
Hartfield Rd, SW19 . . . . .166 C7
  Chessington KT9 . . . . .195 G5
  West Wickham BR4 . . . . . .205 G4
Hartfield Ter, E3 . . . . .114 A2
Hartford Av, Har. HA3 . . . . .68 D3
Hartforde Rd, Borwd. WD6 . . . .38 A2
Hartford Rd, Bex. DA5 . . . . . .159 G6
  Epsom KT19 . . . . .196 A6
Hart Gro, W5 . . . . .126 A1
  Southall UB1 . . . . .103 G5
Hartham Cl, N7 . . . . .93 E5
  Isleworth TW7 . . . . .144 D1
Hartham Rd, N7 . . . . .92 E5
  N17 . . . . .76 C2
  Isleworth TW7 . . . . .144 C1
Harting Rd, SE9 . . . . .174 B4
Hartington Cl, Har. HA1 . . . . . .86 B4
Hartington Ct, W4 . . . . .126 B7
Hartington Rd, E16 . . . . .115 H6
  E17 . . . . .77 H6
  SW8 . . . . .150 E1
  W4 . . . . .126 B7
  W13 . . . . .105 E7
  Southall UB2 . . . . .122 E2
  Twickenham TW1 . . . . .144 E7
Hartismere Rd, SW6 . . . . .128 C7
Hartlake Rd, E9 . . . . .95 G6
Hartland Cl, N21
  off Elmscott Gdns 43 J6
  Edgware HA8 . . . . .54 A3
Hartland Dr, Edg. HA8 . . . . . . .54 A3
  Ruislip HA4 . . . . .84 B3
Hartland Rd, E15 . . . . .97 F7
  N11 . . . . .57 J5
  NW1 . . . . .92 B7
  NW6 . . . . .108 C2

Hartland Rd, Hmptn. (Hmptn H.)
 TW12 ....161 H4
 Isleworth TW7 ....144 D3
 Morden SM4 ....184 D7
Hartlands Cl, Bex. DA5 .....159 F6
Hartland Way, Croy. CR0 ....203 H2
 Morden SM4 ....184 C7
Hartlepool Ct, E16
 off Fishguard Way 136/137 E2
Hartley Av, E6 ....116 B5
 NW7 ....55 F5
Hartley Cl, NW7 ....55 F5
 Bromley BR1 ....192 C2
Hartley Rd, E11 ....97 F1
 Croydon CR0 ....187 H7
 Welling DA16 ....138 C7
Hartley St, E2 ....113 F3
Hartmann Rd, E16 ....136 A1
Hartnoll St, N7 off Eden Gro ..93 F5
Harton Cl, Brom. BR1 ......192 A1
Harton Rd, N9 ....61 C2
Harton St, SE8 ....154 A1
Hartsbourne Av, Bushey (Bushey Hth)
 WD23 ....51 J2
Hartsbourne Cl, Bushey (Bushey Hth)
 WD23 ....52 A2
Hartsbourne Rd, Bushey (Bushey Hth)
 WD23 ....52 A2
Harts Gro, Wdf.Grn. IG8 ....63 G5
Hartshorn All, EC3 ....21 E4
Hartshorn Gdns, E6 ....116 D4
Harts La, SE14 ....133 H7
 Barking IG11 ....98 E6
Hartslock Dr, SE2 ....138 D2
Hartsmead Rd, SE9 ....174 C2
Hart St, EC3 ....20 E5
Hartsway, Enf. EN3 ....45 F4
Hartswood Gdns, W12 .....127 F3
Hartswood Grn, Bushey (Bushey Hth)
 WD23 ....52 A2
Hartswood Rd, W12 ....127 F2
Hartsworth Cl, E13 ....115 F2
Hartville Rd, SE18 ....137 H4
Hartwell Dr, E4 ....62 C6
Hartwell St, E8 off Dalston La ..94 C6
Harvard Hill, W4 ....126 B6
Harvard La, W4 ....126 B5
Harvard Rd, SE13 ....154 C5
 W4 ....126 B5
 Isleworth TW7 ....144 B1
Harvel Cres, SE2 ....138 D5
Harvest Bk Rd, W.Wick. BR4 ..205 F3
Harvesters Cl, Islw. TW7 ...144 A5
Harvest La, Loug. IG10 .....48 A7
 Thames Ditton KT7 .....180 D6
Harvest Rd, Felt. TW13 ....160 A4
Harvey Dr, Hmptn. TW12 ...179 H1
Harvey Gdns, E11
 off Harvey Rd 97 F1
 SE7 ....135 J5
 Loughton IG10 ....49 E3
Harvey Ho, Brent. TW8
 off Green Dragon La 125 H5
Harvey Pt, E16 off Fife Rd ..115 H5
Harvey Rd, E11 ....97 E1
 N8 ....75 F5
 SE5 ....152 A1
 Hounslow TW4 ....143 F7
 Ilford IG1 ....99 E5
 Northolt UB5 ....84 C7
 Walton-on-Thames KT12 ..178 A7
Harvey St, N1 ....112 A1
Harvill Rd, Sid. DA14 ......176 D5
Harvington Wk, E8
 off Wilman Gro 94 D7
Harvist Est, N7 ....93 G4
Harvist Rd, NW6 ....108 A3
Harwater Dr, Loug. IG10 ....48 C2
Harwell Pas, N2 ....73 J4
Harwood Av, Brom. BR1 ....191 H2
 Mitcham CR4 ....185 H3
Harwood Cl, N12
 off Summerfields Av 57 H6
 Wembley HA0
 off Harrowdene Rd 87 G4
Harwood Rd, SW6 ....128 D7
Harwoods Yd, N21
 off Wades Hill 43 G7
Harwood Ter, SW6 ....148 E1
Hascombe Ter, SE5 off Love Wk ..152 A2
Haselbury Rd, N9 ....60 B4
 N18 ....60 B4
Haseley End, SE23 off Tyson Rd ..153 F7
Haselrigge Rd, SW4 ......150 D4
Haseltine Rd, SE26 ....171 J4
Haselwood Dr, Enf. EN2 ....43 H4
Haskard Rd, Dag. RM9 ....100 D4
Hasker St, SW3 ....31 H1
Haslam Av, Sutt. SM3 .....198 A1
Haslam Cl, N1 ....93 G7
Haslam St, SE15 ....132 C7
Haslemere Av, NW4 ....72 A6
 SW18 ....166 E2
 W7 ....124 D3
 W13 ....124 D3
 Barnet EN4 ....57 J1
 Hounslow TW5 ....142 C2

Haslemere Av, Mitch. CR4 ....185 G2
Haslemere Cl, Hmptn. TW12 ..161 F5
 Wallington SM6
 off Stafford Rd 200/201 E5
Haslemere Gdns, N3 ....72 C3
Haslemere Heathrow Est, Houns.
 TW4 ....142 B2
Haslemere Rd, N8 ....74 D7
 N21 ....59 H2
 Bexleyheath DA7 ....159 F2
 Ilford IG3 ....99 J2
 Thornton Heath CR7 ....187 H5
Hasler Cl, SE28 ....118 B7
Hasluck Gdns, Barn. EN5 ....41 F5
Hassard St, E2 ....13 G2
Hassendean Rd, SE3 ......135 H6
Hassett Rd, E9 ....95 G6
Hassocks Cl, SE26 ....171 E3
Hassocks Rd, SW16 ....186 D1
Hassock Wd, Kes. BR2 .....206 A4
Hassop Rd, NW2 ....90 A4
Hassop Wk, SE9 ....174 B4
Hasted Rd, SE7 ....136 A5
Hastings Av, Ilf. IG6 ....81 F4
Hastings Cl, SE15 ....132 D7
 Barnet EN5 off Leicester Rd ..41 F4
 Wembley HA0 ....87 F4
Hastings Dr, Surb. KT6 .....181 F6
Hastings Ho, SE18 ....136 C4
Hastings Rd, N11 ....58 C5
 N17 ....76 A3
 W13 ....104 E7
 Bromley BR2 ....206 B1
 Croydon CR0 ....202 C1
Hastings St, SE18 ....137 F3
 WC1 ....10 A4
Hastingwood Trd Est, N18 ...61 G6
Hastoe Cl, Hayes UB4 .....102 E4
Hat & Mitre Ct, EC1 ....11 H6
Hatch, The, Enf. EN3 ....45 G1
Hatcham Ms Business Cen, SE14
 off Hatcham Pk Rd 153 G1
Hatcham Pk Ms, SE14
 off Hatcham Pk Rd 153 G1
Hatcham Pk Rd, SE14 .....153 G1
Hatcham Rd, SE15 ....133 F6
Hatchard Rd, N19 ....92 D2
Hatchcroft, NW4 ....71 H3
Hatchers Ms, SE1 ....28 E4
Hatch Gro, Rom. RM6 .....83 E4
Hatch La, E4 ....62 D4
 West Drayton UB7 ......120 A7
Hatch Pl, Kings.T. KT2 .....163 H5
Hatch Rd, SW16 ....187 E2
Hatch Side, Chig. IG7 ......64 D5
Hatchwood Cl, Wdf.Grn. IG8
 off Sunset Av 63 F4
Hatcliffe Cl, SE3 ....155 F3
Hatcliffe St, SE10
 off Woolwich Rd 135 F5
Hatfield Cl, SE14 off Reaston St ..133 G7
 Ilford IG6 ....81 E3
 Mitcham CR4 ....185 G4
Hatfield Mead, Mord. SM4
 off Central Rd 184 D5
Hatfield Rd, E15 ....97 E5
 W4 ....126 D2
 W13 ....124 D1
 Dagenham RM9 ....101 G6
Hatfields, SE1 ....27 F1
 Loughton IG10 ....48 E3
Hathaway Cl, Brom. BR2 ...206 C1
 Stanmore HA7 ....52 D5
Hathaway Cres, E12 ....98 C6
Hathaway Gdns, W13 ......104 C5
 Romford RM6 ....82 D5
Hathaway Rd, Croy. CR0 ....187 H7
Hatherleigh Cl, NW7 ....56 A7
 Chessington KT9 ....195 G5
 Morden SM4 ....184 D4
Hatherleigh Rd, Ruis. HA4 ...84 A2
Hatherley Cres, Sid. DA14 ...176 A2
Hatherley Gdns, E6 ....116 A2
 N8 ....74 E6
Hatherley Gro, W2 ....14 A3
Hatherley Ms, E17 ....78 A4
Hatherley Rd, E17 ....77 J4
 Richmond TW9 ....145 J2
 Sidcup DA14 ....176 A4
Hatherley St, SW1 ....33 G1
Hathern Gdns, SE9 ....174 D4
Hatherop Rd, Hmptn. TW12 ..161 F7
Hathorne Cl, SE15 ....153 E2
Hathway St, SE15
 off Gibbon Rd 153 F2
Hathway Ter, SE14 off Kitto Rd ..153 F2
Hatley Av, Ilf. IG6 ....81 F4
Hatley Cl, N11 ....57 J5
Hatley Rd, N4 ....93 F2
Hatteraick St, SE16
 off Brunel Rd 133 F2
Hattersfield Cl, Belv. DA17 ..139 F4
HATTON, Felt. TW14 ....141 J4
Hatton Cl, SE18 ....137 G7
Hatton Ct, E5 off Gilpin Rd ...95 H4
Hatton Gdn, EC1 ....19 F1

Hatton Gdns, Mitch. CR4 ....185 J5
Hatton Grn, Felt. TW14 .....142 A4
Hatton Gro, West Dr. UB7 ...120 A2
Hatton Ho, E1 ....21 J5
Hatton Pl, EC1 ....11 F6
Hatton Rd, Croy. CR0 ......201 G1
 Feltham TW14 ....141 H5
Hatton Row, NW8 ....7 F6
Hatton St, NW8 ....7 F6
Hatton Wall, EC1 ....19 E1
Haul Rd, NW1 ....10 A1
Haunch of Venison Yd, W1 ...16 D4
Havana Rd, SW19 ....166 D2
Havannah St, E14 ....134 A2
Havant Rd, E17 ....78 C3
Havant Way, SE15 ....37 F7
Havelock Rd, N17 ....76 D2
 SW19 ....167 F5
 Belvedere DA17 ....139 F4
 Bromley BR2 ....191 J4
 Croydon CR0 ....202 C1
 Harrow HA3 ....68 B3
 Southall UB2 ....123 F3
Havelock St, N1 ....111 E1
 Ilford IG1 ....98 E2
Havelock Ter, SW8 ....130 B7
Havelock Wk, SE23 ....171 F1
Haven, The, SE26
 off Springfield Rd ..170/171 E5
 Richmond TW9 ....146 A3
 Sunbury-on-Thames TW16 ..160 A7
Haven Cl, SE9 ....174 C3
 SW19 ....166 A3
 Sidcup DA14 ....176 C6
Haven Ct, Esher KT10 .....194 B2
Haven Grn, W5 ....105 G6
Haven Grn Ct, W5
 off Haven Grn 105 G6
Haven Ms, E3
 off St. Pauls Way 113 J5
 N1 off Liverpool Rd 93 G7
Haven Pl, W5
 off The Broadway 105 G7
Haven St, NW1
 off Castlehaven Rd 92 B7
Haven Ter, W5
 off The Broadway 105 G7
Havenwood, Wem. HA9 ....88 B3
Haverfield Gdns, Rich. TW9 ..126 A7
Haverfield Rd, E3 ....113 H3
Haverford Way, Edg. HA8 ....69 J1
Haverhill Rd, E4 ....62 C1
 SW12 ....168 C1
Havering Gdns, Rom. RM6 ...82 C5
Havering St, E1
 off Devonport St 113 G6
Havering Way, Bark. IG11 ...118 B3
Haversfield Est, Brent. TW8 ..125 H5
Haversham Cl, Twick. TW1 ...145 G6
Haversham Pl, N6 ....91 J2
Haverstock Hill, NW3 ......91 H5
Haverstock Pl, N1
 off Haverstock St 111 H2
Haverstock Rd, NW5 ....92 A5
Haverstock St, N1 ....11 H2
Haverthwaite Rd, Orp. BR6 ..207 G2
Havil St, SE5 ....132 B7
Havisham Pl, SE19 ....169 H6
Hawarden Gro, SE24 ......151 J7
Hawarden Hill, NW2 ....89 G3
Hawarden Rd, E17 ....77 G4
Hawbridge Rd, E11 ....96 D1
Hawes La, W.Wick. BR4 ....204 D1
Hawes Rd, N18 ....60 E6
 Bromley BR1 ....191 H1
Hawes St, N1 ....93 H7
Haweswater Ho, Islw. TW7
 off Summerwood Rd 144 C5
Hawgood St, E3 ....114 A5
Hawkdene, E4 ....46 B6
Hawke Pk Rd, N22 ....75 H3
Hawke Pl, SE16
 off Middleton Dr 133 G2
Hawke Rd, SE19 ....170 B6
Hawkesbury Rd, SW15 ....147 H5
Hawkesfield Rd, SE23 .....171 H2
Hawkesley Cl, Twick. TW1 ...162 D4
Hawkes Rd, Felt. TW14 ....142 A7
 Mitcham CR4 ....185 H1
Hawke Twr, SE14
 off Nynehead St 133 H6
Hawkewood Rd, Sun. TW16 ..178 A3
Hawkhurst Gdns, Chess. KT9 ..195 H4
Hawkhurst Rd, SW16 .....186 D1
Hawkhurst Way, N.Mal. KT3 ..182 D5
 West Wickham BR4 .....204 B2
Hawkins Cl, NW7 off Hale La ..54 D5
 Borehamwood WD6
 off Banks Rd 38 C2
 Harrow HA1 ....68 A7
Hawkins Rd, Tedd. TW11 ...163 E6
Hawkins Way, SE6 ....172 A5
Hawkley Gdns, SE27 ......169 H2
Hawkridge Cl, Rom. RM6 ...82 C7

Hawksbrook La, Beck. BR3 ...190 B6
Hawkshaw Cl, SW2
 off Tierney Rd 150/151 E7
Hawkshead Cl, Brom. BR1 ...173 E7
Hawkshead Rd, NW10 ......89 F7
 W4 ....126 E2
Hawkslade Rd, SE15 ......153 G5
Hawksley Rd, N16 ....94 B3
Hawks Ms, SE10 off Luton Pl ..134 C7
Hawksmoor Cl, E6
 off Allhallows Rd 116 B6
 SE18 ....137 H5
Hawksmoor Ms, E1
 off Cable St 112/113 E7
Hawksmoor St, W6 ....128 A6
Hawksmouth, E4 ....46 B7
Hawks Rd, Kings.T. KT1 ....181 J2
Hawkstone Rd, SE16 ......133 F4
Hawk Ter, Ilf. IG5
 off Tiptree Cres 80 D3
Hawkwell Ct, E4
 off Colvin Gdns 62 C3
Hawkwell Ho, Dag. RM8 ....101 G1
Hawkwell Wk, N1 off Basire St ..111 J1
Hawkwood Cres, E4 ....46 B6
Hawkwood La, Chis. BR7 ...193 F1
Hawkwood Mt, E5 ....95 E1
Hawlands Dr, Pnr. HA5 .....66 E7
Hawley Cl, Hmptn. TW12 ...161 F6
Hawley Cres, NW1 ....92 B7
Hawley Ms, NW1 off Hawley St ..92 B7
Hawley Rd, N18 ....61 G5
 NW1 ....92 B7
Hawley St, NW1 ....92 B7
Hawstead Rd, SE6 ....154 B6
Hawsted, Buck.H. IG9 ......47 H7
Hawthorn Av, E3 ....113 J1
 N13 ....59 E6
 Carshalton SM5 ....200 A7
 Richmond TW9 off Kew Rd ..145 H2
 Thornton Heath CR7 ....187 H1
Hawthorn Cen, Har. HA1 ....68 C4
Hawthorn Cl, Hmptn. TW12 ..161 G5
 Hounslow TW5 ....122 B7
 Orpington BR5 ....193 G6
Hawthorn Cotts, Well. DA16
 off Hook La 158 A3
Hawthorn Ct, Rich. TW9
 off West Hall Rd 146 B1
Hawthorn Cres, SW17 .....168 A5
Hawthornden Cl, N12
 off Fallowfields Dr 57 H6
Hawthorndene Cl, Brom. BR2 ..205 F2
Hawthorndene Rd, Brom. BR2 ..205 F2
Hawthorn Dr, Har. HA2 .....67 F6
 West Wickham BR4 .....205 E4
Hawthorne Av, Har. HA3 ....68 D6
 Mitcham CR4 ....185 G2
 Ruislip HA4 ....66 B6
Hawthorne Cl, N1 ....94 B6
 Bromley BR1 ....192 C3
 Sutton SM1
 off Aultone Way 198/199 E2
Hawthorne Ct, Nthwd. HA6
 off Ryefield Cres 66 A2
Hawthorne Cres, West Dr. UB7 ..120 C2
Hawthorne Fm Av, Nthlt. UB5 ..103 E1
Hawthorne Gro, NW9 ......70 C7
Hawthorne Ms, Grnf. UB6
 off Greenford Rd 103 J6
Hawthorne Rd, E17 ....78 A3
 Bromley BR1 ....192 B3
Hawthorne Way, N9 ....60 B2
 Staines (Stanw.) TW19 ..140 A7
Hawthorn Gdns, W5 ....125 G3
Hawthorn Gro, SE20 ......171 E7
 Barnet EN5 ....39 F6
Hawthorn Hatch, Brent. TW8 ..125 E7
Hawthorn Ms, NW7
 off Holders Hill Rd 72 B1
Hawthorn Pl, Erith DA8 ....139 J1
Hawthorn Rd, N8 ....74 D3
 N18 ....60 C5
 NW10 ....89 G7
 Bexleyheath DA6 ......159 F4
 Brentford TW8 ....125 E7
 Buckhurst Hill IG9 .....64 A4
 Sutton SM1 ....199 H6
 Wallington SM6 ....200 B7
Hawthorns, Wdf.Grn. IG8 ....63 G3
Hawthorns, The, Epsom KT17
 off Ewell Bypass 197 F6
 Loughton IG10 ....48 D4
Hawthorn Wk, W10
 off Droop St 108 B4
Hawtrey Av, Nthlt. UB5 .....102 D2
Hawtrey Dr, Ruis. HA4 .....66 A7
Hawtrey Rd, NW3 ....91 H7
Haxted Rd, Brom. BR1
 off North Rd 191 H1
Hay Cl, E15 ....97 E7
 Borehamwood WD6 .....38 C2
Haycroft Gdns, NW10 .....107 G1
Haycroft Rd, SW2 ....151 E5
 Surbiton KT6 ....195 H3
Hay Currie St, E14 ....114 B6
Hayday Rd, E16 ....115 G5

Haydens Pl, W11
  off Portobello Rd 108 C6
Hayden Way, Rom. RM5 ....83 J2
Haydns Ms, W3 off Emanuel Av .106 C1
Haydock Av, Nthlt. UB5 ....85 G6
Haydock Grn, Nthlt. UB5
  off Haydock Av 85 G6
Haydon Cl, NW9 ....70 C4
  Enfield EN1 off Mortimer Dr ..44 B6
Haydon Dr, Pnr. HA5 ....66 A4
Haydon Pk Rd, SW19 ....166 E5
Haydon Rd, Dag. RM8 ....100 C2
Haydons Rd, SW19 ....167 F5
Haydon St, EC3 ....21 F5
Haydon Wk, E1 ....21 G5
Haydon Way, SW11 ....149 G4
HAYES, Brom. BR2 ....205 G2
Hayes Bypass, Hayes UB3, UB4 .102 D4
Hayes Chase, W.Wick. BR4 ...190 E5
Hayes Cl, Brom. BR2 ....205 G2
Hayes Ct, SW2 ....168 E1
  Sutton SM3 ....198 A4
Hayes Cres, NW11 ....72 C5
  Sutton SM3 ....198 A4
Hayesford Pk Dr, Brom. BR2 .191 F5
Hayes Gdn, Brom. BR2 ....205 G2
Hayes Gro, SE15 ....152 C4
Hayes Hill, Brom. BR2 ....204 E1
Hayes Hill Rd, Brom. BR2 ...205 F1
Hayes La, Beck. BR3 ....190 C3
  Bromley BR2 ....191 G5
Hayes Mead Rd, Brom. BR2 .205 E1
Hayes Metro Cen, Hayes UB4 .102 C7
Hayes Pl, NW1 ....7 H6
Hayes Rd, Brom. BR2 ....191 G4
  Southall UB2 ....122 B4
Hayes St, Brom. BR2 ....205 H1
HAYES TOWN, Hayes UB3 ...121 H2
Hayes Way, Beck. BR3 ....190 C4
Hayes Wd Av, Brom. BR2 ...205 H1
Hayfield Pas, E1
  off Stepney Grn 113 F4
Hayfield Yd, E1 off Mile End Rd .113 F4
Haygarth Pl, SW19 ....166 A5
Haygreen Cl, Kings.T. KT2 ..164 B6
Hay Hill, W1 ....17 E6
Hayland Cl, NW9 ....70 D4
Hay La, NW9 ....70 D4
Hayles St, SE11 ....35 G1
Haylett Gdns, Kings.T. KT1
  off Anglesea Rd 181 G4
Hayling Av, Felt. TW13 ....160 A3
Hayling Cl, N16 off Boleyn Rd .94 B5
Hayling Rd, Wat. WD19 ....50 B2
Hayman St, N1 off Cross St ..93 H7
Haymarket, SW1 ....17 H6
Haymarket Arc, SW1 ....17 H6
Haymer Gdns, Wor.Pk. KT4 .197 G3
Haymerle Rd, SE15 ....37 H6
Haymill Cl, Grnf. UB6 ....104 C3
Hayne Rd, Beck. BR3 ....189 J2
Haynes Cl, N11 ....58 A3
  N17 ....60 E7
  SE3 ....155 H1
Haynes Dr, N9 ....60 E3
Haynes La, SE19 ....170 B6
Haynes Rd, Wem. HA0 ....87 H7
Hayne St, EC1 ....19 H1
Haynt Wk, SW20 ....184 B3
★ Hay's Galleria, SE1 ....28 D1
Hay's La, SE1 ....28 D2
Haysleigh Gdns, SE20 ....188 D2
Hay's Ms, W1 ....16 D6
Hay St, E2 ....112 D1
Hayter Ct, E11 ....97 H2
Hayter Rd, SW2 ....151 E5
Hayton Cl, E8
  off Buttermere Wk 94 C6
Hayward Cl, SW19 ....185 E1
★ Hayward Gall, SE1 ....26 D1
Hayward Gdns, SW15 ....147 J6
Hayward Rd, N20 ....57 F2
  Thames Ditton KT7 ....194 D1
Haywards Cl, Rom. (Chad.Hth)
  RM6 ....82 B5
Hayward's Pl, EC1 ....11 G5
Haywood Cl, Pnr. HA5 ....66 D2
Haywood Ri, Orp. BR6 ....207 H4
Haywood Rd, Brom. BR2 ...192 A4
Hayworth Cl, Enf. EN3
  off Green St 45 H2
Hazel Av, West Dr. UB7 ....120 D3
Hazelbank, Surb. KT5 ....196 C1
Hazelbank Rd, SE6 ....172 D2
Hazelbourne Rd, SW12 ....150 B6
Hazelbrouck Gdns, Ilf. IG6 ..65 G7
Hazelbury Cl, SW19 ....184 D2
Hazelbury Grn, N9 ....60 B3
Hazelbury La, N9 ....60 B3
Hazel Cl, N13 ....60 A3
  N19 off Hargrave Pk 92 C2
  NW9 ....71 E2
  SE15 ....152 D2
  Brentford TW8 ....125 E7
  Croydon CR0 ....189 G7
  Mitcham CR4 ....186 D4
  Twickenham TW2 ....143 J7
Hazelcroft, Pnr. HA5 ....51 G6

Hazeldean Rd, NW10 ....88 D7
Hazeldene Dr, Pnr. HA5 ....66 C3
Hazeldene Rd, Ilf. IG3 ....100 B2
  Welling DA16 ....158 C2
Hazeldon Rd, SE4 ....153 H5
Hazeleigh Gdns, Wdf.Grn. IG8 .64 B5
Hazel Gdns, Edg. HA8 ....54 B4
Hazelgreen Cl, N21 ....59 H1
Hazel Gro, SE26 ....171 G4
  Enfield EN1 off Dimsdale Dr ..44 D6
  Orpington BR6 ....206 E3
  Romford RM6 ....82 E3
  Wembley HA0
    off Carlyon Rd 105 H1
Hazel Gro Est, SE26 ....171 G4
Hazelhurst, Beck. BR3 ....190 C1
Hazelhurst Rd, SW17 ....167 F4
Hazel La, Ilf. IG6 ....64 E7
  Richmond TW10 ....163 H2
Hazell Cres, Rom. RM5 ....83 H1
Hazellville Rd, N19 ....74 D7
Hazel Mead, Barn. EN5 ....39 H5
Hazelmere Cl, Felt. TW14 ...141 G6
  Northolt UB5 ....103 F2
Hazelmere Dr, Nthlt. UB5 ...103 F2
Hazelmere Rd, NW6 ....108 D1
  Northolt UB5 ....103 F2
  Orpington BR5 ....193 F4
Hazelmere Wk, Nthlt. UB5 ..103 F2
Hazelmere Way, Brom. BR2 .191 G6
Hazel Ms, N22
  off Alexandra Rd 75 G3
Hazel Rd, E15
  off Wingfield Rd 96/97 E5
  NW10 ....107 J3
Hazeltree La, Nthlt. UB5 ....103 F2
Hazel Wk, Brom. BR2 ....192 D6
Hazel Way, E4 ....61 J6
  SE1 ....37 F1
Hazelwood, Loug. IG10 ....48 A5
Hazelwood Av, Mord. SM4 ..185 E4
Hazelwood Cl, W5 ....125 H2
  Harrow HA2 ....67 H4
Hazelwood Ct, NW10
  off Neasden La N 88/89 E3
Hazelwood Cres, N13 ....59 G4
Hazelwood Cft, Surb. KT6 ...181 H6
Hazelwood Dr, Pnr. HA5 ....66 B2
Hazelwood La, N13 ....59 G4
Hazelwood Pk Cl, Chig. IG7 ..65 H5
Hazelwood Rd, E17 ....77 H5
  Enfield EN1 ....44 C6
Hazlebury Rd, SW6 ....148 E2
Hazledean Rd, Croy. CR0 ....202 A2
Hazledene Rd, W4 ....126 C6
Hazlemere Gdns, Wor.Pk. KT4 .197 H1
Hazlewell Rd, SW15 ....147 H5
Hazlewood Cl, E5
  off Mandeville St 95 H3
Hazlewood Cres, W10 ....108 B4
Hazlitt Cl, Felt. TW13 ....161 E4
Hazlitt Ms, W14 off Hazlitt Rd .128 B3
Hazlitt Rd, W14 ....128 B3
Headcorn Pl, Th.Hth. CR7
  off Headcorn Rd 187 F4
Headcorn Rd, N17 ....60 C7
  Bromley BR1 ....173 F5
  Thornton Heath CR7 ....187 F4
Headfort Pl, SW1 ....24 C4
Headingley Cl, Ilf. IG6 ....65 J6
Headington Rd, SW18 ....167 F2
Headlam Rd, SW4 ....150 D6
Headlam St, E1 ....113 E4
Headley App, Ilf. IG2 ....80 D5
Headley Av, Wall. SM6 ....201 F5
Headley Cl, Epsom KT19 ....196 A6
Headley Ct, SE26 ....171 E5
Headley Dr, Croy. (New Adgtn)
  CR0 ....204 B7
  Ilford IG2 ....80 E6
Head's Ms, W11 off Artesian Rd .108 D6
HEADSTONE, Har. HA2 ....67 J4
Headstone Dr, Har. HA1, HA3 ..68 B3
Headstone Gdns, Har. HA2 ...67 J4
Headstone La, Har. HA2, HA3 ..67 H4
Headstone Rd, Har. HA1 ....68 B5
Head St, E1 ....113 G6
Headway Cl, Rich. TW10
  off Locksmeade Rd 163 F4
Heald St, SE14 ....153 J1
Healey Dr, Orp. BR6 ....207 J4
Healey St, NW1 ....92 B6
Heanor Ct, E5 off Pedro St ...95 G3
Hearne Rd, W4 ....126 A6
Hearn Ri, Nthlt. UB5 ....102 D1
Hearn's Bldgs, SE17 ....36 C2
Hearn St, EC2 ....12 E6
Hearnville Rd, SW12 ....168 A1
Heath, The, W7
  off Lower Boston Rd 124 B1
Heatham Pk, Twick. TW2 ....144 C7
Heath Av, Bexh. DA7 ....138 D6
Heathbourne Rd, Bushey
  (Bushey Hth) WD23 ....52 B2
  Stanmore HA7 ....52 B2
Heath Brow, NW3
  off North End Way 91 F3

Heath Cl, NW11 ....72 E7
  W5 ....105 J4
  Hayes UB3 ....121 G7
Heathcock Ct, WC2
  off Strand 110/111 E7
Heathcote Av, Ilf. IG5 ....80 C2
Heathcote Ct, Ilf. IG5
  off Heathcote Av 80 C2
Heathcote Gro, E4 ....62 C3
Heathcote Pt, E9 off Wick Rd .95 G6
Heathcote Rd, Twick. TW1 ...145 E6
Heathcote St, WC1 ....10 C5
Heathcote Way, West Dr. UB7
  off Tavistock Rd 120 A1
Heath Ct, Houns. TW4 ....143 F4
Heathcroft, NW11 ....91 E1
  W5 ....105 J4
Heathcroft Gdns, E17 ....78 D1
Heathdale Av, Houns. TW4 ...143 E3
Heathdene Dr, Belv. DA17 ...139 H4
Heathdene Rd, SW16 ....169 F7
  Wallington SM6 ....200 B7
Heath Dr, NW3 ....90 E4
  SW20 ....183 J4
Heathedge, SE26 ....170 E2
Heatherbank, SE9 ....156 C2
  Chislehurst BR7 ....192 D2
Heather Cl, E6 ....116 E6
  N7
    off Newington Barrow Way ..93 F3
  SE13 ....154 D6
  SW8 ....150 B3
  Hampton TW12 ....179 F1
  Isleworth TW7
    off Harvesters Cl 144 A5
Heatherdale Cl, Kings.T. KT2 .164 A6
Heatherdene Cl, N12
  off Bow La 73 F1
  Mitcham CR4 ....185 H4
Heather Dr, Enf. EN2
  off Chasewood Av 43 H2
Heather Gdns, NW11 ....72 B6
  Sutton SM2 ....198 D6
Heatherlands, Sun. TW16 ....160 A6
Heatherley Dr, Ilf. IG5 ....80 B3
Heather Pk Dr, Wem. HA0 ....88 A7
Heather Rd, E4 ....61 J6
  NW2 ....89 F2
  SE12 ....173 G2
Heathers, The, Stai. TW19 ...140 C7
Heatherset Gdns, SW16 ....169 F7
Heatherside Rd, Epsom KT19 .196 D7
  Sidcup DA14 off Wren Rd ...176 D3
Heatherton Ter, N3 ....73 E2
Heather Wk, W10 off Droop St .108 B4
  Edgware HA8 ....54 B5
  Twickenham TW2
    off Stephenson Rd 143 G7
Heather Way, Stan. HA7 ....52 C6
Heatherwood Cl, E12 ....97 J2
Heathfield, E4 ....62 C3
  Chislehurst BR7 ....175 F6
Heathfield Av, SW18
  off Heathfield Rd 149 G7
Heathfield Cl, E16 ....116 A5
  Keston BR2 ....205 J5
Heathfield Dr, Mitch. CR4 ...185 H1
Heathfield Gdns, NW11 ....72 A6
  SE3 ....154 E2
  SW18 off Heathfield Rd 149 G6
  W4 ....126 C5
  Croydon CR0
    off Coombe Rd 202 A4
Heathfield La, Chis. BR7 ....175 E6
Heathfield N, Twick. TW2 ....144 C7
Heathfield Pk, NW2 ....89 J6
Heathfield Pk Dr, Rom. (Chad.Hth)
  RM6 ....82 B5
Heathfield Rd, SW18 ....149 F6
  W3 ....126 B2
  Bexleyheath DA6 ....159 F4
  Bromley BR1 ....173 F7
  Croydon CR0 ....202 A4
  Keston BR2 ....205 J5
Heathfields Ct, Houns. TW4
  off Frampton Rd 142/143 E5
Heathfield S, Twick. TW2 ....144 C7
Heathfield Sq, SW18 ....149 G7
Heathfield St, W11
  off Portland Rd 108 B7
Heathfield Ter, SE18 ....137 J6
  W4 ....126 C5
Heath Gdns, Twick. TW1 ....162 C1
Heathgate, NW11 ....72 E6
Heathgate Pl, NW3
  off Agincourt Rd 91 J5
Heath Gro, SE20 off Maple Rd .171 F7
Heath Hurst Rd, NW3 ....91 H4
Heathland Rd, N16 ....94 B1
Heathlands Cl, Sun. TW16 ...178 A2
  Twickenham TW1 ....162 C2
Heathlands Way, Houns. TW4 .143 E5
Heath La, SE3 ....154 D2
Heathlee Rd, SE3 ....155 F4
Heathley End, Chis. BR7 ....175 F6
Heathmans Rd, SW6 ....148 C1
Heath Mead, SW19 ....166 A3

Heath Pk Dr, Brom. BR1 ....192 B3
Heath Pas, NW3 ....91 E2
Heath Ri, SW15 ....148 A6
  Bromley BR2 ....191 F6
Heath Rd, SW8 ....150 B2
  Bexley DA5 ....177 J1
  Harrow HA1 ....67 J7
  Hounslow TW3 ....143 H4
  Romford RM6 ....82 D7
  Thornton Heath CR7 ....187 J3
  Twickenham TW1, TW2 ....162 C1
★ Heathrow Airport, Houns.
  TW6 ....140 E1
Heathrow Ho, Houns. TW5
  off Bath Rd 142 A1
Heathrow Interchange, Hayes
  UB4 ....122 C1
Heathrow Int Trd Est, Houns.
  TW4 ....142 B3
Heathrow Tunnel App, Houns.
  (Hthrw Air.) TW6 ....140 E3
Heathrow Vehicle Tunnel, Houns.
  (Hthrw Air.) TW6 ....140 E1
Heaths Cl, Enf. EN1 ....44 B2
Heath Side, NW3 ....91 G4
Heathside, Esher KT10 ....194 B3
  Hounslow TW4 ....143 F7
Heath Side, Orp. BR5 ....207 F1
Heathside Av, Bexh. DA7 ....159 E1
Heathside Cl, Esher KT10 ....194 B3
  Ilford IG2 ....81 G5
Heathstan Rd, W12 ....107 G6
Heath St, NW3 ....91 F4
Heath Vw, N2 ....73 F4
Heath Vw Cl, N2 ....73 F4
Heathview Ct, SW19 ....166 A2
Heathview Dr, SE2 ....138 D6
Heathview Gdns, SW15 ....147 J6
Heathview Rd, Th.Hth. CR7 ..187 G4
Heath Vil, SE18 ....137 J5
  SW18 off Cargill Rd 167 F1
Heathville Rd, N19 ....74 E7
Heathwall St, SW11 ....149 J3
Heathway, SE3 ....135 F7
  Croydon CR0 ....203 J3
  Dagenham RM9, RM10 ....101 H4
  Woodford Green IG8 ....63 J4
Heathway, Wdf.Grn. IG8 ....63 J4
Heathway Ind Est, Dag. RM10
  off Manchester Way 101 H4
Heathwood Gdns, SE7 ....136 B4
Heathwood Pt, SE23
  off Dacres Rd 171 G3
Heaton Cl, E4 ....62 C3
Heaton Rd, SE15 ....152 D3
  Mitcham CR4 ....168 A7
Heaven Tree Cl, N1 ....93 J5
Heaver Rd, SW11 off Wye St ..149 G3
Heavitree Cl, SE18 ....137 G5
Heavitree Rd, SE18 ....137 G5
Hebden Ct, E2
  off Laburnum St 112 C1
Hebden Ter, N17
  off Commercial Rd 60 B6
Hebdon Rd, SW17 ....167 H3
Heber Rd, NW2 ....90 A5
  SE22 ....152 C6
Hebron Rd, W6 ....127 H3
Hecham Cl, E17 ....77 H2
Heckfield Pl, SW6
  off Fulham Rd 128 D7
Heckford St, E1
  off The Highway 113 G7
Hector St, SE18 ....137 H4
Heddington Gro, N7 ....93 F5
Heddon Cl, Islw. TW7 ....144 D4
Heddon Ct Av, Barn. EN4 ....41 J5
Heddon Ct Par, Barn. EN4
  off Cockfosters Rd 42 A5
Heddon Rd, Barn. EN4 ....41 J5
Heddon St, W1 ....17 F5
Hedge Hill, Enf. EN2 ....43 H3
Hedge La, N13 ....59 H3
Hedgeley, Ilf. IG4 ....80 C4
Hedgemans Rd, Dag. RM9 ...100 D6
Hedgemans Way, Dag. RM9 ..100 E6
Hedgerley Gdns, Grnf. UB6 ..103 J2
Hedgerow La, Barn. EN5 ....39 H5
Hedgers Cl, Loug. IG10
  off Newmans La 48 D4
Hedgers Gro, E9 ....95 H6
Hedger St, SE11 ....35 G1
Hedge Wk, SE6 ....172 B4
Hedgewood Gdns, Ilf. IG5 ....80 D5
Hedgley Ms, SE12
  off Hedgley St 155 F5
Hedgley St, SE12 ....155 F5
Hedingham Cl, N1
  off Popham Rd 93 J7
Hedingham Ho, Kings.T. KT2
  off Kingsgate Rd 181 H1
Hedingham Rd, Dag. RM8 ...100 B5
Hedley Rd, Twick. TW2 ....143 G7
Hedley Row, N5 off Poets Rd ..94 A5
Heenan Cl, Bark. IG11
  off Glenny Rd 99 F6
Heene Rd, Enf. EN2 ....44 A1

Heidegger Cres, SW13
   off Trinity Ch Rd 127 H6
Heigham Rd, E6 ....98 A7
Heighton Gdns, Croy. CR0 ....201 H5
Heights, The, SW7 ....135 J5
  Beckenham BR3 ....172 C7
  Loughton IG10 ....48 C2
  Northolt UB5 ....85 F5
Heights Cl, SW20 ....165 H7
★ Heinz Gall, R.I.B.A., W1 ...16 B3
Heiron St, SE17 ....35 H6
Helby Rd, SW4 ....150 D6
Helder Gro, SE12 ....155 F7
Helder St, S.Croy. CR2 ....202 A6
Heldmann Cl, Houns. TW3 ....144 A4
Helegan Cl, Orp. BR6 ....207 J4
Helena Pl, E9 off Fremont St ..113 F1
Helena Rd, E13 ....115 F2
  E17 ....78 A5
  NW10 ....89 H5
  W5 ....105 G5
Helena Sq, SE16
   off Rotherhithe St 113 H7
Helen Av, Felt. TW14 ....142 B7
Helen Cl, N2
   off Thomas More Way 73 F3
  West Molesey KT8 ....179 H4
Helenslea Av, NW11 ....90 C1
Helen's Pl, E2 off Roman Rd ...113 F3
Helen St, SE18
   off Wilmount St 136/137 E4
Helios Rd, Wall. SM6 ....200 A1
Helix Gdns, SW2 off Helix Rd ..151 F6
Helix Rd, SW2 ....151 F6
Hellen Way, Wat. WD19 ....50 D4
Hellings St, E1 ....29 J2
Helme Cl, SW19 ....166 C5
Helmet Row, EC1 ....12 A5
Helmore Rd, Bark. IG11 ....99 J7
Helmsdale Cl, Hayes UB4 .....102 E4
Helmsdale Rd, SW16 ....186 C1
Helmsley Pl, E8 ....94 E7
Helperby Rd, NW10
   off Mayo Rd 88/89 E6
Helsinki Sq, SE16 ....133 H3
Helston Cl, Pnr. HA5 ....51 F7
Helvetia St, SE6 ....171 J2
Hemans St, SW8 ....33 J7
Hemberton Rd, SW9 ....150 E3
Hemery Rd, Grnf. UB6 ....86 A5
Hemingford Cl, N12 ....57 G5
Hemingford Rd, N1 ....111 F1
  Sutton SM3 ....197 J4
Heming Rd, Edg. HA8 ....54 B7
Hemington Av, N11 ....57 J5
Hemlock Rd, W12 ....107 F7
Hemming Cl, Hmptn. TW12
   off Chandler Cl 179 G1
Hemmings Cl, Sid. DA14 ......176 B2
Hemming St, E1 ....13 J6
Hemp Wk, SE17 ....36 C1
Hemsby Rd, Chess. KT9 ....195 J6
Hemstal Rd, NW6 ....90 D7
Hemswell Dr, NW9 ....70 E1
Hemsworth Ct, N1
   off Hemsworth St 112 B2
Hemsworth St, N1 ....12 D1
Hemus Pl, SW3 ....31 H4
Hen & Chicken Ct, EC4
   off Fleet St 111 G6
Henbury Way, Wat. WD19 ......50 D3
Henchman St, W12 ....107 F6
Hendale Av, NW4 ....71 G3
Henderson Cl, NW10 ....88 C6
Henderson Dr, NW8 ....7 E5
Henderson Rd, E7 ....97 J6
  N9 ....60 E1
  SW18 ....149 H7
  Croydon CR0 ....188 A6
  Hayes UB4 ....102 A3
Hendham Rd, SW17 ....167 H2
HENDON, NW4 ....71 H4
Hendon Av, N3 ....72 B1
Hendon Hall Ct, NW4
   off Parson St 72 A3
Hendon La, N3 ....72 B3
Hendon Pk Row, NW11 ....72 C6
Hendon Rd, N9 ....60 D2
Hendon Way, NW2 ....90 C3
  NW4 ....71 H6
  Staines (Stanw.) TW19 .....140 A6
Hendon Wd La, NW7 ....39 F6
Hendren Cl, Grnf. UB6
   off Dimmock Dr 86 A5
Hendre Rd, SE1 ....36 E2
Hendrick Av, SW12 ....149 J6
Heneage La, EC3 ....20 E4
Heneage St, E1 ....21 G1
Henfield Cl, N19 ....92 C1
  Bexley DA5 ....159 G6
Henfield Rd, SW19 ....184 C1
Hengelo Gdns, Mitch. CR4 ....185 G4
Hengist Rd, SE12 ....155 H7
  Erith DA8 ....139 H7
Hengist Way, Brom. BR2 ......190 E4

Hengrave Rd, SE23 ....153 G7
Hengrove Ct, Bex. DA5
   off Hurst Rd 176/177 E1
Henley Av, Sutt. SM3 ....198 B3
Henley Cl, SE16
   off St. Marychurch St 133 F2
  Greenford UB6 ....103 J2
  Isleworth TW7 ....144 C1
Henley Ct, N14 ....42 C7
Henley Cross, SE3 ....155 H3
Henley Dr, SE1 ....37 G1
  Kingston upon Thames KT2 ..165 F7
Henley Gdns, Pnr. HA5 ....66 B3
  Romford RM6 ....82 E5
Henley Rd, E16 ....136 C1
  N18 ....60 B4
  NW10 ....107 J1
  Ilford IG1 ....99 F4
Henley St, SW11 ....150 A2
Henley Way, Felt. TW13 ....160 D5
Henlow Pl, Rich. TW10
   off Sandpits Rd 163 G2
Hennel Cl, SE23 ....171 F3
Hennessy Rd, N9 ....61 F2
Henniker Gdns, E6 ....116 A3
Henniker Ms, SW3 ....30 E5
Henniker Pt, E15 ....96 E5
Henniker Rd, E15 ....96 D5
Henningham Rd, N17 ....76 A1
Henning St, SW11 ....149 H1
Henrietta Cl, SE8 ....134 A6
Henrietta Ms, WC1 ....10 B5
Henrietta Pl, W1 ....16 D4
Henrietta St, E15 ....96 C5
  WC2 ....18 B5
Henriques St, E1 ....21 J3
Henry Addlington Cl, E6 ......116 E5
Henry Cooper Way, SE9 ......174 A3
Henry Darlot Dr, NW7 ....56 A5
Henry Dent Cl, SE5 ....152 A3
Henry Dickens Ct, W11 ....128 A1
Henry Doulton Dr, SW17 ......168 B4
Henry Jackson Rd, SW15 .....148 A3
Henry Macaulay Av, Kings.T.
  KT2 ....181 G1
Henry Rd, E6 ....116 B2
  N4 ....93 J1
  Barnet EN4 ....41 G5
Henry's Av, Wdf.Grn. IG8 ......63 F5
Henryson Rd, SE4 ....154 A5
Henry St, Brom. BR1 ....191 H1
Henry's Wk, Ilf. IG6 ....65 G7
Henry Tate Ms, SW16 ....169 G5
Hensford Gdns, SE26
   off Wells Pk Rd 170/171 E4
Henshall Pt, E3
   off Bromley High St 114 B3
Henshall St, N1 ....94 A6
Henshawe Rd, Dag. RM8 ......100 D3
Henshaw St, SE17 ....36 B1
Hensley Pt, E9 off Wick Rd 95 G6
Henslowe Rd, SE22 ....152 D5
Henson Av, NW2 ....89 J5
Henson Cl, Orp. BR6 ....207 E2
Henson Path, Har. HA3 ....69 G3
Henson Pl, Nthlt. UB5 ....102 C1
Henstridge Pl, NW8 ....7 G1
Henty Cl, SW11 ....129 H7
Henty Wk, SW15 ....147 H5
Henville Rd, Brom. BR1 ......191 H1
Henwick Rd, SE9 ....156 A3
Henwood Side, Wdf.Grn. IG8
   off Love La 64 C6
Hepburn Gdns, Brom. BR2 ....205 E1
Hepburn Ms, SW11
   off Webbs Rd 149 J5
Hepple Cl, Islw. TW7 ....144 E2
Hepplestone Cl, SW15
   off Dover Pk Dr 147 H6
Hepscott Rd, E9 ....96 A7
Hepworth Ct, Bark. IG11 .....100 A5
Hepworth Gdns, Bark. IG11 ...100 A5
Hepworth Rd, SW16 ....169 E7
Hepworth Wk, NW3
   off Haverstock Hill 91 H5
Heracles Cl, Wall. SM6 ....200 E7
Herald Gdns, Wall. SM6 ......200 B3
Herald's Pl, SE11 ....35 G1
Herald St, E2
   off Three Colts La 112/113 E4
Herbal Hill, EC1 ....11 F6
Herbert Cres, SW1 ....24 A5
Herbert Gdns, NW10 ....107 H2
  W4 off Magnolia Rd 126 B6
  Romford RM6 ....82 D7
Herbert Ms, SW2
   off Bascombe St 151 G6
Herbert Morrison Ho, SW6
   off Clem Attlee Ct 128 C6
Herbert Pl, SE18
   off Plumstead Common
   Rd 136/137 E6
Herbert Rd, E12 ....98 B4
  E17 ....77 J7
  N11 ....58 E7
  N15 ....76 C5
  NW9 ....71 G6

Herbert Rd, SE18 ....136 D7
  SW19 ....166 C7
  Bexleyheath DA7 ....159 E2
  Bromley BR2 ....192 A5
  Ilford IG3 ....99 H2
  Kingston upon Thames KT1 ..181 J3
  Southall UB1 ....123 F1
Herbert St, E13 ....115 G2
  NW5 ....92 A6
Herbert Ter, SE18
   off Herbert Rd 136/137 E6
Herbrand St, WC1 ....10 A5
Hercules Pl, N7
   off Hercules St 92/93 E3
Hercules Rd, SE1 ....26 D6
Hercules St, N7 ....93 E3
Hereford Av, Barn. EN4 ....57 J1
Hereford Ct, Sutt. SM2
   off Worcester Rd 198 D7
Hereford Gdns, SE13
   off Longhurst Rd 154/155 E5
  Ilford IG1 ....80 B7
  Pinner HA5 ....66 E5
  Twickenham TW2 ....161 J1
Hereford Ho, NW6 ....108 D2
Hereford Ms, W2
   off Hereford Rd 108 D6
Hereford Pl, SE14
   off Royal Naval Pl 133 J7
Hereford Retreat, SE15 ....37 H7
Hereford Rd, E11 ....79 H5
  W2 ....108 D6
  W3 ....106 B7
  W5 ....125 F3
  Feltham TW13 ....160 C1
Hereford Sq, SW7 ....30 D2
Hereford St, E2 ....13 H5
Hereford Way, Chess. KT9 ....195 F5
Herent Dr, Ilf. IG5 ....80 B4
Hereward Gdns, N13 ....59 G5
Hereward Grn, Loug. IG10 .....49 F1
Hereward Rd, SW17 ....167 J4
Herga Ct, Har. HA1 ....86 B3
Herga Rd, Har. HA3 ....68 C4
Heriot Av, E4 ....62 A2
Heriot Rd, NW4 ....71 J5
Heriots Cl, Stan. HA7 ....52 D4
Heritage Cl, SW9 ....151 H3
Heritage Hill, Kes. BR2 ....205 J5
Heritage Pl, SW18
   off Earlsfield Rd 167 F1
Heritage Vw, Har. HA1 ....86 C3
Herlwyn Gdns, SW17 ....167 J4
Hermes Cl, W9
   off Chippenham Rd 108 D4
Hermes St, N1 ....10 E2
Hermes Wk, Nthlt. UB5
   off Hotspur Rd 103 G2
Hermes Way, Wall. SM6 ......200 D7
Hermiston Av, N8 ....75 E5
Hermitage, The, SE23 ....171 F1
  SW13 ....147 F1
  Richmond TW10 ....145 G5
Hermitage Cl, E18 ....79 F4
  SE2 off Felixstowe Rd 138 C3
  Enfield EN2 ....43 H2
  Esher (Clay.) KT10 ....194 D6
Hermitage Ct, E18 ....79 G4
  NW2 off Hermitage La 90 D3
Hermitage Gdns, NW2 ....90 D3
  SE19 ....169 J6
Hermitage La, N18 ....60 A5
  NW2 ....90 D3
  SE25 ....188 D6
  SW16 ....169 F7
  Croydon CR0 ....188 D6
Hermitage Path, SW16 ....187 E1
Hermitage Rd, N4 ....75 H7
  N15 ....75 H7
  SE19 ....169 J7
Hermitage Row, E8 ....94 D5
Hermitage St, W2 ....15 E2
Hermitage Wk, E18 ....79 F4
Hermitage Wall, E1 ....29 J2
Hermitage Waterside, E1 ......29 H1
Hermitage Way, Stan. HA7 .....68 D1
Hermit Pl, NW6
   off Belsize Rd 108/109 E1
Hermit Rd, E16 ....115 F5
Hermit St, EC1 ....11 G3
Hermon Gro, Hayes UB3 ......122 A1
Hermon Hill, E11 ....79 G5
  E18 ....79 G5
Herndon Rd, SW18 ....149 F5
Herne Cl, NW10
   off North Circular Rd 88 D5
HERNE HILL, SE24 ....151 J5
Herne Hill, SE24 ....151 J6
Herne Hill Ho, SE24
   off Railton Rd 151 H6
Herne Hill Rd, SE24 ....151 J4
Herne Ms, N18
   off Lyndhurst Rd 60 D4
Herne Pl, SE24 ....151 H5
Herne Rd, Surb. KT6 ....195 G2
Heron Cl, E17 ....77 J2
  NW10 ....89 E6

Heron Cl, Buck.H. IG9 ....63 G1
  Sutton SM1
   off Sandpiper Rd 198 C5
Heron Ct, Brom. BR2 ....191 J4
Heron Cres, Sid. DA14 ....175 H3
Herondale Av, SW18 ....167 G1
Heron Dr, N4 ....93 J2
Herongate Rd, E12 ....97 J2
Heron Hill, Belv. DA17 ....139 F4
Heron Ms, Ilf. IG1
   off Balfour Rd 98/99 E2
Heron Pl, SE16 ....133 H1
Heron Quay, E14 ....134 A1
Heron Rd, SE24 ....151 J4
  Croydon CR0 off Tunstall Rd .202 B2
  Twickenham TW1 ....144 D4
Herons, The, E11 ....79 F6
Heronsforde, W13 ....105 F6
Heronsgate, Edg. HA8 ....54 A5
Heronslea Dr, Stan. HA7 ......53 H5
Heron's Pl, Islw. TW7 ....144 E3
Heron Sq, Rich. TW9
   off Bridge St 145 G5
Herons Ri, Barn. EN4 ....41 H4
Heron Trd Est, W3
   off Alliance Rd 106 B4
Heron Way, Felt. TW14 ....142 A4
Heronway, Wdf.Grn. IG8 ....63 J4
Herrick Rd, N5 ....93 J3
Herrick St, SW1 ....33 J1
Herries St, W10 ....108 B2
Herringham Rd, SE7 ....135 J3
Herrongate Cl, Enf. EN1 ....44 C2
Hersant Cl, NW10 ....107 G1
Herschell Ms, SE5
   off Bicknell Rd 151 J3
Herschell Rd, SE23 ....153 H7
Hersham Cl, SW15 ....147 G7
Hertford Av, SW14 ....146 D5
Hertford Cl, Barn. EN4 ....41 G3
Hertford Pl, W1 ....9 F6
Hertford Rd, N1 ....112 B1
  N2 ....73 H3
  N9 ....60 E2
  Barking IG11 ....98 E7
  Barnet EN4 ....41 F3
  Enfield EN3 ....45 F3
  Ilford IG2 ....81 H6
Hertford Sq, Mitch. CR4
   off Hertford Way 186/187 E4
Hertford St, W1 ....24 D1
Hertford Wk, Belv. DA17
   off Hoddesdon Rd 139 G5
Hertford Way, Mitch. CR4 ....186 E4
Hertslet Rd, N7 ....93 F3
Hertsmere Rd, E14 ....114 A7
Hervey Cl, N3 ....72 D1
Hervey Pk Rd, E17 ....77 H4
Hervey Rd, SE3 ....155 H1
Hesa Rd, Hayes UB3 ....102 A6
Hesewall Cl, SW4
   off Brayburne Av 150 C2
Hesketh Pl, W11 ....108 B7
Hesketh Rd, E7 ....97 G3
Heslop Rd, SW12 ....167 J1
Hesper Ms, SW5 ....30 A3
Hesperus Cres, E14 ....134 B4
Hessel Rd, W13 ....124 D2
Hessel St, E1 ....112 E6
Hestercombe Av, SW6 ....148 B2
Hesterman Way, Croy. CR0 ...201 E1
Hester Rd, N18 ....60 D5
  SW11 ....129 H7
Hester Ter, Rich. TW9
   off Chilton Rd 146 A3
HESTON, Houns. TW5 ....123 F7
Heston Av, Houns. TW5 ......123 E7
Heston Gra La, Houns. TW5 ...123 F6
Heston Ind Mall, Houns. TW5 ..123 F7
Heston Rd, Houns. TW5 ......123 G7
Heston St, SE14 ....153 J1
Heswell Grn, Wat. WD19
   off Fairhaven Cres 50 A3
Hetherington Rd, SW4 ....150 E4
Hetley Gdns, SE19 ....170 C7
Hetley Rd, W12 ....127 H1
Heton Gdns, NW4 ....71 G4
Hevelius Cl, SE10 ....135 F5
Hever Cft, SE9 ....174 D4
Hever Gdns, Brom. BR1 ......192 D3
Heverham Rd, SE18 ....137 H4
Heversham Rd, Bexh. DA7 ...159 G2
Hewer St, W10 ....108 A5
Hewett Cl, Stan. HA7 ....53 E4
Hewett Rd, Dag. RM8 ....100 D5
Hewett St, EC2 ....12 E6
Hewish Rd, N18 ....60 B4
Hewison St, E3 ....113 J2
Hewitt Av, N22 ....75 H2
Hewitt Cl, Croy. CR0 ....204 A3
Hewitt Rd, N8 ....75 G5
Hewlett Rd, E3 ....113 H2
Hexagon, The, N6 ....91 J1
Hexal Rd, SE6 ....172 E3
Hexham Gdns, Islw. TW7 .....124 D7
Hexham Rd, SE27 ....169 J2
  Barnet EN5 ....41 E4

Hexham Rd, Mord. SM4 198 E1
Heybourne Rd, N17 61 E7
Heybridge Av, SW16 169 E7
Heybridge Dr, Ilf. IG6 81 G2
Heybridge Way, E10 77 H7
Heyford Av, SW8 34 B7
SW20 184 C3
Heyford Rd, Mitch. CR4 185 H2
Heyford Ter, SW8
off Heyford Av 130/131 E7
Heygate St, SE17 35 J2
Heylyn Sq, E3
off Malmesbury Rd 113 J3
Heynes Rd, Dag. RM8 100 C4
Heysham Dr, Wat. WD19 50 C5
Heysham La, NW3 91 E3
Heysham Rd, N15 76 A6
Heythorp St, SW18 166 C1
Heywood Av, NW9 70 E1
Heyworth Rd, E5 94 E4
E15 97 F5
Hibbert Rd, E17 77 J7
Harrow HA3 68 C2
Hibbert St, SW11 149 F3
Hibernia Gdns, Houns. TW3 143 G4
Hibernia Pt, SE2
off Wolvercote Rd 138 D2
Hibernia Rd, Houns. TW3 143 G4
Hibiscus Cl, Edg. HA8
off Campion Way 54 C4
Hichisson Rd, SE15 153 F5
Hickin Cl, SE7 136 A4
Hickin St, E14 *off Plevna St* 134 C3
Hickling Rd, Ilf. IG1 99 E5
Hickman Av, E4 62 C6
Hickman Cl, E16 116 A5
Hickman Rd, Rom. RM6 82 C7
Hickmore Wk, SW4 150 C3
Hickory Cl, N9 44 D7
Hicks Av, Grnf. UB6 104 A2
Hicks Cl, SW11 149 H3
Hicks St, SE8 133 H5
Hidcote Gdns, SW20 183 H3
Hide, E6 *off Downings* 116 D6
Hide Pl, SW1 33 H2
Hide Rd, Har. HA1 68 A4
Hides St, N7
off Sheringham Rd 93 F6
Hide Twr, SW1 33 H2
Higgins Wk, Hmptn. TW12
off Abbott Cl 160/161 E6
High Acres, Enf. EN2
off Old Pk Vw 43 H3
HIGHAM HILL, E17 77 H2
Higham Hill Rd, E17 77 H2
Higham Pl, E17 77 H3
Higham Rd, N17 76 A3
Woodford Green IG8 63 G6
Highams Ct, E4 *off Friars Cl* 62 D3
Highams Lo Business Cen, E17 77 H3
HIGHAMS PARK, E4 62 D5
Highams Pk Ind Est, E4 62 C6
Higham Sta Av, E4 62 B6
Higham St, E17 77 H3
Highbanks Cl, Well. DA16 138 B7
Highbanks Rd, Pnr. HA5 51 H5
Highbank Way, N8 75 G6
HIGH BARNET, Barn. EN5 40 A2
Highbarrow Rd, Croy. CR0 188 D7
HIGH BEACH, Loug. IG10 47 G1
High Beech, S.Croy. CR2 202 B7
High Beeches, Sid. DA14 176 E5
High Beech Rd, Loug. IG10 48 A4
High Br, SE10 134 D5
Highbridge Rd, Bark. IG11 116 E1
High Br Wf, SE10 134 D5
Highbrook Rd, SE3 156 A3
High Broom Cres, W.Wick. BR4 190 B7
HIGHBURY, N5 93 H5
Highbury Av, Th.Hth. CR7 187 G2
Highbury Cl, N.Mal. KT3 182 C4
West Wickham BR4 204 B2
Highbury Cor, N5 93 G6
Highbury Cres, N5 93 G5
Highbury Est, N5 93 J5
Highbury Gdns, Ilf. IG3 99 H2
Highbury Gra, N5 93 H4
Highbury Gro, N5 93 H6
Highbury Hill, N5 93 G3
Highbury Ms, N7
off Holloway Rd 93 G6
Highbury New Pk, N5 93 J5
Highbury Pk, N5 93 H3
Highbury Pk Ms, N5
off Highbury Gra 93 J4
Highbury Pl, N5 93 H6
Highbury Quad, N5 93 J3
Highbury Rd, SW19 166 B5
Highbury Sta Rd, N1 93 G6
Highbury Ter, N5 93 H5
Highbury Ter Ms, N5 93 H5
High Cedar Dr, SW20 165 H7
Highclere Rd, N.Mal. KT3 182 D3
Highclere St, SE26 171 H4
Highcliffe Dr, SW15 147 F6
Highcliffe Gdns, Ilf. IG4 80 B5
Highcombe, SE7 135 H6
Highcombe Cl, SE9 174 A1
High Coombe Pl, Kings.T. KT2 164 D7
Highcroft, NW9 70 D5
Highcroft Av, Wem. HA0 106 A1
Highcroft Gdns, NW11 72 C6
Highcroft Rd, N19 74 E7
High Cross Cen, N15 76 D4
High Cross Rd, N17 76 D3
Highcross Way, SW15 165 G1
Highdaun Dr, SW16 187 F4
Highdown, Wor.Pk. KT4 197 E2
Highdown Rd, SW15 147 H6
High Dr, N.Mal. KT3 182 C1
High Elms, Chig. IG7 65 H4
Woodford Green IG8 63 G5
Highfield, Bushey (Bushey Hth)
WD23 52 B2
Feltham TW13 160 A1
Watford WD19 51 F3
Highfield Av, NW9 70 C5
NW11 72 A7
Erith DA8 139 H6
Greenford UB6 86 B5
Orpington BR6 207 J5
Pinner HA5 67 F5
Wembley HA9 87 J3
Highfield Cl, N22 75 G1
NW9 70 C5
SE13 154 D6
Surbiton KT6 195 F1
Highfield Ct, N14 42 C6
Highfield Dr, Brom. BR2 191 E4
Epsom KT19 197 F7
West Wickham BR4 204 B2
Highfield Gdns, NW11 72 B6
Highfield Hill, SE19 170 A7
Highfield Ms, NW6
off Compayne Gdns 90/91 E7
Highfield Rd, N21 59 H2
NW11 72 B6
W3 106 B5
Bexleyheath DA6 159 F5
Bromley BR1 192 C4
Chislehurst BR7 193 J3
Feltham TW13 160 A2
Isleworth TW7 144 C1
Surbiton KT5 182 C7
Sutton SM1 199 H5
Woodford Green IG8 64 B7
Highfields Gro, N6 91 J1
High Foleys, Esher (Clay.)
KT10 194 E7
High Gables, Loug. IG10 48 A5
HIGHGATE, N6 92 A2
Highgate Av, N6 74 B6
★ **Highgate Cem**, N6 92 A1
Highgate Cl, N6 74 A7
Highgate High St, N6 92 A1
Highgate Hill, N6 92 B1
N19 92 B1
Highgate Ho, SE26
off Sydenham Hill 170 D3
Highgate Rd, NW5 92 B4
Highgate Wk, SE23 171 F2
Highgate W Hill, N6 92 A2
High Gro, SE18 137 G7
Bromley BR1 191 J1
Highgrove Cl, N11
off Balmoral Av 58 A5
Chislehurst BR7 192 B1
Highgrove Ms, Cars. SM5 199 J3
Highgrove Rd, Dag. RM8 100 C5
Highgrove Way, Ruis. HA4 66 A6
High Hill Est, E5
off Mount Pleasant La 94/95 E1
High Hill Ferry, E5 95 E1
High Holborn, WC1 18 B3
Highland Av, W7 104 B6
Dagenham RM10 101 J3
Loughton IG10 48 B6
Highland Cotts, Wall. SM6 200 B4
Highland Ct, E18 79 H1
Highland Cft, Beck. BR3 172 B5
Highland Rd, SE19 170 B6
Bexleyheath DA6 159 G5
Bromley BR1, BR2 191 F1
Highlands, Wat. WD19 50 C1
Highlands, The, Edg. HA8 70 B2
Potters Bar EN6 40 E5
Highlands Av, N21 43 F5
W3 106 C7
Highlands Cl, N4
off Mount Vw Rd 74/75 E7
Hounslow TW3 143 H1
Highlands Gdns, Ilf. IG1 98 C1
Highlands Heath, SW15 147 J7
Highlands Rd, Barn. EN5 40 D5
High La, W7 104 A6
High Lawns, Har. HA1 86 B3
Highlea Cl, NW9 71 E1
High Level Dr, SE26 170 D4
Highlever Rd, W10 107 J5
Highmead, SE18 137 J7
High Mead, Chig. IG7 65 F2
Harrow HA1 68 B5
West Wickham BR4 204 D2
Highmead Cres, Wem. HA0 87 J7
High Meadow Cl, Pnr. HA5
off Daymer Gdns 66 B4
High Meadow Cres, NW9 70 D5
High Meadows, Chig. IG7 65 G5
High Meads Rd, E16 116 A6
Highmore Rd, SE3 135 E7
High Mt, NW4 71 G6
High Pk Av, Rich. TW9 146 A1
High Pk Rd, Rich. TW9 146 A1
High Path, SW19 185 E1
High Pt, N6 74 A7
SE9 175 E3
High Rd, N2 73 G1
N11 58 B5
N12 57 F6
N15 76 C6
N17 76 C1
N20 41 F7
N22 75 G3
NW10 (Willesden) 89 H6
Buckhurst Hill IG9 63 H2
Bushey (Bushey Hth) WD23 52 A1
Chigwell IG7 64 C5
Harrow (Har.Wld) HA3 52 B7
Ilford IG1 98 E3
Ilford (Seven Kings) IG3 99 J1
Loughton IG10 47 J7
Pinner HA5 66 B4
Romford (Chad.Hth) RM6 100 B1
Wembley HA0, HA9 87 G5
High Rd Leyton, E10 96 B1
E15 96 C3
High Rd Leytonstone, E11 96 E4
E15 96 E4
High Rd Woodford Grn, E18 63 F7
Woodford Green IG8 63 F7
Highshore Rd, SE15 152 C2
High Silver, Loug. IG10 48 A4
Highstone Av, E11 79 G6
High St, E11 79 G5
E13 115 G2
E15 114 C2
E17 77 J5
N8 74 E4
N14 58 D1
NW7 55 H4
NW10 (Harlesden) 107 F2
SE20 171 E6
SE25 (S.Norwood) 188 C4
W3 126 B1
W5 105 G7
Barnet EN5 40 B3
Beckenham BR3 190 A2
Brentford TW8 125 G6
Bromley BR1 191 G2
Carshalton SM5 200 A4
Chislehurst BR7 174 E6
Croydon CR0 201 J2
Edgware HA8 54 A6
Esher (Clay.) KT10 194 C6
Feltham TW13 160 A3
Hampton TW12 161 J6
Harrow HA1, HA2 86 B1
Harrow (Wldste) HA3 68 B3
Hayes UB3 121 H5
Hounslow TW3 143 J3
Hounslow (Cran.) TW5 122 B7
Ilford (Barkingside) IG6 81 F2
Kingston upon Thames KT1 181 G2
Kingston upon Thames (Hmptn W.)
KT1 181 F1
New Malden KT3 183 E3
Orpington (Farnboro.) BR6 207 E5
Orpington (Grn St Grn) BR6 207 J7
Pinner HA5 66 E3
Southall UB1 123 F1
Staines (Stanw.) TW19 140 A6
Sutton SM1 198 E4
Sutton (Cheam) SM3 198 B6
Teddington TW11 162 D5
Thames Ditton KT7 180 D7
Thornton Heath CR7 187 J4
Twickenham (Whitton) TW2 143 J7
Wembley HA9 87 J4
West Drayton (Harm.) UB7 120 A6
West Drayton (Yiew.) UB7 120 A1
West Molesey KT8 179 G4
West Wickham BR4 204 B1
High St Colliers Wd, SW19 167 G7
High St Ms, SW19 166 B5
High St N, E6 116 B1
E12 98 B5
High St Ponders End, Enf. EN3 45 F4
High St S, E6 116 C2
High St Wimbledon, SW19 166 A5
High Timber St, EC4 19 J5
High Tor Cl, Brom. BR1
off Babbacombe Rd 173 H7
High Tor Vw, SE28
off Hill Vw Dr 137 H1
High Tree Ct, W7 104 B7
High Trees, SW2 169 G1
Barnet EN4 41 H5
Croydon CR0 203 H1
Highview, Nthlt. UB5 103 E3
High Vw, Pnr. HA5 66 C4
Highview Av, Edg. HA8 54 C4
Highview Av, Wall. SM6 201 F5
High Vw Cl, SE19 188 C2
Loughton IG10 47 J5
Highview Gdns, N3 72 B3
N11 58 C5
Edgware HA8 54 C4
Highview Ho, Rom. RM6 83 E4
High Vw Rd, E18 79 F3
SE19 170 A6
Highview Rd, W13 104 D5
Sidcup DA14 176 B4
Highway, The, E1 21 J6
E14 21 J6
Stanmore HA7 68 C1
Highwood, Brom. BR2 190 E3
Highwood Av, N12 57 F4
Highwood Cl, Orp. BR6 207 F2
Highwood Dr, Orp. BR6 207 F2
Highwood Gdns, Ilf. IG5 80 C5
Highwood Gro, NW7 54 D5
HIGHWOOD HILL, NW7 55 G2
Highwood Hill, NW7 55 F2
Highwood La, Loug. IG10 48 D5
Highwood Rd, N19 92 E3
High Worple, Har. HA2 67 F7
Highworth Rd, N11 58 D6
Hilary Av, Mitch. CR4 186 A3
Hilary Cl, SW6 30 A7
Erith DA8 159 J1
Hilary Rd, W12 107 F6
Hilbert Rd, Sutt. SM3 198 A3
Hilborough Way, Orp. BR6 207 G5
Hilda Lockert Wk, SW9
off Fiveways Rd 151 H2
Hilda Rd, E6 98 A7
E16 115 E4
Hilda Ter, SW9 151 G2
Hilda Vale Cl, Orp. BR6 206 E4
Hilda Vale Rd, Orp. BR6 206 D4
Hildenborough Gdns, Brom.
BR1 173 E6
Hildenlea Pl, Brom. BR2 190 E2
Hildreth St, SW12 168 B1
Hildyard Rd, SW6 128 D6
Hiley Rd, NW10 107 J3
Hilgrove Rd, NW6 91 F7
Hiliary Gdns, Stan. HA7 69 F2
Hillary Dr, Islw. TW7 144 C4
Hillary Ri, Barn. EN5 40 D4
Hillary Rd, Sthl. UB2 123 G3
Hillbeck Cl, SE15 133 F7
Hillbeck Way, Grnf. UB6 104 A1
Hillborne Cl, Hayes UB3 122 A5
Hillborough Cl, SW19 167 F7
Hillbrook Rd, SW17 167 J3
Hill Brow, Brom. BR1 192 A1
Hillbrow, N.Mal. KT3 183 F3
Hillbrow Rd, Brom. BR1 172 E7
Hillbury Av, Har. HA3 69 E5
Hillbury Rd, SW17 168 B3
Hill Cl, NW2 89 H3
NW11 72 D6
Barnet EN5 39 J5
Chislehurst BR7 174 E5
Harrow HA1 86 B3
Stanmore HA7 52 E4
Hillcote Av, SW16 169 G7
Hill Ct, Nthlt. UB5 85 G5
Hillcourt Av, N12 56 E6
Hillcourt Est, N16 94 A1
Hillcourt Rd, SE22 152 E6
Hill Cres, N20 56 E2
Bexley DA5 177 J1
Harrow HA1 68 D5
Surbiton KT5 181 J5
Worcester Park KT4 197 J2
Hillcrest, N6 74 A7
N21 43 H7
Hill Crest, Sid. DA15 158 A7
Hillcrest Av, NW11 72 B5
Edgware HA8 54 B4
Pinner HA5 66 D4
Hillcrest Cl, SE26 170 D4
Beckenham BR3 189 J5
Hillcrest Ct, Sutt. SM2
off Eaton Rd 199 G6
Hillcrest Gdns, N3 72 B4
NW2 89 G3
Esher KT10 194 C3
Hillcrest Rd, E17 78 D2
E18 79 F2
W3 126 A1
W5 105 H5
Bromley BR1 173 G5
Loughton IG10 48 A6
Hillcrest Vw, Beck. BR3 189 J6
Hillcroft, Loug. IG10 48 D2
Hillcroft Av, Pnr. HA5 67 F6
Hillcroft Cres, W5 105 H6
Ruislip HA4 84 D3
Watford WD19 50 B1
Wembley HA9 87 J4
Hillcroft Rd, E6 116 E5
Hillcroome Rd, Sutt. SM2 199 G6
Hillcross Av, Mord. SM4 184 C5
Hilldale Rd, Sutt. SM1 198 C4
Hilldown Rd, SW16 169 E7

Hilldown Rd, Brom. BR2 . . . . . . .205 E1
Hill Dr, NW9 . . . . .88 C1
SW16 . . . . .187 F3
Hilldrop Cres, N7 . . . . .92 D5
Hilldrop Est, N7 . . . . .92 D5
Hilldrop La, N7 . . . . .92 D5
Hilldrop Rd, N7 . . . . .92 D5
Bromley BR1 . . . . .173 G6
Hillend, SE18 . . . . .156 D1
Hill End, Orp. BR6
   off The Approach 207 J2
Hillersdon Av, SW13 . . . . .147 H2
Edgware HA8 . . . . .53 J5
Hillery Cl, SE17 . . . . .36 C2
Hill Fm Rd, W10 . . . . .107 F5
Hillfield Av, N8 . . . . .75 E5
NW9 .71 E5
Wembley HA0 . . . . .87 H7
Hillfield Cl, Har. HA2 . . . . .67 J4
Hillfield Ct, NW3 . . . . .91 H5
Hillfield Ms, N8 off Hillfield Av . . .75 E5
Hillfield Par, Mord. SM4 . . . . . . .185 H6
Hillfield Pk, N10 . . . . .74 A3
N21 .59 G2
Hillfield Pk Ms, N10 . . . . .74 A4
Hillfield Rd, NW6 . . . . .90 C5
Hampton TW12 . . . . .161 F7
Hillfoot Av, Rom. RM5 . . . . .83 J1
Hillfoot Rd, Rom. RM5 . . . . .83 J1
Hillgate Pl, SW12 . . . . .150 B7
W8 .128 D1
Hillgate St, W8 . . . . .128 D1
Hill Gate Wk, N6 . . . . .74 C6
Hill Gro, Felt. TW13
   off Watermill Way 161 F2
Hill Ho Av, Stan. HA7 . . . . .52 C7
Hill Ho Cl, N21 . . . . .43 G7
Hill Ho Dr, Hmptn. TW12 . . . . . .179 G1
Hill Ho Rd, SW16 . . . . .169 F5
Hilliards Ct, E1
   off Wapping High St . . .132/133 E1
Hillier Cl, Barn. EN5 . . . . .40 E6
Hillier Gdns, Croy. CR0
   off Crowley Cres 201 G4
Hillier Pl, Chess. KT9 . . . . .195 F6
Hillier Rd, SW11 . . . . .149 J6
Hilliers La, Croy. CR0 . . . . .200 E3
Hillingdon Rd, Bexh. DA7 . . . . . .159 J2
Hillingdon St, SE5 . . . . .35 H6
SE17 . . . . .35 H6
Hillington Gdns, Wdf.Grn. IG8 . . .80 A2
Hillman Dr, W10 . . . . .107 J4
Hillman St, E8 . . . . .95 E6
Hillmarton Rd, N7 . . . . .93 E5
Hillmead Dr, SW9 . . . . .151 H4
Hillmont Rd, Esher KT10 . . . . . . .194 B3
Hillmore Gro, SE26 . . . . .171 G5
Hill Path, SW16 off Valley Rd . . .169 F5
Hillreach, SE18 . . . . .136 C5
Hill Ri, N9 . . . . .45 E6
NW11 . . . . .73 E4
SE23 off London Rd 170/171 E1
Esher KT10 . . . . .194 E2
Greenford UB6 . . . . .85 J7
Richmond TW10 . . . . .145 G5
Hillrise Rd, N19 . . . . .74 E7
Hill Rd, N10 . . . . .73 J1
NW8 . . . . .6 D2
Carshalton SM5 . . . . .199 H6
Harrow HA1 . . . . .68 D5
Mitcham CR4 . . . . .186 B1
Pinner HA5 . . . . .66 E5
Sutton SM1 . . . . .199 E5
Wembley HA0 . . . . .86 E3
Hillsborough Grn, Wat. WD19
   off Ashburnham Dr 50 A3
Hillsborough Rd, SE22 . . . . .152 B5
Hillsgrove, Well. DA16 . . . . .138 C7
Hillside, NW9 . . . . .70 D4
NW10 . . . . .106 C1
SW19 . . . . .166 A6
Barnet EN5 . . . . .41 F5
Hillside Av, N11 . . . . .57 J6
Borehamwood WD6 . . . . .38 A4
Wembley HA9 . . . . .87 J4
Woodford Green IG8 . . . . .63 J5
Hillside Cl, NW8 . . . . .6 B1
Morden SM4 . . . . .184 A4
Woodford Green IG8 . . . . .63 J5
Hillside Cres, Har. HA2 . . . . .85 J1
Northwood HA6 . . . . .66 A1
Hillside Dr, Edg. HA8 . . . . .54 A6
Hillside Est, N15 . . . . .76 C6
Hillside Gdns, E17 . . . . .78 D3
N6 . . . . .74 A6
SW2 . . . . .169 G2
Barnet EN5 . . . . .40 B4
Edgware HA8 . . . . .53 J4
Harrow HA3 . . . . .69 H7
Northwood HA6 . . . . .50 A7
Wallington SM6 . . . . .200 C7
Hillside Gro, N14 . . . . .42 D7
NW7 .55 G7
Hillside La, Brom. BR2 . . . . .205 G2
Hillside Pas, SW2 . . . . .169 F2
Hillside Ri, Nthwd. HA6 . . . . .50 A7
Hillside Rd, N15 . . . . .76 B7

Hillside Rd, SW2 . . . . .169 G2
W5 .105 H5
Bromley BR2 . . . . .191 F3
Croydon CR0 . . . . .201 H5
Northwood HA6 . . . . .50 A7
Pinner HA5 . . . . .50 B7
Southall UB1 . . . . .103 G4
Surbiton KT5 . . . . .181 J5
Sutton SM3 . . . . .198 C7
Hillsleigh Rd, W8 . . . . .128 C1
Hills Ms, W5 . . . . .105 H7
Hills Pl, W1 . . . . .17 F4
Hills Rd, Buck.H. IG9 . . . . .63 H1
Hillstowe St, E5 . . . . .95 F2
Hill St, W1 . . . . .24 C1
Richmond TW9 . . . . .145 G5
Hill Top, NW11 . . . . .73 E4
Loughton IG10 . . . . .48 D2
Morden SM4 . . . . .184 D6
Sutton SM3 . . . . .184 C1
Hilltop Av, NW10 . . . . .88 C7
Hill Top Cl, Loug. IG10 . . . . .48 D3
Hilltop Gdns, NW4 . . . . .71 H2
Orpington BR6 . . . . .207 H2
Hill Top Pl, Loug. IG10 . . . . .48 D3
Hilltop Rd, NW6 . . . . .90 D7
Hill Top Vw, Wdf.Grn. IG8 . . . . . .64 C6
Hilltop Way, Stan. HA7 . . . . .52 D3
Hillview, SW20 . . . . .165 H7
Mitcham CR4 . . . . .186 E4
Hillview Av, Har. HA3 . . . . .69 H5
Hillview Cl, Pnr. HA5 . . . . .51 F6
Wembley HA9 . . . . .87 J2
Hillview Cres, Ilf. IG1 . . . . .80 C6
Hill Vw Cres, Orp. BR6 . . . . .207 J1
Hill Vw Dr, SE28 . . . . .137 H1
Welling DA16 . . . . .157 H2
Hillview Gdns, NW4 . . . . .72 A4
Hill Vw Gdns, NW9 . . . . .70 D5
Hillview Gdns, Har. HA2 . . . . .67 G3
Hillview Rd, NW7 . . . . .56 A4
Chislehurst BR7 . . . . .174 D5
Hill Vw Rd, Esher (Clay.) KT10 . .194 D7
Orpington BR6 . . . . .207 J1
Hillview Rd, Pnr. HA5 . . . . .51 F7
Sutton SM1 . . . . .199 F3
Hill Vw Rd, Twick. TW1 . . . . .144 D6
Hillway, N6 . . . . .92 A2
NW9 .88 E1
Hillworth Rd, SW2 . . . . .151 G7
Hillyard Rd, W7 . . . . .104 B5
Hillyard St, SW9 . . . . .151 G1
Hillyfield, E17 . . . . .77 H2
Hillyfield Cl, E9 off Mabley St . . .95 H5
Hillyfields, Loug. IG10 . . . . .48 D2
Hilly Flds Cres, SE4 . . . . .154 A3
Hilsea Pt, SW15
   off Wanborough Dr 165 H1
Hilsea St, E5 . . . . .95 F4
Hilton Av, N12 . . . . .57 G5
Hilversum Cres, SE22
   off East Dulwich Gro 152 B5
Himley Rd, SW17 . . . . .167 H5
Hinchley Cl, Esher KT10 . . . . . . .194 C3
Hinchley Dr, Esher KT10 . . . . . . .194 C3
Hinchley Way, Esher KT10 . . . . . .194 D3
HINCHLEY WOOD, Esher KT10 . .194 C3
Hinckley Rd, SE15 . . . . .152 D4
Hind Cl, Chig. IG7 . . . . .65 J5
Hind Ct, EC4 . . . . .19 F4
Hinde Ms, W1
   off Marylebone La 110 A6
Hindes Rd, Har. HA1 . . . . .68 A5
Hinde St, W1 . . . . .16 C3
Hind Gro, E14 . . . . .114 A6
Hindhead Cl, N16 . . . . .94 B1
Hindhead Gdns, Nthlt. UB5 . . . .102 E1
Hindhead Grn, Wat. WD19 . . . . . .50 C5
Hindhead Pt, SW15
   off Wanborough Dr 165 H1
Hindhead Way, Wall. SM6 . . . . . .200 E5
Hind Ho, N7 off Harvist Est 93 G4
Hindmans Rd, SE22 . . . . .152 D5
Hindmans Way, Dag. RM9 . . . . .119 F4
Hindmarsh Cl, E1 . . . . .21 J5
Hindon Ct, SW1 off Wilton Rd . .130 C4
Hindrey Rd, E5 . . . . .94 E5
Hindsley's Pl, SE23 . . . . .171 F2
Hinkler Rd, Har. HA3 . . . . .69 G3
Hinksey Path, SE2 . . . . .138 D3
Hinstock Rd, SE18 . . . . .137 F6
Hinton Av, Houns. TW4 . . . . .142 D4
Hinton Cl, SE9 . . . . .174 B1
Hinton Rd, N18 . . . . .60 B4
SE24 . . . . .151 H3
Wallington SM6 . . . . .200 C6
Hippodrome Ms, W11
   off Portland Rd 108 B7
Hippodrome Pl, W11 . . . . .108 B7
Hirst Cres, Wem. HA9 . . . . .87 H3
   off East La 87 H3
Hiscocks Ho, NW10 . . . . .88 C7
Hitcham Rd, E17 . . . . .77 J7
Hitchin Sq, E3 . . . . .113 H2
Hithe Gro, SE16 off Lower Rd . . .133 G3
Hitherbroom Rd, Hayes UB3 . . . .122 A1
Hither Fm Rd, SE3 . . . . .155 J3

Hitherfield Rd, SW16 . . . . .169 F2
Dagenham RM8 . . . . .101 E2
HITHER GREEN, SE13 . . . . .154 E6
Hither Grn La, SE13 . . . . .154 C5
Hitherlands, SW12 . . . . .168 B2
Hitherwell Dr, Har. HA3 . . . . .68 A1
Hitherwood Dr, SE19 . . . . .170 C4
Hive Cl, Bushey (Bushey Hth)
   WD23 . . . . .52 A2
Hive Rd, Bushey (Bushey Hth)
   WD23 . . . . .52 A2
★ H.M.S. Belfast, SE1 . . . . .28 E1
★ H.M.S. President, EC4 . . . . . . .19 F6
★ H.M. Treasury, SW1 . . . . .26 A3
Hoadly Rd, SW16 . . . . .168 D3
Hobart Cl, N20
   off Oakleigh Rd N 57 H2
Hayes UB4 . . . . .102 D4
Hobart Dr, Hayes UB4 . . . . .102 D4
Hobart Gdns, Th.Hth. CR7 . . . . . .188 A3
Hobart La, Hayes UB4 . . . . .102 D4
Hobart Pl, SW1 . . . . .24 D5
Richmond TW10
   off Chisholm Rd 145 J6
Hobart Rd, Dag. RM9 . . . . .100 D4
Hayes UB4 . . . . .102 D4
Ilford IG6 . . . . .81 F2
Worcester Park KT4 . . . . .197 H3
Hobbayne Rd, W7 . . . . .104 A6
Hobbes Wk, SW15 . . . . .147 H5
Hobbs Grn, N2 . . . . .73 F3
Hobbs Ms, Ilf. IG3
   off Ripley Rd 99 J2
Hobbs Pl Est, N1 off Pitfield St . .112 B1
Hobbs Rd, SE27 . . . . .169 J4
Hobday St, E14 . . . . .114 B5
Hobill Wk, Surb. KT5 . . . . .181 J6
Hoblands End, Chis. BR7 . . . . . . .175 H6
Hobsons Pl, E1 . . . . .21 H1
Hobury St, SW10 . . . . .30 D6
Hocker St, E2 . . . . .13 F4
Hockett Cl, SE8 off Grove St 133 J4
Hockley Av, E6 . . . . .116 B2
Hockley Ct, E18
   off Churchfields 79 G1
Hockley Ms, Bark. IG11 . . . . .117 H2
Hocroft Av, NW2 . . . . .90 C3
Hocroft Rd, NW2 . . . . .90 C4
Hocroft Wk, NW2 . . . . .90 C3
Hodder Dr, Grnf. UB6 . . . . .104 C2
Hoddesdon Rd, Belv. DA17 . . . . .139 G5
Hodford Rd, NW11 . . . . .90 C2
Hodgkin Cl, SE28
   off Fleming Way 118 D7
Hodgkins Ms, Stan. HA7 . . . . .52 E5
Hodister Cl, SE5
   off Badsworth Rd 131 J7
Hodnet Gro, SE16 . . . . .133 G4
Hodson Cl, Har. HA2 . . . . .85 F3
Hoe, The, Wat. WD19 . . . . .50 D2
Hoechst, Houns. TW4 . . . . .142 C3
Hoe St, E17 . . . . .78 A4
Hofland Rd, W14 . . . . .128 A3
Hogan Ms, W2 . . . . .14 E1
Hogan Way, E5
   off Geldeston Rd 94 D2
Hogarth Business Pk, W4 . . . . . .127 E6
Hogarth Cl, E16 . . . . .116 A5
W5 .105 H5
Hogarth Ct, EC3 . . . . .20 E5
SE19 off Fountain Dr 170 C4
Hogarth Cres, SW19 . . . . .185 G1
Croydon CR0 . . . . .187 J7
Hogarth Gdns, Houns. TW5 . . . .123 G7
Hogarth Hill, NW11 . . . . .72 C4
Hogarth La, W4 . . . . .126 E6
Hogarth Pl, SW5 . . . . .30 A2
Hogarth Reach, Loug. IG10 . . . . . .48 C5
Hogarth Rd, SW5 . . . . .30 A2
Dagenham RM8 . . . . .100 B5
Edgware HA8 . . . . .70 A2
Hogarth Roundabout, W4 . . . . . .127 F6
Hogarth Roundabout Flyover, W4
   off Burlington La 126/127 E6
★ Hogarth's Ho, W4
   off Hogarth La 126 E6
Hogarth Way, Hmptn. TW12 . . . .179 J1
Hogshead Pas, E1
   off Pennington St 112/113 E7
Hogsmill Way, Epsom KT19 . . . .196 C5
Holbeach Gdns, Sid. DA15 . . . . .157 H6
Holbeach Ms, SW12
   off Harberson Rd 168 B1
Holbeach Rd, SE6 . . . . .154 A7
Holbeck Row, SE15 . . . . .132 D7
Holbein Ms, SW1 . . . . .32 B3
Holbein Pl, SW1 . . . . .32 B2
Holbein Ter, Dag. RM8
   off Marlborough Rd 100 B4
Holberton Gdns, NW10 . . . . .107 H3
HOLBORN, WC2 . . . . .18 C3
Holborn, EC1 . . . . .18 E2
Holborn Circ, EC1 . . . . .19 F2
Holborn Pl, WC1 . . . . .18 C2
Holborn Rd, E13 . . . . .115 H4
Holborn Viaduct, EC1 . . . . .19 F2
Holborn Way, Mitch. CR4 . . . . . .185 J2

Holbrook Cl, N19
   off Dartmouth Pk Hill 92 B1
Enfield EN1 . . . . .44 C1
Holbrooke Ct, N7 . . . . .93 E4
Holbrooke Pl, Rich. TW10
   off Hill Ri 145 G5
Holbrook La, Chis. BR7 . . . . .175 G7
Holbrook Rd, E15 . . . . .115 F2
Holbrook Way, Brom. BR2 . . . . . .192 C6
Holburne Cl, SE3 . . . . .155 J1
Holburne Gdns, SE3 . . . . .156 A1
Holburne Rd, SE3 . . . . .155 J1
Holcombe Hill, NW7 . . . . .55 G3
Holcombe Rd, N17 . . . . .76 C3
Ilford IG1 . . . . .80 D7
Holcombe St, W6 . . . . .127 H5
Holcote Cl, Belv. DA17
   off Blakemore Way 138/139 E3
Holcroft Rd, E9 . . . . .95 F7
Holden Av, N12 . . . . .57 E5
NW9 .88 C1
Holdenby Rd, SE4 . . . . .153 H5
Holden Cl, Dag. RM8 . . . . .100 B3
Holdenhurst Av, N12 . . . . .57 E7
Holden Pt, E15
   off Waddington Rd 96 D6
Holden Rd, N12 . . . . .56 E5
Holden St, SW11 . . . . .150 A2
Holdernesse Cl, Islw. TW7 . . . . . .144 D1
Holdernesse Rd, SW17 . . . . .167 J3
Holderness Way, SE27 . . . . .169 H5
HOLDERS HILL, NW4 . . . . .72 A2
Holders Hill Av, NW4 . . . . .72 A2
Holders Hill Circ, NW7
   off Dollis Rd 56 B7
Holders Hill Cres, NW4 . . . . .72 A2
Holders Hill Dr, NW4 . . . . .72 A3
Holders Hill Gdns, NW4 . . . . .72 B2
Holders Hill Rd, NW4 . . . . .72 A2
NW7 .72 A2
Holegate St, SE7
   off Westmoor St 136 A3
Holford Ms, WC1 . . . . .10 E2
Holford Pl, WC1 . . . . .10 D3
Holford Rd, NW3 . . . . .91 F3
Holford St, WC1 . . . . .10 E3
Holford Yd, WC1 . . . . .10 E2
Holgate Av, SW11 . . . . .149 G3
Holgate Gdns, Dag. RM10 . . . . . .101 G5
Holgate Rd, Dag. RM10 . . . . . . .101 G5
Holland Av, SW20 . . . . .183 F1
Holland Cl, Barn. EN5 . . . . .41 F7
Bromley BR2 . . . . .205 F2
Romford RM7 . . . . .83 J5
Stanmore HA7 . . . . .52 E5
Holland Ct, E17 off Evelyn Rd . . .78 C4
NW7 off Page St 55 G6
Holland Dr, SE23 . . . . .171 H3
Holland Gdns, W14 . . . . .128 B3
Brentford TW8 . . . . .125 H6
Holland Gro, SW9 . . . . .131 G7
★ Holland Ho & Pk, W8 . . . . . . .128 C2
Holland Pk, W11 . . . . .128 C2
W11 .128 B2
Holland Pk Av, W11 . . . . .128 B2
Ilford IG3 . . . . .81 H6
Holland Pk Gdns, W14 . . . . .128 B1
Holland Pk Ms, W11 . . . . .128 C2
Holland Pk Rd, W14 . . . . .128 C3
Holland Pk Roundabout, W11 . . .128 A2
Holland Pas, N1 off Basire St . . .111 J1
Holland Pl, W8 . . . . .22 A3
Holland Rd, E6 . . . . .116 C1
E15 .115 E3
NW10 . . . . .107 G1
SE25 . . . . .188 D5
W14 .128 A2
Wembley HA0 . . . . .87 G6
Hollands, The, Felt. TW13 . . . . . .160 D4
Worcester Park KT4 . . . . .197 F1
Holland St, SE1 . . . . .27 H1
W8 . . . . .22 A3
Holland Vil Rd, W14 . . . . .128 B2
Holland Wk, N19
   off Duncombe Rd 92 D1
W8 .128 C2
Stanmore HA7 . . . . .52 D5
Holland Way, Brom. BR2 . . . . . . .205 F2
Hollar Rd, N16
   off Stoke Newington High St .94 C3
Hollen St, W1 . . . . .17 H3
Holles Cl, Hmptn. TW12 . . . . . . .161 G6
Holles St, W1 . . . . .16 E3
Holley Rd, W3 . . . . .127 E2
Hollickwood Av, N12 . . . . .57 J6
Holliday Sq, SW11
   off Fowler Cl 149 G3
Hollidge Way, Dag. RM10 . . . . . .101 H6
Hollies, The, E11 . . . . .79 G5
N20 off Oakleigh Pk N 57 G1
Harrow HA3 . . . . .68 D4
Hollies Av, Sid. DA15 . . . . .175 J2
Hollies Cl, SW16 . . . . .169 G6
Twickenham TW1 . . . . .162 C2
Hollies End, NW7 . . . . .55 H5
Hollies Rd, W5 . . . . .125 F4

Hollies Way, SW12
off Bracken Av 150 A7
Holligrave Rd, Brom. BR1 . . . .191 G1
Hollingbourne Av, Bexh. DA7 .139 F7
Hollingbourne Gdns, W13 . . . . .104 E5
Hollingbourne Rd, SE24 . . . . .151 J5
Hollingsworth Rd, Croy. CR0 . .203 E6
Hollington Rd, E6 . . . . .116 C3
N17 .76 D2
Hollingworth Cl, W.Mol. KT8 . .179 F4
Hollingworth Rd, Orp. BR5 . . . .192 E6
Hollman Gdns, SW16 . . . . .169 H6
Hollow, The, Wdf.Grn. IG8 . . . . .63 F4
HOLLOWAY, N7 . . . . .92 E4
Holloway Cl, West Dr. UB7 . . . .120 B5
Holloway La, West Dr. UB7 . . . .120 B6
Holloway Rd, E6 . . . . .116 C3
E11 .96 E3
N7 . . . . .93 F4
N19 .92 D2
Holloway St, Houns. TW3 . . . .143 H4
Hollowfield Wk, Nthlt. UB5 . . . .84 E6
Hollows, The, Brent. TW8
off Kew Br Rd 125 J6
Hollow Wk, Rich. TW9
off Kew Rd 125 H7
Holly Av, Stan. HA7 . . . . .69 H2
Hollyberry La, NW3
off Holly Wk 91 F4
Hollybrake Cl, Chis. BR7 . . . .175 G7
Hollybush Cl, E11 . . . . .79 G5
Harrow HA3 . . . . .68 B1
Hollybush Gdns, E2 . . . . .113 E3
Hollybush Hill, E11 . . . . .79 F6
Holly Bush Hill, NW3 . . . . .91 F4
Hollybush Pl, E2
off Bethnal Grn Rd 112/113 E3
Hollybush Rd, Kings.T. KT2 . . .163 H5
Holly Bush Steps, NW3
off Heath St 91 F4
Hollybush St, E13 . . . . .115 H3
Holly Bush Vale, NW3
off Heath St 91 F4
Holly Cl, NW10 . . . . .88 E7
Beckenham BR3 . . . . .190 C4
Buckhurst Hill IG9 . . . . .64 A3
Feltham TW13 . . . . .160 E5
Wallington SM6 . . . . .200 B7
Holly Ct, Sutt. SM2
off Worcester Rd 198 D7
Holly Cres, Beck. BR3 . . . . . .189 J5
Woodford Green IG8 . . . . . . .62 D7
Hollycroft Av, NW3 . . . . .90 D3
Wembley HA9 . . . . .87 J2
Hollycroft Cl, S.Croy. CR2 . . .202 B5
West Drayton UB7 . . . . . . .120 D6
Hollycroft Gdns, West Dr. UB7 .120 D6
Hollydale Cl, Nthlt. UB5
off Dorchester Rd 85 H4
Hollydale Dr, Brom. BR2 . . . . .206 C3
Hollydale Rd, SE15 . . . . .153 F1
Hollydene, SE15 . . . . .152 E1
Hollydown Way, E11 . . . . .96 D3
Holly Dr, E4 . . . . .46 B7
Brentford TW8 . . . . .124 D6
Holly Fm Rd, Sthl. UB2 . . . . . .122 E5
Hollyfield Av, N11 . . . . .57 J5
Hollyfield Rd, Surb. KT5 . . . . .181 J7
Holly Gdns, Bexh. DA7 . . . . . .159 J4
West Drayton UB7 . . . . . . .120 C2
Holly Gro, NW9 . . . . .70 C7
SE15 . . . . .152 C2
Pinner HA5 . . . . .67 E1
Holly Hedge Ter, SE13 . . . . . .154 D5
Holly Hill, N21 . . . . .43 F6
NW3 . . . . .91 F4
Holly Hill Rd, Belv. DA17 . . . . .139 H5
Erith DA8 . . . . .139 H5
Holly Lo Gdns, N6 . . . . .92 A2
Hollymead, Cars. SM5 . . . . . . .199 J3
Holly Ms, SW10 . . . . .30 D4
Holly Mt, NW3
off Holly Bush Hill 91 F4
Hollymount Cl, SE10 . . . . .154 C1
Holly Pk, N3 . . . . .72 C3
N4 . . . . .75 F7
Holly Pk Est, N4
off Blythwood Rd 75 F7
Holly Pk Gdns, N3 . . . . .72 D3
Holly Pk Rd, N11 . . . . .58 A5
W7 . . . . .124 C1
Holly Pl, NW3 off Holly Wk 91 F4
Holly Rd, E11 . . . . .79 F7
W4 off Dolman Rd 126 D4
Hampton (Hmptn H.) TW12 .161 J6
Hounslow TW3 . . . . .143 H4
Twickenham TW1 . . . . .162 D1
Holly St, E8 . . . . .94 C6
Holly Ter, N6
off Highgate W Hill 92 A1
N20 off Swan La 57 F2
Hollytree Cl, SW19 . . . . .166 A1
Holly Vw Cl, NW4 . . . . .71 G6
Holly Village, N6 off Swains La .92 B2

Holly Wk, NW3 . . . . .91 F4
Enfield EN2 . . . . .43 J3
Richmond TW9 . . . . .145 H2
Holly Way, Mitch. CR4 . . . . . . .186 D4
Hollywood Gdns, Hayes UB4 . . .102 B6
Hollywood Ms, SW10 . . . . .30 C4
Hollywood Rd, E4 . . . . .61 H5
SW10 . . . . .30 C4
Hollywood Way, Wdf.Grn. IG8 . . .62 D7
Holman Rd, SW11 . . . . .149 G2
Epsom KT19 . . . . .196 C5
Holmbridge Gdns, Enf. EN3 . . . .45 G4
Holmbrook Dr, NW4 . . . . .72 A5
Holmbury Ct, SW17 . . . . .167 J3
SW19 off Cavendish Rd 167 H7
Holmbury Gdns, Hayes UB3
off Church Rd 121 J1
Holmbury Gro, Croy. CR0 . . . .203 J7
Holmbury Pk, Brom. BR1 . . . . .174 B7
Holmbury Vw, E5 . . . . .95 E1
Holmbush Rd, SW15 . . . . .148 B6
Holmcote Gdns, N5 . . . . .93 J5
Holmcroft Way, Brom. BR2 . . .192 C5
Holmdale Gdns, NW4 . . . . .72 A5
Holmdale Rd, NW6 . . . . .90 D5
Chislehurst BR7 . . . . .175 F5
Holmdale Ter, N15 . . . . .76 B7
Holmdene Av, NW7 . . . . .55 G6
SE24 . . . . .151 J5
Harrow HA2 . . . . .67 H3
Holmdene Cl, Beck. BR3 . . . . .190 C2
Holmead Rd, SW6 . . . . .129 E7
Holmebury Cl, Bushey (Bushey Hth)
WD23 . . . . .52 B2
Holme Ct, Islw. TW7
off Twickenham Rd 144 D3
Holmefield Ct, NW3 . . . . .91 H6
Holme Lacey Rd, SE12 . . . . . .155 F6
Holme Rd, E6 . . . . .116 B1
Holmes Av, E17 . . . . .77 J3
NW7 . . . . .56 B1
Holmesdale Av, SW14 . . . . . . .146 B3
Holmesdale Cl, SE25 . . . . .188 C3
Holmesdale Rd, N6 . . . . .74 B7
SE25 . . . . .188 A5
Bexleyheath DA7 . . . . .158 D2
Croydon CR0 . . . . .188 A5
Richmond TW9 . . . . .145 J1
Teddington TW11 . . . . .163 F6
Holmesley Rd, SE23 . . . . .153 H6
Holmes Pl, SW10 . . . . .30 D5
Holmes Rd, NW5 . . . . .92 B5
SW19 . . . . .167 F7
Twickenham TW1 . . . . .162 C2
Holmes Ter, SE1 . . . . .27 E3
Holme Way, Stan. HA7 . . . . . . .52 C6
Holmewood Gdns, SW2 . . . . . .151 F7
Holmewood Rd, SE25 . . . . . . .188 B3
SW2 . . . . .151 E7
Holmfield Av, NW4 . . . . .72 A5
Holmhurst, Belv. DA17 . . . . . . .139 H5
Holmleigh Rd, N16 . . . . .94 B1
Holmleigh Rd Est, N16
off Holmleigh Rd 94 C1
Holm Oak Cl, SW15
off West Hill 148 C6
Holm Oak Ms, SW4
off King's Av 150/151 E5
Holmshaw Cl, SE26 . . . . .171 H4
Holmside Ri, Wat. WD19 . . . . . .50 B3
Holmside Rd, SW12 . . . . .150 A6
Holmsley Cl, N.Mal. KT3 . . . . .183 F6
Holmsley Ho, SW15
off Tangley Gro 147 F7
Holms St, E2 . . . . .13 H1
Holmstall Av, Edg. HA8 . . . . . . .70 C3
Holm Wk, SE3
off Blackheath Pk 155 G2
Holmwood Cl, Har. HA2 . . . . . . .67 J3
Northolt UB5 . . . . .85 H6
Sutton SM2 . . . . .198 A7
Holmwood Gdns, N3 . . . . .72 D2
Wallington SM6 . . . . .200 B6
Holmwood Gro, NW7 . . . . .54 D5
Holmwood Rd, Chess. KT9 . . .195 G5
Ilford IG3 . . . . .99 H2
Holmwood Vil, SE7
off Woolwich Rd 135 G5
Holne Chase, N2 . . . . .73 F6
Morden SM4 . . . . .184 C6
Holness Rd, E15 . . . . .97 F6
Holroyd Rd, SW15 . . . . .147 J4
Holstein Way, Erith DA18 . . . . .138 E3
Holstock Rd, Ilf. IG1 . . . . .99 F3
Holsworth Cl, Har. HA2 . . . . . . .67 J5
Holsworthy Sq, WC1 . . . . .10 D6
Holsworthy Way, Chess. KT9 . .195 F5
Holt, The, Ilf. IG6 . . . . .65 F6
Wallington SM6 . . . . .200 C4
Holt Cl, N10 . . . . .74 A4
SE28 . . . . .118 B7
Chigwell IG7 . . . . .65 J5
Holt Ct, E15 off Clays La 96 C5
Holton St, E1 . . . . .113 G4
Holt Rd, E16 . . . . .136 B1
Wembley HA0 . . . . .87 E3
Holt Way, Chig. IG7 . . . . .65 J5

Holtwhite Av, Enf. EN2 . . . . . . .43 J2
Holtwhites Hill, Enf. EN2 . . . . . .43 H1
Holwell Pl, Pnr. HA5 . . . . .66 E4
Holwood Pk Av, Orp. BR6 . . . .206 C5
Holwood Pl, SW4 . . . . .150 D4
Holybourne Av, SW15 . . . . . . .147 G7
Holyhead Cl, E3 . . . . .114 A3
E6 off Valiant Way 116 C5
Holyoake Ct, SE16 off Bryan Rd .133 J2
Holyoake Wk, N2 . . . . .73 F3
W5 .105 F4
Holyoak Rd, SE11 . . . . .35 G1
Holyport Rd, SW6 . . . . .127 J7
Holyrood Av, Har. HA2 . . . . .85 E4
Holyrood Gdns, Edg. HA8 . . . . .70 B3
Holyrood Ms, E16
off Wesley Av 135 G1
Holyrood Rd, Barn. EN5 . . . . . . .41 F6
Holyrood St, SE1 . . . . .28 D2
Holywell Cl, SE3 . . . . .28 D2
SE16 off Masters Dr . . .132/133 E5
Holywell La, EC2 . . . . .12 E4
Holywell Row, EC2 . . . . .12 D6
Home Cl, Cars. SM5 . . . . .199 J2
Northolt UB5 . . . . .103 F3
Home Ct, Felt. TW13 . . . . .160 A1
Homecroft Gdns, Loug. IG10 . . . .48 E4
Homecroft Rd, N22 . . . . .75 J1
SE26 . . . . .171 F5
Home Fm Cl, T.Ditt. KT7 . . . . .180 C7
Homefarm Rd, W7 . . . . .104 B6
Homefield Av, Ilf. IG2 . . . . .81 H5
Homefield Cl, NW10 . . . . .88 C6
Hayes UB4 . . . . .102 C5
Homefield Gdns, N2 . . . . .73 G3
Mitcham CR4 . . . . .185 F2
Homefield Ms, Beck. BR3 . . . .190 A1
Homefield Pk, Sutt. SM1 . . . . .198 E6
Homefield Rd, SW19 . . . . .166 A6
W4 .127 E4
Bromley BR1 . . . . .191 J1
Edgware HA8 . . . . .54 D6
Walton-on-Thames KT12 . . .179 E7
Wembley HA0 . . . . .86 D4
Homefield St, N1 . . . . .12 D2
Home Gdns, Dag. RM10 . . . . . .101 J3
Homelands Dr, SE19 . . . . .170 B7
Home Lea, Orp. BR6 . . . . .207 J5
Homeleigh Rd, SE15 . . . . .153 G5
Homemead, SW12 . . . . .168 C2
Home Mead, Stan. HA7 . . . . . . .69 F1
Homemead Rd, Brom. BR2 . . .192 C5
Croydon CR0 . . . . .186 C6
★ Home Office, SW1 . . . . .25 H4
Home Pk Rd, SW19 . . . . .166 D3
Home Pk Wk, Kings.T. KT1 . . . .181 G4
Homer Cl, Bexh. DA7 . . . . .159 J1
Homer Dr, E14 . . . . .134 A4
Home Rd, SW11 . . . . .149 H2
Homer Rd, E9 . . . . .95 H6
Croydon CR0 . . . . .189 G6
Homer Row, W1 . . . . .15 G2
Homersham Rd, Kings.T. KT1 . .182 A2
Homer St, W1 . . . . .15 G2
HOMERTON, E9 . . . . .95 G5
Homerton Gro, E9 . . . . .95 G5
Homerton High St, E9 . . . . .95 F5
Homerton Rd, E9 . . . . .95 H5
Homerton Row, E9 . . . . .95 F5
Homerton Ter, E9
off Morning La 95 F6
Homesdale Cl, E11 . . . . .79 G5
Homesdale Rd, Brom. BR1,
BR2 . . . . .191 J4
Orpington BR5 . . . . .193 H7
Homesfield, NW11 . . . . .72 D5
Homestall Rd, SE22 . . . . .153 F5
Homestead, The, N11 . . . . .58 B4
Homestead Gdns, Esher (Clay.)
KT10 . . . . .194 B5
Homestead Paddock, N14 . . . . .42 B5
Homestead Pk, NW2 . . . . .89 F3
Homestead Rd, SW6 . . . . .128 C2
Dagenham RM8 . . . . .101 F2
Homewillow Cl, N21 . . . . .43 H6
Homewood Cl, Hmptn. TW12
off Fearnley Cres 161 F6
Homewood Cres, Chis. BR7 . . .175 H6
Homildon Ho, SE26
off Sydenham Hill 170 D3
Honduras St, EC1 . . . . .11 J5
Honeybourne Rd, NW6 . . . . .90 E5
Honeybourne Way, Orp. BR5 . . .207 G1
Honeybrook Rd, SW12 . . . . . . .150 C7
Honey Cl, Dag. RM10 . . . . .101 H6
Honeycroft, Loug. IG10 . . . . . . .48 D4
Honeyden Rd, Sid. DA14 . . . . .177 E6
Honey La, EC2 . . . . .20 A4
Honeyman Cl, NW6 . . . . .90 A7
Honeypot Cl, NW9 . . . . .69 J4
Honeypot La, NW9 . . . . .69 J3
Stanmore HA7 . . . . .69 J3
Honeysett Rd, N17
off Reform Row 76 C2
Honeysuckle Cl, Sthl. UB1 . . . .102 E7
Honeysuckle Gdns, Croy. CR0
off Primrose La 203 G1

Honeywell Rd, SW11 . . . . .149 J6
Honeywood Rd, NW10 . . . . . . .107 F2
Isleworth TW7 . . . . .144 D4
Honeywood Wk, Cars. SM5 . . .199 J4
Honister Cl, Stan. HA7 . . . . .69 E1
Honister Gdns, Stan. HA7 . . . . .53 E7
Honister Pl, Stan. HA7 . . . . .69 E1
Honiton Ho, Enf. EN3
off Exeter Rd 45 G3
Honiton Rd, NW6 . . . . .108 C2
Welling DA16 . . . . .157 J2
Honley Rd, SE6 . . . . .154 B7
Honnor Gdns, Islw. TW7 . . . . . .144 A2
HONOR OAK, SE23 . . . . .153 F6
HONOR OAK PARK, SE4 . . . . .153 H6
Honor Oak Pk, SE23 . . . . .153 F6
Honor Oak Ri, SE23 . . . . .153 F6
Honor Oak Rd, SE23 . . . . .171 F1
Hood Av, N14 . . . . .42 B6
SW14 . . . . .146 C5
Hood Cl, Croy. CR0
off Parson's Mead 201 H1
Hoodcote Gdns, N21 . . . . .43 H7
Hood Ct, EC4 . . . . .19 F4
Hood Rd, SW20 . . . . .165 F7
Hood Wk, Rom. RM7 . . . . .83 H1
HOOK, Chess. KT9 . . . . .195 H4
Hook, The, Barn. EN5 . . . . .41 G6
Hookers Rd, E17 . . . . .77 G3
Hook Fm Rd, Brom. BR2 . . . . .192 A5
Hooking Grn, Har. HA2 . . . . .67 H5
Hook La, Well. DA16 . . . . .157 J5
Hook Ri N, Surb. KT6 . . . . .196 A3
Hook Ri S, Surb. KT6 . . . . .196 A3
Hook Ri S Ind Pk, Surb. KT6 . . .196 A3
Hook Rd, Chess. KT9 . . . . .195 G5
Surbiton KT6 . . . . .195 H3
Hooks Cl, SE15
off Woods Rd 152/153 E1
Hooks Hall Dr, Dag. RM10 . . . .101 J3
Hookstone Way, Wdf.Grn. IG8 . . .64 A7
Hooks Way, SE22
off Dulwich Common 170 D1
Hook Wk, Edg. HA8 . . . . .54 C6
Hooper Rd, E16 . . . . .115 G6
Hooper's Ct, SW3 . . . . .23 J4
Hooper's Ms, Bushey WD23 . . . .51 H1
Hooper St, E1 . . . . .21 H5
Hoop La, NW11 . . . . .72 C7
Hope Cl, N1 off Wallace Rd 93 J6
SE12 . . . . .173 H3
Brentford TW8
off Burford Rd 125 H5
Romford (Chad.Hth) RM6 . . .82 C4
Sutton SM1 . . . . .199 F5
Woodford Green IG8
off West Gro 63 J6
Hopedale Rd, SE7 . . . . .135 H6
Hopefield Av, NW6 . . . . .108 B2
Hope Pk, Brom. BR1 . . . . .173 F7
Hopes Cl, Houns. TW5
off Old Cote Dr 123 G6
Hope St, SW11 . . . . .149 G3
Hopetown St, E1 . . . . .21 G2
Hopewell St, SE5 . . . . .132 A7
Hopewell Yd, SE5
off Hopewell St 132 A7
Hope Wf, SE16 . . . . .133 F2
off St. Marychurch St 133 F2
Hop Gdns, WC2 . . . . .18 A6
Hopgood St, W12
off Macfarlane Rd 127 J1
Hopkins Cl, N10 . . . . .58 A1
Hopkins Ms, E15 off West Rd . . .115 F1
Hopkinsons Pl, NW1
off Fitzroy Rd 110 A1
Hopkins St, W1 . . . . .17 G4
Hoppers Rd, N13 . . . . .59 G2
N21 .59 G2
Hoppett Rd, E4 . . . . .62 E3
Hopping La, N1
off St. Mary's Gro 93 H6
Hoppingwood Av, N.Mal. KT3 . .183 E3
Hop St, SE10 . . . . .135 F4
Hopton Gdns, SE1 . . . . .27 H1
New Malden KT3 . . . . .183 G6
Hopton Rd, SE18
off Cadogan Rd 136 E3
SW16 . . . . .168 E5
Hopton St, SE1 . . . . .27 H1
Hoptree Cl, N12
off Woodside Pk Rd 56/57 E4
Hopwood Cl, SW17 . . . . .167 F3
Hopwood Rd, SE17 . . . . .36 C5
Hopwood Wk, E8
off Wilman Gro 94 D7
Horace Av, Rom. RM7 . . . . .101 J1
Horace Rd, E7 . . . . .97 H4
Ilford IG6 . . . . .81 F3
Kingston upon Thames KT1 . .181 J3
Horatio Ct, SE16
off Rotherhithe St 133 F1
Horatio Pl, E14
off Cold Harbour 134 C2
SW19 off Kingston Rd 166 D7
Horatio St, E2 . . . . .13 H2

Horatius Way, Croy. CR0 . . . . . .201 F5
Horbury Cres, W11 . . . . .108 D7
Horbury Ms, W11
   off Ladbroke Rd 108 C7
Horder Rd, SW6 . . . . .148 B1
Hordle Prom E, SE15 . . . . .37 G7
Hordle Prom N, SE15 . . . . .37 E7
Hordle Prom S, SE15 . . . . .37 E7
Hordle Prom W, SE15
   off Blakes Rd 132 B7
Horizon Way, SE7 . . . . .135 H4
Horle Wk, SE5 . . . . .151 H2
Horley Cl, Bexh. DA6 . . . . .159 G5
Horley Rd, SE9 . . . . .174 B4
Hormead Rd, W9 . . . . .108 C4
Hornbeam Cl, NW7 . . . . .55 F3
  SE11 . . . . .34 E1
  Borehamwood WD6 . . . . .38 A1
  Buckhurst Hill IG9
   off Hornbeam Rd 64 A3
  Ilford IG1 . . . . .99 G6
  Northolt UB5 . . . . .85 F5
Hornbeam Cres, Brent. TW8 . . .125 E7
Hornbeam Gro, E4 . . . . .63 E3
Hornbeam La, E4 . . . . .47 E5
  Bexleyheath DA7 . . . . .159 J2
Hornbeam Rd, Buck.H. IG9 . . . . .64 A3
  Hayes UB4 . . . . .102 C5
Hornbeam Sq, E3
   off Hawthorn Av 113 J1
Hornbeams Ri, N11 . . . . .58 A6
Hornbeam Ter, Cars. SM5 . . . . .199 H1
Hornbeam Wk, Rich. TW10 . . . .163 J3
Hornblower Cl, SE16
   off Greenland Quay 133 H4
Hornbuckle Cl, Har. HA2 . . . . . . .86 A2
Hornby Cl, NW3 . . . . .91 G7
Horncastle Cl, SE12 . . . . .155 G7
Horncastle Rd, SE12 . . . . .155 G7
Hornchurch Cl, Kings.T. KT2 . . .163 G4
Horndean Cl, SW15
   off Bessborough Rd 165 G1
Horndon Cl, Rom. RM5 . . . . .83 J1
Horndon Grn, Rom. RM5 . . . . . . .83 J1
Horndon Rd, Rom. RM5 . . . . .83 J1
Horner La, Mitch. CR4 . . . . .185 G2
Horne Way, SW15 . . . . .147 J2
Hornfair Rd, SE7 . . . . .135 J6
Horniman Dr, SE23 . . . . .171 E1
★ Horniman Mus, SE23 . . . . . .170 E1
Horning Cl, SE9 . . . . .174 B4
Horn La, SE10 . . . . .135 G4
  W3 . . . . .106 C7
  Woodford Green IG8 . . . . .63 G6
Horn Link Way, SE10 . . . . .135 G4
Horn Pk Cl, SE12 . . . . .155 H5
Horn Pk La, SE12 . . . . .155 H5
Horns Cft Cl, Bark. IG11
   off Thornhill Gdns 99 H7
Horns End Pl, Pnr. HA5 . . . . .66 C4
HORNSEY, N8 . . . . .75 F3
Hornsey La, N6 . . . . .92 B1
  N19 . . . . .92 C1
Hornsey La Est, N19
   off Hornsey La 74 D7
Hornsey La Gdns, N6 . . . . .74 C7
Hornsey Pk Rd, N8 . . . . .75 F3
Hornsey Ri, N19 . . . . .74 D7
Hornsey Ri Gdns, N19 . . . . .74 D7
Hornsey Rd, N7 . . . . .93 F2
  N19 . . . . .92 E1
Hornsey St, N7 . . . . .93 F5
Hornshay St, SE15 . . . . .133 F6
Horns Rd, Ilf. IG2, IG6 . . . . .81 F5
Hornton Pl, W8 . . . . .22 A4
Hornton St, W8 . . . . .128 D1
Horsa Rd, SE12 . . . . .155 J7
  Erith DA8 . . . . .139 J7
Horse & Dolphin Yd, W1 . . . . . . .17 J5
Horsebridge Cl, Dag. RM9 . . . . .119 E1
Horsecroft Rd, Edg. HA8 . . . . . . .54 D7
Horse Fair, Kings.T. KT1 . . . . . . .181 G2
Horseferry Pl, SE10 . . . . .134 C6
Horseferry Rd, E14 . . . . .113 H7
  SW1 . . . . .25 H6
Horse Guards Av, SW1 . . . . .26 A2
★ Horse Guards Par, SW1 . . . . .25 J2
Horse Guards Rd, SW1 . . . . .25 J2
Horse Leaze, E6 . . . . .116 D6
Horsell Rd, N5 . . . . .93 G5
Horselydown La, SE1 . . . . .29 F3
Horsemongers Ms, SE1 . . . . .28 A4
Horsenden Av, Grnf. UB6 . . . . . . .86 B5
Horsenden Cres, Grnf. UB6 . . . . .86 C5
Horsenden La N, Grnf. UB6 . . . . .86 C6
Horsenden La S, Grnf. UB6 . . . .104 D1
Horse Ride, SW1 . . . . .25 G2
Horse Rd, E7 off Centre Rd 97 H3
Horseshoe Cl, E14 . . . . .134 C5
  NW2 . . . . .89 H2
Horse Shoe Ct, EC1
   off St. John St 111 H4
Horse Shoe Cres, Nthlt. UB5 . . .103 G2
Horse Shoe Grn, Sutt. SM1
   off Aultone Way 198/199 E2
Horseshoe La, N20 . . . . .56 A1

Horseshoe La, Enf. EN2
   off Chase Side 43 J3
Horse Yd, N1 off Essex Rd 111 H1
Horsfeld Gdns, SE9 . . . . .156 B5
Horsfeld Rd, SE9 . . . . .156 A5
Horsford Rd, SW2 . . . . .151 F5
Horsham Av, N12 . . . . .57 H5
Horsham Rd, Bexh. DA6 . . . . . . .159 G5
  Feltham TW14 . . . . .141 F6
Horsley Dr, Croy. (New Adgtn)
  CR0 . . . . .204 C7
  Kingston upon Thames KT2 . .163 G5
Horsley Rd, E4 . . . . .62 C2
  Bromley BR1 off Palace Rd . .191 H1
Horsley St, SE17 . . . . .36 B5
Horsmonden Cl, Orp. BR6 . . . . .193 H7
Horsmonden Rd, SE4 . . . . .153 J5
Hortensia Rd, SW10 . . . . .30 C6
Horticultural Pl, W4
   off Heathfield Ter 126 D5
Horton Av, NW2 . . . . .90 B4
Horton Br Rd, West Dr. UB7 . . . .120 C1
Horton Cl, West Dr. UB7 . . . . . . .120 C1
Horton Ind Pk, West Dr. UB7 . . .120 C1
Horton Rd, E8 . . . . .94 E6
  West Drayton UB7 . . . . .120 D1
Horton St, SE13 . . . . .154 B3
Horton Way, Croy. CR0 . . . . .189 G5
Hortus Rd, E4 . . . . .62 C2
  Southall UB2 . . . . .123 F2
Hosack Rd, SW17 . . . . .167 J2
Hoser Av, SE12 . . . . .173 G2
Hosier La, EC1 . . . . .19 G2
Hoskins Cl, E16 . . . . .115 J6
  Hayes UB3 off Cranford Dr . .121 J5
Hoskins St, SE10 . . . . .134 D5
Hospital Br Rd, Twick. TW2 . . . .143 H7
Hospital Rd, E9
   off Homerton Row 95 G5
  Hounslow TW3 . . . . .143 G3
Hospital Way, SE13
   off Lullingstone La 154 D6
Hotham Cl, W.Mol. KT8
   off Garrick Gdns 179 G3
Hotham Rd, SW15 . . . . .147 J3
  SW19 . . . . .167 F7
Hotham Rd Ms, SW19
   off Haydons Rd 167 F7
Hotham St, E15 . . . . .114 E1
Hothfield Pl, SE16 off Lower Rd .133 F3
Hotspur Rd, Nthlt. UB5 . . . . .103 G2
Hotspur St, SE11 . . . . .34 E3
Houblon Rd, Rich. TW10 . . . . . . .145 H5
Houghton Cl, E8
   off Buttermere Wk 94 C6
  Hampton TW12 . . . . .161 E6
Houghton Rd, N15
   off West Grn Rd 76 C5
Houghton St, WC2 . . . . .18 D4
Houlder Cres, Croy. CR0 . . . . . . .201 H6
Houndsden Rd, N21 . . . . .43 F6
Houndsditch, EC3 . . . . .20 E3
Houndsfield Rd, N9 . . . . .44 E7
HOUNSLOW, TW3 - TW6 . . . . . .143 F4
Hounslow Av, Houns. TW3 . . . . .143 H5
Hounslow Business Pk, Houns.
  TW3 off Alice Way 143 G4
Hounslow Gdns, Houns. TW3 . .143 H5
★ Hounslow Heath, Houns.
  TW4 . . . . .142 E6
Hounslow Rd, Felt. (Feltham)
  TW14 . . . . .160 B1
  Feltham (Han.) TW13 . . . . . .160 D4
  Twickenham TW2 . . . . .143 J6
HOUNSLOW WEST, Houns.
  TW4 . . . . .142 D3
Houseman Way, SE5
   off Hopewell St 132 A7
★ Houses of Parliament, SW1 . .26 B4
Houston Pl, Esher KT10
   off Lime Tree Av 194 B1
Houston Rd, SE23 . . . . .171 H2
  Surbiton KT6 . . . . .181 E6
Hove Av, E17 . . . . .77 J5
Hoveden Rd, NW2 . . . . .90 B5
Hove Gdns, Sutt. SM1 . . . . .199 E1
Hoveton Rd, SE28 . . . . .118 C6
Hoveton Way, Ilf. IG6 . . . . .64 E7
Howard Av, Bex. DA5 . . . . .176 C1
Howard Bldg, SW8
   off Queenstown Rd 130 B6
Howard Cl, N11 . . . . .58 A2
  NW2 . . . . .90 B4
  W3 . . . . .106 B6
  Hampton TW12 . . . . .161 J6
  Loughton IG10 . . . . .48 B6
Howard Dr, Borwd. WD6 . . . . . . .38 D4
Howard Ms, N5
   off Hamilton Pk 93 H4
Howard Rd, E6 . . . . .116 C2
  E11 .97 E3
  E17 .78 A3
  N15 .76 B6
  N16 .94 A4
  NW2 . . . . .90 A4
  SE20 . . . . .189 F1

Howard Rd, SE25 . . . . .188 D5
  Barking IG11 . . . . .117 G1
  Bromley BR1 . . . . .173 G7
  Ilford IG1 . . . . .99 E4
  Isleworth TW7 . . . . .144 C3
  New Malden KT3 . . . . .183 E3
  Southall UB1 . . . . .103 H6
  Surbiton KT5 . . . . .181 J6
Howards Cl, Pnr. HA5 . . . . .66 B2
Howards Crest Cl, Beck. BR3 . . .190 C2
Howards La, SW15 . . . . .147 H5
Howards Rd, E13 . . . . .115 G3
Howard St, T.Ditt. KT7 . . . . .181 E7
Howard Wk, N2 . . . . .73 F4
Howard Way, Barn. EN5 . . . . .40 A5
Howarth Ct, E15 off Clays La 96 C5
Howarth Rd, SE2 . . . . .138 A5
Howberry Cl, Edg. HA8 . . . . .53 G6
Howberry Rd, Edg. HA8 . . . . .53 G6
  Stanmore HA7 . . . . .53 G6
  Thornton Heath CR7 . . . . . .188 A1
Howbury Rd, SE15 . . . . .153 F3
Howcroft Cres, N3 . . . . .56 D7
Howcroft La, Grnf. UB6
   off Cowgate Rd 104 A3
Howden Cl, SE28 . . . . .118 D7
Howden Rd, SE25 . . . . .188 C2
Howden St, SE15 . . . . .152 D3
Howe Cl, Rom. RM7 . . . . .83 G1
Howell Cl, Rom. RM6 . . . . .82 D5
Howell Wk, SE1 . . . . .35 H2
Howes Cl, N3 . . . . .72 D3
Howfield Pl, N17 . . . . .76 C3
Howgate Rd, SW14 . . . . .146 D3
Howick Pl, SW1 . . . . .25 G6
Howie St, SW11 . . . . .129 H7
Howitt Cl, N16 off Allen Rd 94 B4
  NW3 off Howitt Rd 91 H6
Howitt Rd, NW3 . . . . .91 H6
Howland Est, SE16 . . . . .133 F3
Howland Ms E, W1 . . . . .17 G1
Howland St, W1 . . . . .17 F1
Howland Way, SE16 . . . . .133 H2
Howletts Rd, SE24 . . . . .151 J6
Howley Pl, W2 . . . . .14 D1
Howley Rd, Croy. CR0 . . . . .201 H3
Howsman Rd, SW13 . . . . .127 G6
Howson Rd, SE4 . . . . .153 H4
Howson Ter, Rich. TW10 . . . . . . .145 H6
Hows St, E2 . . . . .13 F1
Howton Pl, Bushey (Bushey Hth)
  WD23 . . . . .52 A1
HOXTON, N1 . . . . .12 D2
Hoxton Mkt, N1 . . . . .12 D4
Hoxton Sq, N1 . . . . .12 D4
Hoxton St, N1 . . . . .12 E4
Hoylake Gdns, Mitch. CR4 . . . . .186 C3
  Ruislip HA4 . . . . .84 B1
  Watford WD19 . . . . .50 D4
Hoylake Rd, W3 . . . . .107 E6
Hoyland Cl, SE15
   off Commercial Way . . .132/133 E7
Hoyle Rd, SW17 . . . . .167 H5
Hoy St, E16 . . . . .115 F6
★ H.Q.S. Wellington, Master
  Mariners' Hall, WC2 . . . . .19 E5
Hubbard Dr, Chess. KT9 . . . . . . .195 F6
Hubbard Rd, SE27 . . . . .169 J4
Hubbard St, E15 . . . . .114 E1
Hubbinet Ind Est, Rom. RM7 . . . .83 J3
Hubert Gro, SW9 . . . . .151 E3
Hubert Rd, E6 . . . . .116 A3
Huddart St, E3 . . . . .113 J5
Huddleston Cl, E2 . . . . .113 F2
Huddlestone Rd, E7 . . . . .97 F4
  NW2 . . . . .89 H6
Huddleston Rd, N7 . . . . .92 D4
Hudson Ct, E14
   off Maritime Quay 134 A5
  SW19 . . . . .167 E7
Hudson Gdns, Orp. BR6
   off Superior Dr 207 J6
Hudson Pl, SE18 . . . . .137 F5
Hudson Rd, Bexh. DA7 . . . . .159 F2
  Hayes UB3 . . . . .121 G6
Hudson's Pl, SW1 . . . . .33 E1
Hudson Way, N9 . . . . .61 F3
  NW2 off Gratton Ter 90 A3
Huggin Ct, EC4 . . . . .20 A5
Huggin Hill, EC4 . . . . .20 A5
Huggins Pl, SW2
   off Roupell Rd 169 F1
Hughan Rd, E15 . . . . .96 D5
Hugh Dalton Av, SW6 . . . . .128 C6
Hughenden Av, Har. HA3 . . . . . . .69 E5
Hughenden Gdns, Nthlt. UB5 . . .102 C3
Hughenden Rd, Wor.Pk. KT4 . . .183 G7
Hughendon Ter, E15
   off Westdown Rd 96 C4
Hughes Cl, N12
   off Coleridge Rd 57 F5
Hughes Rd, Hayes UB3 . . . . .102 B7
Hughes Ter, SW9
   off Styles Gdns 151 H3
Hughes Wk, Croy. CR0
   off St. Saviours Rd 187 J7
Hugh Gaitskell Cl, SW6 . . . . . . .128 C6

Hugh Ms, SW1 . . . . .32 E2
Hugh St, SW1 . . . . .32 E2
Hugon Rd, SW6 . . . . .148 E3
Hugo Rd, N19 . . . . .92 C4
Huguenot Pl, E1 . . . . .21 G1
  SW18 . . . . .149 F5
Huguenot Sq, SE15
   off Scylla Rd 152/153 E3
Hullbridge Ms, N1
   off Sherborne St 112 A1
Hull Cl, SE16 . . . . .133 G2
Hull Pl, E16
   off Fishguard Way 136/137 E2
Hull St, EC1 . . . . .11 J4
Hulme Pl, SE1 . . . . .28 A4
Hulse Av, Bark. IG11 . . . . .99 G6
  Romford RM7 . . . . .83 H1
Hulse Ter, Ilf. IG1
   off Buttsbury Rd 99 F5
Humber Cl, West Dr. UB7 . . . . . .120 A1
Humber Dr, W10 . . . . .108 A4
Humber Rd, NW2 . . . . .89 H2
  SE3 . . . . .135 F6
Humberstone Rd, E13 . . . . .115 J3
Humberton Cl, E9
   off Marsh Hill 95 H5
Humbolt Rd, W6 . . . . .128 B6
Humes Av, W7 . . . . .124 B3
Hume Ter, E16
   off Prince Regent La 115 J6
Hume Way, Ruis. HA4 . . . . .66 A6
Humphrey Cl, Ilf. IG5 . . . . .80 C1
Humphrey St, SE1 . . . . .37 F3
Humphries Cl, Dag. RM9 . . . . . .101 F4
Hundred Acre, NW9 . . . . .71 F2
Hungerdown, E4 . . . . .62 C1
Hungerford Br, SE1 . . . . .26 B1
  WC2 . . . . .26 B1
Hungerford La, WC2 . . . . .26 A1
Hungerford Rd, N7 . . . . .92 D5
Hungerford St, E1
   off Commercial Rd 112/113 E6
Hunsdon Cl, Dag. RM9 . . . . .101 E6
Hunsdon Rd, SE14 . . . . .133 G6
Hunslett St, E2 off Royston St . .113 F2
Hunston Rd, Mord. SM4 . . . . . . .198 E1
Hunt Cl, W11 . . . . .128 A1
Hunter Cl, SE1 . . . . .28 C6
  SW12 off Balham Pk Rd 168 A1
  Borehamwood WD6 . . . . .38 C5
  Wallington SM6 . . . . .200 E7
Huntercrombe Gdns, Wat. WD19 .50 C5
Hunter Ho, Felt. TW13 . . . . .160 A1
Hunter Rd, SW20 . . . . .183 J1
  Ilford IG1 . . . . .99 E5
  Thornton Heath CR7 . . . . . .188 A3
Hunters, The, Beck. BR3 . . . . . . .190 C1
Hunters Ct, Rich. TW9
   off Friars La 145 G5
Hunters Gro, Har. HA3 . . . . .69 F4
  Hayes UB3 . . . . .122 A1
  Orpington BR6 . . . . .207 E4
Hunters Hall Rd, Dag. RM10 . . . .101 G4
Hunters Hill, Ruis. HA4 . . . . .84 C3
Hunters Meadow, SE19
   off Dulwich Wd Av 170 B4
Hunters Rd, Chess. KT9 . . . . . . .195 H3
Hunters Sq, Dag. RM10 . . . . . . .101 G4
Hunter St, WC1 . . . . .10 B5
Hunters Way, Croy. CR0 . . . . . . .202 B4
  Enfield EN2 . . . . .43 G1
Hunter Wk, E13 . . . . .115 G2
  Borehamwood WD6
   off Hunter Cl 38 C5
Huntingdon Cl, Mitch. CR4 . . . . .187 E3
Huntingdon Gdns, W4 . . . . .126 C7
  Worcester Park KT4 . . . . . . .197 J3
Huntingdon Rd, N2 . . . . .73 H3
  N9 . . . . .61 F1
Huntingdon St, E16 . . . . .115 F6
  N1 . . . . .93 F7
Huntingfield, Croy. CR0 . . . . .203 J7
Huntingfield Rd, SW15 . . . . .147 G4
Hunting Gate Cl, Enf. EN2 . . . . . .43 G3
Hunting Gate Dr, Chess. KT9 . . .195 H7
Hunting Gate Ms, Sutt. SM1 . . .199 E3
  Twickenham TW2
   off Colne Rd 162 B1
Huntings Rd, Dag. RM10 . . . . . . .101 G6
Huntley Cl, Stai. (Stanw.) TW19
   off Cambria Gdns 140 B7
Huntley Dr, N3 . . . . .56 D6
Huntley St, WC1 . . . . .9 G6
Huntley Way, SW20 . . . . .183 G2
Huntly Rd, SE25 . . . . .188 B4
Hunton St, E1 . . . . .13 H6
Hunt Rd, Sthl. UB2 . . . . .123 G3
Hunt's Cl, SE3 . . . . .155 G2
Hunt's Ct, WC2 . . . . .17 J6
Hunts La, E15 . . . . .114 C2
Huntsmans Cl, Felt. TW13 . . . . .160 B4
Huntsman St, SE17 . . . . .36 C2
Hunts Mead, Enf. EN3 . . . . .45 G3
Hunts Mead Cl, Chis. BR7 . . . . . .174 C7
Huntsmoor Rd, Epsom KT19 . . .196 C5
Huntspill St, SW17 . . . . .167 F3
Hunts Slip Rd, SE21 . . . . .170 B3

Huntsworth Ms, NW1 . . . . .7 J6
Hunt Way, SE22
　off Dulwich Common 170 D1
Hurdwick Pl, NW1
　off Harrington Sq 110 C2
Hurley Cres, SE16
　off Marlow Way 133 G2
Hurley Ho, SE11 . . . . .35 F2
Hurley Rd, Grnf. UB6 . . . . . .103 H6
Hurlingham Business Pk, SW6 .148 D3
Hurlingham Ct, SW6 . . . . . . .148 C3
Hurlingham Gdns, SW6 . . . . .148 C3
★ Hurlingham Ho, SW6 . . . . .148 D3
★ Hurlingham Park, SW6 . . . .148 C2
Hurlingham Retail Pk, SW6
　off Carnwath Rd 148/149 E3
Hurlingham Rd, SW6 . . . . . . .148 C2
　Bexleyheath DA7 . . . . .139 F4
Hurlingham Sq, SW6 . . . . . . .148 C3
Hurlock St, N5 . . . . .93 H3
Hurlstone Rd, SE25 . . . . .188 A5
Hurn Ct Rd, Houns. TW4
　off Renfrew Rd 142 D2
Huron Cl, Orp. BR6
　off Winnipeg Dr 207 J6
Huron Rd, SW17 . . . . .168 A2
Hurren Cl, SE3 . . . . .154 E3
Hurricane Rd, Wall. SM6 . . . .201 E7
Hurry Cl, E15 . . . . .97 E7
Hursley Rd, Chig. IG7
　off Tufter Rd 65 J5
Hurst Av, E4 . . . . .62 A4
　N6 .74 C6
Hurstbourne, Esher (Clay.) KT10 .194 C6
Hurstbourne Gdns, Bark. IG11 . .99 H6
Hurstbourne Ho, SW15
　off Tangley Gro 147 F6
Hurstbourne Rd, SE23 . . . . . .171 H1
Hurst Cl, E4 . . . . .62 A4
　NW11 . . . . .72 E6
　Bromley BR2 . . . . .205 F1
　Chessington KT9 . . . . .196 A5
　Northolt UB5 . . . . .85 F6
Hurstcourt Rd, Sutt. SM1 . . . .198 E2
Hurstdene Av, Brom. BR2 . . . .205 F1
Hurstdene Gdns, N15 . . . . . . .76 B7
Hurst Est, SE2 . . . . .138 C5
Hurstfield, Brom. BR2 . . . . . . .191 G5
Hurstfield Rd, W.Mol. KT8 . . .179 G3
Hurst La, SE2 . . . . .138 C5
　East Molesey KT8 . . . . . . .179 J4
Hurstleigh Gdns, Ilf. IG5 . . . . .80 C1
Hurstmead Ct, Edg. HA8 . . . . .54 B4
Hurst Ri, Barn. EN5 . . . . .40 D3
Hurst Rd, E17 . . . . .78 B3
　N21 . . . . .59 G1
　Bexley DA5 . . . . .176 D1
　Buckhurst Hill IG9 . . . . .64 A1
　Croydon CR0 . . . . .202 A5
　East Molesey KT8 . . . . . . .179 G3
　Erith DA8 . . . . .139 J7
　Sidcup DA15 . . . . .176 A2
　Walton-on-Thames KT12 . . .178 C5
　West Molesey KT8 . . . . . . .179 E3
Hurst Springs, Bex. DA5 . . . . .177 E1
Hurst St, SE24 . . . . .151 H6
Hurst Vw Rd, S.Croy. CR2 . . .202 B7
Hurst Way, S.Croy. CR2 . . . . .202 B6
Hurstway Wk, W11 . . . . .108 A7
Hurstwood Av, E18 . . . . .79 H4
　Bexley DA5 . . . . .176 E1
Hurstwood Dr, Brom. BR1 . . . .192 C3
Hurstwood Rd, NW11 . . . . .72 B4
Hurtwood Rd, Walt. KT12 . . . .179 F7
Huson Cl, NW3 . . . . .91 H7
Hussain Cl, Har. HA1 . . . . .86 C4
Hussars Cl, Houns. TW4 . . . . .142 E3
Husseywell Cres, Brom. BR2 . .205 G1
Hutchings Cl, E14 . . . . .134 A2
Hutchings Wk, NW11 . . . . .73 E4
Hutchins Cl, E15 off Gibbins Rd . .96 C7
Hutchinson Ter, Wem. HA9 . . . .87 G3
Hutchins Rd, SE28 . . . . .118 A7
Hutton Cl, Grnf. UB6
　off Mary Peters Dr 86 A5
　Woodford Green IG8 . . . . . .63 H6
Hutton Gdns, Har. HA3 . . . . . .51 J7
Hutton Gro, N12 . . . . .57 E5
Hutton La, Har. HA3 . . . . .51 J7
Hutton Row, Edg. HA8
　off Pavilion Way 54 C7
Hutton St, EC4 . . . . .19 F4
Hutton Wk, Har. HA3 . . . . .51 J7
Huxbear St, SE4 . . . . .153 J5
Huxley Cl, Nthlt. UB5 . . . . . . .103 E1
Huxley Dr, Rom. RM6 . . . . .82 B7
Huxley Gdns, NW10 . . . . .105 J3
Huxley Par, N18 . . . . .60 A5
Huxley Pl, N13 . . . . .59 H4
Huxley Rd, E10 . . . . .96 C2
　N18 . . . . .60 A4
　Welling DA16 . . . . .157 J3
Huxley Sayze, N18 . . . . .60 A5
Huxley St, W10 . . . . .108 B3
Hyacinth Cl, Hmptn. TW12
　off Gresham Rd 161 G6
　Ilford IG1 . . . . .98 E6

Hyacinth Ct, Pnr. HA5
　off Tulip Ct 66 C3
Hyacinth Rd, SW15 . . . . .165 G1
Hycliffe Gdns, Chig. IG7 . . . . .65 F4
HYDE, THE, NW9 . . . . .71 F4
Hyde, The, NW9 . . . . .71 E5
Hyde Cl, E13 . . . . .115 G2
　Barnet EN5 . . . . .40 C3
Hyde Ct, N20 . . . . .57 G3
Hyde Cres, NW9 . . . . .71 E5
Hyde Est Rd, NW9 . . . . .71 F5
Hyde Fm Ms, SW12
　off Telferscot Rd 168 D1
Hydefield Cl, N21 . . . . .60 A1
Hydefield Ct, N9 . . . . .60 B2
Hyde Ho, NW9 . . . . .71 E5
Hyde La, SW11
　off Battersea Br Rd 149 H1
★ Hyde Park, W2 . . . . .23 G1
Hyde Pk, SW7 . . . . .23 G1
　W1 .23 G1
Hyde Pk Av, N21 . . . . .59 J2
Hyde Pk Cor, W1 . . . . .24 C3
Hyde Pk Cres, W2 . . . . .15 G4
Hyde Pk Gdns, N21 . . . . .59 J1
　W2 .15 F5
Hyde Pk Gdns Ms, W2 . . . . . .15 F5
Hyde Pk Gate, SW7 . . . . .22 D4
Hyde Pk Gate Ms, SW7 . . . . . .22 D4
Hyde Pk Pl, W2 . . . . .15 H5
Hyde Pk Sq, W2 . . . . .15 G4
Hyde Pk Sq Ms, W2 . . . . .15 G4
Hyde Pk St, W2 . . . . .15 G4
Hyderabad Way, E15 . . . . .96 E7
Hyde Rd, N1 . . . . .112 A1
　Bexleyheath DA7 . . . . .159 F2
　Richmond TW10
　off Albert Rd 145 J5
Hydeside Gdns, N9 . . . . .60 C2
Hydes Pl, N1 off Compton Av . .93 H7
Hyde St, SE8
　off Deptford High St 134 A6
Hydethorpe Av, N9 . . . . .60 C2
Hydethorpe Rd, SW12 . . . . . .168 C1
Hyde Vale, SE10 . . . . .134 C7
Hyde Wk, Mord. SM4 . . . . . . .184 D7
Hyde Way, N9 . . . . .60 C2
　Hayes UB3 . . . . .121 J4
Hylands Rd, E17 . . . . .78 D2
Hylton St, SE18 . . . . .137 J4
Hyndewood, SE23 . . . . .171 G3
Hyndman St, SE15 . . . . .132 E6
Hynton Rd, Dag. RM8 . . . . . . .100 C2
Hyrstdene, S.Croy. CR2 . . . . . .201 H4
Hyson Rd, SE16
　off Galleywall Rd 132/133 E4
Hythe Av, Bexh. DA7 . . . . .139 F7
Hythe Cl, N18 . . . . .60 D4
Hythe Path, Th.Hth. CR7 . . . . .188 A3
Hythe Rd, NW10 . . . . .107 G4
　Thornton Heath CR7 . . . . .188 A2
Hythe Rd Ind Est, NW10 . . . . .107 G3
Hyver Hill, NW7 . . . . .38 D6

I

Ian Sq, Enf. EN3
　off Lansbury Rd 45 G1
Ibbetson Path, Loug. IG10 . . . .49 E3
Ibbotson Av, E16 . . . . .115 F6
Ibbott St, E1 off Mantus Rd . . .113 F4
Iberian Av, Wall. SM6 . . . . . . .200 D4
Ibex Ho, E15 off Forest La 96 E6
Ibis La, W4 . . . . .146 C1
Ibis Way, Hayes UB4
　off Cygnet Way 102 D6
Ibscott Cl, Dag. RM10 . . . . . . .101 J6
Ibsley Gdns, SW15 . . . . .165 G1
Ibsley Way, Barn. EN4 . . . . . . .41 H5
★ Ice Ho, Holland Pk, W8 . . . .128 C2
Iceland Rd, E3 . . . . .114 A1
Iceni Ct, E3 off Roman Rd 113 J1
Ice Wf, N1 . . . . .10 B1
Ice Wf Marina, N1
　off New Wf Rd 110/111 E2
Ickburgh Est, E5
　off Ickburgh Rd 94/95 E3
Ickburgh Rd, E5 . . . . .94 E3
Ickleton Rd, SE9 . . . . .174 B4
Icknield Dr, Ilf. IG2 . . . . .81 E5
Ickworth Pk Rd, E17 . . . . .77 H4
Ida Rd, N15 . . . . .76 A5
Ida St, E14 . . . . .114 C6
Iden Cl, Brom. BR2 . . . . .191 E3
Idlecombe Rd, SW17 . . . . . . .168 A6
Idmiston Rd, E15 . . . . .97 F5
　SE27 . . . . .169 J3
　Worcester Park KT4 . . . . . .183 F7
Idmiston Sq, Wor.Pk. KT4 . . . .183 F7
Idol La, EC3 . . . . .20 D6
Idonia St, SE8 . . . . .133 J7
Iffley Rd, W6 . . . . .127 H3
Ifield Rd, SW10 . . . . .30 B5
Ifor Evans Pl, E1
　off Mile End Rd 113 G4
Ightham Rd, Erith DA8 . . . . . .139 G7

Ikea Twr, NW10 . . . . .88 D5
Ilbert St, W10 . . . . .108 A3
Ilchester Gdns, W2 . . . . .14 A5
Ilchester Pl, W14 . . . . .128 C3
Ilchester Rd, Dag. RM8 . . . . . .100 B5
Ildersly Gro, SE21 . . . . .170 A2
Ilderton Rd, SE15 . . . . .133 F7
　SE16 . . . . .133 E5
Ilex Cl, Sun. TW16
　off Oakington Dr 178 C2
Ilex Ho, N4 . . . . .75 F7
Ilex Rd, NW10 . . . . .89 F6
Ilex Way, SW16 . . . . .169 G5
ILFORD, IG1 - IG6 . . . . .99 F3
Ilford Hill, Ilf. IG1 . . . . .98 D3
Ilford La, Ilf. IG1 . . . . .98 E3
Ilfracombe Gdns, Rom. RM6 . .82 B7
Ilfracombe Rd, Brom. BR1 . . . .173 F3
Iliffe St, SE17 . . . . .35 H3
Iliffe Yd, SE17 . . . . .35 H3
Ilkeston Ct, E5 off Overbury St . .95 G4
Ilkley Cl, SE19 . . . . .170 A6
Ilkley Rd, E16 . . . . .115 J5
　Watford WD19 . . . . .50 D5
Illingworth Cl, Mitch. CR4 . . . .185 G3
Illingworth Way, Enf. EN1 . . . . .44 B4
Ilmington Rd, Har. HA3 . . . . . . .69 G6
Ilminster Gdns, SW11 . . . . . . .149 H4
Imber Cl, N14 . . . . .42 C7
　Esher KT10 off Ember La . .194 A1
Imber Ct Trd Est, E.Mol. KT8 . .180 A6
Imber Gro, Esher KT10 . . . . . .180 A7
Imber Pk Rd, Esher KT10 . . . .194 A1
Imber St, N1 . . . . .112 A1
Imer Pl, T.Ditt. KT7 . . . . .180 C7
Imperial Av, N16
　off Victorian Rd 94 C3
Imperial Cl, Har. HA2 . . . . .67 G6
★ Imperial Coll, Uni of London,
　SW7 . . . . .23 E5
Imperial Coll Rd, SW7 . . . . . . .22 E6
Imperial Cres, SW6
　off William Morris Way 149 F2
Imperial Dr, Har. HA2 . . . . .67 G7
Imperial Gdns, Mitch. CR4 . . .186 B3
Imperial Ms, E6
　off Central Pk Rd 115 J2
Imperial Rd, N22 . . . . .74 E1
　SW6 . . . . .149 E1
　Feltham TW14 . . . . .141 H7
Imperial Sq, SW6 . . . . .149 E1
Imperial St, E3 . . . . .114 C3
★ Imperial War Mus, SE1 . . . . .27 F6
Imperial Way, Chis. BR7 . . . . .175 F3
　Croydon CR0 . . . . .201 F6
　Harrow HA3 . . . . .69 H6
Imperial Wf, SW6 . . . . .149 F2
Imprimo Pk, Loug. IG10 . . . . . .49 G4
Imre Cl, W12 off Ellerslie Rd . .127 H1
Inca Dr, SE9 . . . . .156 E7
Inca Ter, N15 off Milton Rd 75 H3
Inchmery Rd, SE6 . . . . .172 B2
Inchwood, Croy. CR0 . . . . .204 B4
Independent Pl, E8
　off Downs Pk Rd 94 C5
Independents Rd, SE3
　off Blackheath Village 155 F3
Inderwick Rd, N8 . . . . .75 F5
Indescon Ct, E14 . . . . .134 B2
India Pl, WC2 . . . . .18 C5
India St, EC3 . . . . .21 F4
India Way, W12 . . . . .107 H7
Indigo Ms, E14 off Ashton St . .114 C7
　N16 . . . . .94 A3
Indus Rd, SE7 . . . . .135 J7
Industry Ter, SW9
　off Canterbury Cres 151 G3
Ingal Rd, E13 . . . . .115 G4
Ingate Pl, SW8 . . . . .150 B1
Ingatestone Rd, E12 . . . . .97 J1
　SE25 . . . . .188 E4
　Woodford Green IG8 . . . . . .63 G7
Ingelow Rd, SW8 . . . . .150 B2
Ingersoll Rd, W12 . . . . .127 H1
　Enfield EN3 . . . . .45 F1
Ingestre Pl, W1 . . . . .17 G4
Ingestre Rd, E7 . . . . .97 G4
　NW5 . . . . .92 B4
Ingham Rd, NW6 . . . . .90 D4
Inglebert St, EC1 . . . . .11 E3
Ingleborough St, SW9 . . . . . . .151 G2
Ingleby Dr, Har. HA1 . . . . .86 A3
Ingleby Rd, N7 off Bryett Rd . .92/93 E3
　Dagenham RM10 . . . . .101 H6
　Ilford IG1 . . . . .98 E1
Ingleby Way, Chis. BR7 . . . . . .174 D5
Ingle Cl, Pnr. HA5 . . . . .67 E3
Ingledew Rd, SE18 . . . . .137 G5
Inglehurst Gdns, Ilf. IG4 . . . . . .80 C5
Inglemere Rd, SE23 . . . . .171 G3
　Mitcham CR4 . . . . .167 J7
Inglesham Wk, E9 . . . . .95 J6
Ingleside Cl, Beck. BR3 . . . . . .172 A7
Ingleside Gro, SE3 . . . . .135 F6
Inglethorpe St, SW6 . . . . .148 A1
Ingleton Av, Well. DA16 . . . . . .158 A5
Ingleton Rd, N18 . . . . .60 D6
Ingleton St, SW9 . . . . .151 G2

Ingleway, N12 . . . . .57 G6
Inglewood Cl, E14 . . . . .134 A4
　Ilford IG6 . . . . .65 J6
Inglewood Copse, Brom. BR1 . .192 B2
Inglewood Rd, NW6 . . . . .90 D5
Inglis Barracks, NW7 . . . . .56 A5
Inglis Rd, W5 . . . . .105 J7
　Croydon CR0 . . . . .202 C1
Inglis St, SE5 . . . . .151 H1
Ingram Av, NW11 . . . . .73 F7
Ingram Cl, SE11 . . . . .34 D1
　Stanmore HA7 . . . . .53 F5
Ingram Rd, N2 . . . . .73 H4
　Thornton Heath CR7 . . . . .187 J1
Ingram Way, Grnf. UB6 . . . . . .104 A1
Ingrave Ho, Dag. RM9 . . . . . . .118 B1
Ingrave St, SW11 . . . . .149 G3
Ingress St, W4
　off Devonshire Rd 126/127 E5
Inigo Jones Rd, SE7 . . . . .136 B7
Inigo Pl, WC2 . . . . .18 A5
Inkerman Rd, NW5 . . . . .92 B6
Inkerman Ter, W8 off Allen St . .128 D3
Inks Grn, E4 . . . . .62 C5
Inkster Ho, SW11
　off Ingrave St 149 H3
Inman Rd, NW10 . . . . .106 E1
　SW18 . . . . .149 F7
Inmans Row, Wdf.Grn. IG8 . . . .63 G4
Inner Circle, NW1 . . . . .8 B4
Inner Pk Rd, SW19 . . . . .166 A1
Inner Ring E, Houns. (Hthrw Air.)
　TW6 . . . . .140 E3
Inner Ring W, Houns. (Hthrw Air.)
　TW6 . . . . .140 D3
Inner Temple La, EC4 . . . . .19 E4
Innes Cl, SW20 . . . . .184 B2
Innes Gdns, SW15 . . . . .147 H6
Innes St, SE15 off Blakes Rd . .132 B7
Innes Yd, Croy. CR0
　off Whitgift St 201 J3
Inniskilling Rd, E13 . . . . .115 J2
Innovation Cl, Wem. HA0 . . . .105 H1
Inskip Cl, E10 . . . . .96 B2
Inskip Rd, Dag. RM8 . . . . .100 D1
★ Institute of Contemporary Arts
　(I.C.A.), SW1 . . . . .25 J1
Institute Pl, E8 . . . . .94 E5
Integer Gdns, E11 . . . . .78 D7
Interchange E Ind Est, E5
　off Grosvenor Way 95 F2
International Av, Houns. TW5 . .122 C5
International Trd Est, Sthl. UB2 .122 A3
Inveraray Pl, SE18
　off Old Mill Rd 137 G6
Inver Cl, E5 off Theydon Rd 95 F2
Inverclyde Gdns, Rom. RM6 . . .82 D4
Inver Ct, W2 . . . . .14 B4
　W6 off Goldhawk Rd 127 G3
Inveresk Gdns, Wor.Pk. KT4 . .197 F3
Inverforth Cl, NW3
　off North End Way 91 F2
Inverforth Rd, N11 . . . . .58 B5
Inverine Rd, SE7 . . . . .135 H5
Invermead Cl, W6
　off Goldhawk Rd 127 G3
Invermore Pl, SE18 . . . . .137 F4
Inverness Av, Enf. EN1 . . . . . . .44 B1
Inverness Dr, Ilf. IG6 . . . . .65 H6
Inverness Gdns, W8 . . . . .22 A2
Inverness Ms, E16 . . . . .137 F1
　W2 .14 B5
Inverness Pl, W2 . . . . .14 B5
Inverness Rd, N18
　off Aberdeen Rd 60/61 E5
　Hounslow TW3 . . . . .143 F4
　Southall UB2 . . . . .123 E4
　Worcester Park KT4 . . . . . .198 A1
Inverness St, NW1 . . . . .110 B1
Inverness Ter, W2 . . . . .14 B5
Inverton Rd, SE15 . . . . .153 G3
Invicta Cl, Chis. BR7 . . . . .174 D5
Invicta Gro, Nthlt. UB5 . . . . . .103 F3
Invicta Plaza, SE1 . . . . .27 G1
Invicta Rd, SE3 . . . . .135 G7
Inville Rd, SE17 . . . . .36 C4
Inwen Ct, SE8 . . . . .133 H5
Inwood Av, Houns. TW3 . . . . . .143 J3
Inwood Cl, Croy. CR0 . . . . .203 H2
Inwood Rd, Houns. TW3 . . . . . .143 H4
Inworth St, SW11 . . . . .149 H2
Inworth Wk, N1 off Popham St . .111 J1
Iona Cl, SE6 . . . . .154 A7
　Morden SM4 . . . . .184 E7
Ionian Bldg, E14 off Narrow St . .113 H7
Ion Sq, E2 . . . . .13 H2
Ipswich Rd, SW17 . . . . .168 A6
Ireland Cl, E6
　off Bradley Stone Rd 116 C5
Ireland Pl, N22
　off Whittington Rd 58/59 E7
Ireland Yd, EC4 . . . . .19 H4
Irene Rd, SW6 . . . . .148 D1
　Orpington BR6 . . . . .193 J7
Ireton Cl, N10 . . . . .58 A7
Ireton St, E3 off Tidworth Rd . .114 A4
Iris Av, Bex. DA5 . . . . .159 E5

Iris Cl, E6 . . . . .116 B4
Iris Cl, Croy. CR0 . . . . .203 G1
  Surbiton KT6 . . . . .181 J7
Iris Ct, Pnr. HA5 . . . . .66 C3
Iris Cres, Bexh. DA7 . . . . .139 F6
Iris Rd, Epsom (W.Ewell) KT19 .196 B5
Iris Wk, Edg. HA8 off Ash Cl . . .54 C4
Iris Way, E4 . . . . .61 J4
Irkdale Av, Enf. EN1 . . . . .44 C1
Iron Br Cl, NW10 . . . . .88 E5
  Southall UB2 . . . . .123 J1
Iron Br Rd, Uxb. UB11 . . . . . . .120 D2
  West Drayton UB7 . . . . .120 D2
Iron Mill Pl, SW18
  off Garratt La 148/149 E6
Iron Mill Rd, SW18 . . . . .149 E6
Ironmonger La, EC2 . . . . .20 B4
Ironmonger Pas, EC1 . . . . .12 A5
Ironmonger Row, EC1 . . . . .12 A4
Ironmongers Pl, E14
  off Spindrift Av 134 A4
Ironside Cl, SE16
  off Kinburn St 133 G2
Irvine Av, Har. HA3 . . . . .68 D3
Irvine Cl, N20 . . . . .57 H2
Irvine Way, Orp. BR6 . . . . .193 J7
Irving Av, Nthlt. UB5 . . . . .102 D1
Irving Gro, SW9 . . . . .151 F2
Irving Ms, N1 off Alwyne Rd . . .93 J6
Irving Rd, W14 . . . . .128 A3
Irving St, WC2 . . . . .17 J6
Irving Way, NW9 . . . . .71 F5
Irwin Av, SE18 . . . . .137 H7
Irwin Gdns, NW10 . . . . .107 H1
Isabel Hill Cl, Hmptn. TW12
  off Upper Sunbury Rd 179 H1
Isabella Cl, N14 . . . . .42 C7
Isabella Ct, Rich. TW10
  off Grove Rd 145 J6
Isabella Dr, Orp. BR6 . . . . .207 F4
Isabella Rd, E9 . . . . .95 F5
Isabella St, SE1 . . . . .27 G2
Isabel St, SW9 . . . . .151 F1
Isambard Ms, E14 . . . . .134 C3
Isambard Pl, SE16
  off Rotherhithe St 133 F1
Isel Way, SE22
  off East Dulwich Gro 152 B5
Isham Rd, SW16 . . . . .186 E2
Isis Cl, SW15 . . . . .147 J4
Isis St, SW18 . . . . .167 F2
Island Fm Av, W.Mol. KT8 . . . .179 F5
Island Fm Rd, W.Mol. KT8 . . . .179 F5
Island Rd, Mitch. CR4 . . . . .167 J7
Island Row, E14 . . . . .113 J6
Isla Rd, SE18 . . . . .137 F6
Islay Gdns, Houns. TW4 . . . . . .142 D5
Islay Wk, N1 off Douglas Rd 93 J7
Isledon Rd, N7 . . . . .93 G3
Islehurst Cl, Chis. BR7 . . . . . . .192 D1
ISLEWORTH, TW7 . . . . .144 C3
Isleworth Business Complex, Islw.
  TW7 off St. John's Rd 144 C2
Isleworth Prom, Twick. TW1 . . .144 E4
ISLINGTON, N1 . . . . .111 F1
Islington Grn, N1 . . . . .111 H1
Islington High St, N1 . . . . .11 F2
Islington Pk Ms, N1
  off Islington Pk St 93 G7
Islington Pk St, N1 . . . . .93 G7
Islip Gdns, Edg. HA8 . . . . .54 D7
  Northolt UB5 . . . . .85 E7
Islip Manor Rd, Nthlt. UB5 . . . . .85 E7
Islip St, NW5 . . . . .92 C5
Ismailia Rd, E7 . . . . .97 H7
★ Ismaili Cen & Zamana Gall,
  SW7 . . . . .31 F1
Isom Cl, E13 off Belgrave Rd . . .115 J4
Ivanhoe Dr, Har. HA3 . . . . .68 D3
Ivanhoe Rd, SE5 . . . . .152 C3
  Hounslow TW4 . . . . .142 D3
Ivatt Pl, W14 . . . . .128 C5
Ivatt Way, N17 . . . . .75 J3
Iveagh Av, NW10 . . . . .106 A2
Iveagh Cl, E9 . . . . .113 G1
  NW10 . . . . .106 A2
Iveagh Ter, NW10
  off Iveagh Av 106 A2
Ivedon Rd, Well. DA16 . . . . .158 C2
Ive Fm Cl, E10 . . . . .96 A2
Ive Fm La, E10 . . . . .96 A2
Iveley Rd, SW4 . . . . .150 C2
Ivere Dr, Barn. EN5 . . . . .40 E6
Iverhurst Cl, Bexh. DA6 . . . . . . .158 D5
Iverna Ct, W8 . . . . .128 D3
Iverna Gdns, W8 . . . . .128 D3
  Feltham TW14 . . . . .141 G5
Iverson Rd, NW6 . . . . .90 C6
Ivers Way, Croy. (New Adgtn)
  CR0 . . . . .204 B7
Ives Rd, E16 . . . . .114 E5
Ives St, SW3 . . . . .31 H1
Ivestor Ter, SE23 . . . . .153 F7
Ivimey St, E2 . . . . .13 J3
Ivinghoe Cl, Enf. EN1 . . . . .44 B2
Ivinghoe Rd, Dag. RM8 . . . . . . .100 B5
Ivor Gro, SE9 . . . . .175 E1

Ivor Pl, NW1 . . . . .7 J6
Ivor St, NW1 . . . . .92 C7
Ivorydown, Brom. BR1 . . . . .173 G4
Ivory Sq, SW11
  off Gartons Way 149 G3
Ivybridge Cl, Twick. TW1 . . . . . .144 D6
Ivybridge Est, Islw. TW7 . . . . . .144 C5
Ivybridge La, WC2 . . . . .18 B6
Ivychurch Cl, SE20 . . . . .171 F7
Ivychurch La, SE17 . . . . .37 F3
Ivy Cl, Har. HA2 . . . . .85 F4
  Pinner HA5 . . . . .66 C7
  Sunbury-on-Thames TW16 . . .178 C2
Ivy Cotts, E14 off Grove Vil 114 B7
Ivy Ct, SE16 . . . . .37 J4
Ivy Cres, W4 . . . . .126 C4
Ivydale Rd, SE15 . . . . .153 G3
  Carshalton SM5 . . . . .199 J2
Ivyday Gro, SW16 . . . . .169 F3
Ivydene, W.Mol. KT8 . . . . .179 F5
Ivydene Cl, Sutt. SM1 . . . . .199 F4
Ivy Gdns, N8 . . . . .74 E6
  Mitcham CR4 . . . . .186 D3
Ivyhouse Rd, Dag. RM9 . . . . . . .100 D6
Ivy La, Houns. TW4 . . . . .143 F4
Ivymount Rd, SE27 . . . . .169 G3
Ivy Pl, Surb. KT5 off Alpha Rd . .181 J6
Ivy Rd, E16 off Pacific Rd 115 G6
  E17 .78 A6
  N14 .42 C7
  NW2 .89 J4
  SE4 . . . . .153 J4
  SW17 off Tooting High St 167 H5
  Hounslow TW3 . . . . .143 H4
  Surbiton KT6 . . . . .196 A1
Ivy St, N1 . . . . .12 D1
Ivy Wk, Dag. RM9 . . . . .100 E6
Ixworth Pl, SW3 . . . . .31 G3
Izane Rd, Bexh. DA6 . . . . .159 F4

J

Jacaranda Cl, N.Mal. KT3 . . . . .182 E3
Jacaranda Gro, E8 . . . . .94 C7
Jackass La, Kes. BR2 . . . . .205 H6
Jack Barnett Way, N22 . . . . .75 F2
Jack Clow Rd, E15 . . . . .115 E2
Jack Cornwell St, E12 . . . . .98 D4
Jack Dash Way, E6 . . . . .116 B4
Jack Goodchild Way, Kings.T. KT1
  off Kingston Rd 182 B3
Jacklin Grn, Wdf.Grn. IG8 . . . . . .63 G4
Jackman Ms, NW10 . . . . .88 E3
Jackman St, E8 . . . . .112 E1
Jackson Cl, E9 . . . . .95 F7
Jackson Ct, E11
  off Brading Cres 97 H1
Jackson Rd, N7 . . . . .93 F4
  Barking IG11 . . . . .117 G1
  Barnet EN4 . . . . .41 H6
  Bromley BR2 . . . . .206 B2
Jacksons La, N6 . . . . .74 A7
Jacksons Pl, Croy. CR0
  off Cross Rd 202 A1
Jacksons Way, Croy. CR0 . . . . . .204 A3
Jackson Way, Sthl. UB2 . . . . . . .123 H2
Jack Walker Ct, N5 . . . . .93 H4
Jacob Ho, Erith DA18
  off Kale Rd 138 D2
Jacobs Cl, Dag. RM10 . . . . .101 H4
Jacobs Ho, E13 . . . . .115 J3
Jacob St, SE1 . . . . .29 G3
Jacob's Well Ms, W1 . . . . .16 C3
Jacqueline Cl, Nthlt. UB5
  off Canford Av 103 F1
Jade Cl, E16 . . . . .116 A6
  NW2 off Marble Dr 72 A7
  Dagenham RM8 . . . . .100 C1
Jaffe Rd, Ilf. IG1 . . . . .99 F1
Jaffray Pl, SE27 off Chapel Rd . .169 H4
Jaffray Rd, Brom. BR2 . . . . .192 A4
Jaggard Way, SW12 . . . . .149 J7
Jago Cl, SE18 . . . . .137 F6
Jago Wk, SE5 . . . . .132 A7
Jamaica Rd, SE1 . . . . .29 G4
  SE16 . . . . .132 C2
  Thornton Heath CR7 . . . . . . .187 H6
Jamaica St, E1 . . . . .113 F6
James Av, NW2 . . . . .89 J5
  Dagenham RM8 . . . . .101 F1
James Bedford Cl, Pnr. HA5 . . . . .66 C2
James Boswell Cl, SW16
  off Curtis Fld Rd 169 G4
James Clavell Sq, SE18
  off Cadogan Rd 136 E3
James Cl, E13
  off Richmond St 115 G2
  NW11 off Woodlands 72 B6
James Collins Cl, W9
  off Fermoy Rd 108 C4
James Ct, N1
  off Morton Rd 93 J7
James Dudson Ct, NW10 . . . . . . .88 C7
James Gdns, N22 . . . . .59 H7
James Hammett Ho, E2 . . . . .13 G2

James Joyce Wk, SE24
  off Shakespeare Rd 151 H4
James La, E10 . . . . .78 D7
James La, E11 . . . . .78 D6
James Newman Ct, SE9
  off Great Harry Dr 174 D3
Jameson Cl, W3 off Acton La . . .126 C2
Jameson Ct, E2 . . . . .113 F2
Jameson St, W8 . . . . .128 D1
James Pl, N17 . . . . .76 C1
James's Cotts, Rich. TW9
  off Kew Rd 126 A7
James Sinclair Pt, E13 . . . . .115 J1
James St, W1 . . . . .16 C3
  WC2 . . . . .18 B5
  Barking IG11 . . . . .99 F7
  Enfield EN1 . . . . .44 C5
  Hounslow TW3 . . . . .144 A3
James Ter, SW14
  off Mullins Path 146 D3
Jamestown Rd, NW1 . . . . .110 B1
Jamestown Way, E14 . . . . .114 D7
James Way, Wat. WD19 . . . . .50 D4
James Yd, E4 . . . . .62 D6
Jamieson Ho, Houns. TW4 . . . . .143 F7
Jamuna Cl, E14 . . . . .113 H5
Jane St, E1
  off Commercial Rd 112/113 E6
Janet St, E14 . . . . .134 A3
Janeway Pl, SE16
  off Janeway St 132/133 E2
Janeway St, SE16 . . . . .29 J4
Janice Ms, Ilf. IG1
  off Oakfield Rd 98/99 E3
Jansen Wk, SW11 off Hope St . .149 G4
Janson Cl, E15
  off Janson Rd 96/97 E5
  NW10 . . . . .88 D3
Janson Rd, E15 . . . . .96 E5
Jansons Rd, N15 . . . . .76 B3
Japan Cres, N4 . . . . .93 F1
Japan Rd, Rom. RM6 . . . . .82 D6
Jardine Rd, E1 . . . . .113 G7
Jarrett Cl, SW2 . . . . .169 H1
Jarrow Cl, Mord. SM4 . . . . .184 E5
Jarrow Rd, N17 . . . . .76 E4
  SE16 . . . . .133 F4
  Romford RM6 . . . . .82 C6
Jarrow Way, E9 . . . . .95 H4
Jarvis Cl, Bark. IG11
  off Westbury Rd 117 G1
  Barnet EN5 . . . . .40 A5
Jarvis Rd, SE22
  off Melbourne Gro 152 B4
  South Croydon CR2 . . . . .202 A6
Jasmine Cl, Ilf. IG1 . . . . .99 E5
  Orpington BR6 . . . . .206 E2
  Southall UB1 . . . . .103 E7
Jasmine Gdns, Croy. CR0 . . . . . .204 B3
  Harrow HA2 . . . . .85 G2
Jasmine Gro, SE20 . . . . .189 E1
Jasmine Ter, West Dr. UB7 . . . . .120 D2
Jasmine Way, E.Mol. KT8
  off Hampton Ct Way 180 B4
Jasmin Rd, Epsom KT19 . . . . . .196 B5
Jason Ct, W1
  off Marylebone La 110 A6
Jason Wk, SE9 . . . . .174 D4
Jasper Pas, SE19 . . . . .170 C6
Jasper Rd, E16 . . . . .116 A6
  SE19 . . . . .170 C5
Jasper Wk, N1 . . . . .12 B3
Javelin Way, Nthlt. UB5 . . . . . . .102 D3
Jaycroft, Enf. EN2
  off The Ridgeway 43 G1
Jay Gdns, Chis. BR7 . . . . .174 C4
Jay Ms, SW7 . . . . .22 E4
Jazzfern Ter, Wem. HA0
  off Maybank Av 86 D5
Jean Batten Cl, Wall. SM6 . . . . .201 F7
Jebb Av, SW2 . . . . .151 E6
Jebb St, E3 . . . . .114 A2
Jedburgh Rd, E13 . . . . .115 J3
Jedburgh St, SW11 . . . . .150 A4
Jeddo Rd, W12 . . . . .127 F2
Jefferson Cl, W13 . . . . .125 E3
  Ilford IG2 . . . . .81 E5
Jefferson Wk, SE18
  off Kempt St 136 D6
Jeffreys Pl, NW1 off Jeffreys St . .92 C7
Jeffreys Rd, SW4 . . . . .150 E2
  Enfield EN3 . . . . .45 J3
Jeffreys St, NW1 . . . . .92 B7
Jeffreys Wk, SW4 . . . . .150 E2
Jeffries Ho, NW10 . . . . .106 D1
Jeffs Cl, Hmptn. TW12
  off Uxbridge Rd 161 H6
Jeffs Rd, Sutt. SM1 . . . . .198 C4
Jeger Av, E2 . . . . .112 C1
Jeken Rd, SE9 . . . . .155 J4
Jelf Rd, SW2 . . . . .151 G5
Jellicoe Gdns, Stan. HA7 . . . . . . .52 C6
Jellicoe Rd, E13 off Jutland Rd . .115 G4
  N17 .60 A7
Jemma Knowles Cl, SW2
  off Neil Wates Cres 169 G1
Jemmett Cl, Kings.T. KT2 . . . . . .182 B1

Jengar Cl, Sutt. SM1 . . . . .199 E4
Jenkins La, E6 . . . . .116 D2
  Barking IG11 . . . . .117 E2
Jenkins Rd, E13 . . . . .115 H4
Jenner Av, W3 . . . . .106 D5
Jenner Cl, Sid. DA14 . . . . .176 A4
Jenner Ho, SE3 . . . . .135 E6
Jenner Pl, SW13 . . . . .127 H6
Jenner Rd, N16 . . . . .94 C2
Jennett Rd, Croy. CR0 . . . . .201 G3
Jennifer Rd, Brom. BR1 . . . . . . .173 F3
Jennings Cl, Surb. KT6 . . . . .181 F7
Jennings Rd, SE22 . . . . .152 C6
Jennings Way, Barn. EN5 . . . . . . .39 J3
Jenningtree Way, Belv. DA17 . . .139 J2
Jenny Hammond Cl, E11
  off Newcomen Rd 97 F3
Jenson Way, SE19 . . . . .170 C7
Jenton Av, Bexh. DA7 . . . . .158 E1
Jephson Rd, E7 . . . . .97 J7
Jephson St, SE5
  off Grove La 152 A1
Jephtha Rd, SW18 . . . . .148 D6
Jeppos La, Mitch. CR4 . . . . .185 J4
Jepson Ho, SW6
  off Pearscroft Rd 148/149 E1
Jerdan Pl, SW6 . . . . .128 D7
Jeremiah St, E14 . . . . .114 B6
Jeremys Grn, N18 . . . . .61 E4
Jermyn St, SW1 . . . . .25 F1
Jerningham Av, Ilf. IG5 . . . . .80 E2
Jerningham Rd, SE14 . . . . .153 H2
Jerome Cres, NW8 . . . . .7 G5
Jerome Pl, Kings.T. KT1
  off Wadbrook St 181 G2
Jerome St, E1 . . . . .21 F1
Jerome Twr, W3 . . . . .126 B2
Jerrard St, N1 . . . . .12 E2
  SE13 . . . . .154 B3
Jersey Av, Stan. HA7 . . . . .69 E2
Jersey Dr, Orp. BR5 . . . . .193 G6
Jersey Par, Houns. TW5 . . . . . . .143 H1
Jersey Rd, E11 . . . . .96 D1
  E16 off Prince Regent La 115 J6
  SW17 . . . . .168 B6
  W7 .124 D2
  Hounslow TW3, TW5 . . . . . . .143 H1
  Ilford IG1 . . . . .99 E4
  Isleworth TW7 . . . . .124 B6
Jersey Sq, E11
  off Prince Regent La 115 J6
Jersey St, E2
  off Bethnal Grn Rd 112/113 E3
Jerusalem Pas, EC1 . . . . .11 G6
Jervis Ct, W1 . . . . .17 E4
Jerviston Gdns, SW16 . . . . .169 G6
Jesmond Av, Wem. HA9 . . . . .87 J6
Jesmond Cl, Mitch. CR4 . . . . . . .186 B3
Jesmond Rd, Croy. CR0 . . . . . . .188 C7
Jesmond Way, Stan. HA7 . . . . . . .53 H5
Jessam Av, E5 . . . . .94 E1
Jessamine Rd, W7 . . . . .124 B1
Jessel Dr, Loug. IG10 . . . . .49 F1
Jesse Rd, E10 . . . . .96 C1
Jessica Rd, SW18 . . . . .149 F6
Jessie Blythe La, N19 . . . . .74 E7
Jessop Av, Sthl. UB2 . . . . .123 F4
Jessop Rd, SE24
  off Milkwood Rd 151 H4
Jessop Sq, E14
  off Heron Quay 134 A1
Jessops Way, Croy. CR0 . . . . . . .186 C6
Jessup Cl, SE18 . . . . .137 F4
Jetstar Way, Nthlt. UB5 . . . . . . .102 E3
Jevington Way, SE12 . . . . .173 H2
Jewel Rd, E17 . . . . .78 A3
★ Jewel Twr, Hos of Parliament,
  SW1 . . . . .26 A5
★ Jewish Mus, NW1
  off Albert St 110 B1
Jewry St, EC3 . . . . .21 F4
Jew's Row, SW18 . . . . .149 E4
Jews Wk, SE26 . . . . .171 E4
Jeymer Av, NW2 . . . . .89 H5
Jeymer Dr, Grnf. UB6 . . . . .103 J1
Jeypore Pas, SW18
  off Jeypore Rd 149 F6
Jeypore Rd, SW18 . . . . .149 F7
Jillian Cl, Hmptn. TW12 . . . . . . .161 G7
Jim Bradley Cl, SE18
  off John Wilson St 136 D4
Jim Griffiths Ho, SW6
  off Clem Attlee Ct 128 C6
Joan Cres, SE9 . . . . .156 A7
Joan Gdns, Dag. RM8 . . . . .100 E2
Joan Rd, Dag. RM8 . . . . .100 E2
Joan St, SE1 . . . . .27 G2
Jocelyn Rd, Rich. TW9 . . . . .145 H3
Jocelyn St, SE15 . . . . .152 D1
Jockey's Flds, WC1 . . . . .18 D1
Jodane St, SE8 . . . . .133 J4
Jodrell Cl, Islw. TW7 . . . . .144 D1
Jodrell Rd, E3 . . . . .113 J1
Joel St, Nthwd. HA6 . . . . .66 A3
  Pinner HA5 . . . . .66 A3
Johanna St, SE1 . . . . .27 E4
John Adam St, WC2 . . . . .18 B6
John Aird Ct, W2 . . . . .14 D1
John Archer Way, SW18 . . . . . . .149 G6

John Ashby Cl, SW2 . . . . .151 E6
John Austin Cl, Kings.T. KT2
  off Queen Elizabeth Rd 181 J1
John Barnes Wk, E15 . . . . .97 F6
John Bradshaw Rd, N14
  . . . . .58 D1
John Burns Dr, Bark. IG11 . . . . .99 H7
John Campbell Rd, N16 . . . . . . .94 B5
John Carpenter St, EC4 . . . . . . .19 G5
John Cornwell VC Ho, E12 . . . . .98 D4
John Drinkwater Cl, E11
  off Browning Rd 79 F7
John Felton Rd, SE16 . . . . .29 H4
John Fisher St, E1 . . . . .21 H5
John Gooch Dr, Enf. EN2 . . . . . .43 H1
John Harrison Way, SE10 . . . . .135 F3
John Horner Ms, N1 . . . . .11 J1
John Islip St, SW1 . . . . .34 A2
John Keats Ho, N22 . . . . .59 F7
John Kennedy Ho, SE16
  off Rotherhithe Old Rd 133 G4
John Maurice Cl, SE17 . . . . .36 B1
John McKenna Wk, SE16 . . . . . .29 J5
John Newton Cl, Well. DA16 . . .158 B3
John Parker Cl, Dag. RM10 . . . .101 H7
John Parker Sq, SW11
  off Thomas Baines Rd 149 G3
John Penn St, SE13 . . . . .154 B1
John Perrin Pl, Har. HA3 . . . . . . .69 H7
John Princes St, W1 . . . . .17 E3
John Rennie Wk, E1
  off Wine Cl 132/133 E1
John Roll Way, SE16 . . . . .29 J5
John Ruskin St, SE5 . . . . .35 G7
Johns Av, NW4 . . . . .71 J4
Johns Ct, Sutt. SM2
  off Mulgrave Rd 198/199 E6
John Silkin La, SE8 . . . . .133 G5
Johns La, Mord. SM4 . . . . .185 F5
John's Ms, WC1 . . . . .10 D6
John Smith Av, SW6 . . . . .128 C7
John Smith Ms, E14
  off Newport Av 114 D7
Johnson Cl, E8 . . . . .112 D1
Johnson Rd, NW10 . . . . .106 D1
  Bromley BR2 . . . . .192 A4
  Croydon CR0 . . . . .188 A7
  Hounslow TW5 . . . . .122 C7
Johnsons Cl, Cars. SM5 . . . . . .199 J3
Johnson's Ct, EC4 off Fleet St . .111 G6
Johnsons Dr, Hmptn. TW12 . . .179 J1
Johnson's Pl, SW1 . . . . .33 F4
Johnson St, E1 off Cable St 113 F7
  Southall UB2 . . . . .122 C3
Johnsons Way, NW10 . . . . .106 B4
John Spencer Sq, N1 . . . . .93 H6
John's Pl, E1
  off Damien St 112/113 E6
John's Ter, Croy. CR0 . . . . .202 A1
Johnston Cl, SW9
  off Hackford Rd 151 F1
Johnstone Rd, E6 . . . . .116 C3
Johnston Rd, Wdf.Grn. IG8 . . . .63 G5
Johnston Ter, NW2
  off Kara Way 90 A3
John St, E15 . . . . .115 F1
  SE25 . . . . .188 D4
  WC1 . . . . .10 D6
  Enfield EN1 . . . . .44 C5
  Hounslow TW3 . . . . .143 E2
John Trundle Ct, EC2
  off The Barbican 111 J5
John Walsh Twr, E11 . . . . .97 F2
John Williams Cl, SE14 . . . . . . .133 G6
  Kingston upon Thames KT2
  off Henry Macaulay Av 181 G1
John Wilson St, SE18 . . . . .136 D3
John Woolley Cl, SE13 . . . . . . .154 E4
Joiner's Arms Yd, SE5
  off Denmark Hill 152 A1
Joiners Pl, N5
  off Leconfield Rd 94 A4
Joiner St, SE1 . . . . .28 C2
Joiners Yd, N1
  off Caledonia St 110 E2
Jollys La, Har. HA2 . . . . .86 A1
  Hayes UB4 . . . . .102 D5
Jonathan Ct, W4
  off Windmill Rd 126/127 E4
Jonathan St, SE11 . . . . .34 C3
Jones Rd, E13 off Holborn Rd . .115 H4
Jones St, W1 . . . . .16 D6
Jones Wk, Rich. TW10
  off Pyrland Rd 145 J6
Jonquil Gdns, Hmptn. TW12
  off Partridge Rd 161 F6
Jonson Cl, Hayes UB4 . . . . . . .102 A5
  Mitcham CR4 . . . . .186 B4
Jordan Cl, Dag. RM10
  off Muggeridge Rd 101 H4
  Harrow HA2
  off Hamilton Cres 85 F3
Jordan Ct, SW15
  off Charlwood Rd 148 A4
Jordan Rd, Grnf. UB6 . . . . .105 E1
Jordans Cl, Islw. TW7 . . . . .144 B1
Joseph Av, W3 . . . . .106 D6

Joseph Hardcastle Cl, SE14 . . . .133 G7
Josephine Av, SW2 . . . . .151 F5
Joseph Powell Cl, SW12
  off Hazelbourne Rd 150 B6
Joseph Ray Rd, E11 . . . . .97 E2
Joseph St, E3 . . . . .113 J4
Joseph Trotter Cl, EC1
  off Myddelton St 111 G3
Joshua Cl, N10 . . . . .58 B7
  South Croydon CR2 . . . . . . .201 H7
Joshua St, E14
  off St. Leonards Rd 114 C6
Joubert St, SW11 . . . . .149 J2
Jowett St, SE15 . . . . .132 C7
Joyce Av, N18 . . . . .60 C5
Joyce Dawson Way, SE28 . . . . .118 A7
  off Thamesmere Dr 118 A7
Joyce Dawson Way Shop Arc, SE28
  off Thamesmere Dr 118 A7
Joyce Page Cl, SE7
  off Lansdowne La 136 A6
Joyce Wk, SW2 . . . . .151 G6
JOYDENS WOOD, Bex. DA5 . . .177 J5
Joydon Dr, Rom. RM6 . . . . .82 B6
Joyners Cl, Dag. RM9 . . . . .101 F4
Jubilee Av, E4 . . . . .62 C6
  Romford RM7 . . . . .83 H5
  Twickenham TW2 . . . . .161 J1
Jubilee Cl, NW9 . . . . .70 D6
  Pinner HA5 . . . . .66 C2
  Romford RM7 . . . . .83 H5
Jubilee Cres, E14 . . . . .134 C3
  N9 . . . . .60 D1
Jubilee Dr, Ruis. HA4 . . . . .84 D4
★ Jubilee Gdns, SE1 . . . . .26 C2
Jubilee Gdns, Sthl. UB1 . . . . . .103 G6
Jubilee La, W5
  off Mountfield Rd 105 H6
Jubilee Pl, SW3 . . . . .31 H3
Jubilee Rd, Grnf. UB6 . . . . .104 E1
  Sutton SM3 . . . . .198 A7
Jubilee St, E1 . . . . .113 F6
Jubilee Wk, Wat. WD19 . . . . . . .50 B1
Jubilee Way, SW19 . . . . .185 E1
  Chessington KT9 . . . . .196 A4
  Sidcup DA14 . . . . .176 A2
Judd St, WC1 . . . . .10 A4
Jude St, E16 . . . . .115 F6
Judge Wk, Esher (Clay.) KT10 . .194 B6
Juer St, SW11 . . . . .129 H7
Jules Thorn Av, Enf. EN1 . . . . . .44 C3
Julia Gdns, Bark. IG11 . . . . . . .118 D2
Julia Garfield Ms, E16
  off Wesley Av 135 H1
Juliana Cl, N2 . . . . .73 F3
Julian Av, W3 . . . . .106 B7
Julian Cl, Barn. EN5 . . . . .40 E3
Julian Hill, Har. HA1 . . . . .86 B2
Julian Pl, E14 . . . . .134 B5
Julian Tayler Path, SE23 . . . . . .170 E2
Julia St, NW5 off Oak Village . . .92 A4
Julien Rd, W5 . . . . .125 F3
Juliette Rd, E13 . . . . .115 F2
Julius Nyerere Cl, N1
  off Copenhagen St 111 G4
Junction App, SE13 . . . . .154 C3
  SW11 . . . . .149 H3
Junction Av, W10
  off Harrow Rd 107 J3
Junction Ms, W2 . . . . .15 G3
Junction Pl, W2 . . . . .15 G3
Junction Rd, E13 . . . . .115 H2
  N9 . . . . .60 D1
  N17 .76 D3
  N19 .92 C4
  W5 .125 G4
  Brentford TW8 . . . . .125 G4
  Harrow HA1 . . . . .68 B6
  South Croydon CR2 . . . . . . .202 A5
Junction Rd E, Rom. RM6
  off Kenneth Rd 82/83 E7
Junction Rd W, Rom. RM6 . . . . .82 E7
Junction Shop Cen, The, SW11
  off St. John's Hill 149 H4
Juniper Cl, Barn. EN5 . . . . .40 A5
  Chessington KT9 . . . . .195 J6
  Wembley HA9 . . . . .87 J5
Juniper Cres, NW1 . . . . .92 A7
Juniper Gdns, SW16
  off Leonard Rd 186 C1
Juniper La, E6 . . . . .116 B5
Juniper Rd, Ilf. IG1 . . . . .98 D4
Juniper St, E1 . . . . .113 F7
Juno Way, SE14 . . . . .133 G6
Jupiter Way, N7 . . . . .93 F6
Jupp Rd, E15 . . . . .96 D7
Jupp Rd W, E15 . . . . .114 C1
Justice Wk, SW3 . . . . .31 G6
Justin Cl, Brent. TW8 . . . . .125 G7
Justin Rd, E4 . . . . .61 J6
Jute La, Enf. EN3 . . . . .45 H2
Jutland Cl, N19
  off Sussex Way 92/93 E1
Jutland Rd, E13 . . . . .115 G4
  SE6 . . . . .154 C7
Jutsums Av, Rom. RM7 . . . . . . .83 H6

Jutsums La, Rom. RM7 . . . . . . .83 H6
Juxon Cl, Har. HA3
  off Augustine Rd 67 H1
Juxon St, SE11 . . . . .34 D1

K

Kaduna Cl, Pnr. HA5 . . . . .66 A5
Kale Rd, Erith DA18 . . . . .138 E2
Kambala Rd, SW11 . . . . .149 G2
Kangley Br Rd, SE26 . . . . .171 J5
Kaplan Dr, N21 . . . . .43 E5
Karanja Ct, NW2 off Walm La . . .89 J6
Kara Way, NW2 . . . . .90 A4
Karen Ct, SE4 off Wickham Rd . .153 J2
  Bromley BR1 off Blyth Rd . . .191 F1
Karen Ter, E11
  off Montague Rd 97 F2
Karenza Ct, Wem. HA9
  off Lulworth Av 69 F7
Kariba Cl, N9 . . . . .61 F3
Karina Cl, Chig. IG7 . . . . .65 H5
Karoline Gdns, Grnf. UB6
  off Oldfield La N 104 A2
Kashgar Rd, SE18 . . . . .137 J5
Kashmir Rd, SE7 . . . . .136 A7
Kassala Rd, SW11 . . . . .149 J1
Katella Trd Est, Bark. IG11 . . . .117 H3
Kates Cl, Barn. EN5 . . . . .39 G5
Katharine St, Croy. CR0 . . . . . .201 J3
Katherine Cl, SE16
  off Rotherhithe St 133 G1
Katherine Gdns, SE9 . . . . .156 A4
  Ilford IG6 . . . . .65 F7
Katherine Rd, E6 . . . . .98 A7
  E7 . . . . .97 J5
  Twickenham TW1
  off London Rd 162 D1
Katherine Sq, W11
  off Wilsham St 128 B1
Kathleen Av, W3 . . . . .106 C5
  Wembley HA0 . . . . .87 H7
Kathleen Rd, SW11 . . . . .149 J3
Kayemoor Rd, Sutt. SM2 . . . . .199 H7
Kay Rd, SW9 . . . . .151 E2
Kays Ter, E18 off Walpole Rd . . .79 F1
Kay St, E2 . . . . .13 J1
  Welling DA16 . . . . .158 B1
Kay Way, SE10
  off Greenwich High Rd 134 B7
Kean St, WC2 . . . . .18 C4
Keatley Grn, E4 . . . . .61 J6
Keats Av, E16 off Wesley Av . . .135 H1
Keats Cl, E11 off Nightingale La . .79 H5
  NW3 off Keats Gro 91 H4
  SE1 .37 F2
  SW19 off North Rd 167 G6
  Chigwell IG7 . . . . .65 F6
  Enfield EN3 . . . . .45 G5
  Hayes UB4 . . . . .102 A5
Keats Gro, NW3 . . . . .91 G4
★ Keats Ho, NW3 . . . . .91 H4
Keats Ho, Beck. BR3 . . . . .172 A6
Keats Pl, EC2 . . . . .20 B2
Keats Way, Belv. DA17 . . . . . . .139 J3
  Welling DA16 . . . . .157 H1
  Croydon CR0 . . . . .189 F6
  Greenford UB6 . . . . .103 H5
  West Drayton UB7 . . . . .120 C4
Keble Cl, Nthlt. UB5 . . . . .85 J5
  Worcester Park KT4 . . . . . . .197 F1
Keble Pl, SW13
  off Somerville Av 127 H6
Keble St, SW17 . . . . .167 F4
Kechill Gdns, Brom. BR2 . . . . .191 G7
Kedelston Ct, E5
  off Redwald Rd 95 G4
Kedeston Ct, Sutt. SM1
  off Hurstcourt Rd 198/199 E1
Kedleston Dr, Orp. BR5 . . . . . .193 J6
Kedleston Wk, E2
  off Middleton St 112/113 E3
Keedonwood Rd, Brom. BR1 . .172 E5
Keel Cl, SE16 . . . . .133 G1
  Barking IG11 . . . . .118 C2
Keel Ct, E14 off Newport Av . . .114 D7
Keeley Rd, Croy. CR0 . . . . .201 J2
Keeley St, WC2 . . . . .18 C4
Keeling Rd, SE9 . . . . .156 A5
Keely Cl, Barn. EN4 . . . . .41 H5
Keemor Cl, SE18
  off Llanover Rd 136 D7
Keens Cl, SW16 . . . . .168 D5
Keens Rd, Croy. CR0 . . . . .201 J4
Keens Yd, N1 off St. Paul's Rd . .93 H6
Keep, The, SE3 . . . . .155 G2
  Kingston upon Thames KT2 . .163 J6
Keep La, N11 off Gardeners Cl . .58 A2
Keetons Rd, SE16 . . . . .132 E3
Keevil Dr, SW19 . . . . .148 A7
Keighley Cl, N7 off Penn Rd . .92/93 E5
Keightley Dr, SE9 . . . . .175 F1
Keildon Rd, SW11 . . . . .149 J4
Keir, The, SW19
  off West Side Common 165 J5

Keir Hardie Est, E5
  off Springfield 94/95 E1
Keir Hardie Ho, W6
  off Lochaline St 127 J6
Keir Hardie Way, Bark. IG11 . . .100 A7
  Hayes UB4 . . . . .102 A3
Keith Connor Cl, SW8
  off Daley Thompson Way . . .150 B3
Keith Gro, W12 . . . . .127 G2
Keith Rd, E17 . . . . .77 J1
  Barking IG11 . . . . .117 G2
  Hayes UB3 . . . . .121 H3
Kelbrook Rd, SE3 . . . . .156 B3
Kelby Path, SE9 . . . . .175 E3
Kelceda Cl, NW2 . . . . .89 G2
Kelfield Gdns, W10 . . . . .107 J6
Kelfield Ms, W10
  off Kelfield Gdns 108 A6
Kelland Cl, N8 off Palace Rd 74 D5
Kelland Rd, E13 . . . . .115 G4
Kellaway Rd, SE3 . . . . .155 J2
Keller Cres, E12 . . . . .98 A4
Kellerton Rd, SE13 . . . . .154 E5
Kellett Rd, SW2 . . . . .151 G4
Kelling Gdns, Croy. CR0 . . . . . .187 H7
Kellino St, SW17 . . . . .167 A4
Kellner Rd, SE28 . . . . .137 J3
Kell St, SE1 . . . . .27 H5
Kelly Av, SE15 . . . . .132 C7
Kelly Cl, NW10 . . . . .88 D3
Kelly Ct, Borwd. WD6 . . . . .38 C2
Kelly Ms, W9 off Woodfield Rd . .108 C5
Kelly Rd, NW7 . . . . .56 B6
Kelly St, NW1 . . . . .92 B6
Kelly Way, Rom. RM6 . . . . .82 E5
Kelman Cl, SW4 . . . . .150 D2
Kelmore Gro, SE22 . . . . .152 D4
Kelmscott Cl, E17 . . . . .77 J2
Kelmscott Gdns, W12 . . . . .127 G3
Kelmscott Rd, SW11 . . . . .149 H5
Kelross Pas, N5 off Kelross Rd . . .93 J4
Kelross Rd, N5 . . . . .93 H4
Kelsall Cl, SE3 . . . . .155 H2
Kelsall Ms, Rich. TW9
  off Melliss Av 146 B1
Kelsey Gate, Beck. BR3 . . . . . .190 B2
Kelsey La, Beck. BR3 . . . . .190 A2
Kelsey Pk Av, Beck. BR3 . . . . . .190 B2
Kelsey Pk Rd, Beck. BR3 . . . . . .190 A2
Kelsey Sq, Beck. BR3 . . . . .190 A2
Kelsey St, E2 . . . . .13 J5
Kelsey Way, Beck. BR3 . . . . . . .190 A3
Kelshall Ct, N4
  off Brownswood Rd 93 J2
Kelsie Way, Ilf. IG6 . . . . .65 H7
Kelson Ho, E14 . . . . .134 C3
Kelso Pl, W8 . . . . .22 B6
Kelso Rd, Cars. SM5 . . . . .185 F7
Kelston Rd, Ilf. IG6 . . . . .81 E2
Kelvedon Cl, Kings.T. KT2 . . . . .163 J6
Kelvedon Ho, SW8 . . . . .150 E1
Kelvedon Rd, SW6 . . . . .128 C7
Kelvedon Way, Wdf.Grn. IG8 . . .64 C6
Kelvin Av, N13 . . . . .59 F6
  Teddington TW11 . . . . .162 B6
Kelvinbrook, W.Mol. KT8 . . . . . .179 H3
Kelvin Cl, Epsom KT19 . . . . . . .196 A6
Kelvin Cres, Har. HA3 . . . . .52 B7
Kelvin Dr, Twick. TW1 . . . . .145 E6
Kelvin Gdns, Croy. CR0 . . . . . .187 E7
  Southall UB1 . . . . .103 G6
Kelvin Gro, SE26 . . . . .170 E3
  Chessington KT9 . . . . .195 H3
Kelvington Cl, Croy. CR0 . . . . . .189 H7
Kelvington Rd, SE15 . . . . .153 G5
Kelvin Ind Est, Grnf. UB6 . . . . . .85 H7
Kelvin Par, Orp. BR6 . . . . .207 H1
Kelvin Rd, N5 . . . . .93 H4
  Welling DA16 . . . . .158 A3
Kember St, N1
  off Carnoustie Dr 93 F7
Kemble Dr, Brom. BR2 . . . . . . .206 B3
Kemble Rd, N17 . . . . .76 D1
  SE23 . . . . .171 G1
  Croydon CR0 . . . . .201 G3
Kemble St, WC2 . . . . .18 C4
Kemerton Rd, SE5 . . . . .151 J3
  Beckenham BR3 . . . . .190 B2
  Croydon CR0 . . . . .188 C2
Kemeys St, E9 . . . . .95 H5
Kemnal Rd, Chis. BR7 . . . . .175 G4
Kempe Rd, NW6 . . . . .108 A2
Kemp Gdns, Croy. CR0
  off St. Saviours Rd 187 J6
Kempis Way, SE22
  off East Dulwich Gro 152 B5
Kemplay Rd, NW3 . . . . .91 G4
Kemp Rd, Dag. RM8 . . . . .100 D1
Kemp's Ct, W1 . . . . .17 G4
Kemps Dr, E14 off Morant St . . .114 A7
Kempsford Gdns, SW5 . . . . . . .128 D5
Kempsford Rd, SE11 . . . . .35 F2
Kemps Gdns, SE13
  off Thornford Rd 154 C5
Kempshott Rd, SW16 . . . . .168 D7
Kempson Rd, SW6 . . . . .148 D1
Kempthorne Rd, SE8 . . . . .133 H4

Kempton Av, Nthlt. UB5 85 G6
Sunbury-on-Thames TW16 178 B1
Kempton Cl, Erith DA8 139 J6
Kempton Ct, E1
off Durward St 112/113 E5
Sunbury-on-Thames TW16 178 B1
★ **Kempton Park Racecourse**, Sun. TW16 160 C7
Kempton Rd, E6 116 C1
Hampton TW12 179 F2
Kempton Wk, Croy. CR0 189 H6
Kempt St, SE18 136 D6
Kemsing Cl, Bex. DA5 159 E7
Bromley BR2 205 F2
Thornton Heath CR7 187 J4
Kemsing Rd, SE10 135 G5
Kemsley, SE13 154 C5
Kenbury Gdns, SE5
off Kenbury St 151 J2
Kenbury St, SE5 151 J2
Kenchester Cl, SW8 131 E7
Kencot Cl, Erith DA18 139 F2
Kendal Av, N18 60 A4
W3 106 A4
Barking IG11 99 H7
Kendal Cl, SW9 35 G7
Woodford Green IG8 63 F2
Kendale Rd, Brom. BR1 172 E5
Kendal Gdns, N18 60 A4
Sutton SM1 199 F2
Kendall Av, Beck. BR3 189 H2
Kendall Ct, SW19
off Byegrove Rd 167 G6
Borehamwood WD6
off Gregson Cl 38 C1
Kendall Pl, W1 16 B2
Kendall Rd, SE18 156 B1
Beckenham BR3 189 H2
Isleworth TW7 144 D2
Kendalmere Cl, N10 74 B1
Kendal Par, N18
off Great Cambridge Rd 60 A4
Kendal Pl, SW15 148 C5
Kendal Rd, NW10 89 G4
Kendal St, W2 15 H4
Kender St, SE14 133 F7
Kendoa Rd, SW4 150 D4
Kendon Cl, E11 *off The Avenue* 79 H5
Kendra Hall Rd, S.Croy. CR2 201 H7
Kendrey Gdns, Twick. TW2 144 B6
Kendrick Ms, SW7 31 E1
Kendrick Pl, SW7 31 E2
Kenelm Cl, Har. HA1 86 D3
Kenerne Dr, Barn. EN5 40 B5
Kenilford Rd, SW12 150 B7
Kenilworth Av, E17 78 A2
SW19 166 D5
Harrow HA2 85 F4
Kenilworth Cl, Borwd. WD6 38 C3
Kenilworth Ct, SW15
off Lower Richmond Rd 148 A3
Kenilworth Cres, Enf. EN1 44 B1
Kenilworth Dr, Borwd. WD6 38 C3
Kenilworth Gdns, SE18 156 E2
Ilford IG3 99 J2
Loughton IG10 48 C6
Southall UB1 103 F3
Watford WD19 50 C5
Kenilworth Rd, E3 113 H2
NW6 108 C1
SE20 189 G1
W5 125 H1
Edgware HA8 54 C3
Epsom KT17 197 G6
Orpington BR5 193 F6
Kenley Av, NW9 70 E1
Kenley Cl, Barn. EN4 41 H4
Bexley DA5 159 G7
Chislehurst BR7 193 H3
Kenley Gdns, Th.Hth. CR7 187 H4
Kenley Rd, SW19 184 C2
Kingston upon Thames KT1 182 B2
Twickenham TW1 144 D6
Kenley Wk, W11 108 B7
Sutton SM3 198 A4
Kenlor Rd, SW17 167 G5
Kenmare Dr, N17 76 C2
Mitcham CR4 167 J7
Kenmare Gdns, N13 59 H4
Kenmare Rd, Th.Hth. CR7 187 G6
Kenmere Gdns, Wem. HA0 106 A1
Kenmere Rd, Well. DA16 158 C2
Kenmont Gdns, NW10 107 H3
Kenmore Av, Har. HA3 68 D4
Kenmore Cl, Rich. TW9
off Kent Rd 126 A7
Kenmore Gdns, Edg. HA8 70 B2
Kenmore Rd, Har. HA3 69 G3
Kenmure Rd, E8 95 E5
Kenmure Yd, E8
off Kenmure Rd 94/95 E5
Kennacraig Cl, E16
off Hanameel St 135 G1
Kennard Rd, E15 96 D7
N11 57 J5
Kennard St, E16 136 C1
SW11 150 A2
Kennedy Av, Enf. EN3 45 F6
Kennedy Cl, E13 115 G2
Mitcham CR4 186 A2
Orpington BR5 207 G1
Pinner HA5 51 F6
Kennedy Path, W7 *off Harp Rd* 104 C4
Kennedy Rd, W7 104 B5
Barking IG11 117 H1
Kennedy Wk, SE17 *off Flint St* 132 A4
Kennet Cl, SW11
off Maysoule Rd 149 G4
Kenneth Av, Ilf. IG1 98 E4
Kenneth Cres, NW2 89 H5
Kenneth Gdns, Stan. HA7 52 D6
Kenneth More Rd, Ilf. IG1
off Oakfield Rd 98/99 E3
Kenneth Rd, Rom. RM6 82 D7
Kenneth Robbins Ho, N17 60 E7
Kennet Rd, W9 108 C4
Isleworth TW7 144 C3
Kennet Sq, Mitch. CR4 185 H1
Kennet St, E1 29 J1
Kennett Dr, Hayes UB4 102 E5
Kennet Wf La, EC4 20 A5
Kenninghall, N18 60 E5
Kenninghall Rd, E5 94 D3
N18 61 F5
Kenning St, SE16
off Railway Av 133 F2
Kennings Way, SE11 35 G3
Kenning Ter, N1 112 B1
KENNINGTON, SE11 35 E6
Kennington Grn, SE11 35 E4
Kennington Gro, SE11 34 D5
Kennington La, SE11 35 F3
Kennington Oval, SE11 34 D5
Kennington Pk, SW9 35 F7
Kennington Pk Est, SE11 35 E6
Kennington Pk Gdns, SE11 35 G5
Kennington Pk Pl, SE11 35 F4
Kennington Pk Rd, SE11 35 F5
Kennington Rd, SE1 27 E5
SE11 27 E6
Kenny Rd, NW7 56 B5
Kenrick Pl, W1 16 B1
KENSAL GREEN, NW10 107 J3
★ **Kensal Green Cem**, W10 107 J3
KENSAL RISE, NW6 108 A2
Kensal Rd, W10 108 B4
KENSAL TOWN, W10 108 A4
Kensal Wf, W10
off Ladbroke Gro 108 A4
KENSINGTON, W8 128 C2
Kensington Av, E12 98 B6
Thornton Heath CR7 187 G1
Kensington Ch Ct, W8 22 A4
Kensington Ch St, W8 128 D1
Kensington Ch Wk, W8 22 A4
Kensington Cl, N11 58 A6
Kensington Ct, NW7
off Grenville Pl 54 D5
W8 22 B4
Kensington Ct Gdns, W8
off Kensington Ct Pl 128/129 E3
Kensington Ct Ms, W8 22 B4
Kensington Ct Pl, W8 22 B5
Kensington Dr, Wdf.Grn. IG8 80 A1
★ **Kensington Gdns**, W2 22 D2
Kensington Gdns, Ilf. IG1 98 C2
Kingston upon Thames KT1
off Portsmouth Rd 181 G3
Kensington Gdns Sq, W2 14 A4
Kensington Gate, W8 22 C5
Kensington Gore, SW7 23 E4
Kensington Hall Gdns, W14
off Beaumont Av 128 C5
Kensington High St, W8 128 D3
W14 128 B4
Kensington Mall, W8 128 D1
★ **Kensington Palace**, W8 22 B2
Kensington Palace Gdns, W8 22 A1
Kensington Pk Gdns, W11 108 C7
Kensington Pk Ms, W11
off Kensington Pk Rd 108 C6
Kensington Pk Rd, W11 108 C7
Kensington Pl, W8 128 D1
Kensington Rd, SW7 23 F4
W8 22 B4
Northolt UB5 103 G3
Romford RM7 83 J6
Kensington Sq, W8 22 A4
Kensington Ter, S.Croy. CR2
off Sanderstead Rd 202 A7
Kensington Village, W14
off Avonmore Rd 128 C4
Kensington Way, Borwd. WD6 38 D3
Kent Av, W13 104 E5
Dagenham RM9 119 G4
Welling DA16 157 J5
Kent Cl, Mitch. CR4 187 E4
Orpington BR6 207 H6
Kent Dr, Barn. EN4 42 A4
Teddington TW11 162 B5
Kentford Way, Nthlt. UB5 102 E1
Kent Gdns, W13 105 E5
Ruislip HA4 66 B6
Kent Gate Way, Croy. CR0 204 A5
Kent Ho La, Beck. BR3 171 H5
Kent Ho Rd, SE26 189 G1
Beckenham BR3 171 H5
Kentish Bldgs, SE1 28 B2
Kentish Rd, Belv. DA17 139 G4
KENTISH TOWN, NW5 92 C6
Kentish Town Rd, NW1 92 B7
NW5 92 B7
Kentish Way, Brom. BR1 191 G2
Kentlea Rd, SE28 137 H2
Kentmere Rd, SE18 137 H4
KENTON, Har. HA3 68 E5
Kenton Av, Har. HA1 68 C7
Southall UB1 103 G7
Sunbury-on-Thames TW16 178 E2
Kenton Ct, W14
off Kensington High St 128 C3
Kenton Gdns, Har. HA3 69 F5
Kenton La, Har. HA3 69 F3
Kenton Pk Av, Har. HA3 69 G4
Kenton Pk Cl, Har. HA3 69 F4
Kenton Pk Cres, Har. HA3 69 G4
Kenton Pk Rd, Har. HA3 69 F4
Kenton Rd, E9 95 G6
Harrow HA1, HA3 69 G5
Kenton St, WC1 10 A5
Kent Pas, NW1 7 J5
Kent Rd, N21 60 A1
W4 126 C3
Dagenham RM10 101 H5
East Molesey KT8 179 J4
Kingston upon Thames KT1
off The Bittoms 181 G3
Richmond TW9 126 A7
West Wickham BR4 204 B1
Kents Pas, Hmptn. TW12 179 F1
Kent St, E2 13 G1
E13 115 J3
Kent Ter, NW1 7 H4
Kent Vw Gdns, Ilf. IG3 99 H2
Kent Way, Surb. KT6 195 H3
Kentwell Cl, SE4 153 H4
Kentwode Grn, SW13 127 G7
Kent Yd, SW7 23 H4
Kenver Av, N12 57 G6
Kenward Rd, SE9 155 J5
Kenway, Rom. RM5 83 J2
Ken Way, Wem. HA9 88 C2
Kenway Rd, SW5 30 A2
Kenwood Av, N14 42 D5
SE14 *off Besson St* 153 G1
Kenwood Cl, NW3 91 G1
West Drayton UB7 120 D6
Kenwood Dr, Beck. BR3 190 C3
Kenwood Gdns, E18 79 H3
Ilford IG2 80 D4
★ **Kenwood Ho (The Iveagh Bequest)**, NW3 91 H1
Kenwood Rd, N6 73 J6
N9 60 D1
Kenworthy Rd, E9 95 H5
Kenwyn Dr, NW2 89 E3
Kenwyn Rd, SW4 150 D4
SW20 183 J1
Kenya Rd, SE7 136 A7
Kenyngton Dr, Sun. TW16 160 A5
Kenyngton Pl, Har. HA3 69 F5
Kenyon St, SW6 148 A1
Keogh Rd, E15 97 E6
Kepler Rd, SW4 150 E4
Keppel Rd, E6 98 C7
Dagenham RM9 100 E4
Keppel Row, SE1 27 J2
Keppel St, WC1 17 J1
Kerbela St, E2 13 H5
Kerbey St, E14 114 B6
Kerfield Cres, SE5 152 A1
Kerfield Pl, SE5 152 A1
Kerri Cl, Barn. EN5 39 J4
Kerridge Ct, N1 94 B6
Kerrison Pl, W5 125 G1
Kerrison Rd, E15 114 D1
SW11 149 H3
W5 125 G1
Kerrison Vil, W5 *off Kerrison Pl* 125 G1
Kerry Av, Stan. HA7 53 G4
Kerry Cl, E16 115 H6
N13 59 F2
Kerry Ct, Stan. HA7 53 G4
Kerry Path, SE14 133 J6
Kerry Rd, SE14 133 J6
Kersey Gdns, SE9 174 B4
Kersfield Rd, SW15 148 A6
Kershaw Cl, SW18
off Westover Rd 149 G6
Kershaw Rd, Dag. RM10 101 G3
Kersley Ms, SW11 149 J2
Kersley Rd, N16 94 B3
Kersley St, SW11 149 J2
Kerswell Cl, N15 76 B5
Kerwick Cl, N7 *off Sutterton St* 93 F7
Keslake Rd, NW6 108 A2
Kessock Cl, N17 76 E5
Kesteven Cl, Ilf. IG6 65 J6
Kestlake Rd, Bex. DA5
off East Rochester Way 158 C6
KESTON, BR2 205 J5
Keston Av, Kes. BR2 205 J5
Keston Cl, N18 60 A3
Welling DA16 138 C7
Keston Gdns, Kes. BR2 205 J4
Keston Pk Cl, Kes. BR2 206 C3
Keston Rd, N17 76 A3
SE15 152 D3
Thornton Heath CR7 187 G6
Kestral Ct, Wall. SM6
off Carew Rd 200 C5
Kestrel Av, E6 *off Swan App* 116 B5
SE24 151 H5
Kestrel Cl, NW9 71 E2
NW10 88 D5
Kingston upon Thames KT2 163 G4
Kestrel Ho, EC1 11 J3
W13 104 C4
Enfield EN3 *off Alma Rd* 45 G5
Kestrel Pl, SE14
off Milton Ct Rd 133 H6
Kestrel Way, Hayes UB3 121 G2
Keswick Av, SW15 164 E5
SW19 184 D2
Keswick Bdy, SW15
off Upper Richmond Rd 148 B5
Keswick Cl, Sutt. SM1 199 F4
Keswick Gdns, Ilf. IG4 80 B5
Wembley HA9 87 H4
Keswick Ms, W5 125 H1
Keswick Rd, SW15 148 B5
Bexleyheath DA7 159 G2
Orpington BR6 207 J1
Twickenham TW2 143 J6
West Wickham BR4 204 E2
Kettering St, SW16 168 C6
Kett Gdns, SW2 151 F5
Kettlebaston Rd, E10 95 J1
Kettlewell Cl, N11 58 A6
Kevan Ho, SE5 131 J7
Kevelioc Rd, N17 75 J1
Kevin Cl, Houns. TW4 142 D2
Kevington Cl, Orp. BR5 193 J4
Kevington Dr, Chis. BR7 193 J4
Orpington BR5 193 J4
KEW, Rich. TW9 126 A6
Kew Br, Brent. TW8 125 J6
Richmond TW9 125 J6
Kew Br Arches, Rich. TW9
off Kew Br 125 J6
Kew Br Ct, W4 126 A5
Kew Br Rd, Brent. TW8 125 J6
★ **Kew Bridge Steam Mus**, Brent. TW8 125 J5
Kew Cres, Sutt. SM3 198 B3
Kew Foot Rd, Rich. TW9 145 H4
Kew Gdns Rd, Rich. TW9 125 J7
Kew Grn, Rich. TW9 126 A7
Kew Meadow Path, Rich. TW9 146 A1
★ **Kew Observatory**, Rich. TW9 145 E3
★ **Kew Palace, Royal Botanic Gdns**, Rich. TW9 125 H7
Kew Retail Pk, Rich. TW9
off Bessant Dr 146 B1
Kew Rd, Rich. TW9 126 A6
Keybridge Ho, SW8 34 B6
Key Cl, E1 113 E4
Keyes Rd, NW2 90 A5
Keymer Rd, SW2 169 F2
Keynes Cl, N2 73 J3
Keynsham Av, Wdf.Grn. IG8 63 E4
Keynsham Gdns, SE9 156 B5
Keynsham Rd, SE9 156 A5
Morden SM4 198 E1
Keynsham Wk, Mord. SM4 198 E1
Keyse Rd, SE1 29 F6
Keysham Av, Houns. TW5
off The Avenue 142 A1
Keystone Cres, N1 10 B2
Keywood Dr, Sun. TW16 160 A6
Keyworth Cl, E5 95 H4
Keyworth St, SE1 27 H5
Kezia St, SE8 *off Trundleys Rd* 133 H5
Khalsa Ct, N22 *off Acacia Rd* 75 H1
Khama Rd, SW17 167 H4
Khartoum Rd, E13 115 H3
SW17 167 G4
Ilford IG1 99 E5
Khyber Rd, SW11 149 H2
Kibworth St, SW8 131 F7
KIDBROOKE, SE3 155 H3
Kidbrooke Gdns, SE3 155 G2
Kidbrooke Gro, SE3 155 G1
Kidbrooke La, SE9 156 B4
Kidbrooke Pk Cl, SE3 155 H1
Kidbrooke Pk Rd, SE3 155 H1
Kidbrooke Way, SE3 155 H2
Kidderminster Pl, Croy. CR0
off Kidderminster Rd 201 H1
Kidderminster Rd, Croy. CR0 201 H1
Kidderpore Av, NW3 90 D4
Kidderpore Gdns, NW3 90 D4
Kidd Pl, SE7 136 B5
Kidlington Way, NW9 70 E2
Kielder Cl, Ilf. IG6 65 J6
Kiffen St, EC2 12 C5
Kilberry Cl, Islw. TW7 144 A1

Kilburn, NW6 .....108 D2
Kilburn Br, NW6
  off Kilburn High Rd 108 D1
Kilburn Gate, NW6 .....6 A1
Kilburn High Rd, NW6 .....90 C7
Kilburn La, W9 .....108 A3
  W10 .....108 A3
Kilburn Pk Rd, NW6 .....108 D3
Kilburn Pl, NW6 .....108 D1
Kilburn Priory, NW6 .....108 E1
Kilburn Sq, NW6 .....108 D1
Kilburn Vale, NW6
  off Belsize Rd 108/109 E1
Kildare Cl, Ruis. HA4 .....84 C1
Kildare Gdns, W2 .....108 D6
Kildare Rd, E16 .....115 G5
Kildare Ter, W2 .....108 D6
Kildare Wk, E14
  off Farrance St 114 A6
Kildoran Rd, SW2 .....150 E5
Kildowan Rd, Ilf. IG3 .....100 A1
Kilgour Rd, SE23 .....153 H6
Kilkie St, SW6 .....149 F2
Killarney Rd, SW18 .....149 F6
Killburns Mill Cl, Wall. SM6
  off London Rd 200 B4
Killearn Rd, SE6 .....172 D1
Killester Gdns, Wor.Pk. KT4 .....197 H4
Killick St, N1 .....10 C1
Killieser Av, SW2 .....168 E2
Killip Cl, E16 .....115 F6
Killowen Av, Nthlt. UB5 .....85 J5
Killowen Rd, E9 .....95 G6
Killyon Rd, SW8 .....150 C2
Killyon Ter, SW8 .....150 C2
Kilmaine Rd, SW6 .....128 B7
Kilmarnock Gdns, Dag. RM8
  off Lindsey Rd 100 C3
Kilmarnock Rd, Wat. WD19 .....50 D4
Kilmarsh Rd, W6 .....127 J4
Kilmartin Av, SW16 .....187 F3
Kilmartin Rd, Ilf. IG3 .....100 A2
Kilmeston Way, SE15 .....37 F7
Kilmington Rd, SW13 .....127 G6
Kilmorey Gdns, Twick. TW1 .....144 E5
Kilmorey Rd, Twick. TW1 .....144 E4
Kilmorie Rd, SE23 .....171 H1
Kiln Cl, Hayes UB3
  off Brickfield La 121 G6
Kilner St, E14 .....114 A5
Kiln Ms, SW17 .....167 G5
Kiln Pl, NW5 .....92 A5
Kilnside, Esher (Clay.) KT10 .....194 D7
Kilpatrick Way, Hayes UB4 .....103 E5
Kilravock St, W10 .....108 B3
Kilsby Wk, Dag. RM9
  off Rugby Rd 100 B6
Kilsha Rd, Walt. KT12 .....178 B6
Kimbell Gdns, SW6 .....148 B1
Kimbell Pl, SE3 *off Tudway Rd* 155 J4
Kimberley Av, E6 .....116 C2
  SE15 .....153 E2
  Ilford IG2 .....81 G7
  Romford RM7 .....83 J6
Kimberley Dr, Sid. DA14 .....176 D2
Kimberley Gdns, N4 .....75 H5
  Enfield EN1 .....44 C3
Kimberley Gate, Brom. BR1
  off Oaklands Rd 173 F7
Kimberley Ind Est, E17 .....77 J1
Kimberley Rd, E4 .....62 E1
  E11 .....96 D2
  E16 .....115 F4
  E17 .....77 J1
  N17 .....76 D2
  N18 .....61 E6
  NW6 .....108 B1
  SW9 .....151 E2
  Beckenham BR3 .....189 G2
  Croydon CR0 .....187 H6
Kimberley Way, E4 .....63 E1
Kimber Rd, SW18 .....148 D7
Kimble Rd, SW19 .....167 G6
Kimbolton Cl, SE12 .....155 F6
Kimbolton Grn, Borwd. WD6 .....38 C4
Kimbolton Row, SW3 .....31 G2
Kimmeridge Gdns, SE9 .....174 B4
Kimmeridge Rd, SE9 .....174 B4
Kimpton Ho, SW15
  off Fontley Way 147 G7
Kimpton Link Business Cen, Sutt.
  SM3 *off Kimpton Rd* 198 C2
Kimpton Rd, SE5 .....152 A1
  Sutton SM3 .....198 C2
Kimpton Trade & Business Cen, Sutt.
  SM3 .....198 C2
Kinburn St, SE16 .....133 G2
Kincaid Rd, SE15 .....132 E7
Kincardine Gdns, W9
  off Harrow Rd 108 C4
Kinch Gro, Wem. HA9 .....69 J7
Kinder Cl, SE28 .....118 D7
Kinder St, E1
  off Cannon St Rd 112/113 E6
Kinfauns Rd, SW2 .....169 G2
  Ilford IG3 .....100 A1
King Alfred Av, SE6 .....172 A3

King & Queen Cl, SE9
  off St. Keverne Rd 174 B4
King & Queen St, SE17 .....36 A2
King & Queen Wf, SE16
  off Rotherhithe St 133 G1
King Arthur Cl, SE15 .....133 F7
King Charles Cres, Surb. KT5 .....181 J7
King Charles Rd, Surb. KT5 .....181 J6
King Charles St, SW1 .....25 J3
King Charles Ter, E1
  off Sovereign Cl 112/113 E7
King Charles Wk, SW19
  off Princes Way 166 B1
Kingcup Cl, Croy. CR0
  off Primrose La 203 G1
King David La, E1 .....113 F7
Kingdon Rd, NW6 .....90 D6
King Edward Dr, Chess. KT9
  off Kelvin Gro 195 H3
King Edward Ms, SW13 .....147 G1
King Edward Rd, E10 .....96 C1
  E17 .....77 H3
  Barnet EN5 .....40 D4
King Edward's Gdns, W3 .....126 A1
King Edwards Gro, Tedd. TW11 .....163 E6
King Edward's Pl, W3
  off King Edward's Gdns 126 A1
King Edward's Rd, E9 .....113 E1
  N9 .....44 E7
  Barking IG11 .....117 G1
King Edward's Rd, Enf. EN3 .....45 G4
King Edward St, EC1 .....19 J3
King Edward III Ms, SE16
  off Paradise St 132/133 E2
King Edward Wk, SE1 .....27 F5
Kingfield Rd, W5 .....105 G4
Kingfield St, E14 .....134 C4
Kingfisher Av, E11
  off Eastern Av 79 H6
Kingfisher Cl, SE28 .....118 C7
  Harrow (Har.Wld) HA3 .....52 C7
Kingfisher Ct, SW19
  off Queensmere Rd 166 B2
  Surbiton KT6 *off Ewell Rd* 181 J7
  Sutton SM1
  off Sandpiper Rd 198 C5
Kingfisher Dr, Rich. TW10 .....163 E4
Kingfisher Ms, SE13 .....154 B4
Kingfisher Pl, N22
  off Clarendon Rd 75 F2
Kingfisher Sq, SE8 .....133 J6
Kingfisher St, E6 .....116 B5
Kingfisher Wk, NW9
  off Eagle Dr 70/71 E2
Kingfisher Way, NW10 .....88 D5
  Beckenham BR3 .....189 G5
King Frederik IX Twr, SE16 .....133 J3
King Gdns, Croy. CR0 .....201 H5
King George Av, E16 .....116 A6
  Ilford IG2 .....81 G5
King George Cl, Rom. RM7 .....83 J3
King Georges Dr, Sthl. UB1 .....103 F5
King George VI Av, Mitch. CR4 .....185 J4
King George Sq, Rich. TW10 .....145 J6
King George's Trd Est, Chess.
  KT9 .....196 A4
King George St, SE10 .....134 C7
Kingham Cl, SW18 .....149 F7
  W11 .....128 B2
King Harolds Way, Bexh. DA7 .....138 D7
King Henry Ms, Orp. BR6
  off Osgood Av 207 J5
King Henry's Reach, W6 .....127 J6
King Henry's Rd, NW3 .....91 H7
  Kingston upon Thames KT1 .....182 B3
King Henry St, N16 .....94 B5
King Henry's Wk, N1 .....94 B6
King Henry Ter, E1
  off Sovereign Cl 112/113 E7
Kinghorn St, EC1 .....19 J2
King James Ct, SE1 .....27 H4
King James St, SE1 .....27 H4
King John Ct, EC2 .....12 E5
King John St, E1 .....113 G5
King Johns Wk, SE9 .....174 A1
Kinglake Est, SE17 .....37 E3
Kinglake St, SE17 .....36 D4
Kinglet Cl, E7 *off Romford Rd* 97 G6
Kingly Ct, W1 .....17 F5
Kingly St, W1 .....17 F4
Kingsand Rd, SE12 .....173 G2
Kings Av, N10 .....74 A3
  N21 .....59 H1
King's Av, SW4 .....150 D7
  SW12 .....168 D1
Kings Av, W5 .....105 G6
  Bromley BR1 .....173 F6
  Buckhurst Hill IG9 .....64 A2
  Carshalton SM5 .....199 H7
  Greenford UB6 .....103 H6
  Hounslow TW3 .....143 H1
  New Malden KT3 .....183 E4
  Romford RM6 .....83 F6

Kings Av, Wdf.Grn. IG8 .....63 H6
Kings Bench St, SE1 .....27 H3
Kings Bench Wk, EC4 .....19 F4
Kingsbridge Av, W3 .....125 J2
Kingsbridge Ct, E14
  off Dockers Tanner Rd 134 A4
Kingsbridge Cres, Sthl. UB1 .....103 F5
Kingsbridge Dr, NW7 .....56 A7
Kingsbridge Rd, W10 .....107 J6
  Barking IG11 .....117 G2
  Morden SM4 .....184 A7
  Southall UB2 .....123 F4
  Walton-on-Thames KT12 .....178 B7
KINGSBURY, NW9 .....70 B6
Kingsbury Circle, NW9 .....70 A5
Kingsbury Rd, N1 .....94 B6
  NW9 .....70 B5
Kingsbury Ter, N1 .....94 B6
Kingsbury Trd Est, NW9 .....70 D6
Kings Butts, SE9
  off Strongbow Cres 156 C5
Kings Chace Vw, Enf. EN2
  off Crofton Way 43 G2
Kings Chase, E.Mol. KT8 .....179 J3
Kingsclere Cl, SW15 .....147 G7
Kingsclere Ct, Barn. EN5
  off Gloucester Rd 41 F5
Kingsclere Pl, Enf. EN2
  off Chase Side 43 J2
Kingscliffe Gdns, SW19 .....166 C1
Kings Cl, E10 .....78 B7
  NW4 .....72 A4
  Thames Ditton KT7 .....180 D6
Kingscote Rd, W4 .....126 D3
  Croydon CR0 .....188 E7
  New Malden KT3 .....182 D3
Kingscote St, EC4 .....19 G5
Kings Ct, E13 .....115 H1
  W6 *off King St* 127 G4
  Wembley HA9 .....88 B2
Kingscourt Rd, SW16 .....168 D3
Kings Ct S, SW3
  off Chelsea Manor Gdns 129 H5
Kings Cres, N4 .....93 J3
Kings Cres Est, N4 .....93 J2
Kingscroft Rd, NW2 .....90 C6
KING'S CROSS, N1 .....110 D1
King's Cross Br, N1 .....10 B3
King's Cross Rd, WC1 .....10 D3
Kingsdale Gdns, W11 .....128 A1
Kingsdale Rd, SE18 .....137 J7
  SE20 .....171 G7
Kingsdown Av, W3 .....107 E7
  W13 .....125 E2
Kingsdown Cl, SE16
  off Masters Dr 132/133 E5
  W10 .....108 A6
Kingsdowne Rd, Surb. KT6 .....181 H7
Kingsdown Rd, E11 .....97 E3
  N19 .....92 E2
  Sutton SM3 .....198 B5
Kingsdown Way, Brom. BR2 .....191 G7
Kings Dr, Edg. HA8 .....53 J4
  Surbiton KT5 .....182 A7
  Teddington TW11 .....162 A5
  Thames Ditton KT7 .....180 E6
  Wembley HA9 .....88 B2
Kings Fm Av, Rich. TW10 .....146 A4
Kingsfield Av, Har. HA2 .....67 H4
Kingsfield Ho, SE9 .....174 A3
Kingsfield Rd, Har. HA1 .....68 A7
Kingsford St, NW5 .....91 J5
Kingsford Way, E6 .....116 C5
Kings Gdns, NW6
  off West End La 90 D7
  Ilford IG1 .....99 G1
King's Garth Ms, SE23
  off London Rd 171 F2
Kingsgate, Wem. HA9 .....88 C3
Kingsgate Av, N3 .....72 D3
Kingsgate Cl, Bexh. DA7 .....158 E1
Kingsgate Pl, NW6 .....90 D7
Kingsgate Rd, NW6 .....90 D7
  Kingston upon Thames KT2 .....181 H1
Kings Grn, Loug. IG10 .....48 B3
Kingsground, SE9 .....156 B7
Kings Gro, SE15 .....133 E7
Kingshall Ms, SE13
  off Lewisham Rd 154 C3
Kings Hall Rd, Beck. BR3 .....171 H7
Kings Head Hill, E4 .....46 B7
Kings Head Yd, SE1 .....28 B2
Kings Highway, SE18 .....137 H6
Kings Hill, Loug. IG10 .....48 B2
Kingshill Av, Har. HA3 .....69 E4
  Northolt UB5 .....102 A3
  Worcester Park KT4 .....183 G7
Kingshill Cl, Hayes UB4 .....102 A3
Kingshill Dr, Har. HA3 .....68 E3
Kingshold Est, E9
  off Victoria Pk Rd 113 F1
Kingshold Rd, E9 .....95 F7
Kingsholm Gdns, SE9 .....156 A4
Kingshurst Rd, SE12 .....155 G7
Kingside Business Pk, SE18
  off Woolwich Ch St 136 B3

Kings Keep, Kings.T. KT1
  off Beaufort Rd 181 H4
KINGSLAND, N1 .....94 B6
Kingsland, NW8
  off Broxwood Way 109 H1
Kingsland Grn, E8 .....94 B6
Kingsland High St, E8 .....94 C5
Kingsland Pas, E8
  off Kingsland Grn 94 B6
Kingsland Rd, E2 .....13 E3
  E8 .....112 B2
  E13 .....115 J3
Kingsland Shop Cen, E8 .....94 C6
Kings La, Sutt. SM1 .....199 G6
Kingslawn Cl, SW15
  off Howards La 147 H5
Kingsleigh Cl, Brent. TW8
  off Brook Rd S 125 G6
Kingsleigh Pl, Mitch. CR4
  off Chatsworth Pl 185 J3
Kingsleigh Wk, Brom. BR2
  off Stamford Dr 191 F4
Kingsley Av, W13 .....104 D6
  Hounslow TW3 .....143 J2
  Southall UB1 .....103 G7
  Sutton SM1 .....199 G4
Kingsley Cl, N2 .....73 F5
  Dagenham RM10 .....101 H4
Kingsley Ct, Edg. HA8 .....54 B2
Kingsley Dr, Wor.Pk. KT4
  off Badgers Copse 197 F2
Kingsley Flats, SE1
  off Old Kent Rd 132 B4
Kingsley Gdns, E4 .....62 A5
Kingsley Ms, E1
  off Wapping La 112/113 E7
  W8 .....22 A5
  Chislehurst BR7 .....175 E6
Kingsley Pl, N6 .....74 A7
Kingsley Rd, E7 .....97 G7
  E17 .....78 C2
  N13 .....59 G4
  NW6 .....108 C1
  SW19 .....167 E5
  Croydon CR0 .....201 G1
  Harrow HA2 .....85 J4
  Hounslow TW3 .....143 J2
  Ilford IG6 .....81 F1
  Loughton IG10 .....49 G3
  Orpington BR6 .....207 J7
  Pinner HA5 .....67 F4
Kingsley St, SW11 .....149 J3
Kingsley Way, N2 .....73 F6
Kingsley Wd Dr, SE9 .....174 C3
Kingslyn Cres, SE19 .....188 B1
Kings Mall, W6 .....127 J4
Kingsman Par, SE18
  off Woolwich Ch St 136 C3
Kingsman St, SE18 .....136 C3
Kingsmead, Barn. EN5 .....40 D4
  Richmond TW10 .....145 J6
Kingsmead Av, N9 .....60 E1
  NW9 .....70 D7
  Mitcham CR4 .....186 C3
  Sunbury-on-Thames TW16 .....178 C2
  Surbiton KT6 .....196 A2
  Worcester Park KT4 .....197 H3
Kingsmead Cl, Epsom KT19 .....196 D7
  Sidcup DA15 .....176 A2
  Teddington TW11 .....162 D6
Kingsmead Dr, Nthlt. UB5 .....85 F7
Kingsmead Est, E9 .....95 H5
Kingsmead Ho, E9
  off Kingsmead Way 95 H4
Kings Mead Pk, Esher (Clay.)
  KT10 .....194 B7
Kingsmead Rd, SW2 .....169 G2
Kingsmead Way, E9 .....95 H4
Kingsmere Cl, SW15
  off Felsham Rd 148 B3
Kingsmere Pk, NW9 .....88 B1
Kingsmere Pl, N16 .....94 A1
Kingsmere Rd, SW19 .....166 A2
Kings Ms, SW4
  off King's Av 150/151 E5
King's Ms, WC1 .....10 D6
Kings Ms, Chig. IG7 .....65 F2
Kingsmill Gdns, Dag. RM9 .....101 F5
Kingsmill Rd, Dag. RM9 .....101 F5
Kingsmill Ter, NW8 .....7 F1
Kingsnympton Pk, Kings.T. KT2 .....164 B6
Kings Oak, Rom. RM7 .....83 G3
King's Orchard, SE9 .....156 B6
Kings Paddock, Hmptn. TW12 .....179 J1
Kings Par, Cars. SM5
  off Wrythe La 199 H3
Kingspark Ct, E18 .....79 G3
King's Pas, E11 .....78 E7
Kings Pas, Kings.T. KT1 .....181 G2
Kings Pl, SE1 .....27 J4
  W4 .....126 C5
  Buckhurst Hill IG9 .....63 J2
  Loughton IG10 .....48 A7
King Sq, EC1 .....11 J4
King's Reach Twr, SE1 .....27 F1
Kings Ride Gate, Rich. TW10 .....146 A4
Kingsridge, SW19 .....166 B2

Kings Rd, E4 . . . .**62** D1
E6 . . . .**115** J1
E11 . . . .**78** E7
King's Rd, N17 . . . .**76** C1
Kings Rd, N18 . . . .**60** D5
N22 . . . .**75** F1
NW10 . . . .**89** H7
SE25 . . . .**188** D3
King's Rd, SW1 . . . .**31** H3
SW3 . . . .**31** H3
SW6 . . . .**148** E1
SW10 . . . .**148** E1
Kings Rd, SW14 . . . .**146** D3
SW19 . . . .**166** B2
W5 . . . .**105** G5
Barking IG11 *off North St* **99** F7
Barnet EN5 . . . .**39** J3
Feltham TW13 . . . .**160** C1
Harrow HA2 . . . .**85** F2
Kingston upon Thames KT1 .**163** H7
Mitcham CR4 . . . .**186** A3
Orpington BR6 . . . .**207** J4
Richmond TW10 . . . .**145** J5
Surbiton KT6 . . . .**195** F1
Teddington TW11 . . . .**162** A6
Twickenham TW1 . . . .**145** E6
West Drayton UB7 . . . .**120** C2
Kings Rd Bungalows, Har. HA2
    off Kings Rd **85** F3
King's Scholars' Pas, SW1 . . . . .**33** F1
King Stairs Cl, SE16
    off Elephant La **132/133** E2
King's Ter, NW1 *off Plender St* . .**110** C1
Kings Ter, Islw. TW7
    off Worple Rd **144** D3
Kingsthorpe Rd, SE26 . . . .**171** G4
Kingston Av, Felt. TW14 . . . . . .**141** H6
Sutton SM3 . . . .**198** B3
Kingston Br, Kings.T. KT1 . . . . .**181** G2
Kingston Bypass, SW15 . . . . . .**165** E4
SW20 . . . .**165** E4
Esher KT10 . . . .**194** D3
New Malden KT3 . . . .**183** F1
Surbiton KT6 . . . .**195** H3
Kingston Cl, Nthlt. UB5 . . . . . .**103** F1
Romford RM6 . . . .**82** E3
Teddington TW11 . . . .**162** E6
Kingston Ct, N4
    off Wiltshire Gdns **75** J3
Kingston Cres, Beck. BR3 . . . . .**189** J1
Kingston Gdns, Croy. CR0
    off Wandle Rd **200/201** E3
Kingston Hall Rd, Kings.T. KT1 .**181** G3
Kingston Hill, Kings.T. KT2 . . . .**164** C6
Kingston Hill Av, Rom. RM6 . . . .**83** E3
Kingston Hill Pl, Kings.T. KT2 . .**164** C4
Kingston La, Tedd. TW11 . . . . .**162** D5
West Drayton UB7 . . . .**120** C2
★ Kingston Mus & Heritage Cen,
    Kings.T. KT1 . . . .**181** H2
Kingston Pk Est, Kings.T. KT2 . .**164** B6
Kingston Pl, Har. HA3
    off Richmond Gdns **52** C7
Kingston Rd, N9 . . . .**60** D2
SW15 . . . .**165** G1
SW19 . . . .**184** C1
SW20 . . . .**183** J2
Barnet EN4 . . . .**41** G5
Epsom KT17, KT19 . . . .**196** E5
Ilford IG1 . . . .**99** E4
Kingston upon Thames KT1 .**182** B3
New Malden KT3 . . . .**182** D4
Southall UB2 . . . .**123** F2
Surbiton KT5 . . . .**196** B2
Teddington TW11 . . . .**162** E5
Worcester Park KT4 . . . .**196** B2
Kingston Sq, SE19 . . . .**170** A5
KINGSTON UPON THAMES, KT1 &
    KT2 . . . .**181** H2
KINGSTON VALE, SW15 . . . . . .**165** E4
Kingston Vale, SW15 . . . .**164** D4
Kingstown St, NW1 . . . .**110** A1
King St, E13 . . . .**115** J4
EC2 . . . .**20** A4
N2 . . . .**73** G3
N17 . . . .**76** C1
SW1 . . . .**25** G2
W3 . . . .**126** B1
W6 . . . .**127** G4
WC2 . . . .**18** A5
Richmond TW9 . . . .**145** G5
Southall UB2 . . . .**123** E3
Twickenham TW1 . . . .**162** D1
King's Wk, Kings.T. KT2 . . . . . .**181** G2
Kings Wk Shop Mall, SW3
    off King's Rd **129** J5
Kingswater Pl, SW11
    off Battersea Ch Rd **129** H7
Kingsway, N12 . . . .**57** F6
SW14 . . . .**146** B3
WC2 . . . .**18** C3
Croydon CR0 . . . .**201** J4
Enfield EN3 . . . .**45** E5
Kings Way, Har. HA1 . . . .**68** B2
Kingsway, N.Mal. KT3 . . . .**183** J4
Orpington BR5 . . . .**193** H5
Wembley HA9 . . . .**87** H4

Kingsway, W.Wick. BR4 . . . . . .**205** E3
Woodford Green IG8 . . . .**63** J5
Kingsway Business Pk, Hmptn.
    TW12 . . . .**179** F1
Kingsway Cres, Har. HA2 . . . . . .**67** J4
Kingsway Pl, EC1 . . . .**11** F5
Kingsway Rd, Sutt. SM3 . . . . . .**198** B7
Kingsway Shop Cen, NW3
    off Hampstead High St **91** F4
Kingswear Rd, NW5 . . . .**92** B3
Ruislip HA4 . . . .**84** A2
Kings Wf, E8 *off Kingsland Rd* . .**112** B1
Kingswood Av, NW6 . . . .**108** B1
Belvedere DA17 . . . .**139** F4
Bromley BR2 . . . .**190** E3
Hampton TW12 . . . .**161** H6
Hounslow TW3 . . . .**143** F1
Thornton Heath CR7 . . . . . .**187** F5
Kingswood Cl, N20 . . . .**41** F6
SW8 . . . .**131** E7
Enfield EN1 . . . .**44** B5
New Malden KT3 . . . .**183** F6
Orpington BR6 . . . .**193** G7
Surbiton KT6 . . . .**181** H7
Kingswood Dr, SE19 . . . .**170** B4
Carshalton SM5 . . . .**199** J1
Kingswood Est, SE21
    off Bowen Dr **170** B4
Kingswood Ms, N15
    off Harringay Rd **75** H5
Kingswood Pk, N3 . . . .**72** C2
Kingswood Pl, SE13 . . . .**155** E4
Kingswood Rd, E11 . . . .**79** E7
SE20 . . . .**171** F6
SW2 . . . .**150** E6
SW19 . . . .**166** C7
W4 . . . .**126** C3
Bromley BR2 . . . .**190** D4
Ilford IG3 . . . .**100** A1
Wembley HA9 . . . .**88** A3
Kingswood Ter, W4
    off Kingswood Rd **126** C3
Kingswood Way, Wall. SM6 . . . .**201** E5
Kingsworth Cl, Beck. BR3 . . . . .**189** H5
Kingsworthy Cl, Kings.T. KT1 . .**181** J3
King's Yd, SW15
    off Stanbridge Rd **147** J3
Kingthorpe Rd, NW10 . . . .**88** D7
Kingthorpe Ter, NW10 . . . .**88** D6
Kingweston Cl, NW2
    off Windmill Dr **90** B3
King William IV Gdns, SE20
    off St. John's Rd **171** F6
King William La, SE10
    off Orlop St **134/135** E5
King William St, EC4 . . . .**20** C6
King William Wk, SE10 . . . . . .**134** C6
Kingwood Rd, SW6 . . . .**148** A1
Kinlet Rd, SE18 . . . .**157** F1
Kinloch Dr, NW9 . . . .**70** E7
Kinloch St, N7 *off Hornsey Rd* . .**93** F3
Kinloss Ct, N3
    off Haslemere Gdns **72** C4
Kinloss Gdns, N3 . . . .**72** C4
Kinloss Rd, Cars. SM5 . . . .**185** F7
Kinnaird Av, W4 . . . .**126** C7
Bromley BR1 . . . .**173** F6
Kinnaird Cl, Brom. BR1 . . . . . .**173** F6
Kinnaird Way, Wdf.Grn. IG8 . . . .**64** C6
Kinnear Rd, W12 . . . .**127** F2
Kinnerton Pl N, SW1 . . . .**24** A4
Kinnerton Pl S, SW1 . . . .**24** A4
Kinnerton St, SW1 . . . .**24** B4
Kinnerton Yd, SW1 . . . .**24** A4
Kinnoul Rd, W6 . . . .**128** B6
Kinross Av, Wor.Pk. KT4 . . . . . .**197** G2
Kinross Cl, Edg. HA8
    off Tayside Dr **54** B2
Harrow HA3 . . . .**69** J5
Kinross Ter, E17 . . . .**77** J2
Kinsale Rd, SE15 . . . .**152** D3
Kintore Way, SE1 . . . .**37** F1
Kintyre Cl, SW16 . . . .**187** F3
Kinveachy Gdns, SE7 . . . .**136** B5
Kinver Rd, SE26 . . . .**171** F4
Kipling Dr, SW19 . . . .**167** G6
Kipling Est, SE1 . . . .**28** C4
Kipling Pl, Stan. HA7
    off Uxbridge Rd **52** C6
Kipling Rd, Bexh. DA7 . . . .**159** E1
Kipling St, SE1 . . . .**28** C4
Kipling Ter, N9 . . . .**60** A3
Kippington Dr, SE9 . . . .**174** A1
Kirby Cl, Epsom KT19 . . . .**197** F5
Ilford IG6 . . . .**65** H6
Loughton IG10 . . . .**48** B7
Kirby Est, SE16 . . . .**132** E3
Kirby Gro, SE1 . . . .**28** D3
Kirby St, EC1 . . . .**19** F1
Kirby Way, Walt. KT12 . . . .**178** C6
Kirchen Rd, W13 . . . .**104** E7
Kirkby Cl, N11
    off Coverdale Rd **58** A6
Kirkcaldy Grn, Wat. WD19
    off Trevose Way **50** C3
Kirkdale, SE26 . . . .**170** E2
Kirkdale Rd, E11 . . . .**97** E1

Kirkfield Cl, W13
    off Broomfield Rd **124/125** E1
Kirkham Rd, E6 . . . .**116** B6
Kirkham St, SE18 . . . .**137** H6
Kirkland Av, Ilf. IG5 . . . .**80** D2
Kirkland Cl, Sid. DA15 . . . .**157** H6
Kirkland Dr, Enf. EN2 . . . .**43** H1
Kirkland Wk, E8 . . . .**94** C6
Kirk La, SE18 . . . .**137** F6
Kirkleas Rd, Surb. KT6 . . . .**195** H1
Kirklees Rd, Dag. RM8 . . . .**100** C5
Thornton Heath CR7 . . . . . .**187** G5
Kirkley Rd, SW19 . . . .**184** D1
Kirkman Pl, W1 . . . .**17** H2
Kirkmichael Rd, E14 *off Dee St* . .**114** C6
Kirk Ri, Sutt. SM1 . . . .**199** E3
Kirk Rd, E17 . . . .**77** J6
Kirkside Rd, SE3 . . . .**135** G6
Kirkstall Av, N17 . . . .**76** A4
Kirkstall Gdns, SW2 . . . .**168** D1
Kirkstall Rd, SW2 . . . .**168** D1
Kirkstead Ct, E5
    off Mandeville St **95** H3
Kirksted Rd, Mord. SM4 . . . . . .**198** E1
Kirkstone Way, Brom. BR1 . . . .**173** E7
Kirk St, WC1 . . . .**10** C6
Kirkton Rd, N15 . . . .**76** B4
Kirkwall Pl, E2 . . . .**113** F3
Kirkwood Rd, SE15 . . . .**153** E2
Kirn Rd, W13
    off Kirchen Rd **104/105** E7
Kirrane Cl, N.Mal. KT3 . . . .**183** F5
Kirtley Rd, SE26 . . . .**171** H4
Kirtling St, SW8 . . . .**33** F7
Kirton Cl, W4 *off Dolman Rd* . .**126** D4
Kirton Gdns, E2 . . . .**13** G4
Kirton Rd, E13 . . . .**115** J2
Kirton Wk, Edg. HA8 . . . .**54** C7
Kirwyn Way, SE5 . . . .**35** H7
Kitcat Ter, E3 . . . .**114** A3
Kitchener Rd, E7 . . . .**97** H6
E17 . . . .**78** B1
N2 . . . .**73** H3
N17 . . . .**76** A3
Dagenham RM10 . . . .**101** H6
Thornton Heath CR7 . . . . . .**188** A3
Kite Pl, E2 . . . .**13** J3
Kite Yd, SW11
    off Cambridge Rd **149** J1
Kitley Gdns, SE19 . . . .**188** C1
Kitson Rd, SE5 . . . .**36** A7
SW13 . . . .**147** G1
Kittiwake Pl, Sutt. SM1
    off Sandpiper Rd **198** C5
Kittiwake Rd, Nthlt. UB5 . . . . . .**102** D3
Kittiwake Way, Hayes UB4 . . . .**102** D5
Kitto Rd, SE14 . . . .**153** G2
Kiver Rd, N19 . . . .**92** D2
Kiwi Cl, Twick. TW1
    off Crown Rd **144/145** E6
Klea Av, SW4 . . . .**150** C6
Knapdale Cl, SE23 . . . .**171** E2
Knapmill Rd, SE6 . . . .**172** A2
Knapmill Way, SE6 . . . .**172** B2
Knapp Cl, NW10 . . . .**89** E6
Knapp Rd, E3 . . . .**114** A4
Knapton Ms, SW17
    off Seely Rd **168** A6
Knaresborough Dr, SW18 . . . . .**166** E1
Knaresborough Pl, SW5 . . . .**30** A1
Knatchbull Rd, NW10 . . . .**106** D1
SE5 . . . .**151** J1
Knebworth Av, E17 . . . .**78** A1
Knebworth Path, Borwd. WD6 . . .**38** D4
Knebworth Rd, N16
    off Nevill Rd **94** B4
Knee Hill, SE2 . . . .**138** C4
Knee Hill Cres, SE2 . . . .**138** C4
Kneller Gdns, Islw. TW7 . . . . . .**144** A5
Kneller Rd, SE4 . . . .**153** H4
New Malden KT3 . . . .**182** E7
Twickenham TW2 . . . .**143** J6
Knight Cl, Dag. RM8 . . . .**100** C2
Knighten St, E1 . . . .**29** J2
Knighthead Pt, E14 . . . .**134** A3
Knightland Rd, E5 . . . .**94** E2
Knighton Cl, S.Croy. CR2 . . . . .**201** H7
Woodford Green IG8 . . . .**63** H4
Knighton Dr, Wdf.Grn. IG8 . . . . .**63** G4
Knighton Grn, Buck.H. IG9
    off High Rd **63** H2
Knighton La, Buck.H. IG9 . . . . . .**63** H2
Knighton Pk Rd, SE26 . . . .**171** G5
Knighton Rd, E7 . . . .**97** G3
Romford RM7 . . . .**83** J6
Knightrider Ct, EC4
    off Godliman St **111** J7
Knightrider St, EC4 . . . .**19** J5
Knights Arc, SW1 . . . .**23** J4
Knights Av, W5 . . . .**125** H2
Knightsbridge, SW1 . . . .**24** A4
SW7 . . . .**23** H4
Knightsbridge Grn, SW1 . . . . . .**23** J4
Knights Cl, E9 *off Churchill Wk* . .**95** F5
Knights Ct, Kings.T. KT1 . . . . . .**181** H3
Romford RM6 . . . .**83** E6
Knights Hill, SE27 . . . .**169** H5

Knights Hill Sq, SE27
    off Knights Hill **169** H4
Knights La, N9 . . . .**60** D3
Knights Ms, Sutt. SM2
    off York Rd **198** D7
Knights Pk, Kings.T. KT1 . . . . . .**181** H3
Knight's Pl, Twick. TW2
    off May Rd **162** B1
Knights Rd, E16 . . . .**135** G2
Stanmore HA7 . . . .**53** F4
Knights Wk, SE11 . . . .**35** G2
Knights Way, Ilf. IG6 . . . .**65** F6
Knightswood Cl, Edg. HA8 . . . . .**54** C2
Knightwood Cres, N.Mal. KT3 . .**182** E6
Knivet Rd, SW6 . . . .**128** D6
Knobs Hill Rd, E15 . . . .**114** B1
Knockholt Rd, SE9 . . . .**156** A5
Knole, The, SE9 . . . .**174** D4
Knole Cl, Croy. CR0
    off Stockbury Rd **189** F6
Knole Gate, Sid. DA15
    off Woodside Cres **175** H3
Knoll, The, W13 . . . .**105** F5
Beckenham BR3 . . . .**190** B1
Bromley BR2 . . . .**205** G2
Knoll Ct, SE19 . . . .**170** C5
Knoll Dr, N14 . . . .**42** A7
Knollmead, Surb. KT5 . . . .**196** C1
Knoll Ri, Orp. BR6 . . . .**207** J1
Knoll Rd, SW18 . . . .**149** F5
Bexley DA5 . . . .**159** G7
Sidcup DA14 . . . .**176** B5
Knolls Cl, Wor.Pk. KT4 . . . .**197** H3
Knollys Cl, SW16 . . . .**169** G3
Knollys Rd, SW16 . . . .**169** G3
Knottisford St, E2 . . . .**113** F3
Knotts Grn Ms, E10 . . . .**78** B6
Knotts Grn Rd, E10 . . . .**78** B6
Knowle Av, Bexh. DA7 . . . .**139** E7
Knowle Cl, SW9 . . . .**151** G3
Knowle Rd, Brom. BR2 . . . .**206** B2
Twickenham TW2 . . . .**162** B1
Knowles Cl, West Dr. UB7 . . . .**120** B1
Knowles Hill Cres, SE13 . . . . .**154** D5
Knowles Ho, SW18
    off Neville Gill Cl **148** E6
Knowles Wk, SW4 . . . .**150** C3
Knowlton Grn, Brom. BR2 . . . . .**191** F5
Knowsley Av, Sthl. UB1 . . . . . .**123** G1
Knowsley Rd, SW11 . . . .**149** J2
Knox Rd, E7 . . . .**97** F6
Knox St, W1 . . . .**15** J1
Knoyle St, SE14 . . . .**133** H6
Kohat Rd, SW19 . . . .**167** E5
Kossuth St, SE10 . . . .**134** E5
Kotree Way, SE1 . . . .**37** J2
Kramer Ms, SW5
    off Kempsford Gdns **128** D5
Kreedman Wk, E8 . . . .**94** D5
Kreisel Wk, Rich. TW9 . . . .**125** J6
Kuala Gdns, SW16 . . . .**187** F1
Kuhn Way, E7 *off Forest La* **97** G5
Kydbrook Cl, Orp. BR5 . . . .**193** G2
Kylemore Cl, E6 *off Parr Rd* . .**116** A2
Kylemore Rd, NW6 . . . .**90** D7
Kymberley Rd, Har. HA1 . . . .**68** B6
Kynance Gdns, Stan. HA7 . . . . .**69** F1
Kynance Ms, SW7 . . . .**22** C6
Kynance Pl, SW7 . . . .**22** D6
Kynaston Av, N16
    off Dynevor Rd **94** C3
Thornton Heath CR7 . . . . . .**187** J5
Kynaston Cl, Har. HA3 . . . .**52** A7
Kynaston Cres, Th.Hth. CR7 . . .**187** J5
Kynaston Rd, N16 . . . .**94** B3
Bromley BR1 . . . .**173** G5
Enfield EN2 . . . .**44** A1
Thornton Heath CR7 . . . . . .**187** J5
Kynaston Wd, Har. HA3 . . . .**52** A7
Kynersley Cl, Cars. SM5
    off William St **199** J3
Kynock Rd, N18 . . . .**61** F4
Kyrle Rd, SW11 . . . .**150** A5
Kyverdale Rd, N16 . . . .**94** C2

L

Laburnham Cl, Wem. HA0
    off Highcroft Av **106** A1
Laburnum Av, N9 . . . .**60** B2
N17 . . . .**60** A7
Sutton SM1 . . . .**199** H3
Laburnum Cl, E4 . . . .**61** J6
N11 . . . .**58** A6
SE15 *off Clifton Way* **133** F7
Laburnum Ct, E2
    off Laburnum St **112** C1
Stanmore HA7 . . . .**53** F4
Laburnum Cres, Sun. TW16
    off Batavia Rd **178** B2
Laburnum Gdns, N21 . . . .**59** J2
Croydon CR0 . . . .**189** G7
Laburnum Gro, N21 . . . .**59** J2
NW9 . . . .**70** C7
Hounslow TW3 . . . .**143** F4
New Malden KT3 . . . .**182** D2

Laburnum Gro, Sthl. UB1 . . . .**103** F4
Laburnum Ho, Dag. RM10
  off Bradwell Av **101** G2
Laburnum Rd, SW19 . . . .**167** F7
  Hayes UB3 . . . .**121** J4
  Mitcham CR4 . . . .**186** A2
Laburnum St, E2 . . . .**112** C1
Laburnum Way, Brom. BR2 . . . . .**192** D2
Lacebark Cl, Sid. DA15 . . . .**157** J7
Lacewing Cl, E13 off Sewell St . .**115** G3
Lacey Cl, N9 . . . .**60** D2
Lacey Dr, Dag. RM8 . . . .**100** B4
  Edgware HA8 . . . .**53** H4
  Hampton TW12 . . . .**179** F1
Lacey Wk, E3 . . . .**114** A2
Lackington St, EC2 . . . .**20** C1
Lacock Cl, SW19 . . . .**167** F6
Lacock Ct, W13
  off Singapore Rd **124** D1
Lacon Rd, SE22 . . . .**152** D4
Lacy Rd, SW15 . . . .**148** A4
Ladas Rd, SE27 . . . .**169** J4
Ladbroke Cres, W11
  off Ladbroke Gro **108** B6
Ladbroke Gdns, W11 . . . .**108** C7
Ladbroke Gro, W10 . . . .**108** A4
  W11 . . . .**108** B6
Ladbroke Ms, W11
  off Ladbroke Rd **128** B1
Ladbroke Rd, W11 . . . .**128** C1
  Enfield EN1 . . . .**44** C6
Ladbroke Sq, W11 . . . .**108** C7
Ladbroke Ter, W11 . . . .**108** C7
Ladbroke Wk, W11 . . . .**128** C1
Ladbrook Cl, Pnr. HA5 . . . .**67** F5
Ladbrooke Cres, Sid. DA14 . . . . .**176** D3
Ladbrook Rd, SE25 . . . .**188** A3
Ladderstile Ride, Kings.T. KT2 . .**164** B5
Ladderswood Way, N11 . . . .**58** C5
Lady Aylesford Av, Stan. HA7 . . . .**52** E5
Lady Booth Rd, Kings.T. KT1 . . . .**181** H2
Ladybower Ct, E5 off Gilpin Rd . . .**95** H4
Ladycroft Gdns, Orp. BR6 . . . . . .**207** F5
Ladycroft Rd, SE13 . . . .**154** B3
Ladycroft Wk, Stan. HA7 . . . .**69** G1
Ladycroft Way, Orp. BR6 . . . .**207** F5
Lady Dock Path, SE16
  off Salter Rd **133** H2
Ladyfield Cl, Loug. IG10 . . . .**49** E4
Ladyfields, Loug. IG10 . . . .**49** E4
Lady Hay, Wor.Pk. KT4 . . . .**197** F2
Lady Margaret Rd, N19 . . . .**92** C4
  NW5 . . . .**92** C5
  Southall UB1 . . . .**103** F5
Ladysmith Av, E6 . . . .**116** B2
  Ilford IG2 . . . .**81** G7
Ladysmith Cl, NW7
  off Colenso Dr **55** G7
Ladysmith Rd, E16 . . . .**115** F3
  N17 . . . .**76** D2
  N18 . . . .**61** E5
  SE9 . . . .**156** D6
  Enfield EN1 . . . .**44** B3
  Harrow HA3 . . . .**68** B2
Lady Somerset Rd, NW5 . . . .**92** B4
LADYWELL, SE13 . . . .**154** A5
Ladywell Cl, SE4
  off Adelaide Av **153** J4
Ladywell Hts, SE4 . . . .**153** J6
Ladywell Rd, SE13 . . . .**154** A5
Ladywell St, E15
  off Plaistow Gro **115** F1
Ladywood Av, Orp. BR5 . . . .**193** H5
Ladywood Rd, Surb. KT6 . . . .**196** A2
Lafone Av, Felt. TW13
  off Alfred Rd **160** C1
Lafone St, SE1 . . . .**29** F3
Lagado Ms, SE16 . . . .**133** G1
Lagonda Av, Ilf. IG6 . . . .**65** J6
Laidlaw Dr, N21 . . . .**43** F4
Laing Cl, Ilf. IG6 . . . .**65** G6
Laing Dean, Nthlt. UB5 . . . .**102** C1
Laings Av, Mitch. CR4 . . . .**185** J2
Lainlock Pl, Houns. TW3
  off Spring Gro Rd **143** H1
Lainson St, SW18 . . . .**148** D7
Lairdale Cl, SE21 . . . .**169** J1
Laird Ho, SE5 . . . .**131** J7
Lairs Cl, N7 off Manger Rd . .**92/93** E6
Laitwood Rd, SW12 . . . .**168** B1
Lake, The, Bushey (Bushey Hth)
  WD23 . . . .**51** J1
Lake Av, Brom. BR1 . . . .**173** G6
Lake Cl, SW19 off Lake Rd **166** C5
  Dagenham RM8 . . . .**100** D3
Lakedale Rd, SE18 . . . .**137** H6
Lake Dr, Bushey (Bushey Hth)
  WD23 . . . .**51** J2
Lakefield Cl, SE20
  off Limes Av **170/171** E7
Lakefield Rd, N22 . . . .**75** H2
Lake Gdns, Dag. RM10 . . . .**101** G5
  Richmond TW10 . . . .**163** E2
  Wallington SM6 . . . .**200** B3
Lakehall Gdns, Th.Hth. CR7 . . . .**187** H5
Lakehall Rd, Th.Hth. CR7 . . . . . .**187** H5
Lake Ho Rd, E11 . . . .**97** G3

Lakehurst Rd, Epsom KT19 . . . .**196** E5
Lakeland Cl, Har. HA3 . . . .**52** A6
Lakenheath, N14 . . . .**42** D6
Lake Rd, SW19 . . . .**166** C5
  Croydon CR0 . . . .**203** J2
  Romford RM6 . . . .**82** D4
Laker Pl, SW15 . . . .**148** C6
Lakeside, N3 . . . .**73** E2
  W13 off Edgehill Rd **105** F6
  Beckenham BR3 . . . .**190** B3
  Enfield EN2 . . . .**42** D4
  Wallington SM6
  off Derek Av **200** B3
Lakeside Cl, SE28 . . . .**138** A1
  Ilford IG4 . . . .**80** A4
Lakeside Cl, SE25 . . . .**188** D2
  Chigwell IG7 . . . .**65** J4
  Sidcup DA15 . . . .**158** C5
Lakeside Ct, N4 . . . .**93** H2
  Borehamwood (Elstree) WD6
  off Cavendish Cres **38** A5
Lakeside Cres, Barn. EN4 . . . .**41** J5
Lakeside Dr, Brom. BR2 . . . .**206** B3
Lakeside Rd, N13 . . . .**59** F4
  W14 . . . .**128** A3
Lakeside Way, Wem. HA9 . . . .**88** A4
Lakes Rd, Kes. BR2 . . . .**205** J5
Lakeswood Rd, Orp. BR5 . . . . . .**193** E6
Lake Vw, Edg. HA8 . . . .**53** J5
Lakeview Rd, SW19
  off Victoria Dr **166** B2
Lakeview Rd, SE27 . . . .**169** G5
  Welling DA16 . . . .**158** B4
Lakis Cl, NW3 off Flask Wk **91** F4
Laleham Av, NW7 . . . .**54** D3
Laleham Rd, SE6 . . . .**154** C6
Lalor St, SW6 . . . .**148** B2
Lambarde Av, SE9 . . . .**174** D4
Lamb Cl, Nthlt. UB5 . . . .**102** E3
Lamberhurst Rd, SE27 . . . .**169** G4
  Dagenham RM8 . . . .**101** F1
Lambert Av, Rich. TW9 . . . .**146** B3
Lambert Jones Ms, EC2
  off The Barbican **111** J5
Lambert Rd, E16 . . . .**115** H6
  N12 . . . .**57** G5
  SW2 . . . .**151** E5
Lamberts Pl, Croy. CR0 . . . .**202** A1
Lamberts Rd, Surb. KT5 . . . .**181** H5
Lambert St, N1 . . . .**93** G7
Lambert Wk, Wem. HA9 . . . .**87** G3
Lambert Way, N12
  off Woodhouse Rd **57** F5
LAMBETH, SE1 . . . .**26** C5
Lambeth Br, SE1 . . . .**34** B1
  SW1 . . . .**34** B1
Lambeth High St, SE1 . . . .**34** C2
Lambeth Hill, EC4 . . . .**19** J5
★ Lambeth Palace, SE1 . . . .**26** C6
Lambeth Palace Rd, SE1 . . . .**26** C6
Lambeth Rd, SE1 . . . .**26** D6
  SE11 . . . .**26** D6
  Croydon CR0 . . . .**187** G7
Lambeth Wk, SE11 . . . .**34** D1
Lamb La, E8 . . . .**94** E7
Lamble St, NW5 . . . .**92** A4
Lambley Rd, Dag. RM9 . . . .**100** B6
Lambolle Pl, NW3 . . . .**91** H6
Lambolle Rd, NW3 . . . .**91** H6
Lambourn Cl, W7 . . . .**124** C2
Lambourne Av, SW19 . . . .**166** C4
Lambourne Ct, Wdf.Grn. IG8
  off Navestock Cres **63** J7
Lambourne Gdns, E4 . . . .**62** A2
  Barking IG11
  off Lambourne Rd **99** J7
  Enfield EN1 . . . .**44** C2
Lambourne Gro, SE16
  off Reculver Rd **133** G2
  Kingston upon Thames KT1
  off Kenley Rd **182** B2
Lambourne Pl, SE3
  off Shooter's Hill Rd **155** H1
Lambourne Rd, E11 . . . .**78** C7
  Barking IG11 . . . .**99** H7
  Chigwell IG7 . . . .**65** H4
  Ilford IG3 . . . .**99** H2
Lambourn Rd, SW4 . . . .**150** B3
Lambrook Ter, SW6 . . . .**148** B1
Lamb's Bldgs, EC1 . . . .**12** B6
Lambs Conduit Pas, WC1 . . . . . .**18** C1
Lamb's Conduit St, WC1 . . . .**10** C6
Lambscroft Av, SE9 . . . .**173** J3
Lambs Meadow, Wdf.Grn. IG8 . . .**80** A2
Lambs Ms, N1
  off Colebrooke Row **111** H1
Lamb's Pas, EC1 . . . .**20** B1
Lambs Ter, N9 . . . .**60** A2
Lamb St, E1 . . . .**21** F1
Lambs Wk, Enf. EN2 . . . .**43** J2
Lambton Ms, N19
  off Lambton Rd **92/93** E1
Lambton Pl, W11
  off Westbourne Gro **108** C6
Lambton Rd, N19 . . . .**92** E1
  SW20 . . . .**183** J1
Lamb Wk, SE1 . . . .**28** D4

Lamerock Rd, Brom. BR1 . . . . . .**173** F4
Lamerton Rd, Ilf. IG6 . . . .**81** E2
Lamerton St, SE8 . . . .**134** A6
Lamford Cl, N17 . . . .**60** A7
Lamington St, W6 . . . .**127** H4
Lamlash St, SE11 . . . .**35** G1
Lammas Av, Mitch. CR4 . . . .**186** A2
Lammas Grn, SE26 . . . .**170** E3
Lammas Pk, W5 . . . .**125** F2
Lammas Pk Gdns, W5 . . . .**125** F2
Lammas Pk Rd, W5 . . . .**125** F1
Lammas Rd, E9 . . . .**95** G7
  E10 . . . .**95** H2
  Richmond TW10 . . . .**163** F4
Lammermoor Rd, SW12 . . . .**150** B7
Lamont Rd, SW10 . . . .**30** D6
Lamont Rd Pas, SW10
  off Lamont Rd **129** G6
LAMORBEY, Sid. DA15 . . . .**175** J1
Lamorbey Cl, Sid. DA15 . . . .**175** J1
Lamorna Cl, E17 . . . .**78** C1
Lamorna Gro, Stan. HA7 . . . .**69** G1
Lampard Gro, N16 . . . .**94** C1
Lampern Sq, E2 . . . .**13** J3
Lampeter Cl, NW9 . . . .**70** E6
Lampeter Sq, W6
  off Humbolt Rd **128** B6
Lamplighter Cl, E1
  off Cleveland Way **113** F4
Lampmead Rd, SE12 . . . .**155** E5
Lamp Office Ct, WC1 . . . .**10** C6
Lamport Cl, SE18 . . . .**136** C4
LAMPTON, Houns. TW3 . . . .**143** H1
Lampton Av, Houns. TW3 . . . . . .**143** H1
Lampton Ho Cl, SW19 . . . .**166** A4
Lampton Pk Rd, Houns. TW3 . . .**143** H2
Lampton Rd, Houns. TW3 . . . . . .**143** H2
Lanacre Av, NW9 . . . .**71** F1
Lanark Cl, W5 . . . .**105** F5
Lanark Ms, W9 . . . .**6** C4
Lanark Pl, W9 . . . .**6** D5
Lanark Rd, W9 . . . .**6** C4
Lanark Sq, E14 . . . .**134** B3
Lanata Wk, Hayes UB4
  off Ramulis Dr **102** D4
Lanbury Rd, SE15 . . . .**153** G4
Lancashire Ct, W1 . . . .**16** E5
Lancaster Av, E18 . . . .**79** H4
  SE27 . . . .**169** H2
  SW19 . . . .**166** A5
  Barking IG11 . . . .**99** H7
  Mitcham CR4 . . . .**186** E5
Lancaster Cl, N1
  off Hertford Rd **94** B7
  N17 off Park La **60** D7
  NW9 . . . .**55** F7
  Bromley BR2 . . . .**191** F4
  Kingston upon Thames KT2
  off Lancaster Rd **163** G5
  Staines (Stanw.) TW19 . . . . .**140** B6
Lancaster Cotts, Rich. TW10
  off Lancaster Pk **145** H6
Lancaster Ct, SE27 . . . .**169** H2
  SW6 . . . .**128** C7
  W2 . . . .**14** D6
  Walton-on-Thames KT12 . . . .**178** A7
Lancaster Dr, E14
  off Prestons Rd **134** C1
  NW3 . . . .**91** H6
  Loughton IG10 . . . .**48** B6
Lancaster Gdns, SW19 . . . .**166** B5
  W13 . . . .**125** E2
  Bromley BR1 . . . .**192** B5
  Kingston upon Thames KT2 . . .**163** G5
Lancaster Gate, W2 . . . .**14** D6
Lancaster Gro, NW3 . . . .**91** G6
★ Lancaster Ho, SW1 . . . .**25** F3
Lancaster Ms, SW18
  off East Hill **148/149** E5
  W2 . . . .**14** D5
  Richmond TW10
  off Richmond Hill **145** H6
Lancaster Pk, Rich. TW10 . . . . . .**145** H5
Lancaster Pl, SW19
  off Lancaster Rd **166** A5
  WC2 . . . .**18** C5
  Hounslow TW4 . . . .**142** C2
  Ilford IG1 off Staines Rd **99** F5
  Twickenham TW1 . . . .**144** D6
Lancaster Rd, E7 . . . .**97** G7
  E11 . . . .**97** E2
  E17 . . . .**77** G2
  N4 . . . .**75** G7
  N11 . . . .**58** D6
  N18 . . . .**60** C5
  NW10 . . . .**89** F5
  SE25 . . . .**188** C2
  SW19 . . . .**166** A5
  W11 . . . .**108** B6
  Barnet EN4 . . . .**41** G5
  Enfield EN2 . . . .**44** A1
  Harrow HA2 . . . .**67** G5
  Northolt UB5 . . . .**85** J6
  Southall UB1 . . . .**103** F2
Lancaster St, SE1 . . . .**27** H4
Lancaster Ter, W2 . . . .**15** E5
Lancaster Wk, W2 . . . .**22** E3
Lancaster Way, Wor.Pk. KT4 . . . .**183** H7

Lancaster W, W11
  off Grenfell Rd **108** A7
Lancastrian Rd, Wall. SM6 . . . . .**201** E7
Lancefield St, W10 . . . .**108** C3
Lancell St, N16
  off Stoke Newington Ch St . .**94** B2
Lancelot Av, Wem. HA0 . . . .**87** G4
Lancelot Cres, Wem. HA0 . . . . . .**87** G4
Lancelot Gdns, Barn. EN4 . . . . . .**42** A7
Lancelot Pl, SW7 . . . .**23** J4
Lancelot Rd, Ilf. IG6 . . . .**65** H6
  Welling DA16 . . . .**158** A4
  Wembley HA0 . . . .**87** G5
Lance Rd, Har. HA1 . . . .**67** J7
Lancer Sq, W8 . . . .**22** A3
Lancey Cl, SE7 off Cleveley Cl . .**136** A4
Lanchester Rd, N6 . . . .**73** J5
Lanchester Way, SE14 . . . .**153** F1
Lancing Gdns, N9 . . . .**60** C1
Lancing Rd, W13
  off Drayton Grn Rd **104/105** E7
  Croydon CR0 . . . .**187** F6
  Ilford IG2 . . . .**81** G6
Lancing St, NW1 . . . .**9** H4
Lancresse Ct, N1 . . . .**112** B1
Landcroft Rd, SE22 . . . .**152** C6
Landells Rd, SE22 . . . .**152** C6
Landford Rd, SW15 . . . .**147** J3
Landgrove Rd, SW19 . . . .**166** D5
Landmann Way, SE14 . . . .**133** G6
Landmark Hts, E5 . . . .**95** H4
Landon Pl, SW1 . . . .**23** J5
Landons Cl, E14 . . . .**134** C1
Landon Wk, E14 off Cottage St . .**114** B7
Landor Rd, SW9 . . . .**150** E3
Landor Wk, W12 . . . .**127** G2
Landport Way, SE15 . . . .**37** G3
Landra Gdns, N21 . . . .**43** H6
Landridge Rd, SW6 . . . .**148** C2
Landrock Rd, N8 . . . .**75** E6
Landscape Rd, Wdf.Grn. IG8 . . . .**63** H7
Landseer Av, E12 . . . .**98** D5
Landseer Cl, SW19
  off Brangwyn Cres **185** F1
  Edgware HA8 . . . .**70** A2
Landseer Rd, N19 . . . .**92** E3
  Enfield EN1 . . . .**44** D5
  New Malden KT3 . . . .**182** D7
  Sutton SM1 . . . .**198** D5
Landstead Rd, SE18 . . . .**137** G7
Lane, The, NW8 . . . .**6** C1
  SE3 . . . .**155** G3
Lane App, NW7 . . . .**56** B5
Lane Cl, NW2 . . . .**89** H3
Lane End, Bexh. DA7 . . . .**159** H3
Lane Gdns, Esher (Clay.) KT10 . .**194** C7
Lane Ms, E12 off Colchester Av . .**98** C3
Lanercost Cl, SW2 . . . .**169** G2
Lanercost Gdns, N14 . . . .**42** E7
Lanercost Rd, SW2 . . . .**169** G2
Lanesborough Pl, SW1 . . . .**24** C3
Laneside, Chis. BR7 . . . .**175** E5
  Edgware HA8 . . . .**54** C5
Laneside Av, Dag. RM8 . . . .**83** F7
Laneway, SW15 . . . .**147** H5
Lanfranc Rd, E3 . . . .**113** H2
Lanfrey Pl, W14
  off North End Rd **128** C5
Langbourne Av, N6 . . . .**92** A2
Langbourne Pl, E14 . . . .**134** B5
Langbourne Way, Esher (Clay.)
  KT10 . . . .**194** D6
Langbrook Rd, SE3 . . . .**156** A3
Langcroft Cl, Cars. SM5 . . . .**199** J3
Langdale Av, Mitch. CR4 . . . .**185** J3
Langdale Cl, SE17 . . . .**35** J5
  SW14 . . . .**146** B4
  Dagenham RM8 . . . .**100** C1
  Orpington BR6
  off Grasmere Rd **206/207** E3
Langdale Cres, Bexh. DA7 . . . . .**139** G7
Langdale Gdns, Grnf. UB6 . . . . .**105** C3
Langdale Rd, SE10 . . . .**134** C7
  Thornton Heath CR7 . . . .**187** G4
Langdale St, E1
  off Burslem St **112/113** E6
Langdon Ct, NW10 . . . .**106** E1
Langdon Cres, E6 . . . .**116** D2
Langdon Dr, NW9 . . . .**88** C1
Langdon Pk, Tedd. TW11 . . . . . .**163** F6
Langdon Pk Rd, N6 . . . .**74** C7
Langdon Pl, SW14
  off Rosemary La **146** C3
Langdon Rd, E6 . . . .**116** D1
  Bromley BR2 . . . .**191** H3
  Morden SM4 . . . .**185** F5
Langdons Ct, Sthl. UB2 . . . .**123** G3
Langdon Shaw, Sid. DA14 . . . . .**175** J5
Langdon Wk, Mord. SM4 . . . . . .**185** F5
Langdon Way, SE1 . . . .**37** J2
Langford Cl, E8 . . . .**94** D5
  N15 . . . .**76** B6
  NW8 . . . .**6** D1
  W3 . . . .**126** B2
Langford Ct, NW8 . . . .**6** C2
Langford Cres, Barn. EN4 . . . .**41** J4
Langford Grn, SE5 . . . .**152** B3

Langford Pl, NW8 ....6 D2
Sidcup DA14 ....176 A3
Langford Rd, SW6 ....149 E2
Barnet EN4 ....41 H4
Woodford Green IG8 ....63 J6
Langham Cl, N15
off Langham Rd 75 H3
Langham Dr, Rom. RM6 ....82 B6
Langham Gdns, N21 ....43 G5
W13 ....105 E7
Edgware HA8 ....54 C7
Richmond TW10 ....163 F4
Wembley HA0 ....87 F2
Langham Ho Cl, Rich. TW10 ....163 G4
Langham Pk Pl, Brom. BR2 ....191 F4
Langham Pl, N15 ....75 H3
W1 ....16 E2
W4 off Hogarth
Roundabout 126/127 E6
Langham Rd, N15 ....75 H3
SW20 ....183 J1
Edgware HA8 ....54 C6
Teddington TW11 ....162 C5
Langham St, W1 ....17 E2
Langhedge Cl, N18
off Langhedge La 60 C6
Langhedge La, N18 ....60 C5
Langhedge La Ind Est, N18 ....60 C6
Langholm Cl, SW12
off King's Av 150 D7
Langholme, Bushey WD23 ....51 J1
Langhorn Dr, Twick. TW2 ....144 B7
Langhorne Rd, Dag. RM10 ....101 G7
Langland Cres, Stan. HA7 ....69 H3
Langland Dr, Pnr. HA5 ....50 E7
Langland Gdns, NW3 ....91 F5
Croydon CR0 ....203 J2
Langler Rd, NW10 ....107 J2
Langley Av, Ruis. HA4 ....84 B1
Surbiton KT6 ....195 G1
Worcester Park KT4 ....198 A2
Langley Cl, WC2 ....18 A5
Beckenham BR3 ....190 B5
Langley Cres, E11 ....79 J7
Dagenham RM9 ....100 C7
Edgware HA8 ....54 C3
Hayes UB3 ....121 J7
Langley Dr, E11 ....79 H7
W3 ....126 B1
Langley Gdns, Brom. BR2 ....191 G4
Dagenham RM9 ....100 C7
Orpington BR5 ....193 E6
Langley Gro, N.Mal. KT3 ....182 E2
Langley La, SW8 ....34 B5
Langley Meadow, Loug. IG10 ....49 G2
Langley Pk, NW7 ....54 E6
Langley Pk Rd, Sutt. SM1, SM2 ....199 F5
Langley Rd, SW19 ....184 C1
Beckenham BR3 ....189 H4
Isleworth TW7 ....144 C2
Surbiton KT6 ....181 H7
Welling DA16 ....138 C6
Langley Row, Barn. EN5 ....40 C1
Langley St, WC2 ....18 A4
Langley Way, W.Wick. BR4 ....204 D1
Langmead Dr, Bushey (Bushey Hth)
WD23 ....52 A1
Langmead St, SE27
off Beadman St 169 H4
Langmore Ct, Bexh. DA6
off Regency Way 158 D3
Langridge Ms, Hmptn. TW12
off Oak Av 161 F6
Langroyd Rd, SW17 ....167 J2
Langside Av, SW15 ....147 G4
Langside Cres, N14 ....58 D3
Langston Hughes Cl, SE24
off Shakespeare Rd 151 H4
Langston Rd, Loug. IG10 ....49 F5
Lang St, E1 ....113 F4
Langthorn Ct, EC2 ....20 B3
Langthorne Rd, E11 ....96 D3
Langthorne St, SW6 ....128 A7
Langton Av, E6 ....116 D3
N20 ....41 F7
Langton Cl, WC1 ....10 D4
Langton Ho, SW16
off Colson Way 168 C4
Langton Pl, SW18
off Merton Rd 166 D1
Langton Ri, SE23 ....152 E7
Langton Rd, NW2 ....89 J3
SW9 ....131 H7
Harrow HA3 ....51 J7
West Molesey KT8 ....179 J4
Langton St, SW10 ....30 D6
Langton Way, SE3 ....155 F1
Croydon CR0 ....202 B4
Langtry Pl, SW6
off Seagrave Rd 128 D6
Langtry Rd, NW8 ....108 E1
Northolt UB5 ....102 D2
Langtry Wk, NW8
off Alexandra Pl 91 F7
Langwood Chase, Tedd. TW11 ....163 F6
Langworth Dr, Hayes UB4 ....102 A6

Lanhill Rd, W9 ....108 D4
Lanier Rd, SE13 ....154 C6
Lanigan Dr, Houns. TW3 ....143 H5
Lankaster Gdns, N2 ....73 G1
Lankers Dr, Har. HA2 ....67 F6
Lankton Cl, Beck. BR3 ....190 C1
Lannock Rd, Hayes UB3 ....121 H1
Lannoy Rd, SE9 ....175 F1
Lanrick Rd, E14 ....114 D6
Lanridge Rd, SE2 ....138 D3
Lansbury Av, N18 ....60 A5
Barking IG11 ....100 A7
Feltham TW14 ....142 B6
Romford RM6 ....83 E5
Lansbury Cl, NW10 ....88 C5
Lansbury Est, E14 ....114 B6
Lansbury Gdns, E14 ....114 D6
Lansbury Rd, Enf. EN3 ....45 G1
Lansbury Way, N18 ....60 B5
Lanscombe Wk, SW8 ....150 E1
Lansdell Rd, Mitch. CR4 ....186 A2
Lansdowne Av, Bexh. DA7 ....138 D7
Orpington BR6 ....207 E1
Lansdowne Cl, SW20 ....166 A7
Surbiton KT5
off Kingston Rd 196 B2
Twickenham TW1
off Lion Rd 162 C1
Lansdowne Copse, Wor.Pk. KT4
off The Avenue 197 G2
Lansdowne Ct, Wor.Pk. KT4
off The Avenue 197 G2
Lansdowne Cres, W11 ....108 B7
Lansdowne Dr, E8 ....94 D6
Lansdowne Gdns, SW8 ....150 E1
Lansdowne Grn, SW8
off Hartington Rd 150/151 E1
Lansdowne Gro, NW10 ....89 E4
Lansdowne Hill, SE27 ....169 H3
Lansdowne La, SE7 ....136 A6
Lansdowne Ms, SE7 ....136 A5
W11 off Lansdowne Rd 128 C1
Lansdowne Pl, SE1 ....28 C6
SE19 ....170 C7
Lansdowne Ri, W11 ....108 B7
Lansdowne Rd, E4 ....62 A2
E11 ....97 F2
E17 ....78 A5
E18 ....79 G3
N3 ....56 C7
N10 ....74 C2
N17 ....76 C1
SW20 ....165 J7
W11 ....108 B7
Bromley BR1 ....173 G7
Croydon CR0 ....202 A2
Epsom KT19 ....196 C7
Harrow HA1 ....68 B7
Hounslow TW3 ....143 H3
Ilford IG3 ....99 J1
Stanmore HA7 ....53 F6
Lansdowne Row, W1 ....24 E1
Lansdowne Ter, WC1 ....10 B6
Lansdowne Wk, W11 ....128 B1
Lansdowne Way, SW8 ....150 D1
Lansdowne Wd Cl, SE27 ....169 H3
Lansdown Rd, E7 ....97 J7
Sidcup DA14 ....176 B3
Lansfield Av, N18 ....60 D4
Lantern Cl, SW15 ....147 G4
Wembley HA0 ....87 G5
Lanterns Ct, E14 ....134 A2
Lantern Way, West Dr. UB7 ....120 B2
Lant St, SE1 ....27 J3
Lanvanor Rd, SE15 ....153 F2
Lapford Cl, W9 ....108 C4
Lapponum Wk, Hayes UB4
off Lochan Cl 102 D5
Lapse Wd Wk, SE23 ....170 E1
Lapstone Gdns, Har. HA3 ....69 F6
Lapwing Ct, Surb. KT6
off Chaffinch Cl 196 A3
Lapwing Twr, SE8
off Abinger Gro 133 J6
Lapwing Way, Hayes UB4 ....102 D6
Lara Cl, SE13 ....154 C6
Chessington KT9 ....195 H7
Larbert Rd, SW16 ....186 C1
Larch Av, W3 ....126 E1
Larch Cl, E13 ....115 H4
N11 ....58 A7
N19 off Bredgar Rd 92 C2
SE8 off Clyde St 133 J6
SW12 ....168 B2
Larch Cres, Epsom KT19 ....196 B6
Hayes UB4 ....102 C4
Larchdene, Orp. BR6 ....206 D2
Larch Dr, W4
off Gunnersbury Av 126 A5
Larches, The, N13 ....59 J3
Larches Av, SW14 ....146 D4
Larch Grn, NW9
off Clayton Fld 70/71 E7
Larch Gro, Sid. DA15 ....175 J1
Larch Rd, E10 off Walnut Rd 96 A2
NW2 ....89 J4
Larch Tree Way, Croy. CR0 ....204 A3

Larch Way, Brom. BR2 ....192 D7
Larchwood Rd, SE9 ....175 E2
Larcombe Cl, Croy. CR0 ....202 C4
Larcom St, SE17 ....36 A2
Larden Rd, W3 ....127 E1
Largewood Av, Surb. KT6 ....196 A2
Larissa St, SE17 ....36 C3
Larkbere Rd, SE26 ....171 H4
Larken Cl, Bushey WD23
off Larken Dr 51 J1
Larken Dr, Bushey WD23 ....51 J1
Larkfield Av, Har. HA3 ....69 E3
Larkfield Cl, Brom. BR2 ....205 F2
Larkfield Rd, Rich. TW9 ....145 H4
Sidcup DA14 ....175 J3
Larkhall La, SW4 ....150 D2
Larkhall Ri, SW4 ....150 C3
Larkhill Ter, SE18 ....156 D1
Lark Row, E2 ....113 F1
Larksfield Gro, Enf. EN1 ....45 E1
Larks Gro, Bark. IG11
off Thornhill Gdns 99 H7
Larkshall Ct, Rom. RM7 ....83 J2
Larkshall Cres, E4 ....62 C4
Larkshall Rd, E4 ....62 C5
Larkspur Cl, E6 ....116 B5
N17 off Fryatt Rd 60 A7
NW9 ....70 B5
Larkspur Gro, Edg. HA8 ....54 C4
Larkspur Way, Epsom KT19 ....196 C5
Larkswood Ct, E4 ....62 D5
Larkswood Leisure Pk, E4 ....62 C4
Larkswood Ri, Pnr. HA5 ....66 C4
Larkswood Rd, E4 ....62 A4
Lark Way, Cars. SM5 ....185 H7
Larkway Cl, NW9 ....70 D4
Larnach Rd, W6 ....128 A6
Larpent Av, SW15 ....147 J5
Larwood Cl, Grnf. UB6 ....86 A5
Lascelles Av, Har. HA1 ....68 A7
Lascelles Cl, E11 ....96 D2
Lascotts Rd, N22 ....59 F6
Lassa Rd, SE9 ....156 B5
Lassell St, SE10 ....134 D5
Lasseter Pl, SE3
off Vanbrugh Hill 135 F6
Latchett Rd, E18 ....79 H1
Latchingdon Ct, E17 ....77 G4
Latchingdon Gdns, Wdf.Grn.
IG8 ....64 B6
Latchmere Cl, Rich. TW10 ....163 H5
Latchmere La, Kings.T. KT2 ....163 J6
Latchmere Pas, SW11
off Cabul Rd 149 H2
Latchmere Rd, SW11 ....149 J2
Kingston upon Thames KT2 ....163 H7
Latchmere St, SW11 ....149 J2
Lateward Rd, Brent. TW8 ....125 G6
Latham Cl, E6 off Oliver Gdns 116 B6
Twickenham TW1 ....144 D7
Latham Ho, E1 ....113 G6
Latham Rd, Bexh. DA6 ....159 G5
Twickenham TW1 ....144 C7
Lathams Way, Croy. CR0 ....201 F1
Lathkill Ct, Enf. EN1 ....44 D7
Lathom Rd, E6 ....98 C5
Latimer, SE17 ....36 D4
Latimer Av, E6 ....116 C1
Latimer Cl, Pnr. HA5 ....66 C1
Worcester Park KT4 ....197 H4
Latimer Gdns, Pnr. HA5 ....66 C1
Latimer Pl, W10 ....107 J6
Latimer Rd, E7 ....97 H4
N15 ....76 B6
SW19 ....166 E6
W10 ....107 J6
Barnet EN5 ....40 E3
Croydon CR0 off Abbey Rd 201 H3
Teddington TW11 ....162 C5
Latona Rd, SE15 ....37 H6
La Tourne Gdns, Orp. BR6 ....207 F3
Lattimer Pl, W4 ....127 E6
Latton Cl, Walt. KT12 ....179 E7
Latymer Ct, W6 ....128 A4
Latymer Rd, N9 ....60 C1
Latymer Way, N9 ....60 A2
Lauder Cl, Nthlt. UB5 ....102 D2
Lauderdale Dr, Rich. TW10 ....163 G3
Lauderdale Pl, EC2 off Beech St 111 J5
Lauderdale Rd, W9 ....6 A4
Lauderdale Twr, EC2 ....19 J1
Laud St, SE11 ....34 C3
Croydon CR0 ....201 J3
Laughton Ct, Borwd. WD6
off Banks Rd 38 D2
Laughton Rd, Nthlt. UB5 ....102 D1
Launcelot Rd, Brom. BR1 ....173 G4
Launcelot St, SE1 ....26 E4
Launceston Gdns, Grnf. UB6 ....105 F1
Launceston Pl, W8 ....22 C5
Launceston Rd, Grnf. UB6 ....105 F1
Launch St, E14 ....134 C3
Laundress La, N16 ....94 D3
Laundry La, N1
off Greenman St 111 J1
Laundry Ms, SE23 ....153 H7
Laundry Rd, W6 ....128 B6

Launton Dr, Bexh. DA6 ....158 D4
Laura Cl, E11 ....79 J5
Enfield EN1 ....44 B5
Lauradale Rd, N2 ....73 J4
Laura Pl, E5 ....95 F4
Laurel Av, Twick. TW1 ....162 C1
Laurel Bk Gdns, SW6
off New Kings Rd 148 C2
Laurel Bk Rd, Enf. EN2 ....43 J1
Laurel Bk Vil, W7
off Lower Boston Rd 124 B1
Laurel Cl, N19 off Hargrave Pk 92 C2
SW17 ....167 H5
Ilford IG6 ....65 F6
Sidcup DA14 ....176 A3
Laurel Cres, Croy. CR0 ....204 A3
Laurel Dr, N21 ....43 G7
Laurel Gdns, E4 ....46 B7
NW7 ....54 D3
W7 ....124 B1
Bromley BR1 ....192 B4
Hounslow TW4 ....142 A4
Laurel Gro, SE20 ....171 E7
SE26 ....171 G4
Laurel La, West Dr. UB7 ....120 B4
Laurel Manor, Sutt. SM2
off Devonshire Rd 199 F7
Laurel Pk, Har. HA3 ....52 C7
Laurel Rd, SW13 ....147 G2
SW20 ....183 H1
Hampton (Hmptn H.) TW12 ....162 A5
Laurel St, E8 ....94 C6
Laurel Vw, N12 ....56 E3
Laurel Way, E18 ....79 F4
N20 ....56 D3
Laurence Ms, W12
off Askew Rd 127 G2
Laurence Pountney Hill, EC4 ....20 B5
Laurence Pountney La, EC4 ....20 B5
Laurie Gro, SE14 ....153 H1
Laurie Rd, W7 ....104 B5
Laurier Rd, NW5 ....92 B3
Croydon CR0 ....188 C7
Laurimel Cl, Stan. HA7
off September Way 52/53 E6
Laurino Pl, Bushey (Bushey Hth)
WD23 ....51 J2
Lauriston Rd, E9 ....113 G1
SW19 ....166 A6
Lausanne Rd, N8 ....75 G4
SE15 ....153 F1
Lavell St, N16 ....94 A4
Lavender Av, NW9 ....88 C1
Mitcham CR4 ....185 H1
Worcester Park KT4 ....197 J3
Lavender Cl, SW3 ....31 F6
Bromley BR2 ....192 B6
Carshalton SM5 ....200 A4
Lavender Ct, W.Mol. KT8
off Molesham Way 179 H3
Lavender Gdns, SW11 ....149 J4
Enfield EN2 ....43 H1
Harrow HA3 off Uxbridge Rd 52 B2
Lavender Gro, E8 ....94 C7
Mitcham CR4 ....185 H1
Lavender Hill, SW11 ....149 H4
Enfield EN2 ....43 G1
Lavender Pl, Ilf. IG1 ....98 E5
Lavender Ri, West Dr. UB7 ....120 D2
Lavender Rd, SE16 ....133 H1
SW11 ....149 G3
Carshalton SM5 ....200 A4
Croydon CR0 ....187 F6
Enfield EN2 ....44 A1
Epsom KT19 ....196 B5
Sutton SM1 ....199 G4
Lavender St, E15
off Manbey Gro 96/97 E6
Lavender Sweep, SW11 ....149 J4
Lavender Ter, SW11
off Falcon Rd 149 H3
Lavender Vale, Wall. SM6 ....200 D6
Lavender Wk, SW11 ....149 J4
Mitcham CR4 ....186 A3
Lavender Way, Croy. CR0 ....189 G6
Lavengro Rd, SE27 ....169 J2
Lavenham Rd, SW18 ....166 C2
Lavernock Rd, Bexh. DA7 ....159 G2
Lavers Rd, N16 ....94 B3
Laverstoke Gdns, SW15 ....147 G7
Laverton Ms, SW5 ....30 B2
Laverton Pl, SW5 ....30 B2
Lavidge Rd, SE9 ....174 B2
Lavina Gro, N1 ....10 C1
Lavington Cl, E9
off Beanacre Cl 95 J6
Lavington Rd, W13 ....125 E1
Croydon CR0 ....201 F3
Lavington St, SE1 ....27 H2
Lawdons Gdns, Croy. CR0 ....201 H4
Lawford Rd, N1 ....94 B7
NW5 ....92 C6
W4 ....126 C7
Law Ho, Bark. IG11 ....118 A2
Lawless St, E14 ....114 B7
Lawley Rd, N14 ....42 B7
Lawley St, E5 ....95 F4

Lawn, The, Sthl. UB2 . . . .**123** G5
Lawn Cl, N9 . . . .**44** C7
  Bromley BR1 . . . .**173** H6
  New Malden KT3 . . . .**182** E2
Lawn Cres, Rich. TW9 . . . .**146** A2
Lawn Fm Gro, Rom. RM6 . . . . .**82** E4
Lawnfield, NW2
  off Coverdale Rd **90** A7
Lawn Gdns, W7 . . . .**124** B1
Lawn Ho Cl, E14 . . . .**134** C2
Lawn La, SW8 . . . .**34** B6
Lawn Rd, NW3 . . . .**91** J5
  Beckenham BR3 . . . .**171** J7
Lawns, The, E4 . . . .**62** A5
  SE3 *off Lee Ter* **154/155** E3
  SE19 . . . .**188** A1
  Pinner HA5 . . . .**51** H7
  Sidcup DA14 . . . .**176** B4
  Sutton SM2 . . . .**198** B7
Lawns Ct, Wem. HA9
  off The Avenue **87** J2
Lawnside, SE3 . . . .**155** F4
Lawn Ter, SE3 . . . .**155** E3
Lawn Vale, Pnr. HA5 . . . .**66** D2
Lawrence Av, E12 . . . .**98** D4
  E17 . . . .**77** G1
  N13 . . . .**59** H4
  NW7 . . . .**55** H4
  NW10 . . . .**106** D1
  New Malden KT3 . . . .**182** D6
Lawrence Bldgs, N16 . . . .**94** C3
Lawrence Campe Cl, N20
  off Friern Barnet La **57** G3
Lawrence Cl, E3 . . . .**114** A2
  N15 *off Lawrence Rd* **76** B3
Lawrence Ct, NW7 . . . .**55** E5
Lawrence Cres, Dag. RM10 . . .**101** H3
  Edgware HA8 . . . .**70** A2
Lawrence Gdns, NW7 . . . .**55** F3
Lawrence Hill, E4 . . . .**62** A2
Lawrence La, EC2 . . . .**20** A4
Lawrence Pl, N1
  off Outram Pl **110/111** E1
Lawrence Rd, E6 . . . .**116** A1
  E13 . . . .**115** H1
  N15 . . . .**76** B3
  N18 . . . .**60** E4
  SE25 . . . .**188** C4
  W5 . . . .**125** G4
  Erith DA8 . . . .**139** H7
  Hampton TW12 . . . .**161** F7
  Hounslow TW4 . . . .**142** C4
  Pinner HA5 . . . .**66** D5
  Richmond TW10 . . . .**163** F4
  West Wickham BR4 . . . . . .**205** G4
Lawrence St, E16 . . . .**115** F5
  NW7 . . . .**55** H4
  SW3 . . . .**31** G6
Lawrence Way, NW10 . . . .**88** C3
Lawrence Weaver Cl, Mord. SM4
  off Green La **184** D6
Lawrie Pk Av, SE26 . . . .**171** E5
Lawrie Pk Cres, SE26 . . . .**171** E5
Lawrie Pk Gdns, SE26 . . . .**171** E4
Lawrie Pk Rd, SE26 . . . .**171** E6
Laws Cl, SE25 . . . .**188** A4
Lawson Cl, E16 . . . .**115** J5
  SW19 . . . .**166** A3
Lawson Est, SE1 . . . .**28** B6
Lawson Gdns, Pnr. HA5 . . . .**66** B3
Lawson Rd, Enf. EN3 . . . .**45** F1
  Southall UB1 . . . .**103** F4
Law St, SE1 . . . .**28** C5
Lawton Rd, E3 . . . .**113** H3
  E10 . . . .**96** C1
  Barnet EN4 . . . .**41** G3
  Loughton IG10 . . . .**48** E3
Laxcon Cl, NW10 . . . .**88** C5
Laxey Rd, Orp. BR6 . . . .**207** J6
Laxley Cl, SE5 . . . .**35** H7
Laxton Pl, NW1 . . . .**9** E5
Layard Rd, SE16 . . . .**133** E4
  Enfield EN1 . . . .**44** C1
  Thornton Heath CR7 . . . . . .**188** A2
Layard Sq, SE16 . . . .**133** E4
Laycock St, N1 . . . .**93** G6
Layer Gdns, W3 . . . .**106** A7
Layfield Cl, NW4 . . . .**71** H7
Layfield Cres, NW4 . . . .**71** H7
Layfield Rd, NW4 . . . .**71** H7
Layhams Rd, Kes. BR2 . . . .**205** F5
  West Wickham BR4 . . . . . .**204** D3
Laymarsh Cl, Belv. DA17 . . . . .**139** F3
Laymead Cl, Nthlt. UB5 . . . .**84** E6
Laystall St, EC1 . . . .**10** E6
Layton Cres, Croy. CR0 . . . . . .**201** G5
Layton Pl, Rich. TW9
  off Station Av **146** A1
Layton Rd, Brent. TW8 . . . .**125** G5
  Hounslow TW3 . . . .**143** H4
Laytons Bldgs, SE1 . . . .**28** A3
Layzell Wk, SE9
  off Mottingham La **174** A1
Lazar Wk, N7 *off Briset Way* . .**93** F2
Leabank Cl, Har. HA1 . . . .**86** B3
Leabank Sq, E9 . . . .**96** A6
Leabank Vw, N15 . . . .**76** D6

Leabourne Rd, N16 . . . .**76** D6
LEA BRIDGE, E5 . . . .**95** G3
Lea Br Business Cen, E10
  off Burwell Rd **95** H1
Lea Br Rd, E5 . . . .**95** F3
  E10 . . . .**95** H1
  E17 . . . .**78** D4
Lea Cl, Twick. TW2 . . . .**143** F7
Leacroft Av, SW12 . . . .**149** J7
Leadale Av, E4 . . . .**62** A2
Leadale Rd, N15 . . . .**76** D6
  N16 . . . .**76** D6
Leadbeaters Cl, N11
  off Goldsmith Rd **57** J5
★ Leadenhall Mkt, EC3 . . . .**20** D4
Leadenhall Pl, EC3 . . . .**20** D4
Leadenhall St, EC3 . . . .**20** D4
Leadenham Ct, E3
  off Spanby Rd **114** A4
Leader Av, E12 . . . .**98** D5
Leadings, The, Wem. HA9 . . . . .**88** C3
Leaf Cl, T.Ditt. KT7 . . . .**180** B5
Leaf Gro, SE27 . . . .**169** G5
Leafield Cl, SW16 . . . .**169** H6
Leafield La, Sid. DA14 . . . .**177** F4
Leafield Rd, SW20 . . . .**184** C3
  Sutton SM1 . . . .**198** D2
Leafy Gro, Kes. BR2 . . . .**205** J5
Leafy Oak Rd, SE12 . . . .**173** J3
Leafy Way, Croy. CR0 . . . .**202** C2
Lea Gdns, Wem. HA9 . . . .**87** H4
Leagrave St, E5 . . . .**95** F3
Lea Hall Rd, E10 . . . .**96** A1
Leahurst Rd, SE13 . . . .**154** D5
Leake St, SE1 . . . .**26** D3
Lealand Rd, N15 . . . .**76** C6
Leamington Av, E17 . . . .**78** A5
  Bromley BR1 . . . .**173** J5
  Morden SM4 . . . .**184** C4
  Orpington BR6 . . . .**207** H4
Leamington Cl, E12 . . . .**98** B5
  Bromley BR1 . . . .**173** J5
  Hounslow TW3 . . . .**143** J5
Leamington Cres, Har. HA2 . . . .**85** E3
Leamington Gdns, Ilf. IG3 . . . . .**99** J2
Leamington Pk, W3 . . . .**106** D5
Leamington Rd, Sthl. UB2 . . . .**122** D4
Leamington Rd Vil, W11 . . . . . .**108** C5
Leamore St, W6 . . . .**127** H4
Leamouth Rd, E6
  off Remington Rd **116** B6
  E14 . . . .**114** D4
Leander Ct, SE8 . . . .**154** A1
Leander Rd, SW2 . . . .**151** F6
  Northolt UB5 . . . .**103** G3
  Thornton Heath CR7 . . . . . .**187** F4
Learner Dr, Har. HA2 . . . .**85** G2
Lea Rd, Beck. BR3
  off Fairfield Rd **190** A2
  Enfield EN2 . . . .**44** A1
  Southall UB2 . . . .**122** E4
Learoyd Gdns, E6 . . . .**116** D7
Leas Cl, Chess. KT9 . . . .**195** J7
Leas Dale, SE9 . . . .**174** D3
Leas Grn, Chis. BR7 . . . .**175** J6
Leaside Av, N10 . . . .**74** A3
Leaside Rd, E5 . . . .**95** F1
Leasowes Rd, E10 . . . .**96** A1
Lea Sq, E3 *off Lefevre Wk* . . .**113** J1
Leatherbottle Grn, Erith DA18 .**139** F3
Leather Bottle La, Belv. DA17 . .**139** E4
Leather Cl, Mitch. CR4 . . . .**186** A2
Leatherdale St, E1
  off Portelet Rd **113** G4
Leather Gdns, E15
  off Abbey Rd **114/115** E1
Leatherhead Cl, N16 . . . .**94** C1
Leather La, EC1 . . . .**19** F2
★ Leather Mkt Bermondsey,
  SE1 . . . .**28** D4
Leathermarket Ct, SE1 . . . .**28** D4
Leathermarket St, SE1 . . . .**28** D4
Leathersellers Cl, Barn. EN5
  off The Avenue **40** B4
Leathsail Rd, Har. HA2 . . . .**85** H3
Leathwaite Rd, SW11 . . . .**149** J4
Leathwell Rd, SE8 . . . .**154** B2
Lea Valley Rd, E4 . . . .**45** G5
  Enfield EN3 . . . .**45** G5
Lea Valley Trd Est, N18 . . . .**61** G5
Lea Valley Viaduct, E4 . . . .**61** G5
  N18 . . . .**61** G5
Lea Valley Wk, E3 . . . .**114** C4
  E5 . . . .**95** H3
  E9 . . . .**95** H3
  E10 . . . .**95** H3
  E14 . . . .**114** B5
  E15 . . . .**114** C3
  E17 . . . .**77** F1
  N9 . . . .**61** H1
  N15 . . . .**76** D6
  N16 . . . .**76** D6
  N17 . . . .**77** F1
  Enfield EN3 . . . .**45** J3
Leaveland Cl, Beck. BR3 . . . . .**190** A4
Leaver Gdns, Grnf. UB6 . . . . . .**104** A2

Leavesden Rd, Stan. HA7 . . . . . .**52** D6
Lea Vw Hos, E5
  off Springfield **94/95** E1
Leaway, E10 . . . .**95** G1
Lebanon Av, Felt. TW13 . . . . . .**160** D5
Lebanon Ct, Twick. TW1 . . . . . .**144** E7
Lebanon Gdns, SW18 . . . .**148** D6
Lebanon Pk, Twick. TW1 . . . . . .**144** E7
Lebanon Rd, SW18 . . . .**148** D5
  Croydon CR0 . . . .**202** B1
Lebrun Sq, SE3 . . . .**155** H3
Lechmere App, Wdf.Grn. IG8 . . .**79** J2
Lechmere Av, Chig. IG7 . . . .**65** F4
  Woodford Green IG8 . . . . . .**80** A2
Lechmere Rd, NW2 . . . .**89** H6
Leckford Rd, SW18 . . . .**167** F2
Leckwith Av, Bexh. DA7 . . . . . .**138** E6
Lecky St, SW7 . . . .**31** E3
Leclair Ho, SE3 *off Gallus Sq* .**155** H3
Leconfield Av, SW13 . . . .**147** F3
Leconfield Rd, N5 . . . .**94** A4
Leda Av, Enf. EN3 . . . .**45** G1
Leda Rd, SE18 . . . .**136** C3
Ledbury Est, SE15 . . . .**132** E7
Ledbury Ms N, W11
  off Ledbury Rd **108** D7
Ledbury Ms W, W11
  off Ledbury Rd **108** D7
Ledbury Pl, Croy. CR0 . . . .**201** J4
Ledbury Rd, W11 . . . .**108** C6
  Croydon CR0 . . . .**201** J4
Ledbury St, SE15 . . . .**37** J7
Ledrington Rd, SE19 . . . .**170** D6
Ledway Dr, Wem. HA9 . . . .**69** J7
LEE, SE12 . . . .**154** E4
Lee Av, Rom. RM6 . . . .**82** E6
Lee Br, SE13 . . . .**154** C3
Leechcroft Av, Sid. DA15 . . . . .**157** J5
Leechcroft Rd, Wall. SM6 . . . . .**200** A3
Lee Ch St, SE13 . . . .**155** E4
Lee Cl, E17 . . . .**77** G1
  Barnet EN5 . . . .**41** F4
Lee Conservancy Rd, E9 . . . . . .**95** J5
Leecroft Rd, Barn. EN5 . . . .**40** B5
Leeds Pl, N4 *off Tollington Pk* . .**93** F2
Leeds Rd, Ilf. IG1 . . . .**99** G1
Leeds St, N18 . . . .**60** D5
Leefern Rd, W12 . . . .**127** G2
Leegate, SE12 . . . .**155** F5
Lee Grn, SE12 *off Lee High Rd* .**155** F5
Lee Gro, Chig. IG7 . . . .**64** D2
Lee High Rd, SE12 . . . .**154** D3
  SE13 . . . .**154** D3
Leeke St, WC1 . . . .**10** C3
Leeland Rd, W13 . . . .**124** D1
Leeland Ter, W13 . . . .**124** D1
Leeland Way, NW10 . . . .**89** F4
Lee Pk, SE3 . . . .**155** F4
Lee Pk Way, N9 . . . .**61** G4
  N18 . . . .**61** G4
Leerdam Dr, E14 . . . .**134** C3
Lee Rd, NW7 . . . .**56** A7
  SE3 . . . .**155** F3
  SW19 . . . .**185** E1
  Enfield EN1 . . . .**44** D6
  Greenford UB6 . . . .**105** F1
Lees, The, Croy. CR0 . . . .**203** J2
Leeside, Barn. EN5 . . . .**40** B5
Leeside Ct, SE16
  off Rotherhithe St **133** G1
Leeside Cres, NW11 . . . .**72** C6
Leeside Rd, N17 . . . .**61** E6
Leeson Rd, SE24 . . . .**151** G4
Leesons Hill, Chis. BR7 . . . . . .**193** H3
Leesons Way, Orp. BR5 . . . . . .**193** J2
Lees Pl, W1 . . . .**16** B5
Lee St, E8 . . . .**112** C1
Lee Ter, SE3 . . . .**154** E3
  SE13 . . . .**154** E3
Lee Valley Pathway, E9 . . . .**95** J3
  E10 . . . .**77** F7
  E17 . . . .**77** F7
Lee Valley Technopark, N17 . . . .**76** D3
Lee Vw, Enf. EN2 . . . .**43** H1
Leeward Gdns, SW19 . . . .**166** C6
Leeway, SE8 . . . .**133** J5
Leeway Cl, Pnr. HA5 . . . .**51** F7
Leewood Cl, SE12
  off Upwood Rd **155** F6
Lefevre Wk, E3 . . . .**113** J1
Lefroy Rd, W12 . . . .**127** F2
Legard Rd, N5 . . . .**93** H3
Legatt Rd, SE9 . . . .**156** A5
Leggatt Rd, E15 . . . .**114** C2
Legge St, SE13 . . . .**154** C5
Leghorn Rd, NW10 . . . .**107** F2
  SE18 . . . .**137** G5
Legion Cl, N1 . . . .**93** G6
Legion Ct, Mord. SM4 . . . .**184** D6
Legion Rd, Grnf. UB6 . . . .**103** J1
Legion Ter, E3 *off Lefevre Wk* .**113** J1
Legion Way, N12 . . . .**57** H7
Legon Av, Rom. RM7 . . . .**101** J1
Legrace Av, Houns. TW4 . . . . . .**142** D2
Leicester Av, Mitch. CR4 . . . . . .**187** E4
Leicester Cl, Wor.Pk. KT4 . . . . .**197** J4
Leicester Ct, WC2 . . . .**17** J5

Leicester Gdns, Ilf. IG3 . . . .**81** H7
Leicester Ms, N2
  off Leicester Rd **73** H3
Leicester Pl, WC2 . . . .**17** J5
Leicester Rd, E11 . . . .**79** H5
  N2 . . . .**73** H3
  Barnet EN5 . . . .**40** E5
  Croydon CR0 . . . .**188** B7
Leicester Sq, WC2 . . . .**17** J6
Leicester St, WC2 . . . .**17** J5
Leigh, The, Kings.T. KT2 . . . . . .**164** E6
Leigham Av, SW16 . . . .**169** E3
Leigham Cl, Wall. SM6
  off Stafford Rd **200** C6
Leigham Ct Rd, SW16 . . . .**169** E2
Leigham Dr, Islw. TW7 . . . .**124** B7
Leigham Vale, SW2 . . . .**169** F3
  SW16 . . . .**169** F3
Leigh Av, Ilf. IG4 . . . .**80** A4
Leigh Cl, N.Mal. KT3 . . . .**182** D4
Leigh Ct, SE4
  off Lewisham Way **154** A2
  Borehamwood WD6
   off Banks Rd **38** D2
  Harrow HA2 . . . .**86** B1
Leigh Cres, Croy. (New Adgtn)
  CR0 . . . .**204** B7
Leigh Gdns, NW10 . . . .**107** J2
Leigh Hunt Dr, N14 . . . .**58** D7
Leigh Hunt St, SE1 . . . .**27** J3
Leigh Orchard Cl, SW16 . . . . . .**169** F3
Leigh Pl, EC1 . . . .**19** E1
  Feltham TW13 . . . .**160** C1
  Welling DA16 . . . .**158** A2
Leigh Rd, E6 . . . .**98** D6
  E10 . . . .**78** C7
  N5 . . . .**93** H4
  Hounslow TW3 . . . .**144** A4
Leigh Rodd, Wat. WD19 . . . .**51** F3
Leigh St, WC1 . . . .**10** A5
Leighton Av, E12 . . . .**98** D5
  Pinner HA5 . . . .**66** E3
Leighton Cl, Edg. HA8 . . . .**70** A2
Leighton Cres, NW5
  off Leighton Gro **92** C5
Leighton Gdns, NW10 . . . .**107** H2
Leighton Gro, NW5 . . . .**92** C5
★ Leighton Ho Mus, W14 . . . . .**128** C3
Leighton Pl, NW5 . . . .**92** C5
Leighton Rd, NW5 . . . .**92** D5
  W13 . . . .**124** D2
  Enfield EN1 . . . .**44** C5
  Harrow (Har.Wld) HA3 . . . . . .**68** A2
Leighton St, Croy. CR0 . . . .**201** H1
Leila Parnell Pl, SE7 . . . .**135** J6
Leinster Av, SW14 . . . .**146** C3
Leinster Gdns, W2 . . . .**14** C4
Leinster Ms, W2 . . . .**14** C5
Leinster Pl, W2 . . . .**14** C4
Leinster Rd, N10 . . . .**74** B4
Leinster Sq, W2 . . . .**108** D6
Leinster Ter, W2 . . . .**14** C5
Leisure Way, N12 . . . .**57** G7
Leith Cl, NW9 . . . .**88** D1
Leithcote Gdns, SW16 . . . .**169** F4
Leithcote Path, SW16 . . . .**169** F3
Leith Rd, N22 . . . .**75** H1
Leith Yd, NW6 *off Quex Rd* . . .**108** D1
Lela Av, Houns. TW4 . . . .**142** C2
Lelitia Cl, E8 *off Pownall Rd* . .**112** D1
Leman St, E1 . . . .**21** G4
Lemark Cl, Stan. HA7 . . . .**53** F5
Le May Av, SE12 . . . .**173** H3
Lemmon Rd, SE10 . . . .**134** E6
Lemna Rd, E11 . . . .**79** E7
Lemonwell Ct, SE9
  off Lemonwell Dr **157** F5
Lemonwell Dr, SE9 . . . .**157** F5
Lemsford Cl, N15 . . . .**76** D5
Lemsford Ct, N4
  off Brownswood Rd **93** J2
  Borehamwood WD6 . . . .**38** C4
Lemuel St, SW18 . . . .**149** E6
Lena Cres, N9 . . . .**61** F2
Lena Gdns, W6 . . . .**127** J3
Lena Kennedy Cl, E4 . . . .**62** B6
Lenanton Steps, E14
  off Manilla St **134** A2
Lendal Ter, SW4 . . . .**150** D3
Lenelby Rd, Surb. KT6 . . . .**196** A1
Len Freeman Pl, SW6
  off John Smith Av **128** C7
Lenham Rd, SE12 . . . .**155** F4
  Bexleyheath DA7 . . . .**139** F6
  Sutton SM1 . . . .**199** E4
  Thornton Heath CR7 . . . . . .**188** A2
Lennard Av, W.Wick. BR4 . . . . .**205** E2
Lennard Cl, W.Wick. BR4 . . . . .**205** E2
Lennard Rd, SE20 . . . .**171** F6
  Beckenham BR3 . . . .**171** G6
  Bromley BR2 . . . .**206** J1
  Croydon CR0 . . . .**201** J1
Lennon Rd, NW2 . . . .**89** J5
Lennox Gdns, NW10 . . . .**89** F4
  SW1 . . . .**23** J6
  Croydon CR0 . . . .**201** H4
  Ilford IG1 . . . .**98** C1

Lennox Gdns Ms, SW1 . . . . .23 J6
Lennox Rd, E17 . . . . .77 J6
  N4 . . . . .93 F2
Lenor Cl, Bexh. DA6 . . . . .159 E4
Lensbury Way, SE2 . . . . .138 C3
Lens Rd, E7 . . . . .97 J7
Lenthall Rd, E8 . . . . .94 D7
  Loughton IG10 . . . . .49 G4
Lenthorp Rd, SE10 . . . . .135 F4
Lentmead Rd, Brom. BR1 . . . . .173 F3
Lenton Path, SE18 . . . . .137 G6
Lenton Ri, Rich. TW9
  off Evelyn Ter 145 H3
Lenton St, SE18 . . . . .137 G4
Leof Cres, SE6 . . . . .172 B5
Leominster Rd, Mord. SM4 . . . .185 F6
Leominster Wk, Mord. SM4 . . . .185 F6
Leonard Av, Mord. SM4 . . . . . .185 F5
Leonard Pl, N16 off Allen Rd . . .94 B4
Leonard Rd, E4 . . . . .62 A6
  E7 . . . . .97 J7
  N9 . . . . .60 C3
  SW16 . . . . .186 C1
  Southall UB2 . . . . .122 D3
Leonard Robbins Path, SE28
  off Tawney Rd 118 B7
Leonard St, E16 . . . . .136 B1
  EC2 . . . . .12 C5
Leontine Cl, SE15 . . . . .132 D7
Leopards Ct, EC1 . . . . .19 E1
Leopold Av, SW19 . . . . .166 C5
Leopold Ms, E9
  off Fremont St 113 F1
Leopold Rd, E17 . . . . .78 A5
  N2 . . . . .73 G3
  N18 . . . . .61 E5
  NW10 . . . . .89 E7
  SW19 . . . . .166 C4
  W5 . . . . .125 J1
Leopold St, E3 . . . . .113 J5
Leopold Ter, SW19 off Dora Rd . .166 D5
Leo St, SE15 . . . . .133 E7
Leo Yd, EC1 . . . . .11 H6
Leppoc Rd, SW4 . . . . .150 D5
Leroy St, SE1 . . . . .36 D1
Lerry Cl, W14 off Thaxton Rd . . .128 C6
Lescombe Cl, SE23 . . . . .171 H3
Lescombe Rd, SE23 . . . . .171 H3
Lesley Cl, Bex. DA5 . . . . .159 H7
Leslie Gdns, Sutt. SM2 . . . . . . .198 D7
Leslie Gro, Croy. CR0 . . . . .202 B1
Leslie Gro Pl, Croy. CR0
  off Leslie Gro 202 A1
Leslie Pk Rd, Croy. CR0 . . . . . .202 B1
Leslie Rd, E11 . . . . .96 C4
  E16 .115 H6
  N2 . . . . .73 G3
Leslie Smith Sq, SE18
  off Nightingale Vale 136 D6
★ Lesnes Abbey (ruins), Erith
  DA18 . . . . .138 D4
Lessar Av, SW4 . . . . .150 C5
Lessingham Av, SW17 . . . . .167 J4
  Ilford IG5 . . . . .80 D3
Lessing St, SE23 . . . . .153 H7
Lessington Av, Rom. RM7 . . . . . .83 J6
Lessness Av, Bexh. DA7 . . . . . .138 D7
LESSNESS HEATH, Belv. DA17 .139 H5
Lessness Pk, Belv. DA17 . . . . . .139 F5
Lessness Rd, Belv. DA17
  off Stapley Rd 139 G5
  Morden SM4 . . . . .185 F6
Lester Av, E15 . . . . .115 E3
Leswin Pl, N16 off Leswin Rd . . .94 C3
Leswin Rd, N16 . . . . .94 C3
Letchford Gdns, NW10 . . . . . . .107 G3
Letchford Ms, NW10
  off Letchford Gdns 107 G3
Letchford Ter, Har. HA3 . . . . . . .67 H1
Letchworth Av, Felt. TW14 . . . . .141 J7
Letchworth Cl, Brom. BR2 . . . . .191 G5
  Watford WD19 . . . . .50 D5
Letchworth Dr, Brom. BR2 . . . . .191 G5
Letchworth St, SW17 . . . . .167 J4
Lethbridge Cl, SE13 . . . . .154 C1
Letterstone Rd, SW6
  off Varna Rd 128 C7
Lettice St, SW6 . . . . .148 C1
Lett Rd, E15 . . . . .96 D7
Lettsom St, SE5 . . . . .152 B2
Lettsom Wk, E13 . . . . .115 G2
Leucha Rd, E17 . . . . .77 H5
Levana Cl, SW19 . . . . .166 B1
Levehurst Way, SW4 . . . . .150 E2
Leven Cl, Wat. WD19 . . . . .50 D5
Levendale Rd, SE23 . . . . .171 H2
Leven Rd, E14 . . . . .114 C5
Leverett St, SW3 . . . . .31 H1
Leverholme Gdns, SE9 . . . . . . .174 D3
Leverson St, SW16 . . . . .168 C6
Lever St, EC1 . . . . .11 H4
Leverton Pl, NW5
  off Leverton St 92 C5
Leverton St, NW5 . . . . .92 C5
Levett Gdns, Ilf. IG3 . . . . .99 J4
Levett Rd, Bark. IG11 . . . . .99 H6
Levine Gdns, Bark. IG11 . . . . . .118 D2

Levison Way, N19
  off Grovedale Rd 92 D2
Lewes Cl, Nthlt. UB5 . . . . .85 G6
Lewesdon Cl, SW19 . . . . .166 A1
Lewes Rd, N12 . . . . .57 H5
  Bromley BR1 . . . . .192 A2
Leweston Pl, N16 . . . . .76 C7
Lewey Ho, E3 . . . . .113 J4
Lewgars Av, NW9 . . . . .70 C6
Lewin Rd, SW14 . . . . .146 D3
  SW16 . . . . .168 D6
  Bexleyheath DA6 . . . . .159 E4
Lewis Av, E17 . . . . .78 A1
Lewis Cl, N14 off Orchid Rd 42 C7
Lewis Cres, NW10 . . . . .88 C5
Lewis Gdns, N2 . . . . .73 G2
Lewis Gro, SE13 . . . . .154 C3
LEWISHAM, SE13 . . . . .154 B4
Lewisham Cen, SE13 . . . . .154 C3
Lewisham High St, SE13 . . . . . .154 C3
Lewisham Hill, SE13 . . . . .154 C2
Lewisham Pk, SE13 . . . . .154 B6
Lewisham Rd, SE13 . . . . .154 B1
Lewisham St, SW1 . . . . .25 J4
Lewisham Way, SE4 . . . . .153 J1
  SE14 . . . . .153 J1
Lewis Pl, E8 . . . . .94 D5
Lewis Rd, Mitch. CR4 . . . . .185 G2
  Richmond TW10
   off Red Lion St 145 G5
  Sidcup DA14 . . . . .176 C3
  Southall UB1 . . . . .123 E2
  Sutton SM1 . . . . .199 E4
  Welling DA16 . . . . .158 C3
Lewis St, NW1 . . . . .92 B6
Lewiston Cl, Wor.Pk. KT4 . . . . .183 H7
Lewis Way, Dag. RM10 . . . . . . .101 H6
Lexden Dr, Rom. RM6 . . . . .82 B6
Lexden Rd, W3 . . . . .106 B7
  Mitcham CR4 . . . . .186 D4
Lexham Ct, Grnf. UB6 . . . . .104 A1
Lexham Gdns, W8 . . . . .30 A1
Lexham Gdns Ms, W8 . . . . .22 B6
Lexham Ho, Bark. IG11
  off St. Margarets 117 G1
Lexham Ms, W8 . . . . .128 D4
Lexham Wk, W8 . . . . .22 B6
Lexington, The, EC1 . . . . .12 B5
Lexington St, W1 . . . . .17 G4
Lexington Way, Barn. EN5 . . . . . .40 A4
Lexton Gdns, SW12 . . . . .168 D1
Leyborne Av, W13 . . . . .125 E2
Leyborne Pk, Rich. TW9 . . . . . .146 A1
Leybourne Cl, Brom. BR2 . . . . .191 G6
Leybourne Rd, E11 . . . . .97 F1
  NW1 .92 B7
  NW9 .70 A5
Leybourne St, NW1
  off Hawley St 92 B7
Leybridge Ct, SE12 . . . . .155 G5
Leyburn Cl, E17 off Church La . . .78 B4
Leyburn Gdns, Croy. CR0 . . . . .202 B2
Leyburn Gro, N18 . . . . .60 D6
Leyburn Rd, N18 . . . . .60 D6
Leycroft Cl, Loug. IG10 . . . . .48 D5
Leyden St, E1 . . . . .21 F2
Leydon Cl, SE16 off Lagado Ms .133 G1
Leyfield, Wor.Pk. KT4 . . . . .197 E1
Leyland Av, Enf. EN3 . . . . .45 H2
Leyland Gdns, Wdf.Grn. IG8 . . . .63 J5
Leyland Rd, SE12 . . . . .155 G5
Leylang Rd, SE14 . . . . .133 G7
Leys, The, N2 . . . . .73 F4
  Harrow HA3 . . . . .69 J6
Leys Av, Dag. RM10 . . . . .101 J7
Leys Cl, Dag. RM10 . . . . .101 J7
  Harrow HA1 . . . . .68 A5
Leysdown Av, Bexh. DA7 . . . . .159 J4
Leysdown Rd, SE9 . . . . .174 B2
Leysfield Rd, W12 . . . . .127 G2
Leys Gdns, Barn. EN4 . . . . .42 A5
Leyspring Rd, E11 . . . . .97 F1
Leys Rd E, Enf. EN3 . . . . .45 H1
Leys Rd W, Enf. EN3 . . . . .45 H1
Ley St, Ilf. IG1, IG2 . . . . .99 E2
Leyswood Dr, Ilf. IG2 . . . . .81 H5
Leythe Rd, W3 . . . . .126 C2
LEYTON, E11 . . . . .96 B1
Leyton Business Cen, E10 . . . . . .96 A2
Leyton Gra, E10
  off Goldsmith Rd 96 B1
Leyton Gra Est, E10 . . . . .96 B1
Leyton Grn Rd, E10 . . . . .78 C6
Leyton Ind Village, E10 . . . . .77 G7
★ Leyton Orient FC, E10 . . . . . . .96 B3
Leyton Pk Rd, E10 . . . . .96 C3
Leyton Rd, E15 . . . . .96 D5
  SW19 . . . . .167 F7
LEYTONSTONE, E11 . . . . .78 D7
Leytonstone Rd, E15 . . . . .96 E5
Leywick St, E15 . . . . .114 E2
Lezayre Rd, Orp. BR6 . . . . .207 J6
Liardet St, SE14 . . . . .133 H6
Liberia Rd, N5 . . . . .93 H6
★ Liberty, W1 . . . . .17 F4
Liberty Av, SW19 . . . . .185 G1
Liberty Ms, SW12 . . . . .150 B6

Liberty St, SW9 . . . . .151 F1
Libra Rd, E3 . . . . .113 J1
  E13 .115 G2
Library Pl, E1 off Cable St . .112/113 E7
Library St, SE1 . . . . .27 G4
Library Way, Twick. TW2
  off Nelson Rd 143 J7
Lichfield Cl, Barn. EN4 . . . . .41 J3
Lichfield Ct, Rich. TW9
  off Sheen Rd 145 H4
Lichfield Gdns, Rich. TW9 . . . . .145 H4
Lichfield Gro, N3 . . . . .72 D1
Lichfield Rd, E3 . . . . .113 H3
  E6 . . . . .116 A3
  N9 off Winchester Rd 60 D2
  NW2 .90 B4
  Dagenham RM8 . . . . .100 B4
  Hounslow TW4 . . . . .142 C3
  Northwood HA6 . . . . .66 A3
  Richmond TW9 . . . . .145 J1
  Woodford Green IG8 . . . . .63 E4
Lichlade Cl, Orp. BR6 . . . . .207 J4
Lidbury Rd, NW7 . . . . .56 B6
Lidcote Gdns, SW9 . . . . .151 G2
Liddall Way, West Dr. UB7 . . . . .120 C1
Liddell Cl, Har. HA3 . . . . .69 G3
Liddell Gdns, NW10 . . . . .107 J2
Liddell Rd, NW6 . . . . .90 D6
Lidding Rd, Har. HA3 . . . . .69 G5
Liddington Rd, E15 . . . . .115 F1
Liddon Rd, E13 . . . . .115 H3
  Bromley BR1 . . . . .191 J3
Liden Cl, E17 off Hitcham Rd 95 J1
Lidfield Rd, N16 . . . . .94 A4
Lidgate Rd, SE15
  off Chandler Way 132 C7
Lidiard Rd, SW18 . . . . .167 F2
Lidlington Pl, NW1 . . . . .9 F2
Lido Sq, N17 . . . . .76 A2
Lidyard Rd, N19 . . . . .92 C1
★ Lifetimes Mus, Croy. CR0 . . .201 J3
Liffler Rd, SE18 . . . . .137 H5
Lifford St, SW15 . . . . .148 A4
Lightcliffe Rd, N13 . . . . .59 G4
Lighter Cl, SE16 . . . . .133 H4
Lighterman Ms, E1 . . . . .113 G6
Lightermans Rd, E14 . . . . .134 A2
Lightfoot Rd, N8 . . . . .74 E5
Lightley Cl, Wem. HA0
  off Stanley Av 87 J7
Ligonier St, E2 . . . . .13 F5
Lilac Cl, E4 . . . . .61 J6
Lilac Gdns, W5 . . . . .125 G3
  Croydon CR0 . . . . .204 A3
Lilac Ms, N8 off Courcy Rd 75 G3
Lilac Pl, SE11 . . . . .34 C2
Lilac St, W12 . . . . .107 G7
Lilburne Gdns, SE9 . . . . .156 B5
Lilburne Rd, SE9 . . . . .156 B5
Lilburne Wk, NW10 . . . . .88 C6
Lile Cres, W7 . . . . .104 B5
Lilestone Est, NW8 . . . . .7 E6
Lilestone St, NW8 . . . . .7 G5
Lilford Rd, SE5 . . . . .151 H2
Lilian Barker Cl, SE12 . . . . .155 G5
Lilian Board Way, Grnf. UB6 . . . .86 A5
Lilian Cl, N16 off Barbauld Rd . . .94 B3
Lilian Gdns, Wdf.Grn. IG8 . . . . . .79 H1
Lilian Rd, SW16 . . . . .186 C1
Lillechurch Rd, Dag. RM8 . . . . .100 B6
Lilleshall Rd, Mord. SM4 . . . . . .185 G6
Lilley Cl, E1 . . . . .29 J2
Lilley La, NW7 . . . . .54 D5
Lillian Av, W3 . . . . .126 A2
Lillian Rd, SW13 . . . . .127 G6
Lillie Rd, SW6 . . . . .128 B7
Lillieshall Rd, SW4 . . . . .150 B3
Lillie Yd, SW6 . . . . .128 D6
Lillingston Ho, N7
  off Harvist Est 93 G4
Lillington Gdns Est, SW1 . . . . . . .33 G2
Lilliput Av, Nthlt. UB5 . . . . .103 F1
Lilyville Rd, SW6 . . . . .148 C1
Limbourne Av, Dag. RM8 . . . . . .83 F7
Limburg Rd, SW11 . . . . .149 J4
Limeburner La, EC4 . . . . .19 G4
Lime Cl, E1 . . . . .29 J1
  Bromley BR1 . . . . .192 B4
  Buckhurst Hill IG9 . . . . .64 A3
  Carshalton SM5 . . . . .199 J2
  Harrow HA3 . . . . .68 C2
  Romford RM7 . . . . .83 J4
Lime Ct, Mitch. CR4
  off Lewis Rd 185 G2
Lime Gdns, Sun. TW16 . . . . . . .178 C2
Limecroft Cl, Epsom KT19 . . . . .196 D7
Limedene Cl, Pnr. HA5 . . . . .66 D1
Lime Gro, E4 . . . . .61 J6
  N20 .56 C1
  W12 . . . . .127 J2
  Ilford IG6 . . . . .65 J6

Lime Gro, N.Mal. KT3 . . . . .182 D3
  Orpington BR6 . . . . .207 E2
  Ruislip HA4 . . . . .66 B7
  Sidcup DA15 . . . . .157 J6
  Twickenham TW1 . . . . .144 C6
Limeharbour, E14 . . . . .134 B3
LIMEHOUSE, E14 . . . . .113 H7
Limehouse Causeway, E14 . . . .113 J7
Limehouse Flds Est, E14 . . . . . .113 H5
Limehouse Link, E14 . . . . .113 H7
Limekiln Dr, SE7 . . . . .135 H6
Limekiln Pl, SE19 . . . . .170 C7
Limerick Cl, SW12 . . . . .150 C7
Limerick Ms, N2 off Bedford Rd . .73 H3
Lime Rd, Rich. TW9
  off St. Mary's Gro 145 J4
Lime Row, Erith DA18
  off Northwood Pl 139 F3
Limerston St, SW10 . . . . .30 D5
Limes, The, W2 off Linden Gdns .108 D7
  Bromley BR2 . . . . .206 B2
Limes Av, E11 . . . . .79 H4
  N12 .57 F4
  NW7 .54 E6
  NW11 . . . . .72 B7
  SE20 . . . . .171 E7
  SW13 . . . . .147 F2
  Carshalton SM5 . . . . .199 J1
  Chigwell IG7 . . . . .65 G6
  Croydon CR0 . . . . .201 G3
Limes Av, The, N11 . . . . .58 B5
Limesdale Gdns, Edg. HA8 . . . . .70 C2
Limes Fld Rd, SW14
  off White Hart La 146/147 E3
Limesford Rd, SE15 . . . . .153 G4
Limes Gdns, SW18 . . . . .148 D6
Limes Gro, SE13 . . . . .154 C4
Limes Pl, Croy. CR0 . . . . .188 A7
Limes Rd, Beck. BR3 . . . . .190 B2
  Croydon CR0 . . . . .188 A6
Limes Row, Orp. BR6
  off Orchard Rd 206/207 E5
Limestone Wk, Erith DA18 . . . .138 D3
Lime St, E17 . . . . .77 H4
  EC3 .20 D4
Lime St Pas, EC3 . . . . .20 D4
Limes Wk, SE15 . . . . .153 E4
  W5 off Chestnut Gro 125 G2
Lime Ter, W7 off Manor Ct Rd . . .104 B7
Lime Tree Av, Esher KT10 . . . . .194 A1
  Thames Ditton KT7 . . . . .194 A1
Limetree Cl, SW2 . . . . .169 F1
Lime Tree Gro, Croy. CR0 . . . . .203 J3
Lime Tree Pl, Mitch. CR4 . . . . . .186 B1
Lime Tree Rd, Houns. TW5 . . . .143 H1
Limetree Ter, Well. DA16
  off Hook La 158 A3
Limetree Wk, SW17
  off Church La 168 A5
Lime Tree Wk, Bushey (Bushey Hth)
  WD23 . . . . .52 B1
  West Wickham BR4 . . . . .205 F4
Lime Wk, E15
  off Church St N 114/115 E1
Limewood Cl, E17 . . . . .77 J4
  W13 off St. Stephens Rd .104/105 E6
  Beckenham BR3 . . . . .190 C5
Limewood Ct, Ilf. IG4 . . . . .80 C5
Limewood Rd, Erith DA8 . . . . . .139 J7
Limpsfield Av, SW19 . . . . .166 A2
  Thornton Heath CR7 . . . . . . .187 F5
Linacre Cl, SE15 . . . . .153 E3
Linacre Ct, W6 . . . . .128 A5
Linacre Rd, NW2 . . . . .89 H6
Linberry Wk, SE8 . . . . .133 J4
Linchmere Rd, SE12 . . . . .155 F7
Lincoln Av, N14 . . . . .58 C3
  SW19 . . . . .166 A3
  Twickenham TW2 . . . . .161 H2
Lincoln Cl, SE25
  off Woodside Grn 188 D6
  Greenford UB6 . . . . .103 J1
  Harrow HA2 . . . . .67 F5
Lincoln Ct, N16 . . . . .76 A7
  Borehamwood WD6 . . . . .38 D5
Lincoln Cres, Enf. EN1 . . . . .44 B5
Lincoln Dr, Wat. WD19 . . . . .50 C3
Lincoln Gdns, Ilf. IG1 . . . . .80 B7
Lincoln Grn Rd, Orp. BR5 . . . . .193 J5
Lincoln Ms, NW6
  off Willesden La 108 C1
  SE21 . . . . .170 A1
Lincoln Rd, E7 . . . . .98 A6
  E13 .115 H4
  E18 off Grove Rd 79 G1
  N2 . . . . .73 H3
  SE25 . . . . .188 D3
  Enfield EN1, EN3 . . . . .44 D5
  Feltham TW13 . . . . .161 F3
  Harrow HA2 . . . . .67 F5
  Mitcham CR4 . . . . .186 E5
  New Malden KT3 . . . . .182 C3
  Sidcup DA14 . . . . .176 B5
  Wembley HA0 . . . . .87 G6
  Worcester Park KT4 . . . . . . .197 G1
Lincolns, The, NW7 . . . . .55 F3
★ Lincoln's Inn, WC2 . . . . .18 D3

Lincoln's Inn Flds, WC2 . . . . .18 C3
Lincoln St, E11 . . . . .96 E2
SW3 . . . . .31 J1
Lincoln Way, Enf. EN1 . . . . .44 E5
Lincombe Rd, Brom. BR1 . . . . . .173 F3
Lindal Cres, Enf. EN2 . . . . .43 E4
Lindales, The, N17
off Brantwood Rd 60 C6
Lindal Rd, SE4 . . . . .153 J5
Linden Av, NW10 . . . . .108 A2
Enfield EN1 . . . . .44 D1
Hounslow TW3 . . . . .143 H5
Ruislip HA4 . . . . .84 A1
Thornton Heath CR7 . . . . .187 H4
Wembley HA9 . . . . .87 J5
Linden Cl, N14 . . . . .42 C6
Ruislip HA4 . . . . .84 A1
Stanmore HA7 . . . . .52 E5
Thames Ditton KT7 . . . . .180 C7
Linden Ct, W12 . . . . .127 J1
Linden Cres, Grnf. UB6 . . . . .86 C6
Kingston upon Thames KT1 . .181 J2
Woodford Green IG8 . . . . .63 H6
Lindenfield, Chis. BR7 . . . . .192 E2
Linden Gdns, W2 . . . . .108 D7
W4 . . . . .126 D5
Enfield EN1 . . . . .44 D1
Linden Gro, SE15 . . . . .153 E3
SE26 . . . . .171 F6
New Malden KT3 . . . . .182 E3
Teddington TW11
off Waldegrave Rd 162 C5
Linden Lawns, Wem. HA9 . . . . . .87 J4
Linden Lea, N2 . . . . .73 F5
Linden Leas, W.Wick. BR4 . . . . .204 D2
Linden Ms, N1 . . . . .94 A5
W2 off Linden Gdns 108 D7
Linden Pas, W4
off Linden Gdns 126 D5
Linden Pl, Mitch. CR4 . . . . .185 H4
Linden Rd, E17 off High St 77 J5
N10 . . . . .74 B4
N11 . . . . .57 J2
N15 . . . . .75 J4
Hampton TW12 . . . . .161 G7
Lindens, The, N12 . . . . .57 F5
W4 off Hartington Rd 146 C1
Croydon (New Adgtn) CR0 . . .204 C6
Loughton IG10 . . . . .48 C5
Linden Wk, N19
off Hargrave Pk 92 C2
Linden Way, N14 . . . . .42 C6
Lindeth Cl, Stan. HA7 . . . . .52 E6
Lindfield Gdns, NW3 . . . . .91 E5
Lindfield Rd, W5 . . . . .105 F4
Croydon CR0 . . . . .188 C6
Lindfield St, E14 . . . . .114 A6
Lindhill Cl, Enf. EN3 . . . . .45 G1
Lindisfarne Rd, SW20 . . . . .165 G7
Dagenham RM8 . . . . .100 C3
Lindisfarne Way, E9 . . . . .95 H4
Lindley Est, SE15 . . . . .37 H7
Lindley Pl, Rich. TW9 . . . . .146 A1
Lindley Rd, E10 . . . . .96 B2
Lindley St, E1 . . . . .113 F5
Lindore Rd, SW11 . . . . .149 J4
Lindores Rd, Cars. SM5 . . . . . . .185 F7
Lindo St, SE15 off Selden Rd . . .153 F2
Lind Rd, Sutt. SM1 . . . . .199 F5
Lindrop St, SW6 . . . . .149 F2
Lindsay Cl, Chess. KT9 . . . . .195 H7
Staines (Stanw.) TW19 . . . . .140 A5
Lindsay Dr, Har. HA3 . . . . .69 H6
Lindsay Rd, Hmptn. (Hmptn H.)
TW12 . . . . .161 H4
Worcester Park KT4 . . . . .197 H2
Lindsay Sq, SW1 . . . . .33 J3
Lindsell St, SE10 . . . . .154 C1
Lindsey Cl, Brom. BR1 . . . . .192 A3
Mitcham CR4 . . . . .187 E4
Lindsey Gdns, Felt. TW14 . . . . . .141 G7
Lindsey Ms, N1 . . . . .93 J7
Lindsey Rd, Dag. RM8 . . . . .100 C4
Lindsey St, EC1 . . . . .19 H1
Lind St, SE8 . . . . .154 B2
Lindum Rd, Tedd. TW11 . . . . . . .163 F7
Lindway, SE27 . . . . .169 H5
Lindwood Cl, E6
off Northumberland Rd 116 B5
Linfield Cl, NW4 . . . . .71 J3
Linford Rd, E17 . . . . .78 C3
Linford St, SW8 . . . . .150 C1
Lingards Rd, SE13 . . . . .154 C4
Lingey Cl, Sid. DA15 . . . . .175 J2
Lingfield Av, Kings.T. KT1 . . . . . .181 H4
Lingfield Cl, Enf. EN1 . . . . .44 B6
Lingfield Cres, SE9 . . . . .157 G4
Lingfield Gdns, N9 . . . . .45 F7
Lingfield Rd, SW19 . . . . .166 A5
Worcester Park KT4 . . . . .197 J3
Lingham St, SW9 . . . . .151 E2
Lingholm Way, Barn. EN5 . . . . . . .40 A5
Lingmere Cl, Chig. IG7 . . . . .65 F2
Ling Rd, E16 . . . . .115 G5
Erith DA8 . . . . .139 J6
Lingrove Gdns, Buck.H. IG9
off Beech La 63 H2

Lings Coppice, SE21 . . . . .170 A2
Lingwell Rd, SW17 . . . . .167 H3
Lingwood Gdns, Islw. TW7 . . . . .124 B7
Lingwood Rd, E5 . . . . .76 D7
Linhope St, NW1 . . . . .7 J5
Link, The, SE9 . . . . .174 D3
W3 .106 B6
Enfield EN3 . . . . .45 H1
Northolt UB5 off Eastcote La . .85 F5
Pinner HA5 . . . . .66 C7
Wembley HA0
off Nathans Rd 87 F1
Linkfield, Brom. BR2 . . . . .191 G6
West Molesey KT8 . . . . .179 G3
Linkfield Rd, Islw. TW7 . . . . .144 C2
Link La, Wall. SM6 . . . . .200 D6
Linklea Cl, NW9 . . . . .55 E7
Link Rd, N11 . . . . .58 A4
Dagenham RM9 . . . . .119 H2
Feltham TW14 . . . . .141 J7
Wallington SM6 . . . . .200 A1
Links, The, E17 . . . . .77 H4
Links Av, Mord. SM4 . . . . .184 D4
Links Dr, N20 . . . . .56 D1
Links Gdns, SW16 . . . . .169 G7
Linkside, N12 . . . . .56 C6
Chigwell IG7 . . . . .65 F5
New Malden KT3 . . . . .183 E2
Linkside Cl, Enf. EN2 . . . . .43 F3
Linkside Gdns, Enf. EN2 . . . . .43 F3
Links Rd, NW2 . . . . .89 F2
SW17 . . . . .167 J6
W3 .106 A6
West Wickham BR4 . . . . .204 C1
Woodford Green IG8 . . . . .63 G5
Links Side, Enf. EN2 . . . . .43 G3
Link St, E9 . . . . .95 F6
Links Vw, N3 . . . . .56 C7
Links Vw Cl, Stan. HA7 . . . . .52 D6
Links Vw Rd, Croy. CR0 . . . . . . .204 A3
Hampton (Hmptn H.) TW12 . .161 J5
Linksway, NW4 . . . . .72 A2
Links Way, Beck. BR3 . . . . .190 A6
Links Yd, E1 . . . . .21 H1
Linkway, N4 . . . . .75 J7
SW20 . . . . .183 H3
Link Way, Brom. BR2 . . . . .192 B7
Linkway, Dag. RM8 . . . . .100 C4
Link Way, Pnr. HA5 . . . . .66 D3
Linkway, Rich. TW10 . . . . .163 E2
Linkway, The, Barn. EN5 . . . . .40 E6
Linkwood Wk, NW1
off Maiden La 92 D7
Linley Cres, Rom. RM7 . . . . .83 H3
Linley Rd, N17 . . . . .76 B2
★ Linley Sambourne Ho, W8 . .128 D2
Linnell Cl, NW11 . . . . .72 E6
Linnell Dr, NW11 . . . . .72 E6
Linnell Rd, N18 off Fairfield Rd . .60 D5
SE5 .152 B2
Linnet Cl, N9 . . . . .61 G1
SE28 . . . . .118 C7
Linnet Ms, SW12 . . . . .150 A7
Linnett Cl, E4 . . . . .62 C4
Linnet Ter, Ilf. IG5
off Tiptree Cres 80 D3
Linom Rd, SW4 . . . . .150 E4
Linscott Rd, E5 . . . . .95 F4
Linsdell Rd, Bark. IG11 . . . . .117 F1
Linsey St, SE16 . . . . .37 H1
Linslade Cl, Houns. TW4
off Frampton Rd 142/143 E5
Pinner HA5 . . . . .66 B3
Linstead St, NW6 . . . . .90 D7
Linstead Way, SW18 . . . . .148 B7
Linsted Ct, SE9 . . . . .157 H6
Linster Gro, Borwd. WD6 . . . . . . .38 C5
Lintaine Cl, W6 off Moylan Rd . .128 B6
Linthorpe Av, Wem. HA0 . . . . .87 F6
Linthorpe Rd, N16 . . . . .76 B7
Barnet EN4 . . . . .41 H3
Linton Cl, Mitch. CR4 . . . . .185 J7
Welling DA16
off Anthony Rd 158 B1
Linton Gdns, E6 . . . . .116 B6
Linton Gro, SE27 . . . . .169 H5
Linton Rd, Bark. IG11 . . . . .99 F7
Lintons, The, Bark. IG11 . . . . .99 F7
Linton St, N1 . . . . .111 J1
Lintott Ct, Stai. (Stanw.) TW19 . .140 A6
Linver Rd, SW6 . . . . .148 D2
Linwood Cl, SE5 . . . . .152 C2
Linwood Cres, Enf. EN1 . . . . .44 D1
Linwood Way, SE15 . . . . .37 F7
Linzee Rd, N8 . . . . .74 E4
Lion Av, Twick. TW1 off Lion Rd .162 C1
Lion Cl, SE4 . . . . .154 A6
Lion Ct, Borwd. WD6 . . . . .38 C1
Lionel Gdns, SE9 . . . . .156 A5
Lionel Ms, W10 off Telford Rd . .108 B5
Lionel Rd, SE9 . . . . .156 A5
Lionel Rd N, Brent. TW8 . . . . . . .125 H4
Lionel Rd S, Brent. TW8 . . . . . . .125 J5
Lion Gate Gdns, Rich. TW9 . . . .145 J3
Lion Gate Ms, SW18
off Merton Rd 148 D7
Lion Pk Av, Chess. KT9 . . . . .196 A4

Lion Plaza, EC2
off Threadneedle St 112 A6
Lion Rd, E6 . . . . .116 C5
N9 . . . . .60 D2
Bexleyheath DA6 . . . . .159 F4
Croydon CR0 . . . . .187 J5
Twickenham TW1 . . . . .162 C1
Lions Cl, SE9 . . . . .173 J3
Lion Way, Brent. TW8 . . . . .125 G7
Lion Wf Rd, Islw. TW7 . . . . .144 E3
Lion Yd, SW4 off Tremadoc Rd .150 D4
Liphook Cres, SE23 . . . . .153 F7
Liphook Rd, Wat. WD19 . . . . .50 D4
Lippitts Hill, Loug. (High Beach)
IG10 .47 E1
Lipton Cl, SE28 off Aisher Rd . . .118 C7
Lipton Rd, E1 off Bower St 113 G6
Lisbon Av, Twick. TW2 . . . . .161 J2
Lisbon Cl, E17 . . . . .77 J2
Lisburne Rd, NW3 . . . . .91 J4
Lisford St, SE15 . . . . .152 C1
Lisgar Ter, W14 . . . . .128 C4
Liskeard Cl, Chis. BR7 . . . . .175 F6
Liskeard Gdns, SE3 . . . . .155 G1
Lisle Cl, SW17 . . . . .168 B4
Lisle St, WC2 . . . . .17 J5
Lismore Circ, NW5 . . . . .92 A5
Lismore Cl, Islw. TW7 . . . . .144 D2
Lismore Rd, N17 . . . . .76 A3
South Croydon CR2 . . . . .202 B6
Lismore Wk, N1
off Clephane Rd 93 J6
Lissant Cl, Surb. KT6
off Lovelace Rd 181 G7
Lissenden Gdns, NW5 . . . . .92 A4
Lisson Grn Est, NW8 . . . . .7 G4
LISSON GROVE, NW8 . . . . .7 F6
Lisson Gro, NW1 . . . . .7 G5
NW8 . . . . .7 F4
Lisson St, NW1 . . . . .15 G1
Liss Way, SE15 . . . . .37 G7
Lister Cl, W3 . . . . .106 D5
Mitcham CR4 . . . . .185 H1
Lister Ct, NW9
off Pasteur Cl 70/71 E2
Lister Gdns, N18 . . . . .59 J5
Lister Ho, SE3 . . . . .135 E6
Lister Rd, E11 . . . . .97 E1
Lister Wk, SE28 off Haldane Rd .118 D7
Liston Rd, N17 . . . . .76 D1
SW4 . . . . .150 C3
Liston Way, Wdf.Grn. IG8
off Navestock Cres 63 J7
Listowel Cl, SW9 . . . . .35 F7
Listowel Rd, Dag. RM10 . . . . . . .101 G3
Listria Pk, N16 . . . . .94 B2
Litchfield Av, E15 . . . . .96 E6
Morden SM4 . . . . .184 C7
Litchfield Gdns, NW10 . . . . .89 G6
Litchfield Rd, Sutt. SM1 . . . . . . .199 F4
Litchfield St, WC2 . . . . .17 J5
Litchfield Way, NW11 . . . . .73 E5
Lithos Rd, NW3 . . . . .91 E6
Little Acre, Beck. BR3 . . . . .190 A3
Little Albany St, NW1 . . . . .8 E4
Little Argyll St, W1 . . . . .17 F4
Little Benty, West Dr. UB7 . . . . . .120 A5
Little Birches, Sid. DA15 . . . . . . .175 H2
Little Boltons, The, SW5 . . . . .30 B3
SW10 . . . . .30 B3
Little Bornes, SE21 . . . . .170 B4
Little Britain, EC1 . . . . .19 J3
Littlebrook Cl, Croy. CR0 . . . . . .189 G6
Little Brownings, SE23 . . . . .170 E2
Littlebury Rd, SW4 . . . . .150 D3
Little Bury St, N9 . . . . .60 A1
Little Cedars, N12
off Woodside Av 57 F4
Little Chester St, SW1 . . . . .24 C5
Little Cloisters, SW1
off Tufton St 130 C3
Little Coll La, EC4
off Upper Thames St 112 A7
Little Coll St, SW1 . . . . .26 A5
Littlecombe, SE7 . . . . .135 H6
Littlecombe Cl, SW15 . . . . .148 A6
Little Common, Stan. HA7 . . . . . . .52 D3
Littlecote Cl, SW19 . . . . .148 A7
Littlecote Pl, Pnr. HA5 . . . . .67 E1
Little Ct, W.Wick. BR4 . . . . .204 E2
Littlecroft, SE9 . . . . .156 D3
Littledale, SE2 . . . . .138 A6
Little Dean's Yd, SW1 . . . . .26 A5
Little Dimocks, SW12 . . . . .168 B2
Little Dorrit Ct, SE1 . . . . .28 A3
Little Dragons, Loug. IG10 . . . . . . .48 A4
LITTLE EALING, W5 . . . . .125 F4
Little Ealing La, W5 . . . . .125 F4
Little Edward St, NW1 . . . . .8 E3
Little Elms, Hayes UB3 . . . . .121 G7
Little Essex St, WC2 . . . . .18 E5
Little Ferry Rd, Twick. TW1
off Ferry Rd 162/163 E1
Littlefield Cl, N19
off Tufnell Pk Rd 92 C4
Kingston upon Thames KT1
off Fairfield W 181 H2

Littlefield Rd, Edg. HA8 . . . . .54 C7
Little Friday Rd, E4 . . . . .62 E2
Little Gearies, Ilf. IG6 . . . . .80 E4
Little George St, SW1 . . . . .26 A4
Little Grn, Grnf. UB6
off Perivale La 104 D3
Little Grn, Rich. TW9 . . . . .145 G4
Little Grn St, NW5
off College La 92 B4
Littlegrove, Barn. EN4 . . . . .41 H6
Little Halliards, Walt. KT12
off Felix Rd 178 A6
Little Heath, SE7 . . . . .136 B6
Romford (Chad.Hth) RM6 . . . .82 B4
Little Heath Rd, Bexh. DA7 . . . . .159 F1
Littleheath Rd, S.Croy. CR2 . . . .202 E7
★ Little Holland Ho, Cars.
SM5 .199 H7
LITTLE ILFORD, E12 . . . . .98 B5
Little Ilford La, E12 . . . . .98 C4
Littlejohn Rd, W7 . . . . .104 C6
Little Marlborough St, W1 . . . . . . .17 F4
Littlemead, Esher KT10 . . . . .194 A4
Littlemede, SE9 . . . . .174 C3
Littlemoor Rd, Ilf. IG1 . . . . .99 G3
Littlemore Rd, SE2 . . . . .138 A2
Little Moss La, Pnr. HA5 . . . . .67 E2
Little Newport St, WC2 . . . . .17 J5
Little New St, EC4 . . . . .19 F3
Little Orchard Cl, Pnr. HA5
off Barrow Pt La 66/67 E2
Little Oxhey La, Wat. WD19 . . . . .50 D5
Little Pk Dr, Felt. TW13 . . . . .160 D2
Little Pk Gdns, Enf. EN2 . . . . .43 J3
Little Plucketts Way, Buck.H. IG9 .63 J1
Little Portland St, W1 . . . . .17 F3
Little Queens Rd, Tedd. TW11 . . .162 C6
Little Redlands, Brom. BR1 . . . . .192 B2
Little Rd, Croy. CR0
off Lower Addiscombe Rd . .202 B1
Hayes UB3 . . . . .121 J2
Littlers Cl, SW19
off Runnymede 185 G1
Little Russell St, WC1 . . . . .18 A2
Little St. James's St, SW1 . . . . . .25 F2
Little St. Leonards, SW14 . . . . . .146 C3
Little Sanctuary, SW1 . . . . .25 J4
Little Smith St, SW1 . . . . .25 J5
Little Somerset St, E1 . . . . .21 F4
Littlestone Cl, Beck. BR3
off Abbey La 172 A6
Little Strand, NW9 . . . . .71 F2
Little Thrift, Orp. BR5 . . . . .193 F4
Little Titchfield St, W1 . . . . .17 F2
Littleton Av, E4 . . . . .63 F1
Littleton Cres, Har. HA1 . . . . .86 C2
Littleton Rd, Har. HA1 . . . . .86 C2
Littleton St, SW18 . . . . .167 F2
Little Trinity La, EC4 . . . . .20 A5
Little Turnstile, WC1 . . . . .18 C3
★ Little Venice (Waterbuses),
W2 . . . . .14 C1
Littlewood, SE13 . . . . .154 C5
Littlewood Cl, W13 . . . . .125 E3
Littleworth Av, Esher KT10 . . . . .194 A5
Littleworth Common Rd, Esher
KT10 . . . . .194 A3
Littleworth La, Esher KT10 . . . . .194 A4
Littleworth Pl, Esher KT10 . . . . .194 A4
Littleworth Rd, Esher KT10 . . . . .194 B4
Livermere Rd, E8 . . . . .112 C1
Liverpool Gro, SE17 . . . . .36 A4
Liverpool Rd, E10 . . . . .78 C6
E16 .115 E5
N1 . . . . .111 G2
N7 . . . . .93 G5
W5 .125 G2
Kingston upon Thames KT2 . .164 A7
Thornton Heath CR7 . . . . . . .187 J3
Liverpool St, EC2 . . . . .20 D2
Livesey Cl, Kings.T. KT1 . . . . . . .181 J3
★ Livesey Mus, SE15 . . . . .132 E6
Livesey Pl, SE15 . . . . .37 J5
Livingstone Ct, E10
off Matlock Rd 78 C6
Barnet EN5
off Christchurch La 40 B2
Livingstone Pl, E14 off Ferry St .134 C5
Livingstone Rd, E15 . . . . .114 C1
E17 . . . . .78 B6
N13 . . . . .59 E6
SW11 off Winstanley Rd 149 G3
Hounslow TW3 . . . . .143 J4
Southall UB1 . . . . .102 D7
Thornton Heath CR7 . . . . . . .187 J2
Livingstone Wk, SW11 . . . . .149 G3
Livonia St, W1 . . . . .17 G4
Livsey Cl, SE28 . . . . .137 F3
Lizard St, EC1 . . . . .12 A4
Lizban St, SE3 . . . . .135 H7
Llanelly Rd, NW2 . . . . .90 C2
Llanover Rd, SE18 . . . . .136 D6
Wembley HA9 . . . . .87 G3
Llanthony Rd, Mord. SM4 . . . . . .185 G6
Llanvanor Rd, NW2 . . . . .90 C2
Llewellyn St, SE16 . . . . .29 J4
Lloyd Av, SW16 . . . . .187 E1

Lloyd Baker St, WC1 . . . . .10 D4
Lloyd Ct, Pnr. HA5 . . . . .66 D5
Lloyd Pk Av, Croy. CR0 . . . . . .202 C4
Lloyd Rd, E6 . . . . .116 C1
E17 . . . . .77 G4
Dagenham RM9 . . . . .101 F6
Worcester Park KT4 . . . . . . .197 J3
Lloyd's Av, EC3 . . . . .21 E4
★ Lloyds of London, EC3 . . . . .20 D4
Lloyds Pl, SE3 . . . . .155 E2
Lloyd Sq, WC1 . . . . .10 E3
Lloyd's Row, EC1 . . . . .11 F4
Lloyd St, WC1 . . . . .10 E3
Lloyds Way, Beck. BR3 . . . . . . .189 H5
Loampit Hill, SE13 . . . . .154 A2
Loampit Vale, SE13 . . . . .154 B3
Loanda Cl, E8 off Clarissa St . .112 C1
Loats Rd, SW2 . . . . .150 E6
Lobelia Cl, E6 off Sorrel Gdns .116 B5
Locarno Rd, W3 . . . . .126 C1
Greenford UB6 . . . . .103 J4
Lochaber Rd, SE13 . . . . .154 E4
Lochaline St, W6 . . . . .127 J6
Lochan Cl, Hayes UB4 . . . . . . .102 E4
Lochinvar St, SW12 . . . . .150 B7
Lochmere Cl, Erith DA8 . . . . . .139 H6
Lochnagar St, E14 . . . . .114 C5
Lock Chase, SE3 . . . . .155 E3
Lock Cl, Sthl. UB2
off Navigator Dr 123 J2
Lockesfield Pl, E14 . . . . .134 B5
Lockesley Dr, Orp. BR5 . . . . . .193 J6
Lockesley Sq, Surb. KT6 . . . . .181 G6
Locket Rd, Har. HA3 . . . . .68 B3
Lockfield Av, Enf. EN3 . . . . .45 H2
Lockgate Cl, E9
off Lee Conservancy Rd 95 J5
Lockhart Cl, N7 . . . . .93 F6
Enfield EN3 off Derby Rd . .44/45 E5
Lockhart St, E3 . . . . .113 J4
Lockhurst St, E5 . . . . .95 G4
Lockie Pl, SE25 . . . . .188 D3
Lockier Wk, Wem. HA9 . . . . . . .87 G4
Lockington Rd, SW8 . . . . .150 B1
Lockmead Rd, N15 . . . . .76 D6
SE13 . . . . .154 C3
Lock Rd, Rich. TW10 . . . . .163 F4
Locks La, Mitch. CR4 . . . . .185 J1
Locksley Est, E14 . . . . .113 J6
Locksley St, E14 . . . . .113 J5
Locksmeade Rd, Rich. TW10 . .163 F4
Lockswood Cl, Barn. EN4 . . . . . .41 J4
Lockton St, W10
off Bramley Rd 108 A7
Lockwood Cl, SE26 . . . . .171 G4
Lockwood Ind Pk, N17 . . . . . . .76 E3
Lockwood Sq, SE16 . . . . .132 E3
Lockwood Way, E17 . . . . .77 G2
Chessington KT9 . . . . .196 A5
Lockyer Est, SE1 . . . . .28 C3
Lockyer St, SE1 . . . . .28 C4
Locomotive Dr, Felt. TW14 . . . .160 A1
Loddiges Rd, E9 . . . . .95 F7
Loder St, SE15 . . . . .153 F1
Lodge Av, SW14 . . . . .146 E3
Croydon CR0 . . . . .201 G3
Dagenham RM8, RM9 . . . . . .118 A1
Harrow HA3 . . . . .69 H4
Lodge Cl, N18 . . . . .59 J5
Edgware HA8 . . . . .53 J6
Isleworth TW7 . . . . .144 E1
Wallington SM6 . . . . .200 A1
Lodge Ct, Wem. HA0 . . . . .87 H5
Lodge Dr, N13 . . . . .59 G4
Lodge Gdns, Beck. BR3 . . . . . .189 J5
Lodge Hill, SE2 . . . . .138 B7
Ilford IG4 . . . . .80 B4
Welling DA16 . . . . .138 B7
Lodgehill Pk Cl, Har. HA2 . . . . . .85 H2
Lodge La, N12 . . . . .57 F5
Bexley DA5 . . . . .158 D6
Croydon (New Adgtn) CR0 . .204 A6
Lodge Pl, Sutt. SM1 . . . . .199 E5
Lodge Rd, NW4 . . . . .71 J4
NW8 .7 F4
Bromley BR1 . . . . .173 H7
Croydon CR0 . . . . .187 H6
Sutton SM1
off Throwley Way 198/199 E5
Wallington SM6 . . . . .200 B5
Lodge Vil, Wdf.Grn. IG8 . . . . . . .63 F7
Lodore Gdns, NW9 . . . . .70 E5
Lodore St, E14 . . . . .114 C6
Lofthouse Pl, Chess. KT9 . . . . .195 F6
Loftie St, SE16 . . . . .29 J4
Lofting Rd, N1 . . . . .93 F7
Loftus Rd, W12 . . . . .127 H1
Logan Cl, Enf. EN3 . . . . .45 G1
Hounslow TW4 . . . . .143 F3
Logan Ms, W8 . . . . .128 D4
Logan Pl, W8 . . . . .128 D4
Logan Rd, N9 . . . . .61 E2
Wembley HA9 . . . . .87 H2
Loggetts, The, SE21 . . . . .170 B2
Logs Hill, Brom. BR1 . . . . .174 B7
Chislehurst BR7 . . . . .174 B7
Logs Hill Cl, Chis. BR7 . . . . . . .192 B1

Lolesworth Cl, E1 . . . . .21 G2
Lollard St, SE11 . . . . .34 D1
Loman St, SE1 . . . . .27 H3
Lomas Cl, Croy. CR0 . . . . .204 C7
Lomas Dr, E8 . . . . .94 C7
Lomas St, E1 . . . . .21 J1
Lombard Av, Enf. EN3 . . . . .45 F1
Ilford IG3 . . . . .99 H1
Lombard Business Pk, SW19 . .185 F2
Lombard Ct, EC3 . . . . .20 C5
W3 off Crown St 126 B1
Lombard La, EC4 . . . . .19 F4
Lombard Rd, N11 . . . . .58 B5
SW11 . . . . .149 G2
SW19 . . . . .185 E2
Lombard St, EC3 . . . . .20 C4
Lombard Wall, SE7 . . . . .135 H3
Lombardy Cl, Ilf. IG6
off Hazel La 64/65 E7
Lombardy Pl, W2 . . . . .14 A6
Lombardy Retail Pk, Hayes
UB3 . . . . .102 B7
Lomond Cl, N15 . . . . .76 B4
Wembley HA0 . . . . .87 J7
Lomond Gdns, S.Croy. CR2 . . .203 H7
Lomond Gro, SE5 . . . . .36 B7
Loncroft Rd, SE5 . . . . .37 E5
Londesborough Rd, N16 . . . . . .94 B4
★ London Aquarium, SE1 . . . . .26 C3
★ London Brass Rubbing Cen,
St. Martin-in-the-Fields Ch,
WC2 .18 A6
London Br, EC4 . . . . .28 C1
SE1 .28 C1
London Br St, SE1 . . . . .28 B2
London Br Wk, SE1 . . . . .28 C1
★ London Broncos R.L.C. (share
Griffin Pk with Brentford F.C.),
Brent. TW8 . . . . .125 G6
★ London Butterfly Ho, Syon Pk,
Brent. TW8 . . . . .145 E1
★ London Canal Mus, The, N1
off New Wf Rd 10 B1
★ London Cen Mosque, NW8 . . .7 H4
★ London City Airport, E16 . . .136 B1
★ London Commodity Exchange,
E1 . . . . .21 G6
★ London Dungeon, SE1 . . . . . .28 C2
★ London Eye, SE1 . . . . .26 C3
London Flds, E8 . . . . .94 E7
London Flds E Side, E8 . . . . . . .94 E7
London Flds W Side, E8 . . . . . .94 D7
★ London Fire Brigade Mus,
SE1 .27 J3
★ London Heathrow Airport,
Houns. TW6 . . . . .140 E1
London La, E8 . . . . .95 E7
Bromley BR1 . . . . .173 F7
★ London Met Archives, EC1 . . .11 H5
London Ms, W2 . . . . .15 F4
★ London Palladium, W1 . . . . . .17 F4
★ London Peace Pagoda,
SW11 . . . . .32 A7
★ London Regatta Cen, E16 . . .116 A7
London Rd, E13 . . . . .115 G2
SE1 .27 G5
SE23 . . . . .170 D1
SW16 . . . . .187 F1
SW17 . . . . .185 J2
Barking IG11 . . . . .98 F7
Brentford TW8 . . . . .125 F7
Bromley BR1 . . . . .173 F7
Croydon CR0 . . . . .187 H7
Enfield EN2 . . . . .44 A3
Harrow HA1 . . . . .86 B2
Hounslow TW3 . . . . .143 J3
Isleworth TW7 . . . . .144 C2
Kingston upon Thames KT2 . .181 J2
Mitcham CR4 . . . . .185 J2
Mitcham (Bedd.Cor.) CR4 . . .186 A7
Morden SM4 . . . . .184 D5
Romford (Abridge) RM4 . . . . .49 J4
Romford (Chad.Hth) RM6,
RM7 . . . . .83 G6
Stanmore HA7 . . . . .53 F5
Sutton SM3 . . . . .198 A3
Thornton Heath CR7 . . . . . . .187 G5
Twickenham TW1 . . . . .144 D5
Wallington SM6 . . . . .200 B4
Wembley HA9 . . . . .87 H6
London Shop Pav, W1 . . . . . . .17 H6
★ London Silver Vaults, WC2 . .18 E2
London Stile, W4
off Wellesley Rd 126 A5
★ London Stone, EC4 . . . . .20 B5
London St, EC3 . . . . .20 E5
W2 . . . . .15 E4
★ London Transport Mus, WC2 .18 B5
London Wall, EC2 . . . . .20 A2
London Wall Bldgs, EC2 . . . . . .20 C2
★ London Wildlife Trust, NW1 .110 D1
★ London Zoo, NW1 . . . . .8 B1
Lonesome Way, SW16 . . . . . . .186 B1
Long Acre, WC2 . . . . .18 A5
Longacre Pl, Cars. SM5
off Beddington Gdns 200 A6
Longacre Rd, E17 . . . . .78 D1

Longbeach Rd, SW11 . . . . .149 J3
Longberrys, NW2 . . . . .90 C3
Longboat Row, Sthl. UB1 . . . . .103 F6
Longbridge Rd, Bark. IG11 . . . .99 F7
Dagenham RM8 . . . . .100 A4
Longbridge Way, SE13 . . . . . . .154 C5
Longcliffe Path, Wat. WD19
off Gosforth La 50 A3
Longcroft, SE9 . . . . .174 C3
Longcrofte Rd, Edg. HA8 . . . . . .53 G7
Longcroft Ri, Loug. IG10 . . . . . .48 D5
Long Deacon Rd, E4 . . . . .62 E1
LONG DITTON, Surb. KT10 . . .195 F1
Longdon Wd, Kes. BR2 . . . . . .206 B4
Longdown Rd, SE6 . . . . .172 A4
Long Dr, W3 . . . . .106 E6
Greenford UB6 . . . . .103 H1
Ruislip HA4 . . . . .84 D4
Long Elmes, Har. HA3 . . . . .67 H1
Longfellow Rd, E17 . . . . .77 J6
Worcester Park KT4 . . . . . . .197 G2
Longfellow Way, SE1 . . . . .37 G2
Long Fld, NW9 . . . . .55 E7
Longfield, Brom. BR1 . . . . .191 F1
Loughton IG10 . . . . .47 J5
Longfield Av, E17 . . . . .77 H4
NW7 .55 G7
W5 .105 F7
Wallington SM6 . . . . .200 A1
Wembley HA9 . . . . .87 H1
Longfield Cres, SE26 . . . . .171 F3
Longfield Dr, SW14 . . . . .146 B5
Mitcham CR4 . . . . .167 H7
Longfield Est, SE1 . . . . .37 G2
Longfield Rd, W5 . . . . .105 F7
Longfield St, SW18 . . . . .148 D7
Longfield Wk, W5 . . . . .105 F6
Longford Av, Felt. TW14 . . . . . .141 H6
Southall UB1 . . . . .103 G7
Longford Cl, Hmptn. (Hmptn H.)
TW12 . . . . .161 G4
Hayes UB4
off Longford Gdns 102 D7
Longford Ct, E5 off Pedro St . . .95 G4
NW4 .72 A4
Epsom KT19 . . . . .196 C4
Longford Gdns, Hayes UB4 . . .102 D7
Sutton SM1 . . . . .199 F3
Longford Rd, Twick. TW2 . . . . .161 G1
Longford St, NW1 . . . . .8 E5
Longford Wk, SW2
off Papworth Way 151 G7
Long Grn, Chig. IG7 . . . . .65 H4
Longhayes Av, Rom. RM6 . . . . .82 D4
Longhayes Ct, Rom. RM6
off Longhayes Av 82 D4
Longheath Gdns, Croy. CR0 . . .189 F5
Longhedge Ho, SE26 . . . . .170 C4
Long Hedges, Houns. TW3 . . . .143 G1
Longhedge St, SW11 . . . . .150 A2
Longhill Rd, SE6 . . . . .172 D2
Longhook Gdns, Nthlt. UB5 . . .102 A2
Longhope Cl, SE15 . . . . .37 E6
Longhurst Rd, SE13 . . . . .154 D5
Croydon CR0 . . . . .189 E6
Longland Ct, SE1 . . . . .37 H3
Longland Dr, N20 . . . . .56 E3
LONGLANDS, Chis. BR7 . . . . .175 F3
Longlands Ct, W11
off Portobello Rd 108 C7
Mitcham CR4
off Summerhill Way 186 A1
Longlands Pk Cres, Sid. DA15 .175 H3
Longlands Rd, Sid. DA15 . . . . .175 H3
Long La, EC1 . . . . .19 H1
N2 . . . . .73 F2
N3 . . . . .56 E7
SE1 .28 B4
Bexleyheath DA7 . . . . .138 D7
Croydon CR0 . . . . .189 F5
Staines (Stanw.) TW19 . . . . .140 C7
Longleat Rd, Enf. EN1 . . . . .44 B5
Longleat Way, Felt. TW14 . . . . .141 G7
Longleigh La, SE2 . . . . .138 C6
Bexleyheath DA7 . . . . .138 C6
Longlents Ho, NW10 . . . . .106 D1
Longley Av, Wem. HA0 . . . . . . .105 J1
Longley Rd, SW17 . . . . .167 H5
Croydon CR0 . . . . .187 H7
Harrow HA1 . . . . .67 J5
Long Leys, E4 . . . . .62 B6
Longley St, SE1 . . . . .37 H2
Longley Way, NW2 . . . . .89 J3
Long Mark Rd, E16
off Fulmer Rd 116 A5
Longmarsh La, SE28
off Hill Vw Dr 137 H1
Long Mead, NW9 . . . . .71 F1
Longmead, Chis. BR7 . . . . .192 D2
Longmead Dr, Sid. DA14 . . . . .176 D2
Long Meadow, NW5
off Torriano Av 92 D5
Long Meadow Cl, W.Wick. BR4 .190 C7
Longmeadow Rd, Sid. DA15 . . .175 H1
Longmead Rd, SW17 . . . . .167 J5
Thames Ditton KT7 . . . . .180 B7
Longmoore St, SW1 . . . . .33 F2

Longmoor Pt, SW15
off Norley Vale 165 H1
Longmore Av, Barn. EN4, EN5 . .41 F6
Longnor Rd, E1 . . . . .113 G3
Long Pond Rd, SE3 . . . . .155 E1
Long Reach Ct, Bark. IG11 . . . .117 G2
Longreach Rd, Bark. IG11 . . . . .117 J4
Longridge La, Sthl. UB1 . . . . . .103 H7
Longridge Rd, SW5 . . . . .128 D4
Long Rd, SW4 . . . . .150 B4
Long's Ct, WC2 . . . . .17 H5
Longs Ct, Rich. TW9
off Crown Ter 145 J4
Longshaw Rd, E4 . . . . .62 D3
Longshore, SE8 . . . . .133 J4
Longstaff Cres, SW18 . . . . .148 D6
Longstaff Rd, SW18 . . . . .148 D6
Longstone Av, NW10 . . . . .89 F7
Longstone Rd, SW17 . . . . .168 B5
Long St, E2 . . . . .13 F3
Longthornton Rd, SW16 . . . . . .186 C2
Longthorpe Ct, W6
off Goldhawk Rd 127 G3
Longton Av, SE26 . . . . .170 D4
Longton Gro, SE26 . . . . .170 E4
Longville Rd, SE11 . . . . .35 G1
Long Wk, SE1 . . . . .28 E5
SE18 . . . . .136 E6
SW13 . . . . .147 E2
New Malden KT3 . . . . .182 C3
Longwalk Rd, Uxb. UB11 . . . . .121 E1
Longwood Dr, SW15 . . . . .147 G6
Longwood Gdns, Ilf. IG5, IG6 . . .80 C4
Longworth Cl, SE28 . . . . .118 D6
Long Yd, WC1 . . . . .10 C6
Lonsdale Av, E6 . . . . .116 A3
Romford RM7 . . . . .83 J6
Wembley HA9 . . . . .87 H5
Lonsdale Cl, E6 off Lonsdale Av .116 A3
SE9 .174 A3
Edgware HA8 off Orchard Dr . .53 J5
Pinner HA5 . . . . .51 E7
Lonsdale Cres, Ilf. IG2 . . . . .80 E6
Lonsdale Dr, Enf. EN2 . . . . .43 E5
Lonsdale Gdns, Th.Hth. CR7 . . .187 F4
Lonsdale Ms, Rich. TW9
off Elizabeth Cotts 146 A1
Lonsdale Pl, N1
off Barnsbury St 93 G7
Lonsdale Rd, E11 . . . . .79 F7
NW6 . . . . .108 C2
SE25 . . . . .188 E4
SW13 . . . . .127 G6
W4 .127 F4
W11 . . . . .108 C6
Bexleyheath DA7 . . . . .159 F2
Southall UB2 . . . . .122 D3
Lonsdale Sq, N1 . . . . .93 G7
Loobert Rd, N15 . . . . .76 B3
Looe Gdns, Ilf. IG6 . . . . .81 E3
Loop Rd, Chis. BR7 . . . . .175 F6
Lopen Rd, N18 . . . . .60 B4
Loraine Cl, Enf. EN3 . . . . .45 F5
Loraine Rd, N7 . . . . .93 F4
W4 .126 B6
Lord Amory Way, E14 . . . . .134 C2
Lord Av, Ilf. IG5 . . . . .80 C4
Lord Chancellor Wk, Kings.T.
KT2 .182 C1
Lordell Pl, SW19 . . . . .165 J6
Lorden Wk, E2 . . . . .13 H4
Lord Gdns, Ilf. IG5 . . . . .80 B4
Lord Hills Br, W2 . . . . .14 B2
Lord Hills Rd, W2 . . . . .14 B1
Lord Holland La, SW9
off St. Lawrence Way 151 G1
Lord Knyvett Cl, Stai. (Stanw.)
TW19 . . . . .140 A6
Lord Knyvetts Ct, Stai. (Stanw.) TW19
off De Havilland Way 140 B6
Lord Napier Pl, W6
off Upper Mall 127 G5
Lord N St, SW1 . . . . .26 A5
Lord Roberts Ms, SW6
off Moore Pk Rd 128/129 E7
Lord Roberts Ter, SE18 . . . . . . .136 D5
★ Lord's, Middlesex County Cricket
Club & Mus, NW8 . . . . .7 F3
Lord's Cl, SE21 . . . . .169 J2
Lords Cl, Felt. TW13 . . . . .161 E2
Lordship Gro, N16 . . . . .94 A2
Lordship La, N17 . . . . .75 J1
N22 .75 G2
SE22 . . . . .152 C6
Lordship La Est, SE22 . . . . . . .170 D1
Lordship Pk, N16 . . . . .93 J2
Lordship Pk Ms, N16
off Allerton Rd 93 J2
Lordship Pl, SW3 . . . . .31 G6
Lordship Rd, N16 . . . . .94 A2
Northolt UB5 . . . . .84 E7
Lordship Ter, N16 . . . . .94 A2
Lordsmead Rd, N17 . . . . .76 B1
Lord St, E16 . . . . .136 B1
Lord's Vw, NW8 . . . . .7 F4
Lord Warwick St, SE18 . . . . . . .136 C3

Lorenzo St, WC1 . . . .**10** C3
Loretto Gdns, Har. HA3 . . . . . .**69** H4
Lorian Cl, N12 . . . .**56** E4
Loring Rd, N20 . . . .**57** H2
  SE14 off St. James's **153** H1
  Isleworth TW7 . . . .**144** C2
Loris Rd, W6 . . . .**127** J3
Lorn Ct, SW9 . . . .**151** G2
Lorne Av, Croy. CR0 . . . .**189** G7
Lorne Cl, NW8 . . . .**7** H4
Lorne Gdns, E11 . . . .**79** J4
  W11 . . . .**128** A2
  Croydon CR0 . . . .**189** G7
Lorne Rd, E7 . . . .**97** H4
  E17 . . . .**78** A5
  N4 . . . .**93** F1
  Harrow HA3 . . . .**68** C2
  Richmond TW10
    off Albert Rd **145** J5
Lorn Rd, SW9 . . . .**151** F2
Lorraine Pk, Har. HA3 . . . .**52** B7
Lorrimore Rd, SE17 . . . .**35** H5
Lorrimore Sq, SE17 . . . .**35** H5
Loseberry Rd, Esher (Clay.)
  KT10 . . . .**194** A5
Lothair Rd, W5 . . . .**125** G2
Lothair Rd N, N4 . . . .**75** H6
Lothair Rd S, N4 . . . .**75** G7
Lothbury, EC2 . . . .**20** B3
Lothian Av, Hayes UB4 . . . .**102** B5
Lothian Cl, Wem. HA0 . . . .**86** D4
Lothian Rd, SW9 . . . .**151** H1
Lothrop St, W10 . . . .**108** B3
Lots Rd, SW10 . . . .**129** F7
Lotus Rd, SE21 . . . .**169** J3
Loubet St, SW17 . . . .**167** J6
Loudoun Av, Ilf. IG6 . . . .**81** E5
Loudoun Rd, NW8 . . . .**6** D1
Loudoun Rd Ms, NW8
  off Loudoun Rd **109** F1
Loudwater Cl, Sun. TW16 . . . . .**178** A4
Loudwater Rd, Sun. TW16 . . . . .**178** A4
Loughborough Est, SW9
  off Loughborough Rd **151** H2
Loughborough Pk, SW9 . . . .**151** H4
Loughborough Rd, SW9 . . . .**151** G2
Loughborough St, SE11 . . . .**34** D3
Lough Rd, N7 . . . .**93** F6
LOUGHTON, IG10 . . . .**48** C5
Loughton Way, Buck.H. IG9 . . . .**64** A1
Louisa Cl, E9 off Wetherell Rd . .**113** G1
Louisa Gdns, E1 off Louisa St . . .**113** G4
Louisa Ho, SW15 . . . .**147** E4
Louisa St, E1 . . . .**113** G4
Louise Aumonier Wk, N19
  off Hillrise Rd **74/75** E7
Louise Bennett Cl, SE24
  off Shakespeare Rd **151** H4
Louise Ct, E11
  off Grosvenor Rd **79** H5
Louise Rd, E15 . . . .**97** E6
Louis Gdns, Chis. BR7 . . . .**174** C4
Louis Ms, N10 . . . .**74** B1
Louisville Rd, SW17 . . . .**168** A3
Louvaine Rd, SW11 . . . .**149** G4
Lovage App, E6 . . . .**116** B5
Lovat Cl, NW2 . . . .**89** F3
Lovat La, EC3 . . . .**20** D6
Lovatt Cl, Edg. HA8 . . . .**54** B6
Lovatt Dr, Ruis. HA4 . . . .**66** A5
Lovatt Wk, Houns. TW5
  off Cranford La **122/123** E7
Loveday Rd, W13 . . . .**125** E1
Lovegrove St, SE1 . . . .**37** J4
Lovegrove Wk, E14 . . . .**134** C1
Lovekyn Cl, Kings.T. KT2
  off Queen Elizabeth Rd **181** J2
Lovelace Av, Brom. BR2 . . . .**192** D6
Lovelace Gdns, Bark. IG11 . . . . .**100** A4
  Surbiton KT6 . . . .**181** G7
Lovelace Grn, SE9 . . . .**156** C3
Lovelace Rd, SE21 . . . .**169** J2
  Barnet EN4 . . . .**41** H7
  Surbiton KT6 . . . .**181** F7
Love La, EC2 . . . .**20** A3
  N17 . . . .**60** C7
  SE18 . . . .**136** E4
  SE25 . . . .**189** E3
  Bexley DA5 . . . .**159** F4
  Mitcham CR4 . . . .**185** H3
  Morden SM4 . . . .**184** D7
  Pinner HA5 . . . .**66** E3
  Surbiton KT6 . . . .**195** G2
  Sutton SM3 . . . .**198** B5
  Woodford Green IG8 . . . .**64** C6
Lovel Av, Well. DA16 . . . .**158** A2
Lovelinch Cl, SE15 . . . .**133** F6
Lovell Ho, E8 . . . .**112** D1
Lovell Pl, SE16
  off Ropemaker Rd **133** H3
Lovell Rd, Rich. TW10 . . . .**163** F3
  Southall UB1 . . . .**103** H6
Loveridge Ms, NW6
  off Loveridge Rd **90** C6
Loveridge Rd, NW6 . . . .**90** C6
Lovers Wk, N3 . . . .**56** D7
  NW7 . . . .**56** C6

Lovers Wk, SE10 . . . .**134** E6
Lover's Wk, W1 . . . .**24** H1
Lovett Dr, Cars. SM5 . . . .**185** F7
Lovett's Pl, SW18
  off Old York Rd **148/149** E4
Lovett Way, NW10 . . . .**88** C5
Love Wk, SE5 . . . .**152** A2
Lovibonds Av, Orp. BR6 . . . .**207** E4
Lowbrook Rd, Ilf. IG1 . . . .**99** E5
Low Cross Wd La, SE21 . . . . . .**170** C3
Lowden Rd, N9 . . . .**61** E1
  SE24 . . . .**151** H4
  Southall UB1 . . . .**102** F7
Lowe Av, E16 . . . .**115** G5
Lowell St, E14 . . . .**113** H6
LOWER ADDISCOMBE RD, Croy.
  CR0 . . . .**202** B1
Lower Addison Rd, W14 . . . .**128** B2
Lower Alderton Hall La, Loug.
  IG10 . . . .**48** D5
Lower Belgrave St, SW1 . . . .**24** D6
Lower Boston Rd, W7 . . . .**124** B1
Lower Broad St, Dag. RM10 . . . .**119** G1
Lower Camden, Chis. BR7 . . . . .**174** C7
Lower Ch St, Croy. CR0
  off Waddon New Rd **201** H2
LOWER CLAPTON, E5 . . . .**95** G4
Lower Clapton Rd, E5 . . . .**95** E5
Lower Clarendon Wk, W11
  off Lancaster Rd **108** B6
Lower Common S, SW15 . . . . . .**147** H3
Lower Coombe St, Croy. CR0 . . .**201** J4
Lower Downs Rd, SW20 . . . . . .**184** A1
Lower Drayton Pl, Croy. CR0
  off Drayton Rd **201** H2
LOWER EDMONTON, N9 . . . .**60** C1
Lower George St, Rich. TW9
  off George St **145** G5
Lower Gravel Rd, Brom. BR2 . . .**206** B1
Lower Grn Gdns, Wor.Pk. KT4 . .**197** G1
Lower Grn W, Mitch. CR4 . . . . . .**185** H3
Lower Grosvenor Pl, SW1 . . . . . .**24** D5
Lower Gro Rd, Rich. TW10 . . . . .**145** J6
Lower Hall La, E4 . . . .**61** H1
Lower Hampton Rd, Sun. TW16 .**178** C3
Lower Ham Rd, Kings.T. KT2 . . .**163** G6
LOWER HOLLOWAY, N7 . . . .**93** F5
Lower James St, W1 . . . .**17** G5
Lower John St, W1 . . . .**17** G5
Lower Kenwood Av, Enf. EN2 . . .**42** D5
Lower Kings Rd, Kings.T. KT2 . . .**163** H7
Lower Lea Crossing, E14 . . . . . .**114** E7
  E16 . . . .**114** E7
Lower Maidstone Rd, N11
  off Telford Rd **58** C6
Lower Mall, W6 . . . .**127** H5
Lower Mardyke Av, Rain. RM13 .**119** J2
Lower Marsh, SE1 . . . .**26** E4
Lower Marsh La, Kings.T. KT1 . .**181** J4
Lower Merton Ri, NW3 . . . .**91** H7
Lower Morden La, Mord. SM4 . .**183** J6
Lower Mortlake Rd, Rich. TW9 . .**145** H4
Lower Pk Rd, N11 . . . .**58** C5
  Belvedere DA17 . . . .**139** G3
  Loughton IG10 . . . .**48** A5
Lower Queens Rd, Buck.H. IG9 . .**64** A2
Lower Richmond Rd, SW14 . . . .**146** B3
  SW15 . . . .**147** J3
  Richmond TW9 . . . .**146** A3
Lower Rd, SE8 . . . .**133** F3
  SE16 . . . .**133** F3
  Belvedere DA17 . . . .**139** G3
  Harrow HA2 . . . .**86** A2
  Loughton IG10 . . . .**48** D2
  Sutton SM1 . . . .**199** F4
Lower Robert St, WC2
  off John Adam St **110/111** E7
Lower Sand Hills, T.Ditt. KT7 . . .**181** F7
Lower Sloane St, SW1 . . . .**32** B2
Lower Sq, Islw. TW7 . . . .**144** E3
Lower Strand, NW9 . . . .**71** F2
Lower Sunbury Rd, Hmptn.
  TW12 . . . .**179** F2
LOWER SYDENHAM, SE26 . . . . .**171** G4
Lower Sydenham Ind Est, SE26 .**171** J5
Lower Tail, Wat. WD19 . . . .**51** E3
Lower Talbot Wk, W11
  off Lancaster Rd **108** B6
Lower Teddington Rd, Kings.T.
  KT1 . . . .**181** G1
Lower Ter, NW3 . . . .**91** F3
Lower Thames St, EC3 . . . .**20** C6
Lower Wd Rd, Esher (Clay.)
  KT10 . . . .**194** D6
Lowestoft Cl, E5
  off Theydon Rd **95** F2
Lowestoft Ms, E16 . . . .**137** E2
Loweswater Cl, Wem. HA9 . . . . .**87** G2
Lowfield Rd, NW6 . . . .**90** D7
  W3 . . . .**106** C6
Low Hall Cl, E4 . . . .**46** A7
Low Hall La, E17 . . . .**77** H6
Lowick Rd, Har. HA1 . . . .**68** B4
Lowlands Dr, Stai. (Stanw.)
  TW19 . . . .**140** A5
Lowlands Gdns, Rom. RM7 . . . . .**83** H6
Lowlands Rd, Har. HA1 . . . .**68** B7

Lowlands Rd, Pnr. HA5 . . . .**66** C7
Lowman Rd, N7 . . . .**93** F4
Lowndes Cl, SW1 . . . .**24** C6
Lowndes Ct, W1 . . . .**17** F4
  Bromley BR1 off Queens Rd .**191** G2
Lowndes Pl, SW1 . . . .**24** B6
Lowndes Sq, SW1 . . . .**24** A4
Lowndes St, SW1 . . . .**24** A5
Lowood Ct, SE19 . . . .**170** C5
Lowood St, E1
  off Dellow St **112/113** E7
Lowry Cres, Mitch. CR4 . . . .**185** H2
Lowry Rd, Dag. RM8 . . . .**100** B4
Lowshoe La, Rom. RM5 . . . .**83** H1
Lowther Dr, Enf. EN2 . . . .**42** E4
Lowther Gdns, SW7 . . . .**23** F4
Lowther Hill, SE23 . . . .**153** H7
Lowther Rd, E17 . . . .**77** H2
  N7 off Mackenzie Rd **93** G5
  SW13 . . . .**147** F1
  Kingston upon Thames KT2 . .**181** J1
  Stanmore HA7 . . . .**69** J3
Lowth Rd, SE5 . . . .**151** J2
LOXFORD, Ilf. IG1 . . . .**99** F5
Loxford Av, E6 . . . .**116** A2
Loxford La, Ilf. IG1, IG3 . . . .**99** F5
Loxford Rd, Bark. IG11 . . . .**99** E6
Loxford Ter, Bark. IG11
  off Fanshawe Av **99** F6
Loxham Rd, E4 . . . .**62** A7
Loxham St, WC1 . . . .**10** B4
Loxley Cl, SE26 . . . .**171** G5
Loxley Rd, SW18 . . . .**167** G1
  Hampton TW12 . . . .**161** F4
Loxton Rd, SE23 . . . .**171** G1
Loxwood Rd, N17 . . . .**76** B3
Lubbock Rd, Chis. BR7 . . . .**174** C7
Lubbock St, SE14 . . . .**133** F7
Lucan Pl, SW3 . . . .**31** G2
Lucan Rd, Barn. EN5 . . . .**40** B3
Lucas Av, E13 . . . .**115** H1
  Harrow HA2 . . . .**85** G2
Lucas Cl, NW10 off Pound La . . .**89** G7
Lucas Ct, Har. HA2 . . . .**85** G1
Lucas Gdns, N2 . . . .**73** F2
Lucas Rd, SE20 . . . .**171** F6
Lucas Sq, NW11
  off Hampstead Way **72** D6
Lucas St, SE8 . . . .**154** A1
Lucerne Cl, N13 . . . .**58** E4
Lucerne Ct, Erith DA18
  off Middle Way **138/139** E3
Lucerne Gro, E17 . . . .**78** D4
Lucerne Ms, W8
  off Kensington Mall **128** D1
Lucerne Rd, N5 . . . .**93** H4
  Orpington BR6 . . . .**207** J1
  Thornton Heath CR7 . . . .**187** H5
Lucey Rd, SE16 . . . .**29** H6
Lucey Way, SE16 . . . .**29** J6
Lucien Rd, SW17 . . . .**168** A4
  SW19 . . . .**166** D2
Lucknow St, SE18 . . . .**137** H7
Lucorn Cl, SE12 . . . .**155** F6
Lucton Ms, Loug. IG10 . . . .**48** E4
Luctons Av, Buck.H. IG9 . . . .**63** J1
Lucy Cres, W3 . . . .**106** C5
Lucy Gdns, Dag. RM8
  off Grafton Rd **100/101** E3
Luddesdon Rd, Erith DA8 . . . . . .**139** G7
Ludford Cl, NW9 . . . .**70** E2
  Croydon CR0
    off Warrington Rd **201** H4
Ludgate Bdy, EC4 . . . .**19** G4
Ludgate Circ, EC4 . . . .**19** G4
Ludgate Hill, EC4 . . . .**19** G4
Ludgate Sq, EC4 . . . .**19** H4
Ludham, SE28
  off Rollesby Way **118** C6
  Ilford IG6 . . . .**80** E1
Ludlow Cl, Brom. BR2
  off Aylesbury Rd **191** G3
  Harrow HA2 . . . .**85** F4
Ludlow Mead, Wat. WD19 . . . . . .**50** B3
Ludlow Rd, W5 . . . .**105** F4
  Feltham TW13 . . . .**160** A4
Ludlow St, EC1 . . . .**11** J5
Ludlow Way, N2 . . . .**73** F4
Ludovick Wk, SW15 . . . .**147** E4
Ludwick Ms, SE14 . . . .**133** H7
Luffield Rd, SE2 . . . .**138** B3
Luffman Rd, SE12 . . . .**173** H3
Lugard Rd, SE15 . . . .**153** E2
Lugg App, E12 . . . .**98** D3
Luke Ho, E1 . . . .**113** E6
Luke St, EC2 . . . .**12** D5
Lukin Cres, E4 . . . .**62** D3
Lukin St, E1 . . . .**113** F6
Lukintone Cl, Loug. IG10 . . . .**48** B6
Lullingstone Cl, Orp. BR5
  off Lullingstone Cres **176** B7
Lullingstone Cres, Orp. BR5 . . . .**176** A7
Lullingstone La, SE13 . . . .**154** D7
Lullingstone Rd, Belv. DA17 . . . .**139** F6
Lullington Garth, N12 . . . .**56** C5
  Borehamwood WD6 . . . .**38** B5
  Bromley BR1 . . . .**173** F7

Lullington Rd, SE20 . . . .**170** D7
  Dagenham RM9 . . . .**100** E7
Lulot Gdns, N19 . . . .**92** B2
Lulworth, SE17 . . . .**36** B3
Lulworth Av, Houns. TW5 . . . . . .**123** H7
  Wembley HA9 . . . .**69** F7
Lulworth Cl, Har. HA2 . . . .**85** F3
Lulworth Cres, Mitch. CR4 . . . . .**185** H2
Lulworth Dr, Pnr. HA5 . . . .**66** D7
Lulworth Gdns, Har. HA2 . . . .**85** E2
Lulworth Rd, SE9 . . . .**174** B2
  SE15 . . . .**153** E2
  Welling DA16 . . . .**157** J2
Lulworth Waye, Hayes UB4 . . . .**102** C6
Lumen Rd, Wem. HA9 . . . .**87** G2
Lumiere Ct, SW17 . . . .**168** A2
Lumley Cl, Belv. DA17 . . . .**139** G6
Lumley Ct, WC2 . . . .**18** B6
Lumley Gdns, Sutt. SM3 . . . . . .**198** B5
Lumley Rd, Sutt. SM3 . . . .**198** B6
Lumley St, W1 . . . .**16** C4
Luna Rd, Th.Hth. CR7 . . . .**187** J3
Lundin Wk, Wat. WD19
  off Woodhall La **50** D4
Lundy Dr, Hayes UB3 . . . .**121** H4
Lundy Wk, N1 off Clephane Rd . .**93** J6
Lunham Rd, SE19 . . . .**170** B6
Lupin Cl, SW2 off Palace Rd **169** H2
  Croydon CR0
    off Primrose La **203** G1
  West Drayton UB7
    off Magnolia St **120** A5
Lupin Cres, Ilf. IG1
  off Bluebell Way **98/99** E5
Lupino Ct, SE11 . . . .**34** D2
Lupton Cl, SE12 . . . .**173** H3
Lupton St, NW5 . . . .**92** C4
Lupus St, SW1 . . . .**33** G4
Luralda Gdns, E14
  off Saunders Ness Rd **134** C5
Lurgan Av, W6 . . . .**128** A6
Lurline Gdns, SW11 . . . .**150** A1
Luscombe Ct, Brom. BR2 . . . . . .**190** E2
Luscombe Way, SW8 . . . .**34** A7
Lushes Ct, Loug. IG10
  off Lushes Rd **48/49** E5
Lushes Rd, Loug. IG10 . . . .**49** E5
Lushington Rd, NW10 . . . .**107** H2
  SE6 . . . .**172** B5
Lushington Ter, E8
  off Wayland Av **94** D5
Luther Cl, Edg. HA8 . . . .**54** C2
Luther King Cl, E17 . . . .**77** H6
Luther Ms, Tedd. TW11
  off Luther Rd **162** C5
Luther Rd, Tedd. TW11 . . . .**162** C5
Luton Pl, SE10 . . . .**134** C7
Luton Rd, E17 . . . .**77** J3
  Sidcup DA14 . . . .**176** C3
Luton St, NW8 . . . .**7** F6
Lutton Ter, NW3 off Flask Wk . . .**91** G4
Luttrell Av, SW15 . . . .**147** H5
Lutwyche Rd, SE6 . . . .**171** J2
Luxborough La, Chig. IG7 . . . . . .**64** B3
Luxborough St, W1 . . . .**16** B1
Luxembourg Ms, E15
  off Leytonstone Rd **96** E5
Luxemburg Gdns, W6 . . . .**128** A4
Luxfield Rd, SE9 . . . .**174** B1
Luxford St, SE16 . . . .**133** G4
Luxmore St, SE4 . . . .**153** J1
Luxor St, SE5 . . . .**151** J3
Lyall Av, SE21 . . . .**170** B3
Lyall Ms, SW1 . . . .**24** B6
Lyall Ms W, SW1 . . . .**24** B6
Lyall St, SW1 . . . .**24** B6
Lyal Rd, E3 . . . .**113** H2
Lycée, The, SE11
  off Stannary St **131** G6
Lycett Pl, W12 off Becklow Rd . .**127** G2
Lyconby Gdns, Croy. CR0 . . . . .**189** H7
Lydd Cl, Sid. DA14 . . . .**175** H3
Lydden Ct, SE9 . . . .**157** H6
Lydden Gro, SW18 . . . .**148** E7
Lydden Rd, SW18 . . . .**148** E7
Lydd Rd, Bexh. DA7 . . . .**139** F7
Lydeard Rd, E6 . . . .**98** C7
Lydford Cl, N16 off Pellerin Rd . . .**94** B5
Lydford Rd, N15 . . . .**76** A5
  NW2 . . . .**90** A6
  W9 . . . .**108** C4
Lydhurst Av, SW2 . . . .**169** F2
Lydney Cl, SE15 . . . .**36** E7
  SW19 off Princes Way **166** B2
Lydon Rd, SW4 . . . .**150** C3
Lydstep Rd, Chis. BR7 . . . .**174** D4
Lyford Rd, SW18 . . . .**149** G7
Lygon Pl, SW1 . . . .**24** D6
Lyham Cl, SW2 . . . .**151** E6
Lyham Rd, SW2 . . . .**150** E5
Lyle Cl, Mitch. CR4 . . . .**186** A7
Lyme Fm Rd, SE12 . . . .**155** G4
Lyme Gro, E9
  off St. Thomas's Sq **95** F7
Lymer Av, SE19 . . . .**170** C5
Lyme Rd, Well. DA16 . . . .**158** B1
Lymescote Gdns, Sutt. SM1 . . .**198** D2

Lyme St, NW1 **92** C7
Lyme Ter, NW1
off Royal Coll St **92** C7
Lyminge Cl, Sid. DA14 **175** J4
Lyminge Gdns, SW18 **167** H1
Lymington Av, N22 **75** G2
Lymington Cl, E6
off Valiant Way **116** C5
SW16 **186** D2
Lymington Gdns, Epsom KT19 **197** F5
Lymington Rd, NW6 **90** E6
Dagenham RM8 **100** D1
Lyminster Cl, Hayes UB4
off West Quay Dr **102/103** E5
Lympstone Gdns, SE15 **37** J7
Lynbridge Gdns, N13 **59** H4
Lynbrook Cl, SE15 **36** E7
Lynbrook Gro, SE15
off Newent Cl **132** B7
Lynchen Cl, Houns. TW5
off The Avenue **142** A1
Lynch Wk, SE8 *off Prince St* **133** J6
Lyncott Cres, SW4 **150** B4
Lyncroft Av, Pnr. HA5 **66** E5
Lyncroft Gdns, NW6 **90** D5
W13 **125** F2
Hounslow TW3 **143** J4
Lyndale, NW2 **90** C4
Lyndale Av, NW2 **90** C3
Lyndale Cl, SE3 **135** F6
Lyndhurst Av, N12 **57** J6
NW7 **54** E6
SW16 **186** D2
Pinner HA5 **66** B1
Southall UB1 **123** H1
Sunbury-on-Thames TW16 **178** A3
Surbiton KT5 **196** B1
Twickenham TW2 **161** F1
Lyndhurst Cl, NW10 **88** D3
Bexleyheath DA7 **159** H3
Croydon CR0 **202** C3
Orpington BR6 **207** E4
Lyndhurst Ct, E18
off Churchfields **79** G1
Sutton SM2
off Overton Rd **198** D7
Lyndhurst Dr, E10 **78** C7
New Malden KT3 **183** E6
Lyndhurst Gdns, N3 **72** B1
NW3 **91** G5
Barking IG11 **99** H6
Enfield EN1 **44** B4
Ilford IG2 **81** G6
Pinner HA5 **66** B1
Lyndhurst Gro, SE15 **152** B2
Lyndhurst Ho, SW15
off Ellisfield Dr **147** G7
Lyndhurst Ri, Chig. IG7 **64** D4
Lyndhurst Rd, E4 **62** C7
N18 **60** D4
N22 **59** F6
NW3 **91** G5
Bexleyheath DA7 **159** H3
Greenford UB6 **103** H4
Thornton Heath CR7 **187** G4
Lyndhurst Sq, SE15 **152** C1
Lyndhurst Ter, NW3 **91** G5
Lyndhurst Way, SE15 **152** C1
Sutton SM2 **198** D7
Lyndon Av, Pnr. HA5 **51** E6
Sidcup DA15 **157** J5
Wallington SM6 **200** A3
Lyndon Rd, Belv. DA17 **139** G4
Lyndon Yd, SW17
off Riverside Rd **167** F4
Lyne Cres, E17 **77** J1
Lyneham Wk, E5 **95** H5
Lynette Av, SW4 **150** B6
Lynett Rd, Dag. RM8 **100** D2
Lynford Cl, Barn. EN5
off Rowley La **39** F5
Edgware HA8 **54** C7
Lynford Gdns, Edg. HA8 **54** B3
Ilford IG3 **99** J2
Lynmere Rd, Well. DA16 **158** B2
Lyn Ms, E3 *off Tredegar Sq* **113** J3
N16 **94** B4
Lynmouth Av, Enf. EN1 **44** C6
Morden SM4 **184** A7
Lynmouth Dr, Ruis. HA4 **84** B2
Lynmouth Gdns, Grnf. UB6 **105** E1
Hounslow TW5 **142** D1
Lynmouth Rd, E17 **77** H6
N2 **73** J3
N16 **94** C1
Greenford UB6 **105** E1
Lynn Cl, Har. HA3 **68** A2
Lynne Cl, Orp. BR6 **207** J6
Lynne Way, NW10 **88** E6
Northolt UB5 **102** D2
Lynn Ms, E11 *off Lynn Rd* **96/97** E2
Lynn Rd, E11 **96** E2
SW12 **150** B7
Ilford IG2 **81** G7
Lynn St, Enf. EN2 **44** A1
Lynsted Cl, Bexh. DA6 **159** H5
Bromley BR1 **191** J2
Lynsted Ct, Beck. BR3
off Churchfields Rd **189** H2
Lynsted Gdns, SE9 **156** A3
Lynton Av, N12 **57** G4
NW9 **71** F4
W13 **104** D6
Romford RM7 **83** G1
Lynton Cl, NW10 **88** E5
Chessington KT9 **195** H4
Isleworth TW7 **144** C4
Lynton Cres, Ilf. IG2 **80** E6
Lynton Est, SE1 **37** H2
Lynton Gdns, N11 **58** D6
Enfield EN1 **44** B7
Lynton Mead, N20 **56** D3
Lynton Rd, E4 **62** B5
N8 **74** D5
NW6 **108** C1
SE1 **37** G2
W3 **106** A7
Croydon CR0 **187** G6
Harrow HA2 **85** E2
New Malden KT3 **182** D5
Lynton Ter, W3 *off Lynton Rd* **106** C6
Lynwood Cl, E18 **79** J1
Harrow HA2 **85** E3
Lynwood Dr, Wor.Pk. KT4 **197** G2
Lynwood Gdns, Croy. CR0 **201** F4
Southall UB1 **103** F6
Lynwood Gro, N21 **59** G1
Orpington BR6 **193** H7
Lynwood Rd, SW17 **167** J3
W5 **105** H4
Thames Ditton KT7 **194** C2
Lynx Way, E16 *off Festoon Way* **116** A7
Lyon Business Pk, Bark. IG11 **117** H2
Lyon Meade, Stan. HA7 **69** F1
Lyon Pk Av, Wem. HA0 **87** H6
Lyon Rd, SW19 **185** F1
Harrow HA1 **68** C6
Lyonsdown Av, Barn. EN5 **41** F6
Lyonsdown Rd, Barn. EN5 **41** F6
Lyons Pl, NW8 **7** E5
Lyon St, N1 *off Caledonian Rd* **93** F7
Lyons Wk, W14 **128** B4
Lyon Way, Grnf. UB6 **104** B1
Lyoth Rd, Orp. BR5 **207** F2
Lyric Dr, Grnf. UB6 **103** H4
Lyric Ms, SE26 **171** F4
Lyric Rd, SW13 **147** F1
★ **Lyric Thea**, W6 **127** J4
Lysander Gdns, Surb. KT6
off Ewell Rd **181** J6
Lysander Gro, N19 **92** D1
Lysander Ms, N19
off Lysander Gro **92** C1
Lysander Rd, Croy. CR0 **201** F6
Lysander Way, Orp. BR6 **207** F3
Lysias Rd, SW12 **150** A6
Lysia St, SW6 **128** A7
Lysons Wk, SW15
off Swinburne Rd **147** G5
Lytchet Rd, Brom. BR1 **173** H7
Lytchet Way, Enf. EN3 **45** F1
Lytchgate Cl, S.Croy. CR2 **202** B7
Lytcott Dr, W.Mol. KT8
off Freeman Dr **179** F3
Lytcott Gro, SE22 **152** C5
Lyte St, E2 *off Bishops Way* **113** F2
Lytham Av, Wat. WD19 **50** D5
Lytham Cl, SE28 **118** E6
Lytham Gro, W5 **105** J3
Lytham St, SE17 **36** B4
Lyttelton Cl, NW3 **91** H7
Lyttelton Rd, E10 **96** B3
N2 **73** F5
Lyttleton Rd, N8 **75** G3
Lytton Av, N13 **59** G2
Lytton Cl, N2 **73** G5
Loughton IG10 **49** G3
Northolt UB5 **85** F7
Lytton Gdns, Wall. SM6 **200** D4
Lytton Gro, SW15 **148** A5
Lytton Rd, E11 **78** E7
Barnet EN5 **41** F4
Pinner HA5 **50** E7
Lytton Strachey Path, SE28
off Titmuss Av **118** B7
Lyveden Rd, SE3 **135** H7
SW17 **167** H6

M

Maberley Cres, SE19 **170** D7
Maberley Rd, SE19 **188** C1
Beckenham BR3 **189** G3
Mabledon Pl, WC1 **9** J4
Mablethorpe Rd, SW6 **128** B7
Mabley St, E9 **95** H6
McAdam Dr, Enf. EN2
off Rowantree Rd **43** H2
Macaret Cl, N20 **41** E7
MacArthur Cl, E7 **97** G6
MacArthur Ter, SE7 **136** B6
Macaulay Av, Esher KT10 **194** B2
Macaulay Ct, SW4 **150** B3
Macaulay Rd, E6 **116** A2
SW4 **150** B3
Macaulay Sq, SW4 **150** B4
Macaulay Way, SE28
off Booth Cl **118** B7
McAuley Cl, SE1 **26** E5
SE9 **156** E5
Macauley Ms, SE13 **154** C2
Macbean St, SE18 **136** D3
Macbeth St, W6 **127** H5
McCall Cl, SW4
off Jeffreys Rd **150/151** E2
McCall Cres, SE7 **136** B5
McCarthy Rd, Felt. TW13 **160** D5
Macclesfield Br, NW1 **7** H1
Macclesfield Rd, EC1 **11** J3
SE25 **189** E5
Macclesfield St, W1 **17** J5
McCoid Way, SE1 **27** J4
McCrone Ms, NW3
off Belsize La **91** G6
McCullum Rd, E3 **113** J1
McDermott Cl, SW11 **149** H3
McDermott Rd, SE15 **152** D3
Macdonald Av, Dag. RM10 **101** H3
Macdonald Rd, E7 **97** G4
E17 **78** C2
N11 **57** J5
N19 **92** C2
McDonough Cl, Chess. KT9 **195** H4
McDowall Cl, E16 **115** F5
McDowall Rd, SE5 **151** J1
Macduff Rd, SW11 **150** A1
Mace Cl, E1 *off Kennet St* **132/133** E1
McEntee Av, E17 **77** H1
Mace St, E2 **113** G2
McEwen Way, E15 **114** D1
Macey Ho, SW11 *off Surrey La* **149** H1
Macfarland Gro, SE15
off Blakes Rd **132** B7
MacFarlane La, Islw. TW7 **124** C6
Macfarlane Rd, W12 **127** J1
Macfarren Pl, NW1 **8** C6
McGrath Rd, E15 **97** F5
Macgregor Rd, E16 **115** J5
McGregor Rd, W11 **108** C6
Machell Rd, SE15 **153** F3
McIntosh Cl, Wall. SM6 **200** E7
Mackay Rd, SW4 **150** B3
McKay Rd, SW20 **165** H7
McKellar Cl, Bushey (Bushey Hth)
WD23 **51** J2
Mackennal St, NW8 **7** H2
Mackenzie Rd, N7 **93** F6
Beckenham BR3 **189** F2
Mackenzie Wk, E14 **134** A1
McKerrell Rd, SE15 **152** D1
Mackeson Rd, NW3 **91** J4
Mackie Rd, SW2 **151** G7
Mackintosh La, E9
off Homerton High St **95** G5
Macklin St, WC2 **18** B3
Mackrow Wk, E14
off Robin Hood La **114** C7
Macks Rd, SE16 **37** J1
Mackworth St, NW1 **9** F3
Maclaren Ms, SW15
off Clarendon Dr **147** J4
Maclean Rd, SE23 **153** H6
Macleod Rd, N21 **43** E5
McLeod Rd, SE2 **138** B4
McLeod's Ms, SW7 **22** B6
Macleod St, SE17 **36** A4
Maclise Rd, W14 **128** B3
McMillan St, SE8 **134** A6
McMillan Student Village, SE8
off Creek Rd **134** A6
Macmillan Way, SW17 **168** B4
McNair Rd, Sthl. UB2 **123** H2
McNeil Rd, SE5 **152** B2
McNicol Dr, NW10 **106** C2
Macoma Rd, SE18 **137** G6
Macoma Ter, SE18 **137** G6
Maconochies Rd, E14 **134** B5
Macquarie Way, E14 **134** B4
McRae La, Mitch. CR4 **185** J7
Macroom Rd, W9 **108** C3
Mac's Pl, EC4 **19** E3
★ **Madame Tussaud's**, NW1 **8** B6
Mada Rd, Orp. BR6 **206** E3
Maddams St, E3 **114** B4
Maddison Cl, Tedd. TW11 **162** C6
Maddocks Cl, Sid. DA14 **176** E5
Maddock Way, SE17 **35** H6
Maddox St, W1 **16** E5
Madeira Av, Brom. BR1 **172** E7
Madeira Gro, Wdf.Grn. IG8 **63** J6
Madeira Rd, E11 **96** D1
N13 **59** H4
SW16 **169** E5
Mitcham CR4 **185** J4
Madeley Rd, W5 **105** H6
Madeline Gro, Ilf. IG1 **99** G5
Madeline Rd, SE20 **188** D1
Madge Gill Way, E6
off Ron Leighton Way **116** B1
Madinah Rd, E8 **94** D6
Madingley, Kings.T. KT1
off St. Peters Rd **182** A2
Madison Cres, Bexh. DA7 **138** C7
Madison Gdns, Bexh. DA7 **138** C7
Bromley BR2 **191** F3
Madras Pl, N7 **93** G6
Madras Rd, Ilf. IG1 **99** E4
Madrid Rd, SW13 **147** G1
Madrigal La, SE5 **131** H7
Madron St, SE17 **36** E3
Mafeking Av, E6 **116** A2
Brentford TW8 **125** H6
Ilford IG2 **81** G7
Mafeking Rd, E16 **115** F4
N17 **76** D2
Enfield EN1 **44** C3
Magdala Av, N19 **92** B2
Magdala Rd, Islw. TW7 **144** D3
South Croydon CR2
off Napier Rd **202** A7
Magdalene Cl, SE15
off Pilkington Rd **152/153** E2
Magdalene Gdns, E6 **116** D4
Magdalen Pas, E1 **21** G5
Magdalen Rd, SW18 **167** F1
Magdalen St, SE1 **28** D2
Magee St, SE11 **35** E5
Magellan Pl, E14
off Maritime Quay **134** A5
Maggie Blakes Causeway, SE1
off Shad Thames **132** C1
Magnet Rd, Wem. HA9 **87** G2
Magnin Cl, E8 *off Wilde Cl* **112** D1
Magnolia Cl, E10 **96** A2
Kingston upon Thames KT2 **164** C6
Magnolia Ct, Har. HA3 **69** J7
Richmond TW9
off West Hall Rd **146** B1
Wallington SM6
off Parkgate Rd **200** B5
Magnolia Gdns, Edg. HA8 **54** C4
Magnolia Pl, SW4 **150** E5
W5 *off Montpelier Rd* **105** H5
Magnolia Rd, W4 **126** B6
Magnolia St, West Dr. UB7 **120** A4
Magnolia Way, Epsom KT19 **196** C5
Magpie All, EC4 **19** F4
Magpie Cl, E7 **97** F5
NW9 *off Eagle Dr* **70/71** E2
Enfield EN1 **44** D1
Magpie Hall Cl, Brom. BR2 **192** B6
Magpie Hall La, Brom. BR2 **192** C5
Magpie Hall Rd, Bushey (Bushey Hth)
WD23 **52** B2
Magpie Pl, SE14
off Milton Ct Rd **133** H6
Magri Wk, E1 *off Ashfield St* **113** F5
Maguire Dr, Rich. TW10 **163** F4
Maguire St, SE1 **29** G3
Mahlon Av, Ruis. HA4 **84** B5
Mahogany Cl, SE16 **133** H1
Mahon Cl, Enf. EN1 **44** C1
Maida Av, E4 **46** B7
W2 **14** D1
MAIDA HILL, W9 **108** C4
Maida Rd, Belv. DA17 **139** G3
MAIDA VALE, W9 **6** B5
Maida Vale, W9 **6** C4
Maida Way, E4 **46** B7
Maiden Erlegh Av, Bex. DA5 **176** E1
Maiden La, NW1 **92** D7
SE1 **28** A1
WC2 **18** B6
Maiden Rd, E15 **97** E7
Maidenstone Hill, SE10 **154** C1
Maids of Honour Row, Rich. TW9
off The Green **145** G5
Maidstone Av, Rom. RM5 **83** J2
Maidstone Bldgs Ms, SE1 **28** A2
Maidstone Ho, E14
off Carmen St **114** B6
Maidstone Rd, N11 **58** C6
Sidcup DA14 **176** D6
Maidstone St, E2 **13** J1
Main Av, Enf. EN1 **44** C5
Main Dr, Wem. HA9 **87** G3
Mainridge Rd, Chis. BR7 **174** D4
Main Rd, Sid. DA14 **175** H3
Main St, Felt. TW13 **160** D5
Maisemore St, SE15 **37** J7
Maitland Cl, Houns. TW4 **143** F3
Maitland Cl Est, SE10
off Greenwich High Rd **134** B7
Maitland Pk Est, NW3 **91** J6
Maitland Pk Rd, NW3 **91** J6
Maitland Pk Vil, NW3 **91** J6
Maitland Pl, E5
off Clarence Rd **94/95** E4
Maitland Rd, E15 **97** F6
SE26 **171** G6
Majendie Rd, SE18 **137** G5
Majestic Way, Mitch. CR4 **185** J2
Major Cl, SW9 *off Styles Gdns* **151** H3
Major Rd, E15 **96** C5
SE16 **29** J5
Makepeace Av, N6 **92** A2
Makepeace Rd, E11 **79** G4

Makepeace Rd, Nthlt. UB5 . . . . .102 E2
Makins St, SW3 . . . . .31 H2
Malabar St, E14 . . . . .134 A2
Malam Gdns, E14 off Wades Pl . .114 B7
Malbrook Rd, SW15 . . . . .147 H4
Malcolm Ct, Stan. HA7 . . . . .53 F5
Malcolm Cres, NW4 . . . . .71 G6
Malcolm Dr, Surb. KT6 . . . . .195 H1
Malcolm Pl, E2 . . . . .113 F4
Malcolm Rd, E1 . . . . .113 F4
  SE20 . . . . .171 F7
  SE25 . . . . .188 D6
  SW19 . . . . .166 B6
Malcolms Way, N14 . . . . .42 C5
Malcolm Way, E11 . . . . .79 G5
Malden Av, SE25 . . . . .188 E4
  Greenford UB6 . . . . .86 B5
Malden Ct, N.Mal. KT3 . . . . .183 H3
  off West Barnes La 183 H3
Malden Cres, NW1 . . . . .92 A6
Malden Grn Av, Wor.Pk. KT4 . .197 F1
Malden Hill, N.Mal. KT3 . . . . .183 F3
Malden Hill Gdns, N.Mal. KT3 .183 F3
Malden Pk, N.Mal. KT3 . . . . .183 F6
Malden Pl, NW5 off Grafton Ter . .92 A5
Malden Rd, NW5 . . . . .92 A5
  Borehamwood WD6 . . . . .38 A3
  New Malden KT3 . . . . .183 E5
  Sutton SM3 . . . . .198 A4
  Worcester Park KT4 . . . . .183 F7
Malden Way, N.Mal. KT3 . . . . .183 F5
Maldon Cl, E15 off David St 96 D5
  N1 off Popham Rd 111 J1
  SE5 . . . . .152 B3
Maldon Ct, Wall. SM6
  off Maldon Rd 200 C5
Maldon Rd, N9 . . . . .60 C7
  W3 . . . . .106 C7
  Romford RM7 . . . . .83 J7
  Wallington SM6 . . . . .200 B5
Maldon Wk, Wdf.Grn. IG8 . . . .63 J6
Malet Pl, WC1 . . . . .9 H6
Malet St, WC1 . . . . .9 H6
Maley Av, SE27 . . . . .169 H2
Malford Ct, E18 . . . . .79 G2
Malford Gro, E18 . . . . .79 F4
Malfort Rd, SE5 . . . . .152 B3
Malham Cl, N11 off Catterick Cl . .58 A6
Malham Rd, SE23 . . . . .171 G1
Malins Cl, Barn. EN5 . . . . .39 H5
Mall, The, E15 . . . . .96 D7
  N14 . . . . .58 E3
  SW1 . . . . .25 G3
  SW14 . . . . .146 C4
  W5 . . . . .105 H7
  Croydon CR0 . . . . .201 J2
  Harrow HA3 . . . . .69 J6
  Surbiton KT6 . . . . .181 G5
Mallams Ms, SW9
  off St. James's Cres 151 H3
Mallard Cl, E9 off Berkshire Rd . .95 J6
  NW6 . . . . .108 D2
  W7 . . . . .124 B2
  Barnet EN5 off The Hook 41 G6
  Twickenham TW2
    off Stephenson Rd 143 G7
Mallard Path, SE28 . . . . .137 G3
Mallard Pl, Twick. TW1 . . . . .162 D3
Mallard Pt, E3 off Rainhill Way . .114 B3
Mallards Rd, Bark. IG11 . . . . .118 A4
  Woodford Green IG8 . . . . .63 H7
Mallard Wk, Beck. BR3 . . . . .189 G5
  Sidcup DA14 . . . . .176 C5
Mallard Way, NW9 . . . . .70 C7
Mallet Dr, Nthlt. UB5 . . . . .85 F5
Mallet Rd, SE13 . . . . .154 D6
Malling, SE13 . . . . .154 C4
Malling Cl, Croy. CR0 . . . . .189 F6
Malling Gdns, Mord. SM4 . . . .185 F6
Malling Way, Brom. BR2 . . . . .191 F7
Mallinson Rd, SW11 . . . . .149 H5
  Croydon CR0 . . . . .200 D3
Mallord St, SW3 . . . . .31 F5
Mallory Cl, SE4 . . . . .153 H4
Mallory Gdns, Barn. EN4 . . . .42 A7
Mallory St, NW8 . . . . .7 H5
Mallow Cl, Croy. CR0
  off Marigold Way 203 G1
Mallow Mead, NW7 . . . . .56 B7
Mallow St, EC1 . . . . .12 B5
Mall Rd, W6 . . . . .127 H5
Malmains Cl, Beck. BR3 . . . . .190 D5
Malmains Way, Beck. BR3 . . . .190 C4
Malmesbury Rd, E3 . . . . .113 J3
  E16 . . . . .115 E5
  E18 . . . . .79 F1
  Morden SM4 . . . . .185 F7
Malmesbury Ter, E16 . . . . .115 F5
Malmsmead Ho, E9
  off Kingsmead Way 95 H5
Malpas Dr, Pnr. HA5 . . . . .66 D5
Malpas Rd, E8 . . . . .94 E6
  SE4 . . . . .153 J2
  Dagenham RM9 . . . . .100 D6
Malta Rd, E10 . . . . .96 A1
Malta St, EC1 . . . . .11 H5

Maltby Rd, Chess. KT9 . . . . .196 A6
Maltby St, SE1 . . . . .29 F4
Malthouse Dr, W4 . . . . .127 E6
  Feltham TW13 . . . . .160 D5
Malthouse Pas, SW13
  off The Terrace 146/147 E2
Malthus Path, SE28
  off Owen Cl 138 C1
Malting Ho, E14 . . . . .113 J7
Maltings, The, Orp. BR6 . . . . .207 J1
Maltings Cl, SW13
  off Cleveland Gdns 146/147 E2
Maltings Ms, Sid. DA15
  off Station Rd 176 A3
Maltings Pl, SW6 . . . . .149 E1
Malting Way, Islw. TW7 . . . . .144 C3
Malton Ms, SE18 off Malton St . .137 H6
  W10 off Cambridge Gdns 108 B6
Malton Rd, W10
  off St. Marks Rd 108 B6
Malton St, SE18 . . . . .137 H6
Maltravers St, WC2 . . . . .18 D5
Malt St, SE1 . . . . .37 H5
Malva Cl, SW18
  off St. Ann's Hill 148/149 E5
Malvern Av, E4 . . . . .62 D7
  Bexleyheath DA7 . . . . .138 E7
  Harrow HA2 . . . . .85 E3
Malvern Cl, SE20
  off Derwent Rd 188 D2
  W10 . . . . .108 C5
  Mitcham CR4 . . . . .186 C4
  Surbiton KT6 . . . . .195 H1
Malvern Ct, SE14
  off Avonley Rd 133 F7
  SW7 . . . . .31 F2
  Sutton SM2 off Overton Rd . .198 D7
Malvern Dr, Felt. TW13 . . . . .160 D5
  Ilford IG3 . . . . .99 J4
  Woodford Green IG8 . . . . .63 J5
Malvern Gdns, NW2 . . . . .90 B2
  Harrow HA3 . . . . .69 H3
  Loughton IG10 . . . . .48 C6
Malvern Ms, NW6
  off Malvern Rd 108 D3
Malvern Pl, NW6 . . . . .108 C3
Malvern Rd, E6 . . . . .116 B1
  E8 . . . . .94 D7
  E11 . . . . .97 E2
  N8 . . . . .75 F3
  N17 . . . . .76 D3
  NW6 . . . . .108 D3
  Hampton TW12 . . . . .161 G7
  Hayes UB3 . . . . .121 H7
  Surbiton KT6 . . . . .195 H2
  Thornton Heath CR7 . . . . .187 G4
Malvern Ter, N1 . . . . .111 G1
  N9 off Latymer Rd 60 C1
Malvern Way, W13
  off Templewood 104/105 E5
Malwood Rd, SW12 . . . . .150 B6
Malyons Rd, SE13 . . . . .154 B5
Malyons Ter, SE13 . . . . .154 B5
Managers St, E14
  off Prestons Rd 134 C1
Manatee Pl, Wall. SM6
  off Croydon Rd 200 D3
Manaton Cl, SE15 . . . . .152 E3
Manaton Cres, Sthl. UB1 . . . . .103 G6
Manbey Gro, E15 . . . . .96 E6
Manbey Pk Rd, E15 . . . . .96 E6
Manbey Rd, E15 . . . . .96 E6
Manbey St, E15 . . . . .96 E6
Manbre Rd, W6 . . . . .127 J6
Manbrough Av, E6 . . . . .116 C3
Manchester Ct, E16 . . . . .115 H6
Manchester Dr, W10 . . . . .108 B4
Manchester Gro, E14 . . . . .134 C5
Manchester Ms, W1 . . . . .16 B2
Manchester Rd, E14 . . . . .134 C5
  N15 . . . . .76 A6
  Thornton Heath CR7 . . . . .187 J3
Manchester Sq, W1 . . . . .16 B3
Manchester St, W1 . . . . .16 B2
Manchester Way, Dag. RM10 . .101 H4
Manchuria Rd, SW11 . . . . .150 A6
Manciple St, SE1 . . . . .28 B4
Mandalay Rd, SW4 . . . . .150 C5
Mandarin St, E14 off Salter St . .114 A7
Mandarin Way, Hayes UB4 . . . .102 D5
Mandela Cl, NW10 . . . . .88 C7
Mandela Rd, E16 . . . . .115 G6
Mandela St, NW1 . . . . .110 C1
  SW9 . . . . .131 G7
Mandela Way, SE1 . . . . .36 E1
Mandeville Cl, SE3
  off Vanbrugh Pk 135 F7
  SW20 . . . . .184 B1
Mandeville Ct, E4 . . . . .61 H4
Mandeville Dr, Surb. KT6 . . . .195 G1
Mandeville Ms, SW4
  off Clapham Pk Rd 150/151 E4
Mandeville Pl, W1 . . . . .16 C3
Mandeville Rd, N14 . . . . .58 B2
  Isleworth TW7 . . . . .144 D2
  Northolt UB5 . . . . .85 G7

Mandeville St, E5 . . . . .95 H3
Mandrake Rd, SW17 . . . . .167 J3
Mandrake Way, E15 . . . . .96 E7
Mandrell Rd, SW2 . . . . .150 E5
Manette St, W1 . . . . .17 J4
Manford Way, Chig. IG7 . . . . .65 H4
Manfred Rd, SW15 . . . . .148 C5
Manger Rd, N7 . . . . .93 E6
Mangold Way, Erith DA18 . . . .138 E3
Manhattan Wf, E16 . . . . .135 G2
Manilla St, E14 . . . . .134 A2
Manister Rd, SE2 . . . . .138 A3
Manitoba Ct, SE16
  off Renforth St 133 F2
Manitoba Gdns, Orp. BR6
  off Superior Dr 207 J6
Manley Ct, N16
  off Stoke Newington High St .94 C3
Manley St, NW1 . . . . .110 A1
Mann Cl, Croy. CR0
  off Salem Pl 201 J3
Manningford Cl, EC1 . . . . .11 G3
Manning Gdns, Har. HA3 . . . .69 G7
Manning Pl, Rich. TW10
  off Grove Rd 145 J6
Manning Rd, E17
  off Southcote Rd 77 H5
  Dagenham RM10 . . . . .101 G6
Manningtree Cl, SW19 . . . . .166 B1
Manningtree Rd, Ruis. HA4 . . . .84 B4
Manningtree St, E1 . . . . .21 H3
Mannin Rd, Rom. RM6 . . . . .82 B7
Mannock Dr, Loug. IG10 . . . . .49 F2
Mannock Ms, E18 . . . . .79 H1
Mannock Rd, N22 . . . . .75 H3
Manns Cl, Islw. TW7 . . . . .144 C5
Manns Rd, Edg. HA8 . . . . .54 A6
Manoel Rd, Twick. TW2 . . . . .161 J2
Manor Av, SE4 . . . . .153 J2
  Hounslow TW4 . . . . .142 D3
  Northolt UB5 . . . . .85 F7
Manorbrook, SE3 . . . . .155 G4
Manor Cl, E17 off Manor Rd 77 H2
  NW7 off Manor Dr 54 D5
  NW9 . . . . .70 B5
  SE28 . . . . .118 C6
  Barnet EN5 . . . . .40 B4
  Worcester Park KT4 . . . . .197 E1
Manor Cotts App, N2 . . . . .73 F2
Manor Ct, E10
  off Grange Pk Rd 96 B1
  N2 . . . . .73 J5
  SW6 off Bagley's La 148/149 E1
  Twickenham TW2 . . . . .161 J2
  Wembley HA9 . . . . .87 H5
Manor Ct Rd, W7 . . . . .104 B7
Manor Cres, Surb. KT5 . . . . .182 A6
Manordene Cl, T.Ditt. KT7 . . . .194 D1
Manordene Rd, SE28 . . . . .118 C6
Manor Dr, N14 . . . . .42 B7
  N20 . . . . .57 H3
  NW7 . . . . .54 D5
  Epsom KT19 . . . . .196 E6
  Esher KT10 . . . . .194 C2
  Feltham TW13
    off Lebanon Av 160 D5
  Sunbury-on-Thames TW16 . .178 A2
  Surbiton KT5 . . . . .181 J6
  Wembley HA9 . . . . .87 J4
Manor Dr, The, Wor.Pk. KT4 . .197 E1
Manor Dr N, N.Mal. KT3 . . . .182 D7
  Worcester Park KT4 . . . . .196 E1
Manor Est, SE16 . . . . .132 E4
Manor Fm Cl, Wor.Pk. KT4 . . .196 E1
Manor Fm Dr, E4 . . . . .63 E3
Manor Fm Rd, Th.Hth. CR7 . . .187 G2
  Wembley HA0 . . . . .105 G2
Manorfield Cl, N19
  off Junction Rd 92 C4
Manor Flds, SW15 . . . . .148 A6
Manorfields Cl, Chis. BR7 . . . .193 J3
Manor Gdns, N7 . . . . .92 E3
  SW20 . . . . .184 C2
  W3 . . . . .126 A4
  W4 off Devonshire Rd . . .126/127 E5
  Hampton TW12 . . . . .161 H7
  Richmond TW9 . . . . .145 J4
  Ruislip HA4 . . . . .84 C5
  South Croydon CR2 . . . . .202 C6
  Sunbury-on-Thames TW16 . .178 A2
Manor Gate, Nthlt. UB5 . . . . .84 E7
Manorgate Rd, Kings.T. KT2 . .182 A1
Manor Gro, SE15 . . . . .133 F6
  Beckenham BR3 . . . . .190 B2
  Richmond TW9 . . . . .146 A4
Manor Hall Av, NW4 . . . . .71 J2
Manor Hall Dr, NW4 . . . . .72 A2
Manorhall Gdns, E10 . . . . .96 A1
Manor Ho Dr, NW6 . . . . .90 A7
Manor Ho Est, Stan. HA7
  off Old Ch La 52/53 E6
Manor Ho Way, Islw. TW7 . . . .144 E3
Manor La, SE12 . . . . .155 E6
  SE13 . . . . .154 E4
  Feltham TW13 . . . . .160 A2
  Hayes UB3 . . . . .121 G6
  Sunbury-on-Thames TW16 . . .178 A2

Manor La, Sutt. SM1 . . . . .199 F5
Manor La Ter, SE13 . . . . .154 E4
Manor Ms, NW6
  off Cambridge Av 108 D2
  SE4 . . . . .153 J2
Manor Mt, SE23 . . . . .171 F1
Manor Par, NW10
  off Station Rd 107 F2
MANOR PARK, E12 . . . . .98 C4
Manor Pk, SE13 . . . . .154 D4
  Chislehurst BR7 . . . . .193 G2
  Richmond TW9 . . . . .145 J4
Manor Pk Cl, W.Wick. BR4 . . .204 B1
Manor Pk Cres, Edg. HA8 . . . .54 A6
Manor Pk Dr, Har. HA2 . . . . .67 H2
Manor Pk Gdns, Edg. HA8 . . . .54 A5
Manor Pk Par, SE13
  off Lee High Rd 154 D4
Manor Pk Rd, E12 . . . . .98 A4
  N2 . . . . .73 G3
  NW10 . . . . .107 F1
  Chislehurst BR7 . . . . .193 F1
  Sutton SM1 . . . . .199 F5
  West Wickham BR4 . . . . .204 B1
Manor Pl, SE17 . . . . .35 H4
  Chislehurst BR7 . . . . .193 G1
  Feltham TW14 . . . . .160 A1
  Mitcham CR4 . . . . .186 C3
  Sutton SM1 . . . . .199 E4
Manor Rd, E10 . . . . .78 A7
  E15 . . . . .114 E3
  E16 . . . . .114 E3
  E17 . . . . .77 H2
  N16 . . . . .94 A2
  N17 . . . . .76 D1
  N22 . . . . .59 E6
  SE25 . . . . .188 D4
  SW20 . . . . .184 C2
  W13 . . . . .104 D7
  Barking IG11 . . . . .99 J6
  Barnet EN5 . . . . .40 B5
  Beckenham BR3 . . . . .190 B2
  Bexley DA5 . . . . .177 H1
  Chigwell IG7 . . . . .64 E5
  Dagenham RM10 . . . . .101 J6
  East Molesey KT8 . . . . .180 A4
  Enfield EN2 . . . . .44 A2
  Harrow HA1 . . . . .68 D6
  Hayes UB3 . . . . .102 A6
  Loughton IG10 . . . . .47 H6
  Loughton (High Beach) IG10 . .47 H1
  Mitcham CR4 . . . . .186 C4
  Richmond TW9 . . . . .145 J3
  Romford (Chad.Hth) RM6 . .82 D6
  Sidcup DA15 . . . . .175 J3
  Sutton SM2 . . . . .198 C7
  Teddington TW11 . . . . .162 E5
  Twickenham TW2 . . . . .161 J2
  Wallington SM6 . . . . .200 B4
  West Wickham BR4 . . . . .204 B2
  Woodford Green IG8 . . . . .64 C6
Manor Rd N, Esher KT10 . . . .194 C3
  Thames Ditton KT7 . . . . .194 D2
  Wallington SM6 . . . . .200 B4
Manor Rd S, Esher KT10 . . . .194 B4
Manorside, Barn. EN5 . . . . .40 B4
Manorside Cl, SE2 . . . . .138 C4
Manor Sq, Dag. RM8 . . . . .100 D2
Manor Vale, Brent. TW8 . . . . .125 F5
Manor Vw, N3 . . . . .72 E2
Manor Way, E4 . . . . .62 D4
  NW9 . . . . .70 E3
  SE3 . . . . .155 F4
  SE23 . . . . .153 F7
  SE28 . . . . .138 C1
  Beckenham BR3 . . . . .190 A2
  Bexley DA5 . . . . .177 G1
  Borehamwood WD6 . . . . .38 C4
  Bromley BR2 . . . . .192 B6
Manorway, Enf. EN1 . . . . .44 B7
Manor Way, Har. HA2 . . . . .67 H4
  Mitcham CR4 . . . . .186 C3
  Orpington BR5 . . . . .193 F4
  South Croydon CR2 . . . . .202 B6
  Southall UB2 . . . . .122 D4
Manorway, Wdf.Grn. IG8 . . . .63 J5
Manor Way, Wor.Pk. KT4 . . . .197 E1
Manor Way, The, Wall. SM6 . .200 B4
Manpreet Ct, E12 off Morris Av . .98 C5
Manresa Rd, SW3 . . . . .31 G4
Mansard Beeches, SW17 . . . .168 A5
Mansard Cl, Pnr. HA5 . . . . .66 D3
Mansbridge Way, NW7 . . . . .56 B7
Manse Cl, Hayes UB3 . . . . .121 G6
Mansel Gro, E17 . . . . .78 A1
Mansell Rd, W3 . . . . .126 D2
  Greenford UB6 . . . . .103 H5
Mansell St, E1 . . . . .21 G6
Mansel Rd, SW19 . . . . .166 B6
Mansergh Cl, SE18 . . . . .136 B7
Manse Rd, N16 . . . . .94 C3
Mansfield Av, N15 . . . . .76 A4
  Barnet EN4 . . . . .41 J6
  Ruislip HA4 . . . . .84 B1
Mansfield Cl, N9 . . . . .44 D6
Mansfield Hill, E4 . . . . .62 B1
Mansfield Ms, W1 . . . . .16 D2

Mansfield Pl, NW3 *off New End* . .91 F4
Mansfield Rd, E11 . . . . .79 H6
E17 . . . . .77 J4
NW3 .91 J5
W3 .106 B4
Chessington KT9 . . . . .195 F5
Ilford IG1 . . . . .98 D2
South Croydon CR2 . . . . .202 A6
Mansfield St, W1 . . . . .16 D2
Mansford St, E2 . . . . .13 J2
Manship Rd, Mitch. CR4 . . . . . .168 A7
Mansion Cl, SW9
off Cowley Rd 151 G1
Mansion Gdns, NW3 . . . . .91 E3
★ **Mansion Ho**, EC4 . . . . .20 B4
Mansion Ho Pl, EC4 . . . . .20 B4
Mansion Ho St, EC4 . . . . .20 B4
Manson Ms, SW7 . . . . .30 D2
Manson Pl, SW7 . . . . .30 E2
Mansted Gdns, Rom. RM6 . . . . . .82 C7
Manston Av, Sthl. UB2 . . . . .123 G4
Manston Cl, SE20
off Garden Rd 189 F1
Manstone Rd, NW2 . . . . .90 B5
Manston Gro, Kings.T. KT2 . . . . .163 G5
Manthorp Rd, SE18 . . . . .137 F5
Mantilla Rd, SW17 . . . . .168 A4
Mantle Rd, SE4 . . . . .153 H3
Mantlet Cl, SW16 . . . . .168 C7
Mantle Way, E15
off Romford Rd 96/97 E7
Manton Av, W7 . . . . .124 C2
Manton Rd, SE2 . . . . .138 A4
Mantua St, SW11 . . . . .149 G3
Mantus Cl, E1 *off Mantus Rd* . . .113 F4
Mantus Rd, E1 . . . . .113 F4
Manus Way, N20
off Blakeney Cl 57 F2
Manville Gdns, SW17 . . . . .168 B2
Manville Rd, SW17 . . . . .168 A2
Manwood Rd, SE4 . . . . .153 J5
Manwood St, E16 . . . . .136 C1
Manygates, SW12 . . . . .168 B2
Mapesbury Ms, NW4
off Station Rd 71 G6
Mapesbury Rd, NW2 . . . . .90 B6
Mapeshill Pl, NW2 . . . . .89 J6
Mape St, E2 . . . . .112 E4
Maple Av, E4 . . . . .61 J5
W3 .127 E1
Harrow HA2 . . . . .85 H2
Maple Cl, N3 . . . . .56 D6
N16 . . . . .76 D6
SW4 . . . . .150 D6
Buckhurst Hill IG9 . . . . .64 A3
Hampton TW12 . . . . .161 F6
Hayes UB4 . . . . .102 D3
Ilford IG6 . . . . .65 H5
Mitcham CR4 . . . . .186 B1
Orpington BR5 . . . . .193 G5
Ruislip HA4 . . . . .66 B6
Maple Ct, N.Mal. KT3 . . . . .182 E3
Maple Cres, Sid. DA15 . . . . . . .158 A6
Maplecroft Cl, E6
off Allhallows Rd 116 B6
Mapledale Av, Croy. CR0 . . . . . .202 D2
Mapledene, Chis. BR7
off Kemnal Rd 175 F5
Mapledene Rd, E8 . . . . .94 C7
Maple Gdns, Edg. HA8 . . . . .54 E7
Maple Gate, Loug. IG10 . . . . .48 D2
Maple Gro, NW9 . . . . .70 C7
W5 .125 G3
Brentford TW8 . . . . .124 E7
Southall UB1 . . . . .103 F5
Maplehurst Cl, Kings.T. KT1 . . . .181 H4
Maple Ind Est, Felt. TW13
off Maple Way 160 A3
Maple Leaf Dr, Sid. DA15 . . . . . .175 J1
Mapleleafe Gdns, Ilf. IG6 . . . . . . .80 E3
Maple Leaf Sq, SE16
off St. Elmos Rd 133 G2
Maple Ms, NW6 . . . . .6 A1
SW16 . . . . .169 F5
Maple Pl, W1 . . . . .9 G6
Maple Rd, E11 . . . . .79 E6
SE20 . . . . .189 E1
Hayes UB4 . . . . .102 C3
Surbiton KT6 . . . . .181 H5
Maples, The, Esher (Clay.) KT10 .194 D7
Maples Pl, E1
off Raven Row 112/113 E5
Maplestead Rd, SW2 . . . . .151 F7
Dagenham RM9 . . . . .118 B1
Maple St, W1 . . . . .17 F1
Romford RM7 . . . . .83 J4
Maplethorpe Rd, Th.Hth. CR7 . . .187 H4
Mapleton Cl, Brom. BR2 . . . . . . .191 G6
Mapleton Cres, SW18 . . . . .148 E6
Mapleton Rd, E4 . . . . .62 C3
SW18 . . . . .148 E6
Enfield EN1 . . . . .45 E2
Maple Wk, W10 *off Droop St* . . .108 A4
Maple Way, Felt. TW13 . . . . .160 A3
Maplin Cl, N21 . . . . .43 F6
Maplin Ho, SE2
off Wolvercote Rd 138 D2
Maplin Rd, E16 . . . . .115 G6
Maplin St, E3 . . . . .113 J3
Mapperley Dr, Wdf.Grn. IG8
off Forest Dr 62/63 E7
Maran Way, Erith DA18 . . . . .138 D2
Marathon Way, SE28 . . . . .137 J2
Marban Rd, W9 . . . . .108 C3
★ **Marble Arch**, W1 . . . . .16 A5
Marble Cl, W3 . . . . .126 B1
Marble Dr, NW2 . . . . .90 A1
Marble Hill Cl, Twick. TW1 . . . . . .144 E7
Marble Hill Gdns, Twick. TW1 . . .144 E7
★ **Marble Hill Ho**, Twick. TW1 . .145 F7
Marble Ho, SE18 *off Felspar Cl* .137 J5
Marble Quay, E1 . . . . .29 H1
Marbrook Ct, SE12 . . . . .173 J3
Marcella Rd, SW9 . . . . .151 G2
Marcellina Way, Orp. BR6 . . . . . .207 H3
Marchant Rd, E11 . . . . .96 D2
Marchant St, SE14 . . . . .133 H6
Marchbank Rd, W14 . . . . .128 C6
Marchmont Gdns, Rich. TW10
off Marchmont Rd 145 J5
Marchmont Rd, Rich. TW10 . . . .145 J5
Wallington SM6 . . . . .200 C7
Marchmont St, WC1 . . . . .10 A5
March Rd, Twick. TW1 . . . . .144 D7
Marchside Cl, Houns. TW5
off Springwell Rd 142 D1
Marchwood Cl, SE5 . . . . .132 B7
Marchwood Cres, W5 . . . . .105 F6
Marcia Rd, SE1 . . . . .37 E2
Marcilly Rd, SW18 . . . . .149 G5
Marconi Rd, E10 . . . . .96 A1
Marconi Way, Sthl. UB1 . . . . . . .103 H6
Marcon Pl, E8 . . . . .94 E6
Marco Rd, W6 . . . . .127 J3
Marcourt Lawns, W5 . . . . .105 H4
Marcus Ct, E15 . . . . .115 E1
Marcus Garvey Ms, SE22
off St. Aidan's Rd 152/153 E5
Marcus Garvey Way, SE24 . . . . .151 G4
Marcus St, E15 . . . . .115 F1
SW18 . . . . .149 E6
Marcus Ter, SW18 . . . . .149 E6
Mardale Dr, NW9 . . . . .70 D5
Mardell Rd, Croy. CR0 . . . . .189 G5
Marden Av, Brom. BR2 . . . . .191 G6
Marden Cres, Bex. DA5 . . . . .159 J5
Croydon CR0 . . . . .187 F6
Marden Rd, N17 . . . . .76 B3
Croydon CR0 . . . . .187 F6
Marden Sq, SE16 . . . . .132 E3
Marder Rd, W13 . . . . .124 D2
Mardyke Cl, Rain. RM13 . . . . . . .119 J2
Marechal Niel Av, Sid. DA15 . . . .175 G3
Maresfield, Croy. CR0 . . . . .202 B3
Maresfield Gdns, NW3 . . . . .91 F5
Mare St, E8 . . . . .113 E1
Marfleet Cl, Cars. SM5 . . . . .199 H2
Margaret Av, E4 . . . . .46 B6
Margaret Bondfield Av, Bark.
IG11 . . . . .100 A7
Margaret Bldgs, N16
off Margaret Rd 94 C1
Margaret Ct, W1 . . . . .17 F3
Margaret Gardner Dr, SE9 . . . . .174 C2
Margaret Ingram Cl, SW6
off John Smith Av 128 C7
Margaret Lockwood Cl, Kings.T.
KT1 .181 J4
Margaret Rd, N16 . . . . .94 C1
Barnet EN4 . . . . .41 G4
Bexley DA5 . . . . .158 D6
Margaret St, W1 . . . . .17 E3
Margaretta Ter, SW3 . . . . .31 G5
Margaretting Rd, E12 . . . . .97 J2
Margaret Way, Ilf. IG4 . . . . .80 B6
Margate Rd, SW2 . . . . .150 E5
Margeholes, Wat. WD19 . . . . .50 E2
Margery Pk Rd, E7 . . . . .97 G6
Margery Rd, Dag. RM8 . . . . .100 D3
Margery St, WC1 . . . . .10 E4
Margin Dr, SW19 . . . . .166 A5
Margravine Gdns, W6 . . . . .128 A5
Margravine Rd, W6 . . . . .128 A5
Marham Gdns, SW18 . . . . .167 H1
Morden SM4 . . . . .185 F6
Maria Cl, SE1 *off Beatrice Rd* . . .132 D4
Marian Cl, Hayes UB4 . . . . .102 D4
Marian Ct, Sutt. SM1 . . . . .198 E5
Marian Pl, E2 . . . . .112 E2
Marian Rd, SW16 . . . . .186 C1
Marian Sq, E2 . . . . .13 J1
Marian St, E2
off Hackney Rd 112/113 E2
Marian Way, NW10 . . . . .89 F7
Maria Ter, E1 . . . . .113 G5
Maria Theresa Cl, N.Mal. KT3 . . .182 D5
Maricas Av, Har. HA3 . . . . .68 A1
Marie Lloyd Gdns, N19
off Hornsey Ri Gdns 74/75 E7
Marie Lloyd Wk, E8
off Forest Rd 94 D6
Marigold All, SE1 . . . . .19 G6
Marigold Cl, Sthl. UB1
off Lancaster Rd 102/103 E7
Marigold Rd, N17 . . . . .61 F7
Marigold St, SE16 . . . . .132 E2
Marigold Way, E4
off Silver Birch Av 61 J6
Croydon CR0 . . . . .203 G1
Marina App, Hayes UB4 . . . . . . .103 E5
Marina Av, N.Mal. KT3 . . . . .183 H5
Marina Cl, Brom. BR2 . . . . .191 G3
Marina Dr, Well. DA16 . . . . .157 H2
Marina Gdns, Rom. RM7 . . . . .83 J6
Marina Way, Tedd. TW11
off Fairways 163 G7
Marine Dr, SE18 . . . . .136 C4
Barking IG11 . . . . .118 B4
Marinefield Rd, SW6 . . . . .149 E2
Mariner Gdns, Rich. TW10 . . . . .163 F3
Mariner Rd, E12
off Dersingham Av 98 C4
Mariners Ms, E14 . . . . .134 D4
Marine St, SE16 . . . . .29 H5
Marine Twr, SE8
off Abinger Gro 133 J6
Marion Cl, Ilf. IG6 . . . . .65 G7
Marion Gro, Wdf.Grn. IG8 . . . . . . .63 E5
Marion Rd, NW7 . . . . .55 G5
Thornton Heath CR7 . . . . . . .187 J5
Marischal Rd, SE13 . . . . .154 D3
Maritime Ho, SE18
off Green's End 136 E4
Barking IG11 *off Linton Rd* 99 F7
Maritime Quay, E14 . . . . .134 A5
Maritime St, E3 . . . . .113 J4
Marius Pas, SW17
off Marius Rd 168 A2
Marius Rd, SW17 . . . . .168 A2
Marjorams Av, Loug. IG10 . . . . . .48 C2
Marjorie Gro, SW11 . . . . .149 J4
Marjorie Ms, E1 *off Arbour Sq* . .113 G6
Mark Av, E4 . . . . .46 B6
Mark Cl, Bexh. DA7 . . . . .158 E1
Southall UB1
off Longford Av 123 H1
Marke Cl, Kes. BR2 . . . . .206 B4
Markeston Grn, Wat. WD19 . . . . . .50 D4
Market, The, Cars. SM5
off Wrythe La 199 F1
Sutton SM1 *off Rose Hill* 199 F1
Market Ct, W1 . . . . .17 F3
Market Est, N7 . . . . .92 E6
Market Hill, SE18 . . . . .136 D3
Market La, Edg. HA8 . . . . .70 C1
Market Ms, W1 . . . . .24 D2
Market Pl, N2 . . . . .73 H3
NW11 .73 F4
SE16 . . . . .37 J1
W1 . . . . .17 F3
W3 . . . . .126 C1
Bexleyheath DA6 . . . . .159 G4
Brentford TW8 . . . . .125 F7
Enfield EN2 *off The Town* 44 A3
Kingston upon Thames KT1 . .181 G2
Market Rd, N7 . . . . .92 E6
Richmond TW9 . . . . .146 A3
Market Row, SW9
off Atlantic Rd 151 G4
Market Service Rd, The, Sutt. SM1
off Rosehill Av 199 F1
Market Sq, E14 *off Chrisp St* . . .114 B6
N9 *off New Rd* 60 D2
Bromley BR1 . . . . .191 G2
Market St, E6 . . . . .116 C2
SE18 . . . . .136 D4
Market Way, E14 *off Kerbey St* . .114 B6
Wembley HA0 *off Turton Rd* . . .87 H5
Market Yd Ms, SE1 . . . . .28 E5
Markfield Gdns, E4 . . . . .46 B7
Markfield Rd, N15 . . . . .76 D4
Markham Pl, SW3 . . . . .31 J3
Markham Sq, SW3 . . . . .31 J3
Markham St, SW3 . . . . .31 H3
Markhole Cl, Hmptn. TW12
off Priory Rd 161 F7
Markhouse Av, E17 . . . . .77 H6
Markhouse Rd, E17 . . . . .77 J5
Markland Ho, W10 . . . . .108 A7
Mark La, EC3 . . . . .20 E6
Markmanor Av, E17 . . . . .77 H7
Mark Rd, N22 . . . . .75 H2
Marksbury Av, Rich. TW9 . . . . . .146 A3
MARK'S GATE, Rom. RM6 . . . . . .82 E2
Mark Sq, EC2 . . . . .12 D5
Marks Rd, Rom. RM7 . . . . .83 J5
Mark St, E15 . . . . .96 E7
EC2 . . . . .12 D5
Markway, Sun. TW16 . . . . .178 C2
Markwell Cl, SE26
off Longton Gro 170/171 E4
Markyate Rd, Dag. RM8 . . . . . . .100 B5
Marlands Rd, Ilf. IG5 . . . . .80 B3
Marlborough, SW3 . . . . .31 H1
Marlborough Av, E8 . . . . .112 D1
N14 . . . . .58 C3
Edgware HA8 . . . . .54 B3
Marlborough Cl, N20
off Marlborough Gdns 57 J3
SE17 . . . . .35 H2
SW19 . . . . .167 H6
Marlborough Cl, Orp. BR6
off Aylesham Rd 193 J7
Marlborough Ct, W1 . . . . .17 F4
W8 .128 D4
Wallington SM6
off Cranley Gdns 200 C7
Marlborough Cres, W4 . . . . .126 D3
Hayes UB3 . . . . .121 G7
Marlborough Dr, Ilf. IG5 . . . . .80 B3
Marlborough Gdns, N20 . . . . .57 J3
Marlborough Gate Ho, W2 . . . . . .14 E5
Marlborough Gro, SE1 . . . . .37 H4
Marlborough Hill, NW8 . . . . .109 F1
Harrow HA1 . . . . .68 C4
★ **Marlborough Ho**, SW1 . . . . . .25 G2
Marlborough La, SE7 . . . . .135 J6
Marlborough Pk Av, Sid. DA15 . .158 A7
Marlborough Pl, NW8 . . . . .6 C2
Marlborough Rd, E4 . . . . .62 A6
E7 . . . . .97 J7
E15 *off Borthwick Rd* 96/97 E4
E18 . . . . .79 G3
N9 . . . . .60 C1
N19 . . . . .92 D2
N22 . . . . .59 E7
SE18 *off Cadogan Rd* 136 E3
SW1 . . . . .25 G2
SW19 . . . . .167 G6
W4 .126 C5
W5 .125 G2
Bexleyheath DA7 . . . . .158 D3
Bromley BR2 . . . . .191 J4
Dagenham RM8 . . . . .100 B4
Feltham TW13 . . . . .160 D2
Hampton TW12 . . . . .161 G6
Isleworth TW7 . . . . .144 E1
Richmond TW10 . . . . .145 H6
Romford RM7 . . . . .83 G4
South Croydon CR2 . . . . .201 J7
Southall UB2 . . . . .122 C3
Sutton SM1 . . . . .198 D3
Marlborough St, SW3 . . . . .31 G2
Marlborough Yd, N19 . . . . .92 D2
Marler Rd, SE23 . . . . .171 H1
Marlescroft Way, Loug. IG10 . . . . .48 E5
Marley Av, Bexh. DA7 . . . . .138 D6
Marley Cl, N15 *off Stanmore Rd* .75 H4
Greenford UB6 . . . . .103 G3
Marley Wk, NW2 *off Lennon Rd* . .89 J5
Marl Fld Cl, Wor.Pk. KT4 . . . . . . .197 G1
Marlingdene Cl, Hmptn. TW12 . .161 G6
Marlings Cl, Chis. BR7 . . . . .193 H4
Marlings Pk Av, Chis. BR7 . . . . .193 H4
Marlins Cl, Sutt. SM1
off Turnpike La 199 F5
Marloes Cl, Wem. HA0 . . . . .87 G4
Marloes Rd, W8 . . . . .22 A6
Marlow Cl, SE20 . . . . .189 E3
Marlow Ct, NW6 . . . . .90 A7
NW9 . . . . .71 F3
Marlow Cres, Twick. TW1 . . . . . .144 C6
Marlow Dr, Sutt. SM3 . . . . .198 A2
Marlowe Cl, Chis. BR7 . . . . .175 G6
Ilford IG6 . . . . .81 F1
Marlowe Ct, SE19 *off Lymer Av* .170 C5
Marlowe Gdns, SE9 . . . . .156 D6
Marlowe Path, SE8
off Glaisher St 134 B6
Marlowe Rd, E17 . . . . .78 C4
Marlowes, The, NW8 . . . . .109 G1
Marlowe Sq, Mitch. CR4 . . . . . . .186 C4
Marlowe Way, Croy. CR0 . . . . . . .201 E2
Marlow Gdns, Hayes UB3 . . . . . .121 G3
Marlow Rd, E6 . . . . .116 C3
SE20 . . . . .189 E3
Southall UB2 . . . . .123 F3
Marlow Way, SE16 . . . . .133 G2
Marl Rd, SW18 . . . . .149 E4
Marl St, SW18 *off Marl Rd* 149 F4
Marlton St, SE10
off Woolwich Rd 135 F5
Marlwood Cl, Sid. DA15 . . . . . . .175 H2
Marmadon Rd, SE18 . . . . .137 J4
Marmion App, E4 . . . . .62 A4
Marmion Av, E4 . . . . .61 J4
Marmion Cl, E4 . . . . .61 J4
Marmion Ms, SW11
off Taybridge Rd 150 A3
Marmion Rd, SW11 . . . . .150 A4
Marmont Rd, SE15 . . . . .152 D1
Marmora Rd, SE22 . . . . .153 F6
Marmot Rd, Houns. TW4 . . . . . . .142 D3
Marne Av, N11 . . . . .58 B4
Welling DA16 . . . . .158 A3
Marnell Way, Houns. TW4 . . . . . .142 D3
Marne St, W10 . . . . .108 B3
Marney Rd, SW11 . . . . .150 A4
Marnfield Cres, SW2 . . . . .169 F1
Marnham Av, NW2 . . . . .90 B4
Marnham Cres, Grnf. UB6 . . . . . .103 H3
Marnock Rd, SE4 . . . . .153 H5
Maroon St, E14 . . . . .113 H5
Maroons Way, SE6 . . . . .172 A5
Marquess Rd, N1 . . . . .94 A6
Marquis Cl, Wem. HA0 . . . . .87 J7
Marquis Rd, N4 . . . . .93 F1
N22 . . . . .59 F6

Marquis Rd, NW1 . . . . .92 D6
Marrabon Cl, Sid. DA15 . . . .176 A1
Marrick Cl, SW15 . . . . .147 G4
Marriott Cl, Felt. TW14 . . . .141 G6
Marriott Rd, E15 . . . . .114 E1
  N4 .93 F1
  N10 . . . . .73 J1
  Barnet EN5 . . . . .40 A3
Marriotts Cl, NW9 . . . . .71 F6
Marryat Cl, Houns. TW4 . . .143 F4
Marryat Pl, SW19 . . . . .166 B4
Marryat Rd, SW19 . . . . . . .166 A5
Marryat Sq, SW6 . . . . .148 B1
Marsala Rd, SE13 . . . . .154 B4
Marsden Rd, N9 . . . . .60 E2
  SE15 . . . . .152 C3
Marsden St, NW5 . . . . .92 A6
Marsden Way, Orp. BR6 . . .207 J4
Marshall Cl, SW18 . . . .
  off Allfarthing La 149 F6
  Harrow HA1 off Bowen Rd 68 A7
  Hounslow TW4 . . . . .143 F5
Marshall Path, SE28 . . . . . .
  off Attlee Rd 118 B7
Marshall Rd, E10 . . . . .96 B3
  N17 . . . . .76 A1
Marshalls Cl, N11 . . . . .58 B4
Marshall's Gro, SE18 . . . . .136 B4
Marshalls Pl, SE16 . . . . .29 G6
Marshall's Rd, Sutt. SM1 . . .198 E4
Marshall St, W1 . . . . .17 G4
Marshalsea Rd, SE1 . . . . . . .28 A3
Marsham Cl, Chis. BR7 . . . .174 E5
Marsham St, SW1 . . . . .25 J6
Marsh Av, Mitch. CR4 . . . . .186 A2
Marshbrook Cl, SE3 . . . . . .156 A3
Marsh Cl, NW7 . . . . .55 F3
Marsh Ct, SW19 . . . . .185 F1
Marsh Dr, NW9 . . . . .71 F6
Marsh Fm Rd, Twick. TW2 . . .162 C1
Marshfield St, E14 . . . . . . .134 C3
Marshgate La, E15 . . . . . . .114 B1
Marshgate Path, SE28 . . . . .
  off Tom Cribb Rd 137 F4
Marshgate Sidings, E15 . . .114 B1
Marsh Grn Rd, Dag. RM10 . . .119 G1
Marsh Hill, E9 . . . . .95 H5
Marsh La, E10 . . . . .96 A2
  N17 . . . . .61 E7
  NW7 . . . . .54 E4
  Stanmore HA7 . . . . .53 F5
Marsh Rd, Pnr. HA5 . . . . . . .66 E4
  Wembley HA0 . . . . .105 G2
Marshside Cl, N9 . . . . .61 F1
Marsh St, E14 off Harbinger Rd . .134 B4
Marsh Wall, E14 . . . . .134 A1
Marsland Cl, SE17 . . . . .35 H4
Marston Av, Chess. KT9 . . .195 H6
  Dagenham RM10 . . . . .101 G2
Marston Cl, NW6 . . . . .91 F7
  Dagenham RM10 . . . . .101 G3
Marston Rd, Ilf. IG5 . . . . . . .80 B1
  Teddington TW11 . . . . .162 E5
Marston Way, SE19 . . . . . .169 H7
Marsworth Av, Pnr. HA5 . . . .66 D1
Marsworth Cl, Hayes UB4 . . .103 E5
Martaban Rd, N16 . . . . .94 B2
Martara Ms, SE17 . . . . .35 J4
Martello St, E8 . . . . .94 E7
Martello Ter, E8 . . . . .94 E7
Martell Rd, SE21 . . . . .170 A3
Martel Pl, E8 off Dalston La . . .94 C6
Marten Rd, E17 . . . . .78 A2
Martens Av, Bexh. DA7 . . . .159 J4
Martens Cl, Bexh. DA7 . . . .159 J4
Martha Ct, E2 . . . . .113 E2
Martham Cl, SE28 . . . . .118 D7
  Ilford IG6 . . . . .80 E1
Martha Rd, E15 . . . . .97 E6
Martha's Bldgs, EC1 . . . . . . .12 B5
Martha St, E1 . . . . .113 E6
Marthorne Cres, Har. HA3 . . . .68 A2
Martina Ter, Chig. IG7 . . . . .
  off Manford Way 65 J5
Martin Bowes Rd, SE9 . . . .156 C3
Martinbridge Trd Est, Enf. EN1 . .44 D5
Martin Cl, N9 . . . . .61 G1
Martin Cres, Croy. CR0 . . . .201 G1
Martindale, SW14 . . . . .146 C5
Martindale Av, E16 . . . . . . .115 G7
Martindale Rd, SW12 . . . . .150 B7
  Hounslow TW4 . . . . .142 E3
Martin Dene, Bexh. DA6 . . .159 F5
Martin Dr, Nthlt. UB5 . . . . . . .85 F5
Martineau Cl, Esher KT10 . . .194 A4
Martineau Ms, N5 . . . .
  off Martineau Rd 93 H4
Martineau Rd, N5 . . . . .93 H4
Martineau St, E1 . . . . .113 F7
Martingales Cl, Rich. TW10 . . .163 G3
Martin Gro, Mord. SM4 . . . .184 D3
Martin La, EC4 . . . . .20 C5
Martin Ri, Bexh. DA6 . . . . . .159 F5
Martin Rd, Dag. RM8 . . . . . .100 C4
Martins Cl, W.Wick. BR4 . . .204 D1

Martinsfield Cl, Chig. IG7 . . . .65 H4
Martins Mt, Barn. EN5 . . . . . .40 D4
Martins Pl, SE28 off Martin St . .137 H1
Martins Rd, Brom. BR2 . . . .191 E2
Martin St, SE28 . . . . .137 H1
Martins Wk, N8 . . . .
  off Alexandra Rd 75 G3
  N10 . . . . .74 A1
  SE28 . . . . .137 H1
  Borehamwood WD6 . . . . . .
  off Siskin Cl 38 A4
Martin Way, SW20 . . . . . . .184 B3
  Morden SM4 . . . . .184 B3
Martlet Gro, Nthlt. UB5 . . . .102 D3
Martlett Ct, WC2 . . . . .18 B4
Martley Dr, Ilf. IG2 . . . . .80 E5
Martock Cl, Har. HA3 . . . . . . .68 D4
Martock Gdns, N11 . . . . .57 J5
Marton Cl, SE6 . . . . .172 A3
Marton Rd, N16 . . . . .94 B2
Martys Yd, NW3 . . . .
  off Hampstead High St 91 G4
Marvell Av, Hayes UB4 . . . .102 A5
Marvels Cl, SE12 . . . . .173 H2
Marvels La, SE12 . . . . .173 H2
Marville Rd, SW6 . . . . .128 C7
Marvin St, E8 . . . .
  off Sylvester Rd 94/95 E6
Marwell Cl, W.Wick. BR4 . . .
  off Deer Pk Way 205 F2
Marwood Cl, Well. DA16 . . .158 B3
Marwood Dr, NW7 . . . . .56 A7
Mary Adelaide Cl, SW15 . . .164 E4
Mary Ann Gdns, SE8 . . . . . .134 A6
Maryatt Av, Har. HA2 . . . . . . .85 H2
Marybank, SE18 . . . . .136 C4
Mary Cl, Stan. HA7 . . . . .69 J4
Mary Datchelor Cl, SE5 . . .152 A1
Mary Grn, NW8 . . . . .109 H1
Maryland Ind Est, E15 . . . . .
  off Maryland Rd 96 D5
Maryland Pk, E15 . . . . .96 E5
Maryland Pt, E15 . . . .
  off Leytonstone Rd 96/97 E6
Maryland Rd, E15 . . . . .96 D5
  N22 . . . . .59 F6
  Thornton Heath CR7 . . . . .187 H1
Maryland Sq, E15 . . . . .97 E5
Marylands Rd, W9 . . . . .108 D4
Maryland St, E15 . . . . .96 D5
Maryland Wk, N1 . . . .
  off Popham St 111 J1
Maryland Way, Sun. TW16 . . .178 A2
Mary Lawrenson Pl, SE3 . . .135 F7
MARYLEBONE, NW1 . . . . . . .15 J3
Marylebone Flyover, NW1 . . .15 F2
  W2 .15 F2
Marylebone High St, W1 . . . .16 C1
Marylebone La, W1 . . . . .16 D4
Marylebone Ms, W1 . . . . . . .16 D2
Marylebone Pas, W1 . . . . . . .17 G3
Marylebone Rd, NW1 . . . . . . .15 H1
Marylebone St, W1 . . . . .16 C2
Marylee Way, SE11 . . . . .34 D3
Mary Macarthur Ho, W6 . . . .
  off Field Rd 128 B6
Maryon Gro, SE7 . . . . .136 B4
Maryon Ms, NW3 . . . .
  off South End Rd 91 H4
Maryon Rd, SE7 . . . . .136 B4
  SE18 . . . . .136 B4
Mary Peters Dr, Grnf. UB6 . . .86 A5
Mary Pl, W11 . . . . .108 B7
Mary Rose Cl, Hmptn. TW12 . . .
  off Ashley Rd 179 G1
Mary Rose Mall, E6 . . . .
  off Frobisher Rd 116 D5
Maryrose Way, N20 . . . . .57 G1
Mary Seacole Cl, E8 . . . . . .
  off Clarissa St 112 C1
Mary's Ter, Twick. TW1 . . . .144 D7
Mary St, E16 off Barking Rd . . .115 F5
  N1 . . . . .111 J1
Mary Ter, NW1 . . . . .110 B1
Mary Way, Wat. WD19 . . . . . .50 D4
Masbro Rd, W14 . . . . .128 A3
Mascalls Ct, SE7 . . . .
  off Victoria Way 135 J6
Mascalls Rd, SE7 . . . . .135 J6
Mascotte Rd, SW15 . . . . . . .148 A4
Mascotts Cl, NW2 . . . . .89 H3
Masefield Av, Borwd. WD6 . . .38 B5
  Southall UB1 . . . . .103 G7
  Stanmore HA7 . . . . .52 C5
Masefield Cres, N14 . . . . . . .42 C6
Masefield Gdns, E6 . . . . . . .116 D4
Masefield La, Hayes UB4 . . .102 B4
Masefield Rd, Hmptn. TW12 . . .
  off Wordsworth Rd 161 F4
Masefield Vw, Orp. BR6 . . . .207 F3
Masham Ho, Erith DA18 . . . .
  off Kale Rd 138 D2
Mashie Rd, W3 . . . . .106 E6
Maskall Cl, SW2 . . . . .169 G1
Maskani Wk, SW16 . . . .
  off Bates Cres 168 C7
Maskell Rd, SW17 . . . . .167 F3

Maskelyne Cl, SW11 . . . . . .149 H1
Mason Bradbear Ct, N1 . . . .
  off St. Paul's Rd 94 A6
Mason Cl, E16 . . . . .115 G7
  SE16 . . . . .37 J3
  SW20 . . . . .184 A1
  Bexleyheath DA7 . . . . .159 H3
  Borehamwood WD6 . . . . . . .38 C2
  Hampton TW12 . . . . .179 F1
Mason Rd, Sutt. SM1 . . . . . .
  off Manor Pl 198/199 E5
  Woodford Green IG8 . . . . . .63 E4
Masons Arms Ms, W1 . . . . . .17 E4
Masons Av, EC2 . . . . .20 B3
  Croydon CR0 . . . . .201 J3
  Harrow HA3 . . . . .68 C4
Masons Ct, Wem. HA9 . . . . .
  off Mayfields 88 A2
Masons Grn La, W3 . . . . . . .106 A5
Masons Hill, SE18 . . . . .137 E4
  Bromley BR1, BR2 . . . . . . .191 G4
Mason's Pl, EC1 . . . . .11 H3
Masons Pl, Mitch. CR4 . . . . .185 J1
Mason St, SE17 . . . . .36 C2
Mason's Yd, SW1 . . . . .25 G1
  SW19 . . . .
  off High St Wimbledon 166 A5
Massey Cl, N11 off Grove Rd . . .58 B5
Massey Ct, E6 . . . . .115 J1
Massie Rd, E8 off Graham Rd . . .94 D6
Massingberd Way, SW17 . . .168 B4
Massinger St, SE17 . . . . .36 D2
Massingham St, E1 . . . . . . .113 G4
Masson Av, Ruis. HA4 . . . . . .84 C6
Master Gunner Pl, SE18 . . . .136 B7
Masterman Ho, SE5 . . . . . . .36 B7
Masterman Rd, E6 . . . . .116 B3
Masters Cl, SW16 . . . .
  off Blegborough Rd 168 C6
Masters Dr, SE16 . . . . .132 E5
Masters St, E1 . . . . .113 G5
Masthouse Ter, E14 . . . . . . .134 A4
Mast Leisure Pk, SE16 . . . . .133 G3
Mastmaker Rd, E14 . . . . . . .134 A2
Maswell Pk Cres, Houns. TW3 . .143 J5
Maswell Pk Rd, Houns. TW3 . .143 H5
Matcham Rd, E11 . . . . .97 E3
Matchless Dr, SE18 . . . . . . .136 D7
Matfield Cl, Brom. BR2 . . . .191 G5
Matfield Rd, Belv. DA17 . . . .139 G6
Matham Gro, SE22 . . . . .152 C4
Matham Rd, E.Mol. KT8 . . . .180 A5
Matheson Rd, W14 . . . . .128 C4
Mathews Av, E6 . . . . .116 D2
Mathews Pk Av, E15 . . . . . . .97 F6
Matilda Cl, SE19 . . . .
  off Elizabeth Way 170 A7
Matilda St, N1 . . . . .111 F1
Matlock Cl, SE24 . . . . .151 J4
  Barnet EN5 . . . . .40 A5
Matlock Ct, SE5 . . . .
  off Denmark Hill Est 152 A4
Matlock Cres, Sutt. SM3 . . .198 B4
  Watford WD19 . . . . .50 C3
Matlock Gdns, Sutt. SM3 . . .198 B4
Matlock Pl, Sutt. SM3 . . . . . .198 B4
Matlock Rd, E10 . . . . .78 C6
Matlock St, E14 . . . . .113 H6
Matlock Way, N.Mal. KT3 . . .182 D1
Matrimony Pl, SW8 . . . . .150 D2
Matson Ct, Wdf.Grn. IG8 . . .
  off The Bridle Path 62/63 E7
Matthew Cl, W10 . . . . .108 A4
Matthew Ct, Mitch. CR4 . . . .186 D5
Matthew Parker St, SW1 . . . .25 J4
Matthews Rd, Grnf. UB6 . . . .86 A5
Matthews St, SW11 . . . . . . .149 J2
Matthews Yd, WC2 . . . . .18 A4
Matthias Rd, N16 . . . . .94 A5
Mattingley Way, SE15 . . . . . .37 F7
Mattison Rd, N4 . . . . .75 G6
Mattock La, W5 . . . . .125 E1
  W13 . . . . .125 E1
Maud Cashmore Way, SE18 . .136 C3
Maude Rd, E17 . . . . .77 H5
  SE5 . . . . .152 B1
Maudesville Cotts, W7 . . . . .
  off The Broadway 124 B1
Maude Ter, E17 . . . . .77 H4
Maud Gdns, E13 . . . . .115 F1
  Barking IG11 . . . . .117 J2
Maudlin's Grn, E1 . . . . .29 H1
Maud Rd, E10 . . . . .96 C3
  E13 . . . . .115 F2
Maudslay Rd, SE9 . . . . .156 C3
Maudsley Ho, Brent. TW8 . . .
  off Green Dragon La 125 H5
Maud St, E16 . . . . .115 F5
Maud Wilkes Cl, NW5 . . . . . .92 C5
Mauleverer Rd, SW2 . . . . . . .150 E5
Maundeby Wk, NW10 . . . . . .
  off Neasden La 88/89 E6
Maunder Rd, W7 . . . . .124 C1
Maunsel St, SW1 . . . . .33 H1
Maurice Av, N22 . . . . .75 H2
Maurice Brown Cl, NW7 . . . .56 A5
Maurice St, W12 . . . . .107 H6

Maurice Wk, NW11 . . . . .73 F4
Maurier Cl, Nthlt. UB5 . . . . .102 C1
Mauritius Rd, SE10 . . . . . . .135 E4
Maury Rd, N16 . . . . .94 D2
Mauveine Gdns, Houns. TW3 . .143 G4
Mavelstone Cl, Brom. BR1 . . .192 B1
Mavelstone Rd, Brom. BR1 . .192 B1
Maverton Rd, E3 . . . . .114 A1
Mavis Av, Epsom KT19 . . . . .197 E5
Mavis Cl, Epsom KT19 . . . . .197 E5
Mavis Wk, E6 . . . . .116 B5
Mawbey Est, SE1 . . . . .37 H4
Mawbey Pl, SE1 . . . . .37 G4
Mawbey Rd, SE1 . . . . .37 G4
Mawbey St, SW8 . . . . .130 E7
Mawney Cl, Rom. RM7 . . . . . .83 H2
Mawney Rd, Rom. RM7 . . . . .83 J4
Mawson Cl, SW20 . . . . .184 B2
Mawson La, W4 off Great W Rd . .127 F6
Maxey Gdns, Dag. RM9 . . . .101 E4
Maxey Rd, SE18 . . . . .137 F4
  Dagenham RM9 . . . . .100 E4
Maxfield Cl, N20 . . . . .41 F7
Maxilla Gdns, W10 . . . .
  off Cambridge Gdns 108 A6
Maxilla Wk, W10 . . . .
  off Kingsdown Cl 108 A6
Maxim Rd, N21 . . . . .43 G6
Maxted Pk, Har. HA1 . . . . . . .68 B7
Maxted Rd, SE15 . . . . .152 C3
Maxwell Cl, Croy. CR0 . . . . .201 E1
  Hayes UB3 . . . . .102 A7
Maxwell Gdns, Orp. BR6 . . .207 J3
Maxwell Rd, SW6 . . . . .128 E7
  Borehamwood WD6 . . . . . . .38 B3
  Welling DA16 . . . . .158 A4
  West Drayton UB7 . . . . . . .120 C4
Maxwelton Av, NW7 . . . . .54 D5
Maxwelton Cl, NW7 . . . . .54 D5
Maya Angelou Ct, E4 . . . . . .
  off Bailey Cl 62 C4
Maya Cl, SE15 . . . . .152 E2
Mayall Rd, SE24 . . . . .151 H5
Maya Pl, N11 . . . . .58 D7
Maya Rd, N2 . . . . .73 F4
Maybank Av, E18 . . . . .79 H2
  Wembley HA0 . . . . .86 C5
Maybank Gdns, Pnr. HA5 . . . .66 A5
Maybank Rd, E18 . . . . .79 H1
May Bate Av, Kings.T. KT2 . . .181 G1
Maybells Commercial Est, Bark.
  IG11 . . . . .118 D2
Mayberry Pl, Surb. KT5 . . . .181 J7
Maybourne Cl, SE26 . . . . . .171 E5
Maybrook Meadow Est, Bark.
  IG11 . . . . .100 A7
Maybury Cl, Loug. IG10 . . . . .48 E4
  Orpington BR5 . . . . .193 E5
Maybury Gdns, NW10 . . . . . .89 H6
Maybury Ms, N6 . . . . .74 C7
Maybury Rd, E13 . . . . .115 J4
  Barking IG11 . . . . .117 J2
Maybury St, SW17 . . . . .167 H5
Maychurch Cl, Stan. HA7 . . . .53 G7
May Cl, Chess. KT9 . . . . . . .195 J6
May Ct, SW19 . . . . .185 F1
Maycroft, Pnr. HA5 . . . . .66 B2
Maycross Av, Mord. SM4 . . .184 C3
Mayday Gdns, SE3 . . . . .156 B2
Mayday Rd, Th.Hth. CR7 . . . .187 H6
Maydew Ho, SE16 . . . .
  off Abbeyfield Rd 133 F4
Mayerne Rd, SE9 . . . . .156 A5
Mayesbrook Rd, Bark. IG11 . .117 J1
  Dagenham RM8 . . . . .100 A3
  Ilford IG3 . . . . .100 A3
Mayesford Rd, Rom. RM6 . . .82 C7
Mayes Rd, N22 . . . . .75 G2
Mayeswood Rd, SE12 . . . . .173 J3
MAYFAIR, W1 . . . . .16 D6
Mayfair Av, Bexh. DA7 . . . . .158 D1
  Ilford IG1 . . . . .98 C2
  Romford RM6 . . . . .82 D6
  Twickenham TW2 . . . . .143 J7
  Worcester Park KT4 . . . . . .197 G1
Mayfair Cl, Beck. BR3 . . . . .190 B1
  Surbiton KT6 . . . . .195 H1
Mayfair Gdns, N17 . . . . .60 A6
  Woodford Green IG8 . . . . . .63 G7
Mayfair Ms, NW1 . . . .
  off Regents Pk Rd 91 J7
Mayfair Pl, W1 . . . . .25 E1
Mayfair Ter, N14 . . . . .42 D7
Mayfield, Bexh. DA7 . . . . . . .159 F3
Mayfield Av, N12 . . . . .57 F4
  N14 . . . . .58 D2
  W4 . . . . .127 E4
  W13 . . . . .124 E3
  Harrow HA3 . . . . .68 E5
  Orpington BR6 . . . . .207 J1
  Woodford Green IG8 . . . . . .63 G7
Mayfield Cl, E8 off Forest Rd . .94 C6
  SW4 . . . . .150 D5
  Thames Ditton KT7 . . . . . . .194 E1
Mayfield Cres, N9 . . . . .44 E6
  Thornton Heath CR7 . . . . .187 F4
Mayfield Dr, Pnr. HA5 . . . . . .67 F4

Mayfield Gdns, NW4 . . . .**72** A6
W7 . . . .**104** A6
Mayfield Mans, SW15
off West Hill **148** A7
Mayfield Rd, E4 . . . .**62** C2
E8 . . . .**94** C7
E13 . . . .**115** F4
E17 . . . .**77** H2
N8 . . . .**75** F6
SW19 . . . .**184** C1
W3 . . . .**106** B7
W12 . . . .**127** E2
Belvedere DA17 . . . .**139** J4
Bromley BR1 . . . .**192** B5
Dagenham RM8 . . . .**100** C1
Enfield EN3 . . . .**45** G2
Sutton SM2 . . . .**199** G6
Thornton Heath CR7 . . . .**187** F4
Mayfields, Wem. HA9 . . . .**88** A2
Mayfields Cl, Wem. HA9 . . . . . .**88** A2
Mayflower Cl, SE16
off Greenland Quay **133** G4
Mayflower Ct, SE16
off St. Marychurch St **133** F2
Mayflower Rd, SW9 . . . .**150** E3
Mayflower St, SE16 . . . .**133** F2
Mayfly Cl, Pnr. HA5 . . . .**66** C7
Mayfly Gdns, Nthlt. UB5
off Ruislip Rd **102** D3
Mayford Cl, SW12 . . . .**149** J7
Beckenham BR3 . . . .**189** G3
Mayford Rd, SW12 . . . .**149** J7
May Gdns, Wem. HA0 . . . .**105** F2
Maygood St, N1 . . . .**10** D1
Maygrove Rd, NW6 . . . .**90** C6
Mayhew Cl, E4 . . . .**62** A3
Mayhill Rd, SE7 . . . .**135** H6
Barnet EN5 . . . .**40** B6
Maylands Dr, Sid. DA14 . . . . . .**176** D3
Maylands Rd, Wat. WD19 . . . . . .**50** C4
Maynard Cl, N15
off Brunswick Rd **76** B4
SW6 *off Cambria St* **128/129** F7
Maynard Path, E17 . . . .**78** C5
Maynard Rd, E17 . . . .**78** C5
Maynards Quay, E1
off Garnet St **113** F7
Maynooth Gdns, Cars. SM5 . . . .**185** J7
Mayola Rd, E5 . . . .**95** F4
Mayo Rd, NW10 . . . .**88** E6
Croydon CR0 . . . .**188** A5
Mayow Rd, SE23 . . . .**171** G3
SE26 . . . .**171** G4
Mayplace Cl, Bexh. DA7 . . . . . .**159** H3
Mayplace La, SE18 . . . .**137** E7
Mayplace Rd E, Bexh. DA7 . . . .**159** H3
Dartford DA1 . . . .**159** J3
Mayplace Rd W, Bexh. DA7 . . . .**159** G4
Maypole Cres, Ilf. IG6 . . . .**65** G2
May Rd, E4 . . . .**62** A6
E13 . . . .**115** G2
Twickenham TW2 . . . .**162** B1
Mayroyd Av, Surb. KT6 . . . .**196** A2
May's Bldgs Ms, SE10
off Crooms Hill **134** D7
Mays Ct, WC2 . . . .**18** A6
Mays Hill Rd, Brom. BR2 . . . . . .**191** E2
Mays La, E4 . . . .**62** D2
Barnet EN5 . . . .**40** B5
Maysoule Rd, SW11 . . . .**149** G4
Mays Rd, Tedd. TW11 . . . .**162** A5
Mayston Ms, SE10
off Westcombe Hill **135** G5
May St, W14 *off North End Rd* . .**128** C5
Mayswood Gdns, Dag. RM10 . . .**101** J6
Mayton St, N7 . . . .**93** F3
Maytree Cl, Edg. HA8 . . . .**54** C3
Maytree Gdns, W5
off South Ealing Rd **125** G2
May Tree La, Stan. HA7 . . . .**52** C7
Maytree Wk, SW2 . . . .**169** G2
Mayville Est, N16
off King Henry St **94** B5
Mayville Rd, E11 . . . .**96** E2
Ilford IG1 . . . .**98** E5
May Wk, E13 . . . .**115** H2
Maywood Rd, Beck. BR3 . . . . . .**172** B7
Maze Hill, SE3 . . . .**134** E6
SE10 . . . .**134** E6
Mazenod Av, NW6 . . . .**90** D7
Maze Rd, Rich. TW9 . . . .**126** A7
Mead, The, N2 . . . .**73** F2
W13 . . . .**104** E5
Beckenham BR3 . . . .**190** C1
Wallington SM6 . . . .**200** D6
Watford WD19 . . . .**50** E3
West Wickham BR4 . . . .**204** D1
Mead Cl, Har. HA3 . . . .**68** A1
Loughton IG10 . . . .**48** E2
Mead Ct, NW9 . . . .**70** C5
Mead Cres, E4 . . . .**62** C4
Sutton SM1 . . . .**199** H4
Meadcroft Rd, SE11 . . . .**35** G6
Meade Cl, W4 . . . .**126** A6
Meadfield, Edg. HA8 . . . .**54** B2
Mead Fld, Har. HA2
off Kings Rd **85** F3

Meadfield Grn, Edg. HA8 . . . . . .**54** B2
Meadfoot Rd, SW16 . . . .**168** C7
Meadgate Av, Wdf.Grn. IG8 . . . .**64** B5
Meadlands Dr, Rich. TW10 . . . .**163** G2
Meadow Av, Croy. CR0 . . . .**189** G6
Meadow Bk, N21 . . . .**43** F6
Meadowbank, NW3 . . . .**91** J7
SE3 . . . .**155** F3
Surbiton KT5 . . . .**181** J6
Meadowbank Cl, SW6 . . . .**127** J7
Meadowbank Gdns, Houns.
TW5 . . . .**142** A2
Meadowbank Rd, NW9 . . . .**70** D7
Meadowbanks, Barn. EN5 . . . . . .**39** F5
Meadow Cl, E4
off Mount Echo Av **62** B1
E9 . . . .**95** J5
SE6 . . . .**172** A5
SW20 . . . .**183** J4
Barking IG11 *off Meadow Rd* . .**99** J7
Barnet EN5 . . . .**40** C6
Bexleyheath DA6 . . . .**159** F5
Chislehurst BR7 . . . .**174** E5
Esher KT10 . . . .**194** C3
Hounslow TW4 . . . .**143** G6
Northolt UB5 . . . .**103** G2
Richmond TW10 . . . .**163** H1
Sutton SM1
off Aultone Way **198/199** E2
Meadowcourt Rd, SE3 . . . .**155** F4
Meadowcroft, Brom. BR1 . . . . .**192** C3
Meadowcroft Rd, N13 . . . .**59** G2
Meadow Dr, N10 . . . .**74** B3
NW4 . . . .**71** J2
Meadow Gdns, Edg. HA8 . . . . . .**54** B6
Meadow Garth, NW10 . . . .**88** C6
Meadowgate Cl, NW7
off Stanhope Gdns **55** F5
Meadow Hill, N.Mal. KT3 . . . . . .**182** E6
Meadowlea Cl, West Dr. UB7 . . .**120** A6
Meadow Ms, SW8 . . . .**34** C6
Meadow Pl, SW8 . . . .**34** B7
W4 *off Edensor Rd* **126/127** E7
Meadow Rd, SW8 . . . .**34** C7
SW19 . . . .**167** F7
Barking IG11 . . . .**99** J7
Borehamwood WD6 . . . .**38** B2
Bromley BR2 . . . .**191** E1
Dagenham RM9 . . . .**101** F6
Esher (Clay.) KT10 . . . .**194** B6
Feltham TW13 . . . .**160** E2
Loughton IG10 . . . .**48** B5
Pinner HA5 . . . .**66** D5
Romford RM7 . . . .**101** J1
Southall UB1 . . . .**103** F7
Sutton SM1 . . . .**199** H5
Meadow Row, SE1 . . . .**27** J6
Meadows Cl, E10 . . . .**96** A2
Meadows End, Sun. TW16 . . . . .**178** A1
Meadowside, SE9 . . . .**155** J4
Meadow Stile, Croy. CR0
off High St **201** J3
Meadowsweet Cl, E16
off Monarch Dr **116** A5
SW20 . . . .**183** J5
Meadow Vw, Har. HA1 . . . .**86** B1
Sidcup DA15 . . . .**158** B7
Meadowview Rd, SE6 . . . .**171** J5
Bexley DA5 . . . .**159** E6
Meadow Vw Rd, Th.Hth. CR7 . . .**187** H5
Meadow Wk, E18 . . . .**79** G4
Dagenham RM9 . . . .**101** F6
Epsom KT17, KT19 . . . .**197** E6
Wallington SM6 . . . .**200** B3
Meadow Way, NW9 . . . .**70** D5
Chessington KT9 . . . .**195** H6
Chigwell IG7 . . . .**65** F3
Orpington BR6 . . . .**206** D3
Ruislip HA4 . . . .**66** B6
Wembley HA9 . . . .**87** G4
Meadow Way, The, Har. HA3 . . . .**68** B2
Meadow Waye, Houns. TW5 . . . .**123** E6
Mead Path, SW17 . . . .**167** F5
Mead Pl, E9 . . . .**95** F6
Croydon CR0 . . . .**201** H1
Mead Plat, NW10 . . . .**88** C6
Mead Rd, Chis. BR7 . . . .**175** F6
Edgware HA8 . . . .**54** A6
Richmond TW10 . . . .**163** F3
Mead Row, SE1 . . . .**27** E5
Meads, The, Edg. HA8 . . . .**54** D6
Sutton SM3 . . . .**198** B3
Meads La, Ilf. IG3 . . . .**81** H7
Meads Rd, N22 . . . .**75** H2
Enfield EN3 . . . .**45** H1
Mead Ter, Wem. HA9
off Meadow Way **87** G4
Meadvale Rd, W5 . . . .**105** E4
Croydon CR0 . . . .**188** C7
Meadway, N14 . . . .**58** D2
NW11 . . . .**72** E6
SW20 . . . .**183** J4
Barnet EN5 . . . .**40** D4
Beckenham BR3 . . . .**190** C1

Mead Way, Brom. BR2 . . . .**191** F6
Croydon CR0 . . . .**203** H2
Meadway, Ilf. IG3 . . . .**99** H4
Surbiton KT5 . . . .**196** C1
Twickenham TW2 . . . .**162** A1
Woodford Green IG8 . . . .**63** J5
Meadway, The, SE3
off Heath La **154** D2
Buckhurst Hill IG9 . . . .**64** A1
Loughton IG10 . . . .**48** C6
Meadway Cl, NW11 . . . .**73** E6
Barnet EN5 . . . .**40** D4
Pinner HA5
off Highbanks Rd **51** H6
Meadway Ct, NW11 . . . .**73** E6
Meadway Gate, NW11 . . . .**72** D6
Meaford Way, SE20 . . . .**171** E7
Meakin Est, SE1 . . . .**28** D5
Meanley Rd, E12 . . . .**98** B4
Meard St, W1 . . . .**17** H4
Meath Rd, E15 . . . .**115** F2
Ilford IG1 . . . .**99** F3
Meath St, SW11 . . . .**150** B1
Mecklenburgh Pl, WC1 . . . .**10** C5
Mecklenburgh Sq, WC1 . . . .**10** C5
Mecklenburgh St, WC1 . . . .**10** C5
Medburn St, NW1 . . . .**9** H1
Medcroft Gdns, SW14 . . . .**146** C4
Medebourne Cl, SE3 . . . .**155** G3
Medesenge Way, N13 . . . .**59** H6
Medfield St, SW15 . . . .**147** H7
Medhurst Cl, E3 *off Arbery Rd* . .**113** H2
Medhurst Rd, E3 *off Arbery Rd* . .**113** H2
Median Rd, E5 . . . .**95** F5
★ Medici Galleries, W1 . . . .**16** E6
Medina Av, Esher KT10 . . . .**194** B3
Medina Gro, N7 *off Medina Rd* . .**93** G3
Medina Rd, N7 . . . .**93** G3
Medland Cl, Wall. SM6 . . . .**200** A1
Medland Ho, E14 *off Branch Rd* . .**113** H7
Medlar St, SE5 . . . .**151** J1
Medley Rd, NW6 . . . .**90** D6
Medora Rd, SW2 . . . .**151** F7
Medusa Rd, SE6 . . . .**154** B6
Medway Bldgs, E3
off Medway Rd **113** H2
Medway Cl, Croy. CR0 . . . .**189** F6
Ilford IG1 . . . .**99** F5
Medway Dr, Grnf. UB6 . . . .**104** C2
Medway Gdns, Wem. HA0 . . . . . .**86** D4
Medway Ms, E3 *off Medway Rd* . .**113** H2
Medway Par, Grnf. UB6 . . . .**104** C2
Medway Rd, E3 . . . .**113** H2
Medway St, SW1 . . . .**25** J6
Medwin St, SW4 . . . .**151** F4
Meerbrook Rd, SE3 . . . .**155** J3
Meeson Rd, E15 . . . .**115** F1
Meeson St, E5 . . . .**95** H4
Meeting Fld Path, E9
off Chatham Pl **95** F6
Meeting Ho All, E1
off Wapping La **132/133** E1
Meeting Ho La, SE15 . . . .**152** E1
Mehetabel Rd, E9 . . . .**95** F6
Meister Cl, Ilf. IG1 . . . .**99** G1
Melancholy Wk, Rich. TW10 . . . .**163** F2
Melanda Cl, Chis. BR7 . . . .**174** C5
Melanie Cl, Bexh. DA7 . . . .**158** E1
Melba Way, SE13 . . . .**154** B1
Melbourne Av, N13 . . . .**59** F6
W13 . . . .**124** D1
Pinner HA5 . . . .**67** H3
Melbourne Cl, Orp. BR6 . . . . . .**193** H7
Wallington SM6
off Melbourne Rd **200** C5
Melbourne Ct, E5
off Daubeney Rd **95** H4
N10 *off Sydney Rd* **58** B7
SE20 . . . .**170** D7
Melbourne Gdns, Rom. RM6 . . . .**82** E5
Melbourne Gro, SE22 . . . .**152** B4
Melbourne Ho, Hayes UB4 . . . .**102** C4
Melbourne Ms, SE6 . . . .**154** C7
SW9 . . . .**151** G1
Melbourne Pl, WC2 . . . .**18** D5
Melbourne Rd, E6 . . . .**116** C1
E10 . . . .**78** B7
E17 . . . .**77** H4
SW19 . . . .**184** D1
Ilford IG1 . . . .**99** E1
Teddington TW11 . . . .**163** F6
Wallington SM6 . . . .**200** B5
Melbourne Sq, SW9
off Melbourne Ms **151** G1
Melbourne Ter, SW6
off Waterford Rd **128/129** E7
Melbourne Way, Enf. EN1 . . . . . .**44** C6
Melbury Av, Sthl. UB2 . . . .**123** H3
Melbury Cl, Chis. BR7 . . . .**174** C6
Esher (Clay.) KT10 . . . .**194** E6
Melbury Ct, W8 . . . .**128** C3
Melbury Dr, SE5
off Sedgmoor Pl **132** B7
Melbury Gdns, SW20 . . . .**183** H1
Melbury Rd, W14 . . . .**128** C3

Melbury Rd, Har. HA3 . . . .**69** J5
Melcombe Gdns, Har. HA3 . . . . .**69** J6
Melcombe Pl, NW1 . . . .**15** J1
Melcombe St, NW1 . . . .**8** A6
Meldex Cl, NW7 . . . .**55** J6
Meldon Cl, SW6
off Bagley's La **148/149** E1
Meldone Cl, Surb. KT5 . . . .**182** B6
Meldrum Rd, Ilf. IG3 . . . .**100** A2
Melfield Gdns, SE6 . . . .**172** B4
Melford Av, Bark. IG11 . . . .**99** H6
Melford Cl, Chess. KT9 . . . .**195** J5
Melford Rd, E6 . . . .**116** C4
E11 . . . .**96** E2
E17 . . . .**77** H4
SE22 . . . .**152** D7
Ilford IG1 . . . .**99** G2
Melfort Av, Th.Hth. CR7 . . . .**187** H3
Melfort Rd, Th.Hth. CR7 . . . .**187** H3
Melgund Rd, N5 . . . .**93** G5
Melina Pl, NW8 . . . .**6** E4
Melina Rd, W12 . . . .**127** H2
Melior Pl, SE1 . . . .**28** D3
Melior St, SE1 . . . .**28** C3
Meliot Rd, SE6 . . . .**172** D2
Meller Cl, Croy. CR0 . . . .**200** E3
Melling Dr, Enf. EN1 . . . .**44** D1
Melling St, SE18 . . . .**137** H6
Mellish Cl, Bark. IG11 . . . .**117** J1
Mellish Gdns, Wdf.Grn. IG8 . . . . .**63** G5
Mellish Ind Est, SE18 . . . .**136** B3
Mellish St, E14 . . . .**134** A3
Mellison Rd, SW17 . . . .**167** H5
Melliss Av, Rich. TW9 . . . .**146** B1
Mellitus St, W12 . . . .**107** F6
Mellor Cl, Walt. KT12 . . . .**179** F7
Mellows Rd, Ilf. IG5 . . . .**80** C3
Wallington SM6 . . . .**200** D5
Mells Cres, SE9 . . . .**174** C4
Mell St, SE10
off Trafalgar Rd **134/135** E5
Melody La, N5 . . . .**93** H5
Melody Rd, SW18 . . . .**149** F5
Melon Pl, W8 . . . .**22** A3
Melon Rd, E11 . . . .**96** E3
SE15 . . . .**152** D1
Melrose Av, N22 . . . .**75** H1
NW2 . . . .**89** H5
SW16 . . . .**187** F3
SW19 . . . .**166** D2
Borehamwood WD6 . . . .**38** B5
Greenford UB6 . . . .**103** H2
Mitcham CR4 . . . .**168** B7
Twickenham TW2 . . . .**143** H7
Melrose Cl, SE12 . . . .**173** G1
Greenford UB6 . . . .**103** H2
Hayes UB4 . . . .**102** A5
Melrose Ct, W13
off Williams Rd **124** D1
Melrose Cres, Orp. BR6 . . . . . .**207** G4
Melrose Dr, Sthl. UB1 . . . .**123** G1
Melrose Gdns, W6 . . . .**127** J3
Edgware HA8 . . . .**70** B2
New Malden KT3 . . . .**182** D3
Melrose Rd, SW13 . . . .**147** F2
SW18 . . . .**148** C6
SW19 . . . .**184** D2
W3 *off Stanley Rd* **126** C3
Pinner HA5 . . . .**67** F4
Melrose Ter, W6 . . . .**127** J2
Melsa Rd, Mord. SM4 . . . .**185** F6
Melthorne Dr, Ruis. HA4 . . . .**84** C3
Melthorpe Gdns, SE3 . . . .**156** B1
Melton Cl, Ruis. HA4 . . . .**84** C1
Melton Ct, SW7 . . . .**31** F2
Sutton SM2 . . . .**199** F7
Melton St, NW1 . . . .**9** G4
Melville Av, SW20 . . . .**165** G7
Greenford UB6 . . . .**86** C5
South Croydon CR2 . . . .**202** C5
Melville Gdns, N13 . . . .**59** H5
Melville Pl, N1 *off Essex Rd* . . .**111** H1
Melville Rd, E17 . . . .**77** J3
NW10 . . . .**88** D7
SW13 . . . .**147** G1
Sidcup DA14 . . . .**176** C2
Melville Vil Rd, W3 *off High St* . .**126** D1
Melvin Rd, SE20 . . . .**189** F1
Melyn Cl, N7 *off Anson Rd* **92** C4
Memel Ct, EC1 . . . .**11** J6
Memel St, EC1 . . . .**11** J6
Memess Path, SE18 . . . .**136** D6
Memorial Av, E15 . . . .**114** E3
Memorial Cl, Houns. TW5 . . . . .**123** F6
Mendip Cl, SE26 . . . .**171** F4
Hayes UB3 . . . .**121** G7
Worcester Park KT4 . . . .**197** J1
Mendip Dr, NW2 . . . .**90** A2
Mendip Ho, N9 *off New Rd* **60** D3
Mendip Rd, SW11 . . . .**149** F3
Ilford IG2 . . . .**81** H5
Mendora Rd, SW6 . . . .**128** B7
Menelik Rd, NW2 . . . .**90** B4
Menlo Gdns, SE19 . . . .**170** A7
Menon Dr, N9 . . . .**60** E3
Menotti St, E2 . . . .**13** J5
Mentmore Cl, Har. HA3 . . . .**69** F6

Mentmore Ter, E8 95 E7
Meon Ct, Islw. TW7 144 B2
Meon Rd, W3 126 C2
Meopham Rd, Mitch. CR4 186 C1
Mepham Cres, Har. HA3 51 J7
Mepham Gdns, Har. HA3 51 J7
Mepham St, SE1 26 D2
Mera Dr, Bexh. DA7 159 G4
Merantun Way, SW19 185 F1
Merbury Cl, SE13 154 C5
SE28 *off Merbury Rd* 137 G1
Merbury Rd, SE28 137 H2
Mercator Pl, E14 *off Napier Av* 134 A5
Mercator Rd, SE13 154 D4
Mercer Cl, T.Ditt. KT7 180 C7
Merceron St, E1 112 E4
Mercer Pl, Pnr. HA5
off Crossway 66 C2
Mercers Cl, SE10 135 F4
Mercers Ms, N19
off Mercers Rd 92 D3
Mercers Pl, W6 127 J4
Mercers Rd, N19 92 D3
Mercer St, WC2 18 A4
Merchants Cl, SE25
off Clifford Rd 188 D4
Merchants Ho, SE10
off Hoskins St 134 D5
Merchant St, E3 113 J3
Merchiston Rd, SE6 172 D2
Merchland Rd, SE9 175 F1
Mercia Gro, SE13 154 C4
Mercier Rd, SW15 148 B5
Mercury Cen, Felt. TW14 142 B5
Mercury Way, SE14 133 G6
Mercy Ter, SE13 154 B4
Merebank La, Croy. CR0 201 F5
Mere Cl, SW15 148 A7
Orpington BR6 206 E2
Meredith Av, NW2 89 J5
Meredith Cl, Pnr. HA5 50 D7
Meredith Ms, SE4 153 J4
Meredith St, E13 115 G3
EC1 11 G4
Meredyth Rd, SW13 147 G2
Mere End, Croy. CR0 189 G7
Mere Side, Orp. BR6 206 D2
Meretone Cl, SE4 153 H4
Merevale Cres, Mord. SM4 185 F6
Mereway Rd, Twick. TW2 162 A1
Merewood Cl, Brom. BR1 192 D2
Merewood Rd, Bexh. DA7 159 J2
Mereworth Cl, Brom. BR2 191 F5
Mereworth Dr, SE18 137 E7
Merganser Gdns, SE28
off Avocet Ms 137 G3
Meriden Cl, Brom. BR1 174 A7
Ilford IG6 81 F1
Meridian Gate, E14 134 C2
Meridian Pl, E14 134 B2
Meridian Rd, SE7 136 A7
Meridian Sq, E15 96 D7
Meridian Trd Est, SE7 135 H4
Meridian Wk, N17
off Commercial Rd 60 B6
Meridian Way, N9 61 F5
N18 61 F6
Enfield EN3 45 G6
Merifield Rd, SE9 155 J4
Merino Cl, E11 79 J4
Merino Pl, Sid. DA15
off Blackfen Rd 158 A6
Merivale Rd, SW15 148 B4
Harrow HA1 67 J7
Merlewood Dr, Chis. BR7 192 C1
Merley Ct, NW9 88 C1
Merlin Cl, Croy. CR0 202 B4
Mitcham CR4 185 H3
Northolt UB5 102 C3
Wallington SM6 201 F6
Merlin Cres, Edg. HA8 69 J1
Merlin Gdns, Brom. BR1 173 G3
Merling Cl, Chess. KT9
off Coppard Gdns 195 G5
Merlin Gro, Beck. BR3 189 J4
Ilford IG6 65 E7
Merlin Ho, Enf. EN3
off Allington Ct 45 G5
Merlin Rd, E12 97 J2
Welling DA16 158 A4
Merlin Rd N, Well. DA16 158 A4
Merlins Av, Har. HA2 85 F3
Merlin St, WC1 11 E4
Mermaid Ct, SE1 28 B3
SE16 133 J1
Mermaid Twr, SE8
off Abinger Gro 133 J6
Merredene St, SW2 151 F6
Merriam Av, E9 95 J6
Merriam Cl, E4 62 C5
Merrick Rd, Sthl. UB2 123 F2
Merrick Sq, SE1 28 A5
Merridale, SE12 155 G5
Merridene, N21 43 H6
Merrielands Cres, Dag. RM9 119 F1
Merrilands Rd, Wor.Pk. KT4 197 J1
Merrilees Rd, Sid. DA15 175 H1
Merrilyn Cl, Esher (Clay.) KT10 194 D6
Merriman Rd, SE3 155 J1
Merrington Rd, SW6 128 D6
Merrion Av, Stan. HA7 53 G5
Merrion Wk, SE17
off Dawes St 132 A5
Merritt Gdns, Chess. KT9 195 F6
Merritt Rd, SE4 153 J5
Merrivale, N14 42 D6
Merrivale Av, Ilf. IG4 80 A4
Merrow St, SE17 36 B5
Merrow Wk, SE17 36 C3
Merrow Way, Croy. (New Adgtn)
CR0 204 C6
Merrydown Way, Chis. BR7 192 B1
Merryfield, SE3 155 F2
Merryfield Gdns, Stan. HA7 53 F5
Merryfield Ho, SE9
off Grove Pk Rd 173 J3
Merryfields Way, SE6 154 B7
MERRY HILL, Bushey WD23 51 G1
Merryhill Cl, E4 46 B7
Merry Hill Mt, Bushey WD23 51 H1
Merry Hill Rd, Bushey WD23 51 H1
Merryhills Ct, N14 42 C5
Merryhills Dr, Enf. EN2 42 D4
Mersea Ho, Bark. IG11 98 E6
Mersey Rd, E17 77 J3
Mersey Wk, Nthlt. UB5
off Brabazon Rd 103 G2
Mersham Dr, NW9 70 A5
Mersham Pl, SE20 189 E1
Mersham Rd, Th.Hth. CR7 188 A3
Merten Rd, Rom. RM6 83 E7
Merthyr Ter, SW13 127 H6
MERTON, SW19 184 D1
Merton Av, W4 127 F4
Northolt UB5 85 J5
Merton Gdns, Orp. BR5 193 E5
Merton Hall Gdns, SW20 184 B1
Merton Hall Rd, SW19 184 B1
Merton High St, SW19 167 E7
Merton Ind Pk, SW19 185 F1
Merton La, N6 91 J2
Merton Mans, SW20 184 A2
MERTON PARK, SW19 184 D2
Merton Pk Par, SW19
off Kingston Rd 184 C1
Merton Ri, NW3 91 H7
Merton Rd, E17 78 C5
SE25 188 D5
SW18 148 D5
SW19 166 E7
Barking IG11 99 J7
Harrow HA2 85 J1
Ilford IG3 81 J7
Merton Way, W.Mol. KT8 179 H4
Merttins Rd, SE15 153 G5
Meru Cl, NW5 92 A4
Mervan Rd, SW2 151 G4
Mervyn Av, SE9 175 F3
Mervyn Rd, W13 124 D3
Messaline Av, W3 106 C6
Messent Rd, SE9 155 J5
Messeter Pl, SE9 156 D6
Messina Av, NW6 90 D7
Metcalf Wk, Felt. TW13
off Gabriel Cl 160/161 E4
Meteor St, SW11 150 A4
Meteor Way, Wall. SM6 200 E7
Metheringham Way, NW9 70 E1
Methley St, SE11 35 F4
★ **Methodist Cen Hall**, SW1 25 J4
Methuen Cl, Edg. HA8 54 A7
Methuen Pk, N10 74 B2
Methuen Rd, Belv. DA17 139 H4
Bexleyheath DA6 159 F4
Edgware HA8 54 A7
Methwold Rd, W10 108 A5
Metro Cen, The, Islw. TW7 144 B2
Metropolis Cen, Borwd. WD6 38 A3
Metropolitan Cen, The, Grnf.
UB6 103 H1
Metropolitan Cl, E14
off Broomfield St 114 A5
Mews, The, N1 *off St. Paul St* 111 J1
N8 *off Turnpike La* 75 G3
Ilford IG4 80 A5
Twickenham TW1
off Bridge Rd 144/145 E6
Mews Deck, E1 113 E7
Mews Pl, Wdf.Grn. IG8 63 G4
Mews St, E1 29 H1
Mexfield Rd, SW15 148 C5
Meyer Rd, Erith DA8 139 J6
Meymott St, SE1 27 G2
Meynell Cres, E9 95 G7
Meynell Gdns, E9 95 G7
Meynell Rd, E9 95 G7
Meyrick Rd, NW10 89 G6
SW11 149 G3
Miah Ter, E1
off Wapping High St 132 D1
Miall Wk, SE26 171 H4
Micawber St, N1 12 A3
Michael Cliffe Ho, EC1
off Skinner St 111 H3
Michael Faraday Ho, SE17 36 C4
Michael Gaynor Cl, W7 124 C1
Michaelmas Cl, SW20 183 J3
Michael Rd, E11 97 E1
SE25 188 B3
SW6 149 E1
Michaels Cl, SE13 154 E4
Micheldever Rd, SE12 155 E6
Michelham Gdns, Twick. TW1 162 C3
Michels Row, Rich. TW9
off Kew Foot Rd 145 H4
Michel Wk, SE18
off Cambridge Row 136 E5
Michigan Av, E12 98 B4
Michleham Down, N12 56 C4
Mickleham Cl, Orp. BR5 193 J2
Mickleham Gdns, Sutt. SM3 198 B6
Mickleham Rd, Orp. BR5 193 J1
Mickleham Way, Croy. (New Adgtn)
CR0 204 D7
Micklethwaite Rd, SW6 128 D6
Midas Met Ind Est, The, Mord. SM4
off Garth Rd 198 A1
Middle Dene, NW7 54 D3
Middle Fld, NW8 109 G1
Middlefielde, W13 104 E5
Middlefield Gdns, Ilf. IG2 81 E6
Middle Grn Cl, Surb. KT5
off Alpha Rd 181 J6
Middleham Gdns, N18 60 D6
Middleham Rd, N18 60 D6
Middle La, N8 74 E5
Teddington TW11 162 C6
Middle La Ms, N8
off Middle La 74/75 E5
Middle Pk Av, SE9 156 A6
Middle Path, Har. HA2
off Middle Rd 86 A1
Middle Rd, E13 *off London Rd* 115 G2
SW16 186 D2
Barnet EN4 41 H6
Harrow HA2 86 A2
Middle Row, W10 108 B4
Middlesborough Rd, N18 60 D6
Middlesex Business Cen, Sthl.
UB2 123 G2
Middlesex Cl, Sthl. UB1 103 H4
Middlesex Ct, W4
off British Gro 127 F4
★ **Middlesex Guildhall**, SW1 26 A4
Middlesex Ho, Wem. HA0 105 G1
Middlesex Pas, EC1 19 H2
Middlesex Rd, Mitch. CR4 186 E5
Middlesex St, E1 20 E2
Middlesex Wf, E5 95 F2
Middle St, EC1 19 J1
Croydon CR0 *off Surrey St* 201 J3
Middle Temple, EC4 19 E5
Middle Temple La, EC4 18 E4
Middleton Av, E4 61 J4
Greenford UB6 104 A2
Sidcup DA14 176 C6
Middleton Cl, E4 61 J3
Middleton Dr, SE16 133 G2
Pinner HA5 66 A3
Middleton Gdns, Ilf. IG2 80 E6
Middleton Gro, N7 92 E5
Middleton Ms, N7
off Middleton Gro 92/93 E5
Middleton Pl, W1 17 F2
Middleton Rd, E8 94 C7
NW11 72 D7
Carshalton SM5 185 H7
Morden SM4 185 F6
Middleton St, E2 112 E3
Middleton Way, SE13 154 D4
Middleway, NW11 73 E5
Middle Way, SW16 186 D2
Erith DA18 138 E3
Hayes UB4 102 C4
Middle Way, The, Har. HA3 68 C2
Middle Yd, SE1 28 C1
Midfield Av, Bexh. DA7 159 J3
Midfield Par, Bexh. DA7 159 J3
Midford Pl, W1 9 G6
Midholm, NW11 72 E4
Wembley HA9 88 A1
Midholm Cl, NW11 72 E4
Midholm Rd, Croy. CR0 203 H2
Midhope St, WC1 10 B4
Midhurst Av, N10 74 A3
Croydon CR0 187 G7
Midhurst Hill, Bexh. DA6 159 G6
Midhurst Rd, W13 124 D2
Midhurst Way, E5 94 D4
Midland Cres, NW3
off Finchley Rd 91 F6
Midland Pl, E14 *off Ferry St* 134 C5
Midland Rd, E10 78 C7
NW1 9 J2
Midland Ter, NW2 90 A3
NW10 107 E4
Midleton Rd, N.Mal. KT3 182 C3
Midlothian Rd, E3
off Burdett Rd 113 J5
Midmoor Rd, SW12 168 C1
SW19 184 A1
Midship Cl, SE16
off Surrey Water Rd 133 G1
Midship Pt, E14 134 A2
Midstrath Rd, NW10 89 E4
Midsummer Av, Houns. TW4 143 F4
Midway, Sutt. SM3 184 C7
Midwinter Cl, Well. DA16
off Hook La 158 A3
Midwood Cl, NW2 89 H3
Miers Cl, E6 116 D1
Mighell Av, Ilf. IG4 80 A5
Milan Rd, Sthl. UB1 123 F2
Milborne Gro, SW10 30 D4
Milborne St, E9 95 F6
Milborough Cres, SE12 155 E6
Milcote St, SE1 27 G4
Mildenhall Rd, E5 95 F4
Mildmay Av, N1 94 A6
Mildmay Gro N, N1 94 A5
Mildmay Gro S, N1 94 A5
Mildmay Pk, N1 94 A5
Mildmay Pl, N16 *off Boleyn Rd* 94 B5
Mildmay Rd, N1 94 B5
Ilford IG1
off Winston Way 98/99 E3
Romford RM7 83 J5
Mildmay St, N1 94 A6
Mildred Av, Borwd. WD6 38 A4
Hayes UB3 121 G4
Northolt UB5 85 H5
MILE END, E1 113 G3
Mile End, The, E17 77 G1
Mile End Pl, E1 113 G4
Mile End Rd, E1 113 F5
E3 113 F5
Mile Rd, Wall. SM6 200 C1
Miles Dr, SE28 137 G1
Milespit Hill, NW7 55 H5
Miles Pl, NW1 15 F1
Surbiton KT5 *off Villiers Av* 181 J4
Miles Rd, N8 75 E3
Mitcham CR4 185 H3
Miles St, SW8 34 A6
Milestone Cl, N9
off Chichester Rd 60 D2
Sutton SM2 199 G6
Milestone Rd, SE19 170 C6
Miles Way, N20 57 H2
Milfoil St, W12 107 G7
Milford Cl, SE2 139 E6
Milford Gdns, Croy. CR0
off Tannery Cl 189 G5
Edgware HA8 54 A7
Wembley HA0 87 G5
Milford Gro, Sutt. SM1 199 F4
Milford La, WC2 18 D5
Milford Ms, SW16 169 F3
Milford Rd, W13 124 E1
Southall UB1 103 G7
Milford Twrs, SE6
off Thomas La 154 B7
Milk St, E16 136 E1
EC2 20 A4
Bromley BR1 173 H6
Milkwell Gdns, Wdf.Grn. IG8 63 H7
Milkwell Yd, SE5 151 J1
Milkwood Rd, SE24 151 H5
Milk Yd, E1 113 F7
Millais Av, E12 98 D5
Millais Cres, Epsom KT19 196 E5
Millais Gdns, Edg. HA8 70 A2
Millais Rd, E11 96 C4
Enfield EN1 44 C5
New Malden KT3 182 E6
Millais Way, Epsom KT19 196 C4
Milland Ct, Borwd. WD6 38 D1
Millard Cl, N16 *off Boleyn Rd* 94 B5
Millard Ter, Dag. RM10
off Church Elm La 101 G6
Millbank, SW1 26 A6
Millbank Twr, SW1 34 A2
Millbank Way, SE12 155 G5
Millbourne Rd, Felt. TW13 161 E4
Millbrook Av, Well. DA16 157 G4
Millbrook Gdns, Rom. (Chad.Hth)
RM6 83 F6
Millbrook Pl, NW1
off Hampstead Rd 110 C2
Millbrook Rd, N9 60 E1
SW9 151 H3
Mill Cl, Cars. SM5 200 A2
West Drayton UB7 120 A3
Mill Cor, Barn. EN5 40 C1
Mill Ct, E10 96 C3
Millcroft Ho, SE6 172 C4
Millender Wk, SE16 133 F4
Millennium Br, EC4 19 J5
SE1 19 J5
Millennium Cl, E16
off Russell Rd 115 G6
Millennium Dr, E14 134 D4
Millennium Harbour, E14 133 J2
Millennium Pl, E2 113 E2
Millennium Sq, SE1 29 G3
Millennium Way, SE10 134 E2
Miller Cl, Mitch. CR4 185 J7
Pinner HA5 66 C2

Miller Rd, SW19 . . . .**167** G6
  Croydon CR0 . . . .**201** F1
Miller's Av, E8 . . . .**94** C5
Millers Cl, NW7 . . . .**55** G4
Millers Ct, W4 off Chiswick Mall .**127** F5
Millers Grn Cl, Enf. EN2 . . . .**43** H3
Millers Meadow Cl, SE3
  off Meadowcourt Rd **155** F5
Miller's Ter, E8 . . . .**94** C5
Miller St, NW1 . . . .**9** F1
Millers Way, W6 . . . .**127** J2
Millet Rd, Grnf. UB6 . . . .**103** H3
Mill Fm Cl, Pnr. HA5 . . . .**66** C2
Mill Fm Cres, Houns. TW4 . . . .**161** E1
Millfield Av, E17 . . . .**77** H1
Millfield La, N6 . . . .**91** J2
Millfield Pl, N6 . . . .**92** A2
Millfield Rd, Edg. HA8 . . . .**70** C2
  Hounslow TW4 . . . .**161** E1
Millfields Est, E5
  off Denton Way **95** G3
Millfields Rd, E5 . . . .**95** G4
Mill Gdns, SE26 . . . .**171** E4
Mill Grn, Mitch. CR4
  off London Rd **186** A7
Mill Grn Business Pk, Mitch. CR4
  off Mill Grn Rd **186** A7
Mill Grn Rd, Mitch. CR4 . . . .**185** J7
Millgrove St, SW11 . . . .**150** A2
Millharbour, E14 . . . .**134** B3
Millhaven Cl, Rom. RM6 . . . .**82** B6
MILL HILL, NW7 . . . .**55** G5
Mill Hill, SW13 off Mill Hill Rd .**147** G2
Mill Hill Circ, NW7
  off Watford Way **55** F5
Mill Hill Gro, W3 off Mill Hill Rd .**126** B1
Mill Hill Rd, SW13 . . . .**147** G2
  W3 . . . .**126** B2
Millhouse Pl, SE27 . . . .**169** H4
Millicent Rd, E10 . . . .**95** J1
Milligan St, E14 . . . .**113** J7
Milliners Ct, Loug. IG10
  off The Croft **48** D2
Milliners Ho, SW18
  off Point Pleasant **148** D4
Milling Rd, Edg. HA8 . . . .**54** D7
Millington Rd, Hayes UB3 . . . .**121** H3
Mill La, E4 . . . .**46** B3
  NW6 . . . .**90** C5
  SE18 . . . .**136** D5
  Carshalton SM5 . . . .**199** J4
  Croydon CR0 . . . .**201** F3
  Romford (Chad.Hth) RM6 . . . .**82** E6
  Woodford Green IG8 . . . .**63** F5
Mill La Trd Est, Croy. CR0 . . . .**201** F3
Millman Ms, WC1 . . . .**10** C6
Millman Pl, WC1 off Millman St .**111** F4
Millman St, WC1 . . . .**10** C6
Millmark Gro, SE14 . . . .**153** H2
Millmarsh La, Enf. EN3 . . . .**45** H2
Mill Mead Rd, N17 . . . .**76** E4
Mill Pl, E14 off Commercial Rd .**113** H6
  Chislehurst BR7 . . . .**192** E1
  Kingston upon Thames KT1 . .**181** J3
Mill Plat, Islw. TW7 . . . .**144** D2
Mill Plat Av, Islw. TW7 . . . .**144** D2
Mill Pond Cl, SW8
  off Crimsworth Rd **130** D7
Millpond Est, SE16
  off West La **132/133** E2
Millpond Pl, Cars. SM5 . . . .**200** A3
Mill Ridge, Edg. HA8 . . . .**53** J5
Mill Rd, E16 . . . .**135** H1
  SW19 . . . .**167** F7
  Erith DA8 . . . .**139** J7
  Ilford IG1 . . . .**98** D3
  Twickenham TW2 . . . .**161** J2
Mill Row, N1 . . . .**112** B1
Mills Ct, EC2 . . . .**12** E4
Mills Gro, E14 off Dewberry St .**114** C5
  NW4 . . . .**72** A3
Mill Shot Cl, SW6 . . . .**127** J7
Millside, Cars. SM5 . . . .**199** J2
Millside Pl, Islw. TW7 . . . .**144** E2
Millsmead Way, Loug. IG10 . . . .**48** C2
Millson Cl, N20 . . . .**57** G2
Mills Row, W4 . . . .**126** D4
Millstream Cl, N13 . . . .**59** G5
Millstream Rd, SE1 . . . .**29** F4
Mill St, SE1 . . . .**29** G4
  W1 . . . .**17** E5
  Kingston upon Thames KT1 . .**181** H3
Mill Vale, Brom. BR2 . . . .**191** F2
Mill Vw Cl, Epsom (Ewell) KT17 .**197** F7
Mill Vw Gdns, Croy. CR0 . . . . .**203** G3
MILLWALL, E14 . . . .**134** B3
Millwall Dock Rd, E14 . . . .**134** A3
★ Millwall FC, SE16 . . . .**133** F5
Millway, NW7 . . . .**54** E5
Mill Way, Felt. TW14 . . . .**142** B5
Millway Gdns, Nthlt. UB5 . . . . .**85** F6
Millwell Cres, Chig. IG7 . . . . . .**65** G5
Millwood Rd, Houns. TW3 . . . .**143** J5
Millwood St, W10
  off St. Charles Sq **108** B5
Mill Yd, E1 . . . .**21** H5

Milman Cl, Pnr. HA5 . . . .**66** D3
Milman Rd, NW6 . . . .**108** B2
Milman's St, SW10 . . . .**31** G6
Milmead Ind Cen, N17 . . . .**76** E2
Milne Ct, E18 off Churchfields . .**79** G1
Milne Feild, Pnr. HA5 . . . .**51** G7
Milne Gdns, SE9 . . . .**156** B5
Milner Dr, Twick. TW2 . . . .**144** A7
Milner Pl, N1 . . . .**111** G1
  Carshalton SM5 off High St .**200** A4
Milner Rd, E15 . . . .**114** E3
  SW19 . . . .**184** E1
  Dagenham RM8 . . . .**100** C2
  Kingston upon Thames KT1 . .**181** G3
  Morden SM4 . . . .**185** G5
  Thornton Heath CR7 . . . .**188** A3
Milner Sq, N1 . . . .**93** H7
Milner St, SW3 . . . .**31** J1
Milner Wk, SE9 . . . .**175** G2
Milnthorpe Rd, W4 . . . .**126** D6
Milo Rd, SE22 . . . .**152** C6
Milroy Wk, SE1 . . . .**27** G1
Milson Rd, W14 . . . .**128** B3
Milton Av, E6 . . . .**98** A7
  N6 . . . .**74** C7
  NW9 . . . .**70** C3
  NW10 . . . .**106** C1
  Barnet EN5 . . . .**40** C5
  Croydon CR0 . . . .**188** A7
  Sutton SM1 . . . .**199** G3
Milton Cl, N2 . . . .**73** F5
  SE1 . . . .**37** F2
  Hayes UB4 . . . .**102** A6
  Sutton SM1 . . . .**199** G3
Milton Ct, EC2 . . . .**20** B1
  Romford (Chad.Hth) RM6
  off Cross Rd **82** C7
Milton Ct Rd, SE14 . . . .**133** H6
Milton Cres, Ilf. IG2 . . . .**81** F7
Milton Dr, Borwd. WD6 . . . .**38** B5
Milton Gdn Est, N16
  off Milton Gro **94** B4
Milton Gro, N11 . . . .**58** C5
  N16 . . . .**94** A4
Milton Pk, N6 . . . .**74** C7
Milton Pl, N7 off George's Rd . .**93** G5
Milton Rd, E17 . . . .**78** A4
  N6 . . . .**74** C7
  N15 . . . .**75** H4
  NW7 . . . .**55** G5
  NW9 off West Hendon Bdy . .**71** G7
  SE24 . . . .**151** H6
  SW14 . . . .**146** D3
  SW19 . . . .**167** F6
  W3 . . . .**126** D1
  W7 . . . .**104** C1
  Belvedere DA17 . . . .**139** G4
  Croydon CR0 . . . .**202** A1
  Hampton TW12 . . . .**161** G7
  Harrow HA1 . . . .**68** B4
  Mitcham CR4 . . . .**168** A4
  Sutton SM1 . . . .**198** D3
  Wallington SM6 . . . .**200** C6
  Welling DA16 . . . .**157** J1
Milton St, EC2 . . . .**20** B1
Milton Way, West Dr. UB7 . . . .**120** C4
Milverton Gdns, Ilf. IG3 . . . .**99** J2
Milverton Ho, SE23 . . . .**171** H3
Milverton Rd, NW6 . . . .**89** J7
Milverton St, SE11 . . . .**35** F4
Milverton Way, SE9 . . . .**174** D4
Milward St, E1
  off Stepney Way **112/113** E5
Milward Wk, SE18
  off Spearman St **136** D6
Mimosa Rd, Hayes UB4 . . . . . .**102** C5
Mimosa St, SW6 . . . .**148** C1
Minard Rd, SE6 . . . .**154** E7
Mina Rd, SE17 . . . .**36** E4
  SW19 . . . .**184** D1
Minchenden Cres, N14 . . . .**58** C3
Mincing La, EC3 . . . .**20** D5
Minden Rd, SE20 . . . .**188** E1
  Sutton SM3 . . . .**198** C2
Minehead Rd, SW16 . . . .**169** F5
  Harrow HA2 . . . .**85** G3
Mineral St, SE18 . . . .**137** H4
Minera Ms, SW1 . . . .**32** C1
Minerva Cl, SW9 . . . .**131** G7
  Sidcup DA14 . . . .**175** H3
Minerva Rd, E4 . . . .**62** B7
  NW10 . . . .**106** C4
  Kingston upon Thames KT1 . .**181** J2
Minerva St, E2 . . . .**112** E2
Minet Av, NW10 . . . .**106** E2
Minet Dr, Hayes UB3 . . . .**122** A1
Minet Gdns, NW10 . . . .**106** E2
  Hayes UB3 . . . .**122** A1
Minet Rd, SW9 . . . .**151** H2
Minford Gdns, W14 . . . .**128** A2
Mingard Wk, N7 off Hornsey Rd .**93** F2
Ming St, E14 . . . .**114** A7
★ Ministry of Defence, SW1 . .**26** A2
Ministry Way, SE9 . . . .**174** C2
Miniver Pl, EC4 off Garlick Hill .**111** J7
Mink Ct, Houns. TW4 . . . .**142** C3
Minniedale, Surb. KT5 . . . .**181** J5

Minnow St, SE17 off East St . . .**132** B4
Minnow Wk, SE17 . . . .**36** E2
Minories, EC3 . . . .**21** F5
Minshull Pl, Beck. BR3 . . . .**172** A7
Minshull St, SW8
  off Wandsworth Rd **150** D1
Minson Rd, E9 . . . .**113** G1
Minstead Gdns, SW15 . . . .**147** F7
Minstead Way, N.Mal. KT3 . . . .**182** E6
Minster Av, Sutt. SM1
  off Leafield Rd **198** D2
Minster Ct, EC3 off Mincing La .**112** A7
Minster Dr, Croy. CR0 . . . .**202** B4
Minster Gdns, W.Mol. KT8 . . . .**179** F4
Minster Pavement, EC3
  off Mincing La **112** A7
Minster Rd, NW2 . . . .**90** B5
  Bromley BR1 . . . .**173** H7
Minster Wk, N8
  off Lightfoot Rd **74/75** E4
Minstrel Gdns, Surb. KT5 . . . . .**181** J4
Mint Business Pk, E16 . . . .**115** G5
Mintern Cl, N13 . . . .**59** H3
Minterne Av, Sthl. UB2 . . . .**123** G4
Minterne Rd, Har. HA3 . . . .**69** J5
Minterne Waye, Hayes UB4 . . .**102** C6
Mintern St, N1 . . . .**12** C1
Minton Ms, NW6
  off Lymington Rd **90/91** E6
Mint Rd, Wall. SM6 . . . .**200** B4
Mint St, SE1 . . . .**27** J3
Mint Wk, Croy. CR0
  off High St **201** J3
Mirabel Rd, SW6 . . . .**128** C7
Miranda Cl, E1 off Sidney St . .**113** F5
Miranda Ct, W3 off Queens Dr .**105** J6
Miranda Rd, N19 . . . .**92** C1
Mirfield St, SE7 . . . .**136** A4
Miriam Rd, SE18 . . . .**137** H5
Mirravale Trd Est, Dag. RM8 . . .**83** F7
Mirren Cl, Har. HA2 . . . .**85** F4
Mirror Path, SE9
  off Lambscroft Av **173** J3
Missenden Gdns, Mord. SM4 . .**185** F6
Mission Gro, E17 . . . .**77** H5
Mission Pl, SE15 . . . .**152** D1
Mission Sq, Brent. TW8 . . . . . .**125** H6
Mistletoe Cl, Croy. CR0
  off Marigold Way **203** G1
Mitali Pas, E1 . . . .**21** H4
MITCHAM, CR4 . . . .**186** A3
Mitcham Gdn Village, Mitch.
  CR4 . . . .**186** A5
Mitcham Ind Est, Mitch. CR4 . .**186** A1
Mitcham La, SW16 . . . .**168** C6
Mitcham Pk, Mitch. CR4 . . . . . .**185** J4
Mitcham Rd, E6 . . . .**116** B3
  SW17 . . . .**167** J5
  Croydon CR0 . . . .**186** E6
  Ilford IG3 . . . .**81** J7
Mitchellbrook Way, NW10 . . . . .**88** D6
Mitchell Cl, SE2 . . . .**138** C4
  Belvedere DA17 . . . .**139** J3
Mitchell Rd, N13 . . . .**59** H5
  Orpington BR6 . . . .**207** J4
Mitchell's Pl, SE21
  off Dulwich Village **152** B7
Mitchell St, EC1 . . . .**11** J5
Mitchell Wk, E6 . . . .**116** B5
Mitchell Way, NW10 . . . .**88** C6
  Bromley BR1 . . . .**191** G1
Mitchison Rd, N1 . . . .**94** A6
Mitchley Rd, N17 . . . .**76** D3
Mitford Cl, Chess. KT9
  off Merritt Gdns **195** F6
Mitford Rd, N19 . . . .**93** E2
Mitre, The, E14 off Three Colt St .**113** J7
Mitre Av, E17 off Greenleaf Rd . . .**77** J3
Mitre Cl, Brom. BR2
  off Beckenham La **191** F2
  Sutton SM2 . . . .**199** F7
Mitre Ct, EC2 . . . .**20** A3
  EC4 . . . .**19** F4
Mitre Rd, E15 . . . .**114** E2
  SE1 . . . .**27** F3
Mitre Sq, EC3 . . . .**21** E4
Mitre St, EC3 . . . .**21** E4
Mitre Way, W10 . . . .**107** H4
Moat, The, N.Mal. KT3 . . . .**182** E1
Moat Cl, Orp. BR6 . . . .**207** J6
Moat Cres, N3 . . . .**72** E3
Moat Cft, Well. DA16 . . . .**158** C4
Moat Dr, E13 off Boundary Rd . .**115** J2
  Harrow HA1 . . . .**67** J4
Moat Fm Rd, Nthlt. UB5 . . . .**85** F6
Moat Pl, SW9 . . . .**151** F3
  W3 . . . .**106** B6
Moatside, Enf. EN3 . . . .**45** G4
  Feltham TW13 . . . .**160** C4
Moberley Rd, SW4 . . . .**150** D7
Modbury Gdns, NW5
  off Queen's Cres **92** A6
Modder Pl, SW15 . . . .**148** A4
Model Cotts, SW14
  off Upper Richmond Rd W . .**146** C4
Model Fm Cl, SE9 . . . .**174** B3
Modling Ho, E2 . . . .**113** G2

Moelwyn Hughes Ct, N7
  off Hilldrop Cres **92** D5
Moelyn Ms, Har. HA1 . . . .**68** D5
Moffat Rd, N13 . . . .**59** E6
  SW17 . . . .**167** H4
  Thornton Heath CR7 . . . . . .**187** J2
Mogden La, Islw. TW7 . . . .**144** B5
Mohmmad Khan Rd, E11
  off Harvey Rd **97** F1
Moira Cl, N17 . . . .**76** B2
Moira Rd, SE9 . . . .**156** C4
Moland Mead, SE16
  off Crane Mead **133** G5
Molasses Row, SW11
  off Cinnamon Row **149** F3
Mole Abbey Gdns, W.Mol. KT8
  off New Rd **179** G3
Mole Ct, Epsom KT19 . . . .**196** C4
Molember Ct, E.Mol. KT8 . . . . .**180** B5
Molember Rd, E.Mol. KT8 . . . . .**180** B5
Molescroft, SE9 . . . .**175** F3
Molesey Av, W.Mol. KT8 . . . . . .**179** F4
Molesey Dr, Sutt. SM3 . . . .**198** B2
Molesey Pk Av, W.Mol. KT8 . . .**179** H5
Molesey Pk Cl, E.Mol. KT8 . . . .**179** J5
Molesey Pk Rd, E.Mol. KT8 . . .**180** A5
  West Molesey KT8 . . . .**179** H5
Molesey Rd, W.Mol. KT8 . . . . . .**179** E5
Molesford Rd, SW6 . . . .**148** D1
Molesham Cl, W.Mol. KT8 . . . . .**179** H3
Molesham Way, W.Mol. KT8 . . .**179** H3
Molesworth St, SE13 . . . .**154** C3
Mollison Av, Enf. EN3 . . . .**45** H5
Mollison Dr, Wall. SM6 . . . .**201** E6
Mollison Sq, Wall. SM6
  off Mollison Dr **200/201** E7
Mollison Way, Edg. HA8 . . . .**70** A2
Molly Huggins Cl, SW12 . . . . . .**150** C7
Molyneux Dr, SW17 . . . .**168** B4
Molyneux St, W1 . . . .**15** H2
Monarch Cl, Felt. TW14 . . . . . .**141** H7
  West Wickham BR4 . . . .**205** H4
Monarch Dr, E16 . . . .**116** A5
Monarch Ms, E17 . . . .**78** B5
  SW16 . . . .**169** G5
Monarch Par, Mitch. CR4
  off London Rd **185** J2
Monarch Pl, Buck.H. IG9 . . . . . .**63** J2
Monarch Rd, Belv. DA17 . . . . . .**139** G3
Monarchs Ct, NW7
  off Grenville Pl **54** D5
Mona Rd, SE15 . . . .**153** F2
Monastery Gdns, Enf. EN2 . . . . .**44** A2
Mona St, E16 . . . .**115** F5
Monaveen Gdns, W.Mol. KT8 . .**179** G3
Monck St, SW1 . . . .**25** J6
Monclar Rd, SE5 . . . .**152** A4
Moncorvo Cl, SW7 . . . .**23** J4
Moncrieff Cl, E6
  off Linton Gdns **116** B6
Moncrieff Pl, SE15 off Rye La . .**152** D2
Moncrieff St, SE15 . . . .**152** D2
Mondial Way, Hayes UB3 . . . . .**121** F7
Monega Rd, E7 . . . .**97** J6
  E12 . . . .**98** A6
Money La, West Dr. UB7 . . . . . .**120** A3
Monier Rd, E3 . . . .**96** A7
Monivea Rd, Beck. BR3 . . . . . .**171** J7
Monkchester Cl, Loug. IG10 . . . .**48** D1
Monk Dr, E16 . . . .**115** G6
MONKEN HADLEY, Barn. EN5 . .**40** C1
Monkfrith Av, N14 . . . .**42** B6
Monkfrith Cl, N14 . . . .**42** B7
Monkfrith Way, N14 . . . .**42** A7
Monkhams Av, Wdf.Grn. IG8 . . .**63** G5
Monkhams Dr, Wdf.Grn. IG8 . . .**63** H4
Monkhams La, Buck.H. IG9 . . . .**63** H3
  Woodford Green IG8 . . . .**63** G5
Monkleigh Rd, Mord. SM4 . . . .**184** B3
Monk Pas, E16 off Monk Dr . . .**115** G7
Monks Av, Barn. EN5 . . . .**41** F6
  West Molesey KT8 . . . .**179** F5
Monks Cl, SE2 . . . .**138** D4
  Enfield EN2 . . . .**43** J2
  Harrow HA2 . . . .**85** H2
  Ruislip HA4 . . . .**84** D4
Monksdene Gdns, Sutt. SM1 . .**199** E3
Monks Dr, W3 . . . .**106** A5
Monksgrove, Loug. IG10 . . . .**48** D5
Monksmead, Borwd. WD6 . . . . .**38** C4
MONKS ORCHARD, Croy. CR0 .**189** J7
Monks Orchard Rd, Beck. BR3 .**204** A1
Monks Pk, Wem. HA9 . . . .**88** C6
Monks Pk Gdns, Wem. HA9 . . . .**88** B6
Monk's Ridge, N20 . . . .**55** H1
Monks Rd, Enf. EN2 . . . .**43** J2
Monk St, SE18 . . . .**136** D4
Monks Way, NW11
  off Hurstwood Rd **72** C4
  Beckenham BR3 . . . .**190** A5
  Orpington BR5 . . . .**207** F1
  West Drayton UB7 . . . .**120** B6
Monkswell Ct, N10
  off Pembroke Rd **74** A1
Monkswood Gdns, Borwd. WD6 .**38** D4
  Ilford IG5 . . . .**80** D3
Monkton Rd, Well. DA16 . . . . . .**157** J2

Monkton St, SE11 . . . . .35 F1
Monkville Av, NW11 . . . . .72 C4
Monkwell Sq, EC2 . . . . .20 A2
Monmouth Av, E18 . . . . .79 H4
  Kingston upon Thames KT1 . .163 F7
Monmouth Cl, W4
  off Beaumont Rd 126 D3
Mitcham CR4
  off Recreation Way 186/187 E4
  Welling DA16 . . . . .158 A4
Monmouth Gro, Brent. TW8
  off Sterling Pl 125 H4
Monmouth Pl, W2
  off Monmouth Rd 108 D6
Monmouth Rd, E6 . . . . .116 C3
  N9 .60 E2
  W2 . . . . .108 C6
  Dagenham RM9 . . . . .101 F5
  Hayes UB3 . . . . .121 H4
Monmouth St, WC2 . . . . .18 A4
Monnery Rd, N19 . . . . .92 C3
Monnow Rd, SE1 . . . . .37 H3
Mono La, Felt. TW13 . . . . .160 B2
Monoux Gro, E17 . . . . .78 A1
Monroe Cres, Enf. EN1 . . . . .44 E1
Monroe Dr, SW14 . . . . .146 B5
Monro Gdns, Har. HA3 . . . . .52 B7
Monro Way, E5 . . . . .94 E4
Monsal Ct, E5 off Redwald Rd 95 G4
Monsell Ct, N4 off Monsell Rd 93 H3
Monsell Rd, N4 . . . . .93 H3
Monson Rd, NW10 . . . . .107 G2
  SE14 . . . . .133 G7
Mons Way, Brom. BR2 . . . . .192 B6
Montacute Rd, SE6 . . . . .153 J7
  Morden SM4 . . . . .185 G6
Montagu Cres, N18 . . . . .61 E4
Montague Av, SE4 . . . . .153 J4
  W7 . . . . .124 C1
Montague Cl, SE1 . . . . .28 B1
  Walton-on-Thames KT12 . . . .178 A7
Montague Gdns, W3 . . . . .106 A7
Montague Pl, WC1 . . . . .17 J1
Montague Rd, E8 . . . . .94 D5
  E11 . . . . .97 F1
  N8 .75 F5
  N15 . . . . .76 D4
  SW19 . . . . .166 E7
  W7 . . . . .124 C1
  W13 . . . . .105 E6
  Croydon CR0 . . . . .201 H1
  Hounslow TW3 . . . . .143 H3
  Richmond TW10 . . . . .145 H6
  Southall UB2 . . . . .122 E4
Montague Sq, SE15
  off Clifton Way 133 F7
Montague St, EC1 . . . . .19 J2
  WC1 . . . . .18 A1
Montague Waye, Sthl. UB2 . . . .122 E3
Montagu Gdns, N18 . . . . .60 E4
  Wallington SM6 . . . . .200 C4
Montagu Mans, W1 . . . . .16 A1
Montagu Ms N, W1 . . . . .16 A2
Montagu Ms S, W1 . . . . .16 A3
Montagu Ms W, W1 . . . . .16 A3
Montagu Pl, W1 . . . . .15 J2
Montagu Rd, N9 . . . . .61 J2
  N18 . . . . .61 E5
  NW4 . . . . .71 G6
Montagu Rd Ind Est, N18 . . . . . .61 F4
Montagu Row, W1 . . . . .16 A2
Montagu Sq, W1 . . . . .16 A2
Montagu St, W1 . . . . .16 A3
Montaigne Cl, SW1 . . . . .33 J1
Montalt Rd, Wdf.Grn. IG8 . . . . . .63 F5
Montana Gdns, SE26 . . . . .171 J5
  Sutton SM1 off Lind Rd 199 F5
Montana Rd, SW17 . . . . .168 A4
  SW20 . . . . .183 J1
Montbelle Rd, SE9 . . . . .174 E3
Montcalm Cl, Brom. BR2 . . . . . .191 G6
  Hayes UB4 off Ayles Rd 102 B3
Montcalm Rd, SE7 . . . . .136 A7
Montclare St, E2 . . . . .13 F4
Monteagle Av, Bark. IG11 . . . . . .99 F6
Monteagle Way, E5
  off Rendlesham Rd 94 D3
  SE15 . . . . .153 E3
Montefiore St, SW8 . . . . .150 B2
Montego Cl, SE24
  off Railton Rd 151 G4
Montem Rd, SE23 . . . . .153 J7
  New Malden KT3 . . . . .182 E4
Montem St, N4
  off Thorpedale Rd 93 F1
Montenotte Rd, N8 . . . . .74 C5
Monterey Cl, Bex. DA5 . . . . .177 J2
Montesole Ct, Pnr. HA5 . . . . .66 C2
Montevetro, SW11 . . . . .149 G1
Montford Pl, SE11 . . . . .34 E4
Montford Rd, Sun. TW16 . . . . . .178 A4
Montfort Gdns, Ilf. IG6 . . . . .65 F6
Montfort Pl, SW19 . . . . .166 A1
Montgolfier Wk, Nthlt. UB5
  off Jetstar Way 102/103 E3
Montgomery Av, Esher KT10 . . . .194 B3
Montgomery Cl, Mitch. CR4 . . . .187 E4

Montgomery Cl, Sid. DA15 . . . .157 J6
Montgomery Ct, W4
  off St. Thomas' Rd 126 C6
Montgomery Rd, W4 . . . . .126 C4
  Edgware HA8 . . . . .53 J6
Montholme Rd, SW11 . . . . .149 J6
Monthope Rd, E1 . . . . .21 H2
Montolieu Gdns, SW15 . . . . . . .147 H5
Montpelier Av, W5 . . . . .105 F5
  Bexley DA5 . . . . .158 D7
Montpelier Gdns, E6 . . . . .116 A3
  Romford RM6 . . . . .82 C7
Montpelier Gro, NW5 . . . . .92 C5
Montpelier Ms, SW7 . . . . .23 H5
Montpelier Pl, E1 . . . . .113 F6
  SW7 . . . . .23 H5
Montpelier Ri, NW11 . . . . .72 B7
  Wembley HA9 . . . . .87 G1
Montpelier Rd, N3 . . . . .73 F1
  SE15 . . . . .153 E1
  W5 . . . . .105 G5
  Sutton SM1 . . . . .199 F4
Montpelier Row, SE3 . . . . .155 F2
  Twickenham TW1 . . . . .145 E7
Montpelier Sq, SW7 . . . . .23 H4
Montpelier St, SW7 . . . . .23 H4
Montpelier Ter, SW7 . . . . .23 H4
Montpelier Vale, SE3 . . . . .155 F2
Montpelier Wk, SW7 . . . . .23 H5
Montpelier Way, NW11 . . . . .72 B7
Montrave Rd, SE20 . . . . .171 F6
Montreal Pl, WC2 . . . . .18 C5
Montreal Rd, Ilf. IG1 . . . . .81 F7
Montrell Rd, SW2 . . . . .169 E1
Montrose Av, NW6 . . . . .108 B2
  Edgware HA8 . . . . .70 C2
  Sidcup DA15 . . . . .158 A7
  Twickenham TW2 . . . . .143 H7
  Welling DA16 . . . . .157 G3
Montrose Cl, Well. DA16 . . . . . .157 J3
  Woodford Green IG8 . . . . . . .63 G4
Montrose Ct, SW7 . . . . .23 F4
Montrose Cres, N12 . . . . .57 F6
  Wembley HA0 . . . . .87 H6
Montrose Gdns, Mitch. CR4 . . . .185 J3
  Sutton SM1 . . . . .199 E2
Montrose Pl, SW1 . . . . .24 C4
Montrose Rd, Felt. TW14 . . . . . .141 G6
  Harrow HA3 . . . . .68 B2
Montrose Way, SE23 . . . . .171 G1
Montserrat Av, Wdf.Grn. IG8 . . . .62 D7
Montserrat Cl, SE19 . . . . .170 A5
Montserrat Rd, SW15 . . . . .148 B4
★ Monument, The, EC3 . . . . . . .20 C6
Monument Gdns, SE13 . . . . . . .154 C5
Monument St, EC3 . . . . .20 C5
Monument Way, N17 . . . . .76 C3
Monza St, E1 . . . . .113 F7
Moodkee St, SE16 . . . . .133 F3
Moody Rd, SE15 . . . . .132 C7
Moody St, E1 . . . . .113 G3
Moon La, Barn. EN5 . . . . .40 C3
Moon St, N1 . . . . .111 H1
Moorcroft Gdns, Brom. BR2
  off Southborough Rd 192 B5
Moorcroft Rd, SW16 . . . . .168 E3
Moorcroft Way, Pnr. HA5 . . . . . . .66 E5
Moordown, SE18 . . . . .156 D1
Moore Cl, SW14
  off Little St. Leonards 146 C3
  Mitcham CR4 . . . . .186 B2
Moore Cres, Dag. RM9 . . . . . . .118 B1
Moorefield Rd, N17 . . . . .76 C2
Moorehead Way, SE3 . . . . .155 H3
Mooreland Rd, Brom. BR1 . . . . .173 F7
Moore Pk Rd, SW6 . . . . .128 E7
Moore Rd, SE19 . . . . .169 J6
Moore St, SW3 . . . . .31 J1
Moore Wk, E7 off Stracey Rd 97 G4
Moore Way, SE22
  off Lordship La 170 D1
Moorey Cl, E15
  off Stephen's Rd 115 F1
Moorfield Av, W5 . . . . .105 G4
Moorfield Rd, Chess. KT9 . . . . .195 H5
  Enfield EN3 . . . . .45 F1
Moorfields, EC2 . . . . .20 B2
Moorfields Highwalk, EC2
  off Fore St 112 A5
Moorgate, EC2 . . . . .20 B3
Moorgate Pl, EC2 . . . . .20 B3
Moorhouse Rd, W2 . . . . .108 D6
  Harrow HA3 . . . . .69 G3
Moorings, SE28 . . . . .118 B7
Moorland Cl, Twick. TW2
  off Telford Rd 143 G7
Moorland Rd, SW9 . . . . .151 H4
Moorlands Av, NW7 . . . . .55 H6
Moorlands Est, SW9 . . . . .151 G4
Moor La, EC2 . . . . .20 B2
  Chessington KT9 . . . . .195 H4
Moormead Dr, Epsom KT19 . . . .197 E5
Moor Mead Rd, Twick. TW1 . . . .144 D6
Moor Pk Gdns, Kings.T. KT2 . . . .165 E7
Moor Pl, EC2 . . . . .20 B2
Moorside Rd, Brom. BR1 . . . . . .173 E3

Moor St, W1 . . . . .17 J4
Moortown Rd, Wat. WD19 . . . . . .50 C4
Moot Ct, NW9 . . . . .70 A5
Morant Pl, N22
  off Commerce Rd 75 F2
Morant St, E14 . . . . .114 A7
Mora Rd, NW2 . . . . .89 J4
Mora St, EC1 . . . . .12 A4
Morat St, SW9 . . . . .151 F1
Moravian Pl, SW10 . . . . .31 F6
Moravian St, E2 . . . . .113 F3
Moray Av, Hayes UB3 . . . . .121 J1
Moray Cl, Edg. HA8
  off Pentland Av 54 B2
Moray Ms, N7
  off Durham Rd 93 F2
Moray Rd, N4 . . . . .93 F2
Mordaunt Gdns, Dag. RM9 . . . .100 E7
Mordaunt Ho, NW10 . . . . .106 D1
Mordaunt Rd, NW10 . . . . .106 D1
Mordaunt St, SW9 . . . . .151 F3
MORDEN, SM4 . . . . .184 D3
Morden Ct, Mord. SM4 . . . . . . .184 E4
Morden Gdns, Grnf. UB6 . . . . . . .86 C5
  Mitcham CR4 . . . . .185 G4
★ Morden Hall Pk N.T., Mord.
  SM4 . . . . .185 E3
Morden Hall Rd, Mord. SM4 . . . .185 E3
Morden Hill, SE13 . . . . .154 C2
Morden La, SE13 . . . . .154 C1
MORDEN PARK, Mord. SM4 . . .184 B5
Morden Rd, SE3 . . . . .155 G2
  SW19 . . . . .185 E1
  Mitcham CR4 . . . . .185 F4
  Romford RM6 . . . . .83 E7
Morden Rd Ms, SE3 . . . . .155 G2
Morden St, SE13 . . . . .154 B1
Morden Way, Sutt. SM3 . . . . . . .184 D7
Morden Wf Rd, SE10 . . . . .134 E3
Mordon Rd, Ilf. IG3 . . . . .81 J7
Mordred Rd, SE6 . . . . .172 E2
Morecambe Cl, E1 . . . . .113 G5
Morecambe Gdns, Stan. HA7 . . . .53 G4
Morecambe St, SE17 . . . . .36 A2
Morecambe Ter, N18 . . . . .60 A4
More Cl, E16 . . . . .115 F6
  W14 . . . . .128 A4
Morecoombe Cl, Kings.T. KT2 . .164 B7
Moree Way, N18 . . . . .60 D4
Moreland St, EC1 . . . . .11 H3
Moreland Way, E4 . . . . .62 B3
Morella Rd, SW12 . . . . .149 J7
Morell Cl, Barn. EN5
  off Galdana Av 41 F3
More La, Esher KT10 . . . . .194 A2
More London Pl, SE1
  off Tooley St 132 B1
More London Riverside, SE1
  off Tooley St 132 B1
Moremead Rd, SE6 . . . . .171 J4
Morena St, SE6 . . . . .154 B7
Moresby Av, Surb. KT5 . . . . .182 B7
Moresby Rd, E5 . . . . .94 E1
Moresby Wk, SW8 . . . . .150 B2
Moreton Av, Islw. TW7 . . . . .144 B1
Moreton Cl, E5 . . . . .95 F2
  N15 . . . . .76 A6
  NW7 . . . . .55 J6
  SW1 . . . . .33 G3
Moreton Gdns, Wdf.Grn. IG8 . . . .64 B5
Moreton Pl, SW1 . . . . .33 G3
Moreton Rd, N15 . . . . .76 A6
  South Croydon CR2 . . . . . . .202 A5
  Worcester Park KT4 . . . . . . .197 G2
Moreton St, SW1 . . . . .33 G3
Moreton Ter, SW1 . . . . .33 G3
Moreton Ter Ms N, SW1 . . . . . . .33 G3
Moreton Ter Ms S, SW1 . . . . . . .33 G3
Moreton Twr, W3 . . . . .126 B1
Morford Cl, Ruis. HA4 . . . . .66 B7
Morford Way, Ruis. HA4 . . . . .66 B7
Morgan Av, E17 . . . . .78 D4
Morgan Cl, Dag. RM10 . . . . . . .101 G7
Morgan Rd, N7 . . . . .93 G5
  W10 . . . . .108 C5
  Bromley BR1 . . . . .173 G7
Morgans La, SE1 . . . . .28 D2
Morgan St, E3 . . . . .113 H3
  E16 . . . . .115 F5
Morgan Way, Wdf.Grn. IG8 . . . . .64 B6
Moriatry Cl, N7 . . . . .92 E4
Morie St, SW18 . . . . .149 E5
Morieux Rd, E10 . . . . .95 J1
Moring Rd, SW17 . . . . .168 A4
Morkyns Wk, SE21 . . . . .170 B3
Morland Av, Croy. CR0 . . . . . . .202 B1
Morland Cl, NW11 . . . . .91 E1
  Hampton TW12 . . . . .161 F5
  Mitcham CR4 . . . . .185 H3
Morland Gdns, NW10 . . . . .88 D7
  Southall UB1 . . . . .123 H1
Morland Ms, N1 off Lofting Rd . . .93 G7
Morland Rd, E17 . . . . .77 G5
  SE20 . . . . .171 G6
  Croydon CR0 . . . . .202 B1
  Dagenham RM10 . . . . .101 G7
  Harrow HA3 . . . . .69 H5
  Ilford IG1 . . . . .98 E2

Morland Rd, Sutt. SM1 . . . . .199 F5
Morley Av, E4 . . . . .62 D7
  N18 . . . . .60 D4
  N22 . . . . .75 G2
Morley Cl, Orp. BR6 . . . . .207 E2
Morley Cres, Edg. HA8 . . . . .54 C2
  Ruislip HA4 . . . . .84 C2
Morley Cres E, Stan. HA7 . . . . . .69 F2
Morley Cres W, Stan. HA7 . . . . . .69 F2
Morley Rd, E10 . . . . .96 C1
  E15 . . . . .115 F2
  SE13 . . . . .154 C4
  Barking IG11 . . . . .117 G1
  Chislehurst BR7 . . . . .193 F1
  Romford RM6 . . . . .82 E5
  Sutton SM3 . . . . .198 C1
  Twickenham TW1 . . . . .145 G6
Morley St, SE1 . . . . .27 F5
Morna Rd, SE5 . . . . .151 J2
Morning La, E9 . . . . .95 F6
Morningside Rd, Wor.Pk. KT4 . . .197 H2
Mornington Av, W14 . . . . .128 C4
  Bromley BR1 . . . . .191 J3
  Ilford IG1 . . . . .80 D7
Mornington Cl, Wdf.Grn. IG8 . . . .63 G4
Mornington Ct, Bex. DA5 . . . . . .177 J1
Mornington Cres, NW1 . . . . .9 F1
  Hounslow TW5 . . . . .142 A1
Mornington Gro, E3 . . . . .114 A3
Mornington Ms, SE5 . . . . .151 J1
Mornington Pl, NW1 . . . . .9 E1
Mornington Rd, E4 . . . . .46 D7
  E11 . . . . .97 F1
  SE8 . . . . .133 J7
  Greenford UB6 . . . . .103 H5
  Loughton IG10 . . . . .49 F3
  Woodford Green IG8 . . . . . . .63 F4
Mornington St, NW1 . . . . .8 E1
Mornington Ter, NW1 . . . . .110 B1
Mornington Wk, Rich. TW10 . . . .163 G4
Morocco St, SE1 . . . . .28 D4
Morpeth Gro, E9 . . . . .113 G1
Morpeth Rd, E9 . . . . .113 F1
Morpeth St, E2 . . . . .113 G3
Morpeth Ter, SW1 . . . . .25 F6
Morpeth Wk, N17
  off West Rd 60/61 E7
Morrab Gdns, Ilf. IG3 . . . . .99 J3
Morris Av, E12 . . . . .98 C5
Morris Cl, Croy. CR0 . . . . .189 H6
  Orpington BR6 . . . . .207 H3
Morris Ct, E4 . . . . .62 B3
Morris Gdns, SW18 . . . . .148 D7
Morrish Rd, SW2 . . . . .151 E7
Morrison Av, E4 . . . . .62 A6
  N17 . . . . .76 B3
Morrison Rd, SW9
  off Marcella Rd 151 G2
  Barking IG11 . . . . .118 E2
  Hayes UB4 . . . . .102 B3
Morrison St, SW11 . . . . .150 A3
Morris Pl, N4 . . . . .93 G2
Morris Rd, E14 . . . . .114 B5
  E15 . . . . .96 E4
  Dagenham RM8 . . . . .101 F2
  Isleworth TW7 . . . . .144 C3
Morris St, E1 . . . . .113 E6
Morriston Cl, Wat. WD19 . . . . . . .50 C5
Morse Cl, E13 . . . . .115 G3
Morshead Rd, W9 . . . . .108 D3
Morson Rd, Enf. EN3 . . . . .45 H6
Morston Gdns, SE9 . . . . .174 C4
Morten Cl, SW4 . . . . .150 D6
Morteyne Rd, N17 . . . . .76 A1
Mortgramit Sq, SE18
  off Powis St 136 D3
Mortham St, E15 . . . . .114 D1
Mortimer Cl, NW2 . . . . .90 C2
  SW16 . . . . .168 D2
Mortimer Cres, NW6 . . . . .108 E1
  Worcester Park KT4 . . . . . . .196 D3
Mortimer Dr, Enf. EN1 . . . . .44 A5
Mortimer Est, NW6 . . . . .108 E1
Mortimer Ho, W11
  off St. Anns Rd 128 A1
Mortimer Mkt, WC1 . . . . .9 G6
Mortimer Pl, NW6 . . . . .108 E1
Mortimer Rd, E6 . . . . .116 C3
  N1 .94 B7
  NW10 . . . . .107 J3
  W13 . . . . .105 F6
  Mitcham CR4 . . . . .185 J1
Mortimer Sq, W11
  off St. Anns Rd 108 A7
Mortimer St, W1 . . . . .17 F3
Mortimer Ter, NW5
  off Gordon Ho Rd 92 B4
MORTLAKE, SW14 . . . . .146 C3
Mortlake Cl, Croy. CR0
  off Richmond Rd 200/201 E3
Mortlake Dr, Mitch. CR4 . . . . . .185 H1
Mortlake High St, SW14 . . . . . . .146 D3
Mortlake Rd, E16 . . . . .115 H6
  Ilford IG1 . . . . .99 F4
  Richmond TW9 . . . . .126 A7
Mortlake Ter, Rich. TW9
  off Kew Rd 126 A7

Mortlock Cl, SE15
   off Cossall Wk 152/153 E1
Morton Cl, Wall. SM6 . . . . . . .201 F7
Morton Cl, Nthlt. UB5 . . . . . . .85 J5
Morton Cres, N14 . . . . .58 D4
Morton Gdns, Wall. SM6 . . . .200 C5
Morton Ms, SW5 . . . . .30 A4
Morton Pl, SE1 . . . . .26 E6
Morton Rd, E15 . . . . .97 F7
  N1 . . . . .93 J7
  Morden SM4 . . . . .185 G5
Morton Way, N14 . . . . .58 C3
Morvale Cl, Belv. DA17 . . . . . .139 F4
Morval Rd, SW2 . . . . .151 G5
Morven Rd, SW17 . . . . .167 J3
Morville Ho, SW18
   off Fitzhugh Gro 149 G6
Morville St, E3 . . . . .114 A2
Morwell St, WC1 . . . . .17 J2
Moscow Pl, W2 . . . . .14 A5
Moscow Rd, W2 . . . . .14 A5
Moseley Row, SE10 . . . . . . .135 F4
Moselle Av, N22 . . . . .75 G2
Moselle Cl, N8 off Miles Rd . . .75 F3
Moselle Ho, N17 off William St . .60 C7
Moselle Pl, N17 off High Rd . . .60 C7
Moselle St, N17 . . . . .60 C7
Mossborough Cl, N12 . . . . . . .57 E6
Mossbury Rd, SW11 . . . . . . .149 H3
Moss Cl, E1 . . . . .21 J1
  Pinner HA5 . . . . .67 F2
Mossdown Cl, Belv. DA17 . . .139 G4
Mossford Ct, Ilf. IG6 . . . . .81 E3
Mossford Grn, Ilf. IG6 . . . . . . .81 E3
Mossford La, Ilf. IG6 . . . . .81 E2
Mossford St, E3 . . . . .113 J4
Moss Gdns, Felt. TW13 . . . . .160 A2
  South Croydon CR2
   off Warren Av 203 G7
Moss Hall Ct, N12 . . . . .57 E6
Moss Hall Cres, N12 . . . . . . .57 E6
Moss Hall Gro, N12 . . . . .56 E6
Mossington Gdns, SE16
   off Abbeyfield Rd 133 F4
Moss La, Pnr. HA5 . . . . .67 F3
Mosslea Rd, SE20 . . . . .171 F6
  Bromley BR2 . . . . .192 A5
  Orpington BR6 . . . . .207 F3
Mossop St, SW3 . . . . .31 H1
Moss Rd, Dag. RM10 . . . . . .101 G7
Mossville Gdns, Mord. SM4 . .184 C3
Moston Cl, Hayes UB3
   off Fuller Way 121 J5
Mostyn Av, Wem. HA9 . . . . . .87 J5
Mostyn Gdns, NW10 . . . . . . .108 A2
Mostyn Gro, E3 . . . . .113 J2
Mostyn Rd, SW9 . . . . .151 G1
  SW19 . . . . .184 C1
  Edgware HA8 . . . . .54 D7
Mosul Way, Brom. BR2 . . . . .192 B6
Motcomb St, SW1 . . . . .24 A5
Moth Cl, Wall. SM6 . . . . .200 E7
Mothers' Sq, E5 . . . . .95 E4
Motley Av, EC2 . . . . .12 D5
Motley St, SW8 off St. Rule St . .150 C2
MOTSPUR PARK, N.Mal. KT3 . .183 G6
Motspur Pk, N.Mal. KT3 . . . .183 F6
MOTTINGHAM, SE9 . . . . . . .173 J2
Mottingham Gdns, SE9 . . . . .174 A1
Mottingham La, SE9 . . . . . . .173 J1
  SE12 . . . . .173 J1
Mottingham Rd, N9 . . . . .45 G6
  SE9 . . . . .174 B2
Mottisfont Rd, SE2 . . . . .138 A3
Mott St, Loug. (High Beach)
  IG10 . . . . .47 F1
Moulins Rd, E9 . . . . .113 F1
Moulsford Ho, N7 . . . . .92 D5
Moulton Av, Houns.TW3 . . . .143 E2
Mound, The, SE9 . . . . .174 D3
Moundfield Rd, N16 . . . . .76 D4
Mount, The, N20 . . . . .57 F2
  NW3 off Heath St 91 F4
  W3 . . . . .126 B1
  New Malden KT3 . . . . . . .183 F3
  Wembley HA9 . . . . .88 B2
  Worcester Park KT4 . . . . .197 H4
Mountacre Cl, SE26 . . . . . . .170 C4
Mount Adon Pk, SE22 . . . . . .152 D7
Mountague Pl, E14 . . . . .114 C7
Mount Angelus Rd, SW15 . . .147 F7
Mount Ararat Rd, Rich.TW10 . .145 H5
Mount Ash Rd, SE26 . . . . . . .170 E3
Mount Av, E4 . . . . .62 A3
  W5 . . . . .105 G5
  Southall UB1 . . . . .103 G6
Mountbatten Cl, SE18 . . . . . .137 H6
  SE19 . . . . .170 B5
Mountbatten Ct, SE16
   off Rotherhithe St 133 F1
  Buckhurst Hill IG9 . . . . . . .64 A2
Mountbatten Gdns, Beck. BR3
   off Balmoral Av 189 H4
Mountbatten Ms, SW18
   off Inman Rd 167 F1
Mountbel Rd, Stan. HA7 . . . . .68 D1
Mount Cl, W5 . . . . .105 F5

Mount Cl, Barn. EN4 . . . . .42 A4
  Bromley BR1 . . . . .192 B1
Mountcombe Cl, Surb. KT6 . .181 H7
Mount Cor, Felt. TW13 . . . . . .160 D2
Mount Ct, SW15 off Weimar St . .148 B3
  West Wickham BR4 . . . . .204 E2
Mount Culver Av, Sid. DA14 . .176 D6
Mount Dr, Bexh. DA6 . . . . . . .158 A5
  Harrow HA2 . . . . .67 F5
  Wembley HA9 . . . . .88 C2
Mountearl Gdns, SW16 . . . . .169 F3
Mount Echo Av, E4 . . . . .62 B2
Mount Echo Dr, E4 . . . . .62 B1
Mount Ephraim La, SW16 . . . .168 D3
Mount Ephraim Rd, SW16 . . . .168 D3
Mount Est, The, E5
   off Mount Pleasant La . . .94/95 E2
Mountfield Cl, SE6 . . . . .154 D7
Mountfield Rd, E6 . . . . .116 D2
  N3 . . . . .72 D3
  W5 . . . . .105 G6
Mountfield Ter, SE6
   off Mountfield Cl 154 D7
Mountford St, E1 . . . . .21 H3
Mountfort Cres, N1
   off Barnsbury Sq 93 G7
Mountfort Ter, N1
   off Barnsbury Sq 93 G7
Mount Gdns, SE26 . . . . .170 E3
Mount Gro, Edg. HA8 . . . . . . .54 C3
Mountgrove Rd, N5 . . . . .93 H3
Mounthurst Rd, Brom. BR2 . . .191 F7
Mountington Pk Cl, Har. HA3 . .69 G6
Mountjoy Cl, SE2 . . . . .138 B2
Mountjoy Ho, EC2
   off The Barbican 111 J5
Mount Ms, Hmptn. TW12 . . . .179 H1
Mount Mills, EC1 . . . . .11 H4
Mount Nod Rd, SW16 . . . . . .169 F3
Mount Pk Av, Har. HA1 . . . . . .86 A2
Mount Pk Cres, W5 . . . . .105 G6
Mount Pk Rd, W5 . . . . .105 G5
  Harrow HA1 . . . . .86 A3
  Pinner HA5 . . . . .66 A5
Mount Pl, W3 off High St 126 B1
Mount Pleasant, SE27 . . . . .169 J4
  WC1 . . . . .10 D6
  Barnet EN4 . . . . .41 H4
  Ruislip HA4 . . . . .84 C2
  Wembley HA0 . . . . .105 H1
Mount Pleasant Cres, N4 . . . .75 F7
Mount Pleasant Hill, E5 . . . . .95 E2
Mount Pleasant La, E5 . . . . . .94 E2
Mount Pleasant Pl, SE18
   off Orchard Rd 137 G4
Mount Pleasant Rd, E17 . . . . .77 H2
  N17 . . . . .76 B2
  NW10 . . . . .89 J7
  SE13 . . . . .154 B6
  W5 . . . . .105 H4
  Chigwell IG7 . . . . .65 G4
  New Malden KT3 . . . . . . .182 C3
Mount Pleasant Vil, N4 . . . . . .75 F7
Mount Pleasant Wk, Bex. DA5 . .159 J5
Mount Rd, NW2 . . . . .89 H3
  NW4 . . . . .71 G7
  SE19 . . . . .170 A6
  SW19 . . . . .166 D2
  Barnet EN4 . . . . .41 H5
  Bexleyheath DA6 . . . . . . .158 D5
  Chessington KT9 . . . . . . .195 J5
  Dagenham RM8 . . . . .101 F1
  Feltham TW13 . . . . .160 E3
  Hayes UB3 . . . . .121 J2
  Ilford IG1 . . . . .98 E5
  Mitcham CR4 . . . . .185 H2
  New Malden KT3 . . . . . . .182 D3
Mount Row, W1 . . . . .16 D6
Mountsfield Ct, SE13 . . . . . . .154 D6
Mountside, Felt. TW13 . . . . . .161 E3
  Stanmore HA7 . . . . .68 C1
Mounts Pond Rd, SE3 . . . . . .154 D2
Mount Sq, The, NW3
   off Heath St 91 F3
Mount Stewart Av, Har. HA3 . . .69 G6
Mount St, W1 . . . . .16 C6
Mount Ter, E1 off New Rd . .112/113 E2
Mount Vernon, NW3 . . . . .91 F4
Mount Vw, NW7 . . . . .54 D3
  W5 . . . . .105 G4
Mountview Cl, NW11 . . . . .91 E1
Mountview Ct, N8
   off Green Las 75 H4
Mount Vw Rd, E4 . . . . .46 C7
  N4 . . . . .75 E7
  NW9 . . . . .70 D4
Mountview Rd, Esher (Clay.)
  KT10 . . . . .194 E7
Mount Vil, SE27 . . . . .169 H3
Mountwood, W.Mol. KT8 . . . .179 G3
Movers La, Bark. IG11 . . . . . .117 G1
Mowatt Cl, N19 . . . . .92 D1
Mowbray Rd, NW6 . . . . .90 B7
  SE19 . . . . .188 C1
  Barnet EN5 . . . . .41 F4
  Edgware HA8 . . . . .54 A4
  Richmond TW10 . . . . .163 F3

Mowbrays Cl, Rom. RM5 . . .83 J1
Mowbrays Rd, Rom. RM5 . . .83 J2
Mowbrey Gdns, Loug. IG10 . . .49 F2
Mowlem St, E2 . . . . .113 E2
Mowlem Trd Est, N17 . . . . . . .61 F7
Mowll St, SW9 . . . . .131 G7
Moxon Cl, E13 off Whitelegg Rd .115 F2
Moxon St, W1 . . . . .16 B2
  Barnet EN5 . . . . .40 C3
Moye Cl, E2 . . . . .13 J1
Moyers Rd, E10 . . . . .78 C7
Moylan Rd, W6 . . . . .128 B6
Moyne Pl, NW10 . . . . .106 A2
Moynihan Dr, N21 . . . . .43 E5
Moys Cl, Croy. CR0 . . . . .186 E6
Moyser Rd, SW16 . . . . .168 B5
Mozart St, W10 . . . . .108 C3
Mozart Ter, SW1 . . . . .32 C2
Muchelney Rd, Mord. SM4 . . .185 F6
Mud La, W5 . . . . .105 G5
Muggeridge Cl, S.Croy. CR2 . .202 A5
Muggeridge Rd, Dag. RM10 . .101 H4
Muirdown Av, SW14 . . . . . . .146 C4
Muir Dr, SW18 . . . . .149 G6
Muirfield, W3 . . . . .107 E6
Muirfield Cl, SE16
   off Ryder Dr 132/133 E5
  Watford WD19 . . . . .50 C4
Muirfield Cres, E14
   off Millharbour 134 B3
Muirfield Grn, Wat. WD19 . . . .50 C4
Muirfield Rd, Wat. WD19 . . . . .50 D4
Muirkirk Rd, SE6 . . . . .172 C1
Muir Rd, E5 . . . . .94 D4
Muir St, E16 off Newland St . .136 C1
Mulberry Business Cen, SE16
   off Quebec Way 133 G2
Mulberry Cl, E4 . . . . .62 A2
  N8 . . . . .74 E5
  NW3 off Hampstead High St . .91 G4
  NW4 . . . . .71 J3
  SE7 off Charlton Pk Rd . . .136 A6
  SE22 . . . . .152 D5
  SW3 off Beaufort St 129 G6
  SW16 . . . . .168 C4
  Barnet EN4 . . . . .41 G4
  Northolt UB5
   off Parkfield Av 102/103 E2
Mulberry Ct, Bark. IG11
   off Westrow Dr 99 J7
Mulberry Cres, Brent. TW8 . . .125 E7
  West Drayton UB7 . . . . . .120 D2
Mulberry La, Croy. CR0 . . . . .202 C1
Mulberry Ms, SE14
   off Lewisham Way 153 J1
  Wallington SM6
   off Ross Rd 200 C6
Mulberry Par, West Dr. UB7 . .120 D3
Mulberry Pl, W6
   off Chiswick Mall 127 G5
Mulberry Rd, E8 . . . . .94 C7
Mulberry St, E1 . . . . .21 H3
Mulberry Wk, SW3 . . . . .31 F5
Mulberry Way, E18 . . . . .79 H2
  Belvedere DA17 . . . . .139 J2
  Ilford IG6 . . . . .81 F4
Mulgrave Rd, NW10 . . . . .89 F4
  SE18 . . . . .136 C4
  SW6 . . . . .128 C6
  W5 . . . . .105 G3
  Croydon CR0 . . . . .202 A3
  Harrow HA1 . . . . .86 D2
  Sutton SM2 . . . . .198 D6
Mulholland Cl, Mitch. CR4 . . .186 B2
Mulkern Rd, N19 . . . . .92 D1
Mullards Cl, Mitch. CR4 . . . . .199 J1
Muller Rd, SW4 . . . . .150 D6
Mullet Gdns, E2 . . . . .13 J3
Mullins Path, SW14 . . . . .146 D3
Mullion Cl, Har. HA3 . . . . .67 H1
Mullion Wk, Wat. WD19
   off Ormskirk Rd 50 D4
Mull Wk, N1 off Clephane Rd . . .93 J6
Mulready St, NW8 . . . . .7 G6
Multi-way, W3
   off Valetta Rd 126/127 E2
Multon Rd, SW18 . . . . .149 G7
Mulvaney Way, SE1 . . . . .28 C4
Mumford Ct, EC2 . . . . .20 A3
Mumford Rd, SE24
   off Railton Rd 151 H5
Muncaster Rd, SW11 . . . . . . .149 J5
Muncies Ms, SE6 . . . . .172 C2
Mundania Rd, SE22 . . . . .153 E6
Munday Rd, E16 . . . . .115 G6
Munden St, W14 . . . . .128 B4
Mundesley Cl, Wat. WD19 . . . .50 C4
Mundford Rd, E5 . . . . .95 F2
Mundon Gdns, Ilf. IG1 . . . . . . .99 G1
Mund St, W14 . . . . .128 C5
Mundy St, N1 . . . . .12 D3
Mungo Pk Cl, Bushey (Bushey Hth)
  WD23 . . . . .51 J2
Munnery Way, Orp. BR6 . . . . .206 D3
Munnings Gdns, Islw. TW7 . . .144 A5
Munro Dr, N11 . . . . .58 C6
Munro Ms, W10 . . . . .108 B5

Munro Ter, SW10 . . . . .31 E5
Munslow Gdns, Sutt. SM1 . . .199 G4
Munster Av, Houns.TW4 . . . .143 F4
Munster Ct, Tedd.TW11 . . . . .163 F6
Munster Gdns, N13 . . . . .59 H4
Munster Ms, SW6 off Lillie Rd . .128 C1
Munster Rd, SW6 . . . . .148 C1
  Teddington TW11 . . . . . . .163 F6
Munster Sq, NW1 . . . . .9 E4
Munton Rd, SE17 . . . . .36 A1
Murchison Av, Bex. DA5 . . . .176 D1
Murchison Rd, E10 . . . . .96 C2
Murdock Cl, E16 off Rogers Rd . .115 F6
Murdock St, SE15 . . . . .132 E6
Murfett Cl, SW19 . . . . .166 B2
Muriel St, N1 . . . . .10 D1
Murillo Rd, SE13 . . . . .154 D4
Murphy St, SE1 . . . . .27 E4
Murray Av, Brom. BR1 . . . . . .191 H2
  Hounslow TW3 . . . . .143 H5
Murray Cres, Pnr. HA5 . . . . . .66 D1
Murray Gro, N1 . . . . .12 A2
Murray Ms, NW1 . . . . .92 D7
Murray Rd, SW19 . . . . .166 A6
  W5 . . . . .125 F4
  Richmond TW10 . . . . .163 E2
Murray Sq, E16 . . . . .115 G6
Murray St, NW1 . . . . .92 D7
Murrays Yd, SE18 . . . . .136 E4
Murray Ter, NW3 off Flask Wk . .91 G4
  W5 off Murray Rd 125 G4
Mursell Est, SW8 . . . . .151 F1
Murtwell Dr, Chig. IG7 . . . . . .65 F6
Musard Rd, W6 . . . . .128 B6
  W14 . . . . .128 B6
Musbury St, E1 . . . . .113 F6
Muscal, W6 . . . . .128 B6
Muscatel Pl, SE5
   off Dalwood St 152 B1
Muschamp Rd, SE15 . . . . . . .152 C3
  Carshalton SM5 . . . . .199 H2
Muscovy Ho, Erith DA18
   off Kale Rd 138/139 E2
Muscovy St, EC3 . . . . .21 E6
★ **Museum in Docklands**, E14
   off Hertsmere Rd 114 A7
★ **Museum Interpretative Cen**, E6
   off Norman Rd 116 C4
Museum La, SW7 . . . . .23 E6
★ **Museum of Artillery, The
  Rotunda**, SE18 . . . . .136 C5
★ **Museum of Gdn History**,
  SE1 . . . . .26 C6
★ **Museum of Instruments, Royal
  Coll of Music**, SW7 . . . . .22 E5
★ **Museum of London**, EC2 . . . .19 J2
★ **Museum of Richmond**, Rich.
  TW9 . . . . .145 G5
Museum Pas, E2
   off Victoria Pk Sq 112/113 E3
Museum St, WC1 . . . . .18 A2
Musgrave Cl, Barn. EN4 . . . . .41 F1
Musgrave Cres, SW6 . . . . . . .148 D1
Musgrave Rd, Islw.TW7 . . . . .144 C1
Musgrove Rd, SE14 . . . . .153 G1
Musjid Rd, SW11
   off Kambala Rd 149 G2
Musket Cl, Barn. EN4
   off East Barnet Rd 41 G5
Musquash Way, Houns.TW4 . .142 C2
Muston Rd, E5 . . . . .94 E2
Mustow Pl, SW6
   off Munster Rd 148 C2
Muswell Av, N10 . . . . .74 B2
MUSWELL HILL, N10 . . . . . . .74 B3
Muswell Hill, N10 . . . . .74 B3
Muswell Hill Bdy, N10 . . . . . . .74 B3
Muswell Hill Pl, N10 . . . . .74 B4
Muswell Hill Rd, N6 . . . . .74 A4
  N10 . . . . .74 A4
Muswell Ms, N10
   off Muswell Rd 74 B3
Muswell Rd, N10 . . . . .74 B3
Mutrix Rd, NW6 . . . . .108 D1
Mutton Pl, NW1
   off Harmood St 92 B6
Muybridge Rd, N.Mal. KT3 . . .182 C2
Myatt Rd, SW9 . . . . .151 H1
Myatt's Flds N, SW9
   off Eythorne Rd 151 G1
Mycenae Rd, SE3 . . . . .135 G7
Myddelton Cl, Enf. EN1 . . . . . .44 C1
Myddelton Gdns, N21 . . . . . . .43 H7
Myddelton Pk, N20 . . . . .57 G3
Myddelton Pas, EC1 . . . . .11 F3
Myddelton Rd, N8 . . . . .75 E4
Myddelton Sq, EC1 . . . . .11 F3
Myddelton St, EC1 . . . . .11 F4
Myddleton Av, N4 . . . . .93 J2
Myddleton Ms, N22 . . . . .59 E7
Myddleton Rd, N22 . . . . .59 E7
Myers La, SE14 . . . . .133 G6
Mylis Cl, SE26 . . . . .171 E4
Mylius Cl, SE14 off Kender St . .153 F1
Mylne St, EC1 . . . . .11 E2
Mynterne Ct, SW19
   off Swanton Gdns 166 A1

Myra St, SE2 138 A5
Myrdle St, E1 21 J2
Myrna Cl, SW19 167 H7
Myron Pl, SE13 154 C3
Myrtle Av, Felt. TW14 141 H4
Ruislip HA4 66 A7
Myrtleberry Cl, E8
off Beechwood Rd 94 C6
Myrtle Cl, Barn. EN4 57 J1
West Drayton UB7 120 C3
Myrtledene Rd, SE2 138 A5
Myrtle Gdns, W7 124 B1
Myrtle Gro, N.Mal. KT3 182 C2
Myrtle Rd, E6 116 B1
E17 77 H6
N13 59 J3
W3 126 C1
Croydon CR0 204 A3
Hampton (Hmptn H.) TW12 161 J6
Hounslow TW3 143 J2
Ilford IG1 99 E2
Sutton SM1 199 F5
Myrtle Wk, N1 12 D2
Mysore Rd, SW11 149 J3
Myton Rd, SE21 170 A3

N

N1 Shop Cen, N1 11 F1
Nadine St, SE7 135 J5
Nafferton Ri, Loug. IG10 48 A5
Nagle Cl, E17 78 D2
Nag's Head Ct, EC1 11 J6
Nags Head La, Well. DA16 158 B3
Nags Head Rd, Enf. EN3 45 F4
Nags Head Shop Cen, N7 93 F4
Nairne Gro, SE24 152 A5
Nairn Grn, Wat. WD19 50 A3
Nairn Rd, Ruis. HA4 84 C6
Nairn St, E14 114 C5
Nallhead Rd, Felt. TW13 160 C5
Namba Roy Cl, SW16 169 F4
Namton Dr, Th.Hth. CR7 187 F4
Nan Clark's La, NW7 55 F2
Nankin St, E14 114 A6
Nansen Rd, SW11 150 A4
Nansen Village, N12 57 E4
Nantes Cl, SW18 149 F4
Nantes Pas, E1 21 F1
Nant Rd, NW2 90 C2
Nant St, E2
off Cambridge Heath Rd 112/113 E3
Naoroji St, WC1 11 E4
Napier Av, E14 134 A5
SW6 148 C3
Napier Cl, SE8
off Amersham Vale 133 J7
W14 *off Napier Rd* 128 C3
West Drayton UB7 120 C3
Napier Ct, SW6
off Ranelagh Gdns 148 C3
Napier Gro, N1 12 A2
Napier Pl, W14 128 C3
Napier Rd, E6 116 D1
E11 96 E4
E15 115 E2
N17 76 B3
NW10 107 H3
SE25 188 E4
W14 128 C3
Belvedere DA17 139 F4
Bromley BR2 191 H4
Enfield EN3 45 G5
Hounslow (Hthrw Air.) TW6 140 A1
Isleworth TW7 144 D4
South Croydon CR2 202 A7
Wembley HA0 87 G5
Napier Ter, N1 93 H7
Napoleon Rd, E5 94 E3
Twickenham TW1 145 E7
Napton Cl, Hayes UB4 102 E4
Narbonne Av, SW4 150 C5
Narborough St, SW6 148 E2
Narcissus Rd, NW6 90 D5
Naresby Fold, Stan. HA7 53 F6
Narford Rd, E5 94 D3
Narrow Boat Cl, SE28
off Ridge Cl 137 G2
Narrow St, E14 113 H7
Narrow Way, Brom. BR2 192 B6
Nascot St, W12 107 J6
Naseberry Ct, E4
off Merriam Cl 62 C5
Naseby Cl, NW6 91 F7
Isleworth TW7 144 B1
Naseby Rd, SE19 170 A6
Dagenham RM10 101 G3
Ilford IG5 80 C1
Nash Cl, Sutt. SM1 199 G3
Nash Ct, E14
off South Colonnade 134 B1
Nash Grn, Brom. BR1 173 G6
Nash La, Kes. BR2 205 G5
Nash Rd, N9 61 F2
SE4 153 G4
Romford RM6 82 D4
Nash St, NW1 8 E4
Nash Way, Har. HA3 69 E6
Nasmyth St, W6 127 H3
Nassau Path, SE28
off Disraeli Cl 138 C1
Nassau Rd, SW13 147 F1
Nassau St, W1 17 F2
Nassington Rd, NW3 91 H4
Natalie Cl, Felt. TW14 141 G7
Natalie Ms, Twick. TW2
off Sixth Cross Rd 162 A3
Natal Rd, N11 58 E6
SW16 168 D6
Ilford IG1 98 E4
Thornton Heath CR7 188 A3
Nathaniel Cl, E1 21 G2
Nathans Rd, Wem. HA0 87 F1
Nathan Way, SE28 137 H4
★ **National Army Mus**, SW3 32 A5
★ **National Gall**, WC2 17 J6
★ **National Maritime Mus**,
SE10 134 D6
★ **National Portrait Gall**, WC2 17 J6
National Ter, SE16
off Bermondsey Wall E 132/133 E2
Nation Way, E4 62 C1
★ **Natural History Mus**, SW7 23 E6
Naval Row, E14 114 C7
Naval Wk, Brom. BR1
off High St 191 G3
Navarino Gro, E8 94 D6
Navarino Rd, E8 94 D6
Navarre Rd, E6 116 B2
Navarre St, E2 13 F5
Navenby Wk, E3
off Rounton Rd 114 A4
Navestock Cl, E4
off Mapleton Rd 62 C3
Navestock Cres, Wdf.Grn. IG8 79 J1
Navestock Ho, Bark. IG11 118 B2
Navigator Dr, Sthl. UB2 123 J2
Navigator Pk, Sthl. UB2
off Southall La 122 C4
Navy St, SW4 150 D3
Naxos Bldg, E14
off Hutchings St 134 A2
Nayim Pl, E8
off Amhurst Rd 94/95 E5
Naylor Gro, Enf. EN3
off South St 45 G5
Naylor Rd, N20 57 F2
SE15 132 E7
Nazareth Gdns, SE15 152 E2
Nazrul St, E2 13 F3
Neagle Cl, Borwd. WD6
off Balcon Way 38 C1
Neal Av, Sthl. UB1 103 F4
Neal Cl, Nthwd. HA6 66 A1
Nealden St, SW9 151 F3
Neale Cl, N2 73 F3
Neal St, WC2 18 A4
Neal's Yd, WC2 18 A4
Near Acre, NW9 71 F1
NEASDEN, NW2 89 E3
Neasden Cl, NW10 89 E5
Neasden La, NW10 89 E4
Neasden La N, NW10 88 D3
Neasham Rd, Dag. RM8 100 B5
Neate St, SE5 37 E5
Neath Gdns, Mord. SM4 185 F6
Neathouse Pl, SW1 33 F1
Neatscourt Rd, E6 116 A5
Nebraska St, SE1 28 B4
Neckinger, SE16 29 G5
Neckinger Est, SE16 29 G5
Neckinger St, SE1 29 G4
Nectarine Way, SE13 154 B2
Needham Rd, W11
off Westbourne Gro 108 D6
Needham Ter, NW2
off Kara Way 90 A3
Needleman St, SE16 133 G2
Neeld Cres, NW4 71 H5
Wembley HA9 88 A5
Neeld Par, Wem. HA9
off Harrow Rd 88 A5
Neil Wates Cres, SW2 169 G1
Nelgarde Rd, SE6 154 A7
Nella Rd, W6 128 A6
Nelldale Rd, SE16 133 F4
Nello James Gdns, SE27 170 A4
Nelson Cl, NW6 108 D2
Croydon CR0 201 H1
Romford RM7 83 H1
Nelson Ct, SE16 *off Brunel Rd* 133 F1
Nelson Gdns, E2 13 J3
Hounslow TW3 143 G6
Nelson Gro Rd, SW19 185 E1
Nelson Mandela Cl, N10 74 A2
Nelson Mandela Rd, SE3 155 J3
Nelson Pas, EC1 12 A4
Nelson Pl, N1 11 H2
Sidcup DA14
off Sidcup High St 176 A4
Nelson Rd, E4 62 B6
E11 79 G4
N8 75 F5
Nelson Rd, N9 61 E2
N15 76 B4
SE10 134 C6
SW19 167 E7
Belvedere DA17 139 F5
Bromley BR2 191 J4
Enfield EN3 45 G6
Harrow HA1 86 A1
Hounslow TW3, TW4 143 G6
Hounslow (Hthrw Air.) TW6 140 C1
New Malden KT3 182 D5
Sidcup DA14
off Sidcup High St 176 A4
Stanmore HA7 53 F6
Twickenham TW2 143 J6
★ **Nelson's Column**, WC2 26 A1
Nelson Sq, SE1 27 G3
Nelson's Row, SW4 150 D4
Nelson St, E1 112 E6
E6 116 C2
E16 *off Huntingdon St* 115 F7
Nelsons Yd, NW1 9 F1
Nelson Ter, N1 11 H2
Nelson Trd Est, SW19 184 E1
Nelson Wk, SE16
off Rotherhithe St 133 H1
Nemoure Rd, W3 106 C7
Nene Gdns, Felt. TW13 161 F2
Nene Rd, Houns. (Hthrw Air.)
TW6 141 E1
Nepaul Rd, SW11 149 H2
Nepean St, SW15 147 G6
Neptune Ct, Borwd. WD6
off Clarendon Rd 38 A3
Neptune Rd, Har. HA1 68 A6
Hounslow (Hthrw Air.) TW6 141 G1
Neptune St, SE16 133 F3
Nero Ct, Brent. TW8
off Justin Cl 125 G7
Nesbit Rd, SE9 156 A4
Nesbitt Cl, SE3
off Hurren Cl 154/155 E3
Nesbitts All, Barn. EN5
off Bath Pl 40 C3
Nesbitt Sq, SE19
off Coxwell Rd 170 B7
Nesham St, E1 29 H1
Ness St, SE16 29 H5
Nesta Rd, Wdf.Grn. IG8 63 E6
Nestles Av, Hayes UB3 121 J3
Nestor Av, N21 43 H6
Netheravon Rd, W4 127 F4
W7 124 C1
Netheravon Rd S, W4 127 F5
Netherbury Rd, W5 125 G3
Netherby Gdns, Enf. EN2 42 E4
Netherby Rd, SE23 153 F7
Nether Cl, N3 56 D7
Nethercourt Av, N3 56 D6
Netherfield Gdns, Bark. IG11 99 G6
Netherfield Rd, N12 57 E5
SW17 168 A3
Netherford Rd, SW4 150 C2
Netherhall Gdns, NW3 91 F6
Netherhall Way, NW3
off Netherhall Gdns 91 F5
Netherlands Rd, Barn. EN5 41 G6
Netherleigh Cl, N6 92 B1
Nether St, N3 72 D1
N12 56 D7
Netherton Gro, SW10 30 D6
Netherton Rd, N15 76 A6
Twickenham TW1 144 E5
Netherwood, N2 73 G2
Netherwood Pl, W14
off Netherwood Rd 128 A3
Netherwood Rd, W14 128 A3
Netherwood St, NW6 90 C7
Netley Cl, Croy. (New Adgtn)
CR0 204 C7
Sutton SM3 198 A5
Netley Dr, Walt. KT12 179 F7
Netley Gdns, Mord. SM4 185 F7
Netley Rd, E17 77 J5
Brentford TW8 125 H6
Hounslow (Hthrw Air.) TW6 141 G1
Ilford IG2 81 G5
Morden SM4 185 F7
Netley St, NW1 9 F4
Nettleden Av, Wem. HA9 88 A6
Nettlefold Pl, SE27 169 H3
Nettlestead Cl, Beck. BR3
off Copers Cope Rd 171 J7
Nettleton Rd, SE14 153 G1
Hounslow (Hthrw Air.) TW6 141 E1
Nettlewood Rd, SW16 168 D7
Neuchatel Rd, SE6 171 J2
Nevada Cl, N.Mal. KT3
off Georgia Rd 182 C4
Nevada St, SE10 134 C6
Nevern Pl, SW5 128 D4
Nevern Rd, SW5 128 D4
Nevern Sq, SW5 128 D4
Neville Av, N.Mal. KT3 182 D1
Neville Cl, E11 97 F3
NW1 9 J2
NW6 108 C2
Neville Cl, SE15 132 D7
W3 *off Acton La* 126 C2
Hounslow TW3 143 H2
Sidcup DA15 175 J4
Neville Dr, N2 73 F6
Neville Gdns, Dag. RM8 100 D3
Neville Gill Cl, SW18 148 D6
Neville Pl, N22 75 F1
Neville Rd, E7 97 G7
NW6 108 C2
W5 105 G4
Croydon CR0 188 A7
Dagenham RM8 100 D2
Ilford IG6 81 F1
Kingston upon Thames KT1 182 A2
Richmond TW10 163 F3
Nevilles Ct, NW2 89 G3
Neville St, SW7 31 E3
Neville Ter, SW7 31 E3
Neville Wk, Cars. SM5
off Green Wrythe La 185 H7
Nevill Rd, N16 94 B4
Nevill Way, Loug. IG10
off Valley Hill 48 B7
Nevin Dr, E4 62 B1
Nevinson Cl, SW18 149 G6
Nevis Rd, SW17 168 A2
New Acres Rd, SE28 137 H2
Newall Rd, Houns. (Hthrw Air.)
TW6 141 F1
Newark Cres, NW10 106 D3
Newark Grn, Borwd. WD6 38 D3
Newark Knok, E6 116 D6
Newark Par, NW4
off Greyhound Hill 71 G3
Newark Rd, S.Croy. CR2 202 A6
Newark St, E1 112 E5
Newark Way, NW4 71 G4
New Ash Cl, N2 *off Oakridge Dr* 73 G3
New Atlas Wf, E14
off Arnhem Pl 133 J3
New Barn Cl, Wall. SM6 201 F6
NEW BARNET, Barn. EN5 41 E4
New Barns Av, Mitch. CR4 186 D4
New Barn St, E13 115 G4
New Barns Way, Chig. IG7 64 E3
NEW BECKENHAM, Beck. BR3 171 J6
Newbiggin Path, Wat. WD19 50 C4
Newbolt Av, Sutt. SM3 197 J5
Newbolt Rd, Stan. HA7 52 C6
New Bond St, W1 16 D4
Newborough Grn, N.Mal. KT3 182 D4
New Brent St, NW4 71 J5
Newbridge Pt, SE23
off Windrush La 171 G3
New Br St, EC4 19 G4
New Broad St, EC2 20 D2
New Bdy, W5 105 F7
Hampton (Hmptn H.) TW12
off Hampton Rd 162 A5
New Bdy Bldgs, W5
off New Bdy 105 G7
Newburgh Rd, W3 126 C1
Newburgh St, W1 17 F4
New Burlington Ms, W1 17 F5
New Burlington Pl, W1 17 F5
New Burlington St, W1 17 F5
Newburn St, SE11 34 D4
Newbury Cl, Nthlt. UB5 85 F6
Newbury Gdns, Epsom KT19 197 F4
Newbury Ho, N22 75 E1
Newbury Ms, NW5
off Malden Rd 92 A6
NEWBURY PARK, Ilf. IG2 81 G5
Newbury Rd, E4 62 C6
Bromley BR2 191 G3
Hounslow (Hthrw Air.) TW6 140 C1
Ilford IG2 81 G6
Newbury St, EC1 19 J2
Newbury Way, Nthlt. UB5 85 E6
New Butt La, SE8 134 A7
New Butt La N, SE8
off Reginald Rd 134 A7
Newby Cl, Enf. EN1 44 B2
Newby Pl, E14 114 C7
Newby St, SW8 150 B3
New Caledonian Wf, SE16 133 J3
Newcastle Cl, EC4 19 G3
Newcastle Pl, W2 15 F2
Newcastle Row, EC1 11 F5
New Cavendish St, W1 17 E1
New Change, EC4 19 J4
New Chapel Sq, Felt. TW13 160 B1
New Charles St, EC1 11 H3
NEW CHARLTON, SE7 135 J4
New Ch Ct, SE19
off Waldegrave Rd 170 D7
New Ch Rd, SE5 36 A7
New City Rd, E13 115 J3
New Cl, SW19 185 F3
Feltham TW13 160 E5
New Coll Ct, NW3
off Finchley Rd 91 F6
New Coll Ms, N1
off Islington Pk St 93 G7
New Coll Par, NW3
off Finchley Rd 91 G6

Newcombe Gdns, SW16 . . . . . .169 E4
  Hounslow TW4 . . . . .143 F4
Newcombe Pk, NW7 . . . . .55 E5
  Wembley HA0 . . . . .105 J1
Newcombe St, W8
  off Kensington Pl 128 D1
Newcomen Rd, E11 . . . . .97 F3
  SW11 . . . . .149 G3
Newcomen St, SE1 . . . . .28 B3
New Compton St, WC2 . . . . . . .17 A4
New Concordia Wf, SE1 . . . . . . .29 H3
New Ct, EC4 . . . . .18 E5
Newcourt St, NW8 . . . . .7 G2
★ New Covent Garden Flower
  Mkt, SW8 . . . . .34 A6
★ New Covent Garden Mkt,
  SW8 . . . . .130 D7
New Crane Pl, E1 off Garnet St .133 F3
NEW CROSS, SE14 . . . . .153 H1
NEW CROSS GATE, SE14 . . . . .153 G1
New Cross Rd, SE14 . . . . .133 F7
Newdales Cl, N9 off Balham Rd . .60 D2
Newdene Av, Nthlt. UB5 . . . . . .102 A2
Newell St, E14 . . . . .113 J6
NEW ELTHAM, SE9 . . . . .174 D1
New End, NW3 . . . . .91 F4
New End Sq, NW3 . . . . .91 G4
Newent Cl, SE15 . . . . .36 D7
  Carshalton SM5 . . . . .199 J1
New Fm Av, Brom. BR2 . . . . . .191 G4
New Ferry App, SE18 . . . . .136 D3
New Fetter La, EC4 . . . . .19 F3
Newfield Cl, Hmptn. TW12
  off Percy Rd 179 G3
Newfield Ri, NW2 . . . . .89 H3
New Forest La, Chig. IG7 . . . . . .64 D6
Newgale Gdns, Edg. HA8 . . . . . .69 J1
New Gdn Dr, West Dr. UB7
  off Drayton Gdns 120 B2
Newgate, Croy. CR0 . . . . .201 J1
Newgate Cl, Felt. TW13 . . . . . .161 E2
Newgate St, E4 . . . . .63 F3
  EC1 . . . . .19 H3
New Globe Wk, SE1 . . . . .27 J1
New Goulston St, E1 . . . . .21 F3
New Grn Pl, SE19
  off Hawke Rd 170 B6
Newhams Row, SE1 . . . . .28 E4
Newham Way, E6 . . . . .115 J5
  E16 . . . . .115 F5
Newhaven Cl, Hayes UB3 . . . . .121 J4
Newhaven Gdns, SE9 . . . . .156 A4
Newhaven La, E16 . . . . .115 F4
Newhaven Rd, SE25 . . . . .188 A5
New Heston Rd, Houns. TW5 . . .123 F7
New Horizons Ct, Brent. TW8
  off Shield Dr 124 D6
Newhouse Av, Rom. RM6 . . . . . .82 D3
Newhouse Cl, N.Mal. KT3 . . . . .183 E7
Newhouse Wk, Mord. SM4 . . . .185 F7
Newick Cl, Bex. DA5 . . . . .159 H6
Newick Rd, E5 . . . . .95 E3
Newing Grn, Brom. BR1 . . . . . .174 A7
NEWINGTON, SE1 . . . . .35 J1
Newington Barrow Way, N7 . . . .93 F3
Newington Butts, SE1 . . . . .35 H2
  SE11 . . . . .35 H2
Newington Causeway, SE1 . . . . .27 H6
Newington Grn, N1 . . . . .94 A5
  N16 . . . . .94 A5
Newington Grn Rd, N1 . . . . .94 A6
New Inn Bdy, EC2 . . . . .12 E5
New Inn Pas, WC2 . . . . .18 D4
New Inn Sq, EC2 . . . . .12 E5
New Inn St, EC2 . . . . .12 E5
New Inn Yd, EC2 . . . . .12 E5
New James Ct, SE15
  off Nunhead La 152/153 E3
New Jersey Ter, SE15
  off Nunhead La 152/153 E3
New Jubilee Ct, Wdf.Grn. IG8
  off Grange Av 63 G7
New Kent Rd, SE1 . . . . .27 J6
New Kings Rd, SW6 . . . . .148 C2
New King St, SE8 . . . . .134 A6
Newland Cl, Pnr. HA5 . . . . .51 E6
Newland Ct, Wem. HA9
  off Forty Av 88 A2
Newland Dr, Enf. EN1 . . . . .44 E1
Newland Gdns, W13 . . . . .124 D2
Newland Rd, N8 . . . . .74 E3
Newlands, The, Wall. SM6 . . . . .200 C7
Newlands Av, T.Ditt. KT7 . . . . . .194 B1
Newlands Cl, Edg. HA8 . . . . . . .53 H3
  Southall UB2 . . . . .122 C5
  Wembley HA0 . . . . .87 F6
Newlands Ct, SE9 . . . . .156 D6
Newlands Pk, SE26 . . . . .171 G5
Newlands Pl, Barn. EN5 . . . . . . .40 A5
Newlands Quay, E1 . . . . .113 F7
Newlands Rd, SW16 . . . . .187 E2
  Woodford Green IG8 . . . . . .63 F2
Newland St, E16 . . . . .136 B1
Newlands Way, Chess. KT9 . . . .195 F5
Newling Cl, E6 off Porter Rd 116 C6
New London St, EC3 . . . . .21 E5
New Lydenburg St, SE7 . . . . . . .135 J3

Newlyn Cl, Orp. BR6 . . . . .207 J4
Newlyn Gdns, Har. HA2 . . . . . . .67 F7
Newlyn Rd, N17 . . . . .76 C1
  NW2 off Tilling Rd 89 J1
  Barnet EN5 . . . . .40 C4
  Welling DA16 . . . . .157 J2
NEW MALDEN, KT3 . . . . .182 D3
Newman Pas, W1 . . . . .17 G2
Newman Rd, E13 . . . . .115 H2
  E17 off Southcote Rd 77 G5
  Bromley BR1 . . . . .191 G1
  Croydon CR0 . . . . .201 F1
  Hayes UB3 . . . . .102 B7
Newmans Cl, Loug. IG10 . . . . . .48 E3
Newman's Ct, EC3 . . . . .20 C4
Newmans La, Loug. IG10 . . . . . .48 D3
  Surbiton KT6 . . . . .181 G6
Newman's Row, WC2 . . . . .18 D2
Newman St, W1 . . . . .17 G2
Newman Yd, W1 . . . . .17 H3
Newmarket Av, Nthlt. UB5 . . . . .85 G5
Newmarket Grn, SE9
  off Middle Pk Av 156 A7
Newmarsh Rd, SE28 . . . . .137 J1
Newminster Rd, Mord. SM4 . . . .185 F6
New Mt St, E15 . . . . .96 D7
Newnes Path, SW15
  off Putney Pk La 147 H4
Newnham Av, Ruis. HA4 . . . . . . .84 C1
Newnham Cl, Loug. IG10 . . . . . .48 A6
  Northolt UB5 . . . . .85 J5
  Thornton Heath CR7 . . . . . .187 J2
Newnham Gdns, Nthlt. UB5 . . . .85 J5
Newnham Ms, N22
  off Newnham Rd 75 F1
Newnham Rd, N22 . . . . .75 F1
Newnhams Cl, Brom. BR1 . . . . .192 C3
Newnham Ter, SE1 . . . . .26 E5
Newnham Way, Har. HA3 . . . . . .69 H5
New N Pl, EC2 . . . . .12 D4
New N Rd, N1 . . . . .12 C2
  Ilford IG6 . . . . .65 G7
New N St, WC1 . . . . .18 C1
Newnton Cl, N4 . . . . .76 A7
New Oak Rd, N2 . . . . .73 F2
New Orleans Wk, N19 . . . . .74 D7
New Oxford St, WC1 . . . . .17 J3
New Pk Av, N13 . . . . .59 J3
New Pk Cl, Nthlt. UB5 . . . . .84 E6
New Pk Ct, SW2 . . . . .151 E7
New Pk Par, SW2
  off Doverfield Rd 150/151 E6
New Pk Rd, SW2 . . . . .168 D1
Newpiece, Loug. IG10 . . . . .48 E3
New Pl Sq, SE16 . . . . .132 E3
New Plaistow Rd, E15 . . . . . . .115 E1
Newport Av, E13 . . . . .115 H4
  E14 . . . . .114 D7
Newport Ct, WC2 . . . . .17 J5
Newport Mead, Wat. WD19
  off Kilmarnock Rd 50 D4
Newport Pl, WC2 . . . . .17 J5
Newport Rd, E10 . . . . .96 C2
  E17 . . . . .77 H4
  SW13 . . . . .147 G1
  Hounslow (Hthrw Air.) TW6 . .140 D1
Newport St, SE11 . . . . .34 C2
New Printing Ho Sq, WC1
  off Gray's Inn Rd 111 F4
New Priory Ct, NW6
  off Mazenod Av 90 D7
New Providence Wf, E14
  off Blackwall Way 134 D1
Newquay Cres, Har. HA2 . . . . . .85 E2
Newquay Gdns, Wat. WD19
  off Fulford Gro 50 B2
Newquay Rd, SE6 . . . . .172 B2
New Quebec St, W1 . . . . .16 A4
New Ride, SW7 . . . . .23 J3
New River Ct, N8 off High St 75 F4
New River Ct, N5 . . . . .94 A4
New River Cres, N13 . . . . .59 H4
New River Head, EC1 . . . . .11 F3
New River Wk, N1 . . . . .93 J6
New River Way, N4 . . . . .76 A7
New Rd, E1 . . . . .112 E5
  E4 . . . . .62 B4
  N8 . . . . .74 E5
  N9 . . . . .60 D3
  N17 . . . . .76 C1
  N22 . . . . .75 J1
  NW7 . . . . .56 B7
  NW7 (Barnet Gate) 39 F7
  SE2 . . . . .138 D4
  Brentford TW8 . . . . .125 G6
  Dagenham RM9, RM10 . . . .119 G1
  Feltham TW14 . . . . .160 B1
  Feltham (E.Bed.) TW14 . . . .141 G6
  Feltham (Han.) TW13 . . . . .160 E5
  Harrow HA1 . . . . .86 C4
  Hayes UB3 . . . . .121 F7
  Hounslow TW3
    off Station Rd 143 H4
  Ilford IG3 . . . . .99 H2
  Kingston upon Thames KT2 . .164 A7
  Mitcham CR4 . . . . .199 J1

New Rd, Rich. TW10 . . . . .163 F4
  Welling DA16 . . . . .158 B2
  West Molesey KT8 . . . . . . .179 G3
New Row, WC2 . . . . .18 A5
Newry Rd, Twick. TW1 . . . . . . .144 D4
Newsam Av, N15 . . . . .76 A5
★ New Scotland Yd, SW1 . . .25 H5
Newsholme Dr, N21 . . . . .43 F5
NEW SOUTHGATE, N11 . . . . . . .58 D4
New Spring Gdns Wk, SE11 . . . .34 B4
New Sq, WC2 . . . . .18 D3
New Sq Pas, WC2 off New Sq . . .111 F6
Newstead Av, Orp. BR6 . . . . . .207 G3
Newstead Rd, SE12 . . . . .155 E7
Newstead Wk, Cars. SM5 . . . . .185 F7
Newstead Way, SW19 . . . . . . .166 A4
New St, EC2 . . . . .20 E2
New St Hill, Brom. BR1 . . . . . . .173 H5
New St Sq, EC4 . . . . .19 F3
Newton Av, N10 . . . . .74 A1
  W3 . . . . .126 C2
Newton Cl, E17 . . . . .77 H6
  Harrow HA2 . . . . .85 G2
Newton Cres, Borwd. WD6 . . . . .38 C4
Newton Gro, W4 . . . . .126 E4
Newton Ho, Enf. EN3
  off Exeter Rd 45 G3
Newton Pl, E14 . . . . .134 A4
Newton Rd, E15 . . . . .96 D5
  N15 . . . . .76 C5
  NW2 . . . . .89 J3
  SW19 . . . . .166 B7
  W2 . . . . .108 D6
  Harrow HA3 . . . . .68 B2
  Isleworth TW7 . . . . .144 C2
  Welling DA16 . . . . .158 A3
  Wembley HA0 . . . . .87 J7
Newton St, WC2 . . . . .18 B3
Newtons Yd, SW18
  off Wandsworth High St .148/149 E5
Newton Wk, Edg. HA8
  off North Rd 70 B1
Newton Way, N18 . . . . .59 J5
Newtown St, SW11
  off Strasburg Rd 150 B1
New Trinity Rd, N2 . . . . .73 G3
New Turnstile, WC1 . . . . .18 C2
New Union Cl, E14 . . . . .134 C3
New Union St, EC2 . . . . .20 B2
New Wanstead, E11 . . . . .79 F6
New Way Rd, NW9 . . . . .71 E4
New Wf Rd, N1 . . . . .10 B1
New Zealand Way, W12 . . . . . .107 H7
Niagara Av, W5 . . . . .125 F4
Niagara Cl, N1 off Cropley St . . .112 A2
Nibthwaite Rd, Har. HA1 . . . . . .68 B5
Nicholas Cl, Grnf. UB6 . . . . . . .103 H2
Nicholas Ct, E13
  off Tunmarsh La 115 H3
Nicholas Gdns, W5 . . . . .125 G2
Nicholas La, EC4 . . . . .20 C5
Nicholas Ms, W4
  off Short Rd 126/127 E6
Nicholas Pas, EC4 . . . . .20 C5
Nicholas Rd, E1 . . . . .113 F4
  Croydon CR0 . . . . .201 F4
  Dagenham RM8 . . . . .101 F2
Nicholay Rd, N19 . . . . .92 D1
Nichol Cl, N14 . . . . .58 D1
Nicholes Rd, Houns. TW3 . . . . .143 G4
Nichol La, Brom. BR1 . . . . .173 G7
Nicholsfield Wk, N7
  off Hillmarton Rd 93 F5
Nicholls Pt, E15 off Park Gro . . .115 G1
Nicholl St, E2 . . . . .112 D1
Nichols Cl, N4 off Osborne Rd . . .93 G1
  Chessington KT9
    off Merritt Gdns 195 F6
Nichols Ct, E2 . . . . .13 F2
Nichols Grn, W5
  off Montpelier Rd 105 H5
Nicholson Rd, Croy. CR0 . . . . . .202 C1
Nicholson St, SE1 . . . . .27 G2
Nickelby Cl, SE28 . . . . .118 C6
Nickols Wk, SW18
  off Jew's Row 148/149 E4
Nicola Cl, Har. HA3 . . . . .68 A2
  South Croydon CR2 . . . . . .201 J6
Nicola Ms, Ilf. IG6 . . . . .65 E7
Nicol Cl, Twick. TW1
  off Cassilis Rd 144/145 E6
Nicoll Pl, NW4 . . . . .71 H6
Nicoll Rd, NW10 . . . . .107 E1
Nicoll Way, Borwd. WD6 . . . . . .38 D5
Nicolson Dr, Bushey (Bushey Hth)
  WD23 . . . . .51 J1
Nicosia Rd, SW18 . . . . .149 H7
Niederwald Rd, SE26 . . . . .171 H4
Nield Rd, Hayes UB3 . . . . .121 J2
Nigel Cl, Nthlt. UB5
  off Church Rd 102/103 E1
Nigel Fisher Way, Chess. KT9 . . .195 F7
Nigel Ms, Ilf. IG1 . . . . .98 E4
Nigel Playfair Av, W6
  off King St 127 H4
Nigel Rd, E7 . . . . .97 J5
  SE15 . . . . .152 D3

Nigeria Rd, SE7 . . . . .135 J7
  Harrow HA1 . . . . .68 E7
Nightingale Av, E4 . . . . .62 E5
  W4 off Grove Pk Ter 126 C6
  Carshalton SM5 . . . . .200 A2
  Pinner HA5 . . . . .66 C5
Nightingale Cl, E11
  off Nightingale La 79 H5
Nightingale Dr, Epsom KT19 . . .196 B6
Nightingale Est, E5 . . . . .94 D3
Nightingale Gro, SE13 . . . . . . .154 D5
Nightingale Hts, SE18
  off Nightingale Vale 136 E6
Nightingale La, E11 . . . . .79 G5
  N6 . . . . .91 H1
  N8 . . . . .74 E4
  SW4 . . . . .149 J7
  SW12 . . . . .149 J7
  Bromley BR1 . . . . .191 J2
  Richmond TW10 . . . . .145 H7
Nightingale Ms, E3
  off Chisenhale Rd 113 H2
  E11 . . . . .79 G5
  SE11 . . . . .35 F1
  Kingston upon Thames KT1
    off South La 181 G3
Nightingale Pl, SE18 . . . . .136 D6
  SW10 . . . . .30 D5
Nightingale Rd, E5 . . . . .94 E3
  N1 . . . . .93 J6
  N9 . . . . .45 F6
  N22 . . . . .75 E1
  NW10 . . . . .107 F2
  W7 . . . . .124 C1
  Carshalton SM5 . . . . .199 J3
  Hampton TW12 . . . . .161 G5
  Orpington BR5 . . . . .193 F6
  Walton-on-Thames KT12 . . .178 B7
  West Molesey KT8 . . . . . . .179 H5
Nightingales, The, Stai. TW19 . . .140 C7
Nightingale Sq, SW12 . . . . . . .150 A7
Nightingale Vale, SE18 . . . . . . .136 D6
Nightingale Wk, SW4 . . . . .150 B6
Nightingale Way, E6 . . . . .116 B5
Nile Cl, N16 off Evering Rd 94 C3
Nile Dr, N9 . . . . .61 F2
Nile Path, SE18 off Jackson St . .136 D6
Nile Rd, E13 . . . . .115 J2
Nile St, N1 . . . . .12 A3
Nile Ter, SE15 . . . . .37 F4
Nimegen Way, SE22 . . . . .152 B5
Nimrod Cl, Nthlt. UB5 . . . . .102 D3
Nimrod Pas, N1
  off Tottenham Rd 94 B6
Nimrod Rd, SW16 . . . . .168 B6
Nina Mackay Cl, E15
  off Arthingworth St 114/115 E1
Nine Acres Cl, E12 . . . . .98 B5
NINE ELMS, SW8 . . . . .33 G7
Nine Elms La, SW8 . . . . .33 G6
Nineteenth Rd, Mitch. CR4 . . . .186 E4
Ninhams Wd, Orp. BR6 . . . . . .206 D4
Ninth Av, Hayes UB3 . . . . .102 A7
Nisbet Ho, E9
  off Homerton High St 95 G5
Nithdale Rd, SE18 . . . . .137 E7
Niton Cl, Barn. EN5 . . . . .40 A6
Niton Rd, Rich. TW9 . . . . .146 A3
Niton St, SW6 . . . . .128 A7
Niven Cl, Borwd. WD6 . . . . .38 C1
N.L.A. Twr, Croy. CR0 . . . . . . .202 A2
Nobel Dr, Hayes UB3 . . . . .121 G7
Nobel Rd, N18 . . . . .61 F5
Noble St, EC2 . . . . .19 J3
NOEL PARK, N22 . . . . .75 G2
Noel Pk Rd, N22 . . . . .75 G2
Noel Rd, E6 . . . . .116 B4
  N1 . . . . .11 G1
  W3 . . . . .106 B6
Noel Sq, Dag. RM8 . . . . .100 C4
Noel St, W1 . . . . .17 G4
Noel Ter, SE23
  off Dartmouth Rd 171 F2
Nolan Way, E5 . . . . .94 D4
Nolton Pl, Edg. HA8 . . . . .69 J1
Nonsuch Cl, Ilf. IG6 . . . . .65 E6
★ Nonsuch Mansion Ho, Sutt.
  SM3 . . . . .197 J6
Nora Gdns, NW4 . . . . .72 A4
NORBITON, Kings.T. KT2 . . . . . .182 B2
Norbiton Av, Kings.T. KT1 . . . . .182 C1
Norbiton Common Rd, Kings.T.
  KT1 . . . . .182 B3
Norbiton Rd, E14 . . . . .113 J6
Norbreck Gdns, NW10
  off Lytham Gro 105 J3
Norbreck Par, NW10
  off Lytham Gro 105 J3
Norbroke St, W12 . . . . .107 F7
Norburn St, W10
  off Chesterton Rd 108 B5
NORBURY, SW16 . . . . .187 G1
Norbury Av, SW16 . . . . .187 F1
  Hounslow TW3 . . . . .144 A5
  Thornton Heath CR7 . . . . . .187 G2
Norbury Cl, SW16 . . . . .187 G1

Norbury Ct Rd, SW16 186 E3
Norbury Cres, SW16 187 F1
Norbury Cross, SW16 186 E3
Norbury Gdns, Rom. RM6 82 D5
Norbury Gro, NW7 54 E3
Norbury Hill, SW16 169 G7
Norbury Ri, SW16 186 E3
Norbury Rd, E4 62 A5
Thornton Heath CR7 187 J2
Norcombe Gdns, Har. HA3 69 F6
Norcott Cl, Hayes UB4 102 C4
Norcott Rd, N16 94 D2
Norcroft Gdns, SE22 152 D7
Norcutt Rd, Twick. TW2 162 B1
Norfield Rd, Dart. DA2 177 J4
Norfolk Av, N13 59 H6
N15 76 C6
Norfolk Cl, N2 *off Park Rd* 73 H3
N13 59 H6
Barnet EN4 42 A4
Twickenham TW1
off Cassilis Rd 144/145 E6
Norfolk Cres, W2 15 H3
Sidcup DA15 157 H7
Norfolk Gdns, Bexh. DA7 159 F1
Borehamwood WD6 38 D4
Norfolk Ho, SE3 135 E6
Norfolk Ho Rd, SW16 168 D3
Norfolk Ms, W10
off Blagrove Rd 108 C5
Norfolk Pl, W2 15 F3
Welling DA16 158 A2
Norfolk Rd, E6 116 C1
E17 77 G2
NW8 109 G1
NW10 88 E7
SW19 167 H7
Barking IG11 99 H7
Barnet EN5 40 D3
Dagenham RM10 101 H5
Enfield EN3 45 E6
Esher (Clay.) KT10 194 B5
Feltham TW13 160 C1
Harrow HA1 67 H5
Ilford IG3 99 H1
Romford RM7 83 J6
Thornton Heath CR7 187 J3
Norfolk Row, SE1 34 C1
Norfolk Sq, W2 15 F4
Norfolk Sq Ms, W2 15 F4
Norfolk St, E7 97 G4
Norfolk Ter, W6 *off Field Rd* 128 B5
Norgrove St, SW12 150 A7
Norhyrst Av, SE25 188 C3
Norland Ho, W11 128 A1
Norland Pl, W11 128 B1
Norland Rd, W11 128 A1
Norlands Cres, Chis. BR7 192 E1
Norlands Gate, Chis. BR7 193 E1
Norland Sq, W11 128 B1
Norley Vale, SW15 165 G1
Norlington Rd, E10 96 C1
E11 96 C1
Norman Av, N22 75 H1
Feltham TW13 161 E2
Southall UB1 103 E7
Twickenham TW1 145 E7
Normanby Cl, SW15
off Manfred Rd 148 C5
Normanby Rd, NW10 89 F4
Norman Cl, Orp. BR6 207 F3
Romford RM5 83 H2
Norman Ct, Ilf. IG2 81 G7
Woodford Green IG8
off Monkhams Av 63 H5
Norman Cres, Houns. TW5 142 D1
Pinner HA5 66 C1
Normand Gdns, W14
off Greyhound Rd 128 B6
Normand Ms, W14
off Normand Rd 128 B6
Normand Rd, W14 128 C6
Normandy Av, Barn. EN5 40 C5
Normandy Cl, SE26 171 H3
Normandy Rd, SW9 151 G1
Normandy Ter, E16 115 H6
Norman Gro, E3 113 H2
Normanhurst Av, Bexh. DA7 158 D1
Normanhurst Dr, Twick. TW1
off St. Margarets Rd 144/145 E5
Normanhurst Rd, SW2 169 F2
Norman Rd, E6 116 C4
E11 96 D2
N15 76 C5
SE10 134 B7
SW19 167 F7
Belvedere DA17 139 H3
Ilford IG1 99 E5
Sutton SM1 198 D5
Thornton Heath CR7 187 H5
Norman's Bldgs, EC1
off Ironmonger Row 111 J3
Normans Cl, NW10 88 D6
Normansfield Av, Tedd. TW11 163 F7
Normanshire Av, E4 62 C4
Normanshire Dr, E4 62 A4
Normans Mead, NW10 88 D6
Norman St, EC1 11 J4
Normanton Av, SW19 166 D2
Normanton Pk, E4 62 E3
Normanton Rd, S.Croy. CR2 202 B6
Normanton St, SE23 171 G2
Norman Way, N14 58 E2
W3 106 B5
Normington Cl, SW16 169 G5
Norrice Lea, N2 73 G5
Norris St, SW1 17 H6
Norroy Rd, SW15 148 A4
Norrys Cl, Barn. EN4 41 J5
Norrys Rd, Barn. EN4 41 J4
Norseman Cl, Ilf. IG3 100 B1
Norseman Way, Grnf. UB6
off Olympic Way 103 H1
Norstead Pl, SW15 165 G2
North Access Rd, E17 77 G6
North Acre, NW9 71 E1
NORTH ACTON, W3 106 D4
North Acton Rd, NW10 106 D3
Northall Rd, Bexh. DA7 159 J2
Northampton Gro, N1 94 A5
Northampton Pk, N1 93 J6
Northampton Rd, EC1 11 F5
Croydon CR0 202 D2
Enfield EN3 45 H4
Northampton Row, EC1 11 F4
Northampton Sq, EC1 11 G4
Northampton St, N1 93 J7
Northanger Rd, SW16 168 E6
North Arc, Croy. CR0
off North End 201 J2
North Audley St, W1 16 B4
North Av, N18 60 D4
W13 104 E6
Carshalton SM5 199 J7
Harrow HA2 67 H6
Hayes UB3 102 A7
Richmond TW9
off Sandycombe Rd 146 A1
Southall UB1 103 F7
North Bk, NW8 7 F4
Northbank Rd, E17 78 C2
NORTH BECKTON, E6 116 B4
North Birkbeck Rd, E11 96 D3
Northborough Rd, SW16 186 D3
Northbourne, Brom. BR2 191 G7
Northbourne Rd, SW4 150 D4
North Branch Av, W10
off Harrow Rd 107 J3
Northbrook Rd, N22 59 E7
SE13 154 D5
Barnet EN5 40 B6
Croydon CR0 188 A5
Ilford IG1 98 D2
Northburgh St, EC1 11 H5
North Carriage Dr, W2 15 G5
NORTH CHEAM, Sutt. SM3 197 J3
Northchurch, SE17 36 C3
Northchurch Rd, N1 94 A7
Wembley HA9 87 J6
Northchurch Ter, N1 94 B7
North Circular Rd, E4 (A406) 61 J7
E6 (A406) 117 E2
E11 (A406) 79 J2
E12 (A406) 98 D5
E17 (A406) 61 J7
E18 (A406) 79 J2
N3 (A406) 72 E3
N11 (A406) 73 G1
N12 (A406) 73 G1
N13 (A406) 59 G5
N18 (A406) 60 B5
NW2 (A406) 88 E3
NW10 (A406) 88 B7
NW11 (A406) 72 B4
W3 (A406) 125 J2
W4 (A406) 125 J2
W5 (A406) 125 J2
Barking (A406) IG11 117 E2
Ilford (A406) IG1, IG4 98 B1
Northcliffe Cl, Wor.Pk. KT4 197 E3
Northcliffe Dr, N20 56 C1
North Cl, Barn. EN5 39 J5
Bexleyheath DA6 158 D4
Dagenham RM10 119 G1
Feltham TW14 *off North Rd* 141 G6
Morden SM4 184 B4
North Colonnade, E14 134 A1
North Common Rd, W5 105 H7
Northcote, Pnr. HA5 66 C2
Northcote Av, W5 105 H7
Isleworth TW7 144 D5
Southall UB1 103 E7
Surbiton KT5 182 A7
Northcote Ms, SW11
off Northcote Rd 149 H4
Northcote Rd, E17 77 H4
NW10 89 E7
SW11 149 H4
Croydon CR0 188 A6
New Malden KT3 182 C3
Sidcup DA14 175 H4
Twickenham TW1 144 D5
Northcott Av, N22 75 E1
North Countess Rd, E17 77 J2
NORTH CRAY, Sid. DA14 177 G3
North Cray Rd, Bex. DA5 177 F3
Sidcup DA14 176 E6
North Cres, E16 114 D4
N3 72 C2
WC1 17 H1
Northcroft Rd, W13 124 E2
Epsom KT19 196 D7
Northcroft Ter, W13
off Northcroft Rd 124/125 E2
North Cross Rd, SE22 152 C5
Ilford IG6 81 F4
North Dene, NW7 54 D3
Northdene, Chig. IG7 65 G5
North Dene, Houns. TW3 143 H1
Northdene Gdns, N15 76 C6
Northdown Gdns, Ilf. IG2 81 H5
Northdown Rd, Well. DA16 158 B2
Northdown St, N1 10 B1
North Dr, SW16 168 C4
Hounslow TW3 143 J2
Orpington BR6 207 H4
North End, NW3 91 F2
Buckhurst Hill IG9 47 J7
Croydon CR0 201 J2
North End Av, NW3 91 F2
North End Cres, W14 128 C4
North End Ho, W14 128 B4
North End Par, W14
off North End Rd 128 B4
North End Rd, NW11 90 D1
SW6 128 C6
W14 128 B4
Wembley HA9 88 A3
North End Way, NW3 91 F2
Northern Av, N9 60 C2
Northernhay Wk, Mord. SM4 184 B4
Northern Perimeter Rd, Houns.
(Hthrw Air.) TW6 141 F1
Northern Perimeter Rd W, Houns.
(Hthrw Air.) TW6 140 A1
Northern Relief Rd, Bark. IG11 99 E7
Northern Rd, E13 115 H1
Northern Service Rd, Barn. EN5 40 B3
North Eyot Gdns, W6 127 G5
Northey St, E14 113 H7
Northfield, Loug. IG10 48 A4
Northfield Av, W5 125 E2
W13 125 E2
Pinner HA5 66 D4
Northfield Cl, Brom. BR1 192 B1
Hayes UB3 121 J3
Northfield Cres, Sutt. SM3 198 B4
Northfield Gdns, Dag. RM9
off Northfield Rd 101 F4
Northfield Ind Est, NW10 106 A3
Northfield Pk, Hayes UB3 121 J3
Northfield Path, Dag. RM9 101 F3
Northfield Rd, E6 98 C7
N16 76 B7
W13 124 E2
Barnet EN4 41 H3
Borehamwood WD6 38 B1
Dagenham RM9 101 F4
Enfield EN3 44 E5
Hounslow TW5 122 D6
Northfields, SW18 148 D4
Northfields Ind Est, Wem. HA0 106 A1
Northfields Rd, W3 106 B5
NORTH FINCHLEY, N12 57 G5
North Flockton St, SE16 29 H3
North Gdn, E14
off Westferry Circ 133 J1
North Gdns, SW19 167 G7
Northgate Dr, NW9 70 E6
Northgate Ind Pk, Rom. RM5 83 F2
North Glade, The, Bex. DA5 159 F7
North Gower St, NW1 9 G4
North Grn, NW9
off Clayton Fld 54/55 E7
North Gro, N6 74 A7
N15 76 A5
NORTH HARROW, Har. HA2 67 G6
North Hatton Rd, Houns.
(Hthrw Air.) TW6 141 G1
North Hill, N6 73 J6
North Hill Av, N6 74 A6
NORTH HYDE, Sthl. UB2 123 E4
North Hyde Gdns, Hayes UB3 122 A4
North Hyde La, Houns. TW5 123 E5
Southall UB2 123 E5
North Hyde Rd, Hayes UB3 121 J3
Northiam, N12 56 D3
Northiam St, E9 113 E1
Northington St, WC1 10 C6
NORTH KENSINGTON, W10 107 J6
Northlands Av, Orp. BR6 207 H4
Northlands St, SE5 151 J2
North La, Tedd. TW11 162 C6
North Lo Cl, SW15
off Westleigh Av 148 A5
North Mall, N9
off St. Martins Rd 60/61 E2
North Ms, WC1 10 D6
Northolm, Edg. HA8 54 D4
Northolme Gdns, Edg. HA8 70 A1
Northolme Ri, Orp. BR6 207 H2
Northolme Rd, N5 93 J4
NORTHOLT, UB5 85 F7
Northolt Av, Ruis. HA4 84 B5
Northolt Gdns, Grnf. UB6 86 C5
Northolt Rd, Har. HA2 85 H4
Hounslow (Hthrw Air.) TW6 140 A1
Northover, Brom. BR1 173 F3
North Par, Chess. KT9 195 H5
North Pk, SE9 156 C6
North Pas, SW18 148 D4
North Peckham Est, SE15 37 E7
North Pl, Mitch. CR4 167 J7
Teddington TW11 162 C6
Northpoint, Brom. BR1
off Sherman Rd 191 G1
North Pole La, Kes. BR2 205 F6
North Pole Rd, W10 107 J5
Northport St, N1 112 A1
North Ride, W2 15 G6
North Rd, N6 74 A7
N7 92 E6
N9 60 E1
SE18 137 H4
SW19 167 F6
W5 125 G3
Belvedere DA17 139 H3
Brentford TW8 125 H6
Bromley BR1 191 H1
Edgware HA8 70 B1
Feltham TW14 141 G6
Ilford IG3 99 H2
Richmond TW9 146 A3
Romford (Chad.Hth) RM6 82 E5
Southall UB1 103 G7
Surbiton KT6 181 G6
West Drayton UB7 120 C3
West Wickham BR4 204 B1
Northrop Rd, Houns. (Hthrw Air.)
TW6 141 H1
North Row, W1 16 A5
North Several, SE3
off Orchard Rd 154 D2
NORTH SHEEN, Rich. TW9 146 A2
Northside Rd, Brom. BR1
off Mitchell Way 191 G1
North Side Wandsworth Common,
SW18 149 F5
Northspur Rd, Sutt. SM1 198 D3
North Sq, N9
off St. Martins Rd 60/61 E2
NW11 72 D5
Northstead Rd, SW2 169 G2
North St, E13 115 G2
NW4 71 J5
SW4 150 C3
Barking IG11 99 E6
Bexleyheath DA7 159 G4
Bromley BR1 191 G1
Carshalton SM5 199 J3
Isleworth TW7 144 D3
North St Pas, E13 115 H2
North Tenter St, E1 21 G4
North Ter, SW3 23 G6
Northumberland All, EC3 21 E4
Northumberland Av, E12 97 J1
WC2 26 A1
Enfield EN1 45 E1
Isleworth TW7 144 C1
Welling DA16 157 G4
Northumberland Cl, Erith DA8 139 J7
Staines (Stanw.) TW19 140 B6
Northumberland Cres, Felt.
TW14 141 H6
Northumberland Gdns, N9 60 C3
Bromley BR1 192 D4
Isleworth TW7 124 D7
Mitcham CR4 186 D5
Northumberland Gro, N17 60 E7
NORTHUMBERLAND HEATH, Erith
DA8 139 J7
Northumberland Pk, N17 60 C7
Erith DA8 139 J7
Northumberland Pl, W2 108 D6
Richmond TW10 145 G5
Northumberland Rd, E6 116 B6
E17 78 A7
Barnet EN5 41 F6
Harrow HA2 67 F5
Northumberland Row, Twick. TW2
off Colne Rd 162 B1
Northumberland St, WC2 26 A1
Northumberland Way, Erith DA8 159 J1
Northumbria St, E14 114 A6
North Verbena Gdns, W6
off St. Peter's Sq 127 G5
Northview, N7 93 E3
North Vw, SW19 165 H5
W5 105 F4
Pinner HA5 66 C7
Northview Cres, NW10 89 F4
North Vw Dr, Wdf.Grn. IG8 80 A2
North Vw Rd, N8 74 D3
North Vil, NW1 92 D6
North Wk, W2 14 C6
Croydon (New Adgtn) CR0 204 B5
North Way, N9 61 F2
N11 58 C6

North Way, NW9 ... 70 B3
Northway, NW11 ... 72 E5
Morden SM4 ... 184 B3
North Way, Pnr. HA5 ... 66 C3
Northway, Wall. SM6 ... 200 C4
Northway Circ, NW7 ... 54 D4
Northway Cres, NW7 ... 54 D4
Northway Ho, N20 ... 57 F1
Northway Rd, SE5 ... 151 J3
Croydon CR0 ... 188 C6
Northways Par, NW3
off Finchley Rd ... 91 G7
Northweald La, Kings.T. KT2 ... 163 G5
NORTH WEMBLEY, Wem. HA0 ... 87 E2
Northwest Pl, N1 ... 11 F1
North Wf Rd, W2 ... 14 E2
Northwick Av, Har. HA3 ... 68 D6
Northwick Circle, Har. HA3 ... 69 F6
Northwick Cl, NW8 ... 6 E5
Harrow HA1
off Nightingale Av ... 68/69 E7
Northwick Pk Rd, Har. HA1 ... 68 C6
Northwick Rd, Wat. WD19 ... 50 C4
Wembley HA0 ... 105 G1
Northwick Ter, NW8 ... 6 E5
Northwick Wk, Har. HA1 ... 68 C7
Northwold Dr, Pnr. HA5
off Cuckoo Hill ... 66 C3
Northwold Est, E5 ... 94 D2
Northwold Rd, E5 ... 94 C2
N16 ... 94 C2
North Wd Ct, SE25
off Regina Rd ... 188 D3
Northwood Gdns, N12 ... 57 G5
Greenford UB6 ... 86 C5
Ilford IG5 ... 80 D4
Northwood Hall, N6 ... 74 C7
Northwood Ho, SE27 ... 170 A4
Northwood Pl, Erith DA18 ... 139 F3
Northwood Rd, N6 ... 74 B7
SE23 ... 171 J1
Carshalton SM5 ... 200 A6
Hounslow (Hthrw Air.) TW6 ... 140 A1
Thornton Heath CR7 ... 187 H2
Northwood Twr, E17 ... 78 C4
Northwood Way, SE19
off Roman Ri ... 170 A6
Northwood HA6 ... 50 A7
NORTH WOOLWICH, E16 ... 136 B2
North Woolwich Rd, E16 ... 135 G1
North Woolwich Roundabout, E16
off North Woolwich Rd ... 136 A1
★ **North Woolwich Sta Mus**,
E16 ... 136 D2
North Worple Way, SW14 ... 146 D3
Norton Av, Surb. KT5 ... 182 B7
Norton Cl, E4 ... 62 A5
Borehamwood WD6 ... 38 A1
Enfield EN1 *off Brick La* ... 44/45 E2
Norton Folgate, E1 ... 21 E1
Norton Gdns, SW16 ... 186 E2
Norton Rd, E10 ... 95 J1
Wembley HA0 ... 87 G6
Norval Rd, Wem. HA0 ... 86 E2
Norway Gate, SE16 ... 133 H3
Norway Pl, E14
off Commercial Rd ... 113 J6
Norway St, SE10 ... 134 B6
Norwich Ho, E14 *off Cordelia St* ... 114 B6
Norwich Ms, Ilf. IG3
off Ashgrove Rd ... 100 A1
Norwich Pl, Bexh. DA6 ... 159 G4
Norwich Rd, E7 ... 97 G5
Dagenham RM9 ... 119 G2
Greenford UB6 ... 103 H1
Thornton Heath CR7 ... 187 J3
Norwich St, EC4 ... 19 E3
Norwich Wk, Edg. HA8 ... 54 C7
NORWOOD, SE19 ... 170 B6
Norwood Av, Wem. HA0 ... 105 J1
Norwood Cl, NW2 ... 90 B3
Southall UB2 ... 123 G4
Twickenham TW2
off Fourth Cross Rd ... 162 A2
Norwood Cres, Houns. (Hthrw Air.)
TW6 ... 141 F1
Norwood Dr, Har. HA2 ... 67 F6
Norwood Gdns, Hayes UB4 ... 102 C4
Southall UB2 ... 123 F4
NORWOOD GREEN, Sthl. UB2 ... 123 G4
Norwood Grn Rd, Sthl. UB2 ... 123 G4
Norwood High St, SE27 ... 169 H3
NORWOOD NEW TOWN, SE19 ... 169 J6
Norwood Pk Rd, SE27 ... 169 J5
Norwood Rd, SE24 ... 169 H1
SE27 ... 169 H2
Southall UB2 ... 123 F4
Norwood Ter, Sthl. UB2
off Tentelow La ... 123 H4
Notley St, SE5 ... 36 B7
Notre Dame Est, SW4 ... 150 C4
Notson Rd, SE25 ... 188 E4
Notting Barn Rd, W10 ... 108 A4
Nottingdale Sq, W11
off Wilsham St ... 128 B1
Nottingham Av, E16 ... 115 J5
Nottingham Ct, WC2 ... 18 A4
Nottingham Pl, W1 ... 8 B6
Nottingham Rd, E10 ... 78 C6
SW17 ... 167 J1
Isleworth TW7 ... 144 C2
South Croydon CR2 ... 201 J4
Nottingham St, W1 ... 16 B1
Nottingham Ter, NW1 ... 8 B6
NOTTING HILL, W11 ... 108 B7
Notting Hill Gate, W11 ... 128 D1
Nova, E14 *off Newton Pl* ... 134 A4
Nova Ms, Sutt. SM3 ... 198 B1
Novar Cl, Orp. BR6 ... 193 J7
Nova Rd, Croy. CR0 ... 187 H7
Novar Rd, SE9 ... 175 F1
Novello St, SW6 ... 148 D1
Novello Way, Borwd. WD6 ... 38 D1
Nowell Rd, SW13 ... 127 G6
Nower Hill, Pnr. HA5 ... 67 F4
Noyna Rd, SW17 ... 167 J3
Nuding Cl, SE13 ... 154 A3
Nugent Rd, N19 ... 93 E1
SE25 ... 188 C3
Nugents Ct, Pnr. HA5
off St. Thomas' Dr ... 66/67 E1
Nugents Pk, Pnr. HA5 ... 67 E1
Nugent Ter, NW8 ... 6 D2
Numa Ct, Brent. TW8
off Justin Cl ... 125 G7
★ **No. 2 Willow Rd**, NW3 ... 91 H4
Nun Ct, EC2 ... 20 B3
Nuneaton Rd, Dag. RM9 ... 100 D7
NUNHEAD, SE15 ... 153 F3
Nunhead Cres, SE15 ... 152 E3
Nunhead Est, SE15 ... 152 E4
Nunhead Grn, SE15 ... 153 E3
Nunhead Gro, SE15 ... 153 E3
Nunhead La, SE15 ... 152 E3
Nunhead Pas, SE15
off Peckham Rye ... 152 D3
Nunnington Cl, SE9 ... 174 B3
Nunns Rd, Enf. EN2 ... 43 J2
Nupton Dr, Barn. EN5 ... 39 J6
Nursery Av, N3 ... 73 F2
Bexleyheath DA7 ... 159 F3
Croydon CR0 ... 203 G2
Nursery Cl, SE4 ... 153 J2
SW15 ... 148 A4
Croydon CR0 ... 203 G2
Enfield EN3 ... 45 G1
Feltham TW14 ... 142 B7
Romford RM6 ... 82 D6
Woodford Green IG8 ... 63 H5
Nursery Ct, N17 *off Nursery St* ... 60 C7
Nursery Gdns, Chis. BR7 ... 174 E6
Enfield EN3 ... 45 G1
Hounslow TW4 ... 143 F5
Nursery La, E2 ... 112 C1
E7 ... 97 G6
W10 ... 107 J5
Nurserymans Rd, N11 ... 58 A2
Nursery Rd, E9 *off Morning La* ... 95 F6
N2 ... 73 G1
N14 ... 42 C7
SW9 ... 151 F4
Loughton IG10 ... 47 J5
Loughton (High Beach) IG10 ... 47 H1
Pinner HA5 ... 66 C3
Sutton SM1 ... 199 F4
Thornton Heath CR7 ... 188 A4
Nursery Rd Merton, SW19 ... 185 E2
Nursery Rd Mitcham, Mitch.
CR4 ... 185 H3
Nursery Rd Wimbledon, SW19
off Worple Rd ... 166 B7
Nursery Row, SE17 ... 36 B2
Barnet EN5 *off St. Albans Rd* ... 40 B3
Nursery St, N17 ... 60 C7
Nursery Wk, NW4 ... 71 H3
Nurstead Rd, Erith DA8 ... 139 G7
Nutbourne St, W10 ... 108 B3
Nutbrook St, SE15 ... 152 D3
Nutbrowne Rd, Dag. RM9 ... 119 F1
Nutcroft Rd, SE15 ... 132 E7
Nutfield Cl, N18 ... 60 D6
Carshalton SM5 ... 199 H3
Nutfield Gdns, Ilf. IG3 ... 99 J2
Northolt UB5 ... 102 C2
Nutfield Rd, E15 ... 96 C4
NW2 ... 89 G2
SE22 ... 152 C5
Thornton Heath CR7 ... 187 H4
Nutfield Way, Orp. BR6 ... 206 D2
Nutford Pl, W1 ... 15 H3
Nuthatch Gdns, SE28 ... 137 G2
Nuthurst Av, SW2 ... 169 F2
Nutley Ter, NW3 ... 91 F6
Nutmead Cl, Bex. DA5 ... 177 J1
Nutmeg Cl, E16
off Cranberry La ... 114/115 E4
Nutmeg La, E14 ... 114 D6
Nuttall St, N1 ... 12 E1
Nutter La, E11 ... 79 J6
Nutt Gro, Edg. HA8 ... 53 G2
Nutt St, SE15 ... 37 G7
Nutwell St, SW17 ... 167 H5
Nuxley Rd, Belv. DA17 ... 139 F6
Nyanza St, SE18 ... 137 G6
Nye Bevan Est, E5 ... 95 G3
Nylands Av, Rich. TW9 ... 146 A1
Nymans Gdns, SW20
off Hidcote Gdns ... 183 H3
Nynehead St, SE14 ... 133 H7
Nyon Gro, SE6 ... 171 J2
Nyssa Cl, Wdf.Grn. IG8
off Gwynne Pk Av ... 64 C6
Nyton Cl, N19
off Courtauld Rd ... 92/93 E1

O

O2 Shop Cen, NW3
off Finchley Rd ... 91 F6
Oak Apple Ct, SE12 ... 173 G2
Oak Av, N8 ... 74 E4
N10 ... 58 B7
N17 ... 60 A7
Croydon CR0 ... 204 A2
Hampton TW12 ... 161 E5
Hounslow TW5 ... 122 D7
West Drayton UB7 ... 120 D3
Oak Bk, Croy. (New Adgtn) CR0 ... 204 C6
Oakbank Av, Walt. KT12 ... 179 F7
Oakbank Gro, SE24 ... 151 J4
Oakbrook Cl, Brom. BR1 ... 173 H4
Oakbury Rd, SW6 ... 149 E2
Oak Cl, N14 ... 42 B7
Sutton SM1 ... 199 F2
Oakcombe Cl, N.Mal. KT3
off Traps La ... 182/183 E1
Oak Cottage Cl, SE6 ... 173 F1
Oak Cres, E16 ... 115 E5
Oakcroft Cl, Pnr. HA5 ... 66 B2
Oakcroft Rd, SE13 ... 154 D2
Chessington KT9 ... 195 J4
Oakcroft Vil, Chess. KT9 ... 195 J4
Oakdale, N14 ... 58 B1
Oakdale Av, Har. HA3 ... 69 H5
Northwood HA6 ... 66 A2
Oakdale Cl, Wat. WD19 ... 50 C4
Oakdale Gdns, E4 ... 62 C5
Oakdale Rd, E7 ... 97 H7
E11 ... 96 D2
E18 ... 79 H2
N4 ... 75 J6
SE15 ... 153 F3
SW16 ... 169 E5
Watford WD19 ... 50 C3
Oakdale Way, Mitch. CR4
off Wolseley Rd ... 186 A7
Oakdene, SE15
off Carlton Gro ... 152/153 E1
Oak Dene, W13
off The Dene ... 104/105 E5
Oakdene Av, Chis. BR7 ... 174 D5
Erith DA8 ... 139 J6
Thames Ditton KT7 ... 194 D1
Oakdene Cl, Pnr. HA5 ... 51 F7
Oakdene Dr, Surb. KT5 ... 182 C7
Oakdene Ms, Sutt. SM3 ... 198 C1
Oakdene Pk, N3 ... 56 C7
Oakdene Rd, Orp. BR5 ... 193 J5
Oakden St, SE11 ... 35 F1
Oake Ct, SW15 ... 148 B5
Oaken Dr, Esher (Clay.) KT10 ... 194 C6
Oakenholt Ho, SE2
off Hartslock Dr ... 138 D2
Oaken La, Esher (Clay.) KT10 ... 194 B5
Oakenshaw Cl, Surb. KT6 ... 181 H7
Oakes Cl, E6 *off Savage Gdns* ... 116 C6
Oakeshott Av, N6 ... 92 A2
Oakey La, SE1 ... 27 E5
Oak Fm, Borwd. WD6 ... 38 C5
Oakfield, E4 ... 62 B5
Oakfield Av, Har. HA3 ... 69 E3
Oakfield Cl, N.Mal. KT3
off Blakes La ... 183 F5
Oakfield Ct, N8 ... 74 E7
NW2 *off Hendon Way* ... 72 A7
Borehamwood WD6 ... 38 B3
Oakfield Gdns, N18 ... 60 B4
SE19 ... 170 B5
Beckenham BR3 ... 190 A5
Carshalton SM5 ... 199 H1
Greenford UB6 ... 104 A4
Oakfield La, Kes. BR2 ... 205 J4
Oakfield Rd, E6 ... 116 B1
E17 ... 77 H2
N3 ... 72 E1
N4 ... 75 G6
N14 ... 58 E3
SE20 ... 171 E7
SW19 ... 166 A3
Croydon CR0 ... 201 J1
Ilford IG1 ... 99 E2
Oakfields Rd, NW11 ... 72 B6
Oakfield St, SW10 ... 30 C5
Oakford Rd, NW5 ... 92 C4
Oak Gdns, Croy. CR0 ... 204 A2
Edgware HA8 ... 70 C2
Oak Gro, NW2 ... 90 B4
Ruislip HA4 ... 66 B7
Sunbury-on-Thames TW16 ... 160 B7
West Wickham BR4 ... 204 C2
Oak Gro Rd, SE20 ... 189 F1
Oakhall Ct, E11 ... 79 H6
Oak Hall Rd, E11 ... 79 H6
Oakham Cl, SE6 *off Rutland Wk* ... 171 J2
Barnet EN4 ... 41 J3
Oakham Dr, Brom. BR2 ... 191 F4
Oakhampton Rd, NW7 ... 56 A7
Oakhill, Esher (Clay.) KT10 ... 194 D6
Oak Hill, Surb. KT6 ... 181 H7
Woodford Green IG8 ... 62 D7
Oakhill Av, NW3 ... 90 E4
Pinner HA5 ... 66 E2
Oak Hill Cl, Wdf.Grn. IG8 ... 62 D7
Oakhill Ct, SW19 ... 166 A7
Oak Hill Cres, Surb. KT6 ... 181 H7
Woodford Green IG8 ... 62 D7
Oakhill Dr, Surb. KT6 ... 181 H7
Oak Hill Gdns, Wdf.Grn. IG8 ... 79 E1
Oak Hill Gro, Surb. KT6 ... 181 H6
Oak Hill Pk, NW3 ... 91 E4
Oak Hill Pk Ms, NW3 ... 91 F4
Oakhill Path, Surb. KT6 ... 181 H6
Oakhill Pl, SW15 *off Oakhill Rd* ... 148 D5
Oakhill Rd, SW15 ... 148 C5
SW16 ... 187 E1
Beckenham BR3 ... 190 C2
Orpington BR6 ... 207 J1
Oak Hill Rd, Surb. KT6 ... 181 H6
Oakhill Rd, Sutt. SM1 ... 199 E3
Oak Hill Way, NW3 ... 91 F4
Oakhouse Rd, Bexh. DA6 ... 159 G5
Oakhurst Av, Barn. EN4 ... 41 H7
Bexleyheath DA7 ... 138 E7
Oakhurst Cl, E17 ... 78 E4
Chislehurst BR7 ... 192 C1
Ilford IG6 ... 81 F1
Teddington TW11 ... 162 B5
Oakhurst Gdns, E4 ... 63 F1
E17 ... 78 E4
Bexleyheath DA7 ... 139 E7
Oakhurst Gro, SE22 ... 152 D4
Oakhurst Rd, Epsom KT19 ... 196 C6
Oakington Av, Har. HA2 ... 67 G7
Hayes UB3 ... 121 G4
Wembley HA9 ... 87 J3
Oakington Cl, Sun. TW16
off Oakington Dr ... 178 C2
Oakington Dr, Sun. TW16 ... 178 C2
Oakington Manor Dr, Wem. HA9 ... 88 A5
Oakington Rd, W9 ... 108 D4
Oakington Way, N8 ... 75 E6
Oakland Pl, Buck.H. IG9 ... 63 G2
Oakland Rd, E15 ... 96 D4
Oaklands, N21 ... 59 F2
Twickenham TW2 ... 143 J7
Oaklands Av, N9 ... 44 E6
Esher KT10 ... 194 A1
Isleworth TW7 ... 124 C6
Sidcup DA15 ... 157 J7
Thornton Heath CR7 ... 187 G4
Watford WD19 ... 50 B1
West Wickham BR4 ... 204 B3
Oaklands Cl, Bexh. DA6 ... 159 F5
Chessington KT9 ... 195 F4
Orpington BR5 ... 193 H6
Oaklands Ct, Wem. HA0 ... 87 G5
Oaklands Est, SW4 ... 150 C6
Oaklands Gro, W12 ... 127 G1
Oaklands La, Barn. EN5 ... 39 H4
Oaklands Pk Av, Ilf. IG1
off High Rd ... 99 G2
Oaklands Pl, SW4
off St. Alphonsus Rd ... 150 C4
Oaklands Rd, N20 ... 40 C7
NW2 ... 90 A4
SW14 ... 146 D3
W7 ... 124 C2
Bexleyheath DA6 ... 159 F4
Bromley BR1 ... 173 E7
Oaklands Way, Wall. SM6 ... 200 D7
Oakland Way, Epsom KT19 ... 196 D6
Oak La, E14 ... 113 J7
N2 ... 73 G2
N11 ... 58 D6
Isleworth TW7 ... 144 B4
Twickenham TW1 ... 144 D7
Woodford Green IG8 ... 63 F4
Oakleafe Gdns, Ilf. IG6 ... 80 E3
Oaklea Pas, Kings.T. KT1 ... 181 G3
Oakleigh Av, N20 ... 57 G2
Edgware HA8 ... 70 B2
Surbiton KT6 ... 196 A1
Oakleigh Cl, N20 ... 57 J3
Oakleigh Ct, Barn. EN4
off Church Hill Rd ... 41 H6
Edgware HA8 ... 70 C2
Oakleigh Cres, N20 ... 57 H2
Oakleigh Gdns, N20 ... 57 F1
Edgware HA8 ... 53 J5
Orpington BR6 ... 207 H4
Oakleigh Ms, N20
off Oakleigh Rd N ... 57 F2
OAKLEIGH PARK, N20 ... 57 G1
Oakleigh Pk Av, Chis. BR7 ... 192 D1
Oakleigh Pk N, N20 ... 57 G1
Oakleigh Pk S, N20 ... 57 H2
Oakleigh Rd, Pnr. HA5 ... 51 F6

Oakleigh Rd N, N20 57 G2
Oakleigh Rd S, N11 58 A3
Oakleigh Way, Mitch. CR4 186 B1
Surbiton KT6 196 A1
Oakley Av, W5 106 A7
Barking IG11 99 J7
Croydon CR0 201 E4
Oakley Cl, E4 62 C3
E6 off Northumberland Rd 116 B6
W7 104 B7
Isleworth TW7 144 A1
Oakley Ct, Loug. IG10
off Hillyfields 48 D2
Mitcham CR4 off London Rd 200 A1
Oakley Cres, EC1 11 H2
Oakley Dr, SE9 175 G1
SE13 154 D6
Bromley BR2 206 B3
Oakley Gdns, N8 75 F5
SW3 31 H5
Oakley Pk, Bex. DA5 158 C7
Oakley Pl, SE1 37 F4
Oakley Rd, N1 94 A7
SE25 188 E5
Bromley BR2 206 B3
Harrow HA1 68 B6
Oakley Sq, NW1 9 G2
Oakley St, SW3 31 G5
Oakley Wk, W6 128 A6
Oakley Yd, E2 13 G5
Oak Lo Av, Chig. IG7 65 G5
Oak Lo Cl, Stan. HA7
off Dennis La 53 F5
Oak Lo Dr, W.Wick. BR4 190 B7
Oak Manor Dr, Wem. HA9
off Oakington Manor Dr 87 J5
Oakmead Av, Brom. BR2 191 G6
Oakmeade, Pnr. HA5 51 G6
Oakmead Gdns, Edg. HA8 54 D4
Oakmead Pl, Mitch. CR4 185 H1
Oakmead Rd, SW12 168 A1
Croydon CR0 186 D6
Oakmere Rd, SE2 138 A6
Oakmoor Way, Chig. IG7 65 H5
Oakmount Pl, Orp. BR6 207 G1
Oak Pk Gdns, SW19 148 A7
Oak Pk Ms, E5 off Brooke Rd 94 C3
Oak Pl, SW18 off East Hill 148/149 E5
Oakridge Dr, N2 73 G3
Oakridge La, Brom. BR1
off Downham Way 172 D5
Oakridge Rd, Brom. BR1 172 D4
Oak Ri, Buck.H. IG9 64 A3
Oak Rd, W5 off The Broadway 105 G7
Erith (Northumb.Hth) DA8 139 J7
New Malden KT3 182 D2
Oak Row, SW16 186 C2
Oaks, The, N12 57 E4
SE18 137 F5
Watford WD19 50 C1
Woodford Green IG8 63 E6
Oaks Av, SE19 170 B5
Feltham TW13 160 E2
Romford RM5 83 J2
Worcester Park KT4 197 H3
Oaksford Av, SE26 170 E3
Oaks Gro, E4 62 E2
Oakshade Rd, Brom. BR1 172 D4
Oakshaw Rd, SW18 149 E7
Oaks La, Croy. CR0 203 F3
Ilford IG2 81 H5
Oaks Rd, Croy. CR0 202 E5
Staines (Stanw.) TW19 140 A6
Oak St, Rom. RM7 83 J5
Oaks Way, Cars. SM5 199 J7
Surbiton KT6 195 G2
Oakthorpe Rd, N13 59 G5
Oaktree Av, N13 59 H3
Oak Tree Cl, W5
off Pinewood Gro 105 F6
Loughton IG10 49 F1
Stanmore HA7 53 F7
Oak Tree Dell, NW9 70 C5
Oak Tree Dr, N20 57 E1
Oak Tree Gdns, Brom. BR1 173 H5
Oaktree Gro, Ilf. IG1 99 G5
Oak Tree Rd, NW8 7 F4
Oakview Gdns, N2 73 G4
Oakview Gro, Croy. CR0 203 H1
Oakview Rd, SE6 172 B5
Oak Village, NW5 92 A4
Oak Wk, Wall. SM6
off Helios Rd 200 A1
Oak Way, N14 42 B7
Oakway, SW20 183 J4
Oak Way, W3 126 E1
Oakway, Brom. BR2 190 D2
Oak Way, Croy. CR0 189 G6
Oakway Cl, Bex. DA5 159 E6
Oakways, SE9 156 E6
OAKWOOD, N14 42 D6
Oakwood Av, N14 42 D7
Beckenham BR3 190 C2
Borehamwood WD6 38 B4
Bromley BR2 191 H3
Mitcham CR4 185 G2
Southall UB1 103 G7
Oakwood Cl, N14 42 C6
Chislehurst BR7 174 C6
Woodford Green IG8
off Green Wk 64 B6
Oakwood Ct, W14 128 C3
Oakwood Cres, N21 43 E6
Greenford UB6 86 D6
Oakwood Dr, SE19 170 A6
Edgware HA8 54 C6
Oakwood Gdns, Ilf. IG3 99 J2
Orpington BR6 207 F2
Sutton SM1 198 D2
Oakwood Hill, Loug. IG10 48 C6
Oakwood Hill Ind Est, Loug.
IG10 49 F5
Oakwood La, W14 128 C3
Oakwood Pk Rd, N14 42 D7
Oakwood Pl, Croy. CR0 187 G6
Oakwood Rd, NW11 72 E5
SW20 183 G1
Croydon CR0 187 G6
Orpington BR6 207 F2
Pinner HA5 66 B2
Oakwood Vw, N14 42 D6
Oakworth Rd, W10 107 J5
Oarsman Pl, E.Mol. KT8 180 B4
Oates Cl, Brom. BR2 190 D3
Oatfield Ho, N15 off Bushey Rd 76 B6
Oatfield Rd, Orp. BR6 207 J1
Oatland Ri, E17 77 H2
Oatlands Rd, Enf. EN3 45 F1
Oat La, EC2 19 J3
Oban Cl, E13 115 J4
Oban Ho, Bark. IG11
off Wheelers Cross 117 G2
Oban Rd, E13 115 J3
SE25 188 A4
Oban St, E14 114 D6
Oberon Cl, Borwd. WD6 38 C1
Oberstein Rd, SW11 149 G4
Oborne Cl, SE24 151 H5
Observatory Gdns, W8 128 D2
Observatory Ms, E14
off Storers Quay 134 D4
Observatory Rd, SW14 146 C4
Occupation La, SE18 156 E1
W5 125 G4
Occupation Rd, SE17 35 J3
W13 124 E2
Ocean Est, E1 113 G4
Ocean St, E1 113 G5
Ocean Wf, E14 134 A2
Ockendon Ms, N1
off Ockendon Rd 94 A6
Ockendon Rd, N1 94 A6
Ockham Dr, Orp. BR5 176 A7
Ockley Ct, Sutt. SM1
off Oakhill Rd 199 F4
Ockley Rd, SW16 168 E3
Croydon CR0 187 F7
Octagon Arc, EC2 20 D2
Octavia Cl, Mitch. CR4 185 H5
Octavia Ms, W9
off Bravington Rd 108 C4
Octavia Rd, Islw. TW7 144 C2
Octavia St, SW11 149 H1
Octavia Way, SE28 off Booth Cl 118 B7
Octavius St, SE8 134 A7
Odard Rd, W.Mol. KT8
off Down St 179 G4
Oddesey Rd, Borwd. WD6 38 B1
Odell Cl, Bark. IG11 99 J7
Odeon, The, Bark. IG11
off Longbridge Rd 99 G7
Odessa Rd, E7 97 F3
NW10 107 G2
Odessa St, SE16 133 J2
Odger St, SW11 149 J2
Odhams Wk, WC2 18 B4
Odyssey Business Pk, Ruis.
HA4 84 B5
Offa's Mead, E9
off Lindisfarne Way 95 H4
Offenbach Ho, E2 113 G2
Offenham Rd, SE9 174 C4
Offers Ct, Kings.T. KT1
off Winery La 181 J3
Offerton Rd, SW4 150 C3
Offham Slope, N12 56 C5
Offley Pl, Islw. TW7 144 A2
Offley Rd, SW9 35 E7
Offord Cl, N17 60 D7
Offord Rd, N1 93 F7
Offord St, N1 93 F7
Ogilby St, SE18 136 C4
Oglander Rd, SE15 152 C4
Ogle St, W1 17 F1
Oglethorpe Rd, Dag. RM10 101 F3
Ohio Rd, E13 115 F4
Oil Mill La, W6 127 G5
Okeburn Rd, SW17 168 A5
Okehampton Cl, N12 57 G5
Okehampton Cres, Well. DA16 158 B1
Okehampton Rd, NW10 107 J1
Olaf St, W11 108 A7
Oldacre Ms, SW12
off Balham Gro 150 B7
★ Old Admiralty Bldgs (M.o.D.),
SW1 25 J2
Old Bailey, EC4 19 H4
Old Barge Ho All, SE1
off Upper Grd 131 G1
Old Barn Cl, Sutt. SM2 198 B7
Old Barrack Yd, SW1 24 B3
Old Barrowfield, E15
off New Plaistow Rd 114/115 E1
Old Bellgate Pl, E14 134 A3
Oldberry Rd, Edg. HA8 54 D6
Old Bethnal Grn Rd, E2 13 H3
OLD BEXLEY, Bex. DA5 159 H7
Old Billingsgate Wk, EC3
off Lower Thames St 112 B6
Old Bond St, W1 17 F6
Oldborough Rd, Wem. HA0 87 F2
Old Brewers Yd, WC2 18 A4
Old Brewery Ms, NW3
off Hampstead High St 91 G4
Old Br Cl, Nthlt. UB5 103 G2
Old Br St, Kings.T. (Hmptn W.)
KT1 181 G2
Old Broad St, EC2 20 C4
Old Bromley Rd, Brom. BR1 172 D5
Old Brompton Rd, SW5 128 D5
SW7 128 D5
Old Bldgs, WC2 18 E3
Old Burlington St, W1 17 F5
Oldbury Pl, W1 16 C1
Oldbury Rd, Enf. EN1 44 D2
Old Canal Ms, SE15 37 G4
Old Castle St, E1 21 F2
Old Cavendish St, W1 16 D3
Old Change Ct, EC4
off Carter La 111 J6
Old Chelsea Ms, SW3 31 F6
Old Ch La, NW9 88 C2
Greenford UB6
off Perivale La 104 D3
Stanmore HA7 53 F7
Old Ch Rd, E1 113 G6
E4 62 A4
Old Ch St, SW3 31 F4
Old Claygate La, Esher (Clay.)
KT10 194 D6
Old Clem Sq, SE18
off Kempt St 136 D6
Old Coal Yd, SE28
off Pettman Cres 137 G4
Old Compton St, W1 17 H5
Old Cote Dr, Houns. TW5 123 G6
Old Ct Pl, W8 22 A3
★ Old Curiosity Shop, WC2 18 C3
Old Dairy Ms, SW12
off Chestnut Gro 150 A7
Old Deer Pk Gdns, Rich. TW9 145 H3
Old Devonshire Rd, SW12 150 B7
Old Dock Cl, Rich. TW9
off Watcombe Cotts 126 A6
Old Dover Rd, SE3 135 G7
Old Fm Av, N14 42 C7
Sidcup DA15 175 G1
Old Fm Cl, Houns. TW4 143 F4
Old Fm Pas, Hmptn. TW12 179 J1
Old Fm Rd, N2 73 G1
Hampton TW12 161 F6
West Drayton UB7 120 A2
Old Fm Rd E, Sid. DA15 176 A2
Old Fm Rd W, Sid. DA15 175 J2
Oldfield Cl, Brom. BR1 192 C4
Greenford UB6 86 B5
Stanmore HA7 52 D5
Oldfield Fm Gdns, Grnf. UB6 104 A1
Oldfield Gro, SE16 133 G4
Oldfield La N, Grnf. UB6 86 B6
Oldfield La S, Grnf. UB6 103 J4
Oldfield Ms, N6 74 C7
Oldfield Rd, N16 94 B3
NW10 89 F7
SW19 166 B6
W3 off Valetta Rd 127 F2
Bexleyheath DA7 159 E2
Bromley BR1 192 C4
Hampton TW12 179 F1
Oldfields Circ, Nthlt. UB5 85 J6
Oldfields Rd, Sutt. SM1 198 C3
Oldfields Trd Est, Sutt. SM1 198 D3
Old Fish St Hill, EC4 19 J5
Old Fleet La, EC4 19 G3
Old Fold Cl, Barn. EN5
off Old Fold La 40 C1
Old Fold La, Barn. EN5 40 C1
Old Fold Vw, Barn. EN5 39 J3
OLD FORD, E3 95 J7
Old Ford Rd, E2 113 F2
E3 113 H2
Old Forge Cl, Stan. HA7 52 D4
Old Forge Ms, W12
off Goodwin Rd 127 H2
Old Forge Rd, N19
off Elthorne Rd 92 D2
Old Forge Way, Sid. DA14 176 B4
Old Fox Footpath, S.Croy. CR2
off Essenden Rd 202 B7
Old Gloucester St, WC1 18 B1
Old Hall Cl, Pnr. HA5 67 E1
Old Hall Dr, Pnr. HA5 66 E1
Oldham Ter, W3 126 C1
Old Hill, Chis. BR7 192 D1
Orpington BR6 207 G6
Oldhill St, N16 94 D1
Old Homesdale Rd, Brom. BR2 191 J4
Old Hosp Cl, SW12 167 J1
Old Ho Cl, SW19 166 B5
Old Ho Gdns, Twick. TW1 145 F5
Old Jamaica Rd, SE16 29 H5
Old James St, SE15 152 E3
Old Jewry, EC2 20 B4
Old Kenton La, NW9 70 B5
Old Kent Rd, SE1 28 C6
SE15 37 J5
Old Kingston Rd, Wor.Pk. KT4 196 C3
Old Lo Pl, Twick. TW1
off St. Margarets Rd 144/145 E6
Old Lo Way, Stan. HA7 52 D5
Old London Rd, Kings.T. KT2 181 H2
Old Maidstone Rd, Sid. DA14 177 F7
OLD MALDEN, Wor.Pk. KT4 196 D1
Old Malden La, Wor.Pk. KT4 196 D2
Old Manor Dr, Islw. TW7 143 J6
Old Manor Rd, Sthl. UB2 122 D4
Old Manor Way, Chis. BR7 174 C5
Old Manor Yd, SW5
off Earls Ct Rd 128/129 E4
Old Mkt Sq, E2 13 F3
Old Marylebone Rd, NW1 15 H2
Old Ms, Har. HA1 off Hindes Rd 68 B5
Old Mill Ct, E18 79 J3
Old Mill Rd, SE18 137 G6
Old Mitre Ct, EC4 off Fleet St 111 G6
Old Montague St, E1 21 H2
Old Nichol St, E2 13 F5
Old N St, WC1 18 C1
Old Oak Cl, Chess. KT9 195 J4
OLD OAK COMMON, NW10 107 F5
Old Oak Common La, NW10 107 E5
W3 107 E5
Old Oak La, NW10 107 E3
Old Oak Rd, W3 107 F7
★ Old Operating Thea Mus & Herb
Garret, SE1 28 C2
Old Orchard, Sun. TW16 178 C2
Old Orchard, The, NW3
off Nassington Rd 91 J4
Old Palace La, Rich. TW9 145 F5
Old Palace Rd, Croy. CR0 201 H3
Old Palace Ter, Rich. TW9
off King St 145 G5
Old Palace Yd, SW1 26 A5
Richmond TW9 145 F5
Old Paradise St, SE11 34 C1
Old Pk Av, SW12 150 A6
Enfield EN2 43 J4
Old Pk Gro, Enf. EN2 43 J4
Old Pk La, W1 24 C2
Old Pk Ms, Houns. TW5 123 F7
Old Pk Ridings, N21 43 H6
Old Pk Rd, N13 59 F4
SE2 138 A5
Enfield EN2 43 H3
Old Pk Rd S, Enf. EN2 43 H4
Old Pk Vw, Enf. EN2 43 G3
Old Perry St, Chis. BR7 175 H7
Old PO La, SE3
off Kidbrooke Pk Rd 155 H3
Old Pound Cl, Islw. TW7 144 D1
Old Pye St, SW1 25 H5
Old Quebec St, W1 16 A4
Old Queen St, SW1 25 J4
Old Rectory Gdns, Edg. HA8 54 A6
Old Redding, Har. HA3 51 J4
Oldridge Rd, SW12 150 A7
Old River Lea Towpath, E15
off City Mill River Towpath 96 B7
Old Rd, SE13 155 E4
Enfield EN3 45 F1
Old Rope Wk, Sun. TW16
off The Avenue 178 B3
Old Royal Free Pl, N1
off Liverpool Rd 111 G1
Old Royal Free Sq, N1 111 G1
Old Ruislip Rd, Nthlt. UB5 102 D2
Old Savill's Cotts, Chig. IG7
off The Chase 65 F4
Old Sch Cl, SE10 135 E3
SW19 184 D2
Beckenham BR3 189 G2
Old Sch Cres, E7 97 F6
Old Sch Pl, Croy. CR0 201 G4
Old Sch Sq, E14 off Pelling St 114 A6
Thames Ditton KT7 180 C6
Old Seacoal La, EC4 19 G3
Old S Cl, Pnr. HA5 66 D1
Old S Lambeth Rd, SW8 34 B7
★ Old Spitalfields Mkt, E1 21 F1
Old Sq, WC2 18 D3
Old Sta Rd, Hayes UB3 121 J3
Loughton IG10 48 B5
Old Sta Yd, Brom. BR2
off Bourne Way 205 F1
Oldstead Rd, Brom. BR1 172 D4
Old Stockley Rd, West Dr. UB7 120 E2
Old St, E13 115 H2

Old St, EC1 11 J5
Old Swan Yd, Cars. SM5 199 J4
Old Town, SW4 150 C3
Croydon CR0 201 H3
Old Tram Yd, SE18
off Lakedale Rd 137 H4
Old Woolwich Rd, SE10 134 D6
Old York Rd, SW18 149 E5
Oleander Cl, Orp. BR6 207 G5
O'Leary Sq, E1 113 F5
Olga St, E3 113 H2
Olinda Rd, N16 76 C6
Oliphant St, W10 108 A3
Oliver Av, SE25 188 C3
Oliver Cl, W4 126 B6
Oliver Gdns, E6 116 B6
Oliver-Goldsmith Est, SE15 152 D1
Oliver Gro, SE25 188 C4
Oliver Ms, SE15 152 D2
Olive Rd, E13 115 J3
NW2 89 J4
SW19 *off Norman Rd* 167 F7
W5 125 G3
Oliver Rd, E10 96 B2
E17 78 C5
NW10 106 C2
New Malden KT3 182 C2
Sutton SM1 199 G4
Olivers Yd, EC1 12 C5
Olivette St, SW15 148 A3
Ollards Gro, Loug. IG10 48 A4
Ollerton Grn, E3 113 J1
Ollerton Rd, N11 58 D5
Olley Cl, Wall. SM6 200 E7
Ollgar Cl, W12 127 F1
Olliffe St, E14 134 C3
Olmar St, SE1 37 H5
Olney Rd, SE17 35 J5
Olron Cres, Bexh. DA6 158 D5
Olven Rd, SE18 137 F7
Olveston Wk, Cars. SM5 185 G6
Olwen Ms, Pnr. HA5 66 D2
Olyffe Av, Well. DA16 158 A2
Olyffe Dr, Beck. BR3 190 C1
★ **Olympia**, W14 128 B3
Olympia Ms, W2 14 B6
Olympia Way, W14 128 B3
Olympic Way, Grnf. UB6 103 H1
Wembley HA9 88 A4
Olympus Sq, E5 *off Nolan Way* 94 D4
Oman Av, NW2 89 J4
O'Meara St, SE1 28 A2
Omega Cl, E14 *off Tiller Rd* 134 B3
Omega Pl, N1 10 B2
Omega St, SE14 154 A1
Ommaney Rd, SE14 153 G1
Omnibus Way, E17 78 A2
Ondine Rd, SE15 152 C4
Onega Gate, SE16 133 H3
O'Neill Path, SE18 *off Kempt St* 136 D6
One Tree Cl, SE23 153 F6
Ongar Cl, Rom. RM6 82 C5
Ongar Rd, SW6 128 D6
Onra Rd, E17 78 A7
Onslow Av, Rich. TW10 145 H5
Onslow Cl, E4 62 C2
Thames Ditton KT7 194 B1
Onslow Cres, Chis. BR7 192 E1
Onslow Dr, Sid. DA14 176 D2
Onslow Gdns, E18 79 H3
N10 74 B5
N21 43 G5
SW7 30 E2
Thames Ditton KT7 194 B1
Wallington SM6 200 C6
Onslow Ms E, SW7 31 E2
Onslow Ms W, SW7 30 E2
Onslow Rd, Croy. CR0 187 F7
New Malden KT3 183 G4
Richmond TW10 145 H5
Onslow Sq, SW7 31 F1
Onslow St, EC1 11 F6
Onslow Way, T.Ditt. KT7 194 B1
Ontario St, SE1 27 H6
Ontario Way, E14 114 A7
On The Hill, Wat. WD19 50 E2
Onyx Ms, E15 *off Vicarage La* 96 E6
Opal Cl, E16 116 A6
Opal Ms, NW6 *off Priory Pk Rd* 108 C1
Ilford IG1 *off Ley St* 98/99 E2
Opal St, SE11 35 G2
Openshaw Rd, SE2 138 B4
Openview, SW18 167 F1
Ophelia Gdns, NW2
off Hamlet Sq 90 B3
Ophir Ter, SE15 152 D1
Opossum Way, Houns. TW4 142 C2
Oppenheim Rd, SE13 154 C2
Oppidans Ms, NW3
off Meadowbank 91 J7
Oppidans Rd, NW3 91 J7
Orange Ct, E1 29 J2
Orange Gro, E11 96 E3
Chigwell IG7 65 F6
Orange Hill Rd, Edg. HA8 54 C7
Orange Pl, SE16 *off Lower Rd* 133 F3
Orangery, The, Rich. TW10 163 F2
Orangery La, SE9 156 C5
Orange Sq, SW1 32 C2
Orange St, WC2 17 H6
Orange Yd, W1 17 J4
Oransay Rd, N1 93 J6
Oransay Wk, N1
off Clephane Rd 93 J6
Oratory La, SW3 31 F3
Orbain Rd, SW6 128 B7
Orbel St, SW11 149 H1
Orb St, SE17 36 B2
Orchard, The, N14 42 B5
N21 44 A6
NW11 72 D5
SE3 154 D2
W4 126 D4
W5 105 G5
Epsom KT17 197 F7
Hounslow TW3 143 J2
Orchard Av, N3 72 D3
N14 42 C6
N20 57 G2
Belvedere DA17 139 E6
Croydon CR0 189 H7
Feltham TW14 141 G5
Hounslow TW5 123 E7
Mitcham CR4 200 A1
New Malden KT3 183 E2
Southall UB1 123 E1
Thames Ditton KT7 194 D1
Orchard Cl, E4
off Chingford Mt Rd 62 A4
E11 79 H4
N1 *off Morton Rd* 93 J7
NW2 89 G3
SE23 *off Brenchley Gdns* 153 F6
SW20 *off Grand Dr* 183 J4
W10 108 B5
Bexleyheath DA7 158 E1
Bushey (Bushey Hth) WD23 52 A1
Edgware HA8 53 H6
Epsom (W.Ewell) KT19 196 B6
Northolt UB5 85 J5
Surbiton KT6 181 E7
Walton-on-Thames KT12 178 B7
Wembley HA0 105 H1
Orchard Ct, Islw. TW7
off Thornbury Av 144 A1
Twickenham TW2 162 A2
Wallington SM6
off Parkgate Rd 200 B5
Worcester Park KT4 197 G1
Orchard Cres, Edg. HA8 54 C5
Enfield EN1 44 C1
Orchard Dr, SE3
off Orchard Rd 154/155 E2
Edgware HA8 53 J5
Orchard Est, Wdf.Grn. IG8 63 J7
Orchard Gdns, Chess. KT9 195 H4
Sutton SM1 198 D5
Orchard Gate, NW9 70 E4
Esher KT10 194 A1
Greenford UB6 86 E6
Orchard Grn, Orp. BR6 207 H2
Orchard Gro, SE20 170 D7
Croydon CR0 189 H7
Edgware HA8 70 A1
Harrow HA3 69 J5
Orpington BR6 207 J2
Orchard Hill, SE13
off Coldbath St 154 B2
Carshalton SM5 199 J5
Orchard La, SW20 183 H1
East Molesey KT8 180 A6
Woodford Green IG8 63 J4
Orchardleigh Av, Enf. EN3 45 F2
Orchardmede, N21 44 A6
Orchard Ms, N1
off Southgate Gro 94 A7
Orchard Pl, E5 95 E5
E14 114 E7
N17 60 C7
Orchard Ri, Croy. CR0 203 H1
Kingston upon Thames KT2 182 C1
Richmond TW10 146 B4
Orchard Ri E, Sid. DA15 157 J5
Orchard Ri W, Sid. DA15 157 H5
Orchard Rd, N6 74 B7
SE3 154 E2
SE18 137 G4
Barnet EN5 40 C4
Belvedere DA17 139 G4
Brentford TW8 125 F6
Bromley BR1 191 J1
Chessington KT9 195 H4
Dagenham RM10 119 G1
Enfield EN3 45 F5
Hampton TW12 161 F7
Hounslow TW4 143 F5
Kingston upon Thames KT1 181 H2
Mitcham CR4 200 A1
Orpington (Farnboro.) BR6 207 E5
Richmond TW9 146 A3
Romford RM7 83 H1
Sidcup DA14 175 H4
Sunbury-on-Thames TW16
off Hanworth Rd 160 B7
Orchard Rd, Sutt. SM1 198 D5
Twickenham TW1 144 D5
Welling DA16 158 B3
Orchardson St, NW8 7 E6
Orchard Sq, W14 *off Sun Rd* 128 C5
Orchard St, E17 77 H4
W1 16 B4
Orchard Ter, Enf. EN1
off Great Cambridge Rd 44 D6
Orchard Vil, Sid. DA14 176 C6
Orchard Way, Beck. BR3 189 H5
Croydon CR0 203 H1
Enfield EN1 44 B3
Sutton SM1 199 G4
Orchid Cl, E6 116 B5
Chessington KT9 195 F7
Southall UB1 103 E6
Orchid Rd, N14 42 C7
Orchid St, W12 107 G7
Orde Hall St, WC1 10 C6
Ordell Rd, E3 113 J2
Ordnance Cl, Felt. TW13 160 A3
Ordnance Cres, SE10 134 D2
Ordnance Hill, NW8 109 G1
Ordnance Ms, NW8 7 F1
Ordnance Rd, E16 115 F5
SE18 136 D6
Oregano Dr, E14 114 D6
Oregon Av, E12 98 C4
Oregon Cl, N.Mal. KT3
off Georgia Rd 182 C4
Oregon Sq, Orp. BR6 207 G1
Orestes Ms, NW6 *off Aldred Rd* 90 D5
Orford Ct, SE27 169 H2
Orford Gdns, Twick. TW1 162 C2
Orford Rd, E17 78 A5
E18 79 H3
SE6 172 B3
Organ La, E4 62 C2
Oriel Cl, Mitch. CR4 186 D4
Oriel Ct, NW3 *off Heath St* 91 F4
Oriel Dr, SW13 127 H6
Oriel Gdns, Ilf. IG5 80 C3
Oriel Pl, NW3 *off Heath St* 91 F4
Oriel Rd, E9 95 G6
Oriel Way, Nthlt. UB5 85 H7
Oriental Rd, E16 136 A1
Oriental St, E14 *off Morant St* 114 A7
Orient Ind Pk, E10 96 A2
Orient St, SE11 35 G1
Orient Way, E5 95 G3
E10 95 H2
Oriole Way, SE28 118 B7
Orion Pt, E14 *off Crews St* 134 A4
Orion Rd, N11 58 B6
Orissa Rd, SE18 137 H5
Orkney St, SW11 150 A2
Orlando Rd, SW4 150 C3
Orleans Cl, Esher KT10 194 A2
★ **Orleans Ho Gall**, Twick. TW1 163 E1
Orleans Rd, SE19 170 A6
Twickenham TW1 145 E7
Orleston Ms, N7 93 G6
Orleston Rd, N7 93 G6
Orley Fm Rd, Har. HA1 86 B3
Orlop St, SE10 134 E5
Ormanton Rd, SE26 170 D4
Orme Ct, W2 14 A6
Orme Ct Ms, W2 14 B6
Orme La, W2 14 A6
Ormeley Rd, SW12 168 B1
Orme Rd, Kings.T. KT1 182 B2
Sutton SM1
off Grove Rd 198/199 E6
Ormerod Gdns, Mitch. CR4 186 A2
Ormesby Cl, SE28
off Wroxham Rd 118 D7
Ormesby Way, Har. HA3 69 J6
Orme Sq, W2 14 A6
Ormiston Gro, W12 127 H1
Ormiston Rd, SE10 135 G5
Ormond Av, Hmptn. TW12 179 H1
Richmond TW10
off Ormond Rd 145 G5
Ormond Cl, WC1 18 B1
Ormond Cres, Hmptn. TW12 179 H1
Ormond Dr, Hmptn. TW12 161 H7
Ormonde Av, Orp. BR6 207 F2
Ormonde Gate, SW3 32 A4
Ormonde Pl, SW1 32 B2
Ormonde Ri, Buck.H. IG9 63 J1
Ormonde Rd, SW14 146 B3
Ormonde Ter, NW8 109 J1
Ormond Ms, WC1 10 B6
Ormond Rd, N19 93 E1
Richmond TW10 145 G5
Ormond Yd, SW1 25 G1
Ormsby, Sutt. SM2
off Grange Rd 198/199 E7
Ormsby Gdns, Grnf. UB6 103 J2
Ormsby Pl, N16
off Victorian Gro 94 C3
Ormsby Pt, SE18
off Troy Ct 136/137 E4
Ormsby St, E2 13 F1
Ormside St, SE15 133 F6
Ormskirk Rd, Wat. WD19 50 D4
Ornan Rd, NW3 91 H5
Orpen Wk, N16 94 B3
Orpheus St, SE5 152 A1
ORPINGTON, BR5 & BR6 207 H1
Orpington Gdns, N18 60 B3
Orpington Rd, N21 59 H1
Chislehurst BR7 193 H3
Orpwood Cl, Hmptn. TW12 161 F5
Orsett St, SE11 34 D3
Orsett Ter, W2 14 B3
Woodford Green IG8 79 J1
Orsman Rd, N1 112 B1
Orton St, E1 29 H2
Orville Rd, SW11 149 G2
Orwell Ct, N5 93 J4
Orwell Rd, E13 115 J2
Osbaldeston Rd, N16 94 D2
Osberton Rd, SE12 155 G5
Osbert St, SW1 33 H2
Osborn Cl, E8 112 D1
Osborne Cl, Barn. EN4 41 J3
Beckenham BR3 189 H4
Feltham TW13 160 D5
Osborne Gdns, Th.Hth. CR7 187 J2
Osborne Gro, E17 77 J4
N4 93 G1
Osborne Ms, E17
off Osborne Gro 77 J4
Osborne Pl, Sutt. SM1 199 G5
Osborne Rd, E7 97 H5
E9 95 J6
E10 96 B3
N4 93 F1
N13 59 G3
NW2 89 H6
W3 126 B3
Belvedere DA17 139 F5
Buckhurst Hill IG9 63 H1
Dagenham RM9 101 F5
Enfield EN3 45 H2
Hounslow TW3 143 F3
Kingston upon Thames KT2 163 H7
Southall UB1 103 J6
Thornton Heath CR7 187 J2
Osborne Sq, Dag. RM9 101 F4
Osborne Ter, SW17
off Church La 168 A5
Osborne Way, Chess. KT9
off Bridge Rd 195 J5
Osborn Gdns, NW7 56 A7
Osborn La, SE23 153 H7
Osborn St, E1 21 G2
Osborn Ter, SE3 *off Lee Rd* 155 F4
Osbourne Av, NW7 56 A7
Oscar Faber Pl, N1
off St. Peter's Way 94 B7
Oscar St, SE8 154 A1
Oseney Cres, NW5 92 C6
Osgood Av, Orp. BR6 207 J5
Osgood Gdns, Orp. BR6 207 J5
OSIDGE, N14 58 B1
Osidge La, N14 58 A1
Osier Cres, N10 73 J1
Osier La, SE10 135 F3
Osier Ms, W4 127 F6
Osiers Rd, SW18 148 D4
Osier St, E1 113 F4
Osier Way, E10 96 B3
Mitcham CR4 185 H5
Oslac Rd, SE6 172 B5
Oslo Ct, NW8 7 G2
Oslo Sq, SE16 133 H3
Osman Cl, N15
off Tewkesbury Rd 76 A6
Osman Rd, N9 60 D3
W6 *off Batoum Gdns* 127 J3
Osmond Cl, Har. HA2 85 J2
Osmond Gdns, Wall. SM6 200 C5
Osmund St, W12
off Braybrook St 107 F6
Osnaburgh St, NW1 9 E6
NW1 (north section) 9 E4
Osnaburgh Ter, NW1 8 E5
Osney Ho, SE2 *off Hartslock Dr* 138 D2
Osney Wk, Cars. SM5 185 G6
Osprey Cl, E6 *off Dove App* 116 B5
E11 79 G4
E17 61 H7
Sutton SM1
off Sandpiper Rd 198 C5
West Drayton UB7 120 A2
Osprey Hts, SW11
off Bramlands Cl 149 H3
Osprey Ms, Enf. EN3 45 E5
Ospringe Cl, SE20 171 F7
Ospringe Ct, SE9
off Alderwood Rd 157 G6
Ospringe Rd, NW5 92 C4
Osram Ct, W6 *off Lena Gdns* 127 J3
Osram Rd, Wem. HA9 87 G3
Osric Path, N1 12 D2
Ossian Ms, N4 75 F7
Ossian Rd, N4 75 F7
Ossington Bldgs, W1 16 B1
Ossington Cl, W2
off Ossington St 108/109 E7
Ossington St, W2 108 D7

Ossory Rd, SE1 . . . . .37 H4
Ossulston St, NW1 . . . . .9 H2
Ossulton Pl, N2 off East End Rd .73 F3
Ossulton Way, N2 . . . . .73 F4
Ostade Rd, SW2 . . . . .151 F7
Osten Ms, SW7 . . . . .22 B6
OSTERLEY, Islw. TW7 . . . . .123 J7
Osterley Av, Islw. TW7 . . . . . . .124 A7
Osterley Ct, Islw. TW7 . . . . . . .144 A1
Osterley Cres, Islw. TW7 . . . . . .144 B1
Osterley Gdns, Th.Hth. CR7 . . . .187 J2
Osterley Ho, E14 off Giraud St . .114 B6
Osterley La, Islw. TW7 . . . . . . .124 B5
Southall UB2 . . . . .123 G6
Osterley Pk, Islw. TW7 . . . . . . .124 A5
★ Osterley Park Ho, Islw. TW7 .123 J5
Osterley Pk Rd, Sthl. UB2 . . . . .123 F3
Osterley Pk Vw Rd, W7 . . . . . . .124 B2
Osterley Rd, N16 . . . . .94 B4
Isleworth TW7 . . . . .124 B7
Ostliffe Rd, N13 . . . . .59 J5
Oswald Rd, Sthl. UB1 . . . . .123 E1
Oswald's Mead, E9
off Lindisfarne Way 95 H4
Oswald St, E5 . . . . .95 G3
Oswald Ter, NW2 off Temple Rd . .89 J3
Osward Pl, N9 . . . . .60 E2
Osward Rd, SW17 . . . . .167 J2
Oswell Ho, E1 . . . . .133 E1
Oswin St, SE11 . . . . .35 H1
Oswyth Rd, SE5 . . . . .152 B2
Otford Cl, SE20 . . . . .189 F1
Bexley DA5
off Southwold Rd 159 H6
Bromley BR1 . . . . .192 D3
Otford Cres, SE4 . . . . .153 J6
Othello Cl, SE11 . . . . .35 G3
Otho Ct, Brent. TW8 . . . . .125 G7
Otis St, E3 . . . . .114 C3
Otley App, Ilf. IG2 . . . . .81 E6
Otley Dr, Ilf. IG2 . . . . .80 E5
Otley Rd, E16 . . . . .115 J6
Otley Ter, E5 . . . . .95 G3
Otley Way, Wat. WD19 . . . . .50 C3
Ottaway St, E5 off Stellman Cl . .94 D3
Ottenden Cl, Orp. BR6
off Southfleet Rd 207 H4
Otterbourne Rd, E4 . . . . .62 D3
Croydon CR0 . . . . .201 J2
Otterburn Gdns, Islw. TW7 . . . .124 D7
Otterburn Ho, SE5 . . . . .35 J7
Otterburn St, SW17 . . . . .167 J6
Otter Cl, E15 . . . . .114 C1
Otterden St, SE6 . . . . .172 A4
Otter Rd, Grnf. UB6 . . . . .103 J4
Otto Cl, SE26 . . . . .170 E3
Otto St, SE17 . . . . .35 G6
Oulton Cl, E5 off Mundford Rd . .95 F2
SE28 off Rollesby Way 118 C6
Oulton Cres, Bark. IG11 . . . . . . .99 J6
Oulton Rd, N15 . . . . .76 A5
Oulton Way, Wat. WD19 . . . . . . .51 E4
Ouseley Rd, SW12 . . . . .167 J1
Outer Circle, NW1 . . . . .8 B6
Outgate Rd, NW10 . . . . .89 F7
Outram Pl, N1 . . . . .111 E1
Outram Rd, E6 . . . . .116 B1
N22 .74 D1
Croydon CR0 . . . . .202 C1
Outwich St, EC3 . . . . .20 E3
★ Oval, The, Surrey County Cricket
Club, SE11 . . . . .34 D5
Oval, The, E2 . . . . .112 E2
Sidcup DA15 . . . . .158 A7
Oval Pl, SW8 . . . . .34 C7
Oval Rd, NW1 . . . . .110 B1
Croydon CR0 . . . . .202 B1
Oval Rd N, Dag. RM10 . . . . . . .119 H1
Oval Rd S, Dag. RM10 . . . . . . .119 H2
Oval Way, SE11 . . . . .34 D4
Overbrae, Beck. BR3 . . . . .172 A6
Overbrook Wk, Edg. HA8 . . . . . .54 A7
Overbury Av, Beck. BR3 . . . . . .190 B3
Overbury Rd, N15 . . . . .76 A6
Overbury St, E5 . . . . .95 G4
Overcliff Rd, SE13 . . . . .154 A3
Overcourt Cl, Sid. DA15 . . . . . .158 B6
Overdale Av, N.Mal. KT3 . . . . . .182 C2
Overdale Rd, W5 . . . . .125 F3
Overdown Rd, SE6 . . . . .172 A4
Overhill Rd, SE22 . . . . .152 D7
Overhill Way, Beck. BR3 . . . . . .190 D5
Overlea Rd, E5 . . . . .76 D7
Overmead, Sid. DA15 . . . . .157 G7
Oversley Ho, W2 . . . . .108 D5
Overstand Cl, Beck. BR3 . . . . . .190 A5
Overstone Gdns, Croy. CR0 . . . .189 J7
Overstone Rd, W6 . . . . .127 J3
Overton Cl, NW10 . . . . .88 C6
Isleworth TW7
off Avenue Rd 144 C1
Overton Ct, E11 . . . . .79 G7
Overton Dr, E11 . . . . .79 H7
Romford RM6 . . . . .82 C7

Overton Ho, SW15
off Tangley Gro 147 F7
Overton Rd, E10 . . . . .95 H1
N14 .42 E5
SE2 . . . . .138 C3
SW9 . . . . .151 G2
Sutton SM2 . . . . .198 D6
Overton Rd E, SE2 . . . . .138 D3
Overtons Yd, Croy. CR0 . . . . . . .201 J3
Ovesdon Av, Har. HA2 . . . . .85 F1
Ovett Cl, SE19 . . . . .170 B6
Ovex Cl, E14 . . . . .134 C2
Ovington Gdns, SW3 . . . . .23 H6
Ovington Ms, SW3 . . . . .23 H6
Ovington Sq, SW3 . . . . .23 H6
Ovington St, SW3 . . . . .23 H6
Owen Cl, SE28 . . . . .138 C1
Croydon CR0 . . . . .188 A6
Hayes UB4 . . . . .102 B3
Owen Gdns, Wdf.Grn. IG8 . . . . .64 B6
Owenite St, SE2 . . . . .138 B4
Owen Rd, N13 . . . . .59 J5
Hayes UB4 . . . . .102 B3
Owen's Ct, EC1 . . . . .11 G3
Owen's Row, EC1 . . . . .11 G3
Owen St, EC1 . . . . .11 G2
Owens Way, SE23 . . . . .153 H7
Owen Wk, SE20
off Sycamore Gro 170 D7
Owen Waters Ho, Ilf. IG5 . . . . . .80 C1
Owgan Cl, SE5 off Benhill Rd . .132 A7
Owl Pk, Loug. (High Beach)
IG10 . . . . .47 F2
Oxberry Av, SW6 . . . . .148 B2
Oxendon St, SW1 . . . . .17 H6
Oxenford St, SE15 . . . . .152 C3
Oxenholme, NW1 . . . . .9 G2
Oxenpark Av, Wem. HA9 . . . . . . .69 H7
Oxestalls Rd, SE8 . . . . .133 H5
Oxford Av, SW20 . . . . .184 B2
Hayes UB3 . . . . .121 J7
Hounslow TW5 . . . . .123 G5
★ Oxford Circ, W1 . . . . .17 F3
Oxford Circ Av, W1 . . . . .17 F4
Oxford Cl, N9 . . . . .60 E2
Mitcham CR4 . . . . .186 D4
Oxford Ct, EC4 . . . . .20 B5
W3 . . . . .106 A6
Feltham TW13
off Oxford Way 160 D4
Oxford Cres, N.Mal. KT3 . . . . . .182 D6
Oxford Dr, SE1 . . . . .28 D2
Ruislip HA4 . . . . .84 C2
Oxford Gdns, N20 . . . . .57 G1
N21 .43 J7
W4 . . . . .126 A5
W10 . . . . .108 B6
Oxford Gate, W6 . . . . .128 A4
Oxford Ms, Bex. DA5 . . . . .159 G7
Oxford Pl, NW10
off Neasden La N 88 D3
Oxford Rd, E15 . . . . .96 D6
N4 . . . . .93 G1
N9 . . . . .61 E2
NW6 . . . . .108 D2
SE19 . . . . .170 A6
SW15 . . . . .148 B4
W5 .105 G7
Carshalton SM5 . . . . .199 H6
Enfield EN3 . . . . .45 E5
Harrow HA1 . . . . .67 J6
Harrow (Wldste) HA3 . . . . . . .68 C3
Ilford IG1 . . . . .99 F4
Sidcup DA14 . . . . .176 B5
Teddington TW11 . . . . .162 A5
Wallington SM6 . . . . .200 C5
Woodford Green IG8 . . . . . . .63 J5
Oxford Rd N, W4 . . . . .126 B5
Oxford Rd S, W4 . . . . .126 A5
Oxford Sq, W2 . . . . .15 H4
Oxford St, W1 . . . . .17 G3
Oxford Wk, Sthl. UB1 . . . . .123 F1
Oxford Way, Felt. TW13 . . . . . . .160 D4
Oxgate Gdns, NW2 . . . . .89 H3
Oxgate La, NW2 . . . . .89 H2
Oxhawth Cres, Brom. BR2 . . . . .192 D5
Oxhey Dr, Nthwd. HA6 . . . . .50 A4
Watford WD19 . . . . .50 C3
Oxhey Dr S, Nthwd. HA6 . . . . . .50 B5
Oxhey La, Har. HA3 . . . . .51 G5
Pinner HA5 . . . . .51 G5
Watford WD19 . . . . .51 F2
Oxhey Ridge Cl, Nthwd. HA6 . . .50 A5
Oxleas, E6 . . . . .116 E6
Oxleas Cl, Well. DA16 . . . . .157 G2
Oxleay Ct, Har. HA2 . . . . .85 G1
Oxleay Rd, Har. HA2 . . . . .85 G1
Oxleigh Cl, N.Mal. KT3 . . . . . . .183 E5
Oxley Cl, SE1 . . . . .37 G3
Oxleys Rd, NW2 . . . . .89 H3
Oxlip Cl, Croy. CR0
off Marigold Way 203 G1
Oxlow La, Dag. RM9, RM10 . . .101 G4
Oxonian St, SE22 . . . . .152 C4
Oxo Twr Wf, SE1 . . . . .19 F6
Oxted Cl, Mitch. CR4 . . . . .185 G3

Oxtoby Way, SW16 . . . . .186 D2
Oyster Catchers Cl, E16
off Freemasons Rd 115 H6
Oyster Catcher Ter, Ilf. IG5
off Tiptree Cres 80 D3
Oystergate Wk, EC4
off Upper Thames St 112 A7
Oyster Row, E1 off Lukin St 113 F6
Oyster Wf, SW11
off Lombard Rd 149 G2
Ozolins Way, E16 . . . . .115 G6

P

Pablo Neruda Cl, SE24
off Shakespeare Rd 151 H4
Pace Pl, E1 off Bigland St . . .112/113 E6
Pacific Rd, E16 . . . . .115 G6
Pacific Wf, SE16
off Rotherhithe St 133 G1
Packham Ct, Wor.Pk. KT4
off Lavender Av 197 J3
Packington Rd, W3 . . . . .126 C3
Packington Sq, N1 . . . . .111 J1
Packington St, N1 . . . . .111 H1
Packmores Rd, SE9 . . . . .157 G5
Padbury, SE17 . . . . .36 D4
Padbury Ct, E2 . . . . .13 G4
Padcroft Rd, West Dr. UB7 . . . .120 A1
Padden Ct, NW7 off Bittacy Hill . .56 B7
Paddenswick Rd, W6 . . . . .127 G3
PADDINGTON, W2 . . . . .14 C2
Paddington Cl, Hayes UB4 . . . .102 D4
Paddington Grn, W2 . . . . .15 F1
Paddington St, W1 . . . . .16 B1
Paddock Cl, SE3 . . . . .155 G2
SE26 . . . . .171 G4
Northolt UB5 . . . . .103 G2
Orpington BR6
off State Fm Av 206/207 E4
Worcester Park KT4 . . . . .196 E1
Paddock Gdns, SE19
off Westow St 170 B6
Paddock Rd, NW2 . . . . .89 G3
Bexleyheath DA6 . . . . .159 E4
Ruislip HA4 . . . . .84 D3
Paddocks, The, NW7 . . . . .56 B6
Barnet EN4 . . . . .41 J3
Wembley HA9 . . . . .88 B2
Paddocks Cl, Har. HA2 . . . . .85 H4
Paddock Way, SW15 . . . . .147 J3
Chislehurst BR7 . . . . .175 G7
Padfield Ct, Wem. HA9
off Forty Av 87 J3
Padfield Rd, SE5 . . . . .151 J3
Padley Cl, Chess. KT9 . . . . .195 J5
Padnall Ct, Rom. RM6
off Padnall Rd 82 D3
Padnall Rd, Rom. RM6 . . . . .82 D4
Padstow Cl, Orp. BR6 . . . . .207 J4
Padstow Rd, Enf. EN2 . . . . .43 H2
Padua Rd, SE20 . . . . .189 F1
Pagden St, SW8 . . . . .150 B1
Pageant Av, NW9 . . . . .70 D1
Pageant Cres, SE16
off Rotherhithe St 133 H1
Pageantmaster Ct, EC4 . . . . . . .19 G4
Pageant Wk, Croy. CR0 . . . . . . .202 B3
Page Av, Wem. HA9 . . . . .88 C3
Page Cl, Dag. RM9 . . . . .101 E5
Hampton TW12 . . . . .161 E6
Harrow HA3 . . . . .69 J6
Page Cres, Croy. CR0 . . . . .201 H5
Page Grn Rd, N15 . . . . .76 D5
Page Grn Ter, N15 . . . . .76 C5
Page Heath La, Brom. BR1 . . . .192 A3
Page Heath Vil, Brom. BR1 . . . .192 A3
Pagehurst Rd, Croy. CR0 . . . . . .188 E7
Page Meadow, NW7 . . . . .55 G7
Page Rd, Felt. TW14 . . . . .141 G6
Pages Hill, N10 . . . . .74 A2
Pages La, N10 . . . . .74 A2
Page St, NW7 . . . . .71 G1
SW1 . . . . .33 J1
Pages Wk, SE1 . . . . .36 D1
Pages Yd, W4 off Church St . .126/127 E6
Paget Av, Sutt. SM1 . . . . .199 G3
Paget Cl, Hmptn. TW12 . . . . . . .162 A4
Paget Gdns, Chis. BR7 . . . . . . .192 E1
Paget La, Islw. TW7 . . . . .144 A3
Paget Pl, Kings.T. KT2 . . . . .164 C6
Thames Ditton KT7
off Brooklands Rd 194 D1
Paget Ri, SE18 . . . . .136 D7
Paget Rd, N16 . . . . .94 A1
Ilford IG1 . . . . .98 E4
Paget St, EC1 . . . . .11 G3
Paget Ter, SE18 . . . . .136 D6
Pagitts Gro, Barn. EN4 . . . . .40 E1
Pagnell St, SE14 . . . . .133 J7
Pagoda Av, Rich. TW9 . . . . .145 J3
Pagoda Gdns, SE3 . . . . .154 D2
Pagoda Vista, Rich. TW9 . . . . . .145 J2
Paignton Rd, N15 . . . . .76 B6
Ruislip HA4 . . . . .84 A3
Paines Cl, Pnr. HA5 . . . . .67 E3

Paines La, Pnr. HA5 . . . . .66 E1
Pains Cl, Mitch. CR4 . . . . .186 B2
Painsthorpe Rd, N16
off Oldfield Rd 94 B3
Painters Ms, SE16 off Macks Rd .132 D4
Painters Rd, Ilf. IG2 . . . . .81 J3
Paisley Rd, N22 . . . . .75 H1
Carshalton SM5 . . . . .199 G1
Pakeman St, N7 . . . . .93 F3
Pakenham Cl, SW12
off Balham Pk Rd 168 A1
Pakenham St, WC1 . . . . .10 D4
Palace Av, W8 . . . . .22 B2
Palace Ct, NW3 . . . . .91 E5
W2 .14 A5
Bromley BR1 off Palace Gro .191 H1
Harrow HA3 . . . . .69 H6
Palace Ct Gdns, N10 . . . . .74 C3
Palace Gdns, Buck.H. IG9 . . . . . .64 A1
Palace Gdns Ms, W8 . . . . .128 D1
Palace Gdns Prec, Enf. EN2
off Sydney Rd 44 A3
Palace Gdns Ter, W8 . . . . .128 D1
Palace Gate, W8 . . . . .22 C4
Palace Gates Rd, N22 . . . . .74 D1
Palace Grn, W8 . . . . .22 B3
Croydon CR0 . . . . .203 J7
Palace Gro, SE19 . . . . .170 C7
Bromley BR1 . . . . .191 H1
Palace Ms, E17 . . . . .77 J4
SW1 . . . . .32 C2
SW6 off Hartismere Rd 128 C7
Palace of Industry, Wem. HA9 . .88 A4
Palace Par, E17 . . . . .78 A4
Palace Pl, SW1 . . . . .25 F5
Palace Rd, N8 . . . . .74 D5
N11 .58 E7
SE19 . . . . .170 C7
SW2 . . . . .169 F1
Bromley BR1 . . . . .191 H1
East Molesey KT8 . . . . .180 A3
Kingston upon Thames KT1 . .181 G4
Ruislip HA4 . . . . .84 E4
Palace Rd Est, SW2 . . . . .169 F1
Palace Sq, SE19 . . . . .170 C7
Palace St, SW1 . . . . .25 F5
Palace Vw, SE12 . . . . .173 G2
Bromley BR1 . . . . .191 G3
Croydon CR0 . . . . .203 J4
Palace Vw Rd, E4 . . . . .62 B5
Palamos Rd, E10 . . . . .96 A1
Palatine Av, N16
off Stoke Newington Rd 94 C4
Palatine Rd, N16 . . . . .94 B4
Palermo Rd, NW10 . . . . .107 G2
Palestine Gro, SW19 . . . . .185 G1
Palewell Common Dr, SW14 . . .146 D5
Palewell Pk, SW14 . . . . .146 D5
Paley Gdns, Loug. IG10 . . . . . . .49 E3
Palfrey Pl, SW8 . . . . .34 D7
Palgrave Av, Sthl. UB1 . . . . .103 G7
Palgrave Gdns, NW1 . . . . .7 H5
Palgrave Rd, W12 . . . . .127 F3
Palissy St, E2 . . . . .13 F4
Palladino Ho, SW17
off Laurel Cl 167 H5
Pallant Way, Orp. BR6 . . . . .206 D3
Pallet Way, SE18 . . . . .156 B1
Palliser Rd, W14 . . . . .128 B5
Pallister Ter, SW15
off Roehampton Vale 165 F3
Pall Mall, SW1 . . . . .25 G2
Pall Mall E, SW1 . . . . .25 J1
Palmar Cres, Bexh. DA7 . . . . . .159 G3
Palmar Rd, Bexh. DA7 . . . . .159 G2
Palm Av, Sid. DA14 . . . . .176 D6
Palm Cl, E10 . . . . .96 B3
Palmeira Rd, Bexh. DA7 . . . . . .158 D3
Palmer Av, Sutt. SM3 . . . . .197 J4
Palmer Cl, Houns. TW5 . . . . . . .143 G1
West Wickham BR4 . . . . .204 D3
Palmer Cres, Kings.T. KT1 . . . . .181 H3
Palmer Gdns, Barn. EN5 . . . . . . .40 A5
Palmer Pl, N7 . . . . .93 G5
Palmer Rd, E13 . . . . .115 H4
Dagenham RM8 . . . . .100 D1
PALMERS GREEN, N13 . . . . .59 G3
Palmers Gro, W.Mol. KT8 . . . . .179 G4
Palmers La, Enf. EN1, EN3 . . . . .45 E1
Palmers Pas, SW14
off Palmers Rd 146 C3
Palmers Rd, E2 . . . . .113 G2
N11 .58 C5
SW14 . . . . .146 C3
SW16 . . . . .187 F2
Borehamwood WD6 . . . . .38 B1
Palmerston Cres, N13 . . . . .59 G5
SE18 . . . . .137 F6
Palmerston Gro, SW19 . . . . . . .166 D7
Palmerston Rd, E7 . . . . .97 H5
E17 .77 J4
N22 .59 F7
NW6 .90 D7
SW14 . . . . .146 C4
SW19 . . . . .166 D7
W3 .126 C3
Buckhurst Hill IG9 . . . . .63 H2

Palmerston Rd, Cars. SM5 . . . . .**199** J4
  Croydon CR0 . . . .**188** A5
  Harrow HA3 . . . .**68** C3
  Hounslow TW3 . . . .**143** J1
  Orpington BR6 . . . .**207** F4
  Sutton SM1 *off Vernon Rd* . . .**199** F5
  Twickenham TW2 . . . .**144** C6
Palmerston Way, SW8
  off Bradmead **130** B7
Palmer St, SW1 . . . .**25** H4
Palm Gro, W5 . . . .**125** G5
Palm Rd, Rom. RM7 . . . .**83** J5
Pamela Gdns, Pnr. HA5 . . . .**66** B5
Pamela Wk, E8
  off Marlborough Av **112** D1
Pampisford Rd, S.Croy. CR2 . . .**201** H7
Pams Way, Epsom KT19 . . . . . .**196** D5
Pancras La, EC4 . . . .**20** A4
Pancras Rd, NW1 . . . .**9** H1
Pandora Rd, NW6 . . . .**90** D6
Panfield Ms, Ilf. IG2
  off Cranbrook Rd **80** D6
Panfield Rd, SE2 . . . .**138** A3
Pangbourne Av, W10 . . . .**107** J5
Pangbourne Dr, Stan. HA7 . . . . . .**53** G5
Pangbourne Ho, N7 . . . .**92** E5
Panhard PI, Sthl. UB1 . . . .**103** H7
Pank Av, Barn. EN5 . . . .**41** F5
Pankhurst Av, E16
  off Wesley Av **135** H1
Pankhurst CI, SE14 *off Briant St* .**133** G7
  Isleworth TW7 . . . .**144** C3
Pankhurst Rd, Walt. KT12 . . . . . .**178** C7
Panmuir Rd, SW20 . . . .**183** H1
Panmure CI, N5 . . . .**93** H4
Panmure Rd, SE26 . . . .**170** E3
Pansy Gdns, W12 . . . .**107** G7
Panther Dr, NW10 . . . .**88** D5
Pantiles, The, NW11
  off Willifield Way **72** C5
  Bexleyheath DA7 . . . .**139** F7
  Bromley BR1 . . . .**192** B3
Pantiles CI, N13 . . . .**59** H5
Panton St, SW1 . . . .**17** H6
Panyer All, EC4 . . . .**19** J4
Papermill CI, Cars. SM5 . . . .**200** A4
Papillons Wk, SE3 . . . .**155** G2
Papworth Gdns, N7
  off Liverpool Rd **93** F5
Papworth Way, SW2 . . . .**151** G7
Parade, The, SW11 . . . .**32** A7
  Esher (Clay.) KT10 . . . .**194** B6
  Hampton TW12
    off Hampton Rd **162** A5
  Watford (Carp.Pk) WD19 . . . . .**50** E3
  Watford (S.Oxhey) WD19
    off Prestwick Rd **50** D3
Parade Ms, SE27
  off Norwood Rd **169** H2
Paradise Path, SE28
  off Birchdene Dr **138** A1
Paradise PI, SE18 *off Woodhill* . .**136** B4
Paradise Rd, SW4 . . . .**150** E2
  Richmond TW9 . . . .**145** G5
Paradise Row, E2
  off Bethnal Grn Rd **112/113** E3
Paradise St, SE16 . . . .**132** E2
Paradise Wk, SW3 . . . .**31** J5
Paragon, The, SE3 . . . .**155** F2
Paragon CI, E16 . . . .**115** G6
Paragon Gro, Surb. KT5 . . . .**181** J6
Paragon Ms, SE1 . . . .**36** C1
Paragon PI, SE3 . . . .**155** F2
  Surbiton KT5
    off Berrylands Rd **181** J6
Paragon Rd, E9 . . . .**95** F6
Parbury Ri, Chess. KT9 . . . .**195** H6
Parbury Rd, SE23 . . . .**153** H6
Parchmore Rd, Th.Hth. CR7 . . . . .**187** H2
Parchmore Way, Th.Hth. CR7 . . . .**187** H2
Pardoner St, SE1 . . . .**28** C5
Pardon St, EC1 . . . .**11** H5
Parfett St, E1 . . . .**21** J2
Parfitt CI, NW3 *off North End* . . .**91** F2
Parfrey St, W6 . . . .**127** J6
Parham Dr, Ilf. IG2 . . . .**80** E6
Parham Way, N10 . . . .**74** C2
Paris Gdn, SE1 . . . .**27** G1
Parish Gate Dr, Sid. DA15 . . . . .**157** H6
Parish La, SE20 . . . .**171** H7
Parish Ms, SE20 . . . .**171** G7
Parish Wf, SE18 *off Woodhill* . .**136** B4
Park, The, N6 . . . .**74** A6
  NW11 . . . .**90** E1
  SE19 . . . .**170** B7
  SE23 *off Park Hill* **170/171** E1
  W5 . . . .**125** G1
  Carshalton SM5 . . . .**199** J5
  Sidcup DA14 . . . .**175** J5
Park App, Well. DA16 . . . .**158** A4
Park Av, E6 . . . .**116** D1
  E15 . . . .**96** E6
  N3 . . . .**73** E1
  N13 . . . .**59** G3
  N18 . . . .**60** D4
  N22 . . . .**75** E2

Park Av, NW2 . . . .**89** H6
  NW10 . . . .**105** J3
  NW11 . . . .**90** E1
  SW14 . . . .**146** D4
  Barking IG11 . . . .**99** F6
  Bromley BR1 . . . .**173** F6
  Carshalton SM5 . . . .**200** A6
  Enfield EN1 . . . .**44** B6
  Hounslow TW3 . . . .**143** H6
  Ilford IG1 . . . .**98** D2
  Mitcham CR4 . . . .**168** B7
  Orpington (Farnboro.) BR6 . .**206** C3
  Southall UB1 . . . .**123** G1
  West Wickham BR4 . . . .**204** C2
  Woodford Green IG8 . . . .**63** H5
Park Av E, Epsom KT17 . . . .**197** G6
Park Av Ms, Mitch. CR4
  off Park Av **168** B7
Park Av N, N8 . . . .**74** D3
  NW10 . . . .**89** H5
Park Av Rd, N17 . . . .**61** E7
Park Av S, N8 . . . .**74** D4
Park Av W, Epsom KT17 . . . .**197** G6
Park Chase, Wem. HA9 . . . .**87** J4
Park CI, E9 . . . .**113** F1
  NW2 . . . .**89** H3
  NW10 . . . .**105** J3
  SW1 . . . .**23** J4
  W4 . . . .**126** D5
  W14 . . . .**128** C3
  Carshalton SM5 . . . .**199** J6
  Hampton TW12 . . . .**179** J1
  Harrow HA3 . . . .**68** B1
  Hounslow TW3 . . . .**143** J5
  Kingston upon Thames KT2 . .**182** A1
Park Ct, SE26 . . . .**171** E6
  Kingston upon Thames (Hmptn W.)
    KT1 . . . .**181** F1
  New Malden KT3 . . . .**182** D4
  Wembley HA9 . . . .**87** H5
Park Cres, N3 . . . .**57** E7
  W1 . . . .**8** D6
  Enfield EN2 . . . .**44** A4
  Erith DA8 . . . .**139** J6
  Harrow HA3 . . . .**68** B1
  Twickenham TW2 . . . .**162** A1
Park Cres Ms E, W1 . . . .**8** E6
Park Cres Ms W, W1 . . . .**16** D1
Park Cft, Edg. HA8 . . . .**70** C1
Parkcroft Rd, SE12 . . . .**155** F7
Park Dale, N11 . . . .**58** D6
Parkdale Cres, Wor.Pk. KT4 . . . .**196** D3
Parkdale Rd, SE18 . . . .**137** H5
Park Dr, N21 . . . .**43** J6
  NW11 . . . .**90** E1
  SE7 . . . .**136** B6
  SW14 . . . .**146** D4
  W3 . . . .**126** A3
  Dagenham RM10 . . . .**101** J3
  Harrow (Har.Wld) HA3 . . . . . .**52** B6
  Harrow (N.Har.) HA2 . . . .**67** G7
Park Dr CI, SE7 . . . .**136** B5
Park End, NW3
  off South Hill Pk **91** H4
  Bromley BR1 . . . .**191** F1
Parker CI, E16 . . . .**136** B1
Parker Ms, WC2 . . . .**18** B3
Parke Rd, SW13 . . . .**147** G1
  Sunbury-on-Thames TW16 . . .**178** A4
Parker Rd, Croy. CR0 . . . .**201** J4
Parkers Row, SE1 . . . .**29** G4
Parker St, E16 . . . .**136** B1
  WC2 . . . .**18** B3
Parkes Rd, Chig. IG7 . . . .**65** H5
Park Fm CI, N2 . . . .**73** F3
  Pinner HA5 *off Field End Rd* . .**66** B5
Park Fm Rd, Brom. BR1 . . . .**192** A1
  Kingston upon Thames KT2 . .**163** H7
Parkfield Av, SW14 . . . .**146** E4
  Feltham TW13 . . . .**160** A3
  Harrow HA2 . . . .**67** J2
  Northolt UB5 . . . .**102** D2
Parkfield CI, Edg. HA8 . . . .**54** B6
  Northolt UB5 . . . .**102** E2
Parkfield Cres, Felt. TW13 . . . . .**160** A3
  Harrow HA2 . . . .**67** J2
  Ruislip HA4 . . . .**84** E3
Parkfield Dr, Nthlt. UB5 . . . .**102** D2
Parkfield Gdns, Har. HA2 . . . .**67** H3
Parkfield Rd, NW10 . . . .**89** G7
  SE14 . . . .**153** J1
  Feltham TW13 . . . .**160** A3
  Harrow HA2 . . . .**85** J3
  Northolt UB5 . . . .**102** E2
Parkfields, SW15 . . . .**147** J4
  Croydon CR0 . . . .**203** J1
Parkfields Av, NW9 . . . .**88** D1
  SW20 . . . .**183** H1
Parkfields CI, Cars. SM5
  off Devonshire Rd **200** A4
Parkfields Rd, Kings.T. KT2 . . . .**163** J5
Parkfield St, N1 . . . .**11** F1
Parkfield Way, Brom. BR2 . . . . .**192** C6
Park Gdns, NW9 . . . .**70** B3
  Kingston upon Thames KT2 . .**163** J5
Park Gate, N2 . . . .**73** G3

Park Gate, N21 . . . .**43** F7
Parkgate, SE3 . . . .**155** F3
Park Gate, W5 . . . .**105** G5
Parkgate Av, Barn. EN4 . . . .**41** F1
Parkgate CI, Kings.T. KT2
  off Warboys App **164** B6
Parkgate Cres, Barn. EN4 . . . . . .**41** F2
Parkgate Gdns, SW14 . . . .**146** D5
Parkgate Ms, N6
  off Stanhope Rd **74** C7
Parkgate Rd, SW11 . . . .**129** H7
  Wallington SM6 . . . .**200** A5
Park Gates, Har. HA2 . . . .**85** G4
Park Gro, E15 . . . .**115** G1
  N11 . . . .**58** D7
  Bexleyheath DA7 . . . .**159** J4
  Bromley BR1 . . . .**191** H1
  Edgware HA8 . . . .**53** J5
Park Gro Rd, E11 . . . .**96** E2
Park Hall Rd, N2 . . . .**73** H4
  SE21 . . . .**169** J3
Parkham Ct, Brom. BR2 . . . .**191** E2
Parkham St, SW11 . . . .**149** H1
Park Hill, SE23 . . . .**171** E2
  SW4 . . . .**150** D5
  W5 . . . .**105** G5
  Bromley BR1 . . . .**192** B4
  Carshalton SM5 . . . .**199** H6
  Loughton IG10 . . . .**48** A5
  Richmond TW10 . . . .**145** J6
Park Hill CI, Cars. SM5 . . . .**199** H5
Park Hill Ct, SW17
  off Beeches Rd **167** J3
Park Hill Ri, Croy. CR0 . . . .**202** B2
Parkhill Rd, E4 . . . .**62** C1
  NW3 . . . .**91** J5
  Bexley DA5 . . . .**159** F7
Park Hill Rd, Brom. BR2 . . . .**190** E2
  Croydon CR0 . . . .**202** B2
Parkhill Rd, Sid. DA15 . . . .**175** G3
Park Hill Rd, Wall. SM6 . . . .**200** B7
Parkhill Wk, NW3 . . . .**91** J5
Parkholme Rd, E8 . . . .**94** C6
Park Ho, N21 . . . .**43** F7
Park Ho Gdns, Twick. TW1 . . . . .**145** F6
Parkhouse St, SE5 . . . .**36** C7
Parkhurst Gdns, Bex. DA5 . . . . .**159** G7
Parkhurst Rd, E12 . . . .**98** D4
  E17 . . . .**77** H4
  N7 . . . .**92** E4
  N11 . . . .**58** A4
  N17 . . . .**76** D2
  N22 . . . .**59** F7
  Bexley DA5 . . . .**159** G7
  Sutton SM1 . . . .**199** G4
Parkland CI, Chig. IG7 . . . .**65** F3
Parkland Gdns, SW19 . . . .**166** A1
Parkland Rd, N22 . . . .**75** F2
  Woodford Green IG8 . . . .**63** G7
Parklands, N6 . . . .**74** B7
  Chigwell IG7 . . . .**65** F3
  Surbiton KT5 . . . .**181** J5
Parklands CI, SW14 . . . .**146** C5
  Ilford IG2 . . . .**81** F7
Parklands Ct, Houns. TW5 . . . . .**142** D2
Parklands Dr, N3 . . . .**72** B3
Parklands Rd, SW16 . . . .**168** B5
Parklands Way, Wor.Pk. KT4 . . .**197** E3
Parkland Wk, N4 . . . .**75** F7
  N6 . . . .**74** D7
  N10 . . . .**74** B4
Park La, E15 *off High St* **114** D1
  N9 . . . .**60** D3
  N17 . . . .**60** D7
  W1 . . . .**24** C2
  Carshalton SM5 . . . .**200** A4
  Croydon CR0 . . . .**202** A3
  Harrow HA2 . . . .**85** H3
  Hounslow TW5 . . . .**122** A7
  Richmond TW9 . . . .**145** J4
  Romford (Chad.Hth) RM6 . . . .**82** D6
  Stanmore HA7 . . . .**52** D3
  Sutton SM3 . . . .**198** B6
  Teddington TW11 . . . .**162** C6
  Wallington SM6 . . . .**200** A4
  Wembley HA9 . . . .**87** H5
Park La CI, N17 . . . .**60** D7
PARK LANGLEY, Beck. BR3 . . . .**190** C5
Park Lawns, Wem. HA9 . . . .**87** J4
Parklea CI, NW9 . . . .**71** E1
Parkleigh Rd, SW19 . . . .**184** E2
Parkleys, Rich. TW10 . . . .**163** G4
Parkmead, SW15 . . . .**147** H6
Park Mead, Har. HA2 . . . .**85** H3
Parkmead, Loug. IG10 . . . .**48** D4
Park Mead, Sid. DA15 . . . .**158** B5
Parkmead Gdns, NW7 . . . .**55** F6
Park Ms, SE24 *off Croxted Rd* . .**151** J6
  Chislehurst BR7 . . . .**175** E6
  East Molesey KT8 . . . .**179** J4
  Hampton (Hmptn H.) TW12
    off Park Rd **161** J5
Parkmore CI, Wdf.Grn. IG8 . . . . .**63** G4
Park Par, NW10 . . . .**107** F2
Park PI, E14 . . . .**134** A1
  SW1 . . . .**25** F2
  W3 . . . .**126** A4

Park PI, W5 . . . .**125** G1
  Hampton (Hmptn H.) TW12 . .**161** J6
  Wembley HA9 . . . .**87** J4
Park PI Vil, W2 . . . .**14** E1
Park Ridings, N8 . . . .**75** G3
Park Ri, SE23 . . . .**171** H1
  Harrow HA3 . . . .**68** B1
Park Ri Rd, SE23 . . . .**171** H1
Park Rd, E6 . . . .**115** J1
  E10 . . . .**96** A1
  E12 . . . .**97** H1
  E15 . . . .**115** J1
  E17 . . . .**77** J5
  N2 . . . .**73** G3
  N8 . . . .**74** C4
  N11 . . . .**58** D7
  N14 . . . .**42** D7
  N15 . . . .**75** H3
  N18 . . . .**60** C4
  NW1 . . . .**7** G3
  NW4 . . . .**71** G7
  NW8 . . . .**7** G3
  NW9 . . . .**70** D7
  NW10 . . . .**106** E1
  SE25 . . . .**188** B4
  SW19 . . . .**167** G6
  W4 . . . .**126** C7
  W7 . . . .**104** C7
  Barnet EN5 . . . .**40** C4
  Barnet (New Barn.) EN4 . . . . .**41** H4
  Beckenham BR3 . . . .**171** J7
  Bromley BR1 . . . .**191** H1
  Chislehurst BR7 . . . .**175** E6
  East Molesey KT8 . . . .**179** J4
  Feltham TW13 . . . .**160** D4
  Hampton (Hmptn H.) TW12 . .**161** J5
  Hounslow TW3 . . . .**143** J4
  Ilford IG1 . . . .**99** G3
  Isleworth TW7 . . . .**144** E2
  Kingston upon Thames KT2 . .**163** J5
  Kingston upon Thames (Hmptn W.)
    KT1 . . . .**181** F1
  New Malden KT3 . . . .**182** D4
  Richmond TW10 . . . .**145** J6
  Sunbury-on-Thames TW16 . .**160** B7
  Surbiton KT5 . . . .**181** J5
  Sutton SM3 . . . .**198** B6
  Teddington TW13 . . . .**162** C6
  Twickenham TW1 . . . .**145** F6
  Wallington SM6 . . . .**200** B5
  Wallington (Hackbr.) SM6 . . .**200** B2
  Wembley HA0 . . . .**87** H6
Park Rd E, W3 . . . .**126** C7
Park Rd N, W3 . . . .**126** B2
  W4 . . . .**126** D5
Park Row, SE10 . . . .**134** D6
PARK ROYAL, NW10 . . . .**106** A3
Park Royal Rd, NW10 . . . .**106** C3
  W3 . . . .**106** C3
Parkshot, Rich. TW9 . . . .**145** H4
Parkside, N3 . . . .**72** E1
  NW2 . . . .**89** G3
  NW7 . . . .**55** G6
  SE3 . . . .**135** F7
  SW19 . . . .**166** A4
  Buckhurst Hill IG9 . . . .**63** H2
  Hampton (Hmptn H.) TW12 . .**162** A5
  Sidcup DA14 . . . .**176** B2
  Sutton SM3 . . . .**198** B6
Parkside Av, SW19 . . . .**166** A5
  Bromley BR1 . . . .**192** B4
Parkside Business Est, SE8
  off Rolt St **133** H6
Parkside CI, SE20 . . . .**171** F7
Parkside Cres, N7 . . . .**93** G3
  Surbiton KT5 . . . .**182** C6
Parkside Dr, Edg. HA8 . . . .**54** A3
Parkside Est, E9 *off Rutland Rd* .**113** F1
Parkside Gdns, SW19 . . . .**166** A4
  Barnet EN4 . . . .**57** J1
Parkside Ho, Dag. RM10 . . . .**101** J3
Parkside Rd, SW11 . . . .**150** A1
  Belvedere DA17 . . . .**139** J4
  Hounslow TW3 . . . .**143** H5
Parkside Ter, N18
  off Great Cambridge Rd **60** A4
  Orpington BR6
    off Willow Wk **206/207** E3
Parkside Wk, SE10 . . . .**134** E5
Parkside Way, Har. HA2 . . . .**67** H4
Park S, SW11 *off Austin Rd* **150** A1
Park Sq E, NW1 . . . .**8** D5
Park Sq Ms, NW1 . . . .**8** D6
Park Sq W, NW1 . . . .**8** D5
Parkstead Rd, SW15 . . . .**147** G5
Parkstone Av, N18 . . . .**60** C5
Parkstone Rd, E17 . . . .**78** C3
  SE15 *off Rye La* **152** D2
Park St, SE1 . . . .**27** J1
  W1 . . . .**16** B5
  Croydon CR0 . . . .**201** J2
  Teddington TW11 . . . .**162** B6
Park Ter, Wor.Pk. KT4 . . . .**197** G1
Parkthorne CI, Har. HA2 . . . .**67** H6
Parkthorne Dr, Har. HA2 . . . .**67** G6
Parkthorne Rd, SW12 . . . .**150** D7
Park Vw, N21 . . . .**43** F7

Park Vw, W3 . . . .**106** C5
  New Malden KT3 . . . .**183** F3
  Pinner HA5 . . . .**.67** F1
  Wembley HA9 . . . .**.88** B5
Parkview Ct, SW18
  off Broomhill Rd **148** D6
Park Vw Ct, Ilf. IG2
  off Brancaster Rd . . . .**.81** H6
Parkview Dr, Mitch. CR4 . . . . .**185** G2
Park Vw Est, E2 . . . .**113** G2
  N5 . . . .**.93** J4
Park Vw Gdns, NW4 . . . .**.71** J5
  Ilford IG4 . . . .**.80** C4
Park Vw Ho, SE24 *off Hurst St* .**151** H6
Park Vw Ms, SW9 . . . .**151** F2
Park Vw Rd, N3 . . . .**.73** E1
  N17 . . . .**.76** D3
  NW10 . . . .**.89** F4
Parkview Rd, SE9 . . . .**174** E2
Park Vw Rd, W5 . . . .**105** H5
Parkview Rd, Croy. CR0 . . . . . .**202** D1
Park Vw Rd, Pnr. HA5 . . . .**.50** B7
  Southall UB1 . . . .**123** G1
  Welling DA16 . . . .**158** C3
Park Vw Rd Est, N17 . . . .**.76** D3
Park Village E, NW1 . . . .**110** B2
Park Village W, NW1 . . . .**.8** D1
Park Vil, Rom. RM6 . . . .**.82** D6
Parkville Rd, SW6 . . . .**128** C7
Park Vista, SE10 . . . .**134** D6
Park Wk, N6 *off North Rd* . . . .**.74** A7
  SE10 *off Crooms Hill* **134** D7
  SW10 . . . .**.30** D5
Parkway, N14 . . . .**.58** E2
Park Way, N20 . . . .**.57** J4
Parkway, NW1 . . . .**110** B1
Park Way, NW11 . . . .**.72** B5
Parkway, SW20 . . . .**184** A4
Park Way, Edg. HA8 . . . .**.70** B1
  Enfield EN1 . . . .**.43** G2
Parkway, Erith DA18 . . . .**139** E3
Park Way, Felt. TW14 . . . .**142** B7
Parkway, Ilf. IG3 . . . .**.99** J3
Park Way, Ruis. HA4 . . . .**.84** A1
  West Molesey KT8 . . . .**179** H3
Parkway, Wdf.Grn. IG8 . . . . . .**.63** J5
Parkway, The, Hayes UB3, UB4 .**102** C6
  Hounslow (Cran.) TW4, TW5 .**142** B2
  Northolt UB5 . . . .**102** D3
  Southall UB2 . . . .**122** A5
Parkway Trd Est, Houns. TW5 . .**122** C6
Park W, W2 . . . .**.15** H4
Park W Pl, W2 . . . .**.15** H3
Parkwood, N20 . . . .**.57** J4
  Beckenham BR3 . . . .**190** A1
Parkwood Gro, Sun. TW16 . . . .**178** A3
Parkwood Ms, N6 . . . .**.74** B6
Parkwood Rd, SW19 . . . .**166** C5
  Bexley DA5 . . . .**159** F7
  Isleworth TW7 . . . .**144** C1
Parliament Ct, E1
  off Sandy's Row **112** B5
Parliament Hill, NW3 . . . .**.91** H4
Parliament Ms, SW14
  off Thames Bk **146** C2
Parliament Sq, SW1 . . . .**.26** A4
Parliament St, SW1 . . . .**.26** A4
Parliament Vw Apartments,
  SE1 . . . .**.34** C1
Parma Cres, SW11 . . . .**149** J4
Parmiter St, E2 . . . .**113** E2
Parmoor Ct, EC1 . . . .**.11** J5
Parnell Cl, W12 . . . .**127** H1
  Edgware HA8 . . . .**.54** B4
Parnell Rd, E3 . . . .**113** J1
Parnham St, E14 *off Blount St* .**113** H6
Parolles Rd, N19 . . . .**.92** C1
Paroma Rd, Belv. DA17 . . . . . .**139** G3
Parr Cl, N9 . . . .**.60** E4
  N18 . . . .**.60** E4
Parr Ct, N1 . . . .**.12** B1
  Feltham TW13 . . . .**160** C4
Parr Pl, W4
  off Chiswick High Rd **127** F4
Parr Rd, E6 . . . .**116** A1
  Stanmore HA7 . . . .**.69** G1
Parrs Pl, Hmptn. TW12 . . . . . .**161** G7
Parr St, N1 . . . .**.12** B1
Parry Av, E6 . . . .**116** C6
Parry Cl, Epsom KT17 . . . .**197** G7
Parry Pl, SE18 . . . .**137** E4
Parry Rd, SE25 . . . .**188** B3
  W10 . . . .**108** B3
Parry St, SW8 . . . .**.34** A5
Parsifal Rd, NW6 . . . .**.90** D5
Parsley Gdns, Croy. CR0
  off Primrose La **203** G1
Parsloes Av, Dag. RM9 . . . . . .**100** D4
Parsonage Gdns, Enf. EN2 . . . .**.43** J2
Parsonage La, Enf. EN1, EN2 . .**.44** A2
  Sidcup DA14 . . . .**177** F4
Parsonage Manorway, Belv.
  DA17 . . . .**139** G6
Parsonage St, E14 . . . .**134** C4
Parsons Cl, Sutt. SM1 . . . .**198** E3
Parsons Cres, Edg. HA8 . . . . . .**.54** A3

PARSONS GREEN, SW6 . . . .**148** D1
Parsons Grn, SW6 . . . .**148** D1
Parsons Grn La, SW6 . . . .**148** D1
Parsons Gro, Edg. HA8 . . . . . .**.54** A3
Parsons Ho, SW2
  off New Pk Rd **150/151** E7
Parson's Ho, W2 . . . .**.7** E6
Parson's Mead, Croy. CR0 . . . .**201** H1
Parsons Mead, E.Mol. KT8 . . . .**179** J3
Parsons Rd, E13 *off Old St* . . .**115** J2
Parson St, NW4 . . . .**.71** J4
Parthenia Rd, SW6 . . . .**148** D1
Partingdale La, NW7 . . . .**.56** A5
Partington Cl, N19 . . . .**.92** D1
Partridge Cl, E16 *off Fulmer Rd* .**116** A5
  Barnet EN5 . . . .**.39** J6
  Bushey WD23 . . . .**.51** H1
  Stanmore HA7 . . . .**.53** H4
Partridge Ct, EC1 *off Percival St* .**111** H4
Partridge Dr, Orp. BR6 . . . . . .**207** F3
Partridge Grn, SE9 . . . .**174** D3
Partridge Rd, Hmptn. TW12 . . .**161** F6
  Sidcup DA14 . . . .**175** H4
Partridge Sq, E6
  off Nightingale Way **116** B5
Partridge Way, N22 . . . .**.75** E1
Parvin St, SW8 . . . .**150** D1
Pasadena Cl, Hayes UB3 . . . . .**122** B2
Pasadena Cl Trd Est, Hayes UB3
  off Pasadena Cl **122** B2
Pascal St, SW8 . . . .**.33** J7
Pascoe Rd, SE13 . . . .**154** D5
Pasley Cl, SE17 . . . .**.35** J4
Pasquier Rd, E17 . . . .**.77** H3
Passey Pl, SE9 . . . .**156** C6
Passfield Dr, E14 *off Uamvar St* .**114** B5
Passfield Path, SE28
  off Booth Cl **118** B7
Passing All, EC1 . . . .**.11** H6
Passmore Gdns, N11 . . . .**.58** D6
Passmore St, SW1 . . . .**.32** B2
★ Passport Office, SW1 . . . . . .**.32** E1
Pasteur Cl, NW9 . . . .**.71** E2
Pasteur Gdns, N18 . . . .**.59** H5
Paston Cl, E5 *off Caldecott Way* .**.95** G3
  Wallington SM6 . . . .**200** C3
Paston Cres, SE12 . . . .**155** H7
Pastor St, SE11 . . . .**.35** H1
Pasture Cl, Wem. HA0 . . . .**.86** E3
Pasture Rd, SE6 . . . .**173** F1
  Dagenham RM9 . . . .**101** F4
  Wembley HA0 . . . .**.86** E2
Pastures, The, N20 . . . .**.56** C5
Patcham Ter, SW8 . . . .**150** B1
Patching Way, Hayes UB4 . . . .**102** E5
Paternoster Row, EC4 . . . .**.19** J4
Paternoster Sq, EC4 . . . .**.19** H4
Pater St, W8 . . . .**128** D3
Pates Manor Dr, Felt. TW14 . . .**141** G7
Path, The, SW19 . . . .**184** E1
Pathfield Rd, SW16 . . . .**168** D5
Pathway, The, Wat. WD19
  off Anthony Cl . . . .**.50** D1
Patience Rd, SW11 . . . .**149** H2
Patio Cl, SW4 . . . .**150** D6
Patmore Est, SW8 . . . .**150** C1
Patmore St, SW8 . . . .**150** C1
Patmos Rd, SW9 . . . .**131** H7
Paton Cl, E3 . . . .**114** A3
Paton St, EC1 . . . .**.11** J4
Patricia Ct, Chis. BR7
  off Manor Pk Rd **193** G1
  Welling DA16 . . . .**138** B7
Patrick Connolly Gdns, E3
  off Talwin St **114** B3
Patrick Rd, E13 . . . .**115** J3
Patriot Sq, E2 . . . .**113** E2
Patrol Pl, SE6 . . . .**154** B6
Patshull Pl, NW5
  off Patshull Rd . . . .**.92** C6
Patshull Rd, NW5 . . . .**.92** C6
Patten All, Rich. TW10
  off The Hermitage **145** G5
Pattenden Rd, SE6 . . . .**171** J1
Patten Rd, SW18 . . . .**149** H7
Patterdale Cl, Brom. BR1 . . . . .**173** F5
Patterdale Rd, SE15 . . . .**133** F7
Patterson Ct, SE19 . . . .**170** C7
Patterson Rd, SE19 . . . .**170** C6
Pattina Wk, SE16 . . . .**133** J1
Pattison Pt, E16 *off Fife Rd* . . .**115** G5
Pattison Rd, NW2 . . . .**.90** D3
Pattison Wk, SE18 . . . .**137** F5
Paul Cl, E15 . . . .**.96** E7
Paulet Rd, SE5 . . . .**151** H2
Paul Gdns, Croy. CR0 . . . .**202** C2
Paulhan Rd, Har. HA3 . . . .**.69** G4
Paulin Dr, N21 . . . .**.43** G7
Pauline Cres, Twick. TW2 . . . . .**161** J1
Paul Julius Cl, E14 . . . .**114** D7
Paul Robeson Cl, E6
  off Eastbourne Rd **116** D3
Paul St, E15 . . . .**114** D1
  EC2 . . . .**.12** C6
Paul's Wk, EC4 . . . .**.19** H5
Paultons Sq, SW3 . . . .**.31** F5
Paultons St, SW3 . . . .**.31** F6

Pauntley St, N19 . . . .**.92** C1
Paved Ct, Rich. TW9 . . . .**145** G5
Paveley Dr, SW11 . . . .**129** H7
Paveley St, NW8 . . . .**.7** H5
Pavement, The, SW4 . . . .**150** C4
  W5 *off Popes La* **125** H3
Pavement Ms, Rom. RM6
  off Clarissa Rd . . . .**.82** D7
Pavement Sq, Croy. CR0 . . . . .**202** D1
Pavet Cl, Dag. RM10 . . . .**101** H6
Pavilion La, Beck. BR3 . . . .**171** J6
Pavilion Ms, N3
  off Windermere Av . . . .**.72** D2
Pavilion Rd, SW1 . . . .**.24** A6
  Ilford IG1 . . . .**.80** C7
Pavilion Sq, SW17 . . . .**167** J3
Pavilion St, SW1 . . . .**.24** A6
Pavilion Ter, E.Mol. KT8 . . . . . .**180** C4
  Ilford IG2
  off Southdown Cres . . . . . .**.81** H5
Pavilion Way, Edg. HA8 . . . . . .**.54** B7
  Ruislip HA4 . . . .**.84** C2
Pawleyne Cl, SE20 . . . .**171** F7
Pawsey Cl, E13 *off Plashet Rd* .**115** G1
Pawson's Rd, Croy. CR0 . . . . .**187** J6
Paxford Rd, Wem. HA0 . . . . . .**.86** D2
Paxton Cl, Rich. TW9 . . . .**145** J2
  Walton-on-Thames KT12 . . .**178** C7
Paxton Pl, SE27 . . . .**170** B4
Paxton Rd, N17 . . . .**.60** C7
  SE23 . . . .**171** H3
  W4 . . . .**126** E6
  Bromley BR1 . . . .**173** G7
Paxton Ter, SW1 . . . .**.33** E5
Payne Cl, Bark. IG11 . . . .**.99** H7
Paynell Ct, E3
  off Lawn Ter **154/155** E3
Payne Rd, E3 . . . .**114** B2
Paynesfield Av, SW14 . . . .**146** D3
Payne St, SE8 . . . .**133** J6
Paynes Wk, W6 . . . .**128** B6
Peabody Av, SW1 . . . .**.32** D3
Peabody Cl, SE10
  off Devonshire Dr **154** B1
  SW1 . . . .**.32** E4
  Croydon CR0 *off Shirley Rd* .**203** F1
Peabody Dws, WC1 . . . .**.10** A5
Peabody Est, EC1 . . . .**.12** A6
  N1 (Islington)
  off Greenman St . . . .**.93** J7
  N17 . . . .**.76** B1
  SE1 . . . .**.27** F2
  SE24 . . . .**151** J7
  SW3 . . . .**.31** H5
  W6 *off The Square* **127** J5
  W10 . . . .**107** J5
Peabody Hill, SE21 . . . .**169** H1
Peabody Hill Est, SE21 . . . . . .**151** H7
Peabody Sq, SE1 . . . .**.27** G4
Peabody Twr, EC1 *off Golden La* .**111** J4
Peabody Trust, SE1 . . . .**.27** J2
Peabody Yd, N1
  off Greenman St **111** J1
Peace Cl, N14 . . . .**.42** B5
  SE25 . . . .**188** B4
Peace Gro, Wem. HA9 . . . .**.88** B3
Peace St, SE18
  off Nightingale Vale **136/137** E6
Peaches Cl, Sutt. SM2 . . . .**198** B7
Peach Rd, W10 . . . .**108** A3
Peachum Rd, SE3 . . . .**135** F6
Peachwalk Ms, E3 *off Grove Rd* .**113** G2
Peacock St, SE17 . . . .**.35** H2
Peacock Wk, E16 . . . .**115** H6
Peacock Yd, SE17 . . . .**.35** H2
Peak, The, SE26 . . . .**171** F3
Peaketon Av, Ilf. IG4 . . . .**.80** A4
Peak Hill, SE26 . . . .**171** F4
Peak Hill Av, SE26 . . . .**171** F4
Peak Hill Gdns, SE26 . . . .**171** F4
Peal Gdns, W13 *off Ruislip Rd E* .**104** D4
Peall Rd, Croy. CR0 . . . .**187** F6
Pearce Cl, Mitch. CR4 . . . .**186** A2
Pearcefield Av, SE23 . . . .**171** F1
Pearce Rd, W.Mol. KT8 . . . . . .**179** H3
Pear Cl, NW9 . . . .**.70** D4
  SE14 *off Southerngate Way* .**133** H7
Pearcroft Rd, E11 . . . .**.96** D2
Peardon St, SW8 . . . .**150** B2
Peareswood Gdns, Stan. HA7 . .**.69** G1
Pearfield Rd, SE23 . . . .**171** H3
Pearl Cl, E6 . . . .**116** D6
  NW2 *off Marble Dr* . . . .**.72** A7
Pearl Rd, E17 . . . .**.78** A3
Pearl St, E1 *off Penang St* .**132/133** E1
Pearman St, SE1 . . . .**.27** F5
Pear Pl, SE1 . . . .**.27** E3
Pear Rd, E11 . . . .**.96** D3
Pearscroft Ct, SW6 . . . .**149** E1
Pearscroft Rd, SW6 . . . .**148** E1
Pearse St, SE15 . . . .**.36** E6
Pearson Cl, SE5 *off Medlar St* .**151** J1
Pearson Ms, SW4
  off Edgeley Rd **150** D3
Pearsons Av, SE14
  off Tanners Hill **154** A1
Pearson St, E2 . . . .**.13** E1

Pears Rd, Houns. TW3 . . . .**143** J3
Peartree Av, SW17 . . . .**167** F3
Pear Tree Cl, E2 . . . .**112** C1
  Chessington KT9 . . . .**196** A5
  Mitcham CR4 . . . .**185** H2
Peartree Ct, E18
  off Churchfields . . . .**.79** H1
Pear Tree Ct, EC1 . . . .**.11** F6
Peartree Gdns, Dag. RM8 . . . .**100** B4
  Romford RM7 . . . .**.83** H2
Peartree La, E1 *off Glamis Rd* .**113** F7
Peartree Rd, Enf. EN1 . . . .**.44** B3
Pear Tree St, EC1 . . . .**.11** H5
Peartree Way, SE10 . . . .**135** G4
Peary Pl, E2 *off Kirkwall Pl* . . .**113** F3
Peatfield Cl, Sid. DA15
  off Woodside Rd **175** H3
Pebble Way, W3 . . . .**126** B1
Pebworth Rd, Har. HA1 . . . . . .**.86** D2
Peckarmans Wd, SE26 . . . . . .**170** D3
Peckett Sq, N5
  off Highbury Gra . . . .**.93** J4
Peckford Pl, SW9 . . . .**151** G2
PECKHAM, SE15 . . . .**.36** E7
Peckham Gro, SE15 . . . .**152** B1
Peckham High St, SE15 . . . . . .**152** D1
Peckham Hill St, SE15 . . . .**.37** H7
Peckham Pk Rd, SE15 . . . .**.37** H7
Peckham Rd, SE5 . . . .**152** B1
  SE15 . . . .**152** B1
Peckham Rye, SE15 . . . .**152** D3
  SE22 . . . .**152** D4
Pecks Yd, E1 . . . .**.21** F1
Peckwater St, NW5 . . . .**.92** C5
Pedlars Wk, N7 . . . .**.93** E6
Pedley Rd, Dag. RM8 . . . .**100** C1
Pedley St, E1 . . . .**.13** G6
Pedro St, E5 . . . .**.95** G3
Pedworth Gdns, SE16
  off Rotherhithe New Rd **133** F4
Peek Cres, SW19 . . . .**166** A5
Peel Cl, E4 . . . .**.62** B2
  N9 *off Plevna Rd* . . . .**.60** D3
Peel Dr, NW9 . . . .**.71** F3
  Ilford IG5 . . . .**.80** B3
Peel Gro, E2 . . . .**113** F2
Peel Pas, W8 *off Peel St* **128** C1
Peel Pl, Ilf. IG5 . . . .**.80** B2
Peel Prec, NW6 . . . .**108** D2
Peel Rd, E18 . . . .**.79** F1
  NW6 . . . .**108** C3
  Harrow (Wldste) HA3 . . . . . .**.68** C3
  Orpington BR6 . . . .**207** F5
  Wembley HA9 . . . .**.87** G3
Peel St, W8 . . . .**128** D1
Peerless St, EC1 . . . .**.12** B4
Pegamoid Rd, N18 . . . .**.61** F3
Pegasus Cl, N16 *off Green Las* . .**94** A4
Pegasus Pl, SE11 . . . .**.35** E5
  SW6 *off Ackmar Rd* **148** D1
Pegasus Rd, Croy. CR0 . . . . . .**201** G6
Pegasus Way, N11 . . . .**.58** B6
Pegg Rd, Houns. TW5 . . . .**122** D7
Pegley Gdns, SE12 . . . .**173** G2
Pegwell St, SE18 . . . .**137** H7
Pekin Cl, E14 *off Pekin St* **114** A6
Pekin St, E14 . . . .**114** A6
Peldon Ct, Rich. TW9 . . . .**145** J4
Peldon Pas, Rich. TW10
  off Worple Way **145** J4
Peldon Wk, N1
  off Britannia Row **111** H1
Pelham Av, Bark. IG11 . . . .**117** J1
Pelham Cl, SE5 . . . .**152** B2
Pelham Cres, SW7 . . . .**.31** G2
Pelham Pl, SW7 . . . .**.31** G2
  W13 *off Ruislip Rd E* **104** C4
Pelham Rd, E18 . . . .**.79** H3
  N15 . . . .**.76** C4
  N22 . . . .**.75** G2
  SW19 . . . .**166** D7
  Beckenham BR3 . . . .**189** F2
  Bexleyheath DA7 . . . .**159** G3
  Ilford IG1 . . . .**.99** G2
Pelham St, SW7 . . . .**.31** F1
Pelican Est, SE15 . . . .**152** C1
Pelican Pas, E1
  off Cambridge Heath Rd . . .**113** F4
Pelier St, SE17 . . . .**.36** A5
Pelinore Rd, SE6 . . . .**172** E2
Pellant Rd, SW6 . . . .**128** B7
Pellatt Gro, N22 . . . .**.75** G1
Pellatt Rd, SE22 . . . .**152** C5
  Wembley HA9 . . . .**.87** G2
Pellerin Rd, N16 . . . .**.94** B5
Pelling St, E14 . . . .**114** A6
Pellipar Cl, N13 . . . .**.59** G3
Pellipar Gdns, SE18 . . . .**136** C5
Pelly Rd, E13 . . . .**115** G2
Pelter St, E2 . . . .**.13** F3
Pelton Rd, SE10 . . . .**134** E5
Pembar Av, E17 . . . .**.77** H3
Pemberley Chase, Epsom (W.Ewell)
  KT19 . . . .**196** B5
Pemberley Cl, Epsom (W.Ewell)
  KT19 . . . .**196** B5
Pember Rd, NW10 . . . .**108** A3

Pemberton Gdns, N19 . . . . .92 C3
Romford RM6 . . . . .82 E5
Pemberton Ho, SE26
off High Level Dr 170 D4
Pemberton Pl, E8
off Mare St 94/95 E7
Pemberton Rd, N4 . . . . .75 G5
East Molesey KT8 . . . . . . .179 J4
Pemberton Row, EC4 . . . . .19 G4
Pemberton Ter, N19 . . . . .92 C3
Pembridge Av, Twick. TW2 . . . .161 F1
Pembridge Cres, W11 . . . . . . .108 D7
Pembridge Gdns, W2 . . . . . . .108 D7
Pembridge Ms, W11 . . . . .108 D7
Pembridge Pl, SW15 . . . . .148 D5
W2 . . . . .108 D7
Pembridge Rd, W11 . . . . .108 D7
Pembridge Sq, W2 . . . . .108 D7
Pembridge Vil, W2 . . . . .108 D7
W11 . . . . .108 D7
Pembroke Av, N1 . . . . .111 E1
Harrow HA3 . . . . .68 D3
Pinner HA5 . . . . .84 D1
Surbiton KT5 . . . . .182 B5
Pembroke Cl, SW1 . . . . .24 C4
Pembroke Cotts, W8
off Pembroke Sq 128 D3
Pembroke Gdns, W8 . . . . .128 C4
Dagenham RM10 . . . . .101 H3
Pembroke Gdns Cl, W8 . . . . . .128 D3
Pembroke Ms, E3 off Morgan St .113 H3
N10 off Pembroke Rd 74 A1
W8 off Earls Wk 128 D3
Pembroke Pl, W8 . . . . .128 D3
Edgware HA8 . . . . .54 A7
Isleworth TW7
off Thornbury Rd 144 B2
Pembroke Rd, E6 . . . . .116 C5
E17 . . . . .78 B5
N8 . . . . .74 E4
N10 . . . . .74 A1
N13 . . . . .59 J3
N15 . . . . .76 C5
SE25 . . . . .188 B4
W8 . . . . .128 D4
Bromley BR1 . . . . .191 J4
Erith DA8 . . . . .139 J5
Greenford UB6 . . . . .103 H4
Ilford IG3 . . . . .99 J1
Mitcham CR4 . . . . .186 A2
Wembley HA9 . . . . .87 G3
Pembroke Sq, W8 . . . . .128 D3
Pembroke St, N1 . . . . .93 E7
Pembroke Studios, W8 . . . . . . .128 C3
Pembroke Vil, W8 . . . . .128 D4
Richmond TW9 . . . . .145 G4
Pembroke Wk, W8 . . . . .128 D4
Pembroke Way, Hayes UB3 . . . .121 F3
Pembry Cl, SW9 . . . . .151 G1
Pembury Av, Wor.Pk. KT4 . . . . .183 G7
Pembury Cl, Brom. BR2 . . . . . .191 F7
Pembury Ct, Hayes UB3 . . . . . .121 G6
Pembury Cres, Sid. DA14 . . . . .176 E2
Pembury Pl, E5 . . . . .94 E5
Pembury Rd, E5 . . . . .94 E5
N17 . . . . .76 C2
SE25 . . . . .188 D4
Bexleyheath DA7 . . . . .139 E7
Pemdevon Rd, Croy. CR0 . . . . .187 G7
Pemell Cl, E1 off Colebert Av . .113 F4
Pemerich Cl, Hayes UB3 . . . . . .121 J5
Pempath Pl, Wem. HA9 . . . . . . .87 G2
Penally Pl, N1
off Shepperton Rd 112 A1
Penang St, E1 . . . . .133 E1
Penard Rd, Sthl. UB2 . . . . .123 G3
Penarth St, SE15 . . . . .133 F6
Penates, Esher KT10 . . . . .194 A4
Penberth Rd, SE6 . . . . .172 C2
Penbury Rd, Sthl. UB2 . . . . . . .123 F4
Pencombe Ms, W11
off Denbigh Rd 108 C7
Pencraig Way, SE15 . . . . .132 E6
Pendall Cl, Barn. EN4 . . . . .41 H4
Penda Rd, Erith DA8 . . . . .139 H7
Pendarves Rd, SW20 . . . . .183 J1
Penda's Mead, E9
off Lindisfarne Way 95 H4
Pendell Av, Hayes UB3 . . . . . . .121 J7
Pendennis Rd, N17 . . . . .76 A3
SW16 . . . . .168 E4
Penderel Rd, Houns. TW3 . . . . .143 G5
Penderry Ri, SE6 . . . . .172 C2
Penderyn Way, N7 . . . . .92 D4
Pendle Rd, SW16 . . . . .168 B6
Pendlestone Rd, E17 . . . . .78 A5
Pendragon Rd, Brom. BR1 . . . .173 F3
Pendragon Wk, NW9 . . . . .70 E6
Pendrell Rd, SE4 . . . . .153 H2
Pendrell St, SE18 . . . . .137 G7
Pendula Dr, Hayes UB4 . . . . . .102 D4
Pendulum Ms, E8
off Birkbeck Rd 94 C5
Penerley Rd, SE6 . . . . .172 B1
Penfold Cl, Croy. CR0
off Epsom Rd 201 G3
Penfold La, Bex. DA5 . . . . .176 D2

Penfold Pl, NW1 . . . . .15 F1
Penfold Rd, N9 . . . . .61 G1
Penfold St, NW1 . . . . .7 F6
NW8 . . . . .7 F6
Penford Gdns, SE9 . . . . .156 A3
Penford St, SE5 . . . . .151 H2
Pengarth Rd, Bex. DA5 . . . . . . .158 D5
PENGE, SE20 . . . . .171 F7
Penge Ho, SW11 off Wye St . . .149 G3
Penge La, SE20 . . . . .171 F7
Penge Rd, E13 . . . . .97 J1
SE20 . . . . .188 D3
SE25 . . . . .188 D3
Penhall Rd, SE7 . . . . .136 A4
Penhill Rd, Bex. DA5 . . . . .158 C7
Penhurst Pl, SE1 . . . . .26 D6
Penhurst Rd, Ilf. IG6 . . . . .65 E7
Penifather La, Grnf. UB6 . . . . . .104 A3
Peninsula Apartments, W2
off Praed St 109 G5
Peninsula Hts, SE1
off Albert Embk 130 E5
Peninsular Cl, Felt. TW14 . . . . .141 G6
Peninsular Pk Rd, SE7 . . . . . . .135 G4
Penistone Rd, SW16 . . . . .168 E7
Penketh Dr, Har. HA1 . . . . .86 A3
Penmon Rd, SE2 . . . . .138 A3
Pennack Rd, SE15 . . . . .37 G6
Pennant Ms, W8 . . . . .30 A1
Pennant Ter, E17 . . . . .77 J2
Pennard Rd, W12 . . . . .127 J2
Pennards, The, Sun. TW16 . . . .178 C2
Penn Cl, Grnf. UB6 . . . . .103 H2
Harrow HA3 . . . . .69 F4
Penner Cl, SW19 . . . . .166 B2
Penners Gdns, Surb. KT6 . . . . .181 H7
Pennethorne Cl, E9
off Victoria Pk Rd 113 F1
Pennethorne Ho, SW11
off Wye St 149 G3
Pennethorne Rd, SE15 . . . . . . .132 E7
Penn Gdns, Chis. BR7 . . . . . . .192 E2
Pennine Dr, NW2 . . . . .90 B2
Pennine Ho, N9 off Plevna Rd . .60 D3
Pennine La, NW2
off Pennine Dr 90 B2
Pennine Way, Hayes UB3 . . . . .121 G7
Pennington Cl, SE27
off Hamilton Rd 170 A4
Pennington Dr, N21 . . . . .43 E5
Pennington St, E1 . . . . .21 J6
Pennington Way, SE12 . . . . . . .173 H2
Penniston Cl, N17 . . . . .75 J2
Penn La, Bex. DA5 . . . . .158 D5
Penn Rd, N7 . . . . .93 E5
Penn St, N1 . . . . .112 A1
Pennyfather La, Enf. EN2 . . . . . .43 J2
Pennyfields, E14 . . . . .114 A7
Penny Ms, SW12 off Caistor Rd .150 B7
Pennymoor Wk, W9
off Ashmore Rd 108 C3
Penny Rd, NW10 . . . . .106 B3
Pennyroyal Av, E6 . . . . .116 D6
Penpoll Rd, E8 . . . . .94 E6
Penpool La, Well. DA16 . . . . . .158 B3
Penrhyn Av, E17 . . . . .77 J1
Penrhyn Cres, E17 . . . . .78 A1
SW14 . . . . .146 C4
Penrhyn Gdns, Kings.T. KT1
off Surbiton Rd 181 G4
Penrhyn Gro, E17 . . . . .78 A1
Penrhyn Rd, Kings.T. KT1 . . . . .181 H3
Penrith Cl, SW15 . . . . .148 B5
Beckenham BR3
off Albemarle Rd 190 B1
Penrith Pl, SE27
off Harpenden Rd 169 H2
Penrith Rd, N15 . . . . .76 A5
Ilford IG6 . . . . .65 J6
New Malden KT3 . . . . .182 D4
Thornton Heath CR7 . . . . . .187 J2
Penrith St, SW16 . . . . .168 C6
Penrose Av, Wat. WD19 . . . . . .50 D2
Penrose Gro, SE17 . . . . .35 J4
Penrose Ho, SE17 . . . . .35 J4
Penrose St, SE17 . . . . .35 J4
Penryn St, NW1 . . . . .9 H1
Penry St, SE1 . . . . .37 E2
Pensbury Pl, SW8 . . . . .150 C2
Pensbury St, SW8 . . . . .150 C2
Penscroft Gdns, Borwd. WD6 . . .38 D4
Pensford Av, Rich. TW9 . . . . . .146 A2
Penshurst Av, Sid. DA15 . . . . . .158 A6
Penshurst Gdns, Edg. HA8 . . . . .54 B5
Penshurst Grn, Brom. BR2 . . . .191 F5
Penshurst Rd, E9 . . . . .95 G7
N17 . . . . .60 C7
Bexleyheath DA7 . . . . .159 F1
Thornton Heath CR7 . . . . . .187 H5
Penshurst Wk, Brom. BR2
off Hayesford Pk Dr 191 F5
Penshurst Way, Sutt. SM2 . . . .198 D7
Pensilver Cl, Barn. EN4 . . . . . . .41 H4
Penstemon Cl, N3 . . . . .56 D7
Penstock Footpath, N22 . . . . . . .75 D3
Pentavia Retail Pk, NW7
off Bunns La 55 F7

Pentelow Gdns, Felt. TW14 . . . .142 A6
Pentire Rd, E17 . . . . .78 D1
Pentland Av, Edg. HA8 . . . . .54 B2
Pentland Cl, N9 . . . . .61 F2
NW11 . . . . .90 B2
Pentland Gdns, SW18
off St. Ann's Hill 149 F6
Pentland Pl, Nthlt. UB5 . . . . . . .102 E1
Pentlands Cl, Mitch. CR4 . . . . .186 B3
Pentland St, SW18 . . . . .149 F6
Pentlow St, SW15 . . . . .147 J3
Pentlow Way, Buck.H. IG9 . . . . .48 B7
Pentney Rd, E4 . . . . .62 D1
SW12 . . . . .168 C1
SW19 off Midmoor Rd 184 B1
Penton Gro, N1 . . . . .11 E2
Penton Ho, SE2 off Hartslock Dr .138 D2
Penton Pl, SE17 . . . . .35 H3
Penton Ri, WC1 . . . . .10 D3
Penton St, N1 . . . . .10 E1
PENTONVILLE, N1 . . . . .10 E2
Pentonville Rd, N1 . . . . .10 C2
Pentridge St, SE15 . . . . .132 C7
Pentyre Av, N18 . . . . .60 A5
Penwerris Av, Islw. TW7 . . . . . .123 J7
Penwith Rd, SW18 . . . . .166 E2
Penwood Ho, SW15
off Tunworth Cres 147 F6
Penwortham Rd, SW16 . . . . . .168 B6
Penylan Pl, Edg. HA8 . . . . .54 A7
Penywern Rd, SW5 . . . . .128 D5
Penzance Pl, W11 . . . . .128 B1
Penzance St, W11 . . . . .128 B1
Peony Ct, Wdf.Grn. IG8
off The Bridle Path 62/63 E7
Peony Gdns, W12 . . . . .107 G7
Pepler Ms, SE5 . . . . .37 F5
Peploe Rd, NW6 . . . . .108 A2
Peplow Cl, West Dr. UB7
off Tavistock Rd 120 A1
Pepper All, Loug. (High Beach)
IG10 . . . . .47 G1
Pepper Cl, E6 . . . . .116 C5
Peppercorn Cl, Th.Hth. CR7 . . .188 A2
Peppermead Sq, SE13 . . . . . . .154 A5
Peppermint Cl, Croy. CR0 . . . . .186 E7
Peppermint Pl, E11
off Birch Gro 96/97 E3
Pepper St, E14 . . . . .134 B3
SE1 . . . . .27 J3
Peppie Cl, N16 off Bouverie Rd . .94 B2
Pepys Cres, E16
off Britannia Gate 135 G1
Barnet EN5 . . . . .39 J5
Pepys Ri, Orp. BR6 . . . . .207 J1
Pepys Rd, SE14 . . . . .153 G1
SW20 . . . . .183 J1
Pepys St, EC3 . . . . .21 E5
Perceval Av, NW3 . . . . .91 H5
Percheron Cl, Islw. TW7 . . . . . .144 D3
Percheron Rd, Borwd. WD6 . . . .38 D6
Perch St, E8 . . . . .94 C4
Percival Ct, N17 off High Rd 60 C7
Northolt UB5 . . . . .85 G5
★ Percival David Foundation of
Chinese Art, WC1
off Gordon Sq 9 J6
Percival Gdns, Rom. RM6 . . . . .82 C6
Percival Rd, SW14 . . . . .146 C4
Enfield EN1 . . . . .44 C4
Orpington BR6 . . . . .207 E2
Percival St, EC1 . . . . .11 G5
Percival Way, Epsom KT19 . . . .196 C4
Percy Bush Rd, West Dr. UB7 . . .120 C3
Percy Circ, WC1 . . . . .10 D3
Percy Gdns, Enf. EN3 . . . . .45 G5
Isleworth TW7 . . . . .144 D4
Worcester Park KT4 . . . . . .196 D1
Percy Ms, W1 . . . . .17 H2
Percy Pas, W1 . . . . .17 G2
Percy Rd, E11 . . . . .78 E7
E16 . . . . .115 E5
N12 . . . . .57 F5
N21 . . . . .43 J7
SE20 . . . . .189 G1
SE25 . . . . .188 D5
W12 . . . . .127 G2
Bexleyheath DA7 . . . . .159 E2
Hampton TW12 . . . . .161 G7
Ilford IG3 . . . . .82 A7
Isleworth TW7 . . . . .144 D4
Mitcham CR4 . . . . .186 A7
Romford RM7 . . . . .83 H3
Twickenham TW2 . . . . .161 H1
Percy St, W1 . . . . .17 H2
Percy Way, Twick. TW2 . . . . . . .161 J1
Percy Yd, WC1 . . . . .10 D3
Peregrine Cl, NW10 . . . . .88 D5
Peregrine Ct, SW16
off Leithcote Gdns 169 F4
Welling DA16 . . . . .157 J1
Peregrine Gdns, Croy. CR0 . . . .203 H2
Peregrine Ho, EC1 . . . . .11 H3
Peregrine Way, SW19 . . . . .165 J7
Perham Rd, W14 . . . . .128 B5
Peridot St, E6 . . . . .116 B5
Perifield, SE21 . . . . .169 J1

Perimeade Rd, Grnf. UB6 . . . . .105 J2
Periton Rd, SE9 . . . . .156 A4
PERIVALE, Grnf. UB6 . . . . .105 F1
Perivale Gdns, W13
off Bellevue Rd 104/105 E4
Perivale Gra, Grnf. UB6 . . . . . .104 D3
Perivale Ind Pk, Grnf. UB6 . . . .104 D3
Perivale La, Grnf. UB6 . . . . . . .104 D3
Perivale New Business Cen, Grnf.
UB6 . . . . .105 E2
Perkin Cl, Houns. TW3 . . . . . . .143 H4
Wembley HA0 . . . . .86 E5
Perkin's Rents, SW1 . . . . .25 H5
Perkins Rd, Ilf. IG2 . . . . .81 G5
Perkins Sq, SE1 . . . . .28 A1
Perks Cl, SE3 off Hurren Cl . .154/155 E3
Perpins Rd, SE9 . . . . .157 H6
Perran Rd, SW2
off Christchurch Rd 169 H5
Perran Wk, Brent. TW8 . . . . . . .125 H5
Perren St, NW5 off Ryland Rd . .92 B6
Perrers Rd, W6 . . . . .127 H4
Perrin Rd, Wem. HA0 . . . . .86 D4
Perrins Ct, NW3
off Hampstead High St 91 F4
Perrins La, NW3 . . . . .91 F4
Perrin's Wk, NW3 . . . . .91 F4
Perrott St, SE18 . . . . .137 F4
Perry Av, W3 . . . . .106 D6
Perry Ct, E14 off Napier Av 134 A5
N15 off Albert Rd 76 B6
Perryfield Way, NW9 . . . . .71 F6
Richmond TW10 . . . . .163 E2
Perry Gdns, N9 off Deansway . .60 B3
Perry Garth, Nthlt. UB5 . . . . . . .102 C1
Perry Hall Rd, Orp. BR6 . . . . . .193 J6
Perry Hill, SE6 . . . . .171 J4
Perry Ho, SW2
off Tierney Rd 150/151 F7
Perry How, Wor.Pk. KT4 . . . . . .197 F1
Perryman Ho, Bark. IG11 . . . . .117 F1
Perrymans Fm Rd, Ilf. IG2 . . . . .81 G6
Perry Mead, Enf. EN2 . . . . .43 H2
Perrymead St, SW6 . . . . .148 D1
Perryn Rd, SE16
off Drummond Rd 132/133 E3
W3 . . . . .106 D7
Perry Ri, SE23 . . . . .171 H3
Perry Rd, Dag. RM9 . . . . .119 F4
Perrys Pl, W1 . . . . .17 H3
Perry St, Chis. BR7 . . . . .175 G6
Perry St Gdns, Chis. BR7
off Old Perry St 175 H6
Perry Vale, SE23 . . . . .171 F2
Persant Rd, SE6 . . . . .172 E2
Perseverance Pl, SW9 . . . . .131 G7
Richmond TW9
off Shaftesbury Rd 145 H3
Pershore Cl, Ilf. IG2 . . . . .81 E5
Pershore Gro, Cars. SM5 . . . . .185 G6
Pert Cl, N10 . . . . .58 B7
Perth Av, NW9 . . . . .70 D7
Hayes UB4 . . . . .102 C4
Perth Cl, SW20 off Huntley Way .183 G2
Perth Rd, E10 . . . . .95 H1
E13 . . . . .115 H2
N4 . . . . .93 G1
N22 . . . . .75 H1
Barking IG11 . . . . .117 G2
Beckenham BR3 . . . . .190 C2
Ilford IG2 . . . . .80 D6
Perth Ter, Ilf. IG2 . . . . .81 F7
Perwell Av, Har. HA2 . . . . .85 F1
Perwell Ct, Har. HA2 . . . . .85 F1
Peter Av, NW10 . . . . .89 H7
Peterboat Cl, SE10
off Tunnel Av 134/135 E4
Peterborough Gdns, Ilf. IG1 . . . .80 B7
Peterborough Ms, SW6 . . . . . . .148 D2
Peterborough Rd, E10 . . . . .78 C5
SW6 . . . . .148 D2
Carshalton SM5 . . . . .185 H6
Harrow HA1 . . . . .86 B1
Peterborough Vil, SW6 . . . . . . .148 E1
Peterchurch Ho, SE15
off Commercial Way 132/133 E6
Petergate, SW11 . . . . .149 F4
Peter Heathfield Ho, E15
off High St 114 D1
Peterhouse Gdns, SW6
off Bagley's La 148/149 E1
Peter James Business Cen, Hayes
UB3 . . . . .122 A2
Peterley Business Cen, E2
off Hackney Rd 112/113 E2
★ Peter Pan Statue, W2 . . . . . . .23 E1
Peters Cl, Dag. RM8 . . . . .100 D1
Stanmore HA7 . . . . .53 G6
Welling DA16 . . . . .157 H2
Petersfield Cl, N18 . . . . .59 J5
Petersfield Ri, SW15 . . . . .165 H1
Petersfield Rd, W3 . . . . .126 C2
PETERSHAM, Rich. TW10 . . . . .163 H1
Petersham Cl, Rich. TW10 . . . . .163 G2
Sutton SM1 . . . . .198 D5
Petersham Dr, Orp. BR5 . . . . . .193 J2
Petersham Gdns, Orp. BR5 . . . .193 J2

Petersham La, SW7 . . . . .22 C5
Petersham Ms, SW7 . . . . .22 C6
Petersham Pl, SW7 . . . . .22 C5
Petersham Rd, Rich. TW10 . . . .145 H6
Petersham Ter, Croy. CR0
    off Richmond Grn 200/201 E3
Peters Hill, EC4 . . . . .19 J5
Peter's La, EC1 . . . . .19 H1
Peters Path, SE26 . . . . .170 E4
Peterstone Rd, SE2 . . . . .138 B3
Peterstow Cl, SW19 . . . . .166 B2
Peter St, W1 . . . . .17 G5
Peto Pl, NW1 . . . . .8 E5
Peto St N, E16
    off Victoria Dock Rd 115 F7
Petrie Cl, NW2 . . . . .90 B6
★ Petrie Mus of Egyptian
    Archaeology, WC1
    off Malet Pl 9 H6
★ Petticoat La (Market), E1 . . .21 E2
Petticoat Sq, E1 . . . . .21 F3
Petticoat Twr, E1
    off Petticoat Sq 112 C6
Pettits Pl, Dag. RM10 . . . . .101 G5
Pettits Rd, Dag. RM10 . . . . .101 G5
Pettiward Cl, SW15 . . . . .147 J4
Pettman Cres, SE28 . . . . .137 G3
Pettsgrove Av, Wem. HA0 . . . . .87 F5
Petts Hill, Nthlt. UB5 . . . . .85 H5
Pett St, SE18 . . . . .136 B4
PETTS WOOD, Orp. BR5 . . . . . .193 F4
Petts Wd Rd, Orp. BR5 . . . . . . .193 F5
Petty France, SW1 . . . . .25 G5
Petty Wales, EC3
    off Lower Thames St 112 B7
Petworth Cl, Nthlt. UB5 . . . . . . .85 F7
Petworth Gdns, SW20
    off Hidcote Gdns 183 H3
Petworth Rd, N12 . . . . .57 H5
    Bexleyheath DA6 . . . . .159 G5
Petworth St, SW11 . . . . .149 H1
Petyt Pl, SW3 . . . . .31 G6
Petyward, SW3 . . . . .31 H2
Pevensey Av, N11 . . . . .58 D5
    Enfield EN1 . . . . .44 A2
Pevensey Cl, Islw. TW7 . . . . . .123 J7
Pevensey Rd, E7 . . . . .97 F4
    SW17 . . . . .167 G4
    Feltham TW13 . . . . .160 E1
Peverel, E6 off Downings 116 D6
Peverel Ho, Dag. RM10 . . . . . . .101 G2
Peveret Cl, N11
    off Woodland Rd 58 B5
Peveril Dr, Tedd. TW11 . . . . . .162 A5
Pewsey Cl, E4 . . . . .62 A5
Peyton Pl, SE10 . . . . .134 C7
Pharaoh Cl, Mitch. CR4 . . . . . .185 J7
Pheasant Cl, E16 off Maplin Rd .115 G6
Phelp St, SE17 . . . . .36 B5
Phelps Way, Hayes UB3 . . . . . .121 J4
Phene St, SW3 . . . . .31 H5
Philbeach Gdns, SW5 . . . . .128 D5
Phil Brown Pl, SW8
    off Daley Thompson Way . .150 B2
Philchurch Pl, E1 . . . . .21 J4
Philimore Cl, SE18 . . . . .137 H5
Philip Gdns, Croy. CR0 . . . . . . .203 J2
Philip La, N15 . . . . .76 A4
Philipot Path, SE9 . . . . .156 C6
Philippa Gdns, SE9 . . . . .156 A5
Philips Cl, Cars. SM5 . . . . .200 A1
Philip St, E13 . . . . .115 G4
Philip Wk, SE15 . . . . .152 D3
Phillimore Gdns, NW10 . . . . . . .107 J1
    W8 . . . . .128 D2
Phillimore Gdns Cl, W8
    off Phillimore Gdns 128 D3
Phillimore Pl, W8 . . . . .128 D2
Phillimore Wk, W8 . . . . .128 D3
Phillipp St, N1 . . . . .112 B1
Philpot La, EC3 . . . . .20 D5
Philpot Path, Ilf. IG1
    off Sunnyside Rd 99 F3
Philpot Sq, SW6
    off Peterborough Rd . . .148/149 E3
Philpot St, E1 . . . . .113 E6
Phineas Pett Rd, SE9 . . . . .156 B3
Phipp's Br Rd, SW19 . . . . .185 F2
    Mitcham CR4 . . . . .185 F2
Phipp's Ms, SW1 . . . . .24 C4
Phipp St, EC2 . . . . .12 D5
Phoebeth Rd, SE4 . . . . .154 A5
Phoenix Cl, E8 off Stean St 112 C1
    E17 . . . . .77 J2
    West Wickham BR4 . . . . . .204 E2
Phoenix Dr, Kes. BR2 . . . . .206 A3
Phoenix Pk, Brent. TW8 . . . . . .125 G5
Phoenix Pl, WC1 . . . . .10 D5
Phoenix Rd, NW1 . . . . .9 H4
    SE20 . . . . .171 F6
Phoenix St, WC2 . . . . .17 J4
Phoenix Way, Houns. TW5 . . . .122 C6
Phoenix Wf, SE10 . . . . .135 F2
Phoenix Wf Rd, SE1 . . . . .29 G4

Phoenix Yd, WC1 . . . . .10 D4
★ Photographers' Gall, WC2 . . .17 J5
Phyllis Av, N.Mal. KT3 . . . . . . .183 H5
★ Physical Energy Statue, W2 . .22 D2
Physic Pl, SW3 . . . . .31 J5
Piazza, The, WC2
    off Covent Gdn 110/111 E7
Picardy Manorway, Belv. DA17 .139 H3
Picardy Rd, Belv. DA17 . . . . . .139 G4
Picardy St, Belv. DA17 . . . . . . .139 G3
Piccadilly, W1 . . . . .24 E2
Piccadilly Arc, SW1 . . . . .25 F1
Piccadilly Circ, W1 . . . . .17 H6
Piccadilly Pl, W1 . . . . .17 G6
Pickard St, EC1 . . . . .11 H3
Pickering Av, E6 . . . . .116 D2
Pickering Cl, E9
    off Cassland Rd 95 G7
Pickering Gdns, N11 . . . . .58 A6
    Croydon CR0 . . . . .188 C6
Pickering Ms, W2 . . . . .14 B3
Pickering Pl, SW1 . . . . .25 G2
Pickering St, N1 off Essex Rd . .111 H1
Pickets Cl, Bushey (Bushey Hth)
    WD23 . . . . .52 A1
Pickets St, SW12 . . . . .150 B7
Pickett Cft, Stan. HA7 . . . . .69 G1
Picketts Lock La, N9 . . . . .61 F2
Pickford Cl, Bexh. DA7 . . . . . . .158 E2
Pickford La, Bexh. DA7 . . . . . . .159 E2
Pickford Rd, Bexh. DA7 . . . . . .158 E3
Pickfords Wf, N1 . . . . .11 J2
Pickhurst Grn, Brom. BR2 . . . .191 F7
Pickhurst La, Brom. BR2 . . . . .205 F1
    West Wickham BR4 . . . . . .191 E6
Pickhurst Mead, Brom. BR2 . . .191 F7
Pickhurst Pk, Brom. BR2 . . . . .191 E5
Pickhurst Ri, W.Wick. BR4 . . . .190 C7
Pickle Herring St, SE1
    off Tooley St 132 B1
Pickwick Cl, Houns. TW4
    off Dorney Way 142/143 E5
Pickwick Ct, SE9 off West Pk . . .174 B1
Pickwick Ms, N18 . . . . .60 B5
Pickwick Pl, Har. HA1 . . . . .68 B7
Pickwick Rd, SE21 . . . . .152 A7
Pickwick St, SE1 . . . . .27 J4
Pickwick Way, Chis. BR7 . . . . .175 F6
Pickworth Cl, SW8
    off Kenchester Cl 130/131 E7
Picton Pl, W1 . . . . .16 C4
    Surbiton KT6 . . . . .196 A1
Picton St, SE5 . . . . .132 A7
Piedmont Rd, SE18 . . . . .137 G5
Pier Head, E1
    off Wapping High St . . .132/133 E1
Piermont Grn, SE22 . . . . .152 E5
Piermont Pl, Brom. BR1 . . . . . .192 B2
Piermont Rd, SE22 . . . . .152 E5
Pier Par, E16 off Pier Rd 136 D1
Pierrepoint Arc, N1
    off Islington High St 111 H2
Pierrepoint Rd, W3 . . . . .106 B7
Pierrepoint Row, N1 . . . . .11 G1
Pier Rd, E16 . . . . .136 C2
    Feltham TW14 . . . . .142 B5
Pier St, E14 . . . . .134 C4
Pier Ter, SW18 off Jew's Row . .149 F4
Pier Way, SE28 . . . . .137 G3
Pigeon La, Hmptn. TW12 . . . . .161 G4
Pigott St, E14 . . . . .114 A6
Pike Cl, Brom. BR1 . . . . .173 H5
Pike Rd, NW7 off Ellesmere Av .54 D4
Pikes End, Pnr. HA5 . . . . .66 B4
Pikestone Cl, Hayes UB4
    off Berrydale Rd 102/103 E4
Pilgrimage St, SE1 . . . . .28 B4
Pilgrim Cl, Mord. SM4 . . . . . . .185 E7
Pilgrim Hill, SE27 . . . . .169 J4
Pilgrims Cl, N13 . . . . .59 F4
    Northolt UB5 . . . . .85 J5
Pilgrims Ct, SE3 . . . . .155 G1
Pilgrim's La, NW3 . . . . .91 G4
Pilgrims Ms, E14
    off Blackwall Way 114 C7
Pilgrims Pl, NW3
    off Hampstead High St 91 G4
Pilgrims Ri, Barn. EN4 . . . . .41 H5
Pilgrim St, EC4 . . . . .19 G4
Pilgrims Way, E6 off High St N . .116 B1
    N19 . . . . .92 D1
    South Croydon CR2 . . . . . .202 C5
Pilgrim's Way, Wem. HA9 . . . . .88 B1
Pilkington Rd, SE15 . . . . .152 E2
    Orpington BR6 . . . . .207 F2
Pilot Cl, SE8 . . . . .133 J6
Pilsdon Cl, SW19
    off Inner Pk Rd 166 A1
Piltdown Rd, Wat. WD19 . . . . . .50 D4
Pilton Est, The, Croy. (Pitlake) CR0
    off Pitlake 201 H2
Pilton Pl, SE17 . . . . .36 A3
Pimento Ct, W5 off Olive Rd . . .125 G3
PIMLICO, SW1 . . . . .33 F3
Pimlico Rd, SW1 . . . . .32 B3
Pimlico Wk, N1 . . . . .12 D3
Pinchbeck Rd, Orp. BR6 . . . . . .207 J6

Pinchin St, E1 . . . . .21 J5
Pincott Pl, SE4 . . . . .153 G4
Pincott Rd, SW19 . . . . .167 F7
    Bexleyheath DA6 . . . . .159 G5
Pindar St, EC2 . . . . .20 D1
Pindock Ms, W9 . . . . .6 B6
Pineapple Ct, SW1 . . . . .25 F5
Pine Av, E15 . . . . .96 D5
    West Wickham BR4 . . . . . .204 B1
Pine Cl, E10 off Walnut Rd 96 B2
    N14 . . . . .42 C1
    N19 off Hargrave Pk 92 C2
    SE20 . . . . .189 F1
    Stanmore HA7 . . . . .52 E2
Pine Coombe, Croy. CR0 . . . . .203 G4
Pinecrest Gdns, Orp. BR6 . . . . .207 E4
Pinecroft Cres, Barn. EN5
    off Hillside Gdns 40 B4
Pinedene, SE15
    off Meeting Ho La 152/153 E1
Pinefield Cl, E14 . . . . .114 A7
Pine Gdns, Ruis. HA4 . . . . .84 B1
    Surbiton KT5 . . . . .182 A6
Pine Glade, Orp. BR6 . . . . .206 C4
Pine Gro, N4 . . . . .93 E2
    N20 . . . . .56 C1
    SW19 . . . . .166 C5
Pinehurst Wk, Orp. BR6 . . . . . .207 H1
Pinelands Cl, SE3
    off St. John's Pk 135 F7
Pinemartin Cl, NW2 . . . . .89 J3
Pine Ms, NW10
    off Clifford Gdns 108 A2
Pine Rd, N11 . . . . .58 A2
    NW2 . . . . .89 J4
Pines, The, N14 . . . . .42 C5
    Sunbury-on-Thames TW16 .178 A3
    Woodford Green IG8 . . . . . .63 G3
Pines Rd, Brom. BR1 . . . . .192 B2
Pine St, EC1 . . . . .11 E5
Pine Tree Cl, Houns. TW5 . . . . .142 B1
Pine Wk, Brom. BR1 . . . . .191 J1
    Surbiton KT5 . . . . .182 A6
Pine Wd, Sun. TW16 . . . . .178 A1
Pinewood Av, Pnr. HA5 . . . . . . .51 H6
    Sidcup DA15 . . . . .175 H1
Pinewood Cl, Borwd. WD6 . . . . .38 D1
    Croydon CR0 . . . . .203 H3
    Northwood HA6 . . . . .50 B5
    Orpington BR6 . . . . .207 G1
    Pinner HA5 . . . . .51 H6
Pinewood Dr, Orp. BR6 . . . . . . .207 H5
Pinewood Gro, W5 . . . . .105 F6
Pinewood Ms, Stai. (Stanw.)
    TW19 . . . . .140 A6
Pinewood Rd, SE2 . . . . .138 D6
    Bromley BR2 . . . . .191 G4
    Feltham TW13 . . . . .160 B3
Pinfold Rd, SW16 . . . . .168 E4
Pinglestone Cl, West Dr. UB7 . .120 B7
Pinkcoat Cl, Felt. TW13
    off Tanglewood Way 160 B3
Pinkerton Pl, SW16
    off Riggindale Rd 168 D4
Pinkham Way, N11 . . . . .58 A7
Pinkwell Av, Hayes UB3 . . . . . .121 G4
Pinkwell La, Hayes UB3 . . . . . .121 F4
Pinley Gdns, Dag. RM9
    off Stamford Rd 118 B1
Pinnacle Hill, Bexh. DA7 . . . . .159 H4
Pinnacle Hill N, Bexh. DA7 . . . .159 H3
Pinnell Rd, SE9 . . . . .156 A4
PINNER, HA5 . . . . .67 E4
Pinner Ct, Pnr. HA5 . . . . .67 G4
PINNER GREEN, Pnr. HA5 . . . . .66 C1
Pinner Grn, Pnr. HA5 . . . . .66 C2
Pinner Gro, Pnr. HA5 . . . . .67 E4
Pinner Hill, Pnr. HA5 . . . . .66 C1
Pinner Hill Rd, Pnr. HA5 . . . . . .66 C2
Pinner Pk, Pnr. HA5 . . . . .67 G1
Pinner Pk Av, Har. HA2 . . . . . . .67 H3
Pinner Pk Gdns, Har. HA2 . . . . .67 J2
Pinner Rd, Har. HA1, HA2 . . . . .67 H5
    Pinner HA5 . . . . .67 F4
Pinner Vw, Har. HA1, HA2 . . . . .67 J6
PINNERWOOD PARK, Pnr. HA5 .50 C7
Pintail Cl, E6 off Swan App 116 B5
Pintail Rd, Wdf.Grn. IG8 . . . . . .63 H7
Pintail Way, Hayes UB4 . . . . . .102 D5
Pinter Ho, SW9
    off Grantham Rd 150/151 E2
Pinto Cl, Borwd. WD6
    off Percheron Rd 38 D6
Pinto Way, SE3 . . . . .155 H4
Pioneers Ind Pk, Croy. CR0 . . .200 E1
Pioneer St, SE15 . . . . .152 D1
Pioneer Way, W12
    off Du Cane Rd 107 H6
Piper Cl, N7 . . . . .93 F6
Piper Rd, Kings.T. KT1 . . . . . . .182 A3
Piper's Gdns, Croy. CR0 . . . . . .189 H7
Pipers Grn, NW9 . . . . .70 C5
Pipers Grn La, Edg. HA8 . . . . . .53 H3
Pipewell Rd, Cars. SM5 . . . . . .185 H6
Pippin Cl, NW2 . . . . .89 H3
    Croydon CR0 . . . . .203 J1
Pippins Cl, West Dr. UB7 . . . . .120 A3

Piquet Rd, SE20 . . . . .189 F2
Pirbright Cres, Croy. (New Adgtn)
    CR0 . . . . .204 C6
Pirbright Rd, SW18 . . . . .166 C1
Pirie Cl, SE5 off Denmark Hill . .152 A3
Pirie St, E16 . . . . .135 H1
Pitcairn Cl, Rom. RM7 . . . . .83 G4
Pitcairn Rd, Mitch. CR4 . . . . . .167 J7
Pitcairn's Path, Har. HA2
    off Eastcote Rd 85 J3
Pitchford St, E15 . . . . .96 D7
Pitfield Cres, SE28 . . . . .138 A1
Pitfield Est, N1 . . . . .12 C3
Pitfield St, N1 . . . . .12 D4
Pitfield Way, NW10 . . . . .88 C6
    Enfield EN3 . . . . .45 F1
Pitfold Cl, SE12 . . . . .155 G6
Pitfold Rd, SE12 . . . . .155 G6
Pitlake, Croy. CR0 . . . . .201 H2
Pitman Ho, SE8 off Tanners Hill .154 A1
Pitman St, SE5 . . . . .35 J7
Pitmaston Ho, SE13
    off Lewisham Rd 154 C2
Pitmaston Rd, SE13
    off Morden Hill 154 C2
Pitsea Pl, E1 off Pitsea St 113 G6
Pitsea St, E1 . . . . .113 G6
Pitshanger La, W5 . . . . .105 E4
★ Pitshanger Manor & Gall,
    W5 . . . . .125 F1
Pitshanger Pk, W13 . . . . .105 F3
Pitt Cres, SW19 . . . . .166 E4
Pittman Gdns, Ilf. IG1 . . . . .99 F5
Pitt Rd, Croy. CR0 . . . . .187 J5
    Orpington BR6 . . . . .207 F4
    Thornton Heath CR7 . . . . .187 J5
Pitt's Head Ms, W1 . . . . .24 C2
Pittsmead Av, Brom. BR2 . . . . .191 G7
Pitt St, W8 . . . . .128 D2
Pittville Gdns, SE25 . . . . .188 D3
Pixfield Ct, Brom. BR2
    off Beckenham La 191 F2
Pixley St, E14 . . . . .113 J6
Place Fm Av, Orp. BR6 . . . . . . .207 G1
PLAISTOW, E13 . . . . .115 F3
PLAISTOW, Brom. BR1 . . . . . . .173 F6
Plaistow Gro, E15 . . . . .115 F1
    Bromley BR1 . . . . .173 H7
Plaistow La, Brom. BR1 . . . . . .173 H7
Plaistow Pk Rd, E13 . . . . .115 H2
Plaistow Rd, E13 . . . . .115 F1
    E15 . . . . .115 F1
Plane St, SE26 . . . . .170 E3
★ Planetarium, W1 . . . . .8 A6
Plane Tree Cres, Felt. TW13 . . .160 B3
Plane Tree Wk, N2 . . . . .73 G3
    SE19 off Central Hill 170 B6
Plantagenet Cl, Wor.Pk. KT4 . .196 D4
Plantagenet Gdns, Rom. RM6 . .82 D7
Plantagenet Pl, Rom. RM6
    off Broomfield Rd 82 D7
Plantagenet Rd, Barn. EN5 . . . .41 F4
Plantain Gdns, E11
    off Hollydown Way 96 D3
Plantain Pl, SE1 . . . . .28 B3
Plantation, The, SE3 . . . . .155 G2
Plantation Wf, SW11 . . . . .149 F3
Plasel Ct, E13 off Plashet Rd . . .115 G1
Plashet Gro, E6 . . . . .115 J1
Plashet Rd, E13 . . . . .115 G1
Plassy Rd, SE6 . . . . .154 B7
Platina St, EC2 . . . . .12 C5
Plato Rd, SW2 . . . . .151 E4
Platt, The, SW15 . . . . .148 A3
Platt's Eyot, Hmptn. TW12 . . . .179 G2
Platt's La, NW3 . . . . .90 D4
Platts Rd, Enf. EN3 . . . . .45 F1
Platt St, NW1 . . . . .9 H1
Plawsfield Rd, Beck. BR3 . . . . .189 G1
Plaxtol Cl, Brom. BR1 . . . . . . .191 J1
Plaxtol Rd, Erith DA8 . . . . .139 G7
Plaxton Ct, E11
    off Woodhouse Rd 97 F3
Playfair St, W6 off Winslow Rd .127 J5
Playfield Av, Rom. RM5 . . . . . . .83 J1
Playfield Cres, SE22 . . . . .152 C5
Playfield Rd, Edg. HA8 . . . . . . .70 C2
Playford Rd, N4 . . . . .93 F2
Playgreen Way, SE6 . . . . .172 A4
Playground Cl, Beck. BR3
    off Churchfields Rd 189 G2
Playhouse Ct, SE1
    off Southwark Br Rd 131 J2
Playhouse Yd, EC4 . . . . .19 G4
Plaza Par, NW6
    off Kilburn High Rd 108/109 E2
Plaza Shop Cen, The, W1 . . . . . .17 G3
Plaza W, Houns. TW3 . . . . .143 H1
Pleasance, The, SW15 . . . . . . .147 H4
Pleasance Rd, SW15 . . . . .147 H5
Pleasant Gro, Croy. CR0 . . . . . .203 J3
Pleasant Pl, N1 . . . . .93 H7
Pleasant Row, NW1 . . . . .110 B1
Pleasant Vw Pl, Orp. BR6
    off High St 206/207 E5
Pleasant Way, Wem. HA0 . . . . .105 F2
Plender St, NW1 . . . . .110 C1

Pleshey Rd, N7 . . . . .92 D4
Plevna Cres, N15 . . . . .76 B3
Plevna Rd, N9 . . . . .60 D3
  Hampton TW12 . . . . .179 H1
Plevna St, E14 . . . . .134 C3
Pleydell Av, SE19 . . . . .170 C7
  W6 . . . . .127 F4
Pleydell Ct, EC4 . . . . .19 F4
Pleydell Est, EC1 off Radnor St .111 J3
Pleydell St, EC4 . . . . .19 F4
Plimsoll Cl, E14 off Grundy St .114 B6
Plimsoll Rd, N4 . . . . .93 G3
Plough Ct, EC3 . . . . .20 C5
Plough La, SE22 . . . . .152 C6
  SW17 . . . . .167 E5
  SW19 . . . . .167 E5
  Teddington TW11 . . . . . . .162 D5
  Wallington SM6 . . . . .200 E4
Plough La Cl, Wall. SM6 . . . . .200 E5
Ploughmans Cl, NW1
  off Crofters Way 110 D7
Ploughmans End, Islw. TW7 . . .144 A5
Ploughmans Wk, N2
  off Long La 73 F2
Plough Ms, SW11
  off Plough Ter 149 G4
Plough Pl, EC4 . . . . .19 F3
Plough Rd, SW11 . . . . .149 G3
Plough St, E1 . . . . .21 H3
Plough Ter, SW11 . . . . .149 G4
Plough Way, SE16 . . . . .133 G4
Plough Yd, EC2 . . . . .12 E6
Plover Way, SE16 . . . . .133 H3
  Hayes UB4 . . . . .102 D6
Plowden Bldgs, EC4
  off Middle Temple La 111 G6
Plowman Cl, N18 . . . . .60 A5
Plowman Way, Dag. RM8 . . . .100 C1
Plumbers Row, E1 . . . . .21 H2
Plumbridge St, SE10
  off Blackheath Hill 154 C1
Plum Cl, Felt. TW13
  off Highfield Rd 160 A1
Plum Garth, Brent. TW8 . . . . .125 G4
Plum La, SE18 . . . . .137 E7
Plummer La, Mitch. CR4 . . . . .185 J2
Plummer Rd, SW4 . . . . .150 D7
Plumpton Cl, Nthlt. UB5 . . . . . .85 G6
Plumpton Way, Cars. SM5 . . . .199 H3
PLUMSTEAD, SE18 . . . . .137 H5
Plumstead Common Rd, SE18 . .136 E6
Plumstead High St, SE18 . . . .137 H4
Plumstead Rd, SE18 . . . . .137 E4
Plumtree Cl, Dag. RM10 . . . . .101 H6
  Wallington SM6 . . . . .200 D7
Plumtree Ct, EC4 . . . . .19 F3
Plumtree Mead, Loug. IG10 . . .48 D3
Plymouth Rd, E16 . . . . .115 G5
  Bromley BR1 . . . . .191 H1
Plymouth Wf, E14 . . . . .134 D4
Plympton Av, NW6 . . . . .90 C7
Plympton Cl, Belv. DA17
  off Halifield Dr 138/139 E3
Plympton Pl, NW8 . . . . .7 G6
Plympton Rd, NW6 . . . . .90 C7
Plympton St, NW8 . . . . .7 G6
Plymstock Rd, Well. DA16 . . . .138 C7
Pocklington Cl, NW9 . . . . .70 E2
Pocock Av, West Dr. UB7 . . . .120 C3
Pocock St, SE1 . . . . .27 G3
Podmore Rd, SW18 . . . . .149 F4
Poets Rd, N5 . . . . .94 A5
Poets Way, Har. HA1
  off Blawith Rd 68 B4
Pointalls Cl, N3 . . . . .73 F2
Point Cl, SE10 off Point Hill . . .154 C1
Pointer Cl, SE28 . . . . .118 D6
Pointers Cl, E14 . . . . .134 B5
Point Hill, SE10 . . . . .134 C7
Point of Thomas Path, E1
  off Glamis Rd 113 F7
Point Pl, Wem. HA9 . . . . .88 B7
Point Pleasant, SW18 . . . . . . .148 D4
Point W, SW7 off Cromwell Rd .128 E4
Point Wf La, Brent. TW8
  off High St 125 H6
Poland Ho, E15 . . . . .114 D1
Poland St, W1 . . . . .17 G4
Polebrook Rd, SE3 . . . . .155 J3
Pole Cat All, Brom. BR2 . . . . .205 F2
Polecroft La, SE6 . . . . .171 J2
Polehamptons, The, Hmptn. TW12
  off High St 161 J7
Pole Hill Rd, E4 . . . . .46 C7
Polesden Gdns, SW20 . . . . . .183 H2
Polesworth Ho, W2 . . . . .108 D5
Polesworth Rd, Dag. RM9 . . . .100 D7
★ Polish Inst & Sikorski Mus, SW7
  off Princes Gate 23 F4
Pollard Cl, E16 . . . . .115 G7
  N7 . . . . .93 F5
Pollard Rd, N20 . . . . .57 H2
  Morden SM4 . . . . .185 G5
Pollard Row, E2 . . . . .13 J3
Pollards Cl, Loug. IG10 . . . . . .47 J5
Pollards Cres, SW16 . . . . .187 E3
Pollards Hill E, SW16 . . . . . . .187 F3

Pollards Hill N, SW16 . . . . . . .187 E3
Pollards Hill S, SW16 . . . . . . .187 E3
Pollards Hill W, SW16 . . . . . . .187 E3
Pollard St, E2 . . . . .13 J3
Pollards Wd Rd, SW16 . . . . . .187 E2
Pollard Wk, Sid. DA14 . . . . . .176 C6
Pollen St, W1 . . . . .17 E4
Pollitt Dr, NW8 . . . . .7 F5
★ Pollock's Toy Mus, W1 . . . . .17 G1
Polperro Cl, Orp. BR6
  off Cotswold Ri 193 J6
Polperro Ms, SE11 . . . . .35 F1
Polsted Rd, SE6 . . . . .153 J7
Polthorne Est, SE18 . . . . .137 G4
Polthorne Gro, SE18 . . . . .137 F4
Polworth Rd, SW16 . . . . .168 E5
Polygon, The, SW4 off Old Town .150 C4
Polygon Rd, NW1 . . . . .9 H2
Polytechnic St, SE18 . . . . .136 D4
Pomell Way, E1 . . . . .21 G3
Pomeroy St, SE14 . . . . .153 F1
Pomfret Rd, SE5
  off Flaxman Rd 151 H3
Pomoja La, N19 . . . . .92 D2
Pond Cl, N12
  off Summerfields Av 57 H6
  SE3 . . . . .155 F2
Pond Cottage La, W.Wick. BR4 . .204 A1
Pond Cotts, SE21 . . . . .170 B1
PONDERS END, Enf. EN3 . . . . .45 F5
Ponders End Ind Est, Enf. EN3 . .45 J4
Pond Fld End, Loug. IG10 . . . . .47 J7
Pondfield Rd, Brom. BR2 . . . . .205 E1
  Dagenham RM10 . . . . . . .101 H5
  Orpington BR6 . . . . .207 E3
Pond Hill Gdns, Sutt. SM3 . . . .198 B6
Pond Mead, SE21 . . . . .152 A6
Pond Path, Chis. BR7
  off Heathfield La 174/175 E6
Pond Pl, SW3 . . . . .31 G2
Pond Rd, E15 . . . . .114 E2
  SE3 . . . . .155 F2
Pondside Cl, Hayes UB3
  off Providence La 121 G7
Pond Sq, N6 off South Gro 92 A1
Pond St, NW3 . . . . .91 H5
Pond Way, Tedd. TW11
  off Holmesdale Rd 163 F6
Pondwood Ri, Orp. BR6 . . . . . .193 H7
Ponler St, E1 . . . . .112 E6
Ponsard Rd, NW10 . . . . .107 H3
Ponsford St, E9 . . . . .95 F6
Ponsonby Pl, SW1 . . . . .33 J3
Ponsonby Rd, SW15 . . . . .147 H7
Ponsonby Ter, SW1 . . . . .33 J3
Pontefract Rd, Brom. BR1 . . . .173 F5
Ponton Rd, SW8 . . . . .33 J6
Pont St, SW1 . . . . .23 J6
Pont St Ms, SW1 . . . . .23 J6
Pontypool Pl, SE1 . . . . .27 G3
Pool Cl, Beck. BR3 . . . . .172 A5
  West Molesey KT8 . . . . . .179 F5
Pool Ct, SE6 . . . . .172 A2
Poole Ct Rd, Houns. TW4
  off Vicarage Fm Rd 142/143 E2
Poole Rd, E9 . . . . .95 G6
  Epsom KT19 . . . . .196 D6
Pooles Bldgs, EC1 . . . . .10 E6
Pooles La, SW10 off Lots Rd . . .129 F7
  Dagenham RM9 . . . . .119 E2
Pooles Pk, N4
  off Seven Sisters Rd 93 G2
Poole St, N1 . . . . .112 A1
Poolmans St, SE16 . . . . .133 G2
Pool Rd, Har. HA1 . . . . .68 A7
  West Molesey KT8 . . . . . .179 F6
Poolsford Rd, NW9 . . . . .71 E4
Poonah St, E1 off Hardinge St . .113 F6
Pope Cl, SW19 . . . . .167 G6
Pope Rd, Brom. BR2 . . . . .192 A5
Popes Av, Twick. TW2 . . . . . . .162 B2
Popes Dr, N3 . . . . .72 D1
Popes Gro, Croy. CR0 . . . . . . .203 J3
  Twickenham TW1, TW2 . . . .162 C2
Pope's Head All, EC3
  off Cornhill 112 A6
Popes La, W5 . . . . .125 G3
Popes Rd, SW9 . . . . .151 G3
Pope St, SE1 . . . . .29 E4
Popham Cl, Felt. TW13 . . . . . .161 F3
Popham Gdns, Rich. TW9
  off Lower Richmond Rd 146 A3
Popham Rd, N1 . . . . .111 J1
Popham St, N1 . . . . .111 H1
POPLAR, E14 . . . . .114 B7
Poplar Av, Mitch. CR4 . . . . . . .185 J1
  Orpington BR6 . . . . .207 E2
  Southall UB2 . . . . .123 H3
Poplar Bath St, E14
  off Lawless St 114 B7
Poplar Business Pk, E14 . . . . .114 C7
Poplar Cl, E9
  off Lee Conservancy Rd 95 J5
  Pinner HA5 . . . . .66 D1
Poplar Ct, SW19 . . . . .166 D5
Poplar Cres, Epsom KT19 . . . .196 C6
Poplar Fm Cl, Epsom KT19 . . .196 C6

Poplar Gdns, N.Mal. KT3 . . . . .182 D2
Poplar Gro, N11 . . . . .58 A6
  W6 . . . . .127 J2
  New Malden KT3 . . . . . . .182 D3
  Wembley HA9 . . . . .88 C3
Poplar High St, E14 . . . . .114 A7
Poplar Mt, Belv. DA17 . . . . . .139 H4
Poplar Pl, SE28 . . . . .118 C7
  W2 . . . . .14 A5
  Hayes UB3 off Central Av . . .102 A7
Poplar Rd, SE24 . . . . .151 J4
  SW19 . . . . .184 D2
  Sutton SM3 . . . . .198 C1
Poplar Rd S, SW19 . . . . .184 D3
Poplars, The, N14 . . . . .42 B5
Poplars Av, NW10 . . . . .89 J6
Poplars Rd, E17 . . . . .78 B6
Poplar St, Rom. RM7 . . . . .83 J4
Poplar Vw, Wem. HA9
  off Magnet Rd 87 G2
Poplar Wk, SE24 . . . . .151 J4
  Croydon CR0 . . . . .201 J2
Poplar Way, Felt. TW13 . . . . . .160 A3
  Ilford IG6 . . . . .81 F4
Poppins Ct, EC4 . . . . .19 G4
Poppleton Rd, E11 . . . . .79 E6
Poppy Cl, Belv. DA17 . . . . . . .139 H3
  Northolt UB5 . . . . .85 F6
  Wallington SM6 . . . . .200 A1
★ Poppy Factory Mus, The, Rich.
  TW10 . . . . .145 G6
Poppy La, Croy. CR0 . . . . .189 F7
Porchester Cl, SE5 . . . . .151 J4
Porchester Gdns, W2 . . . . .14 A5
Porchester Gdns Ms, W2 . . . . . .14 B4
Porchester Mead, Beck. BR3 . .172 B6
Porchester Ms, W2 . . . . .14 B3
Porchester Pl, W2 . . . . .15 H4
Porchester Rd, W2 . . . . .14 A3
  Kingston upon Thames KT1 .182 B2
Porchester Sq, W2 . . . . .14 B3
Porchester Ter, W2 . . . . .14 C4
Porchester Ter N, W2 . . . . .14 B3
Porch Way, N20 . . . . .57 J3
Porcupine Cl, SE9 . . . . .174 B2
Porden Rd, SW2 . . . . .151 F4
Porlock Av, Har. HA2 . . . . .85 J1
Porlock Rd, W10
  off Ladbroke Gro 108 A4
  Enfield EN1 . . . . .44 C7
Porlock St, SE1 . . . . .28 B3
Porrington Cl, Chis. BR7 . . . . .192 C1
Portal Cl, SE27 . . . . .169 G3
  Ruislip HA4 . . . . .84 A4
Portal Way, W3 off Victoria Rd .106 D5
Portbury Cl, SE15
  off Clayton Rd 152 D1
Port Cres, E13 off Jenkins Rd . .115 H4
★ Portcullis Ho, SW1 . . . . .26 A3
Portcullis Lo Rd, Enf. EN2 . . . . .44 A3
Portelet Ct, N1
  off De Beauvoir Est 112 B1
Portelet Rd, E1 . . . . .113 G3
Porten Rd, W14 . . . . .128 B3
Porter Rd, E6 . . . . .116 C6
Porters Av, Dag. RM8, RM9 . . .100 B6
Portersfield Rd, Enf. EN1 . . . . .44 B4
Porter Sq, N19
  off Hornsey Rd 92/93 E1
Porter St, SE1 . . . . .28 A1
  W1 . . . . .16 A1
Porters Wk, E1
  off Pennington St 112/113 J7
Porters Way, West Dr. UB7 . . . .120 C3
Porteus Rd, W2 . . . . .14 D2
Portgate Cl, W9 . . . . .108 C4
Porthallow Cl, Orp. BR6
  off Sevenoaks Rd 207 J4
Porthcawe Rd, SE26 . . . . .171 H4
Porthkerry Av, Well. DA16 . . . .158 A4
Portia Way, E3 . . . . .113 J4
Portinscale Rd, SW15 . . . . . . .148 B5
Portland Av, N16 . . . . .76 C7
  New Malden KT3 . . . . . . .183 F7
  Sidcup DA15 . . . . .158 A6
Portland Cl, Rom. RM6 . . . . . . .82 E5
  Worcester Park KT4 . . . . . .183 H7
Portland Cres, SE9 . . . . .174 B2
  Greenford UB6 . . . . .103 H4
  Stanmore HA7 . . . . .69 G2
Portland Gdns, N4 . . . . .75 H6
  Romford RM6 . . . . .82 D5
Portland Gro, SW8 . . . . .151 F1
Portland Ms, W1 . . . . .17 G4
Portland Pl, W1 . . . . .16 E2
Portland Ri, N4 . . . . .93 H1
Portland Ri Est, N4 . . . . .93 J1
Portland Rd, N15 . . . . .76 C4
  SE9 . . . . .174 B2
  SE25 . . . . .188 D4
  W11 . . . . .108 B7
  Bromley BR1 . . . . .173 J4
  Kingston upon Thames KT1 .181 H3
  Mitcham CR4 . . . . .185 H2
  Southall UB2 . . . . .123 F3
Portland Sq, E1
  off Watts St 132/133 E1

Portland St, SE17 . . . . .36 B3
Portland Ter, Rich. TW9 . . . . . .145 G4
Portland Wk, SE17 . . . . .36 C5
Portman Av, SW14 . . . . .146 D3
Portman Cl, W1 . . . . .16 A3
  Bexleyheath DA7
  off Queen Anne's Gate 158 D3
Portman Dr, Wdf.Grn. IG8 . . . . .80 A2
Portman Gdns, NW9 . . . . .70 D2
Portman Gate, NW1 . . . . .7 H6
Portman Hall, Har. HA3 . . . . . . .52 A4
Portman Ms S, W1 . . . . .16 B4
Portman Pl, E2 . . . . .113 F3
Portman Rd, Kings.T. KT1 . . . . .181 J2
Portman Sq, W1 . . . . .16 A3
Portman St, W1 . . . . .16 B4
Portmeadow Wk, SE2 . . . . . . .138 D2
Portmeers Cl, E17
  off Lennox Rd 77 J6
Portnall Rd, W9 . . . . .108 C2
Portobello Ct, W11
  off Westbourne Gro 108 C7
Portobello Ms, W11
  off Portobello Rd 108 D7
Portobello Rd, W10 . . . . .108 C6
  W11 . . . . .108 C6
Porton Ct, Surb. KT6 . . . . .181 F6
Portpool La, EC1 . . . . .18 C1
Portree Cl, N22
  off Nightingale Rd 59 F7
Portree St, E14 . . . . .114 D6
Portsdown, Edg. HA8
  off Rectory La 54 A5
Portsdown Av, NW11 . . . . .72 C6
Portsdown Ms, NW11 . . . . .72 C6
Portsea Ms, W2 . . . . .15 H4
Portsea Pl, W2 . . . . .15 H4
Portslade Rd, SW8 . . . . .150 C2
Portsmouth Av, T.Ditt. KT7 . . . .180 D7
Portsmouth Ms, E16
  off Wesley Av 135 H1
Portsmouth Rd, SW15 . . . . . . .147 H7
  Kingston upon Thames KT1 .181 F5
  Surbiton KT6 . . . . .181 F5
  Thames Ditton KT7 . . . . . .194 B2
Portsmouth St, WC2 . . . . .18 C4
Portsoken St, E1 . . . . .21 F5
Portugal Gdns, Twick. TW2
  off Fulwell Pk Av 161 J2
Portugal St, WC2 . . . . .18 C4
Portway, E15 . . . . .115 F1
Portway Gdns, SE18
  off Shooter's Hill Rd 136 A7
Postern Grn, Enf. EN2 . . . . .43 G2
Post La, Twick. TW2 . . . . .162 A1
Postmill Cl, Croy. CR0 . . . . . . .203 G3
Post Office App, E7 . . . . .97 H5
Post Office Ct, EC3 . . . . .20 C4
Post Office Way, SW8 . . . . .33 H7
Post Rd, Sthl. UB2 . . . . .123 H3
Postway Ms, Ilf. IG1
  off Clements Rd 98/99 E3
Potier St, SE1 . . . . .28 C6
Potter Cl, Mitch. CR4 . . . . . . .186 B2
Potterne Cl, SW19 . . . . .148 A7
Potters Cl, SE15
  off Chandler Way 132 B7
  Croydon CR0 . . . . .203 H1
  Loughton IG10 . . . . .48 B2
Potters Flds, SE1 . . . . .29 E2
Potters Gro, N.Mal. KT3 . . . . . .182 C4
Potters Hts Cl, Pnr. HA5 . . . . . .50 B7
Potters La, SW16 . . . . .168 D6
  Barnet EN5 . . . . .40 D4
  Borehamwood WD6 . . . . . . .38 C1
Potters Rd, SW6 . . . . .149 F2
  Barnet EN5 . . . . .40 E4
Potter St, Nthwd. HA6 . . . . .66 A1
  Pinner HA5 . . . . .66 B1
Potter St Hill, Pnr. HA5 . . . . . . .50 B6
Pottery La, W11 off Portland Rd .108 B7
Pottery Rd, Bex. DA5 . . . . .177 J2
  Brentford TW8 . . . . .125 H6
Pottery St, SE16 . . . . .132 E2
Pott St, E2 . . . . .113 E3
Poulett Gdns, Twick. TW1 . . . .162 D1
Poulett Rd, E6 . . . . .116 C2
Poulner Way, SE15
  off Daniel Gdns 132 C7
Poulters Wd, Kes. BR2 . . . . . .206 A5
Poulton Av, Sutt. SM1 . . . . . . .199 G3
Poulton Cl, E8
  off Spurstowe Ter 94/95 E5
Poultry, EC2 . . . . .20 B4
Pound Cl, Orp. BR6 . . . . .207 G2
  Surbiton KT6 . . . . .195 F1
Pound Ct Dr, Orp. BR6 . . . . . .207 G2
Pound Fm Cl, Esher KT10 . . . .194 A1
Poundfield Rd, Loug. IG10 . . . . .48 D5
Pound La, NW10 . . . . .89 G6
Pound Pk Rd, SE7 . . . . .136 A4
Pound Pl, SE9 . . . . .156 D6
Pound St, Cars. SM5 . . . . .199 J5
Pound Way, Chis. BR7
  off Royal Par 175 F7
Pountney Rd, SW11 . . . . .150 A3
POVEREST, Orp. BR5 . . . . . . .193 J5

Poverest Rd, Orp. BR5 . . . .**193** J5
Powder Mill La, Twick. TW2 . . . . .**161** F1
Powell Cl, Chess. KT9
   off Coppard Gdns **195** G5
Edgware HA8 . . . .**53** J6
Wallington SM6 . . . .**200** D7
Powell Gdns, Dag. RM10 . . . . . .**101** G4
Powell Rd, E5 . . . .**95** E3
Buckhurst Hill IG9 . . . .**47** J7
Powell's Wk, W4 . . . .**127** E6
Powergate Business Pk, NW10 . .**106** D3
Power Rd, W4 . . . .**126** A4
Powers Ct, Twick. TW1 . . . .**145** G7
Powerscroft Rd, E5 . . . .**95** F4
Sidcup DA14 . . . .**176** C6
Powis Gdns, NW11 . . . .**72** C7
W11 . . . .**108** C6
Powis Ms, W11
   off Westbourne Pk Rd **108** C6
Powis Pl, WC1 . . . .**10** C6
Powis Rd, E3 . . . .**114** B3
Powis Sq, W11 . . . .**108** C6
Powis St, SE18 . . . .**136** D5
Powis Ter, W11 . . . .**108** C6
Powle Ter, Ilf. IG1
   off Oaktree Gro **99** F5
Powlett Pl, NW1
   off Harmood St **92** B6
Pownall Gdns, Houns. TW3 . . . .**143** H4
Pownall Rd, E8 . . . .**112** C1
Hounslow TW3 . . . .**143** H4
Pownsett Ter, Ilf. IG1
   off Buttsbury Rd **99** F5
Powster Rd, Brom. BR1 . . . .**173** H5
Powys Cl, Bexh. DA7 . . . .**138** D6
Powys Ct, Borwd. WD6
   off Kensington Way **38** D3
Powys La, N13 . . . .**58** E5
N14 . . . .**58** E4
Poynders Ct, SW4
   off Poynders Rd **150** C6
Poynders Gdns, SW4 . . . .**150** C7
Poynders Rd, SW4 . . . .**150** C6
Poynings Rd, N19 . . . .**92** C3
Poynings Way, N12 . . . .**56** D5
Poyntell Cres, Chis. BR7 . . . .**193** H2
Poynter Ho, W11 . . . .**128** A1
Poynter Rd, Enf. EN1 . . . .**44** D5
Poynton Rd, N17 . . . .**76** D2
Poyntz Rd, SW11 . . . .**149** J2
Poyser St, E2 . . . .**113** J2
Praed Ms, W2 . . . .**15** F3
Praed St, W2 . . . .**15** G2
Pragel St, E13 . . . .**115** H2
Pragnell Rd, SE12 . . . .**173** H2
Prague Pl, SW2 . . . .**150** E5
Prah Rd, N4 . . . .**93** G2
Prairie St, SW8 . . . .**150** A2
Pratt Ms, NW1 off Pratt St **110** C1
Pratts Pas, Kings.T. KT1
   off Eden St **181** H2
Pratt St, NW1 . . . .**110** C1
Pratt Wk, SE11 . . . .**34** D1
Prayle Gro, NW2 . . . .**90** A1
Prebend Gdns, W4 . . . .**127** F3
W6 . . . .**127** F3
Prebend St, N1 . . . .**111** J1
Precinct, The, W.Mol. KT8
   off Victoria Av **179** H3
Precinct Rd, Hayes UB3 . . . .**102** A7
Precincts, The, Mord. SM4
   off Green La **184** D6
Premier Cor, W9 off Kilburn La .**108** C2
Premiere Pl, E14 off Garford St .**114** A7
Premier Pk, NW10 . . . .**106** B1
Premier Pk Rd, NW10 . . . .**106** B2
Premier Pl, SW15
   off Putney High St **148** A4
Prendergast Rd, SE3 . . . .**155** E3
Prentis Rd, SW16 . . . .**168** D4
Prentiss Ct, SE7 . . . .**136** A4
Presburg Rd, N.Mal. KT3 . . . . . .**183** E5
Presburg St, E5 off Glyn Rd **95** G3
Prescelly Pl, Edg. HA8 . . . .**69** J1
Prescot St, E1 . . . .**21** G5
Prescott Av, Orp. BR5 . . . .**192** E6
Prescott Cl, SW16 . . . .**168** E7
Prescott Grn, Loug. IG10 . . . .**49** F3
Prescott Ho, SE17 . . . .**35** H6
Prescott Pl, SW4 . . . .**150** D3
Presentation Ms, SW2
   off Palace Rd **169** F1
President Dr, E1
   off Waterman Way **132/133** E1
President St, EC1 . . . .**11** J3
Prespa Cl, N9 off Hudson Way . . .**61** F2
Press Rd, NW10 . . . .**88** D3
Prestage Way, E14 . . . .**114** C7
Prestbury Rd, E7 . . . .**97** J7
Prestbury Sq, SE9 . . . .**174** C4
Prested Rd, SW11
   off St. John's Hill **149** H4
Prestige Way, NW4
   off Heriot Rd **71** J5
PRESTON, Wem. HA9 . . . .**69** G7

Preston Av, E4 . . . .**62** D6
Preston Cl, SE1 . . . .**36** D1
Twickenham TW2 . . . .**162** B3
Preston Dr, E11 . . . .**79** J5
Bexleyheath DA7 . . . .**158** D1
Epsom KT19 . . . .**197** E6
Preston Gdns, NW10
   off Church Rd **88/89** E6
Ilford IG1 . . . .**80** B6
Preston Hill, Har. HA3 . . . .**69** J6
Preston Pl, NW2 . . . .**89** G6
Richmond TW10 . . . .**145** H5
Preston Rd, E11 . . . .**79** E6
SE19 . . . .**169** H6
SW20 . . . .**165** F7
Harrow HA3 . . . .**69** H7
Wembley HA9 . . . .**87** H2
Prestons Rd, E14 . . . .**134** C2
Bromley BR2 . . . .**205** G3
Preston Waye, Har. HA3 . . . .**87** H1
Prestwick Cl, Sthl. UB2
   off Ringway **122/123** E5
Prestwick Rd, Wat. WD19 . . . .**50** D5
Prestwood Av, Har. HA3 . . . .**69** E4
Prestwood Cl, SE18 . . . .**138** A7
Harrow HA3 . . . .**69** F4
Prestwood Gdns, Croy. CR0 . . . .**187** J7
Prestwood St, N1 . . . .**12** A2
Pretoria Av, E17 . . . .**77** H4
Pretoria Cl, N17 off Pretoria Rd .**60** C7
Pretoria Cres, E4 . . . .**62** C1
Pretoria Rd, E4 . . . .**62** C1
E11 . . . .**96** D1
E16 . . . .**115** F3
N17 . . . .**60** C7
SW16 . . . .**168** B6
Ilford IG1 . . . .**98** E5
Romford RM7 . . . .**83** J4
Pretoria Rd N, N18 . . . .**60** C6
Prevost Rd, N11 . . . .**58** A2
Price Cl, NW7 . . . .**56** B6
SW17 . . . .**167** A3
Price Rd, Croy. CR0 . . . .**201** H5
Price's Ct, SW11 . . . .**149** G3
Price's St, SE1 . . . .**27** H2
Price's Yd, N1 . . . .**111** F1
Price Way, Hmptn. TW12
   off Victors Dr **160/161** E6
Pricklers Hill, Barn. EN5 . . . .**41** E6
Prickley Wd, Brom. BR2 . . . .**205** F1
Priddy's Yd, Croy. CR0
   off Church St **201** J2
Prideaux Pl, W3 off Friars Pl La .**106** D7
WC1 . . . .**10** D3
Prideaux Rd, SW9 . . . .**151** E3
Pridham Rd, Th.Hth. CR7 . . . . . .**188** A4
Priest Ct, EC2 . . . .**19** J3
Priestfield Rd, SE23 . . . .**171** H3
Priestlands Pk Rd, Sid. DA15 . . .**175** J3
Priestley Cl, N16
   off Ravensdale Rd **76** C7
Priestley Gdns, Rom. RM6 . . . . . .**82** B6
Priestley Rd, Mitch. CR4 . . . .**186** A2
Priestley Way, E17 . . . .**77** G3
NW2 . . . .**89** G2
Priestman Pt, E3
   off Rainhill Way **114** B3
Priest Pk Av, Har. HA2 . . . .**85** G2
Priests Br, SW14 . . . .**147** E4
SW15 . . . .**147** E4
Prima Rd, SW9 . . . .**35** E7
Primrose Av, Enf. EN2 . . . .**44** A1
Romford RM6 . . . .**82** B7
Primrose Cl, N3
   off Rosemary Av **72** E2
SE6 . . . .**172** C5
Harrow HA2 . . . .**85** F4
Wallington SM6 . . . .**200** B1
Primrose Dr, West Dr. UB7 . . . . .**120** A4
Primrose Gdns, NW3 . . . .**91** H6
Ruislip HA4 . . . .**84** C5
PRIMROSE HILL, NW8 . . . .**109** J1
Primrose Hill, EC4 . . . .**19** F4
Primrose Hill Ct, NW3 . . . .**91** J7
Primrose Hill Rd, NW3 . . . .**91** H7
Primrose Hill Studios, NW1
   off Fitzroy Rd **110** A1
Primrose La, Croy. CR0 . . . .**203** G1
Primrose Ms, NW1
   off Sharpleshall St **91** J7
SE3 . . . .**135** H7
W5 off St. Mary's Rd **125** G2
Primrose Rd, E10 . . . .**96** B1
E18 . . . .**79** H2
Primrose Sq, E9 . . . .**95** F7
Primrose St, EC2 . . . .**20** D1
Primrose Wk, SE14
   off Alexandra St **133** H7
Epsom KT17 . . . .**197** F7
Primrose Way, Wem. HA0 . . . . . .**105** G2
Primula St, W12 . . . .**107** G6
Prince Albert Rd, NW1 . . . .**7** H2
NW8 . . . .**7** H2
Prince Arthur Ms, NW3
   off Perrins La **91** F4

Prince Arthur Rd, NW3 . . . .**91** F5
Prince Charles Dr, NW4 . . . .**71** J7
Prince Charles Rd, SE3 . . . .**155** F1
Prince Charles Way, Wall. SM6 . .**200** B3
Prince Consort Dr, Chis. BR7 . . .**193** G1
Prince Consort Rd, SW7 . . . .**22** D6
Princedale Rd, W11 . . . .**128** B1
Prince Edwards Rd, E9 . . . .**95** J6
Prince George Av, N14 . . . .**42** C4
Prince George Duke of Kent Ct,
   Chis. BR7 off Holbrook La . . .**175** G7
Prince George Rd, N16 . . . .**94** B4
Prince George's Av, SW20 . . . . .**183** J2
Prince George's Rd, SW19 . . . . .**185** G1
Prince Henry Rd, SE7 . . . .**136** A7
★ Prince Henry's Room, EC4 . . . .**19** E4
Prince Imperial Rd, SE18 . . . . . .**156** C1
Chislehurst BR7 . . . .**175** E7
Prince John Rd, SE9 . . . .**156** B5
Princelet St, E1 . . . .**21** G1
Prince of Orange La, SE10
   off Greenwich High Rd **134** C7
Prince of Wales Cl, NW4
   off Church Ter **71** H4
Prince of Wales Dr, SW8 . . . .**130** B7
SW11 . . . .**149** J1
Prince of Wales Gate, SW7 . . . . .**23** G3
Prince of Wales Pas, NW1 . . . .**9** F4
Prince of Wales Rd, NW5 . . . .**92** A6
SE3 . . . .**155** F1
Sutton SM1 . . . .**199** G2
Prince of Wales Ter, W4 . . . .**126** E5
W8 . . . .**22** B4
Prince Regent La, E13 . . . .**115** H3
E16 . . . .**115** J5
Prince Regent Ms, NW1 . . . .**9** F4
Prince Regent Rd, Houns. TW3 . .**143** J3
Prince Rd, SE25 . . . .**188** B5
Prince Rupert Rd, SE9 . . . .**156** C4
Prince's Arc, SW1 . . . .**25** G1
Princes Av, N3 . . . .**72** D1
N10 . . . .**74** A3
N13 . . . .**59** G5
N22 . . . .**74** D1
NW9 . . . .**70** B4
W3 . . . .**126** A3
Carshalton SM5 . . . .**199** J7
Greenford UB6 . . . .**103** H6
Orpington BR5 . . . .**193** H5
Surbiton KT6 . . . .**196** A1
Woodford Green IG8 . . . .**63** H4
Princes Cl, N4 . . . .**93** H1
NW9 . . . .**70** A4
SW4 off Old Town **150** C3
Edgware HA8 . . . .**54** A5
Sidcup DA14 . . . .**176** D3
Teddington TW11 . . . .**162** A4
Princes Ct, E1 . . . .**113** E7
SE16 . . . .**133** J3
Wembley HA9 . . . .**87** H5
Princes Dr, Har. HA1 . . . .**68** B3
Princes Gdns, SW7 . . . .**23** F5
W3 . . . .**106** A5
W5 . . . .**105** F4
Princes Gate, SW7 . . . .**23** G4
Princes Gate Ct, SW7 . . . .**23** F4
Princes Gate Ms, SW7 . . . .**23** F5
Princes La, N10 . . . .**74** B3
Princes Ms, W2 . . . .**14** A5
Princes Pk Av, NW11 . . . .**72** B6
Princes Pl, SW1 . . . .**25** G1
W11 . . . .**128** B1
Princes Plain, Brom. BR2 . . . . . .**192** B7
Princes Ri, SE13 . . . .**154** C2
Princes Riverside Rd, SE16 . . . .**133** G1
Princes Rd, N18 . . . .**61** F4
SE20 . . . .**171** G6
SW14 . . . .**146** D3
SW19 . . . .**166** D6
W13 off Broomfield Rd . .**124/125** E1
Buckhurst Hill IG9 . . . .**63** J2
Ilford IG6 . . . .**81** G4
Kingston upon Thames KT2 . .**164** A7
Richmond TW10 . . . .**145** H5
Richmond (Kew) TW9 . . . . . .**125** J7
Teddington TW11 . . . .**162** A4
Princess Alice Way, SE28 . . . . . .**137** G2
Princess Av, Wem. HA9 . . . .**87** H2
Princess Cl, SE28
   off Redbourne Dr **118** D6
Princess Cres, N4 . . . .**93** H2
Princesses Wk, Rich. TW9
   off Kew Rd **125** H7
Princess Louise Cl, W2 . . . .**15** F1
Princess May Rd, N16 . . . .**94** B4
Princess Ms, NW3
   off Belsize Cres **91** G6
Kingston upon Thames KT1 . .**181** J3
Princess Par, Orp. BR6
   off Crofton Rd **206** D3
Princess Pk Manor, N11 . . . .**58** A5
Princes Sq, W2 . . . .**14** A5
Princess Rd, NW1 . . . .**110** A1
NW6 . . . .**108** D2
Croydon CR0 . . . .**187** J6

Princess St, SE1 . . . .**27** H6
Princes St, EC2 . . . .**20** B3
N17 off Queen St **60** B6
W1 . . . .**17** E4
Bexleyheath DA7 . . . .**159** F4
Richmond TW9 off Sheen Rd .**145** H5
Sutton SM1 . . . .**199** G4
Princes Ter, E13 . . . .**115** H1
Prince St, SE8 . . . .**133** J6
Princes Way, SW19 . . . .**148** A7
Buckhurst Hill IG9 . . . .**63** J2
Croydon CR0 . . . .**201** F5
Ruislip HA4 . . . .**84** E4
West Wickham BR4 . . . .**205** F4
Princes Yd, W11
   off Princedale Rd **128** B1
Princethorpe Ho, W2 . . . .**14** A1
Princethorpe Rd, SE26 . . . .**171** G4
Princeton Ct, SW15
   off Felsham Rd **148** A3
Princeton St, WC1 . . . .**18** C1
Principal Sq, E9 off Chelmer Rd . .**95** G5
Pringle Gdns, SW16 . . . .**168** C4
Printers Inn Ct, EC4 . . . .**19** E3
Printers Ms, E3 . . . .**113** H1
Printer St, EC4 . . . .**19** F3
Printing Ho La, Hayes UB3 . . . . .**121** H2
Printing Ho Yd, E2 . . . .**13** E3
Print Village, SE15
   off Chadwick Rd **152** C2
Priolo Rd, SE7 . . . .**135** J5
Prior Av, Sutt. SM2 . . . .**199** H7
Prior Bolton St, N1 . . . .**93** H6
Prioress Rd, SE27 . . . .**169** H3
Prioress St, SE1 . . . .**28** C6
Prior Rd, Ilf. IG1 . . . .**98** D3
Priors Cft, E17 . . . .**77** H2
Priors Fm La, Nthlt. UB5 . . . .**85** F6
Priors Fld, Nthlt. UB5
   off Arnold Rd **84/85** E6
Priors Gdns, Ruis. HA4 . . . .**84** C5
Priors Mead, Enf. EN1 . . . .**44** B1
Priors Shop Cen, The, N12
   off High Rd **57** F5
Prior St, SE10 . . . .**134** C7
Priory, The, SE3 . . . .**155** F4
Priory Av, E4 . . . .**61** J3
E17 . . . .**78** A5
N8 . . . .**74** D4
W4 . . . .**127** E4
Orpington BR5 . . . .**193** G6
Sutton SM3 . . . .**198** A4
Wembley HA0 . . . .**86** C4
Priory Cl, E4 . . . .**61** J3
E18 . . . .**79** G1
N3 off Church Cres **72** C1
N14 . . . .**42** B5
N20 . . . .**40** C7
SW19 off High Path **184/185** E1
Beckenham BR3 . . . .**189** H3
Chislehurst BR7 . . . .**192** C1
Hampton TW12
   off Priory Gdns **179** F1
Hayes UB3 . . . .**102** B7
Stanmore HA7 . . . .**52** C3
Sunbury-on-Thames TW16
   off Staines Rd E **160** A2
Wembley (Sudbury) HA0 . . . . .**86** C4
Priory Ct, E17 . . . .**77** J3
EC4 off Carter La **111** H6
SW8 . . . .**150** D1
Priory Ct Est, E17 off Priory Ct . . .**77** J2
Priory Cres, SE19 . . . .**169** J7
Sutton SM3 . . . .**198** A4
Wembley HA0 . . . .**86** D3
Priory Dr, SE2 . . . .**138** D5
Stanmore HA7 . . . .**52** C3
Priory Fld Dr, Edg. HA8 . . . .**54** B4
Priory Gdns, N6 . . . .**74** B6
SE25 . . . .**188** C4
SW13 . . . .**147** F3
W4 . . . .**127** E4
W5 off Hanger La **105** H3
Hampton TW12 . . . .**161** F7
Wembley HA0 . . . .**86** D4
Priory Grn Est, N1 . . . .**10** D1
Priory Gro, SW8 . . . .**150** E1
Barnet EN5 . . . .**40** D5
Priory Hill, Wem. HA0 . . . .**86** D4
Priory La, SW15 . . . .**147** E6
Richmond TW9 off Forest Rd .**126** A1
West Molesey KT8 . . . .**179** G4
Priory Ms, SW8 . . . .**150** D1
Priory Pk, SE3 . . . .**155** F3
Priory Pk Rd, NW6 . . . .**108** C1
Wembley HA0 . . . .**86** D4
Priory Rd, E6 . . . .**116** A1
N8 . . . .**74** D4
NW6 . . . .**108** E1
SW19 . . . .**167** G7
W4 . . . .**126** D3
Barking IG11 . . . .**99** G7
Chessington KT9 . . . .**195** H3
Croydon CR0 . . . .**187** G7
Hampton TW12 . . . .**161** F7

Priory Rd, Houns. TW3 . . . .**143** J5
  Loughton IG10 . . . .**48** B4
  Richmond TW9 . . . .**126** A6
  Sutton SM3 . . . .**198** A4
Priory St, E3
  off St. Leonards St **114** B3
Priory Ter, NW6 . . . .**108** E1
  Sunbury-on-Thames TW16
  off Staines Rd E **160** A7
Priory Wk, SW10 . . . .**30** D4
Priory Way, Har. HA2 . . . .**67** H4
  Southall UB2 . . . .**122** D3
  West Drayton UB7 . . . .**120** B6
Priscilla Cl, N15 off Conway Rd . . .**75** J5
Pritchard's Rd, E2 . . . .**112** D1
Priter Rd, SE16 . . . .**29** J4
Priter Way, SE16 off Dockley Rd .**132** D3
Private Rd, Enf. EN1 . . . .**44** B5
Probert Rd, SW2 . . . .**151** G5
Probyn Rd, SW2 . . . .**169** H2
Procter St, WC1 . . . .**18** C2
Proctor Cl, Mitch. CR4 . . . .**186** A1
Proctors Cl, Felt. TW14 . . . .**160** A1
Progress Business Pk, Croy.
  CR0 . . . .**201** F2
Progress Way, N22 . . . .**75** G1
  Croydon CR0 . . . .**201** F2
  Enfield EN1 . . . .**44** D5
Promenade, The, W4 . . . .**147** E1
Promenade App Rd, W4 . . . . . .**126** E7
Promenade Mans, Edg. HA8
  off Hale La **54** B5
Prospect Business Pk, Loug.
  IG10 . . . .**49** F4
Prospect Cl, SE26 . . . .**170** E4
  Belvedere DA17 . . . .**139** G4
  Hounslow TW3 . . . .**143** F1
  Ruislip HA4 . . . .**66** D7
Prospect Cotts, SW18
  off Point Pleasant **148** D4
Prospect Cres, Twick. TW2 . . . .**143** J6
Prospect Hill, E17 . . . .**78** B4
Prospect Pl, E1 . . . .**133** F1
  N2 . . . .**73** G4
  N7 off Parkhurst Rd **92/93** E4
  N17 . . . .**76** B1
  NW2 off Ridge Rd **90** C3
  NW3 off Holly Wk **91** F4
  W4 off Chiswick High Rd **126** D5
  Bromley BR2 . . . .**191** H3
  Romford RM5 . . . .**83** J2
Prospect Quay, SW18 . . . .**148** D4
Prospect Ring, N2 . . . .**73** G3
Prospect Rd, NW2 . . . .**90** C3
  Barnet EN5 . . . .**40** D5
  Surbiton KT6 . . . .**181** F6
  Woodford Green IG8 . . . .**63** J5
Prospect St, SE16
  off Jamaica Rd **132/133** E2
Prospect Vale, SE18 . . . .**136** B4
Prospero Rd, N19 . . . .**92** C1
Protea Cl, E16 off Hermit Rd . . .**115** F4
Prothero Gdns, NW4 . . . .**71** H5
Prothero Ho, NW10 . . . .**88** D7
Prothero Rd, SW6 . . . .**128** B7
Prout Gro, NW10 . . . .**89** E4
Prout Rd, E5 . . . .**95** E3
Provence St, N1
  off St. Peters St **111** J2
Providence Cl, E9
  off Wetherell Rd **113** G1
Providence Ct, W1 . . . .**16** C5
Providence La, Hayes UB3 . . . .**121** G7
Providence Pl, N1 off Upper St . .**111** H1
  Romford RM5 . . . .**83** F2
Providence Rd, West Dr. UB7 . . .**120** B1
Providence Row, N1
  off Pentonville Rd **111** F2
Providence Row Cl, E2
  off Ainsley St **112/113** E3
Providence Sq, SE1
  off Jacob St **132** C2
Providence St, N1
  off St. Peters St **111** J2
Providence Yd, E2 . . . .**13** H3
Provident Ind Est, Hayes UB3 . .**122** A2
Provost Est, N1 . . . .**12** B3
Provost Rd, NW3 . . . .**91** J7
Provost St, N1 . . . .**12** B4
Prowse Av, Bushey (Bushey Hth)
  WD23 . . . .**51** J2
Prowse Pl, NW1 off Bonny St . . .**92** B7
Pruden Cl, N14 . . . .**58** C2
Prudent Pas, EC2 . . . .**20** A3
Prusom St, E1 . . . .**133** E1
Pryors, The, NW3 . . . .**91** G3
★ P.S. Tattershall Castle, SW1 . .**26** B2
★ Public Record Office, Rich.
  TW9 . . . .**126** B7
Pudding La, EC3 . . . .**20** C6
  Chigwell IG7 . . . .**65** J1
Pudding Mill La, E15 . . . .**114** B1
Puddle Dock, EC4 . . . .**19** H5
Puffin Cl, Bark. IG11 . . . .**118** B3
  Beckenham BR3 . . . .**189** G5

Puffin Ter, Ilf. IG5
  off Tiptree Cres **80** D3
Pulborough Rd, SW18 . . . .**148** C7
Pulborough Way, Houns. TW4 . .**142** C4
Pulford Rd, N15 . . . .**76** A6
Pulham Av, N2 . . . .**73** F4
Puller Rd, Barn. EN5 . . . .**40** B2
Pulleyns Av, E6 . . . .**116** B3
Pullman Ct, SW2 . . . .**169** E1
Pullman Gdns, SW15 . . . .**147** J6
Pullman Pl, SE9 . . . .**156** B5
Pulross Rd, SW9 . . . .**151** F3
Pulteney Cl, E3 . . . .**113** J1
  Isleworth TW7
  off Gumley Gdns **144** D3
Pulteney Gdns, E18
  off Pulteney Rd **79** H3
Pulteney Rd, E18 . . . .**79** H3
Pulteney Ter, N1 . . . .**111** F1
Pulton Pl, SW6 . . . .**128** D7
Puma Ct, E1 . . . .**21** F1
Pump All, Brent. TW8 . . . .**125** G7
Pump Cl, Nthlt. UB5
  off Union Rd **103** G2
Pump Ct, EC4 . . . .**19** E4
Pumphandle Path, N2
  off Tarling Rd **73** F2
Pump Hill, Loug. IG10 . . . .**48** C2
Pump Ho Cl, SE16
  off Renforth St **133** F2
  Bromley BR2 . . . .**191** F2
Pump Ho Ms, E1 . . . .**21** H5
Pumping Sta Rd, W4 . . . .**127** E7
Pump La, SE14 . . . .**133** F7
  Hayes UB3 . . . .**122** B2
Pump Pail N, Croy. CR0
  off Old Town **201** J3
Pump Pail S, Croy. CR0
  off Southbridge Rd **201** J3
Pundersons Gdns, E2 . . . .**113** E3
Punjab La, Sthl. UB1
  off Herbert Rd **123** F1
Purbeck Av, N.Mal. KT3 . . . .**183** F6
Purbeck Dr, NW2 . . . .**90** B2
Purbrook Est, SE1 . . . .**29** E4
Purbrook St, SE1 . . . .**29** E5
Purcell Cres, SW6 . . . .**128** B7
Purcell Ms, NW10
  off Suffolk Rd **88/89** E7
Purcell Rd, Grnf. UB6 . . . .**103** H5
Purcells Av, Edg. HA8 . . . .**54** A5
Purcell St, N1 . . . .**12** D1
Purchese St, NW1 . . . .**9** J1
Purdy St, E3 . . . .**114** B4
Purelake Ms, SE13 . . . .**154** D3
Purland Cl, Dag. RM8 . . . .**101** F1
Purland Rd, SE28 . . . .**137** J2
Purleigh Av, Wdf.Grn. IG8 . . . . . .**64** B6
Purley Av, NW2 . . . .**90** B3
Purley Cl, Ilf. IG5 . . . .**80** D2
Purley Pl, N1 off Islington Pk St . . .**93** H7
Purley Rd, N9 . . . .**60** A3
  South Croydon CR2 . . . .**202** A7
Purley Way, Croy. CR0 . . . .**187** F7
  Purley CR8 . . . .**201** G7
Purley Way Cres, Croy. CR0
  off Purley Way **187** F7
Purneys Rd, SE9 . . . .**156** A4
Purrett Rd, SE18 . . . .**137** J5
Purser's Cross Rd, SW6 . . . . . .**148** C1
Pursewardens Cl, W13 . . . .**125** F1
Pursley Rd, NW7 . . . .**55** H7
Purves Rd, NW10 . . . .**107** J2
Puteaux Ho, E2 . . . .**113** G2
PUTNEY, SW15 . . . .**148** B4
Putney Br, SW6 . . . .**148** B3
  SW15 . . . .**148** B3
Putney Br App, SW6 . . . .**148** B3
Putney Br Rd, SW15 . . . .**148** B4
  SW18 . . . .**148** B4
Putney Common, SW15 . . . . . .**147** J3
Putney Ex Shop Cen, SW15 . . . .**148** A4
Putney Gdns, Rom. (Chad.Hth) RM6
  off Heathfield Pk Dr **82** B6
PUTNEY HEATH, SW15 . . . .**147** J6
Putney Heath, SW15 . . . .**147** J6
Putney Heath La, SW15 . . . .**148** A6
Putney High St, SW15 . . . .**148** A4
Putney Hill, SW15 . . . .**148** A6
Putney Pk Av, SW15 . . . .**147** G4
Putney Pk La, SW15 . . . .**147** H4
PUTNEY VALE, SW15 . . . .**165** H2
Putney Wf Twr, SW15 . . . .**148** B3
Puttenham Cl, Wat. WD19 . . . . . .**50** C3
Pycroft Way, N9 . . . .**60** D4
Pyecombe Cor, N12 . . . .**56** C4
Pylbrook Rd, Sutt. SM1 . . . .**198** D3
Pylon Way, Croy. CR0 . . . .**201** E1
Pym Cl, Barn. EN4 . . . .**41** G5
Pymers Mead, SE21 . . . .**169** J1
Pymmes Cl, N13 . . . .**59** F5
  N17 . . . .**76** E1
Pymmes Gdns N, N9 . . . .**60** C3
Pymmes Gdns S, N9 . . . .**60** C3
Pymmes Grn Rd, N11 . . . .**58** B4

Pymmes Rd, N13 . . . .**59** E6
Pymms Brook Dr, Barn. EN4 . . . .**41** H4
Pyne Rd, Surb. KT6 . . . .**196** A1
Pyne Ter, SW19
  off Windlesham Gro **166** A1
Pynfolds, SE16
  off Paradise St **132/133** E2
Pynham Cl, SE2 . . . .**138** A3
Pynnacles Cl, Stan. HA7 . . . .**52** E5
Pyrland Rd, N5 . . . .**94** A5
  Richmond TW10 . . . .**145** J6
Pyrles Grn, Loug. IG10 . . . .**48** E1
Pyrles La, Loug. IG10 . . . .**48** E2
Pyrmont Gro, SE27 . . . .**169** H3
Pyrmont Rd, W4 . . . .**126** A6
  Ilford IG1 off High Rd **99** F2
Pytchley Cres, SE19 . . . .**169** J6
Pytchley Rd, SE22 . . . .**152** B3

Q

Quadrangle, The, W2 . . . .**15** G3
Quadrangle Cl, SE1 . . . .**36** D1
Quadrangle Ho, E15
  off Romford Rd **96** E6
Quadrangle Ms, Stan. HA7 . . . . .**53** F7
Quadrant, The, SE24
  off Herne Hill **151** J5
  SW20 . . . .**184** B1
  Bexleyheath DA7 . . . .**138** D1
  Richmond TW9 . . . .**145** H4
  Sutton SM2 . . . .**199** F6
Quadrant Arc, W1 . . . .**17** G6
Quadrant Cl, NW4
  off The Burroughs **71** H5
Quadrant Gro, NW5 . . . .**91** J5
Quadrant Ho, Sutt. SM2 . . . . . .**199** F6
Quadrant Rd, Rich. TW9 . . . . . .**145** G4
  Thornton Heath CR7 . . . .**187** H4
Quad Rd, Wem. HA9
  off Courtenay Rd **87** G3
Quaggy Wk, SE3 . . . .**155** G4
Quainton St, NW10 . . . .**88** D3
Quaker Ct, E1 . . . .**13** F6
Quaker La, Sthl. UB2 . . . .**123** G3
Quakers Course, NW9 . . . .**71** F1
Quakers La, Islw. TW7 . . . .**144** D1
Quaker's Pl, E7 . . . .**98** A5
Quaker St, E1 . . . .**13** F6
Quakers Wk, N21 . . . .**44** A6
Quality Ct, WC2 . . . .**18** E3
Quantock Cl, Hayes UB3 . . . . . .**121** G7
Quantock Dr, Wor.Pk. KT4 . . . . .**197** J2
Quantock Gdns, NW2 . . . .**90** A2
Quantock Ms, SE15
  off Choumert Gro **152** D2
Quarley Way, SE15 . . . .**37** F7
Quarrendon St, SW6 . . . .**148** D2
Quarr Rd, Cars. SM5 . . . .**185** G6
Quarry Pk Rd, Sutt. SM1 . . . . . .**198** C6
Quarry Ri, Sutt. SM1 . . . .**198** C6
Quarry Rd, SW18 . . . .**149** F6
Quarterdeck, The, E14 . . . .**134** A2
Quarter Mile La, E10 . . . .**96** B4
Quayside Wk, Kings.T. KT1
  off Bishop's Hall **181** G2
Quay W, Tedd. TW11 . . . .**162** E5
Quebec Ms, W1 . . . .**16** A4
Quebec Rd, Hayes UB4 . . . .**102** C7
  Ilford IG1, IG2 . . . .**81** E7
Quebec Way, SE16 . . . .**133** G2
Queen Adelaide Rd, SE20 . . . . .**171** F6
Queen Alexandra's Ct, SW19 . . .**166** C5
Queen Anne Av, N15
  off Suffield Rd **76** C5
  Bromley BR2 . . . .**191** F3
Queen Anne Dr, Esher (Clay.)
  KT10 . . . .**194** B7
Queen Anne Ms, W1 . . . .**16** E2
Queen Anne Rd, E9 . . . .**95** G6
Queen Anne's Cl, Twick. TW2 . . .**162** A3
Queen Anne's Gdns, W4 . . . . . .**127** E3
Queen Annes Gdns, W5 . . . . . .**125** H2
  Enfield EN1 . . . .**44** B6
Queen Anne's Gdns, Mitch. CR4 .**185** J3
Queen Anne's Gate, SW1 . . . . . .**25** H4
  Bexleyheath DA7 . . . .**158** D3
Queen Anne's Gro, W4 . . . .**126** E3
Queen Annes Gro, W5 . . . .**125** H2
  Enfield EN1 . . . .**44** A7
Queen Annes Pl, Enf. EN1 . . . . . .**44** B6
Queen Anne St, W1 . . . .**16** D3
Queen Anne's Wk, WC1
  off Guilford St **110/111** E4
Queen Anne Ter, E1
  off Sovereign Cl **112/113** E7
Queenborough Gdns, Chis. BR7 .**175** G6
  Ilford IG2 . . . .**80** D4
Queen Caroline Est, W6 . . . . . .**127** J5
Queen Caroline St, W6 . . . .**127** J4
Queen Elizabeth Gdns, Mord.
  SM4 . . . .**184** D4
**★ Queen Elizabeth Hall & Purcell
  Room**, SE1 . . . .**26** C1

Queen Elizabeth Rd, E17 . . . . . .**77** H3
  Kingston upon Thames KT2 . .**181** J1
Queen Elizabeths Cl, N16 . . . . . .**94** A2
Queen Elizabeths Dr, N14 . . . . . .**58** E4
★ Queen Elizabeth II Conf Cen,
  SW1 . . . .**25** J4
★ Queen Elizabeth's Hunting Lo,
  Epping Forest, E4 . . . .**47** F3
Queen Elizabeth St, SE1 . . . . . .**29** E3
Queen Elizabeths Wk, N16 . . . . .**94** A2
Queen Elizabeth's Wk, Wall.
  SM6 . . . .**200** D4
Queen Elizabeth Wk, SW13 . . . .**147** H1
Queenhithe, EC4 . . . .**20** A5
Queen Margaret's Gro, N1 . . . . .**94** B5
Queen Mary Av, Mord. SM4 . . . .**184** A5
Queen Mary Cl, Surb. KT6 . . . . .**196** A3
Queen Mary Rd, SE19 . . . .**169** H6
Queen Mary's Av, Cars. SM5 . . .**199** J7
★ Queen Mary's Gdns, NW1 . . . . .**8** B4
Queen of Denmark Ct, SE16 . . .**133** J3
Queens Acre, Sutt. SM3 . . . . . .**198** A7
Queens Av, N3 . . . .**57** F7
  N10 . . . .**74** A3
  N20 . . . .**57** G2
Queen's Av, N21 . . . .**59** H1
Queens Av, Felt. TW13 . . . .**160** C4
  Greenford UB6 . . . .**103** H6
  Stanmore HA7 . . . .**69** F3
  Woodford Green IG8 . . . .**63** H5
Queensberry Ms W, SW7 . . . . . .**30** E1
Queensberry Pl, E12 . . . .**98** A5
  SW7 . . . .**30** E1
  Richmond TW9 off Friars La . .**145** G5
Queensberry Way, SW7 . . . .**31** E1
Queensborough Ms, W2 . . . .**14** C5
Queensborough Pas, W2 . . . . . .**14** C5
Queensborough S Bldgs, W2
  off Porchester Ter **109** F7
Queensborough Studios, W2 . . .**14** C5
Queensborough Ter, W2 . . . .**14** B5
Queensbridge Pk, Islw. TW7 . . . .**144** B5
Queensbridge Rd, E2 . . . .**112** C1
  E8 . . . .**94** C7
QUEENSBURY, Har. HA3 . . . .**69** G3
Queensbury Circle Par, Har. HA3
  off Streatfield Rd **69** H3
  Stanmore HA7
  off Streatfield Rd **69** H3
Queensbury Rd, NW9 . . . .**70** D7
  Wembley HA0 . . . .**105** J2
Queensbury Sta Par, Edg. HA8 . .**69** J3
Queensbury St, N1 . . . .**93** J7
Queen's Circ, SW8
  off Queenstown Rd **130** B7
  SW11 off Queenstown Rd . . .**130** B7
Queens Cl, Edg. HA8 . . . .**54** A5
  Wallington SM6
  off Queens Rd **200** B5
★ Queens Club (Tennis Cen),
  W14 . . . .**128** B5
Queens Club Gdns, W14 . . . . . .**128** B6
Queens Ct, SE23 . . . .**171** F1
  Richmond TW10 . . . .**145** J6
Queenscourt, Wem. HA9 . . . .**87** H4
Queen's Cres, NW5 . . . .**92** A6
Queens Cres, Rich. TW10 . . . . .**145** J5
Queenscroft Rd, SE9 . . . .**156** A5
Queensdale Cres, W11 . . . .**128** A1
Queensdale Pl, W11 . . . .**128** B1
Queensdale Rd, W11 . . . .**128** A1
Queensdale Wk, W11 . . . .**128** B1
Queensdown Rd, E5 . . . .**94** E4
Queens Dr, E10 . . . .**78** A7
  N4 . . . .**93** H2
  W3 . . . .**105** J6
  W5 . . . .**105** J6
  Surbiton KT5 . . . .**182** A7
  Thames Ditton KT7 . . . .**180** D7
Queens Elm Par, SW3
  off Old Ch St **129** G5
Queen's Elm Sq, SW3 . . . .**31** F4
Queensferry Wk, N17
  off Jarrow Rd **76/77** E4
★ Queen's Gall, The, SW1 . . . . . .**24** E4
Queens Gdns, NW4 . . . .**71** J5
  W2 . . . .**14** C5
  W5 . . . .**105** F4
Queen's Gdns, Houns. TW5 . . . .**142** E1
Queen's Gate, SW7 . . . .**22** D4
Queen's Gate Gdns, SW7 . . . . . .**22** D6
Queens Gate Gdns, SW15 . . . . .
  off Upper Richmond Rd **147** H4
Queensgate Gdns, Chis. BR7 . .**193** G1
Queen's Gate Ms, SW7 . . . .**22** D4
Queensgate Pl, NW6 . . . .**90** D7
Queen's Gate Pl, SW7 . . . .**22** D6
Queen's Gate Pl Ms, SW7 . . . . . .**22** D6
Queen's Gate Ter, SW7 . . . .**22** C5
Queen's Gro, NW8 . . . .**109** G1
Queen's Gro Ms, NW8 . . . .**109** G1
Queens Gro Rd, E4 . . . .**62** D1
Queen's Head Pas, EC4 . . . .**19** J3
Queen's Head St, N1 . . . .**111** H1
Queens Head Yd, SE1 . . . .**28** B2

Queens Ho, Tedd. TW11 . . . .**162** C6
★ **Queen's Ice Rink**, W2
   off Queensway **14** B6
Queensland Av, N18 . . . .**59** J6
   SW19 . . . .**184** E1
Queensland CI, E17 . . . .**77** J2
Queensland Ho, E16
   off Rymill St **136** D1
Queens La, N10 . . . .**74** B3
Queens Mkt, E13 *off Green St* . .**115** J1
Queensmead, NW8 . . . .**109** G1
Queensmead Rd, Brom. BR2 . .**191** F2
Queensmere CI, SW19 . . . .**166** A2
Queensmere Rd, SW19 . . . . . .**166** A2
Queens Ms, W2 . . . .**14** B5
Queens Par, N11
   off Colney Hatch La **57** J5
   W5 . . . .**105** J6
Queens Par CI, N11
   off Colney Hatch La **57** J5
Queens Pk Ct, W10 . . . .**108** A3
★ **Queens Park Rangers FC**,
   W12 . . . .**127** H1
Queens Pas, Chis. BR7
   off High St **174/175** E6
Queens PI, Mord. SM4 . . . .**184** D4
Queen's Prom, Kings.T. KT1
   off Portsmouth Rd **181** G3
Queen Sq, WC1 . . . .**10** B6
Queen Sq PI, WC1 . . . .**10** B6
Queens Reach, E.Mol. KT8 . . .**180** B3
Queens Ride, SW13 . . . .**147** G3
   SW15 . . . .**147** G3
Queen's Ride, Rich. TW10 . . . .**164** B1
Queens Ri, Rich. TW10 . . . .**145** J6
Queens Rd, E11 . . . .**78** D7
   E13 . . . .**115** H1
Queen's Rd, E17 . . . .**77** J6
Queens Rd, N3 . . . .**73** F1
   N9 . . . .**60** E3
Queen's Rd, N11 . . . .**58** E7
Queens Rd, NW4 . . . .**71** J5
   SE14 . . . .**152** E1
   SE15 . . . .**152** E1
   SW14 . . . .**146** D3
   SW19 . . . .**166** C6
   W5 . . . .**105** H6
   Barking IG11 . . . .**99** F7
   Barnet EN5 . . . .**40** A3
   Beckenham BR3 . . . .**189** H2
   Bromley BR1 . . . .**191** G2
   Buckhurst Hill IG9 . . . .**63** H2
   Chislehurst BR7 . . . .**175** E6
Queen's Rd, Croy. CR0 . . . .**187** H6
Queens Rd, Enf. EN1 . . . .**44** B1
   Feltham TW13 . . . .**160** B1
   Hampton (Hmptn H.) TW12 .**161** H4
Queen's Rd, Houns. TW3 . . . . .**143** H3
   Kingston (Hmptn H.) TW12 .**161** H4
Queen's Rd, Kings.T. KT2 . . . . .**164** A7
   Loughton IG10 . . . .**48** B3
   Mitcham CR4 . . . .**185** G3
   Morden SM4 . . . .**184** D4
   New Malden KT3 . . . .**183** F4
   Richmond TW10 . . . .**145** J5
   Southall UB2 . . . .**122** D2
Queen's Rd, Tedd. TW11 . . . . . .**162** B6
   Thames Ditton KT7 . . . . . .**180** C5
Queens Rd, Twick. TW1 . . . .**162** C1
   Wallington SM6 . . . .**200** B5
Queen's Rd, Well. DA16 . . . . . .**158** B2
Queens Rd, West Dr. UB7 . . . . .**120** C2
Queens Rd W, E13 . . . .**115** G2
Queen's Row, SE17 . . . .**36** B5
Queens Ter, E13 . . . .**115** H1
Queen's Ter, NW8 . . . .**7** E1
Queens Ter, Islw. TW7 . . . .**144** D4
Queens Ter Cotts, W7
   off Boston Rd **124** B2
Queensthorpe Rd, SE26 . . . . .**171** G4
★ **Queen's Twr**, SW7 . . . .**23** E5
Queenstown Ms, SW8
   off Queenstown Rd **150** B2
Queenstown Rd, SW8 . . . .**32** D6
Queen St, EC4 . . . .**20** A5
   N17 . . . .**60** B6
   W1 . . . .**24** D1
   Bexleyheath DA7 . . . .**159** F3
   Croydon CR0 . . . .**201** J4
Queen St PI, EC4 . . . .**20** A6
Queensville Rd, SW12 . . . .**150** D7
Queens Wk, E4
   off The Green Wk **62** D1
   NW9 . . . .**88** C2
Queen's Wk, SE1 . . . .**26** C2
   SW1 . . . .**25** F2
Queens Wk, W5 . . . .**105** F4
Queen's Wk, Har. HA1 . . . .**68** B4
Queens Wk, Ruis. HA4 . . . .**84** D3
Queens Way, NW4 . . . .**71** J5
Queensway, W2 . . . .**14** B4
Queens Way, Croy. CR0 . . . . . .**201** F6
Queensway, Enf. EN3 . . . .**45** E4
Queens Way, Felt. TW13 . . . . . .**160** C4
Queensway, Orp. BR5 . . . .**193** F5

Queensway, Sun. TW16 . . . . . .**178** B2
   West Wickham BR4 . . . . . .**205** E3
Queenswell Av, N20 . . . .**57** H3
Queenswood Av, E17 . . . .**78** C1
   Hampton TW12 . . . .**161** H6
   Hounslow TW3 . . . .**143** F2
   Thornton Heath CR7 . . . . . .**187** G5
   Wallington SM6 . . . .**200** D4
Queenswood Gdns, E11 . . . . . .**97** G1
Queenswood Pk, N3 . . . .**72** B2
Queen's Wd Rd, N10 . . . .**74** B6
Queenswood Rd, SE23 . . . . . .**171** G3
   Sidcup DA15 . . . .**157** J5
Queens Yd, WC1 . . . .**9** G6
Queen Victoria Av, Wem. HA0 . .**87** G7
★ **Queen Victoria Mem**, SW1 . . .**25** F3
Queen Victoria St, EC4 . . . .**19** H5
Queen Victoria Ter, E1
   off Sovereign CI **112/113** E7
Quemerford Rd, N7 . . . .**93** F5
Quentin PI, SE13 . . . .**155** E3
Quentin Rd, SE13 . . . .**155** E3
Quernmore CI, Brom. BR1 . . . .**173** G6
Quernmore Rd, N4 . . . .**75** G6
   Bromley BR1 . . . .**173** G6
Querrin St, SW6 . . . .**149** F2
Quex Ms, NW6 *off Quex Rd* . . .**108** D1
Quex Rd, NW6 . . . .**108** D1
Quick Rd, W4 . . . .**126** E5
Quicks Rd, SW19 . . . .**167** E7
Quick St, N1 . . . .**11** H2
Quick St Ms, N1 . . . .**11** H2
Quickswood, NW3
   off King Henry's Rd **91** H7
Quiet Nook, Brom. BR2
   off Croydon Rd **206** A3
Quill La, SW15 . . . .**148** A4
Quill St, N4 . . . .**93** H3
   W5 . . . .**105** H3
Quilp St, SE1 . . . .**27** J3
Quilter St, E2 . . . .**13** H3
   SE18 . . . .**137** J5
Quilting Ct, SE16
   off Poolmans St **133** G2
Quince Rd, SE13 . . . .**154** B2
Quinta Dr, Barn. EN5 . . . .**39** H5
Quintin Av, SW20 . . . .**184** C1
Quintin CI, Pnr. HA5
   off High Rd **66** B5
Quinton CI, Beck. BR3 . . . .**190** C3
   Hounslow TW5 . . . .**122** B7
   Wallington SM6 . . . .**200** B4
Quinton Rd, T.Ditt. KT7 . . . .**194** D1
Quinton St, SW18 . . . .**167** F2
Quixley St, E14 . . . .**114** D7
Quorn Rd, SE22 . . . .**152** B4

R

Rabbit Row, W8
   off Kensington Mall **128** D1
Rabbits Rd, E12 . . . .**98** B4
Rabournmead Dr, Nthlt. UB5 . . .**84** E5
Raby Rd, N.Mal. KT3 . . . .**182** D4
Raby St, E14 *off Salmon La* . . .**113** H6
Raccoon Way, Houns. TW4 . . . .**142** C2
Rachel CI, IIf. IG6 . . . .**81** G3
Rachel Pt, E5 *off Muir Rd* **94** D4
Rackham CI, Well. DA16 . . . . . .**158** B2
Rackham Ms, SW16
   off Westcote Rd **168** C6
Racton Rd, SW6 . . . .**128** D6
Radbourne Av, W5 . . . .**125** F4
Radbourne CI, E5
   off Overbury St **95** G4
Radbourne Cres, E17 . . . .**78** D2
Radbourne Rd, SW12 . . . .**150** C7
Radcliffe Av, NW10 . . . .**107** G2
   Enfield EN2 . . . .**43** J1
Radcliffe Gdns, Cars. SM5 . . . .**199** H7
Radcliffe Ms, Hmptn. (Hmptn H.)
   TW12 *offTaylor CI* **161** J5
Radcliffe Path, SW8
   off Robertson St **150** B2
Radcliffe Rd, N21 . . . .**59** H1
   SE1 . . . .**29** E5
   Croydon CR0 . . . .**202** C2
   Harrow HA3 . . . .**68** D2
Radcliffe Sq, SW15 . . . .**148** A6
Radcliffe Way, Nthlt. UB5 . . . . .**102** D3
Radcot Pt, SE23 . . . .**171** G3
Radcot St, SE11 . . . .**35** F4
Raddington Rd, W10 . . . .**108** B5
Radfield Way, Sid. DA15 . . . . . .**157** G7
Radford Rd, SE13 . . . .**154** C6
Radford Way, Bark. IG11 . . . . . .**117** J3
Radipole Rd, SW6 . . . .**148** C1
Radius Pk, Felt. TW14 . . . .**141** J4
Radland Rd, E16 . . . .**115** F6
Radlet Av, SE26 . . . .**171** E3
Radlett CI, E7 . . . .**97** F6
Radlett PI, NW8 . . . .**109** H1
Radley Av, IIf. IG3 . . . .**99** J4
Radley Ct, SE16 *offThame Rd* .**133** G2

Radley Gdns, Har. HA3 . . . .**69** H4
Radley Ho, SE2
   off Wolvercote Rd **138** D2
Radley Ms, W8 . . . .**128** D3
Radley Rd, N17 . . . .**76** B2
Radley's La, E18 . . . .**79** G2
Radleys Mead, Dag. RM10 . . . .**101** H6
Radley Sq, E5
   off Dudlington Rd **95** F2
Radlix Rd, E10 . . . .**96** A1
Radnor Av, Har. HA1 . . . .**68** B5
   Welling DA16 . . . .**158** B5
Radnor CI, Chis. BR7
   off Homewood Cres **175** H6
   Mitcham CR4 . . . .**187** E4
Radnor Cres, SE18 . . . .**138** A6
   Ilford IG4 . . . .**80** C5
Radnor Gdns, Enf. EN1 . . . .**44** B1
   Twickenham TW1 . . . .**162** C2
Radnor Ms, W2 . . . .**15** F4
Radnor PI, W2 . . . .**15** G4
Radnor Rd, NW6 . . . .**108** B1
   SE15 . . . .**37** H7
   Harrow HA1 . . . .**68** A5
   Twickenham TW1 . . . .**162** C2
Radnor St, EC1 . . . .**12** A4
Radnor Ter, W14 . . . .**128** C4
Radnor Wk, E14
   off Copeland Dr **134** A4
   SW3 . . . .**31** H4
   Croydon CR0 . . . .**189** G6
Radnor Way, NW10 . . . .**106** B4
Radstock Av, Har. HA3 . . . .**68** D3
Radstock CI, N11
   off Martock Gdns **58** A6
Radstock St, SW11 . . . .**129** H7
Raebarn Gdns, Barn. EN5 . . . . .**39** H5
Raeburn Av, Surb. KT5 . . . .**182** B6
Raeburn CI, NW11 . . . .**73** F6
   Kingston upon Thames KT1 .**163** G7
Raeburn Rd, Edg. HA8 . . . .**70** A2
   Sidcup DA15 . . . .**157** H6
Raeburn St, SW2 . . . .**151** E4
Rafford Way, Brom. BR1 . . . . . .**191** H2
Raft Rd, SW18 *off North Pas* . .**148** D4
★ **Ragged Sch Mus**, E3
   off Copperfield Rd **113** H5
Raggleswood, Chis. BR7 . . . . . .**192** D1
Raglan CI, Houns. TW4
   off Vickers Way **142/143** E5
Raglan Ct, SE12 . . . .**155** G5
   South Croydon CR2 . . . . . .**201** H5
   Wembley HA9 . . . .**87** J4
Raglan Gdns, Wat. WD19 . . . . . .**50** B1
Raglan Rd, E17 . . . .**78** C5
   SE18 . . . .**137** F5
   Belvedere DA17 . . . .**139** F4
   Bromley BR2 . . . .**191** J4
   Enfield EN1 . . . .**44** B7
Raglan St, NW5 . . . .**92** B6
Raglan Ter, Har. HA2 . . . .**85** H4
Raglan Way, Nthlt. UB5 . . . .**85** J6
Ragley CI, W3 *off Church Rd* . .**126** C2
Ragwort Ct, SE26 . . . .**170** E5
Rahere Ho, EC1 *off Central St* . .**111** J3
Raider CI, Rom. RM7 . . . .**83** G1
Railey Ms, NW5 . . . .**92** C5
Railshead Rd, Islw. TW7 . . . . . .**144** E4
Railton Rd, SE24 . . . .**151** G4
Railway App, N4
   off Wightman Rd **75** G6
   SE1 . . . .**28** C1
   Harrow HA3 . . . .**68** C4
   Twickenham TW1 . . . .**144** D7
   Wallington SM6 . . . .**200** B6
Railway Av, SE16 . . . .**133** F2
Railway Children Wk, SE12
   off Baring Rd **173** G2
   Bromley BR1 *off Reigate Rd* .**173** G2
Railway Ms, E3
   off Wellington Way **114** A3
   W10 *off Ladbroke Gro* **108** B6
Railway Pas, Tedd. TW11
   off Victoria Rd **162** D6
Railway PI, SW19
   off Hartfield Rd **166** C6
   Belvedere DA17 . . . .**139** G3
Railway Ri, SE22 *off Grove Vale* .**152** B4
Railway Rd, Tedd. TW11 . . . .**162** C4
Railway Side, SW13 . . . .**147** E3
Railway St, N1 . . . .**10** B2
   Romford RM6 . . . .**100** C1
Railway Ter, SE13
   off Ladywell Rd **154** B5
   Feltham TW13 . . . .**160** A1
Rainborough CI, NW10 . . . .**88** C6
Rainbow Av, E14 . . . .**134** B5
Rainbow Quay, SE16 . . . .**133** H3
Rainbow St, SE5 . . . .**132** B7
Raines Ct, N16
   off Northwold Rd **94** C2
Raine St, E1 . . . .**133** E1
Rainham CI, SE9 . . . .**157** G6
   SW11 . . . .**149** H6
Rainham Rd, NW10 . . . .**107** J3

Rainham Rd N, Dag. RM10 . . . .**101** H2
Rainham Rd S, Dag. RM10 . . . .**101** H4
Rainhill Way, E3 . . . .**114** A3
Rainsborough Av, SE8 . . . .**133** H4
Rainsford CI, Stan. HA7
   off Coverdale CI **53** F5
Rainsford Rd, NW10 . . . .**106** B3
Rainsford St, W2 . . . .**15** G3
Rainton Rd, SE7 . . . .**135** G5
Rainville Rd, W6 . . . .**127** J6
Raisins Hill, Pnr. HA5 . . . .**66** C3
Raith Av, N14 . . . .**58** D3
Raleana Rd, E14 . . . .**134** C1
Raleigh Av, Hayes UB4 . . . .**102** B5
   Wallington SM6 . . . .**200** D4
Raleigh CI, NW4 . . . .**71** J5
   Pinner HA5 . . . .**66** D7
Raleigh Ct, SE16
   off Rotherhithe St **133** G1
   SE19 *off Lymer Av* **170** C5
   Beckenham BR3 . . . .**190** B1
   Wallington SM6 . . . .**200** B6
Raleigh Dr, N20 . . . .**57** H3
   Esher (Clay.) KT10 . . . .**194** A5
   Surbiton KT5 . . . .**196** C1
Raleigh Gdns, SW2
   off Brixton Hill **151** F6
   Mitcham CR4 . . . .**185** J2
Raleigh Ms, N1
   off Queen's Head St **111** H1
   Orpington BR6
   off Osgood Av **207** J5
Raleigh Rd, N8 . . . .**75** G4
   SE20 . . . .**171** G7
   Enfield EN2 . . . .**44** A4
   Richmond TW9 . . . .**145** J3
   Southall UB2 . . . .**122** E5
Raleigh St, N1 . . . .**111** H1
Raleigh Way, N14 . . . .**58** D1
   Feltham TW13 . . . .**160** C5
Ralph Ct, W2 . . . .**14** B3
Ralph Perring Ct, Beck. BR3 . . .**190** A4
Ralston St, SW3 . . . .**31** J4
Ralston Way, Wat. WD19 . . . .**50** D2
Rama CI, SW16 . . . .**168** D7
Rama Ct, Har. HA1 . . . .**86** B2
Ramac Way, SE7 . . . .**135** H4
Rama La, SE19 . . . .**170** C7
Rambler CI, SW16 . . . .**168** C4
Rame CI, SW17 . . . .**168** A5
Ramilles CI, SW2 . . . .**151** E6
Ramillies PI, W1 . . . .**17** F4
Ramillies Rd, NW7 . . . .**54** E2
   W4 . . . .**126** D4
   Sidcup DA15 . . . .**158** B6
Ramillies St, W1 . . . .**17** F4
Rampart St, E1
   off Commercial Rd **112/113** E6
Ram Pas, Kings.T. KT1
   off High St **181** G2
Rampayne St, SW1 . . . .**33** H3
Ram PI, E9 *off Chatham PI* **95** F6
Rampton CI, E4 . . . .**62** A3
Ramsay Ms, SW3 . . . .**31** G5
Ramsay PI, Har. HA1 . . . .**86** B1
Ramsay Rd, E7 . . . .**97** E4
   W3 . . . .**126** C3
Ramscroft CI, N9 . . . .**44** B7
Ramsdale Rd, SW17 . . . .**168** A5
Ramsden Rd, N11 . . . .**57** J5
   SW12 . . . .**150** A6
Ramsey CI, NW9 . . . .**71** F6
   Greenford UB6 . . . .**85** J5
Ramsey Ho, Wem. HA9 . . . .**87** H6
Ramsey Ms, N4 *off Monsell Rd* .**93** H3
Ramsey Rd, Th.Hth. CR7 . . . . . .**187** F6
Ramsey St, E2 . . . .**13** J5
Ramsey Wk, N1 . . . .**94** A6
Ramsey Way, N14 . . . .**42** C7
Ramsgate CI, E16
   off Hanameel St **135** H1
Ramsgate St, E8 *off Dalston La* .**94** C6
Ramsgill App, IIf. IG2 . . . .**81** J4
Ramsgill Dr, IIf. IG2 . . . .**81** J5
Rams Gro, Rom. RM6 . . . .**83** E4
Ram St, SW18 . . . .**148** E5
Ramulis Dr, Hayes UB4 . . . .**102** D4
Ramus Wd Av, Orp. BR6 . . . . . .**207** H5
Rancliffe Gdns, SE9 . . . .**156** B4
Rancliffe Rd, E6 . . . .**116** B2
Randall Av, NW2 . . . .**89** F3
Randall CI, SW11 . . . .**149** H1
   Erith DA8 . . . .**139** J6
Randall Ct, NW7 *of Page St* **55** G7
Randall PI, SE10 . . . .**134** C7
Randall Rd, SE11 . . . .**34** C3
Randall Row, SE11 . . . .**34** C2
Randell's Rd, N1 . . . .**111** E1
Randle Rd, Rich. TW10 . . . .**163** F4
Randlesdown Rd, SE6 . . . .**172** A4
Randolph App, E16 . . . .**116** A6
Randolph Av, W9 . . . .**6** D5
Randolph CI, Bexh. DA7 . . . . . .**159** J3
   Kingston upon Thames KT2 .**164** C5
Randolph Cres, W9 . . . .**6** C6

Randolph Gdns, NW6 . . . . .6 A2
Randolph Ho, Rom. RM6
  off Donald Dr 82 C5
Randolph Ho, Croy. CR0 . . . . . .201 J1
Randolph Ms, W9 . . . . .6 C6
Randolph Rd, E17 . . . . .78 B5
  W9 . . . . .6 C6
  Bromley BR2 . . . . .206 C7
  Southall UB1 . . . . .123 F2
Randolph St, NW1 . . . . .92 C7
Randon Cl, Har. HA2 . . . . .67 H2
Ranelagh Av, SW6 . . . . .148 C3
  SW13 . . . . .147 G3
Ranelagh Br, W2
  off Gloucester Ter 108/109 E5
Ranelagh Cl, Edg. HA8 . . . . .54 A4
Ranelagh Dr, Edg. HA8 . . . . .54 A4
  Twickenham TW1 . . . . .145 E5
★ Ranelagh Gdns, SW3 . . . . .32 B4
Ranelagh Gdns, E11 . . . . .79 J5
  SW6 . . . . .148 C3
  W4 off Grove Pk Gdns 126 C3
  W6 .127 F3
  Ilford IG1 . . . . .98 D1
Ranelagh Gdns Mans, SW6
  off Ranelagh Gdns 148 B3
Ranelagh Gro, SW1 . . . . .32 C4
Ranelagh Ms, W5
  off Ranelagh Rd 125 G2
Ranelagh Pl, N.Mal. KT3 . . . . . .182 E5
Ranelagh Rd, E6 . . . . .116 D1
  E11 .96 E4
  E15 . . . . .115 E1
  N17 .76 B3
  N22 .75 F1
  NW10 . . . . .107 F2
  SW1 .33 G4
  W5 .125 G2
  Southall UB1 . . . . .122 D1
  Wembley HA0 . . . . .87 G5
Ranfurly Rd, Sutt. SM1 . . . . . . .198 D2
Rangefield Rd, Brom. BR1 . . . . .172 E5
Rangemoor Rd, N15 . . . . .76 C5
Rangers Rd, E4 . . . . .47 E7
  Loughton IG10 . . . . .47 E7
Rangers Sq, SE10 . . . . .154 D1
Rangeworthy Pl, Sid. DA15
  off Priestlands Pk Rd 175 J3
Rangoon St, EC3 . . . . .21 F4
Rankin Cl, NW9 . . . . .71 E3
Ranleigh Gdns, Bexh. DA7 . . . . .139 F7
Ranmere St, SW12
  off Ormeley Rd 168 B1
Ranmoor Cl, Har. HA1 . . . . .68 A4
Ranmoor Gdns, Har. HA1 . . . . . . .68 A4
Ranmore Av, Croy. CR0 . . . . . . .202 C3
Rannoch Cl, Edg. HA8 . . . . .54 B2
Rannoch Rd, W6 . . . . .127 A6
Rannock Av, NW9 . . . . .70 E7
Ranskill Rd, Borwd. WD6 . . . . . . .38 A1
Ransome's Dock Business Cen, SW11
  off Parkgate Rd 129 H7
Ransom Rd, SE7 off Floyd Rd . .135 J5
Ransom Wk, SE7
  off Woolwich Rd 135 J5
Ranston St, NW1 . . . . .15 G1
Ranulf Rd, NW2 . . . . .90 C4
Ranwell Cl, E3 off Beale Rd 113 J1
Ranwell St, E3 . . . . .113 J1
Ranworth Rd, N9 . . . . .61 F2
Ranyard Cl, Chess. KT9 . . . . . . .195 J3
Raphael Dr, T.Ditt. KT7 . . . . . . .180 C7
Raphael St, SW7 . . . . .23 J4
Rashleigh St, SW8
  off Peardon St 150 B2
Rasper Rd, N20 . . . . .57 F2
Rastell Av, SW2 . . . . .168 D2
Ratcliffe Cl, SE12 . . . . .155 G7
Ratcliffe Cross St, E1 . . . . .113 G6
Ratcliffe La, E14 . . . . .113 H6
Ratcliffe Orchard, E1 . . . . .113 G7
Ratcliff Rd, E7 . . . . .97 J5
Rathbone Mkt, E16
  off Barking Rd 115 F5
Rathbone Pl, W1 . . . . .17 H3
Rathbone Pt, E5 off Nolan Way . .94 D4
Rathbone St, E16 . . . . .115 F5
  W1 . . . . .17 G2
Rathcoole Av, N8 . . . . .75 F4
Rathcoole Gdns, N8 . . . . .75 F5
Rathfern Rd, SE6 . . . . .171 J1
Rathgar Av, W13 . . . . .125 E1
Rathgar Cl, N3 . . . . .72 C2
Rathgar Rd, SW9
  off Coldharbour La 151 H3
Rathmell Dr, SW4 . . . . .150 D6
Rathmore Rd, SE7 . . . . .135 H5
Rattray Rd, SW2 . . . . .151 G4
Raul Rd, SE15 . . . . .152 D2
Raveley St, NW5 . . . . .92 C4
Raven Cl, NW9 off Eagle Dr . .70/71 G2
Raven Ct, E5 off Stellman Cl 94 D3
Ravenet St, SW11
  off Strasburg Rd 150 B1
Ravenfield Rd, SW17 . . . . .167 J3

Ravenhill Rd, E13 . . . . .115 J2
Ravenna Rd, SW15 . . . . .148 A5
Ravenoak Way, Chig. IG7 . . . . . . .65 H5
Ravenor Pk Rd, Grnf. UB6 . . . . .103 H3
Raven Rd, E18 . . . . .79 J2
Raven Row, E1 . . . . .113 E5
Ravensbourne Av, Beck. BR3 . . .172 D7
  Bromley BR2 . . . . .172 D7
Ravensbourne Gdns, W13 . . . . . .104 E5
  Ilford IG5 . . . . .80 D1
Ravensbourne Pk, SE6 . . . . .154 A7
Ravensbourne Pk Cres, SE6 . . . .153 J7
Ravensbourne Pl, SE13 . . . . . . .154 B2
Ravensbourne Rd, SE6 . . . . .153 J7
  Bromley BR1 . . . . .191 G3
  Twickenham TW1 . . . . .145 F6
Ravensbury Av, Mord. SM4 . . . . .185 F5
Ravensbury Ct, Mitch. CR4
  off Ravensbury Gro 185 G4
Ravensbury Gro, Mitch. CR4 . . . .185 G4
Ravensbury La, Mitch. CR4 . . . . .185 G4
Ravensbury Path, Mitch. CR4 . . .185 G4
Ravensbury Rd, SW18 . . . . .166 D2
  Orpington BR5 . . . . .193 J4
Ravensbury Ter, SW18 . . . . .166 E2
Ravenscar Rd, Brom. BR1 . . . . . .172 E4
  Surbiton KT6 . . . . .195 J2
Ravens Cl, Brom. BR2 . . . . .191 F2
  Chessington KT9 . . . . .181 G6
  Enfield EN1 . . . . .44 B2
Ravenscourt Av, W6 . . . . .127 G4
Ravenscourt Gdns, W6 . . . . .127 G4
Ravenscourt Pk, W6 . . . . .127 G3
Ravenscourt Pl, W6 . . . . .127 H4
Ravenscourt Rd, W6 . . . . .127 H4
Ravenscourt Sq, W6 . . . . .127 G3
Ravenscraig Rd, N11 . . . . .58 B4
Ravenscroft Av, NW11 . . . . .72 C7
  Wembley HA9 . . . . .87 J1
Ravenscroft Cl, E16 . . . . .115 G5
Ravenscroft Cres, SE9 . . . . .174 C3
Ravenscroft Pk, Barn. EN5 . . . . . .40 A4
Ravenscroft Pt, E9
  off Kenton Rd 95 G6
Ravenscroft Rd, E16 . . . . .115 G5
  W4 .126 C4
  Beckenham BR3 . . . . .189 F2
Ravenscroft St, E2 . . . . .13 G2
Ravensdale Av, N12 . . . . .57 F4
Ravensdale Gdns, SE19 . . . . . . .170 A7
  Hounslow TW4 . . . . .142 E3
Ravensdale Rd, N16 . . . . .76 C7
  Hounslow TW4 . . . . .142 E3
Ravensdon St, SE11 . . . . .35 F4
Ravensfield Cl, Dag. RM9 . . . . . .100 D4
Ravensfield Gdns, Epsom KT19 . .197 E5
Ravenshaw St, NW6 . . . . .90 C5
Ravenshill, Chis. BR7 . . . . .192 E1
Ravenshurst Av, NW4 . . . . .71 J4
Ravenside Cl, N18 . . . . .61 G6
Ravenside Retail Pk, N18 . . . . . . .61 G5
Ravenslea Rd, SW12 . . . . .149 J7
Ravensmead Rd, Brom. BR2 . . . .172 D7
Ravensmede Way, W4 . . . . .127 F4
Ravens Ms, SE12
  off Ravens Way 155 G5
Ravenstone, SE17 . . . . .36 E4
Ravenstone Rd, N8 . . . . .75 G3
  NW9 off West Hendon Bdy 71 F6
Ravenstone St, SW12 . . . . .168 A1
Ravens Way, SE12 . . . . .155 G5
Ravenswood, Bex. DA5 . . . . .177 E1
Ravenswood Av, Surb. KT6 . . . . .195 J2
  West Wickham BR4 . . . . .204 C1
Ravenswood Ct, Kings.T. KT2 . . .164 B6
Ravenswood Cres, Har. HA2 . . . . .85 F2
  West Wickham BR4 . . . . .204 C1
Ravenswood Gdns, Islw. TW7 . . .144 B1
Ravenswood Pk, Nthwd. HA6 . . . .50 A6
Ravenswood Rd, E17 . . . . .78 B4
  SW12 . . . . .150 B7
  Croydon CR0 . . . . .201 H3
Ravensworth Rd, NW10 . . . . . . .107 H3
  SE9 .174 C4
Ravey St, EC2 . . . . .12 D5
Ravine Gro, SE18 . . . . .137 H6
Rav Pinter Cl, N16 . . . . .76 B7
Rawlings Cl, Beck. BR3
  off Creswell Dr 190 B5
  Orpington BR6 . . . . .207 J5
Rawlings Cres, Wem. HA9 . . . . . .88 B3
Rawlings St, SW3 . . . . .31 J1
Rawlins Cl, N3 . . . . .72 B3
  South Croydon CR2 . . . . .203 H7
Rawnsley Av, Mitch. CR4 . . . . . . .185 G5
Rawreth Wk, N1 off Basire St . . .111 J1
Rawson St, SW11
  off Strasburg Rd 150 A1
Rawsthorne Cl, E16
  off Kennard St 136 C1
Rawstone Wk, E13 . . . . .115 G2
Rawstorne Pl, EC1 . . . . .11 G3
Rawstorne St, EC1 . . . . .11 G3
Ray Cl, Chess. KT9
  off Merritt Gdns 195 F6

Raydean Rd, Barn. EN5 . . . . .40 E5
Raydons Gdns, Dag. RM9 . . . . . .101 E5
Raydons Rd, Dag. RM9 . . . . .100 E5
Raydon St, N19 . . . . .92 B2
Rayfield Cl, Brom. BR2 . . . . .192 B6
Rayford Av, SE12 . . . . .155 F7
Ray Gdns, Bark. IG11 . . . . .118 A2
  Stanmore HA7 . . . . .53 E5
Rayleas Cl, SE18 . . . . .156 E1
Rayleigh Av, Tedd. TW11 . . . . . . .162 B6
Rayleigh Cl, N13
  off Rayleigh Rd 60 A3
Rayleigh Ct, Kings.T. KT1 . . . . . .181 J2
Rayleigh Ri, S.Croy. CR2 . . . . . .202 B6
Rayleigh Rd, E16 . . . . .135 H1
  N13 .59 J3
  SW19 . . . . .184 C1
  Woodford Green IG8 . . . . .63 J6
Ray Lo Rd, Wdf.Grn. IG8 . . . . . . .63 J6
Ray Massey Way, E6
  off Ron Leighton Way 116 B1
Raymead, NW4
  off Tenterden Gro 71 J4
Raymead Av, Th.Hth. CR7 . . . . . .187 G5
Raymead Pas, Th.Hth. CR7
  off Raymead Av 187 G5
Raymere Gdns, SE18 . . . . .137 G7
Raymond Av, E18 . . . . .79 F3
  W13 . . . . .124 D3
Raymond Bldgs, WC1 . . . . .18 D1
Raymond Cl, SE26 . . . . .171 F5
Raymond Ct, N10
  off Pembroke Rd 58 A7
  Sutton SM2
  off Mulgrave Rd 198/199 E6
Raymond Rd, E13 . . . . .97 J7
  SW19 . . . . .166 B6
  Beckenham BR3 . . . . .189 H4
  Ilford IG2 . . . . .81 G7
Raymond Way, Esher (Clay.)
  KT10 . . . . .194 D6
Raymouth Rd, SE16 . . . . .133 E4
Rayne Ct, E18 . . . . .79 F4
Rayners Cl, Wem. HA0 . . . . .87 G5
Rayners Ct, Har. HA2 . . . . .85 G1
Rayners Cres, Nthlt. UB5 . . . . . .102 B3
Rayners Gdns, Nthlt. UB5 . . . . . .102 B2
RAYNERS LANE, Har. HA2 . . . . . .85 F2
Rayners La, Har. HA2 . . . . .85 H2
  Pinner HA5 . . . . .67 F6
Rayners Rd, SW15 . . . . .148 B5
Rayner Twr, E10 . . . . .78 A7
Raynes Av, E11 . . . . .79 J7
RAYNES PARK, SW20 . . . . .183 H3
Raynham Av, N18 . . . . .60 D6
Raynham Rd, N18 . . . . .60 D5
  W6 .127 H4
Raynham Ter, N18 . . . . .60 D5
Raynor Cl, Sthl. UB1 . . . . .123 F1
Raynor Pl, N1 off Elizabeth Av . . .111 J1
Raynton Cl, Har. HA2 . . . . .85 E1
Ray Rd, W.Mol. KT8 . . . . .179 H5
Rays Av, N18 . . . . .61 F4
Rays Rd, N18 . . . . .61 F4
  West Wickham BR4 . . . . .190 C7
Ray St, EC1 . . . . .11 F6
Ray St Br, EC1 . . . . .11 F6
Ray Wk, N7 off Andover Rd 93 F2
Raywood Cl, Hayes UB3 . . . . . . .121 F7
Reachview Cl, NW1
  off Baynes St 92 C7
Read Cl, T.Ditt. KT7 . . . . .180 D7
Reade Wk, NW10
  off Denbigh Cl 88/89 E7
Reading La, E8 . . . . .94 E6
Reading Rd, Nthlt. UB5 . . . . .85 H5
  Sutton SM1 . . . . .199 F5
Reading Way, NW7 . . . . .56 A5
Reads Cl, Ilf. IG1
  off Chapel Rd 98/99 E3
Reapers Cl, NW1
  off Crofters Way 110 D1
Reapers Way, Islw. TW7
  off Hall Rd 144 A5
Reardon Ct, N21
  off Cosgrove Cl 59 J2
Reardon Path, E1 . . . . .133 E1
Reardon St, E1 . . . . .132 E1
Reaston St, SE14 . . . . .133 F7
Reckitt Rd, W4 . . . . .126 E5
Record St, SE15 . . . . .133 F6
Recovery St, SW17 . . . . .167 H5
Recreation Av, Rom. RM7 . . . . . . .83 J5
Recreation Rd, SE26 . . . . .171 G4
  Bromley BR2 . . . . .191 F2
  Sidcup DA15
  off Woodside Rd 175 H3
  Southall UB2 . . . . .122 C4
Recreation Way, Mitch. CR4 . . . .186 D3
Rector St, N1 . . . . .111 J1
Rectory Cl, E4 . . . . .62 A3
  N3 . . . . .72 C1
  SW20 . . . . .183 J3
  Sidcup DA14 . . . . .176 B4
  Stanmore HA7 . . . . .53 E6

Rectory Cl, Surb. KT6 . . . . .195 F1
Rectory Cres, E11 . . . . .79 J6
Rectory Fld Cres, SE7 . . . . .135 J7
Rectory Gdns, N8 . . . . .74 E4
  SW4 off Fitzwilliam Rd 150 C3
  Northolt UB5 . . . . .103 F1
Rectory Grn, Beck. BR3 . . . . . . .189 J1
Rectory Gro, SW4 . . . . .150 C3
  Croydon CR0 . . . . .201 H2
  Hampton TW12 . . . . .161 F4
Rectory La, SW17 . . . . .168 A6
  Edgware HA8 . . . . .54 A6
  Loughton IG10 . . . . .48 D2
  Sidcup DA14 . . . . .176 B4
  Stanmore HA7 . . . . .52 E5
  Surbiton KT6 . . . . .195 E1
  Wallington SM6 . . . . .200 C4
Rectory Orchard, SW19 . . . . . . .166 B4
Rectory Pk Av, Nthlt. UB5 . . . . . .103 F3
Rectory Pl, SE18 . . . . .136 D4
Rectory Rd, E12 . . . . .98 C5
  E17 .78 B3
  N16 .94 C3
  SW13 . . . . .147 G2
  W3 .126 B1
  Beckenham BR3 . . . . .190 A1
  Dagenham RM10 . . . . .101 G7
  Hayes UB3 . . . . .102 A6
  Hounslow TW4 . . . . .142 B1
  Keston BR2 . . . . .206 A7
  Southall UB2 . . . . .123 F3
  Sutton SM1 . . . . .198 D3
Rectory Sq, E1 . . . . .113 G5
Reculver Ms, N18
  off Lyndhurst Rd 60 D4
Reculver Rd, SE16 . . . . .133 G5
Red Anchor Cl, SW3 . . . . .31 G6
Redan Pl, W2 . . . . .14 A4
Redan St, W14 . . . . .128 A3
Redan Ter, SE5 off Flaxman Rd . .151 J2
Red Barracks Rd, SE18 . . . . .136 C4
Redberry Gro, SE26 . . . . .171 F3
Redbourne Av, N3 . . . . .72 D1
Redbourne Dr, SE28 . . . . .118 D6
REDBRIDGE, Ilf. IG 80 C6
Redbridge Enterprise Cen, Ilf.
  IG1 .99 F2
Redbridge Gdns, SE5 . . . . .132 B7
Redbridge La E, Ilf. IG4 . . . . .80 A6
Redbridge La W, E11 . . . . .79 H6
Redburn St, SW3 . . . . .31 J5
Redcar Cl, Nthlt. UB5 . . . . .85 H5
Redcar St, SE5 . . . . .131 J7
Redcastle Cl, E1 . . . . .113 F7
Redcliffe Cl, SW5
  off Warwick Rd 128/129 E5
Redcliffe Gdns, SW5 . . . . .30 B4
  SW10 . . . . .30 B4
  W4 .126 B7
  Ilford IG1 . . . . .98 D1
Redcliffe Ms, SW10 . . . . .30 B4
Redcliffe Pl, SW10 . . . . .30 C6
Redcliffe Rd, SW10 . . . . .30 C4
Redcliffe Sq, SW10 . . . . .30 B4
Redcliffe St, SW10 . . . . .30 B5
Redclose Av, Mord. SM4 . . . . . . .184 D5
Redclyffe Rd, E6 . . . . .115 J1
Redcroft Rd, Sthl. UB1 . . . . .103 J7
Redcross Way, SE1 . . . . .28 A3
Reddings, The, NW7 . . . . .55 F3
Reddings Cl, NW7 . . . . .55 F4
Reddins Rd, SE15 . . . . .37 H6
Reddons Rd, Beck. BR3 . . . . . . .171 H7
Redenham Ho, SW15
  off Tangley Gro 147 F7
Rede Pl, W2 off Chepstow Pl 108 D6
Redesdale Gdns, Islw. TW7 . . . . .124 D7
Redesdale St, SW3 . . . . .31 H5
Redfern Av, Houns. TW4 . . . . . . .143 G7
Redfern Rd, NW10 . . . . .89 E7
  SE6 .154 C7
Redfield La, SW5 . . . . .128 D4
Redfield Ms, SW5
  off Redfield La 128 D4
Redford Av, Th.Hth. CR7 . . . . . . .187 F4
  Wallington SM6 . . . . .200 E6
Redford Wk, N1
  off Britannia Row 111 H1
Redgate Dr, Brom. BR2 . . . . .205 H2
Redgate Ter, SW15
  off Lytton Gro 148 A6
Redgrave Cl, Croy. CR0 . . . . .188 C6
Redgrave Rd, SW15 . . . . .148 A3
Red Hill, Chis. BR7 . . . . .174 D5
Redhill Dr, Edg. HA8 . . . . .70 C2
Redhill St, NW1 . . . . .8 E3
Red Ho La, Bexh. DA6 . . . . .158 D4
Redhouse Rd, Croy. CR0 . . . . . . .186 D6
Red Ho Sq, N1 off Ashby Gro 93 J6
★ Red Ho (William Morris Ho), The,
  Bexh. DA6 . . . . .158 E4
Redington Gdns, NW3 . . . . .90 E4
Redington Rd, NW3 . . . . .90 E4

Redland Gdns, W.Mol. KT8
  off Dunstable Rd **179** F4
Redlands Ct, Brom. BR1 . . . .**173** F7
Redlands Rd, Enf. EN3 . . . .**45** H1
Redlands Way, SW2 . . . .**151** F7
Red La, Esher (Clay.) KT10 . .**194** D6
Redleaf Cl, Belv. DA17 . . . . . .**139** G6
Redlees Cl, Islw. TW7 . . . .**144** B4
Red Lion Cl, SE17 . . . .**36** A5
Red Lion Ct, EC4 . . . .**19** F3
Red Lion Hill, N2 . . . .**73** G2
Red Lion La, SE18 . . . .**136** D7
Red Lion Pl, SE18
  off Shooter's Hill Rd **156** D1
Red Lion Rd, Surb. KT6 . . . . . .**195** J2
Red Lion Row, SE17 . . . .**36** A5
Red Lion Sq, SW18
  off Wandsworth High St **148** D5
  WC1 . . . .**18** C2
Red Lion St, WC1 . . . .**18** C1
  Richmond TW9 . . . .**145** G5
Red Lion Yd, W1 . . . .**24** C1
Red Lo Rd, Beck. BR3 . . . .**190** D6
  West Wickham BR4 . . . .**204** C1
Redman Cl, Nthlt. UB5 . . . . . .**102** C2
Redman's Rd, E1 . . . .**113** F5
Redmead La, E1 . . . .**29** H2
Redmead Rd, Hayes UB3 . . . .**121** H4
Redmore Rd, W6 . . . .**127** H4
Red Oak Cl, Orp. BR6 . . . .**207** E3
Red Path, E9 . . . .**95** J6
Red Pl, W1 . . . .**16** B5
Redpoll Way, Erith DA18 . . . .**138** D3
Red Post Hill, SE21 . . . .**152** A5
  SE24 . . . .**152** A4
Redriffe Rd, E13 . . . .**115** F1
Redriff Est, SE16 . . . .**133** J3
Redriff Rd, SE16 . . . .**133** G4
  Romford RM7 . . . .**83** H2
Redroofs Cl, Beck. BR3 . . . . . .**190** B1
Redruth Cl, N22
  off Palmerston Rd **59** F7
Redruth Rd, E9 . . . .**113** G1
Redvers St, N1 . . . .**13** E3
Redvers Rd, N22 . . . .**75** G2
Redwald Rd, E5 . . . .**95** G4
Redway Dr, Twick. TW2 . . . . .**143** J7
Redwing Path, SE28 . . . .**137** G2
Redwing Rd, Wall. SM6 . . . . .**201** E7
Redwood Cl, E3 . . . .**114** A2
  N14 *off The Vale* **42** D7
  SE16 . . . .**133** H1
  Buckhurst Hill IG9
    off Beech La **63** H2
  Sidcup DA15 . . . .**158** A7
  Watford WD19 . . . .**50** C4
Redwood Ct, NW6
  off The Avenue **90** B7
Redwood Est, Houns. TW5 . .**122** B6
Redwood Gdns, E4 . . . .**46** B6
Redwood Ms, SW4
  off Hannington Rd **150** B3
Redwoods, SW15 . . . .**165** G1
Redwood Wk, Surb. KT6 . . . .**195** G1
Redwood Way, Barn. EN5 . . . .**40** A5
Reece Ms, SW7 . . . .**30** E1
Reed Av, Orp. BR6 . . . .**207** H3
Reed Cl, E16 . . . .**115** G5
  SE12 . . . .**155** G5
Reede Gdns, Dag. RM10 . . . .**101** H5
Reede Rd, Dag. RM10 . . . . . .**101** G6
Reede Way, Dag. RM10 . . . . .**101** H6
Reedham Cl, N17 . . . .**76** E4
Reedham St, SE15 . . . .**152** D2
Reedholm Vil, N16
  off Winston Rd **94** A4
Reed Rd, N17 . . . .**76** C2
Reeds Pl, NW1 *off Royal Coll St* . .**92** C7
Reedworth St, SE11 . . . .**35** F2
Ree La Cotts, Loug. IG10
  off Englands La **48** D2
Reenglass Rd, Stan. HA7 . . . . .**53** G4
Rees Dr, Stan. HA7 . . . .**53** H4
Rees Gdns, Croy. CR0 . . . . . .**188** C6
Reesland Cl, E12 . . . .**98** D6
Rees St, N1 . . . .**111** J1
Reets Fm Cl, NW9 . . . .**71** E6
Reeves Av, NW9 . . . .**70** D7
Reeves Cor, Croy. CR0
  off Roman Way **201** H2
Reeves Ms, W1 . . . .**16** B6
Reeves Rd, E3 . . . .**114** B4
  SE18 . . . .**136** E6
Reflection, The, E16
  off Woolwich Manor
    Way **136/137** E2
Reform Row, N17 . . . .**76** C2
Reform St, SW11 . . . .**149** J2
Regal Cl, E1 . . . .**21** J1
  W5 . . . .**105** G5

Regal Ct, N18 *off College Cl* **60** C5
Regal Cres, Wall. SM6 . . . . . .**200** B3
Regal Dr, N11 . . . .**58** B5
Regal La, NW1
  off Regents Pk Rd **110** A1
Regal Pl, E3 *off Coborn St* **113** J3
  SW6 *off Maxwell Rd* **128/129** E7
Regal Row, SE15
  off Astbury Rd **153** F1
Regal Way, Har. HA3 . . . .**69** H6
Regan Way, N1 . . . .**12** D2
Regatta Ho, Tedd. TW11
  off Twickenham Rd **162** D4
Regency Cl, W5 . . . .**105** H6
  Chigwell IG7 . . . .**65** F5
  Hampton TW12 . . . .**161** F5
Regency Ct, Sutt. SM1
  off Brunswick Rd **198/199** E4
Regency Cres, NW4 . . . .**72** A2
Regency Ho, SW6
  off The Boulevard **149** F1
Regency Lo, Buck.H. IG9 . . . . .**64** A2
Regency Ms, NW10 *off High Rd* . .**89** G6
  SW9 *off Lothian Rd* **131** H7
  Beckenham BR3 . . . .**190** C1
  Isleworth TW7
    off Queensbridge Pk **144** B5
Regency Pl, SW1 . . . .**33** J1
Regency St, SW1 . . . .**33** H1
Regency Ter, SW7
  off Fulham Rd **129** G5
Regency Wk, Croy. CR0 . . . . .**189** H6
  Richmond TW10
    off Grosvenor Rd **145** H5
Regency Way, Bexh. DA6 . . . .**158** D3
Regent Cl, N12 *off Nether St* **57** F5
  Harrow HA3 . . . .**69** H6
  Hounslow TW4 . . . .**142** B1
Regent Gdns, Ilf. IG3 . . . .**82** A6
Regent Pl, SW19
  off Haydons Rd **166/167** E5
  W1 . . . .**17** G5
  Croydon CR0 *off Grant Rd* . .**202** C1
Regent Rd, SE24 . . . .**151** H6
  Surbiton KT5 . . . .**181** J5
Regents Av, N13 . . . .**59** F5
Regents Br Gdns, SW8 . . . .**34** B7
Regents Cl, S.Croy. CR2 . . . . .**202** B6
Regents Dr, Kes. BR2 . . . .**206** A5
  Woodford Green IG8 . . . . . .**64** D7
Regents Ms, NW8 . . . .**6** D1
REGENT'S PARK, NW1 . . . .**8** C2
 ★ Regent's Park, NW1 . . . .**7** J3
Regent's Pk Est, NW1 . . . .**9** F4
Regents Pk Rd, N3 . . . .**72** C3
  NW1 . . . .**109** J1
Regents Pk Ter, NW1
  off Oval Rd **110** B1
Regent's Pl, SE3 . . . .**155** G2
Regents Pl, Loug. IG10 . . . . . .**48** A7
Regent Sq, E3 . . . .**114** B3
  WC1 . . . .**10** B4
  Belvedere DA17 . . . .**139** H4
Regents Row, E8 . . . .**112** D1
Regent St, NW10
  off Wellington Rd **108** A3
  SW1 . . . .**17** H6
  W1 . . . .**17** E3
  W4 . . . .**126** A5
Regents Wf, N1 . . . .**10** C1
Regina Cl, Barn. EN5 . . . .**40** A3
Reginald Rd, E7 . . . .**97** G7
  SE8 . . . .**134** A7
Reginald Sq, SE8 . . . .**134** A7
Regina Pt, SE16 *off Renforth St* .**133** F3
Regina Rd, N4 . . . .**93** F1
  SE25 . . . .**188** D3
  W13 . . . .**124** D1
  Southall UB2 . . . .**122** E4
Regina Ter, W13 . . . .**124** D1
Regis Pl, SW2 . . . .**151** F4
Regis Rd, NW5 . . . .**92** B5
Regnart Bldgs, NW1 . . . .**9** G5
Reid Cl, Pnr. HA5 . . . .**66** A4
Reidhaven Rd, SE18 . . . .**137** H4
Reigate Av, Sutt. SM1 . . . .**198** D1
Reigate Rd, Brom. BR1 . . . . . .**173** F3
  Ilford IG3 . . . .**99** J2
Reigate Way, Wall. SM6 . . . . .**201** E5
Reighton Rd, E5 . . . .**94** D3
Reinickendorf Av, SE9 . . . . . .**157** F5
Reizel Cl, N16 . . . .**94** C1
Relay Rd, W12 . . . .**107** J2
Relf Rd, SE15 . . . .**152** D3
Reliance Sq, EC2 . . . .**13** E5
Relko Gdns, Sutt. SM1 . . . . . .**199** G5
Relton Ms, SW7 . . . .**23** H5
Rembrandt Cl, E14 . . . .**134** D3
  SW1 . . . .**32** B2
Rembrandt Ct, Epsom KT19 . .**197** F6
Rembrandt Rd, SE13 . . . .**154** E4
  Edgware HA8 . . . .**70** A2
Remington Rd, E6 . . . .**116** B6
  N15 . . . .**76** A6
Remington St, N1 . . . .**11** H2

Remnant St, WC2 . . . .**18** C3
Remus Rd, E3 *off Monier Rd* . . .**96** A7
Renaissance Wk, SE10
  off Teal St **135** F3
Rendle Cl, Croy. CR0 . . . .**188** C5
Rendlesham Rd, E5 . . . .**94** D4
  Enfield EN2 . . . .**43** H1
Renforth St, SE16 . . . .**133** F2
Renfrew Cl, E6 . . . .**116** D7
Renfrew Rd, SE11 . . . .**35** G1
  Hounslow TW4 . . . .**142** D2
  Kingston upon Thames KT2 .**164** B7
Renmuir St, SW17 . . . .**167** J6
Rennell St, SE13 . . . .**154** C3
Rennels Way, Islw. TW7
  off St. John's Rd **144** B2
Renness Rd, E17 . . . .**77** H3
Rennets Cl, SE9 . . . .**157** H5
Rennets Wd Rd, SE9 . . . .**157** G5
Rennie Est, SE16 . . . .**133** E4
Rennie St, SE1 . . . .**27** G1
Renovation, The, E16
  off Woolwich Manor
    Way **136/137** E2
Renown Cl, Croy. CR0 . . . .**201** H1
  Romford RM7 . . . .**83** G1
Rensburg Rd, E17 . . . .**77** G5
Renshaw Cl, Belv. DA17
  off Grove Rd **139** F6
Renters Av, NW4 . . . .**71** J6
Renwick Ind Est, Bark. IG11 .**118** B1
Renwick Rd, Bark. IG11 . . . . .**118** B1
Repens Way, Hayes UB4
  off Stipularis Dr **102** D4
Rephidim St, SE1 . . . .**28** D6
Replingham Rd, SW18 . . . . . .**166** C1
Reporton Rd, SW6 . . . .**148** B1
Repository Rd, SE18 . . . .**136** C6
Repton Av, Hayes UB3 . . . . . .**121** G4
  Wembley HA0 . . . .**87** F4
Repton Cl, Cars. SM5 . . . .**199** H5
Repton Ct, Beck. BR3 . . . .**190** B1
  Ilford IG5 *off Repton Gro* . . .**80** C1
Repton Gro, Ilf. IG5 . . . .**80** C1
Repton Rd, Har. HA3 . . . .**69** J4
  Orpington BR6 . . . .**207** J3
Repton St, E14 . . . .**113** H6
Repulse Cl, Rom. RM5 . . . .**83** H1
Reservoir Cl, Th.Hth. CR7 . . . .**188** A4
Reservoir Rd, N14 . . . .**42** C5
  SE4 . . . .**153** H2
Resham Cl, Sthl. UB2 . . . .**122** C3
Resolution Wk, SE18 . . . .**136** C5
Resolution Way, SE8
  off Deptford High St **134** A7
Restell Cl, SE3 . . . .**135** E6
Restmor Way, Wall. SM6 . . . .**200** A2
Reston Pl, SW7 . . . .**22** C4
Restons Cres, SE9 . . . .**157** G6
Restormel Cl, Houns. TW3 . . .**143** G5
Retcar Cl, N19
  off Dartmouth Pk Hill **92** B2
Retcar Pl, N19 . . . .**92** B2
Retford St, N1 . . . .**13** E2
Retingham Way, E4 . . . .**62** B2
Retreat, The, NW9 . . . .**70** D5
  SW14
    off South Worple Way . .**146/147** E3
  Harrow HA2 . . . .**67** G7
  Surbiton KT5 . . . .**181** J6
  Thornton Heath CR7 . . . . . .**188** A4
  Worcester Park KT4 . . . . . .**197** H3
Retreat Cl, Har. HA3 . . . .**69** F5
Retreat Pl, E9 . . . .**95** F6
Retreat Rd, Rich. TW9 . . . . . .**145** G5
Reunion Row, E1
  off Pennington St **112/113** E7
Reveley Sq, SE16
  off Howland Way **133** H2
Revell Ri, SE18 . . . .**137** J6
Revell Rd, Kings.T. KT1 . . . . .**182** B1
  Sutton SM1 . . . .**198** C6
Revelon Rd, SE4 . . . .**153** H4
Revelstoke Rd, SW18 . . . .**166** C2
Reventlow Rd, SE9 . . . .**175** F1
Reverdy Rd, SE1 . . . .**37** H2
Reverend Cl, Har. HA2 . . . .**85** H3
Revesby Rd, Cars. SM5 . . . . . .**185** G6
Review Rd, NW2 . . . .**89** F2
  Dagenham RM10 . . . .**119** H1
Rewell St, SW6 . . . .**129** F7
Rewley Rd, Cars. SM5 . . . .**185** G6
Rex Pl, W1 . . . .**16** C6
Reydon Av, E11 . . . .**79** J6
Reynard Cl, SE4 *off Foxwell St* .**153** H3
  Bromley BR1 . . . .**192** C3
Reynard Dr, SE19 . . . .**170** C7
Reynard Pl, SE14
  off Milton Ct Rd **133** H6
Reynardson Rd, N17 . . . .**59** J7
Reynolah Gdns, SE7
  off Rathmore Rd **135** H5
Reynolds Av, E12 . . . .**98** D5
  Chessington KT9 . . . .**195** H7
  Romford RM6 . . . .**82** C7
Reynolds Cl, NW11 . . . .**72** E7

Reynolds Cl, SW19 . . . .**185** G1
  Carshalton SM5 . . . .**199** J1
Reynolds Ct, E11
  off Cobbold Rd **97** F3
  Romford RM6 . . . .**82** D3
Reynolds Dr, Edg. HA8 . . . . . .**69** J3
Reynolds Pl, SE3 . . . .**135** H7
  Richmond TW10
    off Cambrian Rd **145** J6
Reynolds Rd, SE15 . . . .**153** F5
  W4 . . . .**126** C3
  Hayes UB4 . . . .**102** C4
  New Malden KT3 . . . .**182** D7
Reynolds Way, Croy. CR0 . . . .**202** B4
Rheidol Ms, N1 . . . .**11** J1
Rheidol Ter, N1 . . . .**11** H1
Rheola Cl, N17 . . . .**76** C1
Rhoda St, E2 . . . .**13** G5
Rhodes Av, N22 . . . .**74** C1
Rhodesia Rd, E11 . . . .**96** D2
  SW9 . . . .**151** E2
Rhodes Moorhouse Ct, Mord.
  SM4 . . . .**184** D6
Rhodes St, N7
  off Mackenzie Rd **93** F5
Rhodeswell Rd, E14 . . . .**113** H5
Rhodrons Av, Chess. KT9 . . . .**195** H5
Rhondda Gro, E3 . . . .**113** H3
Rhyl Rd, Grnf. UB6 . . . .**104** C2
Rhyl St, NW5 . . . .**92** A6
Rhys Av, N11 . . . .**58** D7
Rialto Rd, Mitch. CR4 . . . .**186** A2
Ribble Cl, Wdf.Grn. IG8
  off Prospect Rd **63** J6
Ribblesdale Av, N11 . . . .**58** A6
  Northolt UB5 . . . .**85** H6
Ribblesdale Rd, N8 . . . .**75** F4
  SW16 . . . .**168** B6
Ribbon Dance Ms, SE5
  off Camberwell Gro **152** A1
Ribchester Av, Grnf. UB6 . . . .**104** C3
Ribston Cl, Brom. BR2 . . . . . .**206** C1
Ricardo Path, SE28 *off Byron Cl* .**138** C1
Ricardo St, E14 . . . .**114** B6
Ricards Rd, SW19 . . . .**166** C5
Richard Cl, SE18 . . . .**136** B4
Richard Fell Ho, E12
  off Walton Rd **98** D4
Richard Foster Cl, E17 . . . .**77** J7
Richard Ho Dr, E16 . . . .**116** A6
Richards Av, Rom. RM7 . . . . . .**83** J5
Richards Pl, Har. HA1 . . . .**68** D5
  Hayes UB3 . . . .**121** G6
Richardson Cl, E8
  off Clarissa St **112** C1
Richardson Rd, E15 . . . .**114** E2
Richardson's Ms, W1 . . . .**9** F6
Richards Pl, E17 . . . .**78** A3
  SW3 . . . .**31** H1
Richard St, E1
  off Commercial Rd **112/113** E6
Richbell Pl, WC1 . . . .**18** C1
Richborne Ter, SW8 . . . .**34** D7
Richborough Rd, NW2 . . . .**90** A4
Richens Cl, Houns. TW3 . . . . .**144** A2
Riches Rd, Ilf. IG1 . . . .**99** F2
Richford Rd, E15 . . . .**115** F1
Richford St, W6 . . . .**127** J2
Richlands Av, Epsom KT17 . . .**197** G4
Rich La, SW5 . . . .**30** A4
RICHMOND, TW9 & TW10 . . .**145** H6
Richmond Av, E4 . . . .**62** D5
  N1 . . . .**111** F1
  NW10 . . . .**89** J6
  SW20 . . . .**184** B1
  Feltham TW14 . . . .**141** H6
Richmond Br, Rich. TW9 . . . .**145** G6
  Twickenham TW1 . . . .**145** G6
Richmond Bldgs, W1 . . . .**17** H4
Richmond Cl, E17 . . . .**77** J6
  Borehamwood WD6 . . . .**38** D5
Richmond Cres, E4 . . . .**62** D5
  N1 . . . .**111** F1
  N9 . . . .**60** D1
Richmond Dr, Wdf.Grn. IG8 . . .**64** D7
Richmond Gdns, NW4 . . . .**71** G5
  Harrow HA3 . . . .**52** C6
Richmond Grn, Croy. CR0 . . .**201** E3
Richmond Gro, N1 . . . .**93** H7
  Surbiton KT5 . . . .**181** J6
Richmond Hill, Rich. TW10 . .**145** H6
Richmond Hill Ct, Rich. TW10 .**145** H6
Richmond Ms, W1 . . . .**17** H4
  Teddington TW11
    off Broad St **162** C6
 ★ Richmond Palace (remains),
    Rich. TW9 . . . .**145** F5
 ★ Richmond Park, Rich. TW10 .**164** A1
Richmond Pk, Kings.T. KT2 . .**164** A1
  Loughton IG10
    off Fallow Flds **47** J7
  Richmond TW10 . . . .**164** A1
Richmond Pk Rd, SW14 . . . . .**146** C5
  Kingston upon Thames KT2 .**163** H7
Richmond Pl, SE18 . . . .**137** F4

Richmond Rd, E4 . . . . .62 D1
  E7 . . . . .97 H5
  E8 . . . . .94 C7
  E11 .96 D2
  N2 . . . . .73 F2
  N11 .58 E6
  N15 .76 B6
  SW20 . . . . .183 H1
  W5 .125 H2
  Barnet EN5 . . . . .41 G5
  Croydon CR0 . . . . .200 E3
  Ilford IG1 . . . . .99 F3
  Isleworth TW7 . . . . .144 D3
  Kingston upon Thames KT2 .163 G5
  Thornton Heath CR7 . . . . . .187 H3
  Twickenham TW1 . . . . .145 H4
Richmond St, E13 . . . . .115 G2
Richmond Ter, SW1 . . . . .26 A3
Richmond Ter Ms, SW1
  off Parliament St 130/131 E2
Richmond Way, E11 . . . . .97 G2
  W12 . . . . .128 A2
  W14 . . . . .128 A3
Richmount Gdns, SE3 . . . . .155 G3
Rich St, E14 . . . . .113 J7
Rickard Cl, NW4 . . . . .71 H4
  SW2 . . . . .169 F1
  West Drayton UB7 . . . . .120 A3
Rickards Cl, Surb. KT6 . . . . . . .195 H1
Rickett St, SW6 . . . . .128 D6
Rickman St, E1 off Mantus Rd . .113 F3
Rickmansworth Rd, Pnr. HA5 . .66 B2
Rick Roberts Way, E15 . . . . . . .114 C1
Rickthorne Rd, N19
  off Landseer Rd 92/93 E2
Rickyard Path, SE9 . . . . .156 B4
Ridding La, Grnf. UB6 . . . . .86 C5
Riddons Rd, SE12 . . . . .173 J3
Ride, The, Brent. TW8 . . . . . . .125 E5
  Enfield EN3 . . . . .45 F3
Rideout St, SE18 . . . . .136 C4
Rider Cl, Sid. DA15 . . . . .157 H6
Ridgdale St, E3 . . . . .114 B2
Ridge, The, Bex. DA5 . . . . .159 F7
  Orpington BR6 . . . . .207 G2
  Surbiton KT5 . . . . .182 A5
  Twickenham TW2 . . . . .144 A5
Ridge Av, N21 . . . . .43 J7
Ridgebrook Rd, SE3 . . . . .155 J4
Ridge Cl, NW4 . . . . .72 A2
  NW9 . . . . .70 D4
  SE28 . . . . .137 G2
Ridge Crest, Enf. EN2 . . . . .43 F1
Ridgecroft Cl, Bex. DA5 . . . . . .177 J1
Ridge Hill, NW11 . . . . .90 B1
Ridgemont Gdns, Edg. HA8 . . . .54 C4
Ridgemont Av, Croy. CR0 . . . . .203 G1
Ridgemont Cl, SE20 . . . . .170 E7
Ridgemount Gdns, Enf. EN2 . . .43 H2
Ridge Rd, N8 . . . . .75 F6
  N21 . . . . .59 J1
  NW2 . . . . .90 C3
  Mitcham CR4 . . . . .168 B7
  Sutton SM3 . . . . .198 B1
Ridgeview Cl, Barn. EN5 . . . . . .40 A6
Ridgeview Rd, N20 . . . . .57 E3
Ridge Way, SE19
  off Central Hill 170 B6
Ridgeway, SE28
  off Pettman Cres 137 G4
  Bromley BR2 . . . . .205 G2
Ridge Way, Felt. TW13 . . . . . . .160 E3
Ridgeway, Wdf.Grn. IG8 . . . . . .63 J4
Ridgeway, The, E4 . . . . .62 B2
  N3 .56 E7
  N11 . . . . .57 J4
  N14 . . . . .59 E2
  NW7 . . . . .55 G4
  NW9 . . . . .70 E4
  NW11 . . . . .90 C1
  W3 . . . . .126 A3
  Croydon CR0 . . . . .201 F3
  Enfield EN2 . . . . .43 G1
  Harrow (Kenton) HA3 . . . . .69 F5
  Harrow (N.Har.) HA2 . . . . . .67 G6
  Ruislip HA4 . . . . .66 A7
  Stanmore HA7 . . . . .53 F6
Ridgeway Av, Barn. EN4 . . . . . .41 J6
Ridgeway Cres, Orp. BR6 . . . . .207 H3
Ridgeway Cres Gdns, Orp. BR6 .207 H3
Ridgeway Dr, Brom. BR1 . . . . .173 H4
Ridgeway E, Sid. DA15 . . . . . . .157 J5
Ridgeway Gdns, N6 . . . . .74 C7
  Ilford IG4 . . . . .80 B5
Ridgeway Rd, SW9 . . . . .151 H3
  Isleworth TW7 . . . . .124 B7
Ridgeway Rd N, Islw. TW7 . . . .124 B6
Ridgeway Wk, Nthlt. UB5
  off Fortunes Mead 84/85 E6
Ridgeway W, Sid. DA15 . . . . . .157 H5
Ridgewell Cl, N1 off Basire St . .111 J1
  SE26 . . . . .171 J4
  Dagenham RM10 . . . . .119 H1
Ridgmount Gdns, WC1 . . . . .9 H6
Ridgmount Pl, WC1 . . . . .17 H1

Ridgmount Rd, SW18 . . . . .149 E5
Ridgmount St, WC1 . . . . .17 H1
Ridgway, SW19 . . . . .166 A6
Ridgway, The, Sutt. SM2 . . . . .199 G7
Ridgway Gdns, SW19 . . . . .166 A7
Ridgway Pl, SW19 . . . . .166 B6
Ridgwell Rd, E16 . . . . .115 J5
Riding, The, NW11
  off Golders Grn Rd 72 C7
Riding Ho St, W1 . . . . .17 F2
Ridings, The, E11
  off Malcolm Way 79 G5
  W5 . . . . .105 J4
  Sunbury-on-Thames TW16 .178 A1
  Surbiton KT5 . . . . .182 A5
Ridings Av, N21 . . . . .43 H4
Ridings Cl, N6
  off Hornsey La Gdns 74 C7
Ridley Av, W13 . . . . .124 E3
Ridley Cl, Bark. IG11 . . . . .99 J7
Ridley Rd, E7 . . . . .97 J4
  E8 .94 C5
  NW10 . . . . .107 G2
  SW19 . . . . .166 E7
  Bromley BR2 . . . . .191 F3
  Welling DA16 . . . . .158 B1
Ridsdale Rd, SE20 . . . . .188 E1
Riefield Rd, SE9 . . . . .157 F4
Riesco Dr, Croy. CR0 . . . . .203 F6
Riffel Rd, NW2 . . . . .89 J5
Rifle Pl, SE11 . . . . .35 F5
Rifle St, E14 . . . . .114 B5
Rigault Rd, SW6 . . . . .148 B2
Rigby Cl, Croy. CR0 . . . . .201 G3
Rigby La, Hayes UB3 . . . . .121 G2
Rigby Ms, Ilf. IG1
  off Cranbrook Rd 98/99 E2
Rigden St, E14 . . . . .114 B6
Rigeley Rd, NW10 . . . . .107 G3
Rigg App, E10 . . . . .95 G1
Rigge Pl, SW4 . . . . .150 D4
Riggindale Rd, SW16 . . . . .168 D5
Riley Rd, SE1 . . . . .29 E5
Riley St, SW10 . . . . .31 E7
Rinaldo Rd, SW12 . . . . .150 B7
Ring, The, W2 . . . . .15 G5
Ring Cl, Brom. BR1
  off Garden Rd 173 H7
Ringcroft St, N7 . . . . .93 G5
Ringers Rd, Brom. BR1 . . . . . . .191 G3
Ringford Rd, SW18 . . . . .148 C5
Ringlet Cl, E16 . . . . .115 H5
Ringlewell Cl, Enf. EN1
  off Central Av 44/45 E2
Ringmer Av, SW6 . . . . .148 B1
Ringmer Gdns, N19
  off Sussex Way 92/93 E2
Ringmer Pl, N21 . . . . .44 A5
Ringmer Way, Brom. BR1 . . . . .192 C5
Ringmore Ri, SE23 . . . . .153 E7
Ring Rd, W12 . . . . .107 J2
Ringslade Rd, N22 . . . . .75 F2
Ringstead Rd, SE6 . . . . .154 B7
  Sutton SM1 . . . . .199 G4
Ringway, N11 . . . . .58 C6
  Southall UB2 . . . . .123 E5
Ringwold Cl, Beck. BR3 . . . . . .171 H7
Ringwood Av, N2 . . . . .73 J2
  Croydon CR0 . . . . .187 E7
Ringwood Cl, Pnr. HA5 . . . . . . .66 C3
Ringwood Gdns, E14
  off Inglewood Cl 134 A4
  SW15 . . . . .165 G2
Ringwood Rd, E17 . . . . .77 J6
Ringwood Way, N21 . . . . .59 H1
  Hampton (Hmptn H.) TW12 .161 G4
Ripley Cl, Brom. BR1
  off Ringmer Way 192 C5
  Croydon (New Adgtn) CR0 . .204 C6
Ripley Gdns, SW14 . . . . .146 D3
  Sutton SM1 . . . . .199 F4
Ripley Ms, E11
  off Wadley Rd 78/79 E7
Ripley Rd, E16 . . . . .115 J6
  Belvedere DA17 . . . . .139 G4
  Enfield EN2 . . . . .43 J1
  Hampton TW12 . . . . .161 G7
  Ilford IG3 . . . . .99 J2
Ripley Vil, W5 off Castlebar Rd . .105 F6
Riplington Ct, SW15
  off Longwood Dr 147 G7
Ripon Cl, Nthlt. UB5 . . . . .85 G5
Ripon Gdns, Chess. KT9 . . . . . .195 G5
  Ilford IG1 . . . . .80 B6
Ripon Rd, N9 . . . . .44 E7
  N17 . . . . .76 A3
  SE18 . . . . .136 E6
Ripon Way, Borwd. WD6 . . . . . .38 C5
Rippersley Rd, Well. DA16 . . . .158 A1
Ripple Rd, Bark. IG11 . . . . .99 F7
  Dagenham RM9 . . . . .118 A7
Rippleside Commercial Est, Bark.
  IG11 . . . . .118 C2
Ripplevale Gro, N1 . . . . .93 F7
Rippolson Rd, SE18 . . . . .137 J5

Risborough Dr, Wor.Pk. KT4 . . .183 G7
Risborough St, SE1 . . . . .27 H3
Risdon St, SE16 . . . . .133 F2
Rise, The, E11 . . . . .79 G5
  N13 . . . . .59 G4
  NW7 . . . . .55 F6
  NW10 . . . . .88 D4
  Bexley DA5 . . . . .158 C7
  Buckhurst Hill IG9 . . . . .48 A7
  Edgware HA8 . . . . .54 B5
  Greenford UB6 . . . . .86 D5
Risedale Rd, Bexh. DA7 . . . . . .159 H3
Riseldine Rd, SE23 . . . . .153 H6
Risinghill St, N1 . . . . .10 E1
Risingholme Cl, Har. HA3 . . . . .68 B1
Risingholme Rd, Har. HA3 . . . . .68 B2
Risings, The, E17 . . . . .78 D4
Rising Sun Ct, EC1 . . . . .19 H2
Risley Av, N17 . . . . .75 J1
Rita Rd, SW8 . . . . .34 B6
Ritches Rd, N15 . . . . .75 J5
Ritchie Rd, Croy. CR0 . . . . .189 E6
Ritchie St, N1 . . . . .11 F1
Ritchings Av, E17 . . . . .77 H4
Ritherdon Rd, SW17 . . . . .168 A2
Ritson Rd, E8 . . . . .94 D6
Ritter St, SE18 . . . . .136 D6
Ritz Par, W5 off Connell Cres . .105 J4
Rivaz Pl, E9 . . . . .95 F6
Rivenhall Gdns, E18 . . . . .79 F4
River Av, N13 . . . . .59 H3
  Thames Ditton KT7 . . . . . .180 D7
River Bk, N21 . . . . .43 J7
  East Molesey KT8 . . . . . . .180 B3
  Thames Ditton KT7 . . . . . .180 C5
  West Molesey KT8 . . . . . . .179 F3
Riverbank Way, Brent. TW8 . . .125 F6
River Barge Cl, E14
  off Stewart St 134 C2
River Brent Business Pk, W7 . . .124 B3
River Cl, E11 . . . . .79 J6
  Southall UB2 . . . . .123 J2
  Surbiton KT6
   off Catherine Rd 181 G5
Rivercourt Rd, W6 . . . . .127 H4
River Crane Wk, Felt. TW13 . . .160 D1
  Hounslow TW4 . . . . .160 D1
River Crane Way, Felt. TW13
  off Watermill Way 161 F2
Riverdale, SE13 . . . . .154 C3
  off Lewisham High St 154 C3
Riverdale Cl, Bark. IG11 . . . . . .118 B4
Riverdale Dr, SW18
  off Strathville Rd 166/167 E1
Riverdale Gdns, Twick. TW1 . . .145 F6
Riverdale Rd, SE18 . . . . .137 J5
  Bexley DA5 . . . . .159 F7
  Erith DA8 . . . . .139 H5
  Feltham TW13 . . . . .161 E4
  Twickenham TW1 . . . . .145 F6
Riverdene, Edg. HA8 . . . . .54 C3
Riverdene Rd, Ilf. IG1 . . . . .98 D3
River Front, Enf. EN1 . . . . .44 A3
River Gdns, Cars. SM5 . . . . . . .200 A2
  Feltham TW14 . . . . .142 A5
River Gro Pk, Beck. BR3 . . . . . .189 J1
Riverhead Cl, E17 . . . . .77 G2
River La, Rich. TW10 . . . . .163 G1
Rivermead, E.Mol. KT8 . . . . . . .179 J3
Rivermead, Tedd. TW11 . . . . . .163 E5
Rivermead Ct, SW6 . . . . .148 C3
Rivermead Ho, E9
  off Kingsmead Way 95 H5
Rivermead Rd, N18 . . . . .61 G6
Rivermeads Av, Twick. TW2 . . .161 G3
Rivermill, SW1
  off Grosvenor Rd 130 D5
Rivernook Cl, Walt. KT12 . . . . .178 C5
River Pk Gdns, Brom. BR2 . . . .172 D7
River Pk Rd, N22 . . . . .75 F2
River Pl, N1 . . . . .93 J7
River Reach, Tedd. TW11 . . . . .163 F5
River Rd, Bark. IG11 . . . . .117 H2
  Buckhurst Hill IG9 . . . . .64 B1
River Rd Business Pk, Bark. IG11 .117 J3
Riversdale Rd, N5 . . . . .93 H3
  Thames Ditton KT7 . . . . . .180 D5
Riversfield Rd, Enf. EN1 . . . . . .44 B3
Riverside, NW4 . . . . .71 H7
  SE7 . . . . .135 H3
  Twickenham TW1 . . . . .162 E1
Riverside, The, E.Mol. KT8 . . . .180 A3
Riverside Av, E.Mol. KT8 . . . . .180 A5
Riverside Business Cen, SW18 .167 E1
Riverside Cl, E5 . . . . .95 F1
  W7 . . . . .104 B4
  Kingston upon Thames KT1 .181 G4
  Wallington SM6 . . . . .200 B3
Riverside Ct, E4
  off Chelwood Cl 46 B6
  SW8 . . . . .33 J4
Riverside Dr, NW11 . . . . .72 B6
  W4 . . . . .126 D7
  Mitcham CR4 . . . . .185 H5
  Richmond TW10 . . . . .162 E2

Riverside Gdns, N3 . . . . .72 B3
  W6 . . . . .127 H5
  Enfield EN2 . . . . .43 J2
  Wembley HA0 . . . . .105 H2
Riverside Ind Est, Bark. IG11 . . .118 A3
  Enfield EN3 . . . . .45 H6
Riverside Mans, E1 off Milk Yd . .113 F7
Riverside Ms, Croy. CR0
  off Wandle Rd 200/201 E3
Riverside Pl, Stai. (Stanw.) TW19 .140 A6
Riverside Rd, E15 . . . . .114 C2
  N15 . . . . .76 D6
  SW17 . . . . .167 E4
  Sidcup DA14 . . . . .177 E3
  Staines (Stanw.) TW19 . . . .140 A5
Riverside Twr, SW6 . . . . .149 F2
Riverside Wk, E14 off Ferry St . .134 C5
  Bexley DA5 . . . . .158 C7
  Isleworth TW7 . . . . .144 B3
  Kingston upon Thames KT1
   off High St 181 G2
  Loughton IG10 . . . . .48 E6
  West Wickham BR4
   off The Alders 204 B1
Riverside W, SW18
  off Smugglers Way 148/149 E4
Riverside Yd, SW17
  off Riverside Rd 167 F4
River St, EC1 . . . . .11 E3
River Ter, W6 off Crisp Rd 127 J5
Riverton Cl, W9 . . . . .108 C3
River Vw, Enf. EN2
  off Chase Side 43 J3
Riverview Gdns, SW13 . . . . . . .127 H6
  Twickenham TW1 . . . . .162 C2
Riverview Gro, W4 . . . . .126 B6
River Vw Hts, SE16 . . . . .29 H3
Riverview Pk, SE6 . . . . .172 A2
Riverview Rd, W4 . . . . .126 B6
  Epsom KT19 . . . . .196 C4
River Wk, Walt. KT12 . . . . .178 A6
Riverway, N13 . . . . .59 G5
River Way, Epsom KT19 . . . . . .196 D5
  Loughton IG10 . . . . .48 D6
  Twickenham TW2 . . . . .161 H2
Riverwood La, Chis. BR7 . . . . . .193 G1
Rivington Av, Wdf.Grn. IG8 . . . .80 A2
Rivington Ct, NW10 . . . . .107 G1
Rivington Cres, NW7 . . . . .55 F7
Rivington Pl, EC2 . . . . .12 E4
Rivington St, EC2 . . . . .12 D4
Rivington Wk, E8 off Wilde Cl . .112 D1
Rivulet Rd, N17 . . . . .59 J7
Rixon Ho, SE18
  off Barnfield Rd 136/137 E6
Rixon St, N7 . . . . .93 G3
Rixsen Rd, E12 . . . . .98 B5
Roach Rd, E3 . . . . .96 A7
Roads Pl, N19
  off Hornsey Rd 92/93 E2
Roan St, SE10 . . . . .134 C6
Robarts Cl, Pnr. HA5
  off Field End Rd 66 B5
Robb Rd, Stan. HA7 . . . . .52 D6
Robert Adam St, W1 . . . . .16 B3
Roberta St, E2 . . . . .13 H3
Robert Burns Ms, SE24
  off Mayall Rd 151 H5
Robert Cl, W9 . . . . .6 D6
  Chigwell IG7 . . . . .65 J5
Robert Dashwood Way, SE17 . . .35 J2
Robert Keen Cl, SE15
  off Cicely Rd 152 D1
Robert Lowe Cl, SE14 . . . . . . .133 G7
Roberton Dr, Brom. BR1 . . . . . .191 J1
Robert Owen Ho, SW6 . . . . . . .148 A1
Robertsbridge Rd, Cars. SM5 . .199 F1
Roberts Cl, SE9 . . . . .175 G1
  SE16 . . . . .133 G2
  Sutton SM3 . . . . .198 A7
  Thornton Heath CR7
   off Kitchener Rd 188 A3
  West Drayton UB7 . . . . .120 B1
Roberts Ms, SW1 . . . . .24 B6
Robertson Rd, E15 . . . . .114 C1
Robertson St, SW8 . . . . .150 B3
Robert's Pl, EC1 . . . . .11 F5
Robert Sq, SE13
  off Bonfield Rd 154 C4
Roberts Rd, E17 . . . . .78 B1
  NW7 . . . . .56 B6
  Belvedere DA17 . . . . .139 G5
Robert St, E16 . . . . .136 E1
  NW1 . . . . .8 E4
  SE18 . . . . .137 G4
  WC2 . . . . .18 B6
  Croydon CR0 off High St . . .201 J3
Robeson St, E3 off Ackroyd Dr . .113 J5
Robeson Way, Borwd. WD6 . . . .38 C1
Robina Cl, Bexh. DA6 . . . . .158 D4
Robin Cl, NW7 . . . . .54 E3
  Hampton TW12 . . . . .161 E5
Robin Ct, SE16 . . . . .37 H1
  Wallington SM6
   off Carew Rd 200 C6

Robin Cres, E6 .... 116 A5
Robin Gro, N6 .... 92 A2
　Brentford TW8 .... 125 F6
　Harrow HA3 .... 69 J6
Robin Hill Dr, Chis. BR7 .... 174 B6
Robinhood Cl, Mitch. CR4 .... 186 C3
Robin Hood Dr, Har. HA3 .... 52 C7
Robin Hood Gdns, E14
　off Woolmore St 114 C7
Robin Hood La, E14 .... 114 C7
　SW15 .... 164 E4
　Bexleyheath DA6 .... 159 E5
Robinhood La, Mitch. CR4 .... 186 C3
Robin Hood La, Sutt. SM1 .... 198 D5
Robin Hood Rd, SW19 .... 165 H5
Robin Hood Way, SW15 .... 165 E4
　SW20 .... 165 E4
　Greenford UB6 .... 86 C6
Robin Ho, NW8
　off Newcourt St 109 H2
Robinia Cl, SE20
　off Sycamore Gro 188 D1
　Ilford IG6 .... 65 H6
Robinia Cres, E10 .... 96 B2
Robins Ct, SE12 .... 173 J3
Robinscroft Ms, SE10
　off Sparta St 154 B1
Robins Gro, W.Wick. BR4 .... 205 G3
Robinson Cl, E11 .... 97 E3
Robinson Cres, Bushey (Bushey Hth)
　WD23 .... 51 J1
Robinson Rd, E2 .... 113 F2
　SW17 .... 167 H6
　Dagenham RM10 .... 101 G4
Robinsons Cl, W13 .... 104 D5
Robinson St, SW3 .... 31 J5
Robinwood Pl, SW15 .... 164 D4
Robsart St, SW9 .... 151 F2
Robson Av, NW10 .... 107 G1
Robson Cl, E6 off Linton Gdns 116 B6
　Enfield EN2 .... 43 H2
Robson Rd, SE27 .... 169 H3
Rocastle Rd, SE4
　off Turnham Rd 153 H5
Roch Av, Edg. HA8 .... 69 J2
Rochdale Rd, E17 .... 78 A7
　SE2 .... 138 B5
Rochdale Way, SE8
　off Octavius St 134 A7
Rochelle Cl, SW11 .... 149 G4
Rochelle St, E2 .... 13 F4
Rochemont Wk, E8
　off Pownall Rd 112 C1
Roche Rd, SW16 .... 187 F1
Rochester Av, E13 .... 115 J1
　Bromley BR1 .... 191 H2
Rochester Cl, SW16 .... 169 E7
　Enfield EN1 .... 44 B1
　Sidcup DA15 .... 158 B6
Rochester Dr, Bex. DA5 .... 159 F6
　Pinner HA5 .... 66 D5
Rochester Gdns, Croy. CR0 .... 202 B2
　Ilford IG1 .... 80 C7
Rochester Ms, NW1 .... 92 C7
Rochester Pl, NW1 .... 92 C6
Rochester Rd, NW1 .... 92 C6
　Carshalton SM5 .... 199 J4
Rochester Row, SW1 .... 33 G1
Rochester Sq, NW1 .... 92 C7
Rochester St, SW1 .... 25 H6
Rochester Ter, NW1 .... 92 C6
Rochester Wk, SE1 .... 28 B1
Rochester Way, SE3 .... 155 H1
　SE9 .... 156 C3
Rochester Way Relief Rd, SE3 .... 155 H1
　SE9 .... 156 B4
Roche Wk, Cars. SM5 .... 185 G6
Rochford Av, Loug. IG10 .... 49 F3
　Romford RM6 .... 82 C5
Rochford Cl, E6 off Boleyn Rd 116 A2
Rochford Grn, Loug. IG10 .... 49 F3
Rochford St, NW5 .... 91 J5
Rochford Wk, E8
　off Wilman Gro 94 D7
Rochford Way, Croy. CR0 .... 186 E6
Rock Av, SW14
　off South Worple Way 146 D3
Rockbourne Rd, SE23 .... 171 G1
★ Rock Circ, W1 .... 17 H6
Rockells Pl, SE22 .... 153 E6
Rockford Av, Grnf. UB6 .... 104 D2
Rock Gdns, Dag. RM10 .... 101 H5
Rock Gro Way, SE16 .... 37 J1
Rockhall Rd, NW2 .... 90 A4
Rockhall Way, NW2
　off Midland Ter 90 A3
Rockhampton Cl, SE27
　off Rockhampton Rd 169 G4
Rockhampton Rd, SE27 .... 169 G4
　South Croydon CR2 .... 202 B6
Rock Hill, SE26 .... 170 C4
Rockingham Cl, SW15 .... 147 F4
Rockingham Est, SE1 .... 27 J6
Rockingham St, SE1 .... 27 J6
Rockland Rd, SW15 .... 148 B4

Rocklands Dr, Stan. HA7 .... 69 E2
Rockley Rd, W14 .... 128 A2
Rockmount Rd, SE18 .... 137 J5
　SE19 .... 170 A6
Rocks La, SW13 .... 147 G1
Rock St, N4 .... 93 G2
Rockware Av, Grnf. UB6 .... 104 A1
Rockways, Barn. EN5 .... 39 F6
Rockwell Gdns, SE19 .... 170 B5
Rockwell Rd, Dag. RM10 .... 101 H5
Rockwood Pl, W12 .... 127 J2
Rocliffe St, N1 .... 11 H2
Rocombe Cres, SE23 .... 153 F7
Rocque La, SE3 .... 155 F3
Rodborough Rd, NW11 .... 90 D1
Roden Ct, N6 off Hornsey La 74 D7
Roden Gdns, Croy. CR0 .... 188 B6
Rodenhurst Rd, SW4 .... 150 C6
Roden St, N7 .... 93 F3
　Ilford IG1 .... 98 D3
Roderick Rd, NW3 .... 91 J4
Roding Av, Wdf.Grn. IG8 .... 64 B6
Roding Gdns, Loug. IG10 .... 48 B6
Roding La, Buck.H. IG9 .... 64 B1
　Chigwell IG7 .... 64 D1
Roding La N, Wdf.Grn. IG8 .... 80 A2
Roding La S, Ilf. IG4 .... 80 A4
　Woodford Green IG8 .... 80 A4
Roding Ms, E1 .... 29 J1
Roding Rd, E5 .... 95 G4
　E6 .... 116 E5
　Loughton IG10 .... 48 B5
Rodings, The, Wdf.Grn. IG8 .... 63 J6
Rodings Row, Barn. EN5
　off Leecroft Rd 40 B5
Roding Trd Est, Bark. IG11 .... 98 E7
Roding Vw, Buck.H. IG9 .... 64 A1
Rodmarton St, W1 .... 16 A2
Rodmell Cl, Hayes UB4 .... 102 E4
Rodmell Slope, N12 .... 56 C5
Rodmere St, SE10
　off Trafalgar Rd 134/135 E5
Rodmill La, SW2 .... 151 E7
Rodney Cl, Croy. CR0 .... 201 H1
　New Malden KT3 .... 182 E5
　Pinner HA5 .... 66 E7
Rodney Ct, W9 .... 6 D5
Rodney Gdns, Pnr. HA5 .... 66 B5
　West Wickham BR4 .... 205 G4
Rodney Pl, E17 .... 77 H2
　SE17 .... 36 A1
　SW19 .... 185 F1
Rodney Rd, E11 .... 79 H4
　SE17 .... 36 A1
　Mitcham CR4 .... 185 H2
　New Malden KT3 .... 182 E5
　Twickenham TW2 .... 143 G6
Rodney St, N1 .... 10 D1
Rodney Way, Rom. RM7 .... 83 G1
Rodway Rd, SW15 .... 147 G7
　Bromley BR1 .... 191 H1
Rodwell Cl, Ruis. HA4 .... 84 C1
Rodwell Pl, Edg. HA8
　off Whitchurch La 54 A6
Rodwell Rd, SE22 .... 152 C6
Roebourne Way, E16 .... 136 D2
Roebuck Cl, Felt. TW13 .... 160 B4
Roebuck La, N17 off High Rd 60 C6
　Buckhurst Hill IG9 .... 47 J7
Roebuck Rd, Chess. KT9 .... 196 A5
Roedean Av, Enf. EN3 .... 45 F1
Roedean Cl, Enf. EN3 .... 45 F1
Roedean Cres, SW15 .... 146 E6
Roe End, NW9 .... 70 C4
Roe Grn, NW9 .... 70 C5
ROEHAMPTON, SW15 .... 147 G5
Roehampton Cl, SW15 .... 147 G4
Roehampton Dr, Chis. BR7 .... 175 F6
Roehampton Gate, SW15 .... 146 E6
Roehampton High St, SW15 .... 147 H7
Roehampton La, SW15 .... 147 G4
Roehampton Vale, SW15 .... 165 E3
Roe La, NW9 .... 70 B4
Roe Way, Wall. SM6 .... 201 E6
Roffey St, E14 .... 134 C2
Rogate Ho, E5 off Muir Rd 94 D3
Roger Dowley Ct, E2 .... 113 F2
Rogers Gdns, Dag. RM10 .... 101 G5
Rogers Rd, E16 .... 115 F6
　SW17 .... 167 G4
　Dagenham RM10 .... 101 G5
Roger St, WC1 .... 10 D6
Rogers Wk, N12
　off Brook Meadow 56/57 E3
Rojack Rd, SE23 .... 171 G1
Rokeby Gdns, Wdf.Grn. IG8 .... 79 G1
Rokeby Pl, SW20 .... 165 H7
Rokeby Rd, SE4 .... 153 J2
Rokeby St, E15 .... 114 E1
Rokell Cl, Well. DA16 .... 157 G2
Rokesby Pl, Wem. HA0 .... 87 G5
Rokesly Av, N8 .... 74 E5
Roland Gdns, SW7 .... 30 D3
　Feltham TW13 .... 161 E3
Roland Ms, E1 off Stepney Grn 113 G5

Roland Rd, E17 .... 78 D4
Roland Way, SE17 .... 36 C4
　SW7 .... 30 D3
　Worcester Park KT4 .... 197 F2
Roles Gro, Rom. RM6 .... 82 D4
Rolfe Cl, Barn. EN4 .... 41 H4
Rolinsden Way, Kes. BR2 .... 206 A4
Rollesby Rd, Chess. KT9 .... 196 A6
Rollesby Way, SE28 .... 118 C7
Rolleston Av, Orp. BR5 .... 192 E6
Rolleston Cl, Orp. BR5 .... 193 E7
Rolleston Rd, S.Croy. CR2 .... 202 A7
Roll Gdns, Ilf. IG2 .... 80 D5
Rollins St, SE15 .... 133 F6
Rollit Cres, Houns. TW3 .... 143 G5
Rollit St, N7 off Hornsey Rd 93 F5
Rolls Bldgs, EC4 .... 19 E3
Rollscourt Av, SE24 .... 151 J5
Rolls Pk Av, E4 .... 62 A6
Rolls Pk Rd, E4 .... 62 B5
Rolls Pas, EC4 .... 18 E3
Rolls Rd, SE1 .... 37 G3
Rolt St, SE8 .... 133 H6
Rolvenden Gdns, Brom. BR1 .... 174 A7
Rolvenden Pl, N17
　off Manor Rd 76 D1
★ Roman Bath, WC2
　off Strand La 18 D5
Roman Cl, W3 off Avenue Gdns 126 B2
　Feltham TW14 .... 142 C5
Romanfield Rd, SW2 .... 151 F7
Romanhurst Av, Brom. BR2 .... 191 E4
Romanhurst Gdns, Brom. BR2 .... 190 E4
Roman Ind Est, Croy. CR0 .... 188 B7
Roman Ri, SE19 .... 170 A6
Roman Rd, E2 .... 113 F3
　E3 .... 113 H2
　E6 .... 116 B4
　N10 .... 58 B7
　NW2 .... 89 J3
　W4 .... 127 E4
　Ilford IG1 .... 99 E6
Roman Sq, SE28 .... 138 A1
Roman Way, N7 .... 93 F6
　SE15 off Clifton Way 133 F7
　Croydon CR0 .... 201 H2
　Enfield EN1 .... 44 C5
Roman Way Ind Est, N1
　off Offord Rd 93 F7
Romany Gdns, E17
　off McEntee Av 77 H1
　Sutton SM3 .... 184 D7
Romany Ri, Orp. BR5 .... 207 F1
Roma Read Cl, SW15
　off Bessborough Rd 147 H7
Roma Rd, E17 .... 77 H3
Romberg Rd, SW17 .... 168 A3
Romborough Gdns, SE13 .... 154 C5
Romborough Way, SE13 .... 154 C5
Romero Cl, SW9
　off Stockwell Rd 151 F3
Romero Sq, SE3 .... 155 J4
Romeyn Rd, SW16 .... 169 F3
Romford Rd, E7 .... 97 H5
　E12 .... 98 B4
　E15 .... 96 E7
Romford St, E1 .... 21 J2
Romilly Dr, Wat. WD19 .... 51 E4
Romilly Rd, N4 .... 93 H2
Romilly St, W1 .... 17 H5
Rommany Rd, SE27 .... 170 A4
Romney Cl, N17 .... 76 E1
　NW11 .... 91 F1
　SE14 off Kender St 133 F7
　Chessington KT9 .... 195 H4
　Harrow HA2 .... 67 G7
Romney Dr, Brom. BR1 .... 174 A7
　Harrow HA2 .... 67 G7
Romney Gdns, Bexh. DA7 .... 159 F1
Romney Ms, W1 .... 16 B1
Romney Rd, SE10 .... 134 C6
　New Malden KT3 .... 182 D6
Romney Row, NW2
　off Brent Ter 90 A2
Romney St, SW1 .... 25 J6
Romola Rd, SE24 .... 169 H1
Romsey Cl, Orp. BR6 .... 207 E4
Romsey Gdns, Dag. RM9 .... 118 D1
Romsey Rd, W13 .... 104 D1
　Dagenham RM9 .... 118 D1
Romulus Ct, Brent. TW8
　off Justin Cl 125 G7
Ronald Av, E15 .... 115 E3
Ronald Cl, Beck. BR3 .... 189 J4
Ronald Ho, SE3
　off Cambert Way 155 J4
Ronalds Rd, N5 .... 93 G5
　Bromley BR1 .... 191 G1
Ronaldstone Rd, Sid. DA15 .... 157 H6
Ronald St, E1 off Devonport St 113 F6
Rona Rd, NW3 .... 92 A4
Ronart St, Har. (Wldste) HA3
　off Stuart Rd 68 C3
Rona Wk, N1 off Ramsey Wk 94 A6
Rondu Rd, NW2 .... 90 B5

Ronelean Rd, Surb. KT6 .... 195 J3
Ron Leighton Way, E6 .... 116 B1
Ronnie La, E12 off Walton Rd 98 C2
Ronver Rd, SE12 .... 155 F7
Rood La, EC3 .... 20 C5
Rookby Ct, N21
　off Carpenter Gdns 59 H2
Rook Cl, Wem. HA9 .... 88 B3
Rookeries Cl, Felt. TW13 .... 160 B3
Rookery Cl, NW9 .... 71 F5
Rookery Cres, Dag. RM10 .... 101 H7
Rookery Dr, Chis. BR7 .... 192 D1
Rookery La, Brom. BR2 .... 192 A6
Rookery Rd, SW4 .... 150 C4
Rookery Way, NW9 .... 71 F5
Rooke Way, SE10 .... 135 F5
Rookfield Av, N10 .... 74 C4
Rookfield Cl, N10
　off Cranmore Way 74 C4
Rookstone Rd, SW17 .... 167 J5
Rook Wk, E6 off Allhallows Rd 116 B6
Rookwood Av, Loug. IG10 .... 49 F3
　New Malden KT3 .... 183 G4
　Wallington SM6 .... 200 D4
Rookwood Gdns, E4
　off Whitehall Rd 63 F1
　Loughton IG10 .... 49 F3
Rookwood Ho, Bark. IG11
　off St. Marys 117 G2
Rookwood Rd, N16 .... 76 C7
★ Roosevelt Mem, W1 .... 16 C5
Rootes Dr, W10 .... 108 A4
Ropemaker Rd, SE16 .... 133 H3
Ropemakers Flds, E14
　off Narrow St 113 J7
Ropemaker St, EC2 .... 20 B1
Roper La, SE1 .... 29 E4
Ropers Av, E4 .... 62 C5
Ropers Orchard, SW3 .... 31 F6
Roper St, SE9 .... 156 C6
Ropers Wk, SW2
　off Brockwell Pk Gdns 151 G7
Roper Way, Mitch. CR4 .... 186 A2
Ropery St, E3 .... 113 J4
Rope St, SE16 .... 133 H4
Rope Wk, Sun. TW16 .... 178 C3
Rope Wk Gdns, E1 .... 21 J4
Ropewalk Ms, E8
　off Middleton Rd 94 C7
Rope Yd Rails, SE18 .... 136 E3
Ropley St, E2 .... 13 H2
Rosa Alba Ms, N5
　off Kelross Rd 93 J4
Rosaline Rd, SW6 .... 128 B7
Rosamond St, SE26 .... 170 E3
Rosamund Cl, S.Croy. CR2 .... 202 A4
Rosamun St, Sthl. UB2 .... 123 E4
Rosary Cl, Houns. TW3 .... 142 E2
Rosary Gdns, SW7 .... 30 C2
Rosaville Rd, SW6 .... 128 C7
Roscoe St, EC1 .... 12 A6
Roscoff Cl, Edg. HA8 .... 70 C1
Roseacre Cl, W13
　off Middlefielde 104/105 E5
Roseacre Rd, Well. DA16 .... 158 B3
Rose All, EC2 off Bishopsgate 112 B5
　SE1 .... 28 A1
Rose & Crown Ct, EC2 .... 19 J3
Rose & Crown Yd, SW1 .... 25 G1
Roseary Cl, West Dr. UB7 .... 120 A4
Rose Av, E18 .... 79 H2
　Mitcham CR4 .... 185 J1
　Morden SM4 .... 185 F5
Rosebank, SE20 .... 170 E7
Rosebank Av, Wem. HA0 .... 86 C4
Rosebank Cl, N12 .... 57 H5
　Teddington TW11 .... 162 D6
Rosebank Gdns, E3 .... 113 J2
Rosebank Gro, E17 .... 77 J3
Rosebank Rd, E17 .... 78 B6
　W7 .... 124 B2
Rosebank Vil, E17 .... 78 A4
Rosebank Wk, NW1
　off Maiden La 92 D7
　SE18 off Woodhill 136 B4
Rosebank Way, W3 .... 106 D6
Rose Bates Dr, NW9 .... 70 A4
Roseberry Gdns, N4 .... 75 H6
　Orpington BR6 .... 207 H3
Roseberry Pl, E8 .... 94 C6
Roseberry St, SE16 .... 132 E4
Rosebery Av, E12 .... 98 B6
　EC1 .... 10 E6
　N17 .... 76 D2
　Harrow HA2 .... 85 F4
　New Malden KT3 .... 183 F2
　Sidcup DA15 .... 157 H7
　Thornton Heath CR7 .... 187 J2
Rosebery Cl, Mord. SM4 .... 184 A6
Rosebery Ct, EC1
　off Rosebery Av 111 G4
Rosebery Gdns, N8 .... 74 E5
　W13 .... 104 D6
　Sutton SM1 .... 199 E4
Rosebery Ms, N10 .... 74 C2

Rosebery Ms, SW2
   off Rosebery Rd 150/151 E6
Rosebery Rd, N9 . . . . .60 D3
  N10 . . . . .74 C2
  SW2 . . . . .150 E6
  Hounslow TW3 . . . . .143 J5
  Kingston upon Thames KT1 . .182 B2
  Sutton SM1 . . . . .198 C6
Rosebery Sq, EC1 . . . . .10 E6
  Kingston upon Thames KT1 . .182 A2
Rosebine Av, Twick. TW2 . . . . . .144 A7
Rosebury Rd, SW6 . . . . .149 E2
Rosebury Sq, Wdf.Grn. IG8 . . . . .64 D7
Rose Ct, E1 . . . . .21 F7
  Pinner HA5 off Nursery Rd . .66 C3
Rosecourt Rd, Croy. CR0 . . . . . .187 F6
Rosecroft Av, NW3 . . . . .90 D3
Rosecroft Gdns, NW2 . . . . .89 G3
  Twickenham TW2 . . . . .162 A1
Rosecroft Rd, Sthl. UB1 . . . . . . .103 G4
Rosecroft Wk, Pnr. HA5 . . . . . . .66 C6
  Wembley HA0 . . . . .87 G5
Rose Dale, Orp. BR6 . . . . .207 E2
Rosedale Cl, SE2 . . . .
  off Finchale Rd 138 B3
  W7 off Boston Rd 124 C2
  Stanmore HA7 . . . . .53 E6
Rosedale Ct, N5 . . . . .93 H4
Rosedale Gdns, Dag. RM9 . . . . .100 B7
Rosedale Pl, Croy. CR0 . . . . . . .189 G2
Rosedale Rd, E7 . . . . .97 J5
  Dagenham RM9 . . . . .100 B7
  Epsom KT17 . . . . .197 G6
  Richmond TW9 . . . . .145 H4
  Romford RM1 . . . . .83 J2
Rosedale Ter, W6 off Dalling Rd .127 H3
Rosedene, NW6 . . . . .108 A1
Rosedene Av, SW16 . . . . .169 F3
  Croydon CR0 . . . . .187 F7
  Greenford UB6 . . . . .103 G3
  Morden SM4 . . . . .184 D5
Rosedene Gdns, Ilf. IG2 . . . . .80 D4
Rosedene Ter, E10 . . . . .96 B2
Rosedew Rd, W6 . . . . .128 A6
Rose End, Wor.Pk. KT4 . . . . .198 A1
Rosefield Cl, Cars. SM5 . . . . . . .199 H5
Rosefield Gdns, E14 . . . . .114 A7
Roseford Ct, W12 . . . . .128 A2
Rose Gdn Cl, Edg. HA8 . . . . .53 H6
Rose Gdns, W5 . . . . .125 G3
  Feltham TW13 . . . . .160 A2
  Southall UB1 . . . . .103 G4
  Staines (Stanw.) TW19 . . . .
   off Diamedes Av 140 A7
Rose Glen, NW9 . . . . .70 D4
Rosehart Ms, W11 . . . .
  off Westbourne Gro 108 D6
Rosehatch Av, Rom. RM6 . . . . . . .82 D3
Roseheath Rd, Houns. TW4 . . . .143 F5
ROSEHILL, Sutt. SM1 . . . . .198 E1
Rosehill, Esher (Clay.) KT10 . . . .194 D6
  Hampton TW12 . . . . .179 G1
Rose Hill, Sutt. SM1 . . . . .199 E3
Rosehill Av, Sutt. SM1 . . . . .199 F1
Rosehill Gdns, Grnf. UB6 . . . . . . .86 C5
  Sutton SM1 . . . . .199 E2
Rosehill Pk W, Sutt. SM1 . . . . . .199 F1
Rosehill Rd, SW18 . . . . .149 F6
Roseland Cl, N17 off Cavell Rd . .60 A7
Rose La, Rom. RM6 . . . . .82 D3
Rose Lawn, Bushey (Bushey Hth) . . .
  WD23 . . . . .51 J1
Roseleigh Av, N5 . . . . .93 H4
Roseleigh Cl, Twick. TW1 . . . . . .145 G6
Rosemary Av, N3 . . . . .73 E2
  N9 . . . . .60 E1
  Enfield EN2 . . . . .44 A1
  Hounslow TW4 . . . . .142 D2
  West Molesey KT8 . . . . .179 G3
Rosemary Cl, Croy. CR0 . . . . . . .186 E6
Rosemary Dr, E14 . . . . .114 D6
  Ilford IG4 . . . . .80 A5
Rosemary Gdns, SW14 . . . .
  off Rosemary La 146 C3
  Chessington KT9 . . . . .195 H4
  Dagenham RM8 . . . . .101 F1
Rosemary La, SW14 . . . . .146 C3
Rosemary Rd, SE15 . . . . .37 G7
  SW17 . . . . .167 F3
  Welling DA16 . . . . .157 J1
Rosemary St, N1 . . . .
  off Shepperton Rd 112 A1
Rosemead, NW9 . . . . .71 F7
Rosemead Av, Mitch. CR4 . . . . . .186 C2
  Wembley HA9 . . . . .87 H5
Rosemont Av, N12 . . . . .57 F6
Rosemont Rd, NW3 . . . . .91 F6
  W3 .106 B7
  New Malden KT3 . . . . .182 C3
  Richmond TW10 . . . . .145 H6
  Wembley HA0 . . . . .105 H1
Rosemoor St, SW3 . . . . .31 J2
Rosemount Cl, Wdf.Grn. IG8 . . . .
  off Chapelmount Rd 64 C6
Rosemount Dr, Brom. BR1 . . . . .192 C4

Rosemount Pt, SE23 . . . .
  off Dacres Rd 171 G3
Rosemount Rd, W13 . . . . .104 D6
Rosenau Cres, SW11 . . . . .149 H1
Rosenau Rd, SW11 . . . . .149 H1
Rosendale Rd, SE21 . . . . .151 J7
  SE24 . . . . .151 J7
Roseneath Av, N21 . . . . .59 H1
Roseneath Rd, SW11 . . . . .150 A6
Roseneath Wk, Enf. EN1 . . . . .44 B4
Rosens Wk, Edg. HA8 . . . . .54 B3
Rosenthal Rd, SE6 . . . . .154 B6
Rosenthorpe Rd, SE15 . . . . .153 G5
Rose Pk Cl, Hayes UB4 . . . . .102 C4
Rosepark Ct, Ilf. IG5 . . . . .80 C2
Roserton St, E14 . . . . .134 C2
Rosery, The, Croy. CR0 . . . . .189 G6
Roses, The, Wdf.Grn. IG8 . . . . . . .63 F7
Rose Sq, SW3 . . . . .31 F3
Rose St, EC4 . . . . .19 H3
  WC2 . . . . .18 A5
Rosethorn Cl, SW12 . . . . .150 C7
Rosetta Cl, SW8 . . . . .131 E7
Rosetti Ter, Dag. RM8 . . . .
  off Marlborough Rd 100 B4
Roseveare Rd, SE12 . . . . .173 J4
Roseville Av, Houns. TW3 . . . . . .143 G5
Roseville Rd, Hayes UB3 . . . . . . .122 A5
Rosevine Rd, SW20 . . . . .183 J1
Rose Wk, Surb. KT5 . . . . .182 B5
  West Wickham BR4 . . . . . . .204 D2
Rose Way, SE12 . . . . .155 G5
Roseway, SE21 . . . . .152 A6
Rose Way, Edg. HA8 . . . . .54 C4
Rosewell Cl, SE20 . . . . .170 E7
Rosewood, Esher KT10 . . . . .194 D2
Rosewood Av, Grnf. UB6 . . . . .86 D5
Rosewood Cl, Sid. DA14 . . . . . . .176 C3
Rosewood Ct, Brom. BR1 . . . . . .191 J1
  Romford RM6 . . . . .82 C5
Rosewood Gdns, SE13 . . . .
  off Morden Hill 154 C2
Rosewood Gro, Sutt. SM1 . . . . . .199 F2
Rosewood Sq, W12 . . . .
  off Primula St 107 G6
Rosewood Ter, SE20 . . . .
  off Laurel Gro 171 F7
Rosher Cl, E15 . . . . .96 D7
Rosina St, E9 . . . . .95 G5
Roskell Rd, SW15 . . . . .148 A3
Roslin Rd, W3 . . . . .126 B3
Roslin Sq, W3 . . . . .126 B3
Roslin Way, Brom. BR1 . . . . .173 G5
Roslyn Cl, Mitch. CR4 . . . . .185 G2
Roslyn Rd, N15 . . . . .76 A5
Rosmead Rd, W11 . . . . .108 B7
Rosoman Pl, EC1 . . . . .11 F5
Rosoman St, EC1 . . . . .11 F4
Rossall Cres, NW10 . . . . .105 J3
Ross Av, NW7 . . . . .56 B5
  Dagenham RM8 . . . . .101 F2
Ross Cl, Har. HA3 . . . . .51 J7
  Hayes UB3 . . . . .121 G4
  Northolt UB5 . . . . .86 A4
Ross Ct, SW15 . . . . .148 A7
Rossdale, Sutt. SM1 . . . . .199 H5
Rossdale Dr, N9 . . . . .45 F6
  NW9 . . . . .88 C1
Rossdale Rd, SW15 . . . . .147 J4
Rosse Ms, SE3 . . . . .155 H1
Rossendale St, E5 . . . . .94 E2
Rossendale Way, NW1 . . . . .92 C7
Rossetti Rd, SE16 . . . . .132 E5
Rossignol Gdns, Cars. SM5 . . . .200 A2
Rossindel Rd, Houns. TW3 . . . . .143 G5
Rossington St, E5 . . . . .94 D2
Rosslyn Av, E4 . . . . .63 F2
  SW13 . . . . .147 E3
  Barnet EN4 . . . . .41 H6
  Dagenham RM8 . . . . .83 F7
  Feltham TW14 . . . . .142 A6
Rosslyn Cl, W.Wick. BR4 . . . . . . .205 F3
Rosslyn Cres, Har. HA1 . . . . .68 C5
  Wembley HA9 . . . . .87 H4
Rosslyn Gdns, Wem. HA9 . . . .
  off Rosslyn Cres 87 H3
Rosslyn Hill, NW3 . . . . .91 G4
Rosslyn Ms, NW3 . . . .
  off Rosslyn Hill 91 G4
Rosslyn Pk Ms, NW3 . . . .
  off Lyndhurst Rd 91 G5
Rosslyn Rd, E17 . . . . .78 C4
  Barking IG11 . . . . .99 G7
  Twickenham TW1 . . . . .145 F6
Rossmore Ct, NW1 . . . . .7 J5
Rossmore Rd, NW1 . . . . .7 H6
Ross Par, Wall. SM6 . . . . .200 B6
Ross Rd, SE25 . . . . .188 A3
  Twickenham TW2 . . . . .161 H1
  Wallington SM6 . . . . .200 C5
Ross Way, SE9 . . . . .156 B3
Rosswood Gdns, Wall. SM6 . . . .200 C6

Rostella Rd, SW17 . . . . .167 G4
Rostrevor Av, N15 . . . . .76 C6
Rostrevor Gdns, Hayes UB3 . . . .121 H1
  Southall UB2 . . . . .122 E5
Rostrevor Ms, SW6 . . . . .148 C1
Rostrevor Rd, SW6 . . . . .148 C1
  SW19 . . . . .166 D5
Rotary St, SE1 . . . . .27 G5
Rothbury Gdns, Islw. TW7 . . . . . .124 D7
Rothbury Rd, E9 . . . . .95 J7
Rothbury Wk, N17 . . . . .60 D7
Rotherfield Rd, Cars. SM5 . . . . . .200 A4
Rotherfield St, N1 . . . . .93 J7
Rotherham Wk, SE1 . . . . .27 G2
Rotherhill Av, SW16 . . . . .168 D6
ROTHERHITHE, SE16 . . . . .133 G3
★ Rotherhithe Heritage Mus, ...
  SE16 . . . . .133 H1
Rotherhithe New Rd, SE16 . . . . . .37 J4
Rotherhithe Old Rd, SE16 . . . . . .133 G4
Rotherhithe St, SE16 . . . . .133 F2
Rotherhithe Tunnel, E1 . . . . .133 F1
Rotherhithe Tunnel App, E14 . . . .113 H7
  SE16 . . . . .133 F2
Rothermere Rd, Croy. CR0 . . . . . .201 F5
Rotherwick Hill, W5 . . . . .105 J4
Rotherwick Rd, NW11 . . . . .72 D7
Rotherwood Cl, SW20 . . . . .184 B1
Rotherwood Rd, SW15 . . . . .148 A3
Rothery St, N1 off Gaskin St 111 H1
Rothery Ter, SW9 . . . . .131 H7
Rothesay Av, SW20 . . . . .184 B2
  Greenford UB6 . . . . .86 A6
  Richmond TW10 . . . . .146 B4
Rothesay Rd, SE25 . . . . .188 B4
Rothsay Rd, E7 . . . . .97 J6
Rothsay St, SE1 . . . . .28 D5
Rothsay Wk, E14 . . . .
  off Charnwood Gdns 134 A4
Rothschild Rd, W4 . . . . .126 C4
Rothschild St, SE27 . . . . .169 H4
Roth Wk, N7 off Durham Rd 93 F3
Rothwell Gdns, Dag. RM9 . . . . . .100 C7
Rothwell Rd, Dag. RM9 . . . . .118 C1
Rothwell St, NW1 . . . . .109 J1
Rotten Row, SW1 . . . . .24 B3
  SW7 . . . . .23 G3
Rotterdam Dr, E14 . . . . .134 C2
Rouel Rd, SE16 . . . . .29 H6
Rougemont Av, Mord. SM4 . . . . .184 D6
Roundacre, SW19 . . . .
  off Inner Pk Rd 166 A2
Roundaway Rd, Ilf. IG5 . . . . .80 C2
Roundel Cl, SE4 . . . .
  off Adelaide Av 153 J4
Round Gro, Croy. CR0 . . . . .189 G2
Roundhay Cl, SE23 . . . . .171 G2
Round Hill, SE26 . . . . .171 F2
Roundhill Dr, Enf. EN2 . . . . .43 F4
Roundmead Av, Loug. IG10 . . . . . .48 D3
Roundmead Cl, Loug. IG10 . . . . . .48 D3
Roundshaw Cen, Wall. SM6 . . . .
  off Meteor Way 200/201 E7
Roundtable Rd, Brom. BR1 . . . . .173 F3
Roundtree Rd, Wem. HA0 . . . . . . .86 E5
Roundway, The, N17 . . . . .75 J1
  Esher (Clay.) KT10 . . . . .194 C5
Roundwood, Chis. BR7 . . . . .192 E2
Roundwood Av, Uxb. UB11 . . . . .121 F1
Roundwood Rd, NW10 . . . . .89 F6
Rounton Rd, E3 . . . . .114 A4
Roupell Rd, SW2 . . . . .169 F1
Roupell St, SE1 . . . . .27 F2
Rousden St, NW1 . . . . .92 C7
Rouse Gdns, SE21 . . . . .170 B4
Rous Rd, Buck.H. IG9 . . . . .64 B1
Routemaster Cl, E13 . . . . .115 H3
Routh Rd, SW18 . . . . .149 H7
Routh St, E6 . . . . .116 C5
Routledge Cl, N19 . . . . .92 D1
Rover Av, Ilf. IG6 . . . . .65 J6
Rowallan Rd, SW6 . . . . .128 B7
Rowan Av, E4 . . . . .61 J6
Rowan Cl, SW16 . . . . .186 C1
  W5 .125 H2
  Ilford IG1 . . . . .99 G5
  New Malden KT3 . . . . .182 E2
  Stanmore HA7 . . . .
   off Woodlands Dr 52 C6
  Wembley HA0 . . . . .86 D4
Rowan Cres, SW16 . . . . .186 C1
Rowan Dr, NW9 . . . . .71 G4
Rowan Gdns, Croy. CR0 . . . .
  off Radcliffe Rd 202 C3
Rowan Rd, SW16 . . . . .186 C2
  W6 .128 A4
  Bexleyheath DA7 . . . . .159 E3
  Brentford TW8 . . . . .125 E7
  West Drayton UB7 . . . . .120 A4
Rowans, The, N13 . . . . .59 H3
Rowans Way, Loug. IG10 . . . . .48 C4
Rowan Ter, SE20 . . . .
  off Sycamore Gro 188 D1
  W6 off Bute Gdns 128 A4
Rowantree Cl, N21 . . . . .60 A1

Rowantree Rd, N21 . . . . .60 A1
  Enfield EN2 . . . . .43 H2
Rowan Wk, N2 . . . . .73 F6
  N19 off Bredgar Rd 92 C2
  W10 off Droop St 108 B4
  Barnet EN5 off Station Rd .40/41 E5
  Bromley BR2 . . . . .206 C3
Rowan Way, Rom. RM6 . . . . .82 C3
Rowanwood Av, Sid. DA15 . . . . .176 A1
Rowanwood Ms, Enf. EN2 . . . . . . .43 H2
Rowben Cl, N20 . . . . .56 E1
Rowberry Cl, SW6 . . . . .127 A7
Rowcross St, SE1 . . . . .37 F3
Rowdell Rd, Nthlt. UB5 . . . . .103 G1
Rowden Pk Gdns, E4 . . . .
  off Rowden Rd 62 A6
Rowden Rd, E4 . . . . .62 A6
  Beckenham BR3 . . . . .189 H1
  Epsom KT19 . . . . .196 B4
Rowditch La, SW11 . . . . .150 A2
Rowdon Av, NW10 . . . . .89 H7
Rowdowns Rd, Dag. RM9 . . . . . .119 F1
Rowe Gdns, Bark. IG11 . . . . .117 J2
Rowe La, E9 . . . . .95 F5
Rowena Cres, SW11 . . . . .149 H2
Rowe Wk, Har. HA2 . . . . .85 G3
Rowfant Rd, SW17 . . . . .168 A1
Rowhill Rd, E5 . . . . .95 E4
Rowington Cl, W2 . . . . .14 A1
Rowland Av, Har. HA3 . . . . .69 F4
Rowland Ct, E16 . . . . .115 F4
Rowland Cres, Chig. IG7 . . . . .65 H4
Rowland Gro, SE26 . . . .
  off Dallas Rd 170/171 E3
Rowland Hill Av, N17 . . . . .59 J7
Rowland Hill St, NW3 . . . . .91 H5
Rowlands Av, Pnr. HA5 . . . . .51 G6
Rowlands Cl, N6 . . . .
  off North Hill 74 A6
  NW7 . . . . .55 G7
Rowlands Rd, Dag. RM8 . . . . . . .101 F2
Rowland Way, SW19 . . . .
  off Hayward Cl 184/185 E1
Rowley Av, Sid. DA15 . . . . .158 B7
Rowley Cl, Wem. HA0 . . . . .87 J7
Rowley Gdns, N4 . . . . .75 J7
ROWLEY GREEN, Barn. EN5 . . . .39 F4
Rowley Grn Rd, Barn. EN5 . . . . . .39 F5
Rowley Ind Pk, W3 . . . . .126 B3
Rowley La, Barn. EN5 . . . . .39 F5
  Borehamwood WD6 . . . . . . .38 D1
Rowley Rd, N15 . . . . .75 J5
Rowley Way, NW8 . . . . .109 E1
Rowlheys Pl, West Dr. UB7 . . . . .120 B3
Rowlls Rd, Kings.T. KT1 . . . . .181 J3
Rowney Gdns, Dag. RM9 . . . . . .100 C6
Rowney Rd, Dag. RM9 . . . . .100 B6
Rowntree Clifford Cl, E13 . . . .
  off Liddon Rd 115 H3
Rowntree Path, SE28 . . . .
  off Booth Cl 118 B7
Rowntree Rd, Twick. TW2 . . . . . .162 B1
Rowse Cl, E15 . . . . .96 C7
Rowsley Av, NW4 . . . . .71 J3
Rowstock Gdns, N7 . . . . .92 D5
Rowton Rd, SE18 . . . . .137 F7
Roxborough Av, Har. HA1 . . . . . . .68 A7
  Isleworth TW7 . . . . .124 C7
Roxborough Pk, Har. HA1 . . . . . . .68 A5
Roxborough Rd, Har. HA1 . . . . . . .68 A5
Roxbourne Cl, Nthlt. UB5 . . . . . . .84 D6
Roxburgh Rd, SE27 . . . . .169 H5
Roxby Pl, SW6 . . . . .128 D6
ROXETH, Har. HA2 . . . . .86 A2
Roxeth Grn Av, Har. HA2 . . . . . . .85 H3
Roxeth Gro, Har. HA2 . . . . .85 H4
Roxeth Hill, Har. HA2 . . . . .86 A2
Roxley Rd, SE13 . . . . .154 B6
Roxton Gdns, Croy. CR0 . . . . . . .204 A5
Roxwell Rd, W12 . . . . .127 G2
  Barking IG11 . . . . .118 A2
Roxwell Trd Pk, E10 . . . . .77 H7
Roxwell Way, Wdf.Grn. IG8 . . . . . .63 J7
Roxy Av, Rom. RM6 . . . . .82 C7
★ Royal Acad of Arts, W1 . . . . . . .17 F6
★ Royal Acad of Dramatic Art . . . .
  (R.A.D.A.), WC1 . . . . .17 H1
★ Royal Acad of Music, NW1 . . . .8 C6
★ Royal Air Force Museums, ...
  NW9 . . . . .71 G2
Royal Albert Dock, E16 . . . . .116 C7
★ Royal Albert Hall, SW7 . . . . . . .22 E4
Royal Albert Roundabout, E16 . . . . . .
  off Royal Albert Way 116 B7
Royal Albert Way, E16 . . . . .116 A7
Royal Arc, W1 . . . . .17 F6
Royal Artillery Barracks, SE18 . . . . . .
  off Repository Rd 136 D5
Royal Av, SW3 . . . . .31 J3
  Worcester Park KT4 . . . . . . .197 E2
★ Royal Botanic Gdns, Kew, Rich. . . . .
  TW9 . . . . .125 H7
Royal Circ, SE27 . . . . .169 G3
Royal Cl, N16 off Manor Rd 94 B1
  SE8 . . . . .133 J6

Royal Cl, SW19 . . . . .166 A2
Ilford IG3 . . . . .82 A7
Orpington BR6 . . . . .206 E4
Worcester Park KT4 . . . . . .196 E2
★ Royal Coll of Art, SW7 . . . .22 D4
★ Royal Coll of Music, SW7 . .22 E5
★ Royal Coll of Surgeons, WC2 .18 D3
Royal Coll St, NW1 . . . . .92 C7
Royal Ct, EC3 off Cornhill 112 A6
SE16 . . . . .133 J3
★ Royal Courts of Justice,
WC2 . . . . .18 D4
Royal Cres, W11 . . . . .128 A1
Ruislip HA4 . . . . .84 E4
Royal Cres Ms, W11
off Queensdale Rd 128 A1
Royal Docks Rd, E6 . . . . .117 C4
Royal Dr, N11 . . . . .58 A5
Royal Duchess Ms, SW12
off Dinsmore Rd 150 B7
Royale Leisure Pk, W3 . . . . . .106 A4
★ Royal Exchange, EC3 . . . . .20 C4
Royal Ex Av, EC3 . . . . .20 C4
Royal Ex Bldgs, EC3 . . . . .20 C4
Royal Ex Steps, EC3
off Cornhill 112 A6
★ Royal Festival Hall, SE1 . . . .26 C1
Royal Gdns, W7 . . . . .124 D3
★ Royal Geographical Society,
SW7 . . . . .23 E4
Royal Herbert Pavilions, SE18 .156 C1
Royal Hill, SE10 . . . . .134 C7
★ Royal Horticultural Society
(Lawrence Hall), SW1 . . . . .25 H6
★ Royal Horticultural Society
(Lindley Hall), SW1 . . . . . . .33 H1
★ Royal Hosp Chelsea & Mus,
SW3 . . . . .32 B4
Royal Hosp Rd, SW3 . . . . .31 J5
Royal London Est, The, N17 . .60 E6
★ Royal Mews, The, SW1 . . . .24 E5
★ Royal Military Acad, SE18 .136 C7
Royal Mint Ct, EC3 . . . . .21 G6
Royal Mint Pl, E1 . . . . .21 G5
Royal Mint St, E1 . . . . .21 G5
Royal Mt Ct, Twick. TW2 . . . .162 B3
★ Royal Nat Thea, SE1 . . . . . .26 C1
Royal Naval Pl, SE14 . . . . . . .133 J7
Royal Oak Ct, N1 off Pitfield St .112 B3
Royal Oak Pl, SE22 . . . . .153 E6
Royal Oak Rd, E8 . . . . .94 E6
Bexleyheath DA6 . . . . .159 F5
Royal Oak Yd, SE1 . . . . .28 E4
Royal Opera Arc, SW1 . . . . . . .25 H1
★ Royal Opera Ho, WC2 . . . . .18 B4
Royal Orchard Cl, SW18 . . . . .148 B7
Royal Par, SE3 . . . . .155 E2
SW6 off Dawes Rd 128 B7
W5 off Western Av 105 H3
Chislehurst BR7 . . . . .175 F7
Richmond TW9
off Station App 146 A1
Royal Par Ms, SE3 off Royal Par .155 F2
Chislehurst BR7 . . . . .175 F7
Royal Pl, SE10 . . . . .134 C7
Royal Quarter, Kings.T. KT2
off Seven Kings Way 181 H1
Royal Rd, E16 . . . . .116 A6
SE17 . . . . .35 G5
Sidcup DA14 . . . . .176 D3
Teddington TW11 . . . . . . .162 A5
Royal Route, Wem. HA9 . . . . . .87 J4
Royal St, SE1 . . . . .26 D5
Royalty Ms, W1 . . . . .17 H4
Royal Victoria Dock, E16 . . . . .116 H7
Royal Victoria Patriotic Bldg, SW18
off Fitzhugh Gro 149 G6
Royal Victoria Pl, E16
off Wesley Av 135 H1
Royal Victoria Sq, E16
off Western Gateway 115 H7
Royal Victor Pl, E3 . . . . .113 G2
Royal Wk, Wall. SM6
off Prince Charles Way 200 B3
Roycraft Av, Bark. IG11 . . . . . .117 J2
Roycraft Cl, Bark. IG11 . . . . . .117 J2
Roycroft Cl, E18 . . . . .79 H1
SW2 . . . . .169 G1
Roydene Rd, SE18 . . . . .137 H6
Roydon Cl, SW11 off Reform St .149 J2
Loughton IG10 . . . . .48 B7
Roydon St, SW11
off Southolm St 150 B1
Roy Gdns, Ilf. IG2 . . . . .81 H4
Roy Gro, Hmptn. TW12 . . . . . .161 H6
Royle Cres, W13 . . . . .104 D4
Roy Sq, E14 off Narrow St 113 H7
Royston Av, E4 . . . . .62 A5
Sutton SM1 . . . . .199 G3
Wallington SM6 . . . . .200 D4
Royston Cl, Houns. TW5 . . . . .142 B1
Royston Ct, SE24
off Burbage Rd 151 J6
Richmond TW9
off Lichfield Rd 145 J1

Royston Ct, Surb. KT6
off Hook Ri N 196 A3
Royston Gdns, Ilf. IG1 . . . . . . .80 A6
Royston Gro, Pnr. HA5 . . . . . . .51 F6
Royston Par, Ilf. IG1 . . . . .80 A6
Royston Pk Rd, Pnr. HA5 . . . . .51 F6
Royston Rd, SE20 . . . . .189 G1
Richmond TW10 . . . . .145 H5
Roystons, The, Surb. KT5 . . . .182 B5
Royston St, E2 . . . . .113 F2
Rozel Ct, N1 . . . . .112 B1
Rozel Rd, SW4 . . . . .150 C2
Rubastic Rd, Sthl. UB2 . . . . . .122 B3
Rubens Pl, SW4 off Dolman St .151 F4
Rubens Rd, Nthlt. UB5 . . . . . .102 C2
Rubens St, SE6 . . . . .171 J2
Ruby Ms, E17 off Ruby Rd 78 A3
Ruby Rd, E17 . . . . .78 A3
Ruby St, NW10 off Diamond St .88 D7
SE15 . . . . .132 E6
Ruby Triangle, SE15
off Sandgate St 132/133 E6
Ruckholt Cl, E10 . . . . .96 B3
Ruckholt Rd, E10 . . . . .96 A4
Rucklidge Av, NW10 . . . . .107 F2
Rudall Cres, NW3
off Willoughby Rd 91 G4
Ruddington Cl, E5 . . . . .95 H4
Ruddock Cl, Edg. HA8 . . . . . . .54 C7
Ruddstreet Cl, SE18 . . . . .137 E4
Rudgwick Ter, NW8
off Avenue Rd 109 H1
Rudland Rd, Bexh. DA7 . . . . . .159 H3
Rudloe Rd, SW12 . . . . .150 C7
Rudolf Pl, SW8 . . . . .34 B6
Rudolph Ct, SE22 . . . . .152 D7
Rudolph Rd, E13 . . . . .115 F2
NW6 . . . . .108 D2
Rudyard Gro, NW7 . . . . .54 C6
Ruffetts, The, S.Croy. CR2 . . . .203 E7
Ruffetts Cl, S.Croy. CR2 . . . . .202 E7
Ruffle Cl, West Dr. UB7 . . . . . .120 B2
Rufford Cl, Har. HA3 . . . . .68 D6
Rufford St, N1 . . . . .111 E1
Rufford Twr, W3 . . . . .126 B1
Rufus Cl, Ruis. HA4 . . . . .84 E3
Rufus St, N1 . . . . .12 D4
Rugby Av, N9 . . . . .60 C1
Greenford UB6 . . . . .86 A6
Wembley HA0 . . . . .87 E5
Rugby Cl, Har. HA1 . . . . .68 B5
★ Rugby Football Union
Twickenham, Twick. TW2 . . . .144 B6
Rugby Gdns, Dag. RM9 . . . . . .100 C6
Rugby Rd, NW9 . . . . .70 B4
W4 . . . . .126 E2
Dagenham RM9 . . . . .100 B7
Twickenham TW1 . . . . . . .144 B6
Rugby St, WC1 . . . . .10 C6
Rugg St, E14 . . . . .114 A7
Ruislip Cl, Grnf. UB6 . . . . .103 H4
RUISLIP MANOR, Ruis. HA4 . .84 A2
Ruislip Rd, Grnf. UB6 . . . . . . .103 G3
Northolt UB5 . . . . .102 D2
Southall UB1 . . . . .103 G3
Ruislip Rd E, W7 . . . . .104 A4
W13 . . . . .104 A4
Greenford UB6 . . . . .104 A4
Ruislip St, SW17 . . . . .167 J4
Rumbold Rd, SW6 . . . . .129 E7
Rum Cl, E1 . . . . .113 F7
Rumsey Cl, Hmptn. TW12 . . . .161 F6
Rumsey Ms, N4 off Monsell Rd .93 H3
Rumsey Rd, SW9 . . . . .151 F3
Runbury Circle, NW9 . . . . .88 D2
Runcorn Cl, N17 . . . . .76 E4
Runcorn Pl, W11 . . . . .108 B7
Rundell Cres, NW4 . . . . .71 H5
Runes Cl, Mitch. CR4 . . . . . . .185 G4
Runnel Fld, Har. HA1 . . . . .86 B3
Running Horse Yd, Brent. TW8
off Pottery Rd 125 H6
Runnymede, SW19 . . . . .185 G1
Runnymede Cl, Twick. TW2 . . .143 H6
Runnymede Ct, Croy. CR0 . . . .202 C2
Runnymede Cres, SW16 . . . . .186 D1
Runnymede Gdns, Grnf. UB6 .104 A2
Twickenham TW2 . . . . . . .143 H6
Runnymede Ho, E9
off Kingsmead Way 95 H4
Runnymede Rd, Twick. TW2 . .143 H6
Runway, The, Ruis. HA4 . . . . . .84 B5
Rupack St, SE16
off St. Marychurch St 133 F2
Rupert Av, Wem. HA9 . . . . . . .87 H5
Rupert Ct, W1 . . . . .17 H5
West Molesey KT8
off St. Peter's Rd 179 G4
Rupert Gdns, SW9 . . . . .151 H2
Rupert Rd, N19
off Holloway Rd 92 D3
NW6 . . . . .108 C2
W4 . . . . .127 E3
Rupert St, W1 . . . . .17 H5
Rural Way, SW16 . . . . .168 B7

Rusbridge Cl, E8
off Amhurst Rd 94 D5
Ruscoe Rd, E16 . . . . .115 F6
Ruscombe Way, Felt. TW14 . . .141 J7
Rush, The, SW19
off Kingston Rd 184 C1
Rusham Rd, SW12 . . . . .149 J6
Rushbrook Cres, E17 . . . . .77 J1
Rushbrook Rd, SE9 . . . . .175 F2
Rush Common Ms, SW2 . . . . .151 F7
Rushcroft Rd, E4 . . . . .62 A7
SW2 . . . . .151 G4
Rushden Cl, SE19 . . . . .170 A7
Rushdene, SE2 . . . . .138 D3
Rushdene Av, Barn. EN4 . . . . .41 H7
Rushdene Cl, Nthlt. UB5 . . . . .102 C3
Rushdene Cres, Nthlt. UB5 . . .102 C2
Rushdene Rd, Pnr. HA5 . . . . . .66 D6
Rushden Gdns, NW7 . . . . .55 J6
Ilford IG5 . . . . .80 D3
Rushen Wk, Cars. SM5
off Paisley Rd 199 G1
Rushett Cl, T.Ditt. KT7 . . . . . .194 E1
Rushett Rd, T.Ditt. KT7 . . . . . .180 E7
Rushey Cl, N.Mal. KT3 . . . . . .182 D4
Rushey Grn, SE6 . . . . .154 B7
Rushey Hill, Enf. EN2 . . . . . . .43 F4
Rushey Mead, SE4 . . . . .154 A5
Rushford Rd, SE4 . . . . .153 J6
RUSH GREEN, Rom. RM7 . . . .83 J7
Rush Grn Gdns, Rom. RM7 . . .101 J1
Rush Grn Rd, Rom. RM7 . . . . .101 J1
Rushgrove Av, NW9 . . . . .71 F5
Rush Gro St, SE18 . . . . .136 C4
Rush Hill Ms, SW11
off Rush Hill Rd 150 A3
Rush Hill Rd, SW11 . . . . .150 A3
Rushley Cl, Kes. BR2 . . . . . . .206 A4
Rushmead, E2
off Florida St 112/113 E3
Richmond TW10 . . . . .163 E3
Rushmead Cl, Croy. CR0 . . . . .202 C4
Rushmere Ct, Wor.Pk. KT4
off The Avenue 197 G2
Rushmere Ho, SW15
off Fontley Way 165 G1
Rushmere Pl, SW19 . . . . .166 A5
Rushmoor Cl, Pnr. HA5 . . . . . .66 B4
Rushmore Cl, Brom. BR1 . . . .192 B3
Rushmore Cres, E5
off Rushmore Rd 95 G4
Rushmore Rd, E5 . . . . .95 F4
Rusholme Av, Dag. RM10 . . . .101 G3
Rusholme Gro, SE19 . . . . . . .170 B5
Rusholme Rd, SW15 . . . . .148 A6
Rushout Av, Har. HA3 . . . . .68 E6
Rushton St, N1 . . . . .12 C1
Rushworth Av, NW4
off Rushworth Gdns 71 G3
Rushworth Gdns, NW4 . . . . . .71 G3
Rushworth St, SE1 . . . . .27 H3
Rushy Meadow La, Cars. SM5 .199 H2
Ruskin Av, E12 . . . . .98 B6
Feltham TW14 . . . . .141 J6
Richmond TW9 . . . . .126 A7
Welling DA16 . . . . .158 A3
Ruskin Cl, NW11 . . . . .72 E6
Ruskin Dr, Orp. BR6 . . . . .207 H3
Welling DA16 . . . . .158 A3
Worcester Park KT4 . . . . . .197 H2
Ruskin Gdns, W5 . . . . .105 G4
Harrow HA3 . . . . .69 J4
Ruskin Gro, Well. DA16 . . . . . .158 A2
Ruskin Pk Ho, SE5 . . . . .152 A3
Ruskin Rd, N17 . . . . .76 C1
Belvedere DA17 . . . . .139 G4
Carshalton SM5 . . . . .199 J5
Croydon CR0 . . . . .201 H2
Isleworth TW7 . . . . .144 C3
Southall UB1 . . . . .102 E7
Ruskin Wk, N9 off Durham Rd . .60 D2
SE24 . . . . .151 J5
Bromley BR2 . . . . .192 C6
Ruskin Way, SW19 . . . . .185 G1
Rusland Av, Orp. BR6 . . . . . . .207 G3
Rusland Hts, Har. HA1
off Rusland Pk Rd 68 B4
Rusland Pk Rd, Har. HA1 . . . . .68 B4
Rusper Cl, NW2 . . . . .89 J3
Stanmore HA7 . . . . .53 F4
Rusper Rd, N22 . . . . .75 J2
Dagenham RM9 . . . . .100 C6
Russell Av, N22 . . . . .75 H2
Russell Cl, NW10 . . . . .88 C7
SE7 . . . . .135 J7
W4 . . . . .127 F6
Beckenham BR3 . . . . .190 B3
Bexleyheath DA7 . . . . .159 G4
Ruislip HA4 . . . . .84 C2
Russell Ct, SW1 . . . . .25 G2
Russell Dr, Stai. (Stanw.) TW19 .140 A6
Russell Gdns, N20 . . . . .57 H2
NW11 . . . . .72 B6
W14 . . . . .128 B3
Richmond TW10 . . . . .163 F2

Russell Gdns, West Dr. UB7 . . .120 D5
Russell Gdns Ms, W14 . . . . . .128 B3
Russell Gro, NW7 . . . . .54 E5
SW9 . . . . .131 G7
Russell Kerr Cl, W4
off Burlington La 126 C7
Russell La, N20 . . . . .57 H2
Russell Mead, Har. (Har.Wld)
HA3 . . . . .68 C1
Russell Par, NW11
off Golders Grn Rd 72 B6
Russell Pl, NW3 off Aspern Gro .91 H5
SE16 off Onega Gate 133 H3
Russell Rd, E4 . . . . .61 J4
E10 . . . . .78 B6
E16 . . . . .115 G6
E17 . . . . .77 J3
N8 . . . . .74 D6
N13 . . . . .59 F6
N15 . . . . .76 B5
N20 . . . . .57 H2
NW9 . . . . .71 F6
SW19 . . . . .166 D7
W14 . . . . .128 B3
Buckhurst Hill IG9 . . . . . . .63 H1
Mitcham CR4 . . . . .185 H3
Northolt UB5 . . . . .85 J5
Twickenham TW2 . . . . . . .144 C6
Walton-on-Thames KT12 . . .178 A6
Russell's Footpath, SW16 . . . .169 E5
Russell Sq, WC1 . . . . .10 A6
Russell St, WC2 . . . . .18 B5
Russell Wk, Rich. TW10
off Park Hill 145 J6
Russell Way, Sutt. SM1 . . . . . .198 D5
Russet Cres, N7
off Stock Orchard Cres 93 F5
Russet Dr, Croy. CR0 . . . . . . .203 H1
Russets Cl, E4 off Larkshall Rd . .62 D4
Russett Way, SE13 . . . . .154 B2
Russia Ct, EC2 . . . . .20 A3
Russia Dock Rd, SE16 . . . . . .133 H1
Russia La, E2 . . . . .113 F2
Russia Row, EC2 . . . . .20 A4
Russia Wk, SE16 . . . . .133 H2
Rusthall Av, W4 . . . . .126 D4
Rusthall Cl, Croy. CR0 . . . . . .189 F6
Rustic Av, SW16 . . . . .168 B7
Rustic Pl, Wem. HA0 . . . . .87 G4
Rustic Wk, E16 off Lambert Rd .115 H6
Rustington Wk, Mord. SM4 . . .184 C7
Ruston Av, Surb. KT5 . . . . . . .182 B7
Ruston Gdns, N14
off Farm La 42 A6
Ruston Ms, W11
off St. Marks Rd 108 B6
Ruston Rd, SE18 . . . . .136 B3
Ruston St, E3 . . . . .113 J1
Rust Sq, SE5 . . . . .36 B7
Rutford Rd, SW16 . . . . .168 E5
Ruth Cl, Stan. HA7 . . . . .69 J4
Rutherford Cl, Borwd. WD6 . . .38 C2
Sutton SM2 . . . . .199 G6
Rutherford St, SW1 . . . . .33 H1
Rutherford Twr, Sthl. UB1 . . . .103 H6
Rutherford Way, Bushey (Bushey Hth)
WD23 . . . . .52 A1
Wembley HA9 . . . . .88 A4
Rutherglen Rd, SE2 . . . . .138 A6
Rutherwyke Cl, Epsom KT17 . .197 G6
Ruthin Cl, NW9 . . . . .70 E6
Ruthin Rd, SE3 . . . . .135 G6
Ruthven St, E9 off Lauriston Rd .113 G1
Rutland Av, Sid. DA15 . . . . . . .158 A7
Rutland Cl, SW14 . . . . .146 C1
SW19 off Rutland Rd 167 H7
Bexley DA5 . . . . .176 D1
Chessington KT9 . . . . .195 J6
Rutland Ct, Enf. EN3 . . . . .45 F5
Rutland Dr, Mord. SM4 . . . . . .184 C6
Richmond TW10 . . . . .163 G4
Rutland Gdns, N4 . . . . .75 H6
SW7 . . . . .23 H4
W13 . . . . .104 D5
Croydon CR0 . . . . .202 B4
Dagenham RM8 . . . . .100 C5
Rutland Gdns Ms, SW7 . . . . . .23 H4
Rutland Gate, SW7 . . . . .23 H4
Belvedere DA17 . . . . .139 H5
Bromley BR2 . . . . .191 F4
Rutland Gate Ms, SW7 . . . . . .23 G4
Rutland Gro, W6 . . . . .127 H5
Rutland Ms, NW8
off Boundary Rd 108/109 E1
Rutland Ms E, SW7 . . . . .23 G5
Rutland Ms S, SW7 . . . . .23 G5
Rutland Ms W, SW7
off Ennismore St 129 H3
Rutland Pk, NW2 . . . . .89 J6
SE6 . . . . .171 J2
Rutland Pk Gdns, NW2
off Rutland Pk 89 J6
Rutland Pk Mans, NW2
off Walm La 89 J6
Rutland Pl, EC1 . . . . .11 J6

Rutland Pl, Bushey (Bushey Hth)
   WD23 *off The Rutts* **52** A1
Rutland Rd, E7 . . . .**98** A7
  E9 . . . .**113** H7
  E11 . . . .**79** H5
  E17 . . . .**78** A6
  SW19 . . . .**167** H7
  Harrow HA1 . . . .**67** J6
  Hayes UB3 . . . .**121** G4
  Ilford IG1 . . . .**99** E4
  Southall UB1 . . . .**103** G4
  Twickenham TW2 . . . .**162** A2
Rutland St, SW7 . . . .**23** H5
Rutland Wk, SE6 . . . .**171** J2
Rutley Cl, SE17 . . . .**35** G5
Rutlish Rd, SW19 . . . .**184** D1
Rutter Gdns, Mitch. CR4 . . . . . .**185** F4
Rutters Cl, West Dr. UB7 . . . . . .**120** D2
Rutts, The, Bushey (Bushey Hth)
  WD23 . . . .**52** A1
Rutts Ter, SE14 . . . .**153** C5
Ruvigny Gdns, SW15 . . . .**148** A3
Ruxley Cl, Epsom KT19 . . . .**196** B5
  Sidcup DA14 . . . .**176** D6
Ruxley Cor Ind Est, Sid. DA14 .**176** D6
Ruxley Cres, Esher (Clay.) KT10 .**194** E6
Ruxley La, Epsom KT19 . . . .**196** B5
Ruxley Ms, Epsom KT19 . . . . . .**196** B5
Ruxley Ridge, Esher (Clay.) KT10 .**194** D7
Ryalls Ct, N20 . . . .**57** J3
Ryan Cl, SE3 . . . .**155** J4
  Ruislip HA4 . . . .**84** B1
Ryan Dr, Brent. TW8 . . . .**124** D6
Ryarsh Cres, Orp. BR6 . . . .**207** H4
Rycott Path, SE22
   off Lordship La **152** D7
Ryculff Sq, SE3 . . . .**155** F2
Rydal Cl, NW4 . . . .**72** B1
Rydal Cres, Grnf. UB6 . . . .**105** E3
Rydal Dr, Bexh. DA7 . . . .**159** G1
  West Wickham BR4 . . . .**205** E2
Rydal Gdns, NW9 . . . .**71** E5
  SW15 . . . .**164** E5
  Hounslow TW3 . . . .**143** H6
  Wembley HA9 . . . .**87** F1
Rydal Rd, SW16 . . . .**168** D4
Rydal Way, Enf. EN3 . . . .**45** F6
  Ruislip HA4 . . . .**84** C4
Ryde Pl, Twick. TW1 . . . .**145** F6
Ryder Cl, Brom. BR1 . . . .**173** H5
Ryder Ct, SW1 . . . .**25** G1
Ryder Dr, SE16 . . . .**132** E5
Ryder Ms, E9
   off Homerton High St **95** F5
Ryders Ter, NW8 . . . .**6** C1
Ryder St, SW1 . . . .**25** G1
Ryder Yd, SW1 . . . .**25** G1
Ryde Vale Rd, SW12 . . . .**168** B2
Rydons Cl, SE9 . . . .**156** B3
Rydon St, N1 *off St. Paul St* **111** J1
Rydston Cl, N7 *off Sutterton St* . .**93** F7
Rye, The, N14 . . . .**42** C7
Rye Cl, Bex. DA5 . . . .**159** H6
Ryecotes Mead, SE21 . . . .**170** B1
Ryecroft Av, Ilf. IG5 . . . .**80** E2
  Twickenham TW2 . . . .**143** H7
Ryecroft Cres, Barn. EN5 . . . . . .**39** H5
Ryecroft Rd, SE13 . . . .**154** C5
  SW16 . . . .**169** G6
  Orpington BR5 . . . .**193** G6
Ryecroft St, SW6 . . . .**148** E1
Ryedale, SE22 . . . .**152** E6
Ryefield Ct, Nthwd. HA6
   off Ryefield Cres **66** A2
Ryefield Cres, Nthwd. HA6 . . . . .**66** A2
Ryefield Par, Nthwd. HA6
   off Ryefield Cres **66** A2
Ryefield Path, SW15 . . . .**165** G1
Ryefield Rd, SE19 . . . .**169** J6
Ryegates, SE15
   off Caulfield Rd **152/153** E2
Rye Hill Pk, SE15 . . . .**153** F4
Ryelands Cres, SE12 . . . .**155** J6
Rye La, SE15 . . . .**152** D1
Rye Pas, SE15 . . . .**152** D3
Rye Rd, SE15 . . . .**153** G4
Rye Wk, SW15 *off Chartfield Av* .**148** A5
Rye Way, Edg. HA8
   off Canons Dr **53** J6
Ryfold Rd, SW19 . . . .**166** D3
Ryhope Rd, N11 . . . .**58** B4
Rylandes Rd, NW2 . . . .**89** G3
Ryland Ho, Croy. CR0 . . . .**201** J3
Ryland Rd, NW5 . . . .**92** B6
Rylett Cres, W12 . . . .**127** F3
Rylett Rd, W12 . . . .**127** F2
Rylston Rd, N13 . . . .**60** A3
  SW6 . . . .**128** C6
Rymer Rd, Croy. CR0 . . . .**188** B7
Rymer St, SE24 . . . .**151** H6
Rymill St, E16 . . . .**136** D1
Rysbrack St, SW3 . . . .**23** J5
Rythe Cl, Chess. KT9
   off Nigel Fisher Way **195** F7

Rythe Ct, T.Ditt. KT7 . . . .**180** D7
Rythe Rd, Esher (Clay.) KT10 . . .**194** A5

S

★ **Saatchi Gall**, SE1 . . . .**26** C4
Sabbarton St, E16
   off Victoria Dock Rd **115** F6
Sabella Ct, E3 . . . .**113** J2
Sabine Rd, SW11 . . . .**149** J3
Sable Cl, Houns. TW4 . . . .**142** C3
Sable St, N1 . . . .**93** H7
Sach Rd, E5 . . . .**95** E2
Sackville Av, Brom. BR2 . . . . . .**205** G1
Sackville Cl, Har. HA2 . . . .**86** A3
Sackville Est, SW16 . . . .**169** E3
Sackville Gdns, Ilf. IG1 . . . .**98** C1
Sackville Rd, Sutt. SM2 . . . .**198** D7
Sackville St, W1 . . . .**17** G6
Sackville Way, SE22
   off Dulwich Common **170** D1
Saddlers Cl, Barn. (Arkley) EN5 . .**39** H5
  Borehamwood WD6
   off Farriers Way **38** D6
  Pinner HA5 . . . .**51** G6
Saddlers Ms, SW8
   off Portland Gro **151** F1
  Kingston upon Thames (Hmptn W.)
   KT1 . . . .**181** F1
  Wembley HA0
   off The Boltons **86** C4
Saddlers Path, Borwd. WD6 . . . .**38** D5
Saddlescombe Way, N12 . . . . . .**56** D5
Saddle Yd, W1 . . . .**24** D1
Sadler Cl, Mitch. CR4 . . . .**185** J2
Sadlers Ride, W.Mol. KT8 . . . . .**179** J2
★ **Sadler's Wells Thea**, EC1 . . . .**11** G3
Saffron Av, E14 . . . .**114** D7
Saffron Cl, NW11 . . . .**72** C5
  Croydon CR0 . . . .**186** E6
Saffron Ct, Felt. TW14
   off Staines Rd **141** F7
Saffron Hill, EC1 . . . .**11** F6
Saffron Rd, Rom. RM5 . . . .**83** J2
Saffron St, EC1 . . . .**19** F1
Saffron Way, Surb. KT6 . . . .**195** G1
Sage Cl, E6
   off Bradley Stone Rd **116** C5
Sage Ms, SE22 *off Lordship La* .**152** C5
Sage St, E1 *off Cable St* **113** F7
Sage Way, WC1 . . . .**10** C4
Saigasso Cl, E16 *off Royal Rd* . .**116** A6
Sail Ct, E14 *off Newport Av* **114** D7
Sailmakers Ct, SW6
   off William Morris Way **149** F3
Sail St, SE11 . . . .**34** D1
Sainfoin Rd, SW17 . . . .**168** A2
Saini Ms, N8
   off Harringay Gdns **75** H3
Sainsbury Rd, SE19 . . . .**170** B5
St. Agatha's Dr, Kings.T. KT2 . . .**163** J6
St. Agathas Gro, Cars. SM5 . . . .**199** J1
St. Agnes Cl, E9 *off Gore Rd* . . .**113** F1
St. Agnes Pl, SE11 . . . .**35** G6
St. Agnes Well, EC1 *off Old St* . .**112** A4
St. Aidans Ct, W13
   off St. Aidans Rd **124/125** E2
  Barking IG11 *off Choats Rd* . .**118** B3
St. Aidan's Rd, SE22 . . . .**152** E6
St. Aidans Rd, W13 . . . .**125** E2
St. Alban's Av, E6 . . . .**116** C3
St. Albans Av, W4 . . . .**126** D4
St. Albans Av, Felt. TW13 . . . . . .**160** D5
St. Albans Cl, NW11 . . . .**90** D1
St. Albans Ct, EC2 . . . .**20** A3
St. Albans Cres, N22 . . . .**75** G1
St. Alban's Cres, Wdf.Grn. IG8 . .**63** G7
St. Alban's Gdns, Tedd. TW11 . .**162** D5
St. Albans Gro, W8 . . . .**22** B5
St. Alban's Gro, Cars. SM5 . . . .**185** H7
St. Albans La, NW11
   off West Heath Dr **90** D1
St. Alban's Pl, N1 . . . .**111** H1
St. Albans Rd, NW5 . . . .**92** A3
  NW10 . . . .**106** E1
  Barnet EN5 . . . .**40** A1
  Ilford IG3 . . . .**99** J1
St. Alban's Rd, Kings.T. KT2 . . . .**163** H6
  Sutton SM1 . . . .**198** C4
  Woodford Green IG8 . . . .**63** G7
St. Albans St, SW1 . . . .**17** H6
St. Albans Ter, W6
   off Margravine Rd **128** B6
St. Alban's Vil, NW5
   off Highgate Rd **92** A3
St. Alfege Pas, SE10 . . . .**134** C6
St. Alfege Rd, SE7 . . . .**136** A6
St. Alphage Gdns, EC2 . . . .**20** A2
St. Alphage Highwalk, EC2 . . . . .**20** B2
St. Alphage Wk, Edg. HA8 . . . . . .**70** C2
St. Alphege Rd, N9 . . . .**45** F7
St. Alphonsus Rd, SW4 . . . .**150** C4
St. Amunds Cl, SE6 . . . .**172** A4
St. Andrews Av, Wem. HA0 . . . . .**86** D4

St. Andrew's Cl, N12
   off Woodside Av **57** F4
St. Andrews Cl, NW2 . . . .**89** H3
  SE16 *off Ryder Dr* **132/133** E5
  SE28 . . . .**118** D6
St. Andrew's Cl, Islw. TW7 . . . . .**144** A1
St. Andrews Cl, Ruis. HA4 . . . . . .**84** D2
  Stanmore HA7 . . . .**69** F2
  Thames Ditton KT7 . . . .**194** E1
St. Andrew's Ct, SW18
   off Waynflete St **167** F2
St. Andrews Dr, Stan. HA7 . . . . .**69** F1
St. Andrew's Gro, N16 . . . .**94** A1
St. Andrew's Hill, EC4 . . . .**19** H5
St. Andrew's Ms, N16 . . . .**94** B1
St. Andrews Ms, SE3
   off Mycenae Rd **135** G7
St. Andrews Pl, NW1 . . . .**8** E5
St. Andrew's Rd, E11 . . . .**78** E6
  E13 . . . .**115** H3
  E17 . . . .**77** G2
  N9 . . . .**45** F7
  NW9 . . . .**88** D1
  NW10 . . . .**89** H6
  NW11 . . . .**72** C6
  W3 . . . .**107** E7
  W7 *off Churchfield Rd* **124** B1
  W14 . . . .**128** B6
  Carshalton SM5 . . . .**199** H3
  Croydon CR0
   off Lower Coombe St **201** J4
  Enfield EN1 . . . .**44** A3
  Ilford IG1 . . . .**80** C7
  Sidcup DA14 . . . .**176** D3
St. Andrew's Rd, Surb. KT6 . . . .**181** G6
St. Andrews Sq, W11
   off St. Marks Rd **108** B6
St. Andrew's Sq, Surb. KT6 . . . .**181** G6
St. Andrews Twr, Sthl. UB1 . . . .**103** J7
St. Andrew St, EC4 . . . .**19** F2
St. Andrews Way, E3 . . . .**114** B4
St. Anna Rd, Barn. EN5
   off Sampson Av **40** A5
St. Anne's Av, Stai. (Stanw.)
  TW19 . . . .**140** A7
St. Anne's Cl, N6
   off Highgate W Hill **92** A3
  Watford WD19 . . . .**50** C4
St. Anne's Ct, W1 . . . .**17** H4
St. Annes Gdns, NW10 . . . .**105** J3
St. Annes Pas, E14
   off Newell St **113** J6
St. Annes Rd, E11 . . . .**96** D2
St. Anne's Rd, Wem. HA0 . . . . . .**87** G5
St. Anne's Row, E14
   off Commercial Rd **113** J6
St. Anne St, E14
   off Commercial Rd **113** J6
St. Ann's, Bark. IG11 . . . .**117** F1
St. Ann's Cres, SW18 . . . .**149** F6
St. Ann's Gdns, NW5
   off Queen's Cres **92** A6
St. Ann's Hill, SW18 . . . .**149** E5
St. Ann's La, SW1 . . . .**25** J5
St. Ann's Pk Rd, SW18 . . . .**149** F6
St. Ann's Pas, SW13 . . . .**147** E3
St. Anns Rd, N9 . . . .**60** C2
St. Ann's Rd, N15 . . . .**75** H5
  SW13 . . . .**147** F2
St. Anns Rd, W11 . . . .**108** A7
St. Ann's Rd, Bark. IG11
   off Axe St **117** F1
  Harrow HA1 . . . .**68** B6
St. Ann's Shop Cen, Har. HA1 . . .**68** B6
St. Ann's St, SW1 . . . .**25** J5
St. Ann's Ter, NW8 . . . .**7** F1
St. Anns Vil, W11 . . . .**128** A1
St. Anns Way, S.Croy. CR2 . . . .**201** H6
St. Anselm's Pl, W1 . . . .**16** D4
St. Anselms Rd, Hayes UB3 . . . .**121** J2
St. Anthonys Av, Wdf.Grn. IG8 . .**63** J6
St. Anthonys Cl, E1 . . . .**29** H1
  SW17 *off College Gdns* **167** H2
St. Anthony's Way, Felt. TW14 . .**141** J4
St. Antony's Rd, E7 . . . .**97** H7
St. Arvans Cl, Croy. CR0 . . . . . .**202** B3
St. Asaph Rd, SE4 . . . .**153** G3
St. Aubins Ct, N1
   off De Beauvoir Est **112** A1
St. Aubyn's Av, SW19 . . . .**166** C5
St. Aubyns Av, Houns. TW3 . . . .**143** G5
St. Aubyns Cl, Orp. BR6 . . . .**207** J3
St. Aubyns Gdns, Orp. BR6 . . . .**207** J2
St. Aubyn's Rd, SE19 . . . .**170** C6
St. Audrey Av, Bexh. DA7 . . . . . .**159** G2
St. Augustine's Av, W5 . . . .**105** H2
St. Augustines Av, Brom. BR2 . .**192** B5
St. Augustine's Av, S.Croy. CR2 .**201** J6
St. Augustines Av, Wem. HA9 . . .**87** H4
St. Augustine's Path, N5
   off Highbury New Pk **93** J4
St. Augustines Rd, NW1 . . . .**92** D7
St. Augustine's Rd, Belv. DA17 . .**139** F4
St. Austell Cl, Edg. HA8 . . . .**69** J2

St. Austell Rd, SE13 . . . .**154** C2
St. Awdry's Rd, Bark. IG11 . . . . .**99** G7
St. Awdry's Wk, Bark. IG11
   off Station Par **99** F7
St. Barnabas Cl, SE22
   off East Dulwich Gro **152** B5
  Beckenham BR3 . . . .**190** C2
St. Barnabas Ct, Har. HA3 . . . . . .**67** J1
St. Barnabas Gdns, W.Mol. KT8 .**179** G5
St. Barnabas Rd, E17 . . . .**78** A6
  Mitcham CR4 . . . .**168** A7
  Sutton SM1 . . . .**199** G5
  Woodford Green IG8 . . . .**79** H1
St. Barnabas St, SW1 . . . .**32** C3
St. Barnabas Ter, E9 . . . .**95** G5
St. Barnabas Vil, SW8 . . . .**151** E1
St. Bartholomews Cl, SE26 . . . .**171** F4
St. Bartholomew's Rd, E6 . . . . .**116** B1
★ **St. Bartholomew-the-Great Ch**,
  EC1 . . . .**19** H2
St. Benedict's Cl, SW17
   off Church La **168** A5
St. Benet's Cl, SW17
   off College Gdns **167** H2
St. Benet's Gro, Cars. SM5 . . . .**185** F7
St. Benet's Pl, EC3 . . . .**20** C5
St. Bernards, Croy. CR0 . . . .**202** B3
St. Bernard's Cl, SE27
   off St. Gothard Rd **170** A4
St. Bernard's Rd, E6 . . . .**116** A1
St. Blaise Av, Brom. BR1 . . . . . .**191** H2
St. Botolph Row, EC3 . . . .**21** F4
St. Botolph St, EC3 . . . .**21** F4
St. Brides Av, EC4 . . . .**19** G4
  Edgware HA8 . . . .**69** J1
★ **St. Bride's Ch & Crypt Mus**,
  EC4 . . . .**19** G4
St. Brides Cl, Erith DA18
   off St. Katherines Rd **138** D2
St. Bride's Pas, EC4 . . . .**19** G4
St. Bride St, EC4 . . . .**19** G3
St. Catherines Cl, SW17
   off College Gdns **167** H2
St. Catherines Dr, SE14
   off Kitto Rd **153** G2
St. Catherine's Ms, SW3 . . . .**31** J1
St. Catherines Rd, E4 . . . .**62** A2
St. Catherines Twr, E10
   off Kings Cl **78** B7
St. Cecilia's Cl, Sutt. SM3 . . . . .**198** B1
St. Chads Cl, Surb. KT6 . . . .**181** F7
St. Chad's Gdns, Rom. RM6 . . . .**82** E7
St. Chad's Pl, WC1 . . . .**10** B3
St. Chad's Rd, Rom. RM6 . . . . . .**82** E6
St. Chad's St, WC1 . . . .**10** B3
St. Charles Pl, W10
   off Chesterton Rd **108** B5
St. Charles Sq, W10 . . . .**108** B5
St. Christopher's Cl, Islw. TW7 . .**144** B1
St. Christopher's Dr, Hayes UB3 .**102** B7
St. Christophers Gdns, Th.Hth.
  CR7 . . . .**187** G3
St. Christophers Ms, Wall.
  SM6 . . . .**200** C5
St. Christopher's Pl, W1 . . . .**16** C3
St. Clair Dr, Wor.Pk. KT4 . . . . . .**197** H3
St. Clair Rd, E13 . . . .**115** H2
St. Clair's Rd, Croy. CR0 . . . . . .**202** B2
St. Clare Business Pk, Hmptn.
  TW12 . . . .**161** J6
St. Clare Cl, Ilf. IG5 . . . .**80** C2
St. Clare St, EC3 . . . .**21** F4
★ **St. Clement Danes Ch**, WC2 . .**18** D4
St. Clements Ct, EC4
   off Clements La **112** A7
  N7 *off Arundel Sq* **93** G6
St. Clements Hts, SE26 . . . .**170** D3
St. Clement's La, WC2 . . . .**18** D4
St. Clements La, N7 . . . .**93** G6
St. Clements Yd, SE22
   off Archdale Rd **152** C5
St. Cloud Rd, SE27 . . . .**169** J4
St. Crispins Cl, NW3 . . . .**91** H4
  Southall UB1 . . . .**103** F6
St. Cross St, EC1 . . . .**19** F1
St. Cuthberts Gdns, Pnr. HA5
   off Westfield Pk **51** F7
St. Cuthberts Rd, N13 . . . .**59** G6
  NW2 . . . .**90** C6
St. Cyprian's St, SW17 . . . .**167** J4
St. Davids Cl, SE16
   off Masters Dr **132/133** E5
  Wembley HA9 . . . .**88** C3
St. David's Cl, W.Wick. BR4 . . . .**190** B7
St. Davids Ct, E17 . . . .**78** C2
St. Davids Dr, Edg. HA8 . . . .**69** J1
St. Davids Ms, E3
   off Morgan St **113** H3
St. Davids Pl, NW4 . . . .**71** H7
St. Davids Sq, E14 . . . .**134** B5
St. Denis Rd, SE27 . . . .**170** A4
St. Dionis Rd, SW6 . . . .**148** C2
St. Donatts Rd, SE14 . . . .**153** J1
St. Dunstan's All, EC3 . . . .**20** D5
St. Dunstans Av, W3 . . . .**106** D7

St. Dunstans Cl, Hayes UB3 ....121 J4
St. Dunstan's Ct, EC4
   off Fleet St 111 G6
St. Dunstans Gdns, W3
   off St. Dunstans Av 106 D7
St. Dunstan's Hill, EC3 ....20 D6
Sutton SM1 ....198 B5
St. Dunstan's La, EC3 ....20 D6
Beckenham BR3 ....190 C6
St. Dunstan's Rd, E7 ....97 J6
St. Dunstans Rd, SE25 ....188 C4
W6 ....128 A5
W7 ....124 B2
Hounslow TW4 ....142 C2
St. Edmunds Cl, NW8
   off St. Edmunds Ter 109 J1
SW17 off College Gdns 167 H2
Erith DA18
   off St. Katherines Rd 138 D2
St. Edmunds Dr, Stan. HA7 ....68 D1
St. Edmund's La, Twick. TW2 ..143 H7
St. Edmunds Rd, N9 ....44 D7
Ilford IG1 ....80 C6
St. Edmunds Sq, SW13 ......127 J6
St. Edmunds Ter, NW8 ....7 H1
St. Edwards Cl, NW11 ....72 D6
St. Egberts Way, E4 ....62 C1
St. Elmo Rd, W12 ....127 F1
St. Elmos Rd, SE16 ....133 G2
St. Erkenwald Ms, Bark. IG11
   off St. Erkenwald Rd 117 G1
St. Erkenwald Rd, Bark. IG11 ..117 G1
St. Ermin's Hill, SW1 ....25 H5
St. Ervans Rd, W10 ....108 B5
St. Faiths Cl, Enf. EN2 ....43 J1
St. Faith's Rd, SE21 ....169 H1
St. Fillans Rd, SE6 ....172 C1
St. Francis Cl, Orp. BR5 ......193 H6
Watford WD19 ....50 B1
St. Francis Rd, SE22 ....152 B4
St. Francis Way, Ilf. IG1 ....99 H4
St. Frideswides Ms, E14
   off Lodore St 114 C6
St. Gabriel's Cl, E11 ....97 H2
St. Gabriels Rd, NW2 ....90 A5
St. Georges Av, E7 ....97 H7
N7 ....92 D4
NW9 ....70 C4
St. George's Av, W5 ....125 G2
St. Georges Av, Sthl. UB1 ....103 F7
St. Georges Cen, Har. HA1
   off St. Ann's Rd 68 B6
St. Georges Circ, SE1 ....27 G5
St. Georges Cl, NW11 ....72 C6
SE28 off Redbourne Dr 118 D6
St. George's Cl, SW8
   off Patmore St 150 C1
St. Georges Cl, Wem. HA0 .....86 D3
St. Georges Ct, E6 ....116 C4
EC4 ....19 G3
SW7 ....22 C5
St. George's Dr, SW1 ....33 F2
St. Georges Dr, Wat. WD19 ....50 E3
St. Georges Flds, W2 ....15 H4
St. George's Gdns, Surb. KT6
   off Hamilton Av 196 B2
St. Georges Gro, SW17 ......167 G3
St. Georges Gro Est, SW17 ...167 G3
St. Georges Ind Est, Kings.T. KT2
   off Richmond Rd 163 G5
St. Georges La, EC3 ....20 D5
St. Georges Ms, NW1
   off Regents Pk Rd 91 J7
SE1 ....27 F5
St. Georges Pl, Twick. TW1
   off Church St 162 D1
St. Georges Rd, E7 ....97 H6
E10 ....96 C3
N9 ....60 D3
N13 ....59 F3
NW11 ....72 C6
SE1 ....27 F5
St. George's Rd, SW19 ....166 E2
St. Georges Rd, W4 ....126 E2
W7 ....124 C1
St. George's Rd, Beck. BR3 ...190 B1
St. Georges Rd, Brom. BR1 ...192 C4
Dagenham RM9 ....100 E5
St. George's Rd, Felt. TW13 ..160 D4
St. Georges Rd, Ilf. IG1 ....80 C7
St. George's Rd, Kings.T. KT2 .164 A7
Mitcham CR4 ....186 B3
Orpington BR5 ....193 J6
St. Georges Rd, Rich. TW9 ...145 J3
St. George's Rd, Sid. DA14 ...176 D4
St. Georges Rd, Twick. TW1 ..145 E5
Wallington SM6 ....200 B5
St. Georges Rd W, Brom. BR1 .192 B1
St. Georges Sq, E7 ....97 H7
E14 off Narrow St 113 H7
SE8 ....133 J4
St. George's Sq, SW1 ....33 H3
New Malden KT3
   off High St 182/183 E3
St. George's Sq Ms, SW1 .....33 H4

St. Georges Ter, NW1
   off Regents Pk Rd 91 J7
St. George St, W1 ....17 E4
St. Georges Wk, Croy. CR0 ...201 J3
St. Georges Way, SE15 ....36 D6
St. George Wf, SW8 ....34 A4
St. Gerards Cl, SW4 ....150 C5
St. German's Pl, SE3 ....155 G1
St. Germans Rd, SE23 ....171 H1
St. Giles Av, Dag. RM10 ......101 H7
St. Giles Cl, Dag. RM10 ......101 H7
   off St. Giles Av
Hounslow TW5
   off Vicarage Fm Rd 123 F7
Orpington BR6 ....207 G5
St. Giles Ct, WC2
   off St. Giles High St ...110/111 E6
St. Giles High St, WC2 ....17 J3
St. Giles Pas, WC2 ....17 J4
St. Giles Rd, SE5 ....132 B7
St. Gilles Ho, E2 ....113 G2
St. Gothard Rd, SE27 ....170 A4
St. Gregory Cl, Ruis. HA4 ......84 C4
St. Helena Rd, SE16 ....133 G4
St. Helena St, WC1 ....10 E4
St. Helens Cres, SW16
   off St. Helens Rd 187 F1
St. Helens Gdns, W10 ....108 A6
St. Helens Pl, EC3 ....20 D3
St. Helens Rd, SW16 ....187 F1
St. Helen's Rd, W13
   off Dane Rd 124/125 E1
St. Helens Rd, Erith DA18 ....138 D2
Ilford IG1 ....80 C6
ST. HELIER, Cars. SM5 ......185 G7
St. Helier Av, Mord. SM4 .....185 F7
St. Heliers Av, Houns. TW3 ...143 G5
St. Heliers Rd, E10 ....78 C6
St. Hildas Cl, NW6 ....90 A7
SW17 ....167 H2
St. Hilda's Rd, SW13 ....127 H6
St. Hughe's Cl, SW17
   off College Gdns 167 H2
St. Hughs Rd, SE20
   off Ridsdale Rd 188/189 E1
St. James Av, N20 ....57 H3
W13 ....124 D1
Sutton SM1 ....198 D5
St. James Cl, N20 ....57 H3
SE18 off Congleton Gro 137 F5
Barnet EN4 ....41 G4
New Malden KT3 ....183 F5
Ruislip HA4 ....84 C2
St. James Gdns, Rom. (Lt.Hth)
RM6 ....82 B4
Wembley HA0 ....87 G7
St. James Gate, NW1
   off St. Paul's Cres 92 D7
St. James Gro, SW11
   off Reform St 149 J2
St. James Ms, E14 ....134 C4
E17 off St. James's St 77 H5
St. James Rd, E15 ....97 F5
N9 off Queens Rd 60/61 M2
Carshalton SM5 ....199 H3
Kingston upon Thames KT1 .181 H2
Mitcham CR4 ....168 A7
Surbiton KT6 ....181 G6
Sutton SM1 ....198 D5
ST. JAMES'S, SW1 ....25 G2
St. James's, SE14 ....153 H1
St. James's Av, E2 ....113 F2
Beckenham BR3 ....189 H3
Hampton (Hmptn H.) TW12 .161 J5
St. James's Cl, SW17
   off St. James's Dr 167 J2
St. James's Cotts, Rich. TW9
   off Paradise Rd 145 G5
St. James's Ct, SW1 ....25 G5
St. James's Cres, SW9 ....151 G3
St. James's Dr, SW12 ....167 J1
SW17 ....167 J1
St. James's Gdns, SW11 .....128 B1
St. James's La, N10 ....74 B4
St. James's Mkt, SW1 ....17 H6
★ St. James's Palace, SW1 ...25 G3
★ St. James's Park, SW1 .....25 H3
St. James's Pk, Croy. CR0 ...187 J7
St. James's Pas, EC3 ....21 E4
St. James's Pl, SW1 ....25 F2
St. James's Rd, SE1 ....37 J3
SE16 ....29 J5
Croydon CR0 ....187 H7
Hampton (Hmptn H.) TW12 .161 J5
St. James's Sq, SW1 ....25 G1
St. James's St, E17 ....77 H5
SW1 ....25 F1
St. James's Ter, NW8 ....7 J1
St. James's Ter Ms, NW8 .....109 J1
St. James St, W6 ....127 J5
St. James's Wk, EC1 ....11 G5
St. James Way, Sid. DA14 ...177 E5
St. Joans Rd, N9 ....60 C1
St. John Fisher Rd, Erith DA18 .138 D3
ST. JOHN'S, SE8 ....154 A2

St. Johns Av, N11 ....57 J5
St. John's Av, N10 ....107 F1
SW15 ....148 A5
St. John's Ch Rd, E9 ....95 F5
St. Johns Cl, N14 off Chase Rd .42 C6
St. John's Cl, SW6
   off Dawes Rd 128 D7
Wembley HA9 ....87 H5
St. John's Cotts, SE20
   off Maple Rd 171 F7
St. Johns Cotts, Rich. TW9
   off Kew Foot Rd 145 H4
St. Johns Ct, Buck.H. IG9 .....63 H1
St. John's Ct, Islw. TW7 ......144 C2
St. John's Cres, SW9 ....151 G3
St. Johns Dr, SW18 ....166 E1
St. John's Gdns, W11 ....108 C7
★ St. John's Gate & Mus of the
Order of St. John, EC1 ......11 G6
St. Johns Gro, N19 ....92 C2
SW13 off Terrace Gdns 147 F2
Richmond TW9
   off Kew Foot Rd 145 H4
St. John's Hill, SW11 ....149 G4
St. John's Hill Gro, SW11 ....149 G4
St. John's La, EC1 ....11 G6
St. John's Ms, W11
   off Ledbury Rd 108 D6
St. Johns Par, Sid. DA14 .....176 A4
St. John's Pk, SE3 ....135 F7
St. John's Pas, SW19
   off Ridgway Pl 166 B6
St. John's Path, EC1 ....11 G6
St. Johns Pathway, SE23
   off Devonshire Rd 171 F1
St. John's Pl, EC1 ....11 G6
St. John's Rd, E4 ....62 B3
E6 off Ron Leighton Way ...116 B1
St. Johns Rd, E16 ....115 G6
St. John's Rd, E17 ....78 B2
N15 ....76 B6
St. Johns Rd, N11 ....72 C6
St. John's Rd, SE20 ....171 F7
SW11 ....149 H4
SW19 ....166 B7
Barking IG11 ....117 H1
Carshalton SM5 ....199 H3
St. Johns Rd, Croy. CR0
   off Sylverdale Rd 201 H3
East Molesey KT8 ....180 A4
St. John's Rd, Felt. TW13 ....161 E4
Harrow HA1 ....68 C6
St. Johns Rd, Ilf. IG2 ....81 G7
St. John's Rd, Islw. TW7 .....144 B2
Kingston upon Thames (Hmptn W.)
KT1 ....181 F2
St. Johns Rd, Loug. IG10 .....48 C2
New Malden KT3 ....182 C3
St. John's Rd, Orp. BR5 ......193 G6
Richmond TW9 ....145 H4
St. Johns Rd, Sid. DA14 .....176 B4
Southall UB2 ....122 E3
Sutton SM1 ....198 D2
St. John's Rd, Well. DA16 ....158 B3
Wembley HA9 ....87 G4
St. John's Sq, EC1 ....11 G6
St. Johns Ter, E7 ....97 H6
SE18 ....137 F6
SW15 off Kingston Vale 164 D4
W10 off Harrow Rd 108 A4
St. John St, EC1 ....11 H6
St. Johns Vale, SE8 ....154 A2
St. Johns Vil, N19 ....92 D2
St. Johns Vil, W8 ....22 B6
St. Johns Way, N19 ....92 D1
ST. JOHN'S WOOD, NW8 ....6 E3
St. John's Wd Ct, NW8 ....7 F4
St. John's Wd High St, NW8 ....7 F2
St. John's Wd Pk, NW8 ....109 G1
St. John's Wd Rd, NW8 ....6 E5
St. John's Wd Ter, NW8 ....7 G1
St. Josephs Cl, W10
   off Bevington Rd 108 B5
St. Joseph's Cl, Orp. BR6 ....207 J4
St. Josephs Ct, SE7 ....135 H6
St. Josephs Dr, Sthl. UB1 ....123 E1
St. Joseph's Gro, NW4 ....71 H4
St. Josephs Rd, N9 ....45 E7
St. Josephs St, SW8
   off Battersea Pk Rd 150 B1
St. Joseph's Vale, SE3 ....154 D2
St. Jude's Rd, E2 ....113 E2
St. Jude St, N16 ....94 B5
St. Julian's Cl, SW16 ....169 G4
St. Julian's Fm Rd, SE27 .....169 G4
St. Julian's Rd, NW6 ....90 C7
★ St. Katharine's Dock, E1 ....21 G6
St. Katharines Prec, NW1 ......8 E2
St. Katharine's Way, E1 ....29 G1
St. Katherine's Rd, Erith DA18 .138 D2
St. Katherine's Row, EC3 .....21 E4
St. Katherine's Wk, W11
   off Freston Rd 108 A7

St. Keverne Rd, SE9 ....174 B4
St. Kilda Rd, W13 ....124 D1
Orpington BR6 ....207 J1
St. Kilda's Rd, N16 ....94 A1
Harrow HA1 ....68 B6
St. Kitts Ter, SE19 ....170 B5
St. Laurence Cl, NW6 ....108 A1
St. Lawrence Cl, Edg. HA8 ....53 J7
St. Lawrence Dr, Pnr. HA5 ....66 B6
★ St. Lawrence Jewry Ch, EC2 .20 A3
St. Lawrence St, E14 ....134 C1
St. Lawrence Ter, W10 ......108 B5
St. Lawrence Way, SW9 .....151 G1
St. Leonards Av, E4 ....62 D6
Harrow HA3 ....69 F4
St. Leonard's Av, Well. DA16
   off Hook La 158 A3
St. Leonards Ct, N1 ....12 A3
St. Leonard's Gdns, Houns.
TW5 ....122 E7
St. Leonards Gdns, Ilf. IG1 ....99 F5
St. Leonards Ri, Orp. BR6 ....207 H4
St. Leonards Rd, E14 ....114 B5
NW10 ....106 D4
St. Leonard's Rd, SW14 .....146 B3
W13 ....105 F7
Croydon CR0 ....201 H3
Esher (Clay.) KT10 ....194 C6
St. Leonard's Rd, T.Ditt. KT7 .180 D6
St. Leonards Sq, NW5 ....92 A6
St. Leonard's Sq, Surb. KT6
   off St. Leonard's Rd 181 G5
St. Leonards St, E3 ....114 B3
St. Leonard's Ter, SW3 ....31 J4
St. Leonards Wk, SW16 ......169 F7
St. Loo Av, SW3 ....31 H5
St. Louis Rd, SE27 ....169 J4
St. Loy's Rd, N17 ....76 B2
St. Lucia Dr, E15 ....115 F1
ST. LUKE'S, EC1 ....12 A5
St. Luke's Av, SW4 ....150 D4
Ilford IG1 ....99 E5
St. Luke's Cl, EC1 ....12 A5
SE25 ....189 E6
St. Lukes Est, EC1 ....12 B4
St. Lukes Ms, W11 off Basing St .108 C5
St. Lukes Rd, W11 ....108 C5
St. Lukes Sq, E16 ....115 F6
St. Luke's St, SW3 ....31 G3
St. Luke's Yd, W9 ....108 C2
St. Malo Av, N9 ....61 F3
ST. MARGARETS, Twick. TW1 .144 D5
St. Margarets, Bark. IG11 ....117 G1
St. Margarets Av, N15 ....75 H4
N20 ....57 F2
Harrow HA2 ....85 J3
Sidcup DA15 ....175 G3
St. Margaret's Av, Sutt. SM3 .198 B3
St. Margarets Cl, EC2
   off Lothbury 112 A6
St. Margaret's Ct, SE1 ....28 A2
St. Margaret's Cres, SW15 ...147 H5
St. Margaret's Dr, Twick. TW1 .144 E5
St. Margaret's Gro, E11 ....97 F3
SE18 ....137 F6
St. Margarets Gro, Twick. TW1 .144 E5
St. Margarets La, W8 ....22 A6
St. Margarets Pas, SE13
   off Church Ter 154/155 E3
St. Margarets Path, SE18 ....137 F5
St. Margaret's Rd, E12 ....97 J2
St. Margaret's Rd, N17 ....76 B3
NW10 ....107 J3
St. Margarets Rd, SE4 ....153 J4
W7 ....124 B2
Edgware HA8 ....54 B5
Isleworth TW7 ....144 E4
Twickenham TW1 ....144 E4
St. Margarets Sq, SE4
   off Adelaide Av 153 J4
St. Margaret's St, SW1 ....26 A4
St. Margaret's Ter, SE18 .....137 F5
St. Marks Cl, SE10
   off Ashburnham Gro 134 C7
SW6 off Ackmar Rd 148 D1
W11 off Lancaster Rd 108 B6
St. Mark's Cl, Barn. EN5 ......40 E3
St. Marks Cl, Har. HA1
   off Nightingale Av 68/69 E7
St. Marks Cres, NW1 ....110 A1
St. Mark's Gate, E9
   off Cadogan Ter 95 J7
St. Mark's Gro, SW10 ....30 B7
St. Mark's Hill, Surb. KT6 ....181 H6
St. Mark's Pl, SW19
   off Wimbledon Hill Rd 166 C6
St. Marks Pl, W11 ....108 B6
St. Marks Ri, E8 ....94 C5
St. Marks Rd, SE25
   off Coventry Rd 188 D4
St. Mark's Rd, W5
   off The Common 125 H1
St. Marks Rd, W7 ....124 B2
W10 ....108 A6

St. Marks Rd, W11 . . . . .108 B6
Bromley BR2 . . . . .191 H3
Enfield EN1 . . . . .44 C6
Mitcham CR4 . . . . .185 J2
St. Mark's Rd, Tedd. TW11 . . . . .163 E7
St. Marks Sq, NW1 . . . . .110 A1
St. Mark St, E1 . . . . .21 G4
★ St. Martin-in-the-Fields Ch,
    WC2 . . . . .18 A6
St. Martins Av, E6 . . . . .116 A2
St. Martins Cl, NW1 . . . . .110 A1
Enfield EN1 . . . . .44 E1
Erith DA18
    off St. Helens Rd 138 D2
St. Martin's Cl, Wat. WD19
    off Muirfield Rd 50 C4
West Drayton UB7
    off St. Martin's Rd 120 A3
St. Martin's Ct, WC2
    off St. Martin's La 110 D7
St. Martins Est, SW2 . . . . .169 G1
St. Martin's La, WC2 . . . . .18 A5
St. Martins La, Beck. BR3 . . . . . .190 B5
St. Martin's-le-Grand, EC1 . . . . . .19 J3
St. Martin's Ms, WC2 . . . . .18 A5
St. Martin's Pl, WC2 . . . . .18 A6
St. Martins Rd, N9 . . . . .60 E2
St. Martin's Rd, SW9 . . . . .151 F2
West Drayton UB7 . . . . .120 A3
St. Martin's St, WC2 . . . . .17 J6
St. Martins Ter, N10
    off Pages La 74 A2
St. Martins Way, SW17 . . . . .167 F3
St. Mary Abbots Pl, W8 . . . . . . .128 C3
St. Mary Abbots Ter, W14
    off Holland Pk Rd 128 C3
St. Mary at Hill, EC3 . . . . .20 D6
★ St. Mary at Hill Ch, EC3 . . . . . .20 D6
St. Mary Av, Wall. SM6 . . . . .200 A3
St. Mary Axe, EC3 . . . . .20 D4
St. Marychurch St, SE16 . . . . . . .133 F2
★ St. Mary-le-Bow Ch, EC2 . . . . . .20 A4
St. Mary Rd, E17 . . . . .78 A4
St. Marys, Bark. IG11 . . . . .117 G1
St. Marys App, E12 . . . . .98 C5
St. Marys Av, E11 . . . . .79 H6
St. Mary's Av, N3 . . . . .72 B2
Bromley BR2 . . . . .191 E3
Staines (Stanw.) TW19 . . . . . .140 A7
Teddington TW11 . . . . .162 C6
St. Mary's Av Cen, Sthl. UB2 . . .123 H4
St. Mary's Av N, Sthl. UB2 . . . . .123 H4
St. Mary's Av S, Sthl. UB2 . . . . .123 H4
St. Mary's Cl, N17
    off Kemble Rd 76 C1
St. Marys Cl, Chess. KT9 . . . . . .195 J7
Epsom KT17 . . . . .197 G7
St. Mary's Cl, Stai. (Stanw.)
    TW19 . . . . .140 A7
Sunbury-on-Thames TW16
    off Green Way 178 A4
St. Mary's Copse, Wor.Pk. KT4 . .196 E2
St. Marys Ct, E6 . . . . .116 C4
St. Mary's Ct, SE7 . . . . .136 A7
W5 off St. Mary's Rd 125 G2
St. Mary's Cres, NW4 . . . . .71 H4
St. Marys Cres, Islw. TW7 . . . . .124 A7
St. Mary's Cres, Stai. (Stanw.)
    TW19 . . . . .140 A7
St. Marys Dr, Felt. TW14 . . . . . .141 F7
St. Mary's Gdns, SE11 . . . . .35 F1
St. Mary's Gate, W8 . . . . .22 A6
St. Marys Grn, N2
    off Thomas More Way 73 F3
St. Mary's Gro, N1 . . . . .93 H6
SW13 . . . . .147 H3
W4 . . . . .126 B6
Richmond TW9 . . . . .145 J4
St. Marys Mans, W2 . . . . .14 E1
St. Mary's Ms, NW6
    off Priory Rd 90/91 E7
Richmond TW10 . . . . .163 F2
St. Marys Path, N1 . . . . .111 H1
St. Mary's Pl, SE9
    off Eltham High St 156 D6
W5 off St. Mary's Rd 125 G2
W8 . . . . .22 A6
St. Marys Rd, E10 . . . . .96 C3
E13 . . . . .115 H2
N8 off High St 74/75 E4
N9 . . . . .61 F1
St. Mary's Rd, NW10 . . . . .107 E1
St. Marys Rd, NW11 . . . . .72 B7
St. Marys Rd, SE15 . . . . .153 F1
SE25 . . . . .188 B3
SW19 (Wimbledon) 166 B5
W5 . . . . .125 G2
Barnet EN4 . . . . .41 J7
Bexley DA5 . . . . .177 J1
St. Mary's Rd, E.Mol. KT8 . . . . .180 A5
Ilford IG1 . . . . .99 F2
Surbiton KT6 . . . . .181 G6
Surbiton (Long Dit.) KT6 . . . . .181 F7
St. Mary's Rd, Wor.Pk. KT4 . . . .197 E2
St. Marys Sq, W2 . . . . .14 E1

St. Mary's Sq, W5
    off St. Mary's Rd 125 G2
St. Marys Ter, W2 . . . . .14 E1
St. Mary's Twr, EC1
    off Fortune St 111 J4
St. Mary St, SE18 . . . . .136 C4
St. Marys Vw, Har. HA3 . . . . .69 F5
St. Mary's Wk, SE11 . . . . .35 F1
St. Mary's Way, Chig. IG7 . . . . . . .64 D5
St. Matthew's Av, Surb. KT6 . . . .195 H1
St. Matthew's Dr, Brom. BR1 . . . .192 C3
St. Matthew's Rd, SW2 . . . . .151 F4
St. Matthews Rd, W5
    off The Common 125 H1
St. Matthew's Row, E2 . . . . .13 H4
St. Matthew St, SW1 . . . . .25 H4
St. Matthias Cl, NW9 . . . . .71 F5
St. Maur Rd, SW6 . . . . .148 C1
St. Mellion Cl, SE28
    off Redbourne Dr 118 D6
St. Merryn Cl, SE18 . . . . .137 G7
St. Michael's All, EC3 . . . . .20 C4
St. Michaels Av, N9 . . . . .45 F7
St. Michael's Av, Wem. HA9 . . . . . .88 A6
St. Michaels Cl, E16
    off Fulmer Rd 116 A5
St. Michael's Cl, N3 . . . . .72 C2
St. Michaels Cl, N12 . . . . .57 H5
Bromley BR1 . . . . .192 B3
Erith DA18 off St. Helens Rd . .138 D2
Worcester Park KT4 . . . . .197 F2
St. Michaels Cres, Pnr. HA5 . . . . .67 E6
St. Michaels Gdns, W10
    off St. Lawrence Ter 108 B5
St. Michaels Rd, NW2 . . . . .89 J4
St. Michael's Rd, SW9 . . . . .151 F2
St. Michaels Rd, Croy. CR0 . . . . .201 J1
Wallington SM6 . . . . .200 C6
Welling DA16 . . . . .158 B3
St. Michaels St, W2 . . . . .15 F3
St. Michaels Ter, N22 . . . . .75 E2
St. Mildred's Ct, EC2 off Poultry .112 A6
St. Mildreds Rd, SE12 . . . . .155 E7
St. Nicholas Cen, Sutt. SM1
    off St. Nicholas Way 198/199 E4
St. Nicholas Glebe, SW17 . . . . .168 A6
St. Nicholas Pl, Loug. IG10 . . . . . .48 D4
St. Nicholas Rd, SE18 . . . . .137 J5
Sutton SM1 . . . . .199 E5
Thames Ditton KT7 . . . . .180 C6
St. Nicholas St, SE8
    off Lucas St 154 A1
St. Nicholas Way, Sutt. SM1 . . . .198 E4
St. Nicolas La, Chis. BR7 . . . . . .192 B1
St. Ninian's Ct, N20 . . . . .57 J3
St. Norbert Grn, SE4 . . . . .153 H4
St. Norbert Rd, SE4 . . . . .153 H4
St. Olaf's Rd, SW6 . . . . .128 B7
St. Olaves Ct, EC2 . . . . .20 B4
St. Olaves Est, SE1 . . . . .29 E3
St. Olaves Gdns, SE11 . . . . .34 E1
St. Olave's Rd, E6 . . . . .116 D1
St. Olave's Wk, SW16 . . . . .186 C2
St. Olav's Sq, SE16 . . . . .133 F3
St. Oswald's Pl, SE11 . . . . .34 C4
St. Oswald's Rd, SW16 . . . . .187 H1
St. Oswulf St, SW1 . . . . .33 J2
ST. PANCRAS, WC1 . . . . .10 A4
St. Pancras Way, NW1 . . . . .92 C7
St. Patrick's Ct, Wdf.Grn. IG8 . . . .63 E7
St. Paul's All, EC4
    off St. Paul's Chyd 111 H6
St. Paul's Av, NW2 . . . . .89 H6
SE16 . . . . .133 G1
St. Pauls Av, Har. HA3 . . . . .69 J5
★ St. Paul's Cath, EC4 . . . . .19 J4
St. Paul's Chyd, EC4 . . . . .19 H4
St. Paul's Cl, SE7 . . . . .136 A5
W5 . . . . .125 J2
Carshalton SM5 . . . . .199 H1
St. Pauls Cl, Chess. KT9 . . . . . .195 G4
Hayes UB3 . . . . .121 G5
St. Paul's Cl, Houns. TW3 . . . . . .143 E2
St. Paul's Ct, W14
    off Colet Gdns 128 A4
St. Pauls Ctyd, SE8
    off Deptford High St 134 A7
St. Pauls Cray Rd, Chis. BR7 . . . .193 G1
St. Paul's Cres, NW1 . . . . .92 D7
St. Pauls Dr, E15 . . . . .96 D5
St. Paul's Ms, NW1
    off St. Paul's Cres 92 D7
St. Paul's Pl, N1 . . . . .94 A6
St. Pauls Ri, N13 . . . . .59 H6
St. Paul's Rd, N1 . . . . .93 H6
N17 . . . . .60 D7
Barking IG11 . . . . .117 F1
Brentford TW8 . . . . .125 G6
Erith DA8 . . . . .139 J7
Richmond TW9 . . . . .145 J3
Thornton Heath CR7 . . . . .187 J3
St. Paul's Shrubbery, N1 . . . . . . .94 A6
St. Pauls Sq, Brom. BR2 . . . . . . .191 G2
St. Paul's Ter, SE17 . . . . .35 H5
St. Pauls Twr, E10 . . . . .78 B7

St. Paul St, N1 . . . . .111 J1
St. Pauls Wk, Kings.T. KT2
    off Alexandra Rd 164 A7
St. Pauls Way, E3 . . . . .113 J5
E14 . . . . .113 J5
St. Paul's Way, N3 . . . . .56 E7
St. Pauls Wd Hill, Orp. BR5 . . . . .193 H2
St. Peter's All, EC3 . . . . .20 C4
St. Peter's Av, E2 . . . . .13 J2
E17 . . . . .78 E4
St. Peters Av, N18 . . . . .60 D4
St. Petersburgh Ms, W2 . . . . .14 A5
St. Petersburgh Pl, W2 . . . . .14 A5
St. Peter's Cl, E2 . . . . .13 J2
St. Peters Cl, SW17
    off College Gdns 167 H2
St. Peter's Cl, Barn. EN5 . . . . . . .39 H5
St. Peters Cl, Bushey (Bushey Hth)
    WD23 . . . . .52 A1
Chislehurst BR7 . . . . .175 G7
Ilford IG2 . . . . .81 H4
St. Peter's Cl, Ruis. HA4 . . . . . . .84 D2
St. Peter's Ct, NW4 . . . . .71 J5
St. Peters Ct, SE3
    off Eltham Rd 155 F4
SE4 off Wickham Rd 153 J2
West Molesey KT8 . . . . .179 G4
St. Peter's Gdns, SE27 . . . . .169 G3
St. Peter's Gro, W6 . . . . .127 G4
St. Peters Ms, N4
    off Warham Rd 75 H5
St. Peter's Pl, W9 . . . . .6 A6
St. Peter's Rd, N9 . . . . .61 F1
St. Peter's Rd, W6 . . . . .127 G5
Croydon CR0 . . . . .202 A4
St. Peters Rd, Kings.T. KT1 . . . . .182 A2
Southall UB1 . . . . .103 G5
Twickenham TW1 . . . . .145 E5
St. Peter's Rd, W.Mol. KT8 . . . . .179 G4
St. Peter's Sq, E2 . . . . .13 J2
W6 . . . . .127 G5
St. Peters St, N1 . . . . .111 H1
St. Peter's St, S.Croy. CR2 . . . . .202 A5
St. Peters Ter, SW6 . . . . .128 B7
St. Peter's Vil, W6 . . . . .127 G4
St. Peter's Way, N1 . . . . .94 B7
St. Peters Way, W5 . . . . .105 G5
Hayes UB3 . . . . .121 G5
St. Philip's Av, Wor.Pk. KT4 . . . . .197 H2
St. Philips Gate, Wor.Pk. KT4 . . . .197 H2
St. Philip Sq, SW8 . . . . .150 B2
St. Philip's Rd, E8 . . . . .94 D6
St. Philips Rd, Surb. KT6 . . . . . . .181 G6
St. Philip St, SW8 . . . . .150 B2
St. Philip's Way, N1
    off Linton St 111 J1
St. Quentin Ho, SW18
    off Fitzhugh Gro 149 G6
St. Quentin Rd, Well. DA16 . . . . .157 J3
St. Quintin Av, W10 . . . . .107 J5
St. Quintin Gdns, W10 . . . . .107 J5
St. Quintin Rd, E13 . . . . .115 H2
St. Raphael's Way, NW10 . . . . . . .88 C5
St. Regis Cl, N10 . . . . .74 B2
St. Ronans Cres, Wdf.Grn. IG8 . . .63 G7
St. Rule St, SW8 . . . . .150 C2
St. Saviour's Est, SE1 . . . . .29 F5
St. Saviour's Rd, SW2 . . . . .151 F5
St. Saviours Rd, Croy. CR0 . . . . .187 J6
Saints Cl, SE27
    off Wolfington Rd 169 H4
Saints Dr, E7 . . . . .98 A5
St. Silas Pl, NW5 . . . . .92 A6
St. Silas St Est, NW5 . . . . .92 A6
St. Simon's Av, SW15 . . . . .147 J5
St. Stephens Av, E17 . . . . .78 C5
W12 . . . . .127 H2
W13 . . . . .104 E6
St. Stephens Cl, E17 . . . . .78 B5
NW8 off Avenue Cl 109 H1
Southall UB1 . . . . .103 G5
St. Stephens Cres, W2 . . . . .108 D6
Thornton Heath CR7 . . . . .187 G3
St. Stephens Gdn Est, W2
    off Shrewsbury Rd 108 D6
St. Stephens Gdns, SW15
    off Manfred Rd 148 C5
W2 . . . . .108 D6
Twickenham TW1 . . . . .145 F6
St. Stephens Gro, SE13 . . . . . . .154 C3
St. Stephens Ms, W2
    off Chepstow Rd 108 D5
St. Stephen's Par, E7
    off Green St 97 J7
St. Stephen's Pas, Twick. TW1
    off Richmond Rd 145 F6
St. Stephen's Rd, E3 . . . . .113 J2
St. Stephen's Rd, E6 . . . . .97 J7
St. Stephen's Rd, E17
    off Grove Rd 78 B5
St. Stephens Rd, W13 . . . . .105 E6
St. Stephen's Rd, Barn. EN5 . . . . .40 A5
St. Stephens Rd, Houns. TW3 . . .143 G6
St. Stephen's Rd, West Dr. UB7 . .120 A1
St. Stephens Row, EC4 . . . . .20 B4

St. Stephens Ter, SW8 . . . . .131 F7
St. Stephen's Wk, SW7 . . . . .30 C1
St. Swithin's La, EC4 . . . . .20 B5
St. Swithun's Rd, SE13 . . . . .154 D5
St. Theresa's Rd, Felt. TW14 . . . .141 J4
St. Thomas' Cl, Surb. KT6 . . . . . .195 J1
St. Thomas Ct, Bex. DA5 . . . . . .159 G7
St. Thomas Dr, Orp. BR5 . . . . . .207 F1
St. Thomas' Dr, Pnr. HA5 . . . . . . .67 E1
St. Thomas Gdns, Ilf. IG1 . . . . . . .99 F6
St. Thomas Pl, NW1
    off Maiden La 92 D7
St. Thomas Rd, E16 . . . . .115 G6
N14 . . . . .42 D7
St. Thomas' Rd, W4 . . . . .126 C5
St. Thomas Rd, Belv. DA17 . . . . .139 J2
St. Thomas's Gdns, NW5
    off Queen's Cres 92 A6
St. Thomas's Pl, E9 . . . . .95 F7
St. Thomas's Rd, N4 . . . . .93 G2
NW10 . . . . .107 E1
St. Thomas's Sq, E9 . . . . .95 E7
St. Thomas St, SE1 . . . . .28 C2
St. Thomas's Way, SW6 . . . . . . .128 C7
St. Timothy's Ms, Brom. BR1
    off Wharton Rd 191 H1
St. Ursula Gro, Pnr. HA5 . . . . . . .66 D5
St. Ursula Rd, Sthl. UB1 . . . . . . .103 G6
St. Vincent Cl, SE27 . . . . .169 H5
St. Vincent Rd, Twick. TW2 . . . . .143 J6
St. Vincent St, W1 . . . . .16 C2
St. Wilfrids Cl, Barn. EN4 . . . . . . .41 H5
St. Wilfrids Rd, Barn. EN4 . . . . . . .41 G5
St. Winefride's Av, E12 . . . . .98 C5
St. Winifreds Cl, Chig. IG7 . . . . . .65 F5
St. Winifred's Rd, Tedd. TW11 . . .163 E6
Sala Ho, SE3 off Pinto Way 155 H1
Salamanca Pl, SE1 . . . . .34 C2
Salamanca St, SE1 . . . . .34 B2
Salamander Cl, Kings.T. KT2 . . . .163 F5
Salcombe Dr, Mord. SM4 . . . . . .198 A1
Romford RM6 . . . . .83 F6
Salcombe Gdns, NW7 . . . . .55 J6
Salcombe Pk, Loug. IG10 . . . . . . .48 A5
Salcombe Rd, E17 . . . . .77 J7
N16 . . . . .94 B5
Salcombe Way, Ruis. HA4 . . . . . . .84 A2
Salcott Rd, SW11 . . . . .149 H5
Croydon CR0 . . . . .201 E3
Salehurst Cl, Har. HA3 . . . . .69 H5
Salehurst Rd, SE4 . . . . .153 J6
Salem Pl, Croy. CR0 . . . . .201 J3
Salem Rd, W2 . . . . .14 B5
Sale Pl, W2 . . . . .15 G2
Sale St, E2 . . . . .13 H5
Salford Rd, SW2 . . . . .168 D1
Salhouse Cl, SE28
    off Rollesby Way 118 C6
Salisbury Av, N3 . . . . .72 C3
Barking IG11 . . . . .99 H7
Sutton SM1 . . . . .198 C6
Salisbury Cl, SE17 . . . . .36 B1
Worcester Park KT4 . . . . .197 F3
Salisbury Ct, EC4 . . . . .19 G4
Salisbury Gdns, SW19 . . . . .166 B7
Buckhurst Hill IG9 . . . . .64 A2
Salisbury Hall Gdns, E4 . . . . .62 A6
Salisbury Ho, E14
    off Hobday St 114 B6
Salisbury Ms, SW6
    off Dawes Rd 128 C7
Bromley BR2
    off Salisbury Rd 192 B5
Salisbury Pl, SW9 . . . . .131 H7
W1 . . . . .15 J1
Salisbury Rd, E4 . . . . .62 A3
E7 . . . . .97 G6
E10 . . . . .96 C2
E12 . . . . .98 A5
E17 . . . . .78 C5
N4 . . . . .75 H5
N9 . . . . .60 D3
N22 . . . . .75 H1
SE25 . . . . .188 D6
SW19 . . . . .166 B7
W13 . . . . .124 D2
Barnet EN5 . . . . .40 B3
Bexley DA5 . . . . .177 G1
Bromley BR2 . . . . .192 B5
Carshalton SM5 . . . . .199 J6
Dagenham RM10 . . . . .101 H6
Feltham TW13 . . . . .160 C1
Harrow HA1 . . . . .68 A5
Hounslow TW4 . . . . .142 C3
Hounslow (Hthrw Air.) TW6 . . .141 F5
Ilford IG3 . . . . .99 H2
New Malden KT3 . . . . .182 D3
Pinner HA5 . . . . .66 A4
Richmond TW9 . . . . .145 H4
Southall UB2 . . . . .123 E4
Worcester Park KT4 . . . . .197 F3
Salisbury Sq, EC4 . . . . .19 F4
Salisbury St, NW8 . . . . .7 G5
W3 . . . . .126 C2
Salisbury Ter, SE15 . . . . .153 F3

Salisbury Wk, N19 . . . . .92 C2
Salix Cl, Sun. TW16
off Oak Gro 160 B7
Salliesfield, Twick. TW2 . . . . . .144 A6
Sally Murrey Cl, E12
off Grantham Rd 98 D4
Salmen Rd, E13 . . . . .115 F2
Salmond Cl, Stan. HA7
off Robb Rd 52 D6
Salmon La, E14 . . . . .113 H6
Salmon Rd, Belv. DA17 . . . . . .139 G5
Salmons Rd, N9 . . . . .60 D1
Chessington KT9 . . . . .195 G6
Salmon St, E14 off Salmon La . .113 J6
NW9 . . . . .88 B1
Salomons Rd, E13 off Chalk Rd .115 J5
Salop Rd, E17 . . . . .77 G6
Saltash Cl, Sutt. SM1 . . . . . . .198 C4
Saltash Rd, Ilf. IG6 . . . . .65 G7
Welling DA16 . . . . .158 C1
Saltcoats Rd, W4 . . . . .126 E2
Saltcroft Cl, Wem. HA9 . . . . . . .88 B1
Salterford Rd, SW17 . . . . .168 A6
Salter Rd, SE16 . . . . .133 G1
Salters Hall Ct, EC4 . . . . .20 B5
Salters Hill, SE19 . . . . .170 A5
Salters Rd, E17 . . . . .78 D4
W10 . . . . .108 A4
Salter St, E14 . . . . .114 A7
NW10 . . . . .107 G3
Salterton Rd, N7 . . . . .93 E3
Saltley Cl, E6 off Dunnock Rd . .116 B6
Saltoun Rd, SW2 . . . . .151 G4
Saltram Cl, N15 . . . . .76 C4
Saltram Cres, W9 . . . . .108 C3
Saltwell St, E14 . . . . .114 A7
Saltwood Gro, SE17 . . . . .36 B4
Salusbury Rd, NW6 . . . . .108 B1
Salutation Rd, SE10 . . . . .135 E4
Salvia Gdns, Grnf. UB6
off Selborne Gdns 104 D2
Salvin Rd, SW15 . . . . .148 A3
Salway Cl, Wdf.Grn. IG8 . . . . . .63 F7
Salway Pl, E15
off Broadway 96/97 E6
Salway Rd, E15
off Great Eastern Rd 96 D6
Samantha Cl, E17 . . . . .77 J7
Sam Bartram Cl, SE7 . . . . .135 J5
Sambruck Ms, SE6 . . . . .172 B1
Samels Ct, W6
off South Black Lion La 127 G5
Samford St, NW8 . . . . .7 F6
Samira Cl, E17
off Colchester Rd 78 A6
Samos Rd, SE20 . . . . .189 E2
Sampson Av, Barn. EN5 . . . . . . .40 A5
Sampson Cl, Belv. DA17
off Carrill Way 138 D3
Sampson St, E1 . . . . .29 J2
Samson St, E13 . . . . .115 J2
Samuel Cl, E8 off Pownall Rd . .112 C1
SE14 . . . . .133 G6
SE18 . . . . .136 B4
Samuel Gray Gdns, Kings.T. KT2 .181 G1
Samuel Johnson Cl, SW16
off Curtis Fld Rd 169 G4
Samuel Lewis Trust Dws, E8
off Amhurst Rd 94 D4
N1 off Liverpool Rd 93 G7
SW3 . . . . .31 G2
SW6 . . . . .128 D7
Samuels Cl, W6
off South Black Lion La 127 G5
Samuel St, SE15 . . . . .37 F7
SE18 . . . . .136 C4
Sancroft Cl, NW2 . . . . .89 H3
Sancroft Rd, Har. HA3 . . . . .68 C2
Sancroft St, SE11 . . . . .34 D3
Sanctuary, The, SW1 . . . . .25 J4
Bexley DA5 . . . . .158 A4
Morden SM4 . . . . .184 D6
Sanctuary Rd, Houns. (Hthrw Air.)
TW6 . . . . .140 D6
Sanctuary St, SE1 . . . . .28 A4
Sandale Cl, N16
off Stoke Newington Ch St . . .94 A3
Sandall Cl, W5 . . . . .105 H4
Sandall Rd, NW5 . . . . .92 C6
W5 . . . . .105 H4
Sandal Rd, N18 . . . . .60 D5
New Malden KT3 . . . . .182 D5
Sandal St, E15 . . . . .114 E1
Sandalwood Cl, E1
off Solebay St 113 H4
Sandalwood Rd, Felt. TW13 . . . .160 B3
Sandbach Pl, SE18 . . . . .137 F4
Sandbourne Av, SW19 . . . . . . .184 E3
Sandbourne Rd, SE4 . . . . .153 H2
Sandbrook Cl, NW7 . . . . .54 D6
Sandbrook Rd, N16 . . . . .94 B3
Sandby Grn, SE9 . . . . .156 B3
Sandcroft Cl, N13 . . . . .59 H6
Sandell St, SE1 . . . . .27 E3

Sanders Cl, Hmptn. (Hmptn H.)
TW12 . . . . .161 J5
Sanders La, NW7 . . . . .56 A7
Sanderson Cl, NW5 . . . . .92 B4
Sanderstead Av, NW2 . . . . .90 B2
Sanderstead Cl, SW12
off Atkins Rd 150 C7
Sanderstead Rd, E10 . . . . .95 H1
South Croydon CR2 . . . . . . .202 A7
Sanders Way, N19
off Sussex Way 92 D1
Sandfield Gdns, Th.Hth. CR7 . . .187 H3
Sandfield Pas, Th.Hth. CR7 . . . .187 J3
Sandfield Rd, Th.Hth. CR7 . . . . .187 H3
Sandford Av, N22 . . . . .59 J7
Loughton IG10 . . . . .49 F3
Sandford Cl, E6 . . . . .116 C4
Sandford Ct, N16 . . . . .94 B1
Sandford Rd, E6 . . . . .116 B4
Bexleyheath DA7 . . . . .159 E4
Bromley BR2 . . . . .191 G4
Sandford St, SW6
off King's Rd 128/129 E7
Sandgate La, SW18 . . . . .167 H1
Sandgate Rd, Well. DA16 . . . . . .138 C7
Sandgate St, SE15 . . . . .132 E6
Sandhills, Wall. SM6 . . . . .200 D4
Sandhurst Av, Har. HA2 . . . . . . .67 H6
Surbiton KT5 . . . . .182 B7
Sandhurst Cl, NW9 . . . . .70 A3
Sandhurst Dr, Ilf. IG3 . . . . .99 J4
Sandhurst Rd, N9 . . . . .45 F6
NW9 . . . . .70 A3
SE6 . . . . .172 D1
Bexley DA5 . . . . .158 D5
Sidcup DA15 . . . . .175 J3
Sandhurst Way, S.Croy. CR2 . . .202 B7
Sandifer Dr, NW2 . . . . .90 A3
Sandiford Rd, Sutt. SM3 . . . . . .198 C2
Sandiland Cres, Brom. BR2 . . . .205 F2
Sandilands, Croy. CR0 . . . . . . .202 D2
Sandilands Rd, SW6 . . . . .148 E1
Sandison St, SE15 . . . . .152 C3
Sandland St, WC1 . . . . .18 D2
Sandling Ri, SE9 . . . . .174 D3
Sandlings, The, N22 . . . . .75 G2
Sandlings Cl, SE15
off Pilkington Rd 152/153 E2
Sandmartin Way, Wall. SM6 . . . .200 A1
Sandmere Rd, SW4 . . . . .150 E4
Sandon Cl, Esher KT10 . . . . . . .180 A7
Sandow Cres, Hayes UB3 . . . . .121 J3
Sandown Av, Dag. RM10 . . . . . .101 J6
Sandown Cl, Houns. TW5 . . . . .142 A1
Sandown Ct, Sutt. SM2
off Grange Rd 198/199 E7
Sandown Rd, SE25 . . . . .188 E5
Sandown Way, Nthlt. UB5 . . . . . .85 E6
Sandpiper Cl, E17 . . . . .77 G1
SE16 . . . . .133 J2
Sandpiper Rd, Sutt. SM1 . . . . . .198 C5
Sandpit Pl, SE7 . . . . .136 B5
Sandpit Rd, Brom. BR1 . . . . . . .172 E5
Sandpits Rd, Croy. CR0 . . . . . .203 G4
Richmond TW10 . . . . .163 G2
Sandra Cl, N22 off New Rd 75 J1
Hounslow TW3 . . . . .143 H5
Sandridge Cl, Har. HA1 . . . . .68 B4
Sandridge St, N19 . . . . .92 C2
Sandringham Av, SW20 . . . . . . .184 B2
Sandringham Cl, SW19 . . . . . . .166 A1
Enfield EN1 . . . . .44 B2
Ilford IG6 . . . . .81 F3
Sandringham Ct, W9 . . . . .6 D4
Sandringham Cres, Har. HA2 . . . .85 G2
Sandringham Dr, Well. DA16 . . .157 H2
Sandringham Gdns, N8 . . . . . . .75 E6
N12 . . . . .57 F6
Hounslow TW5 . . . . .142 A1
Ilford IG6 . . . . .81 F3
West Molesey KT8
off Rosemary Av 179 G4
Sandringham Ms, W5
off High St 105 G7
Hampton TW12
off Oldfield Rd 179 F1
Sandringham Rd, E7 . . . . .97 J5
E8 . . . . .94 C5
E10 . . . . .78 D6
N22 . . . . .75 J3
NW2 . . . . .89 H6
NW11 . . . . .72 B7
Barking IG11 . . . . .99 J6
Bromley BR1 . . . . .173 G5
Hounslow (Hthrw Air.) TW6 . .140 B5
Northolt UB5 . . . . .85 G7
Thornton Heath CR7 . . . . . . .187 J5
Worcester Park KT4 . . . . . . .197 G3
Sandrock Pl, Croy. CR0 . . . . . . .203 G4
Sandrock Rd, SE13 . . . . .154 A3
SANDS END, SW6 . . . . .149 F1
Sand's End La, SW6 . . . . .149 E1
Sandstone La, E16 . . . . .115 H7

Sandstone Pl, N19 . . . . .92 B2
Sandstone Rd, SE12 . . . . .173 H2
Sands Way, Wdf.Grn. IG8 . . . . . .64 B6
Sandtoft Rd, SE7 . . . . .135 H6
Sandwell Cres, NW6 . . . . .90 D6
Sandwich St, WC1 . . . . .10 A4
Sandwick Cl, NW7
off Sebergham Grn 55 G7
Sandy Bury, Orp. BR6 . . . . .207 G3
Sandycombe Rd, Felt. TW14 . . . .160 A1
Richmond TW9 . . . . .146 A3
Sandycoombe Rd, Twick. TW1 . . .145 F6
Sandycroft, SE2 . . . . .138 A6
Sandy Hill Av, SE18 . . . . .136 E5
Sandy Hill Rd, SE18 . . . . .136 E5
Sandyhill Rd, Ilf. IG1 . . . . .98 E4
Sandy La, Har. HA3 . . . . .69 J6
Kingston upon Thames KT1 . .162 D7
Mitcham CR4 . . . . .186 A1
Northwood HA6 . . . . .50 A5
Richmond TW10 . . . . .163 F2
Sidcup DA14 . . . . .176 D7
Sutton SM2 . . . . .198 B7
Teddington TW11 . . . . .162 D7
Walton-on-Thames KT12 . . . .178 B6
Sandy La Est, Rich. TW10 . . . . .163 G2
Sandy La N, Wall. SM6 . . . . . . .200 D6
Sandy La S, Wall. SM6 . . . . . . .200 D6
Sandymount Av, Stan. HA7 . . . . .53 F5
Sandy Ridge, Chis. BR7 . . . . . .174 D6
Sandy Rd, NW3 . . . . .90 E3
Sandy Way, Croy. CR0 . . . . .203 J3
Sanford La, N16
off Lawrence Bldgs 94 C2
Sanford St, SE14 . . . . .133 H6
Sanford Ter, N16 . . . . .94 C3
Sanford Wk, N16
off Sanford Ter 94 C2
SE14 off Cold Blow La 133 H6
Sanger Av, Chess. KT9 . . . . . . .195 H5
Sangley Rd, SE6 . . . . .154 B7
SE25 . . . . .188 B4
Sangora Rd, SW11 . . . . .149 G4
Sansom Rd, E11 . . . . .97 E2
Sansom St, SE5 . . . . .132 A7
Sans Wk, EC1 . . . . .11 F5
Santley St, SW4 . . . . .151 F4
Santos Rd, SW18 . . . . .148 D5
Santway, The, Stan. HA7 . . . . . . .52 B5
Sapcote Trd Cen, NW10 . . . . . . .89 F5
Saperton Wk, SE11 . . . . .34 D1
Saphora Cl, Orp. BR6
off Oleander Cl 207 G5
Sapperton Ct, EC1 . . . . .11 J5
Sapphire Cl, E6 . . . . .116 D6
Dagenham RM8 . . . . .100 C1
Sapphire Rd, SE8 . . . . .133 H4
Saracen Cl, Croy. CR0 . . . . .188 A6
Saracen's Head Yd, EC3 . . . . . . .21 E4
Saracen St, E14 . . . . .114 A6
Sara Ct, Beck. BR3
off Albemarle Rd 190 B1
Sarah Ho, SW15 . . . . .147 F4
Saratoga Rd, E5 . . . . .95 F4
Sardinia St, WC2 . . . . .18 C4
Sarita Cl, Har. HA3 . . . . .68 A2
Sarjant Path, SW19
off Queensmere Rd 166 A2
Sark Cl, Houns. TW5 . . . . .123 G7
Sark Wk, E16 . . . . .115 H6
Sarnesfield Ho, SE15
off Pencraig Way 132/133 E6
Sarnesfield Rd, Enf. EN2
off Church St 44 A3
Sarre Rd, NW2 . . . . .90 C5
Sarsen Av, Houns. TW3 . . . . . . .143 F2
Sarsfeld Rd, SW12 . . . . .167 J1
Sarsfield Rd, Grnf. UB6 . . . . . . .105 E2
Sartor Rd, SE15 . . . . .153 G4
Sarum Ter, E3
off Bow Common La 113 H4
Satanita Cl, E16 off Fulmer Rd . .116 A6
Satchell Mead, NW9 . . . . .71 F1
Satchwell Rd, E2 . . . . .13 H4
Sattar Ms, N16 off Clissold Rd . . .94 A3
Sauls Grn, E11
off Napier Rd 96/97 E3
Saunders Cl, E14
off Limehouse Causeway 113 J7
Saunders Ness Rd, E14 . . . . . . .134 C5
Saunders Rd, SE18 . . . . .137 J5
Saunders St, SE11 . . . . .34 E1
Saunders Way, SE28
off Oriole Way 118 B7
Saunderton Rd, Wem. HA0 . . . . .86 E5
Saunton Av, Hayes UB3 . . . . . .121 J7
Savage Gdns, E6 . . . . .116 C6
EC3 . . . . .21 E5
Savannah Cl, SE15
off Chandler Way 132 C7
Savernake Rd, N9 . . . . .44 D6
NW3 . . . . .91 J4
Savery Dr, Surb. KT6 . . . . .181 F7
Savile Cl, N.Mal. KT3 . . . . .183 E5

Savile Cl, T.Ditt. KT7 . . . . .194 C1
Savile Gdns, Croy. CR0 . . . . . . .202 C2
Savile Row, W1 . . . . .17 F5
Saville Rd, E16 . . . . .136 C5
W4 . . . . .126 D3
Romford RM6 . . . . .83 F6
Twickenham TW1 . . . . .162 C1
Saville Row, Brom. BR2 . . . . . . .205 F1
Enfield EN3 . . . . .45 G2
Savill Gdns, SW20
off Bodnant Gdns 183 G3
Savill Row, Wdf.Grn. IG8 . . . . . .63 F6
Savona Cl, SW19 . . . . .166 B7
Savona Est, SW8 . . . . .130 C7
Savona St, SW8 . . . . .130 C7
Savoy Av, Hayes UB3 . . . . .121 H5
Savoy Bldgs, WC2 . . . . .18 C6
Savoy Cl, E15
off Arthingworth St 114/115 E1
Edgware HA8 . . . . .54 A5
Savoy Ct, WC2 . . . . .18 B6
Savoy Hill, WC2 . . . . .18 C6
Savoy Ms, SW9
off Clapham Rd 150 E3
Savoy Pl, WC2 . . . . .18 B6
Savoy Row, WC2 . . . . .18 C5
Savoy Steps, WC2 off Savoy St .111 F7
Savoy St, WC2 . . . . .18 C5
Savoy Way, WC2 . . . . .18 C6
Sawbill Cl, Hayes UB4 . . . . . . .102 D5
Sawkins Cl, SW19 . . . . .166 B2
Sawley Rd, W12 . . . . .127 F1
Sawmill Yd, E3 . . . . .113 H1
Sawtry Cl, Cars. SM5 . . . . .185 H7
Sawyer Cl, N9 off Lion Rd 60 D2
Sawyers Cl, Dag. RM10 . . . . . . .101 J6
Sawyer's Hill, Rich. TW10 . . . . .146 B7
Sawyers Lawn, W13 . . . . .104 C6
Sawyer St, SE1 . . . . .27 J3
Saxby Rd, SW2 . . . . .150 E7
Saxham Rd, Bark. IG11 . . . . . . .117 H2
Saxlingham Rd, E4 . . . . .62 D3
Saxon Av, Felt. TW13 . . . . .161 E2
Saxonbury Av, Sun. TW16 . . . . .178 B3
Saxonbury Cl, Mitch. CR4 . . . . .185 G3
Saxonbury Gdns, Surb. KT6 . . . .195 F1
Saxon Cl, E17 . . . . .78 A7
Surbiton KT6 . . . . .181 G6
Saxon Dr, W3 . . . . .106 B6
Saxonfield Cl, SW2 . . . . .151 F7
Saxon Gdns, Sthl. UB1
off Saxon Rd 102/103 E7
Saxon Rd, E3 . . . . .113 J2
E6 . . . . .116 C4
N22 . . . . .75 H1
SE25 . . . . .188 A5
Bromley BR1 . . . . .173 F7
Ilford IG1 . . . . .99 E6
Kingston upon Thames KT2 . .181 H1
Southall UB1 . . . . .123 E1
Wembley HA9 . . . . .88 C3
Saxon Wk, Sid. DA14 . . . . .176 C6
Saxon Way, N14 . . . . .42 D6
Saxton Cl, SE13 . . . . .154 D3
Sayers Wk, Rich. TW10
off Stafford Pl 145 J7
Sayesbury La, N18 . . . . .60 D5
Sayes Ct, SE8 off Sayes Ct St . .133 J6
Sayes Ct St, SE8 . . . . .133 J6
Scadbury Pk, Chis. BR7 . . . . . . .175 J6
Scads Hill Cl, Orp. BR6 . . . . . . .193 J6
Scala St, W1 . . . . .17 G1
Scales Rd, N17 . . . . .76 C3
Scampston Ms, W10 . . . . .108 A6
Scampton Rd, Houns. (Hthrw Air.)
TW6 off Southampton Rd . . .140 C6
Scandrett St, E1 . . . . .132 E1
Scarba Wk, N1 off Marquess Rd . .94 A6
Scarborough Rd, E11 . . . . .96 D1
N4 . . . . .75 G7
N9 . . . . .45 F7
Hounslow (Hthrw Air.) TW6
off Southern Perimeter Rd . . .141 F6
Scarborough St, E1 . . . . .21 G4
Scarbrook Rd, Croy. CR0 . . . . . .201 J3
Scarle Rd, Wem. HA0 . . . . .87 G6
Scarlet Rd, SE6 . . . . .172 E3
Scarlette Manor Way, SW2
off Papworth Way 151 G7
Scarsbrook Rd, SE3 . . . . .156 A3
Scarsdale Pl, W8 . . . . .22 A5
Scarsdale Rd, Har. HA2 . . . . .85 J3
Scarsdale Vil, W8 . . . . .128 D3
Scarth Rd, SW13 . . . . .147 F3
Scawen Cl, Cars. SM5 . . . . .200 A4
Scawen Rd, SE8 . . . . .133 H5
Scawfell St, E2 . . . . .13 G2
Scaynes Link, N12 . . . . .56 D5
Sceaux Est, SE5 . . . . .152 B1
Sceptre Rd, E2 . . . . .113 F3
Schofield Wk, SE3
off Dornberg Cl 135 H7
Scholars Pl, N16 off Oldfield Rd . .94 B3
Scholars Rd, E4 . . . . .62 C1
SW12 . . . . .168 C1

Scholefield Rd, N19 92 D1
Schonfeld Sq, N16 94 A2
Schoolbank Rd, SE10 135 F4
Schoolbell Ms, E3 *off Arbery Rd* 113 H2
Schoolhouse Gdns, Loug. IG10 48 E4
Schoolhouse La, E1 113 G7
School Ho La, Tedd. TW11 163 E7
School La, Chig. IG7 65 J4
Kingston upon Thames KT1
off School Rd 181 F1
Pinner HA5 66 E4
Surbiton KT6 196 A1
Welling DA16 158 B3
School Pas, Kings.T. KT1 181 J2
Southall UB1 123 F1
School Rd, E12 *off Sixth Av* 98 C4
NW10 106 D4
Chislehurst BR7 193 F1
Dagenham RM10 119 G1
East Molesey KT8 180 A4
Hampton (Hmptn H.) TW12 161 J6
Hounslow TW3 143 J3
Kingston upon Thames KT1 181 F1
West Drayton UB7 120 A6
School Rd Av, Hmptn. (Hmptn H.) TW12 161 J6
School Way, N12 *off High Rd* 57 F4
Schoolway, N12 (Woodhouse Rd) 57 G6
School Way, Dag. RM8 100 C3
Schooner Cl, E14 134 D3
SE16 *off Kinburn St* 133 G2
Barking IG11 118 B3
Schubert Rd, SW15 148 C5
★ **Science Mus**, SW7 23 F6
Sclater St, E1 13 F5
Scoble Pl, N16 *off Amhurst Rd* 94 C4
Scoles Cres, SW2 169 G1
Scope Way, Kings.T. KT1 181 H4
Scoresby St, SE1 27 G2
Scorton Av, Grnf. UB6 104 D2
Scotch Common, W13 104 D5
Scoter Cl, Wdf.Grn. IG8
off Mallards Rd 63 H7
Scot Gro, Pnr. HA5 50 D7
Scotia Rd, SW2 151 G7
Scotland Grn, N17 76 C2
Scotland Grn Rd, Enf. EN3 45 G5
Scotland Grn Rd N, Enf. EN3 45 G4
Scotland Pl, SW1 26 A1
Scotland Rd, Buck.H. IG9 63 J1
Scotney Cl, Orp. BR6 206 D4
Scotsdale Cl, Orp. BR5 193 H4
Sutton SM3 198 B7
Scotsdale Rd, SE12 155 H5
Scotswood St, EC1 11 F5
Scotswood Wk, N17 60 D7
Scott Cl, SW16 187 F1
Epsom KT19 196 C5
West Drayton UB7 120 C4
Scott Ct, W3 *off Petersfield Rd* 126 C2
Scott Cres, Har. HA2 85 H1
Scott Ellis Gdns, NW8 6 E4
Scottes La, Dag. RM8
off Valence Av 100 D1
Scott Fm Cl, T.Ditt. KT7 194 E1
Scott Gdns, Houns. TW5 122 D7
Scott Ho, E13 *off Queens Rd W* 115 G2
N18 60 D5
Scott Lidgett Cres, SE16 29 H4
Scott Russell Pl, E14
off Westferry Rd 134 B5
Scotts Av, Brom. BR2 190 D2
Scotts Dr, Hmptn. TW12 161 H7
Scotts Fm Rd, Epsom KT19 196 C6
Scotts La, Brom. BR2 190 D3
Scotts Pas, SE18 *off Spray St* 136 E4
Scotts Rd, E10 96 C1
W12 127 H2
Bromley BR1 173 G7
Southall UB2 122 C3
Scott St, E1 112 E4
Scott Trimmer Way, Houns. TW3 143 E2
Scottwell Dr, NW9 71 F5
Scoulding Rd, E16 115 F6
Scouler St, E14 *off Quixley St* 114 D7
Scout App, NW10 88 E4
Scout La, SW4 *off Old Town* 150 C3
Scout Way, NW7 54 D4
Scovell Cres, SE1 27 J4
Scovell Rd, SE1 27 J4
Scrattons Ter, Bark. IG11 118 D2
Scriven St, E8 112 C1
Scrooby St, SE6 154 B6
Scrubs La, NW10 107 G3
W10 107 G3
Scrutton Cl, SW12 150 D7
Scrutton St, EC2 12 D6
Scudamore La, NW9 70 C3
Scutari Rd, SE22 153 F5
Scylla Cres, Houns. (Hthrw Air.) TW6 141 E7
Scylla Rd, SE15 152 E3
Hounslow (Hthrw Air.) TW6 141 E6
Seabright St, E2
off Bethnal Grn Rd 112/113 E3
Seabrook Dr, W.Wick. BR4 204 E2
Seabrook Gdns, Rom. RM7 83 G7
Seabrook Rd, Dag. RM8 100 D3
Seacole Cl, W3 106 D5
Seacon Twr, E14
off Hutchings St 134 A2
Seacourt Rd, SE2 138 D2
Seacroft Gdns, Wat. WD19 50 D3
Seafield Rd, N11 58 D4
Seaford Rd, E17 78 B3
N15 76 A5
W13 124 E1
Enfield EN1 44 B4
Hounslow (Hthrw Air.) TW6 140 A5
Seaford St, WC1 10 B4
Seaforth Av, N.Mal. KT3 183 H5
Seaforth Cres, N5 93 J5
Seaforth Gdns, N21 43 F7
Epsom KT19 197 F4
Woodford Green IG8 63 J5
Seaforth Pl, SW1
off Buckingham Gate 130 C3
Seagrave Rd, SW6 128 D6
Seagry Rd, E11 79 G6
Seagull Cl, Bark. IG11 118 A3
Seagull La, E16 115 G7
Sealand Rd, Houns. (Hthrw Air.) TW6 140 D6
Sealand Wk, Nthlt. UB5
off Wayfarer Rd 102/103 E3
Seal St, E8 94 C4
Searle Pl, N4 *off Evershot Rd* 93 F1
Searles Cl, SW11 129 H7
Searles Dr, E6 116 E5
Searles Rd, SE1 36 C1
Sears St, SE5 36 B7
Seasprite Cl, Nthlt. UB5 102 D3
Seaton Av, Ilf. IG3 99 H5
Seaton Cl, E13 *off New Barn St* 115 H4
SE11 35 F3
SW15 165 H1
Twickenham TW2 144 A6
Seaton Gdns, Ruis. HA4 84 A3
Seaton Pt, E5 *off Nolan Way* 94/95 E4
Seaton Rd, Hayes UB3 121 G4
Mitcham CR4 185 H2
Twickenham TW2 143 J6
Welling DA16 138 C7
Wembley HA0 105 H2
Seaton Sq, NW7
off Tavistock Av 56 A7
Seaton St, N18 60 D5
Sebastian Ct, Bark. IG11
off Meadow Rd 99 J7
Sebastian St, EC1 11 H4
Sebastopol Rd, N9 60 D4
Sebbon St, N1 93 H7
Sebergham Gro, NW7 55 G7
Sebert Rd, E7 97 H5
Sebright Pas, E2 13 J2
Sebright Rd, Barn. EN5 40 A2
Secker Cres, Har. HA3 67 J1
Secker St, SE1 27 E2
Second Av, E12 98 B4
E13 115 G3
E17 78 A5
N18 61 F4
NW4 72 A4
SW14 146 E3
W3 127 F1
W10 108 B4
Dagenham RM10 119 H1
Enfield EN1 44 C5
Hayes UB3 121 J1
Romford RM6 82 C5
Walton-on-Thames KT12 178 B6
Wembley HA9 87 G2
Second Cl, W.Mol. KT8 179 J4
Second Cross Rd, Twick. TW2 162 B2
Second Way, Wem. HA9 88 B4
Sedan Way, SE17 36 D3
Sedcombe Cl, Sid. DA14
off Knoll Rd 176 B4
Sedcote Rd, Enf. EN3 45 F5
Sedding St, SW1 32 B1
Seddon Highwalk, EC2
off Beech St 111 J5
Seddon Ho, EC2
off The Barbican 111 J5
Seddon Rd, Mord. SM4 185 G5
Seddon St, WC1 10 D4
Sedgebrook Rd, SE3 156 A2
Sedgecombe Av, Har. HA3 69 F5
Sedgeford Rd, W12 127 F1
Sedgehill Rd, SE6 172 A4
Sedgemere Av, N2 73 F3
Sedgemere Rd, SE2 138 C3
Sedgemoor Dr, Dag. RM10 101 G4
Sedge Rd, N17 61 F7
Sedgeway, SE6 173 F1
Sedgewood Cl, Brom. BR2 191 F7
Sedgmoor Pl, SE5 132 B7
Sedgwick Rd, E10 96 C2
Sedgwick St, E9 95 G5
Sedleigh Rd, SW18 148 C6
Sedlescombe Rd, SW6 128 C6
Sedley Pl, W1 16 D4
Sedley Ri, Loug. IG10 48 C2
Sedum Cl, NW9 70 B5
Seeley Dr, SE21 170 B4
Seelig Av, NW9 71 G7
Seely Rd, SW17 168 A6
Seething La, EC3 21 E6
Seething Wells La, Surb. KT6 181 F6
Sefton Av, NW7 54 D5
Harrow HA3 68 A1
Sefton Cl, Orp. BR5 193 J4
Sefton Rd, Croy. CR0 202 D1
Orpington BR5 193 J4
Sefton St, SW15 147 J2
Segal Cl, SE23 153 H7
Sekforde St, EC1 11 G6
Sekhon Ter, Felt. TW13 161 G3
Selan Gdns, Hayes UB4 102 B5
Selbie Av, NW10 89 F5
Selborne Av, E12 *off Walton Rd* 98 D4
Bexley DA5 176 E1
Selborne Gdns, NW4 71 G4
Greenford UB6 104 D1
Selborne Rd, E17 77 J5
N14 58 E3
N22 75 F1
SE5 *off Denmark Hill* 152 A2
Croydon CR0 202 B3
Ilford IG1 98 D2
New Malden KT3 182 E2
Sidcup DA14 176 B4
Selbourne Av, E17 77 J4
Surbiton KT6 195 J2
Selbourne Wk, E17
off Selbourne Wk Shop Cen 77 J4
Selbourne Wk Shop Cen, E17 77 J4
Selby Chase, Ruis. HA4 84 B2
Selby Cl, E6 *off Linton Gdns* 116 B5
Chessington KT9 195 H7
Chislehurst BR7 174 D6
Selby Gdns, Sthl. UB1 103 G4
Selby Grn, Cars. SM5 185 H7
Selby Rd, E11 96 E3
E13 115 H5
N17 60 B6
SE20 188 D2
W5 105 E4
Carshalton SM5 185 H7
Selby St, E1 13 J6
Selden Rd, SE15 153 F2
Selden Wk, N7 *off Durham Rd* 93 F2
★ **Selfridges**, W1 16 C4
SELHURST, SE25 188 B6
Selhurst Cl, SW19 166 A1
Selhurst New Rd, SE25 188 B6
Selhurst Pl, SE25 188 B6
Selhurst Rd, N9 60 A3
SE25 188 B5
Selinas La, Dag. RM8 83 E7
Selkirk Rd, SW17 167 H4
Twickenham TW2 161 J2
Sellers Cl, Borwd. WD6 38 C1
Sellers Hall Cl, N3 56 D7
Sellincourt Rd, SW17 167 H5
Sellindge Cl, Beck. BR3 171 J7
Sellons Av, NW10 107 F1
Sellwood Dr, Barn. EN5 40 A5
Sellwood St, SW2 *off Tulse Hill* 151 G7
Selsdon Av, S.Croy. CR2 202 A6
Selsdon Cl, Rom. RM5 83 J1
Surbiton KT6 181 H5
Selsdon Rd, E11 79 G7
E13 115 J1
NW2 89 F2
SE27 169 H3
South Croydon CR2 202 A5
Selsdon Rd Ind Est, S.Croy. CR2
off Selsdon Rd 202 A6
Selsdon Way, E14 134 B3
Selsea Pl, N16 *off Crossway* 94 B5
Selsey Cres, Well. DA16 158 D1
Selsey St, E14 114 A5
Selvage La, NW7 54 D5
Selway Cl, Pnr. HA5 66 B4
Selwood Pl, SW7 30 E3
Selwood Rd, Chess. KT9 195 G4
Croydon CR0 202 E2
Sutton SM3 198 C1
Selwood Ter, SW7 31 E3
Selworthy Cl, E11 79 G5
Selworthy Ho, SW11 149 G1
Selworthy Rd, SE6 171 J3
Selwyn Av, E4 62 C6
Ilford IG3 81 H6
Richmond TW9 145 H3
Selwyn Cl, Houns. TW4 143 E4
Selwyn Ct, SE3 155 E3
Edgware HA8
off Camrose Av 54 B7
Selwyn Cres, Well. DA16 158 B4
Selwyn Rd, E3 113 J2
E13 115 H1
NW10 88 D7
New Malden KT3 182 D5
Semley Pl, SW1 32 C2
Semley Rd, SW16 187 E2
Senate St, SE15 153 F2
Senator Wk, SE28
off Broadwater Rd 137 G3
Sendall Ct, SW11 149 G3
Seneca Rd, Th.Hth. CR7 187 J4
Senga Rd, Wall. SM6 200 A1
Senhouse Rd, Sutt. SM3 198 A3
Senior St, W2 14 A1
Senlac Rd, SE12 173 H1
Sennen Rd, Enf. EN1 44 C7
Sennen Wk, SE9 174 B3
Senrab St, E1 113 G6
Sentinel Cl, Nthlt. UB5 103 E4
Sentinel Sq, NW4 71 J4
September Way, Stan. HA7 53 E6
Sequoia Cl, Bushey (Bushey Hth)
WD23 *off Giant Tree Hill* 52 A1
Sequoia Gdns, Orp. BR6 193 J7
Sequoia Pk, Pnr. HA5 51 H6
Serbin Cl, E10 78 C7
Serenaders Rd, SW9 151 G2
Serjeants Inn, EC4 19 F4
Serle St, WC2 18 D3
Sermon La, EC4 19 J4
★ **Serpentine, The**, W2 23 G2
★ **Serpentine Gall**, W2 23 F2
Serpentine Rd, W2 23 J2
Serviden Dr, Brom. BR1 192 A1
Setchell Rd, SE1 37 F1
Setchell Way, SE1 37 F1
Seth St, SE16 *off Swan Rd* 133 F2
Seton Gdns, Dag. RM9 100 C7
Settle Pt, E13 *off London Rd* 115 G2
Settle Rd, E13 *off London Rd* 115 G2
Settlers Ct, E14 *off Newport Av* 114 D7
Settles St, E1 21 J2
Settrington Rd, SW6 148 E2
Seven Acres, Cars. SM5 199 H2
Northwood HA6 50 A6
SEVEN KINGS, Ilf. IG3 81 H7
Seven Kings Rd, Ilf. IG3 99 J2
Seven Kings Way, Kings.T. KT2 181 H1
Sevenoaks Cl, Bexh. DA7 159 J4
Sevenoaks Ho, SE25 188 D3
Sevenoaks Rd, SE4 153 H6
Orpington BR6 207 J5
Orpington (Grn St Grn) BR6 207 J7
Sevenoaks Way, Orp. BR5 176 C7
Sidcup DA14 176 C7
Seven Sisters Rd, N4 93 F3
N7 93 F3
N15 75 J7
Seven Stars Cor, W12
off Goldhawk Rd 127 G3
Seven Stars Yd, E1 21 G1
Seventh Av, E12 98 C4
Hayes UB3 122 A1
Severnake Cl, E14 134 A4
Severn Dr, Esher KT10 194 D2
Severn Way, NW10 89 F5
Severus Rd, SW11 149 H4
Seville Ms, N1 94 B7
Seville St, SW1 24 A4
Sevington Rd, NW4 71 H6
Sevington St, W9 6 A6
Seward Rd, W7 124 D2
Beckenham BR3 189 G2
SEWARDSTONE, E4 46 C1
SEWARDSTONEBURY, E4 47 E4
Sewardstone Gdns, E4 46 B5
Sewardstone Grn, E4 46 E4
Sewardstone Rd, E2 113 F2
E4 46 B7
Seward St, EC1 11 H5
Sewdley St, E5 95 G3
Sewell Rd, SE2 138 A3
Sewell St, E13 115 G3
Sextant Av, E14 134 D4
Sexton Ct, E14 *off Newport Av* 114 D7
Seymour Av, N17 76 D2
Morden SM4 184 A7
Seymour Cl, E.Mol. KT8 179 J5
Loughton IG10 48 B6
Pinner HA5 67 F1
Seymour Ct, E4 63 F2
Seymour Dr, Brom. BR2 206 C1
Seymour Gdns, SE4 153 H3
Feltham TW13 160 C4
Ilford IG1 98 C1
Ruislip HA4 84 D1
Surbiton KT5 181 J5
Twickenham TW1 144 E7
Seymour Ms, W1 16 B3
Seymour Pl, SE25 188 E4
W1 15 J2
Seymour Rd, E4 62 B1
E6 116 A2
E10 95 J1
N3 57 E7
N8 75 G5
N9 61 E2
SW18 148 C7
SW19 166 A2

Seymour Rd, W4 . . . .**126** C4
  Carshalton SM5 . . . .**200** A5
  East Molesey KT8 . . . .**179** J5
  Hampton (Hmptn H.) TW12 .**161** J5
  Kingston upon Thames KT1 .**181** G1
  Mitcham CR4 . . . .**186** A7
Seymours, The, Loug. IG10 . . . .**48** D1
Seymour St, SE18 . . . .**137** F3
  W1 . . . .**15** J4
  W2 . . . .**15** J4
Seymour Ter, SE20 . . . .**188** E1
Seymour Vil, SE20 . . . .**188** E1
Seymour Wk, SW10 . . . .**30** C5
Seyssel St, E14 . . . .**134** C4
Shaa Rd, W3 . . . .**106** D7
Shacklegate La, Tedd. TW11 . .**162** B4
Shackleton Cl, SE23
  off Featherstone Av **170/171** E2
Shackleton Ct, E14
  off Maritime Quay **134** A5
  W12 . . . .**127** H2
Shackleton Rd, Sthl. UB1 . . . .**103** F7
SHACKLEWELL, N16 . . . .**94** C4
Shacklewell Grn, E8 . . . .**94** C4
Shacklewell La, E8 . . . .**94** C5
Shacklewell Rd, N16 . . . .**94** C4
Shacklewell Row, E8 . . . .**94** C4
Shacklewell St, E2 . . . .**13** G5
Shadbolt Av, E4 . . . .**61** H5
Shadbolt Cl, Wor.Pk. KT4 . . . .**197** F2
Shad Thames, SE1 . . . .**29** F2
SHADWELL, E1 . . . .**113** F7
Shadwell Ct, Nthlt. UB5
  off Shadwell Dr **103** F2
Shadwell Dr, Nthlt. UB5 . . . . .**103** F3
Shadwell Gdns Est, E1
  off Martha St **113** F6
Shadwell Pierhead, E1
  off Glamis Rd **113** F7
Shadwell Pl, E1 off Sutton St . .**113** F7
Shaef Way, Tedd. TW11 . . . . . .**162** D7
Shafter Rd, Dag. RM10 . . . . . .**101** J6
Shaftesbury, Loug. IG10 . . . . . .**48** A3
Shaftesbury Av, W1 . . . .**17** H5
  WC2 . . . .**17** H5
  Barnet EN5 . . . .**41** F4
  Enfield EN3 . . . .**45** G2
  Feltham TW14 . . . .**142** A6
  Harrow HA2 . . . .**85** H1
  Harrow (Kenton) HA3 . . . . . .**69** G6
  Southall UB2 . . . .**123** G4
Shaftesbury Circle, Har. HA2
  off Shaftesbury Av **85** J1
Shaftesbury Ct, N1
  off Shaftesbury St **112** A2
Shaftesbury Gdns, NW10 . . . .**107** E4
Shaftesbury Ms, SW4
  off Clapham Common S
  Side **150** C5
  W8 off Stratford Rd **128** D3
Shaftesbury Pl, W14
  off Warwick Rd **128** C4
Shaftesbury Pt, E13 off High St .**115** H2
Shaftesbury Rd, E4 . . . .**62** D1
  E7 . . . .**97** J7
  E10 . . . .**96** A1
  E17 . . . .**78** B6
  N18 . . . .**60** B6
  N19 . . . .**92** E1
  Beckenham BR3 . . . .**189** J2
  Carshalton SM5 . . . .**185** G7
  Richmond TW9 . . . .**145** H3
Shaftesburys, The, Bark. IG11 .**117** F1
Shaftesbury St, N1 . . . .**12** A2
Shaftesbury Way, Twick. TW2 . .**162** A3
Shaftesbury Waye, Hayes UB4 .**102** B5
Shafto Ms, SW1 . . . .**23** J4
Shafton Rd, E9 . . . .**113** G1
Shakespeare Av, N11 . . . .**58** C5
  NW10 . . . .**106** D1
  Feltham TW14 . . . .**142** A6
  Hayes UB4 . . . .**102** B4
Shakespeare Cres, E12 . . . .**98** C6
  NW10 . . . .**106** D1
Shakespeare Dr, Har. HA3 . . . . .**69** J6
Shakespeare Gdns, N2 . . . .**73** J4
Shakespeare Ho, N14
  off High St **58** D2
Shakespeare Rd, E17 . . . .**77** G2
  N3 off Popes Dr **72** D1
  NW7 . . . .**55** F4
  SE24 . . . .**151** H5
  W3 . . . .**126** C1
  W7 . . . .**104** C7
  Bexleyheath DA7 . . . .**158** E1
★ Shakespeare's Globe Thea,
  SE1 . . . .**19** J6
Shakespeare Sq, Ilf. IG6 . . . . . .**65** F6
Shakespeare Twr, EC2 . . . .**20** A1
Shakespeare Way, Felt. TW13 . .**160** C4
Shakspeare Ms, N16
  off Shakspeare Wk **94** B4
Shakspeare Wk, N16 . . . .**94** B4
Shalbourne Sq, E9 . . . .**95** J6
Shalcomb St, SW10 . . . .**30** D6

Shalden Ho, SW15
  off Tunworth Cres **147** F6
Shaldon Dr, Mord. SM4 . . . . . .**184** B5
  Ruislip HA4 . . . .**84** C3
Shaldon Rd, Edg. HA8 . . . .**69** J1
Shalfleet Dr, W10 . . . .**108** A7
Shalford Cl, Orp. BR6 . . . .**207** F4
Shalimar Gdns, W3 . . . .**106** C7
Shalimar Rd, W3
  off Hereford Rd **106** C7
Shallons Rd, SE9 . . . .**174** E4
Shalstone Rd, SW14 . . . .**146** B3
Shalston Vil, Surb. KT6 . . . . . .**181** J6
Shamrock Ho, SE26
  off Talisman Sq **170** D4
Shamrock Rd, Croy. CR0 . . . . .**187** F6
Shamrock St, SW4 . . . .**150** D3
Shamrock Way, N14 . . . .**58** B1
Shandon Rd, SW4 . . . .**150** C6
Shand St, SE1 . . . .**28** D3
Shandy St, E1 . . . .**113** G5
Shanklin Gdns, Wat. WD19 . . . .**50** C4
Shanklin Rd, N8 . . . .**74** D5
  N15 . . . .**76** D4
Shanklin Way, SE15
  off Pentridge St **132** C7
Shannon Cl, NW2 . . . .**90** A3
  Southall UB2 . . . .**122** D5
Shannon Gro, SW9 . . . .**151** F4
Shannon Pl, NW8 . . . .**7** H1
Shannon Way, Beck. BR3 . . . . .**172** B6
Shap Cres, Cars. SM5 . . . .**199** J1
Shapland Way, N13 . . . .**59** F5
Shapwick Cl, N11
  off Friern Barnet Rd **57** J5
Shardcroft Av, SE24 . . . .**151** H5
Shardeloes Rd, SE4 . . . .**153** J3
  SE14 . . . .**153** J3
Sharland Cl, Th.Hth. CR7
  off Dunheved Rd N **187** G6
Sharman Ct, Sid. DA14 . . . . . .**176** A4
Sharnbrooke Cl, Well. DA16 . .**158** C3
Sharon Cl, Surb. KT6 . . . .**195** G1
Sharon Gdns, E9 . . . .**113** F1
Sharon Rd, W4 . . . .**126** D5
  Enfield EN3 . . . .**45** H2
Sharpe Cl, W7
  off Templeman Rd **104** C5
Sharpleshall St, NW1 . . . .**91** J7
Sharpness Cl, Hayes UB4 . . . .**102** E5
Sharratt St, SE15 . . . .**133** F6
Sharsted St, SE17 . . . .**35** G4
Sharvel La, Nthlt. UB5 . . . . . .**102** A1
Shavers Pl, SW1 . . . .**17** H6
Shaw Av, Bark. IG11 . . . .**118** E2
Shawbrooke Rd, SE9 . . . .**155** J5
Shawbury Rd, SE22 . . . .**152** C5
Shaw Cl, SE28 . . . .**138** B1
  Bushey (Bushey Hth) WD23 . .**52** B2
Shaw Ct, SW11 . . . .**149** G3
Shaw Dr, Walt. KT12 . . . .**178** C7
Shawfield Ct, West Dr. UB7 . . .**120** B3
Shawfield Pk, Brom. BR1 . . . . .**192** A2
Shawfield St, SW3 . . . .**31** H4
Shawford Ct, SW15 . . . .**147** G7
Shawford Rd, Epsom KT19 . . .**196** D6
Shaw Gdns, Bark. IG11 . . . . . .**118** E2
Shaw Rd, SE22 . . . .**152** B4
  Bromley BR1 . . . .**173** F3
  Enfield EN3 . . . .**45** G1
Shaws Cotts, SE23 . . . .**171** H3
Shaw Sq, E17 . . . .**77** H1
Shaw Way, Wall. SM6 . . . .**200** E7
Shearing Dr, Cars. SM5
  off Stavordale Rd **185** F7
Shearling Way, N7 . . . .**93** E6
Shearman Rd, SE3 . . . .**155** F4
Shearsmith Ho, E1 . . . .**21** J5
Shearwater Cl, Bark. IG11 . . . .**118** A3
Shearwater Rd, Sutt. SM1 . . . .**198** C5
Shearwater Way, Hayes UB4 . .**102** D6
Sheaveshill Av, NW9 . . . .**71** E4
Sheen Common Dr, Rich. TW10 .**146** A4
Sheen Ct, Rich. TW10 . . . .**146** A4
Sheen Ct Rd, Rich. TW10 . . . . .**146** A4
Sheendale Rd, Rich. TW9 . . . .**145** J4
Sheenewood, SE26 . . . .**171** E5
Sheen Gate Gdns, SW14 . . . . .**146** C4
Sheen Gro, N1
  off Richmond Av **111** G1
Sheen La, SW14 . . . .**146** C3
Sheen Pk, Rich. TW9 . . . .**145** J4
Sheen Rd, Orp. BR5 . . . .**193** J4
  Richmond TW9, TW10 . . . . .**145** H5
Sheen Way, Wall. SM6 . . . .**201** F5
Sheen Wd, SW14 . . . .**146** C5
Sheepcote Cl, Houns. TW5 . . .**122** A7
Sheepcote La, SW11 . . . .**149** J2
Sheepcote Rd, Har. HA1 . . . . . .**68** C6
Sheepcotes Rd, Rom. RM6 . . . .**82** D4
Sheephouse Way, N.Mal. KT3 . .**182** E7
Sheep La, E8 . . . .**112** E1
Sheep Wk Ms, SW19 . . . .**166** A6
Sheerness Ms, E16 . . . .**137** E2
Sheerwater Rd, E16 . . . .**116** A5

Sheffield Rd, Houns. (Hthrw Air.) TW6
  off Southern Perimeter Rd . .**141** G5
Sheffield Sq, E3
  off Malmesbury Rd **113** J3
Sheffield St, WC2 . . . .**18** C4
Sheffield Ter, W8 . . . .**128** D1
Shefton Ri, Nthwd. HA6 . . . . . .**50** A7
Shelbourne Cl, Pnr. HA5 . . . . . .**67** F3
Shelbourne Pl, Beck. BR3 . . . .**171** J7
Shelbourne Rd, N17 . . . .**76** E2
Shelburne Dr, Houns. TW4
  off Hanworth Rd **143** G6
Shelburne Rd, N7 . . . .**93** F4
Shelbury Cl, Sid. DA14 . . . . . .**176** A3
Shelbury Rd, SE22 . . . .**153** E5
Sheldon Av, N6 . . . .**73** H7
  Ilford IG5 . . . .**80** E2
Sheldon Cl, SE12 . . . .**155** H5
  SE20 . . . .**189** E1
Sheldon Rd, N18 . . . .**60** B4
  NW2 . . . .**90** A4
  Bexleyheath DA7 . . . .**159** F1
  Dagenham RM9 . . . .**100** E7
Sheldon Sq, W2 . . . .**14** D2
Sheldon St, Croy. CR0 . . . .**201** J3
Sheldrake Cl, E16 . . . .**136** C1
Sheldrake Pl, W8 . . . .**128** C2
Sheldrick Cl, SW19 . . . .**185** G2
Shelduck Cl, E15 . . . .**97** F5
Sheldwich Ter, Brom. BR2 . . . .**192** B6
Shelford Pl, N16
  off Stoke Newington Ch St . .**94** A3
Shelford Ri, SE19 . . . .**170** C7
Shelford Rd, Barn. EN5 . . . .**39** J6
Shelgate Rd, SW11 . . . .**149** H5
★ Shell Cen, SE1 . . . .**26** D2
Shell Cl, Brom. BR2 . . . .**192** C6
Shellduck Cl, NW9
  off Swan Dr **70/71** E2
Shelley Av, E12 . . . .**98** B6
  Greenford UB6 . . . .**104** A3
Shelley Cl, SE15 . . . .**153** E2
  Edgware HA8 . . . .**54** A4
  Greenford UB6 . . . .**104** A3
  Hayes UB4 . . . .**102** A5
  Orpington BR6 . . . .**207** H3
Shelley Cres, Houns. TW5 . . . .**142** D2
  Southall UB1 . . . .**103** F6
Shelley Dr, Well. DA16 . . . . . .**157** H1
Shelley Gdns, Wem. HA0 . . . . . .**87** F2
Shelley Gro, Loug. IG10 . . . . . .**48** C4
Shelley Rd, NW10 . . . .**106** D1
Shelley Way, SW19 . . . .**167** G6
Shellgrove Est, N16 . . . .**94** B5
Shellness Rd, E5 . . . .**95** E5
Shell Rd, SE13 . . . .**154** B3
Shellwood Rd, SW11 . . . .**149** J2
Shelmerdine Cl, E3 . . . .**114** A5
Shelton Rd, SW19 . . . .**184** D1
Shelton St, WC2 . . . .**18** A4
Shenfield Ho, SE18
  off Shooter's Hill Rd **136** A7
Shenfield Rd, Wdf.Grn. IG8 . . . .**63** H7
Shenfield St, N1 . . . .**12** E2
Shenley Rd, SE5 . . . .**152** B1
  Borehamwood WD6 . . . .**38** A4
  Hounslow TW5 . . . .**142** E1
Shepcot Ho, N14 . . . .**42** C6
Shepherd Cl, W1 off Lees Pl . . .**110** A7
  Feltham (Han.) TW13 . . . . .**160** E4
Shepherdess Pl, N1 . . . .**12** A3
Shepherdess Wk, N1 . . . .**12** A1
Shepherd Mkt, W1 . . . .**24** D1
SHEPHERD'S BUSH, W12 . . . . .**127** J1
Shepherds Bush Grn, W12 . . . .**127** J2
Shepherds Bush Mkt, W12 . . . .**127** J2
Shepherds Bush Pl, W12 . . . . .**128** A2
Shepherds Bush Rd, W6 . . . . .**127** J4
Shepherds Cl, N6 . . . .**74** B6
  Orpington BR6
  off Stapleton Rd **207** J3
  Romford RM6 . . . .**82** D5
  Stanmore HA7 . . . .**52** E5
Shepherds Ct, W12
  off Shepherds Bush Grn . . .**128** A2
Shepherds Grn, Chis. BR7 . . . .**175** G7
Shepherds Hill, N6 . . . .**74** B6
Shepherds La, E9 . . . .**95** G5
  SE28 off Hill Vw Dr **137** H1
Shepherds Path, Nthlt. UB5
  off Fortunes Mead **84/85** E6
Shepherd's Pl, W1 . . . .**16** B5
Shepherd St, W1 . . . .**24** D1
Shepherds Wk, NW2 . . . .**89** G2
  NW3 . . . .**91** G5
  Bushey (Bushey Hth) WD23 . . .**52** A2
Shepherds Way, S.Croy. CR2 . .**203** G7
Shepiston La, Hayes UB3 . . . .**121** G4
  West Drayton UB7 . . . .**121** F4
Shepley Cl, Cars. SM5 . . . .**200** A3
Sheppard Cl, Enf. EN1 . . . .**45** E1
  Kingston upon Thames KT1
  off Beaufort Rd **181** H4
Sheppard Dr, SE16 . . . .**132** E5
Sheppard St, E16 . . . .**115** F4

Shepperton Cl, Borwd. WD6 . . . .**38** D1
Shepperton Rd, N1 . . . .**111** J1
  Orpington BR5 . . . .**193** F6
Sheppey Gdns, Dag. RM9
  off Sheppey Rd **100** C7
Sheppey Rd, Dag. RM9 . . . . . .**100** B7
Sheppey Wk, N1 off Ashby Gro . .**93** J7
Sherard Ct, N7
  off Manor Gdns **92/93** E3
Sherard Rd, SE9 . . . .**156** B5
Sheraton Business Cen, Grnf.
  UB6 . . . .**105** E2
Sheraton St, W1 . . . .**17** H4
Sherborne Av, Enf. EN3 . . . .**45** F2
  Southall UB2 . . . .**123** G4
Sherborne Cl, Hayes UB4 . . . .**102** C6
Sherborne Cres, Cars. SM5 . . .**185** H7
Sherborne Gdns, NW9 . . . .**70** A3
  W13 . . . .**105** E6
Sherborne La, EC4 . . . .**20** B5
Sherborne Rd, Chess. KT9 . . . .**195** H5
  Feltham TW14 . . . .**141** G7
  Orpington BR5 . . . .**193** J4
  Sutton SM3 . . . .**198** D2
Sherborne St, N1 . . . .**112** A1
Sherboro Rd, N15
  off Ermine Rd **76** C6
Sherbourne Pl, Stan. HA7 . . . . .**52** D6
Sherbrooke Cl, Bexh. DA6 . . . .**159** G4
Sherbrooke Rd, SW6 . . . .**128** C7
Sherbrooke Way, Wor.Pk. KT4 .**183** H7
Sherbrook Gdns, N21 . . . .**43** H7
Shere Cl, Chess. KT9 . . . .**195** G5
Sheredan Rd, E4 . . . .**62** D5
Shere Rd, Ilf. IG2 . . . .**80** D5
Sherfield Cl, N.Mal. KT3 . . . . .**182** B4
Sherfield Gdns, SW15 . . . .**147** F6
Sheridan Ct, Houns. TW4
  off Vickers Way **143** H5
  Northolt UB5 . . . .**85** H5
Sheridan Cres, Chis. BR7 . . . .**192** E2
Sheridan Gdns, Har. HA3 . . . . .**69** G6
Sheridan Ms, E11
  off Woodbine Pl **79** G6
Sheridan Pl, SW13
  off Brookwood Av **147** F2
  Hampton TW12 . . . .**179** H1
Sheridan Rd, E7 . . . .**97** F3
  E12 . . . .**98** B5
  SW19 . . . .**184** C1
  Belvedere DA17 . . . .**139** G4
  Bexleyheath DA7 . . . .**158** E3
  Richmond TW10 . . . .**163** F3
Sheridan St, E1
  off Watney St **112/113** E6
Sheridan Ter, Nthlt. UB5
  off Whitton Av W **85** H5
Sheridan Wk, NW11 . . . .**72** D6
  Carshalton SM5
  off Carshalton Pk Rd **199** J5
Sheridan Way, Beck. BR3
  off Turners Meadow Way . . .**189** J1
Sheringham Av, E12 . . . .**98** C4
  N14 . . . .**42** D5
  Feltham TW13 . . . .**160** A3
  Romford RM7 . . . .**83** J6
  Twickenham TW2 . . . .**161** F1
Sheringham Dr, Bark. IG11 . . . .**99** J6
Sheringham Rd, N7 . . . .**93** F6
  SE20 . . . .**189** E3
Sheringham Twr, Sthl. UB1 . . .**103** H7
Sherington Av, Pnr. HA5 . . . . . .**51** G7
Sherington Rd, SE7 . . . .**135** H6
Sherland Rd, Twick. TW1 . . . . .**162** C1
Sherlies Av, Orp. BR6 . . . .**207** H2
★ Sherlock Holmes Mus, NW1 . .**8** A6
Sherlock Ms, W1 . . . .**16** B1
Sherman Rd, Brom. BR1 . . . . .**191** G1
Shernhall St, E17 . . . .**78** C5
Sherrard Rd, E7 . . . .**97** J6
  E12 . . . .**98** A6
Sherrards Way, Barn. EN5 . . . . .**40** D5
Sherrick Grn Rd, NW10 . . . .**89** H5
Sherriff Rd, NW6 . . . .**90** D6
Sherringham Av, N17 . . . .**76** D2
Sherrin Rd, E10 . . . .**96** A4
Sherrock Gdns, NW4 . . . .**71** G4
Sherry Ms, Bark. IG11
  off Cecil Av **99** G7
Sherwin Rd, SE14 . . . .**153** G1
Sherwood Av, E18 . . . .**79** H3
  SW16 . . . .**168** D7
  Greenford UB6 . . . .**86** B6
  Hayes UB4 . . . .**102** B4
Sherwood Cl, SW13
  off Lower Common S **147** H3
  W13 . . . .**124** E1
  Bexley DA5 . . . .**158** C6
Sherwood Gdns, E14 . . . .**134** A4
  SE16 . . . .**37** J4
  Barking IG11 . . . .**99** G7
Sherwood Pk Av, Sid. DA15 . . .**158** A7
Sherwood Pk Rd, Mitch. CR4 . .**186** C4
  Sutton SM1 . . . .**198** D5
Sherwood Rd, NW4 . . . .**71** J3

Sherwood Rd, SW19 . . . .**166** C7
  Croydon CR0 . . . .**189** J7
  Hampton (Hmptn H.) TW12 . .**161** J5
  Harrow HA2 . . . .**85** J2
  Ilford IG6 . . . .**81** G4
  Welling DA16 . . . .**157** H2
Sherwood St, N20 . . . .**57** G3
  W1 . . . .**17** G5
Sherwood Ter, N20
  off Green Rd **57** G3
Sherwood Way, W.Wick. BR4 . .**204** B2
Shetland Cl, Borwd. WD6
  off Percheron Rd **38** D6
Shetland Rd, E3 . . . .**113** J2
Shield Dr, Brent. TW8 . . . .**124** D6
Shieldhall St, SE2 . . . .**138** C4
Shifford Path, SE23 . . . .**171** G3
Shillibeer Pl, W1 . . . .**15** H1
Shillibeer Wk, Chig. IG7 . . . .**65** J3
Shillingford Cl, NW7 . . . .**56** A7
Shillingford St, N1
  off Cross St **93** H7
Shinfield St, W12 . . . .**107** J6
Shinglewell Rd, Erith DA8 . . . . .**139** G7
Shinners Cl, SE25 . . . .**188** D5
Ship All, W4 *off Thames Rd* **126** A6
Ship & Mermaid Row, SE1 . . . . .**28** C3
Shipka Rd, SW12 . . . .**168** B1
Shipman Rd, E16 . . . .**115** H6
  SE23 . . . .**171** G2
Ship St, SE8 . . . .**154** A1
Ship Tavern Pas, EC3 . . . .**20** D5
Shipton Cl, Dag. RM8 . . . .**100** D3
Shipton St, E2 . . . .**13** G3
Shipwright Rd, SE16 . . . .**133** H2
Shipwright Yd, SE1 . . . .**28** D2
Ship Yd, E14 *off Napier Av* **134** B5
Shirburn Cl, SE23 *off Tyson Rd* . .**153** F7
Shirbutt St, E14 . . . .**114** B7
Shirebrook Rd, SE3 . . . .**156** A3
Shire Ct, Epsom KT17 . . . .**197** F7
  Erith DA18
  off St. John Fisher Rd **138** D3
Shirehall Cl, NW4 . . . .**72** A6
Shirehall Gdns, NW4 . . . .**72** A6
Shirehall La, NW4 . . . .**72** A6
Shirehall Pk, NW4 . . . .**72** A6
Shire Horse Way, Islw. TW7 . . . .**144** C3
Shire La, Kes. BR2 . . . .**206** C7
  Orpington BR6 . . . .**207** G6
Shire Pl, SW18
  off Swaffield Rd **148/149** E7
Shires, The, Rich. TW10 . . . .**163** H4
Shirland Ms, W9 . . . .**108** C3
Shirland Rd, W9 . . . .**108** D3
SHIRLEY, Croy. CR0 . . . .**203** G3
Shirley Av, Bex. DA5 . . . .**158** D7
  Croydon CR0 . . . .**203** F1
  Sutton SM1 . . . .**199** H4
Shirley Ch Rd, Croy. CR0 . . . . . .**203** G3
Shirley Cl, E17 *off Addison Rd* . .**78** B5
  Hounslow TW3 . . . .**143** J5
Shirley Ct, Croy. CR0 . . . .**203** G3
Shirley Cres, Beck. BR3 . . . .**189** H4
Shirley Dr, Houns. TW3 . . . .**143** J5
Shirley Gdns, W7 . . . .**124** C1
  Barking IG11 . . . .**99** H6
Shirley Gro, N9 . . . .**45** F7
  SW11 . . . .**150** A3
Shirley Hills Rd, Croy. CR0 . . . . .**203** G5
Shirley Ho Dr, SE7 . . . .**135** J7
Shirley Oaks Rd, Croy. CR0 . . . . .**203** G1
Shirley Pk Rd, Croy. CR0 . . . . . .**203** E1
Shirley Rd, E15 . . . .**97** E7
  W4 . . . .**126** D2
  Croydon CR0 . . . .**189** E7
  Enfield EN2 . . . .**43** J4
  Sidcup DA15 . . . .**175** H3
Shirley St, E16 . . . .**115** F6
Shirley Way, Croy. CR0 . . . .**203** H3
Shirlock Rd, NW3 . . . .**91** J4
Shirwell Cl, NW7 . . . .**56** A7
Shobden Rd, N17 . . . .**76** A1
Shobroke Cl, NW2 . . . .**89** J3
Shoebury Rd, E6 . . . .**98** C7
Shoe La, EC4 . . . .**19** F3
Sholto Rd, Houns. (Hthrw Air.)
  TW6 . . . .**140** C5
SHOREDITCH, E1 . . . .**13** F6
Shoreditch High St, E1 . . . .**13** E6
Shoreditch Ho, N1 . . . .**12** C4
Shore Gro, Felt. TW13 . . . .**161** G2

Shoreham Cl, SW18
  off Ram St **148/149** E5
  Bexley DA5 . . . .**176** D1
  Croydon CR0 . . . .**189** F6
Shoreham Rd E, Houns. (Hthrw Air.)
  TW6 . . . .**140** B5
Shoreham Rd W, Houns. (Hthrw Air.)
  TW6 . . . .**140** B5
Shoreham Way, Brom. BR2 . . . . .**191** G6
Shore Pl, E9 . . . .**95** F7
Shore Rd, E9 . . . .**95** F7
Shorncliffe Rd, SE1 . . . .**37** F3
Shorndean St, SE6 . . . .**172** C1
Shorne Cl, Sid. DA15 . . . .**158** B6
Shornefield Cl, Brom. BR1 . . . . .**192** D3
Shornells Way, SE2
  off Willrose Cres **138** C5
Shorrolds Rd, SW6 . . . .**128** C7
Shortcroft Rd, Epsom KT17 . . . . .**197** F7
Shortcrofts Rd, Dag. RM9 . . . . .**101** F6
Shorter St, E1 . . . .**21** F5
Shortgate, N12 . . . .**56** C4
Short Hedges, Houns. TW3, TW5 .**143** H1
Short Hill, Har. HA1 *off High St* . .**86** B1
SHORTLANDS, Brom. BR1 . . . . .**190** E3
Shortlands, W6 . . . .**128** A4
  Hayes UB3 . . . .**121** G6
Shortlands Cl, N18 . . . .**60** A3
  Belvedere DA17 . . . .**139** F3
Shortlands Gdns, Brom. BR2 . . .**191** E2
Shortlands Gro, Brom. BR2 . . . .**190** D3
Shortlands Rd, E10 . . . .**78** B7
  Bromley BR2 . . . .**190** D3
  Kingston upon Thames KT2 . . . .**163** J7
Short Path, SE18
  off Westdale Rd **136/137** E6
Short Rd, E11 . . . .**96** E2
  E15 . . . .**114** D1
  W4 . . . .**126** E6
  Hounslow (Hthrw Air.) TW6 . . .**140** B6
Shorts Cft, NW9 . . . .**70** B4
Shorts Gdns, WC2 . . . .**18** A4
Shorts Rd, Cars. SM5 . . . .**199** H4
Short St, NW4
  off New Brent St **71** J4
  SE1 . . . .**27** F3
Short Wall, E15 . . . .**114** C3
Shortway, N12 . . . .**57** H6
Short Way, SE9 . . . .**156** B3
  Twickenham TW2 . . . .**143** J7
Shotfield, Wall. SM6 . . . .**200** B6
Shott Cl, Sutt. SM1
  off Turnpike La **199** F5
Shottery Cl, SE9 . . . .**174** B3
Shottendane Rd, SW6 . . . .**148** D1
Shottfield Av, SW14 . . . .**146** E4
Shoulder of Mutton All, E14
  off Narrow St **113** H7
Shouldham St, W1 . . . .**15** H2
Showers Way, Hayes UB3 . . . . .**122** A1
Shrapnel Cl, SE18 . . . .**136** B7
Shrapnel Rd, SE9 . . . .**156** C3
Shrewsbury Av, SW14 . . . .**146** C4
  Harrow HA3 . . . .**69** H4
Shrewsbury Cl, Surb. KT6 . . . . . .**195** H2
Shrewsbury Ct, EC1
  off Whitecross St **111** J4
Shrewsbury Cres, NW10 . . . . . .**106** D1
Shrewsbury La, SE18 . . . .**156** E1
Shrewsbury Ms, W2
  off Chepstow Rd **108** D5
Shrewsbury Rd, E7 . . . .**98** A5
  N11 . . . .**58** C6
  W2 . . . .**108** D6
  Beckenham BR3 . . . .**189** H3
  Carshalton SM5 . . . .**185** H6
  Hounslow (Hthrw Air.) TW6 . . .**141** F6
Shrewsbury St, W10 . . . .**107** J4
Shrewsbury Wk, Islw. TW7
  off South St **144** D3
Shrewton Rd, SW17 . . . .**167** J7
Shroffold Rd, Brom. BR1 . . . . . .**173** E4
Shropshire Cl, Mitch. CR4 . . . . .**187** E4
Shropshire Ho, N18
  off Cavendish Rd **60/61** E5
Shropshire Pl, WC1 . . . .**9** G6
Shropshire Rd, N22 . . . .**59** F7
Shroton St, NW1 . . . .**15** G1
Shrubberies, The, E18 . . . .**79** G2
  Chigwell IG7 . . . .**65** F5
Shrubbery, The, E11 . . . .**79** H5
Shrubbery Cl, N1 *off St. Paul St* . .**111** J1
Shrubbery Gdns, N21 . . . .**43** H7
Shrubbery Rd, N9 . . . .**60** D3
  SW16 . . . .**168** E4
  Southall UB1 . . . .**123** F1
Shrubland Gro, Wor.Pk. KT4 . . . .**197** J3
Shrubland Rd, E8 . . . .**112** D1
  E10 . . . .**78** A7
  E17 . . . .**78** A5
Shrublands Av, Croy. CR0 . . . . . .**204** A4
Shrublands Cl, N20 . . . .**57** G1
  SE26 . . . .**171** F3
  Chigwell IG7 . . . .**65** J5
Shrubsall Cl, SE9 . . . .**174** B1

Shuna Wk, N1 *off St. Paul's Rd* . .**94** A6
Shurland Av, Barn. EN4 . . . .**41** G6
Shurland Gdns, SE15 . . . .**37** G7
Shurlock Dr, Orp. BR6 . . . .**207** F4
Shuters Sq, W14 *off Sun Rd* . . .**128** C5
Shuttle Cl, Sid. DA15 . . . .**157** J7
Shuttlemead, Bex. DA5 . . . .**159** F7
Shuttle St, E1 . . . .**13** H6
Shuttleworth Rd, SW11 . . . .**149** H2
Siamese Ms, N3 *off Station Rd* . .**72** D1
Sibella Rd, SW4 . . . .**150** D2
Sibley Cl, Bexh. DA6 . . . .**159** E5
  Bromley BR1
  off Southborough Rd **192** B5
Sibley Gro, E12 . . . .**98** B7
Sibthorpe Rd, SE12 . . . .**155** H6
Sibton Rd, Cars. SM5 . . . .**185** H7
Sicilian Av, WC1 . . . .**18** B2
Sidbury St, SW6 . . . .**148** B1
SIDCUP, DA14 & DA15 . . . .**175** J4
Sidcup Bypass, Chis. BR7 . . . . . .**175** H4
  Orpington BR5 . . . .**176** D2
  Sidcup DA14 . . . .**175** H4
Sidcup High St, Sid. DA14 . . . . .**176** A4
Sidcup Hill, Sid. DA14 . . . .**176** B4
Sidcup Hill Gdns, Sid. DA14
  off Sidcup Hill **176** C5
Sidcup Pl, Sid. DA14 . . . .**176** A5
Sidcup Rd, SE9 . . . .**156** A7
  SE12 . . . .**155** H5
Sidcup Tech Cen, Sid. DA14 . . . .**176** D5
Siddeley Dr, Houns. TW4 . . . . . .**142** E3
Siddons La, NW1 . . . .**8** A4
Siddons Rd, N17 . . . .**76** D1
  SE23 . . . .**171** H2
  Croydon CR0 . . . .**201** G3
Side Rd, E17 . . . .**77** J5
Sidewood Rd, SE9 . . . .**175** G1
Sidford Pl, SE1 . . . .**26** D6
Sidi Ct, N15 *off Milton Rd* **75** H3
Sidings, The, E11 . . . .**96** C1
  Loughton IG10 . . . .**48** B6
Sidings Ms, N7 . . . .**93** G3
Sidmouth Av, Islw. TW7 . . . .**144** B2
Sidmouth Cl, Wat. WD19 . . . .**50** B2
Sidmouth Dr, Ruis. HA4 . . . .**84** A3
Sidmouth Par, NW2
  off Sidmouth Rd **89** J7
Sidmouth Rd, E10 . . . .**96** C3
  NW2 . . . .**89** J7
  Welling DA16 . . . .**138** C7
Sidmouth St, WC1 . . . .**10** B4
Sidney Av, N13 . . . .**59** F5
Sidney Elson Way, E6
  off Edwin Av **116** D2
Sidney Gdns, Brent. TW8 . . . . . .**125** F6
Sidney Gro, EC1 . . . .**11** G2
Sidney Rd, E7 . . . .**97** G3
  N22 . . . .**59** F7
  SE25 . . . .**188** D5
  SW9 . . . .**151** F2
  Beckenham BR3 . . . .**189** H2
  Harrow HA2 . . . .**67** J3
  Twickenham TW1 . . . .**144** D6
  Walton-on-Thames KT12 . . . . .**178** A7
Sidney Sq, E1 . . . .**113** F6
Sidney St, E1 . . . .**113** E5
Sidworth St, E8 . . . .**95** E7
Siebert Rd, SE3 . . . .**135** G6
Siemens Rd, SE18 . . . .**136** A3
Sigdon Rd, E8 . . . .**94** D5
Sigers, The, Pnr. HA5 . . . .**66** B6
Signmakers Yd, NW1
  off Delancey St **110** B1
Sigrist Sq, Kings.T. KT2 . . . .**181** H1
Silbury Av, Mitch. CR4 . . . .**185** H1
Silbury Ho, SE26
  off Sydenham Hill **170** D3
Silbury St, N1 . . . .**12** B3
Silchester Rd, W10 . . . .**108** A6
Silecroft Rd, Bexh. DA7 . . . .**159** G1
Silesia Bldgs, E8
  off London La **94/95** E7
Silex St, SE1 . . . .**27** H4
Silk Cl, SE12 . . . .**155** G5
Silkfield Rd, NW9 . . . .**71** E5
Silkin Ho, Wat. WD19 . . . .**50** C3
Silk Mills Pas, SE13
  off Russett Way **154** B2
Silk Mills Path, SE13
  off Lewisham Rd **154** C2
Silk Mills Sq, E9 . . . .**95** J6
Silkstream Rd, Edg. HA8 . . . .**70** C1
Silk St, EC2 . . . .**20** A1
Silsoe Rd, N22 . . . .**75** F2
Silver Birch Av, E4 . . . .**61** J6
Silver Birch Cl, N11 . . . .**58** A6
  SE6 . . . .**171** J3
  SE28 . . . .**138** A1
Silver Birch Gdns, E6 . . . .**116** C4
Silver Birch Ms, Ilf. IG6
  off Fencepiece Rd **65** F6
Silverbirch Wk, NW3
  off Queen's Cres **92** A4
Silvercliffe Gdns, Barn. EN4 . . . . .**41** H4

Silver Cl, SE14
  off Southerngate Way **133** H7
  Harrow HA3 . . . .**52** A7
Silver Cres, W4 . . . .**126** B4
Silverdale, SE26 . . . .**171** F4
  Enfield EN2 . . . .**43** E4
Silverdale Av, Ilf. IG3 . . . .**81** H5
Silverdale Cl, W7 . . . .**124** B1
  Northolt UB5 . . . .**85** F5
  Sutton SM1 . . . .**198** C4
Silverdale Dr, SE9 . . . .**174** B2
  Sunbury-on-Thames TW16 . . . .**178** B3
Silverdale Gdns, Hayes UB3 . . . .**122** A2
Silverdale Rd, E4 . . . .**62** D6
  Bexleyheath DA7 . . . .**159** J2
  Hayes UB3 . . . .**122** A2
  Orpington (Petts Wd) BR5 . . . .**193** F4
Silvergate, Epsom KT19 . . . .**196** C5
Silverhall St, Islw. TW7 . . . .**144** D3
Silverholme Cl, Har. HA3 . . . .**69** G7
Silver Jubilee Way, Houns. TW4 .**142** B2
Silverland St, E16 . . . .**136** C1
Silver La, W.Wick. BR4 . . . .**204** D2
Silverleigh Rd, Th.Hth. CR7 . . . . .**187** F4
Silvermead, E18
  off Churchfields **63** G7
Silvermere Dr, N18 . . . .**61** G6
Silvermere Rd, SE6 . . . .**154** B6
Silver Pl, W1 . . . .**17** G5
Silver Rd, SE13 . . . .**154** B3
  W12 . . . .**108** A7
Silver Spring Cl, Erith DA8 . . . . .**139** H6
Silverston Way, Stan. HA7 . . . . . .**53** F6
Silver St, N18 . . . .**60** B4
  Enfield EN1 . . . .**44** A3
Silverthorne Rd, SW8 . . . .**150** B2
Silverthorn Gdns, E4 . . . .**62** A2
SILVERTOWN, E16 . . . .**135** J2
Silverton Rd, W6 . . . .**128** A6
Silvertown Way, E16 . . . .**115** F6
Silvertree La, Grnf. UB6
  off Cowgate Rd **104** A3
Silver Wk, SE16 . . . .**133** J1
Silver Way, Rom. RM7 . . . .**83** H3
Silverwood Cl, Beck. BR3 . . . . . .**172** A7
Silvester Rd, SE22 . . . .**152** C5
Silvester St, SE1 . . . .**28** A4
Silvocea Way, E14 . . . .**114** D6
Silwood Est, SE16 . . . .**133** F4
Silwood St, SE16 . . . .**133** F4
Simla Ho, SE1 . . . .**28** C4
Simmil Rd, Esher (Clay.) KT10 . . .**194** B5
Simmons Cl, N20 . . . .**57** H1
  Chessington KT9 . . . .**195** F7
Simmons La, E4 . . . .**62** D2
Simmons Rd, SE18 . . . .**136** E5
Simmons Way, N20 . . . .**57** H2
Simms Cl, Cars. SM5 . . . .**199** H2
Simms Gdns, N2 . . . .**73** F2
Simms Rd, SE1 . . . .**37** H2
Simnel Rd, SE12 . . . .**155** H7
Simon Cl, W11
  off Portobello Rd **108** C7
Simonds Rd, E10 . . . .**96** A2
Simone Cl, Brom. BR1 . . . .**192** A1
Simons Wk, E15
  off Waddington Rd **96** D5
Simpson Cl, N21
  off Macleod Rd **42/43** E5
Simpson Dr, W3 . . . .**106** D6
Simpson Rd, Houns. TW4 . . . . . .**143** F6
  Richmond TW10 . . . .**163** F4
Simpsons Rd, E14 . . . .**114** B7
  Bromley BR2 . . . .**191** G3
Simpson St, SW11 . . . .**149** H2
Simrose Ct, SW18
  off Wandsworth High St **148** D5
Sims Wk, SE3 . . . .**155** F4
Sinclair Ct, Beck. BR3 . . . .**172** A7
Sinclair Gdns, W14 . . . .**128** A2
Sinclair Gro, NW11 . . . .**72** A6
Sinclair Pl, SE4 . . . .**154** A6
Sinclair Rd, E4 . . . .**61** J5
  W14 . . . .**128** A2
Sinclare Cl, Enf. EN1 . . . .**44** C1
Singapore Rd, W13 . . . .**124** D1
Singer St, EC2 . . . .**12** C4
Singleton Cl, SW17 . . . .**167** J7
  Croydon CR0
  off St. Saviours Rd **187** J7
Singleton Rd, Dag. RM9 . . . .**101** F5
Singleton Scarp, N12 . . . .**56** D5
Sinnott Rd, E17 . . . .**77** G1
Sion Rd, Twick. TW1 . . . .**162** E1
SIPSON, West Dr. UB7 . . . .**120** D6
Sipson Cl, West Dr. UB7 . . . .**120** D6
Sipson La, Hayes UB3 . . . .**120** D6
  West Drayton UB7 . . . .**120** D6
Sipson Rd, West Dr. UB7 . . . . . .**120** D5
Sipson Way, West Dr. UB7 . . . . .**120** D7
Sir Alexander Cl, W3 . . . .**127** F1
Sir Alexander Rd, W3 . . . .**127** F1
Sir Cyril Black Way, SW19 . . . . .**166** D7
Sirdar Rd, N22 . . . .**75** H3
  W11 . . . .**108** A7

Sirdar Rd, Mitch. CR4
  off Grenfell Rd **168** A6
Sirinham Pt, SW8 . . . .**34** G6
Sirius Rd, Nthwd. HA6 . . . .**50** A5
Sir John Kirk Cl, SE5 . . . .**35** J7
★ Sir John Soane's Mus, WC2
  off Lincoln's Inn Flds **18** C3
Sir Thomas More Est, SW3 . . . .**31** F6
Sise La, EC4 . . . .**20** B4
Siskin Cl, Borwd. WD6 . . . .**38** A4
Sisley Rd, Bark. IG11 . . . .**117** H1
Sispara Gdns, SW18 . . . .**148** C6
Sissinghurst Rd, Croy. CR0 . . .**188** D7
Sissulu Ct, E6 . . . .**115** J1
Sister Mabel's Way, SE15 . . . . .**37** H7
Sisters Av, SW11 . . . .**149** J4
Sistova Rd, SW12 . . . .**168** B1
Sisulu Pl, SW9 . . . .**151** G3
Sittingbourne Av, Enf. EN1 . . . .**44** A6
Sitwell Gro, Stan. HA7 . . . .**52** A5
Siverst Cl, Nthlt. UB5 . . . .**85** H6
Sivill Ho, E2 . . . .**13** G3
Siviter Way, Dag. RM10 . . . . . .**101** H7
Siward Rd, N17 . . . .**76** A1
  SW17 . . . .**167** F3
  Bromley BR2 . . . .**191** H3
Six Acres Est, N4 . . . .**93** G2
Six Bridges Trd Est, SE1 . . . . . .**37** J4
Sixth Av, E12 . . . .**98** C4
  W10 . . . .**108** B3
  Hayes UB3 . . . .**121** J1
Sixth Cross Rd, Twick. TW2 . . .**161** H3
Skardu Rd, NW2 . . . .**90** B5
Skeena Hill, SW18 . . . .**148** B7
Skeffington Rd, E6 . . . .**116** B1
Skeffington St, SE18 . . . .**137** F3
Skelbrook St, SW18 . . . .**167** E2
Skelgill Rd, SW15 . . . .**148** C4
Skelley Rd, E15 . . . .**97** F7
Skelton Cl, E8
  off Buttermere Wk **94** C6
Skelton Rd, E7 . . . .**97** G6
Skeltons La, E10 . . . .**78** B7
Skelwith Rd, W6 . . . .**127** J6
Skenfrith Ho, SE15
  off Commercial Way . . .**132/133** E6
Skerne Rd, Kings.T. KT2 . . . . .**181** G1
Skerne Wk, Kings.T. KT2 . . . . .**181** G1
Sketchley Gdns, SE16 . . . .**133** G5
Sketty Rd, Enf. EN1 . . . .**44** B3
Skiers St, E15 . . . .**114** E1
Skiffington Cl, SW2 . . . .**169** G1
Skinner Ct, E2
  off Parmiter St **112/113** E2
★ Skinners' Hall, EC4
  off Dowgate Hill **20** B5
Skinners La, EC4 . . . .**20** A4
  Hounslow TW5 . . . .**143** H1
Skinner St, EC1 . . . .**11** F4
Skipsea Ho, SW18
  off Fitzhugh Gro **149** G6
Skipsey Av, E6 . . . .**116** C3
Skipton Cl, N11
  off Ribblesdale Av **58** A6
Skipton Dr, Hayes UB3 . . . . . .**121** F3
Skipworth Rd, E9 . . . .**113** F1
Skomer Wk, N1 off Ashby Gro . .**93** J6
Slade, The, SE18 . . . .**137** H6
Sladebrook Rd, SE3 . . . .**156** A3
Sladedale Rd, SE18 . . . .**137** H5
Slade Ho, Hounslow TW4 . . . .**143** F6
Slades Cl, Enf. EN2 . . . .**43** G3
Slades Dr, Chis. BR7 . . . .**175** F3
Slades Gdns, Enf. EN2 . . . .**43** G2
Slades Hill, Enf. EN2 . . . .**43** G3
Slades Ri, Enf. EN2 . . . .**43** G3
Slade Twr, E10 . . . .**96** B2
Slade Wk, SE17 . . . .**35** H6
Slagrove Pl, SE13 . . . .**154** A5
Slaidburn St, SW10 . . . .**30** D6
Slaithwaite Rd, SE13 . . . .**154** C4
Slaney Pl, N7 off Hornsey Rd . . .**93** G5
Slater Cl, SE18
  off Woolwich New Rd **136** D5
Slattery Rd, Felt. TW13 . . . . . .**160** C1
Sleaford Grn, Wat. WD19 . . . . .**50** D3
Sleaford Ho, E3 off Chiltern Rd . .**114** A4
Sleaford St, SW8 . . . .**33** F7
Slievemore Cl, SW4
  off Voltaire Rd **150** D3
Slingsby Pl, WC2 . . . .**18** A5
Slippers Pl, SE16 . . . .**133** E3
Sloane Av, SW3 . . . .**31** G1
Sloane Ct E, SW3 . . . .**32** B3
Sloane Ct W, SW3 . . . .**32** B3
Sloane Gdns, SW1 . . . .**32** B2
  Orpington BR6 . . . .**207** F3
Sloane Sq, SW1 . . . .**32** B2
Sloane St, SW1 . . . .**24** A5
Sloane Ter, SW1 . . . .**32** A1
Sloane Wk, Croy. CR0 . . . .**189** J6

Slocum Cl, SE28 . . . .**118** C7
Slough La, NW9 . . . .**70** C6
Sly St, E1
  off Cannon St Rd **112/113** E6
Smaldon Cl, West Dr. UB7
  off Walnut Av **120** D3
Smallberry Av, Islw. TW7 . . . . .**144** C2
Smallbrook Ms, W2 . . . .**14** E4
Smalley Cl, N16 . . . .**94** C3
Smalley Rd Est, N16
  off Smalley Cl **94** C3
Smallwood Rd, SW17 . . . .**167** G4
Smardale Rd, SW18
  off Alma Rd **149** F5
Smarden Cl, Belv. DA17
  off Essenden Rd **139** G5
Smarden Gro, SE9 . . . .**174** C4
Smarts La, Loug. IG10 . . . .**48** A4
Smarts Pl, N18 off Fore St **60** D5
Smart's Pl, WC2 . . . .**18** B3
Smart St, E2 . . . .**113** G3
Smeaton Cl, Chess. KT9
  off Merritt Gdns **195** G6
Smeaton Rd, SW18 . . . .**148** D7
  Woodford Green IG8 . . . . . .**64** C5
Smeaton St, E1 . . . .**132** E1
Smedley St, SW4 . . . .**150** D2
  SW8 . . . .**150** D2
Smeed Rd, E3 . . . .**96** A7
Smiles Pl, SE13 . . . .**154** C2
Smith Cl, SE16 . . . .**133** G1
★ Smithfield Cen Mkt, EC1 . . .**19** H2
Smithfield St, EC1 . . . .**19** G2
Smithies Ct, E15 . . . .**96** C5
Smithies Rd, SE2 . . . .**138** B4
Smith's Ct, W1 . . . .**17** G5
Smiths Fm Est, Nthlt. UB5 . . . .**103** G2
Smithson Rd, N17 . . . .**76** A1
Smiths Pt, E13 off Brooks Rd . .**115** G1
Smith Sq, SW1 . . . .**26** A6
Smith St, SW3 . . . .**31** J3
  Surbiton KT5 . . . .**181** J6
Smiths Yd, SW18
  off Summerley St **167** F2
Smith's Yd, Croy. CR0
  off St. Georges Wk **201** J3
Smith Ter, SW3 . . . .**31** J4
Smithwood Cl, SW19 . . . .**166** B1
Smithy St, E1 . . . .**113** F5
Smock Wk, Croy. CR0 . . . .**187** J6
Smokehouse Yd, EC1 . . . .**19** H1
Smugglers Way, SW18 . . . . . .**149** E4
Smyrks Rd, SE17 . . . .**36** E4
Smyrna Rd, NW6 . . . .**90** D7
Smythe St, E14 . . . .**114** B7
Snakes La, Barn. EN4 . . . .**42** B3
Snakes La E, Wdf.Grn. IG8 . . . .**63** J6
Snakes La W, Wdf.Grn. IG8 . . . .**63** G6
SNARESBROOK, E11 . . . .**79** E5
Snaresbrook Dr, Stan. HA7 . . . .**53** G4
Snaresbrook Rd, E11 . . . .**78** E4
Snarsgate St, W10 . . . .**107** J5
Sneath Av, NW11 . . . .**72** C7
Snells Pk, N18 . . . .**60** C6
Sneyd Rd, NW2 . . . .**89** J4
Snowberry Cl, E15 . . . .**96** D4
Snowbury Rd, SW6 . . . .**149** E2
Snowden St, EC2 . . . .**12** D6
Snowdon Cres, Hayes UB3 . . .**121** F3
Snowdon Dr, NW9 . . . .**70** E6
Snowdon Rd, Houns. (Hthrw Air.) TW6
  off Southern Perimeter Rd . . .**141** F5
Snowdown Cl, SE20 . . . .**189** G1
Snowdrop Cl, Hmptn. TW12
  off Gresham Rd **161** G6
Snow Hill, EC1 . . . .**19** G2
Snow Hill Ct, EC1 . . . .**19** H3
Snowman Ho, NW6 . . . .**109** E1
Snowsfields, SE1 . . . .**28** C3
Snowshill Rd, E12 . . . .**98** B5
Snowy Fielder Waye, Islw. TW7 .**144** E2
Soames St, SE15 . . . .**152** C3
Soames Wk, N.Mal. KT3 . . . . .**182** E1
Soane Cl, W5 . . . .**125** G2
Soap Ho La, Brent. TW8 . . . . .**125** H7
Socket La, Brom. BR2 . . . .**191** H6
SOHO, W1 . . . .**17** H5
Soho Sq, W1 . . . .**17** H3
Soho St, W1 . . . .**17** H3
Sojourner Truth Cl, E8
  off Richmond Rd **94/95** E6
Solander Gdns, E1
  off Dellow St **112/113** E7
Solebay St, E1 . . . .**113** H4
Solent Ri, E13 . . . .**115** G3
Solent Rd, NW6 . . . .**90** D5
  Hounslow (Hthrw Air.) TW6 . .**140** C6
Soley Ms, WC1 . . . .**10** E3
Solna Av, SW15 . . . .**147** J5
Solna Rd, N21 . . . .**60** A1
Solomon Av, N9 . . . .**60** D4
Solomon's Pas, SE15 . . . .**152** E4
Solon New Rd, SW4 . . . .**150** E4
Solon New Rd Est, SW4
  off Solon New Rd **150/151** E4

Solon Rd, SW2 . . . .**151** E4
Solway Cl, E8
  off Buttermere Wk **94** C6
  Hounslow TW4 . . . .**143** E3
Solway Rd, N22 . . . .**75** H1
  SE22 . . . .**152** D4
Somaford Gro, Barn. EN4 . . . . .**41** G6
Somali Rd, NW2 . . . .**90** C4
Somborne Ho, SW15
  off Fontley Way **147** G7
Somerby Rd, Bark. IG11 . . . . . .**99** G7
Somercoates Cl, Barn. EN4 . . . .**41** H3
Somerfield Rd, N4 . . . .**93** H2
  SE16 off Oldfield Gro **133** G5
Somerford Cl, Pnr. HA5 . . . .**66** A4
Somerford Gro, N16 . . . .**94** C4
  N17 . . . .**60** D7
Somerford Gro Est, N16
  off Somerford Gro **94** C4
Somerford St, E1 . . . .**112** E4
Somerford Way, SE16 . . . .**133** H2
Somerhill Av, Sid. DA15 . . . . . .**158** B7
Somerhill Rd, Well. DA16 . . . . .**158** B2
Somerleyton Pas, SW9 . . . . . .**151** H4
Somerleyton Rd, SW9 . . . .**151** G4
Somersby Gdns, Ilf. IG4 . . . . . .**80** C5
Somers Cl, NW1 . . . .**9** H1
Somers Cres, W2 . . . .**15** G4
Somerset Av, SW20 . . . .**183** H2
  Chessington KT9 . . . .**195** G4
  Welling DA16 . . . .**157** J5
Somerset Cl, N17 . . . .**76** A2
  New Malden KT3 . . . .**183** E6
  Woodford Green IG8 . . . . . .**79** G1
Somerset Est, SW11 . . . .**149** G1
Somerset Gdns, N6 . . . .**74** A7
  N17 . . . .**60** B7
  SE13 . . . .**154** B2
  SW16 . . . .**187** F3
  Teddington TW11 . . . .**162** B5
★ Somerset Ho, WC2 . . . .**18** C5
Somerset Ho, SW19 . . . .**166** A3
Somerset Rd, E17 . . . .**78** A5
  N17 . . . .**76** C3
  N18 . . . .**60** C5
  NW4 . . . .**71** J4
  SW19 . . . .**166** B4
  W4 . . . .**126** D3
  W13 . . . .**125** E1
  Barnet EN5 . . . .**41** E5
  Brentford TW8 . . . .**125** F6
  Harrow HA1 . . . .**67** J5
  Kingston upon Thames KT1 . .**181** J3
  Southall UB1 . . . .**103** F5
  Teddington TW11 . . . .**162** B5
Somerset Sq, W14 . . . .**128** B2
Somerset Waye, Houns. TW5 . .**122** E6
Somersham Rd, Bexh. DA7 . . .**159** E2
Somers Ms, W2 . . . .**15** G4
Somers Pl, SW2 . . . .**151** F7
Somers Rd, E17 . . . .**77** J4
  SW2 . . . .**151** F6
SOMERS TOWN, NW1 . . . .**9** J3
Somerton Av, Rich. TW9 . . . . .**146** B3
Somerton Rd, NW2 . . . .**90** B3
  SE15 . . . .**153** E4
Somertrees Av, SE12 . . . .**173** H2
Somervell Rd, Har. HA2 . . . . . .**85** F5
Somerville Av, SW13 . . . .**127** H6
Somerville Rd, SE20 . . . .**171** G7
  Romford RM6 . . . .**82** C6
Sonderburg Rd, N7 . . . .**93** F2
Sondes St, SE17 . . . .**36** B5
Sonia Ct, Har. HA1 . . . .**68** C6
Sonia Gdns, N12
  off Woodside Av **57** F4
  NW10 . . . .**89** F4
  Hounslow TW5 . . . .**123** G7
Sonning Gdns, Hmptn. TW12 . .**161** E6
Sonning Rd, SE25 . . . .**188** D6
Soper Cl, E4 . . . .**61** J5
  SE23 . . . .**171** G1
Sophia Cl, N7 off Mackenzie Rd . .**93** F6
Sophia Rd, E10 . . . .**96** B1
  E16 . . . .**115** H6
Sophia Sq, SE16
  off Rotherhithe St **113** H7
Sopwith Av, Chess. KT9 . . . . . .**195** H5
Sopwith Cl, Kings.T. KT2 . . . . .**163** J5
Sopwith Rd, Houns. TW5 . . . . .**122** C7
Sopwith Way, SW8 . . . .**32** D7
  Kingston upon Thames KT2 . .**181** H1
Sorrel Cl, SE28 . . . .**138** A1
Sorrel Gdns, E6 . . . .**116** B5
Sorrel La, E14 . . . .**114** D6
Sorrell Cl, SE14
  off Southerngate Way **133** H7
Sorrento Rd, Sutt. SM1 . . . . . .**198** E3
Sotheby Rd, N5 . . . .**93** H3
Sotheran Cl, E8 . . . .**112** D1
Sotheron Rd, SW6 . . . .**129** E7
Soudan Rd, SW11 . . . .**149** J1
Souldern Rd, W14 . . . .**128** A3
South Access Rd, E17 . . . .**77** H7
Southacre Way, Pnr. HA5 . . . . .**66** C1

SOUTH ACTON, W3 . . . .**126** A3
South Acton Est, W3 . . . .**126** B2
South Africa Rd, W12 . . . .**127** H1
SOUTHALL, UB1 & UB2 . . . . .**122** D1
Southall La, Houns. TW5 . . . . .**122** B6
  Southall UB2 . . . .**122** B6
Southall Pl, SE1 . . . .**28** B4
Southampton Bldgs, WC2 . . . .**18** C3
Southampton Gdns, Mitch. CR4 .**186** E5
Southampton Ms, E16
  off Wesley Av **135** H1
Southampton Pl, WC1 . . . .**18** B2
Southampton Rd, NW5 . . . .**91** J5
  Hounslow (Hthrw Air.) TW6 .**140** C6
Southampton Row, WC1 . . . . .**18** B1
Southampton St, WC2 . . . .**18** B5
Southampton Way, SE5 . . . . . .**36** C7
Southam St, W10 . . . .**108** B4
South Audley St, W1 . . . .**16** C6
South Av, E4 . . . .**46** B7
  Carshalton SM5 . . . .**199** J7
  Richmond TW9
   off Sandycombe Rd **146** A2
  Southall UB1 . . . .**103** F7
South Av Gdns, Sthl. UB1 . . . .**103** F7
South Bk, Chis. BR7 . . . .**175** F4
  Surbiton KT6 . . . .**181** H6
Southbank, T.Ditt. KT7 . . . . . .**180** E7
Southbank Business Cen, SW8 . .**33** J6
South Bk Ter, Surb. KT6 . . .**181** H6
SOUTH BEDDINGTON, Wall.
  SM6 . . . .**200** D6
South Birkbeck Rd, E11 . . . . . .**96** D3
South Black Lion La, W6 . . . . .**127** G5
SOUTHBOROUGH, Brom. BR2 .**192** C6
Southborough Cl, Surb. KT6 . .**195** G1
Southborough La, Brom. BR2 . .**192** B5
Southborough Rd, E9 . . . .**113** F1
  Bromley BR1 . . . .**192** B3
  Surbiton KT6 . . . .**195** H1
Southbourne, Brom. BR2 . . . . .**191** G7
Southbourne Av, NW9 . . . .**70** C3
Southbourne Cl, Pnr. HA5 . . . . .**67** E7
Southbourne Cres, NW4 . . . . . .**72** B4
Southbourne Gdns, SE12 . . . .**155** H5
  Ilford IG1 . . . .**99** F5
  Ruislip HA4 . . . .**84** B1
Southbridge Pl, Croy. CR0 . . .**201** J4
Southbridge Rd, Croy. CR0 . . .**201** J4
Southbridge Way, Sthl. UB2 . . .**123** E2
Southbrook Ms, SE12 . . . .**155** F6
Southbrook Rd, SE12 . . . .**155** F6
  SW16 . . . .**187** E1
Southbury Av, Enf. EN1 . . . .**44** D5
Southbury Rd, Enf. EN1, EN3 . . .**44** A3
South Carriage Dr, SW1 . . . . . .**23** J3
  SW7 . . . .**23** F4
SOUTH CHINGFORD, E4 . . . . . .**61** J5
Southchurch Rd, E6 . . . .**116** C2
South Circular Rd, SE6 (A205) .**154** D7
  SE9 (A205) **156** C3
  SE12 (A205) **155** H6
  SE18 (A205) **136** D6
  SE21 (A205) **170** D3
  SE22 (A205) **171** E1
  SE23 (A205) **171** J1
  SW2 (A205) **169** G1
  SW4 (A205) **150** A5
  SW11 (A3) **149** H5
  SW12 (A205) **169** G1
  SW14 (A205) **147** E4
  SW15 (A205) **147** J4
  SW18 (A3) **149** H5
  W4 (A205) **126** A5
  Brentford (A205) TW8 . . . .**126** A5
  Richmond (A205) TW9 . . .**146** B2
South Cl, N6 . . . .**74** B6
  Barnet EN5 . . . .**40** C3
  Bexleyheath DA6 . . . .**158** D4
  Dagenham RM10 . . . .**119** G1
  Morden SM4 . . . .**184** D6
  Pinner HA5 . . . .**67** F7
  Twickenham TW2 . . . .**161** G3
  West Drayton UB7 . . . . . .**120** C3
South Colonnade, E14 . . . .**134** A1
Southcombe St, W14 . . . .**128** B4
Southcote Av, Surb. KT5 . . . . .**182** B7
Southcote Rd, E17 . . . .**77** G5
  N19 . . . .**92** C4
  SE25 . . . .**189** E6
Southcott Ms, NW8 . . . .**7** G2
South Countess Rd, E17 . . . . . .**77** J3
South Cres, E16 . . . .**114** D4
  WC1 . . . .**17** H2
Southcroft Av, Well. DA16 . . . .**157** H3
  West Wickham BR4 . . . . . .**204** C2
Southcroft Rd, SW16 . . . .**168** A6
  SW17 . . . .**168** A6
  Orpington BR6 . . . .**207** H3
South Cross Rd, Ilf. IG6 . . . .**81** F5
South Croxted Rd, SE21 . . . . .**170** A3
SOUTH CROYDON, CR2 . . . . .**201** J6
Southdale, Chig. IG7 . . . .**65** G6
Southdean Gdns, SW19 . . . . . .**166** C2

South Dene, NW7 . . . . .54 D3
Southdown Av, W7 . . . . .124 D3
Southdown Cres, Har. HA2 . . . . . .85 H1
Ilford IG2 . . . . .81 H5
Southdown Dr, SW20
off Crescent Rd 166 A7
Southdown Rd, SW20 . . . . .184 A1
South Dr, Orp. BR6 . . . . .207 H5
South Ealing Rd, W5 . . . . .125 G2
South Eastern Av, N9 . . . . .60 C3
South Eaton Pl, SW1 . . . . .32 C1
South Eden Pk Rd, Beck. BR3 . . .190 B4
South Edwardes Sq, W8 . . . . . .128 C3
SOUTHEND, SE6 . . . . .172 B4
South End, W8 . . . . .22 B5
Croydon CR0 . . . . .201 J4
South End Cl, NW3 . . . . .91 H4
Southend Cl, SE9 . . . . .156 E1
Southend Cres, SE9 . . . . .156 D6
South End Grn, NW3
off South End Rd 91 H4
Southend La, SE6 . . . . .171 J4
SE26 . . . . .171 J4
Southend Rd, E4 . . . . .61 H5
E6 . . . . .98 C7
E17 . . . . .78 B1
E18 . . . . .79 G1
South End Rd, NW3 . . . . .91 H4
Southend Rd, Beck. BR3 . . . . . .172 A7
Woodford Green IG8 . . . . . . .79 J2
South End Row, W8 . . . . .22 B5
Southern Av, SE25 . . . . .188 C3
Feltham TW14 . . . . .160 A4
Southern Dr, Loug. IG10 . . . . . . .48 C6
Southerngate Way, SE14 . . . . . .133 H7
Southern Gro, E3 . . . . .113 J3
Southernhay, Loug. IG10 . . . . . . .48 A5
Southern Perimeter Rd, Houns.
(Hthrw Air.) TW6 . . . . .141 G5
Southern Rd, E13 . . . . .115 H2
N2 . . . . .73 J4
Southern Row, W10 . . . . .108 B4
Southern St, N1 . . . . .10 C1
Southern Way, SE10 . . . . .135 F4
Romford RM7 . . . . .83 G6
Southerton Rd, W6 . . . . .127 J3
South Esk Rd, E7 . . . . .97 J6
Southey Ms, E16
off Wesley Av 135 G1
Southey Rd, N15 . . . . .76 B5
SW9 . . . . .151 G1
SW19 . . . . .166 D7
Southey St, SE20 . . . . .171 G7
Southfield, Barn. EN5 . . . . .40 A6
Southfield Cotts, W7
off Oaklands Rd 124 C2
Southfield Gdns, Twick. TW1 . . .162 C4
Southfield Pk, Har. HA2 . . . . .67 H4
Southfield Rd, N17
off The Avenue 76 B2
W4 . . . . .126 D3
Chislehurst BR7 . . . . .193 J3
Enfield EN3 . . . . .45 E6
SOUTHFIELDS, SW18 . . . . .166 D1
Southfields, NW4 . . . . .71 G3
East Molesey KT8 . . . . .180 B6
Southfields Ct, SW19 . . . . .166 B1
Sutton SM1
off Sutton Common Rd 198 D2
Southfields Ms, SW18
off Southfields Rd 148 D6
Southfields Pas, SW18 . . . . . . .148 D6
Southfields Rd, SW18 . . . . .148 D6
Southfleet Rd, Orp. BR6 . . . . . .207 H3
South Gdns, SW19 . . . . .167 G2
SOUTHGATE, N14 . . . . .58 C2
Southgate Circ, N14
off The Bourne 58 D1
Southgate Gro, N1 . . . . .94 A7
Southgate Rd, N1 . . . . .112 A1
South Gipsy Rd, Well. DA16 . . . .158 D3
South Glade, The, Bex. DA5 . . . .177 F1
South Grn, NW9
off Clayton Fld 70/71 E1
South Gro, E17 . . . . .77 J5
N6 . . . . .92 A1
N15 . . . . .76 A5
South Gro Ho, N6
off Highgate W Hill 92 A1
SOUTH HACKNEY, E9 . . . . .95 F7
SOUTH HAMPSTEAD, NW6 . . . .91 E7
SOUTH HARROW, Har. HA2 . . . .85 H3
South Hill, Chis. BR7 . . . . .174 C6
South Hill Av, Har. HA1, HA2 . . . .85 J3
South Hill Gro, Har. HA1 . . . . . . .86 B4
South Hill Pk, NW3 . . . . .91 H4
South Hill Pk Gdns, NW3 . . . . . .91 H4
South Hill Rd, Brom. BR2 . . . . .190 E3
Southholme Cl, SE19 . . . . .188 B1
South Huxley, N18 . . . . .60 A5
Southill La, Pnr. HA5 . . . . .66 A4
Southill Rd, Chis. BR7 . . . . .174 B7
Southill St, E14 off Chrisp St . . .114 B6
South Island Pl, SW9 . . . . .131 F7
SOUTH KENSINGTON, SW7 . . . .30 C2

South Kensington Sta Arc, SW7
off Pelham St 129 G4
SOUTH LAMBETH, SW8 . . . . . .151 E1
South Lambeth Pl, SW8 . . . . . . .34 B5
South Lambeth Rd, SW8 . . . . . . .34 B6
Southland Rd, SE18 . . . . .137 J7
Southlands Av, Orp. BR6 . . . . . .207 G4
Southlands Dr, SW19 . . . . .166 A2
Southlands Gro, Brom. BR1 . . . .192 B3
Southlands Rd, Brom. BR1, BR2 .191 J5
Southland Way, Houns. TW3 . . . .144 A5
South La, Kings.T. KT1 . . . . .181 G3
New Malden KT3 . . . . .182 D4
South La W, N.Mal. KT3 . . . . . .182 D4
South Lo Av, Mitch. CR4 . . . . . .186 E4
South Lo Cres, Enf. EN2 . . . . . . .42 A4
South Lo Dr, N14 . . . . .42 E5
★ South London Art Gall, SE5 .152 B1
Southly Cl, Sutt. SM1 . . . . .198 D3
South Mall, N9
off Edmonton Grn Shop Cen .60 D3
South Mead, NW9 . . . . .71 F1
Epsom KT19 . . . . .197 E7
South Meadows, Wem. HA9 . . . . .87 J5
Southmead Rd, SW19 . . . . .166 B1
South Molton La, W1 . . . . .16 D4
South Molton Rd, E16 . . . . .115 G6
South Molton St, W1 . . . . .16 D4
Southmont Rd, Esher KT10 . . . .194 B2
Southmoor Way, E9 . . . . .95 J6
SOUTH NORWOOD, SE25 . . . . .188 C3
South Norwood Hill, SE25 . . . . .188 B2
South Oak Rd, SW16 . . . . .169 F4
Southold Ri, SE9 . . . . .174 C3
Southolm St, SW11 . . . . .150 B1
Southover, N12 . . . . .56 D4
Bromley BR1 . . . . .173 G5
SOUTH OXHEY, Wat. WD19 . . . .50 C3
South Par, SW3 . . . . .31 F3
W4 . . . . .126 D4
South Pk, SW6 . . . . .148 D2
South Pk Cres, SE6 . . . . .173 F1
Ilford IG1 . . . . .99 G3
South Pk Dr, Bark. IG11 . . . . . . .99 H4
Ilford IG3 . . . . .99 H4
South Pk Gro, N.Mal. KT3 . . . . .182 C4
South Pk Hill Rd, S.Croy. CR2 . . .202 A5
South Pk Ms, SW6 . . . . .148 E3
South Pk Rd, SW19 . . . . .166 D6
Ilford IG1 . . . . .99 G3
South Pk Ter, Ilf. IG1 . . . . .99 G3
South Pk Way, Ruis. HA4 . . . . . .84 C6
South Penge Pk Est, SE20 . . . . .188 E2
South Pl, EC2 . . . . .20 C1
Enfield EN3 . . . . .45 F5
Surbiton KT5 . . . . .181 J7
South Pl Ms, EC2 . . . . .20 C1
South Pt, Sutt. SM1 . . . . .199 F6
Southport Rd, SE18 . . . . .137 G4
South Quay Plaza, E14
off Marsh Wall 134 B2
Southridge Pl, SW20 . . . . .166 A7
South Ri Way, SE18 . . . . .137 G5
South Rd, N9 . . . . .60 D1
SE23 . . . . .171 G2
SW19 . . . . .167 F6
W5 . . . . .125 G4
Edgware HA8 . . . . .70 B1
Feltham TW13 . . . . .160 D5
Hampton TW12 . . . . .161 E6
Romford (Chad.Hth) RM6 . . .82 E6
Romford (Lt.Hth) RM6 . . . . . .82 C5
Southall UB1 . . . . .123 F2
Twickenham TW2 . . . . .162 A3
West Drayton UB7 . . . . . . .120 C3
South Row, SE3 . . . . .155 F2
SOUTH RUISLIP, Ruis. HA4 . . . .84 C4
Southsea Rd, Kings.T. KT1 . . . . .181 H4
South Sea St, SE16 . . . . .133 J3
South Side, W6 . . . . .127 F3
Southside Common, SW19 . . . . .165 J6
Southspring, Sid. DA15 . . . . . . .157 G7
South Sq, NW11 . . . . .72 E6
WC1 . . . . .18 E2
South St, W1 . . . . .24 C1
Bromley BR1 . . . . .191 G2
Enfield EN3 . . . . .45 G5
Isleworth TW7 . . . . .144 D3
Rainham RM13 . . . . .119 J2
South Tenter St, E1 . . . . .21 G5
South Ter, SW7 . . . . .31 G1
Surbiton KT6 . . . . .181 H6
SOUTH TOTTENHAM, N15 . . . . .76 B5
South Vale, SE19 . . . . .170 B6
Harrow HA1 . . . . .86 B4
Southvale Rd, SE3 . . . . .155 E2
South Vw, Brom. BR1 . . . . .191 H2
Southview Av, NW10 . . . . .89 F5
Southview Cl, SW17 . . . . .168 A5
Bexley DA5 . . . . .159 F6
Southview Cres, Ilf. IG2 . . . . . . .80 E6
South Vw Dr, E18 . . . . .79 H3
Southview Gdns, Wall. SM6 . . .200 C7
South Vw Rd, N8 . . . . .74 D3
Southview Rd, Brom. BR1 . . . . .172 D4

South Vw Rd, Loug. IG10 . . . . . . .48 C6
Pinner HA5 . . . . .50 B6
South Vil, NW1 . . . . .92 D6
Southville, SW8 . . . . .150 D1
Southville Rd, T.Ditt. KT7 . . . . . .180 E7
South Wk, W.Wick. BR4 . . . . . .204 E3
SOUTHWARK, SE1 . . . . .27 H2
Southwark Br, EC4 . . . . .28 A1
SE1 . . . . .28 A1
★ Southwark Cath, SE1 . . . . . .28 B1
Southwark Br Rd, SE1 . . . . .27 H5
Southwark Pk Est, SE16 . . . . . .133 E4
Southwark Pk Rd, SE16 . . . . . . .37 G1
Southwark Pl, Brom. BR1
off St. Georges Rd 192 C3
Southwark St, SE1 . . . . .27 H1
Southwater Cl, E14 . . . . .113 J6
Beckenham BR3 . . . . .172 B7
South Way, N9 . . . . .61 F2
N11 off Ringway 58 C6
Southway, N20 . . . . .56 D2
NW11 . . . . .72 E6
SW20 . . . . .183 J4
South Way, Brom. BR2 . . . . . . .191 G7
Croydon CR0 . . . . .203 H3
Harrow HA2 . . . . .67 G4
Southway, Wall. SM6 . . . . .200 C4
South Way, Wem. HA9 . . . . .88 A5
Southway Cl, W12
off Scott's Rd 127 H2
Southwell Av, Nthlt. UB5 . . . . . . .85 G6
Southwell Gdns, SW7 . . . . .30 C1
Southwell Gro Rd, E11 . . . . .96 E2
Southwell Rd, SE5 . . . . .151 J3
Croydon CR0 . . . . .187 G6
Harrow HA3 . . . . .69 G6
South Western Rd, Twick. TW1 . .144 D6
Southwest Rd, E11 . . . . .96 D1
South Wf Rd, W2 . . . . .15 E3
Southwick Ms, W2 . . . . .15 F3
Southwick Pl, W2 . . . . .15 G4
Southwick St, W2 . . . . .15 G3
SOUTH WIMBLEDON, SW19 . . .166 E7
Southwold Dr, Bark. IG11 . . . . . .100 A5
Southwold Rd, E5 . . . . .95 E2
Bexley DA5 . . . . .159 H6
Southwood Av, N6 . . . . .74 B7
Kingston upon Thames KT2 . .182 C1
Southwood Cl, Brom. BR1 . . . . .192 C4
Worcester Park KT4 . . . . . . .198 A1
Southwood Dr, Surb. KT5 . . . . .182 C7
SOUTH WOODFORD, E18 . . . . . .79 F2
South Woodford to Barking Relief Rd,
E11 . . . . .79 J4
E12 . . . . .98 D3
E18 . . . . .79 J4
Barking IG11 . . . . .98 D3
Ilford IG1, IG4 . . . . .98 D3
Southwood Gdns, Esher KT10 . .194 D3
Ilford IG2 . . . . .80 E4
Southwood La, N6 . . . . .74 A7
Southwood Lawn Rd, N6 . . . . . . .74 A7
Southwood Rd, SE9 . . . . .174 E2
SE28 . . . . .138 B1
Southwood Smith St, N1
off Old Royal Free Sq 111 G1
South Worple Av, SW14 . . . . . . .146 E3
South Worple Way, SW14 . . . . .146 D3
Sovereign Cl, E1 . . . . .21 J5
W5 . . . . .105 F5
Barnet EN4 . . . . .41 J3
Sovereign Ct, W.Mol. KT8 . . . . .179 F4
Sovereign Cres, SE16
off Rotherhithe St 133 H1
Sovereign Gro, Wem. HA0 . . . . .87 G3
Sovereign Ms, E2
off Pearson St 13 F1
Barnet EN4 off Bournwell Cl . .41 J3
Sovereign Pk, NW10 . . . . .106 B4
Sovereign Pl, Har. HA1 . . . . .68 C5
Sovereign Rd, Bark. IG11 . . . . . .118 C3
Sowerby Cl, SE9 . . . . .156 B5
Space Waye, Felt. TW14 . . . . . .142 A5
Spa Cl, SE25 . . . . .188 B1
Spafield St, EC1 . . . . .11 E5
Spa Grn Est, EC1 . . . . .11 F3
Spa Hill, SE19 . . . . .188 A1
Spalding Cl, Edg. HA8
off Blundell Rd 54/55 E7
Spalding Rd, NW4 . . . . .71 J6
SW17 . . . . .168 B5
Spanby Rd, E3 . . . . .114 A4
Spaniards Cl, NW11 . . . . .91 G1
Spaniards End, NW3 . . . . .91 F1
Spaniards Rd, NW3 . . . . .91 F1
Spanish Pl, W1 . . . . .16 C3
Spanish Rd, SW18 . . . . .149 F5
Spareleaze Hill, Loug. IG10 . . . . .48 C5
Sparkbridge Rd, Har. HA1 . . . . . .68 B4
Sparkford Gdns, N11
off Friern Barnet Rd 58 A5
Sparkford Ho, SW11 . . . . .149 G1
Sparks Cl, W3 off Joseph Av 106 D6
Dagenham RM8 . . . . .100 D2
Hampton TW12
off Victors Dr 160/161 E6
Spa Rd, SE16 . . . . .29 F6
Sparrow Cl, Hmptn. TW12 . . . . .160 E6

Sparrow Dr, Orp. BR5 . . . . .207 F1
Sparrow Fm Dr, Felt. TW14 . . . .142 D1
Sparrow Fm Rd, Epsom KT17 . .197 G4
Sparrow Grn, Dag. RM10 . . . . . .101 H3
Sparrows La, SE9 . . . . .157 F1
Sparsholt Rd, N19 . . . . .93 F1
Barking IG11 . . . . .117 H1
Sparta St, SE10 . . . . .154 B1
★ Speaker's Cor, W2 . . . . .16 A5
Speaker's Ct, Croy. CR0
off St. James's Rd 202 A1
Spearman St, SE18 . . . . .136 D6
Spear Ms, SW5 . . . . .128 D4
Spearpoint Gdns, Ilf. IG2 . . . . . .81 J4
Spears Rd, N19 . . . . .92 E1
Speart La, Houns. TW5 . . . . . . .122 E7
Spedan Cl, NW3 . . . . .91 E3
Speechly Ms, E8
off Alvington Cres 94 C5
Speed Highwalk, EC2
off Beech St 111 J5
Speed Ho, EC2 . . . . .20 B1
Speedwell St, SE8
off Comet St 134 A7
Speedy Pl, WC1 . . . . .10 A4
Speer Rd, T.Ditt. KT7 . . . . .180 C5
Speirs Cl, N.Mal. KT3 . . . . .183 F6
Spekehill, SE9 . . . . .174 C3
Speke Ho, SE5 . . . . .131 J7
Speke Rd, Th.Hth. CR7 . . . . . . .188 A2
Speldhurst Cl, Brom. BR2 . . . . .191 F5
Speldhurst Rd, E9 . . . . .95 G3
W4 . . . . .126 D3
Spellbrook Wk, N1 off Basire St .111 J1
Spelman St, E1 . . . . .21 H1
Spence Cl, SE16
off Vaughan St 133 J2
Spencer Av, N13 . . . . .59 F6
Hayes UB4 . . . . .102 A5
Spencer Cl, N3 . . . . .72 C2
NW10 . . . . .105 J3
Orpington BR6 . . . . .207 H2
Woodford Green IG8 . . . . . . .63 J5
Spencer Ct, NW8
off Marlborough Pl 109 F2
Spencer Dr, N2 . . . . .73 F6
Spencer Gdns, SE9 . . . . .156 C5
SW14 . . . . .146 C5
Spencer Hill, SW19 . . . . .166 B6
Spencer Hill Rd, SW19 . . . . . . .166 B7
★ Spencer Ho, SW1 . . . . .25 F2
Spencer Ms, SW8
off Lansdowne Way 151 F1
W6 off Greyhound Rd 128 B6
Spencer Pk, SW18 . . . . .149 G5
Spencer Pas, E2
off Pritchard's Rd 112/113 E2
Spencer Pl, N1
off Canonbury La 93 H7
Croydon CR0
off Gloucester Rd 188 A7
Spencer Ri, NW5 . . . . .92 B4
Spencer Rd, E6 . . . . .116 A1
E17 . . . . .78 C1
N8 . . . . .75 F5
N11 . . . . .58 B4
N17 . . . . .76 D1
SW18 . . . . .149 G4
SW20 . . . . .183 H1
W3 . . . . .126 C1
W4 . . . . .126 C7
Bromley BR1 . . . . .173 E7
East Molesey KT8 . . . . .179 J5
Harrow HA3 . . . . .68 B2
Ilford IG3 . . . . .99 J1
Isleworth TW7 . . . . .144 A1
Mitcham CR4 . . . . .186 A3
Mitcham (Bedd.Cor.) CR4 . . .186 A7
South Croydon CR2 . . . . . . .202 B5
Twickenham TW2 . . . . .162 B3
Wembley HA0 . . . . .87 F2
Spencer St, EC1 . . . . .11 G4
Southall UB2 . . . . .122 D2
Spencer Wk, NW3 . . . . .91 G4
SW15 . . . . .148 A4
Spencer Yd, SE3
off Blackheath Village 155 F2
Spenser Gro, N16 . . . . .94 B4
Spenser Ms, SE21
off Croxted Rd 170 A1
Spenser Rd, SE24 . . . . .151 G5
Spenser St, SW1 . . . . .25 G5
Spensley Wk, N16
off Clissold Rd 94 A3
Speranza St, SE18 . . . . .137 J5
Sperling Rd, N17 . . . . .76 B2
Spert St, E14 . . . . .113 H7
Speyside, N14 . . . . .42 C6
Spey St, E14 . . . . .114 C5
Spezia Rd, NW10 . . . . .107 G2
Spice Quay Hts, SE1 . . . . .29 G2
Spicer Cl, SW9 . . . . .151 H2
Walton-on-Thames KT12 . . .178 C6
Spice's Yd, Croy. CR0 . . . . .201 J4
Spigurnell Rd, N17 . . . . .76 A1

Spikes Br Moorings, Hayes
UB4 . . . . .102 E6
Spikes Br Rd, Sthl. UB1 . . . . .103 E6
Spilsby Cl, NW9
off Kenley Av 70/71 E2
Spindle Cl, SE18 . . . . .136 B3
Spindlewood Gdns, Croy. CR0 . .202 B4
Spindrift Av, E14 . . . . .134 B4
Spinel Cl, SE18 . . . . .137 J5
Spinnaker Cl, Bark. IG11 . . . . . .118 B3
Spinnells Rd, Har. HA2 . . . . . .85 F1
Spinney, The, N21 . . . . .43 G7
SW16 . . . . .168 D3
Barnet EN5 . . . . .41 E2
Sidcup DA14 . . . . .176 E5
Stanmore HA7 . . . . .53 H4
Sunbury-on-Thames TW16 . . .197 A1
Sutton SM3 . . . . .197 J4
Wembley HA0 . . . . .86 D3
Spinney Cl, Beck. BR3 . . . . . . .190 B4
New Malden KT3 . . . . .182 E5
Worcester Park KT4 . . . . . . .197 F3
Spinney Dr, Felt. TW14 . . . . . .141 F7
Spinney Gdns, SE19 . . . . .170 C5
Dagenham RM9 . . . . .101 E5
Spinney Oak, Brom. BR1 . . . . .192 B2
Spinneys, The, Brom. BR1 . . . .192 C2
Spire Ho, W2
off Lancaster Gate 109 F7
Spires Shop Cen, The, Barn.
EN5 . . . . .40 B3
Spirit Quay, E1 . . . . .29 J1
★ **Spitalfields Comm Fm**, E1 . .13 H6
Spital Sq, E1 . . . . .21 E1
Spital St, E1 . . . . .21 H1
Spital Yd, E1 . . . . .21 E1
Spitfire Est, Houns. TW5 . . . . .122 C5
Spitfire Rd, Wall. SM6 . . . . . .200 E7
Spitfire Way, Houns. TW5 . . . .122 C5
Spode Wk, NW6
off Lymington Rd 90/91 E6
Spondon Rd, N15 . . . . .76 D4
Spoonbill Way, Hayes UB4
off Cygnet Way 102 D5
Spooners Ms, W3
off Churchfield Rd 126 D1
Spooner Wk, Wall. SM6 . . . . . .200 D5
Sporle Ct, SW11 . . . . .149 G3
Sportsbank St, SE6 . . . . .154 C7
Spotted Dog Path, E7
off Upton La 97 G6
Spottons Gro, N17
off Gospatrick Rd 75 J1
Spout Hill, Croy. CR0 . . . . . . .204 A5
Spratt Hall Rd, E11 . . . . .79 G6
Spray La, Twick. TW2 . . . . . . .144 B6
Spray St, SE18 . . . . .137 E4
Spreighton Rd, W.Mol. KT8 . . .179 H4
Sprimont Pl, SW3 . . . . .31 J3
Springall St, SE15 . . . . .133 E7
Springbank, N21 . . . . .43 F6
Springbank Rd, SE13 . . . . . . .154 D6
Springbank Wk, NW1
off St. Paul's Cres 92 D7
Springbourne Ct, Beck. BR3 . . .190 C1
Spring Br Ms, W5
off Spring Br Rd 105 G7
Spring Br Rd, W5 . . . . .105 G7
Spring Cl, Barn. EN5 . . . . .40 A5
Borehamwood WD6 . . . . . . .38 A1
Dagenham RM8 . . . . .100 D1
Springclose La, Sutt. SM3 . . . .198 B6
Spring Cotts, Surb. KT6
off St. Leonard's Rd 181 G5
Spring Ct, Sid. DA15
off Station Rd 176 A3
Springcroft Av, N2 . . . . .73 J4
Springdale Ms, N16
off Springdale Rd 94 A4
Springdale Rd, N16 . . . . .94 A4
Spring Dr, Pnr. HA5
off Eastcote Rd 66 A6
Springfield, E5 . . . . .94 E1
Bushey (Bushey Hth) WD23 . .52 A1
Springfield Av, N10 . . . . .74 C3
SW20 . . . . .184 C3
Hampton TW12 . . . . .161 H6
Springfield Cl, N12 . . . . .56 E5
Stanmore HA7 . . . . .52 D3
Springfield Dr, Wall. SM6
off Springdale Rd 200 B5
Springfield Dr, Ilf. IG2 . . . . . . .81 F6
Springfield Gdns, E5 . . . . .95 E1
NW9 . . . . .70 D5
Bromley BR1 . . . . .192 C4
Ruislip HA4 . . . . .84 B1
West Wickham BR4 . . . . . . .204 B2
Woodford Green IG8 . . . . . . .63 J7
Springfield Gro, SE7 . . . . .135 J6
Springfield La, NW6 . . . . .108 E1
Springfield Mt, NW9 . . . . .70 E5
Springfield Pl, N.Mal. KT3 . . . .182 C4
Springfield Ri, SE26 . . . . .170 E3
Springfield Rd, E4 . . . . .62 E1
E6 . . . . .98 C7

Springfield Rd, E15 . . . . .115 E3
E17 . . . . .77 J6
N11 . . . . .58 B5
N15 . . . . .76 D4
NW8 . . . . .109 F1
SE26 . . . . .171 E5
SW19 . . . . .166 C5
W7 . . . . .124 B1
Bexleyheath DA7 . . . . .159 H3
Bromley BR1 . . . . .192 C4
Harrow HA1 . . . . .68 B4
Hayes UB4 . . . . .122 C1
Kingston upon Thames KT1 . .181 H3
Teddington TW11 . . . . .162 D5
Thornton Heath CR7 . . . . . .187 J1
Twickenham TW2 . . . . .161 G1
Wallington SM6 . . . . .200 B5
Welling DA16 . . . . .158 B3
Springfield Wk, NW6 . . . . . . .108 E1
Orpington BR6
off Place Fm Av 207 G1
Spring Gdns, N5
off Grosvenor Av 93 J5
SW1 . . . . .25 J1
Romford RM7 . . . . .83 J5
Wallington SM6 . . . . .200 C5
West Molesey KT8 . . . . .179 J5
Woodford Green IG8 . . . . . . .63 J7
Spring Gdns Ind Est, Rom. RM7 . .83 J5
Spring Gro, SE19 off Alma Pl . . .170 C7
W4 . . . . .126 A5
Hampton TW12
off Plevna Rd 179 H1
Loughton IG10 . . . . .48 A6
Mitcham CR4 . . . . .186 A1
Spring Gro Cres, Houns. TW3 . .143 J1
Spring Gro Rd, Houns. TW3 . . .143 H1
Isleworth TW7 . . . . .143 H1
Richmond TW10 . . . . .145 J5
Spring Hill, E5 . . . . .76 D7
SE26 . . . . .171 F4
Springhill Cl, SE5 . . . . .152 A3
Springhurst Cl, Croy. CR0 . . . .203 J4
Spring Lake, Stan. HA7 . . . . . .52 E4
Spring La, E5 . . . . .95 E1
N10 . . . . .74 A3
SE25 . . . . .188 E6
Spring Ms, W1 . . . . .16 A1
Richmond TW9
off Rosedale Rd 145 H4
Spring Pk Av, Croy. CR0 . . . . . .203 G2
Spring Pk Dr, N4 . . . . .93 J1
Springpark Dr, Beck. BR3 . . . . .190 C3
Spring Pk Rd, Croy. CR0 . . . . . .203 G2
Spring Pas, SW15
off Embankment 148 A3
Spring Path, NW3 . . . . .91 G5
Spring Pl, N3
off Windermere Av 72 D2
NW5 . . . . .92 B5
Springpond Rd, Dag. RM9 . . . .101 E5
Springrice Rd, SE13 . . . . .154 C6
Spring St, W2 . . . . .15 E4
Spring Ter, Rich. TW9 . . . . . . .145 H5
Springtide Cl, SE15
off Staffordshire St 152 D1
Spring Vale, Bexh. DA7 . . . . . .159 H4
Springvale Av, Brent. TW8 . . . .125 G5
Springvale Est, W14
off Blythe Rd 128 B3
Springvale Ter, W14 . . . . .128 A3
Spring Vil Rd, Edg. HA8 . . . . . .54 A7
Spring Wk, E1 . . . . .21 H1
Springwater Cl, SE18 . . . . . . .156 D1
Springwell Av, NW10 . . . . . . .107 F1
Springwell Cl, SW16
off Etherstone Rd 169 G4
Springwell Ct, Houns. TW4 . . . .142 D2
Springwell Rd, SW16 . . . . . . .169 G4
Hounslow TW4, TW5 . . . . . .142 D2
Springwood Cres, Edg. HA8 . . .54 B2
Sprowston Ms, E7 . . . . .97 G6
Sprowston Rd, E7 . . . . .97 G5
Spruce Ct, W5
off Elderberry Rd 125 H3
Sprucedale Gdns, Croy. CR0 . .203 G4
Spruce Hills Rd, E17 . . . . .78 C2
Spruce Pk, Brom. BR2
off Cumberland Rd 191 F4
Sprules Rd, SE4 . . . . .153 H2
Spurfield, W.Mol. KT8 . . . . . . .179 H3
Spurgeon Av, SE19 . . . . .188 A1
Spurgeon Rd, SE19 . . . . .188 A1
Spurgeon St, SE1 . . . . .28 B6
Spurling Rd, SE22 . . . . .152 C4
Dagenham RM9 . . . . .101 F6
Spur Rd, N15 off Philip La 76 A4
SE1 . . . . .26 E3
SW1 . . . . .25 F4
Barking IG11 . . . . .117 F2
Edgware HA8 . . . . .53 H4
Feltham TW14 . . . . .142 B5
Isleworth TW7 . . . . .124 E7

Spur Rd Est, Edg. HA8 . . . . . . .53 J4
Spurstowe Rd, E8
off Marcon Pl 94/95 E6
Spurstowe Ter, E8 . . . . .94 E5
Square, The, W6 . . . . .127 J5
Carshalton SM5 . . . . .200 A5
Hayes UB3 . . . . .121 G1
Ilford IG1 . . . . .80 D7
Richmond TW9 . . . . .145 G5
Woodford Green IG8 . . . . . . .63 G5
Square Rigger Row, SW11
off York Pl 149 F3
Squarey St, SW17 . . . . .167 F3
Squire Gdns, NW8 . . . . .7 E4
Squires, The, Rom. RM7 . . . . . .83 J6
Squires Ct, SW19 . . . . .166 D4
Squires La, N3 . . . . .73 E2
Squires Mt, NW3
off East Heath Rd 91 G3
Squires Wd Dr, Chis. BR7 . . . . .174 B7
Squirrel Cl, Houns. TW4 . . . . . .142 C2
Squirrel Ms, W13 . . . . .104 D7
Squirrels, The, SE13
off Belmont Hill 154 D3
Pinner HA5 . . . . .67 F3
Squirrels Cl, N12
off Woodside Av 57 F4
Squirrels Grn, Wor.Pk. KT4 . . . .197 F1
Squirrels La, Buck.H. IG9 . . . . .64 A3
Squirrels Trd Est, The, Hayes
UB3 . . . . .122 A3
Squirries St, E2 . . . . .13 J3
Stable Cl, Nthlt. UB5 . . . . .103 G2
Stable Ms, Twick. TW1 . . . . . .162 C1
Stables, The, Buck.H. IG9 . . . . .47 J7
Stables End, Orp. BR6 . . . . . . .207 F3
Stables Ms, SE27 . . . . .169 J5
Stables Way, SE11 . . . . .35 E3
Stable Wk, N1 off Wharfdale Rd . .110 E2
N2 off Old Fm Rd 73 G1
Stable Way, W10 off Latimer Rd . .107 J6
Stable Yd, SW1 . . . . .25 F3
SW9 off Broomgrove Rd 151 F2
SW15 off Danemere St 147 J3
Stable Yd Rd, SW1 . . . . .25 F2
Stacey Av, N18 . . . . .61 F4
Stacey Cl, E10 off Halford Rd . . .78 D5
Stacey St, N7 . . . . .93 G3
WC2 . . . . .17 J4
Stackhouse St, SW3 . . . . .23 J5
Stacy Path, SE5 off Harris St . . .132 B7
Stadium Business Cen, Wem.
HA9 . . . . .88 B3
Stadium Retail Pk, Wem. HA9
off Wembley Pk Dr 88 A3
Stadium Rd, NW2 . . . . .71 H7
SE18 . . . . .136 B6
Stadium Rd E, NW2 . . . . .71 J7
Stadium St, SW10 . . . . .129 F7
Stadium Way, Wem. HA9 . . . . .87 J4
Staffa Rd, E10 . . . . .95 H1
Stafford Cl, E17 . . . . .77 J6
N14 . . . . .42 C7
NW6 . . . . .108 D3
Sutton SM3 . . . . .198 B6
Stafford Ct, W8 . . . . .128 D3
Stafford Cross, Croy. CR0 . . . . .201 F5
Stafford Gdns, Croy. CR0 . . . . .201 F5
Stafford Pl, SW1 . . . . .25 F5
Richmond TW10 . . . . .145 J7
Stafford Rd, E3 . . . . .113 J2
E7 . . . . .97 J7
NW6 . . . . .108 D3
Croydon CR0 . . . . .201 G4
Harrow HA3 . . . . .51 J7
New Malden KT3 . . . . .182 C3
Sidcup DA14 . . . . .175 H4
Wallington SM6 . . . . .200 C6
Staffordshire St, SE15 . . . . . . .152 D1
Stafford St, W1 . . . . .25 F1
Stafford Ter, W8 . . . . .128 D3
Staff St, EC1 . . . . .12 C4
Stag Cl, Edg. HA8 . . . . .70 B2
Staggart Grn, Chig. IG7 . . . . . .65 J6
Stag La, NW9 . . . . .70 C3
SW15 . . . . .165 F2
Buckhurst Hill IG9 . . . . .63 H2
Edgware HA8 . . . . .70 B2
Stag Pl, SW1 . . . . .25 F5
Stag Ride, SW19 . . . . .165 F3
Stags Way, Islw. TW7 . . . . . . .124 C6
Stainbank Rd, Mitch. CR4 . . . .186 B3
Stainby Cl, West Dr. UB7 . . . . .120 B3
Stainby Rd, N15 . . . . .76 C4
Stainer Ho, SE3 off Ryan Cl 155 J4
Stainer St, SE1 . . . . .28 C2
Staines Av, Sutt. SM3 . . . . . . .198 A2
Staines Rd, Felt. TW14 . . . . . .141 G7
Hounslow TW3, TW4 . . . . . .143 H3
Ilford IG1 . . . . .99 F4
Twickenham TW2 . . . . .161 G3
Staines Rd E, Sun. TW16 . . . . .160 A7
Staines Wk, Sid. DA14
off Evry Rd 176 C6
Stainforth Rd, E17 . . . . .78 A4

Stainforth Rd, Ilf. IG2 . . . . .81 G7
Staining La, EC2 . . . . .20 A3
Stainmore Cl, Chis. BR7 . . . . . .193 G1
Stainsbury St, E2
off Royston St 113 F2
Stainsby Pl, E14
off Stainsby Rd 114 A6
Stainsby Rd, E14 . . . . .114 A6
Enfield EN3 . . . . .45 F1
Stalbridge St, NW1 . . . . .15 H1
Stalham St, SE16 . . . . .133 E3
Stalham Way, Ilf. IG6 . . . . .80 E1
Stambourne Way, SE19 . . . . . .170 B7
West Wickham BR4 . . . . . . .204 C3
Stamford Brook Av, W6 . . . . . .127 F3
Stamford Brook Gdns, W6
off Stamford Brook Rd 127 F3
Stamford Brook Rd, W6 . . . . . .127 F3
Stamford Cl, N15 . . . . .76 D4
Harrow HA3 . . . . .52 B7
Southall UB1 . . . . .103 G7
Stamford Cotts, SW10 . . . . . . .30 B7
Stamford Ct, W6
off Goldhawk Rd 127 F4
Stamford Dr, Brom. BR2 . . . . . .191 F4
Stamford Gdns, Dag. RM9 . . . .100 C7
Stamford Gro E, N16
off Oldhill St 94 D1
Stamford Gro W, N16
off Oldhill St 94 D1
STAMFORD HILL, N16 . . . . . . .94 B1
Stamford Hill, N16 . . . . .94 C2
Stamford Hill Est, N16 . . . . . . .94 C1
Stamford Rd, E6 . . . . .116 B1
N1 . . . . .94 B7
N15 . . . . .76 D5
Dagenham RM9 . . . . .118 B1
Stamford St, SE1 . . . . .27 E2
Stamp Pl, E2 . . . . .13 F3
Stanard Cl, N16 . . . . .76 B7
Stanborough Cl, Hmptn. TW12 . .161 F6
Stanborough Pas, E8
off Abbot St 94 C6
Stanborough Rd, Houns. TW3 . .144 A3
Stanbridge Pl, N21 . . . . .59 H2
Stanbridge Rd, SW15 . . . . . . .147 J3
Stanbrook Rd, SE2 . . . . .138 B2
Stanbury Rd, SE15 . . . . .153 E1
Stancroft, NW9 . . . . .70 E4
Standard Ind Est, E16 . . . . . . .136 C2
Standard Pl, EC2 . . . . .12 E4
Standard Rd, NW10 . . . . .106 C4
Belvedere DA17 . . . . .139 G5
Bexleyheath DA6 . . . . .159 E4
Hounslow TW4 . . . . .143 E3
Standen Rd, SW18 . . . . .148 C7
Standfield Gdns, Dag. RM10
off Standfield Rd 101 G6
Standfield Rd, Dag. RM10 . . . . .101 G5
Standish Ho, SE3 off Elford Cl . .155 F1
Standish Rd, W6 . . . . .127 G4
Standlake Pt, SE23 . . . . .171 G3
Stane Cl, SW19
off Hayward Cl 184/185 E1
Stane Way, SE18 . . . . .136 A7
Stanfield Rd, E3 . . . . .113 H2
Stanford Cl, Hmptn. TW12 . . . .161 F6
Romford RM7 . . . . .83 H6
Woodford Green IG8 . . . . . . .64 B5
Stanford Ct, SW6
off Bagley's La 148/149 E1
Stanford Ho, Bark. IG11 . . . . . .118 B2
Stanford Pl, SE17 . . . . .36 D2
Stanford Rd, N11 . . . . .57 J5
SW16 . . . . .186 E1
W8 . . . . .22 B5
Stanford St, SW1 . . . . .33 H2
Stanford Way, SW16 . . . . .186 D2
Stangate Cres, Borwd. WD6 . . .38 E5
Stangate Gdns, Stan. HA7 . . . . .53 E4
Stanger Rd, SE25 . . . . .188 D4
Stanhope Av, N3 . . . . .72 C3
Bromley BR2 . . . . .205 F1
Harrow HA3 . . . . .68 A1
Stanhope Cl, SE16
off Middleton Dr 133 G2
Stanhope Gdns, N4 . . . . .75 H6
N6 . . . . .74 B6
NW7 . . . . .55 F5
SW7 . . . . .30 D1
Dagenham RM8 . . . . .101 F3
Ilford IG1 . . . . .98 C1
Stanhope Gate, W1 . . . . .24 C1
Stanhope Gro, Beck. BR3 . . . . .189 J5
Stanhope Ms E, SW7 . . . . .30 D1
Stanhope Ms S, SW7 . . . . .30 D2
Stanhope Ms W, SW7 . . . . . . .30 D1
Stanhope Par, NW1 . . . . .9 F3
Stanhope Pk Rd, Grnf. UB6 . . .103 J4
Stanhope Pl, W2 . . . . .15 J4
Stanhope Rd, E17 . . . . .78 B5
N6 . . . . .74 C6
N12 . . . . .57 F5
Barnet EN5 . . . . .39 J6

Stanhope Rd, Bexh. DA7 ....159 E2
Carshalton SM5 ....200 A7
Croydon CR0 ....202 B3
Dagenham RM8 ....101 F2
Greenford UB6 ....103 J5
Sidcup DA15 ....176 A4
Stanhope Row, W1 ....24 D2
Stanhope St, NW1 ....9 F4
Stanhope Ter, W2 ....15 F5
Stanier Cl, W14 *off Aisgill Av* 128 C5
Stanlake Ms, W12 ....127 J1
Stanlake Rd, W12 ....127 H1
Stanlake Vil, W12 ....127 H1
Stanley Av, Bark. IG11 ....117 J2
Beckenham BR3 ....190 C2
Dagenham RM8 ....101 F1
Greenford UB6 ....103 J1
New Malden KT3 ....183 G5
Wembley HA0 ....87 H7
Stanley Cl, SW8 ....34 C6
Wembley HA0 ....87 H7
Stanley Ct, Cars. SM5
off Stanley Pk Rd 200 A7
Stanley Cres, W11 ....108 C7
Stanleycroft Cl, Islw. TW7 ....144 B1
Stanley Gdns, NW2 ....89 J5
W3 ....126 E1
W11 ....108 C7
Mitcham CR4
off Ashbourne Rd 168 A6
Wallington SM6 ....200 C6
Stanley Gdns Ms, W11
off Stanley Cres 108 C7
Stanley Gdns Rd, Tedd. TW11 ....162 B5
Stanley Gro, SW8 ....150 A2
Croydon CR0 ....187 G6
Stanley Pk Dr, Wem. HA0 ....87 J7
Stanley Pk Rd, Cars. SM5 ....199 J7
Wallington SM6 ....200 B6
Stanley Rd, E4 ....62 D1
E10 ....78 B6
E12 ....98 B5
E15 ....114 D1
E18 ....79 F1
N2 ....73 G3
N9 ....60 C1
N10 ....58 B7
N11 ....58 D6
N15 ....75 H4
NW9 *off West Hendon Bdy* 71 G7
SW14 ....146 B4
SW19 ....166 D7
W3 ....126 C3
Bromley BR2 ....191 H4
Carshalton SM5 ....200 A7
Croydon CR0 ....187 G7
Enfield EN1 ....44 B3
Harrow HA2 ....85 J2
Hounslow TW3 ....143 J4
Ilford IG1 ....99 G2
Mitcham CR4 ....168 A7
Morden SM4 ....184 D4
Northwood HA6 ....66 A1
Sidcup DA14 ....176 A3
Southall UB1 ....102 E7
Sutton SM2 ....198 E6
Teddington TW11 ....162 B4
Twickenham TW2 ....162 A3
Wembley HA9 ....87 J6
Stanley St, SE8 ....133 J7
Stanley Ter, N19 ....92 E2
Stanmer St, SW11 ....149 H1
STANMORE, HA7 ....52 D5
Stanmore Gdns, Rich. TW9 ....145 J3
Sutton SM1 ....199 F3
Stanmore Hall, Stan. HA7 ....52 E3
Stanmore Hill, Stan. HA7 ....52 D3
Stanmore Pl, NW1
off Arlington Rd 110 B1
Stanmore Rd, E11 ....97 F1
N15 ....75 H4
Belvedere DA17 ....139 J4
Richmond TW9 ....145 J3
Stanmore St, N1
off Caledonian Rd 111 F1
Stanmore Ter, Beck. BR3 ....190 A2
Stanmore Way, Loug. IG10 ....48 D1
Stannard Ms, E8 ....94 D6
Stannard Rd, E8 ....94 D6
Stannary Pl, SE11 ....35 F4
Stannary St, SE11 ....35 F5
Stannet Way, Wall. SM6 ....200 C4
Stannington Path, Borwd. WD6 ....38 A1
Stansfeld Rd, E6 ....116 A5
Stansfield Rd, SW9 ....151 F3
Hounslow TW4 ....142 B2
Stansgate Rd, Dag. RM10 ....101 G2
Stanstead Cl, Brom. BR2 ....191 F5
Stanstead Gro, SE6
off Stanstead Rd 171 J1
Stanstead Manor, Sutt. SM1 ....198 D6
Stanstead Rd, E11 ....79 H5
SE6 ....171 G1
SE23 ....171 G1
Hounslow (Hthrw Air.) TW6 ....140 C6
Stansted Cres, Bex. DA5 ....176 D1
Stanswood Gdns, SE5 ....132 B7
Stanthorpe Cl, SW16 ....168 E5
Stanthorpe Rd, SW16 ....168 E5
Stanton Av, Tedd. TW11 ....162 B5
Stanton Cl, Epsom KT19 ....196 B5
Worcester Park KT4 ....198 A1
Stanton Ho, SE16
off Rotherhithe St 133 J2
Stanton Rd, SE26
off Stanton Way 171 J4
SW13 ....147 F2
SW20 ....184 A2
Croydon CR0 ....187 J7
Stanton Sq, SE26
off Stanton Way 171 J4
Stanton Way, SE26 ....171 J4
Stanway Cl, Chig. IG7 ....65 H5
Stanway Ct, N1 ....13 E2
Stanway Gdns, W3 ....126 A1
Edgware HA8 ....54 C5
Stanway St, N1 ....12 E1
STANWELL, Stai. TW19 ....140 B7
Stanwell Cl, Stai. (Stanw.) TW19 ....140 A6
Stanwell Gdns, Stai. (Stanw.)
TW19 ....140 A6
Stanwell Rd, Felt. TW14 ....141 F7
Stanwick Rd, W14 ....128 C4
Stanworth St, SE1 ....29 F4
Stanwyck Dr, Chig. IG7 ....65 F5
Stapenhill Rd, Wem. HA0 ....86 E3
Staplefield Cl, SW2 ....169 E1
Pinner HA5 ....50 E7
Stapleford Av, Ilf. IG2 ....81 H5
Stapleford Cl, E4 ....62 C3
SW19 ....148 B7
Kingston upon Thames KT1 ....182 A3
Stapleford Rd, Wem. HA0 ....87 G7
Stapleford Way, Bark. IG11 ....118 B3
Staplehurst Rd, SE13 ....154 E5
Carshalton SM5 ....199 H7
Staple Inn, WC1 ....19 E2
Staple Inn Bldgs, WC1 ....18 E2
Staples Cl, SE16 ....133 H1
Staples Cor, NW2 ....89 H1
Staples Cor Business Pk, NW2 ....89 H1
Staples Rd, Loug. IG10 ....48 B3
Staple St, SE1 ....28 C4
Stapleton Gdns, Croy. CR0 ....201 G5
Stapleton Hall Rd, N4 ....75 F7
Stapleton Rd, SW17 ....168 A3
Bexleyheath DA7 ....139 F7
Orpington BR6 ....207 J3
Stapley Rd, Belv. DA17 ....139 G5
Stapylton Rd, Barn. EN5 ....40 B3
Star All, EC3 ....20 E5
Star & Garter Hill, Rich. TW10 ....163 H1
Starboard Way, E14 ....134 A3
Starch Ho La, Ilf. IG6 ....81 G2
Starcross St, NW1 ....9 G4
Starfield Rd, W12 ....127 G2
Star La, E16 ....115 E4
Starling Cl, Buck.H. IG9 ....63 G1
Pinner HA5 ....66 C3
Starling Wk, Hmptn. TW12
off Oak Av 160/161 E6
Starmans Cl, Dag. RM9 ....119 E1
Star Path, Nthlt. UB5
off Brabazon Rd 103 G2
Star Pl, E1 ....21 G6
Star Rd, W14 ....128 C6
Isleworth TW7 ....144 A2
Star St, E16 ....115 F5
W2 ....15 F3
Starts Cl, Orp. BR6 ....206 D3
Starts Hill Av, Orp. BR6 ....207 E4
Starts Hill Rd, Orp. BR6 ....206 D3
Starveall Cl, West Dr. UB7 ....120 C3
Star Yd, WC2 ....18 E3
State Fm Av, Orp. BR6 ....207 E4
Staten Gdns, Twick. TW1 ....162 C1
Statham Gro, N16
off Green Las 93 J4
N18 ....60 B5
Station App, E4 (Highams Pk)
off The Avenue 62 D6
E7 *off Woodford Rd* 97 H4
E11 (Snaresbrook)
off High St 79 G5
N11 *off Friern Barnet Rd* 58 B5
N12 (Woodside Pk) 56 E4
N16 (Stoke Newington)
off Stamford Hill 94 C2
NW10 *off Station Rd* 107 F3
SE1 ....26 D2
SE3 *off Kidbrooke Pk Rd* 155 H3
SE9 (Mottingham) 174 C1
SE26 (Lwr Sydenham)
off Worsley Br Rd 171 J5
SE26 (Sydenham)
off Sydenham Rd 171 F4
SW6 ....148 B3
SW16 ....168 D5
W7 ....124 B1
Barnet EN5 ....41 F4
Station App, Bex. DA5
off Bexley High St 159 G7
Bexleyheath DA7
off Avenue Rd 158/159 E2
Bexleyheath (Barne.) DA7 ....159 J2
Bromley (Hayes) BR2 ....205 G1
Buckhurst Hill IG9
off Cherry Tree Ri 64 A4
Chislehurst BR7 ....192 D1
Chislehurst (Elm.Wds) BR7 ....174 B6
Epsom (Stoneleigh) KT19 ....197 G5
Esher (Hinch.Wd) KT10 ....194 C3
Greenford UB6 ....86 A7
Hampton TW12 *off Milton Rd* 179 G1
Harrow HA1 ....68 B7
Hayes UB3 ....121 J2
Kingston upon Thames KT1 ....182 A1
Loughton IG10 ....48 B5
Loughton (Debden) IG10 ....49 F4
Orpington BR6 ....207 J2
Pinner HA5 ....66 E3
Pinner (Hatch End) HA5
off Uxbridge Rd 51 G7
Richmond TW9 ....146 A1
Ruislip (S.Ruis.) HA4 ....84 B5
Sunbury-on-Thames TW16 ....178 A1
Sutton (Cheam) SM2 ....198 B7
Watford (Carp.Pk) WD19
off Prestwick Rd 50 D3
Welling DA16 ....157 J2
Wembley HA0 ....87 E6
West Drayton UB7 ....120 B1
Worcester Park KT4 ....197 G1
Station App N, Sid. DA15 ....176 A2
Station App Path, SE9
off Glenlea Rd 156 C5
Station App Rd, W4 ....126 C7
Station Av, SW9
off Coldharbour La 151 H3
New Malden KT3 ....183 E3
Richmond TW9 ....146 A1
Station Cl, N3 ....72 D1
N12 (Woodside Pk) 56 E4
Hampton TW12 ....179 H1
Station Ct, SW6
off Townmead Rd 149 F1
Station Cres, N15 ....76 A4
SE3 ....135 G5
Wembley HA0 ....87 E6
Stationers Hall Ct, EC4
off Ludgate Hill 111 H6
Station Est, Beck. BR3
off Elmers End Rd 189 G4
Station Est Rd, Felt. TW14 ....160 B1
Station Gar Ms, SW16
off Estreham Rd 168 D6
Station Gdns, W4 ....126 C7
Station Gro, Wem. HA0 ....87 H6
Station Hill, Brom. BR2 ....205 G2
Station Ho Ms, N9 *off Fore St* 60 D4
Station Par, E11 ....79 G5
N14 *off High St* 58 D1
NW2 ....89 J6
SW12 *off Balham High Rd* 168 A1
W3 ....106 A6
Barking IG11 ....99 F7
Barnet EN4
off Cockfosters Rd 42 A4
Feltham TW14 ....142 B7
Richmond TW9 ....146 A1
Station Pas, E18
off Maybank Rd 79 H2
SE15 ....153 F1
Station Path, E8
off Amhurst Rd 94/95 E6
Station Pl, N4
off Seven Sisters Rd 93 G2
Station Ri, SE27
off Norwood Rd 169 H2
Station Rd, E4 (Chingford) 62 D1
E7 ....97 G4
E12 ....98 A4
E17 ....77 H6
N3 ....72 D1
N11 ....58 B5
N17 ....76 D3
N19 ....92 C3
N21 ....59 H1
N22 ....75 F2
NW4 ....71 G6
NW7 ....55 E5
NW10 ....107 F2
SE13 ....154 C3
SE20 ....171 F6
SE25 (Norwood Junct.) 188 C4
SW13 ....147 G3
SW19 ....185 F1
W5 ....105 J6
W7 (Hanwell) 124 B1
Barnet EN5 ....40 E5
Belvedere DA17 ....139 G3
Bexleyheath DA7 ....159 E3
Borehamwood WD6 ....38 A4
Brentford TW8 ....125 F6
Bromley BR1 ....191 G1
Station Rd, Brom. (Short.) BR2 ....191 E2
Carshalton SM5 ....199 J4
Chessington KT9 ....195 H5
Chigwell IG7 ....64 E3
Croydon (E.Croy.) CR0 ....202 A2
Croydon (W.Croy.) CR0 ....201 J1
Edgware HA8 ....54 A6
Esher KT10 ....194 A2
Esher (Clay.) KT10 ....194 A5
Hampton TW12 ....179 G1
Harrow HA1 ....68 C7
Harrow (N.Har.) HA2 ....67 H5
Hayes UB3 ....121 J3
Hounslow TW3 ....143 H4
Ilford IG1 ....98 E3
Ilford (Barkingside) IG6 ....81 G3
Kingston upon Thames KT2 ....182 A1
Kingston upon Thames (Hmptn W.)
KT1 ....181 F1
Loughton IG10 ....48 B4
New Malden (Mots.Pk) KT3 ....183 H5
Orpington BR6 ....207 J2
Romford (Chad.Hth) RM6 ....82 D7
Sidcup DA15 ....176 A4
Sunbury-on-Thames TW16 ....160 A7
Teddington TW11 ....162 C5
Thames Ditton KT7 ....180 C7
Twickenham TW1 ....162 C1
West Drayton UB7 ....120 A1
West Wickham BR4 ....204 C1
Station Rd N, Belv. DA17 ....139 H3
Station Sq, Orp. (Petts Wd) BR5 ....193 F5
Station St, E15 ....96 D7
E16 ....136 E1
Station Ter, NW10 ....108 A2
SE5 ....151 J1
Station Vw, Grnf. UB6 ....104 A1
Station Way, Buck.H. (Rod.Val.)
IG9 ....63 J4
Esher (Clay.) KT10 ....194 B6
Sutton (Cheam) SM3 ....198 B6
Station Yd, Twick. TW1 ....144 D7
Staunton Rd, Kings.T. KT2 ....163 H6
Staunton St, SE8 ....133 J6
★ **Stave Hill Ecological Pk**,
SE16 ....133 H2
Staveley Cl, E9
off Churchill Wk 95 F5
N7 *off Penn Rd* 92/93 E4
SE15 *off Asylum Rd* 152/153 E1
Staveley Gdns, W4 ....146 D1
Staveley Rd, W4 ....126 D7
Staverton Rd, NW2 ....89 J7
Stave Yd Rd, SE16 ....133 H1
Stavordale Rd, N5 ....93 H4
Carshalton SM5 ....185 F7
Stayner's Rd, E1 ....113 G4
Stayton Rd, Sutt. SM1 ....198 D3
Steadfast Rd, Kings.T. KT1 ....181 G1
Stead St, SE17 ....36 B2
Steam Fm La, Felt. TW14 ....141 J4
Stean St, E8 ....112 C1
Stebbing Ho, W11 ....128 A1
Stebbing Way, Bark. IG11 ....118 A2
Stebondale St, E14 ....134 C5
Stedham Pl, WC1 ....18 A3
Steedman St, SE17 ....35 J2
Steeds Rd, N10 ....73 J1
Steeds Way, Loug. IG10 ....48 B3
Steele Rd, E11 ....96 E4
N17 ....76 B3
NW10 ....106 C2
W4 ....126 C3
Isleworth TW7 ....144 D4
Steeles Ms N, NW3
off Steeles Rd 91 J6
Steeles Ms S, NW3
off Steeles Rd 91 J6
Steeles Rd, NW3 ....91 J6
Steele Wk, Erith DA8 ....139 H6
Steel's La, E1 *off Devonport St* 113 F6
Steelyard Pas, EC4
off Upper Thames St 112 A7
Steen Way, SE22
off East Dulwich Gro 152 B5
Steep Cl, Orp. BR6 ....207 J6
Steep Hill, SW16 ....168 D3
Croydon CR0 ....202 B4
Steeple Cl, SW6 ....148 B2
SW19 ....166 B5
Steeple Ct, E1
off Coventry Rd 112/113 E4
Steeplestone Cl, N18 ....59 J5
Steeple Wk, N1 *off Basire St* 111 J1
Steerforth St, SW18 ....167 E2
Steers Mead, Mitch. CR4 ....185 J1
Steers Way, SE16 ....133 H2
Stellar Ho, N17 ....60 C6
Stella Rd, SW17 ....167 J6
Stellman Cl, E5 ....94 D3
Stembridge Rd, SE20 ....188 E2
Stephan Cl, E8 ....112 D1
Stephen Cl, Orp. BR6 ....207 J3
Stephendale Rd, SW6 ....149 E2
Stephen Ms, W1 ....17 H2

Stephen Pl, SW4
  off Rectory Gro 150 C3
Stephen Rd, Bexh. DA7 ....159 J4
Stephenson Rd, E17 ....77 H5
  W7 ....104 C6
  Twickenham TW2 ....143 G7
Stephenson St, E16 ....114 E4
  NW10 ....107 E3
Stephenson Way, NW1 ......9 G5
Stephen's Rd, E15 ....115 H1
Stephen St, W1 ....17 H2
STEPNEY, E1 ....113 F5
Stepney Causeway, E1 .....113 G6
Stepney Grn, E1 ....113 F5
Stepney High St, E1 ......113 G5
Stepney Way, E1 ....112 E5
Sterling Av, Edg. HA8 ....53 J4
Sterling Cl, N9 ....61 F1
  NW10 ....89 G6
Sterling Gdns, SE14 .....133 H6
Sterling Ho, SE3
  off Cambert Way 155 H4
Sterling Ind Est, Dag. RM10 .101 H4
Sterling Pl, W5 ....125 H4
Sterling St, SW7 ....23 H5
Sterling Way, N18 ....60 A5
★ Sternberg Cen, N3 ......72 E2
Stern Cl, Bark. IG11 .....118 C2
Sterndale Rd, W14 ....128 A3
Sterne St, W12 ....128 A2
Sternhall La, SE15 ......152 D3
Sternhold Av, SW2 ....168 D2
Sterry Cres, Dag. RM10
  off Alibon Rd 101 G5
Sterry Dr, Epsom KT19 ....196 E4
  Thames Ditton KT7 ......180 B6
Sterry Gdns, Dag. RM10 ...101 G6
Sterry Rd, Bark. IG11 ....117 J1
  Dagenham RM10 ....101 G4
Sterry St, SE1 ....28 B4
Steucers La, SE23 ....153 H7
Steve Biko La, SE6 ......172 A4
Steve Biko Rd, N7 ....93 G3
Steve Biko Way, Houns. TW3 .143 G3
Stevedale Rd, Well. DA16 .158 C2
Stevedore St, E1
  off Waterman Way ...132/133 E1
Stevenage Rd, E6 ....98 D6
  SW6 ....128 A7
Stevens Av, E9 ....95 F6
Stevens Cl, Beck. BR3 ....172 A6
  Hampton TW12 ....161 E6
  Pinner HA5 off Bridle Rd .66 C5
Stevens Grn, Bushey (Bushey Hth)
  WD23 ....51 J1
Stevens La, Esher (Clay.) KT10 .194 D7
Stevenson Cl, Barn. EN5 ..41 J5
Stevenson Cres, SE16 .....37 J3
Stevens Rd, Dag. RM8 ....100 B3
Stevens St, SE1 ....29 E5
Steventon Rd, W12 ....107 F7
Stewards Holte Wk, N11
  off Coppies Gro 58 B4
Steward St, E1 ....21 E1
Stewart Cl, NW9 ....70 C6
  Chislehurst BR7 ....175 E5
  Hampton TW12 ....161 E5
Stewart Rainbird Ho, E12 ..98 D5
Stewart Rd, E15 ....96 C4
Stewartsby Cl, N18 ....59 J5
Stewart's Gro, SW3 ....31 F3
Stewart's Rd, SW8 ....130 C7
Stewart St, E14 ....134 C2
Stew La, EC4 ....19 J5
Steyne Rd, W3 ....126 C1
Steyning Gro, SE9 ....174 C4
Steynings Way, N12 ....56 D5
Steyning Way, Houns. TW4 .142 C4
Steynton Av, Bex. DA5 ....176 D2
Stickland Rd, Belv. DA17
  off Picardy Rd 139 G4
Stickleton Cl, Grnf. UB6 ..103 H3
Stilecroft Gdns, Wem. HA0 .86 E3
Stile Hall Gdns, W4 .....126 A5
Stile Hall Par, W4
  off Chiswick High Rd 126 A5
Stile Path, Sun. TW16 ....178 A4
Stiles Cl, Brom. BR2 .....192 C6
  Erith DA8 off Riverdale Rd .139 H5
Stillingfleet Rd, SW13 ...127 G6
Stillington St, SW1 ......33 G1
Stillness Rd, SE23 ......153 H6
Stipularis Dr, Hayes UB4 .102 D4
Stirling Av, Pnr. HA5 .....66 E7
  Wallington SM6 ....200 E7
Stirling Cl, SW16 ....186 C1
Stirling Cor, Barn. EN5 ...38 D6
  Borehamwood WD6 ....38 D6
Stirling Gro, Houns. TW3 .143 J2
Stirling Rd, E13 ....115 H2
  E17 ....77 H3
  N17 ....76 D1
  N22 ....75 H1
  SW9 ....150 E2

Stirling Rd, W3 ....126 B3
  Harrow HA3 ....68 C3
  Hayes UB3 ....102 B7
  Hounslow (Hthrw Air.) TW6 .140 C6
  Twickenham TW2 ....143 G7
Stirling Rd Path, E17 .....77 H3
Stirling Wk, N.Mal. KT3 ..182 C5
  Surbiton KT5 ....182 B6
Stirling Way, Borwd. WD6 ..38 D6
  Croydon CR0 ....186 E7
Stiven Cres, Har. HA2 .....85 F3
Stockbury Rd, Croy. CR0 ..189 F6
Stockdale Rd, Dag. RM8 ...101 F2
Stockdove Way, Grnf. UB6 .104 C3
Stocker Gdns, Dag. RM9 ...100 C7
★ Stock Exchange, EC2 ....19 H3
Stockfield Rd, SW16 .....169 F3
  Esher (Clay.) KT10 .....194 B5
Stockholm Ho, E1 ....112 D7
Stockholm Rd, SE16 .....133 F5
Stockholm Way, E1 ....29 H1
Stockhurst Cl, SW15 .....147 J2
Stockingswater La, Enf. EN3 .45 H3
Stockley Cl, West Dr. UB7 .120 E2
Stockley Fm Rd, West Dr. UB7
  off Stockley Rd 120/121 E3
Stockley Pk, Uxb. UB11 ...121 E1
Stockley Pk Roundabout, Uxb.
  UB11 ....120 E1
Stockley Rd, West Dr. UB7 .120 E4
Stock Orchard Cres, N7 ...93 F5
Stock Orchard St, N7 .....93 F5
Stockport Rd, SW16 .....186 D1
Stocksfield Rd, E17 ....78 C3
Stocks Pl, E14 off Grenade St .113 J7
Stock St, E13 ....115 G2
Stockton Cl, Barn. EN5 ....41 F4
Stockton Gdns, N17
  off Stockton Rd 59 J7
  NW7 ....54 E3
Stockton Rd, N17 ....59 J7
  N18 ....60 D6
STOCKWELL, SW9 ....151 F1
Stockwell Av, SW9 ....151 F3
Stockwell Cl, Brom. BR1 ..191 H2
  Edgware HA8
  off Burnt Oak Bdy 70 C2
Stockwell Gdns, SW9 .....151 F2
Stockwell Gdns Est, SW9 ..151 E2
Stockwell Grn, SW9 .....151 F2
Stockwell La, SW9 ......151 F2
Stockwell Ms, SW9
  off Stockwell Rd 151 F2
Stockwell Pk Cres, SW9 ..151 F2
Stockwell Pk Est, SW9 ...151 F2
Stockwell Pk Rd, SW9 ....151 F1
Stockwell Pk Wk, SW9 ....151 F3
Stockwell Rd, SW9 ......151 F2
Stockwell St, SE10 ......134 C6
Stockwell Ter, SW9 ......151 F1
Stodart Rd, SE20 ....189 F1
Stofield Gdns, SE9
  off Aldersgrove Av 174 A3
Stoford Cl, SW19 ....148 B7
Stokenchurch St, SW6 ....148 E1
STOKE NEWINGTON, N16 ...94 B2
Stoke Newington Ch St, N16 .94 A3
Stoke Newington Common, N16 .94 C3
Stoke Newington High St, N16 .94 C3
Stoke Newington Rd, N16 ..94 C5
Stoke Pl, NW10 ....107 F3
Stoke Rd, Kings.T. KT2 ...164 C7
Stokesby Rd, Chess. KT9 .195 J6
Stokesley St, W12 ....107 F6
Stokes Rd, E6 ....116 B4
  Croydon CR0 ....189 G6
Stoll Cl, NW2 ....89 J3
Stonard Rd, N13 ....59 G3
  Dagenham RM8 ....100 B5
Stonards Hill, Loug. IG10 .48 C6
Stondon Pk, SE23 ....153 H7
Stondon Wk, E6 ....116 A2
Stonebanks, Walt. KT12 ..178 A7
STONEBRIDGE, NW10 .....106 B1
Stonebridge Common, E8
  off Mayfield Rd 94 C7
Stonebridge Pk, NW10 .....88 D7
Stonebridge Rd, N15 ......76 B5
Stonebridge Way, Wem. HA9 .88 B6
Stone Bldgs, WC2 ....18 D2
Stonechat Sq, E6 off Peridot St .116 B5
Stone Cl, SW4 off Larkhall Ri .150 C2
  Dagenham RM8 ....101 F2
  West Drayton UB7 ......120 C1
Stonecot Cl, Sutt. SM3 ...198 B1
Stonecot Hill, Sutt. SM3 ..198 B1
Stone Cres, Felt. TW14 ...141 J7
Stonecroft Cl, Barn. EN5 ..39 H4
Stonecroft Rd, Erith DA8 .139 J7
Stonecroft Way, Croy. CR0 .187 E7
Stonecrop Cl, NW9 ....70 D3
Stonecutter Ct, EC4
  off Stonecutter St 111 H6
Stonecutter St, EC4 ......19 G3
Stonefield Cl, Bexh. DA7 .159 G3

Stonefield Cl, Ruis. HA4 ...84 E5
Stonefield St, N1 ....111 G1
Stonefield Way, SE7
  off Greenbay Rd 136 A7
  Ruislip HA4 ....84 E4
Stonegrove, Edg. HA8 .....53 H4
Stonegrove Est, Edg. HA8 ..53 J4
Stonegrove Gdns, Edg. HA8 .53 J4
Stonehall Av, Ilf. IG1 .....80 B6
Stone Hall Gdns, W8 ......22 A6
Stone Hall Pl, W8 ....22 A6
Stone Hall Rd, N21 ....43 F7
Stoneham Rd, N11 ....58 C6
Stonehill Cl, SW14 ......146 D5
Stonehill Grn, Dart. DA2 .177 J7
Stonehill Rd, SW14 ......146 C5
  W4 off Wellesley Rd 126 A5
Stonehills Business Pk, N18
  off Silvermere Dr 61 G6
Stonehills Ct, SE21 .....170 B3
Stonehill Wds Pk, Sid. DA14 .177 H6
Stonehorse Rd, Enf. EN3 ...45 F5
Stone Ho Ct, EC3 ....20 D3
Stone Lake Retail Pk, SE7 .135 H4
STONELEIGH, Epsom KT17 .197 G5
Stoneleigh Av, Enf. EN1 ...45 E1
  Worcester Park KT4 ....197 G4
Stoneleigh Bdy, Epsom KT17 .197 G5
Stoneleigh Cres, Epsom KT19 .197 F5
Stoneleigh Ms, E3
  off Stanfield Rd 113 H2
Stoneleigh Pk Av, Croy. CR0 .189 G6
Stoneleigh Pk Rd, Epsom KT19 .197 F6
Stoneleigh Pl, W11 ......108 A7
Stoneleigh Rd, N17 ....76 C3
  Carshalton SM5 ....185 H7
  Ilford IG5 ....80 B3
Stoneleigh St, W11 ......108 A7
Stoneleigh Ter, N19 ......92 B2
Stonells Rd, SW11
  off Chatham Rd 149 J5
Stonemasons Cl, N15 ......76 A4
Stonenest St, N4 ....93 F1
Stone Pk Av, Beck. BR3 ..190 A4
Stone Pl, Wor.Pk. KT4 ....197 G2
Stone Rd, Brom. BR2 .....191 F5
Stones End St, SE1 ....27 J4
Stone St, Croy. CR0 .....201 G5
Stonewall, E6 ....116 D5
Stoney All, SE18 ....156 D2
Stoneyard La, E14
  off Poplar High St 114 B7
Stoneycroft Cl, SE12 ....155 F7
Stoneycroft Rd, Wdf.Grn. IG8 .64 B6
Stoneydeep, Tedd. TW11
  off Twickenham Rd 162 D4
Stoneydown, E17 ....77 H4
Stoneydown Av, E17 ......77 H4
Stoneyfields Gdns, Edg. HA8 .54 C4
Stoneyfields La, Edg. HA8 .54 C5
Stoney La, E1 ....21 E3
  SE19 off Church Rd 170 C6
Stoney St, SE1 ....28 B1
Stonhouse St, SW4 ......150 D3
Stonor Rd, W14 ....128 C4
Stonycroft Cl, Enf. EN3
  off Brimsdown Av 45 H2
Stony Path, Loug. IG10 ....48 C2
Stopes St, SE15 ....132 C7
Stopford Rd, E13 ....115 G1
  SE17 ....35 H4
Store Rd, E16 ....136 D2
Storers Quay, E14 ....134 D4
Store St, E15 ....96 D5
  WC1 ....17 H2
Storey Rd, E17 ....77 J4
  N6 ....73 J6
Storey's Gate, SW1 ....25 J4
Storey St, E16 ....136 D1
Stories Ms, SE5 ....152 B2
Stories Rd, SE5 ....152 B3
Stork Rd, E7 ....97 F6
Storksmead Rd, Edg. HA8 ..54 E7
Storks Rd, SE16 ....29 J6
Stormont Rd, N6 ....73 J7
  SW11 ....150 A3
Stormont Way, Chess. KT9 .195 F5
Stormount Dr, Hayes UB3 .121 F2
Storrington Rd, Croy. CR0 .202 C1
Story St, N1 off Carnoustie Dr .93 F7
Stothard Pl, EC2
  off Bishopsgate 112 B5
Stothard St, E1 off Colebert Av .113 F4
Stott Cl, SW18 ....149 G6
Stoughton Av, Sutt. SM3 .198 A5
Stoughton Cl, SE11 ....34 D2
  SW15 off Bessborough Rd .165 G1
Stour Av, Sthl. UB2 .....123 G3
Stourcliffe St, W1 ....15 J4
Stour Cl, Kes. BR2 ......205 J4
Stourhead Cl, SW19
  off Castlecombe Dr 148 A7
Stourhead Gdns, SW20 ...183 G3
Stour Rd, E3 ....96 A7
  Dagenham RM10 ....101 G2

Stourton Av, Felt. TW13 ..161 F4
Stowage, SE8 ....134 A6
Stow Cres, E17 ....61 H7
Stowe Gdns, N9 ....60 C1
Stowe Pl, N15 ....76 B3
Stowe Rd, W12 ....127 H2
Stowting Rd, Orp. BR6 ...207 H4
Stox Mead, Har. HA3 ......68 A1
Stracey Rd, E7 ....97 G4
  NW10 ....106 D1
Strachan Pl, SW19
  off Woodhayes Rd 165 J6
Stradbroke Dr, Chig. IG7 ..64 D6
Stradbroke Gro, Buck.H. IG9 .64 A1
  Ilford IG5 ....80 B3
Stradbroke Pk, Chig. IG7 ..64 E6
Stradbroke Rd, N5 ....93 J4
Stradbrook Cl, Har. HA2
  off Stiven Cres 85 F3
Stradella Rd, SE24 ......151 J6
Strafford Av, Ilf. IG5 .....80 D2
Strafford Rd, W3 ....126 C2
  Barnet EN5 ....40 B3
  Hounslow TW3 ....143 F3
  Twickenham TW1 ....144 D7
Strafford St, E14 ....134 A2
Strahan Rd, E3 ....113 H3
Straight, The, Sthl. UB1 .122 D2
Straightsmouth, SE10 ...134 C7
Strait Rd, E6 ....116 B7
Straker's Rd, SE22 ......152 E4
STRAND, WC2 ....18 A5
Strand, WC2 ....18 A6
Strand Ct, SE18
  off Strandfield Cl 137 H5
Strand Dr, Rich. TW9
  off Bessant Dr 126 B7
Strandfield Cl, SE18 ....137 H5
Strand La, WC2 ....18 D5
Strand on the Grn, W4 ...126 A6
Strand Pl, N18 ....60 A4
Strand Sch App, W4
  off Thames Rd 126 A6
Strangways Ter, W14
  off Melbury Rd 128 C3
Stranraer Rd, Houns. (Hthrw Air.)
  TW6 ....140 B6
Stranraer Way, N1 ....93 E7
Strasburg Rd, SW11 .....150 B1
Stratfield Pk Cl, N21 .....43 H7
Stratfield Rd, Borwd. WD6 .38 A3
STRATFORD, E15 ....96 C6
Stratford Av, W8
  off Stratford Rd 128 D3
Stratford Cen, The, E15 ...96 D7
Stratford Cl, Bark. IG11 ..100 A7
  Dagenham RM10 ....101 J7
Stratford Ct, N.Mal. KT3
  off Kingston Rd 182 D4
Stratford Gro, SW15 .....148 A4
Stratford Ho Av, Brom. BR1 .192 B3
Stratford Pl, W1 ....16 D4
Stratford Rd, E13 ....115 F1
  NW4 ....72 A4
  W8 ....128 D3
  Hayes UB4 ....102 B4
  Hounslow (Hthrw Air.) TW6 .141 E6
  Southall UB2 ....122 E4
  Thornton Heath CR7 ....187 G4
Stratford Vil, NW1 ....92 C7
Strathan Cl, SW18 ......148 B6
Strathaven Rd, SE12 ....155 H6
Strathblaine Rd, SW11 ..149 G4
Strathbrook Rd, SW16 ...169 F7
Strathcona Rd, Wem. HA9 .87 G2
Strathdale, SW16 ....169 F5
Strathdon Dr, SW17 .....167 G3
Strathearn Av, Hayes UB3 .121 J7
  Twickenham TW2 ....161 H1
Strathearn Pl, W2 ....15 F5
Strathearn Rd, SW19 ....166 D5
  Sutton SM1 ....198 D5
Stratheden Par, SE3
  off Stratheden Rd 135 G7
Stratheden Rd, SE3 .....155 G1
Strathfield Gdns, Bark. IG11 .99 G6
Strathleven Rd, SW2 ....151 E5
Strathmore Gdns, N3 .....72 E1
  W8 off Palace Gdns Ter .128 D1
  Edgware HA8 ....70 B2
Strathmore Rd, SW19 ...166 D3
  Croydon CR0 ....187 J7
  Teddington TW11 ......162 B4
Strathnairn St, SE1 ......37 J2
Strathray Gdns, NW3 .....91 H6
Strath Ter, SW11 ....149 H4
Strathville Rd, SW18 ....166 E2
Strathyre Av, SW16 .....187 G3
Stratton Cl, SW19 ......184 D2
  Bexleyheath DA7 ....159 E3
  Edgware HA8 ....53 J6
  Hounslow TW3 ....143 F1
Strattondale St, E14 ....134 C3
Stratton Dr, Bark. IG11 ...99 J5
Stratton Gdns, Sthl. UB1 .103 F6

Stratton Rd, SW19 . . . .**184** D2
  Bexleyheath DA7 . . . .**159** A3
Stratton St, W1 . . . .**25** E1
Strauss Rd, W4 . . . .**126** D2
STRAWBERRY HILL, Twick. TW1 .**162** B3
Strawberry Hill, Twick. TW1 . . .**162** C3
Strawberry Hill Cl, Twick. TW1 . .**162** C3
Strawberry Hill Rd, Twick. TW1 . .**162** C3
Strawberry La, Cars. SM5 . . . . .**199** J3
Strawberry Vale, N2 . . . .**73** G1
  Twickenham TW1 . . . .**162** D3
Streakes Fld Rd, NW2 . . . .**89** G2
Streamdale, SE2 . . . .**138** A6
Stream La, Edg. HA8 . . . .**54** B5
Streamline Ms, SE22 . . . .**170** D1
Streamside Cl, N9 . . . .**60** C1
  Bromley BR2 . . . .**191** G4
Streamway, Belv. DA17 . . . .**139** G6
Streatfield Av, E6 . . . .**116** C1
Streatfield Rd, Har. HA3 . . . .**69** G3
STREATHAM, SW16 . . . .**169** E4
Streatham Cl, SW16 . . . .**169** E2
Streatham Common N, SW16 . . .**168** E5
Streatham Common S, SW16 . . .**169** E6
Streatham Ct, SW16 . . . .**168** E3
Streatham High Rd, SW16 . . . . .**168** E5
STREATHAM HILL, SW2 . . . . . .**151** E7
Streatham Hill, SW2 . . . .**169** E2
STREATHAM PARK, SW16 . . . . .**168** C4
Streatham Pl, SW2 . . . .**150** E7
Streatham Rd, SW16 . . . .**186** A1
  Mitcham CR4 . . . .**186** A1
Streatham St, WC1 . . . .**17** J3
STREATHAM VALE, SW16 . . . . .**168** D7
Streatham Vale, SW16 . . . .**168** C7
Streathbourne Rd, SW17 . . . . . .**168** A2
Streatley Pl, NW3
  off New End Sq **91** F4
Streatley Rd, NW6 . . . .**90** C7
Streeters La, Wall. SM6 . . . .**200** D3
Streetfield Ms, SE3 . . . .**155** G3
Streimer Rd, E15 . . . .**114** C2
Strelley Way, W3 . . . .**106** E7
Stretton Mans, SE8
  off Glaisher St **134** A6
Stretton Rd, Croy. CR0 . . . .**188** B7
  Richmond TW10 . . . .**163** F2
Strickland Row, SW18 . . . .**149** G7
Strickland St, SE8 . . . .**154** A2
Strickland Way, Orp. BR6 . . . . . .**207** J4
Stride Rd, E13 . . . .**115** F2
Strimon Cl, N9 . . . .**61** F2
Strode Cl, N10
  off Pembroke Rd **58** A7
Strode Rd, E7 . . . .**97** G4
  N17 . . . .**76** B2
  NW10 . . . .**89** G6
  SW6 . . . .**128** A7
Strone Rd, E7 . . . .**97** J6
  E12 . . . .**98** A6
Strone Way, Hayes UB4 . . . .**102** E4
Strongbow Cres, SE9 . . . .**156** C5
Strongbow Rd, SE9 . . . .**156** C5
Strongbridge Cl, Har. HA2 . . . . . .**85** G1
Stronsa Rd, W12 . . . .**127** F2
Stroud Cres, SW15 . . . .**165** G3
Stroudes Cl, Wor.Pk. KT4 . . . . . .**183** E7
Stroud Fld, Nthlt. UB5 . . . .**84** E6
Stroud Gate, Har. HA2 . . . .**85** H4
STROUD GREEN, N4 . . . .**75** F6
Stroud Grn Gdns, Croy. CR0 . . . .**189** F7
Stroud Grn Rd, N4 . . . .**93** F1
Stroud Grn Way, Croy. CR0 . . . .**189** E7
Stroudley Wk, E3 . . . .**114** B3
Stroud Rd, SE25 . . . .**188** D6
  SW19 . . . .**166** D3
Strouds Cl, Rom. (Chad.Hth)
  RM6 . . . .**82** B5
Strouts Pl, E2 . . . .**13** F3
Strutton Grd, SW1 . . . .**25** H5
Strype St, E1 . . . .**21** F1
Stuart Av, NW9 . . . .**71** G7
  W5 . . . .**125** J1
  Bromley BR2 . . . .**205** G1
  Harrow HA2 . . . .**85** F3
Stuart Cres, N22 . . . .**75** F1
  Croydon CR0 . . . .**203** J3
Stuart Evans Cl, Well. DA16 . . . .**158** C3
Stuart Gro, Tedd. TW11 . . . .**162** B5
Stuart Pl, Mitch. CR4 . . . .**185** J1
Stuart Rd, NW6 . . . .**108** D3
  SE15 . . . .**153** F4
  SW19 . . . .**166** D3
  W3 . . . .**126** C1
  Barking IG11 . . . .**99** J7
  Barnet EN4 . . . .**41** H7
  Harrow HA3 . . . .**68** C2
  Richmond TW10 . . . .**163** E2
  Thornton Heath CR7 . . . .**187** J4
  Welling DA16 . . . .**158** B1
Stuart Twr, W9 . . . .**6** C4
Stubbs Cl, NW9 . . . .**70** C5
Stubbs Dr, SE16 . . . .**132** E5
Stubbs Ms, Dag. RM8
  off Marlborough Rd **100** B4

Stubbs Pt, E13 . . . .**115** H4
Stubbs Way, SW19
  off Brangwyn Cres **185** G1
Stucley Pl, NW1
  off Hawley Cres **92** B7
Stucley Rd, Houns. TW5 . . . . . .**123** J7
Studdridge St, SW6 . . . .**148** D2
Studd St, N1 . . . .**111** H1
Studholme Ct, NW3 . . . .**90** D4
Studholme St, SE15 . . . .**132** E7
Studio Pl, SW1 . . . .**24** A4
Studio Way, Borwd. WD6 . . . .**38** C2
Studland, SE17 . . . .**36** B3
Studland Cl, Sid. DA15 . . . .**175** J3
Studland Rd, SE26 . . . .**171** G5
  W7 . . . .**104** A6
  Kingston upon Thames KT2 .**163** H6
Studland St, W6 . . . .**127** H4
Studley Av, E4 . . . .**62** D7
Studley Cl, E5 . . . .**95** H5
Studley Ct, E14 off Newport Av .**114** D7
  Sidcup DA14 . . . .**176** B3
Studley Dr, Ilf. IG4 . . . .**80** A6
Studley Est, SW4 . . . .**151** E1
Studley Gra Rd, W7 . . . .**124** B2
Studley Rd, E7 . . . .**97** H6
  SW4 . . . .**150** E1
  Dagenham RM9 . . . .**100** D7
Stukeley Rd, E7 . . . .**97** H7
Stukeley St, WC2 . . . .**18** B3
Stumps Hill La, Beck. BR3 . . . . .**172** A6
Sturdy Rd, SE15 . . . .**153** E2
Sturge Av, E17 . . . .**78** B2
Sturgeon Rd, SE17 . . . .**35** J4
Sturges Fld, Chis. BR7 . . . .**175** G6
Sturgess Av, NW4 . . . .**71** H7
Sturge St, SE1 . . . .**27** J3
Sturmer Way, N7 . . . .**93** F5
Sturminster Cl, Hayes UB4 . . . .**102** C6
Sturrock Cl, N15 . . . .**76** A4
Sturry St, E14 . . . .**114** B6
Sturt St, N1 . . . .**12** A2
Stutfield St, E1 . . . .**21** J4
Styles Gdns, SW9 . . . .**151** H3
Styles Way, Beck. BR3 . . . .**190** C4
Sudbourne Rd, SW2 . . . .**151** E5
Sudbrooke Rd, SW12 . . . .**149** J6
Sudbrook Gdns, Rich. TW10 . . .**163** G3
Sudbrook La, Rich. TW10 . . . . .**163** H1
SUDBURY, Wem. HA0 . . . .**86** D5
Sudbury, E6 off Newark Knok . .**116** D6
Sudbury Av, Wem. HA0 . . . .**87** G3
Sudbury Ct Dr, Har. HA1 . . . .**86** C3
Sudbury Ct Rd, Har. HA1 . . . .**86** C3
Sudbury Cres, Brom. BR1 . . . . .**173** G6
  Wembley HA0 . . . .**87** E5
Sudbury Cft, Wem. HA0 . . . .**86** C4
Sudbury Gdns, Croy. CR0 . . . . .**202** B4
Sudbury Hts Av, Grnf. UB6 . . . . .**86** C5
Sudbury Hill, Har. HA1 . . . .**86** B2
Sudbury Hill Cl, Wem. HA0 . . . . .**86** C4
Sudbury Ho, SW18
  off Wandsworth High St **148** E5
Sudbury Rd, Bark. IG11 . . . .**99** J5
Sudeley St, N1 . . . .**11** H2
Sudlow Rd, SW18 . . . .**148** D4
Sudrey St, SE1 . . . .**27** J4
Suez Av, Grnf. UB6 . . . .**104** C2
Suez Rd, Enf. EN3 . . . .**45** H4
Suffield Rd, E4 . . . .**62** B3
  N15 . . . .**76** C5
  SE20 . . . .**189** F2
Suffolk Cl, Borwd. WD6
  off Clydesdale Cl **38** D5
Suffolk Ct, E10 . . . .**78** A7
  Ilford IG3 . . . .**81** H6
Suffolk La, EC4 . . . .**20** B5
Suffolk Pk Rd, E17 . . . .**77** H4
Suffolk Pl, SW1 . . . .**25** J1
Suffolk Rd, E13 . . . .**115** F3
  N15 . . . .**76** A6
  NW10 . . . .**89** E7
  SE25 . . . .**188** C4
  SW13 . . . .**127** F7
  Barking IG11 . . . .**99** G7
  Dagenham RM10 . . . .**101** J5
  Enfield EN3 . . . .**45** E5
  Harrow HA2 . . . .**67** F6
  Ilford IG3 . . . .**81** H6
  Sidcup DA14 . . . .**176** C6
  Worcester Park KT4 . . . .**197** F2
Suffolk St, E7 . . . .**97** G5
  SW1 . . . .**25** J1
Sugar Bakers Ct, EC3
  off Creechurch La **112** B6
Sugar Ho La, E15 . . . .**114** C2
Sugar Loaf Wk, E2
  off Victoria Pk Sq **113** F3
Sugar Quay Wk, EC3 . . . .**20** E6
Sugden Rd, SW11 . . . .**150** A3
  Thames Ditton KT7 . . . .**194** E1
Sugden Way, Bark. IG11 . . . . . .**117** J2
Sulgrave Gdns, W6
  off Sulgrave Rd **127** J2
Sulgrave Rd, W6 . . . .**127** J2

Sulina Rd, SW2 . . . .**150** E7
Sulivan Ct, SW6 . . . .**148** D3
Sulivan Rd, SW6 . . . .**148** D3
Sullivan Av, E16 . . . .**116** A5
Sullivan Cl, SW11 . . . .**149** H3
  Hayes UB4 . . . .**102** A5
  West Molesey KT8
   off Victoria Av **179** G3
Sullivan Rd, SE11 . . . .**35** F1
Sultan Rd, E11 . . . .**79** H4
Sultan St, SE5 . . . .**35** J7
  Beckenham BR3 . . . .**189** G2
Sultan Ter, N22 off Vincent Rd . .**75** G2
Sumatra Rd, NW6 . . . .**90** D5
Sumburgh Rd, SW12 . . . .**150** A6
Summer Av, E.Mol. KT8 . . . .**180** B5
Summercourt Rd, E1 . . . .**113** F6
Summerene Cl, SW16 . . . .**168** C7
Summerfield Av, NW6 . . . .**108** B2
Summerfield La, Surb. KT6 . . . .**195** G2
Summerfield Rd, W5 . . . .**105** E4
  Loughton IG10 . . . .**48** A6
Summerfields Av, N12 . . . .**57** H6
Summerfield St, SE12 . . . .**155** F7
Summer Gdns, E.Mol. KT8 . . . . .**180** B5
Summer Hill, Borwd. (Elstree)
  WD6 . . . .**38** A5
  Chislehurst BR7 . . . .**192** D2
Summerhill Cl, Orp. BR6 . . . . . .**207** H3
Summerhill Gro, Enf. EN1 . . . . . .**44** B6
Summerhill Rd, N15 . . . .**76** A4
Summer Hill Vil, Chis. BR7 . . . .**192** D1
Summerhill Way, Mitch. CR4 . . .**186** A1
Summerhouse Av, Houns. TW5 .**142** E1
Summerhouse La, West Dr. UB7 .**120** A6
Summerhouse Rd, N16 . . . .**94** B2
Summerland Gdns, N10 . . . .**74** B3
Summerlands Av, W3 . . . .**106** C7
Summerlee Av, N2 . . . .**73** J4
Summerlee Gdns, N2 . . . .**73** J4
Summerley St, SW18 . . . .**167** E2
Summer Rd, E.Mol. KT8 . . . .**180** B5
  Thames Ditton KT7 . . . .**180** C5
Summersby Rd, N6 . . . .**74** B6
Summers Cl, Sutt. SM2
  off Overton Rd **198** D7
  Wembley HA9 . . . .**88** B1
Summerskille Cl, N9
  off Plevna Rd **60/61** E2
Summers La, N12 . . . .**57** G7
Summers Row, N12 . . . .**57** H6
SUMMERSTOWN, SW17 . . . . . .**166** E3
Summerstown, SW17 . . . .**167** F3
Summer St, EC1 . . . .**11** E6
Summerton Way, SE28 . . . .**118** D6
Summer Trees, Sun. TW16
  off The Avenue **178** B1
Summerville Gdns, Sutt. SM1 . .**198** C6
Summerwood Rd, Islw. TW7 . . .**144** C5
Summit, The, Loug. IG10 . . . .**48** C1
Summit Av, NW9 . . . .**70** D5
Summit Cl, N14 . . . .**58** C2
  NW9 . . . .**70** D4
  Edgware HA8 . . . .**54** A7
Summit Ct, NW2 . . . .**90** B5
Summit Dr, Wdf.Grn. IG8 . . . .**80** A2
Summit Est, N16 . . . .**76** D7
Summit Rd, E17 . . . .**78** B4
  Northolt UB5 . . . .**85** G7
Summit Way, N14 . . . .**58** B2
  SE19 . . . .**170** B7
Sumner Av, SE15
  off Peckham Rd **152** C1
Sumner Cl, Orp. BR6 . . . .**207** F4
Sumner Est, SE15 . . . .**132** C7
Sumner Gdns, Croy. CR0 . . . . . .**201** G1
Sumner Pl, SW7 . . . .**31** F2
Sumner Pl Ms, SW7 . . . .**31** F2
Sumner Rd, SE15 . . . .**37** G6
  Croydon CR0 . . . .**201** G1
  Harrow HA1 . . . .**67** J7
Sumner Rd S, Croy. CR0 . . . . . .**201** G1
Sumner St, SE1 . . . .**27** H1
Sumpter Cl, NW3 . . . .**91** F6
Sun All, Rich. TW9 off Kew Rd . .**145** H4
Sunbeam Cres, W10 . . . .**107** J4
Sunbeam Rd, NW10 . . . .**106** C4
Sunbury Av, NW7 . . . .**54** D5
  SW14 . . . .**146** D4
Sunbury Cl, Walt. KT12 . . . .**178** A6
Sunbury Ct, Sun. TW16 . . . .**178** D2
Sunbury Ct Island, Sun. TW16 . .**178** D3
Sunbury Ct Ms, Sun. TW16
  off Lower Hampton Rd **178** D2
Sunbury Ct Rd, Sun. TW16 . . . . .**178** C2
Sunbury Gdns, NW7 . . . .**54** D5
Sunbury La, SW11 . . . .**149** G1
  Walton-on-Thames KT12 . . . .**178** A6
Sunbury Lock Ait, Walt. KT12 . . .**178** B4
Sunbury Rd, Sutt. SM3 . . . .**198** A3
Sunbury St, SE18 . . . .**136** C3
Sunbury Way, Felt. TW13 . . . . . .**160** C5
Sun Ct, EC3 . . . .**20** C4
Suncroft Pl, SE26 . . . .**171** F3
Sunderland Ct, SE22 . . . .**152** D7

Sunderland Mt, SE23
  off Sunderland Rd **171** G2
Sunderland Rd, SE23 . . . .**171** G1
  W5 . . . .**125** G3
Sunderland Ter, W2 . . . .**14** A3
Sunderland Way, E12 . . . .**98** A2
Sundew Av, W12 . . . .**107** G7
Sundial Av, SE25 . . . .**188** C3
Sundorne Rd, SE7 . . . .**135** H5
Sundra Wk, E1
  off Beaumont Gro **113** G4
SUNDRIDGE, Brom. BR1 . . . . . .**173** J6
Sundridge Av, Brom. BR1 . . . . .**192** A1
  Chislehurst BR7 . . . .**174** A7
  Welling DA16 . . . .**157** G3
Sundridge Ho, Brom. BR1
  off Burnt Ash La **173** H5
Sundridge Pl, Croy. CR0
  off Inglis Rd **202** D1
Sundridge Rd, Croy. CR0 . . . . . .**188** C7
Sunfields Pl, SE3 . . . .**135** H7
Sunken Rd, Croy. CR0 . . . .**203** F5
Sunland Av, Bexh. DA6 . . . .**159** E4
Sun La, SE3 . . . .**135** H7
Sunleigh Rd, Wem. HA0 . . . .**105** H1
Sunley Gdns, Grnf. UB6 . . . .**104** D1
Sunlight Cl, SW19 . . . .**167** F6
Sunlight Sq, E2 . . . .**113** E3
Sunmead Rd, Sun. TW16 . . . . . .**178** A3
Sunna Gdns, Sun. TW16 . . . . . .**178** B2
Sunningdale, N14
  off Wilmer Way **58** D5
Sunningdale Av, W3 . . . .**107** E7
  Barking IG11 . . . .**117** G1
  Feltham TW13 . . . .**160** E2
  Ruislip HA4 . . . .**84** C1
Sunningdale Cl, E6 . . . .**116** C3
  SE16 off Ryder Dr **132/133** E5
  SE28 . . . .**118** C6
  Stanmore HA7 . . . .**52** D7
  Surbiton KT6 off Culsac Rd .**195** H2
Sunningdale Gdns, NW9 . . . .**70** C5
  W8 off Lexham Ms **128** D3
Sunningdale Rd, Brom. BR1 . . . .**192** B4
  Sutton SM1 . . . .**198** C4
Sunningfields Cres, NW4 . . . . . .**71** H2
Sunningfields Rd, NW4 . . . .**71** H2
Sunninghill Rd, SE13 . . . .**154** B2
Sunny Bk, SE25 . . . .**188** D3
Sunny Cres, NW10 . . . .**88** C7
Sunnycroft Rd, SE25 . . . .**188** D3
  Hounslow TW3 . . . .**143** H2
  Southall UB1 . . . .**103** G5
Sunnydale, Orp. BR6 . . . .**206** D2
Sunnydale Gdns, NW7 . . . .**54** D6
Sunnydale Rd, SE12 . . . .**155** H5
Sunnydene Av, E4 . . . .**62** D5
  Ruislip HA4 . . . .**84** A2
Sunnydene Gdns, Wem. HA0 . . . .**87** F6
Sunnydene St, SE26 . . . .**171** H4
Sunnyfield, NW7 . . . .**55** F4
Sunny Gdns Par, NW4
  off Great N Way **71** J2
Sunny Gdns Rd, NW4 . . . .**71** H2
Sunny Hill, NW4 . . . .**71** H3
Sunnyhill Cl, E5 . . . .**95** H4
Sunnyhill Rd, SW16 . . . .**168** E4
Sunnyhurst Cl, Sutt. SM1 . . . . . .**198** D3
Sunnymead Av, Mitch. CR4 . . . .**186** C3
Sunnymead Rd, NW9 . . . .**70** D7
  SW15 . . . .**147** H5
Sunnymede Dr, Ilf. IG6 . . . .**80** E5
Sunny Nook Gdns, S.Croy. CR2 .**202** A6
Sunny Rd, The, Enf. EN3 . . . .**45** G1
Sunnyside, NW2 . . . .**90** C3
  SW19 . . . .**166** B6
  Walton-on-Thames KT12 . . . .**178** C5
Sunnyside Dr, E4 . . . .**46** C7
Sunnyside Pas, SW19 . . . .**166** B6
Sunnyside Pl, SW19
  off Sunnyside **166** B6
Sunnyside Rd, E10 . . . .**96** A1
  N19 . . . .**74** D7
  W5 . . . .**125** G1
  Ilford IG1 . . . .**99** F3
  Teddington TW11 . . . .**162** A4
Sunnyside Rd E, N9 . . . .**60** D3
Sunnyside Rd N, N9 . . . .**60** C3
Sunnyside Rd S, N9 . . . .**60** C3
Sunnyside Ter, NW9
  off Edgware Rd **70** D3
Sunny Vw, NW9 . . . .**70** D5
Sunny Way, N12 . . . .**57** H7
Sun Pas, SE16 . . . .**29** H5
Sunray Av, SE24 . . . .**152** A4
  Bromley BR2 . . . .**192** B6
  Surbiton KT5 . . . .**196** B2
  West Drayton UB7 . . . .**120** A2
Sunrise Cl, Felt. TW13
  off Exeter Rd **161** F3
Sun Rd, W14 . . . .**128** C5
Sunset Av, E4 . . . .**62** B1
  Woodford Green IG8 . . . .**63** F4
Sunset Ct, Wdf.Grn. IG8
  off Navestock Cres **63** J7

Sunset Gdns, SE25 . . . . .188 C2
Sunset Rd, SE5 . . . . .151 J4
  SE28 . . . . .138 A2
Sunset Vw, Barn. EN5 . . . . .40 B2
Sunshine Way, Mitch. CR4 . . . .185 J2
Sun St, EC2 . . . . .20 D2
Sun St Pas, EC2 . . . . .20 D2
Sun Wk, E1 . . . . .21 H6
Sunwell Cl, SE15
  off Cossall Wk 152/153 E1
Superior Dr, Orp. BR6 . . . . . . .207 J6
SURBITON, KT6 . . . . .181 J7
Surbiton Ct, Surb. KT6 . . . . . . .181 F6
Surbiton Cres, Kings.T. KT1 . . . .181 H4
Surbiton Hall Cl, Kings.T. KT1 . .181 H4
Surbiton Hill Pk, Surb. KT5 . . . .182 A5
Surbiton Hill Rd, Surb. KT6 . . . .181 H4
Surbiton Par, Surb. KT6
  off St. Mark's Hill 181 H6
Surbiton Rd, Kings.T. KT1 . . . . .181 H4
Surlingham Cl, SE28 . . . . .118 D7
Surma Cl, E1 . . . . .112 C4
Surmans Cl, Dag. RM9 . . . . . . .118 C1
Surrendale Pl, W9 . . . . .108 D4
Surrey Canal Rd, SE14 . . . . . . .133 F6
  SE15 . . . . .133 F6
★ Surrey Docks City Fm, SE16 .133 J2
Surrey Gdns, N4
  off Finsbury Pk Av 75 J6
Surrey Gro, SE17 . . . . .36 D4
  Sutton SM1 . . . . .199 G3
Surrey La, SW11 . . . . .149 H1
Surrey La Est, SW11 . . . . .149 H1
Surrey Lo, SE1 . . . . .26 E6
Surrey Ms, SE27
  off Hamilton Rd 170 B4
Surrey Mt, SE23 . . . . .171 E1
Surrey Quays Retail Cen, SE16 .133 G3
Surrey Quays Rd, SE16 . . . . . . .133 F3
Surrey Rd, SE15 . . . . .153 G5
  Barking IG11 . . . . .117 H1
  Dagenham RM10 . . . . .101 H5
  Harrow HA1 . . . . .67 J5
  West Wickham BR4 . . . . . . .204 B1
Surrey Row, SE1 . . . . .27 H3
Surrey Sq, SE17 . . . . .36 D3
Surrey St, E13 . . . . .115 H3
  WC2 . . . . .18 D5
  Croydon CR0 . . . . .201 J3
Surrey Ter, SE17 . . . . .36 E3
Surrey Water Rd, SE16 . . . . . . .133 G1
Surridge Gdns, SE19
  off Hancock Rd 170 A6
Surr St, N7 . . . . .92 E5
Sury Basin, Kings.T. KT2 . . . . . .181 H1
Susan Cl, Rom. RM7 . . . . .83 J3
Susan Constant Ct, E14
  off Newport Av 114 D7
Susannah St, E14 . . . . .114 B6
Susan Rd, SE3 . . . . .155 H2
Susan Wd, Chis. BR7 . . . . .192 D1
Sussex Av, Islw. TW7 . . . . .144 B3
Sussex Cl, N19
  off Cornwallis Rd 92/93 E2
  Ilford IG4 . . . . .80 C6
  New Malden KT3 . . . . .183 E4
  Twickenham TW1
  off Westmorland Cl 144/145 E6
Sussex Cres, Nthlt. UB5 . . . . . . .85 G6
Sussex Gdns, N4 . . . . .75 J5
  N6 *off Great N Rd* 73 J5
  W2 . . . . .15 E5
  Chessington KT9 . . . . .195 G6
Sussex Ms, SE6
  off Ravensbourne Pk 154 A7
Sussex Ms E, W2 . . . . .15 F4
Sussex Ms W, W2 . . . . .15 F5
Sussex Pl, NW1 . . . . .7 J4
  W2 . . . . .15 F4
  W6 . . . . .127 J5
  Erith DA8 . . . . .139 H7
  New Malden KT3 . . . . .183 E4
Sussex Ring, N12 . . . . .56 D5
Sussex Rd, E6 . . . . .116 D1
  Carshalton SM5 . . . . .199 H7
  Erith DA8 . . . . .139 H7
  Harrow HA1 . . . . .67 J5
  Mitcham CR4
  off Lincoln Rd 186/187 E5
  New Malden KT3 . . . . .183 E4
  Sidcup DA14 . . . . .176 B5
  South Croydon CR2 . . . . . . .202 A6
  Southall UB2 . . . . .122 A6
  West Wickham BR4 . . . . . . .204 B1
Sussex Sq, W2 . . . . .15 F5
Sussex St, E13 . . . . .115 H3
  SW1 . . . . .32 E4
Sussex Way, N7 . . . . .93 G2
  N19 . . . . .92 E1
  Barnet EN4 . . . . .42 A5
Sutcliffe Cl, NW11 . . . . .73 E5
Sutcliffe Ho, Hayes UB3 . . . . . .102 A6

Sutcliffe Rd, SE18 . . . . .137 H6
  Welling DA16 . . . . .158 C2
Sutherland Av, W9 . . . . .6 C4
  W13 . . . . .104 E6
  Hayes UB3 . . . . .122 A4
  Orpington BR5 . . . . .193 J6
  Welling DA16 . . . . .157 H4
Sutherland Cl, Barn. EN5 . . . . . .40 B4
Sutherland Ct, NW9 . . . . .70 B5
Sutherland Dr, SW19 . . . . .185 G1
Sutherland Gdns, SW14 . . . . . .147 E3
  Worcester Park KT4 . . . . . . .197 H1
Sutherland Gro, SW18 . . . . . . .148 B6
  Teddington TW11 . . . . .162 B5
Sutherland Pl, W2 . . . . .108 D6
Sutherland Rd, E17 . . . . .77 G2
  N9 . . . . .60 D1
  N17 . . . . .60 D7
  W4 . . . . .126 E6
  W13 . . . . .104 D6
  Belvedere DA17 . . . . .139 G3
  Croydon CR0 . . . . .187 G7
  Enfield EN3 . . . . .45 G5
  Southall UB1 . . . . .103 F6
Sutherland Rd Path, E17 . . . . . . .77 G3
Sutherland Row, SW1 . . . . .32 E3
Sutherland Sq, SE17 . . . . .35 J4
Sutherland St, SW1 . . . . .32 D3
Sutherland Wk, SE17 . . . . .36 A4
Sutlej Rd, SE7 . . . . .135 J7
Sutterton St, N7 . . . . .93 F6
SUTTON, SM1 - SM3 . . . . .198 E6
Sutton Cl, Beck. BR3
  off Albemarle Rd 190 B1
  Loughton IG10 . . . . .48 B7
  Pinner HA5 . . . . .66 A5
Sutton Common Rd, Sutt. SM1,
  SM3 . . . . .184 C7
Sutton Ct, W4 . . . . .126 C6
  Sutton SM2 . . . . .199 F6
Sutton Ct Rd, E13 . . . . .115 J3
  W4 . . . . .126 C7
  Sutton SM1 . . . . .199 F6
Sutton Cres, Barn. EN5 . . . . . . .40 A5
Sutton Dene, Houns. TW3 . . . . .143 H1
Sutton Est, SW3 . . . . .31 H3
  W10 . . . . .107 J5
Sutton Est, The, N1 . . . . .93 H7
Sutton Gdns, Bark. IG11
  off Sutton Rd 117 H1
  Croydon CR0 . . . . .188 C5
Sutton Grn, Bark. IG11
  off Sutton Rd 117 H1
Sutton Gro, Sutt. SM1 . . . . . . .199 G4
Sutton Hall Rd, Houns. TW5 . . .123 G7
★ Sutton Heritage Cen, Cars.
  SM5 . . . . .199 J4
★ Sutton Ho, E9 . . . . .95 F5
Sutton La, EC1 . . . . .11 H6
  Hounslow TW3 . . . . .143 F3
Sutton La N, W4 . . . . .126 C5
Sutton La S, W4 . . . . .126 C6
Sutton Par, NW4 *off Church Rd* .71 J4
Sutton Pk Rd, Sutt. SM1 . . . . . .198 E6
Sutton Path, Borwd. WD6
  off Stratfield Rd 38 A2
Sutton Pl, E9 . . . . .95 F5
Sutton Rd, E13 . . . . .115 F4
  E17 . . . . .77 G1
  N10 . . . . .74 A2
  Barking IG11 . . . . .117 H2
  Hounslow TW5 . . . . .143 G1
Sutton Row, W1 . . . . .17 J3
Sutton Sq, E9 *off Urswick Rd* . .95 F5
  Hounslow TW5 . . . . .143 F1
Sutton St, E1 . . . . .113 F6
Sutton's Way, EC1 . . . . .12 A6
Sutton Wk, SE1 . . . . .26 D2
Sutton Way, W10 . . . . .107 J5
  Hounslow TW5 . . . . .143 F1
Swaby Rd, SW18 . . . . .167 F1
Swaffham Way, N22
  off White Hart La 59 H7
Swaffield Rd, SW18 . . . . .149 E7
Swain Cl, SW16 . . . . .168 B6
Swain Rd, Th.Hth. CR7 . . . . . . .187 J5
Swains Cl, West Dr. UB7 . . . . . .120 B2
Swains La, N6 . . . . .92 A3
Swainson Rd, W3 . . . . .127 F2
Swains Rd, SW17 . . . . .167 J7
Swain St, NW8 . . . . .7 G5
Swaledale Cl, N11
  off Ribblesdale Av 58 A6
Swallands Rd, SE6 . . . . .172 A3
Swallow Cl, SE14 . . . . .153 F1
  Bushey WD23 . . . . .51 J1
Swallow Dr, NW10
  off Kingfisher Way 88 D6
  Northolt UB5 . . . . .103 G2
Swallowfield Rd, SE7 . . . . .135 H5
Swallowfield Way, Hayes UB3 . .121 G2
Swallow Gdns, SW16 . . . . .168 D5
Swallow Ho, NW8
  off Allitsen Rd 109 H2
Swallow Pas, W1 . . . . .17 E4

Swallow Pl, W1 . . . . .17 E4
Swallow St, E6 . . . . .116 B5
  W1 . . . . .17 G6
Swanage Rd, E4 . . . . .62 C7
  SW18 . . . . .149 F6
Swanage Waye, Hayes UB4 . . . .102 C6
Swan App, E6 . . . . .116 B5
Swanbridge Rd, Bexh. DA7 . . . .159 G1
Swan Cl, E17 . . . . .77 H1
  Croydon CR0 . . . . .188 B7
  Feltham TW13 . . . . .161 E4
Swan Ct, SW3 . . . . .31 H4
Swandon Way, SW18 . . . . .149 E4
Swan Dr, NW9 . . . . .70 E2
Swanfield St, E2 . . . . .13 F4
Swan La, EC4 . . . . .20 B6
  N20 . . . . .57 F3
  Loughton IG10 . . . . .47 J7
Swanley Rd, Well. DA16 . . . . . .158 C1
Swan Mead, SE1 . . . . .28 D6
Swan Pas, E1 *off Cartwright St* .112 C7
Swan Path, E10 *off Jesse Rd* . . .96 C1
Swan Pl, SW13 . . . . .147 F2
Swan Rd, SE16 . . . . .133 F2
  SE18 . . . . .136 A3
  Feltham TW13 . . . . .160 E5
  Southall UB1 . . . . .103 H6
  West Drayton UB7 . . . . .120 A2
Swanscombe Ho, W11
  off St. Anns Rd 128 A1
Swanscombe Rd, W4 . . . . .127 E5
  W11 . . . . .128 A1
Swansea Ct, E16
  off Fishguard Way 136/137 E1
Swansea Rd, Enf. EN3 . . . . .45 F4
  Hounslow (Hthrw Air.) TW6
  off Southern Perimeter Rd . .141 F6
Swanshope, Loug. IG10 . . . . . . .49 E2
Swansland Gdns, E17
  off McEntee Av 77 H1
Swanston Path, Wat. WD19 . . . .50 C3
Swan St, SE1 . . . . .28 A4
  Isleworth TW7 . . . . .144 E3
Swanton Gdns, SW19 . . . . . . .166 A1
Swanton Rd, Erith DA8 . . . . . . .139 H7
Swan Wk, SW3 . . . . .31 J5
Swan Way, Enf. EN3 . . . . .45 G2
Swanwick Cl, SW15 . . . . .147 F7
Swan Yd, N1
  off Highbury Sta Rd 93 H6
Swaton Rd, E3 . . . . .114 A4
Swaylands Rd, Belv. DA17 . . . . .139 G6
Swaythling Cl, N18 . . . . .61 E4
Swaythling Ho, SW15
  off Tunworth Cres 147 F6
Swedenborg Gdns, E1 . . . . .21 J5
Sweden Gate, SE16 . . . . .133 H3
Sweeney Cres, SE1 . . . . .29 G4
Sweet Briar Grn, N9 . . . . .60 C3
Sweet Briar Gro, N9 . . . . .60 C3
Sweet Briar Wk, N18 . . . . .60 C4
Sweetmans Av, Pnr. HA5 . . . . . .66 D3
Sweets Way, N20 . . . . .57 G2
Swetenham Wk, SE18
  off Sandbach Pl 137 F5
Swete St, E13 . . . . .115 G2
Sweyn Pl, SE3 . . . . .155 G2
Swift Cl, E17 . . . . .61 H7
  Harrow HA2 . . . . .85 H2
Swift Rd, Felt. TW13 . . . . .161 E3
  Southall UB2 . . . . .123 F3
Swiftsden Way, Brom. BR1 . . . .173 E6
Swift St, SW6 . . . . .148 C1
Swinbrook Rd, W10 . . . . .108 B5
Swinburne Ct, SE5
  off Basingdon Way 152 A4
Swinburne Cres, Croy. CR0 . . . .189 F6
Swinburne Rd, SW15 . . . . .147 G4
Swinderby Rd, Wem. HA0 . . . . .87 H6
Swindon Cl, Ilf. IG3
  off Salisbury Rd 99 H2
Swindon Rd, Houns. (Hthrw Air.)
  TW6 . . . . .141 F5
Swindon St, W12 . . . . .127 H1
Swinfield Cl, Felt. TW13 . . . . . .160 E4
Swinford Gdns, SW9 . . . . .151 H3
Swingate La, SE18 . . . . .137 H6
Swinnerton St, E9 . . . . .95 H5
Swinton Cl, Wem. HA9 . . . . . . .88 B1
Swinton Pl, WC1 . . . . .10 C3
Swinton St, WC1 . . . . .10 C3
Swires Shaw, Kes. BR2 . . . . . . .206 A4
Swiss Ct, W1 . . . . .17 J6
Swiss Ter, NW6 . . . . .91 G7
Switch Ho, E14
  off Blackwall Way 114 D7
Swithland Gdns, SE9 . . . . .174 D4
Swyncombe Av, W5 . . . . .125 E4
Swynford Gdns, NW4
  off Handowe Cl 71 G4
Sybil Ms, N4 *off Lothair Rd N* . .75 H6
Sybil Phoenix Cl, SE8 . . . . .133 G5
Sybourn St, E17 . . . . .77 J7
Sycamore Av, E3 . . . . .113 J1
  W5 . . . . .125 G3

Sycamore Av, Sid. DA15 . . . . . .157 J6
Sycamore Cl, E16
  off Clarence Rd 114/115 E4
  N9 *off Pycroft Way* 60 D4
  SE9 . . . . .174 B2
  W3 *off Bromyard Av* 126/127 H1
  Barnet EN4 . . . . .41 G6
  Carshalton SM5 . . . . .199 J4
  Edgware HA8 *off Ash Cl* 54 C4
  Feltham TW13 . . . . .160 A3
  Loughton IG10
  off Cedar Dr 48/49 E2
  Northolt UB5 . . . . .103 E1
  South Croydon CR2 . . . . . . .202 B5
Sycamore Ct, Surb. KT6
  off Penners Gdns 181 H7
Sycamore Gdns, W6 . . . . .127 H2
  Mitcham CR4 . . . . .185 G2
Sycamore Gro, NW9 . . . . .70 C7
  SE6 . . . . .154 C6
  SE20 . . . . .170 D7
  New Malden KT3 . . . . .182 D3
Sycamore Hill, N11 . . . . .58 A6
Sycamore Ms, SW4 . . . . .150 C3
Sycamore Rd, SW19 . . . . .165 J6
Sycamore St, EC1 . . . . .11 J6
Sycamore Wk, W10 *off Fifth Av* .108 B4
  Ilford IG6 *off Civic Way* 81 F4
Sycamore Way, Tedd. TW11 . . . .163 F6
  Thornton Heath CR7 . . . . . .187 G5
SYDENHAM, SE26 . . . . .171 F5
Sydenham Av, N21
  off Fleming Dr 43 F5
  SE26 . . . . .171 E5
Sydenham Cotts, SE12 . . . . . . .173 J2
Sydenham Hill, SE23 . . . . .170 E1
  SE26 . . . . .170 D3
Sydenham Hill Est, SE26 . . . . . .170 D3
Sydenham Pk, SE26 . . . . .171 F3
Sydenham Pk Rd, SE26 . . . . . . .171 F3
Sydenham Ri, SE23 . . . . .170 E2
Sydenham Rd, SE26 . . . . .171 F5
  Croydon CR0 . . . . .188 A7
Sydmons Ct, SE23 . . . . .153 F7
Sydner Ms, N16 *off Sydner Rd* . .94 C4
Sydner Rd, N16 . . . . .94 C4
Sydney Cl, SW3 . . . . .31 F2
Sydney Gro, NW4 . . . . .71 J5
Sydney Ms, SW3 . . . . .31 F2
Sydney Pl, SW7 . . . . .31 F2
Sydney Rd, E11 *off Mansfield Rd* .79 H5
  N8 . . . . .75 G4
  N10 . . . . .74 A1
  SE2 . . . . .138 C3
  SW20 . . . . .184 A2
  W13 . . . . .124 D1
  Bexleyheath DA6 . . . . .158 D4
  Enfield EN2 . . . . .44 A4
  Feltham TW14 . . . . .160 A1
  Ilford IG6 . . . . .81 F2
  Richmond TW9 . . . . .145 H4
  Sidcup DA14 . . . . .175 H4
  Sutton SM1 . . . . .198 D5
  Teddington TW11 . . . . .162 C5
  Woodford Green IG8 . . . . . . .63 G6
Sydney St, SW3 . . . . .31 G3
Sylvan Av, N3 . . . . .72 D2
  N22 . . . . .59 F5
  NW7 . . . . .55 F6
  Romford RM6 . . . . .83 F6
Sylvan Ct, N12
  off Holden Rd 56/57 E4
Sylvan Est, SE19 . . . . .188 C1
Sylvan Gdns, Surb. KT6 . . . . . .181 G7
Sylvan Gro, NW2 . . . . .90 A4
  SE15 . . . . .133 E6
Sylvan Hill, SE19 . . . . .188 B1
Sylvan Rd, E7 . . . . .97 G6
  E11 . . . . .79 G5
  E17 . . . . .78 A5
  SE19 . . . . .188 C1
  Ilford IG1 *off Hainault St* 99 F3
Sylvan Wk, Brom. BR1 . . . . . . .192 C3
Sylvan Way, Dag. RM8 . . . . . . .100 B3
  West Wickham BR4 . . . . . . .204 E4
Sylverdale Rd, Croy. CR0 . . . . . .201 H3
Sylvester Av, Chis. BR7 . . . . . . .174 C6
Sylvester Path, E8
  off Sylvester Rd 94/95 E6
Sylvester Rd, E8 . . . . .95 E6
  E17 . . . . .77 J7
  N2 . . . . .73 F2
  Wembley HA0 . . . . .87 F5
Sylvestrus Cl, Kings.T. KT1 . . . .182 A1
Sylvia Av, Pnr. HA5 . . . . .51 F6
Sylvia Ct, Wem. HA9
  off Harrow Rd 88 B7
Sylvia Gdns, Wem. HA9 . . . . . . .88 B7
Symes Ms, NW1 . . . . .9 F1
Symington Ms, E9
  off Coopersale Rd 95 G5
Symister Ms, N1 . . . . .12 D4
Symons St, SW3 . . . . .32 A2
Symphony Ms, W10
  off Third Av 108 B3

Syon Gate Way, Brent. TW8 . . . .124 D7
★ **Syon Ho & Pk**, Brent. TW8 . .145 F1
Syon La, Islw. TW7 . . . . .124 E7
Syon Pk Gdns, Islw. TW7 . . . . . .124 C7
Syon Vista, Rich. TW9 . . . . .145 G1

T

Tabard Cen, SE1 *off Prioress St* .132 A3
Tabard Gdn Est, SE1 . . . . .28 C4
Tabard St, SE1 . . . . .28 B4
Tabernacle Av, E13
off Barking Rd 115 G4
Tabernacle St, EC2 . . . . .12 C6
Tableer Av, SW4 . . . . .150 D5
Tabley Rd, N7 . . . . .92 E4
Tabor Gdns, Sutt. SM3 . . . . .198 C6
Tabor Gro, SW19 . . . . .166 B7
Tabor Rd, W6 . . . . .127 H3
Tachbrook Est, SW1 . . . . .33 J4
Tachbrook Ms, SW1 . . . . .33 F1
Tachbrook Rd, Felt. TW14 . . . . . .141 J7
Southall UB2 . . . . .122 D4
Tachbrook St, SW1 . . . . .33 G2
Tack Ms, SE4 . . . . .154 A3
Tadema Rd, SW10 . . . . .30 D7
Tadmor St, W12 . . . . .128 A1
Tadworth Av, N.Mal. KT3 . . . . . .183 F5
Tadworth Rd, NW2 . . . . .89 G2
Taeping St, E14 . . . . .134 B4
Taffy's How, Mitch. CR4 . . . . . . .185 H3
Taft Way, E3 *off St. Leonards St* .114 B3
Tagg's Island, Hmptn. TW12 . . . .180 A2
Tailworth St, E1 . . . . .21 H2
Tait Rd, Croy. CR0 . . . . .188 B7
Takhar Ms, SW11 *off Cabul Rd* . .149 H2
Talacre Rd, NW5 . . . . .92 A6
Talbot Av, N2 . . . . .73 G3
Talbot Cl, N15 . . . . .76 C4
Talbot Ct, EC3 . . . . .20 C5
Talbot Cres, NW4 . . . . .71 G5
Talbot Gdns, Ilf. IG3 . . . . .100 A2
Talbot Ho, E14 *off Giraud St* 114 B6
N7 *off Harvist Est* 93 G3
Talbot Pl, SE3 . . . . .154 E2
Talbot Rd, E6 . . . . .116 D2
E7 . . . . .97 G4
N6 . . . . .74 A6
N15 . . . . .76 C4
N22 . . . . .74 C2
SE22 .152 B4
W2 . . . . .108 C6
W11 . . . . .108 C6
W13 . . . . .104 D7
Bromley BR2 *off Masons Hill* .191 H4
Carshalton SM5 . . . . .200 A5
Dagenham RM9 . . . . .101 F6
Harrow HA3 . . . . .68 C2
Isleworth TW7 . . . . .144 D4
Southall UB2 . . . . .123 E4
Thornton Heath CR7 . . . . . . .188 A4
Twickenham TW2 . . . . .162 B1
Wembley HA0 . . . . .87 G5
Talbot Sq, W2 . . . . .15 F4
Talbot Wk, NW10
off Garnet Rd 88/89 E6
W11 . . . . .108 B6
Talbot Yd, SE1 . . . . .28 B2
Talfourd Pl, SE15 . . . . .152 C1
Talfourd Rd, SE15 . . . . .152 C1
Talgarth Rd, W6 . . . . .128 B5
W14 . . . . .128 B5
Talgarth Wk, NW9 . . . . .70 E5
Talisman Cl, Ilf. IG3 . . . . .100 B1
Talisman Sq, SE26 . . . . .170 D4
Talisman Way, Wem. HA9 . . . . . . .87 J3
Tallack Cl, Har. HA3
off College Hill Rd 52 B7
Tallack Rd, E10 . . . . .95 J1
Tall Elms Cl, Brom. BR2 . . . . . . .191 F5
Tallis Cl, E16 . . . . .115 H6
Tallis Gro, SE7 . . . . .135 H6
Tallis St, EC4 . . . . .19 F5
Tallis Vw, NW10 . . . . .88 D6
Tall Trees, SW16 . . . . .187 F3
Tally Ho Cor, N12 . . . . .57 F5
Talma Gdns, Twick. TW2 . . . . . . .144 B6
Talmage Cl, SE23 *off Tyson Rd* . .153 F7
Talman Gro, Stan. HA7 . . . . .53 G6
Talma Rd, SW2 . . . . .151 G4
Talwin St, E3 . . . . .114 B3
Tamar Cl, E3 *off Lefevre Wk* 113 J1
Tamarind Yd, E1 . . . . .29 J1
Tamarisk Sq, W12 . . . . .107 F7
Tamar Sq, Wdf.Grn. IG8 . . . . .63 H6
Tamar St, SE7 *off Woolwich Rd* .136 B3
Tamar Way, N17 . . . . .76 D3
Tamesis Gdns, Wor.Pk. KT4 . . . .196 E1
Tamian Way, Houns. TW4 . . . . . .142 C4
Tamworth Av, Wdf.Grn. IG8 . . . . .63 E6
Tamworth La, Mitch. CR4 . . . . . .186 B2
Tamworth Pk, Mitch. CR4 . . . . . .186 B4
Tamworth Pl, Croy. CR0 . . . . . . .201 J2
Tamworth Rd, Croy. CR0 . . . . . .201 H2
Tamworth St, SW6 . . . . .128 D6
Tancred Rd, N4 . . . . .75 H6
Tandem Cen, SW19
off Prince George's Rd 185 G1
Tandem Way, SW19 . . . . .185 G1
Tandridge Dr, Orp. BR6 . . . . .207 G1
Tandridge Pl, Orp. BR6
off Tandridge Dr 193 G7
Tanfield Av, NW2 . . . . .89 F4
Tanfield Rd, Croy. CR0 . . . . .201 J4
Tangier Rd, Rich. TW10 . . . . .146 B3
Tanglebury Cl, Brom. BR1 . . . . .192 C4
Tangle Tree Cl, N3 . . . . .73 E2
Tanglewood Cl, Croy. CR0 . . . . .203 F3
Stanmore HA7 . . . . .52 B2
Tanglewood Way, Felt. TW13 . . .160 B3
Tangley Gro, SW15 . . . . .147 F7
Tangley Pk Rd, Hmptn. TW12 . . .161 F6
Tangmere Gdns, Nthlt. UB5 . . . . .102 C2
Tangmere Gro, Kings.T. KT2 . . . .163 G5
Tangmere Way, NW9 . . . . .71 E2
Tanhurst Wk, SE2 *off Alsike Rd* .138 D3
Tankerton Rd, Surb. KT6 . . . . . . .195 J2
Tankerton St, WC1 . . . . .10 B4
Tankerville Rd, SW16 . . . . .168 D6
Tankridge Rd, NW2 . . . . .89 H2
Tanner Pt, E13 *off Pelly Rd* 115 G1
Tanners Cl, Walt. KT12 . . . . .178 B6
Tanners End La, N18 . . . . .60 B4
Tanners Hill, SE8 . . . . .153 J1
Tanners La, Ilf. IG6 . . . . .81 F3
Tanners Ms, SE8
off Tanners Hill 153 J1
Tanner St, SE1 . . . . .28 E4
Barking IG11 . . . . .99 F6
Tannery Cl, Beck. BR3 . . . . .189 G5
Dagenham RM10 . . . . .101 H3
Tannington Ter, N5 . . . . .93 G3
Tannsfeld Rd, SE26 . . . . .171 G5
Tansley Cl, N7 *off Hilldrop Rd* . . .92 D5
Tanswell Est, SE1 . . . . .27 F4
Tanswell St, SE1 . . . . .27 E4
Tansy Cl, E6 . . . . .116 D6
Tantallon Rd, SW12 . . . . .168 A1
Tant Av, E16 . . . . .115 F6
Tantony Gro, Rom. RM6 . . . . .82 D3
Tanworth Gdns, Pnr. HA5 . . . . . . .66 B2
Tanyard La, Bex. DA5 . . . . .159 G7
Tanza Rd, NW3 . . . . .91 J4
Tapestry Cl, Sutt. SM2 . . . . .198 E7
Taplow, NW3 . . . . .91 G7
SE17 . . . . .36 D4
Taplow Rd, N13 . . . . .59 J4
Taplow St, N1 . . . . .12 A2
Tappesfield Rd, SE15 . . . . .153 F3
Tapp St, E1 . . . . .113 E4
Tapster St, Barn. EN5 . . . . .40 C4
Tara Ms, N8 *off Edison Rd* 74 D6
Taransay Wk, N1 *off Essex Rd* . . .94 A6
Tarbert Ms, N15 *off Roslyn Rd* . . .76 B5
Tarbert Rd, SE22 . . . . .152 B5
Tarbert Wk, E1 *off Juniper St* . . .113 F7
Target Cl, Felt. TW14 . . . . .141 H6
Tariff Cres, SE8 . . . . .133 J4
Tariff Rd, N17 . . . . .60 D6
Tarleton Gdns, SE23 . . . . .171 E1
Tarling Cl, Sid. DA14 . . . . .176 B3
Tarling Rd, E16 . . . . .115 F6
N2 . . . . .73 F2
Tarling St, E1 . . . . .113 E6
Tarling St Est, E1 . . . . .113 F6
Tarnbank, Enf. EN2 . . . . .43 E5
Tarn St, SE1 . . . . .27 J6
Tarnwood Pk, SE9 . . . . .174 C1
Tarquin Ho, SE26 . . . . .170 D4
Tarragon Cl, SE14 . . . . .133 H7
Tarragon Gro, SE26 . . . . .171 G6
Tarrant Pl, W1 . . . . .15 J2
Tarrington Cl, SW16 . . . . .168 D3
Tarver Rd, SE17 . . . . .35 H4
Tarves Way, SE10 . . . . .134 B7
Tash Pl, N11 *off Woodland Rd* . . .58 B5
Tasker Cl, Hayes UB3 . . . . .121 F7
Tasker Ho, Bark. IG11
off Dovehouse Mead 117 G2
Tasker Rd, NW3 . . . . .91 J5
Tasman Ct, E14
off Westferry Rd 134 B4
Tasmania Ter, N18 . . . . .59 J6
Tasman Rd, SW9 . . . . .151 E3
Tasman Wk, E16 *off Royal Rd* . . .116 A6
Tasso Rd, W6 . . . . .128 B6
Tatam Rd, NW10 . . . . .88 C7
Tatchbury Ho, SW15
off Tunworth Cres 147 F6
Tate & Lyle Jetty, E16 . . . . .136 B2
★ **Tate Britain**, SW1 . . . . .34 A2
★ **Tate Modern**, SE1 . . . . .27 H1
Tate Rd, E16 *off Newland St* 136 C1
Sutton SM1 . . . . .198 D5
Tatham Pl, NW8 *off Acacia Rd* . .109 G2
Tatnell Rd, SE23 . . . . .153 H6
Tattersall Cl, SE9 . . . . .156 B5
Tatton Cres, N16
off Clapton Common 76 C7
Tatum St, SE17 . . . . .36 C2
Tauheed Cl, N4 . . . . .93 J2
Taunton Av, SW20 . . . . .183 H2
Hounslow TW3 . . . . .143 J2
Taunton Cl, Ilf. IG6 . . . . .65 J6
Sutton SM3 . . . . .198 D1
Taunton Dr, N2 . . . . .73 F2
Enfield EN2 . . . . .43 G3
Taunton Ms, NW1 . . . . .7 J6
Taunton Pl, NW1 . . . . .7 J5
Taunton Rd, SE12 . . . . .155 E5
Greenford UB6 . . . . .103 H1
Taunton Way, Stan. HA7 . . . . .69 H3
Tavern Cl, Cars. SM5 . . . . .185 H7
Taverners Cl, W11
off Addison Av 128 B1
Taverner Sq, N5
off Highbury Gra 93 J4
Taverners Way, E4
off Douglas Rd 62/63 E1
Tavern La, SW9 . . . . .151 G2
Tavistock Av, E17 . . . . .77 H3
NW7 . . . . .56 A7
Greenford UB6 . . . . .104 D2
Tavistock Cl, N16 *off Crossway* . .94 B5
Tavistock Ct, WC2
off Tavistock St 110/111 E7
Tavistock Cres, W11 . . . . .108 C5
Mitcham CR4 . . . . .186 E4
Tavistock Gdns, Ilf. IG3 . . . . .99 H4
Tavistock Gate, Croy. CR0 . . . . .202 A1
Tavistock Gro, Croy. CR0 . . . . . .188 A7
Tavistock Ms, E18 *off Avon Way* . .79 G4
W11 *off Lancaster Rd* 108 C6
Tavistock Pl, E18 *off Avon Way* . . .79 G3
N14 *off Chase Side* 42 B7
WC1 . . . . .9 J5
Tavistock Rd, E7 . . . . .97 F4
E15 . . . . .97 F6
E18 . . . . .79 G3
N4 . . . . .76 A6
NW10 .107 F2
W11 . . . . .108 C6
Bromley BR2 . . . . .191 F4
Carshalton SM5 . . . . .199 G1
Croydon CR0 . . . . .202 A1
Edgware HA8 . . . . .70 A1
Welling DA16 . . . . .158 C1
West Drayton UB7 . . . . .120 A1
Tavistock Sq, WC1 . . . . .9 J5
Tavistock St, WC2 . . . . .18 B5
Tavistock Ter, N19 . . . . .92 D3
Tavistock Twr, SE16
off Finland St 133 H3
Tavistock Wk, Cars. SM5
off Tavistock Rd 199 G1
Taviton St, WC1 . . . . .9 H5
Tavy Cl, SE11 . . . . .35 F3
Tawney Rd, SE28 . . . . .118 B7
Tawny Cl, W13 . . . . .124 E1
Feltham TW13 *off Chervil Cl* . .160 A3
Tawny Way, SE16 . . . . .133 G4
Tayben Av, Twick. TW2 . . . . .144 B6
Taybridge Rd, SW11 . . . . .150 A3
Tayburn Cl, E14 . . . . .114 C6
Taylor Av, Rich. TW9 . . . . .146 B2
Taylor Cl, N17 . . . . .60 D7
SE8 . . . . .133 J6
Hampton (Hmptn H.) TW12 . .161 J5
Hounslow TW3 . . . . .143 J1
Orpington BR6 . . . . .207 J4
Taylor Ct, E15 *off Clays La* 96 C5
Taylor Rd, Mitch. CR4 . . . . .167 H7
Wallington SM6 . . . . .200 B5
Taylors Bldgs, SE18
off Spray St 136/137 E4
Taylors Cl, Sid. DA14 . . . . .175 J4
Taylors Grn, W3
off Long Dr 106/107 E6
Taylors La, NW10 . . . . .88 E7
SE26 .170 E4
Barnet EN5 . . . . .40 C1
Taymount Ri, SE23 . . . . .171 F2
Tayport Cl, N1 . . . . .93 E7
Tayside Dr, Edg. HA8 . . . . .54 B3
Taywood Rd, Nthlt. UB5 . . . . . . .103 F3
Teak Cl, SE16 . . . . .133 H1
Teal Cl, E16 *off Fulmer Rd* 116 A5
Teal Ct, Wall. SM6
off Carew Rd 200 C6
Teale St, E2 . . . . .13 J1
Tealing Dr, Epsom KT19 . . . . . . .196 D4
Teal Pl, Sutt. SM1
off Sandpiper Rd 198 C5
Teal St, SE10 . . . . .135 F3
Teasel Cl, Croy. CR0 . . . . .203 G1
Teasel Cres, SE28 . . . . .137 H1
Teasel Way, E15 . . . . .114 E3
Tebworth Rd, N17 . . . . .60 C7
Teck Cl, Islw. TW7 . . . . .144 D2
Tedder Cl, Chess. KT9 . . . . .195 F5
Ruislip HA4 *off West End Rd* . .84 B5
Tedder Rd, S.Croy. CR2 . . . . . . .203 F7
TEDDINGTON, TW11 . . . . .162 D6
Teddington Lock, Tedd. TW11 . . .162 E4
Teddington Pk, Tedd. TW11 . . . . .162 C5
Teddington Pk Rd, Tedd. TW11 . .162 C4
Tedworth Gdns, SW3 . . . . .31 J4
Tedworth Sq, SW3 . . . . .31 J4
Tee, The, W3 . . . . .106 E6
Tees Av, Grnf. UB6 . . . . .104 B2
Teesdale Av, Islw. TW7 . . . . .144 D1
Teesdale Cl, E2 . . . . .13 J2
Teesdale Gdns, SE25 . . . . .188 B2
Isleworth TW7 . . . . .144 D1
Teesdale Rd, E11 . . . . .79 F6
Teesdale St, E2 . . . . .112 E2
Teesdale Yd, E2 . . . . .13 J1
Teeswater Ct, Erith DA18
off Middle Way 138 D3
Teevan Cl, Croy. CR0 . . . . .188 D7
Teevan Rd, Croy. CR0 . . . . .188 D7
Teignmouth Cl, SW4 . . . . .150 D4
Edgware HA8 . . . . .69 J2
Teignmouth Gdns, Grnf. UB6 . . .104 C2
Teignmouth Rd, NW2 . . . . .90 A5
Welling DA16 . . . . .158 C2
Telcote Way, Ruis. HA4
off Woodlands Av 66 C7
★ **Telecom Twr**, W1 . . . . .17 F1
Telegraph Hill, NW3 . . . . .90 E3
Telegraph La, Esher (Clay.) KT10 .194 C6
Telegraph Ms, Ilf. IG3 . . . . .100 A1
Telegraph Path, Chis. BR7 . . . . .174 E5
Telegraph Pl, E14 . . . . .134 B4
Telegraph Rd, SW15 . . . . .147 H7
Telegraph St, EC2 . . . . .20 B3
Telemann Sq, SE3 . . . . .155 H3
Telephone Pl, SW6 *off Lillie Rd* .128 C6
Telfer Cl, W3 *off Church Rd* 126 C2
Telferscot Rd, SW12 . . . . .168 D1
Telford Av, SW2 . . . . .168 E1
Telford Cl, E17 . . . . .77 H7
SE19 *off St. Aubyn's Rd* 170 C6
Telford Dr, Walt. KT12 . . . . .178 C7
Telford Rd, N11 . . . . .58 C6
NW9 *off West Hendon Bdy* . . .71 G6
SE9 . . . . .175 G2
W10 . . . . .108 B5
Southall UB1 . . . . .103 H7
Twickenham TW2 . . . . .143 G7
Telfords Yd, E1 . . . . .21 J6
Telford Ter, SW1 . . . . .33 F5
Telford Way, W3 . . . . .106 E5
Hayes UB4 . . . . .102 E5
Telham Rd, E6 . . . . .116 D2
Tell Gro, SE22 . . . . .152 C4
Tellson Av, SE18 . . . . .156 B1
Telscombe Cl, Orp. BR6 . . . . . . .207 H2
Temeraire Pl, Brent. TW8
off Green Dragon La 125 J5
Temeraire St, SE16
off Albion St 133 F2
Temperley Rd, SW12 . . . . .150 A7
Templar Dr, SE28 . . . . .118 D6
Templar Ho, NW2
off Shoot Up Hill 90 C6
Templar Pl, Hmptn. TW12 . . . . . .161 G7
Templars Av, NW11 . . . . .72 C6
Templars Cres, N3 . . . . .72 D2
Templars Dr, Har. HA3 . . . . .52 A6
Templar St, SE5 . . . . .151 H2
Temple, EC4 . . . . .111 G7
★ **Temple, The**, EC4 . . . . .19 E5
Temple Av, EC4 . . . . .19 F5
N20 . . . . .41 G7
Croydon CR0 . . . . .203 J2
Dagenham RM8 . . . . .101 G1
★ **Temple Bar**, EC4 . . . . .18 E4
Temple Cl, E11
off Wadley Rd 78/79 E7
N3 *off Cyprus Rd* 72 C2
SE28 .137 F3
Templecombe Rd, E9 . . . . .113 F1
Templecombe Way, Mord. SM4 .184 B5
Temple Ct, E1 *off Rectory Sq* . . .113 G5
Temple Fortune Hill, NW11 . . . . . .72 D5
Temple Fortune La, NW11 . . . . . .72 D6
Temple Fortune Par, NW11
off Finchley Rd 72 C5
Temple Gdns, N21
off Barrowell Grn 59 H2
NW11 .72 C6
Dagenham RM8 . . . . .100 D3
Temple Gro, NW11 . . . . .72 D6
Enfield EN2 . . . . .43 H3
Templehof Av, NW2 . . . . .71 J7
Temple La, EC4 . . . . .19 F4
Templeman Rd, W7 . . . . .104 C5
Templemead Cl, W3 . . . . .106 E6
Temple Mead Cl, Stan. HA7 . . . . .52 E6
Templemead Ho, E9
off Kingsmead Way 95 H4
Temple Mill La, E15 . . . . .96 B4
★ **Temple of Mithras**, EC4
off Queen Victoria St 20 B4
Temple Pl, WC2 . . . . .18 D5
Temple Rd, E6 . . . . .116 B1
N8 . . . . .75 F4
NW2 . . . . .89 J4

Temple Rd, W4 . . . . .126 C3
W5 . . . . .125 G3
Croydon CR0 . . . . .202 A4
Hounslow TW3 . . . . .143 H4
Richmond TW9 . . . . .145 J3
Temple Sheen, SW14 . . . . . .146 C5
Temple Sheen Rd, SW14 . . . .146 B4
Temple St, E2 . . . . .112 E2
Templeton Av, E4 . . . . .62 A4
Templeton Cl, N16
off Boleyn Rd 94 B5
SE19 . . . . .188 A1
Templeton Ct, NW7
off Kingsbridge Dr 56 A7
Templeton Pl, SW5 . . . . .128 D4
Templeton Rd, N15 . . . . .76 A6
Temple Way, Sutt. SM1 . . . . .199 J3
Temple W Ms, SE11 . . . . .27 G6
Templewood, W13 . . . . .105 E5
Templewood Av, NW3 . . . . . . .90 E3
Templewood Gdns, NW3 . . . . .91 E3
Templewood Pt, NW2
off Granville Rd 90 C2
Temple Yd, E2 off Temple St . . .112 E3
Tempsford Av, Borwd. WD6 . . .38 D4
Tempsford Cl, Enf. EN2
off Gladbeck Way 43 J3
Temsford Rd, Har. HA2 . . . . . .67 J2
Tenbury Cl, E7 off Romford Rd . .98 A5
Tenbury Ct, SW2 . . . . .168 D1
Tenby Av, Har. HA3 . . . . .68 E2
Tenby Cl, N15 off Hanover Rd . . .76 C4
Romford RM6 . . . . .82 E6
Tenby Gdns, Nthlt. UB5 . . . . . .85 G6
Tenby Rd, E17 . . . . .77 H5
Edgware HA8 . . . . .69 J1
Enfield EN3 . . . . .45 F3
Romford RM6 . . . . .83 E6
Welling DA16 . . . . .158 D1
Tench St, E1 . . . . .132 E1
Tenda Rd, SE16
off Roseberry St 132/133 E4
Tendring Way, Rom. RM6 . . . . .82 C5
Tenham Av, SW2 . . . . .168 D1
Tenison Ct, W1 . . . . .17 F5
Tenison Way, SE1 . . . . .26 E2
Tenniel Cl, W2 . . . . .14 C4
Tennis Ct La, E.Mol. KT8
off Hampton Ct Way 180 C3
Tennison Av, Borwd. WD6 . . . .38 A5
Tennison Rd, SE25 . . . . .188 C4
Tennis St, SE1 . . . . .28 B3
Tenniswood Rd, Enf. EN1 . . . . .44 C1
Tennyson Av, E11 . . . . .79 G7
E12 . . . . .98 B7
NW9 . . . . .70 C3
New Malden KT3 . . . . . . .183 H5
Twickenham TW1 . . . . . . .162 C1
Tennyson Cl, Enf. EN3 . . . . . . .45 G5
Feltham TW14 . . . . .141 J6
Welling DA16 . . . . .157 H1
Tennyson Rd, E10 . . . . .96 B2
E15 . . . . .96 E7
E17 . . . . .77 J6
NW6 . . . . .108 C1
NW7 . . . . .55 G5
SE20 . . . . .171 G7
SW19 . . . . .167 F6
W7 . . . . .104 C7
Hounslow TW3 . . . . .143 J2
Tennyson St, SW8 . . . . .150 B2
Tensing Rd, Sthl. UB2 . . . . . .123 G3
Tentelow La, Sthl. UB2 . . . . . .123 G5
Tenterden Cl, NW4 . . . . .72 A3
SE9 . . . . .174 C4
Tenterden Dr, NW4 . . . . .72 A3
Tenterden Gdns, NW4 . . . . . . .72 A3
Croydon CR0 . . . . .188 D7
Tenterden Gro, NW4 . . . . .72 A4
Tenterden Rd, N17 . . . . .60 C7
Croydon CR0 . . . . .188 D7
Dagenham RM8 . . . . .101 F2
Tenterden St, W1 . . . . .16 E4
Tenter Grd, E1 . . . . .21 F2
Tenter Pas, E1 . . . . .21 G4
Tent Peg La, Orp. BR5 . . . . . .193 F5
Tent St, E1 . . . . .112 E4
Terborch Way, SE22
off East Dulwich Gro 152 B5
Teredo St, SE16 . . . . .133 G3
Terence Ct, Belv. DA17
off Nuxley Rd 139 F6
Teresa Ms, E17 . . . . .78 A4
Teresa Wk, N10
off Connaught Gdns 74 B5
Terling Cl, E11 . . . . .97 F3
Terling Rd, Dag. RM8 . . . . . . .101 G2
Terling Wk, N1
off Britannia Row 111 J1
Terminus Pl, SW1 . . . . .25 E6
Terrace, The, E4
off Chingdale Rd 62/63 E3
N3 off Hendon La 72 C2
NW6 . . . . .108 D1
SW13 . . . . .147 E2

Terrace, The, Wdf.Grn. IG8
off Broadmead Rd 63 G6
Terrace Gdns, SW13 . . . . . . .147 F2
Terrace La, Rich. TW10 . . . . . .145 H6
Terrace Rd, E9 . . . . .95 F7
E13 . . . . .115 G1
Walton-on-Thames KT12 . . .178 A7
Terrace Wk, Dag. RM9 . . . . . .101 E5
Terrapin Rd, SW17 . . . . .168 B3
Terretts Pl, N1 off Upper St 93 H7
Terrick Rd, N22 . . . . .75 E1
Terrick St, W12 . . . . .107 H6
Terrilands, Pnr. HA5 . . . . .67 F3
Terront Rd, N15 . . . . .75 J5
Tersha St, Rich. TW9 . . . . . . .145 J4
Tessa Sanderson Pl, SW8 . . . .150 B3
Tessa Sanderson Way, Grnf. UB6
off Lilian Board Way 86 A5
Testerton Wk, W11 . . . . .108 A7
Tetbury Pl, N1 off Upper St . . .111 H1
Tetcott Rd, SW10 . . . . .30 C7
Tetherdown, N10 . . . . .74 A3
Tetty Way, Brom. BR2 . . . . . .191 G2
Teversham La, SW8 . . . . .151 E1
Teviot Cl, Well. DA16 . . . . . . .158 B1
Teviot St, E14 . . . . .114 C5
Tewkesbury Av, SE23 . . . . . . .171 E1
Pinner HA5 . . . . .67 E5
Tewkesbury Cl, N15
off Tewkesbury Rd 76 A6
Barnet EN4 off Approach Rd . .41 G4
Loughton IG10 . . . . .48 B6
Tewkesbury Gdns, NW9 . . . . . .70 B3
Tewkesbury Rd, N15 . . . . .76 A6
W13 . . . . .104 D7
Carshalton SM5 . . . . .199 G1
Tewkesbury Ter, N11 . . . . .58 C6
Tewson Rd, SE18 . . . . .137 H5
Teynham Av, Enf. EN1 . . . . . . .44 A6
Teynham Grn, Brom. BR2 . . . .191 G5
Teynton Ter, N17 . . . . .75 J1
Thackeray Av, N17 . . . . .76 D2
Thackeray Cl, SW19 . . . . .166 A7
Harrow HA2 . . . . .85 G1
Isleworth TW7 . . . . .144 D2
Thackeray Dr, Rom. RM6 . . . . .82 A7
Thackeray Rd, E6 . . . . .116 A2
SW8 . . . . .150 B2
Thackeray St, W8 . . . . .22 B4
Thakeham Cl, SE26 . . . . .170 E5
Thalia Cl, SE10 . . . . .134 D6
Thame Rd, SE16 . . . . .133 G2
Thames Av, SW10 . . . . .149 F1
Dagenham RM9 . . . . .119 H4
Greenford UB6 . . . . .104 C2
Thames Bk, SW14 . . . . .146 C2
Thamesbank Pl, SE28 . . . . . .118 C6
Thames Circle, E14
off Westferry Rd 134 A4
Thames Cl, Hmptn. TW12 . . . .179 H2
Thames Ct, W.Mol. KT8 . . . . .179 H2
Thames Cres, W4
off Corney Rd 126/127 E7
THAMES DITTON, KT7 . . . . . .180 C6
Thames Ditton Island, T.Ditt.
KT7 . . . . .180 D5
★ Thames Flood Barrier & Visitors
Cen, SE18 . . . . .136 A2
Thamesgate Cl, Rich. TW10
off Locksmeade Rd 162/163 E4
Thames Gateway, Dag. RM9 . .119 F2
Thameshill Av, Rom. RM5 . . . . .83 J2
★ Thames Ho, SW1 . . . . .34 A1
Thameside, Tedd. TW11 . . . . .163 G7
Thameside Ind Est, E16 . . . . .136 B2
Thameside Wk, SE28 . . . . . . .117 J6
THAMESMEAD, SE28 . . . . . .137 J1
Thamesmead, Walt. KT12 . . . .178 A7
THAMESMEAD NORTH, SE28 . .118 C6
Thames Meadow, W.Mol. KT8 . .179 G2
Thamesmead Spine Rd, Belv.
DA17 . . . . .139 H2
THAMESMEAD WEST, SE18 . .137 E3
Thamesmere Dr, SE28 . . . . . .118 A7
Thames Pl, SW15 . . . . .148 A3
Thames Pt, SW6
off The Boulevard 149 F1
Thames Quay, SW10
off Harbour Av 149 F1
Thames Rd, E16 . . . . .136 A1
W4 . . . . .126 A6
Barking IG11 . . . . .117 J3
Thames Side, Kings.T. KT1 . . .181 G1
Thames St, SE10 . . . . .134 B6
Hampton TW12 . . . . .179 H1
Kingston upon Thames KT1 . .181 G2
Sunbury-on-Thames TW16 . .178 B4
Thames Tunnel Mills, SE16
off Rotherhithe St 133 F2
Thamesvale Cl, Houns. TW3 . .143 G3
Thames Village, W4 . . . . .146 C1
Thames Wf, E16 . . . . .135 F1
Thanescroft Gdns, Croy. CR0 . .202 B3
Thanet Dr, Kes. BR2
off Phoenix Dr 206 A3

Thanet Pl, Croy. CR0 . . . . . . .201 J4
Thanet Rd, Bex. DA5 . . . . . . .159 G7
Thanet St, WC1 . . . . .10 A4
Thane Vil, N7 . . . . .93 F3
Thane Wks, N7 . . . . .93 F3
Thanington Ct, SE9 . . . . .157 H6
Thant Cl, E10 . . . . .96 B3
Tharp Rd, Wall. SM6 . . . . . . .200 D5
Thatcham Gdns, N20 . . . . .41 F7
Thatcher Cl, West Dr. UB7
off Classon Cl 120 B2
Thatchers Cl, Loug. IG10 . . . . .49 F2
Thatchers Way, Islw. TW7 . . . .144 A5
Thatches Gro, Rom. RM6 . . . . .82 E4
Thavies Inn, EC1 . . . . .19 F3
Thaxted Ct, N1 . . . . .12 B2
Thaxted Ho, Dag. RM10 . . . . .101 H7
Thaxted Pl, SW20 . . . . .166 A7
Thaxted Rd, SE9 . . . . .175 F2
Buckhurst Hill IG9 . . . . .48 B7
Thaxton Rd, W14 . . . . .128 C6
Thayers Fm Rd, Beck. BR3 . . .189 H1
Thayer St, W1 . . . . .16 C2
★ Theatre Mus, WC2
off Russell St 18 B5
★ Theatre Royal, WC2 . . . . . .18 B4
Theatre Sq, E15
off Great Eastern Rd 96 D6
Theatre St, SW11 . . . . .149 J3
Theberton St, N1 . . . . .111 G1
Theed St, SE1 . . . . .27 E2
Thelma Gdns, SE3 . . . . .156 A1
Feltham TW13 . . . . .161 E3
Thelma Gro, Tedd. TW11 . . . .162 D6
Theobald Cres, Har. HA3 . . . . .67 H1
Theobald Rd, E17 . . . . .77 J7
Croydon CR0 . . . . .201 H2
Theobalds Av, N12 . . . . .57 F4
Theobalds Ct, N4
off Queens Dr 93 J2
Theobald's Rd, WC1 . . . . .18 C1
Theobald St, SE1 . . . . .28 B6
Theodore Rd, SE13 . . . . .154 C6
Therapia La, Croy. CR0 . . . . . .187 G6
Therapia Rd, SE22 . . . . .153 F6
Theresa Rd, W6 . . . . .127 G4
Therfield Ct, N4
off Brownswood Rd 93 J2
Thermopylae Gate, E14 . . . . .134 B4
Theseus Wk, N1 . . . . .11 H2
Thesiger Rd, SE20 . . . . .171 G7
Thessaly Rd, SW8 . . . . .130 C7
Thetford Cl, N13 . . . . .59 H6
Thetford Gdns, Dag. RM9 . . . .100 D7
Thetford Rd, Dag. RM9 . . . . . .118 D7
New Malden KT3 . . . . .182 D6
Thetis Ter, Rich. TW9
off Kew Grn 126 A6
Theydon Gro, Wdf.Grn. IG8 . . .63 J6
Theydon Pk Rd, Epp. (They.B.)
CM16 . . . . .49 H1
Theydon Rd, E5 . . . . .95 F2
Theydon St, E17 . . . . .77 J7
Thicket Cres, Sutt. SM1 . . . . .199 F4
Thicket Gro, SE20
off Anerley Rd 170 D7
Dagenham RM9 . . . . .100 C6
Thicket Rd, SE20 . . . . .170 D7
Sutton SM1 . . . . .199 F4
Third Av, E12 . . . . .98 B4
E13 . . . . .115 G3
E17 . . . . .78 A5
W3 . . . . .127 F1
W10 . . . . .108 B3
Dagenham RM10 . . . . . . .119 H1
Enfield EN1 . . . . .44 C5
Hayes UB3 . . . . .121 J1
Romford RM6 . . . . .82 C6
Wembley HA9 . . . . .87 G2
Third Cl, W.Mol. KT8 . . . . . . .179 H4
Third Cross Rd, Twick. TW2 . . .162 A2
Third Way, Wem. HA9 . . . . . . .88 B4
Thirleby Rd, SW1 . . . . .25 G6
Edgware HA8 . . . . .70 D1
Thirlmere Av, Grnf. UB6 . . . . .105 F3
Thirlmere Gdns, Wem. HA9 . . .87 F1
Thirlmere Ho, Islw. TW7
off Summerwood Rd 144 C5
Thirlmere Ri, Brom. BR1 . . . . .173 F6
Thirlmere Rd, N10 . . . . .74 B1
SW16 . . . . .168 D4
Bexleyheath DA7 . . . . .159 J2
Thirsk Cl, Nthlt. UB5 . . . . .85 G6
Thirsk Rd, SE25 . . . . .188 A4
SW11 . . . . .150 A3
Mitcham CR4 . . . . .168 A7
Thirston Path, Borwd. WD6 . . . .38 A2
Thistlebrook, SE2 . . . . .138 C3
Thistlebrook Ind Est, SE2 . . . .138 C2
Thistlecroft Gdns, Stan. HA7 . . .69 G1
Thistledene, T.Ditt. KT7 . . . . .180 B6
Thistledene Av, Har. HA2 . . . . .85 E3
Thistlefield Cl, Bex. DA5 . . . . .176 D1
Thistle Gro, SW10 . . . . .30 D3
Thistlemead, Chis. BR7 . . . . .192 E2

Thistle Mead, Loug. IG10 . . . . .48 D3
Thistlewaite Rd, E5 . . . . .95 E3
Thistlewood Cl, N7 . . . . .93 F2
Thistleworth Cl, Islw. TW7 . . .124 A7
Thistley Cl, N12
off Summerfields Av 57 H6
Thistley Ct, SE8 off Glaisher St . .134 B6
Thomas a'Beckett Cl, Wem. HA0 . .86 C4
Thomas Baines Rd, SW11 . . . .149 G3
Thomas Cribb Ms, E6 . . . . . . .116 C6
Thomas Darby Ct, W11 . . . . . .108 B6
Thomas Dean Rd, SE26
off Kangley Br Rd 171 J4
Thomas Dinwiddy Rd, SE12 . . .173 H2
Thomas Doyle St, SE1 . . . . . . .27 G5
Thomas Hardy Ho, N22 . . . . . .59 F7
Thomas La, SE6 . . . . .154 A7
Thomas More Ho, EC2
off The Barbican 111 J5
Thomas More St, E1 . . . . .21 H6
Thomas More Way, N2 . . . . . . .73 F3
Thomas Pl, W8 . . . . .22 A6
Thomas Rd, E14 . . . . .113 J6
Thomas St, SE18 . . . . .136 D4
Thomas Wall Cl, Sutt. SM1
off Clarence Rd 198/199 E5
Thompson Av, Rich. TW9 . . . .146 A3
Thompson Cl, Ilf. IG1
off High Rd 99 F2
Sutton SM3
off Barrington Rd 198 D1
Thompson Rd, SE22 . . . . .152 C6
Dagenham RM9 . . . . .101 F3
Hounslow TW3 . . . . .143 H4
Thompson's Av, SE5 . . . . .35 J7
Thompson's La, Loug. (High Beach)
IG10 . . . . .47 F1
Thomson Cres, Croy. CR0 . . . .201 G1
Thomson Rd, Har. HA3 . . . . . .68 B3
Thorburn Sq, SE1 . . . . .37 H2
Thorburn Way, SW19 . . . . . . .185 F1
Thoresby St, N1 . . . . .12 A3
Thorkhill Gdns, T.Ditt. KT7 . . .194 D1
Thorkhill Rd, T.Ditt. KT7 . . . . .180 E7
Thornaby Gdns, N18 . . . . .60 D6
Thorn Av, Bushey (Bushey Hth)
WD23 . . . . .51 J1
Thornbury Av, Islw. TW7 . . . . .124 A7
Thornbury Cl, N16
off Boleyn Rd 94 B5
NW7 off Kingsbridge Dr 56 A7
Thornbury Gdns, Borwd. WD6 . .38 C4
Thornbury Rd, SW2 . . . . .150 E6
Isleworth TW7 . . . . .144 A1
Thornbury Sq, N6 . . . . .92 C1
Thornby Rd, E5 . . . . .95 F3
Thorncliffe Rd, SW2 . . . . .150 E6
Southall UB2 . . . . .123 F5
Thorn Cl, Brom. BR2 . . . . . . .192 D6
Northolt UB5 . . . . .103 F3
Thorncombe Rd, SE22 . . . . . .152 B5
Thorncroft Rd, Sutt. SM1 . . . .198 E4
Thorncroft St, SW8 . . . . .130 E7
Thorndean St, SW18 . . . . . . .167 F2
Thorndike Av, Nthlt. UB5 . . . .102 D1
Thorndike Cl, SW10 . . . . .30 C7
Thorndike Rd, N1 . . . . .93 J6
Thorndike St, SW1 . . . . .33 H3
Thorndon Cl, Orp. BR5 . . . . . .193 J2
Thorndon Gdns, Epsom KT19 . .196 E4
Thorndon Rd, Orp. BR5 . . . . .193 J2
Thorndyke Ct, Pnr. HA5
off Westfield Pk 51 F7
Thorne Cl, E11 . . . . .96 E4
E16 . . . . .115 G6
Erith DA8 . . . . .139 J6
Thorneloe Gdns, Croy. CR0 . . .201 G5
Thorne Pas, SW13 . . . . .147 E2
Thorne Rd, SW8 . . . . .130 E7
Thornes Cl, Beck. BR3 . . . . . .190 C3
Thorne St, E16 . . . . .115 F6
SW13 . . . . .147 E3
Thornet Wd Rd, Brom. BR1 . . .192 D3
Thorney Cres, SW11 . . . . . . .129 G7
Thorneycroft Cl, Walt. KT12 . . .178 C6
Thorney Hedge Rd, W4 . . . . . .126 B4
Thorney St, SW1 . . . . .34 A1
Thornfield Av, NW7 . . . . .72 B1
Thornfield Rd, W12 . . . . .127 H2
Thornford Rd, SE13 . . . . .154 C5
Thorngate Rd, W9 . . . . .108 D4
Thorngrove Rd, E13 . . . . .115 H1
Thornham Gro, E15 . . . . .96 D5
Thornham St, SE10 . . . . .134 B6
Thornhaugh Ms, WC1 . . . . .9 J6
Thornhaugh St, WC1 . . . . .17 J1
Thornhill Av, SE18 . . . . .137 H7
Surbiton KT6 . . . . .195 H2
Thornhill Br Wf, N1
off Caledonian Rd 111 F1
Thornhill Cres, N1 . . . . .93 F7
Thornhill Gdns, E10 . . . . .96 B2
Barking IG11 . . . . .99 H7
Thornhill Gro, N1 off Lofting Rd . .93 F7

Thornhill Rd, E10 . . . . .96 B2
N1 . . . . .93 G7
Croydon CR0 . . . . .187 J7
Surbiton KT6 . . . . .195 H2
Thornhill Sq, N1 . . . . .93 F7
Thorn Ho, Beck. BR3 . . . . . .189 H1
Thornlaw Rd, SE27 . . . . .169 G4
Thornley Cl, N17 . . . . .60 D7
Thornley Dr, Har. HA2 . . . . . . .85 H2
Thornley Pl, SE10
    off Caradoc St 134/135 E5
Thornsbeach Rd, SE6 . . . . . .172 C1
Thornsett Pl, SE20 . . . . .188 E2
Thornsett Rd, SE20 . . . . .188 E2
    SW18 . . . . .167 E2
Thornside, Edg. HA8
    off High St 54 A6
Thorn Ter, SE15
    off Nunhead Gro 153 F3
Thornton Av, SW2 . . . . .168 D1
    W4 . . . . .127 A4
    Croydon CR0 . . . . .187 F6
    West Drayton UB7 . . . . . .120 C3
Thornton Cl, West Dr. UB7 . . .120 C3
Thornton Ct, SW20 . . . . .184 A5
Thornton Dene, Beck. BR3 . . .190 A2
Thornton Gdns, SW12 . . . . . .168 D1
Thornton Gro, Pnr. HA5 . . . . . .51 G6
THORNTON HEATH, CR7 . . . .187 H4
Thornton Hill, SW19 . . . . . . .166 B7
Thornton Pl, W1 . . . . .16 A1
Thornton Rd, E11 . . . . .96 D2
    N18 . . . . .61 F3
    SW12 . . . . .150 D7
    SW14 . . . . .146 D3
    SW19 . . . . .166 A6
    Barnet EN5 . . . . .40 B3
    Belvedere DA17 . . . . .139 H4
    Bromley BR1 . . . . .173 G5
    Carshalton SM5 . . . . .199 G6
    Croydon CR0 . . . . .187 F7
    Ilford IG1 . . . . .98 E4
    Thornton Heath CR7 . . . . .187 F7
Thornton Rd E, SW19
    off Thornton Rd 166 A6
Thornton Rd Retail Pk, Croy.
    CR0 . . . . .187 F6
Thornton Row, Th.Hth. CR7
    off London Rd 187 G5
Thornton St, SW9 . . . . .151 G2
Thornton Way, NW11 . . . . . . .73 E5
Thorntree Rd, SE7 . . . . .136 A5
Thornville Gro, Mitch. CR4 . . .185 F2
Thornville St, SE8 . . . . .154 A1
Thornwood Cl, E18 . . . . .79 H2
Thornwood Rd, SE13 . . . . . . .154 E5
Thorogood Gdns, E15 . . . . . . .97 E5
Thorold Rd, N22 . . . . .59 E7
    Ilford IG1 . . . . .98 E2
Thorparch Rd, SW8 . . . . .150 D1
Thorpebank Rd, W12 . . . . . . .127 G1
Thorpe Cl, W10
    off Cambridge Gdns 108 B6
    Orpington BR6 . . . . .207 H2
Thorpe Cres, E17 . . . . .77 J2
Thorpedale Gdns, Ilf. IG2, IG6 . .80 D4
Thorpedale Rd, N4 . . . . .93 E1
Thorpe Hall Rd, E17 . . . . .78 C1
Thorpe Rd, E6 . . . . .116 C1
    E7 . . . . .97 F4
    E17 . . . . .78 C2
    N15 . . . . .76 B6
    Barking IG11 . . . . .99 G7
    Kingston upon Thames KT2 . .163 H7
Thorpe Wk, Grnf. UB6 . . . . . .104 B2
Thorpewood Av, SE26 . . . . . .171 E2
Thorsden Way, SE19
    off Oaks Av 170 B4
Thorverton Rd, NW2 . . . . .90 B3
Thoydon Rd, E3 . . . . .113 H2
Thrale Rd, SW16 . . . . .168 C5
Thrale St, SE1 . . . . .28 A2
Thrasher Cl, E8 off Stean St . . .112 C1
Thrawl St, E1 . . . . .21 G2
Threadneedle St, EC2 . . . . . . .20 C4
Three Barrels Wk, EC4 . . . . . . .20 A5
Three Colts Cor, E2 . . . . .13 H5
Three Colts La, E2 . . . . .113 E4
Three Colt St, E14 . . . . .113 J7
Three Cors, Bexh. DA7 . . . . . .159 H2
Three Cranes Wk, EC4
    off Upper Thames St 111 J7
Three Cups Yd, WC1 . . . . .18 D2
Three Kings Rd, Mitch. CR4 . . .186 A3
Three Kings Yd, W1 . . . . .16 D5
Three Mill La, E3 . . . . .114 C3
Three Oak La, SE1 . . . . .29 F3
Three Quays Wk, EC3 . . . . . . .20 E6
Threshers Pl, W11 . . . . .108 B7
Thriffwood, SE26 . . . . .171 F3
Thrift Fm La, Borwd. WD6 . . . . .38 B2
Thrigby Rd, Chess. KT9 . . . . .195 H6
Throckmorten Rd, E16 . . . . . .115 H6
Throgmorton Av, EC2 . . . . . . .20 C3
Throgmorton St, EC2 . . . . . . .20 C3

Throwley Cl, SE2 . . . . .138 C3
Throwley Rd, Sutt. SM1 . . . . .199 E5
Throwley Way, Sutt. SM1 . . . .199 E4
Thrupp Cl, Mitch. CR4 . . . . . .186 B2
Thrush Grn, Har. HA2 . . . . .67 G4
Thrush St, SE17 . . . . .35 J3
Thruxton Way, SE15 . . . . .37 G7
Thunderer Rd, Dag. RM9 . . . .118 E4
Thurbarn Rd, SE6 . . . . .172 B5
Thurland Rd, SE16 . . . . .29 H5
Thurlby Cl, Har. HA1
    off Gayton Rd 68 D6
    Woodford Green IG8 . . . . . .64 C5
Thurlby Rd, SE27 . . . . .169 G4
    Wembley HA0 . . . . .87 G6
Thurleigh Av, SW12 . . . . .150 A6
Thurleigh Rd, SW12 . . . . .150 A6
Thurleston Av, Mord. SM4 . . . .184 B5
Thurlestone Av, N12 . . . . .57 J6
    Ilford IG3 . . . . .99 J4
Thurlestone Rd, SE27 . . . . . . .169 G3
Thurloe Cl, SW7 . . . . .31 G1
Thurloe Pl, SW7 . . . . .31 F1
Thurloe Pl Ms, SW7 . . . . .31 F1
Thurloe Sq, SW7 . . . . .31 G1
Thurloe St, SW7 . . . . .31 F1
Thurlow Cl, E4
    off Higham Sta Av 62 B6
Thurlow Gdns, Ilf. IG6 . . . . . . .65 G6
    Wembley HA0 . . . . .87 G5
Thurlow Hill, SE21 . . . . .169 J1
Thurlow Pk Rd, SE21 . . . . . . .169 H1
Thurlow Rd, NW3 . . . . .91 G5
    W7 . . . . .124 D2
Thurlow St, SE17 . . . . .36 C3
Thurlow Ter, NW5 . . . . .92 A5
Thurlstone Rd, Ruis. HA4 . . . . .84 A3
Thurnby Cl, Twick. TW2 . . . . . .162 B3
Thursland Rd, Sid. DA14 . . . . .176 E5
Thursley Cres, Croy. (New Adgtn)
    CR0 . . . . .204 D7
Thursley Gdns, SW19 . . . . . . .166 A2
Thursley Rd, SE9 . . . . .174 C3
Thurso St, SW17 . . . . .167 G4
Thurstan Rd, SW20 . . . . .165 H7
Thurston Rd, SE13 . . . . .154 B2
    Southall UB1 . . . . .103 F6
Thurston Rd Ind Est, SE13
    off Jerrard St 154 B3
Thurtle Rd, E2 . . . . .112 C1
Thwaite Cl, Erith DA8 . . . . . . .139 J6
Thyer Cl, Orp. BR6
    off Isabella Dr 207 F4
Thyme Cl, SE3
    off Nelson Mandela Rd 155 J3
Thyra Gro, N12 . . . . .57 E6
Tibbatts Rd, E3 . . . . .114 B4
Tibbenham Pl, SE6 . . . . .172 A2
Tibbenham Wk, E13 . . . . .115 F2
Tibberton Sq, N1
    off Popham Rd 93 J7
Tibbets Cl, SW19 . . . . .166 A1
Tibbet's Cor, SW15 . . . . .148 A7
Tibbet's Cor Underpass, SW15
    off West Hill 148 A7
Tibbet's Ride, SW15 . . . . .148 A7
Tiber Gdns, N1
    off Copenhagen St 111 F1
Ticehurst Cl, Orp. BR5
    off Grovelands Rd 176 A7
Ticehurst Rd, SE23 . . . . .171 H2
Tickford Cl, SE2
    off Ampleforth Rd 138 C2
Tidal Basin Rd, E16 . . . . .115 F7
Tidenham Gdns, Croy. CR0 . . .202 B3
Tideswell Rd, SW15 . . . . .147 J5
    Croydon CR0 . . . . .204 A3
Tideway Cl, Rich. TW10
    off Locksmeade Rd . . .162/163 E4
Tideway Ind Est, SW8 . . . . . . .33 G6
Tideway Wk, SW8
    off Cringle St 130 C7
Tidey St, E3 . . . . .114 A5
Tidford Rd, Well. DA16 . . . . . .157 J2
Tidworth Rd, E3 . . . . .114 A4
Tiepigs La, Brom. BR2 . . . . . .205 E2
    West Wickham BR4 . . . . . .205 E2
Tierney Rd, SW2 . . . . .168 E1
Tiger La, Brom. BR2 . . . . .191 H4
Tiger Way, E5 . . . . .94 E4
Tigris Cl, N9 . . . . .61 F2
Tilbrook Rd, SE3 . . . . .155 J3
Tilbury Cl, SE15 . . . . .37 G7
Tilbury Rd, E6 . . . . .116 C2
    E10 . . . . .78 C7
Tildesley Rd, SW15 . . . . .147 J6
Tile Fm Rd, Orp. BR6 . . . . . . .207 G3
Tilehurst Pt, SE2
    off Yarnton Way 138 C2
Tilehurst Rd, SW18 . . . . .167 G1
    Sutton SM3 . . . . .198 B5
Tile Kiln La, N6 . . . . .92 B1
    N13 . . . . .59 J5
    Bexley DA5 . . . . .177 J2

Tile Yd, E14 off Commercial Rd .113 J6
Tileyard Rd, N7 . . . . .92 F7
Tilford Gdns, SW19 . . . . .166 A2
Tilia Cl, Sutt. SM1 . . . . .198 C5
Tilia Rd, E5 off Clarence Rd . .94/95 E4
Tilia Wk, SW9 off Moorland Rd .151 H4
Tiller Rd, E14 . . . . .134 A3
Tillett Cl, NW10 . . . . .88 C6
Tillett Sq, SE16
    off Howland Way 133 H2
Tillett Way, E2 . . . . .13 H3
Tillingbourne Gdns, N3 . . . . . . .72 C3
Tillingbourne Way, N3
    off Tillingbourne Gdns 72 C3
Tillingham Way, N12 . . . . .56 D4
Tilling Rd, NW2 . . . . .89 J1
Tilling Way, Wem. HA9 . . . . . . .87 G2
Tillman St, E1
    off Bigland St 112/113 E6
Tilloch St, N1 off Carnoustie Dr . .93 F7
Tillotson Rd, N9 . . . . .60 C2
    Harrow HA3 . . . . .51 H7
    Ilford IG1 . . . . .80 D7
Tilney Ct, EC1 . . . . .12 A5
Tilney Dr, Buck.H. IG9 . . . . . . .63 E2
Tilney Gdns, N1 . . . . .94 A6
Tilney Rd, Dag. RM9 . . . . .101 F6
    Southall UB2 . . . . .122 C4
Tilney St, W1 . . . . .24 C1
Tilson Cl, SE5 off Coleman Rd .132 B7
Tilson Gdns, SW2 . . . . .150 E7
Tilson Ho, SW2
    off Tilson Gdns 150/151 E7
Tilson Rd, N17 . . . . .76 D1
Tilston Cl, E11 off Matcham Rd . .97 F3
Tilton St, SW6 . . . . .128 B6
Tiltwood, The, W3 off Acacia Rd .106 C7
Tilt Yd App, SE9 . . . . .156 C6
Timber Cl, Chis. BR7 . . . . . . .192 D2
Timbercroft, Epsom KT19 . . . .196 E4
Timbercroft La, SE18 . . . . . . .137 H6
Timberdene, NW4 . . . . .72 A2
Timberdene Av, Ilf. IG6 . . . . . . .81 E1
Timberland Cl, SE15
    off Peckham Hill St 132 D7
Timberland Rd, E1 . . . . .113 E6
Timber Mill Way, SW4 . . . . . .150 D3
Timber Pond Rd, SE16 . . . . . .133 G2
Timber St, EC1 . . . . .11 J5
Timberwharf Rd, N16 . . . . .76 D6
Timbrell Pl, SE16 off Silver Wk .133 J1
Time Sq, E8 . . . . .94 C5
Times Sq, Sutt. SM1 . . . . . . .199 E5
Times Sq Shop Cen, Sutt. SM1
    off High St 198/199 E5
Timothy Cl, SW4 off Elms Rd . .150 C5
    Bexleyheath DA6 . . . . . . .158 E5
Timothy Ho, Erith DA18
    off Kale Rd 138/139 E2
Timothy Rd, E3 . . . . .113 J5
Timsbury Wk, SW15 . . . . .165 G1
Tindal St, SW9 . . . . .151 H1
Tinderbox All, SW14 . . . . .146 D3
Tine Rd, Chig. IG7 . . . . .65 H5
Tinniswood Cl, N5
    off Drayton Pk 93 G5
Tinsley Rd, E1 . . . . .113 F5
Tintagel Cres, SE22 . . . . .152 C4
Tintagel Dr, Stan. HA7 . . . . . . .53 G4
Tintagel Gdns, SE22
    off Oxonian St 152 C4
Tintern Av, NW9 . . . . .70 B3
Tintern Cl, SW15 . . . . .148 B5
    SW19 . . . . .167 F7
Tintern Ct, W13
    off Green Man La 104 D7
Tintern Gdns, N14 . . . . .43 E7
Tintern Path, NW9
    off Ruthin Cl 70/71 E6
Tintern Rd, N22 . . . . .75 J1
    Carshalton SM5 . . . . .199 G1
Tintern St, SW4 . . . . .151 E4
Tintern Way, Har. HA2 . . . . . . .85 H1
Tinto Rd, E16 . . . . .115 G4
Tinwell Ms, Borwd. WD6
    off Cranes Way 38 C5
Tinworth St, SE11 . . . . .34 B3
Tippetts Cl, Enf. EN2 . . . . .43 J1
Tipthorpe Rd, SW11 . . . . .150 A3
Tipton Dr, Croy. CR0 . . . . . . .202 B4
Tiptree Cl, E4 off Mapleton Rd . .62 C3
Tiptree Cres, Ilf. IG5 . . . . .80 D3
Tiptree Dr, Enf. EN2 . . . . .44 A4
Tiptree Est, Ilf. IG5 . . . . .80 D3
Tiptree Rd, Ruis. HA4 . . . . .84 B4
Tirlemont Rd, S.Croy. CR2 . . .201 J7
Tirrell Rd, Croy. CR0 . . . . . . .187 J6
Tisbury Ct, W1 off Rupert St . . .110 D7
Tisbury Rd, SW16 . . . . .186 E2
Tisdall Pl, SE17 . . . . .36 C2
Titchborne Row, W2 . . . . .15 H4
Titchfield Rd, NW8 . . . . .109 J1
    Carshalton SM5 . . . . .199 G1
Titchfield Wk, Cars. SM5
    off Titchfield Rd 185 G7

Titchwell Rd, SW18 . . . . .149 G7
Tite St, SW3 . . . . .31 J4
Tithe Barn Cl, Kings.T. KT2 . . .181 J1
Tithe Barn Way, Nthlt. UB5 . . .102 B3
Tithe Cl, NW7 . . . . .71 G1
    Walton-on-Thames KT12 . . .178 B6
Tithe Fm Av, Har. HA2 . . . . . . .85 G3
Tithe Fm Cl, Har. HA2 . . . . . . .85 G3
Tithe Wk, NW7 . . . . .71 G1
Titley Cl, E4 . . . . .62 A5
Titmuss Av, SE28 . . . . .118 B7
Titmuss St, W12
    off Goldhawk Rd 127 J2
Tiverton Av, Ilf. IG5 . . . . .80 D3
Tiverton Cl, Croy. CR0
    off Exeter Rd 188 C7
Tiverton Dr, SE9 . . . . .175 F1
Tiverton Ho, Enf. EN3 . . . . .45 G3
Tiverton Rd, N15 . . . . .76 A6
    N18 . . . . .60 B5
    NW10 . . . . .108 A1
    Edgware HA8 . . . . .69 J2
    Hounslow TW3 . . . . .143 J2
    Ruislip HA4 . . . . .84 A3
    Thornton Heath CR7
        off Willett Rd 187 G5
    Wembley HA0 . . . . .105 H2
Tiverton St, SE1 . . . . .27 J6
Tiverton Way, NW7 . . . . .56 A7
    Chessington KT9 . . . . . . .195 F5
Tivoli Ct, SE16 . . . . .133 J2
Tivoli Gdns, SE18 . . . . .136 B4
Tivoli Rd, N8 . . . . .74 D5
    SE27 . . . . .169 J5
    Hounslow TW4 . . . . .142 E4
Toad La, Houns. TW4 . . . . . . .143 F4
Tobacco Dock, E1 . . . . .112 E7
Tobacco Quay, E1
    off Wapping La 112/113 E7
Tobago St, E14 off Manilla St . .134 A2
Tobin Cl, NW3 . . . . .91 H7
Toby La, E1 . . . . .113 H4
Toby Way, Surb. KT5 . . . . . . .196 B2
Todds Wk, N7 off Andover Rd . .93 F2
Tokenhouse Yd, EC2 . . . . .20 B3
Token Yd, SW15
    off Montserrat Rd 148 B4
TOKYNGTON, Wem. HA9 . . . . .88 B6
Tokyngton Av, Wem. HA9 . . . . .88 A6
Toland Sq, SW15 . . . . .147 G5
Tolcarne Dr, Pnr. HA5 . . . . .66 B3
Toley Av, Wem. HA9 . . . . .88 B3
Tollbridge Cl, W10 off Kensal Rd .108 B4
Tollesbury Gdns, Ilf. IG6 . . . . . .81 G3
Tollet St, E1 . . . . .113 G4
Tollgate Dr, SE21 . . . . .170 B2
    Hayes UB4 . . . . .102 D7
Tollgate Gdns, NW6 . . . . .6 A1
Tollgate Rd, E6 . . . . .116 A5
    E16 . . . . .115 J5
Tollhouse Way, N19 . . . . .92 C2
Tollington Pk, N4 . . . . .93 F2
Tollington Pl, N4 . . . . .93 F2
Tollington Rd, N7 . . . . .93 F4
Tollington Way, N7 . . . . .92 E3
Tolmers Sq, NW1 . . . . .9 G5
Tolpuddle Av, E13
    off Rochester Av 115 J1
Tolpuddle St, N1 . . . . .10 E1
Tolsford Rd, E5 . . . . .95 E5
Tolson Rd, Islw. TW7 . . . . . . .144 D3
Tolverne Rd, SW20 . . . . .183 J1
TOLWORTH, Surb. KT6 . . . . .196 A2
Tolworth Bdy, Surb. KT6 . . . . .196 B1
Tolworth Cl, Surb. KT6 . . . . . .196 B1
Tolworth Gdns, Rom. RM6 . . . .82 D5
Tolworth Pk Rd, Surb. KT6 . . .195 J2
Tolworth Ri N, Surb. KT5
    off Elmbridge Av 182 C7
Tolworth Ri S, Surb. KT5
    off Warren Dr S 196 C1
Tolworth Rd, Surb. KT6 . . . . . .195 H2
Tolworth Twr, Surb. KT6 . . . . .196 B2
Tomahawk Gdns, Nthlt. UB5
    off Javelin Way 102 D3
Tom Coombs Cl, SE9
    off Well Hall Rd 156 B4
Tom Cribb Business Cen, SE28
    off Tom Cribb Rd 137 G3
Tom Cribb Rd, SE28 . . . . .137 F3
Tom Gros Cl, E15
    off Maryland St 96 D5
Tom Hood Cl, E15
    off Maryland St 96 D5
Tom Jenkinson Rd, E16 . . . . .135 G1
Tomlins Gro, E3 . . . . .114 A3
Tomlinson Cl, E2 . . . . .13 G4
    W4 . . . . .126 B5
Tomlins Orchard, Bark. IG11 . .117 F1
Tomlins Ter, E1
    off Rhodeswell Rd 113 J5
Tomlins Wk, N7 off Briset Way . .93 F2
Tom Mann Cl, Bark. IG11 . . . .117 H1
Tom Nolan Cl, E15 . . . . .114 E2
Tompion St, EC1 . . . . .11 G4

Tom Smith Cl, SE10
  off Maze Hill 134/135 E6
Tomswood Ct, Ilf. IG6 . . . . .81 F1
Tomswood Hill, Ilf. IG6 . . . . . . .E7
Tomswood Rd, Chig. IG7 . . . .64 D6
Tom Thumbs Arch, E3
  off Malmesbury Rd 114 A2
Tom Williams Ho, SW6
  off Clem Attlee Ct 128 C6
Tonbridge Cres, Har. HA3 . . . . .69 H4
Tonbridge Ho, SE25 . . . . .188 D3
Tonbridge Rd, W.Mol. KT8 . . .179 E4
Tonbridge St, WC1 . . . . .10 A3
Tonbridge Wk, WC1
  off Tonbridge St 110/111 E3
Tonfield Rd, Sutt. SM3 . . . . . .198 C1
Tonge Cl, Beck. BR3 . . . . .190 A5
Tonsley Hill, SW18 . . . . .149 E5
Tonsley Pl, SW18 . . . . .149 E5
Tonsley Rd, SW18 . . . . .149 E5
Tonsley St, SW18 . . . . .149 E5
Tonstall Rd, Mitch. CR4 . . . . .186 A2
Tony Cannell Ms, E3
  off Maplin St 113 J3
Tooke Cl, Pnr. HA5 . . . . .66 E1
Tookey Cl, Har. HA3 . . . . .69 J7
Took's Ct, EC4 . . . . .19 E3
Tooley St, SE1 . . . . .28 C1
Toorack Rd, Har. HA3 . . . . . . .68 A2
Tooting Bec Gdns, SW16 . . . .168 D4
Tooting Bec Rd, SW16 . . . . . .168 A3
  SW17 . . . . .168 A3
TOOTING GRAVENEY, SW17 . .167 H6
Tooting Gro, SW17 . . . . .167 H5
Tooting High St, SW17 . . . . . .167 H6
Tootswood Rd, Brom. BR2 . . .190 E5
Topaz Ho, E15 *off Romford Rd* .97 F6
Topaz Wk, NW2 *off Marble Dr* . .72 A7
Topcliffe Dr, Orp. BR6 . . . . . .207 G4
Topham Sq, N17 . . . . .75 J1
Topham St, EC1 . . . . .11 E5
Top Ho Ri, E4 *off Parkhill Rd* . . .46 C7
Topiary Sq, Rich. TW9 . . . . . .145 J3
Topley St, SE9 . . . . .156 A4
Topmast Pt, E14 . . . . .134 A2
Top Pk, Beck. BR3 . . . . .190 E5
Topp Wk, NW2 . . . . .89 J2
Topsfield Cl, N8
  off Wolseley Rd 74 D5
Topsfield Par, N8
  off Tottenham La 74/75 E5
Topsfield Rd, N8 . . . . .74 E5
Topsham Rd, SW17 . . . . .167 J3
Torbay Rd, NW6 . . . . .90 C7
  Harrow HA2 . . . . .84 E2
Torbay St, NW1 *off Hawley Rd* . . .92 B7
Torbitt Way, Ilf. IG2 . . . . .81 J5
Torbridge Cl, Edg. HA8 . . . . . .53 H7
Torbrook Cl, Bex. DA5 . . . . . .159 E6
Torcross Dr, SE23 . . . . .171 F2
Torcross Rd, Ruis. HA4 . . . . . .84 B3
Tor Gdns, W8 . . . . .128 D2
Tor Gro, SE28 . . . . .137 H1
Tormead Cl, Sutt. SM1 . . . . . .198 D6
Tormount Rd, SE18 . . . . .137 H6
Toronto Av, E12 . . . . .98 C4
Toronto Rd, E11 . . . . .96 D4
  Ilford IG1 . . . . .99 E1
Torquay Gdns, Ilf. IG4 . . . . . . .80 A4
Torquay St, W2 . . . . .14 A2
Torrance Cl, SE7 . . . . .136 A6
Torrens Rd, E15 . . . . .97 F6
  SW2 . . . . .151 F5
Torrens Sq, E15 . . . . .97 E6
Torrens St, EC1 . . . . .11 F2
Torres Sq, E14
  off Maritime Quay 134 A5
Torre Wk, Cars. SM5 . . . . . . .199 H1
Torrey Dr, SW9 *off Overton Rd* . .151 G2
Torriano Av, NW5 . . . . .92 D5
Torriano Cotts, NW5
  off Torriano Av 92 C5
Torriano Ms, NW5
  off Torriano Av 92 D5
Torridge Gdns, SE15 . . . . . . .153 F4
Torridge Rd, Th.Hth. CR7 . . . .187 H5
Torridon Rd, SE6 . . . . .172 D1
  SE13 . . . . .154 D7
Torrington Av, N12 . . . . .57 G5
Torrington Cl, N12 . . . . .57 G4
  Esher (Clay.) KT10 . . . . . . .194 B6
Torrington Dr, Har. HA2 . . . . . .85 H4
  Loughton IG10 . . . . .49 F4
Torrington Gdns, N11 . . . . . . .58 C6
  Greenford UB6 . . . . .87 F7
  Loughton IG10 . . . . .49 F4
Torrington Gro, N12 . . . . .57 H5
Torrington Pk, N12 . . . . .57 F5
Torrington Pl, E1 . . . . .29 J1
  WC1 . . . . .17 G1
Torrington Rd, E18 . . . . .79 G3
  Dagenham RM8 . . . . .101 F1
  Esher (Clay.) KT10 . . . . . . .194 B6
  Greenford UB6 . . . . .105 F1
Torrington Sq, WC1 . . . . .9 J6

Torrington Sq, Croy. CR0
  off Tavistock Gro 188 A7
Torrington Way, Mord. SM4 . .184 D6
Tor Rd, Well. DA16 . . . . .158 C1
Torr Rd, SE20 . . . . .171 G7
Torver Rd, Har. HA1 . . . . .68 B4
Torver Way, Orp. BR6 . . . . . . .207 G3
Torwood Rd, SW15 . . . . .147 G5
Tothill St, SW1 . . . . .25 H4
Totnes Rd, Well. DA16 . . . . . .138 B7
Totnes Wk, N2 . . . . .73 G4
Tottan Ter, E1 . . . . .113 G6
Tottenhall Rd, N13 . . . . .59 G6
TOTTENHAM, N17 . . . . .76 B1
Tottenham Ct Rd, W1 . . . . .9 G6
Tottenham Grn E, N15 . . . . . .76 C4
TOTTENHAM HALE, N17 . . . . .76 E3
Tottenham Hale Retail Pk, N15 .76 D4
Tottenham La, N8 . . . . .74 E5
Tottenham Ms, W1 . . . . .17 G1
Tottenham Rd, N1 . . . . .94 B6
Tottenham St, W1 . . . . .17 G2
Totterdown St, SW17 . . . . . . .167 J4
TOTTERIDGE, N20 . . . . .56 B1
Totteridge Common, N20 . . . .55 G2
Totteridge Grn, N20 . . . . .56 D2
Totteridge Ho, SW11 . . . . . . .149 G2
Totteridge La, N20 . . . . .56 D2
Totteridge Village, N20 . . . . . .56 B1
Totternhoe Cl, Har. HA3 . . . . .69 F5
Totton Rd, Th.Hth. CR7 . . . . .187 G3
Toulmin St, SE1 . . . . .27 J4
Toulon St, SE5 . . . . .35 J7
Tournay Rd, SW6 . . . . .128 C7
Tours Pas, SW11 . . . . .149 G4
Toussaint Wk, SE16 . . . . .29 J5
Tovil Cl, SE20 . . . . .188 D2
Towcester Rd, E3 . . . . .114 B4
Tower 42, EC2 . . . . .20 D3
Tower Br, E1 . . . . .29 F2
  SE1 . . . . .29 F2
Tower Br App, E1 . . . . .29 F1
★ Tower Br Exhib, SE1 . . . . . .29 F2
Tower Br Piazza, SE1 . . . . . . .29 F2
Tower Br Rd, SE1 . . . . .28 D6
Tower Br Wf, E1 . . . . .29 H2
Tower Cl, NW3
  off Lyndhurst Rd 91 G5
  SE20 . . . . .170 F7
  Ilford IG6 . . . . .65 E6
  Orpington BR6 . . . . .207 J2
Tower Ct, WC2 . . . . .18 A4
Tower Gdns, Esher (Clay.) KT10 .194 D7
Tower Gdns Rd, N17 . . . . .75 J1
Tower Hamlets Rd, E7 . . . . . . .97 F4
  E17 . . . . .78 A3
Tower Hill, EC3 . . . . .21 E6
Tower Hill Ter, EC3
  off Tower Hill 112 B7
Tower La, Wem. HA9
  off Main Dr 87 G3
Tower Ms, E17 . . . . .78 A4
★ Tower Millennium Pier, EC3 .29 E5
Tower Mill Rd, SE15 . . . . .36 D6
★ Tower of London, EC3 . . . . .21 F6
Tower Pl, EC3 . . . . .20 E6
Tower Pt, Enf. EN2 . . . . .44 A4
Tower Ri, Rich. TW9
  off Jocelyn Rd 145 H3
Tower Rd, NW10 . . . . .89 G7
  Belvedere DA17 . . . . .139 J4
  Bexleyheath DA7 . . . . .159 H4
  Orpington BR6 . . . . .207 J2
  Twickenham TW1 . . . . .162 C3
Tower Royal, EC4 . . . . .20 A5
Towers Pl, Rich. TW9
  off Eton St 145 H5
Towers Rd, Pnr. HA5 . . . . .66 E1
  Southall UB1 . . . . .103 G4
Tower St, WC2 . . . . .17 J4
Tower Ter, N22 *off Mayes Rd* . .75 F2
  SE4 *off Foxberry Rd* 153 H4
Tower Vw, Croy. CR0 . . . . . . .189 G7
Towfield Rd, Felt. TW13 . . . . .161 F2
Towing Path Wk, N1 . . . . .10 A1
Town, The, Enf. EN2 . . . . .44 A3
Towncourt Cres, Orp. BR5 . . .193 F5
Towncourt La, Orp. BR5 . . . . .193 G6
Town Ct Path, N4 . . . . .93 J1
Towney Mead, Nthlt. UB5 . . . .103 F2
Towney Mead Ct, Nthlt. UB5
  off Towney Mead 103 F2
Town Fm Way, Stai. (Stanw.) TW19
  off Town La 140 A7
Townfield Rd, Hayes UB3 . . . .121 J1
Townfield Sq, Hayes UB3 . . . .121 J1
Town Fld Way, Islw. TW7 . . . .144 D2
Town Hall App, N16
  off Milton Gro 94 B4
Town Hall App Rd, N15 . . . . . .76 C4
Town Hall Av, W4 . . . . .126 D5
Town Hall Rd, SW11 . . . . .149 J3
Townholm Cres, W7 . . . . .124 C3
Town La, Stai. (Stanw.) TW19 .140 A6

Townley Ct, E15 . . . . .97 F6
Townley Rd, SE22 . . . . .152 B5
  Bexleyheath DA6 . . . . .159 F5
Townley St, SE17 . . . . .36 B3
Townmead Business Cen, SW6
  off William Morris Way 149 F3
Town Meadow, Brent. TW8 . . .125 G7
Townmead Rd, SW6 . . . . .149 F2
  Richmond TW9 . . . . .146 B2
Town Quay, Bark. IG11 . . . . . .117 E1
Town Rd, N9 . . . . .60 E2
Townsend Av, N14 . . . . .58 D4
Townsend Ind Est, NW10 . . . .106 D2
Townsend La, NW9 . . . . .70 D7
Townsend Rd, N15 . . . . .76 C5
  Southall UB1 . . . . .122 E1
Townsend St, SE17 . . . . .36 C2
Townsend Yd, N6 . . . . .92 B1
Townshend Cl, Sid. DA14 . . . .176 B6
Townshend Est, NW8 . . . . .7 G1
Townshend Rd, NW8 . . . . . . .109 H1
  Chislehurst BR7 . . . . .174 E5
  Richmond TW9 . . . . .145 J4
Townshend Ter, Rich. TW9 . . .145 J4
Townson Av, Nthlt. UB5 . . . . .102 A3
Townson Way, Nthlt. UB5
  off Townson Av 102 A2
Towpath Rd, N18 . . . . .61 G6
Towpath Wk, E9 . . . . .95 J5
Towpath Way, Croy. CR0 . . . .188 C6
Towton Rd, SE27 . . . . .169 J2
Toynbec Cl, Chis. BR7
  off Beechwood Ri 174/175 E4
★ Toynbee Hall, E1 . . . . .21 F4
Toynbee Rd, SW20 . . . . .184 B1
Toynbee St, E1 . . . . .21 F2
Toyne Way, N6 *off Gaskell Rd* . .73 J6
Tracey Av, NW2 . . . . .89 J5
Tracy Ct, Stan. HA7 . . . . .53 F7
Trade Cl, N13 . . . . .59 G4
Trader Rd, E6 . . . . .116 E6
Tradescant Rd, SW8 . . . . .131 E7
Trading Est Rd, NW10 . . . . . .106 C4
Trafalgar Av, N17 . . . . .60 B6
  SE15 . . . . .37 G4
  Worcester Park KT4 . . . . . .198 A1
Trafalgar Business Cen, Bark.
  IG11 . . . . .117 J4
Trafalgar Cl, SE16
  off Greenland Quay 133 H4
Trafalgar Ct, E1 *off Glamis Rd* .113 F7
Trafalgar Gdns, E1 . . . . .113 G5
  W8 .22 B5
Trafalgar Gro, SE10 . . . . .134 D6
Trafalgar Ms, E9 . . . . .95 J6
Trafalgar Pl, E11 . . . . .79 G4
  N18 . . . . .60 D5
Trafalgar Rd, SE10 . . . . .134 D6
  SW19 . . . . .167 E7
  Twickenham TW2 . . . . .162 A2
Trafalgar Sq, SW1 . . . . .25 J1
  WC2 . . . . .25 J1
Trafalgar St, SE17 . . . . .36 B3
Trafalgar Ter, Har. HA1
  off Nelson Rd 86 B1
Trafalgar Way, E14 . . . . .134 C1
  Croydon CR0 . . . . .201 F2
Trafford Cl, E15 . . . . .96 B5
  Ilford IG6 . . . . .65 J6
Trafford Rd, Th.Hth. CR7 . . . .187 F5
Tralee Ct, SE16
  off Masters Dr 132/133 E5
Tramsheds Ind Est, Croy. CR0 .186 D7
Tramway Av, E15 . . . . .96 E7
  N9 .45 E7
Tramway Cl, SE20 . . . . .189 F1
Tramway Path, Mitch. CR4 . . .185 J5
Tranby Pl, E9
  off Homerton High St 95 G5
Tranley Ms, NW3 *off Fleet Rd* . .91 H5
Tranmere Rd, N9 . . . . .44 C7
  SW18 . . . . .167 F2
  Twickenham TW2 . . . . .143 H7
Tranquil Pas, SE3
  off Tranquil Vale 155 F2
Tranquil Vale, SE3 . . . . .155 E2
Transept St, NW1 . . . . .15 G2
Transmere Cl, Orp. BR5 . . . . .193 F6
Transmere Rd, Orp. BR5 . . . .193 F6
Transom Cl, SE16
  off Plough Way 133 H4
Transom Sq, E14 . . . . .134 B4
Transport Av, Brent. TW8 . . . .124 D5
Tranton Rd, SE16 . . . . .29 J5
Traps Hill, Loug. IG10 . . . . . . .48 C3
Traps La, N.Mal. KT3 . . . . . . .182 E1
Travellers Way, Houns. TW4 . .142 C2
Travers Cl, E17 . . . . .77 G1
Travers Rd, N7 . . . . .93 G3
Treacy Cl, Bushey (Bushey Hth)
  WD23 . . . . .51 J2
Treadgold St, W11 . . . . .108 A7
Treadway St, E2 . . . . .112 E2
Treadway St, E2 . . . . .112 E2
Treasury Cl, Wall. SM6 . . . . . .200 D5
Treaty Cen, Houns. TW3 . . . .143 H3

Treaty Rd, Houns. TW3
  off Hanworth Rd 143 H3
Treaty St, N1 . . . . .111 F1
Trebeck St, W1 . . . . .24 D1
Trebovir Rd, SW5 . . . . .128 D5
Treby St, E3 . . . . .113 J4
Trecastle Way, N7
  off Carleton Rd 92 D4
Tredegar Ms, E3 *off Tredegar Ter* .113 J3
Tredegar Rd, E3 . . . . .113 J2
  N11 . . . . .58 D7
Tredegar Sq, E3 . . . . .113 J3
Tredegar Ter, E3 . . . . .113 J3
Trederwen Rd, E8 . . . . .112 D1
Tredown Rd, SE26 . . . . .171 F5
Tredwell Cl, SW2 *off Hillside Rd* .169 F2
  Bromley BR2 . . . . .192 B4
Tredwell Rd, SE27 . . . . .169 H4
Tree Cl, Rich. TW10 . . . . .163 G1
Treen Av, SW13 . . . . .147 F3
Tree Rd, E16 . . . . .115 J6
Treeside Cl, West Dr. UB7 . . .120 A4
Treetops Cl, SE2 . . . . .138 E5
Treetops Vw, Loug. IG10 . . . . .48 A7
Treeview Cl, SE19 . . . . .188 B1
Treewall Gdns, Brom. BR1 . . .173 H4
Trefgarne Rd, Dag. RM10 . . . .101 G2
Trefil Wk, N7 . . . . .93 E4
Trefoil Ho, Erith DA18
  off Kale Rd 138/139 E2
Trefoil Rd, SW18 . . . . .149 F5
Tregaron Av, N8 . . . . .74 E6
Tregaron Gdns, N.Mal. KT3
  off Avenue Rd 182/183 E4
Tregarvon Rd, SW11 . . . . . . .150 A4
Tregenna Av, Har. HA2 . . . . . .85 F4
Tregenna Cl, N14 . . . . .42 C5
Tregenna Ct, Har. HA2 . . . . . .85 G4
Tregony Rd, Orp. BR6 . . . . . .207 J4
Trego Rd, E9 . . . . .96 A7
Tregothnan Rd, SW9 . . . . . . .151 E3
Tregunter Rd, SW10 . . . . .30 C5
Trehearn Rd, Ilf. IG6 . . . . .65 G7
Treherne Ct, SW9
  off Eythorne Rd 151 G1
  SW17 . . . . .168 A4
Trehern Rd, SW14 . . . . .146 D3
Trehurst St, E5 . . . . .95 H5
Trelawney Cl, E17 *off Orford Rd* .78 B4
Trelawney Est, E9 . . . . .95 F6
Trelawney Rd, Ilf. IG6 . . . . . . .65 G7
Trelawn Rd, E10 . . . . .96 C3
  SW2 . . . . .151 G5
Trellick Twr, W10 . . . . .108 C4
Trellis Sq, E3
  off Malmesbury Rd 113 J3
Treloar Gdns, SE19
  off Hancock Rd 170 A6
Tremadoc Rd, SW4 . . . . .150 D4
Tremaine Cl, SE4 . . . . .154 A2
Tremaine Rd, SE20 . . . . .189 E2
Trematon Pl, Tedd. TW11 . . . .163 F7
Tremlett Gro, N19 . . . . .92 C3
Tremlett Ms, N19 . . . . .92 C3
Trenance Gdns, Ilf. IG3 . . . . .100 A3
Trenance, N9
  off Fulbeck Dr 70/71 E4
  Stanmore HA7 . . . . .52 D6
Trenchard Av, Ruis. HA4 . . . . .84 B4
Trenchard Cl, NW9
  off Fulbeck Dr 70/71 E4
  Stanmore HA7 . . . . .52 D6
Trenchard Ct, Mord. SM4
  off Green La 184 D6
Trenchard St, SE10 . . . . .134 D5
Trenchold St, SW8 . . . . .34 A6
Trenholme Cl, SE20 . . . . .171 E7
Trenholme Rd, SE20 . . . . . . .170 E7
Trenholme Ter, SE20 . . . . . . .170 E7
Trenmar Gdns, NW10 . . . . . .107 H3
Trent Av, W5 . . . . .125 F3
Trentbridge Cl, Ilf. IG6 . . . . . .65 J6
Trent Gdns, N14 . . . . .42 B6
Trentham St, SW18 . . . . .166 D1
★ Trent Park Country Pk, Barn.
  EN4 . . . . .42 B2
Trent Rd, SW2 . . . . .151 F5
  Buckhurst Hill IG9 . . . . .63 H1
Trent Way, Wor.Pk. KT4 . . . . .197 J3
Trentwood Side, Enf. EN2 . . . .43 F3
Treport St, SW18 . . . . .149 E7
Tresco Cl, Brom. BR1 . . . . . . .172 E6
Trescoe Gdns, Har. HA2 . . . . .67 E7
Tresco Gdns, Ilf. IG3 . . . . . . .100 A3
Tresco Rd, SE15 . . . . .153 E4
Tresham Cres, NW8 . . . . .7 G4
Tresham Rd, Bark. IG11 . . . . . .99 J7
Tresham Wk, E9
  off Churchill Wk 95 F5
Tresilian Av, N21 . . . . .43 F5
Tressell Cl, N1 *off Sebbon St* . .93 H7
Tressillian Cres, SE4 . . . . . . .154 A3
Tressillian Rd, SE4 . . . . .153 J4
Trestis Cl, Hayes UB4
  off Jollys La 102/103 E5
Treswell Rd, Dag. RM9 . . . . . .119 E1
Tretawn Gdns, NW7 . . . . .55 E4
Tretawn Pk, NW7 . . . . .55 E4

Trevanion Rd, W14 . . . .**128** B5
Treve Av, Har. HA1 . . . .**67** J7
Trevelyan Av, E12 . . . .**98** C4
Trevelyan Cres, Har. HA3 . . . .**69** G7
Trevelyan Gdns, NW10 . . . .**107** J1
Trevelyan Rd, E15 . . . .**97** E4
   SW17 . . . .**167** H5
Treveris St, SE1 . . . .**27** G2
Treverton St, W10 . . . .**108** A4
Treves Cl, N21 . . . .**43** F5
Treville St, SW15 . . . .**147** H7
Treviso Rd, SE23 off Farren Rd .**171** G2
Trevithick St, SE8 . . . .**134** A5
Trevone Gdns, Pnr. HA5 . . . .**67** E6
Trevor Cl, Barn. EN4 . . . .**41** G5
   Bromley BR2 . . . .**191** F7
   Harrow HA3 off Kenton La . . .**52** C7
   Isleworth TW7 . . . .**144** C5
   Northolt UB5 . . . .**102** C2
Trevor Gdns, Edg. HA8 . . . .**70** D1
   Northolt UB5 . . . .**102** C2
Trevor Pl, SW7 . . . .**23** H4
Trevor Rd, SW19 . . . .**166** B7
   Edgware HA8 . . . .**70** D1
   Hayes UB3 . . . .**121** H2
   Woodford Green IG8 . . . .**63** G7
Trevor Sq, SW7 . . . .**23** J4
Trevor St, SW7 . . . .**23** H4
Trevor Wk, SW7 off Trevor Sq . .**129** J4
Trevose Rd, E17 . . . .**78** D1
Trevose Way, Wat. WD19 . . . . . .**50** C3
Trewenna Dr, Chess. KT9 . . . . . .**195** G5
Trewince Rd, SW20 . . . .**183** J1
Trewint St, SW18 . . . .**167** F2
Trewsbury Ho, SE2
   off Hartslock Dr **138** D2
Trewsbury Rd, SE26 . . . .**171** G5
Triandra Way, Hayes UB4 . . . . . .**102** D5
Triangle, The, EC1 . . . .**11** H5
   N13 off Lodge Dr **59** G4
   Barking IG11 off Tanner St . . .**99** F8
   Hampton TW12 off High St . .**179** J1
   Kingston upon Thames KT1
     off Kenley Rd **182** C2
Triangle Business Cen, NW10
   off Enterprise Way **107** G3
Triangle Ct, E16 off Tollgate Rd .**116** A5
Triangle Est, SE11 . . . .**35** E4
Triangle Pas, Barn. EN4
   off Station App **41** F4
Triangle Pl, SW4 . . . .**150** D4
Triangle Rd, E8 . . . .**112** E1
Trident Gdns, Nthlt. UB5
   off Jetstar Way **102** D3
Trident St, SE16 . . . .**133** G4
Trident Way, Sthl. UB2 . . . .**122** B3
Trig La, EC4 . . . .**19** J5
Trigon Rd, SW8 . . . .**34** D7
Trilby Rd, SE23 . . . .**171** G2
Trimmer Wk, Brent. TW8 . . . . . .**125** H6
Trim St, SE14 . . . .**133** J6
Trinder Gdns, N19
   off Trinder Rd **92/93** E1
Trinder Ms, Tedd. TW11 . . . .**162** D5
Trinder Rd, N19 . . . .**93** E1
   Barnet EN5 . . . .**39** J5
Tring Av, W5 . . . .**125** J1
   Southall UB1 . . . .**103** F6
   Wembley HA9 . . . .**88** A6
Tring Cl, Ilf. IG2 . . . .**81** F5
Trinidad St, E14 . . . .**113** J7
Trinity Av, N2 . . . .**73** G3
   Enfield EN1 . . . .**44** C6
Trinity Buoy Wf, E14 . . . .**115** F7
Trinity Ch Pas, SW13 . . . .**127** H6
Trinity Ch Rd, SW13 . . . .**127** H6
Trinity Ch Sq, SE1 . . . .**28** A5
Trinity Cl, E8 . . . .**94** C6
   E11 . . . .**97** E2
   NW3 off Hampstead High St . .**91** G4
   SE13 off Wisteria Rd **154** D4
   SW4 off The Pavement **150** C4
   Bromley BR2 . . . .**206** B1
   Hounslow TW4 . . . .**143** E4
Trinity Cotts, Rich. TW9
   off Trinity Rd **145** J3
Trinity Ct, N1 off Downham Rd .**94** B7
   NW2 off Anson Rd **89** J5
   SE7 off Charlton La **136** A4
Trinity Cres, SW17 . . . .**167** J2
Trinity Gdns, E16 off Cliff Wk . .**115** F4
   SW9 . . . .**151** F4
Trinity Gro, SE10 . . . .**154** C1
 ★ **Trinity Ho**, EC3 . . . .**21** E5
Trinity Ms, SE20 . . . .**189** E1
   W10 off Cambridge Gdns . . .**108** A6
Trinity Path, SE26 . . . .**171** F3
Trinity Pl, EC3 . . . .**21** F6
   Bexleyheath DA6 . . . .**159** F4
Trinity Ri, SW2 . . . .**169** G1
Trinity Rd, N2 . . . .**73** G3
   N22 . . . .**75** E1
   SW17 . . . .**167** J2
   SW18 . . . .**149** G5
   SW19 . . . .**166** D6

Trinity Rd, Ilf. IG6 . . . .**81** F3
   Richmond TW9 . . . .**145** J3
   Southall UB1 . . . .**122** E1
Trinity Sq, EC3 . . . .**21** E6
Trinity St, E16 off Vincent St **115** G5
   SE1 . . . .**28** A4
   Enfield EN2 . . . .**43** J2
Trinity Wk, NW3 . . . .**91** F6
Trinity Way, E4 . . . .**61** J6
   W3 . . . .**107** F6
Trio Pl, SE1 . . . .**28** A4
Tristan Sq, SE3 . . . .**155** E3
Tristram Cl, E17 . . . .**78** D3
Tristram Dr, N9 off Barbot Cl **60** D3
Tristram Rd, Brom. BR1 . . . .**173** F4
Triton Sq, NW1 . . . .**9** F5
Tritton Av, Croy. CR0 . . . .**201** E4
Tritton Rd, SE21 . . . .**170** A3
Triumph Cl, Hayes UB3 . . . .**121** F7
Triumph Ho, Bark. IG11 . . . .**118** B3
Triumph Rd, E6 . . . .**116** C6
Trocadero Cen, W1 . . . .**17** H6
Trojan Ct, NW6
   off Willesden La **90** B7
Trojan Way, Croy. CR0 . . . .**201** F3
Troon Cl, SE16
   off Masters Dr **132/133** E5
   SE28 off Fairway Dr **118** D6
Troon St, E1 off White Horse Rd .**113** H6
Trosley Rd, Belv. DA17 . . . .**139** G6
Trossachs Rd, SE22 . . . .**152** B5
Trothy Rd, SE1 . . . .**37** J1
Trott Rd, N10 . . . .**57** J7
Trott St, SW11 . . . .**149** H1
Trotwood, Chig. IG7 . . . .**65** G6
Troughton Rd, SE7 . . . .**135** H5
Troutbeck Rd, SE14 . . . .**153** H1
Trout Rd, West Dr. UB7 . . . .**120** A1
Trouville Rd, SW4 . . . .**150** C6
Trowbridge Est, E9
   off Osborne Rd **95** J6
Trowbridge Rd, E9 . . . .**95** J6
Trowlock Av, Tedd. TW11 . . . . . .**163** F6
Trowlock Island, Tedd. TW11 . . .**163** G5
Trowlock Way, Tedd. TW11 . . . . .**163** G6
Troy Ct, SE18 . . . .**137** E4
Troy Rd, SE19 . . . .**170** A6
Troy Town, SE15 . . . .**152** D3
Trubshaw Rd, Sthl. UB2
   off Havelock Rd **123** H3
Truesdale Rd, E6 . . . .**116** C6
Trulock Ct, N17 . . . .**60** D7
Trulock Rd, N17 . . . .**60** D7
Truman Cl, Edg. HA8
   off Pavilion Way **54** B7
Truman's Rd, N16 . . . .**94** B5
Trumpers Way, W7 . . . .**124** B3
Trumpington Rd, E7 . . . .**97** F4
Trump St, EC2 . . . .**20** A4
Trundlers Way, Bushey (Bushey Hth)
   WD23 . . . .**52** B1
Trundle St, SE1 . . . .**27** J3
Trundleys Rd, SE8 . . . .**133** G5
Trundleys Ter, SE8 . . . .**133** G4
Truro Gdns, Ilf. IG1 . . . .**80** B7
Truro Rd, E17 . . . .**77** J4
   N22 . . . .**59** E7
Truro St, NW5 . . . .**92** A6
Truslove Rd, SE27 . . . .**169** G5
Trussley Rd, W6 . . . .**127** J3
Trust Wk, SE21 off Peabody Hill .**169** H1
Tryfan Cl, Ilf. IG4 . . . .**80** A5
Tryon Cres, E9 . . . .**113** F1
Tryon St, SW3 . . . .**31** J3
Trystings Cl, Esher (Clay.) KT10 .**194** D6
Tuam Rd, SE18 . . . .**137** G6
Tubbenden Cl, Orp. BR6 . . . .**207** H2
Tubbenden Dr, Orp. BR6 . . . .**207** G4
Tubbenden La, Orp. BR6 . . . .**207** H3
Tubbenden La S, Orp. BR6 . . . . .**207** G5
Tubbs Rd, NW10 . . . .**107** F2
Tudor Av, Hmptn. TW12 . . . .**161** G6
   Worcester Park KT4 . . . .**197** H3
Tudor Cl, N6 . . . .**74** C7
   NW3 . . . .**91** H5
   NW7 . . . .**55** G6
   NW9 . . . .**88** C2
   SW2 off Elm Pk **151** F6
   Chessington KT9 . . . .**195** H5
   Chigwell IG7 . . . .**64** D4
   Chislehurst BR7 . . . .**192** C1
   Pinner HA5 . . . .**66** A5
   Sutton SM3 . . . .**198** A5
   Wallington SM6 . . . .**200** C7
   Woodford Green IG8 . . . .**63** H5
Tudor Ct, E17 . . . .**77** H7
   Feltham TW13 . . . .**160** C4
Tudor Ct N, Wem. HA9 . . . .**88** A5
Tudor Ct S, Wem. HA9 . . . .**88** A5
Tudor Cres, Enf. EN2 . . . .**43** H1
   Ilford IG6 . . . .**65** H6
Tudor Dr, Kings.T. KT2 . . . .**163** H5
   Morden SM4 . . . .**184** A6
Tudor Est, NW10 . . . .**106** B2
Tudor Gdns, NW9 . . . .**88** C2

Tudor Gdns, SW13
   off Treen Av **146/147** E3
   W3 . . . .**106** A6
   Harrow HA3 off Tudor Rd **68** A2
   Twickenham TW1 . . . .**162** C1
   West Wickham BR4 . . . .**204** C3
Tudor Gro, E9 . . . .**95** F7
   N20 off Church Cres **57** H3
Tudor Ho, Surb. KT6
   off Lenelby Rd **196** A1
Tudor Pl, Mitch. CR4 . . . .**167** H7
Tudor Rd, E4 . . . .**62** B6
   E6 . . . .**115** J1
   E9 . . . .**113** E1
   N9 . . . .**45** E7
   SE19 . . . .**170** C7
   SE25 . . . .**189** E5
   Barking IG11 . . . .**117** J1
   Barnet EN5 . . . .**40** D3
   Beckenham BR3 . . . .**190** B3
   Hampton TW12 . . . .**161** G7
   Harrow HA3 . . . .**68** A2
   Hounslow TW3 . . . .**144** A4
   Kingston upon Thames KT2 . .**164** A1
   Pinner HA5 . . . .**66** C2
   Southall UB1 . . . .**102** E7
Tudor St, EC4 . . . .**19** F5
Tudor Wk, Bex. DA5 . . . .**159** E6
Tudor Way, N14 . . . .**58** D1
   W3 . . . .**126** A2
   Orpington BR5 . . . .**193** G6
Tudor Well Cl, Stan. HA7 . . . .**53** E5
Tudway Rd, SE3 . . . .**155** H3
TUFNELL PARK, N7 . . . .**92** D4
Tufnell Pk Rd, N7 . . . .**92** C4
   N19 . . . .**92** C4
Tufter Rd, Chig. IG7 . . . .**65** J5
Tufton Gdns, W.Mol. KT8 . . . . . .**179** H2
Tufton Rd, E4 . . . .**62** A4
Tufton St, SW1 . . . .**25** J5
Tugboat St, SE28 . . . .**137** H2
Tugela Rd, Croy. CR0 . . . .**188** A6
Tugela St, SE6 . . . .**171** J2
Tugmutton Cl, Orp. BR6
   off Acorn Way **206/207** E4
Tuilerie St, E2 . . . .**13** H1
Tulip Cl, E6
   off Bradley Stone Rd **116** C5
   Croydon CR0 . . . .**203** G1
   Hampton TW12
     off Partridge Rd **161** F6
   Southall UB2 off Chevy Rd . .**123** J2
Tulip Ct, Pnr. HA5 . . . .**66** C3
Tulip Gdns, Ilf. IG1 . . . .**98** E6
Tulip Way, West Dr. UB7 . . . .**120** A4
Tull St, Mitch. CR4 . . . .**185** J7
Tulse Cl, Beck. BR3 . . . .**190** C3
TULSE HILL, SE21 . . . .**169** J1
Tulse Hill, SW2 . . . .**151** G6
Tulse Hill Est, SW2 . . . .**151** G6
Tulsemere Rd, SE27 . . . .**169** J2
Tumbling Bay, Walt. KT12 . . . . . .**178** A6
Tummons Gdns, SE25 . . . .**188** B2
Tuncombe Rd, N18 . . . .**60** B4
Tunis Rd, W12 . . . .**127** H1
Tunley Grn, E14 off Burdett Rd . .**113** J5
Tunley Rd, NW10 . . . .**106** E1
   SW17 . . . .**168** A1
Tunmarsh La, E13 . . . .**115** J3
Tunnan Leys, E6 . . . .**116** D6
Tunnel Av, SE10 . . . .**134** D2
Tunnel Gdns, N11 . . . .**58** C7
Tunnel Rd, SE16
   off St. Marychurch St **133** F2
Tunstall Cl, Orp. BR6 . . . .**207** H4
Tunstall Rd, SW9 . . . .**151** F4
   Croydon CR0 . . . .**202** B1
Tunstall Wk, Brent. TW8 . . . .**125** H6
Tunstock Way, Belv. DA17 . . . . .**139** E3
Tunworth Cl, NW9 . . . .**70** C6
Tunworth Cres, SW15 . . . .**147** F6
Tun Yd, SW8 off Peardon St **150** B2
Tupelo Rd, E10 . . . .**96** B2
Tuppy St, SE28 . . . .**137** F3
Turenne Cl, SW18 . . . .**149** F4
Turin Rd, N9 . . . .**45** F7
Turin St, E2 . . . .**13** H4
Turkey Oak Cl, SE19 . . . .**188** B1
Turk's Head Yd, EC1 . . . .**19** G1
Turks Row, SW3 . . . .**32** A3
Turle Rd, N4 . . . .**93** F2
   SW16 . . . .**186** F2
Turlewray Cl, N4 . . . .**93** F1
Turley Cl, E15 . . . .**115** E1
Turnagain La, EC4 . . . .**19** G3
Turnage Rd, Dag. RM8 . . . .**100** E1
Turnberry Cl, NW4 . . . .**72** A2
   SE16 off Ryder Dr **132/133** E5
Turnberry Ct, Wat. WD19 . . . .**50** C3
Turnberry Quay, E14
   off Pepper St **134** B3
Turnberry Way, Orp. BR6 . . . . . .**207** G1
Turnbury Cl, SE28 . . . .**118** D6
Turnchapel Ms, SW4
   off Cedars Rd **150** B3

Turner Av, N15 . . . .**76** B4
   Mitcham CR4 . . . .**185** J1
   Twickenham TW2 . . . .**161** J3
Turner Cl, NW11 . . . .**72** E6
   SW9 . . . .**151** H1
   Wembley HA0 . . . .**87** G5
Turner Dr, NW11 . . . .**72** E6
Turner Pl, SW11 off Cairns Rd . .**149** H5
Turner Rd, E17 . . . .**78** C3
   Edgware HA8 . . . .**69** J3
   New Malden KT3 . . . .**182** D7
Turners Meadow Way, Beck.
   BR3 . . . .**189** J1
Turners Rd, E3 . . . .**113** J5
Turner St, E1 . . . .**112** E5
   E16 . . . .**115** F6
Turners Way, Croy. CR0 . . . .**201** G2
Turners Wd, NW11 . . . .**73** F7
Turneville Rd, W14 . . . .**128** C6
Turney Grn, E14
   off Wallwood St **113** J5
Turney Rd, SE21 . . . .**152** A7
Turnham Grn Ter, W4 . . . .**126** E4
Turnham Grn Ter Ms, W4
   off Turnham Grn Ter **126/127** E4
Turnham Rd, SE4 . . . .**153** H5
Turnmill St, EC1 . . . .**11** F6
Turnpike Cl, SE8
   off Amersham Vale **133** J7
Turnpike Ho, EC1 . . . .**11** H4
Turnpike La, N8 . . . .**75** F4
   Sutton SM1 . . . .**199** F5
Turnpike Link, Croy. CR0 . . . . . .**202** B2
Turnpike Ms, N8 off Turnpike La .**75** G3
Turnpike Way, Islw. TW7 . . . . . .**144** D1
Turnpin La, SE10 . . . .**134** C6
Turnstone Cl, E13 . . . .**115** G3
   NW9 off Kestrel Cl **70/71** E2
Turpentine La, SW1 . . . .**32** E3
Turpington Cl, Brom. BR2 . . . . . .**192** B6
Turpington La, Brom. BR2 . . . . . .**192** B7
Turpin Rd, Felt. TW14
   off Staines Rd **141** J6
Turpins La, Wdf.Grn. IG8 . . . .**64** C5
Turpin Way, N19
   off Elthorne Rd **92** D2
   Wallington SM6 . . . .**200** B7
Turquand St, SE17 . . . .**36** A2
Turret Gro, SW4 . . . .**150** C3
Turton Rd, Wem. HA0 . . . .**87** H5
Turville St, E2 . . . .**13** F5
Tuscan Rd, SE18 . . . .**137** G5
Tuskar St, SE10 . . . .**134** E5
Tustin Est, SE15 . . . .**133** F6
Tuttlebee La, Buck.H. IG9 . . . . . .**63** G2
Tweedale Ct, E15 . . . .**96** C5
Tweeddale Rd, Cars. SM5 . . . . .**199** G1
Tweedmouth Rd, E13 . . . .**115** H2
Tweedy Cl, Enf. EN1 . . . .**44** C5
Tweedy Rd, Brom. BR1 . . . .**191** F1
Tweezer's All, WC2 . . . .**18** E5
Twelve Acre Ho, E12
   off Grantham Rd **98** D3
Twelvetrees Cres, E3 . . . .**114** C4
Twentyman Cl, Wdf.Grn. IG8 . . . .**63** G5
TWICKENHAM, TW1 & TW2 . . . . .**162** D2
Twickenham Br, Rich. TW9 . . . . .**145** F5
   Twickenham TW1 . . . .**145** F5
Twickenham Cl, Croy. CR0 . . . . .**201** F3
Twickenham Gdns, Grnf. UB6 . . .**86** D5
   Harrow HA3 . . . .**52** B7
Twickenham Rd, E11 . . . .**96** D2
   Feltham TW13 . . . .**161** F3
   Isleworth TW7 . . . .**144** D3
   Richmond TW9 . . . .**145** F4
   Teddington TW11 . . . .**162** D5
Twickenham Trd Est, Twick. TW1 .**144** C6
Twig Folly Cl, E2 off Roman Rd . .**113** G2
Twilley St, SW18 . . . .**148** E7
Twine Cl, Bark. IG11
   off Thames Rd **118** B3
Twine Ct, E1 . . . .**113** F7
Twineham Grn, N12
   off Tillingham Way **56** D4
Twine Ter, E3 off Ropery St **113** J4
Twining Av, Twick. TW2 . . . .**161** J3
Twinn Rd, NW7 . . . .**56** B6
Twin Tumps Way, SE28 . . . .**118** A7
Twisden Rd, NW5 . . . .**92** B4
Twybridge Way, NW10 . . . .**88** C7
Twycross Ms, SE10
   off Blackwall La **134/135** E4
Twyford Abbey Rd, NW10 . . . . . .**105** J3
Twyford Av, N2 . . . .**73** J3
   W3 . . . .**106** A7
Twyford Cres, W3 . . . .**126** A1
Twyford Ho, N15 off Chisley Rd .**76** B6
Twyford Pl, WC2 . . . .**18** C3
Twyford Rd, Cars. SM5 . . . .**199** G1
   Harrow HA2 . . . .**85** H1
   Ilford IG1 . . . .**99** F5
Twyford St, N1 . . . .**111** F1
Tyas Rd, E16 . . . .**115** F4
Tybenham Rd, SW19 . . . .**184** D3
Tyberry Rd, Enf. EN3 . . . .**45** E3

Tyburn La, Har. HA1 . . . . **68** B7
Tyburn Way, W1 . . . . **16** A5
Tycehurst Hill, Loug. IG10 . . . . . **48** C4
Tye La, Orp. BR6 . . . . **207** F5
Tyers Est, SE1 . . . . **28** D3
Tyers Gate, SE1 . . . . **28** D3
Tyers St, SE11 . . . . **34** C3
Tyers Ter, SE11 . . . . **34** C4
Tyeshurst Cl, SE2 . . . . **139** E5
Tylecroft Rd, SW16 . . . . **186** E2
Tylehurst Gdns, Ilf. IG1 . . . . . . **99** F5
Tyler Cl, E2 . . . . **13** F1
   Erith DA8 off Brook St **139** H7
Tyler Cl, Sthl. UB2
   off McNair Rd **123** H3
Tylers Cl, Loug. IG10 . . . . **48** B7
Tyler's Ct, W1 . . . . **17** H4
Tylers Gate, Har. HA3 . . . . **69** H6
Tylers Path, Cars. SM5
   off Rochester Rd **199** J4
Tyler St, SE10 . . . . **135** E5
Tylney Av, SE19 . . . . **170** C5
Tylney Rd, E7 . . . . **97** J4
   Bromley BR1 . . . . **192** A2
Tymperley Ct, SW19
   off Windlesham Gro **166** B1
Tynan Cl, Felt. TW14
   off Sandycombe Rd **160** A1
Tyndale Ct, E14 . . . . **134** B5
Tyndale La, N1 off Upper St . . . **93** H7
Tyndale Ter, N1
   off Canonbury La **93** H7
Tyndall Rd, E10 . . . . **96** C2
   Welling DA16 . . . . **157** J3
Tyneham Cl, SW11
   off Shirley Gro **150** A3
Tyneham Rd, SW11 . . . . **150** A2
Tynemouth Cl, E6
   off Covelees Wall **116/117** E6
Tynemouth Rd, N15 . . . . **76** C4
   SE18 . . . . **137** J5
   Mitcham CR4 . . . . **168** A7
Tynemouth St, SW6 . . . . **149** F2
Tyne St, E1 . . . . **21** G3
Tynsdale Rd, NW10
   off Mayo Rd **88/89** E6
Tynwald Ho, SE26
   off Sydenham Hill **170** D3
Type St, E2 . . . . **113** G2
Tyrawley Rd, SW6 . . . . **148** E1
Tyre La, NW9
   off Sheaveshill Av **70/71** E4
Tyrell Cl, Har. HA1 . . . . **86** B4
Tyrell Ct, Cars. SM5 . . . . **199** J4
Tyrols Rd, SE23 off Wastdale Rd **171** G1
Tyrone Rd, E6 . . . . **116** C2
Tyron Way, Sid. DA14 . . . . **175** H4
Tyrrell Av, Well. DA16 . . . . **158** A5
Tyrrell Rd, SE22 . . . . **152** D4
Tyrrell Sq, Mitch. CR4 . . . . . . **185** H1
Tyrrel Way, NW9 . . . . **71** F7
Tyrwhitt Rd, SE4 . . . . **154** A3
Tysoe St, EC1 . . . . **11** E4
Tyson Rd, SE23 . . . . **153** F7
Tyssen Pas, E8 . . . . **94** C6
Tyssen Rd, N16 . . . . **94** C3
Tyssen St, E8 . . . . **94** C6
   N1 . . . . **12** E1
Tytherton Rd, N19 . . . . **92** D3

U

Uamvar St, E14 . . . . **114** B5
Uckfield Gro, Mitch. CR4 . . . . . **186** A1
Udall St, SW1 . . . . **33** G2
Udney Pk Rd, Tedd. TW11 . . . . **162** D5
Uffington Rd, NW10 . . . . **107** G1
   SE27 . . . . **169** G4
Ufford Cl, Har. HA3
   off Ufford Rd **51** H7
Ufford Rd, Har. HA3 . . . . **51** H7
Ufford St, SE1 . . . . **27** F3
Ufton Gro, N1 . . . . **94** A7
Ufton Rd, N1 . . . . **94** A7
Uhura Sq, N16 . . . . **94** B3
Ujima Ct, SW16
   off Sunnyhill Rd **168/169** E4
Ullathorne Rd, SW16 . . . . **168** C4
Ulleswater Rd, N14 . . . . **59** E4
Ullin St, E14 . . . . **114** C5
   off St. Leonards Rd **114** C5
Ullswater Cl, SW15 . . . . **164** D4
   Bromley BR1 . . . . **173** E6
Ullswater Ct, Har. HA2
   off Oakington Av **67** G7
Ullswater Cres, SW15 . . . . **164** D4
Ullswater Rd, SE27 . . . . **169** H2
   SW13 . . . . **127** G7
Ulster Gdns, N13 . . . . **59** J4
Ulster Pl, NW1 . . . . **8** D6
Ulster Ter, NW1 . . . . **8** D5
Ulundi Rd, SE3 . . . . **135** E6
Ulva Rd, SW15 off Ravenna Rd **148** A5
Ulverscroft Rd, SE22 . . . . **152** C5

Ulverstone Rd, SE27 . . . . **169** H2
Ulverston Rd, E17 . . . . **78** D2
Ulysses Rd, NW6 . . . . **90** C5
Umberston St, E1
   off Hessel St **112/113** E6
Umbria St, SW15 . . . . **147** G6
Umfreville Rd, N4 . . . . **75** H6
Undercliff Rd, SE13 . . . . **154** A3
UNDERHILL, Barn. EN5 . . . . . . **40** D5
Underhill, Barn. EN5 . . . . **40** D5
Underhill Pas, NW1
   off Camden High St **110** B1
Underhill Rd, SE22 . . . . **152** E6
Underhill St, NW1
   off Camden High St **110** B1
Underne Av, N14 . . . . **58** B2
Undershaft, EC3 . . . . **20** D4
Undershaw Rd, Brom. BR1 . . . **173** E3
Underwood, Croy. (New Adgtn)
   CR0 . . . . **204** C5
Underwood, The, SE9 . . . . **174** C2
Underwood Rd, E1 . . . . **13** H6
   E4 . . . . **62** B5
   Woodford Green IG8 . . . . **64** A7
Underwood Row, N1 . . . . **12** A3
Underwood St, N1 . . . . **12** A3
Undine Rd, E14 . . . . **134** B4
Undine St, SW17 . . . . **167** J5
Uneeda Dr, Grnf. UB6 . . . . **104** A1
Unicorn Ho, Brom. BR1
   off Elmfield Rd **191** G3
Union Cl, E11 . . . . **96** D4
Union Cotts, E15
   off Welfare Rd **96/97** E7
Union Ct, EC2 . . . . **20** D3
   Richmond TW9 off Eton St . . **145** H5
Union Dr, E1 off Canal Cl **113** H4
Union Gro, SW8 . . . . **150** D2
Union Jack Club, SE1
   off Waterloo Rd **131** G2
Union Rd, N11 . . . . **58** D6
   SW4 . . . . **150** D2
   SW8 . . . . **150** D2
   Bromley BR2 . . . . **192** A5
   Croydon CR0 . . . . **187** J7
   Northolt UB5 . . . . **103** G3
   Wembley HA0 . . . . **87** H6
Union Sq, N1 . . . . **111** J1
Union St, E15 . . . . **114** C1
   SE1 . . . . **27** H2
   Barnet EN5 . . . . **40** B4
   Kingston upon Thames KT1 . **181** G2
Union Wk, E2 . . . . **13** E3
Union Wf, N1 . . . . **11** J2
Unity Cl, NW10 . . . . **89** G6
   SE19 off Crown Dale **169** J5
Unity Ter, Har. HA2
   off Scott Cres **85** H2
Unity Trd Est, Wdf.Grn. IG8 . . . **80** A3
Unity Way, SE18 . . . . **136** A3
Unity Wf, SE1 . . . . **29** G3
University Cl, NW7 . . . . **55** F7
★ **University Coll London**, WC1 . . **9** H5
University Gdns, Bex. DA5 . . . . **159** F7
★ **University of London**, WC1 . . . **9** J6
University Pl, Erith DA8
   off Belmont Rd **139** H7
University Rd, SW19 . . . . **167** G6
University St, WC1 . . . . **9** G6
University Way, E16 . . . . **116** D7
Unwin Av, Felt. TW14 . . . . **141** H5
Unwin Cl, SE15 . . . . **37** H6
Unwin Rd, SW7 . . . . **23** F5
   Isleworth TW7 . . . . **144** B3
Upbrook Ms, W2 . . . . **14** D4
Upcerne Rd, SW10 . . . . **129** F7
Upchurch Cl, SE20 . . . . **171** E7
Upcroft Av, Edg. HA8 . . . . **54** C5
Updale Rd, Sid. DA14 . . . . **175** J4
Upfield, Croy. CR0 . . . . **203** E2
Upfield Rd, W7 . . . . **104** C4
Upgrove Manor Way, SW2
   off Trinity Ri **151** G7
Uphall Rd, Ilf. IG1 . . . . **99** E5
Upham Pk Rd, W4 . . . . **127** E4
Uphill Dr, NW7 . . . . **55** E5
   NW9 . . . . **70** C5
Uphill Gro, NW7 . . . . **55** E4
Uphill Rd, NW7 . . . . **54** E4
Upland Ms, SE22
   off Upland Rd **152** D5
Upland Rd, E13 off Sutton Rd . **115** F4
   SE22 . . . . **152** D5
   Bexleyheath DA7 . . . . **159** F3
   South Croydon CR2 . . . . . . **202** A5
   Sutton SM2 . . . . **199** G7
Uplands, Beck. BR3 . . . . **190** A2
Uplands, The, Loug. IG10 . . . . . **48** C3
   Ruislip HA4 . . . . **84** A1
Uplands Av, E17
   off Blackhorse La **77** G2
Uplands Business Pk, E17 . . . . **77** G2
Uplands Cl, SW14
   off Monroe Dr **146** B5

Uplands Pk Rd, Enf. EN2 . . . . . **43** G3
Uplands Rd, N8 . . . . **75** F5
   Barnet EN4 . . . . **58** A1
   Romford RM6 . . . . **82** D3
   Woodford Green IG8 . . . . **64** B7
Uplands Way, N21 . . . . **43** G5
Upney La, Bark. IG11 . . . . **99** H6
Upnor Way, SE17 . . . . **37** E3
Uppark Dr, Ilf. IG2 . . . . **81** F6
Upper Abbey Rd, Belv. DA17 . . **139** F4
Upper Addison Gdns, W14 . . . . **128** B2
Upper Bk St, E14 . . . . **134** B1
Upper Bardsey Wk, N1
   off Clephane Rd **93** J6
Upper Belgrave St, SW1 . . . . . . **24** C5
Upper Berkeley St, W1 . . . . **15** J3
Upper Beulah Hill, SE19 . . . . . **188** B1
Upper Brighton Rd, Surb. KT6 . **181** G6
Upper Brockley Rd, SE4 . . . . . **153** J2
Upper Brook St, W1 . . . . **16** B6
Upper Butts, Brent. TW8 . . . . . **125** F6
Upper Caldy Wk, N1
   off Clephane Rd **93** J6
Upper Camelford Wk, W11
   off Lancaster Rd **108** B6
Upper Cavendish Av, N3 . . . . . . **72** D3
Upper Cheyne Row, SW3 . . . . . **31** G6
UPPER CLAPTON, E5 . . . . **94** E1
Upper Clapton Rd, E5 . . . . **94** E1
Upper Clarendon Wk, W11
   off Lancaster Rd **108** B6
Upper Dengie Wk, N1
   off Popham Rd **111** J1
UPPER EDMONTON, N18 . . . . . **60** D6
UPPER ELMERS END, Beck.
   BR3 . . . . **189** J6
Upper Elmers End Rd, Beck.
   BR3 . . . . **189** H4
Upper Fm Rd, W.Mol. KT8 . . . . **179** F4
Upper Fosters, NW4
   off New Brent St **71** J5
Upper Grn E, Mitch. CR4 . . . . . **185** J3
Upper Grn W, Mitch. CR4
   off London Rd **185** J3
Upper Grenfell Wk, W11
   off Whitchurch Rd **108** A7
Upper Grosvenor St, W1 . . . . . . **16** B6
Upper Grotto Rd, Twick. TW1 . . **162** C2
Upper Grd, SE1 . . . . **26** E1
Upper Gro, SE25 . . . . **188** B4
Upper Gro Rd, Belv. DA17 . . . . **139** F6
Upper Gulland Wk, N1
   off Clephane Rd **93** J6
Upper Ham Rd, Kings.T. KT2 . . **163** G4
   Richmond TW10 . . . . **163** G4
Upper Handa Wk, N1
   off Clephane Rd **94** A6
Upper Hawkwell Wk, N1
   off Popham Rd **111** J1
Upper Hitch, Wat. WD19 . . . . . . **51** E1
UPPER HOLLOWAY, N19 . . . . . **92** C2
Upper Holly Hill Rd, Belv. DA17 **139** H5
Upper James St, W1 . . . . **17** G5
Upper John St, W1 . . . . **17** G5
Upper Lismore Wk, N1
   off Clephane Rd **93** J6
Upper Mall, W6 . . . . **127** G5
Upper Marsh, SE1 . . . . **26** D5
Upper Montagu St, W1 . . . . **15** J1
Upper Mulgrave Rd, Sutt. SM2 **198** B7
Upper N St, E14 . . . . **114** A5
UPPER NORWOOD, SE19 . . . . **170** A7
Upper Palace Rd, E.Mol. KT8 . . **179** J3
Upper Pk, Loug. IG10 . . . . **48** A4
Upper Pk Rd, N11 . . . . **58** B5
   NW3 . . . . **91** J5
   Belvedere DA17 . . . . **139** H4
   Bromley BR1 . . . . **191** H1
   Kingston upon Thames KT2 . **164** A6
Upper Phillimore Gdns, W8 . . . **128** D2
Upper Ramsey Wk, N1
   off Clephane Rd **94** A6
Upper Rawreth Wk, N1
   off Popham Rd **111** J1
Upper Richmond Rd, SW15 . . . **148** B4
Upper Richmond Rd W, SW14 . **146** B4
   Richmond TW10 . . . . **146** A4
Upper Rd, E13 . . . . **115** G3
   Wallington SM6 . . . . **200** D5
Upper St. Martin's La, WC2 . . . . **18** A5
Upper Selsdon Rd, S.Croy.
   CR2 . . . . **202** C7
Upper Sheppey Wk, N1
   off Clephane Rd **93** J7
Upper Sheridan Rd, Belv. DA17
   off Coleman Rd **139** G4
Upper Shirley Rd, Croy. CR0 . . **203** F2
Upper Sq, Islw. TW7 . . . . **144** D3
Upper St, N1 . . . . **11** F1
Upper Sunbury Rd, Hmptn.
   TW12 . . . . **179** E1
Upper Sutton La, Houns. TW5 . **123** G7
UPPER SYDENHAM, SE26 . . . . **170** D4
Upper Tachbrook St, SW1 . . . . . **33** F1
Upper Tail, Wat. WD19 . . . . **51** E3

Upper Talbot Wk, W11
   off Lancaster Rd **108** B6
Upper Teddington Rd, Kings.T.
   KT1 . . . . **181** F1
Upper Ter, NW3 . . . . **91** F3
Upper Thames St, EC4 . . . . **19** H5
Upper Tollington Pk, N4 . . . . . . **93** G1
Upperton Rd, Sid. DA14 . . . . . . **175** J5
Upperton Rd E, E13 . . . . **115** J3
   off Inniskilling Rd **115** J3
Upperton Rd W, E13 . . . . **115** J3
UPPER TOOTING, SW17 . . . . . **167** H3
Upper Tooting Pk, SW17 . . . . . **167** J2
Upper Tooting Rd, SW17 . . . . . **167** J4
Upper Town Rd, Grnf. UB6 . . . . **103** H4
Upper Tulse Hill, SW2 . . . . **151** F7
Upper Vernon Rd, Sutt. SM1 . . **199** G5
UPPER WALTHAMSTOW, E17 . . **78** B4
Upper Walthamstow Rd, E17 . . . **78** D4
Upper Wickham La, Well. DA16 **138** B7
Upper Wimpole St, W1 . . . . **16** D1
Upper Woburn Pl, WC1 . . . . **9** J4
Uppingham Av, Stan. HA7 . . . . . **69** E1
Upsdell Av, N13 . . . . **59** G6
Upstall St, SE5 . . . . **151** H1
UPTON, E7 . . . . **97** H7
Upton Av, E7 . . . . **97** G7
Upton Cl, NW2
   off Somerton Rd **90** B3
   Bexley DA5 . . . . **159** F6
Upton Ct, SE20 off Blean Gro . **171** F7
Upton Dene, Sutt. SM2 . . . . . . **198** E7
Upton Gdns, Har. HA3 . . . . **69** E5
Upton La, E7 . . . . **97** G7
UPTON PARK, E6 . . . . **115** J1
Upton Pk Rd, E7 . . . . **97** H7
Upton Rd, N18 . . . . **60** D5
   SE18 . . . . **137** F6
   Bexley DA5 . . . . **159** F6
   Bexleyheath DA6 . . . . **158** E4
   Hounslow TW3 . . . . **143** G3
   Thornton Heath CR7 . . . . . . **188** A2
Upton Rd S, Bex. DA5 . . . . **159** F6
Upway, N12 . . . . **57** H7
Upwood Rd, SE12 . . . . **155** F6
   SW16 . . . . **187** E1
Urlwin St, SE5 . . . . **35** J6
Urlwin Wk, SW9 . . . . **151** G2
Urmston Dr, SW19 . . . . **166** B1
Ursula Ms, N4 off Portland Ri . . **93** J1
Ursula St, SW11 . . . . **149** H1
Urswick Gdns, Dag. RM9
   off Urswick Rd **100/101** G1
Urswick Rd, E9 . . . . **95** F5
   Dagenham RM9 . . . . **100** D7
Usborne Ms, SW8 . . . . **34** C7
Usher Rd, E3 . . . . **113** J2
Usk Rd, SW11 . . . . **149** F4
Usk St, E2 . . . . **113** G3
Utopia Village, NW1
   off Chalcot Rd **110** A1
Uvedale Rd, Dag. RM10 . . . . . . **101** G3
   Enfield EN2 . . . . **44** A5
Uverdale Rd, SW10 . . . . **129** F7
Uxbridge Gdns, Felt. TW13
   off Marlborough Rd **160** D2
Uxbridge Rd, W3 . . . . **105** H7
   W5 . . . . **105** H7
   W5 (Ealing Com.) **105** H7
   W7 . . . . **124** B1
   W12 . . . . **127** G1
   W13 . . . . **124** E1
   Feltham TW13 . . . . **160** C2
   Hampton (Hmptn H.) TW12 . **161** G4
   Harrow HA3 . . . . **51** J7
   Hayes UB4 . . . . **102** C7
   Kingston upon Thames KT1 . **181** G4
   Pinner HA5 . . . . **51** H7
   Southall UB1 . . . . **123** G1
   Stanmore HA7 . . . . **52** C6
Uxbridge St, W8 . . . . **128** D1
Uxendon Cres, Wem. HA9 . . . . . **87** H1
Uxendon Hill, Wem. HA9 . . . . . . **87** J1

V

Valance Av, E4 . . . . **63** F1
Valan Leas, Brom. BR2 . . . . **191** E3
Vale, The, N10 . . . . **74** A1
   N14 . . . . **42** D7
   NW11 . . . . **90** A3
   SW3 . . . . **31** E5
   W3 . . . . **126** D1
   Croydon CR0 . . . . **203** G2
   Feltham TW14 . . . . **142** B6
   Hounslow TW5 . . . . **122** E6
   Ruislip HA4 . . . . **84** C4
   Sunbury-on-Thames TW16
      off Ashridge Way **160** A6
   Woodford Green IG8 . . . . **63** G7
Vale Av, Borwd. WD6 . . . . **38** B5
Vale Cl, N2 off Church Vale **73** J3
   W9 . . . . **6** C4
   Orpington BR6 . . . . **206** D4

Vale Cotts, SW15
  off Kingston Vale 164 D4
Vale Ct, W9 ....6 C4
Vale Cres, SW15 ....165 E3
Vale Cft, Esher (Clay.) KT10 ...194 B7
  Pinner HA5 ....66 E5
Vale Dr, Barn. EN5 ....40 C4
Vale End, SE22 off Grove Vale ..152 B4
Vale Gro, N4 ....75 J7
  W3 off The Vale 126 D1
Vale La, W3 ....106 A5
Valence Av, Dag. RM8 ....100 D3
Valence Circ, Dag. RM8 ......100 D3
★ Valence Ho Mus, Dag. RM8 ..100 E2
Valence Wd Rd, Dag. RM8 ....100 D3
Valencia Rd, Stan. HA7 ......53 F4
Valentia Pl, SW9
  off Brixton Sta Rd 151 G4
Valentine Av, Bex. DA5 ......176 E2
Valentine Ct, SE23 ....171 G2
Valentine Pl, SE1 ....27 G3
Valentine Rd, E9 ....95 G6
  Harrow HA2 ....85 J3
Valentine Row, SE1 ....27 G4
Valentines Rd, Ilf. IG1 ......98 E1
Vale of Health, NW3
  off East Heath Rd 91 G3
Vale Par, SW15
  off Kingston Vale 164 D4
Valerian Way, E15 ....115 E3
Valerie Ct, Sutt. SM2
  off Stanley Rd 198/199 E7
Vale Ri, NW11 ....90 C1
Vale Rd, E7 ....97 H6
  N4 ....75 J7
  Bromley BR1 ....192 D2
  Epsom KT19 ....197 F4
  Mitcham CR4 ....186 D3
  Sutton SM1 ....198 E4
  Worcester Park KT4 ....197 F4
Vale Rd N, Surb. KT6 ....195 H2
Vale Rd S, Surb. KT6 ....195 H2
Vale Row, N5 off Gillespie Rd ..93 H3
Vale Royal, N7 ....92 E7
Valery Pl, Hmptn. TW12 ......161 G7
Vale St, SE27 ....170 A3
Valeswood Rd, Brom. BR1 ....173 F5
Vale Ter, N4 ....75 J6
Valetta Gro, E13 ....115 G2
Valetta Rd, W3 ....126 E2
Valette St, E9 ....95 E6
Valiant Cl, Nthlt. UB5
  off Ruislip Rd 102 D3
  Romford RM7 ....83 G2
Valiant Ho, SE7 ....135 J5
Valiant Path, NW9
  off Blundell Rd 54/55 E7
Valiant Way, E6 ....116 C5
Vallance Rd, E1 ....13 J4
  E2 ....13 J4
  N22 ....74 C2
Vallentin Rd, E17 ....78 C4
Valley Av, N12 ....57 G4
Valley Cl, Loug. IG10 ....48 C6
  Pinner HA5 off Alandale Dr ..66 B2
Valley Dr, NW9 ....70 A6
Valleyfield Rd, SW16 ....169 F5
Valley Flds Cres, Enf. EN2 ...43 G2
Valley Gdns, SW19 ....167 G7
  Wembley HA0 ....87 J7
Valley Gro, SE7 ....135 J5
Valley Hill, Loug. IG10 ......48 B7
Valley Link Ind Est, Enf. EN3 ..45 H6
Valley Ms, Twick. TW1
  off Cross Deep 162 D2
Valley Rd, SW16 ....169 F4
  Belvedere DA17 ....139 H4
  Bromley BR2 ....191 E2
Valley Side, E4 ....62 A2
Valley Side Par, E4
  off Valley Side 62 A2
Valley Vw, Barn. EN5 ....40 B6
Valley Wk, Croy. CR0 ....203 F2
Valliere Rd, NW10 ....107 H3
Valliers Wd Rd, Sid. DA15 ...175 G1
Vallis Way, W13 ....104 D5
  Chessington KT9 ....195 G4
Valmar Rd, SE5 ....151 J1
Val McKenzie Av, N7
  off Parkside Cres 93 G3
Valnay St, SW17 ....167 J5
Valognes Av, E17 ....77 H1
Valonia Gdns, SW18 ....148 C6
Vambery Rd, SE18 ....137 F6
Vanbrough Cres, Nthlt. UB5 ..102 C1
Vanbrugh Cl, E16 off Fulmer Rd ..116 A5
Vanbrugh Dr, Walt. KT12 .....178 C7
Vanbrugh Flds, SE3 ....135 F7
Vanbrugh Hill, SE3 ....135 F5
  SE10 ....135 F5
Vanbrugh Pk, SE3 ....135 F7
Vanbrugh Pk Rd, SE3 ....135 F7
Vanbrugh Pk Rd W, SE3 .....135 F7
Vanbrugh Rd, W4 ....126 D3
Vanbrugh Ter, SE3 ....155 F1

Vanburgh Cl, Orp. BR6 ......207 H1
Vancouver Cl, Orp. BR6 ......207 J4
Vancouver Rd, SE23 ....171 H2
  Edgware HA8 ....70 B1
  Hayes UB4 ....102 B4
  Richmond TW10 ....163 F4
Vanderbilt Rd, SW18 ....167 F1
Vanderville Gdns, N2
  off Tarling Rd 73 F2
Vandome Cl, E16 ....115 H6
Vandon Pas, SW1 ....25 G5
Vandon St, SW1 ....25 G5
Van Dyck Av, N.Mal. KT3 ....182 D7
Vandyke Cl, SW15 ....148 A7
Vandyke Cross, SE9 ....156 B5
Vandy St, EC2 ....12 D6
Vane Cl, NW3 ....91 G4
  Harrow HA3 ....69 J6
Vanessa Cl, Belv. DA17 .....139 G5
Vane St, SW1 ....33 G1
Van Gogh Cl, Islw. TW7
  off Twickenham Rd 144 D3
Vanguard Cl, E16 ....115 G5
  Croydon CR0 ....201 H1
  Romford RM7 ....83 H2
Vanguard St, SE8 ....154 A1
Vanguard Way, Wall. SM6 ...200 E7
Vanneck Sq, SW15 ....147 G5
Vanner Pt, E9 off Wick Rd ...95 G6
Vanoc Gdns, Brom. BR1 .....173 G3
Vansittart Rd, E7 ....97 F4
Vansittart St, SE14 ....133 H7
Vanston Pl, SW6 ....128 D7
Vantage Ms, E14
  off Prestons Rd 134 C1
Vantage Pl, W8
  off Abingdon Rd 128 D3
Vant Rd, SW17 ....167 J5
Varcoe Rd, SE16 ....133 E5
Vardens Rd, SW11 ....149 G4
Varden St, E1 ....112 E6
Vardon Cl, W3 ....106 D6
Varley Par, NW9 ....70 E4
Varley Rd, E16 ....115 H6
Varley Way, Mitch. CR4 .....185 G2
Varna Rd, SW6 ....128 B7
  Hampton TW12 ....179 H1
Varndell St, NW1 ....9 F3
Varnishers Yd, N1
  off Caledonian Rd 110 E2
Varsity Dr, Twick. TW1 ......144 B5
Varsity Row, SW14
  off William's La 146 C2
Vartry Rd, N15 ....76 A6
Vassall Rd, SW9 ....131 G7
Vauban Est, SE16 ....29 G6
Vauban St, SE16 ....29 G6
Vaughan Av, NW4 ....71 G5
  W6 ....127 F4
Vaughan Cl, Hmptn. TW12
  off Oak Av 160/161 E6
Vaughan Gdns, Ilf. IG1 .....80 C7
Vaughan Rd, E15 ....97 F6
  SE5 ....151 J3
  Harrow HA1 ....67 J7
  Thames Ditton KT7 ....180 E7
  Welling DA16 ....157 J2
Vaughan St, SE16 ....133 J2
Vaughan Way, E1 ....21 H6
Vaughan Williams Cl, SE8
  off Watson's La 134 A7
VAUXHALL, SE11 ....34 B4
Vauxhall Br, SE1 ....34 A4
  SW1 ....34 A4
Vauxhall Br Rd, SW1 ....33 G1
Vauxhall Gdns, S.Croy. CR2 ..201 J6
Vauxhall Gdns Est, SE11 ....34 D4
Vauxhall Gro, SW8 ....34 C5
Vauxhall St, SE11 ....34 D4
Vauxhall Wk, SE11 ....34 C3
Vawdrey Cl, E1 ....113 F4
Veals Mead, Mitch. CR4 .....185 H1
Vectis Gdns, SW17
  off Vectis Rd 168 B6
Vectis Rd, SW17 ....168 B6
Veda Rd, SE13 ....154 A4
Veldene Way, Har. HA2 ......85 F3
Velde Way, SE22
  off East Dulwich Gro 152 B5
Velletri Ho, E2 ....113 G2
Vellum Dr, Cars. SM5 ....200 A3
Venables Cl, Dag. RM10 ....101 H4
Venables St, NW8 ....15 F1
Vencourt Pl, W6 ....127 G4
Venetian Rd, SE5 ....151 J2
Venetia Rd, N4 ....75 H6
  W5 ....125 G2
Venner Rd, SE26 ....171 F6
Venn St, SW4 ....150 C4
Ventnor Av, Stan. HA7 ......69 E1
Ventnor Dr, N20 ....56 E3
Ventnor Gdns, Bark. IG11 ...99 H6
Ventnor Rd, SE14 ....133 G7
  Sutton SM2 ....199 E7
Venture Cl, Bex. DA5 ....158 E7

Venue St, E14 ....114 C5
Venus Ho, E14 off Crews St ..134 A4
Venus Rd, SE18 ....136 C3
Vera Av, N21 ....43 G5
Vera Lynn Cl, E7 off Dames Rd ..97 G4
Vera Rd, SW6 ....148 B1
Verbena Cl, E16 off Pretoria Rd ..115 F4
  West Drayton UB7
  off Magnolia St 120 A5
Verbena Gdns, W6 ....127 G5
Verdant La, SE6 ....173 E1
Verdayne Av, Croy. CR0 .....203 G1
Verdun Rd, SE18 ....138 A6
  SW13 ....127 G6
Vereker Dr, Sun. TW16 ......178 A3
Vereker Rd, W14 ....128 B5
Vere Rd, Loug. IG10 ....49 F4
Vere St, W1 ....16 C4
Verity Cl, W11 ....108 B6
Vermeer Gdns, SE15
  off Elland Rd 153 F4
Vermont Cl, Enf. EN2 ....43 H4
Vermont Rd, SE19 ....170 A6
  SW18 ....149 E6
  Sutton SM1 ....198 E3
Verney Gdns, Dag. RM9 .....100 E4
Verney Rd, SE16 ....37 J5
  Dagenham RM9 ....100 E5
Verney St, NW10 ....88 D3
Verney Way, SE16 ....132 E5
Vernham Rd, SE18 ....137 F6
Vernon Av, E12 ....98 C4
  SW20 ....184 A2
  Woodford Green IG8 ......63 H7
Vernon Cl, Epsom KT19 .....196 C5
Vernon Ct, Stan. HA7
  off Vernon Dr 68/69 E1
Vernon Cres, Barn. EN4 .....42 A6
Vernon Dr, Stan. HA7 ....68 D1
Vernon Ms, E17 off Vernon Rd ..77 J5
  W14 off Vernon St 128 B4
Vernon Pl, WC1 ....18 B2
Vernon Ri, WC1 ....10 D3
  Greenford UB6 ....86 A5
Vernon Rd, E3 ....113 J2
  E11 ....97 E1
  E15 ....97 E7
  E17 ....77 J5
  N8 ....75 G3
  SW14 ....146 D3
  Ilford IG3 ....99 J1
  Sutton SM1 ....199 F5
Vernon Sq, WC1 ....10 D3
Vernon St, W14 ....128 B4
Vernon Yd, W11
  off Portobello Rd 108 C7
Veroan Rd, Bexh. DA7 ......158 E2
Verona Ct, W4
  off Chiswick La 126/127 E5
Verona Dr, Surb. KT6 ....195 H2
Verona Rd, E7 off Upton La ..97 G7
Veronica Gdns, SW16 ....186 C1
Veronica Rd, SW17 ....168 B3
Veronique Gdns, Ilf. IG6 ....81 E5
Verran Rd, SW12
  off Balham Gro 150 B7
Versailles Rd, SE20 ....170 D7
Verulam Av, E17 ....77 J6
Verulam Bldgs, WC1 ....18 D1
Verulam Pl, Grnf. UB6 ......103 G4
Verulam St, WC1 ....18 E1
Verwood Dr, Barn. EN4 .....41 J3
Verwood Rd, Har. HA2 ......67 J2
Vesey Path, E14
  off East India Dock Rd 114 B6
Vespan Rd, W12 ....127 G2
Vesta Rd, SE4 ....153 H2
Vestris Rd, SE23 ....171 G2
Vestry Ms, SE5 ....152 B1
Vestry Rd, E17 ....78 B4
  SE5 ....152 B1
Vestry St, N1 ....12 B3
Vevey St, SE6 ....171 J2
Veysey Gdns, Dag. RM10 ...101 G3
Viaduct Pl, E2
  off Viaduct St 112/113 E3
Viaduct St, E2 ....112 E3
Vian St, SE13 ....154 B3
Vibart Gdns, SW2 ....151 F7
Vibart Wk, N1 off Outram Pl ..110/111 E1
Vicarage Av, SE3 ....155 G1
Vicarage Cl, Erith DA8 ......139 J6
  Northolt UB5 ....85 F7
  Worcester Park KT4 ....196 F1
Vicarage Ct, W8 ....22 A3
  Feltham TW14 ....141 F7
Vicarage Cres, SW11 ....149 G1
Vicarage Dr, SW14 ....146 D5
  Barking IG11 ....99 F7
  Beckenham BR3 ....190 A1
Vicarage Fm Rd, Houns. TW3,
  TW5 ....142 E2
Vicarage Flds, Walt. KT12 ...178 C6
Vicarage Fld Shop Cen, Bark.
  IG11 ....99 F7

Vicarage Gdns, SW14
  off Vicarage Rd 146 C5
  W8 ....128 D1
  Mitcham CR4 ....185 H3
Vicarage Gate, W8 ....22 A1
Vicarage Gro, SE5 ....152 A1
Vicarage La, E6 ....116 C3
  E15 ....97 E7
  Chigwell IG7 ....65 F2
  Ilford IG1 ....99 G1
  SE18 ....137 F5
Vicarage Pk, SE18 ....137 F5
Vicarage Path, N8 ....74 F7
Vicarage Rd, E10 ....96 B1
  E15 ....97 F7
  N17 ....60 D7
  NW4 ....71 G6
  SE18 ....137 F5
  SW14 ....146 C5
  Bexley DA5 ....177 H1
  Croydon CR0 ....201 G3
  Dagenham RM10 ....101 H6
  Kingston upon Thames KT1 ..181 G2
  Kingston upon Thames (Hmptn W.)
  KT1 ....181 F1
  Sutton SM1 ....198 E4
  Teddington TW11 ....162 D5
  Twickenham TW2 ....162 B2
  Twickenham (Whitton) TW2 ..143 J6
  Woodford Green IG8 ......64 B7
Vicarage Wk, SW11
  off Battersea Ch Rd 149 G1
Vicarage Way, NW10 ....88 D3
  Harrow HA2 ....67 G7
Vicars Br Cl, Wem. HA0 ....105 H2
Vicars Cl, E9 off Northiam St ..113 F1
  E15 ....115 G1
  Enfield EN1 ....44 B2
Vicars Hill, SE13 ....154 B4
Vicars Moor La, N21 ....43 G7
Vicars Oak Rd, SE19 ....170 B6
Vicars Rd, NW5 ....92 A5
Vicars Wk, Dag. RM8 ......100 B3
Viceroy Cl, N2 off Market Pl ..73 H4
Viceroy Ct, NW8 ....7 H1
Viceroy Par, N2 off High Rd ..73 H3
Viceroy Rd, SW8 ....150 E1
Vickers Cl, Wall. SM6 ......201 F7
Vickers Way, Houns. TW4 ...143 F5
Victor Gro, Wem. HA0 .....87 H7
★ Victoria & Albert Mus, SW7 ..23 F6
Victoria Arc, SW1
  off Terminus Pl 130 B3
Victoria Av, E6 ....116 A1
  EC2 ....20 E2
  N3 ....72 C1
  Barnet EN4 ....41 G4
  Hounslow TW3 ....143 F5
  Surbiton KT6 ....181 G7
  Wallington SM6 ....200 A3
  Wembley HA9 ....88 B6
  West Molesey KT8 ....179 G3
Victoria Cl, Barn. EN4 ......41 G4
  West Molesey KT8
  off Victoria Av 179 G3
★ Victoria Coach Sta, SW1 ..32 D2
Victoria Cotts, Rich. TW9 ...145 J1
Victoria Ct, Wem. HA9 .....88 A6
Victoria Cres, N15 ....76 B5
  SE19 ....170 B6
  SW19 ....166 C7
Victoria Dock Rd, E16 .....115 F6
Victoria Dr, SW19 ....148 A7
  SW1 ....26 B3
  WC2 ....18 C6
★ Victoria Embankment Gdns,
  WC2 ....18 B6
Victoria Gdns, W11 ....128 D1
  Hounslow TW5 ....142 E1
Victoria Gro, N12 ....57 F5
  W8 ....22 C5
Victoria Gro Ms, W2
  off Ossington St 108/109 E7
Victoria Ind Est, NW10 ....106 E4
Victoria La, Barn. EN5 .....40 C4
  Hayes UB3 ....121 F5
Victoria Ms, E8 off Dalston La ..94 D5
  NW6 ....108 D1
  SW4 off Victoria Ri 150 B4
  SW18 ....167 F1
Victorian Gro, N16 ....94 B3
Victorian Rd, N16 ....94 B3
★ Victoria Park, E9 ....95 H7
Victoria Pk Rd, E9 ....113 F1
Victoria Pk Sq, E2 ....113 F3
Victoria Pas, NW8 ....7 E5
Victoria Pl, SE22
  off Underhill Rd 152 D5
  SW1 ....32 E1
  Richmond TW9 ....145 G5
Victoria Pt, E13 off Victoria Rd ..115 G2
Victoria Retail Pk, Ruis. HA4 ..84 E5
Victoria Ri, SW4 ....150 B3
Victoria Rd, E4 ....63 E1
  E11 ....96 E4

Victoria Rd, E13 . . . .**115** G2
E17 . . . .**78** C2
E18 . . . .**79** H2
N4 . . . .**75** F7
N9 . . . .**60** C4
N15 . . . .**76** D4
N18 . . . .**60** C4
N22 . . . .**74** C1
NW4 . . . .**71** J4
NW6 . . . .**108** C1
NW7 . . . .**55** F5
NW10 . . . .**106** D5
SW14 . . . .**146** D3
W3 . . . .**106** D5
W5 . . . .**105** E5
W8 . . . .**22** C6
Barking IG11 . . . .**99** E6
Barnet EN4 . . . .**41** G4
Bexleyheath DA6 . . . .**159** G4
Bromley BR2 . . . .**192** A5
Buckhurst Hill IG9 . . . .**64** A2
Bushey WD23 . . . .**51** H1
Chislehurst BR7 . . . .**174** D5
Dagenham RM10 . . . .**101** H5
Feltham TW13 . . . .**160** B1
Kingston upon Thames KT1 . .**181** J2
Mitcham CR4 . . . .**167** H7
Ruislip HA4 . . . .**84** C5
Sidcup DA15 . . . .**175** J3
Southall UB2 . . . .**123** F3
Surbiton KT6 . . . .**181** G6
Sutton SM1 . . . .**199** G5
Teddington TW11 . . . .**162** D6
Twickenham TW1 . . . .**144** D7
Victoria Sq, SW1 . . . .**24** E5
Victoria Sta, SW1 . . . .**33** E1
Victoria Steps, Brent. TW8
off Kew Br Rd **125** J6
Victoria St, E15 . . . .**96** E7
SW1 . . . .**25** F6
Belvedere DA17 . . . .**139** F5
Victoria Ter, N4 . . . .**93** G1
NW10 _off Old Oak La_ **106/107** E3
Harrow HA1 . . . .**86** B1
★ **Victoria Twr**, SW1 . . . .**26** A5
Victoria Vil, Rich. TW9 . . . . . .**145** J3
Victoria Way, SE7 . . . .**135** H5
Victoria Wf, E14 . . . .**113** H7
Victoria Yd, E1 _off Fairclough St_ .**112** D6
Victor Rd, NW10 . . . .**107** H3
SE20 . . . .**171** G7
Harrow HA2 . . . .**67** J3
Teddington TW11 . . . .**162** B4
Victors Dr, Hmptn. TW12 . . . .**161** E6
Victors Way, Barn. EN5 . . . . . .**40** C3
Victor Vil, N9 . . . .**60** A3
Victor Wk, NW9 . . . .**70** E1
Victory Av, Mord. SM4 . . . . . .**185** G2
Victory Business Cen, Islw. TW7 .**144** C3
Victory Pl, E14 _off Northey St_ . .**113** H7
SE17 . . . .**36** A1
SE19 _off Westow St_ **170** B6
Victory Rd, E11 . . . .**79** H4
SW19 . . . .**167** F7
Victory Rd Ms, SW19
off Victory Rd **167** F7
Victory Wk, SE8 _off Ship St_ . . .**154** A1
Victory Way, SE16 . . . .**133** H2
Hounslow TW5 . . . .**122** C5
Romford RM7 . . . .**83** H2
Vidler Cl, Chess. KT9
off Merritt Gdns **195** F6
Vienna Cl, Ilf. IG5 . . . .**80** A3
View, The, SE2 . . . .**139** E5
View Cl, N6 . . . .**73** J7
Chigwell IG7 . . . .**65** G5
Harrow HA1 . . . .**68** A4
Viewfield Cl, Har. HA3 . . . .**69** H7
Viewfield Rd, SW18 . . . .**148** C6
Bexley DA5 . . . .**176** C1
Viewland Rd, SE18 . . . .**137** J5
View Rd, N6 . . . .**73** J7
Viga Rd, N21 . . . .**43** G6
Vigilant Cl, SE26 . . . .**170** D4
Vignoles Rd, Rom. RM7 . . . . . .**83** G7
Vigo St, W1 . . . .**17** F5
Viking Cl, E3 _off Selwyn Rd_ . . .**113** H2
Viking Ct, SW6 . . . .**128** D6
Viking Gdns, E6
off Jack Dash Way **116** B4
Viking Pl, E10 . . . .**95** J1
Viking Rd, Sthl. UB1 . . . .**103** E7
Viking Way, Erith DA8 . . . .**139** J3
Villacourt Rd, SE18 . . . .**138** A7
Village, The, SE7 . . . .**135** J6
Village Arc, E4 _off Station Rd_ . .**62** D1
Village Cl, E4 . . . .**62** C5
NW3 _off Belsize La_ **91** G5
Village Ct, E17 _off Eden Rd_ . . .**78** B5
Village Hts, Wdf.Grn. IG8 . . . . .**63** F5
Village Ms, NW9 . . . .**88** D2
Village Pk Cl, Enf. EN1 . . . .**44** B6
Village Rd, N3 . . . .**72** B2
Enfield EN1 . . . .**44** B6
Village Row, Sutt. SM2 . . . . . .**198** D7

Village Way, NW10 . . . .**88** D4
SE21 . . . .**152** A6
Beckenham BR3 . . . .**190** A2
Pinner HA5 . . . .**67** E7
Village Way E, Har. HA2 . . . . . .**67** F7
Villa Rd, SW9 . . . .**151** G3
Villas Rd, SE18 . . . .**137** F4
Villa St, SE17 . . . .**36** C4
Villiers Av, Surb. KT5 . . . .**181** J5
Twickenham TW2 . . . .**161** F1
Villiers Cl, E10 . . . .**96** A2
Surbiton KT5 . . . .**181** J4
Villiers Ct, N20
off Buckingham Av **41** F7
Villiers Path, Surb. KT5 . . . . . .**181** J5
Villiers Rd, NW2 . . . .**89** G6
Beckenham BR3 . . . .**189** G2
Isleworth TW7 . . . .**144** B2
Kingston upon Thames KT1 .**181** J3
Southall UB1 . . . .**123** F1
Villiers St, WC2 . . . .**18** A6
Vincam Cl, Twick. TW2 . . . . . .**143** G7
Vincent Av, Surb. KT5 . . . .**196** B1
Vincent Cl, SE16 . . . .**133** H2
Barnet EN5 . . . .**40** D3
Bromley BR2 . . . .**191** H4
Ilford IG6 . . . .**65** F6
Sidcup DA15 . . . .**175** H1
West Drayton UB7 . . . .**120** D6
Vincent Gdns, NW2 . . . .**89** F3
Vincent Ms, E3 . . . .**114** A2
Vincent Rd, E4 . . . .**62** D6
N15 . . . .**75** J4
N22 . . . .**75** G2
SE18 . . . .**137** E4
W3 . . . .**126** C3
Croydon CR0 . . . .**188** B7
Dagenham RM9 . . . .**100** E7
Hounslow TW4 . . . .**142** D2
Isleworth TW7 . . . .**144** A1
Kingston upon Thames KT1 .**182** A3
Wembley HA0 . . . .**87** J7
Vincent Row, Hmptn. (Hmptn H.)
TW12 . . . .**161** J6
Vincents La, NW7 . . . .**55** J4
Vincents Path, Nthlt. UB5
off Arnold Rd **84/85** E6
Vincent Sq, SW1 . . . .**33** G1
Vincent St, E16 . . . .**115** F5
SW1 . . . .**33** H1
Vincent Ter, N1 . . . .**11** G1
Vince St, EC1 . . . .**12** C4
Vine Cl, Surb. KT5 . . . .**181** J6
Sutton SM1 . . . .**199** F3
West Drayton UB7 . . . .**120** D4
Vine Ct, E1 . . . .**21** J2
Harrow HA3 . . . .**69** H6
Vine Gdns, Ilf. IG1 . . . .**99** F5
Vinegar All, E17 . . . .**78** B4
Vinegar St, E1
off Reardon St **132/133** E1
Vinegar Yd, SE1 . . . .**28** D3
Vine Hill, EC1 . . . .**10** E6
Vine La, SE1 . . . .**28** E2
Vine Pl, W5 _off The Common_ . .**125** H1
Hounslow TW3 . . . .**143** H4
Viner Cl, Walt. KT12 . . . .**178** C6
Vineries, The, N14 . . . .**42** C6
Enfield EN1 . . . .**44** B3
Vineries Bk, NW7 . . . .**55** H5
Vineries Cl, Dag. RM9
off Heathway **101** G6
West Drayton UB7 . . . .**120** D6
Vine Rd, E15 . . . .**97** F7
SW13 . . . .**147** F3
East Molesey KT8 . . . .**179** J4
Orpington BR6 . . . .**207** J6
Vines Av, N3 . . . .**72** E1
Vine Sq, W14 . . . .**128** C5
Vine St, EC3 . . . .**21** F5
W1 . . . .**17** G6
Romford RM7 . . . .**83** J5
Vine St Br, EC1 . . . .**11** F6
Vine Yd, SE1 . . . .**28** A3
Vineyard, The, Rich. TW10 . . . .**145** H5
Vineyard Av, NW7 . . . .**56** B7
Vineyard Cl, SE6 . . . .**172** A1
Kingston upon Thames KT1 .**181** J3
Vineyard Gro, N3 . . . .**73** E1
Vineyard Hill Rd, SW19 . . . . . .**166** D4
Vineyard Pas, Rich. TW9
off Paradise Rd **145** H5
Vineyard Path, SW14 . . . .**146** D3
Vineyard Rd, Felt. TW13 . . . . . .**160** A3
Vineyard Row, Kings.T. (Hmptn W.)
KT1 . . . .**181** F1
Vineyard Wk, EC1 . . . .**11** E5
Viney Rd, SE13 . . . .**154** B3
Vining St, SW9 . . . .**151** G4
★ **Vinopolis**, SE1 . . . .**28** A1
Vintners Ct, EC4 . . . .**20** A5
Vintners Pl, EC4
off Upper Thames St **111** J7
Vintry Ms, E17
off Cleveland Pk Cres **78** A4

Viola Av, SE2 . . . .**138** B4
Feltham TW14 . . . .**142** C6
Viola Sq, W12 . . . .**107** F7
Violet Cl, E16 . . . .**115** E4
SE8 _off Dorking Cl_ **133** J6
Sutton SM3 . . . .**198** B1
Wallington SM6 . . . .**200** B3
Violet Gdns, Croy. CR0 . . . . . .**201** H5
Violet Hill, NW8 . . . .**6** C2
Violet La, Croy. CR0 . . . .**201** H5
Violet Rd, E3 . . . .**114** B4
E17 . . . .**78** A6
E18 . . . .**79** H2
Violet St, E2
off Three Colts La **112/113** E4
Virgil Pl, W1 . . . .**15** J2
Virgil St, SE1 . . . .**26** D5
Virginia Cl, N.Mal. KT3
off Willow Rd **182** C4
Virginia Gdns, Ilf. IG6 . . . .**81** F2
Virginia Rd, E2 . . . .**13** F4
Thornton Heath CR7 . . . . .**187** H1
Virginia St, E1 . . . .**21** H6
Virginia Wk, SW2 . . . .**151** F6
Viscount Cl, N11 . . . .**58** B5
Viscount Dr, E6 . . . .**116** C5
Viscount Gro, Nthlt. UB5 . . . . .**102** D3
Viscount St, EC1 . . . .**11** J6
Viscount Way, Houns. (Hthrw Air.)
TW6 . . . .**141** H4
Vista, The, E4 _off Forest Vw_ . . .**46** D7
SE9 . . . .**156** A6
Sidcup DA14
off Langdon Shaw **175** J5
Vista Av, Enf. EN3 . . . .**45** G2
Vista Bldg, The, SE18
off Calderwood St **136** D3
Vista Dr, Ilf. IG4 . . . .**80** A5
Vista Way, Har. HA3 . . . .**69** H6
Viveash Cl, Hayes UB3 . . . . . .**121** J3
Vivian Av, NW4 . . . .**71** H5
Wembley HA9 . . . .**88** A5
Vivian Cl, Wat. WD19 . . . .**50** A1
Vivian Comma Cl, N4
off Blackstock Rd **93** H3
Vivian Gdns, Wat. WD19 . . . . . .**50** A1
Wembley HA9 . . . .**88** A5
Vivian Rd, E3 . . . .**113** H2
Vivian Sq, SE15
off Scylla Rd **152/153** E3
Vivian Way, N2 . . . .**73** G5
Vivien Cl, Chess. KT9 . . . .**195** H7
Vivienne Cl, Twick. TW1 . . . . .**145** F6
Voce Rd, SE18 . . . .**137** G7
Voewood Cl, N.Mal. KT3 . . . . .**183** F6
Volta Cl, N9 _off Hudson Way_ . . .**61** F3
Voltaire Rd, SW4 . . . .**150** D3
Volt Av, NW10 . . . .**106** D3
Volta Way, Croy. CR0 . . . .**201** F1
Voluntary Pl, E11 . . . .**79** G6
Vorley Rd, N19 . . . .**92** C2
Voss Ct, SW16 . . . .**169** E6
Voss St, E2 . . . .**13** J4
Voyagers Cl, SE28 . . . .**118** C6
Voysey Cl, N3 . . . .**72** B3
Vulcan Cl, E6 . . . .**116** D6
Vulcan Gate, Enf. EN2 . . . .**43** G2
Vulcan Rd, SE4 . . . .**153** J2
Vulcan Sq, E14 _off Britannia Rd_ .**134** A4
Vulcan Ter, SE4 . . . .**153** J2
Vulcan Way, N7 . . . .**93** F6
Vyne, The, Bexh. DA7 . . . .**159** H3
Vyner Rd, W3 . . . .**106** D7
Vyner St, E2 . . . .**113** E1
Vyse Cl, Barn. EN5 . . . .**39** J4

W

Wadbrook St, Kings.T. KT1 . . . .**181** G2
Wadding St, SE17 . . . .**36** B2
Waddington Cl, Enf. EN1 . . . . . .**44** B4
Waddington Rd, E15 . . . .**96** D5
Waddington St, E15 . . . .**96** D6
Waddington Way, SE19 . . . . . .**169** J7
WADDON, Croy. CR0 . . . .**201** G2
Waddon Cl, Croy. CR0 . . . .**201** G3
Waddon Ct Rd, Croy. CR0 . . . . .**201** G4
Waddon Marsh Way, Croy.
CR0 . . . .**201** F1
Waddon New Rd, Croy. CR0 . . .**201** H3
Waddon Pk Av, Croy. CR0 . . . . .**201** G3
Waddon Rd, Croy. CR0 . . . .**201** G3
Waddon Way, Croy. CR0 . . . . . .**201** H6
Wades Gro, N21 . . . .**43** G7
Wades Hill, N21 . . . .**43** G6
Wades La, Tedd. TW11
off High St **162** D5
Wades Ms, N21 _off Wades Hill_ . .**43** G7
Wadeson St, E2 . . . .**113** E2
Wades Pl, E14 . . . .**114** B7
Wadeville Av, Rom. RM6 . . . . . .**83** F7
Wadeville Cl, Belv. DA17 . . . . .**139** G6
Wadham Av, E17 . . . .**62** B7
Wadham Gdns, NW3 . . . .**109** H1

Wadham Gdns, Grnf. UB6 . . .**86** A6
Wadham Rd, E17 . . . .**78** B1
SW15 . . . .**148** B4
Wadhurst Cl, SE20 . . . .**188** E2
Wadhurst Rd, SW8 . . . .**150** C1
W4 . . . .**126** D3
Wadley Rd, E11 . . . .**78** E7
Wadsworth Business Cen, Grnf.
UB6 . . . .**105** F2
Wadsworth Cl, Enf. EN3 . . . . .**45** G5
Greenford UB6 . . . .**105** F2
Wadsworth Rd, Grnf. UB6 . . .**105** E2
Wager St, E3 . . . .**113** J4
Waggon Ms, N14
off Chase Side **58** C1
Waghorn Rd, E13 . . . .**115** J1
Harrow HA3 . . . .**69** G3
Waghorn St, SE15 . . . .**152** D3
Wagner St, SE15 . . . .**133** F7
Wagstaff Gdns, Dag. RM9 . . .**100** C6
Wagtail Cl, NW9 _off Swan Dr_ .**70/71** E2
Wagtail Wk, Beck. BR3 . . . . . .**190** C5
Waights Ct, Kings.T. KT2 . . . .**181** H1
Wainfleet Av, Rom. RM5 . . . . .**83** J2
Wainford Cl, SW19
off Windlesham Gro **166** A1
Wainwright Gro, Islw. TW7 . . .**144** A4
Waite Davies Rd, SE12 . . . . . .**155** F7
Waite St, SE15 . . . .**37** F5
Waithman St, EC4 . . . .**19** G4
Wakefield Gdns, SE19 . . . . . .**170** B7
Ilford IG1 . . . .**80** B6
Wakefield Ms, WC1 . . . .**10** B4
Wakefield Rd, N11 . . . .**58** D5
N15 . . . .**76** C5
Richmond TW10 . . . .**145** G5
Wakefield St, E6 . . . .**116** A1
N18 . . . .**60** D5
WC1 . . . .**10** B5
Wakeford Cl, SW4
off Clapham Common S
Side **150** C5
Wakehams Hill, Pnr. HA5 . . . . .**67** F3
Wakeham St, N1 . . . .**94** A6
Wakehurst Rd, SW11 . . . .**149** H5
Wakeling Rd, W7 . . . .**104** C5
Wakeling St, E14 . . . .**113** H6
Wakelin Rd, E15 . . . .**114** E2
Wakeman Rd, NW10 . . . .**107** J3
Wakemans Hill Av, NW9 . . . . . .**70** D5
Wakering Rd, Bark. IG11 . . . . . .**99** F6
Wakerley Cl, E6
off Truesdale Rd **116** C6
Wakley St, EC1 . . . .**11** G3
Walberswick St, SW8 . . . .**131** E7
Walbrook, EC4 . . . .**20** B5
Walbrook Ho, N9 . . . .**61** F1
Walbrook Wf, EC4
off Upper Thames St **111** J7
Walburgh St, E1
off Bigland St **112/113** E6
Walcorde Av, SE17 . . . .**36** A2
Walcot Rd, Enf. EN3 . . . .**45** J2
Walcot Sq, SE11 . . . .**35** F1
Walcott St, SW1 . . . .**33** G1
Waldair Ct, E16
off Barge Ho Rd **136/137** E2
Waldair Wf, E16 . . . .**136** E2
Waldeck Gro, SE27 . . . .**169** H3
Waldeck Rd, N15 . . . .**75** H4
SW14
off Lower Richmond Rd . . .**146** C3
W4 . . . .**126** A6
W13 . . . .**104** E6
Waldeck Ter, SW14
off Lower Richmond Rd . . .**146** C3
Waldegrave Av, Tedd. TW11
off Waldegrave Rd **162** C5
Waldegrave Gdns, Twick. TW1 .**162** C2
Waldegrave Pk, Twick. TW1 . . .**162** C4
Waldegrave Rd, N8 . . . .**75** G3
SE19 . . . .**170** C7
W5 . . . .**105** J6
Bromley BR1 . . . .**192** B4
Dagenham RM8 . . . .**100** C2
Teddington TW11 . . . .**162** C4
Twickenham TW1 . . . .**162** C4
Waldegrove, Croy. CR0 . . . . . .**202** C3
Waldemar Av, SW6 . . . .**148** B1
W13 . . . .**125** F1
Waldemar Rd, SW19 . . . .**166** D5
Walden Av, N13 . . . .**59** J4
Chislehurst BR7 . . . .**174** C4
Walden Cl, Belv. DA17 . . . .**139** F5
Walden Gdns, Th.Hth. CR7 . . . .**187** F3
Walden Par, Chis. BR7
off Walden Rd **174** C6
Walden Rd, N17 . . . .**76** A1
Chislehurst BR7 . . . .**174** C6
Waldenshaw Rd, SE23 . . . . . .**171** F1
Walden St, E1 . . . .**112** E6
Walden Way, NW7 . . . .**56** A6
Ilford IG6 . . . .**65** H7
Waldo Cl, SW4 . . . .**150** C5
Waldo Pl, Mitch. CR4 . . . .**167** H7

Waldo Rd, NW10 . . . .**107** G3
  Bromley BR1 . . . .**192** A3
Waldram Cres, SE23 . . . .**171** F1
Waldram Pk Rd, SE23 . . . .**171** G1
Waldram Pl, SE23
  off Waldram Cres **171** F1
Waldrist Way, Erith DA18 . . . . .**139** F2
Waldron Gdns, Brom. BR2 . . . . .**190** D3
Waldronhyrst, S.Croy. CR2 . . . .**201** H4
Waldron Ms, SW1 . . . .**31** H5
Waldron Rd, SW18 . . . .**167** F3
  Harrow HA1, HA2 . . . .**86** B1
Waldrons, The, Croy. CR0 . . . . .**201** H4
Waldrons Path, S.Croy. CR2 . . .**201** J4
Waldstock Rd, SE28 . . . .**118** A7
Waleran Cl, Stan. HA7 . . . .**52** C6
Walerand Rd, SE13 . . . .**154** C2
Waleran Flats, SE1
  off Old Kent Rd **132** B4
Wales Av, Cars. SM5 . . . .**199** J5
Wales Cl, SE15 . . . .**132** E7
Wales Fm Rd, W3 . . . .**106** D5
Waleton Acres, Wall. SM6 . . . . .**200** C6
Waley St, E1 . . . .**113** G5
Walfield Av, N20 . . . .**41** E7
Walford Rd, N16 . . . .**94** B4
Walfrey Gdns, Dag. RM9 . . . . . .**101** F7
WALHAM GREEN, SW6 . . . .**128** E7
Walham Grn Ct, SW6
  off Waterford Rd **128/129** E7
Walham Gro, SW6 . . . .**128** D7
Walham Ri, SW19 . . . .**166** B6
Walham Yd, SW6
  off Walham Gro **128** D7
Walkden Rd, Chis. BR7 . . . .**174** D5
Walker Cl, N11 . . . .**58** C4
  SE18 . . . .**137** F4
  W7 . . . .**124** B1
  Hampton TW12
  off Fearnley Cres **161** F6
Walker Ms, SW2 *off Effra Rd* . .**151** G5
Walkers Ct, E8 *off Wilton Way* . .**94** D6
  W1 . . . .**17** H5
Walkerscroft Mead, SE21 . . . . .**169** J1
Walkers Pl, SW15
  off Felsham Rd **148** B3
Walkford Way, SE15
  off Daniel Gdns **132** C7
Walks, The, N2 . . . .**73** G3
Walkynscroft, SE15
  off Firbank Rd **152/153** E2
Wallace Cl, SE28
  off Haldane Rd **118** D7
★ **Wallace Collection**, W1 . . . . . .**16** B3
Wallace Cres, Cars. SM5 . . . . . .**199** J5
Wallace Rd, N1 . . . .**93** J6
Wallace Way, N19
  off Giesbach Rd **92** D2
Wallbutton Rd, SE4 . . . .**153** H2
Wallcote Av, NW2 . . . .**90** A1
Wall End Rd, E6 . . . .**98** C7
Waller Dr, Nthwd. HA6 . . . .**66** A2
Waller Rd, SE14 . . . .**153** G1
Wallers Cl, Dag. RM9 . . . .**119** E1
  Woodford Green IG8 . . . .**64** C6
Wallers Hoppit, Loug. IG10 . . . .**48** B2
Waller Way, SE10
  off Greenwich High Rd **134** B7
Wallflower St, W12 . . . .**107** F7
Wallgrave Rd, SW5 . . . .**30** A1
Wallingford Av, W10 . . . .**108** A5
WALLINGTON, SM6 . . . .**200** C5
Wallington Cor, Wall. SM6
  off Manor Rd N **200** B4
Wallington Rd, Ilf. IG3 . . . .**81** J7
Wallington Sq, Wall. SM6
  off Woodcote Rd **200** B6
Wallis All, SE1 . . . .**28** A3
Wallis Cl, SW11 . . . .**149** G3
Wallis Ms, N22
  off Brampton Pk Rd **75** G3
Wallis Rd, E9 . . . .**95** J6
  Southall UB1 . . . .**103** H6
Wallis's Cotts, SW2 . . . .**150** E7
Wallman Pl, N22
  off Bounds Grn Rd **75** F1
Wallorton Gdns, SW14 . . . .**146** D4
Wallside, EC2 . . . .**20** A2
Wall St, N1 . . . .**94** A6
Wallwood Rd, E11 . . . .**96** D1
Wallwood St, E14 . . . .**113** J5
Walmar Cl, Barn. EN4 . . . .**41** G1
Walmer Cl, E4 . . . .**62** B2
  Orpington BR6
  off Tubbenden La S **207** G4
  Romford RM7 . . . .**83** H2
Walmer Gdns, W13 . . . .**124** D2
Walmer Ho, N9 . . . .**44** C7
Walmer Pl, W1 . . . .**15** J1
Walmer Rd, W10 *off Latimer Rd* .**107** J6
  W11 . . . .**108** B7
Walmer St, W1 . . . .**15** J1
Walmer Ter, SE18 . . . .**137** F4
Walmgate Rd, Grnf. UB6 . . . . . .**104** E1
Walmington Fold, N12 . . . .**56** D6

Walm La, NW2 . . . .**90** A5
Walmsley Ho, SW16
  off Colson Way **168** C4
Walney Wk, N1 *off St. Paul's Rd* .**93** J6
Walnut Av, West Dr. UB7 . . . . . .**120** D3
Walnut Cl, SE8 *off Clyde St* **J6
  Carshalton SM5 . . . .**199** J5
  Ilford IG6 *off Civic Way* **81** F4
Walnut Ct, W5 . . . .**125** H2
Walnut Gdns, E15
  off Burgess Rd **96/97** E4
Walnut Gro, Enf. EN1 . . . .**44** A5
Walnut Ms, Sutt. SM2 . . . .**199** F7
Walnut Rd, E10 . . . .**96** A2
Walnut Tree Av, Mitch. CR4
  off De'Arn Gdns **185** H3
Walnut Tree Cl, SW13 . . . .**147** F1
  Chislehurst BR7 . . . .**193** F1
Walnut Tree Cotts, SW19
  off Church Rd **166** B4
Walnut Tree Rd, SE10 . . . .**135** E5
  Brentford TW8 . . . .**125** H6
  Dagenham RM8 . . . .**100** D2
  Hounslow TW5 . . . .**123** F6
Walnut Tree Wk, SE11 . . . .**34** E1
Walnut Way, Buck.H. IG9 . . . . . .**64** A3
  Ruislip HA4 . . . .**84** C6
Walpole Av, Rich. TW9 . . . .**145** J2
Walpole Cl, W13 . . . .**125** F2
  Pinner HA5 . . . .**51** G6
Walpole Cres, Tedd. TW11 . . . .**162** C5
Walpole Gdns, W4 . . . .**126** C5
  Twickenham TW2 . . . .**162** B2
Walpole Ms, NW8
  off Queen's Gro **109** G1
  SW19 *off Walpole Rd* **167** G6
Walpole Pk, W5 . . . .**125** F1
Walpole Pl, SE18
  off Brookhill Rd **136/137** E4
  Teddington TW11 . . . .**162** C5
Walpole Rd, E6 . . . .**97** J7
  E17 . . . .**77** H4
  E18 . . . .**79** F1
  N17 (Downhills Way) **75** J3
  N17 (Lordship La) **75** J2
  SW19 . . . .**167** G6
  Bromley BR2 . . . .**192** A5
  Croydon CR0 . . . .**202** A2
  Surbiton KT6 . . . .**181** H6
  Teddington TW11 . . . .**162** C5
  Twickenham TW2 . . . .**162** B2
Walpole St, SW3 . . . .**31** J3
Walrond Av, Wem. HA9 . . . .**87** H5
Walsham Cl, N16
  off Braydon Rd **76** D7
  SE28 . . . .**118** D7
Walsham Rd, SE14 . . . .**153** G2
  Feltham TW14 . . . .**142** B7
Walsingham Gdns, Epsom KT19 .**197** E4
Walsingham Pk, Chis. BR7 . . . . .**193** G2
Walsingham Pl, SW4
  off Clapham Common W
  Side **149** J4
  SW11 . . . .**150** A6
Walsingham Rd, E5 . . . .**94** D3
  W13 . . . .**124** D1
  Enfield EN2 . . . .**44** A4
  Mitcham CR4 . . . .**185** J5
Walsingham Wk, Belv. DA17 . . .**139** G6
Walter Hurford Par, E12
  off Walton Rd **98** D4
Walter Rodney Cl, E6
  off Stevenage Rd **98** C6
Walters Cl, SE17 . . . .**36** A2
  Hayes UB3
  off St. Anselms Rd **121** J2
Walters Ho, SE17 . . . .**35** G6
Walters Rd, SE25 . . . .**188** B4
  Enfield EN3 . . . .**45** F5
Walter St, E2 . . . .**113** G3
  Kingston upon Thames KT2
  off Sopwith Way **181** H1
Walters Way, SE23 . . . .**153** G6
Walters Yd, Brom. BR1 . . . .**191** G2
Walter Ter, E1 . . . .**113** G6
Walterton Rd, W9 . . . .**108** C4
Walter Wk, Edg. HA8 . . . .**54** C6
Waltham Av, NW9 . . . .**70** A6
  Hayes UB3 . . . .**121** F3
Waltham Dr, Edg. HA8 . . . .**70** A2
Waltham Pk Way, E17 . . . .**78** A1
Waltham Rd, Cars. SM5 . . . . . .**185** G7
  Southall UB2 . . . .**122** E3
  Woodford Green IG8 . . . .**64** B6
WALTHAMSTOW, E17 . . . .**78** B2
Walthamstow Av, E4 . . . .**62** A7
Walthamstow Business Cen,
  E17 . . . .**78** C2
Waltham Way, E4 . . . .**61** J4
Waltheof Av, N17 . . . .**76** A1
Waltheof Gdns, N17 . . . .**76** A1
Walton Av, Har. HA2 . . . .**85** F5
  New Malden KT3 . . . .**183** F4
  Sutton SM3 . . . .**198** C3
  Wembley HA9 . . . .**88** B3

Walton Cl, E5 *off Orient Way* **95** G3
  NW2 . . . .**89** H2
  SW8 . . . .**34** B7
  Harrow HA1 . . . .**68** A4
Walton Cres, Har. HA2 . . . .**85** F4
Walton Dr, NW10
  off Mitchellbrook Way **88** D6
  Harrow HA1 . . . .**68** A4
Walton Gdns, W3 . . . .**106** B5
  Wembley HA9 . . . .**87** H2
Walton Grn, Croy. (New Adgtn)
  CR0 . . . .**204** C7
Walton Pl, SW3 . . . .**23** J5
Walton Rd, E12 . . . .**98** D4
  E13 . . . .**115** J2
  N15 . . . .**76** C5
  East Molesey KT8 . . . .**179** G4
  Harrow HA1 . . . .**68** A4
  Sidcup DA14 . . . .**176** C2
  Walton-on-Thames KT12 . . . .**178** C5
  West Molesey KT8 . . . .**179** E5
Walton St, SW3 . . . .**31** H1
  Enfield EN2 . . . .**44** A1
Walton Way, W3 . . . .**106** B5
  Mitcham CR4 . . . .**186** C4
Walt Whitman Cl, SE24
  off Shakespeare Rd **151** H4
WALWORTH, SE17 . . . .**35** J3
★ **Walworth Garden Fm -**
  Horticultural Training Cen,
  SE17 . . . .**35** H4
Walworth Pl, SE17 . . . .**36** A4
Walworth Rd, SE1 . . . .**35** J1
  SE17 . . . .**35** J1
Walwyn Av, Brom. BR1 . . . .**192** A3
Wanborough Dr, SW15 . . . .**165** H1
Wanderer Dr, Bark. IG11 . . . . . .**118** B3
Wandle Bk, SW19 . . . .**167** G6
  Croydon CR0 . . . .**200** E3
Wandle Ct, Epsom KT19 . . . . . .**196** C4
Wandle Ct Gdns, Croy. CR0 . . . .**200** E4
Wandle Rd, SW17 . . . .**167** H2
  Croydon CR0 . . . .**201** J3
  Croydon (Waddon) CR0 . . . . .**201** G3
  Morden SM4 . . . .**185** F4
  Wallington SM6 . . . .**200** B2
Wandle Side, Croy. CR0 . . . . . .**201** F3
  Wallington SM6 . . . .**200** B3
Wandle Tech Pk, Mitch. CR4
  off Goat Rd **185** J7
Wandle Trd Est, Mitch. CR4
  off Budge La **185** J7
Wandle Way, SW18 . . . .**166** E1
  Mitcham CR4 . . . .**185** J5
Wandon Rd, SW6 . . . .**129** E7
WANDSWORTH, SW18 . . . .**148** C5
Wandsworth Br, SW6 . . . .**149** E3
  SW18 . . . .**149** E3
Wandsworth Br Rd, SW6 . . . . . .**148** E1
Wandsworth Common, SW12 . .**149** H6
Wandsworth Common W Side,
  SW18 . . . .**149** F5
Wandsworth High St, SW18 . . . .**148** D5
★ **Wandsworth Mus**, SW18
  off Garratt La **148** E5
Wandsworth Plain, SW18 . . . . .**148** E5
Wandsworth Rd, SW8 . . . .**34** A5
Wandsworth Shop Cen, SW18 . .**148** E6
Wangey Rd, Rom. RM6 . . . .**82** D7
Wanless Rd, SE24 . . . .**151** J3
Wanley Rd, SE5 . . . .**152** A4
Wanlip Rd, E13 . . . .**115** H4
Wannock Gdns, Ilf. IG6 . . . .**65** E7
Wansbeck Rd, E3 . . . .**95** J7
  E9 . . . .**95** J7
Wansdown Pl, SW6 . . . .**30** A7
Wansey St, SE17 . . . .**35** J2
Wansford Pk, Borwd. WD6 . . . . .**38** E4
Wansford Rd, Wdf.Grn. IG8 . . . . .**79** J1
WANSTEAD, E11 . . . .**79** H7
Wanstead Cl, Brom. BR1 . . . . . .**191** J2
Wanstead La, Ilf. IG1 . . . .**80** A6
Wanstead Pk, E11 . . . .**80** A7
Wanstead Pk Av, E12 . . . .**98** A2
Wanstead Pk Rd, Ilf. IG1 . . . . . .**98** C1
Wanstead Pl, E11 . . . .**79** G6
Wanstead Rd, Brom. BR1 . . . . .**191** J2
Wansunt Rd, Bex. DA5 . . . .**177** J1
Wantage Rd, SE12 . . . .**155** F5
Wantz Rd, Dag. RM10 . . . .**101** H4
WAPPING, E1 . . . .**29** J1
Wapping Dock St, E1
  off Cinnamon St **132/133** E1
Wapping High St, E1 . . . .**29** H2
Wapping La, E1 . . . .**113** E7
Wapping Wall, E1 . . . .**133** F1
Warbank La, Kings.T. KT2 . . . . .**165** F7
Warbeck Rd, W12 . . . .**127** H1
Warberry Rd, N22 . . . .**75** F2
Warboys App, Kings.T. KT2 . . . .**164** B6
Warboys Cres, E4 . . . .**62** C5
Warboys Rd, Kings.T. KT2 . . . . .**164** B6
Warburton Cl, N1
  off Culford Rd **94** B6
  Harrow HA3 . . . .**52** A6

Warburton Rd, E8 . . . .**95** E1
  Twickenham TW2 . . . .**161** H1
Warburton St, E8
  off Warburton Rd **112/113** E1
Warburton Ter, E17 . . . .**78** B2
Wardalls Gro, SE14 . . . .**133** F7
Ward Cl, S.Croy. CR2 . . . .**202** B5
Wardell Cl, NW7 . . . .**55** E7
Wardell Fld, NW9 . . . .**71** E1
Warden Av, Har. HA2 . . . .**85** F1
Warden Rd, NW5 . . . .**92** A6
Wardens Fld Cl, Orp. BR6 . . . . .**207** H6
Wardens Gro, SE1 . . . .**27** J2
Wardle St, E9 . . . .**95** G5
Wardley St, SW18
  off Garratt La **148/149** E7
Wardo Av, SW6 . . . .**148** B1
Wardour Ms, W1 . . . .**17** G4
Wardour St, W1 . . . .**17** H5
Ward Rd, E15 . . . .**114** D1
  N19 . . . .**92** C3
Wardrobe Pl, EC4 *off Carter La* .**111** H6
Wardrobe Ter, EC4 . . . .**19** H4
Wards Rd, Ilf. IG2 . . . .**81** G7
Wards Wf App, E16 . . . .**136** A2
Wareham Cl, Houns. TW3 . . . . .**143** H4
Waremead Rd, Ilf. IG2 . . . .**80** E5
Warenford Way, Borwd. WD6 . . .**38** A1
Warfield Rd, NW10 . . . .**108** A3
  Feltham TW14 . . . .**141** H7
  Hampton TW12 . . . .**179** H1
Warfield Yd, NW10
  off Warfield Rd **108** A3
Wargrave Av, N15 . . . .**76** C6
Wargrave Rd, Har. HA2 . . . .**85** J3
Warham Rd, N4 . . . .**75** G7
  Harrow HA3 . . . .**68** C2
  South Croydon CR2 . . . .**201** J5
Warham St, SE5 . . . .**35** H7
Waring Cl, Orp. BR6 . . . .**207** J6
Waring Dr, Orp. BR6 . . . .**207** J6
Waring Rd, Sid. DA14 . . . .**176** C6
Waring St, SE27 . . . .**169** J4
Warkworth Gdns, Islw. TW7 . . .**124** D7
Warkworth Rd, N17 . . . .**60** A7
Warland Rd, SE18 . . . .**137** G7
Warley Av, Dag. RM8 . . . .**83** F7
  Hayes UB4 . . . .**102** A5
Warley Cl, E10 *off Millicent Rd* . .**95** J1
Warley Rd, N9 . . . .**61** F2
  Hayes UB4 . . . .**102** A6
  Ilford IG5 . . . .**80** D1
  Woodford Green IG8 . . . .**63** H7
Warley St, E2 . . . .**113** G3
Warlingham Rd, Th.Hth. CR7 . . .**187** H4
Warlock Rd, W9 . . . .**108** D4
Warlters Cl, N7
  off Warlters Rd **92/93** E4
Warlters Rd, N7 . . . .**93** E4
Warltersville Rd, N19 . . . .**74** E7
Warmington Cl, E5
  off Orient Way **95** G3
Warmington Rd, SE24 . . . .**151** J6
Warmington St, E13
  off Barking Rd **115** G4
Warminster Gdns, SE25 . . . . . .**188** D2
Warminster Rd, SE25 . . . .**188** C2
Warminster Sq, SE25 . . . .**188** D2
Warminster Way, Mitch. CR4 . . .**186** B1
Warndon St, SE16 . . . .**133** G4
Warneford Rd, Har. HA3 . . . .**69** G3
Warneford St, E9 . . . .**113** E1
Warne Pl, Sid. DA15
  off Westerham Dr **158** B6
Warner Av, Sutt. SM3 . . . .**198** B2
Warner Cl, E15 . . . .**97** E5
  NW9 . . . .**71** F7
  Hampton TW12
  off Tangley Pk Rd **161** F5
  Hayes UB3 . . . .**121** G7
Warner Ho, SE13
  off Conington Rd **154** B2
Warner Par, Hayes UB3 . . . . . .**121** G7
Warner Pl, E2 . . . .**13** J2
Warner Rd, E17 . . . .**77** H4
  N8 . . . .**74** D4
  SE5 . . . .**151** J1
  Bromley BR1 . . . .**173** F7
Warners Cl, Wdf.Grn. IG8 . . . . . .**63** G5
Warners La, Kings.T. KT2 . . . . . .**163** G4
Warners Path, Wdf.Grn. IG8 . . . .**63** G5
Warner St, EC1 . . . .**11** E6
Warner Ter, E14
  off Broomfield St **114** A5
Warner Yd, EC1 . . . .**10** E6
Warnford Ho, SW15
  off Tunworth Cres **147** F6
Warnford Ind Est, Hayes UB3 . .**121** H2
Warnford Rd, Orp. BR6 . . . .**207** J5
Warnham Ct Rd, Cars. SM5 . . . .**199** J7
Warnham Rd, N12 . . . .**57** H5
Warple Ms, W3
  off Warple Way **126/127** E2
Warple Way, W3 . . . .**126** E1

Warren, The, E12 . . . .**98** B4
Hayes UB4 . . . .**102** A6
Hounslow TW5 . . . .**123** F7
Worcester Park KT4 . . . .**196** D4
Warren Av, E10 . . . .**96** C3
Bromley BR1 . . . .**172** E7
Orpington BR6 . . . .**207** J5
Richmond TW10 . . . .**146** B4
South Croydon CR2 . . . .**203** G7
Warren Cl, N9 . . . .**45** G7
SE21 off Lairdale Cl **151** J7
Bexleyheath DA6 . . . .**159** G5
Hayes UB4 . . . .**102** C5
Wembley HA9 . . . .**87** G2
Warren Ct, SE7
off Charlton Ch La **135** J5
Chigwell IG7 . . . .**65** G4
Warren Cres, N9 . . . .**44** C7
Warren Cutting, Kings.T. KT2 . .**164** D7
Warrender Rd, N19 . . . .**92** C3
Warrender Way, Ruis. HA4 . . . . .**66** A7
Warren Dr, Grnf. UB6 . . . .**103** H4
Ruislip HA4 . . . .**66** D7
Warren Dr, The, E11 . . . .**79** J7
Warren Dr N, Surb. KT5 . . . .**196** B1
Warren Dr S, Surb. KT5 . . . .**196** C1
Warren Flds, Stan. HA7
off Valencia Rd **53** F4
Warren Footpath, Twick. TW1 . . .**163** F1
Warren Gdns, E15
off Ashton Rd **96** D5
Warren Gro, Borwd. WD6 . . . . . .**38** D4
Warren Hts, Loug. IG10 . . . .**47** J5
Warren Hill, Loug. IG10 . . . .**47** J6
Warren Ho, E3
off Bromley High St **114** B3
Warren La, SE18 . . . .**136** E3
Stanmore HA7 . . . .**52** C3
Warren La Gate, SE18 . . . .**136** E3
Warren Ms, W1 . . . .**9** F6
Warren Pk, Kings.T. KT2 . . . . . .**164** C6
Warren Pk Rd, Sutt. SM1 . . . . . .**199** G6
Warren Pond Rd, E4 . . . .**63** F1
Warren Rd, E4 . . . .**62** C2
E10 . . . .**96** C3
E11 . . . .**97** J1
NW2 . . . .**89** F2
SW19 . . . .**167** H6
Bexleyheath DA6 . . . .**159** G5
Bromley BR2 . . . .**205** G4
Bushey (Bushey Hth) WD23 . .**51** J1
Croydon CR0 . . . .**202** B1
Ilford IG6 . . . .**81** G5
Kingston upon Thames KT2 . .**164** C6
Orpington BR6 . . . .**207** J5
Sidcup DA14 . . . .**176** C3
Twickenham TW2 . . . .**143** J6
Warrens Shawe La, Edg. HA8 . . .**54** B1
Warren St, W1 . . . .**9** E6
Warren Ter, Rom. RM6 . . . .**82** D4
Warren Wk, SE7 . . . .**135** J6
Warren Way, NW7 . . . .**56** B6
Warren Wd Cl, Brom. BR2 . . . . .**205** F2
Warriner Dr, N9 . . . .**60** D3
Warriner Gdns, SW11 . . . .**149** J1
Warrington Cres, W9 . . . .**6** C6
Warrington Gdns, W9 . . . .**6** C6
Warrington Pl, E14
off Yabsley St **134** C1
Warrington Rd, Croy. CR0 . . . . .**201** H3
Dagenham RM8 . . . .**100** D2
Harrow HA1 . . . .**68** B5
Richmond TW10 . . . .**145** G5
Warrington Sq, Dag. RM8 . . . . .**100** D2
Warrior Sq, E12 . . . .**98** D4
Warsaw Cl, Ruis. HA4
off Glebe Av **84** B6
Warsdale Dr, NW9
off Mardale Dr **70** D5
Warspite Rd, SE18 . . . .**136** B3
Warton Rd, E15 . . . .**96** C7
Warwall, E6 . . . .**116** E6
Warwick Av, W2 . . . .**6** C6
W9 . . . .**6** C6
Edgware HA8 . . . .**54** B3
Harrow HA2 . . . .**85** F4
Warwick Bldg, SW8
off Queenstown Rd **130** B6
Warwick Cl, Barn. EN4 . . . .**41** G5
Bexley DA5 . . . .**159** F7
Hampton TW12 . . . .**161** J7
Warwick Ct, SE15 . . . .**152** D2
WC1 . . . .**18** D2
Surbiton KT6 off Hook Rd . . .**195** H2
Warwick Cres, W2 . . . .**14** C1
Warwick Dene, W5 . . . .**125** H1
Warwick Dr, SW15 . . . .**147** H3
Warwick Est, W2 . . . .**14** B2
Warwick Gdns, N4 . . . .**75** J5
W14 . . . .**128** C3
Ilford IG1 . . . .**99** E1
Thames Ditton KT7 . . . .**180** C5
Warwick Gro, E5 . . . .**94** E1
Surbiton KT5 . . . .**181** J7

Warwick Ho St, SW1 . . . .**25** J1
Warwick La, EC4 . . . .**19** H4
Warwick Pas, EC4 . . . .**19** H3
Warwick Pl, W5 off Warwick Rd .**125** G2
W9 . . . .**14** C1
Warwick Pl N, SW1 . . . .**33** F2
Warwick Rd, E4 . . . .**62** A5
E11 . . . .**79** H5
E12 . . . .**98** B5
E15 . . . .**97** F6
E17 . . . .**77** J1
N11 . . . .**58** D6
N18 . . . .**60** B4
SE20 . . . .**189** E3
SW5 . . . .**128** C4
W5 . . . .**125** G2
W14 . . . .**128** C4
Barnet EN5 . . . .**40** E4
Borehamwood WD6 . . . .**38** D3
Hounslow TW4 . . . .**142** B3
Kingston upon Thames KT1 . .**181** F1
New Malden KT3 . . . .**182** C3
Sidcup DA14 . . . .**176** B5
Southall UB2 . . . .**123** F3
Sutton SM1 . . . .**199** F4
Thames Ditton KT7 . . . .**180** C5
Thornton Heath CR7 . . . .**187** G3
Twickenham TW2 . . . .**162** B1
Welling DA16 . . . .**158** C3
West Drayton UB7 . . . .**120** B2
Warwick Row, SW1 . . . .**25** F5
Warwickshire Path, SE8 . . . .**133** J7
Warwick Sq, EC4 . . . .**19** H3
SW1 . . . .**33** F3
Warwick Sq Ms, SW1 . . . .**33** F2
Warwick St, W1 . . . .**17** G5
Warwick Ter, SE18 . . . .**137** G6
Warwick Way, SW1 . . . .**33** F2
Warwick Yd, EC1 . . . .**12** A6
Washington Av, E12 . . . .**98** B4
Washington Cl, E3
off St. Leonards St **114** B3
Washington Rd, E6
off St. Stephens Rd **97** J7
E18 . . . .**79** F2
SW13 . . . .**127** G7
Kingston upon Thames KT1 . .**182** A2
Worcester Park KT4 . . . .**197** H2
Wastdale Rd, SE23 . . . .**171** G1
Watchfield Ct, W4 . . . .**126** C5
Watcombe Cotts, Rich. TW9 . . . .**126** A6
Watcombe Pl, SE25
off Albert Rd **188/189** E5
Watcombe Rd, SE25 . . . .**188** E5
Waterbank Rd, SE6 . . . .**172** B3
Waterbeach Rd, Dag. RM9 . . . . .**100** C6
Waterbrook La, NW4 . . . .**71** J5
Watercress Pl, N1
off Hertford Rd **94** B7
Waterdale Rd, SE2 . . . .**138** A6
Waterden Rd, E15 . . . .**96** A5
Waterer Ri, Wall. SM6 . . . .**200** D6
Waterfall Cl, N14 . . . .**58** C3
Waterfall Cotts, SW19 . . . .**167** G6
Waterfall Rd, N11 . . . .**58** B4
N14 . . . .**58** C3
SW19 . . . .**167** G6
Waterfall Ter, SW17 . . . .**167** H6
Waterfield Cl, SE28 . . . .**138** B1
Belvedere DA17 . . . .**139** G3
Waterfield Gdns, SE25 . . . .**188** B5
Waterford Rd, SW6 . . . .**149** E1
Waterfront Studios Business Cen,
E16 off Dock Rd **135** F1
Water Gdns, Stan. HA7 . . . .**53** E6
Water Gdns, The, W2 . . . .**15** H3
Watergardens, The, Kings.T. KT2 .**164** C6
Watergate, EC4 . . . .**19** G5
Watergate, The, Wat. WD19 . . . . .**50** D2
Watergate St, SE8 . . . .**134** A6
Watergate Wk, WC2 . . . .**26** B1
Waterhall Av, E4 . . . .**62** E4
Waterhall Cl, E17 . . . .**77** G1
Waterhouse Cl, E16 . . . .**116** A5
NW3 off Lyndhurst Rd **91** G5
W6 off Great Ch La **128** A4
Waterhouse Sq, EC1 . . . .**19** E2
Wateridge Cl, E14
off Westferry Rd **134** A3
Water La, E15 . . . .**97** E6
EC3 . . . .**20** D6
N9 . . . .**60** E1
NW1 off Kentish Town Rd **92** B7
SE14 . . . .**133** F7
Ilford IG3 . . . .**99** H3
Kingston upon Thames KT1 . .**181** G1
Richmond TW9 . . . .**145** G4
Sidcup DA14 . . . .**177** F2
Twickenham TW1
off The Embankment **162** D1
Water Lily Ct, Sthl. UB2
off Navigator Dr **123** J2
Waterloo Br, SE1 . . . .**18** C6
WC2 . . . .**18** C6
Waterloo Cl, E9 off Churchill Wk .**95** F5

Waterloo Est, E2 . . . .**113** F2
Waterloo Gdns, E2 . . . .**113** F2
N1 off Barnsbury St **93** H7
Waterloo Pas, NW6 . . . .**90** C7
Waterloo Pl, SW1 . . . .**25** H1
Richmond TW9 off Sheen Rd .**145** H5
Richmond (Kew) TW9 . . . . . .**126** A6
Waterloo Rd, E6 . . . .**97** J7
E7 off Wellington Rd **97** F5
E10 . . . .**78** A7
NW2 . . . .**89** D1
SE1 . . . .**27** E3
Ilford IG6 . . . .**81** F2
Sutton SM1 . . . .**199** G5
Waterloo Ter, N1 . . . .**93** H7
Waterlow Ct, NW11
off Heath Cl **72/73** E7
Waterlow Rd, N19 . . . .**92** C1
★ **Watermans Art Cen**, Brent.
TW8 . . . .**125** H6
Waterman's Cl, Kings.T. KT2
off Woodside Rd **163** H7
Waterman St, SW15 . . . .**148** A3
Waterman's Wk, EC4
off Upper Thames St **112** A4
Watermans Wk, SE16 . . . .**133** H3
Waterman Way, E1 . . . .**132** E1
Watermead Ho, E9
off Kingsmead Way **95** H5
Watermead La, Cars. SM5
off Middleton Rd **185** J7
Watermeadow La, SW6 . . . .**149** F2
Watermead Rd, SE6 . . . .**172** C4
Watermead Way, N17 . . . .**76** D3
Watermen's Sq, SE20 . . . .**171** F7
Water Ms, SE15 . . . .**153** F4
Watermill Cl, Rich. TW10 . . . .**163** F3
Watermill La, N18 . . . .**60** B5
Watermill Way, SW19 . . . .**185** F1
Feltham TW13 . . . .**161** F2
Watermint Quay, N16 . . . .**76** D7
Water Rd, Wem. HA0 . . . .**105** J1
Watersedge, Epsom KT19 . . . . . .**196** C4
Watersfield Way, Edg. HA8 . . . . .**53** G7
Waters Gdns, Dag. RM10 . . . . . .**101** G5
Waterside, Beck. BR3 . . . .**190** A1
Waterside Av, Beck. BR3
off Creswell Dr **190** B5
Waterside Cl, E3 . . . .**113** J1
SE16 . . . .**29** J4
SE28 off Barnham Dr **137** J1
Barking IG11 . . . .**100** A4
Northolt UB5 . . . .**103** F3
Surbiton KT6 off Culsac Rd . .**195** H2
Waterside Ct, SE13
off Weardale Rd **154** D4
Waterside Dr, Walt. KT12 . . . . . .**178** A5
Waterside Path, SW18
off Smugglers Way **148/149** E4
Waterside Pl, NW1
off Princess Rd **110** A1
Waterside Pt, SW11 . . . .**31** H7
Waterside Rd, Sthl. UB2 . . . .**123** G3
Waterside Twr, SW6 . . . .**149** F1
Waterside Trd Cen, W7 . . . .**124** B3
Waterside Way, SW17 . . . .**167** F4
Watersmeet Way, SE28 . . . .**118** C2
Waterson St, E2 . . . .**13** E3
Waters Pl, SW15
off Danemere St **147** J2
Watersplash Cl, Kings.T. KT1 . . .**181** H3
Watersplash La, Hayes UB3 . . . .**122** A4
Hounslow TW5 . . . .**122** B5
Waters Rd, SE6 . . . .**172** E3
Kingston upon Thames KT1 . .**182** B2
Waters Sq, Kings.T. KT1 . . . .**182** B3
Water St, WC2 . . . .**18** D5
Water Twr Hill, Croy. CR0 . . . . . .**202** A4
Water Twr Pl, N1
off Old Royal Free Sq **111** G1
Waterview Ho, E14 . . . .**113** H5
Waterworks Cor, E18 . . . .**79** E1
Waterworks La, E5 . . . .**95** G2
Waterworks Rd, SW2 . . . .**151** F6
Waterworks Yd, Croy. CR0
off Surrey St **201** J3
Watery La, SW20 . . . .**184** C2
Northolt UB5 . . . .**102** C2
Sidcup DA14 . . . .**176** B6
Wates Way, Mitch. CR4 . . . .**185** J6
Wates Way Ind Est, Mitch. CR4
off Wates Way **185** J6
Wateville Rd, N17 . . . .**75** J1
WATFORD HEATH, Wat. WD19 . . .**50** E1
Watford Cl, SW11
off Petworth St **149** H1
Watford Rd, E16 . . . .**115** G5
Harrow HA1 . . . .**86** D2
Wembley HA0 . . . .**86** D2
Watford Way, NW4 . . . .**71** G4
NW7 . . . .**71** G4
Watkin Rd, Wem. HA9 . . . .**88** B3
Watkinson Rd, N7 . . . .**93** F6
Watling Av, Edg. HA8 . . . .**54** D7
Watling Ct, EC4 . . . .**20** A4

Watling Fm Cl, Stan. HA7 . . . . . .**53** F1
Watling Gdns, NW2 . . . .**90** B6
Watlings Cl, Croy. CR0 . . . .**189** H6
Watling St, EC4 . . . .**19** J4
SE15 . . . .**36** E6
Bexleyheath DA6 . . . .**159** H4
Watlington Gro, SE26 . . . .**171** H5
Watney Mkt, E1
off Commercial Rd **112/113** E6
Watney Rd, SW14 . . . .**146** C3
Watneys Rd, Mitch. CR4 . . . .**186** D5
Watney St, E1 . . . .**113** E6
Watson Av, E6 . . . .**98** D7
Sutton SM3 . . . .**198** B2
Watson Cl, N16 off Matthias Rd . .**94** A5
SW19 . . . .**167** H6
Watson's Ms, W1 . . . .**15** H2
Watsons Rd, N22 . . . .**75** F1
Watson's St, SE8 . . . .**134** A7
Watson St, E13 . . . .**115** H2
Watsons Yd, NW2
off North Circular Rd **89** F2
Wattisfield Rd, E5 . . . .**95** F3
Watts Cl, N15 off Seaford Rd **76** B5
Watts Gro, E3 . . . .**114** B5
Watts La, Chis. BR7 . . . .**193** E1
Teddington TW11 . . . .**162** D5
Watts Rd, T.Ditt. KT7 . . . .**180** D7
Watts St, E1 . . . .**133** E1
SE15 . . . .**152** C1
Watts Way, SW7 . . . .**23** F5
Wat Tyler Rd, SE3 . . . .**154** C2
SE10 . . . .**154** C2
Wauthier Cl, N13 . . . .**59** H5
Wavel Dr, Sid. DA15 . . . .**157** H6
Wavel Ms, N8 . . . .**74** D4
NW6 off Acol Rd **90/91** E7
Wavel Pl, SE26
off Sydenham Hill **170** C4
Wavendon Av, W4 . . . .**126** D5
Waveney Av, SE15 . . . .**153** E4
Waveney Cl, E1 . . . .**29** J1
Waverley Av, E4 . . . .**61** J4
E17 . . . .**78** D3
Surbiton KT5 . . . .**182** B6
Sutton SM1 . . . .**199** E2
Twickenham TW2 . . . .**161** F1
Wembley HA9 . . . .**87** J5
Waverley Cl, E18 . . . .**79** J1
Bromley BR2 . . . .**192** A5
Hayes UB3 . . . .**121** G4
West Molesey KT8 . . . .**179** G5
Waverley Cres, SE18 . . . .**137** G5
Waverley Gdns, E6
off Oliver Gdns **116** B5
NW10 . . . .**105** J3
Barking IG11 . . . .**117** H2
Ilford IG6 . . . .**81** F2
Northwood HA6 . . . .**66** A1
Waverley Gro, N3 . . . .**72** B3
Waverley Ind Est, Har. HA1 . . . . .**68** A3
Waverley Pl, N4
off Adolphus Rd **93** H2
NW8 . . . .**6** E1
Waverley Rd, E17 . . . .**78** C3
E18 . . . .**79** J1
N8 . . . .**74** D6
N17 . . . .**60** D7
SE18 . . . .**137** F5
SE25 . . . .**188** E4
Enfield EN2 . . . .**43** H4
Epsom KT17 . . . .**197** H5
Harrow HA2 . . . .**85** F1
Southall UB1 . . . .**103** H7
Waverley Vil, N17 . . . .**76** C2
Waverley Wk, W2 . . . .**108** D5
Waverley Way, Cars. SM5 . . . . . .**199** H6
Waverton Ho, E3 . . . .**113** J1
Waverton Rd, SW18 . . . .**149** F7
Waverton St, W1 . . . .**24** C1
Wavertree Ct, SW2
off Streatham Hill **169** F1
Wavertree Rd, E18 . . . .**79** G2
SW2 . . . .**169** E1
Waxlow Cres, Sthl. UB1 . . . .**103** G6
Waxlow Rd, NW10 . . . .**106** C2
Waxwell Cl, Pnr. HA5 . . . .**66** D2
Waxwell La, Pnr. HA5 . . . .**66** D2
Waye Av, Houns. TW5 . . . .**142** A1
Wayfarer Rd, Nthlt. UB5 . . . .**102** D4
Wayfield Link, SE9 . . . .**157** G6
Wayford St, SW11 . . . .**149** H2
Wayland Av, E8 . . . .**94** D5
Waylands Mead, Beck. BR3 . . . .**190** B1
Wayleave, The, SE28 . . . .**118** B7
Waylett Pl, SE27 . . . .**169** H3
Wembley HA0 . . . .**87** G4
Wayman Ct, E8 . . . .**94** E6
Wayne Cl, Orp. BR6 . . . .**207** J3
Waynflete Av, Croy. CR0 . . . .**201** H3
Waynflete Sq, W10 . . . .**108** A7
Waynflete St, SW18 . . . .**167** F2
Wayside, NW11 . . . .**90** B1
SW14 . . . .**146** C5
Croydon CR0 off Field Way . .**204** B6

Wayside Cl, N14 ....42 C6
Wayside Commercial Est, Bark.
  IG11 ....118 A1
Wayside Ct, Twick. TW1 ......145 F6
  Wembley HA9
    off Oakington Av 88 A3
Wayside Gdns, SE9
  off Wayside Gro 174 C4
  Dagenham RM10 ....101 A5
Wayside Gro, SE9 ....174 C4
Wayside Ms, Ilf. IG2
  off Gaysham Av 80 D5
Weald, The, Chis. BR7 ....174 C6
Weald Cl, SE16
  off Stevenson Cres ...132/133 E5
  Bromley BR2 ....206 B2
Weald La, Har. HA3 ....68 A2
Weald Ri, Har. HA3 ....52 C7
Weald Sq, E5
  off Rossington St 94/95 E2
WEALDSTONE, Har. HA3 .....68 C3
Wealdstone Rd, Sutt. SM3 ...198 C2
Weald Way, Rom. RM7 ....83 H6
Wealdwood Gdns, Pnr. HA5
  off Highbanks Rd 51 H6
Weale Rd, E4 ....62 D3
Weardale Gdns, Enf. EN2 .....44 A1
Weardale Rd, SE13 ....154 D4
Wear Pl, E2 ....112 E3
Wearside Rd, SE13 ....154 B4
Weatherley Cl, E3 ....113 J5
Weaver Cl, E6 off Trader Rd .116/117 E7
  Croydon CR0 ....202 C4
Weavers Cl, Islw. TW7 ......144 B4
Weavers Ter, SW6 ....128 D6
Weaver St, E1 ....13 H6
Weavers Way, NW1 ....110 D1
Weaver Wk, SE27 ....169 H4
Webb Cl, W10 ....107 A4
Webber Row, SE1 ....27 F5
Webber St, SE1 ....27 F3
Webb Est, E5 ....76 D7
Webb Gdns, E13 off Kelland Rd 115 G4
Webb Pl, NW10 off Old Oak La .107 F3
Webb Rd, SE3 ....135 F6
Webbscroft Rd, Dag. RM10 ...101 H4
Webbs Rd, SW11 ....149 J5
  Hayes UB4 ....102 B3
Webb St, SE1 ....28 D6
Webheath Est, NW6 ....90 C7
Webster Gdns, W5 ....125 G1
Webster Rd, E11 ....96 C3
  SE16 ....29 J6
Wedderburn Rd, NW3 ....91 G5
  Barking IG11 ....117 G1
Wedgewood Wk, NW6
  off Lymington Rd 90/91 E5
Wedgwood Ms, W1 ....17 J4
Wedgwood Wk, NW6
  off Dresden Cl 90 E5
Wedgwood Way, SE19 ......169 J7
Wedlake St, W10 off Kensal Rd 108 B4
Wedmore Av, Ilf. IG5 ....80 D1
Wedmore Gdns, N19 ....92 D2
Wedmore Ms, N19
  off Wedmore St 92 D3
Wedmore Rd, Grnf. UB6 .....104 A3
Wedmore St, N19 ....92 D3
Weech Rd, NW6 ....90 D4
Weedington Rd, NW5 ....92 A5
Weekley Sq, SW11
  off Thomas Baines Rd ...149 G3
Weigall Rd, SE12 ....155 G4
Weighhouse St, W1 ....16 C4
Weighton Rd, SE20 ....188 E2
  Harrow HA3 ....68 A1
Weihurst Gdns, Sutt. SM1 ...199 G5
Weimar St, SW15 ....148 B3
Weirdale Av, N20 ....57 J2
Weir Est, SW12 ....150 C7
Weir Hall Av, N18 ....60 A6
Weir Hall Gdns, N18 ....60 A5
Weir Hall Rd, N17 ....60 A5
  N18 ....60 A5
Weir Rd, SW12 ....150 C7
  SW19 ....167 E3
  Bexley DA5 ....159 H1
  Walton-on-Thames KT12 .178 A6
Weirside Gdns, West Dr. UB7 .120 A1
Weir's Pas, NW1 ....9 J3
Weiss Rd, SW15 ....148 A3
Welbeck Av, Brom. BR1 .....173 G4
  Hayes UB4 ....102 B4
  Sidcup DA15 ....176 A1
Welbeck Cl, N12
  off Torrington Pk 57 G5
  Borehamwood WD6 ....38 A3
  Epsom KT17 ....197 G7
  New Malden KT3 ......183 F5
Welbeck Rd, E6 ....116 A3
  Barnet EN4 ....41 G6
  Carshalton SM5 ....199 H1
  Harrow HA2 ....85 H1
  Sutton SM1 ....199 G2
Welbeck St, W1 ....16 D3

Welbeck Wk, Cars. SM5
  off Welbeck Rd 199 H1
Welbeck Way, W1 ....16 D3
Welby St, SE5 ....151 H1
Welch Pl, Pnr. HA5 ....66 C1
Weldon Cl, Ruis. HA4 ....84 B6
Weldon Dr, W.Mol. KT8 .....179 F4
Weld Pl, N11 ....58 B5
Welfare Rd, E15 ....97 E7
Welford Cl, E5 off Denton Way .95 G3
Welford Pl, SW19 ....166 B4
Welham Rd, SW16 ....168 A5
  SW17 ....168 A5
Welhouse Rd, Cars. SM5 ....199 H1
Wellacre Rd, Har. HA3 ......69 E6
Wellan Cl, Sid. DA15 ....158 B5
Welland Gdns, Grnf. UB6 ....104 C2
Welland Ms, E1 ....29 J1
Wellands Cl, Brom. BR1 .....192 C2
Welland St, SE10 ....134 C6
Well App, Barn. EN5 ....39 J5
Wellbrook Rd, Orp. BR6 ....206 D4
Well Cl, SW16 ....169 F4
  Ruislip HA4
  off Parkfield Cres 84/85 E3
Wellclose Sq, E1 ....21 J5
Wellclose St, E1 ....21 J6
★ Wellcome Trust, NW1 .....9 G5
Well Cottage Cl, E11 ....79 J7
Well Ct, EC4 ....20 A4
  SW16 ....169 F4
Welldon Cres, Har. HA1 .....68 B6
Weller St, SE1 ....27 J3
Wellesley Av, W6 ....127 H3
Wellesley Cl, SE7
  off Wellington Gdns ...135 J5
Wellesley Ct, W9 ....6 C3
Wellesley Ct Rd, Croy. CR0 ..202 A2
Wellesley Cres, Twick. TW2 ..162 B2
Wellesley Gro, Croy. CR0 ....202 A2
Wellesley Pas, Croy. CR0
  off Wellesley Rd 201 J2
Wellesley Pl, NW1 ....9 H4
Wellesley Rd, E11 ....79 G5
  E17 ....78 A6
  N22 ....75 G2
  NW5 ....92 A5
  W4 ....126 A5
  Croydon CR0 ....201 J1
  Harrow HA1 ....68 B5
  Ilford IG1 ....98 E2
  Sutton SM2 ....199 F6
  Twickenham TW2 ......162 A3
Wellesley St, E1 ....113 G5
Wellesley Ter, N1 ....12 A3
Wellfield Av, N10 ....74 B3
Wellfield Rd, SW16 ....169 E4
Wellfields, Loug. IG10 ......48 D3
Wellfield Wk, SW16 ....169 F5
Wellfit St, SE24 off Hinton Rd .151 H3
Wellgarth, Grnf. UB6 ....86 E6
Wellgarth Rd, NW11 ....91 E1
Well Gro, N20 ....41 F7
Well Hall Par, SE9
  off Well Hall Rd 156 C4
Well Hall Rd, SE9 ....156 C3
Wellhouse La, Barn. EN5 ....39 J4
Wellhouse Rd, Beck. BR3 ...189 J4
WELLING, DA16 ....158 A3
Welling High St, Well. DA16 .158 B3
Wellings Ho, Hayes UB3 ....122 B1
★ Wellington Arch, W1 ......24 C3
Wellington Av, E4 ....62 A2
  N9 ....61 E3
  N15 ....76 C6
  Hounslow TW3 ....143 G5
  Pinner HA5 ....67 F1
  Sidcup DA15 ....158 A6
  Worcester Park KT4 ...197 J3
Wellington Bldgs, SW1 .....32 C4
Wellington Cl, SE14
  off Rutts Ter 153 G1
  W11 off Ledbury Rd ...108 D6
  Dagenham RM10 ......101 J7
  Watford WD19 off Highfield .51 F3
Wellington Ct, NW8 ....7 E2
  Staines TW19 off Clare Rd .140 B7
Wellington Cres, N.Mal. KT3 .182 C3
Wellington Dr, Dag. RM10 ...101 J7
Wellington Gdns, SE7 ......135 J6
  Twickenham TW2 ......162 A4
Wellington Gro, SE10
  off Crooms Hill 134 D7
Wellington Ms, SE7 ....135 J6
  SE22 off Peckham Rye ..152 D4
  SW16 off Woodbourne Av .168 A5
Wellington Pk Est, NW2 ....89 G2
Wellington Pas, E11
  off Wellington Rd 79 G5
Wellington Pl, N2
  off Great N Rd 73 H5
  NW8 ....7 F3
Wellington Rd, E6 ....116 C2
  E7 ....97 F4

Wellington Rd, E10 ....95 H1
  E11 ....79 G5
  E17 ....77 H3
  NW8 ....7 E1
  NW10 ....108 A3
  SW19 ....166 D2
  W5 ....125 F3
  Belvedere DA17 ......139 F3
  Bexley DA5 ....158 D5
  Bromley BR2 ....191 J4
  Croydon CR0 ....187 H7
  Enfield EN1 ....44 B4
  Feltham TW14 ....141 H5
  Hampton TW12 ....162 A5
  Harrow HA3 ....68 B3
  Pinner HA5 ....67 F1
  Twickenham TW2 ......162 A5
Wellington Rd N, Houns. TW4 .143 F4
Wellington Rd S, Houns. TW4 .143 F4
Wellington Row, E2 ....13 G3
Wellington Sq, SW3 ....31 J3
Wellington St, SE18 ....136 D4
  WC2 ....18 B5
  Barking IG11 off Axe St ...117 F1
Wellington Ter, E1 ....132 E1
  W2 off Notting Hill Gate .108/109 E7
  Harrow HA1 off West St ...86 A1
Wellington Way, E3 ....114 A3
Welling Way, SE9 ....157 G3
  Welling DA16 ....157 G3
Well La, SW14 ....146 C5
Wellmeadow Rd, SE6 ......155 E7
  SE13 ....154 E6
  W7 ....124 D4
Wellow Wk, Cars. SM5 .....199 G1
Well Pas, NW3 ....91 G3
Well Rd, NW3 ....91 G3
  Barnet EN5 ....39 J5
Wells, The, N14 ....42 D7
Wells Cl, Nthlt. UB5
  off Yeading La 102 C3
  South Croydon CR2 ...202 B5
Wells Dr, NW9 ....88 D1
Wells Gdns, Dag. RM10 ....101 H5
  Ilford IG1 ....80 B7
Wells Ho Rd, NW10 ....106 E5
Wellside Cl, Barn. EN5 ......39 J4
Wellside Gdns, SW14
  off Well La 146 C5
Wells Ms, W1 ....17 G2
Wellsmoor Gdns, Brom. BR1 .192 D3
Wells Pk Rd, SE26 ....170 D3
Wells Pl, SW18 ....149 F7
Wells Ri, NW8 ....109 J1
Wells Rd, W12 ....127 J2
  Bromley BR1 ....192 C2
Wells Sq, WC1 ....10 C4
Wells St, W1 ....17 F2
Wellstead Av, N9 ....45 F7
Wellstead Rd, E6 ....116 D2
Wells Ter, N4 ....93 G2
Well St, E9 ....95 E7
  E15 ....96 E6
Wells Way, SE5 ....36 C5
  SW7 ....22 E5
Wells Yd S, N7 off George's Rd .93 G5
Well Wk, NW3 ....91 G4
Wellwood Rd, Ilf. IG3 ....100 A1
Welmar Ms, SW4
  off Clapham Pk Rd 150 D4
Welsford St, SE1 ....37 H3
Welsh Cl, E13 ....115 G3
Welshpool Ho, E8
  off Benjamin Cl 112 D1
Welshpool St, E8
  off Broadway Mkt 112/113 E1
Welshside Wk, NW9
  off Fryent Gro 70/71 E6
Welstead Way, W4 ....127 F4
Weltje Rd, W6 ....127 G5
Welton Rd, SE18 ....137 H7
Welwyn Av, Felt. TW14 .....141 J6
Welwyn St, E2 off Globe Rd ...113 F3
WEMBLEY, HA0 & HA9 ......87 H5
Wembley Commercial Cen, Wem.
  HA9 ....87 G2
★ Wembley Conf Cen, Wem.
  HA9 ....87 J4
Wembley Hill Rd, Wem. HA9 .87 J5
WEMBLEY PARK, Wem. HA9 .87 J2
Wembley Pk Business Cen, Wem.
  HA9 ....88 B3
Wembley Pk Dr, Wem. HA9 ..87 J3
Wembley Pt, Wem. HA9 .....88 B7
Wembley Rd, Hmptn. TW12 .161 G7
★ Wembley Stadium (under
  redevelopment), Wem. HA9 .88 A4
Wembley Way, Wem. HA9 ...88 B6
Wemborough Rd, Stan. HA7 .53 F7
Wembury Ms, N6
  off Wembury Rd 74 B7
Wembury Rd, N6 ....74 B7
Wemyss Rd, SE3 ....155 F2
Wendela Ct, Har. HA1 ......86 B3
Wendell Rd, W12 ....127 F2

Wendle Ct, SW8 ....34 A6
Wendling Rd, Sutt. SM1 ....199 G1
Wendon St, E3 ....113 J1
Wendover, SE17 ....36 D4
Wendover Cl, Hayes UB4 ...102 E4
Wendover Dr, N.Mal. KT3 ...183 F6
Wendover Rd, NW10 ....107 F2
  SE9 ....156 A3
  Bromley BR2 ....191 H3
Wendover Way, Well. DA16 .158 A5
Wendy Cl, Enf. EN1 ....44 C6
Wendy Way, Wem. HA0 ....105 H1
Wenlock Ct, N1 ....12 C2
Wenlock Gdns, NW4
  off Rickard Cl 71 G4
Wenlock Rd, N1 ....11 J1
  Edgware HA8 ....54 B7
Wenlock St, N1 ....12 A2
Wennington Rd, E3 ....113 G2
Wensley Av, Wdf.Grn. IG8 ..63 F7
Wensley Cl, N11
  off Pickering Gdns 58 A6
  SE9 ....156 C6
Wensleydale Av, Ilf. IG5 .....80 B2
Wensleydale Gdns, Hmptn.
  TW12 ....161 H7
Wensleydale Pas, Hmptn.
  TW12 ....179 G5
Wensleydale Rd, Hmptn.
  TW12 ....161 G6
Wensley Rd, N18 ....60 E6
Wentland Cl, SE6 ....172 D2
Wentland Rd, SE6 ....172 D2
Wentworth Av, N3 ....56 D7
Wentworth Cl, N3 ....56 E7
  SE28 ....118 D6
  Bromley BR2 off Hillside La .205 D4
  Morden SM4 ....184 D7
  Orpington BR6 ....207 H5
  Surbiton KT6 ....195 G2
Wentworth Ct, Surb. KT6
  off Culsac Rd 195 H2
Wentworth Cres, SE15 .....132 D7
  Hayes UB3 ....121 G3
Wentworth Dr, Pnr. HA5 ....66 A5
Wentworth Gdns, N13 .....59 H4
Wentworth Hill, Wem. HA9 ..87 J1
Wentworth Ms, E3 off Eric St .113 J4
Wentworth Pk, N3 ....56 D7
Wentworth Pl, Stan. HA7
  off Greenacres Dr 52/53 E6
Wentworth Rd, E12 ....98 A4
  NW11 ....72 C6
  Barnet EN5 ....40 A3
  Croydon CR0 ....187 G7
  Southall UB2 ....122 C4
Wentworth St, E1 ....21 F3
Wentworth Way, Pnr. HA5 ..66 D4
Wenvoe Av, Bexh. DA7 .....159 H2
Wepham Cl, Hayes UB4 ....102 D5
Wernbrook St, SE18 ....137 F6
Werndee Rd, SE25 ....188 D4
Werneth Hall Rd, Ilf. IG5 ....80 C3
Werrington St, NW1 ....9 G2
Werter Rd, SW15 ....148 B4
Wesleyan Pl, NW5
  off Gordon Ho Rd 92 B4
Wesley Av, E16 ....135 G1
  NW10 ....106 D3
  Hounslow TW3 ....143 E2
Wesley Cl, N7 ....93 F2
  SE17 ....35 H2
  Harrow HA2 ....85 J2
Wesley Rd, E10 ....78 C7
  NW10 ....106 C1
  Hayes UB3 ....102 A2
★ Wesley's Ho, EC1 ....12 C5
Wesley Sq, W11 off Bartle Rd .108 B6
Wesley St, W1 ....16 C2
Wessex Av, SW19 ....184 D2
Wessex Cl, Ilf. IG3 ....81 H6
  Kingston upon Thames KT1
  off Gloucester Rd 182 B1
  Thames Ditton KT7 ...194 C2
Wessex Ct, Wem. HA9
  off The Avenue 87 J2
Wessex Dr, Pnr. HA5 ......51 E7
Wessex Gdns, NW11 ......90 B1
Wessex La, Grnf. UB6 ......104 A2
Wessex St, E2 ....113 F3
Wessex Way, NW11 ....72 B7
West 12 Shop Cen, W12
  off Shepherds Bush Grn ...128 A2
Westacott Cl, N19 ....92 D1
WEST ACTON, W3 ....106 A6
Westall Rd, Loug. IG10 .....49 E3
West App, Orp. BR5 ....193 F5
West Arbour St, E1 ....113 G6
West Av, E17 ....78 B4
  N3 ....56 D6
  NW4 ....72 A5
  Pinner HA5 ....67 F6
  Southall UB1 ....103 F7
  Wallington SM6 ....201 E5
West Av Rd, E17 ....78 A4

West Bk, N16 . . . . .76 B7
Barking IG11
off Highbridge Rd 116/117 E1
Enfield EN2 . . . . .43 J2
Westbank Rd, Hmptn. (Hmptn H.)
TW12 . . . . .161 J6
WEST BARNES, N.Mal. KT3 . . . .183 G5
West Barnes La, SW20 . . . . .183 H3
New Malden KT3 . . . . .183 H3
Westbeech Rd, N22 . . . . .75 G3
Westbere Dr, Stan. HA7 . . . . . . .53 G4
Westbere Rd, NW2 . . . . .90 B4
Westbourne Av, W3 . . . . .106 D6
Sutton SM3 . . . . .198 B2
Westbourne Br, W2 . . . . .14 C2
Westbourne Cl, Hayes UB4 . . . . .102 B4
Westbourne Cres, W2 . . . . .14 E5
Westbourne Cres Ms, W2 . . . . . . .14 E5
Westbourne Dr, SE23 . . . . .171 G2
Westbourne Gdns, W2 . . . . .14 A3
WESTBOURNE GREEN, W2 . . . .108 D5
Westbourne Gro, W2 . . . . .108 D6
W11 .108 C7
Westbourne Gro Ms, W11
off Westbourne Gro 108 D6
Westbourne Gro Ter, W2 . . . . .14 A3
Westbourne Pk Ms, W2 . . . . .14 A3
Westbourne Pk Pas, W2
off Westbourne Pk Vil 108 D5
Westbourne Pk Rd, W2 . . . . .108 D5
W11 .108 B6
Westbourne Pk Vil, W2 . . . . .108 D5
Westbourne Pl, N9
off Eastbournia Av 60/61 E3
Westbourne Rd, N7 . . . . .93 G6
SE26 . . . . .171 G6
Bexleyheath DA7 . . . . .138 E7
Croydon CR0 . . . . .188 C6
Westbourne St, W2 . . . . .15 E5
Westbourne Ter, SE23
off Westbourne Dr 171 G2
W2 . . . . .14 D3
Westbourne Ter Ms, W2 . . . . .14 C3
Westbourne Ter Rd, W2 . . . . .14 C2
Westbridge Rd, SW11 . . . . .149 G1
WEST BROMPTON, SW10 . . . . . .30 A5
Westbrook Av, Hmptn. TW12 . . .161 F7
Westbrook Cl, Barn. EN4 . . . . . . .41 G3
Westbrook Cres, Barn. EN4 . . . . .41 G3
Westbrooke Cres, Well. DA16 . . .158 C3
Westbrooke Rd, Sid. DA15 . . . . .175 G2
Welling DA16 . . . . .158 B3
Westbrook Rd, SE3 . . . . .155 H1
Hounslow TW5 . . . . .123 F7
Thornton Heath CR7 . . . . . . .188 A1
Westbrook Sq, Barn. EN4
off Westbrook Cres 41 G3
Westbury Av, N22 . . . . .75 H3
Esher (Clay.) KT10 . . . . .194 C6
Southall UB1 . . . . .103 G4
Wembley HA0 . . . . .87 H7
Westbury Cl, Ruis. HA4 . . . . .66 A7
Westbury Gro, N12 . . . . .56 D6
Westbury La, Buck.H. IG9 . . . . . .63 J2
Westbury Lo Cl, Pnr. HA5 . . . . . . .66 D3
Westbury Par, SW12
off Balham Hill 150 B6
Westbury Pl, Brent. TW8 . . . . . .125 G6
Westbury Rd, E7 . . . . .97 H5
E17 . . . . .78 A4
N11 . . . . .58 E6
N12 . . . . .56 D6
SE20 . . . . .189 G1
W5 . . . . .105 H6
Barking IG11 . . . . .117 G1
Beckenham BR3 . . . . .189 H3
Bromley BR1 . . . . .192 A1
Buckhurst Hill IG9 . . . . .63 J2
Croydon CR0 . . . . .188 A6
Feltham TW13 . . . . .160 D1
Ilford IG1 . . . . .98 C2
New Malden KT3 . . . . .182 D4
Wembley HA0 . . . . .87 H7
Westbury St, SW8 . . . . .150 C2
Westbury Ter, E7 . . . . .97 H6
West Carriage Dr, W2 . . . . .23 F2
West Cen St, WC1 . . . . .18 A3
West Cen Av, W10
off Harrow Rd 107 H3
West Chantry, Har. HA3
off Chantry Rd 67 H1
Westchester Dr, NW4 . . . . .72 A3
Westcliffe Apartments, W2
off Praed St 109 G5
West Cl, N9 . . . . .60 C3
Barnet EN5 . . . . .39 H5
Barnet (Cockfos.) EN4 . . . . . . .42 A4
Greenford UB6 . . . . .103 J2
Hampton TW12
off Oak Av 160/161 E6
Wembley HA9 . . . . .87 J1
Westcombe Av, Croy. CR0 . . . . .187 E6
Westcombe Ct, SE3
off Westcombe Pk Rd 135 F7
Westcombe Dr, Barn. EN5 . . . . . .40 D5
Westcombe Hill, SE3 . . . . .135 G5
SE10 . . . . .135 G5
Westcombe Pk Rd, SE3 . . . . . . .135 E6
West Common Rd, Brom. BR2 . .205 G2
Keston BR2 . . . . .205 H4
Westcoombe Av, SW20 . . . . . . .183 F1
Westcote Rd, SW16 . . . . .168 C5
West Cotts, NW6 . . . . .90 D5
Westcott Cl, N15 *off Ermine Rd* . .76 C6
Bromley BR1
off Ringmer Way 192 B5
Westcott Cres, W7 . . . . .104 B6
Westcott Rd, SE17 . . . . .35 G5
West Ct, SE18
off Prince Imperial Rd 156 C1
Westcourt, Sun. TW16 . . . . .178 B2
West Ct, Wem. HA0 . . . . .87 F2
Westcroft Cl, NW2 . . . . .90 B4
Westcroft Gdns, Mord. SM4 . . . .184 C3
Westcroft Rd, Cars. SM5 . . . . . .200 A4
Wallington SM6 . . . . .200 A4
Westcroft Sq, W6 . . . . .127 G4
Westcroft Way, NW2 . . . . .90 B4
West Cromwell Rd, SW5 . . . . . .128 C4
W14 .128 C4
West Cross Cen, Brent. TW8 . . . .124 D6
West Cross Route, W10 . . . . . .108 A7
W11 .108 A7
West Cross Way, Brent. TW8 . . .124 E6
Westdale Pas, SE18 . . . . .136 E6
Westdale Rd, SE18 . . . . .137 E6
Westdean Av, SE12 . . . . .173 H1
Westdean Cl, SW18 . . . . .149 E6
West Dene, Sutt. SM3
off Park La 198 B6
Westdown Rd, E15 . . . . .96 C4
SE6 .154 A7
WEST DRAYTON, UB7 . . . . .120 A3
West Drayton Pk Av, West Dr.
UB7 .120 B3
West Dr, SW16 . . . . .168 C4
Harrow HA3 . . . . .52 A6
West Dr Gdns, Har. HA3 . . . . .52 A6
WEST DULWICH, SE21 . . . . . . .170 A3
West Eaton Pl, SW1 . . . . .32 B1
West Eaton Pl Ms, SW1 . . . . .32 B1
West Ella Rd, NW10 . . . . .88 E7
West End Av, E10 . . . . .78 C5
Pinner HA5 . . . . .66 D4
West End Cl, NW10 . . . . .88 C7
West End Ct, Pnr. HA5 . . . . .66 D4
West End Gdns, Nthlt. UB5
off Edward Cl 102 C2
West End La, NW6 . . . . .90 D7
Barnet EN5 . . . . .40 A4
Hayes UB3 . . . . .121 F7
Pinner HA5 . . . . .66 D3
West End Rd, Nthlt. UB5 . . . . . . .84 C7
Ruislip HA4 . . . . .84 B5
Southall UB1 . . . . .122 E1
Westerdale Rd, SE10 . . . . .135 G5
Westerfield Rd, N15 . . . . .76 C5
Westergate Rd, SE2 . . . . .138 E5
Westerham Av, N9 . . . . .60 A3
Westerham Dr, Sid. DA15 . . . . .158 B6
Westerham Rd, E10 . . . . .78 B7
Keston BR2 . . . . .206 A6
Westerley Cres, SE26 . . . . .171 J5
Westerley Ware, Rich. TW9
off Kew Grn 126 A6
Western Av, NW11 . . . . .72 A6
W3 . . . . .106 D5
W5 . . . . .105 J3
Dagenham RM10 . . . . .101 J6
Greenford UB6 . . . . .104 C3
Northolt UB5 . . . . .103 F1
Western Av Business Pk, W3
off Mansfield Rd 106 B4
Western Av Underpass, W5
off Western Av 105 J3
Western Beach Apartments, E16
off Hanover Av 135 G1
Western Ct, N3 *off Huntley Dr* . . .56 D6
Western Gdns, W5 . . . . .106 A7
Western Gateway, E16 . . . . .115 G7
Western La, SW12 . . . . .150 A7
Western Ms, W9
off Great Western Rd 108 C4
Western Par, Barn. EN5
off Great N Rd 40 D5
Western Pl, SE16
off Canon Beck Rd 133 F2
Western Rd, E13 . . . . .115 J1
E17 . . . . .78 C5
N2 . . . . .73 J4
N22 . . . . .75 F2
NW10 . . . . .106 C4
SW9 . . . . .151 G3
SW19 . . . . .185 G1
W5 . . . . .105 G7
Mitcham CR4 . . . . .185 G1
Southall UB2 . . . . .122 D3
Sutton SM1 . . . . .198 D5
Western Ter, W6
off Chiswick Mall 127 G5
Western Trd Est, NW10 . . . . . . .106 C4
Western Vw, Hayes UB3 . . . . . . .121 J2
Westernville Gdns, Ilf. IG2 . . . . . .81 F7
Western Way, SE28 . . . . .137 G3
Barnet EN5 . . . . .40 D6
WEST EWELL, Epsom KT19 . . . .196 E7
Westferry Circ, E14 . . . . .133 J1
Westferry Rd, E14 . . . . .134 A1
Westfield, Loug. IG10 . . . . .47 J5
Westfield Cl, NW9 . . . . .70 C3
SW10 . . . . .129 F7
Enfield EN3 . . . . .45 H3
Sutton SM1 . . . . .198 C4
Westfield Dr, Har. HA3 . . . . .69 G5
Westfield Gdns, Har. HA3 . . . . . . .69 G4
Westfield La, Har. HA3 . . . . .69 G4
Westfield Pk, Pnr. HA5 . . . . .51 F7
Westfield Pk Dr, Wdf.Grn. IG8 . . .64 B6
Westfield Rd, NW7 . . . . .54 D3
W13 .124 D1
Beckenham BR3 . . . . .189 J2
Bexleyheath DA7 . . . . .159 J2
Croydon CR0 . . . . .201 H2
Dagenham RM9 . . . . .101 E4
Mitcham CR4 . . . . .185 J2
Surbiton KT6 . . . . .181 G5
Sutton SM1 . . . . .198 C4
Walton-on-Thames KT12 . . . .179 E7
Westfields, SW13 . . . . .147 F3
Westfields Av, SW13 . . . . .147 E3
Westfields Rd, W3 . . . . .106 B5
Westfield St, SE18 . . . . .136 A3
Westfield Way, E1 . . . . .113 H3
West Gdn Pl, W2 . . . . .15 H4
West Gdns, E1 . . . . .113 E7
SW17 . . . . .167 H6
West Gate, W5 . . . . .105 H3
Westgate Ho, Brent. TW8 . . . . . .125 G5
Westgate Rd, SE25 . . . . .188 E4
Beckenham BR3 . . . . .190 B2
Westgate St, E8 . . . . .112 E1
Westgate Ter, SW10 . . . . .30 B4
Westglade Ct, Har. HA3 . . . . .69 G5
WEST GREEN, N15 . . . . .75 J3
West Grn Pl, Grnf. UB6
off Uneeda Dr 104 A1
West Grn Rd, N15 . . . . .75 H4
West Gro, SE10 . . . . .154 C1
Woodford Green IG8 . . . . .63 J6
Westgrove La, SE10 . . . . .154 C1
West Halkin St, SW1 . . . . .24 B5
West Hallowes, SE9 . . . . .174 A1
West Hall Rd, Rich. TW9 . . . . . .146 B1
WEST HAM, E15 . . . . .97 F7
West Ham La, E15 . . . . .96 E7
West Ham Pk, E7 . . . . .97 G7
WEST HAMPSTEAD, NW6 . . . . . .90 E5
West Hampstead Ms, NW6 . . . . . .90 E6
★ **West Ham United FC**, E13 . .115 J2
West Harding St, EC4 . . . . .19 F3
WEST HARROW, Har. HA1 . . . . . .67 J7
Westhay Gdns, SW14 . . . . .146 B5
WEST HEATH, SE2 . . . . .138 D6
West Heath Av, NW11 . . . . .90 D1
West Heath Cl, NW3 . . . . .90 D3
West Heath Dr, NW11 . . . . .90 D1
West Heath Gdns, NW3 . . . . .90 D3
West Heath Rd, NW3 . . . . .90 D2
SE2 .138 D6
WEST HENDON, NW9 . . . . .71 E7
West Hendon Bdy, NW9 . . . . . . .71 F6
West Hill, SW15 . . . . .148 A7
SW18 . . . . .148 D5
Harrow HA2 . . . . .86 B2
Wembley HA9 . . . . .87 J1
West Hill Ct, N6 . . . . .92 A3
West Hill Pk, N6 *off Merton La* . . .91 J2
West Hill Rd, SW18 . . . . .148 D6
West Hill Way, N20 . . . . .56 E1
Westholm, NW11 . . . . .72 E4
West Holme, Erith DA8 . . . . .159 J1
Westholme, Orp. BR6 . . . . .193 H7
Westholme Gdns, Ruis. HA4 . . . .84 A1
Westhorne Av, SE9 . . . . .155 J6
SE12 . . . . .155 G7
Westhorpe Gdns, NW4 . . . . .71 J3
Westhorpe Rd, SW15 . . . . .147 J3
West Ho Cl, SW19 . . . . .166 B1
Westhurst Dr, Chis. BR7 . . . . . . .175 E5
West India Av, E14 . . . . .134 A1
West India Dock Rd, E14 . . . . . . .113 J6
WEST KILBURN, W9 . . . . .108 C3
Westlake Cl, N13 . . . . .59 G3
Hayes UB4
off Lochan Cl 102/103 E4
Westlake Rd, Wem. HA9 . . . . .87 G2
Westland Cl, Stai. (Stanw.)
TW19 . . . . .140 B6
Westland Dr, Brom. BR2 . . . . . .205 F2
Westland Ho, E16 *off Rymill St* .136 D1
Westland Pl, N1 . . . . .12 B3
Westlands Cl, Hayes UB3
off Granville Rd 122 A4
Westlands Ter, SW12
off Gaskarth Rd 150 C6
West La, SE16 . . . . .132 E2
Westlea Rd, W7 . . . . .124 D3
Westleigh Av, SW15 . . . . .147 H5
Westleigh Dr, Brom. BR1 . . . . . .192 B1
Westleigh Gdns, Edg. HA8 . . . . . .70 A1
Westlinks, Wem. HA0
off Alperton La 105 G3
Westlinton Cl, NW7 . . . . .56 B6
West Lo Av, W3 . . . . .126 A1
West Mall, W8
off Palace Gdns Ter 128 D1
Westmark Pt, SW15
off Norley Vale 165 H1
Westmead, SW15 . . . . .147 H6
West Mead, Epsom KT19 . . . . . .197 E6
Ruislip HA4 . . . . .84 C4
Westmead Cor, Cars. SM5
off Colston Av 199 H4
Westmead Rd, Sutt. SM1 . . . . . .199 G4
Westmede, Chig. IG7 . . . . .65 F6
Westmere Dr, NW7 . . . . .54 D3
West Mersea Cl, E16
off Hanameel St 135 H1
West Ms, N17 . . . . .60 E6
SW1 . . . . .33 E2
Westmill Ct, N4
off Brownswood Rd 93 J2
WESTMINSTER, SW1 . . . . .25 F5
★ **Westminster Abbey**, SW1 . . .26 A5
★ **Westminster Abbey Mus**,
SW1 . . . . .26 A5
Westminster Av, Th.Hth. CR7 . . .187 H2
Westminster Br, SE1 . . . . .26 B4
SW1 . . . . .26 B4
Westminster Br Rd, SE1 . . . . .26 D4
★ **Westminster Cath**, SW1 . . . . .25 F6
★ **Westminster City Hall**, SW1 .25 G5
Westminster Cl, Felt. TW14 . . . .160 A1
Ilford IG6 . . . . .81 G2
Teddington TW11 . . . . .162 D5
Westminster Dr, N13 . . . . .58 E5
Westminster Gdns, E4 . . . . .63 E1
SW1 . . . . .34 A1
Barking IG11 . . . . .117 H2
Ilford IG6 . . . . .81 F2
★ **Westminster Millennium Pier**,
SW1 . . . . .26 B3
Westminster Rd, N9 . . . . .61 E1
W7 . . . . .124 B1
Sutton SM1 . . . . .199 G2
Westmoat Cl, Beck. BR3 . . . . . .172 C7
WEST MOLESEY, KT8 . . . . .179 F5
Westmont Rd, Esher KT10 . . . . .194 B2
Westmoor Gdns, Enf. EN3 . . . . . .45 G2
Westmoor Rd, Enf. EN3 . . . . .45 G2
Westmoor St, SE7 . . . . .135 J3
Westmoreland Av, Well. DA16 . . .157 H3
Westmoreland Bldgs, EC1
off Bartholomew Cl 111 J5
Westmoreland Pl, SW1 . . . . .33 E4
W5 . . . . .105 G5
Bromley BR1 . . . . .191 G3
Westmoreland Rd, NW9 . . . . .70 A4
SE17 .36 A5
SW13 . . . . .147 F1
Bromley BR1, BR2 . . . . .191 E5
Westmoreland St, W1 . . . . .16 C2
Westmoreland Ter, SW1 . . . . .32 E4
Westmoreland Wk, SE17 . . . . . . .36 C5
Westmorland Cl, E12 . . . . .98 A2
Twickenham TW1 . . . . .144 E6
Westmorland Rd, E17 . . . . .78 A6
Harrow HA1 . . . . .67 H5
Westmorland Sq, Mitch. CR4
off Westmorland Way . .186/187 E5
Westmorland Ter, SE20 . . . . .171 E7
Westmorland Way, Mitch. CR4 . .186 D4
Westmount Rd, SE9 . . . . .156 C2
WEST NORWOOD, SE27 . . . . . . .169 J3
West Oak, Beck. BR3 . . . . .190 D1
Westoe Rd, N9 . . . . .61 E2
Weston Av, T.Ditt. KT7 . . . . .180 B7
West Molesey KT8 . . . . .179 E3
Weston Ct, N4 *off Queens Dr* . . .93 J3
N20 *off Farnham Cl* 41 F7
Weston Dr, Stan. HA7 . . . . .68 E1
West One Shop Cen, W1 . . . . . . .16 C4
Weston Gdns, Islw. TW7 . . . . . . .144 A1
WESTON GREEN, T.Ditt. KT7 . . .194 C1
Weston Grn, Dag. RM9 . . . . .101 F4
Thames Ditton KT7 . . . . .194 B1
Weston Grn Rd, Esher KT10 . . . .194 A1
Thames Ditton KT7 . . . . .194 B1
Weston Gro, Brom. BR1 . . . . . . .191 F1
Weston Pk, N8 . . . . .75 E6
Kingston upon Thames KT1
off Fairfield W 181 H2
Thames Ditton KT7 . . . . .194 B1
Weston Pk Cl, T.Ditt. KT7
off Weston Pk 194 B1
Weston Ri, WC1 . . . . .10 D2
Weston Rd, W4 . . . . .126 C3
Bromley BR1 . . . . .173 F7
Dagenham RM9 . . . . .101 E4
Enfield EN2 . . . . .44 A1

Weston Rd, T.Ditt. KT7 . . . .**194** B1
Weston St, SE1 . . . .**28** C5
Weston Wk, E8 off Mare St . .**94/95** E7
Westover Hill, NW3 . . . .**90** D2
Westover Rd, SW18 . . . .**149** F6
Westow Hill, SE19 . . . .**170** B6
Westow St, SE19 . . . .**170** B6
West Pk, SE9 . . . .**174** B2
West Pk Av, Rich. TW9 . . . .**146** A1
West Pk Cl, Houns. TW5
  off Heston Gra La **123** F6
  Romford RM6 . . . .**82** D5
West Pk Rd, Rich. TW9 . . . .**146** A1
  Southall UB2 . . . .**123** J1
West Parkside, SE10 . . . .**135** E2
West Pier, E1
  off Wapping High St . . .**132/133** E1
West Pl, SW19 . . . .**165** J5
Westpoint Trd Est, W3 . . . .**106** B5
Westport Rd, E13 . . . .**115** H4
Westport St, E1 . . . .**113** G6
West Poultry Av, EC1 . . . .**19** G2
West Quarters, W12 . . . .**107** G6
West Quay Dr, Hayes UB4 . . . .**102** E5
West Ramp, Houns. (Hthrw Air.)
  TW6 . . . .**140** D1
West Ridge Gdns, Grnf. UB6 . . .**103** J2
West Rd, E15 . . . .**115** F1
  N17 . . . .**60** E6
  SW3 . . . .**32** A4
  SW4 . . . .**150** D5
  W5 . . . .**105** H5
  Barnet EN4 . . . .**58** A1
  Feltham TW14 . . . .**141** G6
  Kingston upon Thames KT2 . . .**182** C1
  Romford (Chad.Hth) RM6 . . . . .**82** D6
  West Drayton UB7 . . . .**120** C3
Westrow, SW15 . . . .**147** J5
West Row, W10 . . . .**108** B4
Westrow Dr, Bark. IG11 . . . .**99** J6
Westrow Gdns, Ilf. IG3 . . . .**99** J2
West Sheen Vale, Rich. TW9 . . .**145** J4
Westside, NW4 . . . .**71** H2
West Side Common, SW19 . . . .**165** J5
West Smithfield, EC1 . . . .**19** G2
West Sq, SE11 . . . .**27** G6
West St, E2 . . . .**113** E2
  E11 . . . .**96** E3
  E17 off Grove Rd **78** B5
  WC2 . . . .**17** J4
  Bexleyheath DA7 . . . .**159** F4
  Brentford TW8 . . . .**125** F6
  Bromley BR1 . . . .**191** G1
  Carshalton SM5 . . . .**199** J3
  Croydon CR0 . . . .**201** J4
  Harrow HA1 . . . .**86** A1
  Sutton SM1 . . . .**198** E5
West St La, Cars. SM5 . . . .**199** J4
West Temple Sheen, SW14 . . . .**146** B4
West Tenter St, E1 . . . .**21** G1
West Thamesmead Business Pk,
  SE28 . . . .**137** J3
West Twrs, Pnr. HA5 . . . .**66** D6
Westvale Ms, W3 . . . .**127** E1
West Vw, NW4 . . . .**71** J4
  Feltham TW14 . . . .**141** F7
  Loughton IG10 . . . .**48** C3
Westview Cl, NW10 . . . .**89** F5
  W7 . . . .**104** B6
  W10 . . . .**107** J6
Westview Cres, N9 . . . .**44** B7
Westview Dr, Wdf.Grn. IG8 . . . . .**80** A2
Westville Rd, W12 . . . .**127** G2
  Thames Ditton KT7 . . . .**194** D1
West Wk, W5 . . . .**105** H5
  Barnet EN4 . . . .**42** A7
  Hayes UB3 . . . .**122** A1
West Walkway, The, Sutt. SM1
  off Cheam Rd **198/199** E5
Westward Rd, E4 . . . .**61** J5
Westward Way, Har. HA3 . . . .**69** H6
West Warwick Pl, SW1 . . . .**33** F2
West Way, N18 . . . .**60** A4
  NW10 . . . .**88** D3
Westway, SW20 . . . .**183** H3
  W2 . . . .**108** D5
  W9 . . . .**108** D5
  W10 . . . .**108** B6
  W12 . . . .**107** G7
West Way, Croy. CR0 . . . .**203** H2
  Edgware HA8 . . . .**54** B6
  Hounslow TW5 . . . .**143** F1
Westway, Orp. BR5 . . . .**193** G5
West Way, Pnr. HA5 . . . .**66** D4
  West Wickham BR4 . . . .**190** D6
Westway Cl, SW20 . . . .**183** H3
Westway Cross Shop Pk, Grnf.
  UB6 . . . .**104** B1
West Way Gdns, Croy. CR0 . . . .**203** G2
Westways, Epsom KT19 . . . .**197** F4
Westwell Rd, SW16 . . . .**168** E6
Westwell Rd App, SW16
  off Westwell Rd **168/169** E6
Westwick Gdns, W14 . . . .**128** A2

Westwick Gdns, Houns. TW4 . .**142** B2
WEST WICKHAM, BR4 . . . .**204** C2
Westwood Av, SE19 . . . .**187** J1
  Harrow HA2 . . . .**85** H4
Westwood Cl, Brom. BR1 . . . . . .**192** A3
Westwood Gdns, SW13 . . . . . .**147** F3
Westwood Hill, SE26 . . . .**170** D5
Westwood La, Sid. DA15 . . . . . .**158** A5
  Welling DA16 . . . .**157** J3
Westwood Pk, SE23 . . . .**153** E7
Westwood Pl, SE26 . . . .**170** D4
Westwood Rd, E16 . . . .**135** H1
  SW13 . . . .**147** F3
  Ilford IG3 . . . .**99** J1
West Woodside, Bex. DA5 . . . . .**159** E7
West World, W5 . . . .**105** H3
Wetheral Dr, Stan. HA7 . . . .**69** E1
Wetherby Cl, Nthlt. UB5 . . . .**85** H6
Wetherby Gdns, SW5 . . . .**30** A3
Wetherby Ms, SW5 . . . .**30** A3
Wetherby Pl, SW7 . . . .**30** C2
Wetherby Rd, Enf. EN2 . . . .**43** J1
Wetherby Way, Chess. KT9 . . . .**195** H7
Wetherden St, E17 . . . .**77** J7
Wetherell Rd, E9 . . . .**113** G1
Wetherill Rd, N10 . . . .**74** A1
Wexford Rd, SW12 . . . .**149** J7
Weybourne St, SW18 . . . .**167** F2
Weybridge Ct, SE16 . . . .**37** J4
Weybridge Pt, SW11 . . . .**150** A2
Weybridge Rd, Th.Hth. CR7 . . . .**187** G3
Wey Ct, Epsom KT19 . . . .**196** C4
Weydown Cl, SW19 . . . .**166** B1
Weyhill Rd, E1 . . . .**21** J3
Weyland Rd, Dag. RM8 . . . .**101** F3
Weyman Rd, SE3 . . . .**155** J1
Weymouth Av, NW7 . . . .**54** E5
  W5 . . . .**125** F3
Weymouth Cl, E6
  off Covelees Wall **116/117** E6
Weymouth Ct, Sutt. SM2 . . . . . .**198** D7
Weymouth Ms, W1 . . . .**16** D1
Weymouth St, W1 . . . .**16** C2
Weymouth Ter, E2 . . . .**13** G1
Weymouth Wk, Stan. HA7 . . . . . .**52** D6
Whadcote St, N4
  off Seven Sisters Rd **93** G2
Whalebone Av, Rom. RM6 . . . . . .**83** F6
Whalebone Ct, EC2 . . . .**20** C3
Whalebone Gro, Rom. RM6 . . . . .**83** F6
Whalebone La, E15
  off West Ham La **96/97** E7
Whalebone La N, Rom. RM6 . . . .**83** E5
Whalebone La S, Dag. RM8 . . . . .**83** F7
  Romford RM6 . . . .**83** F7
Whales Yd, E15
  off West Ham La **96** E7
Wharfdale Cl, N11
  off Ribblesdale Av **58** A6
Wharfdale Ct, E5
  off Rushmore Rd **95** G4
Wharfdale Rd, N1 . . . .**10** B1
Wharfedale Gdns, Th.Hth. CR7 . .**187** F4
Wharfedale St, SW10 . . . .**30** A4
Wharf La, Twick. TW1 . . . .**162** D1
Wharf Pl, E2 . . . .**112** D1
Wharf Rd, E15 . . . .**114** D1
  N1 . . . .**11** J1
  Enfield EN3 . . . .**45** H6
Wharfside Rd, E16 . . . .**114** E5
Wharf St, E16 . . . .**114** E5
Wharncliffe Dr, Sthl. UB1 . . . . . .**124** A1
Wharncliffe Gdns, SE25 . . . . . .**188** B2
Wharncliffe Rd, SE25 . . . .**188** B2
Wharton Cl, NW10 . . . .**89** E6
Wharton Cotts, WC1
  off Wharton St **111** F3
Wharton Rd, Brom. BR1 . . . .**191** H1
Wharton St, WC1 . . . .**10** D4
Whateley Rd, SE20 . . . .**171** G7
  SE22 . . . .**152** C5
Whatley Av, SW20 . . . .**184** B3
Whatman Rd, SE23 . . . .**153** G7
Wheatfields, E6 off Oxleas . .**116/117** E6
  Enfield EN3 . . . .**45** H2
Wheatfield Way, Kings.T. KT1 . .**181** H2
Wheathill Rd, SE20 . . . .**188** E3
Wheatlands, Houns. TW5 . . . . . .**123** G6
Wheatlands Rd, SW17
  off Stapleton Rd **168** A3
Wheatley Cl, NW4 . . . .**71** G2
Wheatley Cres, Hayes UB3 . . . .**102** A7
Wheatley Gdns, N9 . . . .**60** B2
Wheatley Ho, SW15
  off Tangley Gro **147** G7
Wheatley Rd, Islw. TW7 . . . .**144** C3
Wheatley's Ait, Sun. TW16 . . . . .**178** A5
Wheatley St, W1 . . . .**16** C2
Wheat Sheaf Cl, E14 . . . .**134** A4
Wheatsheaf Cl, Nthlt. UB5 . . . . . .**84** E5
Wheatsheaf La, SW6 . . . .**127** J7
  SW8 . . . .**34** B7
Wheatsheaf Ter, SW6 . . . .**128** C7
Wheatstone Cl, Mitch. CR4 . . . .**185** H1

Wheatstone Rd, W10 . . . .**108** B5
Wheeler Cl, Wdf.Grn. IG8
  off Chigwell Rd **64** C5
Wheeler Gdns, N1
  off Outram Pl **110/111** E1
Wheelers Cross, Bark. IG11 . . . .**117** G2
Wheel Fm Dr, Dag. RM10 . . . . . .**101** J3
Wheelock Cl, Erith DA8 . . . .**139** H7
Wheelwright St, N7 . . . .**93** F7
Whelan Way, Wall. SM6 . . . .**200** D3
Wheler St, E1 . . . .**13** F6
Whellock Rd, W4 . . . .**126** E3
Whenman Av, Bex. DA5 . . . .**177** J2
Whernside Cl, SE28 . . . .**118** C7
WHETSTONE, N20 . . . .**57** E2
Whetstone Cl, N20
  off Oakleigh Rd N **57** G2
Whetstone Pk, WC2 . . . .**18** C3
Whetstone Rd, SE3 . . . .**155** J2
Whewell Rd, N19 . . . .**93** F2
Whichcote St, SE1 . . . .**26** E2
Whidborne Cl, SE8 off Cliff Ter . .**154** B2
Whidborne St, WC1 . . . .**10** B4
Whimbrel Cl, SE28 . . . .**118** C7
Whimbrel Way, Hayes UB4 . . . .**102** D6
Whinchat Rd, SE28 . . . .**137** G3
Whinfell Cl, SW16 . . . .**168** D5
Whinyates Rd, SE9 . . . .**156** B3
Whipps Cross Rd, E11 . . . .**78** D5
Whiskin St, EC1 . . . .**11** G4
Whisperwood Cl, Har. HA3 . . . . . .**52** B7
Whistler Gdns, Edg. HA8 . . . .**69** J2
Whistler Ms, SE15 off Kelly Av . .**132** C7
  Dagenham RM8
  off Fitzstephen Rd **100** B5
Whistlers Av, SW11 . . . .**129** G7
Whistler St, N5 . . . .**93** H4
Whistler Wk, SW10 . . . .**30** D7
Whiston Rd, E2 . . . .**13** F1
Whitacre Ms, SE11
  off Stannary St **131** G5
Whitakers Way, Loug. IG10 . . . . .**48** C1
Whitbread Cl, N17 . . . .**76** D1
Whitbread Rd, SE4 . . . .**153** H4
Whitburn Rd, SE13 . . . .**154** B4
Whitby Av, NW10 . . . .**106** B3
Whitby Gdns, NW9 . . . .**70** A3
  Sutton SM1 . . . .**199** G2
Whitby Rd, SE18 . . . .**136** C4
  Harrow HA2 . . . .**85** J3
  Ruislip HA4 . . . .**84** B3
  Sutton SM1 . . . .**199** G2
Whitby St, E1 . . . .**13** F5
Whitcher Cl, SE14 . . . .**133** H6
Whitcher Pl, NW1
  off Rochester Rd **92** C7
Whitchurch Av, Edg. HA8 . . . . . .**53** J7
Whitchurch Cl, Edg. HA8 . . . .**53** J6
Whitchurch Gdns, Edg. HA8 . . . .**53** J6
Whitchurch La, Edg. HA8 . . . . . .**53** G7
Whitchurch Rd, W11 . . . .**108** A7
Whitcomb Ct, WC2
  off Whitcomb St **110** D7
Whitcombe Ms, Rich. TW9 . . . . .**146** B1
Whitcomb St, WC2 . . . .**17** J6
Whiteadder Way, E14 . . . .**134** B4
Whitear Wk, E15 . . . .**96** D6
Whitebarn La, Dag. RM10 . . . . .**119** G1
Whitebeam Av, Brom. BR2 . . . . .**192** D6
Whitebeam Cl, SW9
  off Clapham Rd **131** F7
Whitebeams, Hat. AL10 . . . .**121** H3
White Bear Pl, NW3
  off New End Sq **91** G4
White Br Av, Mitch. CR4 . . . .**185** G4
Whitebridge Cl, Felt. TW14 . . . . .**141** J6
White Butts Rd, Ruis. HA4 . . . . . .**84** D3
WHITECHAPEL, E1 . . . .**21** H4
★ **Whitechapel Art Gall**, E1 . . . . .**21** G3
Whitechapel High St, E1 . . . .**21** G3
Whitechapel Rd, E1 . . . .**21** H3
White Ch La, E1 . . . .**21** H3
White Ch Pas, E1 . . . .**21** H3
White City Cl, W12 . . . .**107** J7
White City Est, W12 . . . .**107** H7
White City Rd, W12 . . . .**107** H7
White Conduit St, N1 . . . .**11** F1
Whitecote Rd, Sthl. UB1 . . . .**103** H6
White Craig Cl, Pnr. HA5 . . . .**51** G5
Whitecroft Cl, Beck. BR3 . . . . . .**190** D4
Whitecroft Way, Beck. BR3 . . . .**190** C5
Whitecross Pl, EC2 . . . .**20** C1
Whitecross St, EC1 . . . .**12** A5
Whitefield Av, NW2 . . . .**71** J7
Whitefield Cl, SW15 . . . .**148** B6
Whitefoot La, Brom. BR1 . . . . . .**172** C4
Whitefoot Ter, Brom. BR1 . . . . . .**173** E3
Whitefriars Av, Har. HA3 . . . .**68** A2
Whitefriars Dr, Har. HA3 . . . .**68** A2
Whitefriars St, EC4 . . . .**19** F4
White Gdns, Dag. RM10 . . . .**101** G6
Whitegate Gdns, Har. HA3 . . . . . .**52** C7
Whitehall, SW1 . . . .**26** A1
Whitehall Ct, SW1 . . . .**26** A2
Whitehall Cres, Chess. KT9 . . . .**195** G5

Whitehall Gdns, E4 . . . .**62** E1
  SW1 . . . .**26** A2
  W3 . . . .**126** A1
  W4 . . . .**126** B6
Whitehall La, Buck.H. IG9 . . . .**63** G2
Whitehall Pk, N19 . . . .**92** C1
Whitehall Pk Rd, W4 . . . .**126** B6
Whitehall Pl, E7 off Station Rd **97** G5
  SW1 . . . .**26** A2
  Wallington SM6
  off Bernard Rd **200** B4
Whitehall Rd, E4 . . . .**62** E2
  W7 . . . .**124** D2
  Bromley BR2 . . . .**192** A5
  Harrow HA1 . . . .**68** B7
  Thornton Heath CR7 . . . .**187** G5
  Woodford Green IG8 . . . .**62** E2
Whitehall St, N17 . . . .**60** C7
White Hart Av, SE18
  off North Rd **137** J2
White Hart Ct, EC2
  off Bishopsgate **112** B6
White Hart La, N17 . . . .**60** A7
  N22 . . . .**75** G1
  NW10 off Church Rd **89** F6
  SW13 . . . .**147** E3
  Romford RM7 . . . .**83** G1
White Hart Rd, SE18 . . . .**137** H4
White Hart Slip, Brom. BR1
  off Market Sq **191** G2
White Hart St, EC4 . . . .**19** H3
  SE11 . . . .**35** F3
White Hart Yd, SE1 . . . .**28** B2
Whitehaven Cl, Brom. BR2 . . . . .**191** G4
Whitehaven St, NW8 . . . .**7** G6
Whitehead Cl, N18 . . . .**60** A5
  SW18 . . . .**149** F7
Whitehead's Gro, SW3 . . . .**31** H3
White Heron Ms, Tedd. TW11 . . .**162** C6
Whitehills Rd, Loug. IG10 . . . .**48** D3
White Horse All, EC1 . . . .**19** G1
White Horse Hill, Chis. BR7 . . . .**174** D4
White Horse La, E1 . . . .**113** G4
  SE25 . . . .**188** A4
White Horse Ms, SE1 . . . .**27** F4
White Horse Rd, E1 . . . .**113** H6
  E6 . . . .**116** C3
Whitehorse Rd, Croy. CR0 . . . . .**188** A4
  Thornton Heath CR7 . . . .**188** A6
White Horse St, W1 . . . .**24** D2
White Horse Yd, EC2 . . . .**20** B3
Whitehouse Av, Borwd. WD6 . . . .**38** B3
White Ho Dr, Stan. HA7 . . . .**53** F4
Whitehouse Way, N14 . . . .**58** B2
Whitehurst Dr, N18 . . . .**61** G5
White Kennett St, E1 . . . .**21** E3
Whiteledges, W13 . . . .**105** F6
Whitelegg Rd, E13 . . . .**115** F2
Whiteley Rd, SE19 . . . .**170** A5
Whiteleys Shop Cen, W2 . . . .**14** A4
Whiteleys Way, Felt. TW13 . . . . .**161** G3
White Lion Ct, EC3 . . . .**20** D4
White Lion Hill, EC4 . . . .**19** H5
White Lion St, N1 . . . .**11** E2
White Lo, SE19 . . . .**169** H7
White Lo Cl, N2 . . . .**73** G6
  Isleworth TW7 . . . .**144** D2
  Sutton SM2 . . . .**199** F7
White Lyon Ct, EC2
  off Fann St **111** J4
White Oak Dr, Beck. BR3 . . . . . .**190** C2
White Oak Gdns, Sid. DA15 . . . .**157** J7
Whiteoaks La, Grnf. UB6 . . . . . .**104** A2
White Orchards, N20 . . . .**40** C7
  Stanmore HA7 . . . .**52** D5
White Post La, E9 . . . .**95** J7
  SE13 . . . .**154** A3
White Post St, SE15 . . . .**133** F7
White Rd, E15 . . . .**97** E7
Whites Av, Ilf. IG2 . . . .**81** H6
Whites Grds, SE1 . . . .**28** E4
Whites Grds Est, SE1 . . . .**28** E3
White's Row, E1 . . . .**21** F2
White's Sq, SW4
  off Nelson's Row **150** D4
Whitestile Rd, Brent. TW8 . . . . . .**125** F5
Whitestone La, NW3
  off Heath St **91** F3
Whitestone Wk, NW3
  off North End Way **91** F3
White St, Sthl. UB1 . . . .**122** D2
White Swan Ms, W4
  off Bennett St **126/127** E6
Whitethorn Gdns, Croy. CR0 . . .**203** E2
  Enfield EN2 . . . .**44** A5
Whitethorn St, E3 . . . .**114** A4
Whitewebbs Way, Orp. BR5 . . . .**193** J1
Whitfield Pl, W1 . . . .**9** F6
Whitfield Rd, E6 . . . .**97** J3
  SE3 . . . .**154** D1
  Bexleyheath DA7 . . . .**139** F7
Whitfield St, W1 . . . .**17** H2
Whitford Gdns, Mitch. CR4 . . . . .**185** J3
Whitgift Av, S.Croy. CR2 . . . . . .**201** J5
Whitgift Cen, Croy. CR0 . . . .**201** J2

Whitgift Ho, SW11
  off Westbridge Rd **149** H1
Whitgift St, SE11 . . . . **34** C1
  Croydon CR0 . . . . **201** J3
Whiting Av, Bark. IG11 . . . . **99** E7
Whitings, Ilf. IG2 . . . . **81** G5
Whitings Rd, Barn. EN5 . . . . **39** J5
Whitings Way, E6 . . . . **116** D5
Whitland Rd, Cars. SM5 . . . . . . **199** E4
Whitley Cl, Stai. (Stanw.) TW19 . **140** B6
Whitley Rd, N17 . . . . **76** B2
Whitlock Dr, SW19 . . . . **148** B7
Whitman Rd, E3
  off Mile End Rd **113** H4
Whitmead Cl, S.Croy. CR2 . **202** B6
Whitmore Cl, N11 . . . . **58** B5
Whitmore Est, N1 . . . . **112** B1
Whitmore Gdns, NW10 . . . . . . **107** J2
Whitmore Rd, N1 . . . . **112** B1
  Beckenham BR3 . . . . **189** J4
  Harrow HA1 . . . . **67** J7
Whitnell Way, SW15 . . . . **148** A5
Whitney Av, Ilf. IG4 . . . . **80** A4
Whitney Rd, E10 . . . . **78** B7
Whitney Wk, Sid. DA14 . . . . . . **176** E6
Whitstable Cl, Beck. BR3 . . . . . **189** J1
Whitstable Ho, W10 . . . . **108** A6
Whitstable Pl, Croy. CR0 . . . . . **201** J4
Whitstone La, Beck. BR3 . . . . . **190** B5
Whittaker Av, Rich. TW9
  off Hill St **145** G5
Whittaker Rd, E6 . . . . **97** J7
  Sutton SM3 . . . . **198** C3
Whittaker St, SW1 . . . . **32** B2
Whittaker Way, SE1 . . . . **37** J2
Whitta Rd, E12 . . . . **98** A4
Whittell Gdns, SE26 . . . . **171** F3
Whittingstall Rd, SW6 . . . . **148** C1
Whittington Av, EC3 . . . . **20** D4
Whittington Ct, N2 . . . . **73** J1
Whittington Ms, N12
  off Fredericks Pl **57** F4
Whittington Rd, N22 . . . . **58** E7
Whittington Way, Pnr. HA5 . . . . **67** E5
Whittlebury Cl, Cars. SM5 . . . . **199** J7
Whittle Cl, E17 . . . . **77** H6
  Southall UB1 . . . . **103** H6
Whittle Rd, Houns. TW5 . . . . . . **122** C7
  Southall UB2 *off Post Rd* . . **123** H2
Whittlesea Cl, Har. HA3 . . . . **51** J4
Whittlesea Path, Har. HA3 . . . . . **67** J1
Whittlesea Rd, Har. HA3 . . . . . . **67** J1
Whittlesey St, SE1 . . . . **27** E2
WHITTON, Twick. TW2 . . . . . . **143** H7
Whitton Av E, Grnf. UB6 . . . . . . **86** B5
Whitton Av W, Grnf. UB6 . . . . . . **85** J5
  Northolt UB5 . . . . **85** J5
Whitton Cl, Grnf. UB6 . . . . **87** E6
Whitton Dene, Houns. TW3 . . . **143** H5
  Isleworth TW7 . . . . **144** A5
Whitton Dr, Grnf. UB6 . . . . **86** D6
Whitton Manor Rd, Islw. TW7 . . **143** H4
Whitton Rd, Houns. TW3 . . . . . **143** H4
  Twickenham TW1, TW2 . . . . **144** C6
Whitton Wk, E3 . . . . **114** A2
Whitton Waye, Houns. TW3 . . . **143** G6
Whitwell Rd, E13 . . . . **115** G3
Whitworth Pl, SE18 . . . . **137** E4
Whitworth Rd, SE18 . . . . **136** D7
  SE25 . . . . **188** B3
Whitworth St, SE10 . . . . **135** E5
Whorlton Rd, SE15 . . . . **152** E3
Whychcote Pt, NW2
  off Claremont Rd **71** J7
Whymark Av, N22 . . . . **75** G3
Whytecroft, Houns. TW5 . . . . . **122** D7
Whyteville Rd, E7 . . . . **97** H6
Wickersley Rd, SW11 . . . . **150** A2
Wickers Oake, SE19 . . . . **170** C4
Wicker St, E1
  off Burslem St **112/113** E6
Wicket, The, Croy. CR0 . . . . . . **204** A5
Wicket Rd, Grnf. UB6 . . . . **104** D3
Wickets Way, Ilf. IG6 . . . . **65** J6
Wickford St, E1 . . . . **113** F4
Wickford Way, E17 . . . . **77** G4
Wickham Av, Croy. CR0 . . . . . . **203** H2
  Sutton SM3 . . . . **197** J5
Wickham Chase, W.Wick. BR4 . **190** D7
Wickham Cl, E1 . . . . **113** F5
  Enfield EN3 . . . . **45** E3
  New Malden KT3 . . . . **183** F5
Wickham Ct Rd, W.Wick. BR4 . . **204** C2
Wickham Cres, W.Wick. BR4 . . **204** C2
Wickham Gdns, SE4 . . . . **153** J3
Wickham La, SE2 . . . . **138** A5
  Welling DA16 . . . . **138** A5
Wickham Ms, SE4 . . . . **153** J2
Wickham Rd, E4 . . . . **62** C7
  SE4 . . . . **153** J4
  Beckenham BR3 . . . . **190** B2
  Croydon CR0 . . . . **203** G2
  Harrow HA3 . . . . **68** A2
Wickham St, SE11 . . . . **34** C3
  Welling DA16 . . . . **157** H2

Wickham Way, Beck. BR3 . . . . . **190** C4
Wick La, E3 . . . . **114** A2
Wickliffe Av, N3 . . . . **72** B2
Wickliffe Gdns, Wem. HA9 . . . . . **88** B2
Wicklow St, WC1 . . . . **10** C3
Wick Rd, E9 . . . . **95** G6
  Teddington TW11 . . . . **163** E7
Wicks Cl, SE9 . . . . **174** A4
Wicksteed Ho, Brent. TW8
  off Green Dragon La **125** J5
Wickwood St, SE5 . . . . **151** H2
Widdecombe Av, Har. HA2 . . . . . **84** E2
Widdenham Rd, N7 . . . . **93** F4
Widdin St, E15 . . . . **96** D7
Widecombe Gdns, Ilf. IG4 . . . . . . **80** B4
Widecombe Rd, SE9 . . . . **174** B3
Widecombe Way, N2 . . . . **73** G5
Widegate St, E1 . . . . **21** E2
Widenham Cl, Pnr. HA5
  off Bridle Rd **66** C5
Wide Way, Mitch. CR4 . . . . **186** D3
Widewing Cl, Tedd. TW11 . . . . . **163** E7
Widgeon Cl, E16 *off Maplin Rd* . **115** H6
Widley Rd, W9 . . . . **108** D3
WIDMORE, Brom. BR1 . . . . . . **191** H3
WIDMORE GREEN, Brom. BR1 . **191** J1
Widmore Lo Rd, Brom. BR1 . . . **192** A2
Widmore Rd, Brom. BR1 . . . . . **191** G2
Wieland Rd, Nthwd. HA6 . . . . . . **50** A7
Wigan Ho, E5
  off Warwick Gro **94/95** E1
Wigeon Path, SE28 . . . . **137** G3
Wigeon Way, Hayes UB4 . . . . . **102** D6
Wiggins La, Rich. TW10 . . . . . . **163** F2
Wiggins Mead, NW9 . . . . **55** F7
Wigginton Av, Wem. HA9 . . . . . . **88** B6
Wigham Ho, Bark. IG11 . . . . **99** F7
Wightman Rd, N4 . . . . **75** G5
  N8 . . . . **75** G4
Wigley Rd, Felt. TW13 . . . . **160** D1
Wigmore Ct, W13
  off Singapore Rd **124** D1
Wigmore Pl, W1 . . . . **16** D3
Wigmore Rd, Cars. SM5 . . . . . **199** G2
Wigmore St, W1 . . . . **16** B4
Wigmore Wk, Cars. SM5 . . . . . **199** G2
Wigram Rd, E11 . . . . **79** J6
Wigram Sq, E17 . . . . **78** C2
Wigston Cl, N18 . . . . **60** B5
Wigston Rd, E13 . . . . **115** H4
Wigton Gdns, Stan. HA7 . . . . . . **69** H1
Wigton Pl, SE11 . . . . **35** F4
Wigton Rd, E17 . . . . **77** J1
Wilberforce Ms, SW4
  off Stonhouse St **150** D4
Wilberforce Rd, N4 . . . . **93** H2
  NW9 . . . . **71** G6
Wilberforce Way, SW19 . . . . . . **166** A6
Wilbraham Pl, SW1 . . . . **32** A1
Wilbury Way, N18 . . . . **60** A5
Wilby Ms, W11 . . . . **128** C1
Wilcox Cl, SW8 . . . . **34** B7
  Borehamwood WD6 . . . . **38** C1
Wilcox Pl, SW1 . . . . **25** G6
Wilcox Rd, SW8 . . . . **34** A7
  Sutton SM1 . . . . **198** E4
  Teddington TW11 . . . . **162** A4
Wild Ct, WC2 . . . . **18** C3
Wildcroft Gdns, Edg. HA8 . . . . . **53** G6
Wildcroft Rd, SW15 . . . . **147** J7
Wilde Cl, E8 . . . . **112** D1
Wilde Pl, N13
  off Medesenge Way **59** H6
  SW18 *off Heathfield Rd* . . . **149** G7
Wilder Cl, Ruis. HA4 . . . . **84** B1
Wilderness, The, E.Mol. KT8 . . **179** J5
  Hampton (Hmptn H.) TW12
  off Park Rd **161** H4
Wilderness Ms, SW4
  off The Chase **150** B4
Wilderness Rd, Chis. BR7 . . . . **175** E7
Wilde Rd, Erith DA8 . . . . **139** H7
Wilderton Rd, N16 . . . . **76** B7
Wildfell Rd, SE6 . . . . **154** B7
Wild Goose Dr, SE14 . . . . **153** F1
Wild Hatch, NW11 . . . . **72** D6
Wild's Rents, SE1 . . . . **28** D5
Wild St, WC2 . . . . **18** B4
Wildwood Cl, SE12 . . . . **155** F7
Wildwood Gro, NW3
  off North End Way **91** F1
Wildwood Ri, NW11 . . . . **91** F1
Wildwood Rd, NW11 . . . . **73** F7
Wildwood Ter, NW3 . . . . **91** F1
Wilford Cl, Enf. EN2 . . . . **44** A3
Wilfred Owen Cl, SW19
  off Tennyson Rd **167** F6
Wilfred St, SW1 . . . . **25** F5
Wilfred Turney Est, W6
  off Hammersmith Gro **127** J3
Wilfrid Gdns, W3 . . . . **106** C5
Wilkes Rd, Brent. TW8 . . . . **125** H6
Wilkes St, E1 . . . . **21** G1
Wilkie Way, SE22
  off Lordship La **170** D1

Wilkins Cl, Hayes UB3 . . . . **121** J5
  Mitcham CR4 . . . . **185** H1
Wilkinson Rd, E16 . . . . **115** J6
Wilkinson St, SW8 . . . . **131** F7
Wilkinson Way, W4 . . . . **126** D2
Wilkin St, NW5 . . . . **92** B6
Wilkin St Ms, NW5 *off Wilkin St* . **92** B6
Wilks Gdns, Croy. CR0 . . . . . . **203** H1
Wilks Pl, N1 . . . . **12** E2
Willan Rd, N17 . . . . **76** A2
Willan Wall, E16
  off Victoria Dock Rd **115** F7
Willard St, SW8 . . . . **150** B3
Willcocks Cl, Chess. KT9 . . . . . **195** H3
Willcott Rd, W3 . . . . **126** B1
Will Crooks Gdns, SE9 . . . . . . **155** J4
Willen Fld Rd, NW10 . . . . **106** C2
Willenhall Av, Barn. EN5 . . . . . . **41** F6
Willenhall Rd, SE18 . . . . **136** E5
Willersley Av, Orp. BR6 . . . . . . **207** G3
  Sidcup DA15 . . . . **175** J1
Willersley Cl, Sid. DA15 . . . . . . **175** J1
WILLESDEN, NW10 . . . . **89** F6
WILLESDEN GREEN, NW10 . . . **89** H7
Willesden La, NW2 . . . . **90** A6
  NW6 . . . . **90** A6
Willes Rd, NW5 . . . . **92** B6
Willett Cl, Nthlt. UB5
  off Broomcroft Av **102** C3
  Orpington BR5 . . . . **193** H6
Willett Ho, E13
  off Queens Rd W **115** G2
Willett Pl, Th.Hth. CR7
  off Willett Rd **187** G5
Willett Rd, Th.Hth. CR7 . . . . . . **187** G5
Willett Way, Orp. BR5 . . . . **193** G5
William Barefoot Dr, SE9 . . . . . **174** D4
William Bonney Est, SW4 . . . . **150** D4
William Booth Rd, SE20 . . . . . . **188** D1
William Carey Way, Har. HA1 . . **68** B7
  SE13 . . . . **154** C2
William Cl, N2 *off King St* **73** G3
  Romford RM5 . . . . **83** J1
  Southall UB2
  off Windmill Av **123** J2
William Dr, Stan. HA7 . . . . **52** E5
William Dunbar Ho, NW6 . . . . . **108** C2
William Dyce Ms, SW16
  off Babington Rd **168** D4
William Ellis Way, SE16 . . . . **29** J6
William IV St, WC2 . . . . **18** A6
William Gdns, SW15 . . . . **147** H5
William Guy Gdns, E3
  off Talwin St **114** B3
William Harvey Ho, SW19
  off Whitlock Dr **166** B1
William Henry Wk, SW8 . . . . **33** H6
William Margrie Cl, SE15
  off Moncrieff St **152** D2
William Ms, SW1 . . . . **24** A4
William Morley Cl, E6 . . . . **116** A1
William Morris Cl, E17 . . . . **77** J3
★ William Morris Gall, Lloyd Pk,
  E17 . . . . **78** A3
William Morris Way, SW6 . . . . . **149** F3
William Perkin Ct, Grnf. UB6
  off Greenford Rd **86** B6
William Pl, E3 *off Roman Rd* . . **113** J2
William Rd, NW1 . . . . **9** E4
  SW19 . . . . **166** B7
  Sutton SM1 . . . . **199** F5
Williams Av, E17 . . . . **77** J1
William Saville Ho, NW6 . . . . . **108** C2
Williams Bldgs, E2 . . . . **113** F4
Williams Cl, N8
  off Coolhurst Rd **74** D6
  SW6 *off Pellant Rd* **128** B7
Williams Dr, Houns. TW3 . . . . . **143** G4
Williams Gro, N22 . . . . **75** G1
  Surbiton KT6 . . . . **181** F6
William's La, SW14 . . . . **146** C3
Williams La, Mord. SM4 . . . . . . **185** F5
Williamson Cl, SE10
  off Lenthorp Rd **135** F4
Williamson Rd, N4 . . . . **75** H6
Williamson St, N7 . . . . **93** E4
Williamson Way, NW7 . . . . **56** B6
William Sq, SE16
  off Rotherhithe St **113** H7
Williams Rd, W13 . . . . **104** D7
  Southall UB2 . . . . **122** E4
Williams Ter, Croy. CR0 . . . . . . **201** G6
William St, E10 . . . . **78** B6
  N17 . . . . **60** C7
  SW1 . . . . **24** A4
  Barking IG11 . . . . **99** F7
  Carshalton SM5 . . . . **199** H3
Willifield Way, NW11 . . . . **72** C4
Willingale Cl, Loug. IG10
  off Willingale Rd **49** F2
  Woodford Green IG8 . . . . **64** A6
Willingale Rd, Loug. IG10 . . . . . **49** F3
Willingdon Rd, N22 . . . . **75** H2
Willingham Cl, NW5
  off Leighton Rd **92** C5

Willingham Ter, NW5
  off Leighton Rd **92** C5
Willingham Way, Kings.T. KT1 . **182** A3
Willington Ct, E5
  off Mandeville St **95** H3
Willington Rd, SW9 . . . . **150** E3
Willis Av, Sutt. SM2 . . . . **199** H6
Willis Ho, E12 *off Grantham Rd* . **98** D3
Willis Rd, E15 . . . . **115** F1
  Croydon CR0 . . . . **187** J7
  Erith DA8 . . . . **139** J4
Willis St, E14 . . . . **114** B6
Willmore End, SW19 . . . . **184** E1
Willoughby Av, Croy. CR0 . . . . **201** F4
Willoughby Gro, N17 . . . . **60** E7
Willoughby Ho, EC2
  off The Barbican **111** J5
Willoughby La, N17 . . . . **61** E7
Willoughby Ms, SW4
  off Wixs La **150** B4
Willoughby Pk Rd, N17 . . . . **60** E7
Willoughby Pas, E14 . . . . **134** A1
Willoughby Rd, N8 . . . . **75** G3
  NW3 . . . . **91** G4
  Kingston upon Thames KT2 . **181** J1
  Twickenham TW1 . . . . **145** G6
Willoughbys, The, SW14
  *off Upper Richmond Rd
  W* **146/147** E4
Willoughby St, WC1 . . . . **18** A2
Willoughby Way, SE7 . . . . **135** H4
Willow Av, SW13 . . . . **147** F2
  Sidcup DA15 . . . . **158** A6
Willow Bk, SW6 . . . . **148** B3
  Richmond TW10 . . . . **163** E3
Willowbay Cl, Barn. EN5
  off Chesterfield Rd **40** A6
Willow Br Rd, N1 . . . . **93** J6
Willowbrook Est, SE15
  off Sumner Rd **132** C7
Willowbrook Rd, SE15 . . . . **37** G6
  Southall UB2 . . . . **123** G3
Willow Business Cen, Mitch. CR4
  off Willow La **185** J5
Willow Cl, SE6 *off Verdant La* . **172** E1
  Bexley DA5 . . . . **159** F6
  Brentford TW8 . . . . **125** F6
  Bromley BR2 . . . . **192** C5
  Buckhurst Hill IG9 . . . . **64** A3
  Thornton Heath CR7 . . . . . . **187** H6
Willow Cotts, Mitch. CR4 . . . . . **186** C4
  Richmond TW9 *off Kew Grn* . **126** A6
Willow Ct, EC2 . . . . **12** D5
  Edgware HA8 . . . . **53** H4
Willowcourt Av, Har. HA3 . . . . . . **69** E5
Willowdene, N6
  off Denewood Rd **73** J7
Willow Dene, Pnr. HA5 . . . . **66** D2
Willowdene Cl, Twick. TW2 . . . . **143** J7
Willow Dr, Barn. EN5 . . . . **40** B4
Willow End, N20 . . . . **56** D2
  Northwood HA6 . . . . **50** A6
  Surbiton KT6 . . . . **195** H1
Willow Fm La, SW15
  off Queens Ride **147** H3
Willowfield Cl, SE18 . . . . **137** H5
Willow Gdns, Houns. TW3 . . . . **143** G1
Willow Grn, NW9
  off Clayton Fld **70/71** E1
  Borehamwood WD6 . . . . **38** D5
Willow Gro, E13 *off Libra Rd* . . **115** G2
  Chislehurst BR7 . . . . **174** D6
Willowhayne Dr, Walt. KT12 . . . **178** B7
Willowhayne Gdns, Wor.Pk.
  KT4 . . . . **197** J3
Willow La, SE18 . . . . **136** C4
  Mitcham CR4 . . . . **185** J5
Willowmead Cl, W5 . . . . **105** G5
Willow Mt, Croy. CR0
  off Langton Way **202** B3
Willow Pl, SW1 . . . . **33** G1
Willow Rd, NW3 . . . . **91** G4
  W5 . . . . **125** H2
  Enfield EN1 . . . . **44** B3
  New Malden KT3 . . . . **182** C4
  Romford RM6 . . . . **83** E6
  Wallington SM6 . . . . **200** B7
Willows, The, Buck.H. IG9 . . . . . **64** A3
  Esher (Clay.) KT10 . . . . **194** B6
Willows Av, Mord. SM4 . . . . . . **185** E5
Willows Cl, Pnr. HA5 . . . . **66** C2
Willow St, E4 . . . . **46** D7
  EC2 . . . . **12** D5
  Romford RM7 . . . . **83** J4
Willow Tree Cl, E3
  off Birdsfield La **113** J1
  SW18 *off Cargill Rd* **166/167** E1
  Hayes UB4 . . . . **102** C4
Willow Tree La, Hayes UB4 . . . **102** C4
Willowtree Marina, Hayes UB4 . **103** E6
Willow Tree Wk, Brom. BR1 . . . **191** H1
Willowtree Way, Th.Hth. CR7
  off Kensington Av **187** G1
Willow Vale, W12 . . . . **127** G1
  Chislehurst BR7 . . . . **174** E6

Willow Vw, SW19 . . . . .185 G1
Willow Wk, E17 . . . . .77 J5
  N2 . . . . .73 G2
  N15 . . . . .75 H4
  N21 . . . . .43 F6
  SE1 . . . . .37 E1
  Orpington BR6 . . . . .206 E3
  Sutton SM3 . . . . .198 C3
Willow Way, N3 . . . . .56 E7
  SE26 . . . . .171 E3
  W11 off Freston Rd 128 A1
  Epsom KT19 . . . . .196 D6
  Sunbury-on-Thames TW16 .178 A4
  Twickenham TW2 . . . . . . .161 H2
  Wembley HA0 . . . . .86 D3
Willow Wd Cres, SE25 . . . . . .188 B6
Willrose Cres, SE2 . . . . .138 C5
Wills Cres, Houns. TW3 . . . . .143 H6
Wills Gro, NW7 . . . . .55 G5
Wilman Gro, E8 . . . . .94 D7
Wilmar Gdns, W.Wick. BR4 . . .204 B1
Wilmcote Ho, W2 . . . . .14 A1
Wilmer Cl, Kings.T. KT2 . . . . .163 J5
Wilmer Cres, Kings.T. KT2 . . .163 J5
Wilmer Gdns, N1 . . . . .112 B1
Wilmer Lea Cl, E15 . . . . .96 C7
Wilmer Pl, N16
  off Stoke Newington Ch St . .94 C2
Wilmer Way, N14 . . . . .58 D5
Wilmington Av, W4 . . . . .126 D7
Wilmington Gdns, Bark. IG11 . .99 G6
Wilmington Sq, WC1 . . . . .11 E4
Wilmington St, WC1 . . . . .11 E4
Wilmot Cl, N2 . . . . .73 F2
  SE15 . . . . .132 D7
Wilmot Pl, NW1 . . . . .92 C7
  W7 off Boston Rd 124 B1
Wilmot Rd, E10 . . . . .96 B2
  N17 . . . . .76 A3
  Carshalton SM5 . . . . .199 J5
Wilmot St, E2 . . . . .112 E4
Wilmount St, SE18 . . . . .136 E4
Wilna Rd, SW18 . . . . .149 F7
Wilsham St, W11 . . . . .128 A1
Wilshaw Cl, NW4 . . . . .71 G3
Wilshaw St, SE14 . . . . .154 A1
Wilsmere Dr, Har. HA3 . . . . . .52 C7
  Northolt UB5 . . . . .85 E6
Wilson Av, Mitch. CR4 . . . . . .167 H7
Wilson Cl, S.Croy. CR2
  off Bartlett St 202 A5
  Wembley HA9 . . . . .69 J7
Wilson Dr, Wem. HA9 . . . . . . .69 J7
Wilson Gdns, Har. HA1 . . . . . .67 J7
Wilson Gro, SE16 . . . . .132 E2
Wilson Rd, E6 . . . . .116 A3
  SE5 . . . . .152 B1
  Chessington KT9 . . . . .195 H4
  Ilford IG1 . . . . .80 C7
Wilsons Pl, E14 off Salmon La . .113 J6
Wilsons Rd, W6 . . . . .128 A5
Wilson St, E17 . . . . .78 C5
  EC2 . . . . .20 C1
  N21 . . . . .43 G7
Wilstone Cl, Hayes UB4 . . . . .102 E4
Wilthorne Gdns, Dag. RM10
  off Acre Rd 101 H7
Wilton Av, W4 . . . . .127 E5
Wilton Cl, West Dr. UB7 . . . . .120 A6
Wilton Cres, SW1 . . . . .24 B4
  SW19 . . . . .184 C1
Wilton Gdns, W.Mol. KT8 . . . .179 G3
Wilton Gro, SW19 . . . . .184 C1
  New Malden KT3 . . . . . . .183 F6
Wilton Ms, SW1 . . . . .24 C5
Wilton Par, Felt. TW13
  off Highfield Rd 160 A2
Wilton Pk Ct, SE18
  off Prince Imperial Rd 156 D1
Wilton Pl, SW1 . . . . .24 B4
Wilton Rd, N10 . . . . .74 A2
  SE2 . . . . .138 C3
  SW1 . . . . .25 E6
  SW19 . . . . .167 H7
  Barnet (Cockfos.) EN4 . . . . .41 J4
  Hounslow TW4 . . . . .142 D3
  Ilford IG1 off Ilford La . . .98/99 J3
Wilton Row, SW1 . . . . .24 B4
Wilton Sq, N1 . . . . .112 A1
Wilton St, SW1 . . . . .24 D5
Wilton Ter, SW1 . . . . .24 B5
Wilton Vil, N1 . . . . .112 A1
Wilton Way, E8 . . . . .94 D6
Wiltshire Cl, NW7 . . . . .55 F5
  SW3 . . . . .31 J1
Wiltshire Gdns, N4 . . . . .75 J6
  Twickenham TW2 . . . . . . .161 J1
Wiltshire Rd, SW9 . . . . .151 G3
  Thornton Heath CR7 . . . . .187 G3
Wiltshire Row, N1 . . . . .112 A1
Wilverley Cres, N.Mal. KT3 . . .183 E6
Wimbart Rd, SW2 . . . . .151 F7
WIMBLEDON, SW19 . . . . . . .166 B6
★ Wimbledon (All England Tenn &
  Croquet Club), SW19 . . . . .166 B4

Wimbledon Br, SW19 . . . . . . .166 C6
★ Wimbledon Common,
  SW19 . . . . .165 F4
Wimbledon Hill Rd, SW19 . . . .166 B6
WIMBLEDON PARK, SW19 . . .166 C3
Wimbledon Pk, SW19 . . . . . .166 C2
Wimbledon Pk Est, SW19 . . . .166 B1
Wimbledon Pk Rd, SW18 . . . .148 C7
  SW19 . . . . .166 C1
Wimbledon Pk Side, SW19 . . .166 A2
Wimbledon Rd, SW17 . . . . . . .167 F4
Wimbledon Stadium Business Cen,
  SW17 off Riverside Rd 166 E3
Wimbledon Sta, SW19 . . . . . .166 C6
★ Wimbledon Windmill Mus,
  SW19 . . . . .165 H2
Wimbolt St, E2 . . . . .13 H3
Wimborne Av, Hayes UB4 . . . .102 B6
  Southall UB2 . . . . .123 G4
Wimborne Cl, SE12 . . . . .155 F5
  Buckhurst Hill IG9 . . . . .63 H2
  Worcester Park KT4 . . . . . .197 J1
Wimborne Dr, NW9 . . . . .70 A3
  Pinner HA5 . . . . .66 D7
Wimborne Gdns, W13 . . . . . .105 E6
Wimborne Rd, N9 . . . . .60 D2
  N17 . . . . .76 B2
Wimborne Way, Beck. BR3 . . .189 G3
Wimbourne Av, Chis. BR7 . . . .193 J4
  Orpington BR5 . . . . .193 J4
Wimbourne Ct, N1 . . . . .12 B1
Wimbourne St, N1 . . . . .12 B1
Wimpole Cl, Brom. BR2 . . . . .191 J4
  Kingston upon Thames KT1 .181 J2
Wimpole Ms, W1 . . . . .16 D1
Wimpole Rd, West Dr. UB7 . . .120 A1
Wimpole St, W1 . . . . .16 D3
Wimshurst Cl, Croy. CR0 . . . .201 E1
Winans Wk, SW9 . . . . .151 G2
Wincanton Cres, Nthlt. UB5 . . .85 G5
Wincanton Gdns, Ilf. IG6 . . . . .80 E3
Wincanton Rd, SW18 . . . . . . .148 C7
Winchcombe Rd, Cars. SM5 . .185 G7
Winchcomb Gdns, SE9 . . . . . .156 A3
Winchelsea Av, Bexh. DA7 . . .139 F7
Winchelsea Cl, SW15 . . . . . . .148 A5
Winchelsea Rd, E7 . . . . .97 G3
  N17 . . . . .76 B3
  NW10 . . . . .106 D1
Winchelsey Ri, S.Croy. CR2 . . .202 C6
Winchendon Rd, SW6 . . . . . .128 C7
  Teddington TW11 . . . . . . .162 A4
Winchester Av, NW6 . . . . . . .108 B1
  NW9 . . . . .70 A3
  Hounslow TW5 . . . . .123 F6
Winchester Cl, E6
  off Boultwood Rd 116 B6
  SE17 . . . . .35 H2
  Bromley BR2 . . . . .191 F3
  Enfield EN1 . . . . .44 B5
  Kingston upon Thames KT2 .164 B7
Winchester Ct, E17 off Billet Rd . .77 H1
Winchester Dr, Pnr. HA5 . . . . .66 D5
Winchester Ho, SE18
  off Shooter's Hill Rd 136 A7
Winchester Ms, NW3
  off Winchester Rd 91 G7
Winchester Pk, Brom. BR2 . . .191 F3
Winchester Pl, E8
  off Kingsland High St 94 C5
  N6 . . . . .92 B1
  W3 off Avenue Rd 126 C2
Winchester Rd, E4 . . . . .62 C7
  N6 . . . . .92 B1
  N9 . . . . .60 D1
  NW3 . . . . .91 G7
  Bexleyheath DA7 . . . . . . .158 D2
  Bromley BR2 . . . . .191 F3
  Feltham TW13 . . . . .161 F3
  Harrow HA3 . . . . .69 H4
  Hayes UB3 . . . . .121 H7
  Ilford IG1 . . . . .99 G3
  Twickenham TW1 . . . . . . .144 E6
Winchester Sq, SE1 . . . . .28 B1
Winchester St, SW1 . . . . .32 E3
  W3 . . . . .126 C1
Winchester Wk, SE1 . . . . .28 B1
Winchet Wk, Croy. CR0 . . . . .189 F6
Winchfield Cl, Har. HA3 . . . . . .69 F6
Winchfield Ho, SW15
  off Highcliffe Dr 147 F6
Winchfield Rd, SE26 . . . . . . .171 H5
Winchilsea Cres, W.Mol. KT8 . .179 J2
WINCHMORE HILL, N21 . . . . .43 F7
Winchmore Hill Rd, N14 . . . . . .58 D1
  N21 . . . . .58 D1
Winckley Cl, Har. HA3 . . . . . . .69 J5
Wincott St, SE11 . . . . .35 F1
Wincrofts Dr, SE9 . . . . .157 G4
Windall Cl, SE19 . . . . .188 D1
Windborough Rd, Cars. SM5 . .200 A7
Windermere Av, N3 . . . . .72 D3
  NW6 . . . . .108 B1
  SW19 . . . . .184 E3
  Harrow HA3 . . . . .69 H3

Windermere Av, Ruis. HA4 . . . .66 C7
  Wembley HA9 . . . . .69 F7
Windermere Cl, Orp. BR6 . . . .206 E3
Windermere Ct, SW13 . . . . . .127 F6
  Wembley HA9
  off Windermere Av 69 F7
Windermere Gdns, Ilf. IG4 . . . .80 B5
Windermere Gro, Wem. HA9
  off Windermere Av 87 F1
Windermere Ho, Islw. TW7
  off Summerwood Rd 144 C5
Windermere Pt, SE15
  off Ilderton Rd 133 F7
Windermere Rd, N10 . . . . .74 B1
  N19 off Holloway Rd 92 C2
  SW15 . . . . .164 E4
  SW16 . . . . .186 C1
  W5 . . . . .125 F3
  Bexleyheath DA7 . . . . . . .159 J2
  Croydon CR0 . . . . .202 C1
  Southall UB1 . . . . .103 F5
  West Wickham BR4 . . . . . .204 E2
Windermere Way, West Dr. UB7
  off Providence Rd 120 C1
Winders Rd, SW11 . . . . .149 H2
Windfield Cl, SE26 . . . . .171 G4
Windham Rd, Rich. TW9 . . . . .145 J3
Winding Way, Dag. RM8 . . . . .100 C3
  Harrow HA1 . . . . .86 B4
Windlass Pl, SE8 . . . . .133 H4
Windlesham Gro, SW19 . . . . .166 A1
Windley Cl, SE23 . . . . .171 F2
Windmill All, W4
  off Windmill Rd 126/127 E4
Windmill Av, Sthl. UB2 . . . . . .123 J2
Windmill Br Ho, Croy. CR0 . . .202 B1
Windmill Cl, SE1 . . . . .37 J1
  SE13 . . . . .154 C2
  Surbiton KT6 . . . . .195 E1
Windmill Ct, NW2 . . . . .90 B6
Windmill Dr, NW2 . . . . .90 B3
  SW4 . . . . .150 C5
  Keston BR2 . . . . .205 J4
Windmill Gdns, Enf. EN2 . . . . .43 G3
Windmill Gro, Croy. CR0 . . . .187 J7
Windmill Hill, NW3 . . . . .91 F3
  Enfield EN2 . . . . .43 H3
Windmill Ho, E14
  off Westferry Rd 134 A4
Windmill La, E15 . . . . .96 D6
  Barnet EN5 . . . . .39 F6
  Bushey (Bushey Hth) WD23 . .52 B1
  Greenford UB6 . . . . .103 J5
  Isleworth TW7 . . . . .124 B4
  Southall UB2 . . . . .123 J3
  Surbiton KT6 . . . . .181 E6
Windmill Ms, W4
  off Windmill Rd 126/127 E4
Windmill Pas, W4 . . . . .126 E4
Windmill Ri, Kings.T. KT2 . . . .164 B7
Windmill Rd, N18 . . . . .60 A4
  SW18 . . . . .149 G6
  SW19 . . . . .165 H1
  W4 . . . . .126 E4
  W5 . . . . .125 F4
  Brentford TW8 . . . . .125 G5
  Croydon CR0 . . . . .187 J7
  Hampton (Hmptn H.) TW12 .161 H5
  Mitcham CR4 . . . . .186 C5
Windmill Row, SE11 . . . . .35 E4
Windmill St, W1 . . . . .17 H2
  Bushey (Bushey Hth) WD23 . .52 B1
Windmill Wk, SE1 . . . . .27 F2
Windmore Cl, Wem. HA0 . . . . .86 D5
Windover Av, NW9 . . . . .70 D4
Windrose Cl, SE16 . . . . .133 G2
Windrush, N.Mal. KT3 . . . . . .182 B4
Windrush Cl, SW11
  off Maysoule Rd 149 G4
  W4 . . . . .146 C1
Windrush La, SE23 . . . . .171 G3
Windrush Rd, NW10 . . . . .106 D1
Windrush Sq, SW2
  off Rushcroft Rd 151 G4
Windsock Cl, SE16 . . . . .133 J4
Windsor Av, E17 . . . . .77 H2
  SW19 . . . . .185 F1
  Edgware HA8 . . . . .54 B4
  New Malden KT3 . . . . . . .182 C5
  Sutton SM3 . . . . .198 B3
  West Molesey KT8 . . . . . .179 G3
Windsor Cen, The, SE27
  off Advance Rd 169 J4
Windsor Cl, N3 . . . . .72 B2
  SE27 . . . . .169 J4
  Borehamwood WD6 . . . . . .38 A1
  Brentford TW8 . . . . .124 E6
  Chislehurst BR7 . . . . .175 E5
  Harrow HA2 . . . . .85 G3
  Northwood HA6 . . . . .66 A2
Windsor Ct, N14 . . . . .42 C7
  Sunbury-on-Thames TW16
  off Windsor Rd 160 A6
Windsor Cres, Har. HA2 . . . . . .85 G4
  Wembley HA9 . . . . .88 B3

Windsor Dr, Barn. EN4 . . . . . .41 J6
Windsor Gdns, W9 . . . . .108 D5
  Croydon CR0
  off Richmond Rd 200/201 E3
  Hayes UB3 . . . . .121 G3
Windsor Gro, SE27 . . . . .169 J4
  SE23 . . . . .171 H1
Windsor Ms, SE6 . . . . .172 C1
  SE23 . . . . .171 H1
Windsor Pk Rd, Hayes UB3 . . .121 J7
Windsor Pl, SW1 . . . . .25 G6
Windsor Rd, E4 off Chivers Rd . .62 B4
  E7 . . . . .97 H5
  E10 . . . . .96 B2
  E11 . . . . .97 G1
  N3 . . . . .72 B2
  N7 . . . . .93 E3
  N13 . . . . .59 G3
  N17 . . . . .76 D2
  NW2 . . . . .89 H6
  W5 . . . . .105 H7
  Barnet EN5 . . . . .40 B6
  Bexleyheath DA6 . . . . . . .158 E4
  Dagenham RM8 . . . . .101 E3
  Harrow HA3 . . . . .68 A1
  Hounslow TW4 . . . . .142 B2
  Ilford IG1 . . . . .99 E4
  Kingston upon Thames KT2 .163 H7
  Richmond TW9 . . . . .145 J2
  Southall UB2 . . . . .123 F3
  Sunbury-on-Thames TW16 .160 A6
  Teddington TW11 . . . . . . .162 A5
  Thornton Heath CR7 . . . . .187 H2
  Worcester Park KT4 . . . . . .197 G2
Windsors, The, Buck.H. IG9 . . .64 B2
Windsor St, N1 . . . . .111 H1
Windsor Ter, N1 . . . . .12 A3
Windsor Wk, SE5 . . . . .152 A2
Windsor Way, W14 . . . . .128 A4
Windsor Wf, E9 . . . . .95 J5
Windspoint Dr, SE15
  off Ethnard Rd 132/133 E6
Windus Rd, N16 . . . . .94 C1
Windus Wk, N16 . . . . .94 C1
Windy Ridge, Brom. BR1 . . . .192 B1
Windyridge Cl, SW19 . . . . . . .166 A5
Wine Cl, E1 . . . . .113 F7
Wine Office Ct, EC4 . . . . .19 F3
Winery La, Kings.T. KT1 . . . . .181 J3
Winey Cl, Chess. KT9
  off Nigel Fisher Way 195 F7
Winford Ho, E3 . . . . .95 J7
Winford Par, Sthl. UB1
  off Telford Rd 103 H6
Winforton St, SE10 . . . . .154 C1
Winfrith Rd, SW18 . . . . .149 F7
Wingate Cres, Croy. CR0 . . . .186 D6
Wingate Rd, W6 . . . . .127 H3
  Ilford IG1 . . . . .99 E6
  Sidcup DA14 . . . . .176 C5
Wingate Trd Est, N17 . . . . . . .60 D7
Wingfield Ct, E14
  off Newport Av 114 D7
Wingfield Ms, SE15
  off Wingfield St 152 D3
Wingfield Rd, E15 . . . . .96 E5
  E17 . . . . .78 B5
  Kingston upon Thames KT2 .164 A6
Wingfield St, SE15 . . . . .152 D3
Wingfield Way, Ruis. HA4 . . . . .84 B6
Wingford Rd, SW2 . . . . .150 E6
Wingrave Rd, W6 . . . . .127 J6
Wingrove Rd, SE6 . . . . .173 E2
Wings Cl, Sutt. SM1 . . . . .198 D4
Winifred Cl, Barn. EN5 . . . . . . .39 F6
Winifred Gro, SW11 . . . . .149 J4
Winifred Pl, N12 off High Rd . . .57 F5
Winifred Rd, SW19 . . . . .184 D1
  Dagenham RM8 . . . . .101 E2
  Hampton (Hmptn H.) TW12 .161 G4
Winifred St, E16 . . . . .136 C1
Winifred Ter, E13 off Victoria Rd .115 G2
  Enfield EN1
  off Great Cambridge Rd 44 C7
Winkfield Rd, E13 . . . . .115 H2
  N22 . . . . .75 G1
Winkley St, E2 . . . . .112 E2
Winlaton Rd, Brom. BR1 . . . . .172 D4
Winmill Rd, Dag. RM8 . . . . . .101 F3
Winn Common Rd, SE18 . . . . .137 H6
Winnett St, W1 . . . . .17 H5
Winningales Ct, Ilf. IG5
  off Vienna Cl 80 B3
Winnings Wk, Nthlt. UB5
  off Arnold Rd 84/85 E6
Winnington Cl, N2 . . . . .73 G6
Winnington Rd, N2 . . . . .73 G7
Winnipeg Dr, Orp. BR6 . . . . . .207 J6
Winnock Rd, West Dr. UB7 . . .120 A1
Winn Rd, SE12 . . . . .173 G1
Winns Av, E17 . . . . .77 H3
Winns Ms, N15 off Grove Pk Rd .76 B4
Winns Ter, E17 . . . . .78 A2
Winsbeach, E17 . . . . .78 D3
Winscombe Cres, W5 . . . . . . .105 G4

Winscombe St, N19 . . . . .92 B2
Winscombe Way, Stan. HA7 . . .52 D5
Winsford Rd, SE6 . . . . .171 J3
Winsford Ter, N18 . . . . .60 A5
Winsham Gro, SW11 . . . . .150 A5
Winsland Ms, W2 . . . . .15 E3
Winsland St, W2 . . . . .15 E3
Winsley St, W1 . . . . .17 F3
Winslow, SE17 . . . . .36 D4
Winslow Cl, NW10
    off Neasden La N 88/89 E3
    Pinner HA5 . . . . .66 B6
Winslow Gro, E4 . . . . .62 E2
Winslow Rd, W6 . . . . .127 J6
Winslow Way, Felt. TW13 . . . .160 D3
Winsor Ter, E6 . . . . .116 D5
Winsor Ter Roundabout, E6
    off Royal Docks Rd 116/117 E5
Winstanley Est, SW11 . . . . . . .149 G3
Winstanley Rd, SW11 . . . . . . .149 G3
Winstead Gdns, Dag. RM10 . . .101 J5
Winston Av, NW9 . . . . .70 E7
Winston Cl, Har. HA3 . . . . .52 C6
    Romford RM7 . . . . .83 H4
Winston Ct, Har. HA3 . . . . .51 H7
Winston Rd, N16 . . . . .94 A4
Winston Way, W4
    off Beaconsfield Rd 126 D4
Winston Way, Ilf. IG1 . . . . .99 E3
Winstre Rd, Borwd. WD6 . . . . .38 A1
Winter Av, E6 . . . . .116 B1
Winterborne Av, Orp. BR6 . . .207 G3
Winterbourne Rd, SE6 . . . . . .171 J1
    Dagenham RM8 . . . . .100 C2
    Thornton Heath CR7 . . . . .187 G3
Winter Box Wk, Rich. TW10 . . .145 J4
Winterbrook Rd, SE24 . . . . . .151 J6
Winterburn Cl, N11 . . . . .58 A6
Winterfold Cl, SW19 . . . . .166 B2
Wintergreen Cl, E6
    off Yarrow Cres 116 B5
Winters Rd, T.Ditt. KT7 . . . . . .180 E7
Winterstoke Gdns, NW7 . . . . . .55 G5
Winterstoke Rd, SE6 . . . . . . .171 J1
Winterton Ho, E1 . . . . .113 E6
Winterton Pl, SW10 . . . . .30 D5
Winterwell Rd, SW2 . . . . .151 E5
Winthorpe Rd, SW15 . . . . . . .148 B4
Winthrop St, E1 . . . . .112 E5
Winthrop Wk, Wem. HA9
    off Everard Way 87 H3
Winton Av, N11 . . . . .58 C7
Winton Cl, N9 . . . . .45 G7
Winton Gdns, Edg. HA8 . . . . . .53 J7
Winton Rd, Orp. BR6 . . . . . . .206 E4
Winton Way, SW16 . . . . .169 H5
Wirrall Ho, SE26
    off Sydenham Hill 170 D3
Wisbeach Rd, Croy. CR0 . . . . .188 A5
Wisdons Cl, Dag. RM10 . . . . .101 H1
Wise La, NW7 . . . . .55 H6
    West Drayton UB7 . . . . . . .120 A4
Wiseman Ct, SE19 . . . . .170 B5
Wiseman Rd, E10 . . . . .96 A2
Wise Rd, E15 . . . . .114 D1
Wiseton Rd, SW17 . . . . .167 H1
Wishart Rd, SE3 . . . . .156 A1
Wisley Rd, SW11 . . . . .150 A5
    Orpington BR5 . . . . .176 A7
Wisteria Cl, NW7 . . . . .55 F6
    Ilford IG1 . . . . .98 E5
    Orpington BR6 . . . . .207 E2
Wisteria Rd, SE13 . . . . .154 D4
Witan St, E2 . . . . .113 E3
Witham Cl, Loug. IG10 . . . . . . .48 B3
Witham Rd, SE20 . . . . .189 F3
    W13 . . . . .124 D1
    Dagenham RM10 . . . . . . .101 G5
    Isleworth TW7 . . . . .144 A1
Witherby Cl, Croy. CR0 . . . . . .202 B5
Witherington Rd, N5 . . . . .93 G5
Withers Cl, Chess. KT9
    off Coppard Gdns 195 F6
Withers Mead, NW9 . . . . .71 F1
Witherston Way, SE9 . . . . . . .174 D2
Withycombe Rd, SW19 . . . . . .148 A4
Withy Mead, E4 . . . . .62 D3
Witley Cres, Croy. (New Adgtn)
    CR0 . . . . .204 C6
Witley Gdns, Sthl. UB2 . . . . . .123 F4
Witley Pt, SW15
    off Wanborough Dr 165 H1
Witley Rd, N19 off Holloway Rd . .92 C2
Witney Cl, Pnr. HA5 . . . . .51 F6
Witney Path, SE23 . . . . .171 G3
Wittenham Way, E4 . . . . .62 D3
Wittering Cl, Kings.T. KT2 . . . .163 G5
Wittersham Rd, Brom. BR1 . . .173 F5
Wivenhoe Cl, SE15 . . . . .152 E3
Wivenhoe Ct, Houns. TW3 . . .143 F4
Wivenhoe Rd, Bark. IG11 . . . .118 A2
Wiverton Rd, SE26 . . . . .171 F6

Wixom Ho, SE3 off Romero Sq . .155 J4
Wix Rd, Dag. RM9 . . . . .118 D1
Wixs La, SW4 . . . . .150 B4
Woburn Cl, SE28
    off Summerton Way 118 D6
    SW19 off Tintern Cl 167 F6
Woburn Ct, SE16
    off Masters Dr 132/133 E5
Woburn Pl, WC1 . . . . .9 J5
Woburn Rd, Cars. SM5 . . . . . .199 H1
    Croydon CR0 . . . . .201 J1
Woburn Sq, WC1 . . . . .9 J6
Woburn Wk, WC1 . . . . .9 J4
Wodehouse Av, SE5 . . . . .152 C1
Woffington Cl, Kings.T. KT1 . . .181 F1
Woking Cl, SW15 . . . . .147 F4
Woldham Pl, Brom. BR2 . . . . .191 H4
Woldham Rd, Brom. BR2 . . . . .191 H4
Wolds Dr, Orp. BR6 . . . . .206 D4
Wolfe Cl, Brom. BR2 . . . . .191 G6
    Hayes UB4 off Ayles Rd . . .102 B3
Wolfe Cres, SE7 . . . . .136 A5
    SE16 . . . . .133 G2
Wolferton Rd, E12 . . . . .98 C4
Wolffe Gdns, E15 . . . . .97 F6
Wolffram Cl, SE13 . . . . .154 E5
Wolfington Rd, SE27 . . . . .169 H4
Wolftencroft Cl, SW11 . . . . . .149 G3
Wollaston Cl, SE1 . . . . .35 J1
Wolmer Cl, Edg. HA8 . . . . .54 B4
Wolmer Gdns, Edg. HA8 . . . . . .54 A3
Wolseley Av, SW19 . . . . .166 D2
Wolseley Gdns, W4 . . . . .126 B6
Wolseley Rd, E7 . . . . .97 H7
    N8 . . . . .74 D6
    N22 . . . . .75 F1
    W4 . . . . .126 C4
    Harrow HA3 . . . . .68 B3
    Mitcham CR4 . . . . .186 A7
Wolseley St, SE1 . . . . .29 G4
Wolsey Av, E6 . . . . .116 D3
    E17 . . . . .77 J3
    Thames Ditton KT7 . . . . . .180 C5
Wolsey Cl, SW20 . . . . .165 H7
    Hounslow TW3 . . . . .143 J4
    Kingston upon Thames KT2 . .182 B1
    Southall UB2 . . . . .123 J3
    Worcester Park KT4 . . . . . .197 G4
Wolsey Cres, Mord. SM4 . . . . .184 B7
Wolsey Dr, Kings.T. KT2 . . . . .163 H5
Wolsey Gdns, Ilf. IG6 . . . . .65 F6
Wolsey Gro, Edg. HA8 . . . . . . .54 D7
Wolsey Ms, NW5 . . . . .92 C6
    Orpington BR6
    off Osgood Av 207 J5
Wolsey Rd, N1 . . . . .94 A5
    East Molesey KT8 . . . . . . .180 A4
    Enfield EN1 . . . . .45 E2
    Hampton (Hmptn H.) TW12 . .161 H6
Wolsey St, E1 off Sidney St 113 F5
Wolsey Way, Chess. KT9 . . . . .196 A5
Wolstonbury, N12 . . . . .56 D5
Wolvercote Rd, SE2 . . . . .138 D2
Wolverley St, E2
    off Bethnal Grn Rd 112/113 E3
Wolverton, SE17 . . . . .36 C3
Wolverton Av, Kings.T. KT2 . . .182 A1
Wolverton Gdns, W5 . . . . .105 J7
    W6 . . . . .128 A4
Wolverton Rd, Stan. HA7 . . . . . .53 E6
Wolverton Way, N14 . . . . .42 C5
Wolves La, N13 . . . . .59 G7
    N22 . . . . .59 G7
Womersley Rd, N8 . . . . .75 F6
Wonford Cl, Kings.T. KT2 . . . . .183 E1
Wontner Cl, N1
    off Greenman St 93 J7
Wontner Rd, SW17 . . . . .167 J2
Woodall Cl, E14 off Lawless St . .114 B7
    Chessington KT9 . . . . .195 G6
Woodall Rd, Enf. EN3 . . . . .45 G6
Woodbank Rd, Brom. BR1 . . . .173 F3
Woodbastwick Rd, SE26 . . . . .171 G5
Woodberry Av, N21 . . . . .59 G2
    Harrow HA2 . . . . .67 H4
Woodberry Cl, NW7 . . . . .56 A7
    Sunbury-on-Thames TW16
    off Ashridge Way 160 A6
Woodberry Cres, N10 . . . . .74 B3
Woodberry Down, N4 . . . . .75 J7
Woodberry Down Est, N4 . . . . .75 J7
Woodberry Gdns, N12 . . . . . . .57 F6
Woodberry Gro, N4 . . . . .75 J7
    N12 . . . . .57 F6
Woodberry Way, E4 . . . . .62 C1
    N12 . . . . .57 F6
Woodbine Cl, Twick. TW2 . . . .162 A2
Woodbine Gro, SE20 . . . . .171 E7
Woodbine La, Wor.Pk. KT4 . . .197 J3
Woodbine Pl, E11 . . . . .79 G6
Woodbine Rd, Sid. DA15 . . . . .175 H1
Woodbines Av, Kings.T. KT1 . .181 G3
Woodbine Ter, E9
    off Morning La 95 F6
Woodborough Rd, SW15 . . . . .147 H4

Woodbourne Av, SW16 . . . . . .168 D3
Woodbourne Cl, SW16
    off Woodbourne Av 168/169 E3
Woodbourne Dr, Esher (Clay.)
    KT10 . . . . .194 C6
Woodbourne Gdns, Wall. SM6 . .200 B7
Woodbridge Cl, N7 . . . . .93 F2
    NW2 . . . . .89 G3
Woodbridge Ct, Wdf.Grn. IG8 . .64 B7
Woodbridge Rd, Bark. IG11 . . .99 J5
Woodbridge St, EC1 . . . . .11 G5
Woodbrook Rd, SE2 . . . . .138 A6
Woodburn Cl, NW4 . . . . .72 A5
Woodbury Cl, E11 . . . . .79 H4
    Croydon CR0 . . . . .202 C2
Woodbury Hill, Loug. IG10 . . . .48 B3
Woodbury Hollow, Loug. IG10 . .48 B2
Woodbury Pk Rd, W13 . . . . . .104 E4
Woodbury Rd, E17 . . . . .78 B4
Woodbury St, SW17 . . . . .167 H5
Woodchester Sq, W2 . . . . .14 A1
Woodchurch Cl, Sid. DA14 . . . .175 G3
Woodchurch Dr, Brom. BR1 . . .174 A7
Woodchurch Rd, NW6 . . . . .90 D7
Wood Cl, E2 . . . . .13 H5
    NW9 . . . . .70 D7
    Harrow HA1 . . . . .68 A7
Woodclyffe Dr, Chis. BR7 . . . .192 D2
Woodcock Ct, Har. HA3 . . . . . . .69 H7
Woodcock Dell Av, Har. HA3 . . .69 G7
Woodcock Hill, Har. HA3 . . . . . .69 G7
Woodcocks, E16 . . . . .115 J5
Woodcombe Cres, SE23 . . . . .171 F1
Woodcote Av, NW7 . . . . .55 J6
    Thornton Heath CR7 . . . . .187 H4
    Wallington SM6 . . . . .200 B7
Woodcote Cl, Enf. EN3 . . . . . . .45 F6
    Kingston upon Thames KT2 . .163 J5
Woodcote Dr, Orp. BR6 . . . . . .207 G1
Woodcote Ms, Loug. IG10 . . . . .48 A7
    Wallington SM6 . . . . .200 B6
Woodcote Pl, SE27 . . . . .169 H5
Woodcote Rd, E11 . . . . .79 H7
    Wallington SM6 . . . . .200 B6
Woodcott Ho, SW15
    off Ellisfield Dr 147 G7
Woodcroft, N21 . . . . .59 F1
    SE9 . . . . .174 C3
    Greenford UB6 . . . . .86 D6
Woodcroft Av, NW7 . . . . .55 E7
    Stanmore HA7 . . . . .68 C1
Woodcroft Ms, SE8 off Croft St . .133 H4
Woodcroft Rd, Th.Hth. CR7 . . .187 H5
Wood Dr, Chis. BR7 . . . . .174 B6
Woodedge Cl, E4 . . . . .63 F1
Woodend, SE19 . . . . .169 J6
    Sutton SM1 . . . . .199 F2
Wood End Av, Har. HA2 . . . . . .85 H4
Wood End Cl, Nthlt. UB5 . . . . . .86 A5
Woodend Gdns, Enf. EN2 . . . . .42 E4
Wood End Gdns, Nthlt. UB5 . . .85 J5
Wood End La, Nthlt. UB5 . . . . .85 H6
Woodend Rd, E17 . . . . .78 C2
Wood End Rd, Har. HA1 . . . . . .86 A4
Wood End Way, Nthlt. UB5 . . . .85 J5
Wooder Gdns, E7 . . . . .97 F4
Wooderson Cl, SE25 . . . . .188 B4
Woodfall Av, Barn. EN5 . . . . . . .40 C5
Woodfall Rd, N4 . . . . .93 G1
Woodfall St, SW3 . . . . .31 J4
Woodfarrs, SE5 . . . . .152 A4
Woodfield Av, NW9 . . . . .71 E4
    SW16 . . . . .168 D3
    W5 . . . . .105 F4
    Carshalton SM5 . . . . .200 A6
    Wembley HA0 . . . . .87 F3
Woodfield Cl, SE19 . . . . .169 J7
    Enfield EN1 . . . . .44 B4
Woodfield Cres, W5 . . . . .105 F4
Woodfield Dr, Barn. EN4 . . . . . .58 A1
Woodfield Gdns, W9
    off Woodfield Rd 108 C5
    New Malden KT3 . . . . .183 F5
Woodfield Gro, SW16 . . . . . . .168 D3
Woodfield La, SW16 . . . . .168 D3
Woodfield Pl, W9 . . . . .108 C4
Woodfield Rd, W5 . . . . .105 F4
    W9 . . . . .108 C5
    Hounslow TW4 . . . . .142 B2
    Thames Ditton KT7 . . . . . .194 C2
Woodfield Way, N11 . . . . .58 D7
WOODFORD, Wdf.Grn. IG8 . . . .63 H6
Woodford Av, Ilf. IG2, IG4 . . . . .80 C5
    Woodford Green IG8 . . . . . .80 A3
WOODFORD BRIDGE, Wdf.Grn.
    IG8 . . . . .64 C7
Woodford Br Rd, Ilf. IG4 . . . . . .80 A3
Woodford Ct, W12
    off Shepherds Bush Grn . . .128 A2
Woodford Cres, Pnr. HA5 . . . . .66 B2
WOODFORD GREEN, IG8 . . . . .63 H4
Woodford New Rd, E17 . . . . . . .78 E4
    E18 . . . . .79 E1
    Woodford Green IG8 . . . . . .79 E1
Woodford Pl, Wem. HA9 . . . . . .87 H1

Woodford Rd, E7 . . . . .97 H4
    E18 . . . . .79 G4
WOODFORD WELLS, Wdf.Grn.
    IG8 . . . . .63 H4
Woodgate Av, Chess. KT9 . . . .195 G5
Woodgate Cres, Nthwd. HA6 . . .50 A5
Woodgate Dr, SW16 . . . . .168 D7
Woodger Rd, W12
    off Goldhawk Rd 127 J2
Woodget Cl, E6
    off Remington Rd 116 B6
Woodgrange Av, N12 . . . . .57 G6
    W5 . . . . .126 A1
    Enfield EN1 . . . . .44 D6
    Harrow HA3 . . . . .69 F5
Woodgrange Cl, Har. HA3 . . . . .69 G5
Woodgrange Gdns, Enf. EN1 . . .44 D6
Woodgrange Rd, E7 . . . . .97 H4
Woodgrange Ter, Enf. EN1
    off Great Cambridge Rd 44 D6
WOOD GREEN, N22 . . . . .74 E1
Wood Grn Shop City, N22 . . . . .75 G2
Woodhall Av, SE21 . . . . .170 C3
    Pinner HA5 . . . . .66 E2
Woodhall Dr, SE21 . . . . .170 C3
    Pinner HA5 . . . . .66 D1
Woodhall Gate, Pnr. HA5 . . . . .50 D7
Woodhall Ho, SW18
    off Fitzhugh Gro 149 G6
Woodhall La, Wat. WD19 . . . . . .50 D4
Woodhall Rd, Pnr. HA5 . . . . . . .50 D5
Woodham Ct, E18 . . . . .79 F4
Woodham Rd, SE6 . . . . .172 C3
Woodhatch Cl, E6
    off Remington Rd 116 B6
Woodhaven Gdns, Ilf. IG6
    off Brandville Gdns 81 F3
Woodhayes Rd, SW19 . . . . . . .165 J7
Woodhead Dr, Orp. BR6
    off Sherlies Av 207 H2
Woodheyes Rd, NW10 . . . . . . .88 D5
Woodhill, SE18 . . . . .136 B4
Woodhill Cres, Har. HA3 . . . . . .69 G6
Wood Ho, SW17 off Laurel Cl . .167 H5
Woodhouse Av, Grnf. UB6 . . . .104 C2
Woodhouse Cl, Grnf. UB6 . . . .104 C2
    Hayes UB3 . . . . .121 H3
Woodhouse Eaves, Nthwd. HA6 . .50 A5
Woodhouse Gro, E12 . . . . .98 B6
Woodhouse Rd, E11 . . . . .97 F3
    N12 . . . . .57 G6
Woodhurst Av, Orp. BR5 . . . . .193 F6
Woodhurst Rd, SE2 . . . . .138 A5
    W3 . . . . .106 C7
Woodington Cl, SE9 . . . . .156 D6
Woodknoll Dr, Chis. BR7 . . . . .192 C1
Woodland App, Grnf. UB6 . . . . .86 D6
Woodland Cl, NW9 . . . . .70 C6
    SE19 off Woodland Hill 170 B6
    Epsom KT19 . . . . .197 E6
    Woodford Green IG8 . . . . . .63 H3
Woodland Cres, SE10 . . . . . . .134 E6
    SE16 . . . . .133 G2
Woodland Gdns, N10 . . . . .74 B5
    Isleworth TW7 . . . . .144 B2
Woodland Gro, SE10 . . . . .134 E5
Woodland Hill, SE19 . . . . .170 B6
Woodland Ms, SW16 . . . . .168 E2
Woodland Ri, N10 . . . . .74 B4
    Greenford UB6 . . . . .86 D6
Woodland Rd, E4 . . . . .62 C1
    N11 . . . . .58 B5
    SE19 . . . . .170 B5
    Loughton IG10 . . . . .48 B3
    Thornton Heath CR7 . . . . .187 G4
WOODLANDS, Islw. TW7 . . . . .144 B2
Woodlands, NW11 . . . . .72 B6
    SW20 . . . . .183 J4
    Harrow HA2 . . . . .67 G4
Woodlands, The, N14 . . . . .58 B1
    SE13 . . . . .154 D7
    SE19 . . . . .169 J7
    Beckenham BR3 . . . . .190 C1
    Isleworth TW7 . . . . .144 C2
Woodlands Av, E11 . . . . .97 H1
    N3 . . . . .57 F7
    W3 . . . . .126 B1
    New Malden KT3 . . . . .182 C1
    Romford RM6 . . . . .82 E6
    Ruislip HA4 . . . . .84 C1
    Sidcup DA15 . . . . .175 H1
    Worcester Park KT4 . . . . . .197 F2
Woodlands Cl, NW11 . . . . .72 B5
    Borehamwood WD6 . . . . . . .38 B4
    Bromley BR1 . . . . .192 C2
    Esher (Clay.) KT10 . . . . . .194 C7
Woodlands Dr, Stan. HA7 . . . . .52 C6
    Sunbury-on-Thames TW16 . .178 C2
Woodlands Gro, Islw. TW7 . . . .144 B2
Woodlands Pk, Bex. DA5 . . . . .177 J4
Woodlands Pk Rd, N15 . . . . . . .75 H5
    SE10 . . . . .134 E6
Woodlands Rd, E11 . . . . .96 E2
    E17 . . . . .78 C3
    N9 . . . . .61 F1

Woodlands Rd, SW13 . . . . .147 F3
  Bexleyheath DA7 . . . . .159 G3
  Bromley BR1 . . . . .192 B2
  Enfield EN2 . . . . .44 A1
  Harrow HA1 . . . . .68 C5
  Ilford IG1 . . . . .99 F3
  Isleworth TW7 . . . . .144 B2
  Southall UB1 . . . . .122 D1
  Surbiton KT6 . . . . .181 G7
Woodlands St, SE13 . . . . .154 E3
Woodland St, E8 off Dalston La . .94 C6
Woodlands Way, SW15
  off Oakhill Rd 148 C5
Woodland Ter, SE7 . . . . .136 B4
Woodland Wk, NW3 . . . . .91 H5
  SE10
  off Woodland Gro 134/135 E5
  Bromley BR1 . . . . .172 E4
  Epsom KT19 . . . . .196 A6
Woodland Way, N21 . . . . .59 G2
  NW7 . . . . .55 E6
  SE2 . . . . .138 D4
  Croydon CR0 . . . . .203 H1
  Mitcham CR4 . . . . .168 A7
  Morden SM4 . . . . .184 C4
  Orpington BR5 . . . . .193 F4
  Surbiton KT5 . . . . .196 B2
  West Wickham BR4 . . . . . . .204 B4
  Woodford Green IG8 . . . . . . .63 H3
Wood La, N6 . . . . .74 B6
  NW9 . . . . .70 E7
  W12 . . . . .107 J6
  Dagenham RM8, RM9, RM10 .100 C4
  Isleworth TW7 . . . . .124 C7
  Stanmore HA7 . . . . .52 D3
  Woodford Green IG8 . . . . . . .63 F5
Woodlawn Cl, SW15 . . . . .148 C5
Woodlawn Cres, Twick. TW2 . . .161 H4
Woodlawn Dr, Felt. TW13 . . . . .160 D2
Woodlawn Rd, SW6 . . . . .128 A7
Woodlea Dr, Brom. BR2 . . . . . .191 E6
Woodlea Rd, N16 . . . . .94 B3
Woodleigh, E18
  off Churchfields 79 G1
Woodleigh Av, N12 . . . . .57 H6
Woodleigh Gdns, SW16 . . . . . .169 E3
Woodley Cl, SW17
  off Arnold Rd 167 J7
Woodley La, Cars. SM5 . . . . . . .199 G3
Wood Lo Gdns, Brom. BR1 . . . .174 B7
Wood Lo La, W.Wick. BR4 . . . . .204 C3
Woodman La, E4 . . . . .46 E5
Woodman Path, Ilf. IG6 . . . . . . .65 H6
Woodmans Gro, NW10 . . . . . . .89 F5
Woodmans Ms, W12 . . . . .107 H5
Woodmansterne Rd, SW16 . . . .186 D1
Woodman St, E16 . . . . .136 D1
Woodmere, SE9 . . . . .174 C1
Woodmere Av, Croy. CR0 . . . . .189 G7
Woodmere Cl, SW11
  off Lavender Hill 150 A3
  Croydon CR0 . . . . .189 G7
Woodmere Gdns, Croy. CR0 . . .189 G7
Woodmere Way, Beck. BR3 . . . .190 D5
Woodnook Rd, SW16 . . . . .168 B5
Woodpecker Cl, N9 . . . . .44 E6
  Bushey WD23 . . . . .51 J1
  Harrow HA3 . . . . .68 C1
Woodpecker Ms, SE13
  off Mercator Rd 154 D4
Woodpecker Rd, SE14 . . . . . . .133 H6
  SE28 . . . . .118 C7
Wood Pt, E16 off Fife Rd 115 G5
Woodquest Av, SE24 . . . . .151 J5
Wood Retreat, SE18 . . . . .137 G7
Wood Ride, Barn. EN4 . . . . .41 G1
  Orpington BR5 . . . . .193 G4
Woodridge Cl, Enf. EN2 . . . . . . .43 G1
Woodridings Av, Pnr. HA5 . . . . .67 F1
Woodridings Cl, Pnr. HA5 . . . . .51 F2
Woodriffe Rd, E11 . . . . .78 D7
Wood Ri, Pnr. HA5 . . . . .66 A5
Wood Rd, NW10 . . . . .88 C7
Woodrow, SE18 . . . . .136 C4
Woodrow Cl, Grnf. UB6 . . . . . . .87 E7
Woodrow Ct, N17
  off Heybourne Rd 60/61 E7
Woodrush Cl, SE14
  off Southerngate Way 133 H7
Woodrush Way, Rom. RM6 . . . . .82 D4
Woods, The, Nthwd. HA6 . . . . . .50 A5
Wood's Bldgs, E1
  off Whitechapel Rd 112/113 E5
Woodseer St, E1 . . . . .21 G1
Woodsford, SE17 . . . . .36 B4
Woodsford Sq, W14 . . . . .128 B2
Woodshire Rd, Dag. RM10 . . . .101 H3
WOODSIDE, Croy. CR0 . . . . . . .188 D6
Woodside, NW11 . . . . .72 D5
  SW19 . . . . .166 C6
  Buckhurst Hill IG9 . . . . .63 J2
Woodside Av, N6 . . . . .73 J5
  N10 .73 J5
  N12 .57 F4
  SE25 . . . . .188 E6

Woodside Av, Chis. BR7 . . . . . .175 F5
  Esher KT10 . . . . .180 B7
  Wembley HA0 . . . . .105 H1
Woodside Cl, Stan. HA7 . . . . . . .52 E5
  Surbiton KT5 . . . . .182 C7
  Wembley HA0 . . . . .105 H1
Woodside Ct, N12
  off Woodside Av 57 F4
Woodside Ct Rd, Croy. CR0 . . . .188 D7
Woodside Cres, Sid. DA15 . . . .175 H3
Woodside End, Wem. HA0 . . . .105 H1
Woodside Gdns, E4 . . . . .62 B5
  N17 .76 B2
Woodside Gra Rd, N12 . . . . .57 E4
Woodside Grn, SE25 . . . . .188 E6
Woodside Gro, N12 . . . . .57 F3
Woodside La, N12 . . . . .57 E3
  Bexley DA5 . . . . .158 D6
Woodside Ms, SE22
  off Heber Rd 152 C6
Woodside Pk, SE25 . . . . .188 D5
Woodside Pk Av, E17 . . . . .78 D4
Woodside Pk Rd, N12 . . . . .57 E4
Woodside Pl, Wem. HA0 . . . . . .105 H1
Woodside Rd, E13 . . . . .115 J4
  N22 .59 F7
  SE25 . . . . .188 E6
  Bromley BR1 . . . . .192 B5
  Kingston upon Thames KT2 . .163 H7
  New Malden KT3 . . . . .182 D2
  Sidcup DA15 . . . . .175 H3
  Sutton SM1 . . . . .199 F3
  Woodford Green IG8 . . . . . . .63 G4
Woodside Way, Croy. CR0 . . . . .189 E6
  Mitcham CR4 . . . . .186 B1
Woods Ms, W1 . . . . .16 A5
Woodsome Rd, NW5 . . . . .92 A3
Woods Pl, SE1 . . . . .28 E6
Woodspring Rd, SW19 . . . . . . .166 B2
Woods Rd, SE15 . . . . .152 E1
Woodstead Gro, Edg. HA8 . . . . .53 H6
Woodstock Av, NW11 . . . . .72 B7
  W13 . . . . .124 D3
  Isleworth TW7 . . . . .144 D5
  Southall UB1 . . . . .103 F3
  Sutton SM3 . . . . .184 C7
Woodstock Cl, Bex. DA5 . . . . . .177 F1
  Stanmore HA7 . . . . .69 H2
Woodstock Ct, SE12 . . . . .155 G6
Woodstock Cres, N9 . . . . .44 E6
Woodstock Gdns, Beck. BR3 . . .190 B1
  Ilford IG3 . . . . .100 A2
Woodstock Gro, W12 . . . . .128 A2
Woodstock La N, Surb. KT6 . . . .195 F2
Woodstock La S, Chess. KT9 . . .195 F4
  Esher (Clay.) KT10 . . . . .194 E5
Woodstock Ms, W1 . . . . .16 C2
Woodstock Ri, Sutt. SM3 . . . . . .184 C7
Woodstock Rd, E7 . . . . .97 J7
  E17 .78 D2
  N4 . . . . .93 G1
  NW11 . . . . .72 D7
  W4 .127 E3
  Carshalton SM5 . . . . .200 A5
  Croydon CR0 . . . . .202 A3
  Wembley HA0 . . . . .87 J7
Woodstock St, W1 . . . . .16 D4
Woodstock Ter, E14 . . . . .114 B7
Woodstock Way, Mitch. CR4 . . .186 B2
Woodstone Av, Epsom KT17 . . .197 G5
Wood St, E17 . . . . .78 C3
  EC2 .20 A4
  W4 .126 E5
  Barnet EN5 . . . . .39 J4
  Kingston upon Thames KT1 . .181 G1
  Mitcham CR4 . . . . .186 A7
Woodsyre, SE26 . . . . .170 C4
Woodthorpe Rd, SW15 . . . . . . .147 H4
Woodtree Cl, NW4
  off Ashley La 71 J2
Wood Vale, N10 . . . . .74 C5
  SE23 . . . . .170 E1
Woodvale Av, SE25 . . . . .188 C3
Wood Vale Est, SE23 . . . . .153 F6
Woodvale Wk, SE27
  off Elder Rd 169 J5
Woodvale Way, NW11
  off The Vale 90 A3
Woodview Av, E4 . . . . .62 C4
Woodview Cl, N4 . . . . .75 H7
  SW15 . . . . .164 D4
  Orpington BR6
  off Crofton Rd 207 F2
Woodville, SE3 . . . . .155 H1
Woodville Cl, SE12 . . . . .155 G5
  Teddington TW11 . . . . .162 D4
Woodville Gdns, NW11 . . . . . . .72 A7
  W5 .105 H6
  Ilford IG6 . . . . .80 E3
Woodville Gro, Well. DA16 . . . .158 A3
Woodville Rd, E11 . . . . .97 F1
  E17 .77 H4
  E18 .79 H2
  N16 .94 B5
  NW6 . . . . .108 C2

Woodville Rd, NW11 . . . . .72 A7
  W5 .105 G6
  Barnet EN5 . . . . .40 E3
  Morden SM4 . . . . .184 D4
  Richmond TW10 . . . . .163 E3
  Thornton Heath CR7 . . . . . . .187 J4
Woodville St, SE18
  off Woodhill 136 B4
Woodward Av, NW4 . . . . .71 G5
Woodward Cl, Esher (Clay.)
  KT10 . . . . .194 C6
Woodwarde Rd, SE22 . . . . .152 B6
Woodward Gdns, Dag. RM9
  off Woodward Rd 100 C7
  Stanmore HA7 . . . . .52 C7
Woodward Rd, Dag. RM9 . . . . .100 B7
Wood Way, Orp. BR6 . . . . .206 D2
Woodway Cres, Har. HA1 . . . . . .68 D6
Woodwell St, SW18
  off Huguenot Pl 149 F5
Wood Wf, SE10 . . . . .134 B6
Woodyard Cl, NW5
  off Gillies St 92 A5
Woodyard La, SE21 . . . . .152 B7
Woodyates Rd, SE12 . . . . .155 G6
Woolacombe Rd, SE3 . . . . .155 J1
Woolacombe Way, Hayes UB3 . .121 H4
Wooler St, SE17 . . . . .36 B4
Woolf Cl, SE28 . . . . .138 B1
Woolf Ms, WC1 . . . . .9 J5
Woollaston Rd, N4 . . . . .75 H6
Woolmead Av, NW9 . . . . .71 G7
Woolmer Gdns, N18 . . . . .60 D5
Woolmer Rd, N18 . . . . .60 D5
Woolmore St, E14 . . . . .114 C7
Woolneigh St, SW6 . . . . .148 E3
Wool Rd, SW20 . . . . .165 H6
Woolstaplers Way, SE16 . . . . . .29 H5
Woolston Cl, E17
  off Riverhead Cl 77 G2
Woolstone Rd, SE23 . . . . .171 H2
WOOLWICH, SE18 . . . . .136 D5
Woolwich Ch St, SE18 . . . . . . .136 B3
★ **Woolwich Common**, SE18 . .136 C7
Woolwich Common, SE18 . . . . .136 D6
Woolwich Ferry Pier, E16 . . . . .136 D2
Woolwich Foot Tunnel, E16 . . .136 D2
  SE18 . . . . .136 D2
Woolwich Garrison, SE18 . . . . .136 C6
Woolwich High St, SE18 . . . . . .136 D3
Woolwich Ind Est, SE28
  off Hadden Rd 137 H3
Woolwich Manor Way, E6 . . . . .116 C4
  E16 . . . . .117 E7
Woolwich Mkt, SE18 . . . . .136 E4
Woolwich New Rd, SE18 . . . . . .136 D5
Woolwich Rd, SE2 . . . . .138 D6
  SE7 . . . . .135 G5
  SE10 . . . . .135 F5
  Belvedere DA17 . . . . .138 D6
  Bexleyheath DA7 . . . . .159 G4
Woolwich Trade Pk, SE28
  off Pettman Cres 137 G3
Wooster Gdns, E14 . . . . .114 D6
Wooster Ms, Har. HA2
  off Fairfield Dr 67 J3
Wooster Pl, SE1 . . . . .36 C1
Wootton Gro, N3 . . . . .72 D1
Wootton St, SE1 . . . . .27 F3
Worbeck Rd, SE20 . . . . .189 E2
Worcester Av, N17 . . . . .60 D7
Worcester Cl, NW2
  off Newfield Ri 89 H3
  Croydon CR0 . . . . .203 J2
  Mitcham CR4 . . . . .186 A2
Worcester Cres, NW7 . . . . .54 E3
  Woodford Green IG8 . . . . . . .63 H5
Worcester Dr, W4 . . . . .127 E2
Worcester Gdns, SW11
  off Grandison Rd 149 J5
  Greenford UB6 . . . . .85 J6
  Ilford IG1 . . . . .80 B7
  Worcester Park KT4 . . . . . . .197 E3
Worcester Ms, NW6
  off Lymington Rd 90/91 E6
WORCESTER PARK, KT4 . . . . . .197 F2
Worcester Pk Rd, Wor.Pk. KT4 . .196 C3
Worcester Rd, E12 . . . . .98 C4
  E17 .77 G2
  SW19 . . . . .166 C5
  Sutton SM2 . . . . .199 E6
Wordsworth Av, E12 . . . . .98 B6
  E18 .79 F3
  Greenford UB6 . . . . .104 A2
Wordsworth Dr, Sutt. SM3 . . . .197 J4
Wordsworth Rd, N16 . . . . .94 B4
  SE1 .37 F2
  SE20 . . . . .171 G7
  Hampton TW12 . . . . .161 F4
  Wallington SM6 . . . . .200 C6
  Welling DA16 . . . . .157 H1
Wordsworth Wk, NW11 . . . . . . .72 D4
Wordsworth Way, West Dr. UB7 .120 B4
Worfield St, SW11 . . . . .129 H7
Worgan St, SE11 . . . . .34 C3

Worgan St, SE16 . . . . .133 G3
Worland Rd, E15 . . . . .97 E7
WORLD'S END, Enf. EN2 . . . . . .43 F3
World's End Est, SW10 . . . . .30 E7
Worlds End La, N21 . . . . .43 F5
  Enfield EN2 . . . . .43 F5
  Orpington BR6 . . . . .207 J6
World's End Pas, SW10 . . . . . . .30 E7
World's End Pl, SW10
  off King's Rd 129 F7
Worlidge St, W6 . . . . .127 J5
Worlingham Rd, SE22 . . . . .152 C4
Wormholt Rd, W12 . . . . .107 G7
Wormwood St, EC2 . . . . .20 D3
Wornington Rd, W10 . . . . .108 B5
Woronzow Rd, NW8 . . . . .109 G1
Worple Av, SW19 . . . . .166 A7
  Isleworth TW7 . . . . .144 D5
Worple Cl, Har. HA2 . . . . .85 F1
Worple Rd, SW19 . . . . .166 B7
  SW20 . . . . .183 J2
  Isleworth TW7 . . . . .144 D4
Worple Rd Ms, SW19 . . . . .166 C6
Worple St, SW14 . . . . .146 D3
Worple Way, Har. HA2 . . . . .85 F1
  Richmond TW10 . . . . .145 H5
Worship St, EC2 . . . . .12 C6
Worslade Rd, SW17 . . . . .167 G4
Worsley Br Rd, SE26 . . . . .171 J4
  Beckenham BR3 . . . . .171 J5
Worsley Gra, Chis. BR7
  off Kemnal Rd 175 F6
Worsley Gro, E5 . . . . .94 D4
Worsley Rd, E11 . . . . .96 E4
Worsopp Dr, SW4 . . . . .150 C5
Worth Cl, Orp. BR6 . . . . .207 H4
Worthfield Cl, Epsom KT19 . . . .196 D7
Worth Gro, SE17 . . . . .36 B4
Worthing Cl, E15
  off Mitre Rd 114/115 E2
Worthing Rd, Houns. TW5 . . . . .123 F6
Worthington Cl, Mitch. CR4 . . . .186 B3
Worthington Rd, Surb. KT6 . . . .195 J1
Worthy Down Ct, SE18
  off Prince Imperial Rd 156 D1
Wortley Rd, E6 . . . . .98 A7
  Croydon CR0 . . . . .187 G7
Worton Gdns, Islw. TW7 . . . . . .144 A2
Worton Hall Ind Est, Islw. TW7 .144 B4
Worton Rd, Islw. TW7 . . . . .144 B3
Worton Way, Houns. TW3 . . . . .144 A2
  Isleworth TW7 . . . . .143 J1
Wotton Rd, NW2 . . . . .89 J4
  SE8 . . . . .133 J6
Wouldham Rd, E16 . . . . .115 F6
Wragby Rd, E11 . . . . .97 E3
Wrampling Pl, N9 . . . . .60 D1
Wrangthorn Wk, Croy. CR0
  off Epsom Rd 201 G4
Wray Av, Ilf. IG5 . . . . .80 D3
Wray Cres, N4 . . . . .93 E2
Wrayfield Rd, Sutt. SM3 . . . . . .198 A3
Wraysbury Cl, Houns. TW4 . . . .142 E5
Wrekin Rd, SE18 . . . . .137 F7
Wren Av, NW2 . . . . .89 J5
  Southall UB2 . . . . .123 F4
Wren Cl, E16 off Ibbotson Av . . .115 F6
  N9 off Chaffinch Cl 61 G1
Wren Cres, Bushey WD23 . . . . .51 J1
Wren Dr, West Dr. UB7 . . . . . . .120 A3
Wren Gdns, Dag. RM9 . . . . . . .100 D5
Wren Landing, E14
  off Cabot Sq 134 A1
Wren Ms, SE13
  off Lee High Rd 154/155 E4
Wren Path, SE28 . . . . .137 G3
Wren Rd, SE5 . . . . .152 A1
  Dagenham RM9 . . . . .100 D5
  Sidcup DA14 . . . . .176 C4
Wren St, WC1 . . . . .10 D5
Wren Ter, Ilf. IG5
  off Tiptree Cres 80 D3
Wrentham Av, NW10 . . . . .108 A2
Wrenthorpe Rd, Brom. BR1 . . .172 E4
Wrenwood Way, Pnr. HA5 . . . . .66 B4
Wrestlers Ct, EC3
  off Camomile St 112 B6
Wrexham Rd, E3 . . . . .114 A2
Wricklemarsh Rd, SE3 . . . . . . .155 H1
Wrigglesworth St, SE14 . . . . . .133 G7
Wright Rd, N1 off Burder Cl 94 B6
  Hounslow TW5 . . . . .122 C7
Wrights All, SW19 . . . . .165 J6
Wrights Cl, SE13
  off Wisteria Rd 154 D4
  Dagenham RM10 . . . . .101 H3
Wrights Grn, SW4
  off Nelson's Row 150 D4
Wrights La, W8 . . . . .22 A5
Wrights Pl, NW10
  off Mitchell Way 88 C6
Wrights Rd, E3 . . . . .113 J2
  SE25 . . . . .188 B3
Wrights Row, Wall. SM6 . . . . . .200 B4
Wrights Wk, SW14 . . . . .146 D3

Wrigley Cl, E4 . . . .**62** D5
Wrotham Rd, NW1 *off Agar Pl* . .**92** C7
 W13 *off Mattock La* **124/125** E1
 Barnet EN5 . . . .**40** B2
 Welling DA16 . . . .**158** C1
Wroths Path, Loug. IG10 . . . . . .**48** C1
Wrottesley Rd, NW10 . . . .**107** G2
 SE18 . . . .**137** F6
Wroughton Rd, SW11 . . . .**149** J6
Wroughton Ter, NW4 . . . .**71** J4
Wroxall Rd, Dag. RM9 . . . .**100** C6
Wroxham Gdns, N11 . . . .**58** C7
Wroxham Rd, SE28 . . . .**118** D7
Wroxham Way, Ilf. IG6 . . . .**80** E1
Wroxton Rd, SE15 . . . .**153** E2
WRYTHE, THE, Cars. SM5 . . . . .**199** H2
Wrythe Grn, Cars. SM5
 off Wrythe Grn Rd **199** J3
Wrythe Grn Rd, Cars. SM5 . . . .**199** J3
Wrythe La, Cars. SM5 . . . .**199** F1
Wulfstan St, W12 . . . .**107** F6
Wyatt Cl, SE16 . . . .**133** J2
 Feltham TW13 . . . .**160** C1
 Hayes UB4 . . . .**102** A5
Wyatt Dr, SW13 . . . .**127** J7
Wyatt Pk Rd, SW2 . . . .**169** E2
Wyatt Rd, E7 . . . .**97** G6
 N5 . . . .**93** J3
Wyatts La, E17 . . . .**78** C3
Wybert St, NW1 . . . .**9**
Wyborne Way, NW10 . . . .**88** C7
Wyburn Av, Barn. EN5 . . . .**40** C3
Wyche Gro, S.Croy. CR2 . . . . . .**201** J7
Wych Elm Dr, Brom. BR1
 off London La **173** F7
Wych Elm Pas, Kings.T. KT2 . . .**163** J7
Wycherley Cl, SE3 . . . .**135** F7
Wycherley Cres, Barn. EN5 . . . . .**40** E6
Wychwood Av, Edg. HA8 . . . . . .**53** G6
 Thornton Heath CR7 . . . .**187** J3
Wychwood Cl, Edg. HA8 . . . .**53** G6
 Sunbury-on-Thames TW16 . . . .**160** A6
Wychwood End, N6 . . . .**74** C7
Wychwood Gdns, Ilf. IG5 . . . . . .**80** C4
Wychwood Way, SE19
 off Roman Ri **170** A6
Wycliffe Cl, Well. DA16 . . . .**157** J1
Wycliffe Rd, SW11 . . . .**150** A2
 SW19 . . . .**167** E6
Wyclif St, EC1 . . . .**11** G4
Wycombe Gdns, NW11 . . . .**90** D2
Wycombe Pl, SW18 . . . .**149** F6
Wycombe Rd, N17 . . . .**76** D1
 Ilford IG2 . . . .**80** C5
 Wembley HA0 . . . .**106** A1
Wycombe Sq, W8
 off Aubrey Wk **128** D1
Wydehurst Rd, Croy. CR0 . . . . .**188** D7
Wydell Cl, Mord. SM4 . . . .**183** J6
Wydeville Manor Rd, SE12 . . . .**173** H4
Wye Cl, Orp. BR6 . . . .**193** J7
Wyemead Cres, E4 . . . .**62** E2
Wye St, SW11 . . . .**149** G2
Wyevale Cl, Pnr. HA5 . . . .**66** A3
Wyfields, Ilf. IG5
 off Ravensbourne Gdns . .**80/81** E1
Wyfold Ho, SE2
 off Wolvercote Rd **138** D2
Wyfold Rd, SW6 . . . .**128** B7
Wyhill Wk, Dag. RM10 . . . .**101** J6
Wyke Cl, Islw. TW7 . . . .**124** C6
Wyke Gdns, W7 . . . .**124** D3
Wykeham Av, Dag. RM9 . . . . . .**100** C6
Wykeham Cl, West Dr. UB7 . . . .**120** D5
Wykeham Grn, Dag. RM9 . . . . .**100** C6
Wykeham Hill, Wem. HA9 . . . . . .**87** J1
Wykeham Ri, N20 . . . .**56** B1
Wykeham Rd, NW4 . . . .**71** J5
 Harrow HA3 . . . .**68** E4
Wyke Rd, E3 . . . .**96** A7
 SW20 . . . .**183** J2
Wyldes Cl, NW11
 off Wildwood Rd **91** F1
Wyldfield Gdns, N9 . . . .**60** C2

Wyleu St, SE23 . . . .**153** H7
Wylie Rd, Sthl. UB2 . . . .**123** G3
Wyllen Cl, E1 . . . .**113** F4
Wylo Dr, Barn. EN5 . . . .**39** G6
Wymering Rd, W9 . . . .**108** D3
Wymond St, SW15 . . . .**147** J3
Wynan Rd, E14 . . . .**134** B5
Wynash Gdns, Cars. SM5 . . . . .**199** H5
Wynaud Ct, N22
 off Palmerston Rd **59** F6
Wyncham Av, Sid. DA15 . . . . . .**175** H1
Wynchgate, N14 . . . .**58** D1
 N21 . . . .**58** E1
 Harrow HA3 . . . .**52** B7
Wyncroft Cl, Brom. BR1 . . . . . .**192** C3
Wyndale Av, NW9 . . . .**70** A6
Wyndcliff Rd, SE7 . . . .**135** H6
Wyndcroft Cl, Enf. EN2 . . . .**43** H3
Wyndham Cl, Orp. BR6 . . . .**207** F1
 Sutton SM2 . . . .**198** D7
Wyndham Cres, N19 . . . .**92** C3
 Hounslow TW4 . . . .**143** G6
Wyndham Est, SE5 . . . .**36** A7
Wyndham Ms, W1 . . . .**15** J2
Wyndham Pl, W1 . . . .**15** J2
Wyndham Rd, E6 . . . .**98** A7
 SE5 . . . .**131** H7
 W13 . . . .**124** E3
 Barnet EN4 . . . .**57** J1
 Kingston upon Thames KT2 . . .**163** J7
Wyndham St, W1 . . . .**15** J1
Wyndham Yd, W1 . . . .**15** J2
Wyneham Rd, SE24 . . . .**152** A5
Wynell Rd, SE23 . . . .**171** G3
Wynford Pl, Belv. DA17 . . . .**139** G6
Wynford Rd, N1 . . . .**10** C1
Wynford Way, SE9 . . . .**174** C3
Wynlie Gdns, Pnr. HA5 . . . .**66** B2
Wynn Br Cl, Wdf.Grn. IG8
 off Chigwell Rd **79** J1
Wynndale Rd, E18 . . . .**79** H1
Wynne Rd, SW9 . . . .**151** G2
Wynns Av, Sid. DA15 . . . .**158** A5
Wynnstay Gdns, W8 . . . .**128** D3
Wynter St, SW11 . . . .**149** F4
Wynton Gdns, SE25 . . . .**188** C5
Wynton Pl, W3 . . . .**106** B6
Wynyard Ter, SE11 . . . .**34** D3
Wynyatt St, EC1 . . . .**11** G4
Wyre Gro, Edg. HA8 . . . .**54** B3
 Hayes UB3 . . . .**122** A4
Wyresdale Cres, Grnf. UB6 . . . .**104** C3
Wythburn Pl, W1 . . . .**15** J4
Wythenshawe Rd, Dag. RM10 . .**101** G4
Wythens Wk, SE9 . . . .**156** E6
Wythes Cl, Brom. BR1 . . . .**192** C2
Wythes Rd, E16 . . . .**136** B1
Wythfield Rd, SE9 . . . .**156** C6
Wyvenhoe Rd, Har. HA2 . . . .**85** J3
Wyvern Est, N.Mal. KT3 . . . . . .**183** G4
Wyvern Gro, Hayes UB3 . . . . . .**121** E7
Wyvil Est, SW8 . . . .**34** A7
Wyvil Rd, SW8 . . . .**34** A6
Wyvis St, E14 . . . .**114** B5

Y

Yabsley St, E14 . . . .**134** C1
Yalding Rd, SE16 . . . .**29** H6
Yale Cl, Houns. TW4 . . . .**143** F5
Yaohan Plaza, NW9 . . . .**70** D3
Yarborough Rd, SW19 . . . .**185** G1
Yardley Cl, E4 . . . .**46** B5
Yardley Ct, Sutt. SM3
 off Hemingford Rd **197** J4
Yardley La, E4 . . . .**46** B5
Yardley St, WC1 . . . .**10** E4
Yarmouth Cres, N17 . . . .**76** E5
Yarmouth Pl, W1 . . . .**24** D2
Yarnfield Sq, SE15
 off Clayton Rd **152** D1
Yarnton Way, SE2 . . . .**138** D2
 Erith DA18 . . . .**139** F3
Yarrow Cres, E6 . . . .**116** B5

Yateley St, SE18 . . . .**136** A3
Yates Ct, NW2 . . . .**90** A6
YEADING, Hayes UB4 . . . .**102** B3
Yeading Av, Har. HA2 . . . .**84** E2
Yeading Fork, Hayes UB4 . . . . .**102** C5
Yeading Gdns, Hayes UB4 . . . . .**102** B5
Yeading La, Hayes UB4 . . . .**102** B6
 Northolt UB5 . . . .**102** C3
Yeames Cl, W13 . . . .**104** D6
Yeate St, N1 . . . .**94** A7
Yeatman Rd, N6 . . . .**73** J6
Yeats Cl, NW10 . . . .**88** E6
Yeats Ct, N15 *off Tynemouth Rd* .**76** C4
Yeldham Rd, W6 . . . .**128** A5
Yellow Hammer Ct, NW9
 off Eagle Dr **70/71** E2
Yelverton Rd, SW11 . . . .**149** G2
Yenston Cl, Mord. SM4 . . . .**184** D6
Yeoman Cl, E6
 off Ferndale St **116/117** E7
 SE27 . . . .**169** H3
Yeoman Rd, Nthlt. UB5 . . . .**85** E7
Yeomans Acre, Ruis. HA4 . . . . . .**66** A6
Yeoman's Ms, Islw. TW7
 off Queensbridge Pk **144** B5
Yeoman's Row, SW3 . . . .**23** H6
Yeoman St, SE8 . . . .**133** H4
Yeomans Way, Enf. EN3 . . . .**45** F2
Yeomans Yd, E1 . . . .**21** G5
Yeomen Way, Ilf. IG6 . . . .**65** F6
Yeo St, E3 . . . .**114** B5
Yeovil Cl, Orp. BR6 . . . .**207** H2
Yeovilton Pl, Kings.T. KT2 . . . . .**163** F5
Yerbury Rd, N19 . . . .**92** D3
Yester Dr, Chis. BR7 . . . .**174** B7
Yester Pk, Chis. BR7 . . . .**174** C7
Yester Rd, Chis. BR7 . . . .**174** C7
Yew Cl, Buck.H. IG9 . . . .**64** A2
Yewdale Cl, Brom. BR1 . . . .**173** E6
Yewfield Rd, NW10 . . . .**89** F7
Yew Gro, NW2 . . . .**90** A4
Yew Tree Cl, N21 . . . .**43** G7
 Welling DA16 . . . .**158** A1
 Worcester Park KT4 . . . .**197** E1
Yew Tree Gdns, Rom. (Chad.Hth)
 RM6 . . . .**83** E5
Yew Tree Rd, W12 . . . .**107** F7
Yewtree Rd, Beck. BR3 . . . .**189** J3
Yew Tree Wk, Houns. TW4 . . . .**143** F5
Yew Wk, Har. HA1 . . . .**86** B1
YIEWSLEY, West Dr. UB7 . . . . .**120** B1
Yoakley Rd, N16 . . . .**94** B2
Yoke Cl, N7 *off Ewe Cl* **92/93** E6
Yolande Gdns, SE9 . . . .**156** B5
Yonge Pk, N4 . . . .**93** G3
York Av, SW14 . . . .**146** C5
 W7 . . . .**124** B1
 Sidcup DA15 . . . .**175** H2
 Stanmore HA7 . . . .**68** E1
York Br, NW1 . . . .**8** B5
York Bldgs, WC2 . . . .**18** B6
York Cl, E6 *off Boultwood Rd* . .**116** C6
 W7 *off York Av* **124** B1
 Morden SM4 . . . .**184** E4
York Cres, Borwd. WD6 . . . .**38** D2
 Loughton IG10 . . . .**48** B3
York Gate, N14 . . . .**42** E7
 NW1 . . . .**8** B6
York Gro, SE15 . . . .**153** F1
York Hill, SE27 . . . .**169** H3
 Loughton IG10 . . . .**48** B3
York Hill Est, SE27 . . . .**169** H3
York Ho, Wem. HA9 . . . .**87** J4
York Ho Pl, W8 . . . .**22** A3
Yorkland Av, Well. DA16 . . . . . .**157** J3
York Ms, NW5
 off Kentish Town Rd **92** B5
 Ilford IG1 *off York Rd* **98** D3
York Par, Brent. TW8 . . . .**125** G5
York Pl, SW11 . . . .**149** G3
 WC2 . . . .**18** B6
 Dagenham RM10 . . . .**101** J6

York Pl, Ilf. IG1 *off York Rd* **98** D2
York Ri, NW5 . . . .**92** B3
 Orpington BR6 . . . .**207** H1
York Rd, E4 . . . .**62** A5
 E7 . . . .**97** G6
 E10 . . . .**96** C3
 E17 . . . .**77** G5
 N11 . . . .**58** D6
 N18 . . . .**60** E6
 N21 . . . .**44** A7
 SE1 . . . .**26** D3
 SW11 . . . .**149** F4
 SW18 . . . .**149** F4
 SW19 . . . .**167** H6
 W3 . . . .**106** C6
 W5 . . . .**125** F3
 Barnet EN5 . . . .**41** G5
 Brentford TW8 . . . .**125** G5
 Croydon CR0 . . . .**187** G2
 Hounslow TW3 . . . .**143** H3
 Ilford IG1 . . . .**98** D3
 Kingston upon Thames KT2 . . . .**181** J7
 Northwood HA6 . . . .**66** A2
 Richmond TW10
 off Albert Rd **145** J5
 Sutton SM2 . . . .**198** D6
 Teddington TW11 . . . .**162** B4
Yorkshire Cl, N16 . . . .**94** B3
Yorkshire Gdns, N18 . . . .**60** E5
Yorkshire Grey Pl, NW3
 off Heath St **91** F4
Yorkshire Grey Yd, WC1 . . . .**18** C2
Yorkshire Rd, E14 . . . .**113** H6
 Mitcham CR4 . . . .**186** E5
York Sq, E14 . . . .**113** H6
York St, W1 . . . .**16** A1
 Barking IG11 *off Abbey Rd* . . .**117** G1
 Mitcham CR4 . . . .**186** A7
 Twickenham TW1 . . . .**162** D1
York Ter, Erith DA8 . . . .**159** J1
York Ter E, NW1 . . . .**8** C6
York Ter W, NW1 . . . .**8** B6
Yorkton St, E2 . . . .**13** H2
York Way, N1 . . . .**111** E1
 N7 . . . .**92** D6
 N20 . . . .**57** J3
 Borehamwood WD6 . . . .**38** D2
 Chessington KT9 . . . .**195** H7
 Feltham TW13 . . . .**161** F3
York Way Ct, N1 . . . .**111** E1
York Way Est, N7
 off York Way **92/93** E6
Youngmans Cl, Enf. EN2 . . . .**43** J1
Young Rd, E16 . . . .**115** J6
Young's Bldgs, EC1 . . . .**12** A5
★ **Young's Ram Brewery**,
 SW18 . . . .**148** E5
Youngs Rd, Ilf. IG2 . . . .**81** G5
Young St, W8 . . . .**22** A4
Yoxley App, Ilf. IG2 . . . .**81** F6
Yoxley Dr, Ilf. IG2 . . . .**81** F6
Yukon Rd, SW12 . . . .**150** B7
Yuletide Cl, NW10 . . . .**88** E7
Yunus Khan Cl, E17 . . . .**78** A5

Z

Zambezie Dr, N9 . . . .**61** F3
Zampa Rd, SE16 . . . .**133** F5
Zander Ct, E2 . . . .**13** J2
Zangwill Rd, SE3 . . . .**156** A1
Zealand Av, West Dr. UB7 . . . . .**120** A7
Zealand Rd, E3 . . . .**113** H2
Zeland Cl, NW2 . . . .**89** J1
Zennor Rd, SW12 . . . .**168** C1
Zenoria St, SE22 . . . .**152** C4
Zermatt Rd, Th.Hth. CR7 . . . . . .**187** J4
Zetland St, E14 . . . .**114** B5
Zion Pl, Th.Hth. CR7 . . . .**188** A4
Zion Rd, Th.Hth. CR7 . . . .**188** A4
Zoar St, SE1 . . . .**27** J1
Zoffany St, N19 . . . .**92** D2